Platinum Edition

USING XHTML™, XML, AND JAVA™ 2

Platinum Edition

USING XHTML™, XML, AND JAVA™ 2

Eric Ladd, Jim O'Donnell

Mike Morgan, Andrew H. Watt

Platinum Edition Using XHTML™, XML, and Java™ 2

International Standard Book Number: 0-7897-2473-1

Library of Congress Catalog Card Number: 00-107938

Printed in the United States of America

First Printing: November 2000

02 01 4 3 2

Trademarks

All terms mentioned in this book that are known to be trademarks or service marks have been appropriately capitalized. Que cannot attest to the accuracy of this information. Use of a term in this book should not be regarded as affecting the validity of any trademark or service mark.

XHTML is a trademark of the World Wide Web Consortium.

Java is a trademark of Sun Microsystems, Inc.

Warning and Disclaimer

Every effort has been made to make this book as complete and as accurate as possible, but no warranty or fitness is implied. The information provided is on an "as is" basis. The authors and the publisher shall have neither liability nor responsibility to any person or entity with respect to any loss or damages arising from the information contained in this book.

ACQUISITIONS EDITOR
Todd Green

DEVELOPMENT EDITOR
Victoria Elzey

TECHNICAL EDITORS
Jonathan Hassell
Andrew H. Watt
Kynn Bartlett
Dave Gulbransen
Vincent Minden
Amr Hassan

MANAGING EDITOR
Thomas Hayes

PROJECT EDITOR
Tonya Simpson

COPY EDITOR
Julie A. McNamee

INDEXER
Rebecca Salerno

PROOFREADERS
Angela Boley
Jeanne Clark

TEAM COORDINATOR
Cindy Teeters

INTERIOR DESIGNER
Ruth Lewis

COVER DESIGNERS
Dan Armstrong
Ruth Lewis

PRODUCTION
Brandon Allen
Darin Crone
Susan Geiselman
Cheryl Lynch

Contents at a Glance

I XHTML

II XML

III JavaScript

IV Dynamic HTML

V Server-Side Processing

VI Java 2

VII Appendixes

Table of Contents

II XML

III Javascript

V Server-Side Processing

About the Authors

Eric Ladd (`eric@rockcreekweb.com`) is the principal of Rock Creek Web Solutions, a Web-based applications development firm with offices in Arlington and Alexandria, Virginia. RCWS specializes in developing dynamic Web sites, primarily with ColdFusion and Active Server Pages, and has served clients such as MCI, Digex, Home/Work Solutions, the Alliance for Investor Education, and the Pan American Health Organization.

In addition to his development work, he is an active Web programming teacher, serving on the faculty of EEI Communications of Alexandria, Virginia, and as a member of the Interactive Multimedia and Web Development faculty at the George Washington University in Washington, D.C. Eric has worked on nearly a dozen titles for Que, including (with co-author Jim O'Donnell) *Platinum Edition Using HTML 4, XML, and Java 1.2* and *Special Edition Using Microsoft Internet Explorer 4*.

Eric earned two degrees in mathematics from Rensselaer Polytechnic Institute in Troy, New York, where he also taught fun subjects such as differential equations and complex variables for several years.

Outside of work and writing, Eric enjoys hitting the gym, biking, country dancing, and being dragged around the Metro D.C. area by his Boxer Zack.

Jim O'Donnell was born on October 17, 1963, in Pittsburgh, Pennsylvania (you may forward birthday greetings to `jim@odonnell.org`). After a number of unproductive years, he went to Rensselaer Polytechnic Institute, where he spent 11 years earning three degrees, graduating for the third (and final) time in 1992. Currently, he works as an aerospace engineer building satellites in metropolitan Washington, D.C.

Jim has been working as an author and technical editor for Macmillan USA for almost six years, contributing to more than 30 books and lead-authoring (with Eric Ladd) six books. When Jim isn't writing or researching for Macmillan, he can often be found on IRC (under the nickname JOD or HockeyJOD); you can also visit The House of JOD at `http://jim.odonnell.org`. When he isn't on the computer, Jim likes to run, work out, play ice hockey, read, collect comic books and PEZ dispensers, and play the best board game ever, Cosmic Encounter.

Contributing Authors

Michael Morgan (`michmor@regent.edu`) is founder and president of DSE, Inc., a full-service Web presence provider and software development shop. The DSE team has developed software for such companies as Intelect, Magnavox, DuPont, the American Biorobotics Company, and Satellite Systems Corporation, as well as for the government of Iceland and the Royal Saudi Air Force. DSE's Web sites are noted for their effectiveness—one of the company's sites generated sales of more than $100,000 within 30 days of being announced.

During the academic year 1989–1990, Mike was invited by retired Navy Admiral Ron Hays to serve as the first Fellow of the Pacific International Center for High Technology Research

(PICHTR) in Honolulu. PICHTR is a spin-off of the University of Hawaii and bridges the gap between academic research and industrial applications. Mike directed the first technology transfer initiatives at PICHTR and helped PICHTR win its first industrial contract. Mike assisted Admiral Hays in presenting PICHTR and its mission to the Hawaii research community, the Hawaii legislature, and Hawaii's representatives to Congress.

Mike is a frequent speaker at seminars on information technology and has taught computer science and software engineering at Chaminade University (the University of Honolulu) and in the graduate program of Hawaii Pacific University. He has given seminars for the IEEE, National Seminars, the University of Hawaii, Purdue University, and the University of Notre Dame.

He holds a Master of Science in Systems Management from the Florida Institute of Technology and a Bachelor of Science in Mathematics from Wheaton College, where he concentrated his studies on computer science. He has taken numerous graduate courses in computer science through the National Technological University. Mike is currently a student in the doctoral program at the Center for Leadership Studies at Regent University, where he is exploring the relationship between software processes and organizational theory.

Mike can usually be found in his office at DSE, drinking Diet Pepsi and writing Java. He lives in Virginia Beach with his wife, Jean, and their six children.

Andrew H. Watt is an independent Web consultant and principal of XMML.com who specializes in XML, Java, and Lotus Domino in addition to Web technologies such as HTML, XHTML, and JavaScript. He started programming in 1984, writing in 6502 assembler and BBC Basic. In 1996, Andrew recognized the power of Lotus Domino—its separation of presentation and content and its cross-platform capabilities—strengths that the combination of XML and Java also show. His Web sites `www.learningXML.com` and `www.learningXSLT.com` provide complementary tutorial materials on XML technologies. Andrew wrote the XML section of this book. He is currently working on projects involving prototype markup languages in the healthcare and pharmaceuticals fields.

Dedication

In memory of my mother, Beth T. Ladd.

—Eric Ladd

For my co-author and friend, Eric… 100,000 books and counting; it wouldn't have been the same without you.

—Jim O'Donnell

Acknowledgments

A tome like this does not write itself. It is the result of the orchestrated efforts of many; all of whom deserve recognition. Eric and Jim would like to thank the entire staff at Macmillan that helped with this book. Special thanks go to Todd Green, Victoria Elzey, and Tonya Simpson. Also, we would like to thank the contributing authors, Mike Morgan and Andrew Watt, and technical editors, without whom this book would be woefully incomplete. Finally, we want to express a special note of thanks to Doshia Stewart, who got us going, and to Jane Brownlow, for helping to make our time spent working with Macmillan a pleasant experience.

Eric is grateful for the support and understanding of many people while he disappeared yet again to write another book. Special thanks go to Dad in Remsen, NY, Brenda in San Diego, and to many good friends and colleagues: Bob Leidich, Erik Jones, Kurt Collins, Randy Bowers, Gordon Vivace, Carolyn McHale, Michele Keen, Kathy Webb, Tara Bridgman, and the members of the Washington Renegades Rugby Football Club. Extra special thanks to Dave Swim for his assistance with the graphics chapter and for holding down the fort at RCWS.

Jim would like to thank his family and friends for their support while he worked on this book. He would like to especially thank his roommate Jason; his beach house roommates Mark (thanks for the use of your laptop!), Kompan, and Matthew; his trainer, Jolm; the Weekly Poker Crew (Chris, Doug, Thom, and Wayne); and his teammates on the D.C. Nationals and Glaciers. Finally, an extra special thank you goes to Anthony Smith, Jim's "Marine Corps Marathon Road Crew" (Emeritus)…Thanks for being there, Anthony, it wouldn't be the same without you!

Tell Us What You Think!

As the reader of this book, *you* are our most important critic and commentator. We value your opinion and want to know what we're doing right, what we could do better, what areas you'd like to see us publish in, and any other words of wisdom you're willing to pass our way.

As an Associate Publisher for Que, I welcome your comments. You can fax, email, or write me directly to let me know what you did or didn't like about this book—as well as what we can do to make our books stronger.

Please note that I cannot help you with technical problems related to the topic of this book, and that due to the high volume of mail I receive, I might not be able to reply to every message.

When you write, please be sure to include this book's title and author as well as your name and phone or fax number. I will carefully review your comments and share them with the author and editors who worked on the book.

Fax: 317-581-4666

Email: que.programming@macmillanusa.com

Mail: Associate Publisher
Que
201 West 103rd Street
Indianapolis, IN 46290 USA

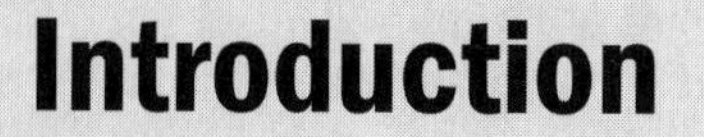

Introduction

The Hypertext Markup Language (HTML) and the World Wide Web altered the face of the Internet and of personal computing forever. One time regarded as the province of universities and government organizations, the Internet has grown to touch more and more lives every day. In addition, the multimedia content that can be provided via HTML (and its successor XHTML) and Web technologies such as JavaScript, Java, XML, CGI, and others makes the Web an exciting place to be.

Through the efforts of standards organizations such as the World Wide Web Consortium, and companies such as Netscape, Microsoft, Macromedia, and Sun Microsystems, HTML and the other languages and technologies used to present information over the Web have continued to develop and evolve. The number of possibilities for providing information content over the Web is astounding, and it's growing every day.

That is where *Platinum Edition Using XHTML, XML, and Java 2* steps in to help. This book is the only source you need to quickly get up to speed and greatly enhance your skill and productivity in providing information on the World Wide Web. ■

How to Use This Book

This book was designed and written from the ground up with two important purposes:

1. First, *Platinum Edition Using XHTML, XML, and Java 2* makes it easy for you to find the most effective means of accomplishing any task or presenting almost any kind of information on the Web.
2. Second, this book covers the major Web technologies—not only HTML, XHTML, XML, and Java, but also JavaScript, Microsoft's VBScript scripting language, CGI, and both Microsoft and Netscape's implementations of Dynamic HTML—in a depth and breadth that you won't find anywhere else. There is also a Web site that goes with the book, where you can find links to Web software, helpful documentation, and code from the examples in this book, at `www.mcp.com`.

With these goals in mind, how do you use this book?

If you are familiar with HTML and with setting up Web pages and Web sites, you can probably skim through the first chapter to see what some of the issues in page and site design are, and you can glance through the basic XHTML elements discussed in the other chapters in the first part of the book. If you are familiar with HTML, a lot of the information in this part will be new to you, as it discusses XHTML, the XML-compliant implementation of the HTML 4.0 standard. You can then read the advanced chapters on XHTML, as well as the sections on other Web technologies, such as JavaScript and Java, XML, ASP, CGI, and Dynamic HTML, to determine which of those elements you want to include in your Web pages.

Platinum Edition Using XHTML, XML, and Java 2 was written with the experienced HTML programmer in mind. Your experience might be limited to a simple Web home page you threw together, or you might be designing and programming professional Web sites. Either way, you will find comprehensive coverage of HTML and other Web technologies. Throughout the book, techniques are described for creating quality, effective Web pages and Web sites.

How This Book Is Organized

Part I: XHTML

Chapter 1, "Web Site and Web Page Design," discusses the issues concerning how to establish a consistent look-and-feel and how to organize your Web pages so they come together to form a coherent whole. It also gives you an overview of some of the issues that need to be considered when designing and laying out your Web pages.

Chapter 2, "Introduction to XHTML," lets you know just what XHTML is, why it is needed, and the differences between XHTML and HTML.

Chapter 3, "XHTML 1.0 Element Reference," gives you a quick reference to all the XHTML 1.0 elements in a format that is easy to understand and use.

Chapter 4, "Image Maps," shows how graphics can be used as image maps—graphic navigation aids formatted to enable the user to link to other URLs by clicking sections of the graphic. The chapter discusses both server-side and client-side image maps.

Chapter 5, "Advanced Graphics," talks about the basic XHTML elements used to include graphics in an XHTML document and discusses the graphics formats and display options supported. The chapter also discusses some of the many uses of graphics.

Chapter 6, "Tables," discusses the use of XHTML tables, both to present data and information in a tabular format and also to achieve greater control of the relative placement and alignment of XHTML text, images, and other objects.

Chapter 7, "Frames," shows you how to split the Web browser window into frames and how to use each frame to display a different XHTML document. Some of the potential uses of frames are also shown and discussed.

Chapter 8, "Forms," discusses XHTML forms—the primary way that user input and interactivity is currently supported in Web pages.

Chapter 9, "Style Sheets," takes a look at a recommended and increasingly popular formatting option available for use with XHTML: Cascading Style Sheets. Style sheets are a way of setting up a custom document template that gives the Web page author a great deal more control over how Web pages will look to those viewing the pages.

Part II: XML

Chapter 10, "Introducing XML," introduces you to XML (and its supporting technologies)—a new markup language that has the potential to provide increased capabilities for formatting information for the Web, the Internet, and beyond.

Chapter 11, "Creating XML Files for Use," describes the component parts of an XML document, so you can create well-formed and valid XML.

Chapter 12, "Parsing and Navigating XML—SAX, DOM, XPath, XPointer, and XLink," describes important technologies that allow you to navigate an XML document or manipulate its content.

Chapter 13, "Transforming XML—XSLT," discusses the important concept of transforming XML documents so that they can be used or displayed in a variety of contexts.

Chapter 14, "Constraining XML—DTDs and XML Schemas," explores the importance of ensuring that the structure of XML documents conforms to the desired format for a particular purpose.

Chapter 15, "Formatting and Displaying XML," shows you some simple techniques for displaying XML using Cascading Style Sheets or XSL Formatting Objects.

Chapter 16, "Exploiting XML—XML and e-Commerce," takes a look at how XML technologies can be used when exchanging data and information between businesses.

Chapter 17, "Moving Forward with XML," looks at some of the exciting XML-related technologies that are currently under development at the World Wide Web Consortium and looks at how you can develop the skills to use them to their full potential.

Part III: JavaScript

Chapter 18, "Introduction to JavaScripting," discusses Netscape's JavaScript Web browser scripting language and shows some ways to use it in a Web page.

Chapter 19, "The Document Object Model," discusses the object model included with Netscape Navigator and Microsoft Internet Explorer. That object model enables you to use scripting languages to interact with XHTML documents.

Chapter 20, "Manipulating Windows and Frames with JavaScript," shows you how to use JavaScript to create and use Web browser windows, dynamically generate XHTML documents, and manipulate and cross-communicate between multiple windows and frames.

Chapter 21, "Using JavaScript to Create Smart Forms," shows you how you can use JavaScript to pre-process information entered into XHTML forms and thus ensure that only valid data is submitted to the Web server.

Chapter 22, "Cookies and State Maintenance," shows you how to interface with and manipulate Web browser cookies with JavaScript. This enables you to remember information from one page to another in a Web site and across multiple visits to a Web site from a single user.

Chapter 23, "Using JavaScript to Control Web Browser Objects," shows you how you can use Netscape's LiveConnect and Microsoft's ActiveX technologies to access and manipulate Java applets, plug-in content, ActiveX Controls, and other objects through JavaScript.

Part IV: Dynamic HTML

Chapter 24, "Introduction to Dynamic HTML," introduces you to the Dynamic HTML implementations of Netscape and Microsoft—two very different ways of adding increased animation and interactivity to Web pages.

Chapter 25, "Advanced Microsoft Dynamic HTML," explores the set of Web technologies that Microsoft has dubbed Dynamic HTML, including extensions to Microsoft's Document Object Model and the use of ActiveX Controls and other Web browser objects to implement new capabilities to Microsoft's Web browser.

Chapter 26, "Advanced Netscape Dynamic HTML," goes into greater depth to show you more of Netscape's two versions of Dynamic HTML. The version of Dynamic HTML in pre-version

6 browsers centers around Netscape's use of manipulating style sheet attributes, the nonstandard <LAYER> element, and Netscape's downloadable font technology. For Navigator version 6, the focus is on implementing the W3C standard Document Object Model.

Chapter 27, "Cross-Browser Dynamic HTML," discusses the increasingly complex techniques required to create Dynamic HTML Web pages that can be successfully viewed using multiple versions of either Netscape Navigator or Microsoft Internet Explorer.

Part V: Server-Side Processing

Chapter 28, "Programming CGI Scripts," describes the basics of the Common Gateway Interface (CGI) and how you can use programs, scripts, and processes that can be run on the Web server with Web browsers.

Chapter 29, "Server-Side Includes," explains server-side includes (SSI)—what they are, how they are used, and some sample applications that show them in action.

Chapter 30, "Server-Side Security Issues," discusses in much greater depth the security issues involved with running and using server-side processing. The discussion also examines what to do with bad data and how to help ensure the safety of your server against malevolent attacks.

Chapter 31, "Survey of Web Databases," discusses some of the tools and utilities you can use to set up databases for access over the Web.

Chapter 32, "Writing Active Server Pages," discusses the Active Server Pages component of Microsoft's Internet Information Server Web server, and how you can use it to dynamically configure and tailor the output of your Web site according to the capabilities of your clients. It also discusses Microsoft's VBScript scripting language, which can be used with the ASP technology.

Chapter 33, "Using ColdFusion," covers Allaire's ColdFusion, a development tool for writing Web-based applications that communicate with server-side, ODBC-compliant databases.

Chapter 34, "Using PHP," discusses PHP, an XHTML-embedded scripting language used to allow Web developers to write dynamically generated pages quickly.

Part VI: Java 2

Chapter 35, "Introduction to Java," gives you an overview of the latest on Java and the technologies that support it. It includes a discussion of all the new features in Java, as well as security and performance enhancements.

Chapter 36, "Developing Java Applets," discusses the basics of designing, writing, and debugging Java applets by using a variety of software development tools.

Chapter 37, "User Input and Interactivity with Java," examines how you can use Java applets to add another way of soliciting user input and adding interactivity between Web pages and users.

Chapter 38, "Graphics and Animation," shows some of the graphics capabilities of Java and how you can use Java to create both static and dynamic images within a Web page.

Chapter 39, "Network Programming," explains how you can use Java sockets to interface Java applets with other sources of data and information anywhere on the Internet.

Chapter 40, "Security," explains some of the special security issues related to writing, providing, and running Java applets over the Web.

Chapter 41, "Server-Side Java," discusses the uses of server-side Java applets, called servlets, in providing greater interactivity and capabilities for Web pages and other applications.

Chapter 42, "Java and XML," talks about the different ways of interfacing Java and XML, and how the combination can be used for many different applications.

Part VII: Appendixes

Appendix A, "JavaScript Language Reference," provides a reference to the most useful properties, functions, and statements included in the JavaScript language.

Appendix B, "General Reference Resource," contains a list of links to Web resources where you can get more information on all the technologies discussed in this book.

Special Features in the Book

Que has more than a decade of experience in writing and developing the most successful computer books available. With that experience, Que has learned which special features help readers most. Look for the following special features throughout the book to enhance your learning experience.

Notes

Notes present interesting or useful information that isn't necessarily essential to the discussion. This secondary track of information enhances your understanding of the material being discussed, but you can safely skip Notes and not be in danger of missing crucial information. Notes look like the following:

NOTE Because XHTML 1.0 is HTML 4.01 with syntax rules enforced, any HTML 4.01-compliant browser should render your XHTML code without a problem. Such a browser might not validate your code to make sure that all the syntax rules are followed, though.

Tips

Tips present advice on quick or often overlooked procedures. These include shortcuts that save you time. A Tip looks like the following:

Using an asterisk (*) as the value of your ALT attribute gives users with nongraphical browsers a bulletlike character in front of each list item.

Cautions

Cautions warn you about potential problems that a procedure might cause, about unexpected results, and mistakes to avoid. Cautions look like the following:

CAUTION

Don't let an animation run indefinitely. An animation that's running constantly can be a distraction from the rest of the content on your page.

Cross References

Throughout the book, you will see references to other sections, chapters, and pages in the book. These cross references point you to related topics and discussions in other parts of the book and look like the following:

▶ For more information about the Web browser objects, **see** "Web Browser Object Model," **p. 461**

Other Features

In addition to the previous special features, several conventions are used in this book to make it easier to read and understand.

Typefaces This book uses the following typeface enhancements to indicate special text, as shown in the following table:

Typeface	Description
italic	Italic is used to indicate new terms.
`computer type`	This typeface is used for onscreen messages, commands, and code. It is also used to indicate text you type and locators in the online world.
`computer italic type`	This typeface is used to indicate placeholders in code and commands.

PART I

XHTML

CHAPTER 1

Web Site and Web Page Design

by Eric Ladd

In this chapter

The Many Facets of Web Design

Designing Web sites is a complex and rewarding activity. Hours of careful thought are needed at the planning stage. You must take the time to think about who will be reading your pages—how they see and understand information, what types of computers they use, what browser software they have, and how fast their connections are. After you have profiled your audience, you must then consider the message you want to communicate through the Web site and how best to convey that message to your target audience. Finally, you need to consider the possibilities and limitations of Web publishing to determine how you will actually create the site. Web site design is a constant struggle among these competing forces. As a designer, you must decide how you will meet the requirements of each one.

This chapter gives you some things to think about during the planning stages both for entire sites and for individual pages. After you have a good handle on site and page planning, you will be ready to move on to later chapters of the book which introduce you to Extensible Hypertext Markup Language (XHTML), the document description language used to author Web pages. With knowledge of XHTML and intelligent design, you can create sites that are accessible to the broadest audience possible and that effectively communicate what you have to say.

TIP Check out the Usenet `comp.infosystems.www.authoring` newsgroups to learn about design concepts, approaches, and philosophies used by other Web designers around the world.

Site Usability and Accessibility

For all the interesting and well-presented content on the Web, probably one hundred times as much is just plain wasteful. Remember that the World Wide Web was invented to foster sharing of information among scientists throughout the world. As more and more people graduated college and clamored to keep their Internet access, Internet service providers popped up to meet the demand. This eventually led to a Web that was more commercial in its purposes than academic.

As the masses continued to pour onto the Web, they began to demand authoring tools that were more like their word processors—programs that enabled them to make up a Web page as they would have it look and then write out the corresponding HTML code. This brought about two unfortunate consequences:

- **Gigabytes of meaningless content.** The sheer volume of meaningless content published to the Web helped to fuel the popularity of early Web sites such as Mirsky's Worst of the Web and the Official Useless WWW Pages List. Even today, users are graced with a Web site and accompanying book called *Web Pages That Suck*—a testament to the fact that there is still a lot of drivel out there on the Web.

- **Gigabytes of poorly designed content.** Because the authoring tools enabled *anyone* to publish *anything* to the Web, without regard for his or her background in design, a great deal of Web content—even the good stuff—is presented in an unintelligible way.

The preponderance of self-indulgent and ill-designed content brought about the necessity for a discipline called *Web usability.* A Web site's usability is a measure of how quickly it gets its message across to the average user, in terms of both download time and the time needed for the user to fully comprehend what is presented on the browser screen. Good usability requires that you simultaneously employ multiple design techniques to keep both of these times to a minimum. This chapter is filled with tips that can make your site more usable. To get you thinking about good usability, the next few sections summarize some of the findings from major usability studies. These ideas should be uppermost in your mind when you are designing an entire Web site or even just a single page within a site.

The Six to Eight Second Rule

Studies have shown that users have little patience with pages that take a long time to download. Specifically, if a download begins to run longer than six to eight seconds, it becomes very likely that the user will abort the download and move on to a different page. This means that it is imperative that you test all your pages to see how long they take to download and render—especially if a substantial fraction of your audience is using a dial-up connection.

The XHTML code for a page is usually not the culprit in a long download. Rather, it is the *dependencies* of the page—images, applets, and other page objects—that require the most time. Therefore, you should keep these to a minimum. You will invariably use some images on your pages, but they should be made as small as possible so that they do not adversely affect total download time.

▶ For tips on minimizing file sizes, **see** "Keeping File Sizes Small," **p. 185**

Web Users Don't Read—They Scan

You might spend hours writing a piece of content for your site, but a typical user only spends a few seconds scanning it. Only in very rare instances does a user read a page completely. This has a profound impact on how people should write for the Web. Specifically, writing for the Web should always make its main point first and then move on to provide more specifics. This way, users pick up a key idea early on in their scan and can then move on to find out more details if they are interested.

Another way you can optimize the scanability of your pages is to highlight key terms and ideas with boldface or italicized text. Alternatively, you can use headings, bulleted or numbered lists, or special indenting to draw attention to critical passages in your content (see Figure 1.1).

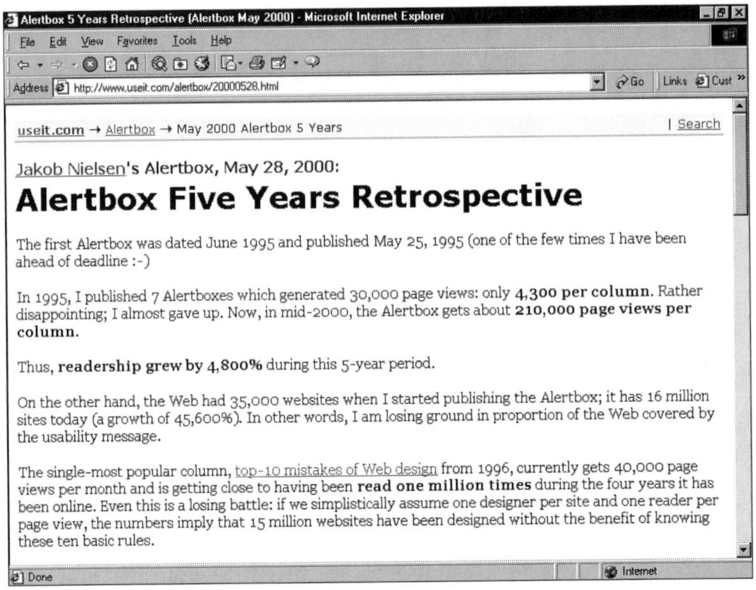

FIGURE 1.1
Usability guru Jakob Nielsen uses headings and boldface text to emphasize important information on his site.

Alertbox 5 Years Retrospective (Alertbox May 2000) - Microsoft Internet Explorer

File Edit View Favorites Tools Help

Address http://www.useit.com/alertbox/20000528.html

useit.com → Alertbox → May 2000 Alertbox 5 Years | Search

Jakob Nielsen's Alertbox, May 28, 2000:

Alertbox Five Years Retrospective

The first Alertbox was dated June 1995 and published May 25, 1995 (one of the few times I have been ahead of deadline :-)

In 1995, I published 7 Alertboxes which generated 30,000 page views: only **4,300 per column**. Rather disappointing; I almost gave up. Now, in mid-2000, the Alertbox gets about **210,000 page views per column**.

Thus, **readership grew by 4,800%** during this 5-year period.

On the other hand, the Web had 35,000 websites when I started publishing the Alertbox; it has 16 million sites today (a growth of 45,600%). In other words, I am losing ground in proportion of the Web covered by the usability message.

The single-most popular column, top-10 mistakes of Web design from 1996, currently gets 40,000 page views per month and is getting close to having been **read one million times** during the four years it has been online. Even this is a losing battle: if we simplistically assume one designer per site and one reader per page view, the numbers imply that 15 million websites have been designed without the benefit of knowing these ten basic rules.

Done Internet

Not All Users Have Visual Browsers

Those users who have good, or at least correctable, eyesight are often biased by their own browsing experience. They think that everyone else in the world has downloaded the latest browser and has a screen resolution of 800×600 pixels with 256 colors. What they forget—or maybe just don't realize—is that some users' browsers don't have a visual component at all. For example, a visually impaired individual might use a browser that synthesizes speech or writes its output to a Braille terminal. For this class of user, visual elements such as images, Flash animations, Java applets, and framed pages are meaningless.

The need to create content that is equally understandable on all types of browsers has given rise to a discipline called *accessibility*. Making your pages accessible is often as simple as taking advantage of the many XHTML elements and attributes that let you specify alternative content. For example, you can use the `<noframes>` element to specify content to be rendered by a browser that can't process a frameset. As you read through the chapters on XHTML, be on the lookout for elements and attributes you can use to optimize the accessibility of your pages.

NOTE The World Wide Web Consortium's Web Accessibility Initiative (WAI) seeks to ensure that all Web-based technologies and standards include features that make content accessible to persons with disabilities. You can read about the WAI at `http://www.w3.org/WAI/`.

Know Your Audience

Web site design should be driven by audience considerations. It doesn't matter how powerful a server you have, how skilled an ASP programmer you are, or how flashy your graphics are if your message is lost on the end user. If you retain just one concept from this chapter, let it be that you keep your audience uppermost in your mind during the design process.

Audience characteristics can fall into many categories. Because most sites must be designed to provide maximum audience appeal, this chapter looks at two broad, yet important, categories:

- **How will users move through the information?** A Web site is different from a single Web page in that a user can visit many major sections within a site. By developing an awareness of how people think about the information you're presenting, you can design a structure that is intuitive and that harnesses the natural associations your audience members are likely to make.
- **What technologies do your users have?** The primary reason that many sites avoid the high-end stuff, such as Java applets or ActiveX controls, is because end users don't have a sufficiently powerful machine, a sufficiently advanced browser, or a sufficiently fast connection to support them. With all the diversity in Web-surfing technology, you should take some time to learn about the tools your audience is using. This enables you to create a more accessible design.

How Will Users Move Through the Information?

You can't know how all your users think, but you can usually make some valid generalizations that can guide you during the design process. As you assess different cognitive characteristics of your audience, think about how you can use those characteristics to achieve the following design objectives:

- **Use association**—*Association* is a mental process in which one concept is paired with another. People in general are prone to making certain associations, whereas other associations might be particular to a specific user group. Identify the associations between informational items you think your audience will make. After you identify the associations, you can express them on your site through the use of hypertext links. A *hypertext link* is highlighted text on a page that, when clicked by the user, instructs the browser to load a new document. Presumably, the new document is related to the hypertext link that the user clicked to load it.
- **Use consistency**—A consistent approach to the many aspects of your site—look and feel, navigation, presentation of information, and so on—reduces the amount of mental effort the user must make to get around. Introduce your approaches to these things as early as you can and carry it through the entire site. Figure 1.2 shows a site that uses a very consistent look that keeps the reader focused on each page's content.

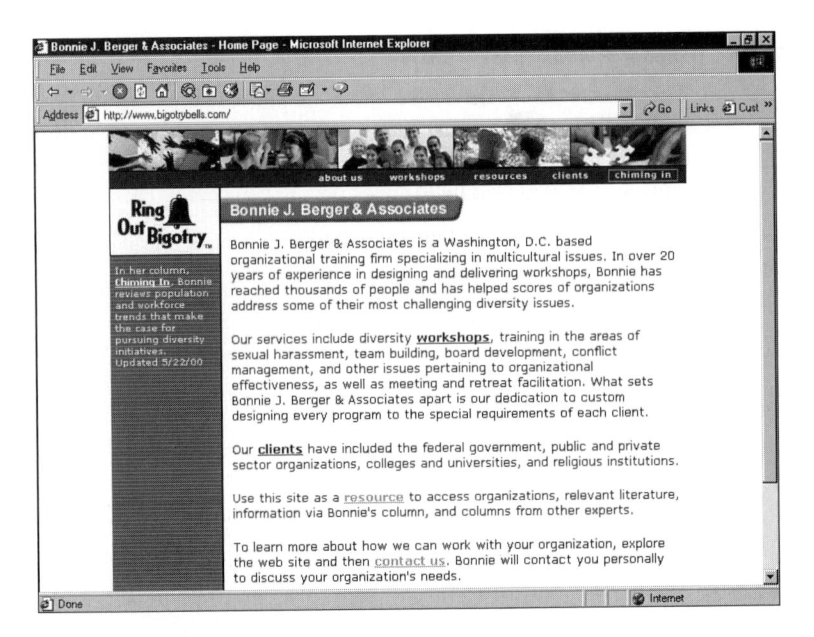

FIGURE 1.2
Bonnie Berger's bigotrybells.com Web site makes strong use of consistency.

- **Use context**—Provide users with a context to which they can relate. Make sure they know where they are and can get to all the important sections of your site from any other section (see Figure 1.3). This is critical because you can never predict on which page a user will enter your site. If you provide context only on the home page, users entering the site at a subordinate page will be unaware of the available options.

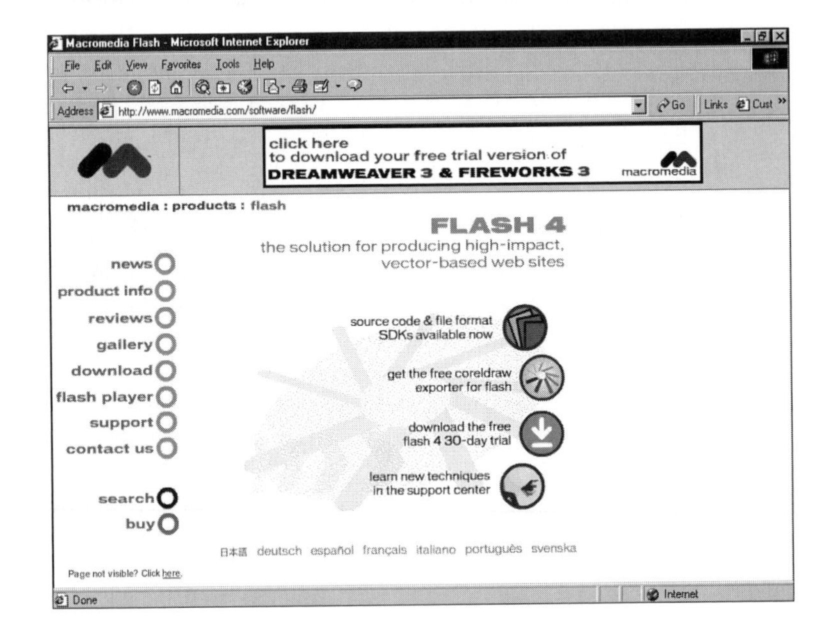

FIGURE 1.3
Macromedia's Web site always provides you with a set of context links–(macromedia: products: flash)–that indicate where you are within the structure of the site.

What Technologies Do Your Users Have?

The equipment your audience has access to is another key characteristic you must assess. Thankfully, XHTML is platform independent, and so the type of machines your audience is using should be largely irrelevant. As long as your audience can run some type of browser program, they should be able to view your pages.

Other technology concerns influence design decisions, as well. These include

- **Monitor**—Because the Web is largely a visual medium, it helps to know for which monitors you are designing. If you are not certain, it is a safe bet to design to a lower-end standard: a 14-inch monitor, set at 640×480 pixels, with a standard 256-color palette. Remember that not everyone has the sophisticated monitors that many designers have, although more and more users tend to have monitors set at 800×600 pixel resolution.

NOTE Lynda Weinman explains the notion of the "browser safe" color palette on her Web site at `http://www.lynda.com/hex.html`. The palette comprises colors that will be rendered the same way on Macintosh and Windows platforms, so you'll have an assurance that all users will see the exact same thing.

- **Browser software**—Netscape Navigator and Microsoft Internet Explorer support all the elements in XHTML, but not every browser does. Some browsers, such as Lynx, are text only, which means users won't be able to see your graphics. Additionally, a good number of your users will be visiting your site from America Online (AOL), CompuServe, Prodigy, or some other online service. Each service's browser has its own quirks that you must consider when designing; AOL's browser could not process the HTML tables for the longest time, for example, so AOL users missed out on some attractive layouts that used tables.

  Visually impaired users might be using Braille- or speech-based browsers, which means that all your visible content is lost on them unless you provide text alternatives for graphics, Flash animations, and other embedded content. The World Wide Web Consortium has expanded the accessibility of many XHTML constructs for users with speech-based browsers. Many of the newer XHTML form elements, for example, were driven by the need for forms to be more usable by the blind or visually impaired.

  Remember that if you design to a higher-end graphical browser, you need to make alternative content available to people using less-capable browsers as well.

- **Helper applications and plug-ins**—Even though many of today's browsers are incredibly powerful, they can't do it all alone. Audio clips, video clips, multimedia content, and some image formats require the use of a separate viewer program (a helper application) or a program that works with the browser to display content inline (a plug-in). Before you load up your site with these elements, make sure your audience has (or at least has access to) the additional software needed to view them.

TIP Many sites notify users of which combinations of browser software and plug-ins the site is best viewed. Many of these notices also include links to pages where you can download the software (see Figure 1.4). This is a helpful service that can maximize a user's experience when visiting your site.

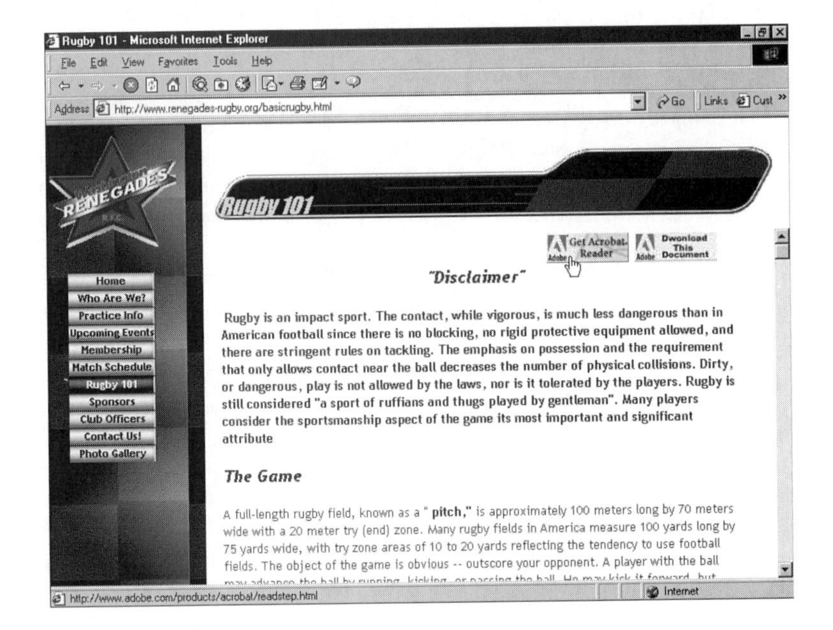

FIGURE 1.4
Providing a link to a supporting program or plug-in is an important user service.

- **Connection speed**—Some designers put together pages on a local drive and browse the pages directly on the same machine. Other designers port finished pages to a server and view them over a high-speed connection. Neither type of designer will appreciate the exasperation of having to wait for a page to download over a 28.8Kbps modem. Consider the types of connections your users might have and design appropriately. This might compel you to scale back on multimedia content and perhaps even some graphics content as well. Another way you can show respect for those with slower connections is to make available versions of your pages that are largely text, with minimal or no graphics.

NOTE More and more Web page authoring programs come with tools that estimate how long it will take a given page to download. The FrontPage Editor, for example, can display an estimated download time over a 28.8Kbps connection for whatever page you are editing. This time displays near the bottom right of the Editor window along the status bar.

Allaire's HomeSite includes a Document Weight function that computes estimated download times for 14.4Kbps, 28.8Kbps, and 57.6Kbps connections.

Set up separate links to large multimedia items and indicate the file size somewhere close to the link (see Figure 1.5). This enables users to decide whether they want to download the file.

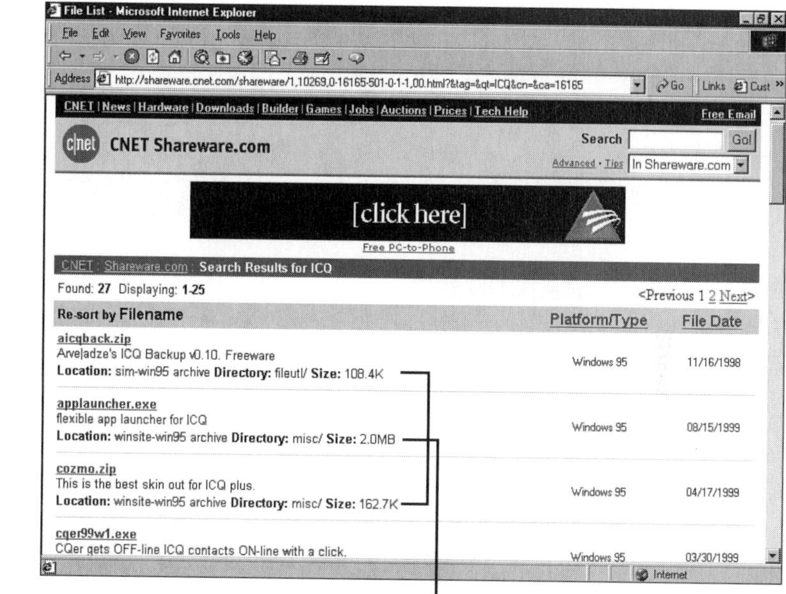

FIGURE 1.5
Shareware.com lets you know the size of a file so you can make a decision about downloading it.

Considering Your Own Objectives

It is possible to spend so much time assessing audience factors that you can forget your reasons for wanting to create a Web site. User considerations are of paramount importance, but during the design process, you should not lose sight of your own motivations.

When planning your site, you should compose a mission statement, requirements document, or list of objectives that articulates why you want to create a Web site. This statement or list is another factor that should contribute to the site's design.

Use your mission statement or objective list to ground yourself during the design process. Keep checking your design against your reasons for designing the site in the first place. By balancing end-user considerations with your own objectives, you will produce a site that has broad appeal and that helps you attain your communications goals.

TIP Post your mission statement, requirements summary, or objective list in a public place on a whiteboard or on newsprint so that you and your design team (if you have one) can always be reminded of why you're doing what you're doing.

Structuring Information

Audience characteristics and your own objectives for creating a site are the human factors that go into Web-site design. As you begin to focus on the site itself, you will discover that two other factors are vying for a visitor's attention: the information you're presenting and the "look and feel" of the site. Just as you had to strike a balance between audience characteristics and your objectives, you must do the same for these site-related factors.

Two approaches for structuring content have emerged during the Web's short history: the drill-down structure (also known as the layered structure) and the flat structure. Additionally, the advent of JavaScript gives you the option to present information in multiple browser windows. Each of these approaches is considered in the next few sections.

The Drill-Down Structure

Most early Web sites used the drill-down structure. A *drill-down structure* means that the information in the site is layered several levels beneath the home page of the site, and users must drill down through those layers to see it. The idea is much like having to navigate down through several folders and subfolders to find a desired file in Windows 98 or Macintosh (or down through several directories and subdirectories to find a desired file in DOS or in a UNIX system). AltaVista's Directory uses this structure on its site (see Figure 1.6). The drilling down occurs as you move from general to specific topics.

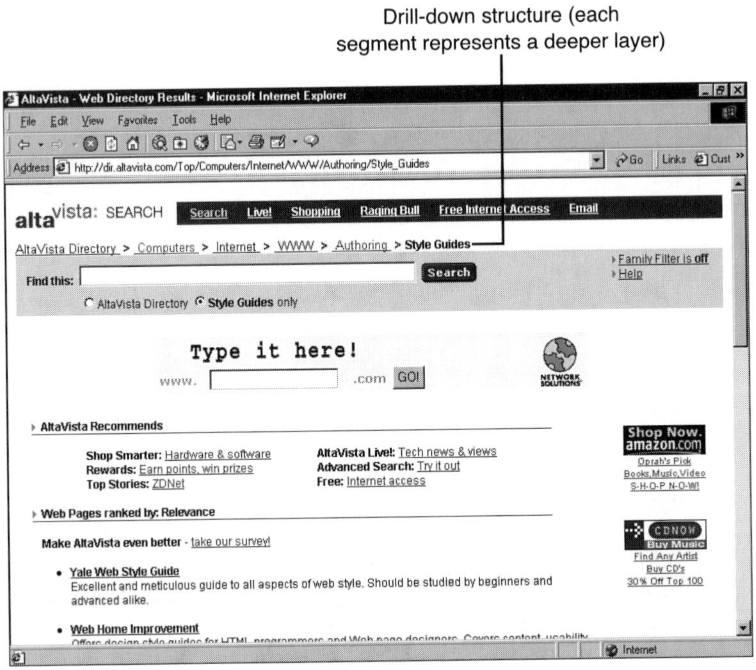

Drill-down structure (each segment represents a deeper layer)

FIGURE 1.6
You drill down through several more general topics as you key in on a specific topic in AltaVista's directory.

NOTE One advantage of the drill-down approach for site administrators is that they can interpret the number of levels a visitor drills down through as a measure of the visitor's interest in the site's content.

The drill-down approach provided a systematic way to structure content on early sites, but users quickly grew tired of plowing through so many levels to get the information they wanted and then navigating back up through the levels to move on to another part of the site. User feedback about so much layering led designers to consider different techniques. The flat structure emerged from these deliberations.

The Flat Structure

The flat structure isn't so much a structure of its own as it is a lessening of the drill-down approach. Every site will probably have one or two levels of drill down (from the home page to any subordinate page, for example), but you can minimize the number of layers so that fewer barriers exist between users and the information they want. There are two ways to do this:

- Limit the number of subdirectories you use. You are more likely to end up with a drill-down structure if you use a lot of subdirectories (or subfolders) on your server to store and organize your XHTML documents. Try to keep your documents up as close to the root level as you can.

TIP Draw out a map of your site hierarchy in outline form and try to identify places in which you can reduce the number of information layers.

- Increase navigation options. Give users access to as much as possible on every page. Figure 1.7 shows the Home Depot home page, which makes available a list of links to all major areas of the site in the form of tabs across the top of the page.

Using Multiple Browser Windows

JavaScript enables a Web developer to pop open new browser instances and populate the new browser windows with content. Although this might seem a compelling thing to do, it can become taxing on both the user (multiple windows competing for the user's attention) and the user's system (each new browser instance consumes resources on the user's computer). Thus, you should avoid gratuitous use of multiple browser windows in an effort to keep your site as intelligible as possible.

There are some instances in which use of a second browser window can be helpful, however. For example, in a Web-based learning setting, you can provide a feedback window to the user based on a specific choice he makes (see Figure 1.8). Additionally, in a Web-based application that supports a particular business process, you can pop open a new window to collect additional information from the user depending on what path he takes through the process. In either case, you should close the pop-up window after the user is done working with the content in it. This can be done in response to an action within the pop-up window (for example, the submission of a form) or by providing the user with a link or a button that can be clicked to close the window.

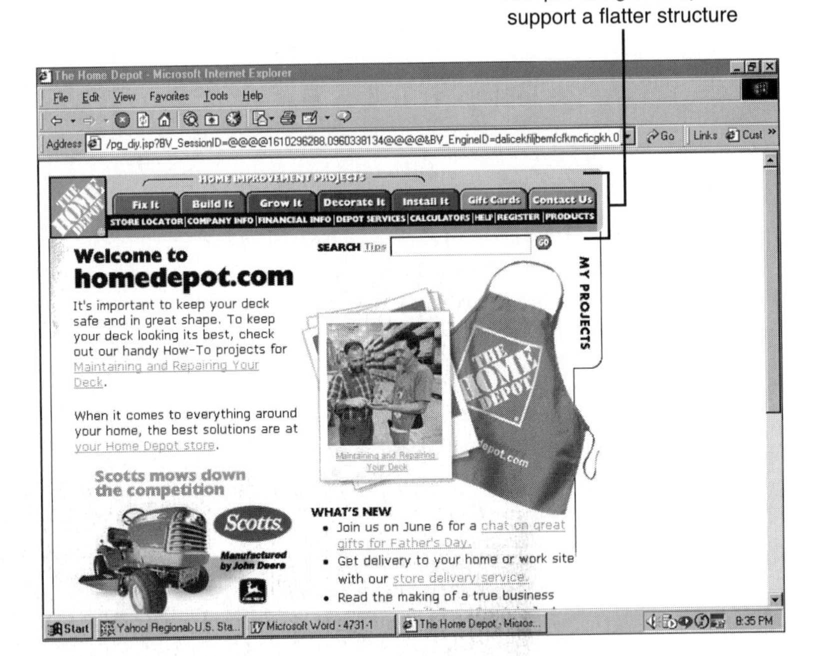

FIGURE 1.7
Providing several navigation options helps visitors avoid having to drill through several layers to get the information they want.

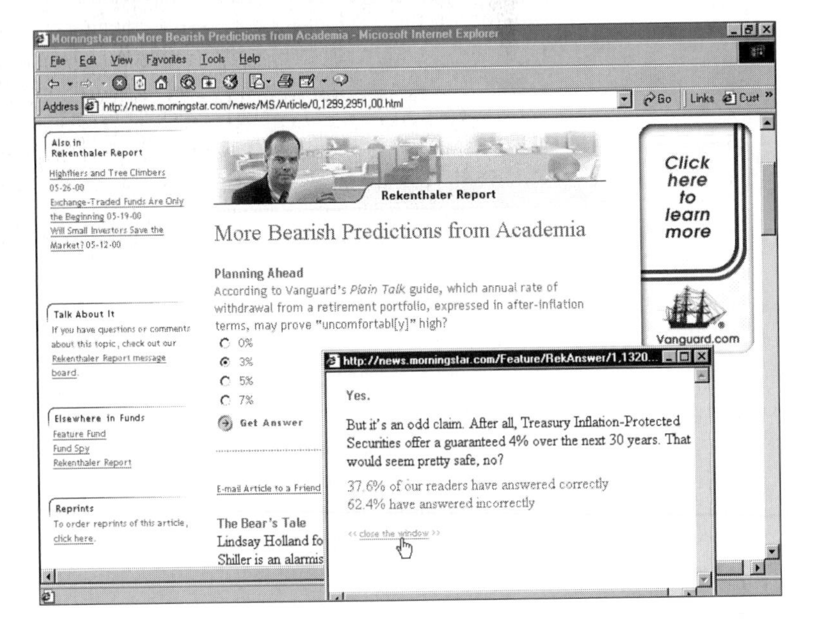

FIGURE 1.8
You get feedback on your answer to a multiple choice question on Morningstar's site in a pop-up browser window.

NOTE You can also pop open a new browser window by using the `"target=_blank"` attribute in an <a> element.

Page Design Follows Site Design

Many of the notions that go into designing a Web site also go into the design of a single Web page, but some page design considerations are unique. Ideally, page design should follow site design; when you get ready to start a page, you should already have a good sense of what the page needs to accomplish, given its place in your site design.

A book the size of this one could be written about all the issues involved in designing a quality Web page. This chapter summarizes only the major concepts and elements of a good design. By looking at the work of others and doing design work yourself, you'll build up good design sense and the skills you need to implement a first-rate Web site.

The cardinal rule for Web site design is also the cardinal rule for page design. Knowing your audience and designing to that audience requires you to gather as much information about them as possible, including

- Equipment configuration (hardware, software, and Internet connection)
- Learning characteristics (how to best present information so they understand it)
- Motivations for surfing the Web (business, professional, personal, entertainment, or educational reasons)
- Demographic factors (age, amount of education, geographic location, language)
- Cultural characteristics (any other factors that could influence how they read a page)

Gather all this information before you start designing pages. As with all things, finding out as much as you can beforehand will save you a lot of headaches later.

In addition to gathering as many user characteristics as you can, you should keep in mind the following two things that are common to all users:

- They are visiting your pages because they are interested in the information you have provided.
- They are using some type of Web browser to visit your site.

NOTE Unless you have the luxury of developing for a homogeneous group of people, you will probably have to design your pages to be accessible to the broadest audience possible. In the absence of proper information about your audience, designing for maximum readability is the best rule.

Corporate Intranets: Designing for a Homogenous Group

If you are working on an intranet page for your company, one thing you can typically take advantage of is a common platform. Many companies that put up intranets get a site license for their browser of choice. After you know that everyone is using the same browser, you can design to that browser's level of performance. If your intranet users are using Netscape Navigator, for example, you can design pages with frames, client-side image maps, Java applets, and the `<layer>` tag (a Netscape extension to standard HTML). If everyone is using Internet Explorer 4, however, you could use one of the Microsoft proprietary tags such as `<marquee>`. Additionally, everyone is most likely running the software on the same platform with the same connection speed, so you can design to those parameters as well.

Another advantage you can harness in a corporate intranet design situation is a common culture. Most firms have a way of doing things that can be captured on the intranet pages. This gives the pages a context to which all your users can relate.

Some cautions go along with intranet design, however. First, you should make your intranet site sufficiently different from your external Web site so that employees can quickly tell the difference between the two. Additionally, because intranets tend to support people in their work, your intranet design should be as task oriented as possible. Many firms make the mistake of using their internal organizational structure as a basis for their intranet information design, but this doesn't provide the best service to the intranet users.

Designing for an audience whose members are more or less the same is a luxury that few people get to experience. If you find yourself in this situation, be sure to make full use of the characteristics common to your users.

Developing a Look

A sharp graphical look is important for your site. Often it's the graphics that hook visitors and influence them to stop and read your content. A consistent look also provides a unique identity for the site.

In general, when you develop a look and feel for your site, make sure it enhances the delivery of your message without overpowering it. A well-done look and feel initially draws in users and then fades into the background as the users move around within the site. If you throw in too much glitz, you run the risk of detracting from your real message.

The next four sections share some other design ideologies to keep in mind as you develop a look and feel for your site.

Less Is Often More The fact that browsers can display images does not justify heaping a bunch of them on all your pages to create a high-impact look. Don't forget that some users have text-only browsers, and others have slow connections. These people will not have the ability or the patience to view a site that relies heavily on a lot of graphics for its look.

Try to keep the number of graphics you use to a minimum. Graphics for logos and navigation are almost essential, but beyond that, give careful consideration to the images you put in your pages. Make sure they add value to the site by enhancing the presentation of your content.

> **TIP** After you decide on a set of images to use, continue to use the same images throughout the site. This helps promote a consistent look. Additionally, after the images are stored in users' caches, users spend less time waiting for pages to download.

Backgrounds A good background should stay there—in the background. If a background is so obtrusive that it interferes with presentation of content in the foreground, you are less likely to get your message across.

Many sites these days have gone to a plain white background. Although this might seem rather ordinary, it supports a clean and professional look that many users appreciate, and it keeps download times to a minimum (see Figure 1.9).

FIGURE 1.9
Lycos employs a plain white background that does not obstruct the content in the foreground.

XHTML supports the use of other colors as backgrounds. If you choose a color other than white, make sure sufficient contrast exists between the background color and all elements in the foreground. If you change the background color to black, for example, you also need to change the color of your body text. If you don't, you will have black text on a black background and your content will be invisible!

You can also use images in the background (see Figure 1.10). Background images are read in and tiled to fill the entire browser window. Again, the critical thing is that the background image does not intrude on the content in the foreground. Additionally, you should design your image so that it tiles seamlessly. Being able to see the boundaries where the tiling occurs can distract users from the information you want them to see.

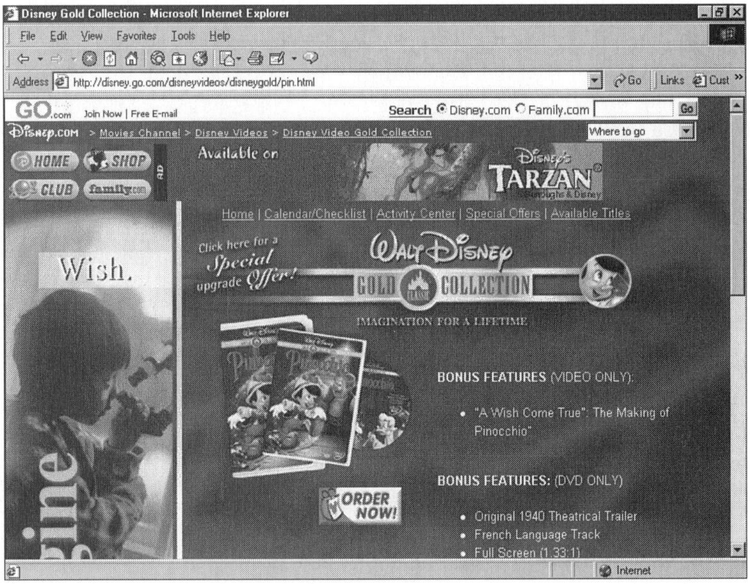

FIGURE 1.10
Disney.com uses an image to provide a textured backdrop for its Gold video series.

> **TIP** You can use a background color and background image simultaneously on your pages; the color you use should be the same as the dominant color in the image. The background color is rendered immediately by the browser, and then the background image is placed and tiled after the image is read in. This way, if a delay occurs in downloading the image, you still have a colored background that approximates the color scheme of the image. After the image has transferred, its appearance onscreen should not be too distracting because of the close match between it and the background color.

Color Choices XHTML provides control over other page colors, too. Controlling background and body text color was mentioned in the preceding section. You can control the color of three types of hypertext links as well: unvisited, visited, and active (a link is active only for the instant that the user clicks it). Choose colors for all three types that contrast well with the background color or image. Beyond that, it is a good visitor service to color visited links a different color from unvisited links because this provides a visual cue as to where users have been in the site.

> **TIP** Hypertext link colors are a nice way to work in your company's color scheme if you're designing for a corporate site. Painting link colors in this way subtly promotes corporate identity throughout the site.

Iconography: Is It Intuitive? Many designers choose to represent major sections of a site with *icons*, small images that are meant to convey what type of content is found in each section. Yahoo!'s main site uses icons for the navigation bar at the top of the home page (see Figure 1.11).

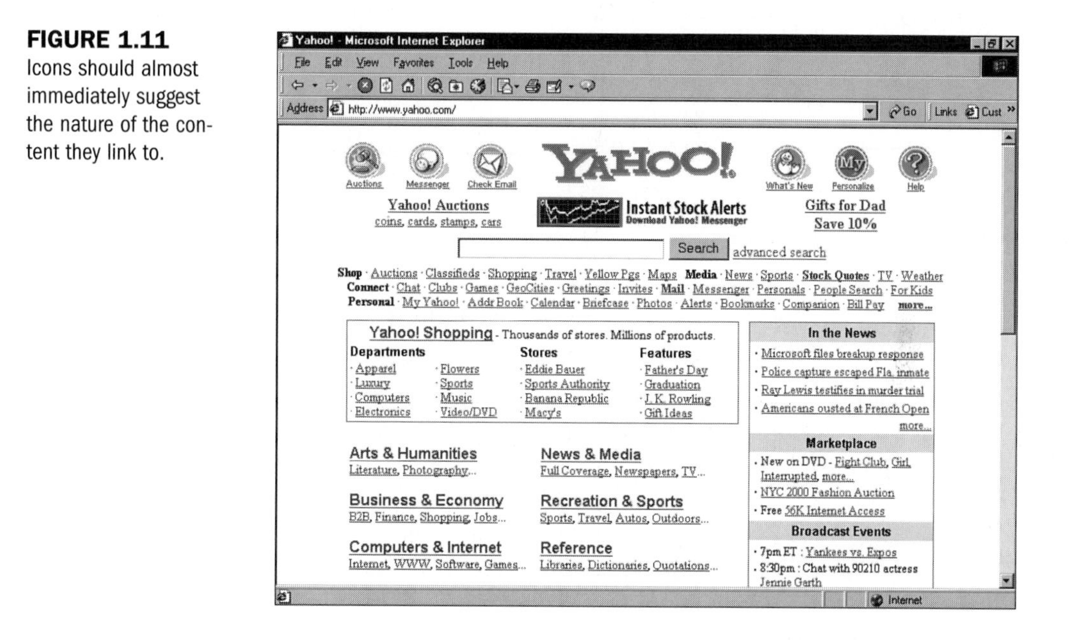

FIGURE 1.11
Icons should almost immediately suggest the nature of the content they link to.

The critical test that icons must pass is the intuitiveness test. Because you are using a small image to communicate a possibly complicated idea, you need to make sure that users can make a quick association between the image and the idea. The best way to do this is to test the icons with potential users. Get some people together who know nothing about the site you're designing and show them your icons. As they see each icon, ask them to write down what Web site information or functionality might be associated with it. After you have gathered their responses, share the icons with them again, this time giving the significance of each icon. Ask for their feedback on whether they think the icon truly represents what you want it to. By combining user responses from the first viewing with feedback from the second viewing, you should be able to make a good assessment of how intuitive your icons are.

Using Prepackaged Graphical Themes

Just because you might not have a dedicated graphic artist to help you come up with a visual identity, you are not necessarily resigned to having a bland site. Many ready-to-use sets of images are available that you can download and use freely in your design.

Perhaps the easiest set of prepackaged themes to use comes as part of the FrontPage Editor. You can choose from one of seven themes, previewing them all in the Themes dialog box. Each theme includes banner, background, button, bullet, horizontal rule, and navigation images, as well as specs to set up heading and body text styles.

If you have a little graphics expertise, it would be a simple matter to import any of the graphics in the theme into a capable graphics program, such as Photoshop or Paint Shop Pro, and customize them for your site. You might, for example, add your company's name to the banner image so that it's always visible to the reader.

If you are having trouble coming up with a look and feel for your site, experiment with a prepackaged theme from one of the many programs such as FrontPage or Microsoft Word that make them available. It's an easy way to put an attractive face on your site with a minimal amount of effort.

Desirable Page Elements

As users traverse the Web, they become accustomed to seeing certain items on pages. They come to rely on these items being present to enhance their Web browsing experience. This section looks at a few common page elements that are also good end-user services.

Search Engines Indexing your site to make it searchable is a great way to make any part of your site available without a lot of drill down. Figure 1.12 shows the AOL home page, which includes a Search field. Many such pages are as simple as the one input field you see in the figure.

Outfitting your site with a search engine may be easier than you think. Some search-engine programs, such as ICE, are publicly available and fairly painless to install. Major server programs, such as Netscape Enterprise Server and Microsoft Internet Information Server, are coming bundled with search-engine software.

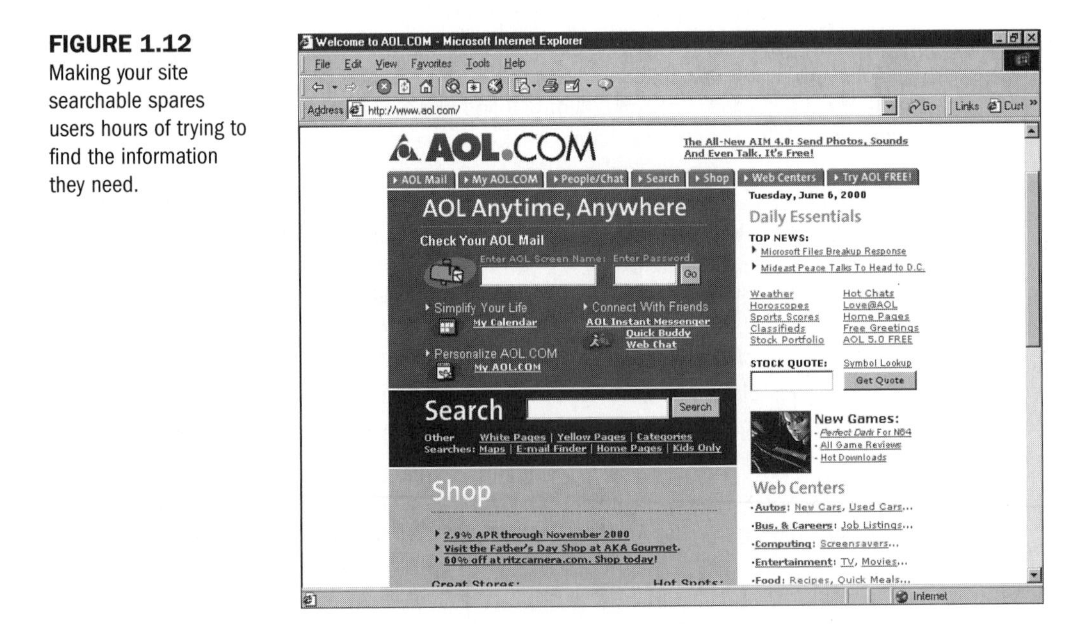

FIGURE 1.12
Making your site searchable spares users hours of trying to find the information they need.

Navigation Tools Navigation tools on your pages will help keep users from getting that frustrating "you can't get there from here" feeling. Depending on where users are, they will have different expectations about which navigation tools should be available.

A visitor hitting the home page of a site will most likely be looking for some type of clickable image or image map that can take her to the major subsections of the site (see Figure 1.13). A well-designed home page will also include a set of hypertext links that duplicate the links on the image map. This enables people with text-only browsers, or people with image loading turned off, to navigate from the home page as well.

▶ To learn how to create image maps, **see** Chapter 4, "Image Maps"

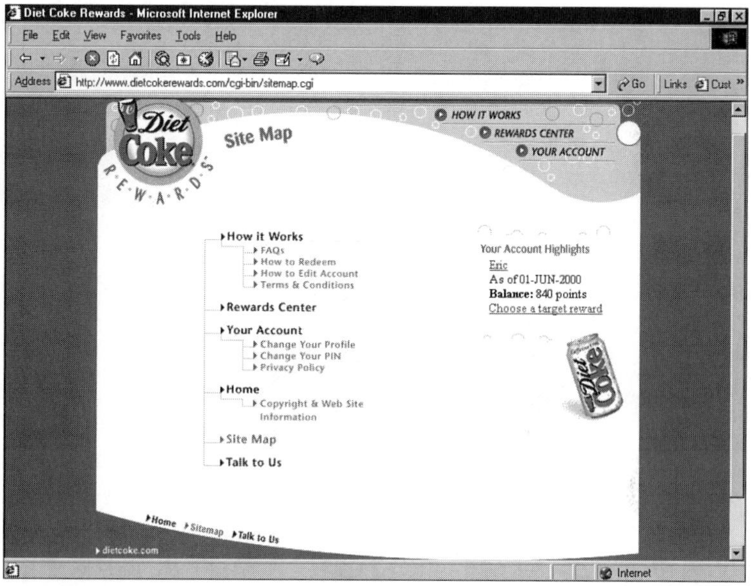

FIGURE 1.13
The site map on the dietcokerewards.com site uses an image map.

When on an inside page of a site, users typically look for navigation bars either at the top or bottom of the page (see Figure 1.14). Some pages have navigation bars at both the top and bottom so the user has the option of using the closest one. In other cases, a page will have a set of links across the top of the page that points to the major areas of the site, and another set along the bottom of the page that points to functional areas.

TIP Try to keep your navigation links as close to the top of the page as you can. This enhances usability by eliminating the need for the user to scroll to find your links.

Last Updated Date Everyone craves fresh content, so it makes sense to have some kind of "freshness dating" on your pages. A last-updated date tells visitors how recently the information on a page has changed (see Figure 1.15). Assuming they remember the last time they visited your page, regular visitors can use the last-updated date to decide whether any new content exists that they need to check out.

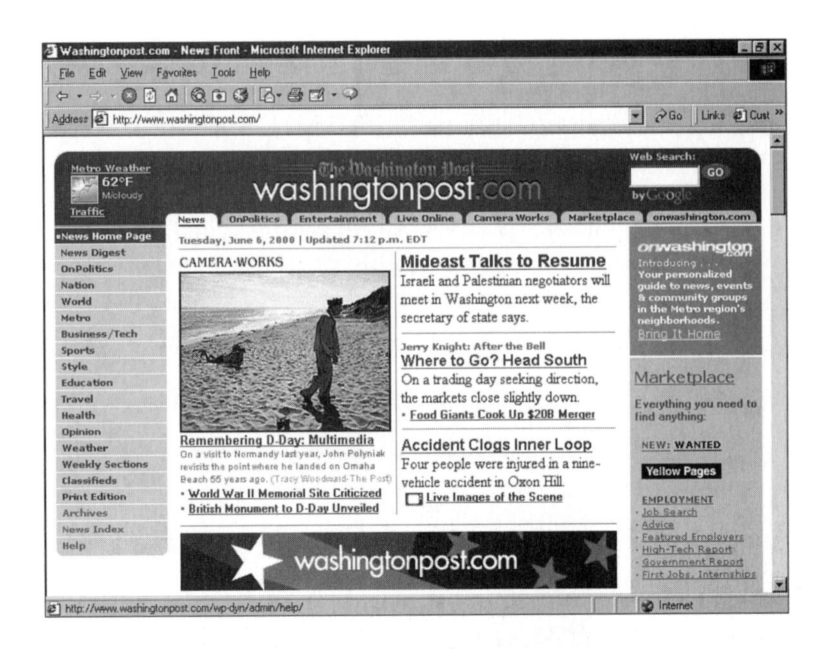

FIGURE 1.14
Washingtonpost.com provides links along the top and down the left side of its home page.

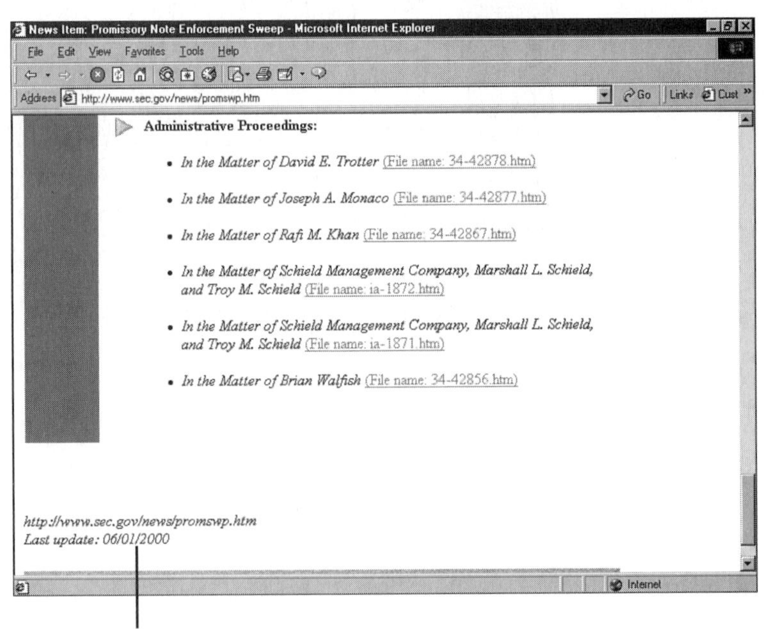

FIGURE 1.15
The Securities and Exchange Commission puts last updated information on all its pages.

TIP Server-side includes are another good way to have the server automatically stamp your pages with last-updated dates. See Chapter 29, "Server-Side Includes," for more information.

CAUTION

Having a last-updated date can create image problems for you if you don't keep refreshing your pages. Users will be unimpressed if they see a last-updated date of six months ago!

Contact Information User feedback is important to your efforts to maintain and improve your pages. Many Web pages have contact information at the bottom, typically the email address of the Webmaster or the page author. Others take you to a separate page to collect feedback (see Figure 1.16). These email addresses are often hyperlinked, so users can click them and compose a feedback message.

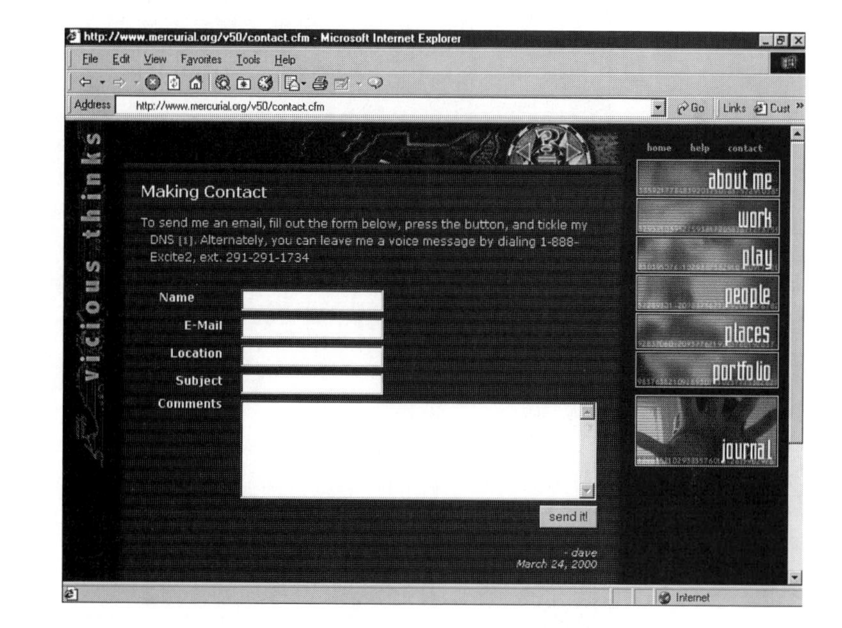

FIGURE 1.16
A feedback form puts you in direct contact with mercurial.org's Webmaster.

NOTE Include your email address directly in the hyperlink so visitors can just click to send mail. That way, if someone is seeing a printout of the page only, she still knows where to send the feedback.

Counters Some people think counters, which are graphical displays of the number of people who have visited a page (see Figure 1.17), are annoying. Counters can be annoying if they are used in a grandstanding or self-indulgent way. Indeed, sites that emblazon themselves with counters featured prominently on every page are often viewed as amateurish.

Counters can be a useful service, however, if they are built into pages in an unobtrusive fashion. Used properly, they are helpful to

- Users, who can get a sense of how many other people are interested in the content on the page.

- Page authors, who can better track the traffic on their pages when HTTP log analysis software is not available.

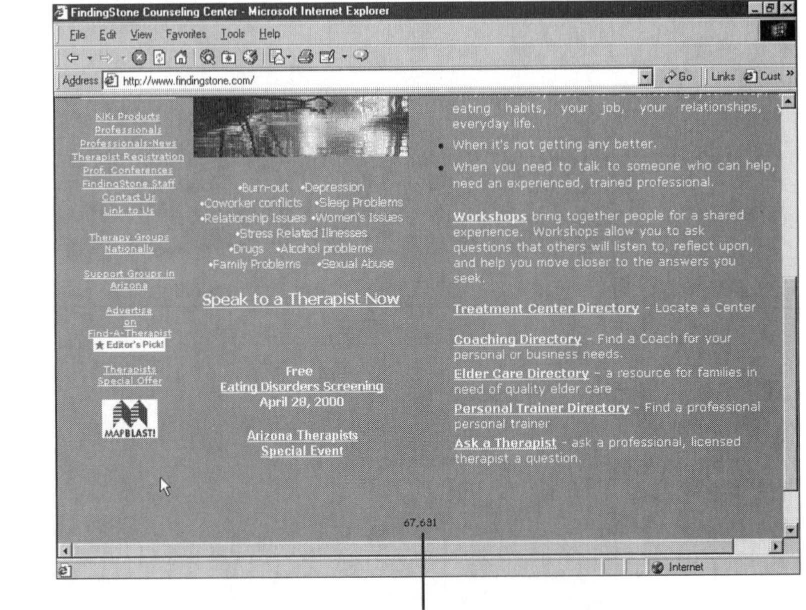

FIGURE 1.17
A discreet counter at the bottom of a page tells a Webmaster about the amount of traffic coming to a site while not detracting from other content.

You can place a counter on a page in two ways. One approach involves programming the counter yourself. This is a fairly straightforward thing to do, but your Web page server must support common gateway interface (CGI) programs. If you want to avoid programming altogether, you can drop the FrontPage Hit Counter Component or a similar preprogrammed object onto your page and let it do all the work for you.

▶ To learn how to create a hit counter using server-side includes, **see** "HitCount," **p. 773**

If you don't have CGI support on your server, you can use one of the online counter services. Figure 1.18 shows you the counter service at `http://www.sitemeter.com/`. The service won't cost you anything, but Site Meter will place an advertising graphic on your page along with the hit count.

CAUTION

When you use an online counter service, the images that make up the counter display must be transferred from your host service. This can delay page loading and make visitors to your Web pages impatient.

Also, don't put a counter on every page you create. Usually a counter on the home page of a site is sufficient. If you need information on subordinate pages of your site, use an HTTP access log analysis tool such as WebTrends (see Figure 1.19) to gather the information you require.

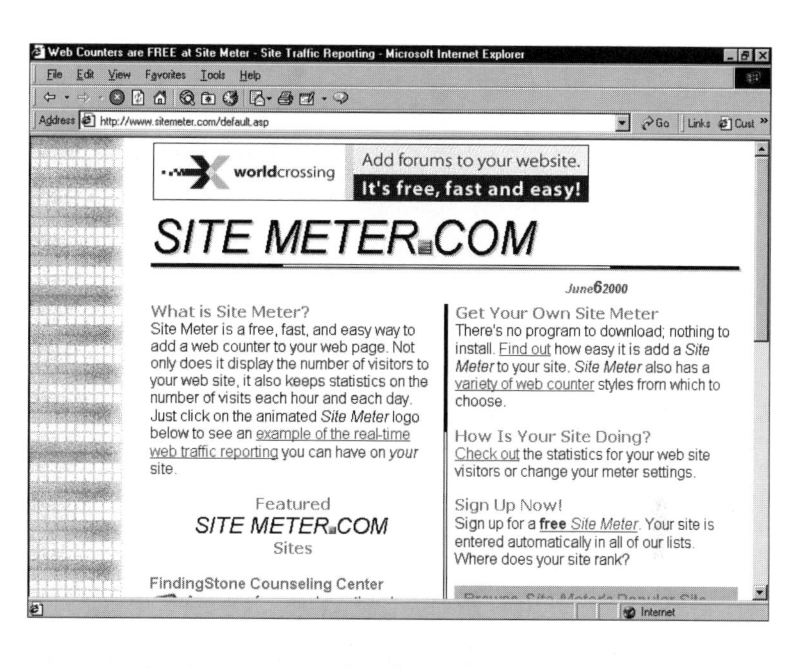

FIGURE 1.18
Sitemeter.com is an online service that provides page counters to sites otherwise unable to implement them.

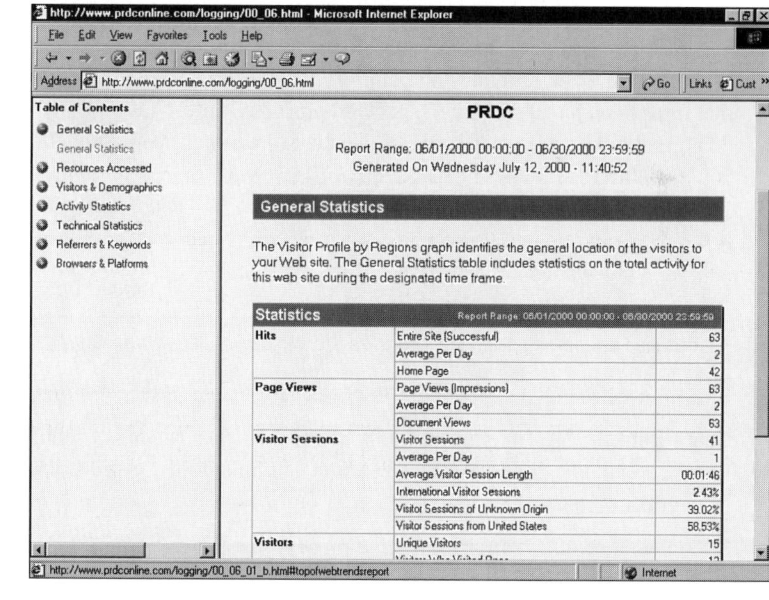

FIGURE 1.19
WebTrends provides thorough reports on Web site traffic in a highly readable report.

What's New People who visit your site frequently will appreciate a What's New section so they can quickly find out what has changed since their last visit (see Figure 1.20). This spares them from having to go through the whole site to discover new content.

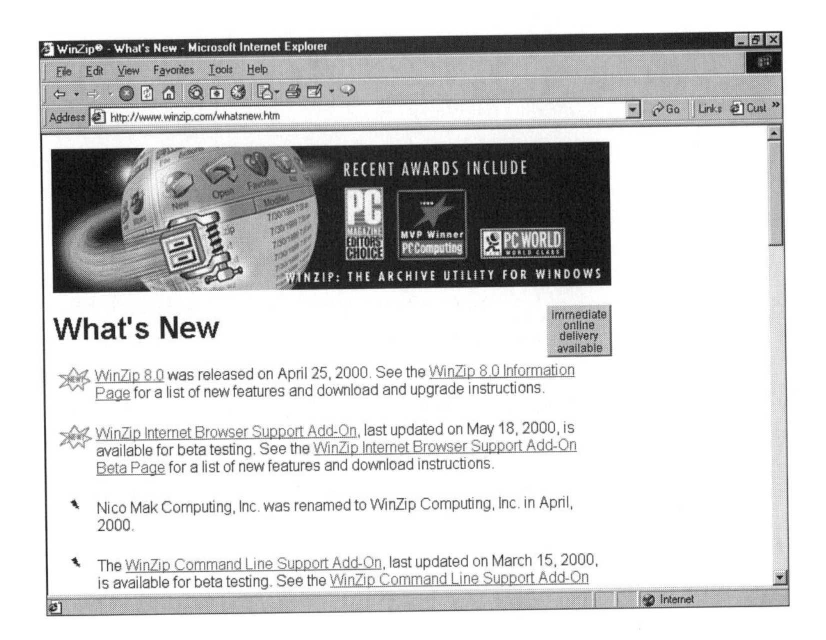

FIGURE 1.20
You can find out what's new with the popular program WinZip from the What's New page at winzip.com.

You can maintain your What's New section manually, or you can have it generated on-the-fly by your Web server by using publicly available common gateway interface (CGI) scripts. These scripts check the files on your site for their last changed dates and display a list of files that have been altered within a specified period of time. The pages generated by these scripts don't tend to be very descriptive, so it's best to maintain your What's New section manually if you have the resources.

NOTE Make sure you include a date with each item on your What's New page so visitors know just how new the information is.

TIP You can also use software such as NetMind's URL Minder to dispatch an email to visitors when something on your site changes.

Guest Books Sign in, please! Guest books provide a record of visitors to the site. Signing the guest book is almost always voluntary, but links to the guest book page from the home page encourage visitors to sign.

▶ To learn how to create an XHTML form, **see** Chapter 8, "Forms"

A guest book uses an XHTML form to gather information about the visitor and then archives the information on the server. Try to keep your guest book form short. Users who are willing to sign might change their minds if they see that they have to fill out an extensive form.

TIP You can use name and address information from your guest book to compile a mailing list for targeted marketing campaigns for your business.

Feedback Mechanism You should always be gathering feedback on your site so you can build on it and improve it. Putting a feedback mechanism on your site is a great way to collect opinions from people as they visit.

Feedback mechanisms can take two forms. A simple way to support user feedback is to place an email hypertext link on your pages. By clicking the link, users open a mail window in their browsers where they can compose and send a feedback message to you.

The second approach is to create an XHTML form that asks specific questions (see Figure 1.21). This requires a bit more effort than setting up an email link, but it does provide the advantage of gathering responses to a standard set of questions.

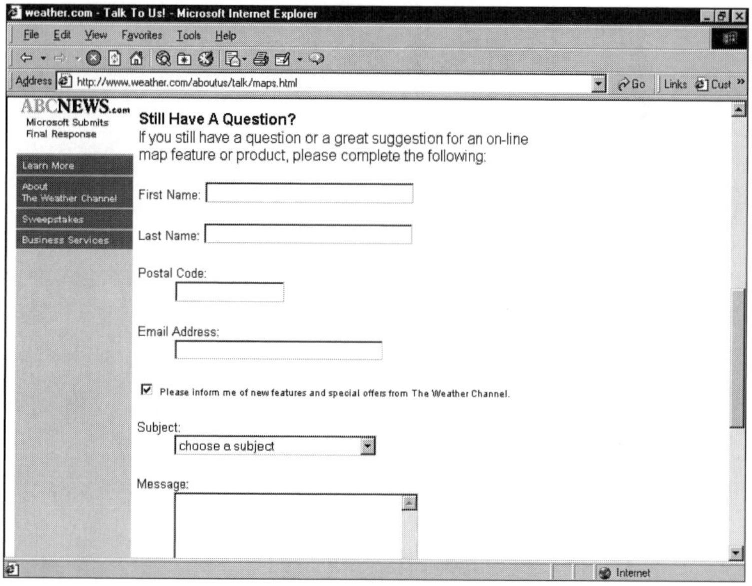

FIGURE 1.21
The Weather Channel seeks feedback on its site through an extensive Web form.

Mailing Lists A mailing list gateway enables users to subscribe to mailing lists that keep them up-to-date on changes to the site or on some other topic of interest. Figure 1.22 shows several mailing lists you can subscribe to if you are interested in HTTP and how it is evolving.

Threaded Discussion Groups Threaded discussion groups are very much like having Usenet newsgroups directly on your site. Users can participate in discussions about the site or about topics relevant to content on the site by posting their ideas and opinions or by responding to posts by others. For example, Morningstar allows its members to post discussion items on various stocks and mutual funds (see Figure 1.23).

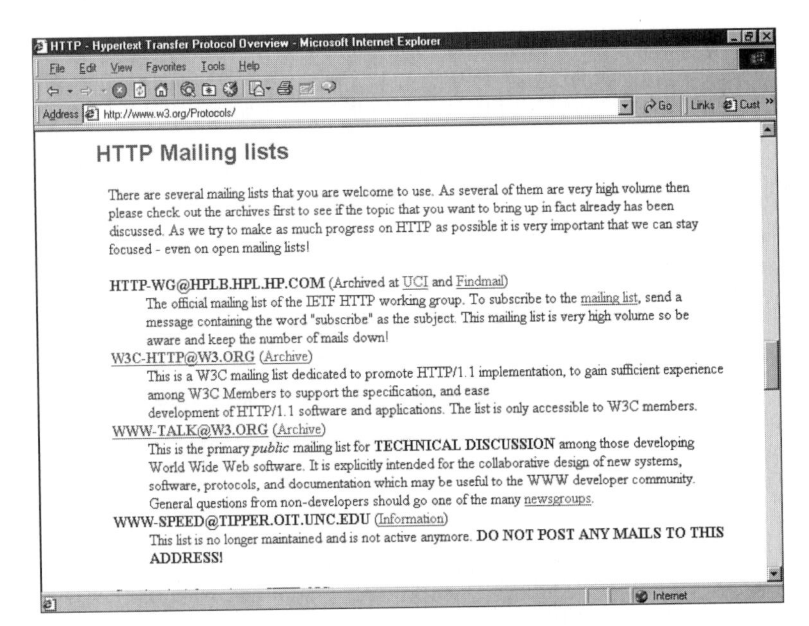

FIGURE 1.22
Mailing lists are a great way to sustain interest in a particular topic.

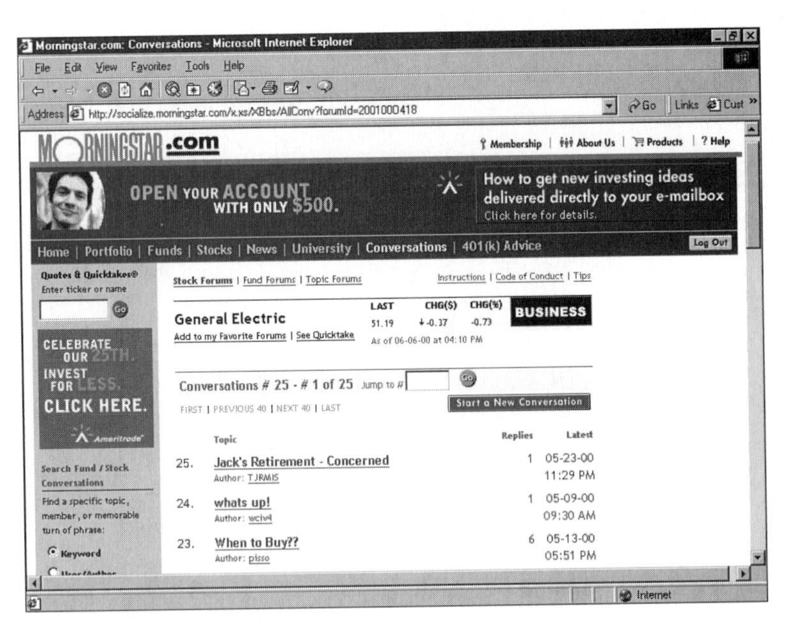

FIGURE 1.23
Morningstar members and analysts interact on discussion forums on the morningstar.com site.

If you aren't sure how to set threaded discussion on your site, you can check out some solutions available from various software vendors. Allaire produces a product called Allaire Forums to support browser-based threaded discussions. By using Forums' ColdFusion engine, users can read and post to any of a number of related groups.

Chat Channels Chat channels enable users to interact in real time. Some sites support a general chat channel on which users can discuss the site or topics that relate to site content. Another application of chat channels is to provide a question-and-answer session with a subject-matter expert or celebrity.

TIP Most chat servers have a feature that enables you to record a chat session. Reviewing the transcripts of a chat is a terrific way to gather feedback and other ideas for improving your site.

Multimedia Content As browsers become better able to display multimedia content inline, you will see more and more of it on Web sites. The biggest impediment continues to be bandwidth. Most multimedia files are quite large and can take several minutes to download.

You have many options when it comes to providing multimedia content, including

- Audio
- Video
- Macromedia Flash movies

Most multimedia files require a helper application or plug-in to view them, so be sure to notify users about which viewer programs they need to download before they get to pages with multimedia content.

Audio clips are especially popular on music sites, where they enable a visitor to preview parts of an album before buying. Audio files come in several formats, including .wav, .au, and .aiff for sound bytes, and .mid for music.

Streamed audio is different from other audio formats in that the sound is played as information is received by the browser, rather than after the entire file is downloaded. Progressive Network's RealAudio (.ra or .ram) is the leading streamed audio format. You can learn more about RealAudio by directing your browser to `http://www.realaudio.com/`.

Computer video files also come in several formats. The most popular are MPEG (.mpg), QuickTime from Apple (.qt or .mov), and Video for Windows from Microsoft (.avi, short for Audio Video Interleave). Computer video files are also huge, usually on the order of 1MB or more of information for a video clip that lasts only a few seconds. Combine this with limited bandwidth, and you can see why Web video hasn't attained the prominence of other multimedia forms.

Nonetheless, progress is being made on the Web video front. Streaming can enable video to be displayed as it is received, although this technique is still in a formative stage. Microsoft made a bold move by making ActiveMovie technology available as part of Internet Explorer 4. ActiveMovie eliminates the need for video helper applications by enabling Internet Explorer to display MPEG, QuickTime, and Video for Windows files inline. Additionally, Real Video by Progressive Networks provides support for streaming video content.

Macromedia Flash is an authoring tool for composing multimedia presentations or movies. A movie draws on text, graphics, audio, and video information to create interactive applications that can be run on Macintosh and Windows platforms or that can be delivered over the Internet (see Figure 1.24).

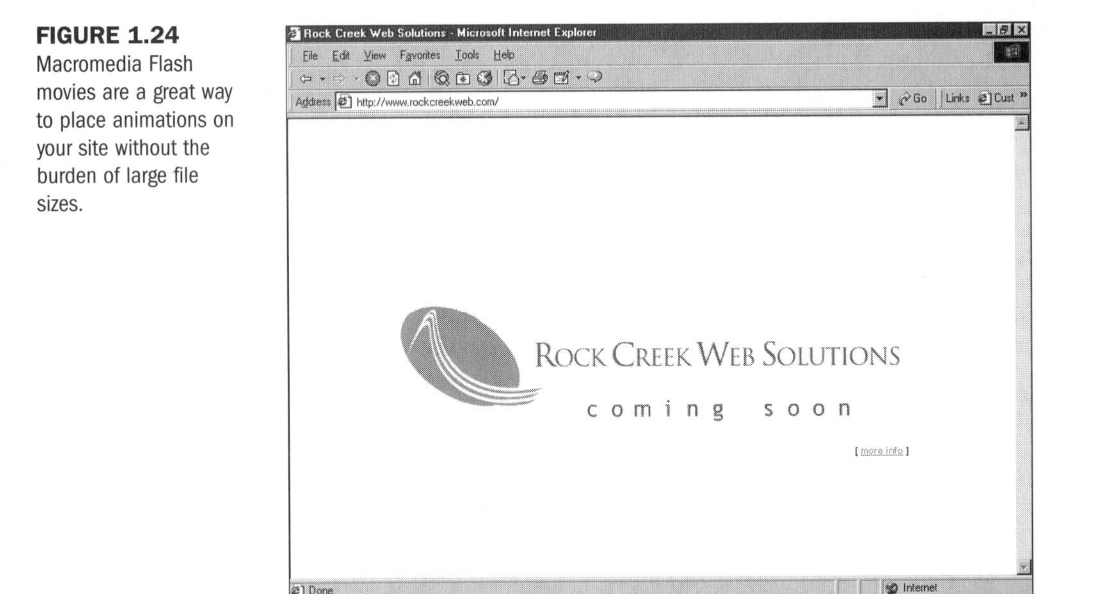

FIGURE 1.24
Macromedia Flash movies are a great way to place animations on your site without the burden of large file sizes.

Breaking Up Long Pages

You should avoid placing too much content on a single page. You read earlier in this chapter that users typically scan a page rather than read it, so most of the content you pack onto a long page will be lost on them. On top of that, forcing users to scroll through large amounts of text serves only to annoy them. If you have a lot of content, you should try to think of ways to divide it over several pages so users can read it in smaller, more digestible chunks.

Sometimes long pages are unavoidable. For those instances, you can use some of the graphics elements techniques, discussed in the following section, to make reading long pages less of an effort for your audience.

Graphic Elements Graphic elements are a terrific way to break up a sea of text. Graphics give users' eyes a break from line after line of content. Intelligent placement of the graphics can also create interesting and attractive layouts.

With the XHTML you will learn in this book, you will be able to use the following three effective graphic elements:

- Horizontal rules
- Images
- Pull quotes

Horizontal Rules A *horizontal rule* is a simple horizontal line across the width of a page (see Figure 1.25). Simple proves very effective in this case because a horizontal rule can break a long page into smaller sections and give the readers' eyes a reprieve from an abundance of text.

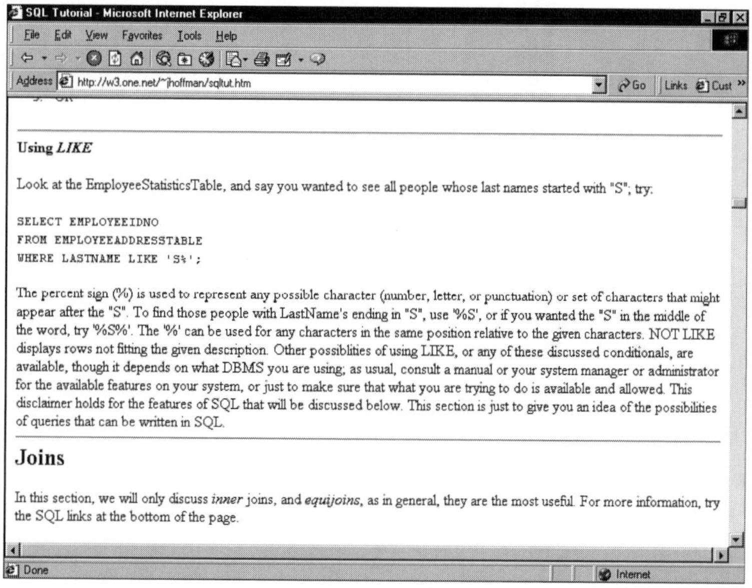

FIGURE 1.25
This SQL tutorial uses horizontal rules between sections to make the document easier to read.

Images Images can break up a lot of text, and they are particularly effective when text wraps around them (see Figure 1.26). XHTML includes instructions for placing "floating images" that permit this kind of text wrapping.

Pull Quotes A *pull quote* is a key phrase or sentence from a manuscript that is repeated in larger, bold text. Pull quotes provide you with a doubly powerful page element: They break up big blocks of text, and they reiterate important points (see Figure 1.27).

You can easily make a pull quote by using XHTML tables. Just float a table in the middle of your document's text and place a large, formatted excerpt from the text in the table. It is also a good idea to have the table borders turned off and to use horizontal lines above and below the excerpted text.

FIGURE 1.26
A photo in the middle of this cnn.com story helps to give the eye a break from large amounts of text.

Microsoft jumps the gun - Jun. 6, 2000 - Microsoft Internet Explorer

Address http://cnnfn.com/2000/06/06/technology/microsoft_filing/

bonds & rates
morning call
after hours report
ipos
continued
Retirement
mutual funds
strategies
401(k)s and IRAs
continued
Consumer
home & auto
investing
recalls
continued
Small Business
electronic
entrepreneur
SOHO
cash flow
continued
Services
broker center
bond center
continued
CNNfn on TV
program schedule
watch cnnfn video
video search
continued

NEW YORK (CNNfn) - Setting the stage for a sooner-than-expected final judgment in its landmark antitrust case, Microsoft on Tuesday submitted its response to the U.S. Justice Department's latest proposal to split the company in two.

The filing, originally expected to be submitted Wednesday, came a day after the government submitted a slightly modified breakup plan. It is expected to be the last filing in the case before the judge hands down a final ruling. Such an action by Judge Thomas Penfield Jackson could come as early as Wednesday, trial watchers said.

In the seven-page brief filed in U.S. District Court in Washington, Microsoft said the comments the government made in its latest proposal "merely confirm that its requested relief is punitive in concept and effect," and that splitting up the company "will inflict severe harm on Microsoft and third parties."

On Monday, government attorneys filed their modified position, advising Jackson to reject almost all of the changes Microsoft wanted to make to their breakup proposal, and agreeing only to a few grammatical and semantic changes. They also advised Jackson to refuse Microsoft's request for a year's time to draft a divestiture plan should such action be ordered.

Judge Jackson

In Tuesday's brief, Microsoft attorneys complain that what concessions the government did make in response to its concerns not only fail to clarify problems that they saw in the breakup plan, but actually makes the situation worse.

Find
Top Stories
Microsoft jumps the gun
Wall St. snaps win streak
DOJ targets credit cards
Viagra rivals may emerge
more
CNN.com
Latest News
Microsoft files final response in antitrust case
D-Day Museum opens: 'Last hurrah' for World War II vets
Lewis testifies against former co-defendants
Campaign finance furor sparked anew as panel releases Justice memos
More

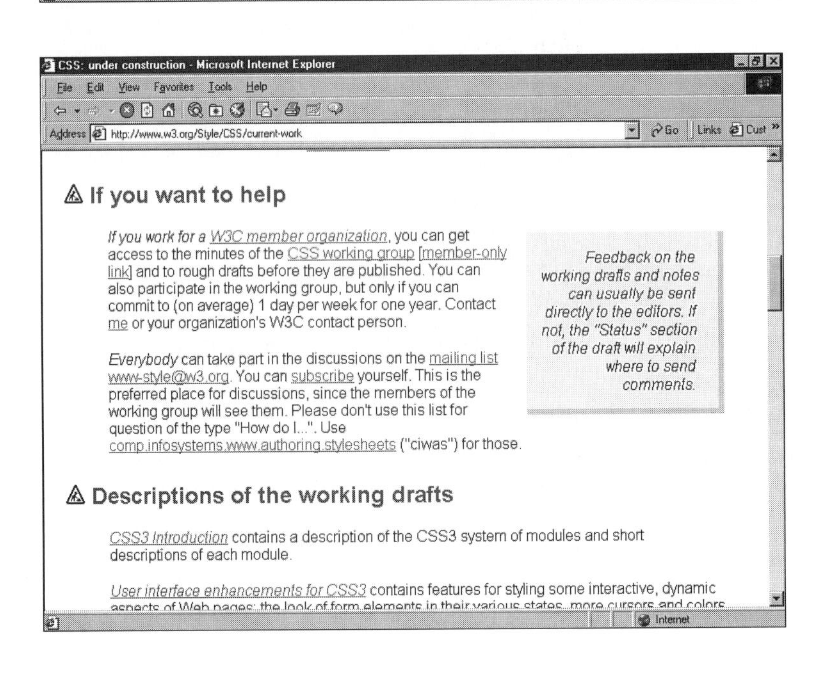
CSS: under construction - Microsoft Internet Explorer

Address http://www.w3.org/Style/CSS/current-work

If you want to help

If you work for a W3C member organization, you can get access to the minutes of the CSS working group [member-only link] and to rough drafts before they are published. You can also participate in the working group, but only if you can commit to (on average) 1 day per week for one year. Contact me or your organization's W3C contact person.

Feedback on the working drafts and notes can usually be sent directly to the editors. If not, the "Status" section of the draft will explain where to send comments.

Everybody can take part in the discussions on the mailing list www-style@w3.org. You can subscribe yourself. This is the preferred place for discussions, since the members of the working group will see them. Please don't use this list for question of the type "How do I...". Use comp.infosystems.www.authoring.stylesheets ("ciwas") for those.

Descriptions of the working drafts

CSS3 Introduction contains a description of the CSS3 system of modules and short descriptions of each module.

User interface enhancements for CSS3 contains features for styling some interactive, dynamic

FIGURE 1.27
Pull quotes enable you to reiterate a key point (from further down the page) and break up a long passage of text.

Text-Based Elements Although it might seem counter-intuitive, you can also use text to help manage a long page. Specifically, you can try either of the following:

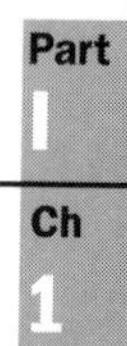

- Develop a table of contents comprised of links that help the user move through the long page.
- Vary the appearance of text by employing bold, italics, and color effects.

Table of Contents If a page is really long, you should make the extra effort to set up a small table of contents at the top of the page (see Figure 1.28). By clicking entries in the table of contents, users can jump right to the section of the document they are interested in and not have to scroll through the document to find it. To make it easy for users to get back to the table of contents, you should include a link back to the top of the page at the end of each major section.

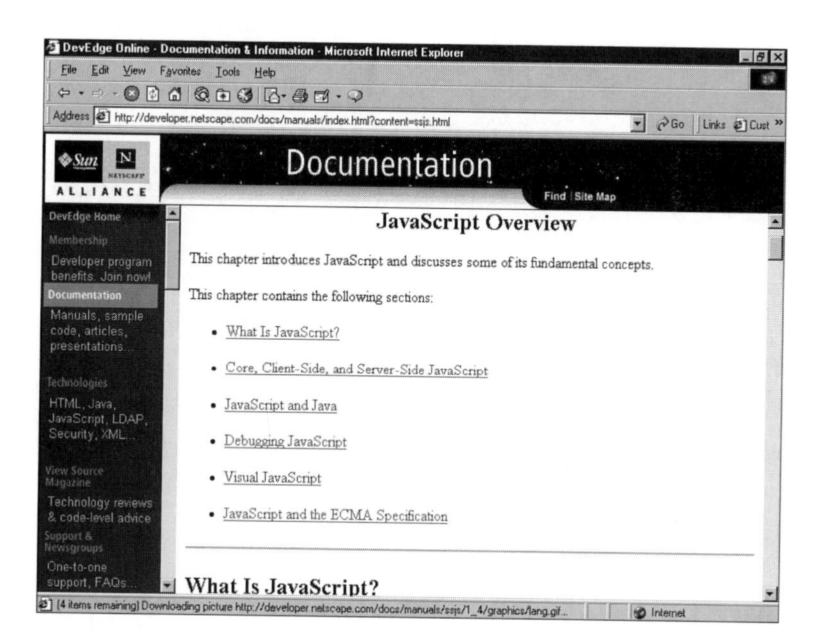

FIGURE 1.28
Long documents placed on a single page should have a table of contents at the top to assist the reader in navigating the document.

Text Effects You can make critical points stand out on long pages by marking them up in boldface or with color. This way, even if users are scanning the long page, the highlighted text will jump right off the page (see Figure 1.29).

NOTE When marking up text you want rendered in boldface, it is best to use the `<strong>` element rather than the `<b>` element. This enables non-visual browsers to understand that the content is to be strongly emphasized and to render the content in a way that lets users know that the content is important.

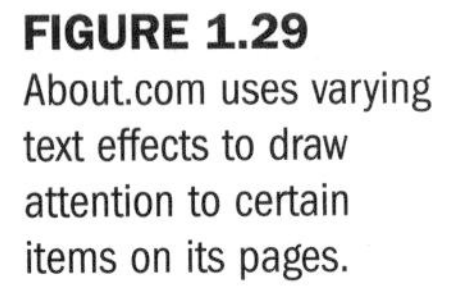

FIGURE 1.29
About.com uses varying text effects to draw attention to certain items on its pages.

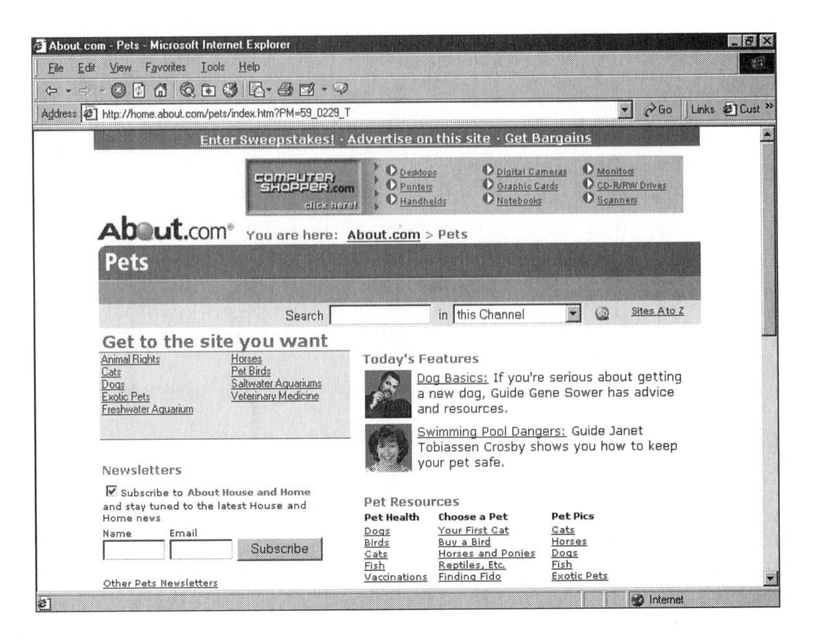

Testing Your Design

After you have completed your design work and have a first cut of your site developed, you should consider testing the design and looking for ways to improve it before final roll-out. The following three sections give you some different tests to try.

Pilot the Site

Taking the site for a test drive with some potential users is a great way to gather ideas for making it better. To do this, round up some people who have some degree of Web-surfing experience but who have not seen the site. Turn them loose on the site and encourage them to look for things they would change. You can even give them a feedback form to fill out with a standard set of questions and an open-ended question for other thoughts they might have.

TIP If you pilot your site with a group of users, watch them as they do it! You'll be amazed at what you can learn from facial expressions and body language.

Try It with Different Browsers and Platforms

As you developed the site, you probably used only one browser. After you are finished, you owe it to your audience to view the site in other browsers, including at least one non-graphical browser, and also on other platforms because Macintoshes and Windows machines vary in how they render Web pages. Record any corrections needed, and then go back to your XHTML files and look for ways to address the problems you find.

> **TIP** As an extension to trying out your site with different browsers, you can also change your monitor's resolution so you can see what your site looks like at 640×480, 800×600, and 1,024×768 pixels.

Try It at Different Connection Speeds

To accomplish this one, you might have to send people home to sign on. It is, however, well worth the effort. Have them check the pages on the site and time how long it takes for each to download. One general rule suggests that it should not take more than six to eight seconds for each page to download. Identify pages that take longer than this and look for ways to scale back the amount of information.

Trends in Web Site Design

When the Web was growing at its fastest rate, new, high-end technologies were being thrown at content providers and users at an alarming rate—so fast, in fact, that few people took the time to think about whether they were really appropriate. Instead, many technologies were used just for the sake of using them. Frequently, the result was disastrous—lengthy download times, unusable pages, and annoyed users. Recently, the Web community demonstrated a move that could be seen as "getting back to basics," in which the high-end stuff is rarely, if ever, used. This chapter closes with a look at this and some of the other site design trends that will feature prominently in the near future.

Server-Side Processing

When Java was released, it was touted as the panacea for Web programming. Several years later, however, Java has not panned out as the "end-all" language for Web-based data processing. Part of the problem was that users were just too impatient to wait for Java applets to load. Security was also a concern as programmers discovered security "holes" in Java that could put a user's machine at risk.

A similar thing has happened with ActiveX technologies. ActiveX controls also take time to download, and they have had their share of security issues. Additionally, only Microsoft Internet Explorer has native support for ActiveX controls, so users with other browsers either miss out on ActiveX technology or have to find a plug-in that enables their browser to work with an ActiveX control.

The common thread in both the Java and ActiveX stories is that they tried to be *client-side* technologies in the face of users wanting short download times and a secure environment. After it was clear that neither technology was really delivering on those counts, the fervor over them subsided. Both are still around, but they are by no means the hot technologies that make the Web interactive.

Rather than shift the burden of interactivity to the browser, support for interactive sites is now being refocused on the server. Indeed, server-side Java is becoming more and more prevalent through Java servlets and Java Server Pages (JSPs). Microsoft Internet Information Server (IIS) can easily work with server-side ActiveX controls. In addition, many server-side application development platforms, such as Allaire ColdFusion and Microsoft Active Server Pages, have emerged and made it a fairly simple matter to develop Web-enabled database applications. All these server-side technologies return XHTML to a browser, enabling fast downloads and the security of knowing that no executable files are being placed on a user's machine.

As time goes on, look for more and more processing to occur on the server side of the HTTP coin. Client-side processing will likely be limited to scripts written in JavaScript or VBScript to perform tasks such as form validation or to support other client-side technologies such as Dynamic HTML.

Personalization

When users personalize a site, they feel more ownership of it and are more likely to return to the site frequently. This is critical for sites that generate revenue through banner ad sales and charge rates commensurate with the amount of traffic they receive.

Web personalization has become a fairly easy thing to implement, thanks to the server-side programming tools that have emerged. All you need to do is ask a user to specify the content she wants on her personalized pages and how the pages should look (layout, colors, images/no images, and so on). You can then store all this information in a server-side database and place a persistent cookie on the user's browser that indicates which database record is hers. When the user subsequently returns to the site, the cookie is handed back over to the server and you can use its value to query the user's profile out of the database. After the profile information is in-hand, you can build the pages you deliver according to those specifications.

Most of the major portal sites have developed personalization schemes for their users and now many smaller, more focused sites are following suit. For example, the Alliance for Investor Education site allows personalization according to life stage (pre-college age, young adult, older adult, retiree) or according to which topics the user is most interested in (see Figure 1.30).

Respecting an International Audience

Site designers and content developers often forget about the "World" in "World Wide Web." As the Internet expands to cover more and more of the globe, you must be aware that your visitors can be coming from anywhere on Earth, not only from your own city, state, or country.

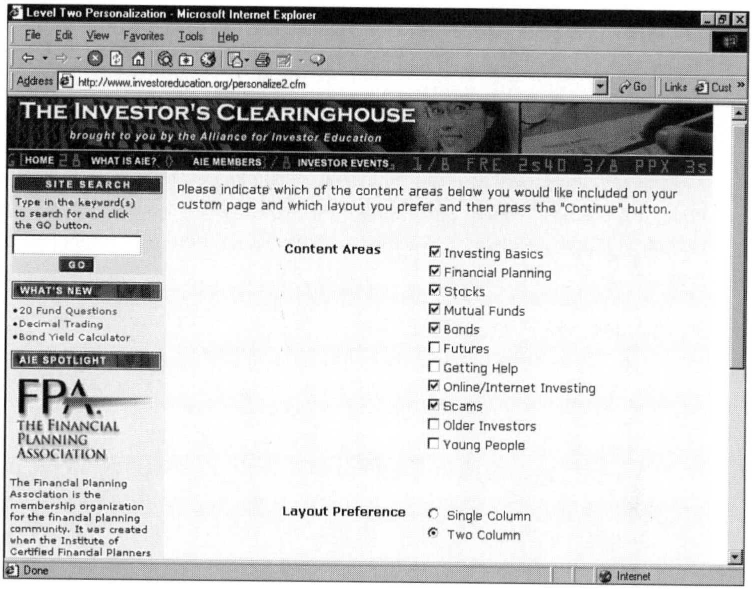

FIGURE 1.30
Users of the Alliance for Investor Education Web site can tailor their pages to their information needs.

You can demonstrate sensitivity to an international audience in several ways:

- Use the XHTML elements that specify the meaning of your content and let the various international versions of browsers handle the language-specific nuances of rendering that content. You can use the <q> element, for example, to mark up a quotation. Then a Spanish-language browser would know to offset the content with << and >> rather than with quotation marks.
- Use the `lang` attribute available for many XHTML elements to specify a language context for a piece of content or for an entire document.
- Use iconography that is not culture specific.
- If you specify dates and times, make sure you note the time zone and/or a reference city so users can deduce when things happened or are going to happen in their time zones.
- Check your server access logs to see what kinds of hits you're getting from countries other than your own. If you're detecting a number of hits from Portugal, you might go so far as to have key content translated into Portuguese so that visitors from Portugal can read your content in their native language.

You should also test your site with an international audience. This can be fairly easy if you work in a corporation with offices around the globe. In that case, just call around and line up some volunteers from each office to walk through the site and offer their feedback.

Respecting a Disabled Audience

XHTML goes a long way toward increasing the accessibility of information published on the Web for people who use browsers that are not screen based. Visually impaired users, for example, might use a browser that renders to Braille or even synthesized speech.

Perhaps the best way to make your pages accessible to non-visual browsers is to make judicious use of the XHTML elements and attributes that support the rendering of non-visual content. These include

- The heading elements (`<h1>`–`<h6>`), which define a hierarchical structure in your document.
- The `alt` attribute to specify a text-based alternative for an image, applet, or other embedded object.
- The `<label>`, `<fieldset>`, and `<legend>` elements, which make it possible to create Web forms that are more accessible to users. Marking up the prompting text in front of a form field, for example, enables a speech-based browser to use that text to prompt a user for input.

In addition to using accessible XHTML, you can also use style sheets that enhance accessibility. You can use relative sizing in your style sheets, for example, rather than absolute sizing, so a user who has set the base font size to a larger value to enhance readability won't have the size reset to an absolute value by your style sheet.

The Cascading Style Sheet level 2 specification also provides support for assigning style information to sound information delivered by an audio browser. You can use these style sheet properties to control volume, pitch, and position of the voice the user hears. By creating the illusion of different people delivering the information, you can simulate a conversation or assign one person to a class of information so that the user comes to associate a specific voice with a specific kind of content. ●

CHAPTER 2

Introduction to XHTML

by Eric Ladd

In this chapter

What Is XHTML?

When XML was first released, you might have heard that it was going to "replace HTML." That was never really a possibility because XML is a *meta-language*, meaning it is a language used to create other markup languages. The real intent has always been to recast HTML according to the rules of XML. The World Wide Web Consortium (W3C) has completed this work and the result is the Extensible Hypertext Markup Language, or XHTML. XHTML 1.0 became a W3C Recommendation in January 2000 and it now falls to the Web community to embrace the new standard. For browser companies, this means reprogramming their browsers to work with XHTML code. For content developers, it means learning the ins and outs of the language.

By and large, XHTML is very much like HTML, so there are not a lot of new elements and attributes to learn. The biggest change for developers will be that all of XHTML's syntax rules must be followed or your document will not be rendered. This is vastly different from the way browsers work now. If you write an HTML document with syntax errors, most browsers will just gloss over them and render the document anyway. This kind of forgiving behavior will no longer be possible with XHTML.

This chapter introduces you to XHTML and what you must know to convert your existing HTML content to conform to the rules of XHTML. After a brief overview of XML and how it's related to XHTML, the chapter focuses on the major rules of XHTML and how you have to change your coding behavior to adhere to those rules.

NOTE All the ideas covered in this chapter are pursued in greater depth in later chapters as well. Chapters 3 through 8 go into the specifics of the XHTML elements and their syntax. Chapters 10 through 17 delve into XML and how developers are using XML to create discipline-specific markup languages. ■

What Is XML?

The Extensible Markup Language, or XML, was developed to provide an alternative to the Standard Generalized Markup Language (SGML). Prior to XML, SGML was the only meta-language available for developing other markup languages. SGML is a powerful language with features that enable you to develop markup languages for a wide variety of media. After you focus on the Web, however, you don't really need many of SGML's features that support markup for other types of publishing. This compelled the W3C to develop XML—a meta-language that preserves the best features of SGML but filters out all the aspects of SGML that aren't necessary in a Web publishing environment.

When you develop a markup language with XML, you are creating an XML application. Even though XML is a relatively new meta-language, several XML applications are already in use. The Synchronized Multimedia Integration Language, or SMIL (pronounced "smile"), is an XML application used to orchestrate presentations for RealPlayer and other multimedia programs. Math Markup Language, or MML, is an XML application that facilitates the publishing of mathematical expressions on the Web. XML applications are also essential to custom business-to-business e-commerce applications.

XHTML is also an XML application. The HTML standard was originally written using SGML, but with XML on the scene, it became prudent to rewrite HTML as an XML application. The result of this effort is the XHTML 1.0 standard.

Where the Last HTML Standard Left Off

The most recent HTML standard—HTML 4.01—did a fine job of updating HTML to reflect contemporary use of the language. It also made great strides in supporting accessibility by introducing several elements and attributes that would allow users with different abilities to consume Web content. These include elements such as `<fieldset>` and `<legend>` for creating forms and the `longdesc` attribute for the `<img>` element.

However, HTML has been lacking the syntactic rigor present in other languages. This has been cultivated in large part by browsers that tolerate HTML syntax errors. After all, why should anyone correct his syntax errors if the documents look fine? While the major browsers have incorporated the capability to look beyond syntax errors, other browsers that rely on all syntax rules being followed have not. This means that people using these other browsers will often have their browsers "broken" by the abundance of erroneous HTML code that's out there.

HTML was also suffering from being extended to include a number of elements and attributes that are solely for presentation purposes and not for indicating the structure of the document. Traditional markup languages only specify structure and have no bearing on how the document looks onscreen. Instead, authors use style sheets to give the content a particular look and feel. In HTML, there was no separation between these two aspects of publishing, contrary to the spirit of how markup languages are implemented.

Applying the Rules of XML to HTML

To help alleviate these problems, the W3C recast HTML as an XML application, resulting in the XHTML standard. XHTML addresses both of the previously noted problems with HTML. First and foremost, an XHTML document cannot be rendered if it is syntactically incorrect. This is a by-product of XML. One of the fundamental concepts in XML is that a document must be syntactically correct or *valid* to be rendered. Thus, if any XHTML document has just one syntax error, it is rejected.

Second, it puts Web authors on the path to using Cascading Style Sheets to indicate how content should look. In its strictest form, XHTML does not allow any of the elements that specify how content should look. Fortunately, the W3C has provided more permissive forms of XHTML for authors to work with initially. You should expect to transition to the strict form of XHTML eventually, however.

NOTE Because XHTML 1.0 is just HTML 4.01 with syntax rules enforced, any HTML 4.01-compliant browser should render your XHTML code without a problem. However, such a browser might not validate your code to make sure that all the syntax rules are followed.

Why Else Do We Need XHTML?

You have already read about two of the benefits of XHTML, but there are more advantages than just the enforcement of syntax and the separation of content and presentation. Before you begin reading about the specific rules of XHTML, here are a few other good reasons to use it:

- **Standardization**—HTML has always been a standardized language, but the standard has been largely ignored by content authors and software companies that create browsers and authoring tools. Indeed, the proprietary tags that Netscape and Microsoft introduced caused trouble for other browsers and prompted the W3C to try to bring some order to the HTML world. With XHTML, everyone is forced to comply with the syntax rules, so there should be no more problems with proprietary code. Additionally, this forces WYSIWYG authoring tools to stop bending the rules of HTML in favor of getting onscreen content to look a certain way.
- **Extensibility**—Because XHTML is an application of XML, it is inherently extensible, meaning you can add new elements and attributes to the language with minimal impact on the syntax of the other elements. This will allow XHTML to adapt to the constantly changing needs of Web publishing.
- **Eliminates Sloppy Coding**—The bad coding habits that have become prevalent make maintaining existing sites nightmarish. Also, search engine indexing programs rely on good coding practices to do the best possible job while cataloging your site. When XHTML forces us into consistently writing good code, things will be easier for both the people and the programs that have to work with the code.
- **Enhanced Linking**—The XML standard provides for a more robust form of linking than standard HTML hyperlinks. For example, one notion within XML linking involves having a single hyperlink point to many resources rather than just one.

Basic Rules of XHTML

Because you now have to follow the rules when writing XHTML, it's important that you spend some time understanding what those rules are. In some cases, following a rule means just a simple behavior change; in others, it seems like you are working with a vastly different language.

Listing 2.1 shows some HTML code that is not XHTML compliant. Indeed, the code is technically not even compliant with the syntax rules put forward in the HTML standard. In spite of this, a browser still renders it with no problem (see Figure 2.1).

Listing 2.1 A Sample HTML Document

```
<HTML>

<HEAD>
<TITLE>OnlinePizza.Com Order Form</TITLE>
<SCRIPT TYPE="text/javascript">
<!--

   function validate(myForm) {
      var rbchecked = 0;
      for (i=0; i<myForm.type.length; i++) {
         if (myForm.type[i].checked) {
            rbchecked = 1;
         }
      }
      if (!rbchecked) {
         alert("Please choose a size for your pizza.");
         return false;
      }
      else {
         return true;
      }
   }

//-->
</SCRIPT>
</HEAD>

<BODY BGCOLOR="WHITE">

<H1>OnlinePizza.Com</H1>

Order your pizza with our handy-dandy form below:<P>

<FORM ACTION="orderprocess.pl" METHOD="POST" onsubmit="return validate(this)">

<TABLE BORDER=0 CELLPADDING=8>
<TR VALIGN="TOP">
    <TD><B>Type:</B></TD>
    <TD>
    <INPUT TYPE="RADIO" NAME="type" VALUE="10"> 10 inch round
    <INPUT TYPE="RADIO" NAME="type" VALUE="12"> 12 inch round
    <INPUT TYPE="RADIO" NAME="type" VALUE="16"> 16 inch round
    </TD>
</TR>
<TR VALIGN="TOP">
    <TD><B>Toppings:</B></TD>
    <TD>
    <SELECT NAME="toppings" SIZE=5 MULTIPLE>
    <OPTION>Mushrooms
    <OPTION>Peppers
```

Listing 2.1 Continued

```
    <OPTION>Onions
    <OPTION>Pepperoni
    <OPTION>Extra Cheese
    </SELECT>
    </TD>
</TR>
<TR><TD COLSPAN=2><INPUT TYPE="SUBMIT" VALUE="Order It!"></TD></TR>
</FORM>

</TABLE>

</BODY>

</HTML>
```

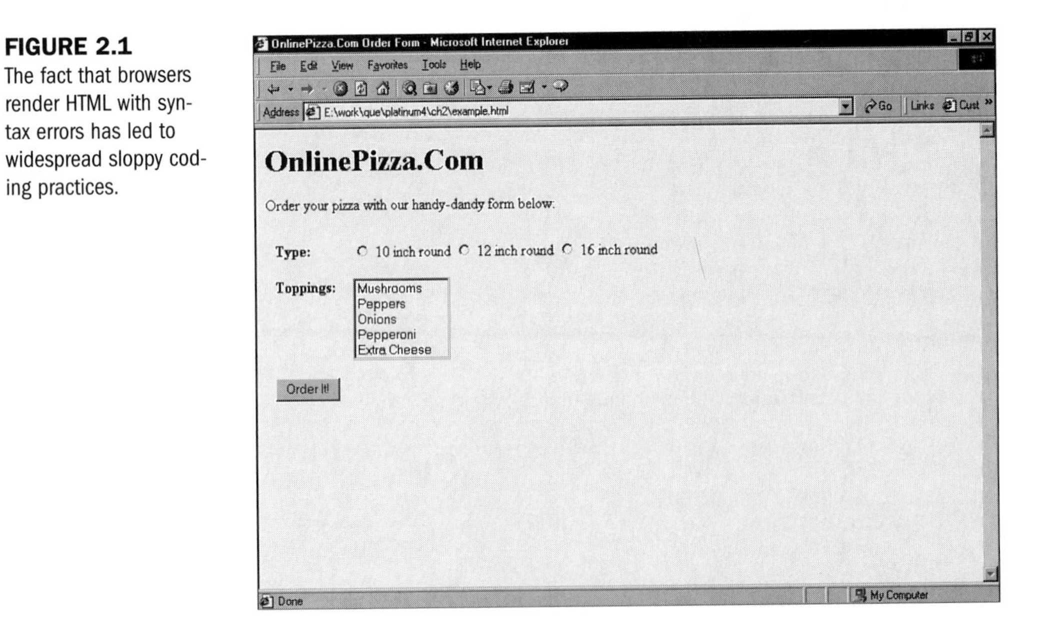

FIGURE 2.1
The fact that browsers render HTML with syntax errors has led to widespread sloppy coding practices.

The following sections about the major rules of XHTML reference sections of the code in Listing 2.1 to give you some context on where and when the rules apply. As you learn about each rule, you can see what needs to be done to the code in Listing 2.1 to make it syntactically correct.

Everything in Lowercase

One change that will have a big impact on some authors and no effect on others is that all element keywords and attribute names must be in lowercase. This rule stems from the fact that

XML is case sensitive. If you already use lowercase letters in your coding, adhering to this rule should not be an issue. However, many HTML coders were taught to write their keywords and attributes in uppercase so they would be easier to go back and edit later on. These developers will most likely have the toughest time with this rule. Fortunately, most authoring tools give you the option of element keywords and attributes being uppercase or lowercase, so it should just be a matter of making the right change in the program options.

The first major step to making Listing 2.1 XHTML compliant, then, is to convert all element keywords and attribute names to lowercase (see Listing 2.2). Although this can be tedious to do by hand, many authoring tools can handle the conversion for you. One such tool is Allaire's HomeSite (see Figure 2.2). You invoke the conversion by choosing the Convert Tag Case option under the Edit menu and then indicating that you want to convert to lowercase.

Listing 2.2 HTML Document with Elements and Attributes in Lowercase

```
<html>

<head>
<title>OnlinePizza.Com Order Form</title>
<script type="text/javascript">
<!--

   function validate(myForm) {
      var rbchecked = 0;
      for (i=0; i<myForm.type.length; i++) {
         if (myForm.type[i].checked) {
            rbchecked = 1;
         }
      }
      if (!rbchecked) {
         alert("Please choose a size for your pizza.");
         return false;
      }
      else {
         return true;
      }
   }
//-->
</script>

</head>

<body bgcolor="WHITE">

<h1>OnlinePizza.Com</h1>

Order your pizza with our handy-dandy form below:<p>

<form action="orderprocess.pl" method="POST" onsubmit="return validate(this)">

<table border=0 cellpadding=8>
<tr valign="TOP">
```

Listing 2.2 Continued

```
        <td><b>Type:</b></td>
        <td>
        <input type="RADIO" name="type" value="10"> 10 inch round
        <input type="RADIO" name="type" value="12"> 12 inch round
        <input type="RADIO" name="type" value="16"> 16 inch round
        </td>
    </tr>
    <tr valign="TOP">
        <td><b>Toppings:</b></td>
        <td>
        <select name="toppings" size=5 multiple>
        <option>Mushrooms
        <option>Peppers
        <option>Onions
        <option>Pepperoni
        <option>Extra Cheese
        </select>
        </td>
    </tr>
    <tr><td colspan=2><input type="SUBMIT" value="Order It!"></td></tr>
    </form>

    </table>

    </body>

    </html>
```

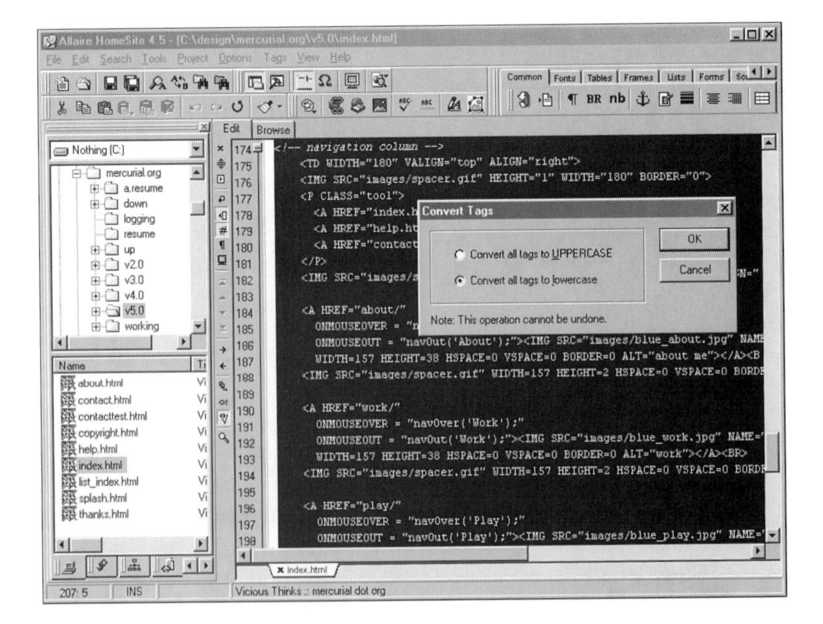

FIGURE 2.2
Authoring tools with tag case converters make your life a lot easier when converting existing content for XHTML compliance.

Note in Listing 2.2 that, although the element keyword and attribute names are in lowercase, the attribute values are not. When specifying an attribute's value, you are free to use uppercase, lowercase, or mixed case as necessary.

Don't Forget the Required Elements

In HTML, the only required element is the `<title>` element. That remains true in XHTML, but there are a few other required elements as well. All of them are related to the document's structure and do not contribute directly to what is displayed in the browser.

One requirement of XML is that each document have a root element. In XHTML, the root element is the `<html>` element, but it is not enough to begin your document with `<html>` and end it with `</html>`. Additionally, you must specify the *XML namespace* you are using inside the `<html>` tag. A namespace is simply a collection of elements and attributes that are permissible to use in a given XML-based language.

For XHTML 1.0, you use the following code to specify the namespace:

```
<html xmlns="http://www.w3.org/1999/xhtml">
```

With the root element in place, you can move on to dealing with the next two required elements: `<head>` and `<body>`. Both of these elements must be contained within the root element, and you are allowed only one of each. The required `<title>` element must reside within the `<head>` element.

Putting all these required elements together, you have a standard document structure that looks like the following:

```
<html xmlns="http://www.w3.org/1999/xhtml">

<head>
<title>Descriptive document title</title>
</head>

<body>
    ... elements and content in the document body ...
</body>

</html>
```

The final thing that needs to be added to the list of required elements is the one that declares the document type you are using. XHTML actually comes in three different versions, each with its own Document Type Definition (DTD). These versions are

- **Strict**—The Strict version of XHTML is the most restrictive because it disallows any elements or attributes that determine how content is presented. This includes popular elements such as `<font>` and `<center>` and attributes such as `bgcolor` and `align`. When you use the Strict DTD, it is assumed that you are using Cascading Style Sheets to specify all your presentation-related parameters and that your XHTML is purely for indicating the structure of the document.

- **Transitional**—The Transitional version of XHTML is meant to make your life a little easier during the transition from HTML 4 to XHTML. The Transitional DTD permits presentation-related tags, so this is the version of XHTML that most people will probably use initially so that fewer revisions to existing code will be necessary to bring it into compliance with the standard.
- **Frameset**—The Frameset version of XHTML is the Transitional version with the frame-related elements added in. If your site uses frames, you will need to use the Frameset DTD instead of the Transitional DTD.

After you've decided which DTD you're using, you need to add a `doctype` declaration as the first line in your file. You must declare this first so that the browser knows which set of rules it should use to validate the document. To declare that you are using the Strict DTD, you would use

```
<!DOCTYPE html PUBLIC "-//W3C//DTD XHTML 1.0 Strict//EN"
"http://www.w3.org/TR/xhtml1/DTD/strict.dtd">
```

The Transitional DTD is indicated by

```
<!DOCTYPE html PUBLIC "-//W3C//DTD XHTML 1.0 Transitional//EN"
"http://www.w3.org/TR/xhtml1/DTD/transitional.dtd">
```

To use the Frameset DTD, the first line in your file would be

```
<!DOCTYPE html PUBLIC "-//W3C//DTD XHTML 1.0 Frameset//EN"
"http://www.w3.org/TR/xhtml1/DTD/frameset.dtd">
```

Adding in the `doctype` declaration for the Transitional DTD into the standard document template, you have

```
<!DOCTYPE html PUBLIC "-//W3C//DTD XHTML 1.0 Transitional//EN"
"http://www.w3.org/TR/xhtml1/DTD/transitional.dtd">

<html xmlns="http://www.w3.org/1999/xhtml">

<head>
<title>Descriptive document title</title>
</head>

<body>
    ... elements and content in the document body ...
</body>

</html>
```

This template should provide you with a helpful starting point for converting existing content or for developing new content that uses presentation-related elements.

All Attribute Values Are Quoted

One place HTML authors can often be sloppy is in the specification of the values of attributes. Technically, attribute values should be enclosed in double quotes, but the browsers' willingness to overlook this syntax mistake has served to magnify the problem. In the earlier Listing 2.2, several tags do not use quotes around the values. For example,

```
<table border=0 cellpadding=8>
```

makes the mistake twice—once with the `border` attribute and once with the `cellpadding` attribute. The correct way to write this element in XHTML is

```
<table border="0" cellpadding="8">
```

Note that the `size` attribute in the `<select>` element and the `colspan` attribute in the final `<td>` element require similar corrections.

This might not be too big of a headache for XHTML authors, but it will certainly create problems for server-side programmers writing scripts to dynamically generate XHTML. For example, an Active Server Page (ASP) programmer might dynamically place an image using the following instruction:

```
<%
Response.Write("<img src=" & queryResults("imgfilename") & "/>")
%>
```

Inside the `Response.Write()` instruction, the programmer has to dynamically build a string that is ultimately incorporated into the document being sent to the browser. If the name of the image file that was queried out of the database is `uglyphoto.jpg`, the element that would end up in the document would be

```
<img src=uglyphoto.jpg>
```

According to XHTML, this is illegal because the value of the `src` attribute is not in double quotes! To accomplish this, the ASP programmer would have to explicitly build the quotes into the string. This is a bit of a challenge because double quotes are already used to delimit the literal parts of the string. Fortunately, VBScript provides the `Chr()` function, which can be used to build the quotes into the string as follows:

```
<%
Response.Write("<img src=" & Chr(22) & queryResults("imgfilename") &  Chr(22)
➥& "/>")
%>
```

The `Chr()` function takes the double quote's ASCII value `(22)` and converts it into the double quote character itself.

TIP Allaire's HomeSite authoring tool can be configured to automatically put in double quotes for you when you type in an attribute. This feature will be invaluable to authors who are prone to "forget" to quote their attribute values.

No Attribute Minimization Is Permitted

Attribute minimization refers to using one-word attributes rather than all attributes having a `name="value"` structure. For example, the `<select>` element in Listing 2.2 uses the standalone attribute `multiple` to indicate that the user should be able to select more than one topping for a pizza. This is illegal in XHTML.

To correct the mistake, the attribute must be written in a `name="value"` format. The W3C suggests repeating the attribute's name as its value as well. Thus, the corrected element would look like this:

```
<select name="toppings" size="5" multiple="multiple">
```

A similar approach should be taken with other attributes that are traditionally written as a single word. These include

- The `checked` attribute for check boxes (`<input type="checkbox" />`) and radio buttons (`<input type="radio" />`).
- The `selected` attribute for the `<option>` element.
- The `ismap` attribute for the `<img />` element.

All Container Elements Must Have a Closing Tag

Most of the elements in XHTML are container elements, meaning they have an opening tag and a corresponding closing tag. In most HTML code, authors are pretty good about using both opening and closing tags where appropriate. There is, however, a handful of HTML container elements that often don't include the necessary closing tag. These elements include

- `<p>`
- `<li>`
- `<dt>`
- `<dd>`
- `<option>`

When writing XHTML, it is absolutely essential that the closing tags for these elements, and any other container element, be used judiciously. The code shown earlier in Listing 2.2 suffers from this problem in a few places. Specifically, the `<p>` element is used to denote where a paragraph break should occur, and none of the `<option>` elements have closing tags. Written correctly, these elements should look like this:

```
<p>Order your pizza with our handy-dandy form below:</p>

...

<select name="toppings" size=5 multiple>
   <option>Mushrooms</option>
   <option>Peppers</option>
   <option>Onions</option>
   <option>Pepperoni</option>
   <option>Extra Cheese</option>
</select>
```

All Standalone Elements Need to Be Explicitly Terminated

A few HTML elements are called empty or standalone elements, meaning they do not have a closing tag associated with them. The most popular standalone elements include

- `<br>`
- `<img>`
- `<input>`
- `<frame>`

In XHTML, you must indicate the termination of standalone elements in one of two ways:

- By placing a forward slash (/) at the end of the element. Thus, to place an image, you might use an element like the following:

  ```
  <img src="corplogo.gif" width="600" height="85" alt="Logo" />
  ```

- By creating a closing tag for the element. In this approach, you simply add on whatever the closing tag would be for the element, if it had one. For example, in setting up a submit button, you might use

  ```
  <input type="submit" value="Send It!"></input>
  ```

CAUTION

If you create a closing tag for the standalone element, make sure you do not put any content between the element's opening and closing tags. This is not permissible because the element is defined to be empty.

The code in Listing 2.2 suffers from this error in the elements that create the radio buttons and the submit button. Written correctly, these elements would look like this:

```
<input type="RADIO" name="type" value="10" /> 10 inch round
<input type="RADIO" name="type" value="12" /> 12 inch round
<input type="RADIO" name="type" value="16" /> 16 inch round
...
<input type="SUBMIT" value="Order It!" />
```

All Elements Must Be Properly Nested

Browsers used to forgive you if you interwove two elements. For example, the following code is technically incorrect because the `<i>` element should have been closed before the `<b>` element:

```
<b><i>boldface and italicized</b></i>
```

This is an example of improper nesting of elements and is illegal in XHTML. To correct the error, the `<i>` element should be closed before the `<b>` element as follows:

```
<b><i>boldface and italicized</i></b>
```

The </form> and </table> tags in Listing 2.2 are improperly nested, because the <form> element was opened first, followed by the <table> element. You can fix this mistake by swapping the positions of the two misplaced tags.

Script and Style Code Require Special Handling

When you place a <script> or <style> element into your document, it is expected that there will be some kind of code inside those elements—JavaScript or VBScript for the <script> element and Cascading Style Sheet code for the <style> element. Because you are embedding one language inside another, you need to denote the embedded language as a CDATA section. Code inside an XML CDATA section will not be interpreted as XML markup, so the browser will not try to apply the rules specified in the DTD to the embedded language code. This is good because client-side script code and CSS code are not subject to the same syntax rules as XHTML code!

The earlier sample code in Listing 2.2 has a JavaScript block that checks to make sure users select a size for their pizzas. To designate the JavaScript code as a CDATA section, you need to wrap the code with `<![CDATA[` and `]]>` markers as follows:

```
<script type="text/javascript">
<!--
<![CDATA[
   function validate(myForm) {
      var rbchecked = 0;
      for (i=0; i<myForm.type.length; i++) {
         if (myForm.type[i].checked) {
            rbchecked = 1;
         }
      }
      if (!rbchecked) {
         alert("Please choose a size for your pizza.");
         return false;
      }
      else {
         return true;
      }
   }
]]>
//-->
</script>
```

This prevents your browser from trying to reconcile the JavaScript code against the syntax rules of XHTML.

NOTE If you use the src attribute of the <script> element to read in your client-side script code from an external source, you do not need to create a CDATA section inside the <script> element. ■

As you can see, a number of these rules require authors to go back and make some fairly substantial changes to their code. Although some changes take more effort than others, all are equally important because it takes only one syntax error for a document to be rejected.

Listing 2.3 shows the corrected, XHTML-compliant version of the original listing. Attribute values in Listing 2.3 have been changed to lowercase or mixed case for enhanced readability.

Listing 2.3 XHTML-Compliant Document

```
<!DOCTYPE html PUBLIC "-//W3C//DTD XHTML 1.0 Transitional//EN"
"http://www.w3.org/TR/xhtml1/DTD/transitional.dtd">

<html xmlns="http://www.w3.org/1999/xhtml">

<head>
<title>OnlinePizza.Com Order Form</title>
<script type="text/javascript">
<!--
<![CDATA[
   function validate(myForm) {
      var rbchecked = 0;
      for (i=0; i<myForm.type.length; i++) {
         if (myForm.type[i].checked) {
            rbchecked = 1;
         }
      }
      if (!rbchecked) {
         alert("Please choose a size for your pizza.");
         return false;
      }
      else {
         return true;
      }
   }
]]>
//-->
</script>

</head>

<body bgcolor="white">

<h1>OnlinePizza.Com</h1>

<p>Order your pizza with our handy-dandy form below:</p>
```

Listing 2.3 Continued

```
<form action="orderprocess.pl" method="post" onsubmit="return validate(this)">

<table border="0" cellpadding="8">
<tr valign="top">
    <td><b>Type:</b></td>
    <td>
    <input type="radio" name="type" value="10"/> 10 inch round
    <input type="radio" name="type" value="12"/> 12 inch round
    <input type="radio" name="type" value="16"/> 16 inch round
    </td>
</tr>
<tr valign="top">
    <td><b>Toppings:</b></td>
    <td>
    <select name="toppings" size="5" multiple="multiple">
    <option>Mushrooms</option>
    <option>Peppers</option>
    <option>Onions</option>
    <option>Pepperoni</option>
    <option>Extra Cheese</option>
    </select>
    </td>
</tr>
<tr><td colspan="2"><input type="submit" value="Order It!"/></td></tr>
</table>

</form>

</body>

</html>
```

Converting Your Existing HTML Content to XHTML

You don't need to rush out and start converting all your HTML content to XHTML right away because it will probably take some time for the browsers to be reprogrammed to work with XHTML code. Even so, you should be thinking about a conversion plan for your existing content, and any new content you are creating should adhere to one of the XHTML DTDs. If you do, you will be well prepared when browsers begin to enforce the rules of XHTML.

TIP For most people, it will probably make sense to use the Transitional DTD for both conversion of existing code and creation of new code. HTML documents that create framed layouts should use the Frameset DTD.

As your long-term approach, you should think about all your content adhering to the Strict DTD while using Cascading Style Sheet instructions to specify how the content should look. CSS level 2 is robust and gives you fine control over how page elements look and where they are placed. Learning CSS might require you to read a book or an online tutorial, but it is well worth the effort.

▶ To learn more about working with style sheets, **see** Chapter 9, "Style Sheets"

Basic Steps

To convert your existing content, you must first decide which DTD you're going to adhere to. Given that most existing HTML code contains presentation-related elements and attributes such as `<font>` and `bgcolor`, it makes the most sense to use the Transitional or Frameset DTD because both allow for the use of such elements and attributes. After you've selected a DTD to use, you can then work through the following checklist to complete the conversion:

- *Convert all element keywords and attribute names to lowercase.* For this step, it would be best to find a software tool that can do the case conversion for you.
- *Make sure you have all required elements.* These include a `doctype` declaration, a root element (`<html>`) that indicates an XML namespace, a `<head>` element, a `<title>` element contained within the `<head>` element, and a `<body>` element.
- *Ensure that all attributes are in a* `name="value"` *format.* This means that you can't have any one-word attributes, and all attribute values must be in double quotes.
- *Make sure that all container elements have closing tags.* The elements that will most likely require correction include `<p>`, `<li>`, and `<option>`.
- *Place a forward slash inside all standalone elements.* For example, all `<br>` elements should be rewritten as `<br />`. Alternatively, you can add a closing tag to standalone elements, in which case a `<br>` element would change to `<br></br>`.
- *Designate client-side script code and style sheet code as CDATA sections.* This prevents XHTML syntax rules from being applied to code written in other languages.

Software Tools

Now that XHTML is an official recommendation, you can expect that software-authoring tools will be retooled to support XHTML syntax. In the meantime, you can use some of the more able existing tools that can assist you with conversion of your current content and creation of new content.

One useful tool is Allaire's HomeSite. You read earlier in the chapter that HomeSite can convert your uppercase element keywords and attributes to lowercase. This alone would make it indispensable, but HomeSite has other useful features as well. These include the capability to automatically place double quotes when writing attributes and to customize the placement of `<script>` and `<style>` tags so that they include the CDATA section markers.

Another helpful tool is HTML Tidy, a free utility written by Dave Raggett of the World Wide Web Consortium. HTML Tidy can do a number of checks and corrections on your code, including

- Determining which HTML standard you are writing to and inserting the appropriate `doctype` declaration
- Fixing unbalanced and mismatched closing tags
- Adding missing forward slash (/) characters in closing tags
- Correcting improperly nested elements
- Adding missing quotes around attribute values
- Identifying elements and attributes that are not standard
- Finding instances of missing “>” characters in a tag

HTML Tidy can also give you suggestions on where you need to improve your coding. To learn more about HTML Tidy, direct your browser to `http://www.w3.org/People/Raggett/tidy/` (see Figure 2.3).

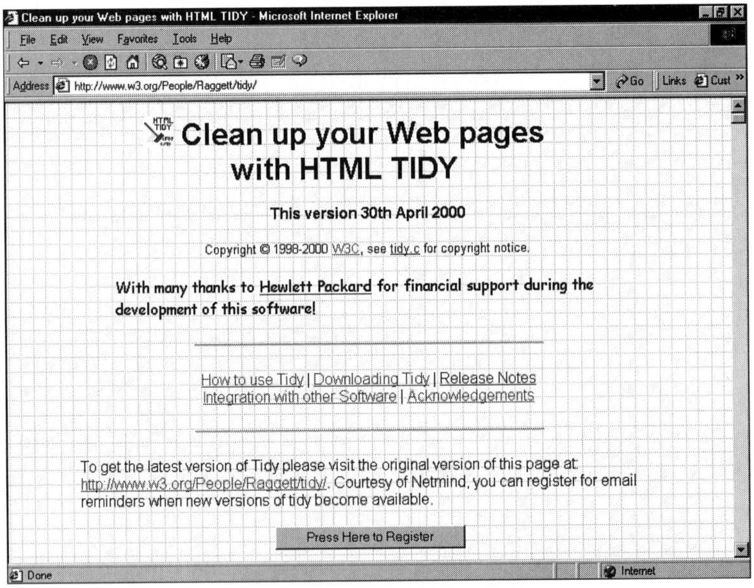

FIGURE 2.3
HTML Tidy can help you make sure that you have met all of XHTML's syntax requirements.

CHAPTER 3

XHTML 1.0 Element Reference

by Eric Ladd

In this chapter

Reference Scope

This chapter is unique in the book because it is written to serve as a reference for all the elements included in the XHTML 1.0 recommendation, as published by the World Wide Web Consortium (W3C). It is a one-stop catalog of each element, including the element's attributes, syntax, and examples of uses. By necessity, this chapter covers a large amount of information, but you'll soon come to appreciate the value of having all the relevant facts about all XHTML elements—together with tips on how to use them—right at your fingertips.

NOTE This chapter covers only the elements included in the recommended XHTML 1.0 Document Type Definition (DTD), as published by the World Wide Web Consortium in January 2000. Browser-specific extensions to HTML 4.0 are beyond the scope of this chapter but might be covered elsewhere in the book. The extended HTML tag `<LAYER>` introduced by Netscape Communications Corporation, for example, is discussed in detail in Chapter 24, "Introduction to Dynamic HTML," and Chapter 26, "Advanced Netscape Dynamic HTML."

For the most up-to-date status of XHTML, consult `http://www.w3.org/TR/xhtml1/`, where you will find links to the most current version of the standard and any version prior to that. ■

How This Chapter Is Organized

Because of the vast coverage of this chapter, the information presented has been carefully structured to make it as easy as possible for you to look up the elements you need. At the highest level, this chapter is organized into major sections that cover a group of related elements. The major sections and the elements they cover include

- Document structure elements (see p. **71**): `<html>`, `<head>`, `<base>`, `<meta>`, `<link>`, `<script>`, `<noscript>`, `<style>`, `<title>`, and `<body>`
- Formatting elements (see p. **80**): `<font>`, `<basefont>`, `<u>`, `<s>`, `<strike>`, `<b>`, `<big>`, `<i>`, `<small>`, `<sub>`, `<sup>`, `<tt>`, `<abbr>`, `<acronym>`, `<address>`, `<cite>`, `<code>`, `<del>`, `<dfn>`, `<em>`, `<ins>`, `<kbd>`, `<q>`, `<samp>`, `<strong>`, `<var>`, `<blockquote>`, `<br>`, `<bdo>`, `<div>`, `<hr>`, `<h1>`–`<h6>`, `<p>`, `<pre>`, and `<span>`
- List elements (see p. **100**): `<li>`, `<dl>`, `<dt>`, `<dd>`, `<ol>`, and `<ul>`
- Hyperlink elements (see p. **106**): `<a>`
- Image and image map elements (see p. **108**): `<img>`, `<map>`, and `<area>`
- Table elements (see p. **112**): `<table>`, `<caption>`, `<thead>`, `<tfoot>`, `<tbody>`, `<colgroup>`, `<col>`, `<tr>`, `<td>`, and `<th>`
- Form elements (see p. **122**): `<form>`, `<input>`, `<select>`, `<option>`, `<optgroup>`, `<textarea>`, `<button>`, `<label>`, `<fieldset>`, and `<legend>`
- Frame elements (see p. **132**): `<frameset>`, `<frame>`, `<noframes>`, and `<iframe>`
- Executable content elements (see p. **137**): `<object>`, `<param>`, and `<applet>`

TIP In some cases, elements covered in this chapter get a more thorough treatment in a later chapter of the book. Look for cross-references to point you to this expanded coverage.

Within a given section, several elements are discussed in detail. Specifically, you'll find the following information about each element:

- **The element's keyword**—For example, the `<input>` element's keyword is `input`.
- **What kind of element it is**—Every XHTML element is either a *container element* or a *standalone element*. A container element activates an effect and has a companion closing element that discontinues the effect. For example, `<i>` is a container element that, together with its companion closing element `</i>`, causes all text found between them to be rendered in italic. The `<i>` element turns on the italic effect, and the `</i>` element turns it off.

  A standalone element does not have a companion element. For example, the `<img/>` element places an image on a page. `<img/>` has no effect that was turned on and needs to be turned off, so no closing element is needed.

NOTE Standalone elements are sometimes called *empty elements*. The rules of XML require that empty elements have a trailing forward slash inside them, which is why you see the forward slash character within the `<img />` element. ■

- **The element's function**—A description of the effect or page element that the element controls.
- **The element's syntax**—XHTML is an application of XML, so adherence to proper syntax is important if you want your documents to be rendered.
- **The element's attributes**—An attribute modifies how an element's effect is applied. Some elements take no attributes, and others might take several. Additionally, attributes can sometimes take on only one of a set number of values. In these cases, the possible values of the attribute are listed along with the attribute. Use of some attributes might be required (such as the `src` attribute for the `<img />` element), and others might be optional. An element's required attributes, if any, are noted in each attribute discussion.
- **Sample use**—You can learn more about how an element is used by looking over the sample code given in the element description.
- **Related elements**—Some elements work in conjunction with others to produce an effect. In these cases, you'll find a listing of the other XHTML elements related to the one being described. Often, you'll find that the related elements are discussed in the same section.

Within a section, elements are listed alphabetically by keyword, unless they need to be used in a certain order, in which case, they are presented in the order that they are typically used.

Global Attributes

Although most element attributes tend to be unique to the element, some are almost universal and usable with any element. Table 3.1 summarizes these attributes, showing which elements do take the attributes and how each attribute is used.

Table 3.1 Global XHTML Attributes

Attribute	Purpose	Used With
`class`	Space-separated list of classes of the element	All elements except `<base />`, `<head>`, `<html>`, `<meta />`, `<param />`, `<script>`, `<style>`, and `<title>`.
`dir`	Direction for weak or neutral text	All elements except `<base />`, ` `, `<frame>`, `<frameset>`, `<hr />`, `<iframe>`, `<param />`, and `<script>`.
`id`	Unique, document-wide identifier	All elements except `<base />`, `<head>`, `<html>`, `<meta />`, `<script>`, `<style>`, and `<title>`.
`lang`	Specifies document language context (for backward compatibility with existing HTML)	All elements except `<base />`, ` `, `<frame>`, `<frameset>`, `<hr />`, `<iframe>`, `<param />`, and `<script>`.
`style`	Binds style information to the element	All elements except `<base />`, `<head>`, `<html>`, `<meta />`, `<param />`, `<script>`, `<style>`, and `<title>`.
`title`	Advisory title	All elements except `<base />`, `<head>`, `<html>`, `<meta />`, `<param />`, `<script>`, and `<title>`.
`xml:lang`	Specifies document language context (as per XML 1.0)	All elements except `<base />`, `<param />`, and `<script>`.

The global attribute you'll probably use most often is the `style` attribute, which is used to assign style information to an element. To color a level 2 heading red, for example, you could use the XHTML:

```
<h2 style="color: red">Red Heading</h2>
```

NOTE Note the use of Cascading Style Sheet instructions in the code above to apply formatting information. One of the intentions of XHTML is to expunge elements like `<font>` which have been used to specify formatting information. ■

The `id` attribute is also useful when you need to have a unique identifier for an element. This situation comes into play when you write scripts to support dynamic HTML documents because you frequently want to change the properties of some object in the document. To do this, you must be able to address the element that marks up the text via JavaScript, JScript, or VBScript, and the best way to do that is to give the element a unique name. Then it becomes fairly simple to address the element via the browser's object model.

▶ To learn more about DHTML, **see** Chapter 24, "Introduction to Dynamic HTML"

`lang` can be helpful in situations in which you are marking up content in multiple languages. The value of `lang` gives browsers a "heads-up" as to what language is being used. `lang` is usually set equal to a two-character language code that denotes the language being used. For example, `fr` denotes French; `de` denotes German, and so on. In cases where variants on a language exist, you'll see expanded language codes, such as `en-US` for English spoken in the United States or `en-Br` for English spoken in Britain. The `xml:lang` attribute can take on the same values but was introduced as a separate attribute for easier compatibility with the XML standard.

`dir` refers to the directionality—left-to-right or right-to-left—of text when it cannot otherwise be deduced from the context of the document. `dir` can take on values of `ltr` (left-to-right) or `rtl` (right-to-left).

The `title` attribute enables you to specify descriptive text to associate with the element. This information might be helpful to nonvisual browsers, such as those that generate speech or Braille output.

Finally, the `class` attribute enables you to create different classes of the same element. For example, you might have

```
<a href="xrefs.html" class="cross-reference"> ... </a>
<a href="defns.html" class="definition"> ... </a>
<a href="biblio.html" class="bibliography"> ... </a>
```

This creates three classes of the `<a>` element. After these classes are established, you can reference them elsewhere in your document. One popular application of this is in a style sheet:

```
a.cross-reference {color: navy}
a.definition {color: yellow}
a.bibliography {color: fuschia}
```

The style information shown here would color cross-reference links navy blue, definition links yellow, and bibliography links fuschia.

Event Handlers

The XHTML 1.0 recommendation also allows for several event handlers that can be used to trigger the execution of script code embedded in an XHTML document. Each event handler is tied to a specific event that can occur during a person's use of a browser. When a user submits a form, for example, you can capture that event and launch a field validation script using the `onsubmit` event handler:

```
<form action="register.cgi" method="post" onsubmit="return validate();">
```

▶ For the specifics on writing scripts for your HTML documents, **see** Chapter 18, "Introduction to JavaScripting," or Chapter 32, "Writing Active Server Pages"

Thus, when a user clicks the Submit button, the scripted function named `validate()` executes and checks the data the user is submitting for appropriate formatting, content, or other validation checks.

Table 3.2 details the event handlers available under XHTML 1.0. Some event handlers must be used within specific elements. These special cases are noted along with the event handler in the table.

Table 3.2 XHTML 1.0 Event Handlers

Event Handler	Triggered When...
`onload`	A document or frameset is loaded; only allowed in the `<body>` and `<frameset>` elements
`onunload`	A document or frameset is unloaded; only allowed in the `<body>` and `<frameset>` elements
`onclick`	The mouse button is clicked once
`ondblclick`	The mouse button is clicked twice
`onmousedown`	The mouse button is pressed
`onmouseup`	The mouse button is released
`onmouseover`	The mouse pointer is over a page element
`onmousemove`	The mouse pointer is moved while over a page element
`onmouseout`	The mouse pointer is moved off a page element
`onfocus`	A form field receives focus by tabbing to it or by clicking it with the mouse pointer; only allowed in the `<input />`, `<select>`, `<textarea>`, `<label>`, and `<button>` elements
`onblur`	A form field loses focus by tabbing out of it or by clicking a different field with the mouse pointer; only allowed in the `<input />`, `<select>`, `<textarea>`, `<label>`, and `<button>` elements

Table 3.2 Continued

Event Handler	Triggered When...
onkeypress	A key is pressed and released over a page element
onkeydown	A key is pressed over a page element
onkeyup	A key is released over a page element
onsubmit	A form is submitted; only allowed in the <form> element
onreset	A form is reset; only allowed in the <form> element
onselect	A user selects some text in a text field; only allowed in the <input /> and <textarea> elements
onchange	A form field loses focus and its value has changed since gaining focus; only allowed in the <input />, <textarea>, and <select> elements

Document Structure Elements

Every XHTML document has three major components: the XHTML declaration, the head, and the body. The document structure elements are those that define each component.

<html>

Type:

Container

Function:

Declares the document to be an XHTML document. All document content and supporting XHTML code goes between the <html> and </html> elements.

Syntax:

```
<html> ... </html>
```

Attributes:

The <html> element can take the xmlns attribute, which specifies the URL that describes the XML namespace for the document (for example, xmlns="http://www.w3.org/1999/xhtml").

Example:

```
<html>
... all content and XHTML code goes here ...
</html>
```

Related Elements:

Although the <html> element is typically the first element in a document, it is sometimes preceded by a <!DOCTYPE> element that specifies which level of HTML conformance the document displays. A document conforming to the XHTML 1.0 standard might have a `<!DOC-TYPE>` element that reads

```
<!DOCTYPE XML PUBLIC "-//W3C//DTD XHTML 1.0//EN">
```

Technically, `<!DOCTYPE>` is an SGML element, not an HTML element, so it is acceptable for it to be outside the `<html>` and `</html>` elements.

<head>

Type:

Container

Function:

Contains the elements that compose the document head.

Syntax:

```
<head> ... </head>
```

Attributes:

`<head>` can take the `profile` attribute, which gets set equal to a space-separated list of URLs that point to meta-data profiles for the document. The profiles could describe the nature of the content, who wrote it, how it was published, and so on.

Example:

```
<html>
<head profile="http://www.server.com/profiles/">
... elements making up the document head go here ...
</head>
... all other content and XHTML code goes here ...
</html>
```

Related Elements:

Several elements can be placed between the `<head>` and `</head>` elements, including `<base/>`, `<link/>`, `<meta/>`, `<script>`, `<style>`, and `<title>`. Each of these is described next.

NOTE The `<ISINDEX>` tag, which has been deprecated from HTML, does not have an equivalent in XHTML. ■

<base />

Type:

Standalone

Function:

Declares a global reference value for `href` and `target` attributes. The reference or base `href` value is used as a basis for computing all relative URL references. The `base target` value indicates which frame in a frameset is targeted by default.

Syntax:

```
<base href="base_url" />
```

or

```
<base target="base_target" />
```

Attributes:

A given `<base />` element takes either the `href` or the `target` attribute, but not both at the same time. The usage of each attribute follows:

- **`href`**—Specifies the reference URL that is used to help compute relative URLs. If the `base href` URL is `http://www.myserver.com/sports/hockey/skates.html` and you use the relative URL `pucks.html` elsewhere in the document, for example, the relative URL will really point to `http://www.myserver.com/sports/hockey/pucks.html`.
- **`target`**—Used to direct the results of a hyperlink click or a form submission to a particular frame in the frameset. A common use of this attribute is to set `target="main"` in a frame that contains navigation links. This results in the linked documents being loaded into the frame called "main" rather than being loaded into the navigation frame itself.

NOTE When used in a `<base>` element, `href` is typically set to the URL of the document. ■

Example:

```
<head>
<base href="http://www.myserver.com/index.html/" />
<base target="main" />
...
</head>
```

This code sets the document's base URL to `http://www.myserver.com/index.html`.

<meta />

Type:

Standalone

Function:

Defines document meta-information, such as keywords, expiration date, author, page-generation software used, and many other document-specific items. It also supports the notion of *client pull*—a dynamic document technique in which the browser loads a new document after a specified delay.

Syntax:

```
<meta http-equiv="header" content="value" />
```

or

```
<meta name="name" content="value" />
```

Attributes:

The `<meta />` element takes the following attributes:

- **`http-equiv`**—Specifies a type of HTTP header to be sent with the document. The value of the header is given by the `content` attribute. The two most commonly used values of `http-equiv` are `refresh`, which refreshes the page after a specified delay, and `expires`, which gives the date after which content in the document is not considered to be reliable.
- **`name`**—Set equal to the name of the document meta-variable you want to specify. The value of the variable is given in the `content` attribute. Typical values for `name` include `author`, `keywords`, `generator`, and `description`. The `keywords` value is particularly useful for specifying words you want a search engine's indexing program to associate with the page.
- **`scheme`**—Provides information on how to interpret the meta-variable. For example, with the following `<meta/>` element:

  ```
  <meta scheme="9-digit-ZipCode" name="zip" content="02134-1078"/>
  ```

  a browser might not know how to interpret `"02134-1078"` without information from the `scheme` attribute.
- **`content`**—Specifies either the HTTP header or the value of the meta-variable.

Example:

```
<head>
<!-- The first <meta/> element instructs the browser
to load a new page after 5 seconds. -->
<!-- This is useful for creating a splash screen effect. -->
<meta http-equiv="refresh"
➥content="5; URL=http://www.myserver.com/index2.html" />
<!-- The remaining <meta /> elements specify author and keyword information. -->
<meta name="author" content="Eric Ladd" />
<meta name="keywords" content="Main page, welcome, neat stuff" />
...
</head>
```

<link />

Type:

Standalone

Function:

Denotes the linking relationship between two files.

Syntax:

```
<link href="url_of_linked_file" title="title"
➥rel="forward_relationship" rev="reverse_relationship" />
```

Attributes:

The `<link />` element takes the following attributes:

- **`charset`**—Denotes which character encoding scheme to use.
- **`href`**—Set equal to the URL of the file to which you're making the linking reference.
- **`hreflang`**—Specifies the language code for the linked file.
- **`media`**—Provides the intended display destination for the linked document. The default value of `media` is `screen`.
- **`rel`**—Specifies the relationship of the linked file to the current file.
- **`rev`**—Specifies how the current file relates to the linked file.
- **`target`**—Specifies which frame to target.
- **`title`**—Gives the link a descriptive title.
- **`type`**—Specifies the MIME type of the linked file.

Table 3.3 shows some possible values for `rel` and `rev` and what these values mean.

Table 3.3 Possible Values for the *rel* and *rev* Attributes

Value	Meaning
`copyright`	Web site's copyright page
`glossary`	Glossary of terms for a site
`help`	Site help page
`home`	Site home page
`index`	Site index page
`made`	Mail to URL pointing to the email address of the page author
`next`	Page that logically follows the current page
`previous`	Page that precedes the current page
`stylesheet`	File containing style information for the page
`toc`	Site table of contents
`up`	Page that is above the current page in a site's hierarchy

NOTE Because so many types of linked files exist, it is permissible to have more than one `<link />` element in a document. ■

Example:

```
<head>
<link href="/style/styles.css" rel="stylesheet" />
<link href="/index.html" rel="home" />
<link href="/help.html" rel="help" />
<link href="back_one.html" rev="previous" />
...
</head>
```

<script>

Type:

Container

Function:

Contains script code referenced in the body of the document.

Syntax:

```
<script type="scripting_language MIME type">
... script code goes here ...
</script>
```

Attributes:

The `<script>` element can take the following attributes:

- **`charset`**—Denotes which character encoding scheme to use.
- **`defer`**—Specifying the `defer` attribute tells the browser that the script does not generate any document content. This enables the browser to continue parsing and rendering the document without having to execute the script.
- **`src`**—Specifies the URL of a file containing the script code, if not contained between the `<script>` and `</script>` elements.
- **`type`**—Set equal to the MIME type of the script code, usually `text/javascript` or `text/vbscript`. When specifying a specific version of a scripting language, you can set `type` equal to a value that includes version information as well (for example, `type="text/javascript1.1"`). `type` is a required attribute under XHTML 1.0.

NOTE The `<script>` element also takes the `xml:space` attribute, which tells processing programs to preserve whitespace within the element. ■

Example:

```
<script type="text/vbscript">

Sub ScriptEx
document.write("<hr/>")
document.write("<h1>Thank you for your submission!</h1>")
document.write("<hr/>")

</script>
```

TIP

Traditionally, script code is often placed between <!-- and --> elements so that browsers that can't process scripts will treat the code as a comment. However, under XHTML, a parser can remove what's contained inside a comment. Therefore, hiding your scripts with comment delimiters will probably not serve you well when writing for XHTML browsers.

Related Elements:

You can use the <noscript> element to specify what a browser should do if it's unable to execute a script contained in the <script> and </script> elements.

<NOSCRIPT>

Type:

Container

Function:

Provides alternative content to use if a script cannot be executed. A browser might not be able to execute a script because the user has turned scripting off or because it does not know the scripting language used to write the script.

Syntax:

```
<noscript>
... alternative to script code goes here ...
</noscript>
```

Attributes:

None.

Example:

```
<script type="text/javascript">
   document.write("Hello, World!");
</script>
<noscript>
   You either have scripting turned off or your browser does not
   understand JavaScript.
</noscript>
```

<style>

Type:

Container

Function:

Specifies style information for the document.

Syntax:

```
<style type="mime_type" media="media_type" title="title">
... style information goes here ...
</style>
```

Attributes:

The `<style>` element takes the following three attributes:

- **`media`**—Specifies what media types the styles are to be used for (visual browser, speech-based browser, Braille browser, and so on).
- **`title`**—Gives the style information a descriptive title.
- **`type`**—Set equal to the Internet content type for the style language. You will most likely use `type="text/css2"` to denote the use of the style language put forward in the Cascading Style Sheets, Level 1 specification. `type` is a required attribute of the `<style>` element.

NOTE The `<style>` element also takes the `xml:space` attribute, which tells processing programs to preserve whitespace within the element. ■

Example:

```
<style type="text/css2">
<!--
   body {font: 10 pt Palatino; color: silver margin-left: 0.25 in}
   h1 {font: 18 pt Palatino; font-weight: bold}
   h2 {font: 16 pt Palatino; font-weight: bold}
   p {font: 12 pt Arial; line-height: 14 pt; text-indent: 0.25 in}
-->
</style>
```

NOTE Style information has traditionally been placed between `<!--` and `-->` elements so browsers that cannot process it will treat the style information as a comment. However, this is not recommended for XHTML documents since an XHTML parser is free to remove contents inside of comments. ■

<title>

Type:

Container

Function:

Gives a descriptive title to a document. Use of the `<title>` element is required by the XHTML 1.0 DTD for many good reasons. Titles show up in browser window title bars and in bookmark and history listings. In each of these cases, you provide an important reader service when you specify a title because otherwise the browser displays just the document's URL. Additionally, Web search engines, such as Yahoo! and AltaVista, frequently look for title information when they index a document.

Syntax:

```
<title> ... document title goes here ... </title>
```

Attributes:

None.

Example:

```
<title>
XHTML Tutorial
</title>
```

TIP Try to keep titles to 40 characters or fewer so that browsers can display them completely.

<body>

Type:

Container

Function:

Contains all content and elements that compose the document body.

Syntax:

```
<body>
 ... document body goes here ...
</body>
```

Attributes:

None.

NOTE The popular <BODY> tag attributes used in HTML--BGCOLOR, BACKGROUND, TEXT, LINK, VLINK, and ALINK—do not have equivalents under the Strict XHTML DTD. You should use style sheets to specify these display characteristics or use the Transitional DTD instead. ■

NOTE The <body> element is not allowed under the XHTML Frameset DTD. ■

Example:

```
<body>
... all document body content and XHTML code goes here ...
</body>
```

Related Elements:

Dozens of elements are allowed inside the <body> element. In fact, with the exception of some of the frame-related elements, any element in the rest of the chapter can be placed between <body> and </body>.

By putting together what you've learned in this section, you can come up with a generic XHTML document template such as the following:

```
<html>
<head>
<title>Document Template</title>
... <meta />, <base />, <link />, <script>, <style> elements ...
</head>
<body>
... document body content and elements ...
</body>
</html>
```

When creating a new document, you can use this code to get started, and then fill in elements and other information according to your needs.

Formatting Elements

XHTML provides a host of elements that you can use to change how text is displayed on a browser screen. After all, 12-point Times Roman or Arial gets a little tiring after a while, and it's nice to give a reader an occasional break from a sea of ordinary text.

You can apply formatting instructions at two levels within a document. The first is at the text level, which means you are marking up at least a single character, but often much more than that. The second is at the paragraph or block level, which means you are formatting a specific logical chunk of the document. This section looks at both types of markup, starting with text-level formatting.

Text-Level Formatting

Text-level formatting can occur in one of two ways. An XHTML element that formats text can make changes to the font properties of the text (*font formatting* or *physical styles*), or it can describe how the text is being used in the context of the document (*phrase formatting* or *logical styles*). The next two sections introduce you to the elements used for each type of formatting.

NOTE The HTML <FONT>, <BASEFONT>, <U>, <S>, and <STRIKE> tags do not have equivalents under the Strict XHTML DTD. You should use style sheets to specify information previously provided through these tags, or you can use the Transitional or Frameset DTD, both of which permit the use of these elements. ■

Font Formatting

<b>

Type:

Container

Function:

Contains text to be rendered in boldface (see Figure 3.1).

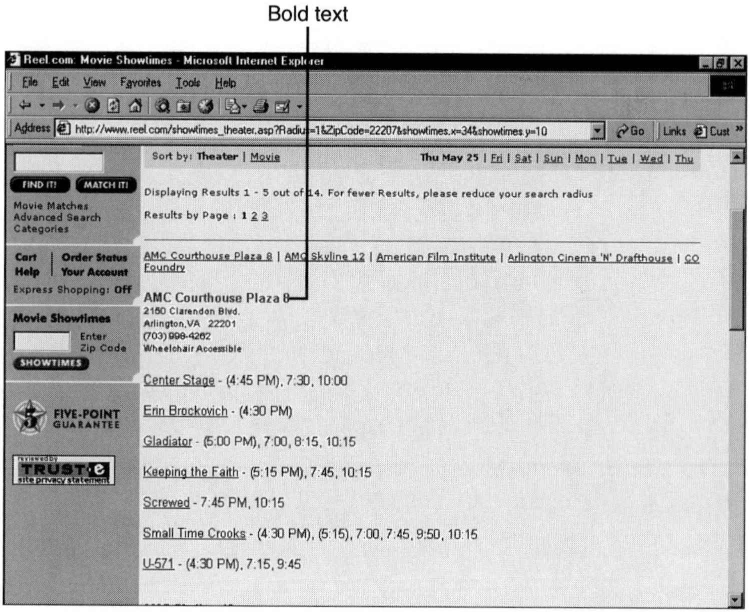

Bold text

FIGURE 3.1
Boldface text stands out from the plain text around it, drawing the reader's attention.

Syntax:

```
<b> ... bold text goes here ... </b>
```

Attributes:

None.

Example:

```
<b>First Name:</b> <input type="text" name="fname" />
```

<big>

Type:

Container

Function:

Contains text to be rendered in a font size bigger than the default font size (see Figure 3.2).

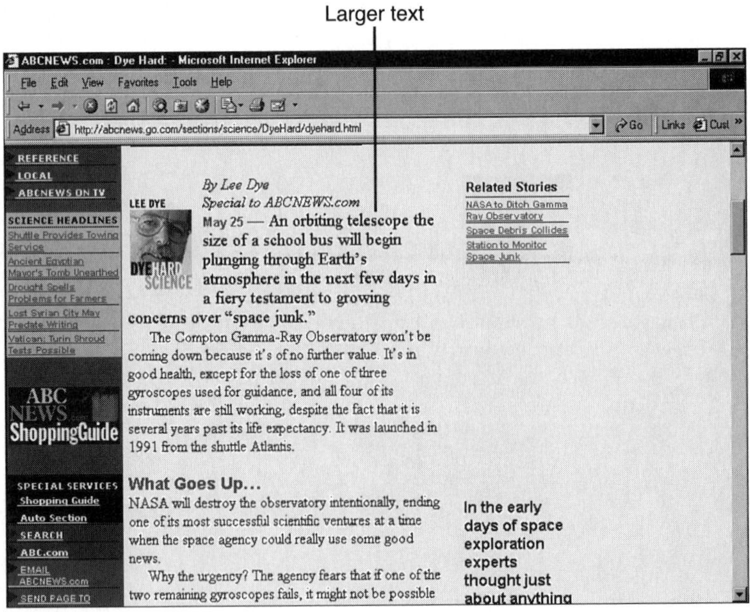

FIGURE 3.2
Using the <big> element increases the point size in which text is rendered.

Example:

```
<big> ... bigger text goes here ... </big>
```

Attributes:

None.

Example:

```
<big>D</big>rop <big>C</big>aps are a nice onscreen effect.
```

Related Elements:

The <small> element has the opposite effect (see later in this chapter).

<i>

Type:

Container

Function:

Contains text to be rendered in italic (see Figure 3.3).

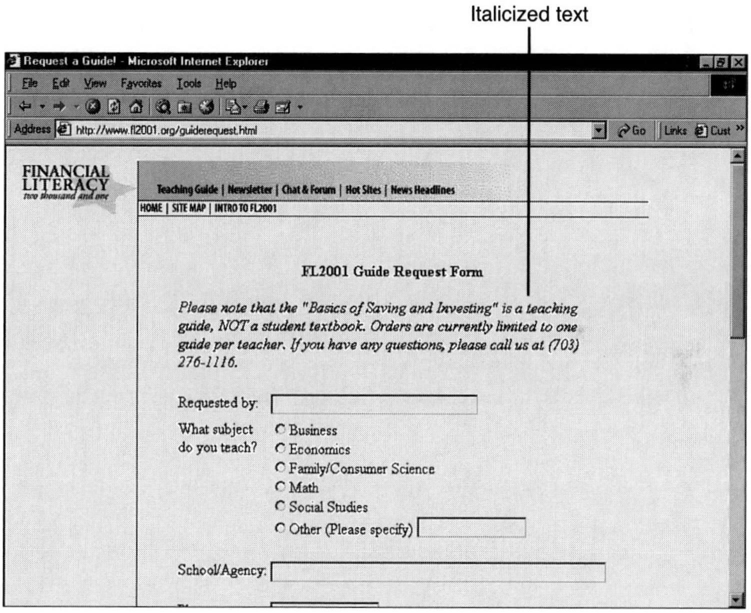

Italicized text

FIGURE 3.3
Italicized text can be used to denote emphasis or the title of something.

Syntax:

```
<i> ... italicized text goes here ... </i>
```

Attributes:

None.

Example:

```
The textbook for the class is Ben Forta's
<i>The ColdFusion 4.0 Web Application Construction Kit</i>.
```

<small>

Type:

Container

Function:

Contains text to be rendered in a font size smaller than the default font size.

Syntax:

```
<small> ... smaller text goes here ... </small>
```

Attributes:

None.

Example:

```
<small>"Sssssssshhh!"</small>, he whispered in a tiny voice.
```

Related Elements:

The `<big>` element has the opposite effect (see the `<big>` element section earlier in the chapter).

<sub>

Type:

Container

Function:

Contains text to be a subscript to the text that precedes it.

Syntax:

```
<sub> ... subscript text goes here ... </sub>
```

Attributes:

None.

Example:

```
a<sub>1</sub>, a<sub>2</sub>, and a<sub>3</sub> are the coefficients of
 the variables x, y, and z.
```

<sup>

Type:

Container

Function:

Contains text to be rendered as a superscript to the text that precedes it (see Figure 3.4).

FIGURE 3.4
Superscripts are useful for indicating trademark or copyright information.

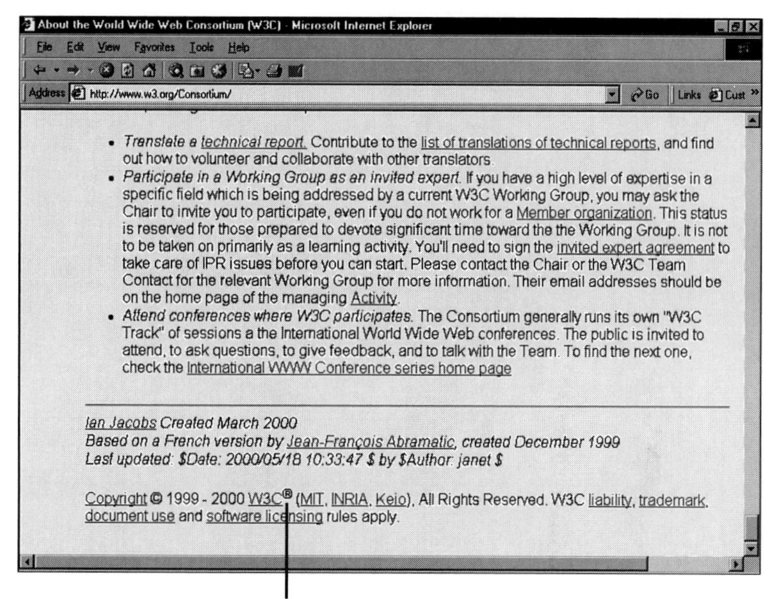

Syntax:

```
<sup> ... superscript text goes here ... </sup>
```

Attributes:

None.

Example:

```
x<sup>2</sup> + y<sup>2</sup> = 1 defines the unit circle.
```

<tt>

Type:

Container

Function:

Contains text to be rendered in a monospace or fixed-width font. Typically, this font is Courier or some kind of typewriter font (see Figure 3.5).

Part I Ch 3

Typewriter text
SQL Tutorial - Microsoft Internet Explorer
File Edit View Favorites Tools Help
Address http://w3.one.net/~jhoffman/sqltut.htm
The WHERE clause is used to specify that only certain rows of the table are displayed, based on the criteria described in that WHERE clause. It is most easily understood by looking at a couple of examples.
If you wanted to see the EMPLOYEEIDNO's of those making at or over $50,000, use the following:
SELECT EMPLOYEEIDNO
FROM EMPLOYEESTATISTICSTABLE
WHERE SALARY >= 50000;
Notice that the >= (greater than or equal to) sign is used, as we wanted to see those who made greater than $50,000, or equal to $50,000, listed together. This displays:
EMPLOYEEIDNO

010
105
152
215
244
The WHERE description, SALARY >= 50000, is known as a condition (an operation which evaluates to True or False). The same can be done for text columns:
SELECT EMPLOYEEIDNO

FIGURE 3.5
Typewriter text is good for displaying computer-related content or for varying the fonts used in the document.

Syntax:

```
<tt> ... text to be in fixed-width font goes here ... </tt>
```

Attributes:

None.

Example:

```
The computer will then display the <t>Login:</tt> prompt.
```

Phrase Formatting Recall that phrase formatting indicates the *meaning* of the text it marks up and not necessarily how the text will be rendered on the browser screen. Nevertheless, text marked with a phrase-formatting element will typically have some kind of special rendering to set it apart from unmarked text.

<abbr>

Type:

Container

Function:

Contains text that is an abbreviation of something. This is useful information for browsers that are not vision-based because it enables them to treat the abbreviation differently. A speech-based browser, for example, could know to look in an abbreviation table for pronunciation if you marked up "Dr." with the <abbr> element. That way, it could say the word "doctor" rather than making the "dr" sound you would get by pronouncing the "d" and the "r" together.

Syntax:

```
<abbr> ... acronym goes here ... </abbr>
```

Attributes:

None.

Example:

```
She got her <abbr>PhD</abbr> from the University of Virginia.
```


<acronym>

Type:

Container

Function:

Contains text that specifies an acronym. This element is also useful for nonvisual browsers. The element might tell a speech-based browser to pronounce the letters in the acronym one at a time, for example, rather than trying to pronounce the acronym as a word.

Syntax:

```
<acronym> ... acronym goes here ... </acronym>
```

Attributes:

None.

Example:

```
Practical Extraction and Reporting Language <acronym>(PERL)</acronym> is
a popular CGI scripting language.
```

<address>

Type:

Container

Function:

Contains either a postal or an email address (see Figure 3.6). Text marked with this element is typically rendered in italic.

FIGURE 3.6
Marking up address information provides a logical marker for programs processing the document and a visual marker for those reading the document.

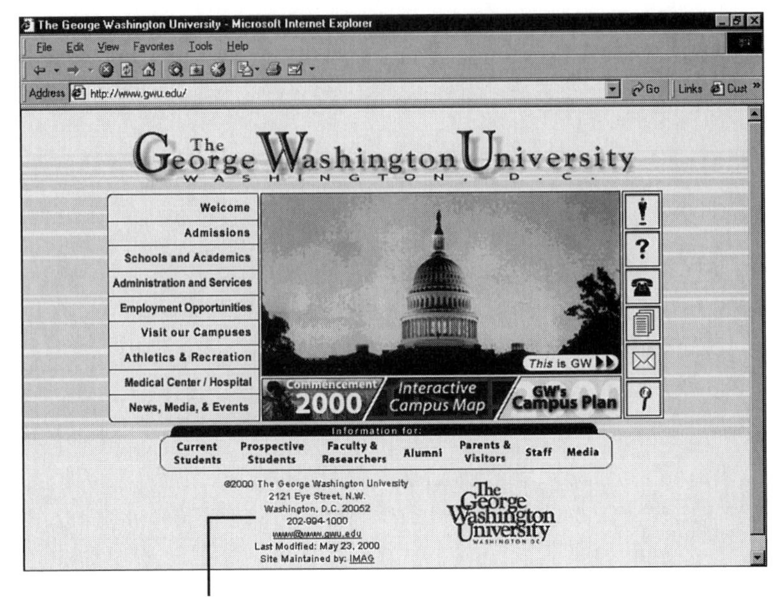

Syntax:

```
<address> ... address goes here ... </address>
```

Attributes:

None.

Example:

```
If you have any comments, please send them to
<address>webmaster@your-isp.com</address>.
```

<cite>

Type:

Container

Function:

Contains the name of a source from which a passage is cited. The source's name is typically rendered in italic.

Syntax:

```
<cite> ... citation source goes here ... </cite>
```

Attributes:

None.

Example:

```
According to the <cite>XHTML 1.0 Recommendation</cite>,
the type attribute of the <script> element
is required.
```

<code>

Type:

Container

Function:

Contains chunks of computer language code. Browsers commonly display text marked with the `<code>` element in a fixed-width font such as Courier.

Syntax:

```
<code> ... code fragment goes here ... </code>
```

Attributes:

None.

Example:

```
<code>
alert("Please fill in the password field.");
return false;
</code>
```

<del>

Type:

Container

Function:

Contains text that has been deleted from the document. The element is intended mainly for documents with multiple authors and editors who would want to see all the content in an original draft, even though it might have been deleted by a reviewer.

NOTE The idea of logically marking up deleted text is similar to the idea of using revision marks in Microsoft Word. When revision marks are turned on, you can see the deleted text even though it is technically no longer part of the document. ■

Syntax:

```
<del cite="url" datetime="YYYYMMDDThh:mm:ss">
... deleted text goes here
</del>
```

Attributes:

`<del>` can take two attributes:

- **`cite`**—Provides the URL of a document that explains why the deletion was necessary.
- **`datetime`**—Puts a "timestamp" on the deletion.

Example:

```
She just got a big<del>, huge</del> raise.
```

In this example, the use of the word "huge" is redundant, so an astute copy editor would delete it.

Related Elements:

The `<ins>` element has a similar function for inserted text.

<dfn>

Type:

Container

Function:

Denotes the defining instance of a term.

Syntax:

```
<dfn> ... term being introduced goes here ... </dfn>
```

Attributes:

None.

Example:

```
Freud proposed the idea of a <dfn>catharsis</dfn> - a release
of psychic tension.
```

<em>

Type:

Container

Function:

Contains text to be emphasized. Most browsers render emphasized text in italic.

Syntax:

```
<em> ... emphasized text goes here ... </em>
```

Attributes:

None.

Example:

```
Please do <em>not</em> feed the animals.
```

<ins>

Type:

Container

Function:

Contains text that has been inserted into the document after its original draft.

Syntax:

```
<ins> ... inserted text goes here ... </ins>
```

Attributes:

Like <del>, <ins> can take two attributes:

- **cite**—Provides the URL of a document that explains why the insertion was necessary.
- **datetime**—Puts a "timestamp" on the insertion.

Example:

```
The New World was discovered by <del>Magellan</del>
<ins>Columbus</ins> in 1492.
```

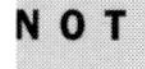

NOTE Note how <del> and <ins> are used together to strike some text and then to insert a correction in its place. ■

Related Elements:

The <del> element logically represents deleted text.

<kbd>

Type:

Container

Function:

Contains text that represents keyboard input. Browsers typically render such text in a fixed-width font.

Syntax:

```
<kbd> ... keyboard input goes here ... </kbd>
```

Attributes:

None.

Example:

```
To begin, type <kbd>go</kbd> and press Enter.
```

<q>

Type:

Container

Function:

Contains a direct quotation to be displayed inline.

Syntax:

```
<q cite="URL_of_cited_document"> ... quotation goes here ... </q>
```

Attributes:

If you're quoting from an online source, you can set the `cite` attribute equal to the source's URL. Also, you might want to consider using the `lang` attribute because quotes are denoted with different characters in many languages.

Related Elements:

The `<blockquote>` element can also be used to mark up quoted text, but block quotes are displayed with increased right and left indents and are not in line with the rest of the body text.

Example:

```
<q>To be or not to be.  That is the question.</q>
is her favorite quote from Shakespeare.
```

<samp>

Type:

Container

Function:

Contains text that represents the literal output from a program. Such output is sometimes referred to as *sample text*. Most browsers render sample text in a fixed-width font.

Syntax:

```
<samp> ... program output goes here ... </samp>
```

Attributes:

None.

Example:

```
A common first exercise in a programming course is to write a program
to produce the message <samp>Hello World</samp>.
```

<strong>

Type:

Container

Function:

Contains text to be strongly emphasized. Browsers typically render strongly emphasized text in boldface (see Figure 3.7).

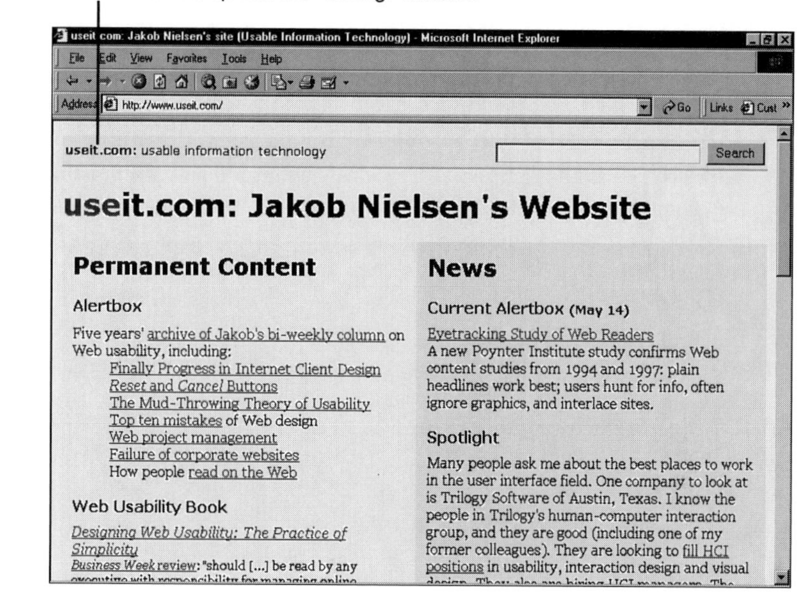

FIGURE 3.7
The `<strong>` element is useful for marking up recommendations with extra emphasis.

Syntax:

```
<strong> ... strongly emphasized text goes here ... </strong>
```

Attributes:

None.

Example:

```
<strong>STOP!</strong> Do not proceed any further.  Contact your system
administrator.
```

<var>

Type:

Container

Function:

Denotes a variable from a computer program. Variables are typically rendered in a fixed-width font.

Syntax:

```
<var> ... program variable goes here ... </var>
```

Attributes:

None.

Example:

```
The <var>RecordCount</var> variable is set to the number of records
that the query retrieved.
```

Block-Level Formatting Elements

Block-level formatting elements are usually applied to larger amounts of content than the text-level formatting elements. As such, the block-level elements define major sections of a document, such as paragraphs, headings, abstracts, chapters, and so on. The elements profiled in this section are the ones to turn to when you want to define the block-level elements in a document you're authoring.

NOTE The HTML <CENTER> tag does not have an equivalent under the Strict XHTML DTD, but is permissible under the Transitional and Frameset DTDs. You should center page elements using the style sheet instructions when writing to the Strict DTD. ■

<blockquote>

Type:

Container

Function:

Contains quoted text that is to be displayed indented from regular body text (see Figure 3.8).

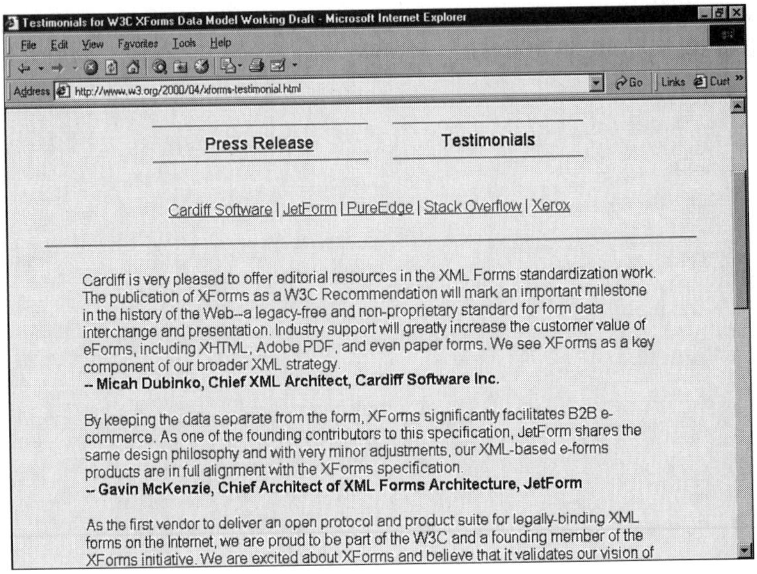

FIGURE 3.8
Blockquotes are used to offset longer quoted passages.

Syntax:

```
<blockquote cite="URL_of_cited_document">
... quoted text goes here ...
</blockquote>
```

Attributes:

If you're quoting from an online source, you can set the `cite` attribute equal to the source's URL.

Example:

```
Fans of Schoolhouse Rock will always be able to recite the preamble
of the United States Constitution:
<blockquote>
We, the people, in order to form a more perfect Union ...
</blockquote>
```

Related Elements:

The `<q>` element is used to denote quoted text that is to be displayed in line with the body text.

*
*

Type:

Standalone

Function:

Inserts a line break in the document. Carriage returns in the XHTML code do not translate to line breaks on the browser screen, so authors often need to insert the breaks themselves. The `<br />` element is indispensable when rendering text with frequent line breaks, such as addresses or poetry. Unlike the `<p>` element or the heading elements, `<br />` adds no additional vertical space after the break.

Syntax:

```
<br/>
```

Attributes:

None.

NOTE The HTML `<BR>` tag takes the `CLEAR` attribute to facilitate breaking to a margin that is free of a "floating" page element such as an image or a table. Under the Strict DTD, XHTML `<br/>` tag does not have a `clear` attribute. You should break to clear margins using style sheet instructions instead. You are free to use the `clear` attribute with the Transitional and Frameset DTDs. ■

Example:

```
First Name: <input type="text" name="fname" /><br />
Last Name: <input type="text" name="lname" /><br />
Telephone: <input type="text" name="phone"/><br />
Email: <input type="text" name="email" />
```

<bdo>

Type:

Container

Function:

When mixing languages in an XHTML document, it sometimes becomes necessary to be sensitive to the direction in which the language is read (left-to-right versus right-to-left). When languages that have mixed directions are used in a document, an approach called the *bidirectional algorithm* is used to ensure proper presentation of the content. In cases where you want to override the bidirectional algorithm for a block of text, you can enclose that text in the `<bdo>` and `</bdo>` elements.

Syntax:

```
<bdo dir="ltr|rtl"> ... directional text goes here ... </bdo>
```

Attributes:

The `<bdo>` element takes the `dir` attribute, which can be set to `ltr` to specify left-to-right directionality or to `rtl` to specify right-to-left directionality.

Example:

```
<body lang="he" ...> <!-- Hebrew language context - RTL directionality>
... <bdo dir="ltr">Here's some English text.</bdo> ...
...
</body>
```

<div>

Type:

Container

Function:

Defines a section or division of a document that requires a special alignment.

Syntax:

```
<div>
... document content ...
</div>
```

Attributes:

None.

NOTE The ALIGN attribute of the HTML <DIV> tag does not have an equivalent under the Strict XHTML DTD. To do alignment within a <div> element, use the style attribute and specify alignment by using a Cascading Style Sheet instruction. You can use the align attribute of the <div> element with the Transitional and Frameset DTDs. ■

Example:

```
<div style="align: right">
Everything in this section is right-justified.  Hard to read, isn't it?
...
</div>
```

<hr />

Type:

Standalone

Function:

Places a horizontal line on the page (see Figure 3.9).

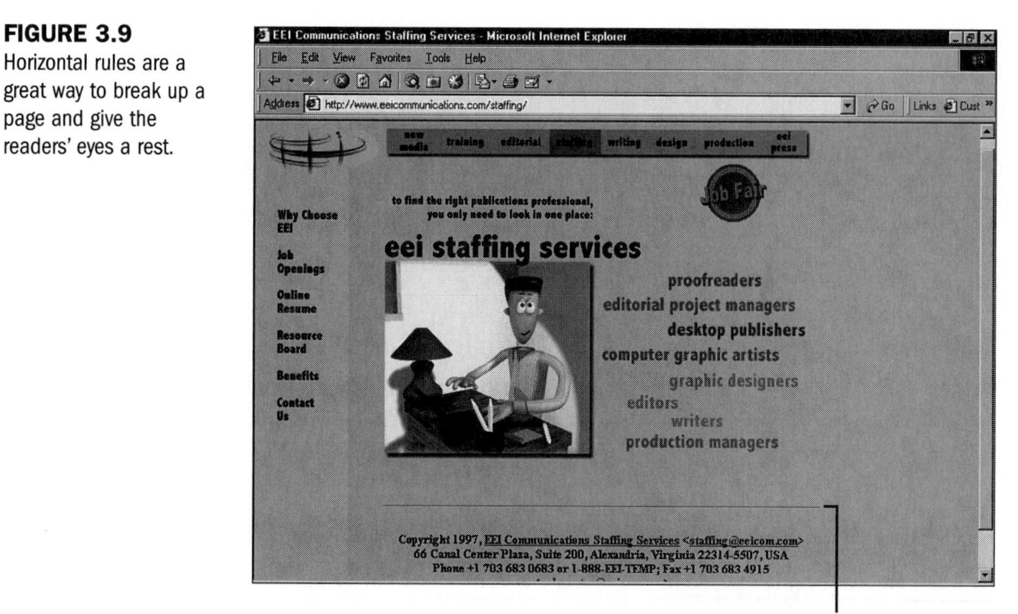

FIGURE 3.9
Horizontal rules are a great way to break up a page and give the readers' eyes a rest.

Syntax:

```
<hr />
```

Attributes:

None.

NOTE The ALIGN, WIDTH, NOSHADE, and SIZE attributes of the HTML <HR> tag do not have equivalents under the Strict XHTML DTD. To modify the appearance of horizontal rule, you should use the style attribute of the <hr /> element. You are free to use these attributes when writing to the Transitional and Frameset DTDs. ■

Example:

```
<hr style="width: 80%" />
```

<h1>–<h6>

Type:

Container

Function:

Establishes a hierarchy of document heading levels. Level 1 has the largest font size. Increasing through the levels causes the font size to decrease. All headings are rendered in boldface and have a little extra line spacing built in above and below them (see Figure 3.10).

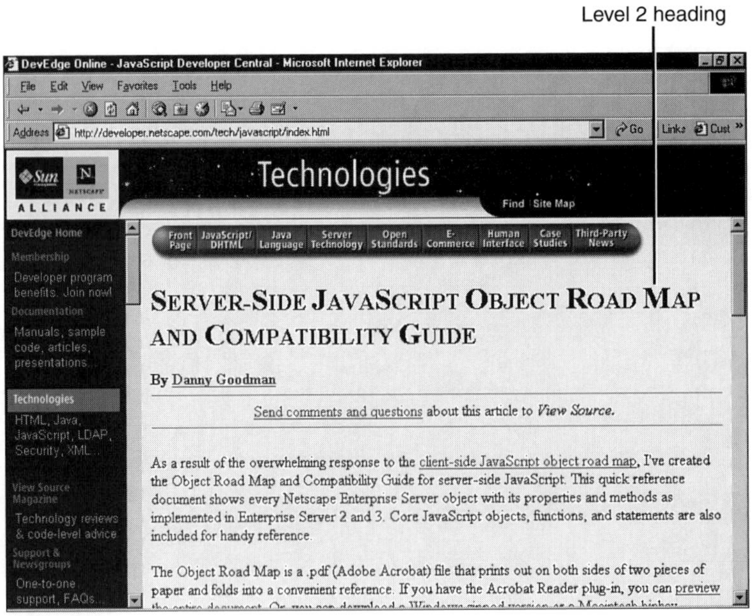

FIGURE 3.10
Headings are rendered in boldface and are usually in a type size different from the body text.

NOTE Although the headings' elements are meant to be used in a strictly hierarchical fashion, many authors use them out of sequence to achieve the formatting effects they want. ■

Syntax:

```
<hn> ... Level n heading ... </hn>
```

where n = 1, 2, 3, 4, 5, or 6.

Attributes:

None.

NOTE The XHTML heading elements do not take an `align` attribute like the corresponding HTML tags do. To align your XHTML headings, you can use the `style` attribute. ■

Example:

```
<h1 style="align: center">Table of Contents</h1>
<h2>Chapter 1 - Introduction</h2>
...
<h2>Chapter 2- Prior Research</h2>
...
```

<p>

Type:

Container

Function:

Denotes a paragraph.

Syntax:

```
<p>
paragraph text
</p>
```

Attributes:

None.

NOTE XHTML does not support an `align` attribute for the <p> element. You should use the `style` attribute together with a style sheet instruction instead. ■

Example:

```
<p style="align: justify">For those of you who scorn ragged right margins.</p>
```

<pre>

Type:

Container

Function:

Denotes text to be treated as preformatted. Browsers render preformatted text in a fixed-width font. Whitespace characters, such as spaces, tabs, and carriage returns, found inside a `<pre>` element are not ignored. This makes preformatted text a viable option for presenting tables of information.

Syntax:

```
<pre>
... preformatted text goes here ...
</pre>
```

Attributes:

The <pre> element's `xml:space` attribute indicates that whitespace should be preserved.

Example:

```
<pre>
Catalog No.  Item          Price
AZ-1390      Polo Shirt    $29.99
FT-0081      Sweater       $52.99
CL-9334      Belt          $16.99
</pre>
```

<span>

Type:

Container

Function:

Generic container element for defining a document block. One popular use is for applying style information.

Syntax:

```
<span style="style information">
range of text over which style is to be applied
</span >
```

Attributes:

If you're assigning style information, you can set the `style` attribute to a sequence of as many `characteristic: value` pairs as you need to specify the style information you're applying. Valid style characteristics are those put forward in the Cascading Style Sheets Level 2 specification.

Example:

```
<span style="font-weight: bold; color: red; text-indent: 0.25 in">
Here is some bold, red, text that's indented by one quarter of an inch.
</span>
```

List Elements

Technically, XHTML lists are a form of block-level formatting, but because lists are such a useful way of presenting content, the list elements merit their own section in the chapter.

Using the elements in this section, you can create the following types of lists:

- Definition lists
- Ordered (numbered) lists
- Unordered (bulleted) lists

Ordered and unordered lists use the list item element, `<li>`, so this element is covered first, followed by the elements you use to create each type of list.

<li>

Type:

Container

Function:

Denotes an item in a list.

Syntax:

```
<li> ... list item goes here ... </li>
```

Attributes:

None.

NOTE The attributes previously used with the HTML `<LI>` tag—`COMPACT`, `TYPE`, and `START`—cannot be used with the XHTML `<li>` tag under the Strict DTD. To modify an `<li>` tag, you should use the `style` attribute. The attributes are permissible under the Transitional and Frameset DTDs. ■

Example:

```
<li>Cookie Dough</li>
<li>Rocky Road</li>
<li>Mint Chocolate Chip</li>
```

Related Elements:

The `<li>` element is always used in conjunction with either the `<ol>` or `<ul>` elements.

> **CAUTION**
> One bad habit from HTML that Web authors will have to shake is using `<li>` as a standalone tag. XHTML syntax rules state that `<li>` is a container tag, so if you try to use it as a standalone tag, your documents will be rejected.

<dl>

Type:

Container

Function:

Denotes a definition list (see Figure 3.11).

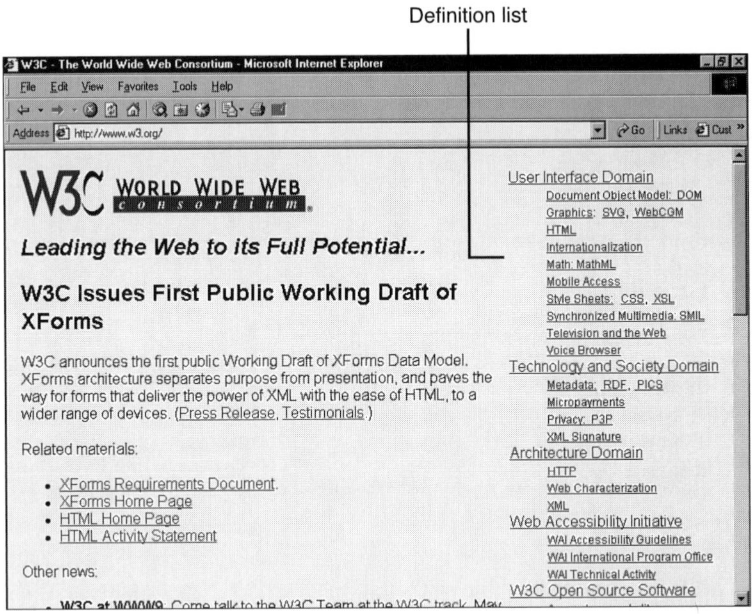

FIGURE 3.11
The World Wide Web Consortium uses a definition list to create the navigation links for its site.

Syntax:

```
<dl>
 ... terms and definitions go here ...
</dl>
```

Attributes:

None.

Example:

```
<dl>
<dt>Browser</dt>
<dd>A program that allows a user to view World Wide Web pages</dd>
<dt>Server</dt>
<dd>A program that fields requests for web pages</dd>
</dl>
```

Related Elements:

Terms in a definition list are specified with the `<dt>` element, and their definitions are specified with the `<dd>` element.

<dt>

Type:

Container

Function:

Contains a term to be defined in a definition list.

NOTE Some browsers automatically render a definition list term in boldface. ■

Syntax:

```
<dt> ... term being defined goes here ... </dt>
```

Attributes:

None.

Example:

```
<dl>
<dt>Creatine</dt>
<dd>A nutritional supplement that promotes muscle development</dd>
...
</dl>
```

Related Elements:

Use of the `<dt>` element makes sense only in the context of a definition list (between the `<dl>` and `</dl>` tags). The `<dd>` element is used to give the term's definition.

<dd>

Type:

Container

Function:

Contains a term's definition. The definition is typically indented from the term, making it easier for the reader to see the term-definition structure of the list.

Syntax:

```
<dd> ... term definition goes here ... </dd>
```

Attributes:

None.

Example:

```
<dl>
<dt>XHTML</dt>
<dd>HTML with the rules of XML applied</dd>
...
</dl>
```

Related Elements:

The `<dd>` element should be used only when contained within a `<dl>`. A term, specified by a `<dt>` element, should precede each definition.

<ol>

Type:

Container

Function:

Creates an ordered or numbered list (see Figure 3.12).

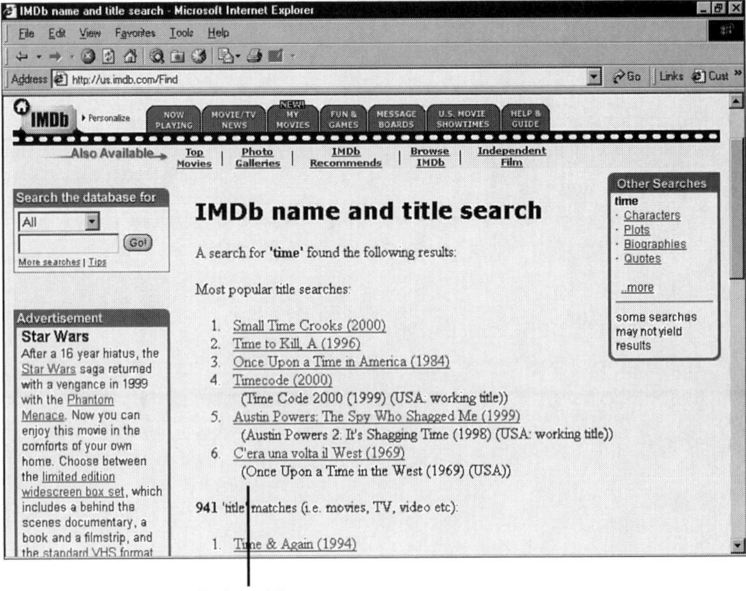

FIGURE 3.12
Ordered and unordered lists are commonly used on Web pages to organize information.

Syntax:

```
<ol>
<li>List item 1</li>
<li>List item 2</li>
...
</ol>
```

Attributes:

None.

NOTE The COMPACT, TYPE, and START attributes of the HTML <OL> tag do not have equivalents under the Strict XHTML DTD. You can use them with the Transitional and Frameset DTDs. ■

Example:

```
Book Outline
<ol>
<li>XHTML</li>
<li>XML</li>
<li>Dynamic HTML</li>
<li>Java</li>
<li>JavaScript</li>
</ol>
```

Related Elements:

List items in an ordered list are specified with the `<li>` element.

<ul>

Type:

Container

Function:

Creates an unordered or bulleted list.

Syntax:

```
<ul>
<li>List item 1</li>
<li>List item 2</li>
...
</ul>
```

Attributes:

None.

NOTE The COMPACT and TYPE attributes of the HTML `<UL>` tag do not have equivalents under the Strict XHTML DTD, but you can use them with the Transitional and Frameset DTDs. ■

Example:

```
Web Browsers
<ul>
<li>Netscape Navigator</li>
<li>Microsoft Internet Explorer</li>
<li>NCSA Mosaic</li>
</ul>
```

Related Elements:

List items in an unordered list are specified with the `<li>` element.

Hyperlink Elements

The capability of linking Web resources is what makes the Web so fascinating. By following links, you can be looking up job opportunities one moment and then be reading up on the latest mixed drink recipes the next! Linking between documents is accomplished with the one simple element described in this section.

<a>

Type:

Container

Function:

The <a> element can do one of two things, depending on which attributes you use. Used with the `href` attribute, the <a> element sets up a hyperlink from whatever content is found within the <a> element and the document at the URL specified by `href` (see Figure 3.13). When you use the <a> element with the `name` attribute, you set up a named anchor within a document that can be targeted by other hyperlinks. This helps make navigating a large document easier because you can set up anchors at the start of major sections and then place a set of links at the top of the document that points to the anchors at the beginning of each section.

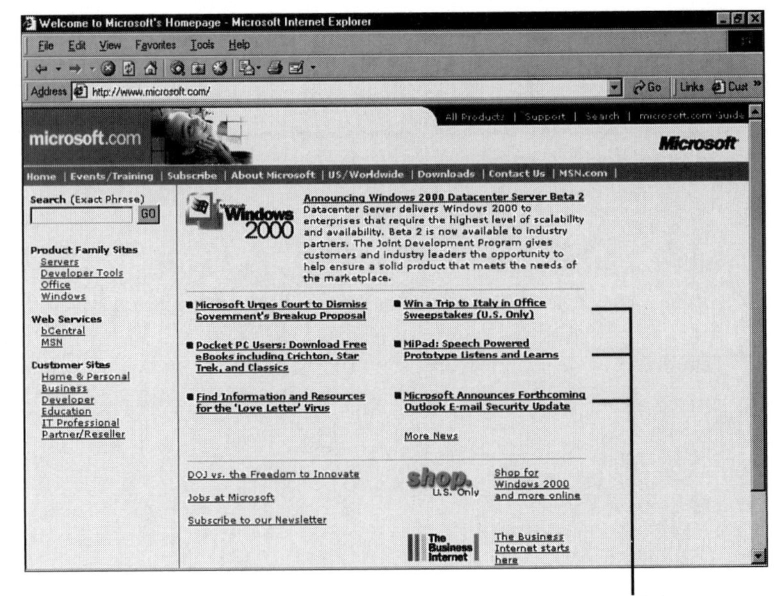

FIGURE 3.13
The hyperlinks on Microsoft's home page are set up using the <a> element.

TIP Hypertext links are typically colored and underlined. A linked graphic is rendered with a colored border. If you don't want a border around your linked image, be sure to specify `style="border: 0 px"` in the `<img />` element you use to place the image.

Syntax:

```
<!-- Setting up a hyperlink -->
<a href="url_of_linked_document" target="frame_name"
   rel="forward_link_type" rev="reverse_link_type"
   accesskey="key_letter" tabindex="tab_order_position">
... hyperlinked element goes here ...
</a>
```

or

```
<!-- Setting up a named anchor -->
<a name="anchor_name">
... text to act as named anchor ...
</a>
```


Attributes:

The `<a>` element can take a host of attributes, including

- **accesskey**—An access key is a shortcut key a reader can use to activate the hyperlink. If you set the access key to the letter `"C"`, for example, Windows users can press Alt+C on their keyboards to activate the link.
- **charset**—Denotes what character encoding to use for the linked document.
- **href**—Gives the URL of the Web resource to which the hyperlink should point.
- **hreflang**—Denotes the language context of the linked resource.
- **name**—Specifies the name of the anchor being set up.
- **rel**—Describes the nature of the forward link (refer to Table 3.3 for possible values).
- **rev**—Describes the nature of the reverse link (refer to Table 3.3 for possible values).
- **tabindex**—Specifies the link's position in the document's tabbing order.
- **target**—Tells the browser into which frame the linked document should be loaded.
- **type**—Specifies the MIME type of the linked resource.

Examples:

The following code sets up a simple hyperlink:

```
You can learn more about our
<a href="prodserv.html target="main" accesskey="p">
products and services</a> as well.
```

To follow the link, a user can click the hypertext `products and services` or press Alt+P (on a Windows machine) or Cmd+P (on a Macintosh).

This code establishes a named anchor within a document:

```
...
<a name="toc">
<h1>Table of Contents</h1>
</a>
...
```

With the anchor set up, you can point a hyperlink to it by using code such as this:

```
<a href="index.html#toc">Back to the Table of Contents</a>
```

Image and Image Map Elements

Without images, the Web would just be another version of Gopher. Web graphics give pages powerful visual appeal and often add significantly to the messages that authors are trying to convey.

Placing an image on a page is as simple as using the XHTML `<img />` element. In its most basic form, the `<img />` element needs only two attributes to do its job. However, `<img />` supports as many as 10 attributes that you can use to modify how the image is presented.

▶ To learn more about placing graphics on Web pages, **see** Chapter 5, "Advanced Graphics"

<img />

Type:

Standalone

Function:

Places an inline image into a document (see Figure 3.14).

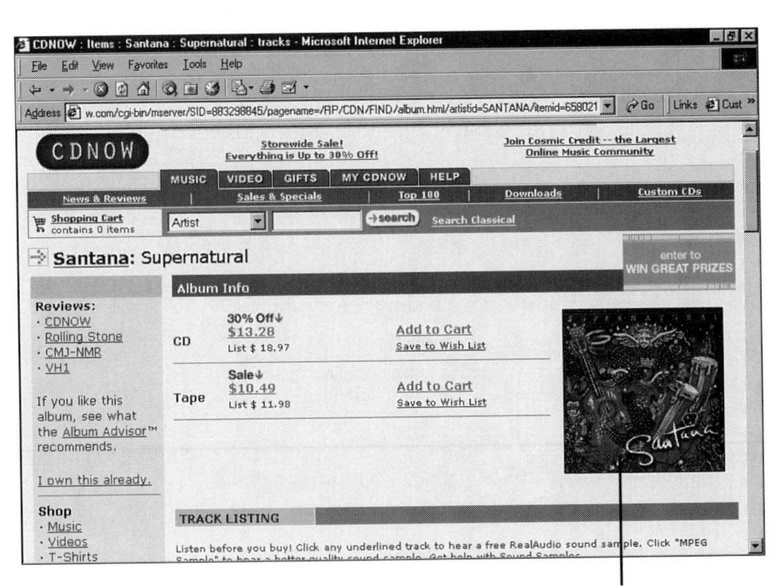

FIGURE 3.14
Photos, logos, and other graphics are placed into a document using the `<img />` element.

Syntax:

```
<img src="URL_of_image_file"
  width="width_in_pixels" height="height_in_pixels"
  alt="text_description"
  longdesc="URL_of_long_description"
  ismap="ismap" usemap="map_name" />
```

Attributes:

As you can see from the element's syntax, `<img />` can take several attributes (each attribute is described in detail in this section):

- **`src`**—Specifies the URL of the file containing the image. `src` is a required attribute of the `<img />` element.
- **`width` and `height`**—Gives the width and height of the image in pixels. Specifying this information in the element means that the browser can allot space for the image and then continue laying out the page while the image file loads.
- **`alt`**—A text-based description of the image content. Using `alt` is an important courtesy to users with nonvisual browsers or with image loading turned off. `alt` is also a required attribute of the `<img />` element.
- **`longdesc`**—Points to a resource that contains a longer description of the image's content.
- **`ismap`**—Identifies the image as being used as part of a server-side image map.
- **`usemap`**—Set equal to the name of the client-side image map to be used with the image.

Part I Ch 3

NOTE The `ALIGN`, `BORDER`, `HSPACE`, and `VSPACE` attributes of the HTML `<IMG>` tag do not have equivalents under the Strict XHTML DTD. You should use cascading style sheet instructions with a `style` attribute to specify these presentation parameters or write your XHTML code using the Transitional or Frameset DTD. ■

Example:

```
<img src="/images/logo.gif" width=600 height=120
  alt="Welcome to XYZ Corporation" usemap="#main" />
```

One popular use of images is to set up *image maps*—clickable images that take users to different URLs, depending on where they click. Image maps are popular page elements on many sites because they provide users with an easy-to-use graphical interface for navigating the site (see Figure 3.15).

Image maps come in two flavors: server-side and client-side. When a user clicks a server-side image map, the coordinates of the click are sent to the server, where a program processes them to determine which URL the browser should load. To accomplish this, the server must have access to a file containing information about which regions on the image are clickable and with which URLs those regions should be paired.

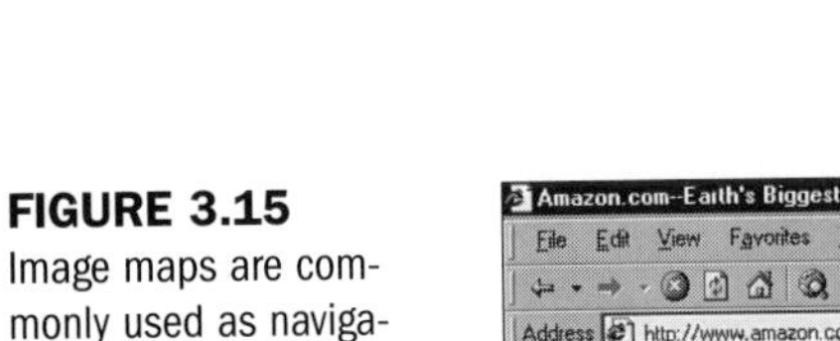

FIGURE 3.15
Image maps are commonly used as navigation interfaces and are usually accompanied by an equivalent set of hypertext links.

With client-side image maps, the client (browser) processes the coordinates of the user's click, rather than passing them to the server for processing. This is a more efficient approach because it reduces the computational load on the server and eliminates the opening and closing of additional HTTP connections. For the browser to be able to process a user's click, it must have access to the same information about the clickable regions and their associated URLs as the server does when processing a server-side image map. The method of choice for getting this information to the client is to pass it in an XHTML file—usually the file that contains the document with the image map, although it does not necessarily have to be this way. XHTML 1.0 supports two elements that enable you to store image map data in your documents: `<map>` and `<area />`. A discussion of these elements rounds out the coverage in this section.

▶ For more information about using image maps, **see** Chapter 4, "Image Maps"

<map>

Type:

Container

Function:

Contains XHTML elements that define the clickable regions (hot regions) of an image map.

Syntax:

```
<map id="map_indentifier">
... hot region definitions go here ...
</map>
```

Attributes:

The required id attribute gives the map information a unique identifier so it can be referenced by the usemap attribute in the <img /> element that places the image map graphic.

Example:

```
<map id="navigation">
<area shape="rect" coords="23,47,58,68" href="search.html" />
<area shape="circle" coords="120,246,150,246" href="about.html" />
...
</map>
```

With the image map data defined by the map named navigation, you would reference the map in an <img /> element as follows:

```
<img src="navigation.gif" usemap="#navigation" />
```

If the map were stored in a file different from the document's XHTML file, you would reference it this way:

```
<img src="navigation.gif" usemap="maps.html#navigation" />
```


TIP Browser support for image map data in a separate file is not yet uniform. Thus, you might want to put image map data in the files in which you need it until support becomes more consistent.

Related Elements:

The <area /> element is used to define the individual hot regions in the image map. The named map is referenced by the usemap attribute of the <img /> element.

<area />

Type:

Standalone

Function:

Defines a hot region in a client-side image map.

Syntax:

```
<area shape="rect|circle|poly|default" coords="coordinate_list"
  href="URL_of_linked_document" target="frame_name"
  alt="text_alternative" tabindex="tab_order_position" nohref
  accesskey="key_letter" />
```

Attributes:

The <area /> element takes several attributes, including

- **accesskey**—Defines a shortcut key combination that the user can press to activate the hot region (see the attribute listing for the <a> element for more details).

- **alt**—Provides a text alternative for the hot region in the event that the image does not load or the user has image loading turned off. alt text is also used by spoken-word browsers for the visually impaired. alt is a required attribute of the <area /> element.
- **coords**—Specifies the coordinates that define the hot region. Coordinates are given as a list of numbers, separated by commas. No coordinates are needed when specifying a default region.
- **href**—Set equal to the URL of the document to associate with the hot region.
- **nohref**—Using the nohref attribute in an <area /> element essentially deactivates the hot region by having it point to nothing.
- **shape**—Specifies the shape of the hot region being defined. Possible values of shape include rect for rectangles (the default value), circle for circles, poly for polygons, and default for any point on the image not part of another hot region.
- **tabindex**—Defines the hot region's position in the tabbing order of the page.
- **target**—Specifies into which frame to load the linked document.

NOTE Each type of hot region has a specific number of coordinate points that you must specify to completely define the hot region. A rectangular region is defined by the coordinates of the upper-left and lower-right corners. A circular region is defined by the coordinates of the center point and either the coordinates of a point on the circle or the radius of the circle. A polygonal region is defined by the coordinates of the polygon's vertices. ■

Example:

```
<map id="main">
<area shape="poly" coords="35,80,168,99,92,145" href="profile.html" />
<area shape="circle" coords="288,306,288,334" href="feedback.html" />
<area shape="default" href="index.html" />
</map>
```

Related Elements:

<area /> elements are allowable only inside the <map> element.

Table Elements

XHTML table elements are not only a great way to present information, but a useful layout tool as well (see Figure 3.16). XHTML 1.0 expands the table elements in several important ways:

- Support for rendering parts of the frame around a table, rather than "all or nothing."
- Control over which boundaries to draw between cells.
- Table header, body, and footer sections can be defined as separate entities.

FIGURE 3.16
Tables make complex page layouts such as AltaVista's possible because of the very fine alignment control you have within the table.

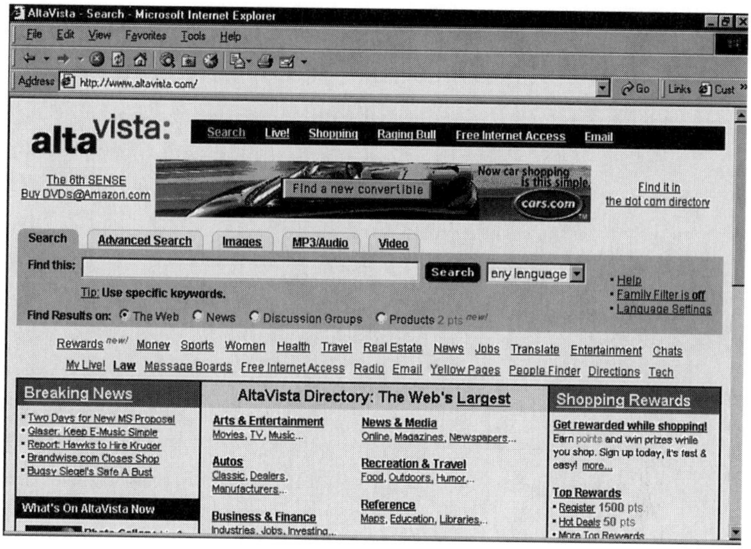

▶ For more information on using tables, **see** Chapter 6, "Tables"

<table>

Type:

Container

Function:

Contains all XHTML elements that compose a table.

Syntax:

```
<table border="thickness_in_pixels"
 width="pixels_or_percentage_of_browser_width"
 cellpadding="pixels" cellspacing="pixels"
 frame="outer_border_rendering" rules="inner_border_rendering"
 summary="description_of_table_contents_and_structure">
...
</table>
```

Attributes:

The `<table>` element can take the following attributes to modify how the table is presented:

- **`border`**—Specifies the thickness of the table border in pixels.
- **`cellpadding`**—Controls the amount of whitespace between the contents of a cell and the edge of the cell.
- **`cellspacing`**—Specifies how many pixels of space to leave between individual cells.
- **`frame`**—Controls which parts of the table's outer border are rendered. `frame` can take on the values shown in Table 3.4.

Table 3.4 Values of the *frame* Attribute of the *<table>* Element

Value	Purpose
`above`	Displays a border on the top of a table frame
`below`	Displays a border at the bottom of a table frame
`border`	Displays a border on all four sides of a table frame
`box`	Same as `border`
`hsides`	Displays a border on the left and right sides of a table frame
`lhs`	Displays a border on the left side of a table frame
`rhs`	Displays a border on the right side of a table frame
`vsides`	Displays a border at the top and bottom of a table frame
`void`	Suppresses the display of all table frame borders

- **`rules`**—Controls which parts of the table's inner borders are displayed. `rules` can be set equal to one of the values shown in Table 3.5.

Table 3.5 Values of the *rules* Attribute of the *<table>* Element

Value	Purpose
`all`	Displays a border between all rows and columns
`cols`	Displays a border between all columns
`groups`	Displays a border between all logical groups (as defined by the `<thead>`, `<tbody>`, `<tfoot>`, and `<colgroup>` elements)
`none`	Suppresses all inner borders
`rows`	Displays a border between all table rows

- **`summary`**—Provides a synopsis of what's in the table and how the table is structured.
- **`width`**—Specifies the width of the table in pixels or as a percentage of the browser screen width.

Example:

```
<table border="2" cellpadding="4" frame="border"
rules="all" style="align: center">
...
</table>
```

Related Elements:

The `<table>` element forms the container for all the other table-related elements. The many elements you can use between `<table>` and `</table>` include `<caption>`, `<thead>`, `<tfoot>`, `<tbody>`, `<colgroup>`, `<col />`, `<tr>`, `<th>`, and `<td>`.

<caption>

Type:

Container

Function:

Specifies a caption for a table.

Syntax:

```
<caption>
... caption text goes here ...
</caption>
```

Attributes:

None.

Example:

```
<caption style="align: bottom">
Table 1 - Return on Investment
</caption>
```


<thead>

Type:

Container

Function:

Defines the header section of a table. Being able to define the header separately enables the browser to duplicate the header when breaking the table across multiple pages.

Syntax:

```
<thead align="left|center|right|justify|char"
 valign="top|middle|bottom|baseline" char="alignment_character"
 charoff="alignment_character_offset">
... rows that comprise the header ...
</thead>
```

Attributes:

The `<thead>` element can take the following four attributes:

- **`align`**—Controls the horizontal alignment within the cells of the table header. `align` can take on values of `left`, `right`, `center`, `justify`, or `char`. `char` is used to align cells by a common character.
- **`char`**—Specifies the alignment character for when `align="char"` is used.
- **`charoff`**—Prescribes the offset distance from the alignment character.
- **`valign`**—Controls the vertical alignment in the header cells. `valign` can take on values of `top`, `middle`, `bottom`, or `baseline`.

Example:

```
<thead align="center" valign="baseline">
<tr>
<th>id #</th>
<th>property</th>
<th>tax assessment</th>
...
</tr>
</thead>
```

Related Elements:

The rows of the table header are built with `<tr>`, `<th>`, and `<td>` elements. Each table header must comprise at least one row.

<tfoot>

Type:

Container

Function:

Defines the footer section of the table.

Syntax:

```
<tfoot align="left|center|right|justify|char"
 valign="top|middle|bottom|baseline" char="alignment_character"
 charoff="alignment_character_offset">
...
</tfoot>
```

Attributes:

`<tfoot>` can take the same `align` and `valign` attributes as the `<thead>` element:

- **`align`**—Controls the horizontal alignment within the cells of the table footer. `align` can take on values of `left`, `right`, `center`, `justify`, or `char`.
- **`char`**—Specifies the alignment character for when `align="char"` is used.
- **`charoff`**—Prescribes the offset distance from the alignment character.
- **`valign`**—Controls the vertical alignment in the footer cells. `valign` can take on values of `top`, `middle`, `bottom`, or `baseline`.

Example:

```
<tfoot align="justify" valign="top">
<tr>
<td>&copy; 2000 - Macmillan Computer Publishing USA</td>
...
</tr>
</tfoot>
```

Related Elements:

You specify the rows and cells in the table footer by using the <tr>, <th>, and <td> elements. A table footer must be made up of at least one row.

<tbody>

Type:

Container

Function:

Defines the body section of the table.

Syntax:

```
<tbody align="left|center|right|justify|char"
 valign="top|middle|bottom|baseline" char="alignment_character"
 charoff="alignment_character_offset">
...
</tbody>
```


Attributes:

<tbody> can take the following attributes:

- **align**—Controls the horizontal alignment within the cells of the table body. align can take on values of left, right, center, justify, and char.
- **char**—Specifies the alignment character for when align="char" is used.
- **charoff**—Prescribes the offset distance from the alignment character.
- **valign**—Controls the vertical alignment in the body cells. valign can take on values of top, middle, bottom, or baseline.

Example:

```
<tbody align="left" valign="baseline">
<tr>
<td>Red Storm Rising</td>
<td>1500 pages (paperback)</td>
<td>$9.95</td>
...
</tr>
</tbody>
```

Related Elements:

You specify the rows and cells in the table body by using the <tr>, <th>, and <td> elements. A table body section must contain at least one row.

<colgroup>

Type:

Container

Function:

Groups a set of columns so properties can be assigned to all columns in the group rather than to each one individually.

Syntax:

```
<colgroup span="number_of_columns" width="width_of_column_group"
  align="left|right|center|justify|char"
 valign="top|middle|bottom|baseline"
 char="alignment_character" charoff="alignment character_offset">
...
</colgroup>
```

A `<colgroup>` element has no content or code inside it if the properties put forward in the `<colgroup>` element are to apply to each column in the group. You can also use the `<col/>` element inside a `<colgroup>` element to specify column properties for a subgroup of the larger group.

Attributes:

`<colgroup>` can take the following attributes:

- **`align`**—Controls the horizontal alignment within the column group. `align` can take on values of `left`, `right`, `center`, `justify`, or `char`.
- **`char`**—Specifies the alignment character for when `align="char"` is used.
- **`charoff`**—Prescribes the offset distance from the alignment character.
- **`span`**—Tells the browser how many columns are in the group. The default value is `1`.
- **`valign`**—Controls the vertical alignment in the column group. `valign` can take on values of `top`, `middle`, `bottom`, or `baseline`.
- **`width`**—Specifies how wide (in pixels or in terms of relative width) the enclosed columns should be.

Example:

```
<colgroup span="3" align="center" valign="top">
</colgroup>
<tr>
<td>Column 1 - center/top alignment</td>
<td>Column 2 - center/top alignment</td>
<td>Column 3 - center/top alignment</td>
<td>Column 4 - default alignment</td>
</tr>
```

Related Elements:

The `<col />` element can be used within the `<colgroup>` element to refine column properties for a subset of the column group.

<col />

Type:

Standalone

Function:

Specifies properties for a column or columns within a group.

Syntax:

```
<col span="number_of_columns" width="width_of_column_subgroup"
 align="left|right|center|justify"
 valign="top|middle|bottom|baseline"
 char="alignment_character" charoff="alignment_character_offset" />
```


Attributes:

`<col />` can take the following attributes:

- **`align`**—Controls the horizontal alignment within the column cells. `align` can take on values of `left`, `right`, `center`, `justify`, or `char`.
- **`char`**—Specifies the alignment character for when `align="char"` is used.
- **`charoff`**—Prescribes the offset distance from the alignment character.
- **`span`**—Tells the browser how many columns to which to apply the property. The default value is `1`.
- **`valign`**—Controls the vertical alignment in the column cells. `valign` can take on values of `top`, `middle`, `bottom`, or `baseline`.
- **`width`**—Specifies the width (in pixels or in terms of relative width) of the column or column group.

Example:

```
<table border="1">
<colgroup>
   <col align="center" />
   <col align="right" />
</colgroup>
<colgroup>
   <col align="center" span="2" />
</colgroup>
<tbody>
   <tr>
      <td>First column in first group, center aligned</td>
      <td>Second column in first group, right aligned</td>
      <td>First column in second group, center aligned</td>
      <td>Second column in second group, center aligned</td>
   </tr>
</tbody>
</table>
```

<tr>

Type:

Container

Function:

Defines a row of a table, table header, table footer, or table body.

Syntax:

```
<tr align="left|right|center|justify|char"
  valign="top|middle|bottom|baseline"
  char="alignment_character" charoff="alignment_character_offset">
...
</tr>
```

Attributes specified in a `<tr>` element apply only to the row that the element is defining and override any default values.

Attributes:

The `<tr>` element can take the following attributes:

- **`align`**—Controls the horizontal alignment within the cells in the row. `align` can take on values of `left`, `right`, `center`, `justify`, or `char`.
- **`char`**—Specifies the alignment character for when `align="char"` is used.
- **`charoff`**—Prescribes the offset distance from the alignment character.
- **`valign`**—Controls the vertical alignment of the cells in the row. `valign` can take on values of `top`, `middle`, `bottom`, or `baseline`.

Example:

```
<tr style="bgcolor:white" valign="top">
<td>Phone</td>
<td>Extension</td>
<td>Fax</td>
...
</tr>
```

Related Elements:

Cells in a row are defined using the `<td>` or `<th>` elements.

<td>, <th>

Type:

Container

Function:

Defines a cell in a table. `<th>` creates a header cell whose contents will be rendered in boldface and with a centered horizontal alignment. `<td>` creates a regular data cell whose contents are aligned flush left and in a normal font weight. Vertical alignment for both types of cells is `middle` by default.

Syntax:

```
<td align="left|right|center|justify|char"
 valign="top|middle|bottom|baseline"
 char="alignment_character" charoff="alignment_character_offset"
 rowspan="number_of_rows"
 colspan="number_of_columns"
 abbr="header_cell_abbreviation" axis="list_of_category_names"
 headers="list_of_id headers" scope="row|col|rowgroup|colgroup">
```

or

```
<th align="left|right|center|justify|char"
 valign="top|middle|bottom|baseline"
 char="alignment_character" charoff="alignment_character_offset"
 rowspan="number_of_rows"
 colspan="number_of_columns"
 abbr="cell_abbreviation" axis="list_of_category_names"
 headers="list_of_id headers" scope="row|col|rowgroup|colgroup">
```


Attributes:

Both the `<th>` and `<td>` elements can take the following attributes:

- **`abbr`**—Specifies an abbreviation form of a cell's contents.
- **`align`**—Controls the horizontal alignment within the cell. `align` can take on values of `left`, `right`, `center`, `justify`, or `char`.
- **`axis`**—Used to group cells into logical categories.
- **`char`**—Specifies the alignment character for when `align="char"` is used.
- **`charoff`**—Prescribes the offset distance from the alignment character.
- **`colspan`**—Specifies the number of columns the cell should occupy. The default value is `1`.
- **`headers`**—Provides a list of IDs of cells that provide header information for the current cell.
- **`rowspan`**—Specifies the number of rows the cell should occupy.
- **`scope`**—A simpler form of the `axis` attribute, `scope` lets you group cells into rows, columns, row groups, or column groups, instead of arbitrarily named logical groups.
- **`valign`**—Controls the vertical alignment of the cell. `valign` can take on values of `top`, `middle`, `bottom`, or `baseline`.

Example:

```
<tr valign="bottom">
<th>Column 1 - center/bottom alignment</th>
<td valign="middle">Column 2 - left/middle alignment</td>
<td align="justify">Column 3 - justify/bottom alignment</td>
<td colspan="2">Columns 4 and 5 - left/bottom alignment</td>
</tr>
```

Form Elements

XHTML forms are a Web surfer's gateway to interactive content. Forms collect information from a user, and then a script or program on a Web server uses the information to compose a custom response to the form submission.

For all the form controls that are available to you as a document author, you need to know surprisingly few XHTML elements to produce them. These elements, together with some new features introduced in the HTML 4.0 recommendation that improve form accessibility for the disabled, are covered in this section.

▶ For more about forms, **see** Chapter 8, "Forms"

<form>

Type:

Container

Function:

Contains the text and elements that compose an XHTML form (see Figure 3.17).

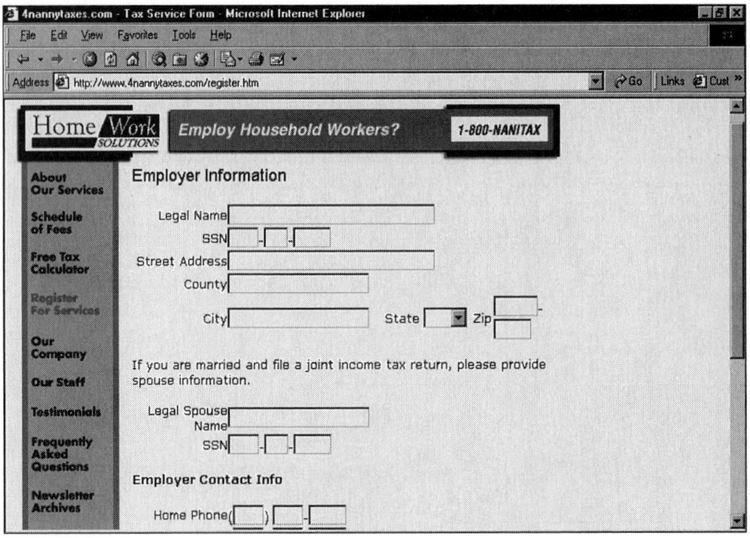

FIGURE 3.17
XHTML forms gather user input and send that information to a server for processing.

Syntax:

```
<form action="URL_of_processing_script" method="get|post"
  target="frame_name" enctype="MIME_type_of_file_to_upload"
  accept-charset="acceptable_character_sets"
  accept="acceptable_MIME_types">
...
</form>
```

The `<form>` element and its attributes are sometimes referred to as the *form header*.

Attributes:

The `<form>` element takes the following attributes:

- **`accept`**—Specifies a list of acceptable content types (MIME types) that a server processing the form can handle correctly.
- **`accept-charset`**—Set equal to a list of character sets that the form's processing script can handle.
- **`action`**—Set equal to the URL of the script or program that will process the form data. `action` is a required attribute of the `<form>` element.
- **`enctype`**—Set equal to `"multipart/form-data"` when you're expecting a file upload as part of the form data submission and is set equal to the expected MIME type of the file. Otherwise the default value of `"application/x-www-form-urlencoded"` is sufficient.
- **`method`**—Refers to the HTTP method used to send the form data to the server. The default `method` is `get`, which appends the data to the end of the processing script URL. If you set `method="post"`, the form data will be sent to the server in a separate HTTP transaction.

CAUTION

URLs are limited in size to 1,024 characters, so be careful about using `"method=get"` when submitting more than a kilobyte of form data.

- **`target`**—Enables you to target the response from the processing script or program to a specific frame.

Example:

```
<form action="shopping_cart.cfm" method="post" target="response">
...
</form>
```

Related Elements:

The following elements are valid only when within a `<form>` element: `<input />`, `<select>`, `<option>`, `<optgroup>`, `<textarea>`, `<button>`, `<label>`, `<fieldset>`, and `<legend>`. Each of these elements is described in this section.

NOTE You can have more than one form on a page, but the `<form>` elements that create them cannot be nested. ■

<input />

Type:

Standalone

Function:

Places one of the following form controls:

- Text, password, or hidden fields
- Check boxes
- Radio buttons
- File-upload fields
- Image-based buttons
- Scripted buttons
- Submit and reset buttons

Syntax:

```
<!-- Text and password fields -->
<input type="text|password" name="field_name" value="default_value"
  size="field_size" maxlength="maximum_input_length"
  disabled="disabled" readonly="readonly" />
```

or

```
<!-- hidden field -->
<input type="hidden" name="field_name" value="field_value" />
```

or

```
<!-- checkbox -->
<input type="checkbox" name="field_name" value="field_value"
  checked="checked" disabled="disabled" />
```

or

```
<!-- radio button -->
<input type="radio" name="field_name" value="field_value"
  checked="checked" disabled="disabled" />
```

or

```
<!-- file upload -->
<input type="file" name="field_name" value="default_value"
  accept="acceptable_mime_types" disabled="disabled" />
```

or

```
<!-- image-based button -->
<input type="image" name="image_name" src="URL_of_image_file"
alt="text_description"  align="top|middle|bottom|left|right" usemap="map_name"
disabled="disabled" />
```

or

```
<!-- scripted button -->
<input type="button" name="button_name" value="button_label"
onclick="script_name"  disabled="disabled"/>
```

or

```
<!-- submit/reset button -->
<input type="submit|reset" name="button_name" value="button_label"
disabled="disabled"/>
```

Attributes:

The `<input />` element is easily the most versatile of all the XHTML elements. It has a large number of attributes, although not all are applicable in every situation. The following list examines each variant of the `<input />` element (which corresponds to changing values of the `type` attribute) and notes what each applicable attribute does in that situation. Note that the `name` attribute is required for all the variations of the `<input />` element.

- **Text and password fields (`type="text|password"`)**—The `name` attribute gives the input field a unique name so it can be identified by the processing script. The `value` attribute is appropriate for a text field when you want to pre-populate the field with a default value. `length` is set equal to the number of characters wide the input field should be onscreen. `maxlength` sets an upper limit on how many characters long the input from the field can be. The `disabled` attribute deactivates the field, and `readonly` leaves the field active while disallowing the user from typing any new input into it.
- **Hidden fields (`type="hidden"`)**—`name` and `value` specify the name of the field and the value to pass to the server.
- **Check box (`type="checkbox"`)**—`name` gives the check box field a unique name, and `value` is set equal to the value you want passed to the server if the box is checked. Including `checked` makes the box preselected, and `disabled` disables the check box altogether.
- **Radio buttons (`type="radio"`)**—`name` gives a name to the entire set of radio buttons. All buttons can have the same `name` because their corresponding `values` have to be mutually exclusive options. The `checked` attribute preselects a radio button and `disabled` shuts down the radio button.
- **File upload (`type="file"`)**—`name` gives the field a unique name, and `value` is set to the default value of the field (presumably a filename). The `accept` attribute provides a set of acceptable MIME types for upload. Specifying the `disabled` attribute deactivates the field.
- **Image-based button (`type="image"`)**—The `SRC` attribute tells the browser where it can find the image file for the button. `alt` provides a text-based alternative to the image, should the image file not be available. You can use `align` to control how the image is aligned on the page. `usemap` is set equal to a client-side image map name, enabling you to take different actions depending on where the user clicks. Using the `disabled` attribute shuts off the button.
- **Scripted button (`type="button"`)**—Whatever you specify for the `value` attribute will be the text that appears on the face of the button. The `onclick` event handler is set

equal to the script code or the name of the script that is to execute when the button is clicked. If you specify the `disabled` attribute, the scripted button will be deactivated.

- **Submit and reset buttons (`type="submit|reset"`)**—The `value` attribute specifies what text to place on the button. If `disabled`, the submit or reset button will be turned off.

> **TIP** Be sure to name your submit buttons when you have more than one of them on a page. That will help you to distinguish which one of them was clicked.

Additionally, you can use the following attributes with the `<input />` element:

- **`accesskey`**—Defines a shortcut key combination that the user can press to give focus to the input field (see the attribute listing for the `<a>` element for more details).
- **`tabindex`**—Defines the input field's position in the tabbing order of the page.

Example:

```
<form action="/cgi-bin/submit_it.pl">
Login Name: <input type="text" name="login" size="12" />
Password: <input type="password" name="passwd" size="12" />
<input type="hidden" name="browser" value="ie4" />
Sex: <input type="radio" name="sex" value="f" />Female
     <input type="radio" name="sex" value="m" />Male
<input type="button" value="Check Data" onclick="validate()" />
<input type="submit" value="Login" />
<input type="reset" value="Clear" />
</form>
```

<select>

Type:

Container

Function:

Sets up a list of choices from which a user can select one or many.

Syntax:

```
<select name="field_name" size="visible_rows" multiple="multiple"
 disabled="disabled" tabindex="tab_position">
...
</select>
```

Attributes:

You can use the following attributes with the `<select>` element:

- **`disabled`**—Deactivates the field.
- **`multiple`**—Enables the user to choose more than one of the options by holding down the Ctrl key and clicking.

- **`name`**—Gives the field a unique name so it can be identified by the processing script.
- **`size`**—Set equal to the number of options that should be visible on the screen.
- **`tabindex`**—Defines the select field's position in the tabbing order of the page.

NOTE If you set `size="1"` and don't use `multiple`, the field is displayed as a drop-down list. Otherwise, the field appears as a scrollable list of options. ■

Example:

```
<p>Please select a size:</p>
<select name="size" size="4">
<option>Small</option>
<option>Medium</option>
<option>Large</option>
<option>X-Large</option>
...
</select>
```

Related Elements:

Individual options in the list are specified using the `<option>` element. You can also use the `<optgroup>` element to place options into logical groups.

<option>

Type:

Container

Function:

Defines an option in a `<select>` field listing.

Syntax:

```
<option value="option_value" selected="selected"
 disabled="disabled" label="label_text">
... option text ...
</option>
```

Attributes:

The `<option>` element takes the following attributes:

- **`disabled`**—Makes the option unavailable.
- **`label`**—Provides a short label for the menu option. If specified, this label is used in place of the option text itself.
- **`selected`**—Preselects an option.
- **`value`**—Specifies a value to pass to the browser if the option is selected. If no `value` is given, the browser passes the option text to the server for processing.

Example:

```
<select name="state" size="5">
<option value="AL">Alabama</option>
<option value="NM" selected>New Mexico</option>
<option value="OK">Oklahoma</option>
...
</select>
```

Related Elements:

The `<option>` element is valid only within a `<select>` element. You can place options into logical groups by using the `<optgroup>` element.

<optgroup>

Type:

Container

Function:

Defines a logical group of select list options. Though it's not supported on browsers currently, it is expected that logically grouped options will be rendered in a special way—most likely by means of a cascading set of choices, similar to what you see with browser bookmarks.

Syntax:

```
<optgroup label="label_text" disabled>
<option> ... </option>
<option> ... </option>
<option> ... </option>
...
</optgroup>
```

Attributes:

`<optgroup>` can take two attributes:

- **`disabled`**—Disables the options in the group.
- **`label`**—Specifies a label for the option group. `label` is a required attribute of the `<optgroup>` element.

Example:

```
<optgroup label="firstquarter">
<option value="Jan">January</option>
<option value="Feb">February</option>
<option value="Mar">March</option>
</optgroup>
...
</option>
```

Related Elements:

The <optgroup> element should be used only inside a <select> element. The only element allowable inside an <optgroup> element is the <option> element.

<textarea>

Type:

Container

Function:

Sets up a multiple-line text input window.

Syntax:

```
<textarea name="field_name" rows="number_of_rows"
  cols="number_of_columns" disabled="disabled" readonly="readonly"
  accesskey="shortcut_key_letter" tabindex="tab_position">
... default text to appear in window ...
</textarea>
```

Attributes:

The <textarea> element can take the following attributes:

- **accesskey**—Defines a shortcut key combination that the user can press to give focus to the text input window (see the attribute listing for the <a> element for more details).
- **cols**—Set equal to the number of columns wide the text window should be. cols is a required attribute of the <textarea> element.
- **disabled**—Deactivates the text window.
- **name**—Assigns a unique name to the input window so that the processing program can identify it.
- **readonly**—Leaves the window active, but the user will not be able to change the default text that is displayed.
- **rows**—Set equal to the number of rows high the text window should be. rows is a required attribute of the <textarea> element.
- **tabindex**—Defines the text window's position in the tabbing order of the page.

Example:

```
<textarea name="feedback" rows="10" cols="40">
We appreciate your comments!  Please delete this
text and type in your feedback.
</textarea>
```

<button>

Type:

Container

Function:

Places a button on the form. This type of button is different from the one rendered by `<input />` because it has improved presentation features, such as three-dimensional rendering and up/down movement when clicked.

Syntax:

```
<button type="submit|reset|button" name="button_name" value="button_value"
  disabled="disabled" accesskey="shortcut_key_letter" tabindex="tab_position">
... text for button face or <img/> element ...
</button>
```

If text is placed within a `<button>` element, that text appears on the face of the button. If an `<img />` element is placed within a `<button>`, the image is used as the button.

Attributes:

You can use the following attributes with the `<button>` element:

- **`accesskey`**—Defines a shortcut key combination that the user can press to click the button (see the attribute listing for the `<a>` element for more details).
- **`disabled`**—Disables the button.
- **`name`**—Gives the button a unique name.
- **`tabindex`**—Defines the button's position in the tabbing order of the page.
- **`type`**—Set to `submit`, `reset`, or `button`, depending on the type of button you're defining. `type="button"` is typically used for defining a scripted button.
- **`value`**—Specifies what is passed to the server when the button is clicked.

Example:

```
<button name="validate" value="form_validation" onclick="validate();">
Click here to validate your input.
</button>
```

<label>

Type:

Container

Function:

Denotes a form field label. Labels are typically text next to the field that prompts the user for the type of input expected. This works fine for text-based browsers, but it makes forms inaccessible for users who are visually impaired and who use speech-based or Braille browsers. Marking field labels with the `<label>` element makes it possible to prompt these users for the necessary input.

Syntax:

```
<LABEL FOR="field_ID" ACCESSKEY="shortcut_key_letter">
... label text goes here ...
</LABEL>
```

Attributes:

The `<label>` element takes the following attributes:

- **accesskey**—Defines a shortcut key combination that the user can press to give focus to the label (see the attribute listing for the `<a>` element for more details).
- **for**—Set equal to the value of the `id` attribute for the field that goes with the label.

Example:

```
<label for="pw" accesskey="p">enter your password:</label>
<input type="password" id="pw" name="passwd" />
```

Related Elements:

`<label>` is typically used with the `<input />`, `<select>`, or `<textarea>` elements.

<fieldset>

Type:

Container

Function:

Groups related form input fields. This is expected to be helpful for browsers used by differently abled Web users. For example, a speech synthesis browser might speak the prompting text from each of the fields in a logical group with the same voice.

Syntax:

```
<fieldset>
... related input fields ...
</fieldset>
```

Attributes:

None.

Example:

```
<fieldset>
Login: <input type="text" name="login"/>
Password: <input type="password" name="passwd"/>
</fieldset>
```

Related Elements:

The `<legend>` element can be used to give a field grouping a specific name.

<legend>

Type:

Container

Function:

Names a group of related form fields. Coupled with the `<fieldset>` element above, `<legend>` further enhances accessibility for differently-abled users.

Syntax:

```
<legend accesskey="shortcut_key_letter">
... legend text goes here ...
</legend>
```

Attributes:

The `<legend>` element takes the `accesskey` attribute, which defines a shortcut key combination that the user can press to give focus to the legend (see the attribute listing for the `<a>` element for more details).

Example:

```
<fieldset>
<legend>User Login Information</legend>
Login: <input type="text" name="login"/>
Password: <input type="password" name="passwd"/>
</fieldset>
```

Related Elements:

`<legend>` gives a name to a set of fields grouped together by the `<fieldset>` element.

Frame Elements

Framed layouts are ones in which the browser window is broken into multiple regions called *frames*. Each frame can contain a distinct XHTML document, enabling you to display several documents at once rather than just one (see Figure 3.18).

You need to know only a few elements to set up a framed page. These elements are covered in this section.

▶ To learn more about using frames, **see** Chapter 7, "Frames"

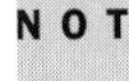

NOTE When implementing framesets in XHTML, make sure you are using the XHTML Frameset Document Type Definition (DTD). ■

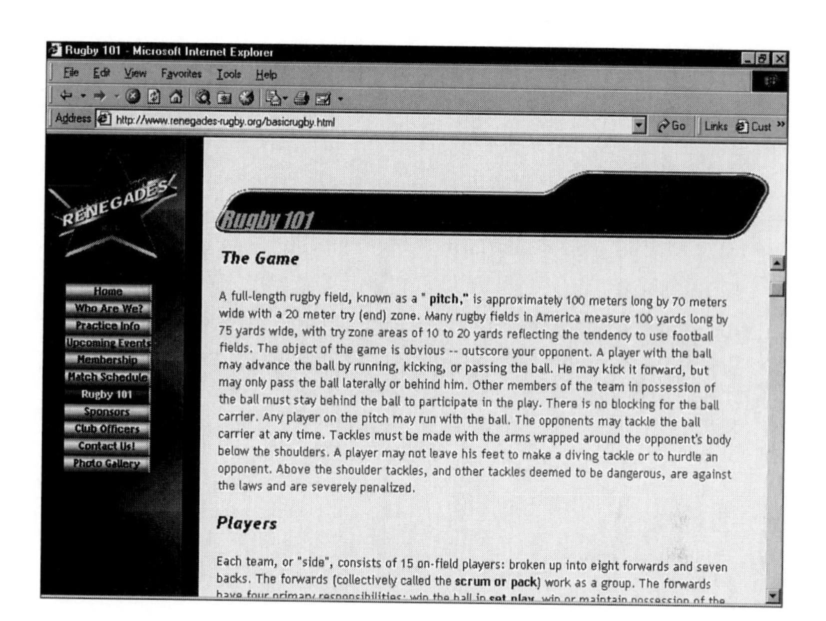

FIGURE 3.18
Frames enable you to keep key page elements (such as navigation) on the screen all the time, while other parts of the page change.

Part I Ch 3

<frameset>

Type:

Container

Function:

Divides the browser window into frames.

Syntax:

```
<frameset rows="list_of_row_sizes" cols="list_of_column_sizes">
...
</frameset>
```

Attributes:

`<frameset>` can take the `rows` or `cols` attribute, but not both at the same time. `rows` specifies how the browser screen should be broken up into multiple rows. `rows` is set equal to a list of values that describe the size of each row. The number of items in the list determines how many rows there will be. The values in the list determine the size of each row. Sizes can be in pixels, percentages of screen depth, or relative to the amount of available space. `cols` works the same way, except it will divide the screen into columns.

NOTE If you try to use `rows` and `cols` in the same `<frameset>` element, a browser typically uses the first attribute it finds and ignores the second. ■

Example:

```
<!-- Divide the screen into four rows: 125 pixels, 30% of screen,
     88 pixels, and whatever is left over. -->
<frameset rows="125,30%,88,*">
...
</frameset>
```

Related Elements:

<frameset> only breaks up the screen into multiple regions. You must use the <frame> element to populate each frame with content. Also, you can use the <noframes> element to specify alternative content for browsers that cannot process frames.

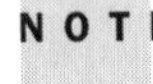

NOTE <frameset> elements can be nested to further subdivide a frame. This enables you to create even more complex layouts. ■

<frame />

Type:

Standalone

Function:

Places content into a frame.

Syntax:

```
<frame src="url_of_document" name="frame_name" frameborder="0|1"
  marginwidth="width_in_pixels" marginheight="height_in_pixels"
  noresize="noresize" scrolling="yes|no|auto" longdesc="url_of_description" />
```

Attributes:

The <frame /> element can take several attributes:

- **frameborder**—Setting frameborder to 1 turns on the frame's borders; setting it to 0 turns them off. The default value is 1.
- **longdesc**—Set equal to the URL of a resource that contains a more detailed description of the frame's content.
- **marginheight**—Specifies the size (in pixels) of the top margin of the frame.
- **marginwidth**—Specifies the size (in pixels) of the left margin of the frame.
- **name**—Gives the frame a unique name so it can be targeted by other elements (such as <a>, <form>, and <area/>).
- **noresize**—Suppresses the user's ability to drag and drop a frame border in a new location.
- **scrolling**—Controls the presence of scrollbars on the frame. Setting scrolling to yes makes the browser always put scrollbars on the frame, setting it to no suppresses the

scrollbars, and setting it to the default of `auto` enables the browser to decide whether the scrollbars are needed. The default value is `yes`.

- **`src`**—Tells the browser the URL of the XHTML file to load into the frame.

Example:

```
<frameset cols="25%,75%"> <!-- make 2 columnar frames -->
   <!-- Populate frame #1 -->
   <frame src="leftframe.html" noresize="noresize"
    name="left" frameborder="0" />
   <!-- Populate frame #2 -->
   <frame src="rightframe.html" noresize="noresize"
    name="right" frameborder="0" />
...
</frameset>
```

Related Elements:

The `<frame />` element is valid only within a `<frameset>` element.

<noframes>

Type:

Container

Function:

Provides an alternative layout for browsers that cannot process frames.

Syntax:

```
<noframes>
... non-frames content goes here ...
</noframes>
```

Attributes:

None.

Example:

```
<frameset cols="25%,75%"> <!-- make 2 columnar frames -->
   <!-- Populate frame #1 -->
   <frame src="leftframe.html" noresize="noresize"
    name="left" frameborder="0"/>
   <!-- Populate frame #2 -->
   <frame src="rightframe.html" noresize="noresize"
    name="right" frameborder="0"/>
<noframes>
<p>Your browser cannot process frames.  Please visit the
<a href="/noframes/index.html">non-frames version</a>
of our site.</p>
</noframes>
</frameset>
```

Related Elements:

`<noframes>` is valid only within a `<frameset>` element, and only one `<noframes>` element is permissible within the `frameset`. Your `<noframes>` content should be specified before any nested `<frameset>` elements.

<iframe>

Type:

Container

Function:

Places a floating frame on a page. *Floating frames* are best described as frames that you can place like images.

Syntax:

```
<iframe src="URL_of_document" name="frame_name" frameborder="0|1"
  width="frame_width_in_pixels_or_percentage"
  height="frame_height_in_pixels_or_percentage"
  marginwidth="margin_width_in_pixels"
  marginheight="margin_height_in_pixels"
  scrolling="yes|no|auto" align="top|middle|bottom|left|right"
  longdesc="URL_of_description">
... text or image alternative to the floating frame ...
</iframe>
```

Attributes:

The `<iframe>` element can take the following attributes:

- **`align`**—Controls how the floating frame is aligned, and can be set to `top`, `middle`, `bottom`, `left`, or `right`. `top`, `middle`, and `bottom` alignments make text appear next to the frame, starting at the top, middle, or bottom of the frame. Setting `align` to `left` or `right` floats the frame in the left or right margin and enables text to wrap around it.
- **`frameborder`**—Setting `frameborder` to `1` turns on the floating frame's borders; setting it to `0` turns them off.
- **`height`**—Specifies the height of the floating frame in pixels.
- **`longdesc`**—Set equal to the URL of a resource that contains more detail about the contents of the floating frame.
- **`marginheight`**—Specifies the size (in pixels) of the top margin of the floating frame.
- **`marginwidth`**—Specifies the size (in pixels) of the left margin of the floating frame.
- **`name`**—Gives the floating frame a unique name so it can be targeted by other elements (such as `<a>`, `<form>`, and `<area>`).
- **`scrolling`**—Controls the presence of scrollbars on the floating frame. Setting `scrolling` to `yes` makes the browser always put scrollbars on the floating frame, setting it to `no` suppresses the scrollbars, and setting it to the default of `auto` enables the browser to decide whether the scrollbars are needed.

- **src**—Tells the browser the URL of the XHTML file to load into the floating frame.
- **width**—Specifies the width of the floating frame in pixels.

Example:

```
<iframe src="float_content.html" width="50%" height="50%" align="right"
  scrolling="no" name="floater" frameborder="1">
<p>Your browser does not support floating frames. :(</p>
</iframe>
```

Executable Content Elements

One of the ways in which Web pages have become more dynamic is through their support of executable content, such as Java applets and ActiveX controls. These page elements are downloaded to the browser and run in its memory space to produce dynamic content on the browser screen.

XHTML 1.0 supports the `<object>` element for placing executable content. This element, along with the supporting `<param/>` element, is profiled in this section.

<object>

Type:

Container

Function:

Places an executable object on a page.

Syntax:

```
<object classid= "implementation_info" codebase="URL_of_object"
  codetype="MIME_type" data="URL_to_data" type="data_MIME_type"
  archive="list_of_archives" usemap="map_name" tabindex="tab_position"
  standby="message_while_loading" declare="declare"
  width="width_in_pixels_or_percentage" name="object_name"
  height="height_in_pixels_or_percentage">
...
</object>
```

Attributes:

The `<object>` element has an exhausting list of attributes, which makes it flexible enough to handle many different types of content (Java applets, ActiveX controls, and so on). These attributes include

- **archive**—Set equal to a comma-delimited list of archive locations.
- **classid**—Identifies which implementation or release of the object you're using.
- **codebase**—Set equal to the URL of the object.
- **codetype**—Describes the code's MIME type.

- **data**—Set equal to list of URLs where data for the object can be found.
- **declare**—Instructs the browser to declare, but not instantiate, a flag for the object.
- **standby**—Enables you to display a message to the user while the object is loading.
- **type**—Specifies the MIME type of the data passed to the object.
- **usemap**—Points to client-side map data, if image maps are used.
- **width and height**—Specifies the size of the object on the page.

Example:

```
<object width="100%" height="100" codetype="application/x-oleobject "
  classid="CLSID: 1A4DA620-6217-11CF-BE62-0080C72EDD2D"
  codebase="http://activex.microsoft.com/controls/iexplorer/marquee.ocx">
  <param name="image" value="greeting.gif"/>
  <param name="speed" value="7"/>
  <param name="repeat" value= "1"/>
...
</object>
```

Related Elements:

Parameters passed to the object are given by the `<param />` element.

<param />

Type:

Standalone

Function:

Passes a parameter to an executable object placed by the `<object>` element.

Syntax:

```
<param id="unique_identifier" name="parameter_name"
 value="parameter_value" valuetype="data|ref|object"
 type="expected_content_type" />
```

Attributes:

The `<param />` element can take the following attributes:

- **id**—Assigns a unique identifying name to the parameter.
- **name**—Provides the name of the parameter.
- **type**—Tells the browser what the parameter's Internet media (MIME) type is.
- **value**—Specifies the value of the parameter.
- **valuetype**—Provides more detail about the nature of the `value` being passed and can be set to `data`, `ref`, or `object`.

Example:

```
<object code="test.class"  name="test">
   <param id="p1" name="tolerance" value="0.001" valuetype="data" />
   <param id="p2" name="pi" value="3.14159" valuetype="data" />
...
</object>
```

Related Elements:

`<param />` elements can be used within an `<object>` element.

NOTE The HTML `<APPLET>` element is not allowed under the Strict XHTML DTD, but you can use it with the Transitional and Frameset DTDs. ■

CHAPTER 4

Image Maps

by Eric Ladd

In this chapter

What Are Image Maps?

If you use an image-capable browser, you have probably noticed that several major Web sites have a large clickable image on their main pages. These images are different from your run-of-the-mill hyperlinked graphic in that your browser loads a different document, depending on where you click. The image is somehow "multilinked" and can take you to several other Web addresses. Such a multilinked image is called an *image map*.

The challenge in preparing an image map is defining which parts of the image are linked to which URLs. Linked regions in an image map are called *hot regions*, and each hot region is associated with the URL of the document that is to be loaded when the hot region is clicked. After you decide the hot regions and their associated URLs, you need to determine whether the Web server or the Web client will make the decision about which document to load, based on the user's click. How this choice is made represents the difference between server-side and client-side image maps. Either approach is easy to implement after you know how to define the hot regions.

This chapter walks you through the necessary steps for creating both client-side and server-side image maps and introduces you to some software programs that make the task of defining hot regions much less tedious.

Client-Side Image Maps

Client-side image maps are a great idea because they permit faster image map processing and enhance the portability of your HTML documents. Client-side image maps involve sending the map data to the browser as part of an HTML file rather than having the browser contact the server each time the map data is needed. This process may add slightly to the transfer time of the HTML file, but the resulting increase in efficiency is well worth it.

The original movement toward client-side image maps was fueled by the promise of several advantages, including the following:

- **Immediate processing**—After the browser has the map file information, it can process a user's click immediately instead of connecting to the server and waiting for a response.
- **Offline viewing of Web pages**—If you're looking at a site from a hard drive or a CD-ROM drive, no server is available to do any image map computations. Client-side image maps enable image maps to be used when you're looking at pages offline.
- **No special configurations based on server program**—Client-side image maps are always implemented the same way. You don't need to format the map data differently, depending on whether a server expects a particular type of image map format, because no server is involved.

Previously, the only disadvantage of using client-side image maps was that it wasn't standard HTML and, therefore, not supported by all browsers. Client-side image maps are part of the

XHTML 1.0 recommendation, so you would be hard pressed to find an image-capable browser that does not support them.

Creating a client-side image map involves three steps:

1. Create the graphic that you want to make into an image map. The graphic can be a GIF or a JPEG file.
2. Define the hot regions for the graphic and place that information between the `<map>` and `</map>` elements in your HTML document. The information for each hot region is stored in an `<area />` element.
3. Use the `<img />` element to insert the graphic for the image map and link it to the hot region information you defined in the `<map>` element.

Defining a Map

A client-side image map is defined using XHTML elements and attributes, usually right in the XHTML file that contains the document with the image map. The map data is stored within the `<map>` element. The `<map>` element has the mandatory attribute `id`, which is used to give the image map data a unique identifier that can be used when referencing the data.

Inside the `<map>` element, hot regions are defined by standalone `<area />` elements—one `<area />` element for each hot region. The `<area />` element takes the attributes shown in Table 4.1.

Part I Ch 4

Table 4.1 Attributes of the *<area />* Element

Attribute	Purpose
`accesskey`	Designates a shortcut key for the region.
`alt`	Provides a text-based alternative to the hot region. This is the only required attribute of the `<area />` element.
`coords`	Lists the coordinates of points needed to define the hot region.
`href`	Supplies the URL to be associated with the hot region.
`nohref`	Specifies that no URL is associated with the hot region.
`shape`	Set equal to the keyword (`rect`, `circle`, `poly`, and `default`) that specifies the shape of the hot region. If no shape is specified, the default value of `rect` is used.
`tabindex`	Specifies the region's position in the page's tabbing order.

NOTE The `shape` attribute can take on values of `rect`, `circle`, `poly`, and `default`. The `point` keyword is not supported in XHTML 1.0.

These regions, as their names suggest, refer to the geometric shape of the hot region. Their defining coordinates are determined as pixel points relative to the upper-left corner of the image map graphic, which is taken to have coordinates 0,0 (see Figure 4.1).

One important difference with client-side image maps is that, when you specify a circular hot region, you need only give the coordinates of the center point and the radius of the circle. This is different from server-side maps, for which you specify the coordinates of the center point and a point on the circle itself. ■

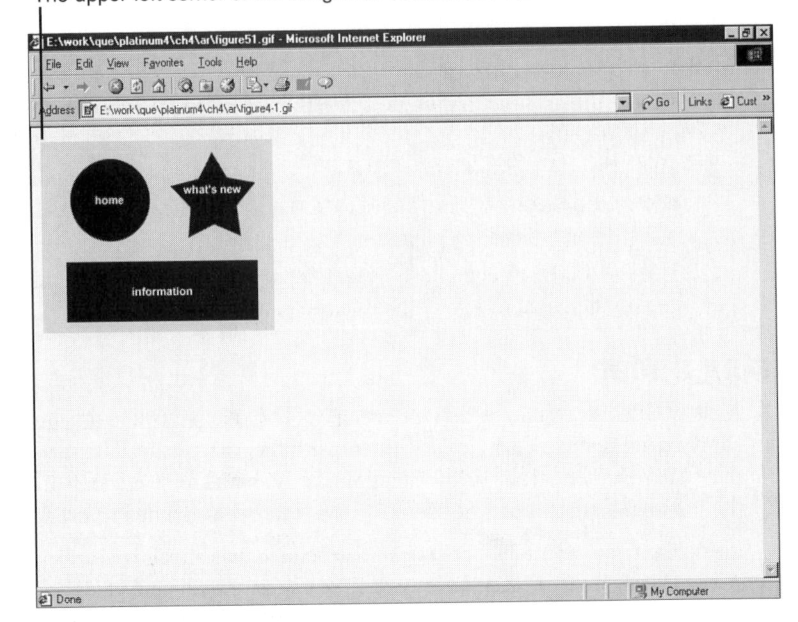

FIGURE 4.1
An image map on a home page typically provides navigation links to all major areas of a site.

To set up a circular hot region, for example, you would use code such as the following:

```
< map id="circle">
<area shape="circle" coords="123,89,49"
href="http://www.yourserver.com/circle.html" alt="Circle Link" />
</map>
```

The preceding XHTML sets up a map with the identifier *circle* that has one hot region. Note that the numbers in the list of coordinates for the coords attribute are all separated by commas. Note also that the coordinates list comprises the coordinates of the center point followed by a single number that represents the radius of the circle.

The <area /> element can also take a nohref attribute, which tells the browser to do nothing if the user clicks the hot region. Any part of the image that is not defined as a hot region is taken to be a nohref region; if users click outside a hot region, they won't go anywhere by default. This approach saves you from setting up an <area shape="default" nohref /> element for all your maps. The nohref attribute is still valuable, though. For example, if you have a donut-shaped hot region, you would need to create an <area /> element with a nohref for the donut hole because you don't want anything to happen if the user clicks there.

NOTE You can have as many <area /> elements as you like. If the hot regions defined by two <area /> elements overlap, the <area /> element listed first has precedence.

Setting Up the Image Map

After the image map data is set up in an XHTML document, you need to set up the image map itself. To do this, you use the `<img />` element along with the `usemap` attribute. `usemap` tells the browser that the image to be used is a client-side image map. It is set equal to the value of the `id` attribute of the map that contains the appropriate map data. For the client-side image map defined previously, the setup would look like this:

```
<img src="images/mainpage.gif" usemap="#circle" alt="Main navigation map" />
```

The pound sign (#) before the map's identifier value indicates that the map data is found in the same HTML file. If the map data is in another file called `maps.html` (which is perfectly legal but not equally supported by all browsers), your `<img />` element would look like the following:

```
<img src="images/mainpage.gif" alt="Main navigation map"
usemap="http://www.yourserver.com/maps.html#circle" />
```

TIP If you have standard navigation image maps on your site, storing the map data for them in a single HTML file makes for easier maintenance. Before you store the data, make certain that your audience is using a browser that can handle map data in a separate file.

NOTE Although the XHTML 1.0 recommendation says that the `usemap` attribute can be set to any valid URL, some browsers do not support the capability to reference another file when looking for map information. In these cases, you can still maintain the map information in a single file and read it into your XHTML files as needed by using a Server-Side Include (SSI). This way, you can still make changes in the map information in one place, and the changes will propagate throughout your site. ■

▶ To learn more about SSIs, **see** Chapter 29, "Server-Side Includes"

Example: A Main Page Image Map

Figure 4.1 showed an image to be used as an image map on the main page of a small corporate site. The coordinates to define the hot regions in the image are given in Table 4.2.

Table 4.2 Coordinates and URLs for Main Page Image Map Example

Shape	Coordinates	URL
Rectangle	(71,127),(218,188)	`http://www.yourserver.com/info.html`
Circle	(66,58), 48 pixel radius	`http://www.yourserver.com/index.html`
Polygon	(174,52), (205,44), (219,17), (236,43), (266,49), (248,73), (250,106), (221,93), (192,106), (195,74)	`http://www.yourserver.com/new.html`

Part I Ch 4

To set up the map information to make the image in Figure 4.1 a client-side image map, you could use the following XHTML:

```
<map id="mainpage">
<area shape="rect" coords="71,127,218,188"
href="http://www.yourserver.com/info.html" alt="Site Map" />
<area shape="circle" coords="66,58,48"
href="http://www.yourserver.com/index.html" alt="search" />
<area shape="poly"
coords="174,52,205,44,219,17,236,43,266,49,248,73,250,106,221,93,192,106,
➥195,74,174,52" href="http://www.yourserver.com/whatsnew.html"
alt="What's New />
</map>
```

Then, to set up the image map, you would use the following if the map information were in the same file:

```
<img src="images/mainpage.gif" usemap="#mainpage" alt="Main navigation map" />
```

If the map information were stored in the file `maps.html`, you would modify the preceding `<img />` element to read as follows:

```
<img src="images/mainpage.gif"
➥usemap="http://www.yourserver.com/maps.html#mainpage" />
```

Example: A Navigation Image Map

Another common use of image maps is for navigation bars at the top or bottom of a Web page. Figure 4.2 shows a typical navigation graphic with the hot regions defined by the information in Table 4.3.

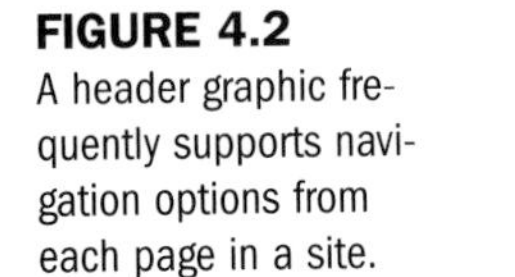

FIGURE 4.2
A header graphic frequently supports navigation options from each page in a site.

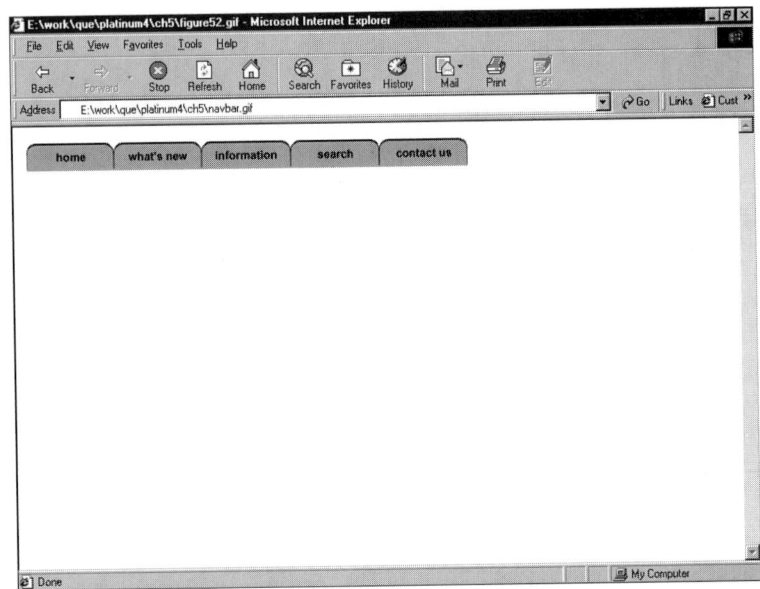

Table 4.3 Coordinates and URLs for Navigation Image Map Example

Shape	Coordinates	URL
Rectangle	(5,0),(98,31)	http://www.yourserver.com/index.html
Rectangle	(99,0),(195,31)	http://www.yourserver.com/whatsnew.html
Rectangle	(196,0),(289,31)	http://www.yourserver.com/info.html
Rectangle	(290,0),(383,31)	http://www.yourserver.com/search.html
Rectangle	(384,0),(480,31)	http://www.yourserver.com/contact.html

To use the navigation bar image in Figure 4.2 as a client-side image map, you first need to set up the map information in an XHTML file:

```
<map id="navigate">
<area shape="rect" coords="5,0,98,31"
 href="http://www.yourserver.com/index.html" alt="Home Page" />
<area shape="rect" coords="99,0,195,31"
 href="http://www.yourserver.com/whatsnew.html" alt="What's New" />
<area shape="rect" coords="195,0,287,31"
 href="http://www.yourserver.com/info.html" alt="Information" />
<area shape="rect" coords="290,0,383,31"
 href="http://www.yourserver.com/search.html" alt="Search" />
<area shape="rect" coords="384,0,480,31"
 href="http://www.yourserver.com/contact.html" alt="Contact Us" />
</map>
```


With the map data in place, you can reference it with the following `<img />` element if the map data is in the same XHTML file:

```
<img src="images/navbar.gif" usemap="#navigate" alt="Navigation links" />
```

Because the same navigation maps are often used on several pages of a site, you might want to consider putting the map data in a single map file and referencing the file each time you need the map as follows:

```
<img src="images/navbar.gif" usemap="maps.html#navigate"
➥alt="Navigation links" />
```

As noted earlier, this is an efficient way to manage image maps common to many pages, provided that your audience is using a browser that can retrieve the map data from the separate file.

Server-Side Image Maps

A server-side image map is one in which the server determines which document should be loaded, based on where the user clicked on the image. To make this determination, the server needs the following information:

- **The coordinates of the user's click**—This information is passed to the server by the client program.

- **A program that takes the click coordinates as input and provides a URL as output**—Most HTTP servers have a routine built in that handles this task.
- **Access to the information that defines the hot regions and their associated URLs**—This information is critical to the processing program that checks the hot regions to see whether the user's click corresponds to a URL. When the program finds a match, it returns the URL paired with the clicked hot region. The file on the server that contains this information is called the *map file*.

Additionally, you need two other "ingredients" to complete a server-side image map:

- **An image**—An image map is like any other graphic in that you need to have a GIF or a JPEG file that contains the image.
- **Proper setup in your XHTML file**—When you place the image map graphic, you use the `<img/>` element with a special attribute to alert the browser that the image is to be used as a server-side image map.

As an XHTML author, you need to be most concerned about two of the items just listed: the map file and the setup in the XHTML file. The next two sections discuss these aspects of creating an image map.

Preparing the Map File

The map file is a text file that contains information about the hot regions of a specific image map graphic. Therefore, a separate map file is necessary for each image map graphic you want to use. The definition specifies the type of hot region as a rectangle, circle, polygon, or point.

The following list identifies basic image map shape keywords and their required coordinates:

- `rect`—Indicates that the hot region is a rectangle. The coordinates required for this type of shape are the upper-left and lower-right pixels in the rectangle. The active region is the area within the rectangle.
- `circle`—Indicates that the hot region is circular. Coordinates required for using a circle are the center-point pixel and one edge-point pixel (a pixel on the circle itself). The active region is the area within the circle.

TIP If you know the center of the circle and its radius, you can simply add the radius to one of the center coordinates to get a point on the circle. For example, if the center of the circle is at (50,61) and the radius is 15 pixels, a point on the edge would be (65,61) or (50,76).

- `poly`—Indicates that the hot region is a polygon. To specify the polygon, you need to provide a list of coordinates for all the polygon's vertices. A polygonal region can have as many as 100 vertices. The active region is the area within the polygon.

NOTE The keyword `poly` will work only for NCSA-type Web servers. If you are using a CERN- or W3C-type server, you should use the keyword `polygon`.

- **`point`**—Indicates that the region is a point on the image. A point coordinate is one specific pixel measured from the upper-left corner of the image map graphic. A point is considered active if the click occurs closest to that point on the graphic, yet not within another active region.
- **`default`**—A catch-all that defines all areas of an image map graphic that are not specified by any other active region.

TIP An image map definition file should, whenever possible, be configured with a default link. The default link corresponds to an area that isn't designated as being an active link and is associated with its own URL. This URL should provide the user with feedback or helpful information about using that particular image map.

CAUTION

An image map definition file should never contain both a point and a default region. If point regions are defined and a user does not click a hot region, the server sends the user to the URL associated with the closest point region and the default URL will never be used.

Following each type of region in the image map definition file is the URL that is returned to the user when a click within that area is recorded. Active regions in the definition file are read from the first line down. If two regions overlap in their coordinates, the image map program uses the first region it encounters in the file.

CAUTION

URLs in map files should always be absolute or fully qualified URLs; that is, the URL should specify a protocol, a server name, and a filename (including the directory path to the file).

NOTE You can use the pound sign (#) to comment on a line in the image map definition file. Any line beginning with a pound sign is ignored by the image map program. Comments are useful for adding information, such as the date of creation, the physical path to the image map graphic, or specific comments about the server configuration.

Two primary types of map file configurations exist: one for the original CERN-style image maps and one for the NCSA server's implementation of image maps. Both use the same types of hot regions and the same coordinates to define each type. However, the formatting of this information in each map file is different. Therefore, you should check with the system administrator about the particular image map setup of the server you are using.

NOTE Most major HTTP servers today use the NCSA map format. This includes Netscape Enterprise Server and Windows 98/NT/2000-based servers, such as Microsoft Internet Information Server (IIS) or Microsoft Peer Web Services (PWS).

CERN Map File Format Lines in a CERN-style map file have the following form:

```
region_type coordinate-pairs URL
```

The coordinates must be in parentheses, and the x and y coordinates must be separated by a comma. The CERN format also doesn't allow for comments about hot regions. A sample CERN-style hot region definition might look like the following:

```
circle (123,89) 49 http://www.yourserver.com/circle.html
```

NSCA Map File Format NCSA developed a slightly different format from CERN's for map file information. Their format is as follows:

```
region_type URL coordinate-pairs
```

The coordinates don't have to be in parentheses, but they do have to be separated by commas. The equivalent of the map data line presented previously in NCSA format is as follows:

```
circle http://www.yourserver.com/circle.html 123,89,146,132
```

Setting Up the Image Map

Because of the differences in image map processing programs on different servers, you can use two techniques for setting up image maps.

Pointing Directly at the Processing Scripting The first approach, most commonly used with NCSA and CERN servers, involves a direct call to the image map processing program on the server. The `href` attribute is set equal to the URL to the image map processing script followed by a slash (/) and the name of the map defined in the server's `imagemap.conf` file. In the following example, the name of the map is `mainpage`. The actual graphic is then placed with the `<img />` element. The `<img />` element also includes the `ismap` attribute, indicating that the image placed by the tag is to be a server-side image map. Using this approach, your image map link might look like this:

```
<a href="/cgi-bin/imagemap/mainpage">
<img src="images/mainpage.gif" ismap="ismap" /></a>
```

NOTE Recall that XHTML does not permit standalone attributes like HTML did. Thus, the `ismap` attribute must be written inside the `<img />` element as `ismap="ismap"` rather than just writing `ismap`.

For this example to work, the `imagemap.conf` file must also include a line pointing to a map file for the image map `mainpage`. That line might look like the following:

```
mainpage : /maps/mainpage.map
```

Entries in the `imagemap.conf` file enable the image map program to find the map files you create. You need a similar entry in the `imagemap.conf` file for each image map you want the server to process.

Pointing Directly at the Map File Linking to the image map script on the server is somewhat easier under Apache, Netscape, and Microsoft HTTP servers. For this program, you just use the following line with an NCSA-style map file:

```
<a href="/maps/mainpage.map">
<img src="images/mainpage.gif" alt="Main navigation map" ismap="ismap"/></a>
```

These servers don't require the `imagemap.conf` file, so you can "eliminate the middleman" and point directly to the map file. When the server detects a call for a map file, it automatically invokes the image map processing program.

Example: A Main Page Image Map

You use the following code to set up the image you saw in Figure 4.1 in a CERN-style map file:

```
rect (71,127)  (218,188) http://www.yourserver.com/info.html
circle (66,58) (114,58) http://www.yourserver.com/index.html
poly (174,52) (205,44) (219,17) (236,43) (266,49) (248,73) (250,106) (221,93)
(192,106) (195,74)  http://www.yourserver.com/new.html
```

For a server that works with the NCSA map file format, you use this:

```
rect http://www.yourserver.com/info.html 71,127 218,188
circle http://www.yourserver.com/index.html 66,58 114,58
poly http://www.yourserver.com/new.html 174,52 205,44 219,17 236,43 266,49
➥248,73
250,106 221,93 192,106 195,74
```

With a map file set up in one style or another, you then set up the image map with this code:

```
<a href="http://www.yourserver.com/cgi-bin/imagemap/mainpage">
<img src="images/mainpage.gif" ismap="ismap" ... /></a>
```

The preceding code is for servers that use an `imagemap.conf` file or with this:

```
<a href="http://www.yourserver.com/maps/mainpage.map">
<img src="images/mainpage.gif" ismap="ismap" ... /></a>
```

This code is for servers that automatically go to the map file.

NOTE If you are using a server with an `imagemap.conf` file, you also need a line in that file matching the name "mainpage" with the map file `mainpage.map`:

```
mainpage : /maps/mainpage.map
```

Example: A Navigation Image Map

The CERN format map file for the image you saw in Figure 4.2 would look like the following:

```
rect (5,0) (98,31) http://www.yourserver.com/index.html
rect (99,0) (195,31) http://www.yourserver.com/whatsnew.html
rect (195,0) (287,31) http://www.yourserver.com/info.html
rect (290,0) (383,31) http://www.yourserver.com/search.html
rect (384,0) (480,31) http://www.yourserver.com/contact.html
```

If you are preparing a map file in NCSA format, use the following:

```
rect http://www.yourserver.com/index.html 5,0 98,31
rect http://www.yourserver.com/new.html 99,0 195,31
rect http://www.yourserver.com/info.html 195,0 287,31
rect http://www.yourserver.com/search/index.html 290,0 383,31
rect http://www.yourserver.com/contact.html 384,0 480,31
```

After your map file is done in the appropriate format, you set up the image map with

```
<a href="http://www.yourserver.com/cgi-bin/imagemap/navigate">
<img src="images/navbar.gif" ismap="ismap" ... /></a>
```

or with

```
<a href="http://www.yourserver.com/maps/navigate.map">
<img src="images/navbar.gif" ismap="ismap" ... /></a>
```

depending on whether the server uses an `imagemap.conf` file.

Using Server-Side and Client-Side Image Maps Together

Client-side image maps are a great idea because they permit faster image map processing and enhance the portability of your XHTML documents. Unfortunately, you can't be certain all image-capable browsers are compliant with the XHTML 1.0 recommendation and support the client-side image map approach described earlier in the chapter. To be on the safe side, you can combine server-side and client-side image maps, essentially implementing both at the same time, to ensure your image maps are accessible to the broadest possible audience.

To combine a server-side image map with a client-side image map for the main page example discussed earlier, you can modify the earlier XHTML as follows:

```
<a href="http://www.server/maps/mainpage.map">
<img src="images/mainpage.gif" usemap="#mainpage" ismap="ismap" ... /></a>
```

Placing the `<img />` element within an `<a>` element makes it point to the `mainpage.map` file on the server. You need to include the `ismap` attribute in the `<img />` element to let the browser know that the image is linked as a server-side image map as well.

NOTE You can link NCSA- and CERN-style server-side image maps to client-side image maps by having the `href` in the `<a>` element point to the `imagemap` script instead of pointing directly to the map file.

Providing a Text Alternative to an Image Map

When you use an image map—in particular, a server-side image map—it's important to provide a text-based alternative to users who have a text-only browser, who have image loading turned off, or who are using a nonvisual browser. These users won't be able to view your image, so the entire image map will be lost on them if a text-based alternative is not supplied.

Additionally, not all Web spiders and robots can follow the links set up in a server-side image map. By providing a text-based set of links that replicate the links in the image map, you give the spiders and robots a way to better index your pages.

NOTE Text-based alternatives are less critical for client-side image maps because of the required `alt` attribute of the `<area />` element. You are still free to include such alternatives, however, if you are willing to make the effort.

Most sites place their text-based alternatives to an image map just below the image map graphic. Usually the links are in a smaller font size and are separated by vertical bars or some such separator character (see Figure 4.3).

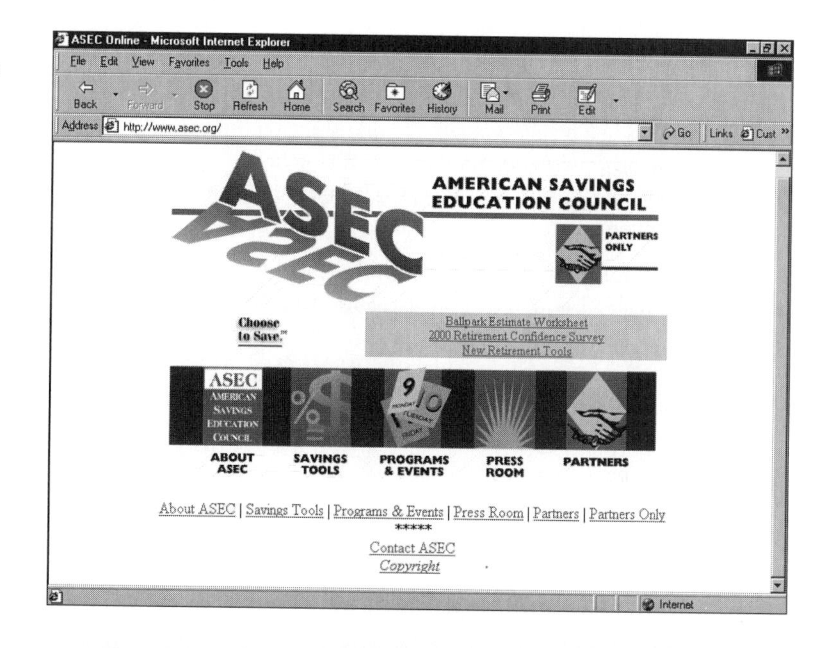

FIGURE 4.3
Duplicating image map links with hypertext links makes it possible for users with text-only browsers to navigate your site.

Image Map Tools

Whether you are creating a server-side or client-side image map, it can be cumbersome determining and typing in all the coordinates of all the points needed to define hot regions. Luckily, programs are available to help you through this process. They enable you to load your image map image, trace out the hot regions onscreen, and then write the appropriate map file or HTML file to implement the image map. The following sections describe two of these programs: Mapedit and LiveImage.

TIP Be sure to check the output of your image map program to make sure that it is XHTML-compliant.

Mapedit

Mapedit is a shareware image map tool produced by Boutell.Com, Inc. This version of Mapedit supports client-side images and targeting of individual frames when you use an image map within a framed document.

Using Mapedit is easy. From the File menu, choose Open HTML Document to begin. In the dialog box that appears, you won't see a choice between doing a server-side and a client-side image map. Instead, you first tell Mapedit which XHTML file contains the image for which you're building the image map. Next, tell Mapedit which file contains the image map image. When you click OK, the image file is loaded into the Mapedit window, and you're ready to start defining hot regions.

You can choose Rectangle, Circle, or Polygon tools from the Mapedit Tools menu or from the toolbar just below the menus. Each tool enables you to trace out a hot region shaped like the name of the tool. To use the Rectangle tool, point your mouse to the upper-left corner of the rectangular hot region and click the left mouse button. Then move your mouse pointer to the lower-right corner of the region. As you do so, a black rectangular outline is dragged along with the pointer, eventually opening up to enclose your hot region (see Figure 4.4).

With the mouse pointer pointing at the lower-right corner, left-click the mouse again. When you do, you see a dialog box like the one shown in Figure 4.5. Type the URL associated with the hot region you are defining into the dialog box, along with any comments you want to include, and click OK. Mapedit puts this information into the file it is building and is then ready to define another hot region or to save the file and exit.

Mapedit's Circle and Polygon tools work similarly. With the Circle tool, you place your mouse pointer at the center of the circular region (which is sometimes difficult to estimate!) and left-click. Then move the pointer to a point on the circle and left-click again to define the region and call up the dialog box. To use the Polygon tool, just left-click the vertices of the polygon in sequence. When you hit the last unique vertex (that is, the next vertex in the sequence is the first one you clicked), right-click instead to define the region and reveal the dialog box.

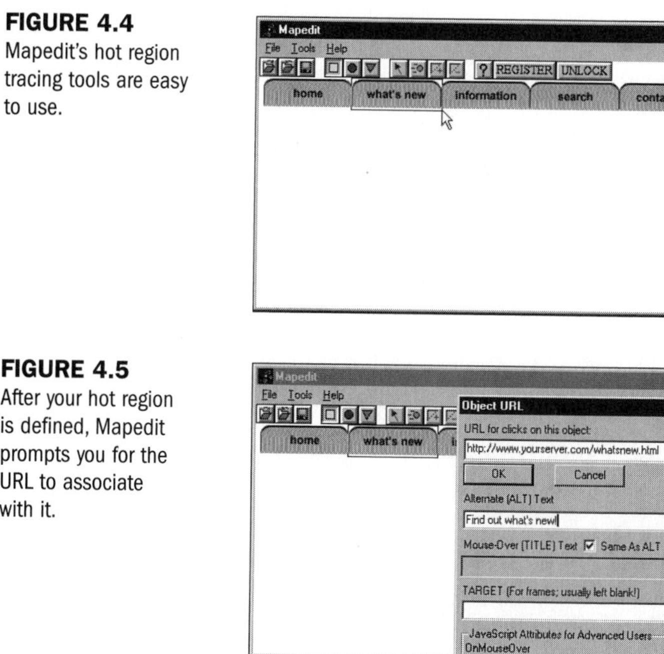

FIGURE 4.4
Mapedit's hot region tracing tools are easy to use.

FIGURE 4.5
After your hot region is defined, Mapedit prompts you for the URL to associate with it.

TIP If you are unhappy with how your trace is coming out, just press the Esc key to erase your trace and start over.

Other Mapedit Tool menu options enable you to move an entire hot region (Move), add points (Add Points), or remove points (Remove Points) from a polygon and test the image map file as it currently stands. The Edit Default URL option, under the File menu, enables you to specify a default URL to go to if a user clicks somewhere other than a hot region. Mapedit's test mode (choose Tools, Test+Edit) presents the image map graphic to you and enables you to click it. If you click a hot region, the URL dialog box opens and displays the URL associated with the region you clicked.

The most recent version of Mapedit for Windows 98 and Windows NT places a heavy emphasis on creating client-side image maps, but you can still use Mapedit to import and export server-side maps as well. Under the File menu, you'll now find Import Old Server Map and Export Old Server Map options that read in or write out a map file.

NOTE Mapedit is available for all Windows platforms, Macintosh, and many kinds of UNIX including Linux. You can find Mapedit on the CD-ROM that comes with this book. After a 30-day evaluation period, you must license Mapedit at a cost of $25. Site licenses are also available. Educational and nonprofit users do not have to pay for a license but should register their copies of Mapedit by mail. For more information, visit `http://www.boutell.com/`. ■

LiveImage

LiveImage is an easy-to-use image mapping tool for Windows 98 and Windows NT. If you have used a program called Map This! in the past, LiveImage might seem very familiar. Indeed, LiveImage is an enhanced version of Map This!, but the enhancements come (literally) with a price. A single-user license for LiveImage will set you back $29.95.

Figure 4.6 shows the LiveImage interface. The image map graphic loads in the large area on the right side of the window. On the left side of the window is a listing of the hot regions you have defined. You can drag the separator bar between the two sides to a new position if you want to change the size of either.

LiveImage's interface is very intuitive, particularly those buttons you use to create hot regions. Just click the button corresponding to the shape of the hot region you want to define, and then trace the hot region with your mouse. When you finish, you will see a dialog box like the one in Figure 4.6 prompting you for a URL, a target frame, and any comments you want to associate with the region. Note also that hot regions are shaded on the graphic.

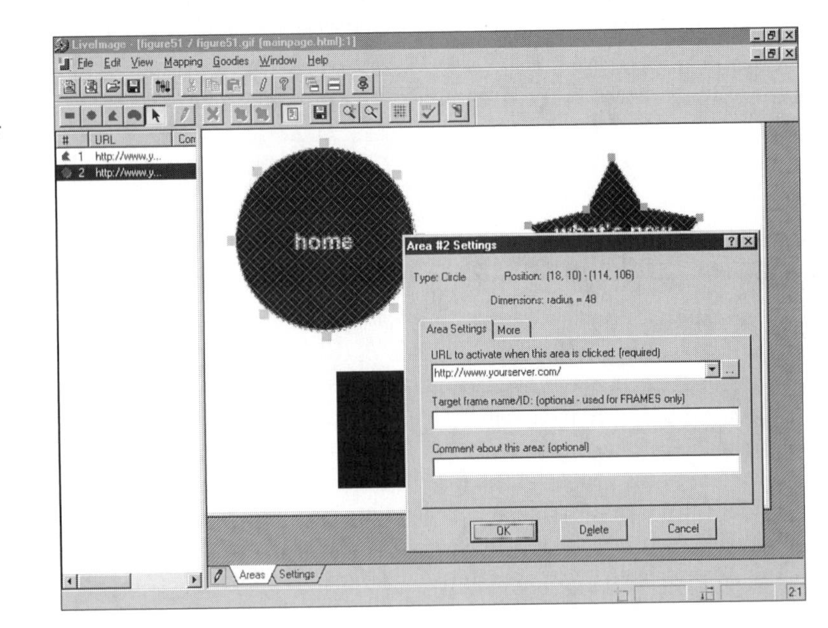

FIGURE 4.6
LiveImage enables you to see both the image map graphics and your hot regions simultaneously.

You also receive a lot of extras in LiveImage that you don't receive in other image map programs. In addition to being able to zoom in and out on the graphic, for example, you can also set up a grid over the image to assist you with very precise hot region traces. You can control the fineness of the grid, and you can even have points in your hot region trace snap to the grid.

LiveImage enables you to test an image map in two ways. The first is through a "simulated browser" built into LiveImage. When you test this way, you move your mouse pointer over the image map graphic, and you will see URLs show up at the bottom of the screen as you pass over a hot region. The second way is to load the HTML file that LiveImage produces into an actual browser and test it there.

Some of the other distinguishing features of LiveImage include the following:

- A URL Checker that tests the URLs you associate with your hot regions to make sure they are valid
- Support for morphing one type of hot region into another
- The ability to work with more advanced types of files, such as ColdFusion templates, Active Server Page files, and Cascading Style Sheets
- JavaScript support for mouse-related events (`onMouseOver` and `onMouseOut`)
- Sample image maps and extensive help files
- A Settings tab where you can specify a map's identifier, author, default URL, and other information

Although you do have to pay a small amount of money for LiveImage, you get quite a lot in return. You can learn more about LiveImage by visiting `http://www.mediatec.com/`.

CHAPTER 5

Advanced Graphics

by Eric Ladd

In this chapter

Sorting Through the Graphic Possibilities

The Web probably wouldn't be so popular if it didn't support graphical content. Graphics give Web pages visual appeal that keeps users surfing for hours. Graphics are also essential for people designing and posting Web pages because graphics often convey a message more powerfully than text alone.

Placing an image on a Web page is a relatively easy matter—you need only one XHTML element, the `<img />` element. This element has many attributes that give you control over how your graphics are presented.

Intelligent use of images requires planning, so you need to think about what idea you want to put forward, how to best represent the idea graphically, and what format is most appropriate for the graphic. You should put at least as much thought into your graphic content as you put into textual content—perhaps even more so because a reader gets a sense of an image just by quickly looking at it, whereas reading and comprehending text-based information requires more time. And making a Web graphic requires more than just creating the illustration. You must consider the appropriateness of one of the many special effects that are possible with the available graphics file formats: GIF, JPG, and PNG. For GIFs, this means asking yourself the following questions:

- Should the GIF be transparent?
- Should it be interlaced?
- Should it be animated?

When considering JPEGs, you can ask

- How much should the JPEG be compressed?
- Should it be a progressive JPEG (analogous to an interlaced GIF)?

Finally, for PNG graphics you can ask

- What level of transparency should be used?
- Will end users be using software that supports the PNG format?

Additionally, you must think about color, depth, textures, filters, drop shadows, embossing, and all the other possible visual effects. Through everything, you also need to keep the size of your graphics files as small as possible so they don't take too long to download. How can you balance all these constraints?

This chapter helps you answer these questions so your graphics content is as effective as it can be; it starts with an examination of the three prevalent graphics storage formats in use on the Web today. Then it moves on to a discussion of how you can implement some of the effects that each format supports using today's most popular graphics tools. Finally, you will learn about the XHTML `<img />` element and how to use it to place images into your documents. Mastering the content of this chapter will not necessarily make you a first-rate, digital-media design guru, but it will make you aware of what is possible in the realm of Web graphics.

Graphic Storage Formats

Technically, Web graphics can be stored in any format, but only three formats display inline on all of today's popular graphical browsers: GIF, JPEG, and PNG.

A third format, PNG, is gaining ground; indeed, PNG is now the native graphics format within all the Microsoft Office applications. Other graphics formats must be displayed by a helper application, which is launched by the browser when it detects a format it can't display.

NOTE Microsoft Internet Explorer supports the inline display of Windows Bitmap (.BMP) graphics in addition to GIFs, JPEGs, and PiNs. ■

Scalable Vector Graphics

Scalable Vector Graphics (SVG) is an emerging, XML-based graphics format that will enable developers to describe two-dimensional graphics. You can store three different types of graphic objects with SVG: simple vector-based shapes (such as lines, curves, and circles), text, and images.

By storing graphics in SVG format, it becomes possible to perform different transformations on the stored graphic objects. Additionally, it is expected that you will be able to script SVG graphics by associating event handlers such as `onMouseOver` and `onClick` with the graphics.

As of this writing, SVG is still in draft form but is getting close to being finalized. Indeed, some graphics packages, such as Adobe Illustrator, are already incorporating rudimentary SVG support. You can keep pace with the development of SVG by periodically visiting `http://www.w3.org/Graphics/SVG/`.

GIF

Graphics Interchange Format (GIF) was originally developed for users of CompuServe as a standard for storing image files. The GIF standards have undergone a couple of revisions since their inception. The current standard is GIF89a.

Graphics stored in GIF are limited to 256 colors. Because full-color photos require many more colors to look lifelike, you shouldn't store full-color photos as GIFs. GIF is best used with line art, logos, and icons. If you do store a full-color photo as a GIF, its palette is reduced to just 256 colors, and the photo will not look as good on your Web page.

CAUTION

When you store a full-color photo as a GIF, much of the color data is irretrievably lost.

In spite of a limited number of colors, the GIF89a standard supports the following three Web page effects:

- **Interlacing**—In an interlaced GIF image, nonadjacent parts of the image are stored together. As a browser reads in an interlaced GIF, the image appears to fade in over several passes. This is useful because the user can get a sense of what the entire image looks like without having to wait for the whole thing to load.

- **Transparency**—In a transparent GIF, one of the colors is designated as transparent, enabling the background of the document to show through. Figure 5.1 provides an example of a transparent GIF. As you move your mouse over the various sections of the pets.com site, an image appears above each button. The transparency effect allows the animal face to appear to sit directly on the background, even though the background is composed of more than one color.

FIGURE 5.1
The background color in a transparent GIF takes on the page's background color.

Transparent GIFs are very popular, and many of the graphics programs available today support the creation of transparent GIFs. As you'll read later, Adobe Photoshop, available for both Windows and Macintosh platforms, makes it easy to export an image as a transparent GIF.

- **Animation**—Animated GIFs are created by storing in one file the sequence of images used to produce the animation. A browser that fully supports the GIF89a standard is designed to present the images in the file one after the other to produce the animation. The programs that enable you to store the multiple images in the GIF file also enable you to specify how much delay should occur before beginning the animation and how many times the animation should repeat. Web designers are making widespread use of animated GIFs because they are much easier to implement than server-push or even Java animations (see Figure 5.2). A server-push animation requires a CGI program to send the individual images down an open HTTP connection.

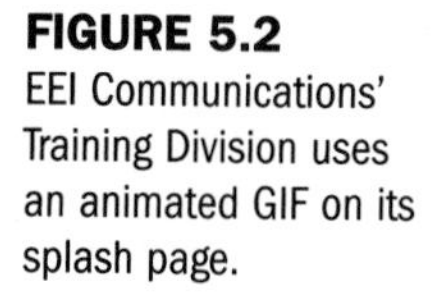

FIGURE 5.2
EEI Communications' Training Division uses an animated GIF on its splash page.

JPEG

Joint Photographic Experts Group (JPEG) refers to a set of formats that supports full-color images and stores them in a compressed form. JPEG is a 24-bit storage format that allows for 2^{24} or 16,777,216 colors! With that much color data, it is easy to see why some form of compression is necessary. Typically, you can control the degree of compression at the time you create the JPEG file. Keep in mind that the more you compress the image, the more information from the original graphic you lose and the less lifelike the JPEG image is likely to appear.

Although JPEG is great for full-color images (see Figure 5.3), it does not permit some of the nice effects that GIF does. Transparency is not possible with JPEG images because the compression tends to make small mathematical changes to the image data. With the exception of a server-push approach, animation is not yet possible with JPEGs. An analogy to interlaced GIFs exists, however. The progressive JPEG (p-JPEG) format has recently emerged, which gives the effect of an image fading in the same way an interlaced GIF would.

PNG

A search for a more open (or less proprietary) graphics format started as far back as 1990 following the demands of Unisys and CompuServe for royalties for use of GIF technology. The rationale behind this announcement was that GIF was developed by CompuServe and used a compression technique developed by Unisys, so the two companies were entitled to compensation. Most of the rest of the world did not share this philosophy, however, and, as part of the fallout, the Portable Network Graphics (PNG, pronounced *ping*) working group was formed and began drafting a proposal for this new, open format. In October 1996, the World Wide Web Consortium accepted the proposed PNG standard as a recommendation.

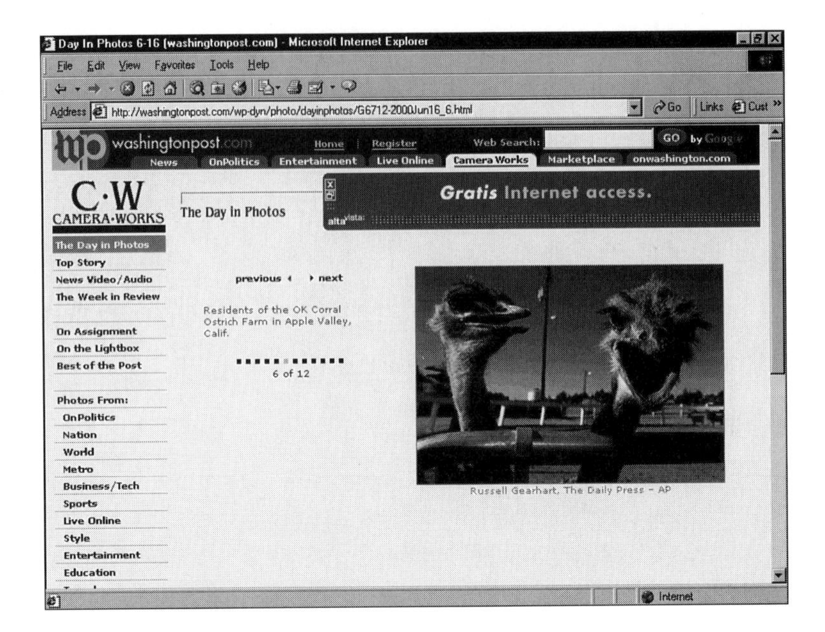

FIGURE 5.3
The photo of these ostriches was converted to a JPEG for publication on the Web.

The PNG format is capable of supporting the two major effects that originally made GIFs so popular: transparency and interlacing. In fact, PNG is an improvement over GIF in that it implements these effects in a more flexible way. Specifically, for transparency, PNG provides for an *alpha channel* that supports up to 254 levels of partial transparency—in contrast to the GIFs approach, which supports only two levels: totally transparent or totally opaque. For interlacing, PNG employs a seven-pass, two-dimensional interlacing scheme that presents initial image data eight times faster than one-dimensional GIF interlacing.

NOTE PNG is also an improvement over GIF when it comes to compression. Compression ratios are typically 5–25% higher, with no data loss, in images that would traditionally be thought suitable for conversion to GIFs.

PNG offers broad support for many kinds of images, including

- **True-color images**—Prior to PNG, your only option for true color (24-bit color) was to use the JPEG format.
- **8-bit palette images**—PNG, like GIF, supports images that are composed of 8-bit color palettes. PNG can also support 1-, 2-, and 4-bit palettes as well, so you can reduce the color depth (and hence the file size) of a PNG graphic if you don't have too many colors.
- **Grayscale images**—PNG allows for 1-, 2-, 4-, 8-, and 16-bit grayscale images.

One thing that PNG does not support, however, is animation. Recall that for animated GIFs, the many images that compose the animation are stored together in one file. PNG was developed as a single-image file format, so no way exists for it to support animation.

NOTE A proposal is under development for a format called MNG that will support storage of multiple images and, therefore, animation. You can track the progress of this effort by regularly visiting `http://www.libpng.org/pub/mng/mngdocs.html`.

Browser- and image-software support for PNG was tentative for the first year, but then Microsoft took the step of making PNG the native format for its Office 97 suite of products and announced its intention to provide inline support for PNG graphics in release 4 of its Internet Explorer browser. Since then, many other companies have followed suit, and PNG is now supported by the following software:

- Netscape Navigator 4.0 and later
- CorelDRAW 7.0 and later
- Macromedia Free Hand Graphics Studio 7.0 and later
- Microsoft Image Composer 1.5 and later
- SoftQuad HoTMetaL 3.0 and later
- Adobe Illustrator 7.0 and later
- Adobe Photoshop 4.0 and later
- Jasc, Inc. Paint Shop Pro 3.01 and later

Thus, it is possible for you to start creating PNG graphics for your Web pages now, and visitors using the most recent releases of Netscape or Microsoft browsers will be able to view them. Alternatively, you can convert your existing GIF and JPEG graphics to PNG using one of the more PNG-compliant conversion tools such as Adobe File Utilities, DeBabelizer Pro (Windows), or DeBabelizer ToolBox (Macintosh). However, keep in mind that the GIF and JPEG images will have lost information compared to the original, so converting an original image to PNG may well give a higher-quality PNG image than an adapted GIF or JPEG image.

NOTE For the latest about PNG, including documentation of the standard, sample images, and a list of PNG-compliant software, consult the PNG home page at `http://www.libpng.org/pub/png/`.

Choosing a Format

The question of which format to use is often daunting for beginning designers. Fortunately, some ways are available to focus your thinking as you make this choice:

- *Do you need to create a transparency effect?* If so, you have your choice of either GIF or PNG.
- *Do you need to produce an animation?* Unless you want to code a server-push animation or use Java applet-based animation, it is easier to place animations on your pages by using animated GIFs.

- *Is your graphic a full-color image?* Full-color images, particularly photographs of things in nature, are best stored in JPEG or PNG formats so that you can harness their support for more than 16 million colors.
- *Does your graphic have any sharp color changes or boundaries?* Some graphics change quickly from one color to another rather than fading gradually over a continuum of colors. Because of the mathematics behind the compression algorithm, JPEGs don't cope well with sudden color changes. Use GIF or PNG to handle images such as these.
- *Do you need a fade-in effect?* This isn't too much of a discriminator because GIF, JPEG, and PNG all support some type of fade-in effect—interlacing for GIF and PNG, and p-JPEG for JPEG.

Using the Browser-Safe Color Palette

Lynda Weinman, a popular author on the topics of Web graphics and color, has advanced the idea of a *browser-safe palette*—a set of colors rendered the same way by ***any*** browser on ***any*** platform.

Netscape Navigator and Microsoft Internet Explorer both use the same default 256-color palette when rendering Web pages, but because of slight differences between the PC and the Macintosh, 40 of these colors can appear differently, depending on the platform. If you remove these 40 colors from the default palette, the remaining 216 colors compose a palette that should appear the same regardless of a user's hardware or software.

The browser-safe color palette is freely available from `http://www.lynda.com/hex.html`, ordered both by hue and by RGB color values. Many popular authoring tools now have the Browser-Safe color palette built in, allowing you to make color selections directly from the palette (see Figure 5.4).

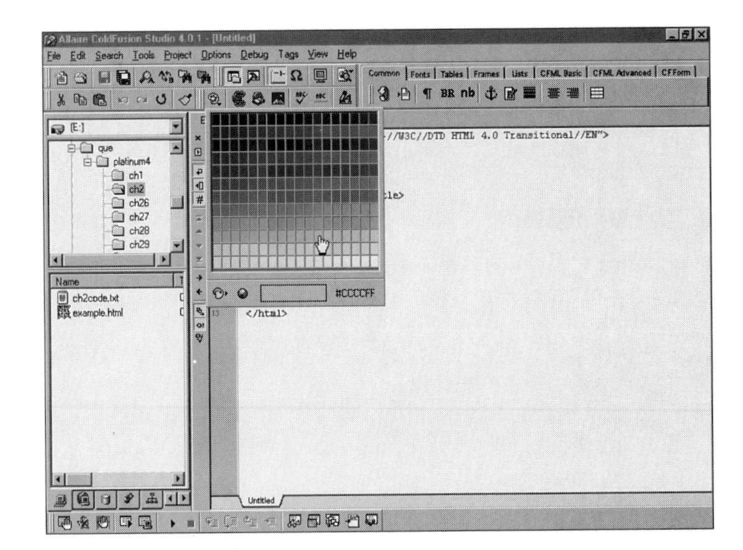

FIGURE 5.4
ColdFusion Studio includes a color palette option that displays the Web Safe Color Palette by default.

TIP If your graphics package does not offer a Web-safe palette (or if you simply want to experiment), but it does offer the capability to numerically adjust color, you can create a Web-safe palette by using multiples of 51 in the RGB color choices. If you use 0, 51, 102, 153, 204, or 255 for each of the red, green, and blue components of screen color, the color will be "Web safe." For example, in RGB order, 153,0,102 is a pleasant maroon color.

Creating Transparent GIFs

When you make a transparent GIF, you designate one color in the image's palette to be the transparent color. Pixels painted with the transparent color enable the background color to show through.

This technique is useful in getting rid of the bounding box that typically surrounds a graphic. When you compose an image in a graphics program, the workspace is almost always rectangular. Your image goes inside this rectangular region (the bounding box), and invariably some amount of space exists between the image and the edges of the box.

By choosing the color of the excess space pixels to be transparent, you make them disappear on the browser screen. This is what happened in Figure 5.1 shown previously. The bounding box pixels in the image using the transparency option were the ones designated as transparent, so they enabled the green background to show through and give the effect of the animal's head sitting right on top of the Web page.

TIP Think twice before putting a border around a transparent GIF because it will outline the bounding box and ruin the transparency effect.

Adobe Photoshop supports GIF images and makes it easy to implement transparency. To create a transparent GIF in Photoshop, follow these steps:

1. Check to make sure the image is displayed using Indexed Color Mode. In Photoshop, choose Image, Mode, Indexed Color (see Figure 5.5). Click the OK button to convert the image to Indexed Color Mode.
2. Choose File, Export, GIF89a Export. Use the Eyedropper tool to select the color that you want to make transparent (the white background in the sample image; see Figure 5.6).
3. After the color is selected, it turns gray to indicate that this color will be transparent after the image is saved.

NOTE You can deselect colors that have been selected by holding down the Control key and clicking with the Eyedropper, either in the color palette or in the image itself. You will see a minus sign (-) next to the bottom of the Eyedropper tool if it's in deselect mode.

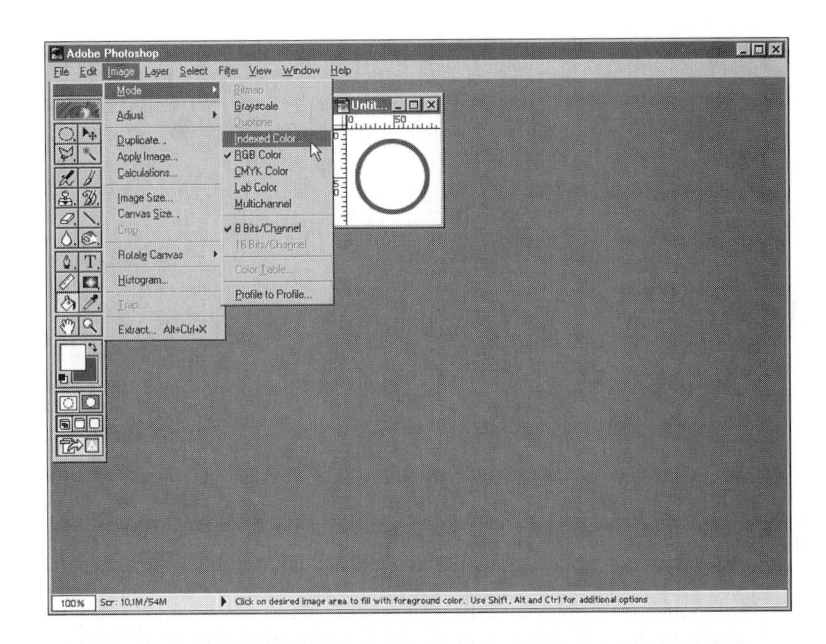

FIGURE 5.5
To create a transparent GIF in Photoshop, you first must be in indexed color mode.

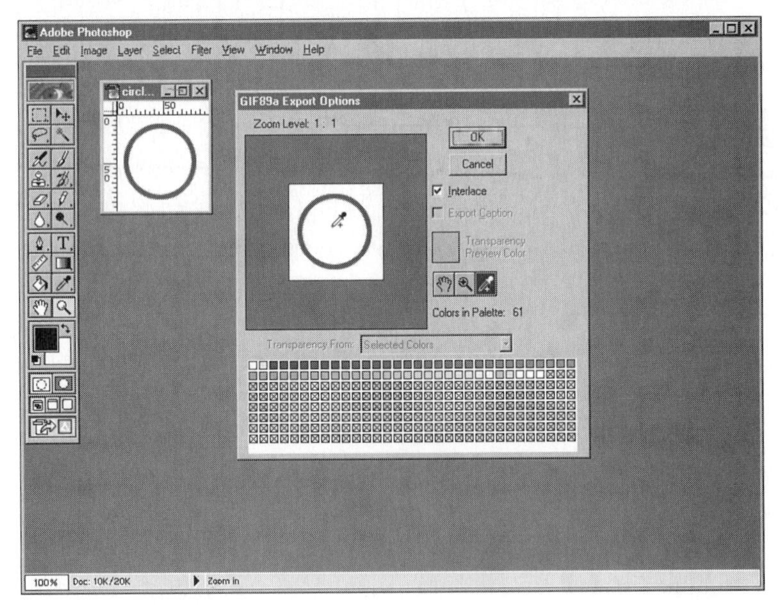

FIGURE 5.6
You use the Eyedropper tool to select the transparent color from the palette.

4. If you want to export the image using interlacing, make sure the Interlace option (beneath the Cancel button) is checked. This option is checked by default. To save an image without using interlacing, uncheck the Interlace option before exporting.
5. Click the OK button to export the transparent GIF.

Making a Transparent PNG

Creating a transparent PNG is a fairly simple matter when you're using Microsoft's Image Composer. To make a transparent PNG, follow these steps:

1. Choose File, Save As to open the Save As dialog box (see Figure 5.7).

FIGURE 5.7
When doing a transparent PNG in Image Composer, you can choose multilevel- or single-color transparency.

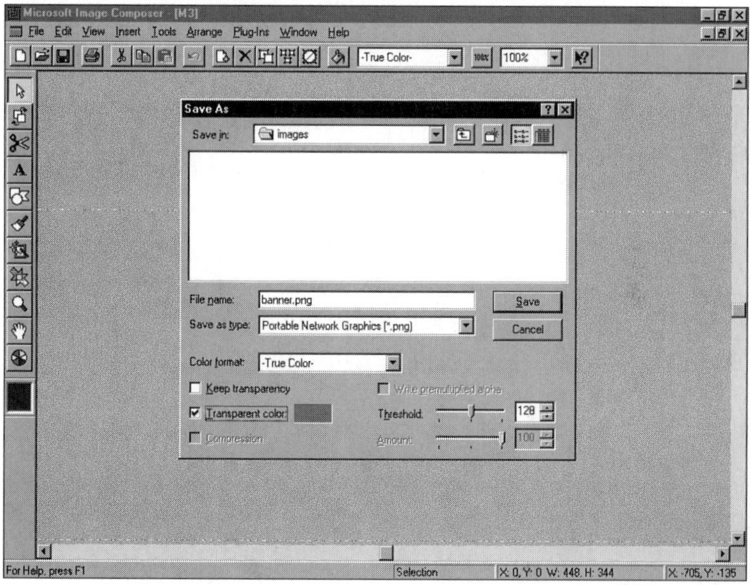

2. From the Save as Type drop-down list, choose the Portable Network Graphics format.
3. Make sure the Color Format selection is set to True Color.
4. Choose the Keep Transparency box if you want to save the image with its alpha channel (this allows for the multiple levels of transparency). Otherwise, click the Transparent Color box and choose a color to act as the transparent color (just as you would with a transparent GIF image).
5. Click the Save button to save the transparent PNG.

Why Aren't There Transparent JPEGs?

Transparency is supported only in the GIF format. A JPEG image cannot use a transparency effect because the algorithm used to compress a JPEG file is lossy. This means that during decompression, some pixels are not painted with the exact same color they had before the compression. These color changes are so small that they are usually imperceptible to the human eye, although you might be able to detect color differences after several cycles of compression and decompression. However, a computer can detect the difference, and therein lies the demise of the transparent JPEG. To understand further, consider the following example:

You scan in a photograph of a field of flowers and you want to save it as a JPEG. The JPEG format supports more than 16.7 million colors. Suppose that you choose color number 3,826,742 as the transparent color and save the file. During the compression and subsequent decompression, some data loss occurs in the file. As a result of the loss, a pixel originally painted with color number 3,826,742 is now colored with color number 3,826,740. The pixel was supposed to be transparent, but because its color number was changed by the compression, it won't be. The pixel will be painted with color number 3,826,740 and not let the background show through.

The reverse situation can happen as well. Suppose a pixel originally colored with color number 3,826,745 ends up being painted with color number 3,826,742. This is the transparent color, so the pixel adopts the background color rather than color number 3,826,745, as originally intended.

As long as JPEG continues to be a lossy format, it will be impossible to use transparency with it. If you have to use a transparent graphic, you must use GIF or PNG.

NOTE If your budget does not permit you to purchase a high-end graphics program like Photoshop, you might want to consider cheaper alternatives such as Corel PhotoPaint 9, Jasc PaintShop Pro 6, and Ulead Photoimpact 5.

Making an Image Fade In

Even when image files are made as small as possible, it can still take a while for them to download. Initially, browsers had to load and process the entire file before it began to present the image onscreen. This meant users had to sit there staring at a blank screen for minutes at a time. Because user attention spans are short, people would often give up in frustration and move on to another page instead of waiting for an image to finish downloading.

Since those early days, two approaches to reducing user frustration have emerged. Both involve having an image "fade in" as the image data is read by the browser. The user sees a blurry, incomplete image at first, but then the image quality improves as more data is read in. The key thing for users is that they immediately see an approximation to the finished image on their screens. This keeps them engaged and makes it less likely that they will move on to another page.

The two approaches to fading an image onto a page are actually variations on the same idea, modified for different storage formats. In each case, the image data is not stored in top-to-bottom order. Instead, the image data is reordered so that adjacent rows of pixel information are no longer stored contiguously in the file. As the browser reads down the file, it places the rows of noncontiguous data up on the screen. The result is an incomplete image that fills itself in as the rest of the image data is read. A GIF or PNG stored in this way is said to be *interlaced*. The same idea applied to a JPEG file yields a *progressive JPEG* or *p-JPEG*.

TIP A different kind of fade-in effect is to have a black-and-white version of an image load first, followed by the full-color version. You can accomplish this by using the `lowsrc` attribute of the `<img />` element. `lowsrc` is set equal to the URL of the black-and-white image file. This file loads and is rendered more quickly because it is generally much smaller than its full-color equivalent (less color information to store means a smaller file size). The full-color version is then rendered in place of the `lowsrc` image after it is read in. This gives the appearance of the black-and-white image being "painted" with color.

Making Interlaced GIFs

You saw in the Photoshop Export GIF89a dialog box that the Interlace option is preselected (refer to Figure 5.6). If you want your GIF to be interlaced, leave this box selected and proceed with the export. If you do not want an interlaced GIF, be sure to deselect the box.

Progressive JPEGs

To create a progressive JPEG, choose the Save for Web option under the Photoshop File menu. This brings up the Save For Web dialog box you see in Figure 5.8. In the upper-right part of the dialog box, you will see a Progressive check box. Make sure this box is checked (it is by default), and Photoshop will save the JPEG in progressive format.

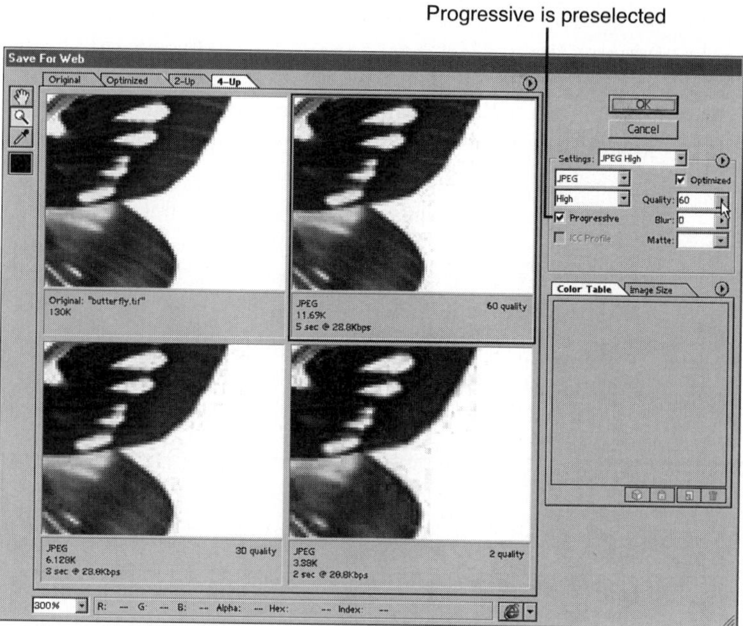

FIGURE 5.8
When saving a JPEG for the Web, Photoshop assumes you want to save it in progressive format.

NOTE The two-dimensional interlacing scheme used in PNG graphics is implemented automatically when you save the file as a PNG.

Creating Animated GIFs

One of the biggest crazes to hit the Web is doing animations with animated GIFs instead of relying on a dynamic document technique such as server push or client pull. The irony is that animated GIFs have been around since 1989—at least in theory. The GIF89a standard has always supported multiple images stored in the same GIF file, but it wasn't until four or five years ago that people caught on that you can do Web animations this way.

It is surprising that this development didn't happen sooner, given that GIF animations are so much easier to implement than server-push animations. A server-push animation requires a server that is CGI-capable, a program to pipe the individual frames of the animation down an open HTTP connection, and a browser that can handle the MIME type used. All you need for a GIF animation is a program to help you set up the GIF file and a browser that is completely compliant with the GIF89a standard. That you don't need any CGI programming is a relief to those publishing on a server that either does not have CGI or that restricts CGI access to certain users.

Adobe now bundles Photoshop with a handy program called ImageReady. ImageReady makes it a snap to create an animated GIF from a layered Photoshop file. To accomplish this, follow these steps:

1. Open the layered file that contains all the individual animation frames. You must have both the Layers palette and the Animation palette open to create your animation (see Figure 5.9). If one or both of these palettes are not visible, use the Window menu in ImageReady to make them appear.
2. Each frame of the animation must be created in the Animation palette. To create a new frame, click the New Frame button next to the Trash button on the bottom of the palette. This button creates a duplicate of the currently selected frame, which appears to the right of that frame.
3. Construct each individual frame of the animation by showing and hiding the combination of layers that makes up the content for that frame. In this example, the final result will show a circle moving from the top to the bottom of the image (see Figure 5.10). The layers are managed using the Layers palette, and each frame of the animation is created by showing the appropriate layer and making the rest non-visible.
4. After all frames of the animation have been created, you can test the animation by clicking the Play button. ImageReady plays the animation one frame at a time, with the current frame highlighted. To stop playback, click the Stop button (located to the left of the Play button). You can also step through the animation one frame at a time by clicking the Forward and Backward buttons, to either side of Play and Stop. The Rewind button will stop playback and select the first frame of the animation.

FIGURE 5.9
Both the Layers palette and the Animation palette must be open for ImageReady to make an animated GIF.

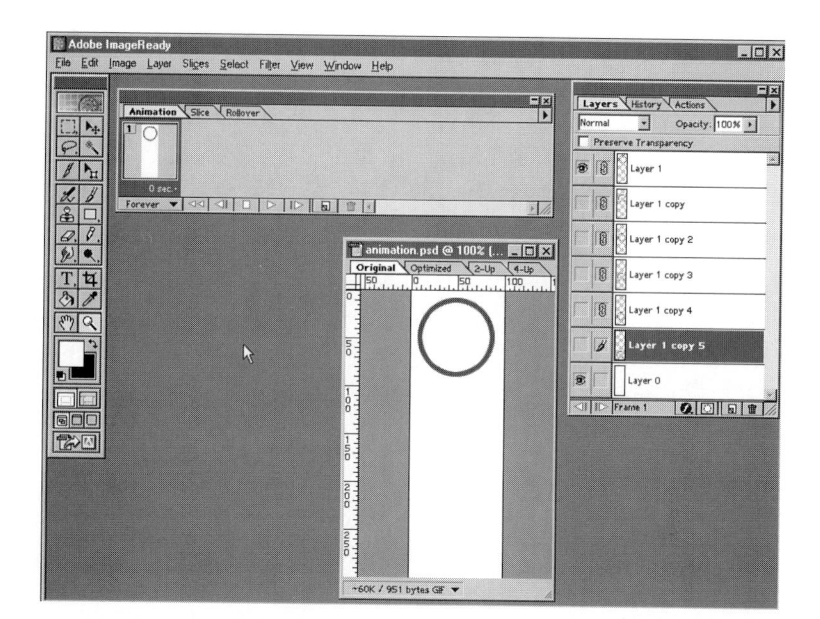

FIGURE 5.10
You build each frame in the animation by selectively displaying layers.

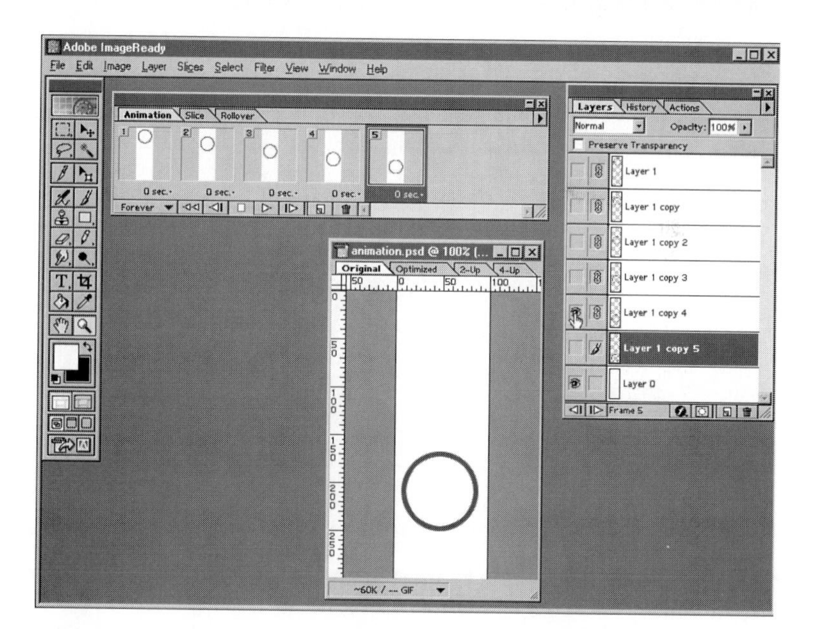

5. Set the time that each frame appears using the Delay menu at the bottom of each frame (see Figure 5.11). Selecting multiple frames allows you to change the delay for all of them at once. Use the Looping options menu to select whether and how many times your animation will loop.

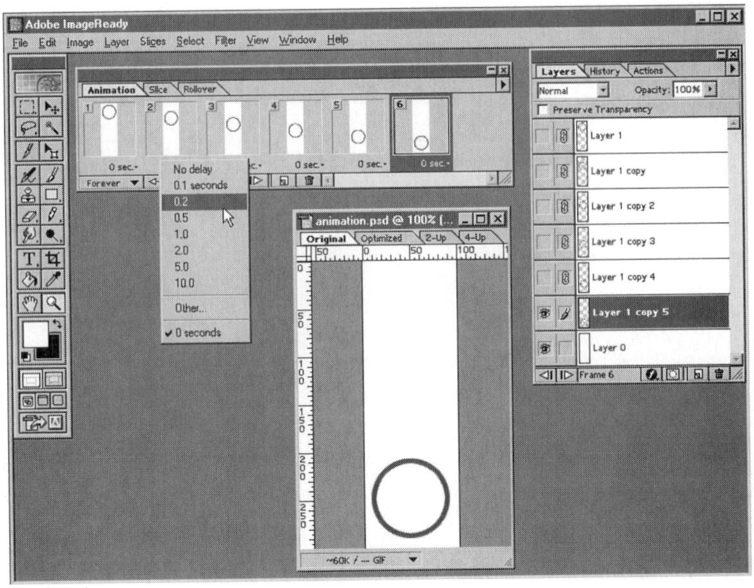

FIGURE 5.11
ImageReady enables you to control how long each frame is displayed and how many times the animation should loop.

6. After your animation has been constructed, use the Optimize palette to specify optimization and color options for your animation (see Figure 5.12). Viewing the original side-by-side with the optimized version and using the 2-up tab will show you how the optimized version looks compared to the original. Beneath each version of the image is information about file format, size, and the download time of the optimized version.

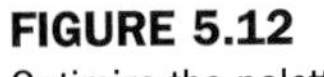

FIGURE 5.12
Optimize the palette only after you are satisfied with the animation.

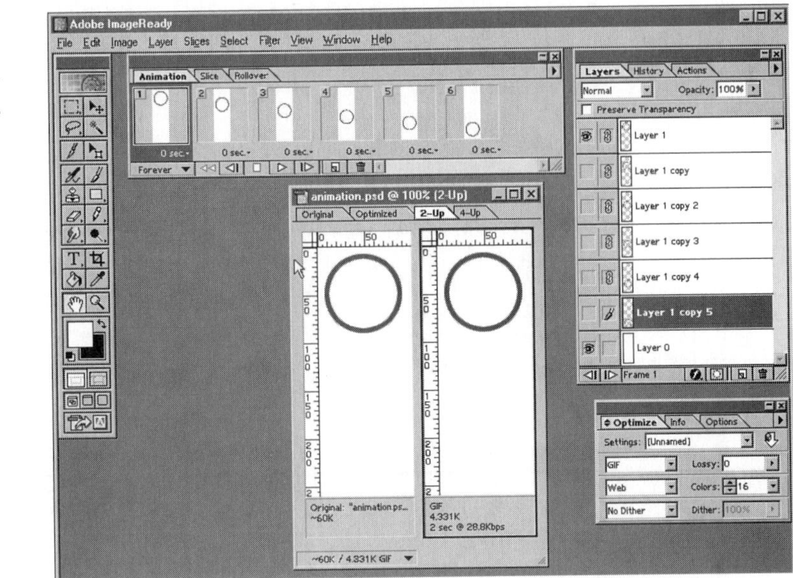

7. When you are ready to save the animation, choose File, Save Optimized. Selecting Save Optimized As will allow you to save the animation with a filename different from the filename of the original layered file.

CAUTION

Don't let an animation run indefinitely. An animation that is going constantly can be a distraction from the rest of the content on your page.

Layout Considerations When Using the *<img />* Element

After you have an image stored and ready to be posted on the Web, you must use the XHTML `<img />` element to place the image on a page. `<img />` is a standalone element that takes the attributes shown in Table 5.1. According to the XHTML 1.0 standard, only the `src` and `alt` attributes are mandatory. You will quickly find, however, that you want to use many of the attributes.

Table 5.1 Attributes of the *<img />* Element

Attribute	Purpose
`alt`	Supplies a text-based alternative for the image
`align`	Controls alignment of text following the image
`border`	Specifies the size of the border to place around the image
`height`	Specifies the height of the image in pixels
`hspace`	Controls the amount of whitespace to the left and right of the image
`ismap`	Denotes an image to be used as part of a server-side image map
`longdesc`	Provides the URL of a link to a longer description of the image's content
`src`	Specifies the URL of the file where the image is stored
`style`	Provides Cascading Style Sheet formatting information for the image
`usemap`	Specifies a client-side image map to use with the image
`vspace`	Controls the amount of whitespace above and below the image
`width`	Specifies the width of the image in pixels

NOTE The XHTML Strict Document Type Definition (DTD) only supports the `alt`, `src`, `longdesc`, `height`, `width`, `usemap`, and `ismap` attributes of the `<img />` element. To use any of the others, you must use the Transitional or Frameset DTDs.

To specify style information when using the Strict DTD, you should use the `style` attribute as follows:

```
<img src="photo.gif" alt="Company Picnic" width="320" height="240"
➥style="align: right" />
```

The Basics

Even though the src and alt attributes are technically the only attributes required in an <img /> element, you should get into the habit of considering two others as mandatory. By providing image height and width information, you speed up the page layout process and enable users to see pages faster. A browser uses the height and width values in the <img /> element to reserve a space for the image, and it actually places the image after it has finished downloading. Without these two attributes, the browser must download the entire image, compute its size, place it on the page, and then continue laying out the rest of the page. If a page has a lot of graphical content, leaving off height and width can seriously delay presentation of the page and annoy visitors.

Your basic <img /> element, then, should look like the following:

```
<img src="URL_of_image_file" width="width_in_pixels"
height="height_in_pixels" alt="alternative_text_description" />
```

Most sites make conscientious use of these attributes in each <img /> element. Figure 5.13, for example, shows a JPEG image on Dell Computer's home page along with the corresponding HTML source code in Listing 5.1.

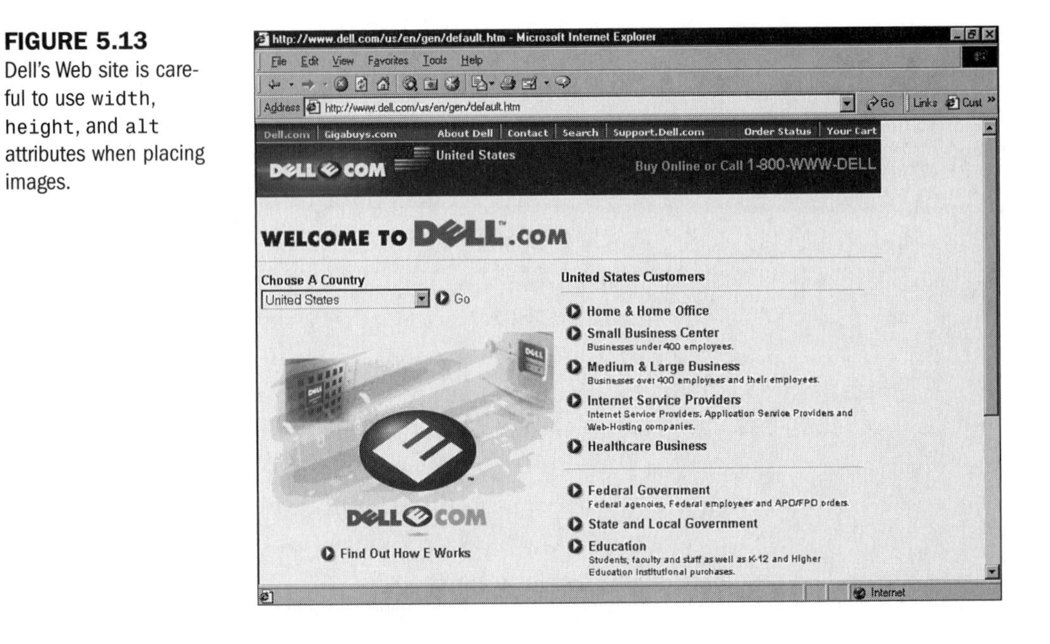

FIGURE 5.13
Dell's Web site is careful to use width, height, and alt attributes when placing images.

Listing 5.1 <img /> Element from Dell's Home Page

```
<td valign="top">
<img src="/images/global/branding/dellecom.jpg" width="320" height="223"
➥alt="DellECom" border="0" />
</td>
```

NOTE You can also use the `height` and `width` attributes to scale the size of your images on some browsers. If you have an image that is 420 pixels wide by 220 pixels high, for example, its dimensions can be halved with the use of the following element:

```
<img src="banner.gif" width="210" height="110" alt="Reduced image" />
```

Similarly, you could scale the image size up by using a `width` greater than 420 and a `height` greater than 220.

Although this is one way to modify the size of images, it is not the best way because bitmapped images tend to lose quality when scaled up or down in size. Additionally, this does not change the download time because the file size is still the same.

Your best bet is to use a program such as Photoshop or Image Composer to resize the graphic before placing it on your Web page. Not only are these programs better suited to resize an image, they also enable you to preserve the aspect ratio (ratio of width to height) during the resize.

Resizing an image can produce loss of information. Be sure to keep a copy of the original in a high-resolution format in case the resized image doesn't meet your needs. If you have kept the original, you can always go back and try again.

Adding a Border

The `border` attribute gives you a simple way to instruct the browser to place a border around an image. `border` is set equal to the number of pixels wide you want the border to be. Figure 5.14 shows an image with a 7-pixel-wide border. The default border is no border.

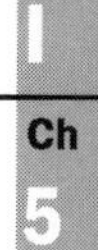

FIGURE 5.14
Borders look good when placed on photos; they give the picture the appearance of being framed.

Adding Space Around Your Image

Whitespace around an image is called *gutter space* or *runaround*. Putting a little extra space around an image is a good way to give it some breathing room on the page and make it stand out better.

Runaround is controlled by the `hspace` and `vspace` attributes. Each is set to the number of pixels of extra space to leave to the right and left of an image (`hspace`) or above and below an image (`vspace`). Figures 5.15 and 5.16 show some images with varying amounts of `hspace` and `vspace`. In each figure, all images have either extra `hspace` (see Figure 5.15) or extra `vspace` (see Figure 5.16) around them. In each figure, both images in a pair have the specified amount of white space along their edges.

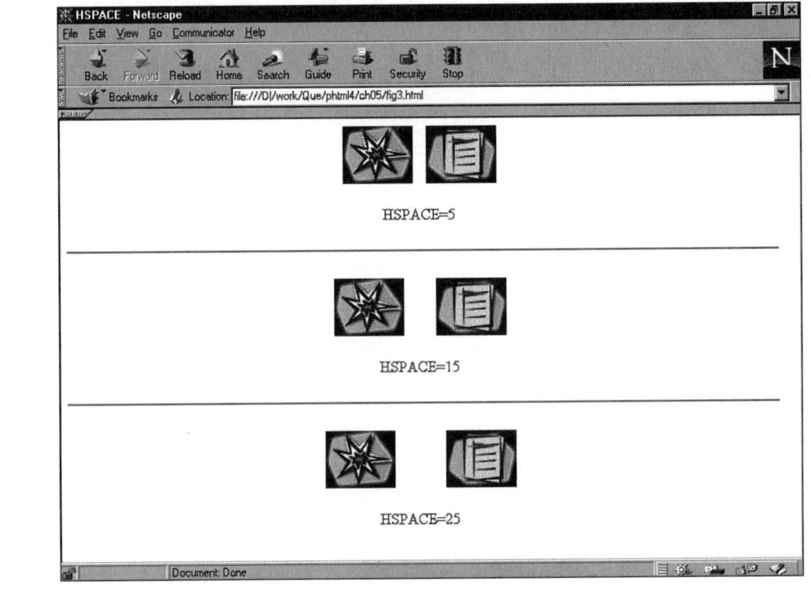

FIGURE 5.15
`hspace` controls the amount of whitespace to the left and right of an image.

NOTE The `hspace` and `vspace` attributes are acceptable only under the Transitional or Frameset XHTML DTDs. If you're using the Strict DTD, you would need to use the `style` attribute and Cascading Style Sheet instructions to control the whitespace around an image.

CAUTION

You cannot increase space on only one side of an image. Remember that `hspace` adds space to both the left and the right of an image, and `vspace` adds space both above and below the image.

FIGURE 5.16
`vspace` lets you specify whitespace above and below an image.

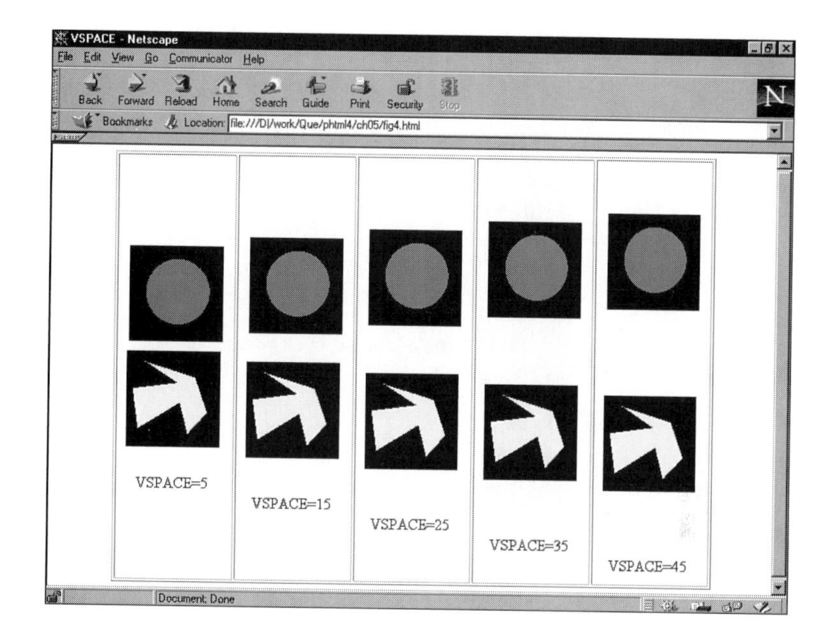

The *align* Attribute and Floating Images

The `align` attribute of the `<img />` element can take on one of the five values summarized in Table 5.2. `top`, `middle`, and `bottom` refer to how text should be aligned following the image. `left` and `right` create floating images in either the left or right margin.

Table 5.2 Values of the *align* Attribute in the *<img />* Element

Value	Purpose
`top`	Aligns the top of subsequent text with the top of the image
`middle`	Aligns the baseline (the line on which the text appears to sit) of subsequent text with the middle of the image
`bottom`	Aligns the baseline of subsequent text with the bottom of the image
`left`	Floats the image in the left margin and enables text to wrap around the right side of the image
`right`	Floats the image in the right margin and enables text to wrap around the left side of the image

Figure 5.17 shows text aligned with `top`, `middle`, and `bottom` (the default alignment). One important thing to note with `top` and `middle` alignments is that after the text reaches a point where it needs to break, it breaks at a point below the image and leaves some whitespace between the lines of text.

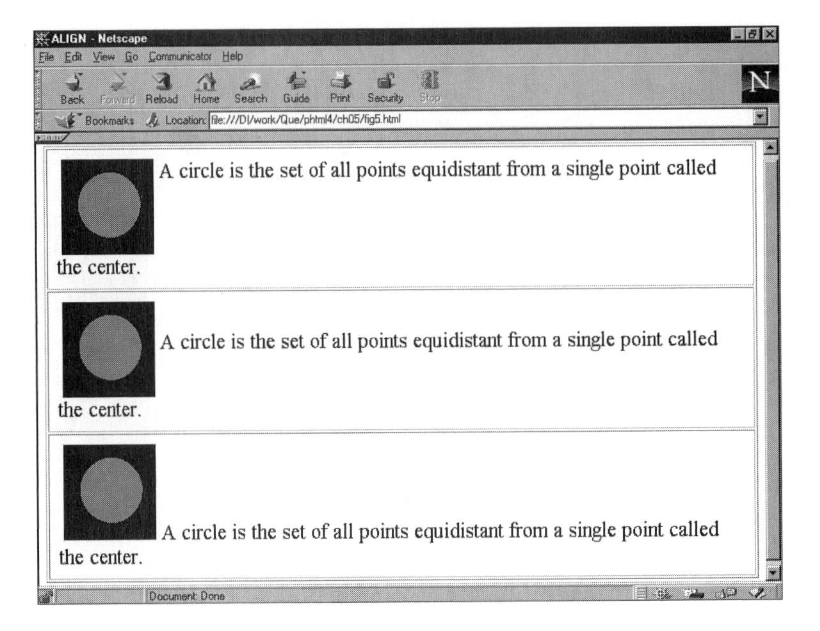

FIGURE 5.17
Of `top`, `middle`, and `bottom` alignments, only `bottom` enables text to properly wrap around an image.

NOTE You are free to use the `align` attribute under the Transitional and Frameset XHTML DTDs but not with the Strict DTD. If you are validating against the Strict DTD, you should use the `style` attribute to specify alignment.

Values of `left` and `right` for the `align` attribute were adopted as part of the HTML 3.2 standard to support floating images that permit text to wrap around them. Figure 5.18 shows an image floating in the right margin with text wrapping around it to the left.

Floating images opened the door to many creative and interesting layouts. It is even possible to overlap images by floating one in the left margin and one in the right margin.

The advent of floating images created a need for a way to break to the first left or right margin that is clear of a floating image. To satisfy this need, the `clear` attribute was added to the `<br />` element. Setting `clear` to `left` breaks to the first instance of a left margin that is clear of floating images. `clear="right"` does the same thing, except it breaks to the first right margin. You can clear both margins by setting `clear="all"`.

ismap and *usemap*

Image maps are clickable images that load different pages depending on where you click the image. They are frequently found on the main page of a site, where they typically serve as a navigational tool to the major sections of the site.

▶ To learn more about image maps, **see** Chapter 4, "Image Maps"

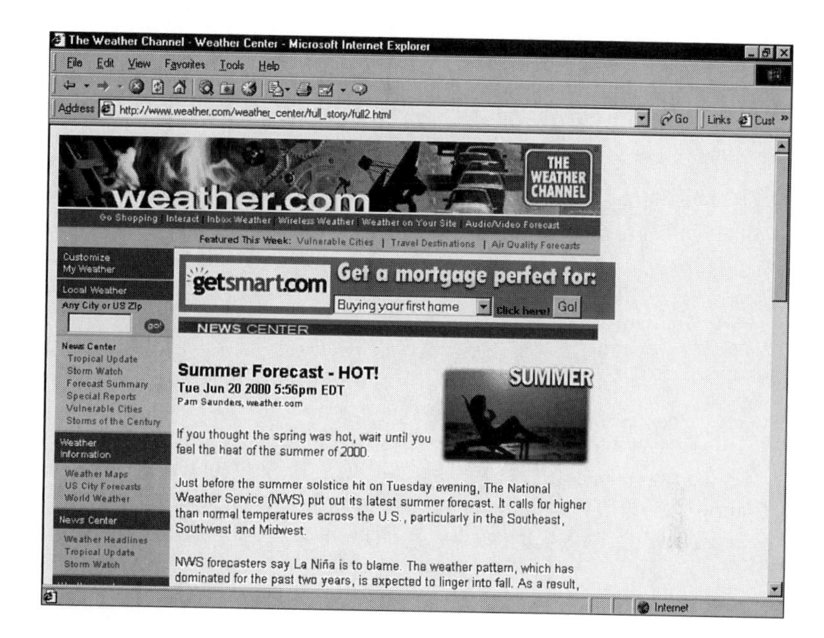

FIGURE 5.18
Floating images sit in one margin and enable text to wrap around them.

The `ismap` attribute of the `<img />` element tells the browser that the image is to be used as part of a server-side image map. `ismap` used to be a standalone attribute in HTML, but in XHTML you must set it equal to a value of `"ismap"` for your code to be well-formed.

The `usemap` attribute of the `<img />` element is set equal to the name of a client-side image map. With client-side image maps, map information is named and sent directly to the browser. Setting `usemap` equal to a map name instructs the browser to use the map information associated with that name.

longdesc

The `longdesc` attribute was added to XHTML as a way of making image content more accessible to users with nonvisual browsers. You set `longdesc` equal to the URL of a document that can provide a longer description of the image's content than you would otherwise put in an `alt` attribute. A speech- or Braille-based browser could then access the URL and furnish a description of the image to the user.

Images as Hyperlink Anchors

As explained in Chapter 3, "XHTML 1.0 Element Reference," the `<a>` container element is used to create hypertext anchors. By clicking the hypertext, you instruct your browser to load the resource at the URL specified in the `href` attribute of the `<a>` element.

No law says that hyperlink anchors can only be text. You will often find images serving as anchors, as well. By linking images to other Web pages, you create a button-like effect—the user clicks the button and the browser loads a new page, submits a form, or performs some other action.

To use a graphic as a hyperlink anchor, put the <img /> element that places the graphic inside the <a> element:

```
<a href="http://www.warnerbrothers.com/">
<img src="daffy2.gif" width=100 height=95 alt="" />
</a>
<p>
<b>Click Daffy's picture to visit the Warner Brother's site ...</b>
</p>
```

This results in the linked image shown in Figure 5.19. Notice that the image has a border although no border attribute was specified. Hyperlinked images automatically receive a border colored with the same colors that you set up for hypertext links using the link, vlink, and alink attributes of the <body> element.

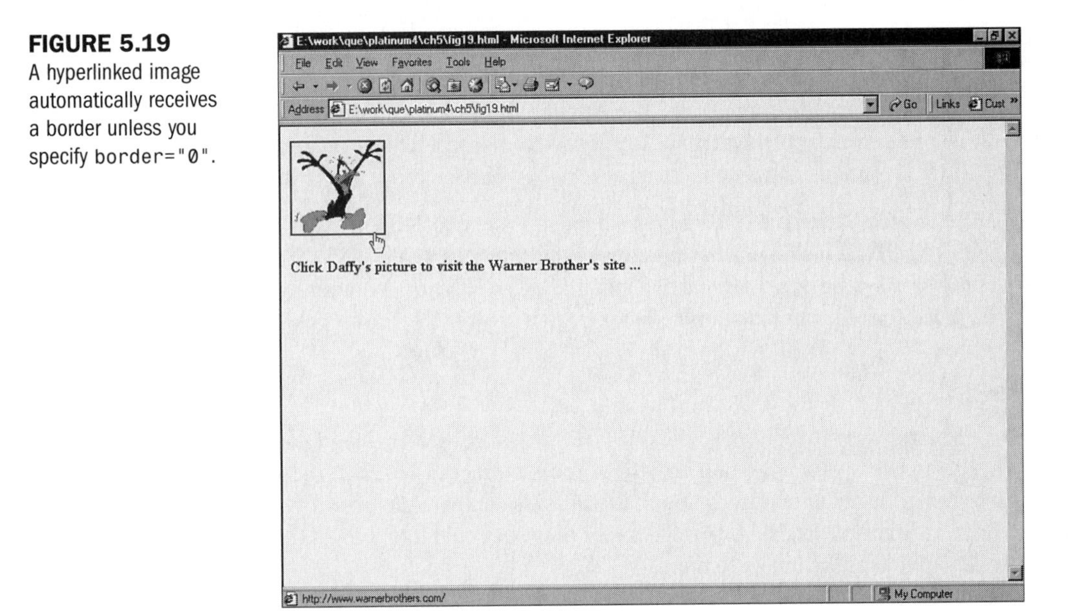

FIGURE 5.19
A hyperlinked image automatically receives a border unless you specify border="0".

TIP Borders around hyperlinked images are usually distracting, especially if the image is a transparent GIF. Notice in Figure 5.19 how the border shows the extent of the otherwise transparent bounding box around the image. To eliminate the border, include border="0" inside the <img /> element.

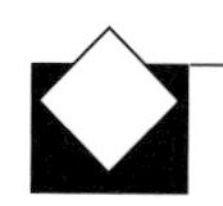

Troubleshooting

A small, hyperlinked line is present at the bottom right of my linked images. How do I get rid of it?

Your problem most likely stems from code such as the following:

```
<a href="boxers.html">
<img src="boxer.jpg" width="300" height="408" alt="Boxer" border="0" />
</a>
```

By having a carriage return after the <img /> element but before the </a> tag, you often get an extraneous line at the bottom-right corner of the linked image (see Figure 5.20). By placing the </a> tag immediately after the <img /> element, you can take care of that annoying little line.

```
<a href="boxers.html">
<img src="boxer.jpg" width="300" height="408" alt="Boxer" border="0" /></a>
```

FIGURE 5.20
Browsers don't always ignore carriage returns, as evidenced by the extraneous line at the bottom right of this linked image.

Images as Bullet Characters

Some people opt to create their own bullet characters for bulleted lists instead of using the characters that browsers provide. To do this, you need to place the bullet graphic with an <img /> element and follow it with a list item:

```
<img src="bullet.gif" width="12" height="12" alt="*">XHTML<br />
<img src="bullet.gif" width="12" height="12" alt="*">XML<br />
<img src="bullet.gif" width="12" height="12" alt="*">Java<br />
<img src="bullet.gif" width="12" height="12" alt="*">JavaScript<br />
```

TIP Using an asterisk (*) as the value of your `alt` attribute gives users with nongraphical browsers a bullet-like character in front of each list item.

Several things should be noted about this code:

- You must have a separate `<img />` element for each bullet.
- You might need to experiment with the `align` attribute to find the best alignment between bullets and list items.
- You must place line breaks manually with a `<br />` element at the end of each list item.

Usually, this is enough to deter many page authors from using their own bullet characters. If you are still determined to use custom bullets, however, you need to be aware of one more alignment issue: If a list item is long enough to break to a new line, the next line starts below the bullet graphic; it is not indented from it (see Figure 5.21). This detracts from the nicely indented presentation that users expect from a bulleted list.

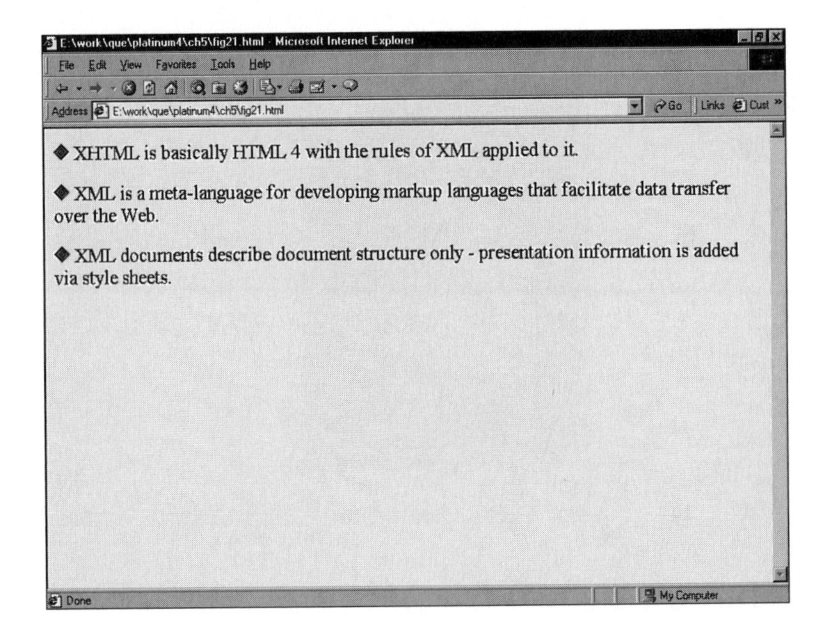

FIGURE 5.21
If you are using a custom bullet graphic, you will also be responsible for things such as text wrapping and alignment.

One way to avoid this problem is to make list items short enough to fit on one line. If that isn't possible, you should consider setting up your list with custom bullets in an XHTML table. By placing the bullet image in its own cell and the list item text in the adjacent cell in the same table row, you can control both alignment and line breaking.

▶ To learn how to use XHTML tables, **see** Chapter 6,"Tables"

Images as Horizontal Rules

Some sites also use a custom graphic in place of a horizontal rule. This is a nice way to subtly reinforce a site's theme (see Figure 5.22).

FIGURE 5.22
Custom rule graphics are strong design elements if implemented carefully.

Alignment problems are less of an issue with a custom rule, but you should keep a couple of rules in mind:

- Assume a screen width of 800 pixels, and keep your rule sized accordingly. Don't let the rule's width exceed 800 pixels.
- The default alignment for a rule placed with the `<hr />` element is centered. You can replicate this effect for your custom rule by placing the `<img />` element for the rule graphic inside a `<div>` element with the `align` attribute set to `center`.
- Use a row of about 70 dashes for your `alt` text in the `<img />` element so text-only users can get a rule effect as well.

Keeping File Sizes Small

One of the greatest courtesies you can extend to your users is to keep your graphics files small. Invariably, the graphics take the longest time to download. By keeping the file sizes small, you minimize the time that users spend waiting to see your pages. Your typical 30KB to

50KB graphics file might load in a few seconds over a T1 connection, but it might take several minutes for users dialing up with a 28.8Kbps or 14.4Kbps connection.

You can enlist several techniques to help keep your file sizes small:

- Crop.
- Make the image dimensions as small as possible.
- Use thumbnail versions of images.
- Save GIFs with natural color gradients as JPEGs or PNGs.
- Increase the amount of JPEG compression.
- Use fewer bits per pixel to store the image.
- Adjust image contrast.
- Suppress dithering.

Each technique is discussed briefly over the next several sections.

Cropping

Cropping refers to reducing the overall size of your image. Most image editing programs have a cropping tool that you can use to do this. You simply trace over the part of the image you want to retain, and the rest is chopped out and discarded. By cropping tightly to the focus of interest, many images can be substantially reduced in size.

Resizing the Image

Larger images take up more disk space—it's as simple as that. The reason for this is straightforward: More pixels are present in a larger image, so more color information must be stored.

The height and width of your graphics should be no larger than they have to be. By keeping the onscreen dimensions of your images small, you contribute to a smaller overall file size.

If you resize an image in a graphics program to make it smaller, be sure to keep the aspect ratio (ratio of width to height) the same. This prevents the image from looking stretched or squashed.

Using Thumbnails

Thumbnails are small versions of an image—usually a photograph. By placing a thumbnail of an image on a page, you reduce file size by using an image that has a smaller width and height than the original.

Thumbnails are usually set up so users can click them to see the full image. If you do this, you should include the size (in kilobytes) of the file that contains the full image so users can make an informed decision about requesting it.

CAUTION

Recall that you can resize an image by reducing the `width` and `height` attributes in the `<img />` element. However, this does not save on download time, and browsers generally don't do the best job of resizing the image.

Storing GIFs as JPEGs or PNGs

JPEGs are created with a very efficient (albeit lossy) compression scheme. The compression works best on images with a lot of natural color gradation. This is why JPEG is the format of choice for color photos placed on the Web.

If you have a GIF with a lot of color gradation, you can experiment with saving as a JPEG to see whether you can compress the file size further. It might not always work, but it's worth a try. You don't have to worry about color loss either because JPEG can accommodate millions of colors to GIF's 256 colors.

Conversely, if you have an image with large blocks of contiguous color, you are better off storing it as a GIF because GIF's compression scheme is geared toward exploiting adjacent pixels painted the same color.

If you're concerned about loss of image quality with the JPEG format, consider converting your GIFs to PNG. PNG compression is more efficient than GIF compression, and PNG is not a lossy format.

Increasing the JPEG Compression Ratio

JPEG compression often achieves impressive compression ratios (on the order of 50:1) with very little loss in image quality. You can crank the ratio higher to make your file size smaller, but the image will not look as good when it is decompressed and decoded. A highly compressed JPEG will take slightly longer to decompress, as well.

Photoshop's Save for Web dialog box enables you to view up to four versions of the file at once so you can compare the visual quality of the image using a variety of compression settings. By comparing different levels of JPG compression for this image of a butterfly (see Figure 5.23), you can see that saving the image at a quality level of 2 results in a much smaller file (3.4KB) than the original (130KB), but the quality is not really good enough to be practical. Quality levels of 30 and 60 (6.13KB and 11.69KB, respectively) offer much more usable image quality and still substantially reduce the size of the original image. Also beneath each image window is the type of compression format being previewed and the approximate download time for the final image.

NOTE Note that the original image in Figure 5.23 is in the TIF format. This is the type of image you would convert for the Web because browsers don't have inline support for TIF images.

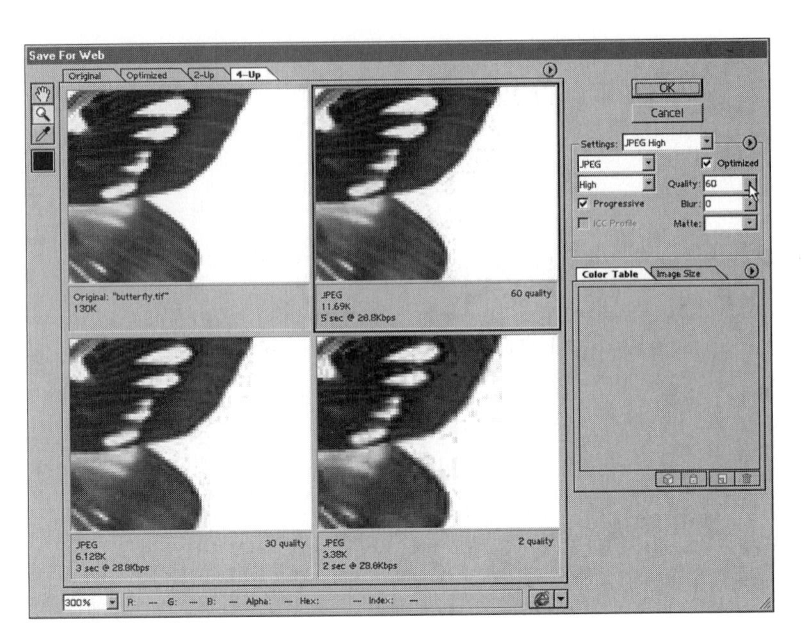

FIGURE 5.23
You can view several different compression levels simultaneously in Photoshop and choose the one that produces the smallest file size without sacrificing image quality.

Reducing Color Depth

GIFs and PNGs can use a palette of up to 256 colors. This corresponds to 8 bits per pixel (2^8 equals 256). But what if you don't need that many colors? Sometimes GIFs and PNGs use just 2 or 3 colors. That small amount of color information can be stored in much less than 8 bits per pixel. It would seem as though some of that storage space could be recovered, resulting in a smaller file size.

You can reduce the number of bits per pixel used to store color information (called reducing the image's color depth). Lowering the color depth is a great way to reduce file size because you can often cut the amount of space you are using in half or better.

Suppose, for example, that you have a GIF that uses six distinct colors. The number six is between four (2^2) and eight (2^3), so you would need 3 bits per pixel to describe the color information. (2 bits per pixel only supports the first four colors, so you must go to the next highest exponent.) By reducing the color depth from 8 bits per pixel to 3 bits, you save over 60%!

Using Photoshop's Save For Web feature to alter the color depth of GIF files is an efficient way to reduce file size. As you can see in Figure 5.24, an existing GIF image with a transparent background looks pretty much the same at 8, 16, and 32 colors, but the overall file size is smallest for the 8-color image. The Save For Web feature doesn't allow you to add transparency to a GIF image; however, you can preserve the transparency of the original image by checking the Transparency option in the Settings box.

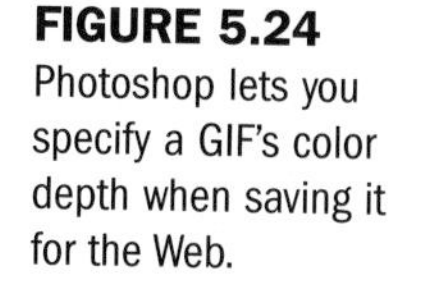

FIGURE 5.24
Photoshop lets you specify a GIF's color depth when saving it for the Web.

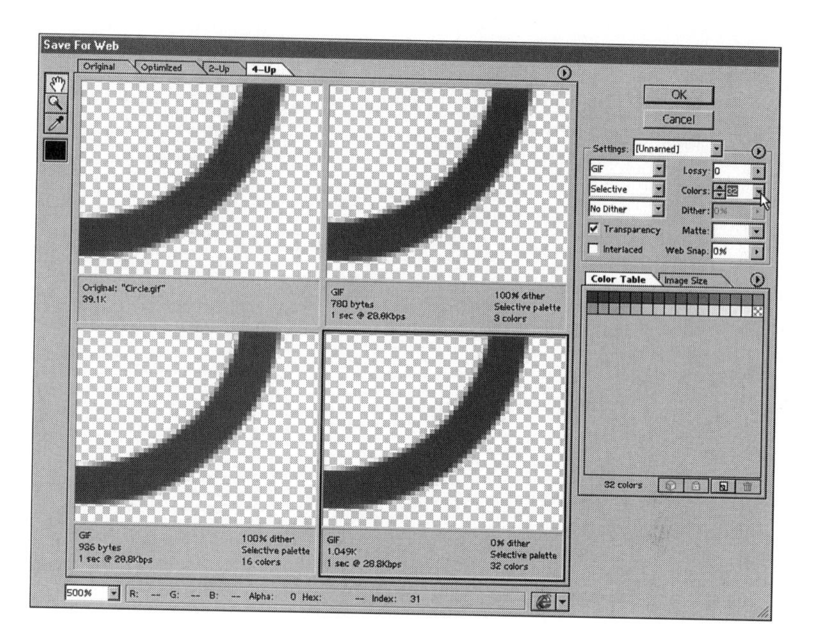

Adjusting Contrast

Contrast in an image refers to the brightness of objects relative to one another. Making changes to the contrast in your image generally affects the size of the resulting image file. If your file is still too big, tweaking the contrast might be a way to bring it down more.

One way to change contrast in your images is to adjust the Gamma correction. Increasing the Gamma correction into positive values tends to brighten the entire image and reduce overall file size because there are fewer colors to store. Conversely, negative Gamma correction values darken an image and increase its file size.

No Dithering

Dithering makes an image appear to have more colors in its palette than it actually does. This is accomplished by combining colors in the existing palette to produce colors that are not in the palette. Dithering can be helpful with GIF images that have a lot of subtle color gradations. Otherwise, for images with just a few solid colors, you probably won't want to use dithering.

One thing to be aware of when using dithering is that it tends to increase file size because fewer pixels in a row have the same color. The compression scheme used with GIF files exploits adjacent pixels that have the same color. When fewer same-colored pixels exist, the compression can't make the file as small.

CAUTION

Dithering can also create an unattractive graininess in your images. If you enable dithering, be sure to look at your image before you put it on the Web to make sure the dithering does not detract from it.

CHAPTER 6

Tables

by Eric Ladd

In this chapter

Introduction to HTML Tables and Their Structure

This chapter introduces you to tables as they have been written into the XHTML 1.0 recommendation. Although tables are intended for the display of columnar data, you'll find that, as you progress through this chapter, tables are much more than that—they are a bona fide page design tool as well.

To understand the basic table elements better, it helps to take a moment to consider how XHTML tables are structured. The fundamental building blocks of an XHTML table are *cells*, which can contain a *data element* of the table or a *heading* for a column of data. Related cells are logically grouped in a *row* of the table. The rows, in turn, combine to make up the entire table.

If you can keep this breakdown in mind as you read the next few sections, the syntax of the table elements will make much more sense to you (see "Table Sections and Column Properties," later in this chapter). Remember the following:

- Cells are the basic units of a table; they can contain data elements or column headers.
- Cells are grouped into rows.
- Rows are grouped together to produce an entire table.

NOTE XHTML 1.0 provides support for the treatment of table columns as well as rows. That means you can treat a column or columns of a table as a logical unit. This is particularly useful when you want to apply formatting instructions to an entire column or columns of data. ■

The Table Elements

Before delving into the more advanced uses of tables, it's instructive to look at a table used for the purpose tables are intended: to display columns of data. The next three sections present the elements you need to create a simple table for this purpose.

All table-related elements occur within the `<table>` element. Any table-related elements occurring outside a `<table>` element are considered invalid and will cause your document to be rejected.

A good habit you should get into immediately is to put the closing `</table>` tag into your XHTML file whenever you start a `<table>` element. If you don't have a closing `</table>` tag and you go to a browser to preview your work, the browser will reject the page because of inappropriate XHTML syntax.

NOTE Before rendering the table, a browser must read through all the table-related code to compute how much space it needs for the table. After the amount of space is known and allocated, the browser goes back and fills in the cells. Without a closing </table> tag, a browser won't know that it has hit the end of a table and, therefore, won't render any of it. ■

TIP

If you're using an XHTML-editing program that enables you to compose a table onscreen, you won't have to worry about the `<table>` and `</table>` tags or any other table-related element. The program writes the code to produce the table for you.

Additionally, many XHTML editors that let you work directly with the code can automatically insert a closing `</table>` tag when you start a `<table>` element. Make sure that this feature is turned on if you're using such an editing tool.

Creating a Table Row

Tables are made up of rows, so you need to know how to define a row. The `<tr>` element is used to contain the XHTML elements that define the individual cells. You can place as many `<tr>` elements as you need inside a `<table>` element. Each `<tr>` accounts for one row of the table.

So far, then, the code for a basic XHTML table with `m` rows looks like

```
<table>
   <tr> ... </tr>   <!-- Row 1 -->
   <tr> ... </tr>   <!-- Row 2 -->
   ...
   <tr> ... </tr>   <!-- Row m -->
</table>
```

TIP

Indenting your table code helps you keep better track of individual cells and rows.

Creating a Table Cell

Table cells come in two varieties: header cells for headers that appear over a column of data and data cells for the individual entries in the table.

A table header cell is defined with a `<th>` element. The contents of a table header cell are automatically centered and appear in boldface, so typically, you don't need to format them further.

In a standard table, headers usually compose the first row so that each column in the table has some type of heading over it. If the basic table you're developing has `n` columns of data, the code for the table would look like the following:

```
<table>
   <tr>    <!-- Row 1 -->
      <th>Header 1</th>
      <th>Header 2</th>
      ...
      <th>Header n</th>
   </tr>
   <tr> ... </tr>   <!-- Row 2 -->
   ...
   <tr> ... </tr>   <!-- Row m -->
</table>
```

Data cells are defined by the <td> element. Text in data cells is left justified by default. Any special formatting, such as boldface or italic, must be done by including the appropriate formatting elements inside the <td> element.

If data cells make up the rest of the basic table you're constructing, you'll have the template shown in Listing 6.1.

Listing 6.1 A Basic Table Template

```
<table>
  <tr>     <!-- Row 1 -->
     <th>Header 1</th>
     <th>Header 2</th>
     ...
     <th>Header n</th>
  </tr>
  <tr>     <!-- Row 2 -->
     <td>Data element 1</td>
     <td>Data element 2</td>
     ...
     <td>Data element n</td>
  </tr>
  ...
  <tr>     <!-- Row m -->
     <td>Data element 1</td>
     <td>Data element 2</td>
     ...
     <td>Data element n</td>
  </tr>
</table>
```

The XHTML shown here makes a nice template that you can use whenever you're starting a table. By filling in the headers and data elements with some genuine information, you can produce a table like the one providing some search results shown in Figure 6.1.

```
<table>
  <tr>     <!-- Row 1 -->
     <th>ID #</th>
     <th>Address</th>
     <th>Bedrooms/Bathrooms</th>
     <th>Heat/AC</th>
     <th>Selling Price</th>
  </tr>
  <tr>     <!-- Row 2 -->
     <td>AR-1897-3</td>
     <td>4692 Fillmore Street</td>
     <td>4 BR, 2 BA</td>
     <td>Electric/Central Air</td>
     <td>$341,500</td>
  </tr>
```

```
    <tr>    <!-- Row 3 -->
       <td>AR-9854-22</td>
       <td>1910 Washington Boulevard</td>
       <td>5 BR, 3.5 BA</td>
       <td>Gas/Central Air</td>
       <td>$437,000</td>
    </tr>
    <tr>    <!-- Row 4 -->
       <td>AR-5634-7</td>
       <td>449 West Harrison Road</td>
       <td>4 BR, 1.5 BA</td>
       <td>Solar/Central Air</td>
       <td>$358,000</td>
    </tr>
</table>
```

Real Estate Search Results - Microsoft Internet Explorer

ID #	Address	Bedrooms/Bathrooms	Heat/AC	Selling Price
AR-1897-3	4692 Fillmore Street	4 BR, 2 BA	Electric/Central Air	$341,500
AR-9854-22	1910 Washington Boulevard	5 BR, 3.5 BA	Gas/Central Air	$437,000
AR-5634-7	449 West Harrison Road	4 BR, 1.5 BA	Solar/Central Air	$358,000

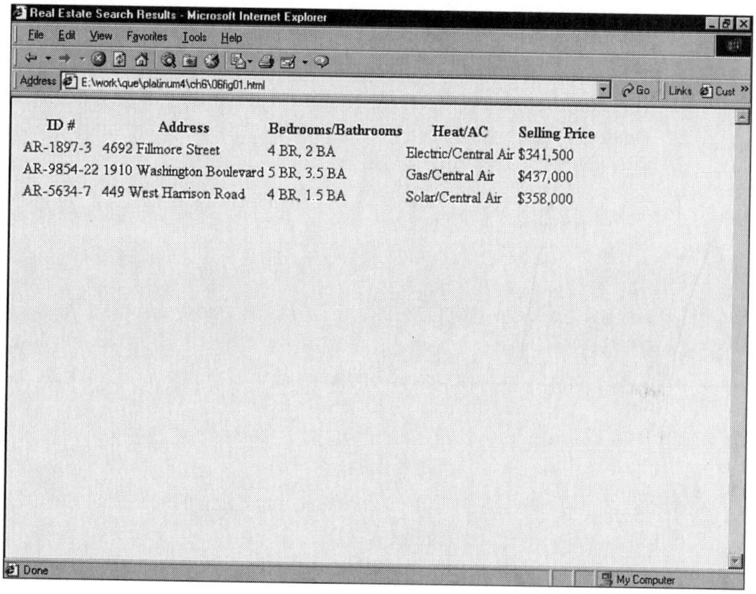

FIGURE 6.1
Results from database searches are typically presented in table form to improve readability.

NOTE If the contents of a table cell are too wide to fit across the cell, the browser breaks the contents onto multiple lines. If you want the content of a cell to be placed on one line with no breaking, include the `nowrap` attribute (for Transitional or Frameset DTDs) or an appropriate `style` attribute (for the Strict DTD) in the `<td>` or `<th>` element that defines the cell.

In addition to the alignment attributes discussed in the next section, both the `<th>` and `<td>` elements take the following attributes:

- **abbr**—Specifies an abbreviation form of a cell's contents.
- **axis**—Used to group cells into logical categories.

- **headers**—Provides a list of IDs of cells that provide header information for the current cell.
- **scope**—A simpler form of the axis attribute, scope lets you group cells into rows, columns, row groups, or column groups, instead of arbitrarily named logical groups.

Alignment

The beauty of XHTML tables is the precise control you have over the alignment of content in individual cells and over the table itself. You can specify two types of alignment:

- **Horizontal alignment**—The alignment of an element across the width of something, such as the alignment of a header across the width of a cell or the alignment of a table across the width of the page. Horizontal alignment is controlled by the `align` attribute. You can set `align` equal to `left`, `center`, `right`, `justify`, or `char` (used to align with respect to a particular character).
- **Vertical alignment**—The alignment of an element between the top and bottom of a cell. Vertical alignment of cell contents is controlled by setting the `valign` attribute to `top`, `middle`, `bottom`, or `baseline`.

CAUTION

If you're using the XHTML 1.0 Strict DTD, you won't be able to use the `align` attribute within a `<table>` element. To horizontally align the table in this case, you should use the `style` attribute along with a cascading style sheet alignment instruction.

NOTE You cannot specify vertical alignment for an entire table because, unlike the page width, a page's length isn't fixed.

Aligning the Entire Table

Provided that you are using the Transitional or Frameset DTD, you can use the `align` attribute in the `<table>` element to specify how the table should be aligned relative to the browser window. Setting `align` to `left` or `right` floats the table in the left or right margin. Floating tables behave much like floating images in that you can wrap text around them. This is how you produce a page element such as the sidebar story you see in Figure 6.2.

Using the `center` value of `align` centers the table in the browser window, although not all browsers support this. If you can't center a table this way, you can enclose the XHTML that produces the table inside a `<div style="align: center">` element. This should become unnecessary, however, as browsers come into compliance with the XHTML 1.0 recommendation.

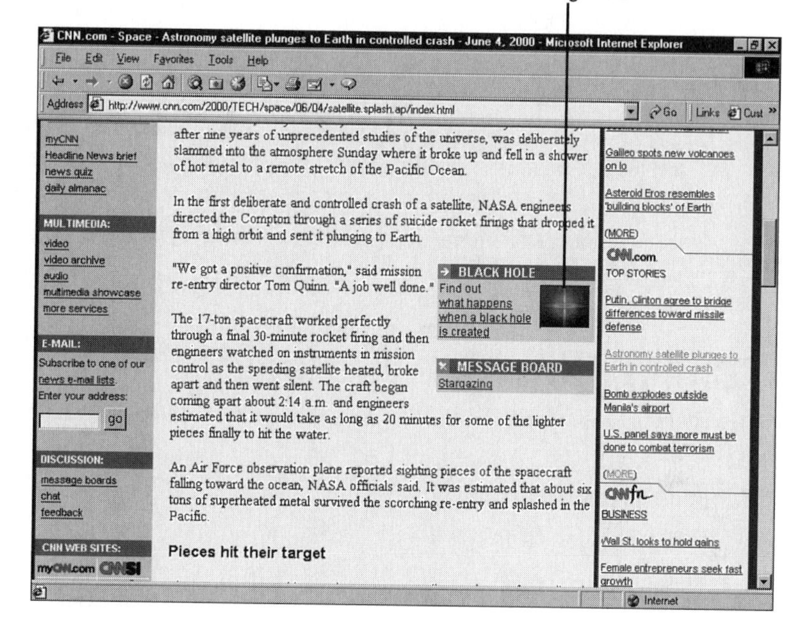

FIGURE 6.2
The sidebar story on black holes that you see on this CNN.com page is indicated by using a floating table.

Alignment Within a Row

If you want the vertical or horizontal alignment to be the same for every cell in a given row, you can use the `valign` and `align` attributes in the row's `<tr>` element. Any alignment specified in a `<tr>` element overrides all default cell alignments.

NOTE The default vertical alignment for both header and data cells is `middle`. The default horizontal alignment depends on the type of cell: Header cells have a `center` alignment and data cells have a `left` alignment.

Alignment Within a Cell

XHTML 1.0 permits alignment control all the way down to the cell level. You can prescribe vertical or horizontal alignments in both header and data cells by using the `valign` or `align` attributes in `<td>` elements. Any alignment specified at the cell level overrides any default alignments and any alignments specified in a `<tr>` element.

Setting alignments in individual cells represents the finest level of control of table alignment. In theory, you can manually specify vertical and horizontal alignments in every single cell of your tables if you need to. Unfortunately, it's easy to get lost among all those `valign` and `align` attributes, especially when it comes to deciding which will take precedence. If you have trouble mastering table alignment, remember the following hierarchy:

- Alignments specified in `<td>` or `<th>` elements override all other alignments but apply only to the cell being defined.
- Alignments specified in a `<tr>` element override default alignments and apply to all cells in a row, unless overridden by an alignment specification in a `<td>` or `<th>` element.
- In the absence of alignment specifications in `<tr>`, `<td>`, or `<th>` elements, default alignments are used.

Controlling Other Table Attributes

In addition to tweaking alignments, you have a say in other aspects of the tables you create. These include

- Content summary
- Background color
- Captions
- Width of the table
- Borders
- Spacing within and between cells

The next six sections walk you through each of these table features and discuss the XHTML elements and attributes you need to know to produce them.

Content Summary

Each revision to the HTML standard has shown increasing support for specialized browsers, such as Braille-based or speech-based browsers. Using these improvements makes your content more accessible to visually impaired users with text-based or speech-based browsers, and you should look for opportunities to work these new elements and attributes into your HTML documents whenever possible.

XHTML 1.0 provides for a `summary` attribute of the `<table>` element. `summary` is set equal to a text string that summarizes the table's content, purpose, and structure. Non-visual browsers can use this information to better communicate the content of your table to their users.

In the real estate listing table shown earlier in Figure 6.1, the `<table>` element might be modified to include a summary such as

```
<table summary="Real estate listings matching your search criteria,
columns include ID number, address, number of bedrooms, number of
bathrooms, and selling price">
```

Background Color

An easy way to add some contrast to your table to make it stand out from the rest of the content on a page is to give the table a background color different from the document's background color. There are two ways to do this, depending on which DTD you are using. If you are using the Transitional or Frameset DTD, you can add the `bgcolor` attribute to the `<table>` element to color the table background with an English-language color name or any RGB hexadecimal triplet. This is done in much the same way as you would specify the document's background color in the `<body>` element.

If you are using the Strict DTD, you can specify a background color using the `style` attribute of the `<table>` element. For example, to make the table background color red, you could use the following:

```
<table style="bgcolor: FF0000">
```

TIP Determining a desired color's RGB hexadecimal code is one of the more tedious tasks in Web-page authoring. Fortunately, many people have made color resources available on the Web that enable you to choose a color and have the RGB hexadecimal code returned to you. For a wide selection of such sites, point your browser to `www.yahoo.com/Arts/Design_Arts/Graphic_Design/Web_Page_Design_and_Layout/Color_Information/`.

Also, most XHTML authoring programs provide some kind of color selection support. Typically, you can choose a color from a palette presented by the program, and the corresponding RGB hexadecimal code is inserted for you.

TIP Many browsers also support the use of `bgcolor` in the `<tr>`, `<td>`, and `<th>` elements (Transitional and Frameset DTDs only), enabling you to present rows and cells in different colors. One effective use of this technique is to paint the top row of the table (presumably the row containing the column headers) with one background color and the remaining rows with a different color. This further distinguishes the items in the top row as column heads. You can make rows of data stand out by alternating a white and gray background color as well (see Figure 6.3).

Adding a Caption

To put a caption on your table, you enclose the caption text within a `<caption>` element. Captions appear centered over the table and the text may be broken to match the table's width (see Figure 6.4). You can also use physical style elements to mark up your caption text. The XHTML to produce Figure 6.4 follows:

```
<table border="1">
   <caption><B>Homes for Sale Matching Your Preferences</B></caption>
<tr>    <!-- Row 1 -->
      <th>ID #</th>
      <th>Address</th>
```

```
            <th>Bedrooms/Bathrooms</th>
            <th>Heat/AC</th>
            <th>Selling Price</th>
        </tr>
        <tr>    <!-- Row 2 -->
            <td>AR-1897-3</td>
            <td>4692 Fillmore Street</td>
            <td>4 BR, 2 BA</td>
            <td>Electric/Central Air</td>
            <td>$341,500</td>
        </tr>
        <tr>    <!-- Row 3 -->
            <td>AR-9854-22</td>
            <td>1910 Washington Boulevard</td>
            <td>5 BR, 3.5 BA</td>
            <td>Gas/Central Air</td>
            <td>$437,000</td>
        </tr>
        <tr>    <!-- Row 4 -->
            <td>AR-5634-7</td>
            <td>449 West Harrison Road</td>
            <td>4 BR, 1.5 BA</td>
            <td>Solar/Central Air</td>
            <td>$358,000</td>
        </tr>
    </table>
```

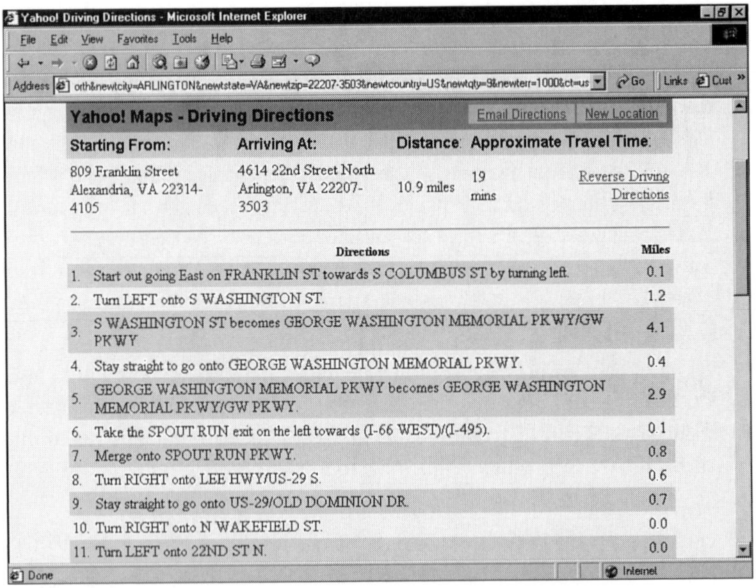

FIGURE 6.3
Alternating background colors makes individual rows easier to read, particularly when several rows of information are present, as in these driving directions.

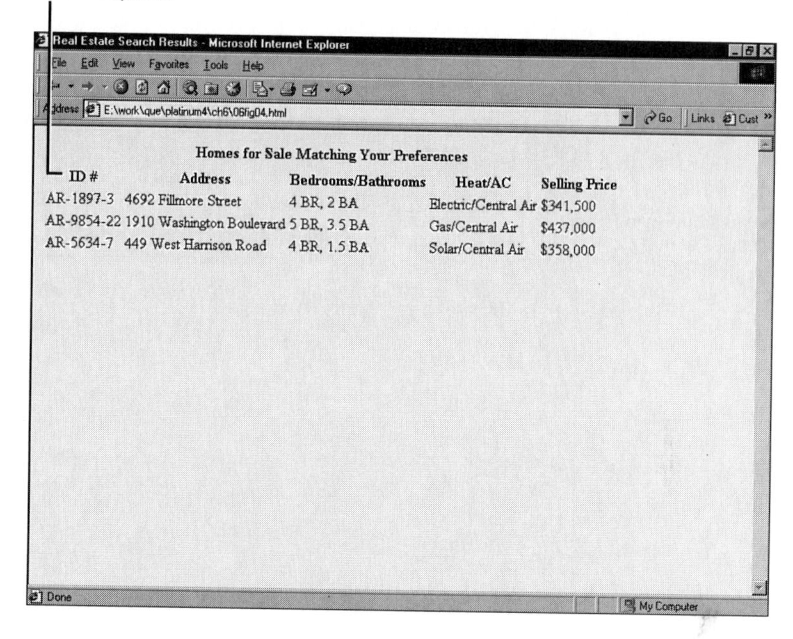

FIGURE 6.4
Captions put the contents of your table into context for the reader.

If you prefer your caption below the table, you can include the `align` attribute in the `<caption>` element and set it equal to a value of `bottom`. You can also left-justify or right-justify your caption by setting `align` equal to `left` or `right`.

NOTE The `align` attribute of the `<caption>` element only works if you are using the Transitional or Frameset DTDs. To specify caption alignment under the Strict DTD, you should use the `style` attribute.

TIP Put your caption immediately after the opening `<table>` tag or immediately before the closing `</table>` tag to prevent your caption from unintentionally becoming part of a table row or cell.

Setting the Width

The `width` attribute of the `<table>` element enables you to specify how wide the table should be in the browser window. You can set `width` to a specific number of pixels or to a percentage of the available screen width.

`width` is often used to force a table to occupy the entire width of the browser window. If we change the `<table>` element in the HTML code in the previous section to

```
<table width="100%">
```

the table is rendered as shown in Figure 6.5. The information is centered in the columns for easier readability. When you compare the table in Figure 6.5 to the one in Figure 6.4, you can see how using the full screen width can enhance the readability of the table.

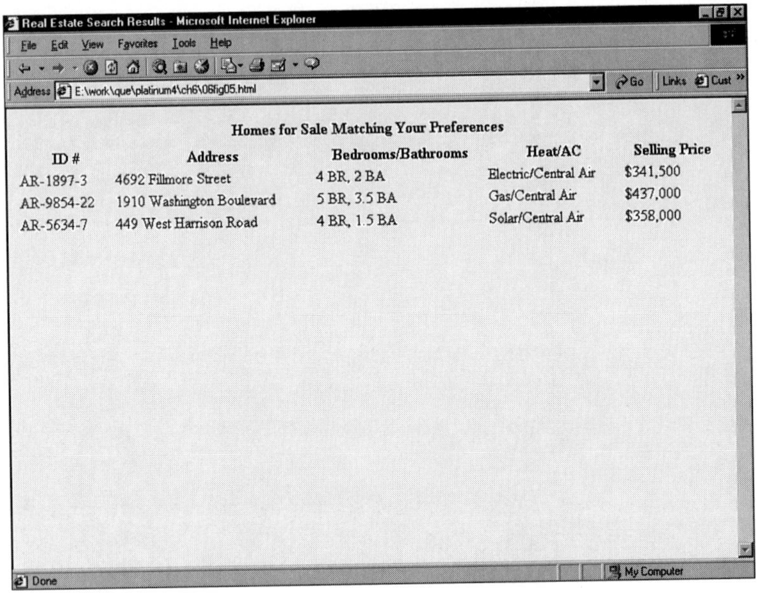

FIGURE 6.5
You have control over how much of the browser screen width a table occupies thanks to the `width` attribute.

> **TIP** Because you can't know how every user has set his or her screen width, you should set `width` equal to a percentage whenever possible. The only exception to this is if the table has to be a certain number of pixels wide to accommodate an image in one of the cells or to achieve a certain layout effect.

Some browsers, such as Netscape Navigator 4 and Internet Explorer 4, support the use of the `width` attribute in a `<td>` or `<th>` element to control the width of individual columns. The use of `width` (as well as `height`) as an attribute of these elements is supported by the XHTML 1.0 Transitional and Frameset DTDs, but not the Strict DTD.

Adding a Border

You can place a border around your table by using the `border` attribute of the `<table>` element. `border` is set to the number of pixels wide you want the border to be. A version of our real estate search table with a 2-pixel border is shown in Figure 6.6. The modified `<table>` element that accomplishes this effect is

```
<table width="100%" border="2">
```

FIGURE 6.6
Table borders create a visual boundary between cells and frequently make your tables easier to read.

Homes for Sale Matching Your Preferences

ID #	Address	Bedrooms/Bathrooms	Heat/AC	Selling Price
AR-1897-3	4692 Fillmore Street	4 BR, 2 BA	Electric/Central Air	$341,500
AR-9854-22	1910 Washington Boulevard	5 BR, 3.5 BA	Gas/Central Air	$437,000
AR-5634-7	449 West Harrison Road	4 BR, 1.5 BA	Solar/Central Air	$358,000

You can also set `border` equal to zero. This means that no border will be used and the browser should give back any space it has reserved to put in a border. This is an especially good approach when you're using a table to position page elements because it enables you to place the elements right up against one another without any 1- or 2-pixel gutters between them.

Spacing Within a Cell

The distance between the content of a cell and the boundaries of a cell is called *cell padding*. The `cellpadding` attribute of the `<table>` element enables you to control the amount of cell padding used in your tables. Typically, Web page authors increase the cell padding from its default value of 1 to put a little extra whitespace between the contents and the edges of a cell (compare the two tables shown in Figure 6.7). This gives the whole table a bit more room to breathe. The `<table>` elements used to produce the tables in Figure 6.7 are

```
<table width="100%" border="2" cellpadding="6">
...
</table>
<table width="100%" border="2" cellpadding="10">
...
</table>
```

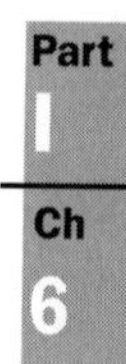

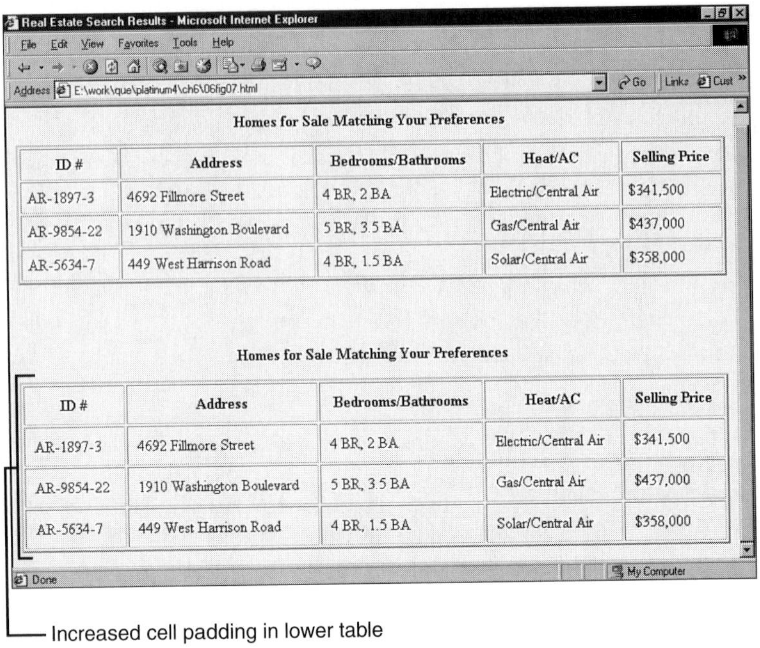

FIGURE 6.7
Increasing cell padding makes your tables appear less cluttered.

Increased cell padding in lower table

Spacing Between Cells

You also have control over the amount of space between cells. By increasing the value of the `cellspacing` attribute of the `<table>` element, you can open up a table even further (see Figure 6.8). Notice that the size of the border used between the cells increases as you increase the cell spacing. The `<table>` element used in Figure 6.8 is

```
<table width="100%" border="2" cellspacing="8">
```

Spanning Multiple Rows or Columns

By default, a cell occupies or *spans* one row and one column. For most tables, this is sufficient. When you start to use tables for layout purposes, however, you'll encounter instances in which you want a cell to span more than one row or column. XHTML 1.0 supports attributes of the `<th>` and `<td>` elements that permit this effect.

Using the *colspan* Attribute

The `colspan` attribute inside a `<th>` or `<td>` element instructs the browser to make the cell defined by the element take up more than one column. You set `colspan` equal to the number of columns the cell is to occupy.

FIGURE 6.8
Increasing the amount of space between cells can give the illusion of your border being thicker than it really is.

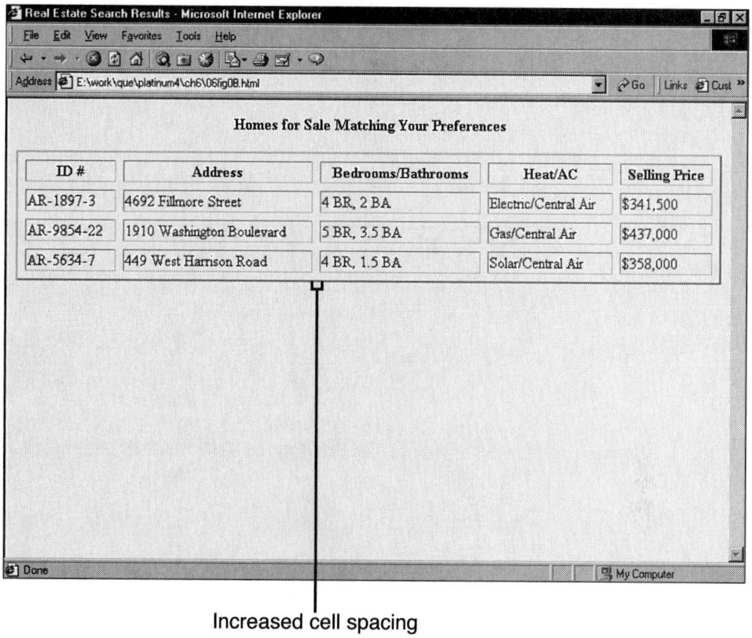

`colspan` is useful when one row of the table is forcing the table to be a certain number of columns wide, and the content in other rows can be accommodated in a smaller number of columns. Figure 6.9 shows the familiar Yahoo! home page, which makes frequent use of the `colspan` attribute. For example, the Yahoo! Shopping box spans the two columns of organized links.

FIGURE 6.9
Forcing a cell to occupy more than one column is helpful in creating more readable page layouts.

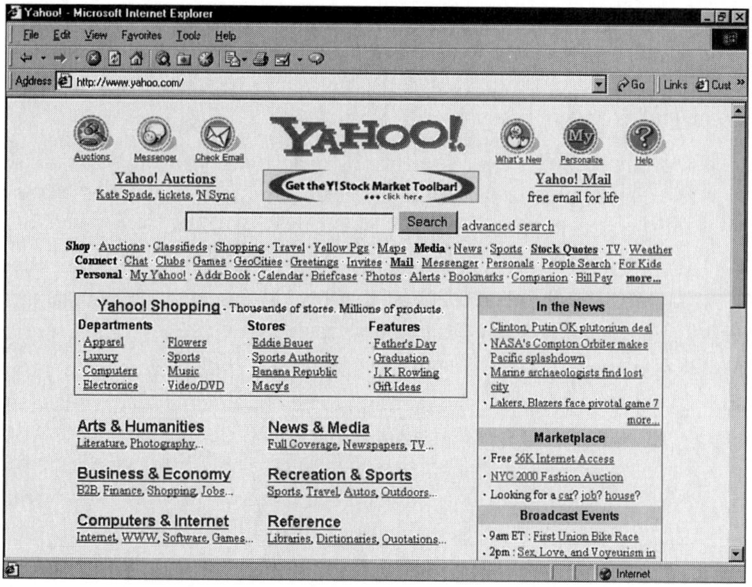

Using the *rowspan* Attribute

`rowspan` works in much the same way as `colspan`, except that it enables a cell to take up more than one row. Figure 6.10 shows the Internet Movie Database home page. The IMDb button and the tabs across the top center of the page are all placed in `<td>` elements with a `rowspan` of 2.

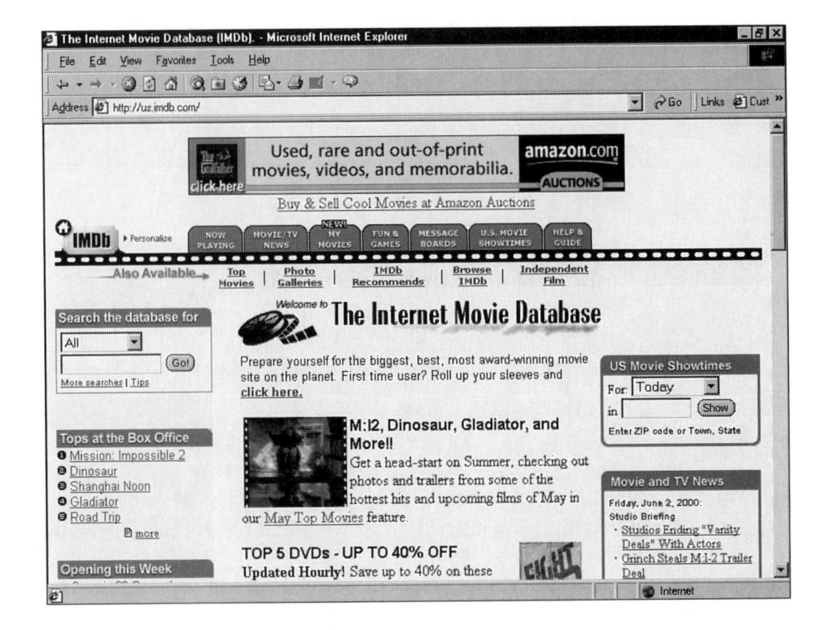

FIGURE 6.10
Table elements can occupy more than one row of the table when you use the `rowspan` attribute.

Which Elements Can Be Placed in a Table Cell?

XHTML tables were developed with the intent of presenting columns of information, but that information does not necessarily have to be text based. You can place many types of page elements in a given table cell:

- **Text**—Text is the most obvious thing to put in a table cell, but don't forget that you can format the text with physical and logical styles, heading styles, list formatting, line and paragraph breaks, and hypertext anchor formatting.
- **Images**—You can place an image in a table cell by enclosing an `<img/>` element within the `<td>` element that defines the cell. This is useful for designing page layout with tables because you aren't constrained only to text.
- **Blank space**—Sometimes it's useful to put a blank cell in a table. You can accomplish this by putting nothing between the cell's defining element (`<td></td>`) or by placing a nonbreaking space inside the element (`<td> </td>`). Use of the nonbreaking space is preferable because, if you have borders turned on, a cell with a nonbreaking space picks up a border, but a cell created with `<td></td>` might not.

- **Form fields**—The ability to place form fields inside a table cell is very important, especially when you consider that the prompting text in front of form fields are of varying lengths. By putting prompting text and form fields in a table, you can align them all and make the form much more readable.
- **Other tables**—You can embed one table inside another, although this can induce quite a headache for many people! Previously, only Netscape Navigator and Microsoft Internet Explorer supported tables within tables; but now that it is part of the XHTML 1.0 standard, other browsers should support it as they come into compliance with the new standard.

TIP If you plan to embed a table within a table, it's helpful to do a pencil-and-paper sketch first. The sketch should help you code the tables more efficiently.

Table Sections and Column Properties

The W3C has included several table-related elements to the XHTML 1.0 recommendation that enable you to split tables into logical sections and to control alignment properties of rows or columns of data.

Table Sections

The `<thead>`, `<tbody>`, and `<tfoot>` container elements denote the start of a table header, body, and footer. By explicitly distinguishing the different parts of your table, you can control your row and column attributes for each section of the table. The separation of the table header and footer also makes it easier for the browser to render and print tables that are broken across several pages. Additionally, it makes it simple to set up a static header or footer in frames at the top and bottom of a browser screen and to place the body of the table in a scrollable frame between the header and footer frame.

A `<thead>` element contains the rows that compose the table header and a `<tfoot>` element contains the rows that compose the footer. In the absence of `<thead>` and `<tfoot>` elements, the `<tbody>` element becomes optional. You can use multiple `<tbody>` elements in long tables to make smaller, more manageable chunks. All three elements can take both the `align` and `valign` attributes to control horizontal and vertical alignment within the sections they define.

NOTE All three elements are only valid within a `<table>` element.

A typical table created with these elements might look like this:

```
<table>
   <thead>
      <tr>
         ...
```

```
        </tr>
    </thead>
    <tbody>
        <tr>
            ...
        </tr>
        <tr>
            ...
        </tr>
        ...
        <tr>
            ...
        </tr>
    </tbody>
    <tfoot>
        <tr>
            ...
        </tr>
    </tfoot>
</table>
```

NOTE In XHTML 1.0, the use of the closing </thead>, </tbody>, and </tfoot> tags is not optional. These tags were optional in HTML 4.0, but XHTML's rigid syntax requirements make it necessary to include the closing tags.

Used in conjunction with the column grouping elements discussed in the next section, the table section elements are an ideal way to control how different properties are applied to different parts of a table.

Setting Column Properties

The <tr> element supports attributes that enable you to specify all sorts of properties for an entire row of a table. In particular, you get very good control over both horizontal and vertical alignment with the `align` and `valign` attributes of the <tr> element. XHTML 1.0 takes this a step further by making it possible to apply horizontal alignment properties to columns of data as well.

You have two options when applying alignment properties to columns. The <colgroup> element is appropriate when applying properties over several columns. It takes the attributes `align`, which can be set to `left`, `center`, `right`, `justify`, or `char`; `valign`, which can be set to `top`, `middle`, `bottom`, or `baseline`; `width`, which is set equal to the desired width of the group; and `span`, which is set to the number of consecutive columns to which the properties apply.

To see how <colgroup> works, consider the following code:

```
<table border="1">
    <colgroup align="left" span="4">
```

```
    <colgroup align="right" span="2">
    <colgroup align="center">
    <tbody>
       <tr>
          <td>First column group, left horizontal alignment</td>
          <td>First column group, left horizontal alignment</td>
          <td>First column group, left horizontal alignment</td>
          <td>First column group, left horizontal alignment</td>
          <td>Second column group, right horizontal alignment</td>
          <td>Second column group, right horizontal alignment</td>
          <td>Third column group, justified horizontal alignment</td>
       </tr>
    </tbody>
</table>
```

The seven columns are split into three groups. The first four columns have left-aligned table entries, the fifth and sixth columns have entries horizontally aligned along the right, and the last column has centered entries (see Figure 6.11).

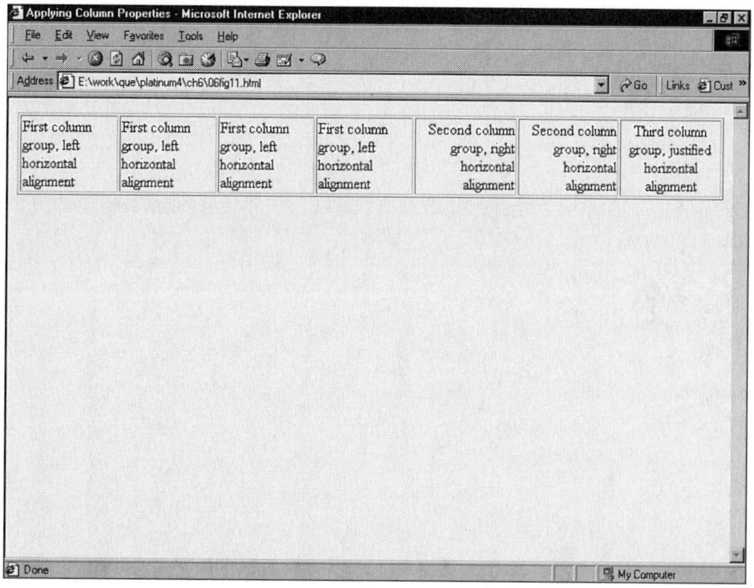

FIGURE 6.11
Grouping columns enables you to assign common alignment properties to several columns simultaneously.

NOTE When you use the `<colgroup>` and `<col>` elements, the default value of the `align`, `valign`, and `span` attributes are `left`, `middle`, and `1`, respectively. `width` has no specific default value. Instead, the width is made as big as it needs to be to accommodate the contents of the cell.

If columns in a group are to have differing properties, you can use `<colgroup>` to set up the group, and then specify the individual properties with the `<col />` element. `<col />` takes the same attributes as `<colgroup>`, but these attributes only apply to a subset of the columns in a group. For example, the following XHTML splits the five columns of the table into two groups:

```
<table border="1" cellpadding="16">
   <colgroup>
      <col align="center" />
      <col align="right" />
      <col align="left" />
   </colgroup>
   <colgroup>
      <col align="center" span="3" />
   </colgroup>
   <tbody>
      <tr>
         <td>First column in first group, center horizontal alignment</td>
         <td>Second column in first group, right horizontal alignment</td>
         <td>Third column in first group, left horizontal alignment</td>
         <td>First column in second group, center horizontal alignment</td>
         <td>Second column in second group, center horizontal alignment</td>
         <td>Third column in second group, center horizontal alignment</td>
      </tr>
   </tbody>
</table>
```

The first group's columns use center, right, and left horizontal alignments, whereas both columns in the second group use only center horizontal alignment (see Figure 6.12).

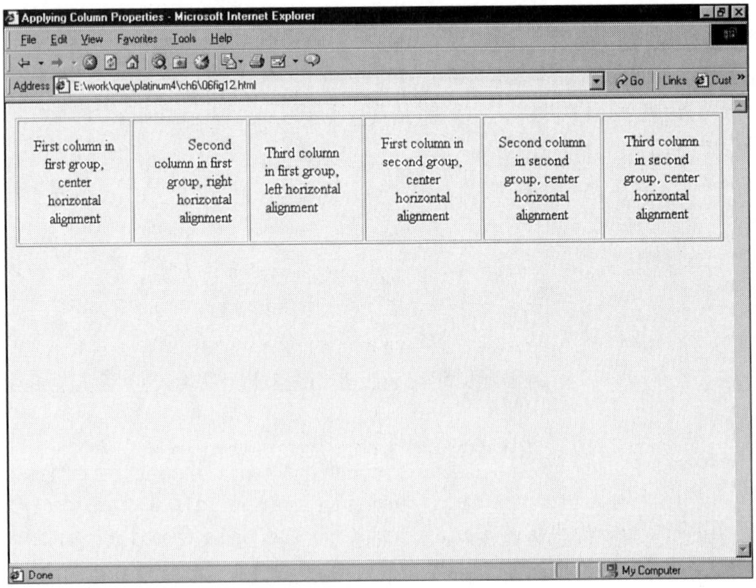

FIGURE 6.12
You can also group columns and still assign alignment parameters on an individual basis.

Other Attributes of the <table> Element

Because of the new support for dividing tables into logical sections and the grouping of columns, the W3C has introduced some new attributes for the `<table>` element that enable you to control inner and outer borders of a table. Inner borders are controlled by the `rules` attribute. You can think of inner borders as the dividing lines between certain components of the table. `rules` can take on the values shown in Table 6.1.

Table 6.1 Values of the *rules* Attribute of the *<table>* Element

Value	Purpose
`all`	Displays a border between all rows and columns
`cols`	Displays a border between all columns
`groups`	Displays a border between all logical groups (as defined by the `<thead>`, `<tbody>`, `<tfoot>`, and `<colgroup>` elements)
`none`	Suppresses all inner borders
`rows`	Displays a border between all table rows

The `frame` attribute controls which sides of the outer borders are displayed. In the context of tables, `frame` refers to the outer perimeter of the entire table and not frames such as those discussed in Chapter 7, "Frames." `frame` can take on the values summarized in Table 6.2.

Table 6.2 Values of the *frame* Attribute of the *<table>* Element

Value	Purpose
`above`	Displays a border on the top of a table frame
`below`	Displays a border at the bottom of a table frame
`border`	Displays a border on all four sides of a table frame
`box`	Same as `border`
`hsides`	Displays a border on the left and right sides of a table frame
`lhs`	Displays a border on the left side of a table frame
`rhs`	Displays a border on the right side of a table frame
`vsides`	Displays a border at the top and bottom of a table frame
`void`	Suppresses the display of all table frame borders

Tables as Design Tools

Although tables were developed for presenting columnar data, they have evolved to do much more. Three primary driving forces are behind the rise of tables as design tools:

- You aren't restricted to only putting text in table cells.
- You can make a cell occupy more than one row or column.
- You get incredibly fine control over the alignment of content in individual cells.

Creating a Complex Layout

The General Electric home page is a complex combination of embedded tables (see Figure 6.13). The overall structure of the page is a three-column table, but content in each column is situated in its own table to control alignment and background colors.

FIGURE 6.13
Sites such as General Electric's often use tables to create a columnar look for the layout.

Aligning Page Elements of Different Sizes

Figure 6.14 shows a portion of United Airlines' home page. Note the boxes labeled Flight status, Quick fare finder, and Mileage summary. Each of these boxes has a different height, so using the default `valign` value of `middle` would mean that the tops of the boxes would not line up. By setting `valign` equal to `top`, the boxes are all forced to the tops of the cells they occupy, producing an attractive alignment.

Aligning Form Fields

The contact form on Impala Communication's Web site would be a mess if it weren't for the different form fields placed in table cells (see Figure 6.15). The prompting text in front of the fields (Name, Company, E-Mail, and Comments) are of varying lengths. If the fields started right after each word, none of them would line up. By placing both the prompting text and the form fields in common table rows, the alignment is perfect.

FIGURE 6.14
Page elements of different sizes can make a page look unaligned. By placing these elements in a table and using alignment attributes, everything lines up cleanly.

United Airlines - Microsoft Internet Explorer
File Edit View Favorites Tools Help
Address http://www.ual.com/
Go Links Cust

UNITED
US AIRWAYS
United and US Airways Plan to Combine
CEO Message
News Release

Planning travel
Create itinerary
E-Fares (Sales)
Award travel
Electronic timetable
Past itineraries
Request upgrade
Special offers
Route maps
Update profile

Travel support
Airport services
Baggage
Destination info
Flight status
In-flight services
Red Carpet Club
Service classes
Special needs
Wireless/Paging

Mileage Plus
Mileage summary
Program info
Awards
Promotions
Partners
MP programs

About United
Products and services
Contact United
Company information
Employment
Alliances
Our United Commitment
Worldwide sites

Flight status
Flight number
Departure date
06/04/2000
Check

Quick fare finder
From To
Departure date
Jun 4 Anytime
Return
Jun 4 Anytime
Number of Passengers 1
Check Full flight search

Mileage summary
Mileage Plus# Password
Check Need registration help?

Gomez Advisors
#1 Airline Web Site
Details
INTERNET SCORECARD Gomez AIRLINE

Internet

FIGURE 6.15
Using a table to align form fields is an essential part of making a form readable and usable.

Impala Communications - Microsoft Internet Explorer
File Edit View Favorites Tools Help
Address http://www.impalacom.com/contact.html
Go Links Cust

Profile
Services
Expertise
Philosophy
HOME CONTACT

Contact Us!

Please feel free to contact Impala by phone, e-mail or fax and expect a speedy response! Your comments and suggestions are greatly appreciated.

Impala Communications LLC
1612 U St NW, Suite 402
Washington, DC 20009

Phone: 202-299-0300
Fax: 202-299-0302
e-mail: fwalter@impalacom.com

Name:
Company:
E-Mail:
Comments:

Submit to Impala

Impala Communications LLC
202.299.0300 phone
202.299.0302 fax

Done
Internet

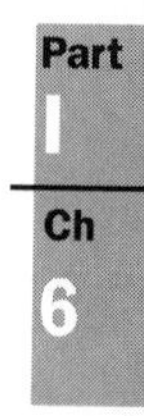

CHAPTER 7

Frames

by Eric Ladd

In this chapter

Introduction to Frames

Netscape introduced the idea of frames way back when it released Netscape Navigator 2.0. At the same time, Netscape proposed frames to the World Wide Web Consortium (W3C) for inclusion in the HTML 3.0 standard. When the HTML 3.2 draft was released, frames were not part of the standard, but W3C indicated it was still considering other proposals that were put forward for HTML 3.0. When it released the HTML 4.0 specification, the W3C included the frame tags as proposed by Netscape, along with a few new twists that Microsoft and other W3C members threw in. Frames have also made the crossover to XHTML as well, so you can continue to implement documents inside a frameset, rather than just the standard browser window.

Since their introduction, frames have evolved much like tables. Initially, a number of browsers implemented both tables and frames, even though they were not part of the HTML standard. Frames are part of the XHTML standard and most major browsers use them now, so you can feel more comfortable about using frames. Used wisely, frames can provide you with an improved interface and a better experience with your site. However, some developers do not use frames wisely, and that has resulted in an outcry from people who try to promote usable Web pages. If you hear dissent about frames these days, it is most likely related to these usability issues and not to frames being nonstandard XHTML.

This chapter introduces you to the basics of frames and how you can best use frames on your site. Before jumping into how to create framed documents, it's helpful to take a moment to get a feel for what they are, what they do, and what advantages they bring.

The main idea behind a framed document is that you can split the browser window into two or more regions called *frames*. After this is done, you can load separate XHTML documents into each frame and enable users to see different pages simultaneously (see Figure 7.1). Each frame can have its own scrollbars if the document is too big to fit in the allocated space.

Additionally, you can resize a frame with your mouse, provided that the content author has not suppressed your ability to do so. To resize a frame, follow these steps:

1. Place your mouse pointer over the border of the frame you want to resize.
2. Click and hold down the left mouse button.
3. Drag the border to its new position and release the mouse button (see Figure 7.2).

After the border is moved to its new position, the browser re-renders any affected frames according to the new distribution of display space.

NOTE In some instances, a document author might include a command in the frame setup that prevents users from resizing the framed layout. You should do this only if it is absolutely essential that your layout be maintained exactly as you specified. This is occasionally the case when you have a page element of a specific size, an image for example, in a frame and you want the entire image showing at all times. ■

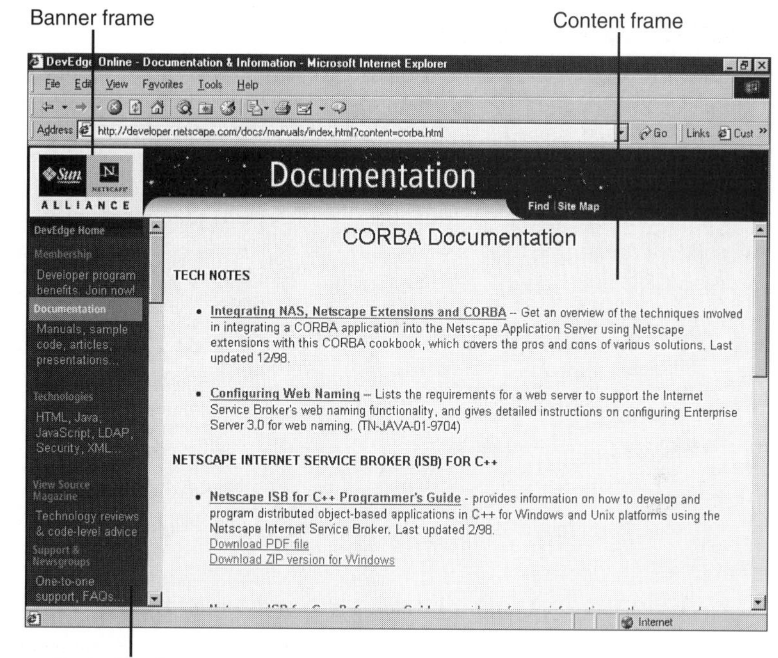

FIGURE 7.1
You can present multiple Web documents simultaneously using frames.

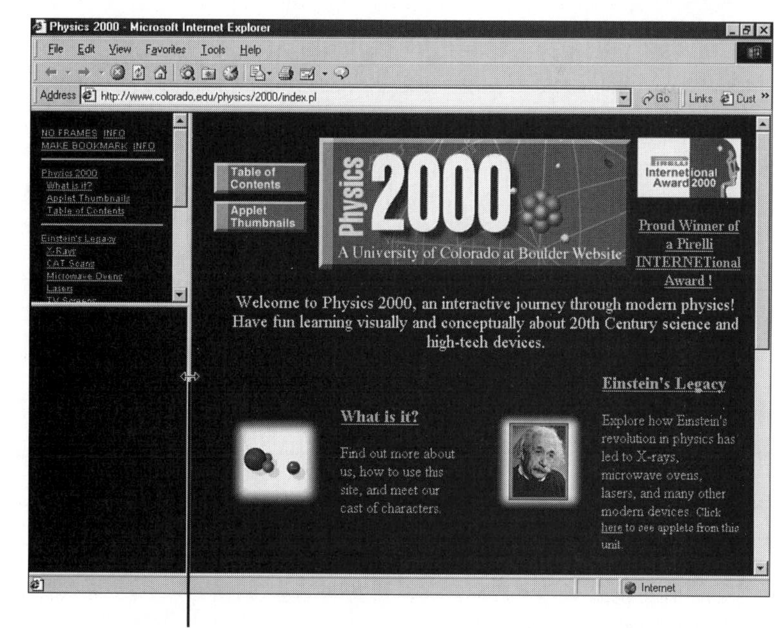

FIGURE 7.2
Unless the content author has specified otherwise, users are free to resize frames to their liking.

Reasons to Use Frames

Like any page element, frames should not be used just because they're cool. Your decision to use frames should be based on the needs and characteristics of your audience and how effective frames will be in communicating your messages.

Frames lend themselves well to applications in which you want one set of content to remain on the browser screen while another set of content changes. This is easily accomplished by splitting the browser window into two frames: one for static content and one for changing content. Items typically found in static content frames include

- Navigation tools (refer to Figure 7.2)
- Tables of content
- Banners and logos
- Search interface forms

In such a frameset, users can interact with the static content (click a hypertext link, enter search criteria into a form, and so on), and the results of their actions appear in the changing content frame.

Another useful application for frames is for documents that are heavy on definitions or footnotes. You can display the main document in a large frame and have a glossary or bibliography file displayed in a secondary frame. A user could then click key terms or footnote indicators in the large frame to cause the appropriate glossary entry or footnote to appear in the secondary frame.

Reasons Not to Use Frames

Frames have come under some heavy criticism by advocates of Web page usability. Specifically, their concerns include

- *Not all users have frames-capable browsers.* Although the number of such users is relatively small, you still need to keep these users in mind. The `<noframes>` element provides a workaround to this concern, so you should use that element diligently.
- *Not all users can print from within a frameset.* Initially, it was difficult to print an individual document within a frameset, but browsers have come a long way in making it possible to print the contents of a particular frame. Even so, there are no assurances that all users are using a browser that can print documents in a frameset, so this concern remains valid.
- *Search engine indexing programs cannot process individual documents within a frameset.* Naturally, everyone wants their sites indexed by all the major search engines. But if the indexing program can't get at your individual documents because they are called within a frameset, then it's less likely that your site will come up in search results.

- *Bookmarking can't be used on all pages.* Users can only bookmark the page that sets up the frameset but not one of the individual pages displayed in the frameset.

Web usability guru Jakob Nielsen explains the advantages and disadvantages of using frames in his highly readable "Alertbox" column. You can read his "Why Frames Suck (Most of the Time)" article at `http://www.useit.com/alertbox/9612.html`.

Setting Up a Frames Document

After you've made the decision to use frames on your site, you need to know the XHTML elements that make it possible. The next several sections show you how to create framed pages and how to provide alternatives for those who can't view frames.

NOTE To implement a frameset in XHTML, you must be using the XHTML 1.0 Frameset Document Type Definition (DTD). The XHTML Strict and Transitional DTDs will not support the frame-related elements.

To incorporate the Frameset DTD into your documents, the first line of code in your XHTML files should be

```
<!DOCTYPE html PUBLIC "-//W3C//DTD XHTML 1.0 Frameset//EN"
"http://www.w3.org/TR/xhtml1/DTD/frameset.dtd">
```

This indicates to the browser that it should use the XHTML Frameset DTD to validate the document and specifies the location of the DTD. ■

TIP A good first step, especially for intricately framed layouts, is to draw a pencil-and-paper sketch of how you want the framed page to look. In addition to helping you think about how to create the most efficient layout, your sketch also helps you determine how to order your `<frameset>` tags, if you have more than one.

The *<frameset>* Element

The first step in creating a framed document is to split the browser screen into the frames you want to use. You accomplish this with an XHTML file that uses the `<frameset>` element instead of the `<body>` element. `<frameset>` and `</frameset>` are not just container elements. Attributes of the `<frameset>` elements are instrumental in defining the frame regions.

Each `<frameset>` element needs one of two attributes: `rows`, to divide the screen into multiple rows, or `cols`, to divide the screen into multiple columns. `rows` and `cols` are set equal to a list of values that instructs a browser how big to make each row or column. The values can be a number of pixels, a percentage of a browser window's dimensions, or an asterisk (*), which acts as a wildcard character and tells the browser to use whatever space it has left.

The following XHTML code, for example, breaks the browser window into five rows (see Figure 7.3):

```
<frameset rows="30%,15%,15%,5%,35%">
...
</frameset>
```

The first row has a height equal to 30% of the browser screen height; the second and third rows each have a height equal to 15% of the browser screen; the fourth row has a height equal to 5% of the screen; and the fifth row has a height equal to 35% of the screen.

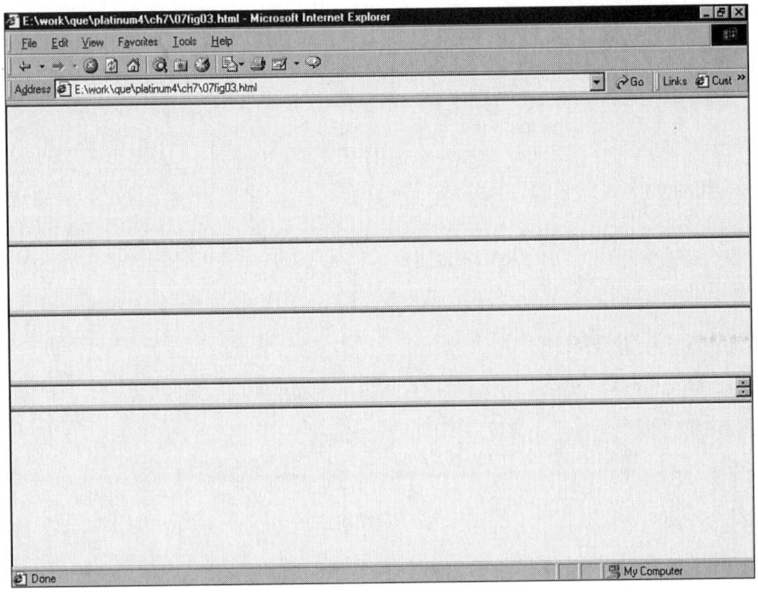

FIGURE 7.3
The <frameset> element enables you to break the browser screen into any number of rows.

Similarly, the following XHTML code splits the window into four columns (see Figure 7.4):

```
<frameset cols="200,120,2*,*">
...
</frameset>
```

The first column is 200 pixels wide; the second is 120 pixels wide; and the remaining space is divided between the third and fourth columns, with the third column twice as wide (2*) as the fourth (*).

CAUTION

Don't put a rows and a cols attribute in the same <frameset> element. Frames-capable browsers can do only one at a time. Normally, these browsers act on the first attribute they encounter.

The <frameset> element can also take two script-related event handlers: onload and onunload. These event handlers execute the script code you assign to them when the framedlayout is loaded and unloaded.

FIGURE 7.4
The `cols` attribute makes it possible to break the browser window into any number of columns. You have control over how big each row or column will be.

Nesting *<frameset>* Elements to Achieve Complex Layouts

To produce really interesting layouts, you can nest `<frameset>` elements. Suppose you want to split the browser window into six equal regions. You can first split the screen into three equal rows with the following XHTML code:

```
<frameset rows="*,*,*">
...
</frameset>
```

This produces the screen shown in Figure 7.5.

Next, you need to divide each row in half. To do this, you need a `<frameset>` element for each row that splits the row into two equal columns. The following XHTML code handles the task of splitting a row into two equal columns:

```
<frameset cols="50%,50%">
...
</frameset>
```

Nesting these tags in the XHTML code at the beginning of this section produces the following:

```
<frameset rows="*,*,*">
     <frameset cols="50%,50%"> <!-- split row 1 into two columns -->
          ...
     </frameset>
     <frameset cols="50%,50%"> <!-- split row 2 into two columns -->
          ...
     </frameset>
```

```
        <frameset cols="50%,50%"> <!-- split row 3 into two columns -->
            ...
        </frameset>
    </frameset>
```

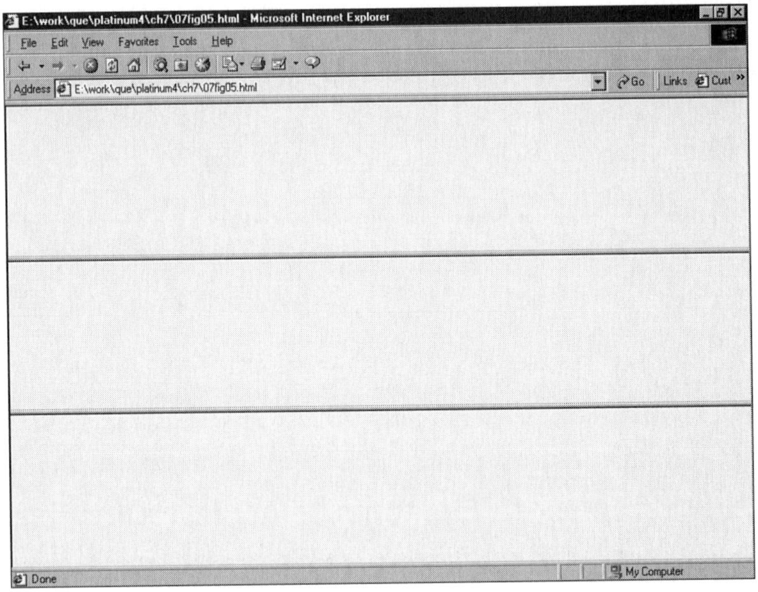

FIGURE 7.5
The first step in producing a complex framed layout is to split the browser screen into rows or columns.

The XHTML shown here completes the task of splitting the window into six equal regions. The resulting screen appears in Figure 7.6.

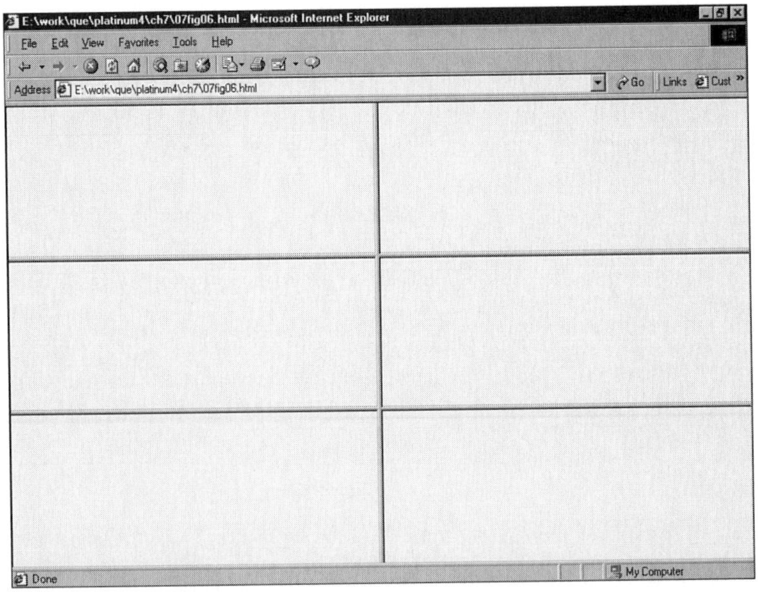

FIGURE 7.6
You further divide the initial rows or columns to produce the final layout.

TIP Not sure whether to do a <frameset> with rows or cols first? Take a look at your sketch of the browser window. If you have unbroken horizontal lines that go from one edge of the window to the other, do your rows first. If you have unbroken vertical lines that go from the top of the window to the bottom, do your cols first.

Of course, you're not limited to making regions that are all the same size. Suppose you want a 225–pixel-wide table of contents frame to appear down the left side of the browser window, and on the right side, you need a 110-pixel row for a logo; the balance of the right side is for changing content. In this case, you could use the XHTML code

```
<frameset cols="225,*">  <!-- split screen into two columns. -->
   ...                  <!-- placeholder for table of contents. -->
   <frameset rows="110,*">  <!-- split column 2 into two rows. -->
         ...    <!-- placeholder for logo. -->
         ...    <!-- placeholder for changing content frame. -->
   </frameset>
</frameset>
```

The ellipses you see in the preceding code are placeholders for the XHTML elements that place the content into the frames that the <frameset> elements create. You put a document in each using the <frame /> element discussed in the next section.

Placing Content in Frames with the *<frame />* Element

Using <frameset> elements is only the beginning of creating a framed page. After the browser window is split into regions, you need to fill each region with content. The keys to doing this are the <frame /> element and its many attributes.

NOTE The <frame /> element is an empty element, meaning there is no closing </frame> or, if you do use </frame>, no content can appear between <frame> and </frame>. This may cause compatibility issues with some framed HTML 4 layouts in which content for the frame is specified between <frame> and </frame> tags. ■

With your frames all set up, you're ready to place content in each frame with the <frame /> element. The most important attribute of the <frame /> element is src, which tells the browser the URL of the document you want to load into the frame. The <frame /> element can also take the attributes summarized in Table 7.1. If you use the name attribute, the name you give the frame must begin with an alphanumeric character.

Table 7.1 Attributes of the *<frame />* Element

Attribute	Purpose
`frameborder="1|0"`	Turns frame borders on (1) or off (0)
`marginheight="n"`	Specifies the amount of whitespace (in pixels) to be left at the top and bottom of the frame
`marginwidth="n"`	Specifies the amount of whitespace (in pixels) to be left along the sides of the frame
`longdesc="url"`	Provides the URL of a document that gives a more detailed description of what's in the frame; useful for nonvisual browsers
`name="frame_name"`	Gives the frame a unique name so it can be targeted from other frames
`noresize="noresize"`	Disables the user's ability to resize the frame
`scrolling="yes|no|auto"`	Controls the appearance of horizontal and vertical scroll-bars in the frame
`src="url"`	Specifies the URL of the document to load into the frame

NOTE Frame names may not start with the underscore (_) character. ■

To place content in each of the regions you created at the end of the previous section, you can use the following XHTML code:

```
<frameset cols="225,*">  <!-- split screen into two columns. -->
   <frame src="toc.html" />   <!-- placeholder for table of contents. -->
   <frameset rows="110,*">  <!-- split column 2 into two rows. -->
          <frame src="logo.html" />    <!-- placeholder for logo. -->
          <frame src="main.html" />    <!-- placeholder for content frame. -->
   </frameset>
</frameset>
```

The resulting screen appears in Figure 7.7.

Certainly, the `src` attribute in a `<frame />` element is essential. Otherwise the browser would not know where to look for the content that is to go into the frame.

You'll probably find that you frequently use the other attributes as well. In particular, `marginwidth` and `marginheight` enable you to set up left and right (`marginwidth`) and top and bottom (`marginheight`) margins within each frame. Putting a little whitespace around the content in each frame enhances readability, especially when you have `frameborder` set to zero.

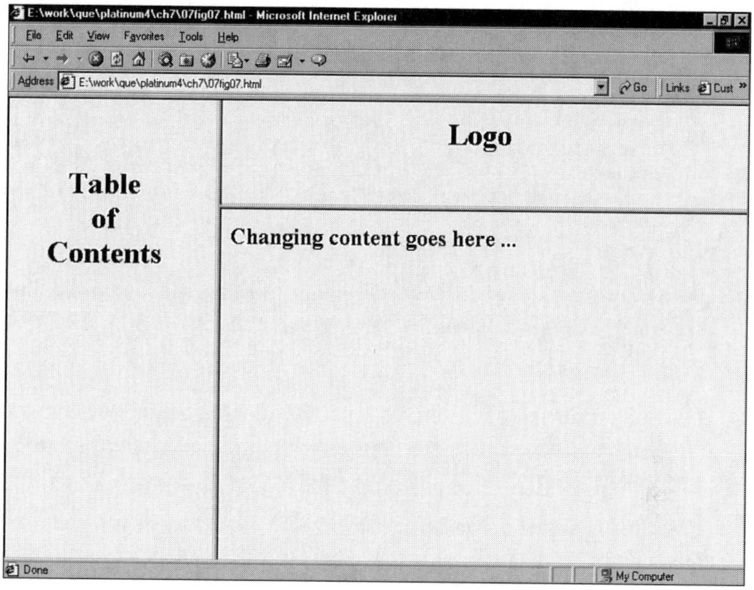

FIGURE 7.7
Each frame in your layout should have a corresponding `<frame />` element that populates it with content or a `<frameset>` element that subdivides it further.

NOTE If you set `frameborder` to zero, there will be no visible boundary between the frames and the layout will appear to be "seamless." The default value of `frameborder` is 1. ■

The `noresize` and `scrolling` attributes are handy when you want to modify the user-controlled aspects of a frame. Recall that a user can change the size of a frame by clicking a border of a frame and dragging it to a new position. `noresize`, when present in a `<frame/>` element, suppresses the user's ability to change the size of the frame. You might want to do this if it's imperative that a frame remain the same size so that it can always accommodate a key piece of content. `scrolling` can be set to `yes` if you always want horizontal and vertical scrollbars on the frame, and to `no` if you never want scrollbars. The default value of `scrolling` is `auto`, in which the browser places scrollbars on the frame if they're needed and leaves them off if they're not needed.

CAUTION

Be careful about setting `scrolling` to `no`. You should do this only if you are absolutely sure that all the content in a frame will always be visible on all browsers and screen resolutions. Otherwise, users might find themselves in a situation in which content runs off the side or bottom of a frame, and they have no way to scroll around to see it.

Targeting Named Frames

Probably the trickiest thing about frames is getting content to appear where you want it to appear. This is where naming the frames you create becomes critical. By naming the changing content frame “main,” you can then use the target attribute in all your <a> elements to direct all hyperlinked documents to be loaded into that frame:

```
<frameset cols="225,*">  <!-- split screen into two columns. -->
   <frame src="toc.html"/>   <!-- placeholder for table of contents. -->
   <frameset rows="110,*">  <!-- split column 2 into two rows. -->
     <frame src="logo.html" />    <!-- placeholder for logo. -->
  <frame src="main.html" name="main" />  <!-- placeholder for content frame -->
   </frameset>
</frameset>
```

With frames set up by the preceding code, an example link in the file toc.html might look like this:

```
<a href="orderform.html" target="main">Order Now!</a>
```

The target attribute tells the browser that the file orderform.html should be loaded into the frame named *main* (the changing content frame) whenever a user clicks the hypertext Order Now! in the table of contents frame.

If all the links in toc.html target the frame named *main*, you can use a <base /> element in the head of the document to set a value for target that applies to all links:

```
<head>
<title>Table of Contents</title>
<base target="main" />
</head>
```

With this <base /> element in place, every hyperlink, image map link, and form submission targets the changing content window named *main.*

Netscape set aside some reserved frame names when it introduced the frame-related tags. These special target names include

- **_blank**—Targets a new blank window that is not named.
- **_self**—Targets the frame where the hyperlink is found.
- **_parent**—Targets the parent <frameset> element of the frame where the hyperlink is found. This defaults to behaving like _self if no parent document exists.
- **_top**—Targets the full window before any frames are introduced. This creates a good way to jump out of a nested sequence of framed documents.

CAUTION

When using the reserved frame names, make sure that the character following the underscore character is lowercase. Otherwise, you are likely to see targeting behavior that you don't expect.

Although the target attribute is useful for targeting the effects of hyperlinks, you can use it in other XHTML elements as well. Placing the target attribute in a <form> element instructs the browser to target the response from the form submission to the specified frame. This enables you to set up a search form in one frame and have the search results appear in a separate frame.

▶ To learn how to author XHTML forms, **see** Chapter 8, "Forms"

Another element that takes the `target` attribute is the `<area />` element, which is used to define a hot region in a client-side image map. This permits the document associated with a hot region to be loaded into the frame of your choice.

▶ To learn how to set up client-side image maps, **see** Chapter 4, "Image Maps"

Finally, you can also use the `target` attribute with the `<link />` element. `<link />` is used to establish links to files that provide supporting information to a browser on how to render a file. You can link a style sheet to a page, for example, using the `<link />` element.

Respecting the Frames-Challenged Browsers

If you create a document with frames, people who are using a browser other than Netscape Navigator 4.0+ or Microsoft Internet Explorer 5.0+ might not be able to see the content you want them to see because their browsers don't understand the `<frameset>` and `<frame />` elements. As a courtesy to users with frames-challenged browsers, you can place alternative XHTML code within the `<noframes>` element. Any XHTML inside a `<noframes>` element is understood and rendered by other browsers. A frames-capable browser, on the other hand, ignores anything inside a `<noframes>` element and works just with the frame-related XHTML.

NOTE You should also consider providing `<noframes>` content for browsers running on screens with a 640×480 monitor. Frames are difficult to use at that resolution. ■

NOTE Only one `<noframes>` element is allowed within a given XHTML document. ■

Some users have a browser that can render frames, but they dislike framed documents. For this portion of your audience, you should consider having a non-frames version of all your pages available (see Figure 7.8). This way, users who like frames can stick with them, and those who don't like frames have a way to view the same content without being burdened with an uncomfortable interface.

TIP When making framed versions of existing pages, don't discard your non-frames content. Very often, you can use the XHTML code in the non-frames documents as the alternative content found within the `<noframes>` element.

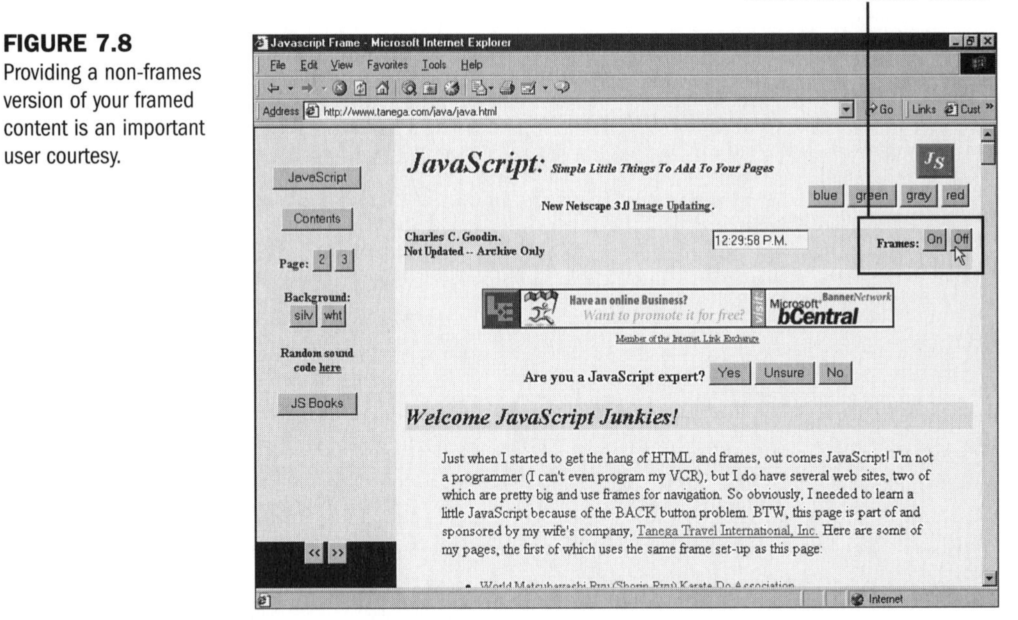

FIGURE 7.8
Providing a non-frames version of your framed content is an important user courtesy.

> **CAUTION**
>
> The `<noframes>` element must occur after the initial `<frameset>` element, but before any nested `<frameset>` elements.

Creating Floating Frames

Microsoft introduced the concept of a floating frame with Internet Explorer 3. You can think of a floating frame as a smaller browser window that you can open in your main browser window—much like the picture-in-picture feature that comes with many television sets. The same as with regular frames, you can load any XHTML document you want into a floating frame. The primary difference is that floating frames can be placed anywhere on a page that you can place an image. In fact, you'll find the XHTML syntax for placing floating frames to be similar to that for placing an image.

You place a floating frame on a page by using the `<iframe>` element. A browser that can do floating frames ignores anything within this element, enabling you to place an alternative to the floating frame (most likely text or an image) on the page as well. This way, browsers that don't know how to render floating frames can ignore the `<iframe>` element and act on what is found inside it. The `<iframe>` element can take the attributes summarized in Table 7.2.

Table 7.2 Attributes of the *<iframe>* Element

Attribute	Purpose
`align="top|middle|bottom|left|right"`	Floats the floating frame in the left or right margin or aligns subsequent content with the top, middle, or bottom of the floating frame
`frameborder="0|1"`	Controls the presence of the beveled border around the floating frame
`height="pixels|percent"`	Specifies the height of the floating frame
`longdesc="url"`	Provides the URL of a document that gives a more detailed description of what's in the floating frame; useful for nonvisual browsers
`marginheight="n"`	Specifies the amount of whitespace (in pixels) to be left at the top and bottom of the floating frame
`marginwidth="n"`	Specifies the amount of whitespace (in pixels) to be left along the sides of the floating frame
`name="frame_name"`	Gives the floating frame a unique name so it can be targeted by hyperlinks
`scrolling="yes|no|auto"`	Controls the presence of scrollbars on the floating frame
`src="url"`	Specifies the URL of the document to load into the floating frame
`width="pixels|percent"`	Specifies the width of the floating frame

The `<iframe>` element has three important attributes that a developer usually specifies: `width`, `height`, and `src`. `width` and `height` specify the width and height of the floating frame in pixels or as a percentage of the browser screen's width and height. `src` tells the browser the URL of the document to load into the floating frame. Thus, your basic floating frame XHTML code looks like this:

```
<iframe width="400 height="225" src="http://www.yourserver.com/floating.html">
Text- or image-based alternative to the floating frame
</iframe>
```

In addition to `height`, `width`, and `src`, the `<iframe>` element takes several other attributes that give you good control over the floating frame's appearance. These include

- **`frameborder`**—By setting `frameborder="1"`, you place a beveled border around the floating frame. This gives the frame the appearance of being slightly recessed on the page. If you prefer a more seamless look (as in Figure 7.9), you can use the `frameborder` attribute in the `<iframe>` element. Setting `frameborder="0"` eliminates the beveled border.

FIGURE 7.9
Floating frames enable you to place a new document right in the middle of the main document. The quote you see on this page is actually randomly selected from within a floating frame.

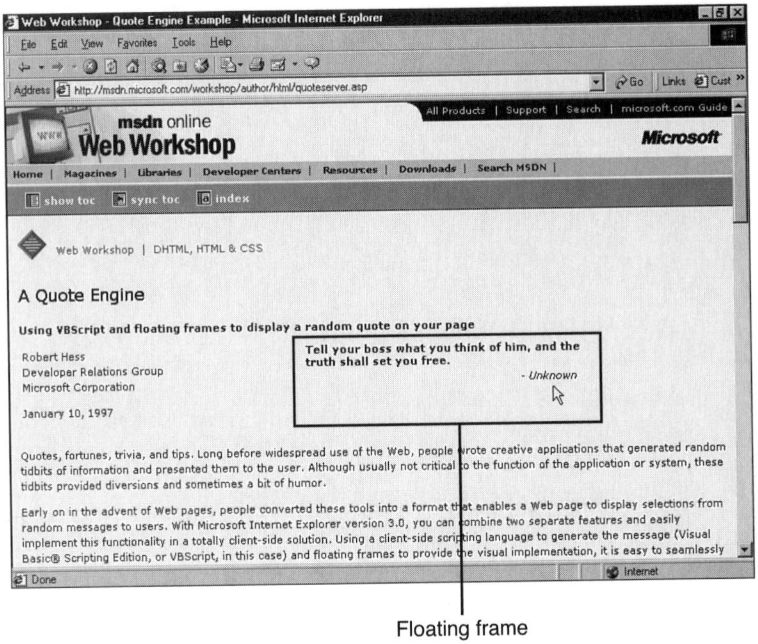

Floating frame

- **`scrolling`**—A browser that can render floating frames puts a scrollbar on the floating frame if the document it contains exceeds the dimensions of the frame. You can suppress the scrollbars by specifying `scrolling="no"` in the `<iframe>` element. If you always want scrollbars present, you can set `scrolling` equal to `yes`.
- **`longdesc`**—Speech- and Braille-based browsers can use the URL specified by the `longdesc` attribute to get more information about what's being presented in the floating frame.
- **`align`**—You can use the `align` attribute in one of two ways, depending on what value you set it equal to. First, you can float the floating frame in the left or right margins by specifying `align="left"` or `align="right"`. Any text following the floated frame wraps around it to the right or left, respectively. You can use the `<br/>` element with the appropriate `clear` attribute to break to the first line clear of floated frames. Second, you can set `align` equal to `top`, `middle`, or `bottom` to align the subsequent content along the top edge, middle, or bottom edge of the floating frame.
- **`name`**—Naming a floating frame enables you to target it with the `target` attribute in an `<a>`, `<area>`, `<link>`, or `<form>` element.

NOTE Early incarnations of the HTML `<iframe>` tag took the `hspace` and `vspace` attributes, but these are not valid attributes of the `<iframe>` element in XHTML. If your floating frame needs some clear space around it, you can use the `style` attribute of the `<iframe>` element, together with cascading style sheet instructions to create the additional whitespace. ■

Using Hidden Frames

A technique that has emerged recently involves the use of hidden frames. Hidden frames are frames that have no size and, therefore, are not visible to a user. You might set up a hidden frame with code such as

```
<frameset rows="30%,70%,*">
   <frame src="frame1.html" name="frame1" />
   <frame src="frame2.html" name="frame2" />
   <frame src="frame3.html" name="hidden_frame" />
</frameset>
```

This creates a frameset with three rows. The first row has a height equal to 30% of the browser window height, the second row a height equal to 70% of the browser screen, and the third row a height of whatever is left over. However, because the entire browser window height is consumed by the first two rows, the third row has a height of zero and is hidden from view.

You might be asking: "If a frame can't be seen, what good is it?" The answer is that it is good for behind-the-scenes kinds of activity such as JavaScripting. When Netscape released its NetHelp online help package with Navigator 4, it used JavaScript tucked away in hidden frames to control aspects of the NetHelp interface such as the processing stack, activity tracking, and error handling. JavaScript code for all these functions is read into a hidden frame named SystemFrame, and a NetHelp application is able to make calls to this frame to invoke script code when needed. Thus, the hidden frame became a library where reusable JavaScript routines were stored.

Another use of hidden frames is in applications developed in ColdFusion or Active Server Pages. With either technology, an XHTML document is dynamically generated and returned to the browser. Occasionally, it is appropriate to build a hidden frame into the XHTML document that contains state information that cannot be stored as a cookie or on the server. Figure 7.10 shows you a multi-part registration form that stores data in a hidden frame as it collects it.

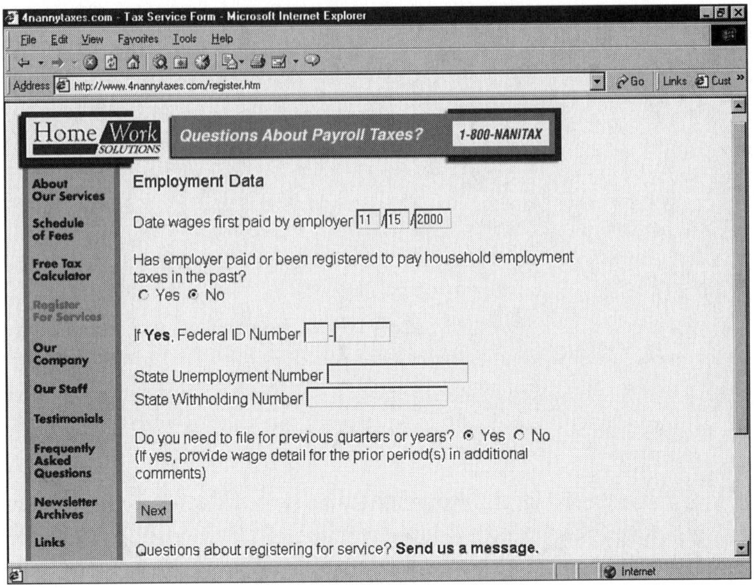

FIGURE 7.10
This registration form collects information over several steps and stores it all in a hidden frame for processing at the end.

▶ To read up on Active Server Page development, **see** Chapter 32, "Writing Active Server Pages"

▶ To learn the basics of ColdFusion Development, **see** Chapter 33, "Using ColdFusion"

CHAPTER 8

Forms

by Eric Ladd

In this chapter

Overview: Forms and CGI

As the Web becomes more interactive, the need for interface components to gather data from users is greater than ever. Fortunately, this was anticipated in earlier versions of HTML and resulted in the introduction of the form elements. *Forms* are the visible or front-end portions of interactive pages. Users enter information into form fields or controls—user interface elements that are similar to those found on Windows and Macintosh operating systems—and click a button to submit the data. The browser then packages the data, opens an HTTP connection, and sends the data to a server. Things then move to the "behind-the-scenes" or back-end part of the process.

Web servers are programs that know how to distribute Web pages. They are not programmed to process data from every possible form, so the best they can do is hand off the form data to a program that does know what to do with it. This handoff occurs with the help of the *common gateway interface* or *CGI*—a set of standards by which HTTP servers communicate with external programs.

The program that processes the form data is called a *CGI script* or a *CGI program*. The script or program performs manipulations of the data and composes a response—typically an XHTML page. The response page is handed back to the server (via CGI), which in turn passes it along to the browser that initiated the request.

NOTE CGI is not the only way to process form data these days. Many other server-side scripting approaches, such as Active Server Pages, ColdFusion, and PHP, can be used to process form submissions. You can learn more about each of these technologies by consulting Chapters 32, 33, and 34, respectively.

▶ To learn more about CGI programming, **see** Chapter 28, "Programming CGI Scripts"

Forms and CGI are opposite sides of the same coin. Both are essential to creating interactive pages, but the user sees the forms side of the coin. This chapter examines how to create Web forms and gives an overview of some of the behind-the-scenes activity that must occur to produce the custom pages, electronic commerce sites, and other dynamic functionality that Web users have come to love.

NOTE When a CGI script or program composes an XHTML page, it is said to be generating XHTML *on-the-fly*. The capability to generate pages on-the-fly is what makes custom responses to form submissions possible.

Creating Forms

XHTML's form support is simple and robust. A handful of XHTML elements create the most popular controls of modern graphical interfaces, including text windows, check boxes and radio buttons, pull-down menus, and push buttons.

Composing XHTML forms might sound complex, but you need to master surprisingly few elements to do it. All form-related elements occur within the `<form>` element. It is possible to have more than one form in an XHTML document, but you must be careful not to nest the `<form>` elements that define them.

TIP Adding a closing `</form>` tag immediately after creating an opening `<form>` tag is a good practice; then you can go back to fill in the contents. Following this procedure helps you avoid leaving off the closing element after you finish. Many of today's popular XHTML editing programs take care of placing the closing `</form>` tag for you, so check to see if the editor you're using does this.

Each XHTML form has three main components: the form header, one or more named input fields, and one or more action buttons.

The *<form>* Element

The form header and the opening `<form>` tag are actually one and the same. The `<form>` element takes the six attributes shown in Table 8.1. The `action` attribute is required in every `<form>` element.

Table 8.1 Attributes of the *<form>* Element

Attribute	Purpose
`accept="MIME_type_list"`	Specifies a list of MIME types that the server will process correctly
`accept-charset="character_set_list"`	Provides a list of character sets that are acceptable to the server
`action="URL"`	Specifies the URL of the processing script
`enctype="encoding type"`	Supplies the MIME type of a file used as form input
`method="get|post"`	Tells the browser how it should send the form data to the server
`target="frame_name"`	Gives the name of the frame where the response from the form submission is to appear

`action` is set equal to the URL of the processing script so the browser knows where to send the form data after it is entered (the HTTP server) and which program on the server should be invoked to process the form data. Without it, the browser has no idea where the form data should go. A full `action` URL has the following form:

```
protocol://server/path/script_file
```

You can also use a relative URL if you are calling a script on the same server.

NOTE If you leave off the `action` attribute, the browser will submit the form data to the same URL used to call up the form. This is often a useful thing to do when using a single-script approach to gathering data. The first call to the script produces the form, and the second call to the script processes the data on the form.

`method` specifies the HTTP method to use when passing the data to the script and can be set to values of `get` or `post`. When you're using the `get` method, the browser appends the form data to the end of the URL of the processing script as a *query string*. The `post` method sends the form data to the server in a separate HTTP transaction.

`method` is not a mandatory attribute of the `<form>` element. In the absence of a specified method, the browser uses the `get` method.

CAUTION

Some servers have operating environment limitations that prevent them from processing a URL that exceeds a certain number of characters—typically 1KB of data. This limitation can be a problem when you're using the `get` method to pass a large amount of form data. Because the `get` method appends the data to the end of the processing script URL, you run a greater risk of passing a URL that's too big for the server to handle. If URL size limitations are a concern on your server, you should use the `post` method to pass form data.

Netscape introduced the `enctype` attribute for the purpose of providing a filename to be uploaded as form input. The default value of `enctype` is `application/x-www-form-urlencoded`, and this is usually sufficient for most form submissions. If you are uploading a file as part of the form submission, however, you need to set `enctype="multipart/form-data"` for the upload to work properly.

NOTE `enctype` does not create the input field for the filename; instead, it gives the browser a cue that a file upload is part of the submission. When prompting for a file to upload, you need to use an `<input />` element with `type` set equal to `file`.

As an example of these three `<form>` element attributes, examine the following HTML:

```
<form action="logo_upload.cgi" method="post" enctype="multipart/form-data">
Please enter the name of the GIF file containing your logo:
<input type="file" name="logo" />
<input type="submit" value="Upload" />
</form>
```

The form header of this short form instructs the server to process the form data using the program named `logo_upload.cgi`. Form data is passed using the `post` method, and the browser knows that it has to upload a file because of the `enctype` attribute.

Newer `<form>` element attributes in XHTML 1.0 include `target`, which is used to direct the response from the processing script to a particular frame; `accept`, which denotes the MIME types of files that the server processing the form can handle correctly (this is useful when a user is submitting a set of files to the server because you can then check to make sure that all the submitted files are of an acceptable MIME type); and `accept-charset`, which specifies the character sets the server understands. Incorporating these attributes, the previous code might look like this:

```
<form action="logo_upload.cgi" method="post" enctype="multipart/form-data"
  accept="image/gif,image/jpeg" target="main"
  accept-charset="euc-jp">
Please enter the name of the GIF file containing your logo:
<input type="file" name="logo" />
<input type="submit" value="Upload" />
</form>
```

The `euc-jp` value for the `accept-charset` attribute suggests the use of a Japanese character set to the server that processes the form.

NOTE Use of the `target` attribute is valid only when you are validating against the XHTML 1.0 Transitional or Frameset DTDs. The `target` attribute is not allowed under the Strict DTD.

The `<form>` element can also take two event handlers: `onsubmit` and `onreset`. This gives you the capability to execute some script code when the form is submitted or reset, respectively. If you write a JavaScript function that validates the data a user enters into a form, for example, you could invoke the script using an event handler as follows:

```
<form action="upload_logo.cgi" onsubmit="return validate(this)">
```

▶ To learn more about using JavaScript to validate form input, **see** Chapter 21, "Using JavaScript to Create Smart Forms"

Named Input Fields

The named input fields typically compose the bulk of a form. The fields appear as standard GUI controls, such as text boxes, check boxes, radio buttons, and menus. You assign each field a unique name that eventually becomes the variable name used in the processing script.

If you are not coding your own processing scripts, be sure to sit down with your programmer to agree on variable names. The names used in the form should exactly match those used in coding the script.

You can use different GUI controls to enter information into forms. The controls for named input fields appear in Table 8.2.

Table 8.2 Types of Named Input Fields

Field Type	XHTML Element(s)
Text box	`<input type="text" />`
Password box	`<input type="password" />`
Check box	`<input type="checkbox" />`
Radio button	`<input type="radio" />`
Hidden field	`<input type="hidden" />`
File	`<input type="file"/>`
Text window	`<textarea>`
Menu	`<select>`, `<option>`

The <*input*> Element

You might notice in Table 8.2 that the `<input />` element handles the majority of named input fields. `<input />` is a standalone element that, thanks to the many values of its `type` attribute, can place most of the fields you need on your forms. `<input />` also takes other attributes depending on which type is in use. These additional attributes are covered for each type, as appropriate, over the next several sections.

NOTE The `<input />` element and other elements that produce named input fields create only the fields themselves. You, as the form designer, must include some descriptive text next to each field so users know what information to enter. You might also need to use line breaks (`<br />`), paragraph breaks (`<p>`), and nonbreaking space (` `) to create the spacing you want between form fields.

TIP Because browsers ignore whitespace, lining up the left edges of text input boxes on multiple lines is difficult because the text to the left of the boxes is of different lengths. In this instance, XHTML tables are invaluable. By setting up the text labels and input fields as cells in the same row of an XHTML table, you can produce a nicely formatted form. To learn more about forms using table conventions, consult Chapter 6, "Tables."

Text and Password Fields Text and password fields are simple data entry fields. The only difference between them is that text typed into a password field appears onscreen as asterisks (*).

CAUTION

Using a password field protects users' passwords from the people looking over their shoulders, but it does not protect the password as it travels over the Internet. To protect password data as it moves from browser to server, you need to use some type of encryption (usually by *Secure Sockets Layer*, or *SSL*, on the Web server) or a similar security measure. Authenticating both the server and client by using signed digital certificates is another way to keep Internet transactions secure.

A text or password field is produced by the XHTML shown here (attributes in square brackets are optional):

```
<input type="text|password" name="name" [value="default_text"]
[size="width"] [maxlength="max_width"] />
```

The `name` attribute is mandatory because it provides a unique identifier for the data entered into the field.

The optional `value` attribute enables you to place some default text in the field, rather than have it initially appear blank. This capability is useful if a majority of users will enter a certain text string into the field. In such cases, you can use `value` to put the text into the field, thereby saving most users the effort of typing it. It is also useful when presenting a form that a user can use to make edits to information stored in a server-side database. You can present the information you currently have inside form fields using the `value` attribute, and the user can simply change whatever pieces of information are outdated.

The optional `size` attribute gives you control over how many characters wide the field should be. The default `size` is typically about 20 characters, although this number can vary from browser to browser. `maxlength` is also optional and enables you to specify the maximum number of characters that can be entered into the field. If `maxlength` is set to a value greater than `size`, the text the user types will scroll off to the left after the field is filled.

Figure 8.1 shows a form on hotmail.com's home page. Password text appears as asterisks. The corresponding XHTML appears in Listing 8.1.

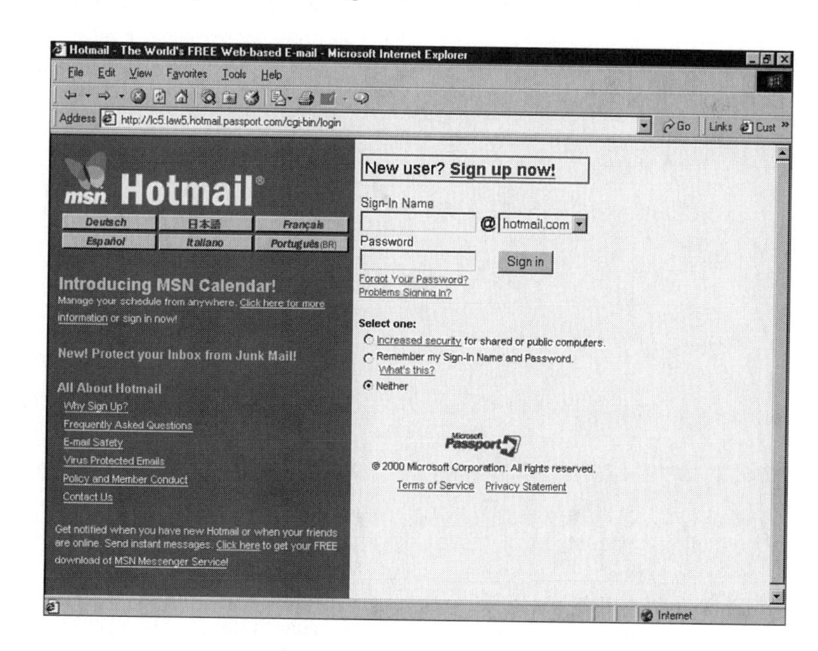

FIGURE 8.1
Text and password fields are frequently used together to produce a login interface.

Listing 8.1 XHTML Code to Produce Text and Password Fields

```
<tr>
<td>
<input type="text" name="login" size="16" maxlength="64" />
</td>
<td valign="middle" align="center" width=22>
<b>@</b>
</td>
<td>
<select name="domain">
<option value="hotmail.com" selected>hotmail.com</option>
</select>
</td>
</tr>
<tr>
<td colspan="3">Password</td>
</tr>
<tr>
<td>
<input type="password" name="passwd" size="16" maxlength="16" />
</td>
<td></td>
<td>
<input type="submit" name="enter" value="Sign in" />
</td>
</tr>
```

Check Boxes Check boxes are used to provide users with several choices from which they can select as many as they want. An `<input />` element that is used to produce a check box option has the following syntax:

```
<input type="checkbox" name="name" value="value" checked="checked" />
```

Each check box option is created by its own `<input />` element and should have its own unique name. If you give multiple check box options the same name, the associated values are all passed under that name, and it might present some programming challenges when creating the processing script.

The `value` attribute specifies what data is sent to the server if the corresponding check box is chosen. This information is transparent to the user. The optional `checked` attribute preselects a commonly selected check box when the form is rendered on the browser screen.

Figure 8.2 shows the customization page of the Alliance for Investor Education site. When customizing the page, you have your choice of several topic areas including stocks, bonds, mutual funds, online investing, and how to avoid scams. Each option has a corresponding check box that you select or deselect, depending on whether you want to see the links for a particular topic. The XHTML that produces the check boxes appears in Listing 8.2.

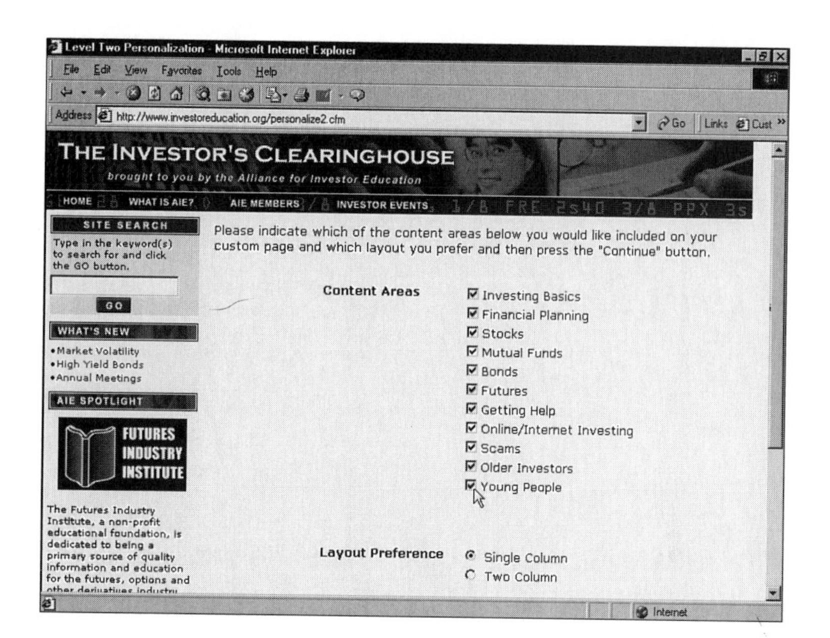

FIGURE 8.2
Users can choose as many check box options as they prefer.

NOTE If they are selected, check box options show up in the form data sent to the server. Options that are not selected do not get sent to the server.

Listing 8.2 XHTML Code to Produce Check Boxes

```
<input type="checkbox" name="content" value="ib" checked="checked" />
Investing Basics<br />
<input type="checkbox" name="content" value="fp" checked="checked" />
Financial Planning<br />
<input type="checkbox" name="content" value="st" checked="checked" />
Stocks<br />
<input type="checkbox" name="content" value="mf" checked="checked" />
Mutual Funds<br />
<input type="checkbox" name="content" value="bo" checked="checked" />
Bonds<br />
<input type="checkbox" name="content" value="fu" checked="checked" />
Futures<br />
<input type="checkbox" name="content" value="gh" checked="checked" />
Getting Help<br />
<input type="checkbox" name="content" value="on" checked="checked" />
Online/Internet Investing<br/>
<input type="checkbox" name="content" value="sc" checked="checked" />
Scams<br />
<input type="checkbox" name="content" value="ol" checked="checked" />
Older Investors<br />
<input type="checkbox" name="content" value="yp" checked="checked" />
Young People<br />
```

Radio Buttons Radio buttons are also used to present users with a set of choices, but they can choose only one. When you set up options with a radio button format, make sure the options are mutually exclusive so a user doesn't try to select more than one.

The XHTML code used to produce a set of three radio button options is as follows:

```
<form ...>
<input type="radio" name="name" value="value1" checked="checked" />
Option 1<br />
<input type="radio" name="name" value="value2" />Option 2<br />
<input type="radio" name="name" value="value3" />Option 3<br />
...
</form>
```

The `value` and `checked` attributes work the same as they do for check boxes, although you should have only one preselected radio button option. A fundamental difference with a set of radio button options is that they all have the same name. This is permissible because the user can select only one of the options.

Figure 8.3 shows a registration form for ordering a teaching guide from the Financial Literacy 2001 site. The person ordering needs to specify his or her area of instruction as given by a set of radio buttons. The corresponding XHTML appears in Listing 8.3.

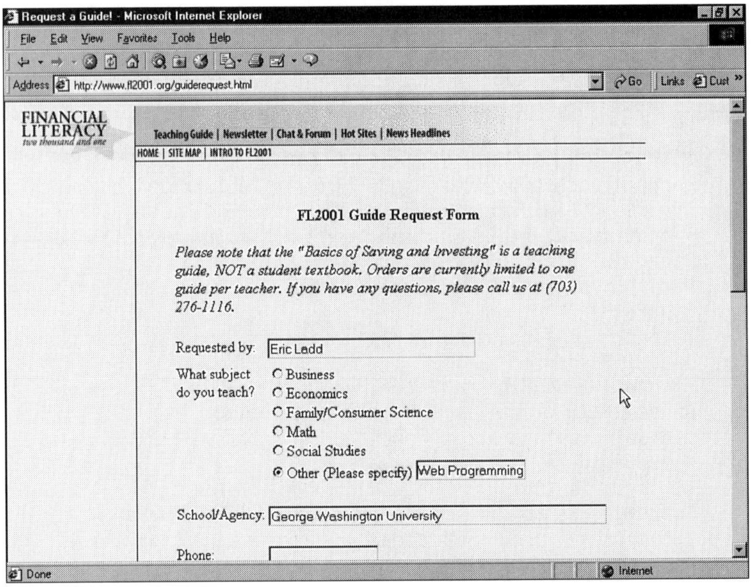

FIGURE 8.3
Users can choose only one of a set of radio button options.

Listing 8.3 XHTML Code to Produce Radio Buttons

```
<td valign="top">What subject do you teach?</td>
<td>
<input type="radio" name="teacher" value="Business" />
Business<br />
<input type="radio" name="teacher" value="Economics" />
Economics<br />
<input type="radio" name="teacher" value="Family/ConsumerScience" />
Family/Consumer Science<br />
<input type="radio" name="teacher" value="Math" />
Math<br />
<input type="radio" name="teacher" value="SocialStudies" />
Social Studies<br />
<input type="radio" name="teacher" value="Other" />
Other (Please specify) 
<input type="text" name="OtherText" size="15" /><br />
</td>
</tr>
```

NOTE Just as with check boxes, values for radio button fields are not sent to the server if no option is selected.

Hidden Fields Technically, hidden fields are not meant for data input. You can send information to the server about a form without displaying that information anywhere on the form itself. The general format for including hidden fields is as follows:

```
<input type="hidden" name="name" value="value" />
```

One possible use of hidden fields is to enable a single general script to process data from different forms. The script needs to know which form is sending the data, and a hidden field can provide this information without requiring anything on the part of the user.

Because HTTP is a stateless protocol (information from the user's session is not tracked), input from one form can't be carried forward to another. However, you can use hidden fields to accomplish that task. You can split a long form into several smaller forms and still keep all the user's input in one place by passing it from one form to the next in the sequence. Suppose, for example, that in the first of a sequence of several forms, you collect a visitor's name and mailing address. That information is passed to the script that processes the form. Because this script also must build the next form in the sequence, it would be easy to have the script include hidden fields in the next form that carry the name and address information forward.

NOTE Because hidden fields are transparent to users, it doesn't matter where you put them in your XHTML code. You need to make sure they occur within the <form> element that defines the form where the hidden fields reside.

Hidden fields are integral in the development of ColdFusion and Active Server Page applications. Additionally, these technologies have server-side features that allow you to store information you might otherwise put in a hidden field. Look for examples of hidden field usage as you read Chapter 32, "Writing Active Server Pages," and Chapter 33, "Using ColdFusion."

Files You can upload an entire file to a server by using a form. The first step is to include the `enctype` attribute in the <form> element. `enctype` should be set to `multipart/form-data` to accomplish the file upload. To enter a filename in a field, the user needs the <input /> element with `type` set equal to `file`:

```
<form action="upload.cgi" enctype="multipart/form-data" method="post">
What file would you like to submit: <input type="file" name="upload_file" />
...
</form>
```

Being able to send an entire file is useful when submitting a document produced by another program—for example, an Excel spreadsheet, a resume in Word format, or a compiled executable file.

NOTE You can also use the `accept` attribute when you have an <input /> field of type `file` to specify the MIME types of files that are acceptable for upload.

File upload fields are usually accompanied by a Browse button, which enables users to browse to the file they want to upload. The Browse button is supplied by the browser, and you don't need to do anything special to place the button there.

CAUTION

Depending on the user's browser version and operating system, it's possible for the name of the file that gets copied to the Web server to not match the name of the source file. That is, a user could submit `budget.xls` from her machine and the file copied onto the server might have some other name. Be sure to test your applications that use file upload fields to verify that the naming stays consistent.

Multiple-Line Text Windows

Text and password boxes are used for simple, one-line input fields. You can create multiline text windows that function in much the same way by using the <textarea> element. The XHTML syntax for a text window is as follows:

```
<textarea name="name" rows="rows" cols="columns">
Default_window_text
</textarea>
```

The name attribute gives the text window a unique identifier, the same as it does with the variations on the <input /> element. The required rows and cols attributes enable you to specify the dimensions of the text window as it appears on the browser screen.

The text that appears within the <textarea> element shows up in the input window by default. To type in something else, users must delete the default text and enter their own text.

Multiline text windows are ideal for entry of long pieces of text, such as feedback comments or email messages (see the Digex job application page in Figure 8.4 and corresponding code in Listing 8.4). Some corporate sites on the Web that collect information on potential employees might ask you to copy and paste your entire resume into multiline text windows!

FIGURE 8.4
A multiline text window is ideal for gathering free-response text, such as comments or feedback.

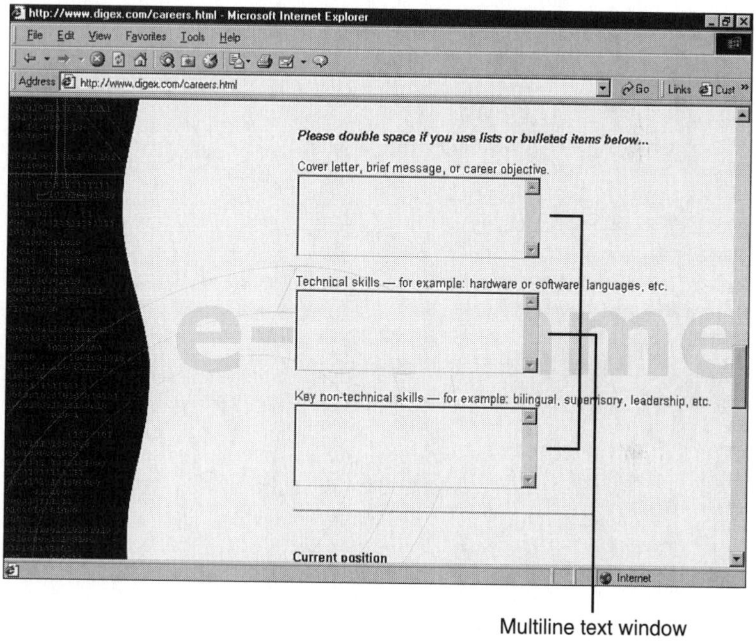

Listing 8.4 XHTML Code to Produce a Multiline Text Window

```
Cover letter, brief message, or career objective.<br />
<textarea rows="5" cols="30" name="letter">
</textarea>
<br />
Technical skills &#151; for example:
hardware or software, languages, etc.<br/>
<textarea rows="5" cols="30" name="tech">
</textarea>
<br />
```

Listing 8.4 Continued

```
Key non-technical skills &#151; for example:
bilingual, supervisory, leadership, etc.<br/>
<textarea rows="5" cols="30" name="nontech">
</textarea>
<br />
```

In addition to name, rows, and cols, the <textarea> element also supports the following attributes:

- **disabled**—Using the disabled attribute disallows the user from typing anything into the text window. This is similar to a field being "grayed out" in the Windows or Macintosh operating system environment.
- **readonly**—The readonly attribute enables you to display text in the text window, but the user cannot modify or delete the text.
- **tabindex**—tabindex specifies the text window's position in the form's tabbing order.
- **accesskey**—You can set up a shortcut key to bring the user to the text window by using the accesskey attribute.

Menus

The final technique for creating a named input field is to use the <select> element to produce pull-down or scrollable option menus (see Figure 8.5 and Listing 8.5). The XHTML code used to create a general menu is as follows:

```
<form ...>
<select name="name" [size="size"] [multiple="multiple"]>
<option [selected="selected"]>Option 1</option>
<option [selected="selected"]>Option 2</option>
<option [selected="selected"]>Option 3</option>
...
<option [selected="selected"]>Option n</option>
</select>
....
</form>
```

In the <select> element, the name attribute again gives the input field a unique identifier. The optional size attribute enables you to specify how many options should be displayed when the menu renders on the browser screen. If you have more options than you have space, you can access them either by using a pull-down window or by scrolling through the window with scrollbars. If you want to let users choose more than one menu option, include the multiple attribute. When multiple is used, users can choose multiple options by holding down the Ctrl key and clicking the options they want.

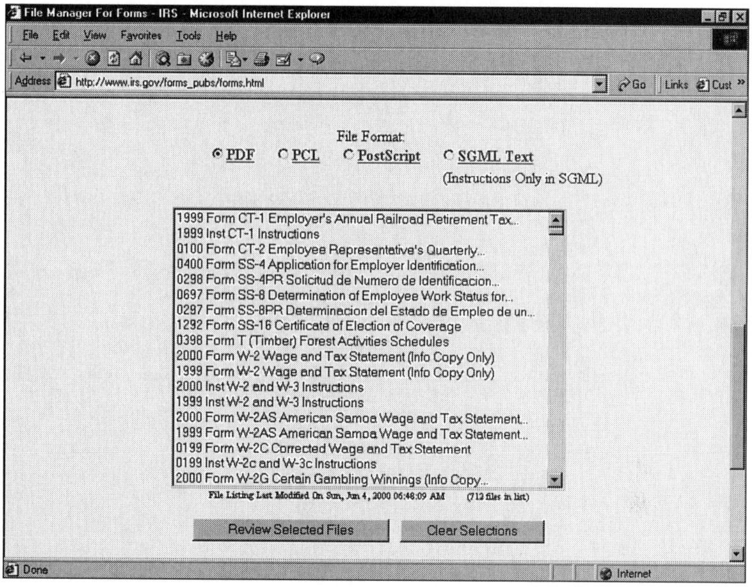

FIGURE 8.5
Taxpayers can download the forms they need from the IRS Web site. The many available forms are presented by means of a scrollable menu.

NOTE If you specify the `multiple` attribute and `size="1"`, a one-line scrollable list box displays instead of a drop-down list box. This box appears because you can select only one item in a drop-down list box.

Listing 8.5 XHTML Code to Produce a Menu

```
<select name="WSYS_query" multiple="multiple" size="18">
<option value="00991">
1999 Form CT-1 Employer's Annual Railroad Retirement Tax...</option>
<option value="01402">1999 Inst CT-1 Instructions</option>
<option value="00992">
0100 Form CT-2 Employee Representative's Quarterly...</option>
<option value="01062">
0400 Form SS-4 Application for Employer Identification...</option>
<option value="01063">
0298 Form SS-4PR Solicitud de Numero de Identificacion...</option>
<option value="01064">
0697 Form SS-8 Determination of Employee Work Status for...</option>
<option value="01065">
0297 Form SS-8PR Determinacion del Estado de Empleo de un...</option>
<option value="01061">
1292 Form SS-16 Certificate of Election of Coverage</option>
<option value="01066">
0398 Form T (Timber) Forest Activities Schedules</option>
<option value="01070">
```

Listing 8.5 Continued

```
2000 Form W-2 Wage and Tax Statement (Info Copy Only)</option>
<option value="01078">
1999 Form W-2 Wage and Tax Statement (Info Copy Only)</option>
<option value="01951">2000 Inst W-2 and W-3 Instructions</option>
<option value="01952">1999 Inst W-2 and W-3 Instructions</option>
...
</select>
```

Each option in the menu is specified inside its own `<option>` element. If you want an option to be preselected, include the `select` attribute in the appropriate `<option>` element. The value passed to the server is the menu item that follows the `<option>` element unless you supply an alternative using the `value` attribute. For example:

```
<form ...>
<select name="state" multiple="multiple">
<option value="NY">New York</option>
<option value="DC">Washington, DC</option>
<option value="FL">Florida</option>
...
</select>
...
</form>
```

In the preceding menu, the user clicks a state name, but it is the state's two-letter abbreviation that passes to the server.

NOTE If multiple menu options are selected, all the values are passed to the server using the name specified by the `name` attribute in the `<select>` element. This means that multiple "copies" of that variable have to be created—one for each value selected.

In the preceding code, for example, a user might choose the states of New York and Florida. In that case, you would have two copies of the form field `state`—one set equal to "NY" and the other set equal to "FL"—and both would be passed on to the server. This means your processing script must be ready to handle multiple instances of a variable if they appear. ■

One other element related to the `<select>` element is `<optgroup>`. `<optgroup>` enables you to create logical groups of menu options. You specify the name to associate with the option group by using the `label` attribute of the `<optgroup>` element.

Grouping related menu options can be invaluable in a long list of options in which it can be difficult for the user to keep track of them all. Consider, for example, the following list of Web server configuration options:

```
<select name="server_options" multiple="multiple">
<option>Windows NT 4.0</option>
<option>Solaris 2.6</option>
<option>Netscape Enterprise Server</option>
```

```
<option>Apache</option>
<option>Microsoft IIS</option>
<option>Firewall server</option>
<option>Pre-production test server</option>
<option>Emergency backup server</option>
</select>
```

Many options are in the list, but they are something of a mixed bag—a collection of operating systems, HTTP servers, and other support computers. You can use the `<optgroup>` element to logically group these options into a more intelligible list:

```
<select name="server_options" multiple="multiple">
<optgroup label="Operating Systems">
   <option>Windows NT 4.0</option>
   <option>Solaris 2.6</option>
</optgroup>
<optgroup label="HTTP Servers">
   <option>Netscape Enterprise Server</option>
   <option>Apache</option>
   <option>Microsoft IIS</option>
</optgroup>
<optgroup label="Other Servers">
   <option>Firewall server</option>
   <option>Pre-production test server</option>
   <option>Emergency backup server</option>
</optgroup>
</select>
```

Although it is not required of browsers, one presentation possibility for menus that use logically grouped options is to present a cascading menu—as of this writing, however, no major browsers have implemented this approach. When users first see the menu, they see only the names of the option groups. Then, by moving their mouse pointers over one of the option group names, they can reveal the individual options under that group. You can see an example of this behavior in the way a browser handles favorite sites or bookmarks. Bookmarks that are grouped into subfolders are presented via cascading menus (see Figure 8.6).

Action Buttons

The handy `<input />` element provides an easy way of creating the form action buttons you see in many of the preceding figures. Action buttons can be of two types: Submit and Reset. Clicking a Submit button instructs the browser to package the form data and send it to the server. Clicking a Reset button clears out any data entered into the form and sets all the named input fields back to their default values.

Regular Submit and Reset Buttons Any form you compose should have a Submit button so that users can submit the data they enter. The one exception to this rule is a form containing only one input field. For such a form, pressing Enter automatically submits the data. Reset buttons are technically not necessary but are usually provided as a user courtesy.

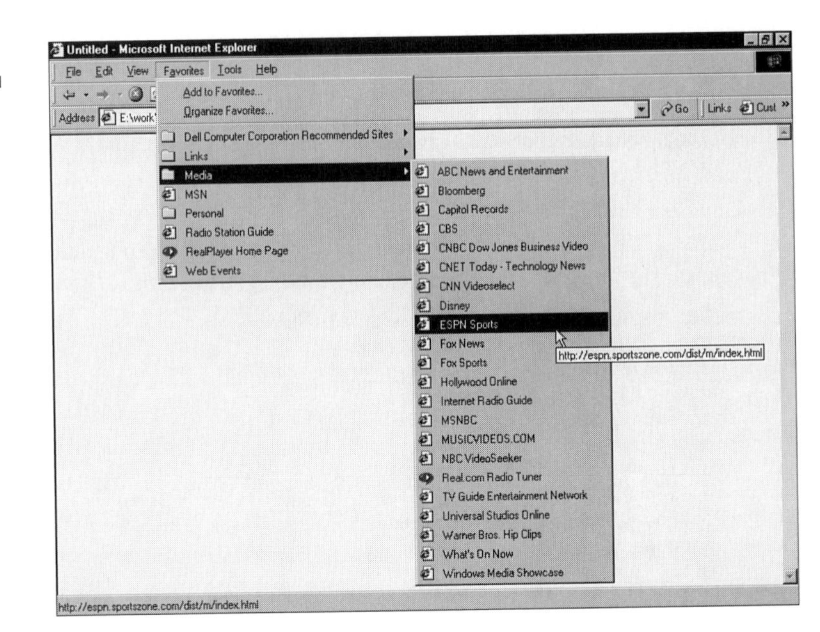

FIGURE 8.6
Logically grouped menu options may someday be available via cascading menus, like Internet Explorer favorites are.

> **TIP** Even though you technically don't need to include a Submit button on a single-field form, you should do so as a guide for users who are less experienced with Web forms.
>
> If you want to get fancy, you can leave the Submit button off and use the JavaScript `submit()` method to submit the form. See Chapter 19, "The Document Object Model," for more details.

To create Submit or Reset buttons, use the `<input />` element as follows:

```
<input type="submit" value="Submit Data" />
<input type="reset" value="Clear Data" />
```

Use the `value` attribute to specify the text that appears on the button. You should set `value` to a text string that concisely describes the function of the button. If `value` is not specified, the button text is "Submit" for Submit buttons and "Reset" for Reset buttons.

Using Images as Submit Buttons You can create a custom image to be a Submit button for your forms, and you can set up the image so that clicking it instructs the browser to submit the form data. To do this, you set `type` equal to `image` in your `<input />` element, and you provide the URL of the image you want to use with the `src` attribute:

```
<input type="image" src="images/submit_button.gif" />
```

Figure 8.7 shows how amazon.com uses a GIF image in place of a standard submit button on its login page. The code to produce the form and the image-based submit button appears in Listing 8.6.

FIGURE 8.7
Clicking this image on amazon.com's site prompts your browser to submit the data collected by the form on the page.

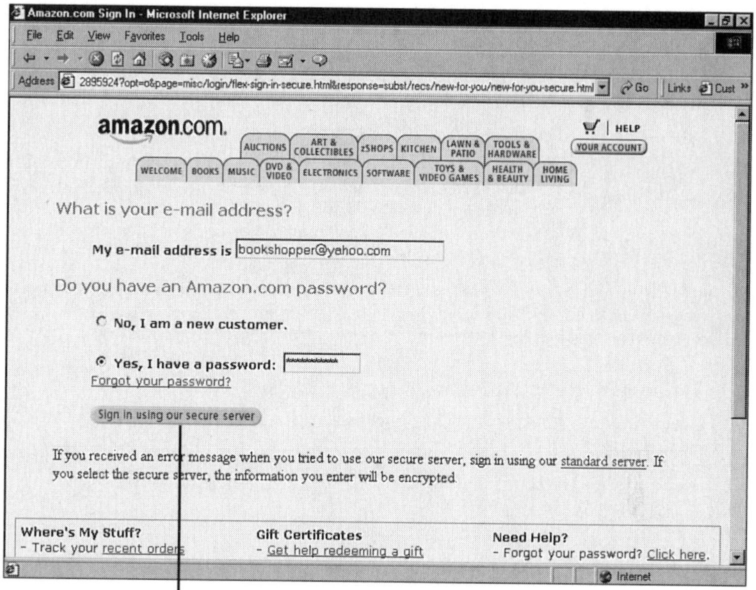

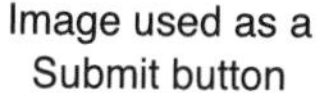

Image used as a Submit button

If you're using the Transitional or Frameset DTD, you can also use the `align` attribute in this variation of the `<input />` element to control how text appears next to the image (`top`, `middle`, or `bottom`), or to float the image in the left or right margin (`left` or `right`).

Image Mapped Submit Buttons

A future possibility for image-based Submit buttons is to include the `usemap` attribute so that clicking different parts of the image would cause different instructions to be sent to the server. The various instructions would be set up using the `<area />` element, the same as you set up different URLs in a client-side image map. Some details about how the browser would gather and pass the coordinates of the click still need to be ironed out, however, before this becomes standard. Until then, the `usemap` attribute has been reserved for use with the `<input type="image"/>` element just for this purpose.

Listing 8.6 XHTML Code to Produce an Image-Based Submit Button

```
<font face="verdana,arial,helvetica" size="-1">
<b>My e-mail address is</b>
</font>
<input name="email" type="text" size="30" maxlength="64" /><br />
<strong><font face="verdana,arial,helvetica" color="#CC6600">
Do you have an Amazon.com password?</font></strong><br/ >
```

Listing 8.6 Continued

```
<input type="radio" name="action" value="continue" />
<font face="verdana,arial,helvetica" size="-1">
<b>No&#44; I am a new customer.</b></font><br />
<input type="radio" name="action" value="sign-in checked" />
<font face="verdana,arial,helvetica" size="-1">
<b>Yes&#44; I have a password:</b></font>
<input type="hidden" name="next-page"
➥value="misc/login/flex-register-secure.html" />
<input name="password" type="password" size="10" maxlength="20" /><br />
<input type="image" src="images/submit_button.gif" />
```

Scripted Buttons A relatively new variant on action buttons is the *scripted button*—one that executes a client-side script when clicked. To create a scripted button, you still use the `<input/>` element, but with `type` set equal to `button`. The `value` attribute still specifies what text should appear on the face of the button.

By default, a button created in this way has no behavior associated with it. To make the button do something when clicked, you need to include the `onclick` event handler. You set `onclick` equal to a name of a script that has presumably been set up using the `<script>` element earlier in the document. Thus, the code to produce a fully defined scripted button might look like this:

```
<input type="button" value="Check data" onclick="checkdata()" />
```

Set up in this way, the button sends an instruction to the browser to execute the scripted function `checkdata` whenever it is clicked.

▶ To learn more about JavaScript-enabled forms, **see** Chapter 21, "Using JavaScript to Create Smart Forms"

The <*button*> Element The `<button>` element was introduced to allow for action buttons with better presentation features. The first thing to note about the `<button>` element is that it is a container element. What goes inside the `<button>` element has everything to do with how the button looks onscreen. If only text is between the elements, that text appears on the face of the button. If an `<img />` element is between them, the image is used as the button.

`<button>` takes the `type` attribute, which can be set to `submit`, `reset`, or `button`. Each of these options produces a button similar to the ones you get by using the `<input />` element with the same `type` values, but subtle differences exist in how the buttons appear onscreen. This is particularly so in the case of image-based buttons, which are rendered three-dimensionally (with a drop shadow) and which move down when clicked and up when released.

`<button>` can take the `name` and `value` attributes as well. You need to assign a name to a button when it is a Submit button in a set of more than one. The `value` attribute gets passed to the server when the button is clicked.

Labeling Input Fields

As noted earlier in the chapter, it's up to you as a form author to include prompting text in front of your form fields to suggest to a user how he or she should fill in the field. The XHTML `<label>` element formalizes the relationship between the prompting text (the label) and the form field it is paired with. `<label>` takes the `for` attribute, where `for` is set equal to the `id` attribute value of the associated form field. In the example

```
<label for="Zip">Enter your 9-digit ZIP code: </label>
<input type="text" name="ZipCode" id="Zip" />
```

the prompting text "Enter your 9-digit ZIP code:" composes the label. Note how the label is associated with the subsequent field with the matching `for` and `id` attributes.

How a label is rendered varies from browser to browser, so you should continue to place labels and their associated form fields in tables for proper alignment. Thus, the preceding example is better done as

```
<form ...>
<table>
<tr>
<td><label for="Zip">Enter your 9-digit ZIP code: </label></td>
<td><input type="text" name="ZipCode" id="Zip" /></td>
</tr>
</table>
...
</form>
```

NOTE You can also implicitly associate a label with a form field by placing the element that created the field inside the `<label>` element. Done this way, the form field in the previous example looks like this:

```
<label>Enter your 9-digit ZIP code:
➥<input type="text" name="ZipCode" /></label>
```

Although this might reduce how much you have to type, it's worth noting that this approach precludes you from putting your labels and form fields in their own table cells.

Although labels might not seem to do much for you, they're important to include for visually impaired users who use speech-based browsers. In this case, the browser knows to treat the label as prompting text for a form field, and it instructs the user accordingly.

Additionally, you can associate an *access key* with your form field label by using the `accesskey` attribute. `accesskey` is set equal to a single letter from the user's keyboard.

After it is set up, users can use the accesskey keystroke to go directly to the associated form field (an action called *giving focus* to the field) and fill it in. Expanding the previous password example to include an access key yields the following:

```
<form ...>
<table>
<tr>
<td>
<label for="Zip" accesskey="Z">Enter your 9-digit <U>Z</U>IP code: </label>
</td>
<td><input type="text" name="ZipCode" id="Zip"/></td>
</tr>
</table>
...
</form>
```

The accesskey attribute in the <label> element associates the letter Z with the form field label. Thus, whenever Windows users type Alt+Z or Macintosh users type Cmd+Z, they give focus to the Password field, which means that the cursor moves there and enables the user to type in a Zip code.

If you assign an accesskey to a form field label, be sure you make the key known to your users. In the preceding example, the letter Z in Zip code was put inside a <u> element so that it would appear underlined. This is consistent with the way Windows programs label their access keys (for example, the underlined F in the File menu means you can press Alt+F to activate the menu).

You can use the accesskey attribute with the <a> element as well. This way, users can jump to a linked document by pressing the access key rather than by clicking the link.

Grouping Related Fields

Two other XHTML form elements that recognize the use of nonvisual browsers are the <fieldset> and <legend> elements. <fieldset> enables you to group related form fields together in a logical group, and <legend> enables you to assign descriptive text to the group of fields. Neither of these might seem necessary on a standard visual browser, but for a visually impaired user with a speech-based browser, these extra features make a form much more usable.

NOTE One advantage of using <fieldset> grouping on a visual browser is that it facilitates tabbing through the form field. After the browser knows about a group of fields, it can tab you through the fields in sequence.

<fieldset> is a container element that does not have any attributes. To create a logical grouping of fields, you place the elements that create the fields inside a <fieldset> element.

Each logical <fieldset> grouping can have a <legend> element associated with it. The text inside the <legend> element captions the grouping. If you are validating against the Transitional or Frameset DTD, you can use the align attribute in the <legend> element to align the legend text with respect to the grouped fields. Possible values for align in this case are top, bottom, left, and right.

NOTE Aligning the legend text produces an effect only on visual browsers.

<legend> can also take the accesskey attribute so that you can set up an access key for the form field grouping.

As an example of how <fieldset> and <legend> work together, consider the following example:

```
<form ...>
<fieldset>
<legend align="left">Shipping Address</legend>
<table>
<tr>
<td colspan="2">Address:</td>
<td colspan="4"><input type="text" name="SH_ADDR" /></td>
</tr>
<tr>
<td>City:</td>
<td><input type="text" name="SH_CITY" /></td>
<td>State:</td>
<td><input type="text" name="SH_STATE" /></td>
<td>Zip:</td>
<td><input type="text" name="SH_ZIP" /></td>
</tr>
</table>
</fieldset>
<fieldset>
<legend align="left">Billing Address</legend>
<table>
<tr>
<td colspan="2">Address:</td>
<td colspan="4"><input type="text" name="BL_ADDR" /></td>
</tr>
<tr>
<td>City:</td>
<td><input type="text" name="BL_CITY" /></td>
<td>State:</td>
<td><input type="text" name="BL_STATE" /></td>
<td>Zip:</td>
<td><input type="text" name="BL_ZIP" /></td>
</tr>
</table>
</fieldset>
...
</form>
```

In the preceding code, the form fields are grouped into two logical groups: shipping address fields and billing address fields. On a visual browser, the legend text Shipping Address and Billing Address appears above each logical grouping.

Disabled and Read-Only Fields

Many of the XHTML 1.0 form elements accept attributes that render the fields they produce as disabled—meaning the field is grayed out—or as read only, which means that the text that initially appears in the field cannot be changed. The `disabled` attribute takes care of disabling a field and can be used with the following elements:

- `<input />`
- `<label>`
- `<select>`
- `<option>`
- `<textarea>`
- `<button>`

You might want to disable an option in a drop-down list, for example, if you know from other information gathered from the user that the option was inappropriate to present.

NOTE Disabled form fields are skipped over as a user tabs through the form. Also, any values assigned to a disabled field are not passed to the server when the form is submitted.

The `readonly` attribute works only for the `<input />` element with `type` set to `text` or `password` and the `<textarea>` element because these are the only elements that can be prepopulated with text. In these cases, the text is presented only for the user's information, not so that it can be changed.

NOTE Read-only form fields are included when a user tabs through a form, and values assigned to these fields are passed to the server upon form submission.

Form Field Event Handlers

The W3C has also added a number of scripting event handlers to work with many of the form elements to facilitate the execution of script code while a user fills out a form. These event handlers include

- `onfocus`
- `onblur`

- onselect
- onchange

Two of the most widely usable event handlers are onfocus and onblur. Recall that a field receives focus when you've tabbed to it or clicked it to make it active. At the moment a field receives focus, you can choose to execute a script by setting the onfocus attribute of the corresponding form field element equal to the name of a script defined in the document.

When you tab out of a form field that has focus, the field is said to blur. You can execute a script when a blur event occurs by setting onblur equal to the name of the script you want to run.

onfocus and onblur can be used with the following XHTML form elements:

- <button>
- <input />
- <label>
- <select>
- <textarea>

Additionally, the <input />, <select>, and <textarea> elements can take the onselect and onchange event handlers that launch scripts when the field is selected or changed.

All these form event handlers are useful for invoking JavaScript functions that validate the data in the form field. Chapter 19 introduces you to the scripting techniques you can employ to perform the validation tests.

Passing Form Data

After a user enters form data and clicks a Submit button, the browser does two things. First, it encodes the form data into a single string. Then it sends the encoded string to the server by either the get or post HTTP method. The next two sections close out the chapter by providing details on each of these steps.

URL Encoding

When a user clicks the Submit button on a form, the browser gathers all the form data and assembles it into a string of name=value pairs, each separated by an ampersand (&) character. This process is called *encoding*. It is done to package the data into one string that is sent to the server.

Consider the following HTML code:

```
<form action="http://www.server.com/cgi-bin/process_it.cgi" method="post">
     Favorite color: <input type="text" name="Color" />
```

```
    Favorite movie: <input type="text" name="Movie" />
    <input type="submit" />
</form>
```

If a user's favorite color is green and his favorite movie is *Fargo*, his browser creates the following data string and sends it to the CGI script:

```
Color=green&Movie=Fargo
```

If the `get` method is used instead of `post`, the same string is appended to the URL of the processing script, producing the following encoded URL:

```
http://www.server.com/cgi-bin/process_it.cgi?Color=green&Movie=Fargo
```

A question mark (?) separates the script URL from the encoded data string. The data you see to the right of the question mark is called the *query string*.

Storing Encoded URLs

As you learned in the previous discussion of URL encoding, packaging form data into a single text string follows a few simple formatting rules. Consequently, you can fake a script into believing that it is receiving form data without using a form. To do so, you send the URL that would be constructed if a form were used. This approach can be useful if you frequently run a script with the same data set.

Suppose, for example, you frequently search the Web index Yahoo! for new documents related to XHTML. If you are interested in checking for new documents several times a day, you could fill out the Yahoo! search query each time. A more efficient way, however, is to store the query URL as a bookmark. Each time you select that item from your bookmarks, a new query generates as if you had filled out the form. The stored URL looks like the following:

```
http://search.yahoo.com/bin/search?p=XHTML
```

Further encoding occurs with data that is more complex than a single word. Such encoding replaces spaces with the plus character (+) and translates any other possibly troublesome character (control characters, ampersand, equal sign, some punctuation, and so on) to a percent sign, followed by its hexadecimal equivalent. Thus, the following string:

```
I love XHTML!
```

becomes

```
I+love+XHTML%21
```

HTTP Methods

You have two ways to read the form data submitted to a CGI script, depending on the method the form used. The type of method the form used—either `get` or `post`—is stored in an environment variable called `REQUEST_METHOD` and, based on that, the data should be read in one of the following ways:

- If the data is sent by the `get` method, the input stream is stored in an environment variable called `QUERY_STRING`. As noted previously, this input stream usually is limited to about 1KB of data. This is why `get` is losing popularity to the more flexible `post`.
- If the data is submitted by the `post` method, the input string waits on the server's input device, with the available number of bytes stored in the environment variable `CONTENT_LENGTH`. `post` accepts data of any length, although it is not yet very common for form submissions to be that large.

▶ To learn more about environment variables, **see** "Standard CGI Environment Variables," **p. 744**

If you are writing your CGI scripts in Perl, you need to be aware of which HTTP method is used to send data to the server and which environment variable to use to help you get at the data. More recent server-side scripting techniques, such as Active Server Pages and ColdFusion, bundle the data for you in certain memory objects, making it much easier for you to reference the data.

▶ To learn how to process forms with Active Server Pages, **see** Chapter 32, "Writing Active Server Pages"

▶ To learn how to handle form data with ColdFusion, **see** Chapter 33, "Using ColdFusion"

CHAPTER 9

Style Sheets

by Eric Ladd

In this chapter

What Are Style Sheets?

Two forces compete in Web page authoring: content and presentation. When HTML was first released, the tags were largely focused on content, and they descriptively defined the various parts of a document: a heading, a paragraph, a list, and so on. Over time, instructions were added to help with presentation issues at the font level. These instructions included tags for boldface, italic, and typewriter styles.

Then, as graphical browsers became standard equipment, a greatly increased focus on presentation began. In particular, Netscape introduced proprietary extensions to HTML that only its browser could render properly. These extensions generally produced attractive effects on pages, and users began using Netscape en masse. Not to be left out, Microsoft began producing its own browser—Internet Explorer—and with it, its own proprietary HTML extensions. Content authors, who could only watch the new tags emerge, were frequently left confused and frustrated because it was hard to tell which browser to write for and how long it would be before the next new set of bells and whistles became available.

With the advent of XHTML, content authors will be forced into a position in which they will have to explicitly separate content from presentation. This is accomplished by use of a *style sheet*—a separate file that associates presentation attributes with particular markup elements. For many authors, the transition to use style sheets will not be terribly difficult because of their experience with Cascading Style Sheets (CSS) for developing HTML pages. The World Wide Web Consortium's first stab at separating content and presentation was the Cascading Style Sheets, level 1 (CSS1) specification—a formal statement on how to specify style information. In 1998, the W3C released Cascading Style Sheets, level 2 (CSS2) as a published recommendation, and that is the prevailing standard for Web-based style sheets. This chapter introduces you to CSS2 and how to use it to apply style information to your existing content.

NOTE The next standard—Cascading Style Sheets, level 3—is in the works. You can read about some of the features expected in CSS3 in a special section at the end of this chapter.

The current CSS level 2 standard can be found at `http://www.w3.org/TR/1998/REC-CSS2-19980512`. ■

Before you look at the different ways to build style information into your pages, it will be helpful to review some of the basics behind the concept of a style sheet.

Style sheets are collections of style information that are applied to plain text. Style information includes font attributes such as type size, special effects (bold, italic, underline), color, and alignment. Style sheets also provide broader formatting instructions by specifying values for quantities such as line spacing and left and right margins.

Style sheets are not really a new concept; word processing programs such as Microsoft Word have been using user-defined style for several years. Figure 9.1 shows a Word style definition in the Style dialog box. Notice how the style accounts for many of the presentation attributes previously mentioned.

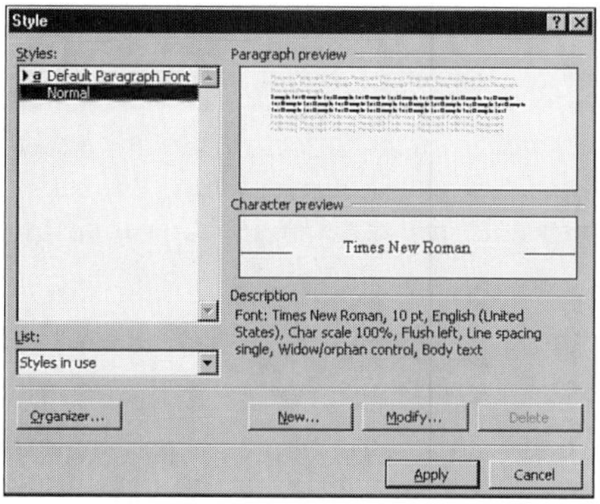

FIGURE 9.1
Word processors enable users to store content presentation attributes together as a style.

Why Style Sheets Are Valuable

Simply put, style sheets separate content and presentation. Apart from being necessary for specifying style information for XHTML documents adhering to the Strict Document Type Definition (DTD), it gives Web page designers precise control over how their content appears onscreen. Other benefits of style sheets include

- **Central repositories of style information**—If you use a standard set of styles on all your pages, you can store the corresponding style information in one file. This way, if you must edit the style information, you have to make the change in only one place instead of in every file.
- **No pressure to extend the markup language**—By capturing all presentation-related information in style sheets, the associated markup language will not be under pressure to evolve to include elements that describe how the content should look. Markup languages are free to be true markup languages that only describe the structure of the content.
- **Consistent rendering of content**—Browsers vary slightly in how they render content, especially the logical text styles (emphasized text [`<em>`], keyboard input [`<kbd>`], and so on). By assigning specific style information to logical style elements in XHTML, Web page authors can be assured that their content will look the same on every browser.

Additionally, Cascading Style Sheets are important for the rendering of general XML documents, not just XHTML documents. Until the XML Style Language (XSL) is finalized, CSS will continue to be the principal means for displaying data in an XML document.

▶ To learn more about how to render XML documents with CSS, **see** Chapter 10, "Introducing XML"

Different Approaches to Style Sheets

The W3C advocates the Cascading Style Sheet proposal for implementing style sheets. *Cascading* refers to a certain set of rules that browsers use, in cascading order, to determine how to use the style information. Such a set of rules is useful in the event of conflicting style information because the rules would give the browser a way to determine which style is given precedence.

The CSS2 recommendation supports three ways of including style information in a document. These approaches include

- **Linked styles**—Style information is read from a separate file that is specified in the `<link />` element.
- **Embedded styles**—Style information is defined in the `<style>` element in the document head.
- **Inline styles**—Style information is placed inside an XHTML element and applies to all content between that tag and its companion closing tag. You can left-indent an entire paragraph one-half inch, for example, by using `<p style="margin-left: .5 in">` to start the paragraph. If the content to which you want to apply style information isn't conveniently grouped by a set of container tags, you can also use the `<span>` element to do the same job.

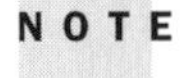

NOTE Note that the remarks apply to all versions of the XHTML DTD—Strict, Transitional, and Frameset. ■

Using Multiple Approaches

You aren't limited to using only one of the described style sheet approaches. You can use all three simultaneously if needed. One case in which you might want to do this is on an intranet site where you have the following:

- **Global styles**—Certain styles used on every page are best stored in a single style sheet file and linked to each page with the `<link />` element. This might apply to styles mandated as a corporate standard, such as the use of a plain white background and a single typeface.
- **Subsection styles**—Intranet sites typically have many subdivisions, each with its own look and feel. To support a subdivision's look, you can store styles within the `<STYLE>` element in the head of each document in the subdivision. The subdivisions might represent different business units within the corporation, or it can just be a set of related documents, such as product specs or white papers.

- **Page-specific styles**—If you need to make a small deviation from your chosen global or subsection styles, you can use an inline style to make the change where you want it. You might use a page-specific style if a page in one of your subdivisions has particular presentation requirements. A key passage in a white paper, for example, might be highlighted by rendering it in bold and in color.

However, you shouldn't use all three approaches in the same document just for the sake of doing it. You should seek to optimize your use of style sheets by choosing the approach or combination of approaches that enables you to apply the styles you want, where you want them, without a lot of unnecessary code.

Remember style precedence when using multiple approaches. The idea behind a Cascading Style Sheet is that browsers apply a set of rules in cascading order to determine which style information takes precedence. You must be aware of these rules so you do not produce unintended style effects on your pages. In general, you'll be fine if you remember the following:

- Inline styles override both linked style sheets and style information stored in the document head with the `<style>` element.
- Styles defined in the document head override linked style sheets.
- Linked style sheets override browser defaults.

Keeping these rules in mind will make troubleshooting your style sheets much easier.

NOTE One important point for content authors to remember is that users can develop style sheets of their own. CSS2 supports the `!important` keyword in the specification of any property, which enables the user's style sheet to override the specification in the author's style sheet. ■

Linking to Style Information in a Separate File

One important thing to realize is that you don't have to store your style sheet information inside each of your XHTML documents. If you anticipate applying the same styles across several XHTML pages, it is much more efficient for you to store the style information in one place and have each XHTML document linked to it. This makes it much easier to change the formatting of all your pages by changing the style sheet instead of changing every page.

Setting Up the Style Information

To set up a linked style sheet, you first need to create the file with the style information. This takes the form of a plain-text file with style information entries. Each entry starts with an XHTML element, followed by a list of presentation attributes to associate with the rendering of the effect of that element. Some sample lines in a style sheet file might look like this:

```
body { bgcolor: white; margin-left: 0.25in}
p {font 10 pt Arial; color: navy}
h1 {font 16 pt Arial; color: CC3366}
```

The first line sets the background color of the document to white and the left margin to a value of one-quarter inch. The second line says that all content within a <p> element should be rendered in navy blue 10-point Arial type, and the third line sets the level 1 16-point Arial type, rendered in the color represented by the hexadecimal triplet CC3366.

NOTE When setting colors in your style sheet file, you can use one of the 16 English-language color names or an RGB hexadecimal triplet to describe the color. The acceptable English-language color names are

aqua	lime	red
black	maroon	silver
blue	navy	teal
fuchsia	olive	white
gray	purple	yellow
green		

Remember that the syntax for specifying a characteristic has the form

```
{characteristic: value}
```

Multiple characteristic/value pairs should be separated by semicolons. For example,

```
em {font: 14 pt Times New Roman; line-height: 16 pt; color: black}
```

CAUTION

When you first start to work with style sheets, you might be tempted to use the syntax "*characteristic=value*." Make sure you use the "*characteristic: value*" syntax previously noted.

The Cascading Style Sheet specification enables you to specify more than fonts, typefaces, and colors. Table 9.1 lists some of the common font and block level style attributes content authors control when using style sheets.

Table 9.1 Font and Block Level Characteristics Permitted in Style Sheets

Characteristic	Possible Values
`font-family`	Any typeface available to the browser through the operating system (the default font is used if one of the specified fonts is not available)
`font-size`	Any size in points (pt), inches (in), centimeters (cm), or pixels (px); larger or smaller (relative-size values); xx-small, x-small, small, medium, large, x-large, xx-large (absolute-size values); or a percentage relative to the parent font's size
`font-weight`	Normal, bold; bolder, lighter, 100, 200, 300, 400, 500 (default weight), 600, 700, 800, 900
`font-style`	Normal, italic, oblique
`font-variant`	Normal, small caps
`color`	Any RGB hexadecimal triplet or English-language color name
`background-attachment`	(Whether the background image stays fixed or scrolls with the content) scroll, fixed
`background-color`	Transparent; any RGB hexadecimal triplet or HTML 4.0 English-language color name
`background-image`	None; URL of image file
`background-repeat`	Repeat-x (tile background image only in the horizontal direction), repeat-y (tile only in the vertical direction), repeat (tile in both directions), no-repeat (no tiling)
`border-color`	Any RGB hexadecimal triplet or English-language color name
`border-style`	None, dashed, dotted, solid, double, groove, ridge, inset, outset
`border-bottom-width`	Thin, medium, thick; any number of points (pt), inches (in), centimeters (cm), or pixels (px)
`border-left-width`	Thin, medium, thick; any number of points (pt), inches (in), centimeters (cm), or pixels (px)
`border-right-width`	Thin, medium, thick; any number of points (pt), inches (in), centimeters (cm), or pixels (px)
`border-top-width`	Thin, medium, thick; any number of points (pt), inches (in), centimeters (cm), or pixels (px)
`border-bottom-color`	Any RGB hexadecimal triplet or English-language color name
`border-left-color`	Any RGB hexadecimal triplet or English-language color name

Table 9.1 Continued

Characteristic	Possible Values
`border-right-color`	Any RGB hexadecimal triplet or English-language color name
`border-top-color`	Any RGB hexadecimal triplet or English-language color name
`float`	Left, right, none; floats positioned content in left or right margin, thereby allowing other content to wrap around it
`padding-bottom`	Any number of points (pt), inches (in), centimeters (cm), or pixels (px); or a percentage of the parent element's width
`padding-left`	Any number of points (pt), inches (in), centimeters (cm), or pixels (px); or a percentage of the parent element's width
`padding-right`	Any number of points (pt), inches (in), centimeters (cm), or pixels (px); or a percentage of the parent element's width
`padding-top`	Any number of points (pt), inches (in), centimeters (cm), or pixels (px); or a percentage of the parent element's width
`text-align`	Left, center, right, justify
`text-decoration`	None, underline, overline, line-through, blink
`text-indent`	Any number of points (pt), inches (in), centimeters (cm), or pixels (px); or a percentage relative to the indentation of the parent element
`text-shadow`	The shadow offset is required and can be set to any number of points (pt), inches (in), centimeters (cm), or pixels (px); specification of blur radius and shadow color is optional
`text-transform`	Capitalize, uppercase, lowercase, none
`line-height`	Normal; any number of points (pt), inches (in), centimeters (cm), or pixels (px); or a percentage of the font size
`letter-spacing`	Normal; any number of points (pt), inches (in), cen timeters (cm), or pixels (px)
`word-spacing`	Normal; any number of points (pt), inches (in), cen timeters (cm), or pixels (px)
`margin-left`	Auto; any number of points (pt), inches (in), centimeters (cm), or pixels (px); or a percentage of the parent element's width

Table 9.1 Continued

Characteristic	Possible Values
`margin-right`	Auto; any number of points (pt), inches (in), centimeters (cm), or pixels (px); or a percentage of the parent element's width
`margin-top`	Auto; any number of points (pt), inches (in), centimeters (cm), or pixels (px); or a percentage of the parent element's width
`margin-bottom`	Auto; any number of points (pt), inches (in), centimeters (cm), or pixels (px); or a percentage of the parent element's width
`vertical-align`	Baseline, sub, super, top, text-top, middle, bottom, text-bottom; or a percentage of the current line-height

NOTE `line-height` in Table 9.1 refers to the leading, or space between lines, that the browser uses. `padding` refers to the amount of space left around all four sides of a page element. ■

You can see from the table that you get control over a large number of presentation characteristics. In addition to the font and block level properties noted in Table 9.1, CSS2 includes characteristics that give you control over how your content is positioned on the browser screen. The common content positioning characteristics, summarized in Table 9.2, enable you to precisely place any portion of your content, even overlapping other content in some cases.

Table 9.2 Content Positioning Characteristics Permitted in Style Sheets

Characteristic	Purpose and Possible Values
`position`	Specifies how content is to be positioned; possible values are static (content cannot be positioned or repositioned), absolute (content is positioned with respect to the upper-left corner of the browser window), and relative (content is positioned with respect to its natural position in the document)
`top`	Specifies the vertical displacement of the positioned content from the top edge of its container; values can be in points (pt), pixels (px), centimeters (cm), or inches (in) and can have negative values (a negative value moves content above its reference point on the screen)
`left`	Specifies the horizontal displacement of positioned content from the left edge of its container; values can be in points (pt), pixels (px), centimeters (cm), or inches (in) and can have negative values (a negative value moves content to the left of its reference point on the screen)

Table 9.2 Continued

Characteristic	Purpose and Possible Values
`bottom`	Specifies the vertical displacement of the positioned content from bottom edge of its container; values can be in points (pt), pixels (px), centimeters (cm), or inches (in) and can have negative values (a negative value moves content above its reference point on the screen)
`right`	Specifies the horizontal displacement of positioned content from the right edge of its container; values can be in points (pt), pixels (px), centimeters (cm), or inches (in) and can have negative values (a negative value moves content to the left of its reference point on the screen)
`clip:rect(x1,y1,x2,y2)`	Defines the size of the clipping region (rectangular area in which the positioned content appears); (x1,y1) are the coordinates of the upper-left corner of the rectangle and (x2,y2) are the coordinates of the lower-right corner
`overflow`	Tells the browser how to handle positioned content that overflows the space allocated for it; possible values are visible, hidden, auto, and scroll
`visibility`	Enables the document author to selectively display or conceal positioned content; possible values are visible or hidden
`z-index`	Permits stacking of positioned content in the browser screen so that content overlaps; z-index is set to an integer value of 0 or higher (content with a smaller z-index will be positioned below content with higher z-index values)

Both Netscape and Microsoft have bundled their support for content positioning as part of the "Dynamic HTML" capabilities of their browsers. Although both browsers support content positioning by means of Cascading Style Sheets, Netscape initially tried to implement positioned content through the proprietary `<layer>` element. Currently, Navigator 4.0 supports both the CSS and the `<element>` tag approaches.

NOTE Content positioning is discussed in great detail in Chapter 24, "Introduction to Dynamic HTML," Chapter 25, "Advanced Microsoft Dynamic HTML," and Chapter 26, "Advanced Netscape Dynamic HTML." ■

Using the *<link />* Element

After you create your style sheet file, save it in text format with a `.css` extension and place it on your server. Then you can reference it by using the `<link />` element in the head of each of your XHTML documents, as follows:

```
<head>
<title>A Document that Uses Style Sheets</title>
<link rel="stylesheet" href="styles/sitestyles.css" />
</head>
```

The `rel` attribute describes the relationship of the linked file to the current file, namely that the linked file is a style sheet. `href` specifies the URL of the style sheet file.

CAUTION

Style sheet files are of MIME type `text/css`, although not all servers and browsers register this automatically. If you set up a site that uses style sheets, be sure to configure your server to handle the MIME type `text/css`.

Embedded Style Information

Figure 9.2 shows the W3C's page for the Extensible Stylesheet Language (XSL). The style information is stored in the document head, as shown in the excerpt of XHTML source code in Listing 9.1. The first line says that the `<div>` element of class `main` should have a 40-pixel top margin. Next, it says that level 1 headings should have a 24-pixel bottom margin, and finally that terms in a definition list should be rendered in italics. The rest of the style information is devoted to setting up style classes. These classes can then be referenced by multiple tags by using the `class` attribute.

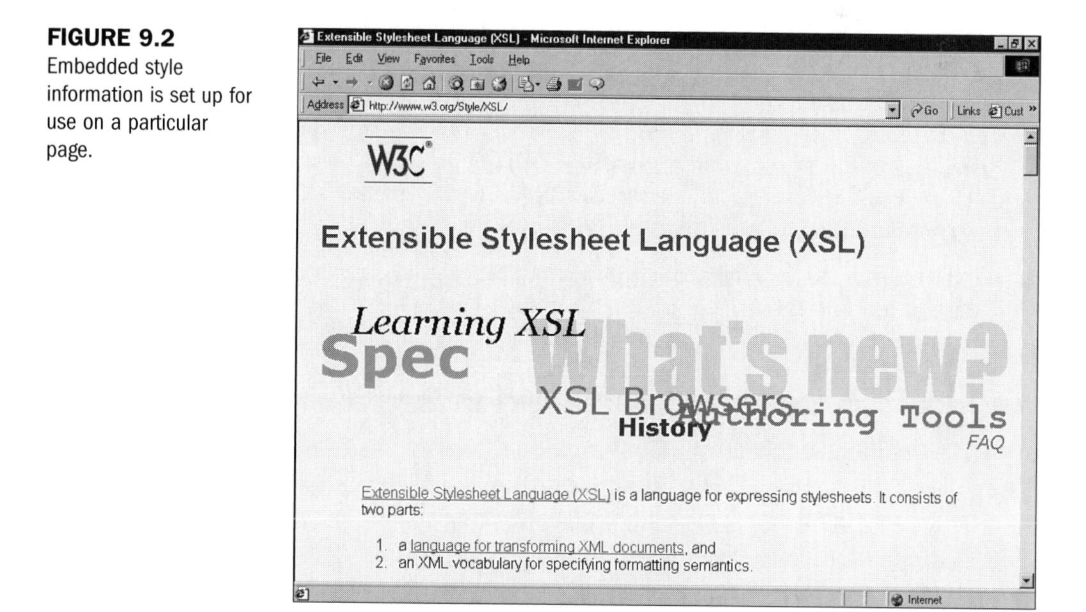

FIGURE 9.2
Embedded style information is set up for use on a particular page.

Listing 9.1 Embedded Style Information in the W3C's XSL Home Page

```
<style type="text/css">
<!--
div.main { margin-top: 40px }
h1 { margin-bottom: 24px }
dt { font-style: italic }
.date {color: #063; font-style: italic }
.xslj { font-style: italic }
-->
</style>
```

Using the <*style*> Element

As you can see in Listing 9.1, embedded style information is placed inside the `<style>` element. When the W3C released HTML 3.2, it reserved the use of this element specifically for the purpose of embedded style information. The XHTML 1.0 recommendation now formalizes the use of the `<style>` element.

The `type` attribute tells a browser what type of style information setup is used and is most often set equal to `text/css`. Specifying other types allows for some flexibility in the implementation of other style information specification schemes in the future. This also makes it easier for browsers that do not support style sheets to ignore the style information between the two tags.

Style information of the MIME type `text/css` is set up the same way that style information is set up in a linked style sheet file. The first entry on each line names an XHTML element and is followed by a list of characteristic/value pairs enclosed in curly braces. You can use any of the characteristics shown in Tables 9.1 or 9.2 when specifying your embedded style information.

NOTE Note that the style information you see in Listing 9.1 is enclosed in comment markers (`<!--` and `-->`), so browsers that do not understand style sheets will ignore the style information rather than presenting it onscreen.

Also, you need to conceal your style sheet code from the XML parser by enclosing it between `<![CDATA[` and `]]>` markers. These declared the code to be part of a character data section that is not parsed as markup. ■

▶ To learn more about XML character data sections, **see** Chapter 10, "Introducing XML"

> **TIP**
>
> Style information that is specified in the head of a document by using the `<style>` element can be used only in that document. If you want to use the same styles in another document, you need to embed the style information in the head of that document as well.
>
> Only use embedded style information for page-specific styles. If you have global style elements you want to implement, place them in a file and link the file as a style sheet in all your documents. Centralizing as much style information as possible is the best way to ensure a consistent implementation.

Inline Style Information

You can specify inline styles inside an XHTML element. The style information given applies to the document content up until the defining tag's companion closing tag is encountered. Consider the Morgan Stanley Dean Witter site in Figure 9.3. The code for one of the links down the left side of the screen is

```
<a href="institutional/clientlink/index.html"
onmouseout="out('link')" onmouseover="over('link')"
style="COLOR: #ffffff" target="top">
<b>ClientLink</b>
</a>
```

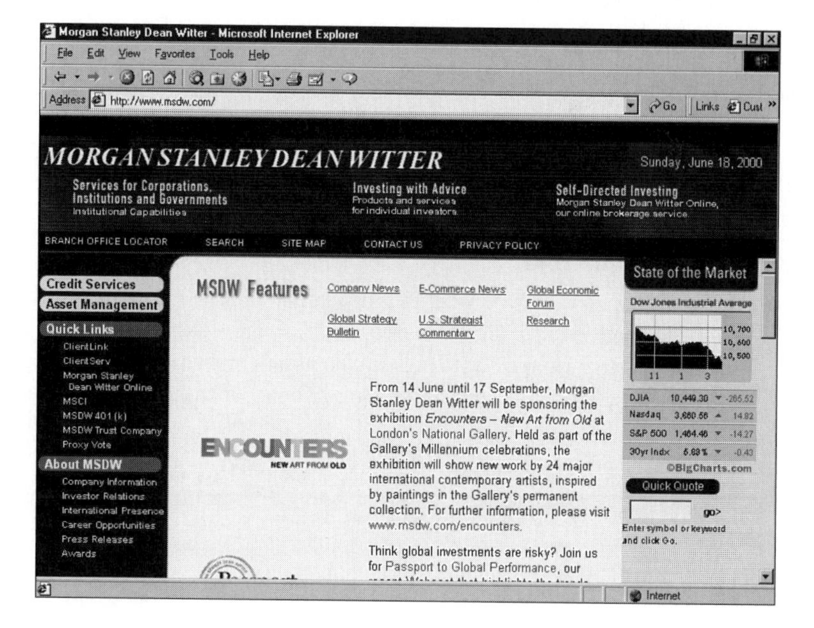

FIGURE 9.3
Many XHTML elements take the `style` attribute that specifies style information to apply to content contained within the element.

The `style` attribute in the <a> element causes the hypertext to be rendered in white. This helps it to show up better against the dark blue background.

CAUTION

Don't forget the closing tag when embedding style information in an XHTML element. Otherwise, the effects of the style might extend beyond the point in the document where you wanted them to stop. Additionally, the document will not be valid if you leave off the closing tag and are using a DTD.

XHTML Elements That Take the *style* Attribute

You saw in the preceding example that the <a> tag can take the `style` attribute to define an inline style. Many other tags can take the style attribute as well, including the following:

- **Physical style tags**—`<tt>`, `<i>`, `<b>`, `<u>`, `<s>`, `<strike>`, `<big>`, `<small>`, `<sub>`, `<sup>`
- **Logical style tags**—`<em>`, `<strong>`, `<dfn>`, `<code>`, `<samp>`, `<kbd>`, `<var>`, `<cite>`, `<abbr>`, `<acronym>`, `<ins>`, `<del>`, `<q>`
- **Block formatting tags**—`<body>`, `<br />`, `<blockquote>`, `<address>`, `<div>`, `<hr />`, `<center>`, `<h1>`, `<h2>`, `<h3>`, `<h4>`, `<h5>`, `<h6>`, `<pre>`, `<span>`, `<p>`
- **List tags**—`<ul>`, `<ol>`, `<li>`, `<dl>`, `<dt>`, `<dd>`
- **Image and linking tags**—`<img />`, `<map>`, `<a>`, `<area>`
- **Form tags**—`<form>`, `<label>`, `<input>`, `<select>`, `<optgroup>`, `<option>`, `<textarea>`, `<fieldset>`, `<legend>`, `<button>`
- **Table tags**—`<table>`, `<caption>`, `<colgroup>`, `<col />`, `<thead>`, `<tbody>`, `<tfoot>`, `<tr>`, `<th>`, `<td>`

The *<span>* Element

For those times when you want to apply a style to part of a document that is not nicely contained between two tags, you can use the <span> element to set up the part of the document that is to have the style applied. You assign style characteristics to the area set up by the <span> element by using the `style` attribute, as in the previous example with the <a> element.

As an example of how you might use the <span> element, consider the following code from the W3C's XSL home page:

```
<li>
<span class="date">000529</span>
<a href="http://users.ox.ac.uk/~rahtz/">Sebastian Rahtz</a> announces a new
release of <a href="http://users.ox.ac.uk/~rahtz/passivetex/">PassiveTeX</a>,
an implementation of the March 2000 draft.
</li>
```

The <span> element creates the colored, italicized dates seen on the W3C Web site shown in Figure 9.4.

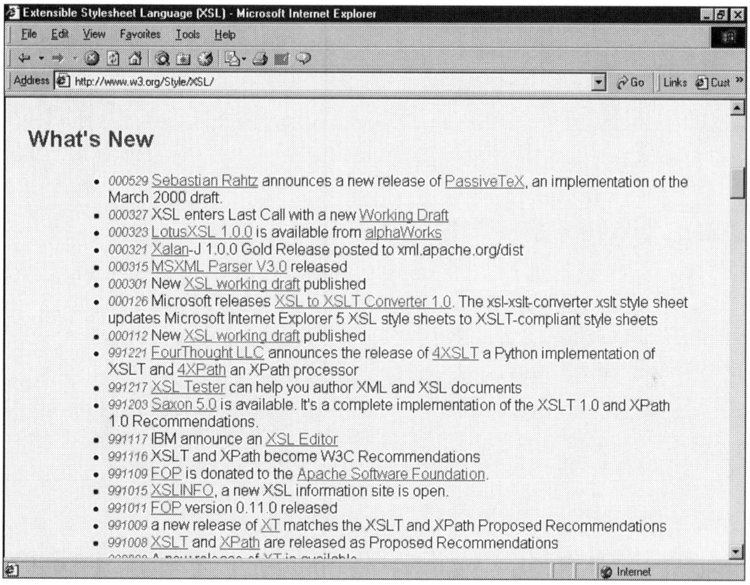

FIGURE 9.4
The <span> element enables you to assign style characteristics to content that is not neatly contained within another element.

> **TIP** Using inline styles is fine for changes to small sections of your document. However, you should consider using a linked style sheet or the <style> element if your styles are to be more widely used.

Tips for Style Sheet Users

Now that style sheets have been around for a few years, Web authors have had the chance to use them and identify a number of best practices. The next few sections share some of these helpful hints.

Harnessing Inheritance

Inheritance refers to the fact that XHTML documents are essentially set up as hierarchies, and styles applied at one level of the hierarchy necessarily apply to all subordinate levels (except where explicitly overridden by a more local style) as well.

Therefore, if you assign style information in a <ul> element, the information also applies to all the items in the unordered list because the <li> elements are subordinate to the <ul> element.

If you weren't using embedded style information (the `<style>` element), you can make broader use of inheritance by setting up as much common style information in the `<body>` element as you can. Because every tag within the `<body>` element is subordinate to the `<body>` element, these tags will inherit the style information you specify in the `<body>` element, and you should be spared from having to repeat it throughout the rest of the document.

Additionally, under CSS2, all presentation properties can take the keyword `inherit`, which forces an element to inherit the same value of the property as its parent element.

Grouping Style Information

If you want to assign the same style characteristics to several tags, you can do so in just one line rather than using a separate line for each tag. If you want all three kinds of links—unvisited, visited, and active—to be rendered in the same style, for example, you can list them all individually:

```
a:link {font-size: 10 pt; color: 00FF00; font-decoration: underline}
a:visited {font-size: 10 pt; color: 00FF00; font-decoration: underline}
a:active {font-size: 10 pt; color: 00FF00; font-decoration: underline}
```

Or you can define them all at once:

```
A:link A:visited A:active {font-size: 10 pt; color: 00FF00;
font-decoration: underline}
```

Either set of code will make all hypertext links appear in 10-point type that is green and underlined.

You can also group style information applied to only one tag. For example, if you redefined your level 2 headings as

```
h2 {font-size: 16 pt; line-height: 18 pt; font-family: "Helvetica";
font-weight: bold}
```

you can express the same thing as

```
H2 {font: 16pt/18pt "Helvetica" bold}
```

and save yourself a bit of typing.

Creating Tag Classes

The proposed style sheet specifications enable you to subdivide a tag into named classes and to specify different style information for each class. If you want three colors of unvisited links, for example, you can set them up as

```
a:link.red {color: red}
a:link.yellow {color: yellow}
a:link.fuschia {color: fuschia}
```

The period and color name that follow each `a:link` sets up a class of the `a:link` tag. The class name is whatever follows the period. You use the class names in the <a> element to specify which type of unvisited link you want to create, as follows:

```
Here's a <a class="red" href="red.html">red</a> link!
And a <a class="yellow" href="yellow.html">yellow</a> one ...
And a <a class="fuschia" href="fuschia.html">fuschia</a> one!
```

TIP If you use multiple style sheet approaches, make sure you define the same set of classes in all of them so the same set of class names is available to the browser in each case.

Using the *id* Attribute

You can also set up your own style names if setting up a named class doesn't suit your needs. For example, you can write

```
<style type="text/css">
<!--
...
#style1    { font-size: 16 pt; text-decoration: underline }
#style2    { font-size: 20 pt; text-decoration: blink}
...
-->
</style>
```

and then reference these styles using an `id` attribute in an element that can take the `style` attribute; for example,

```
<body id="style1" ...>
...
<p id="style2">
Here is a paragraph done in style2 ...
</p>
...
</body>
```

In this code excerpt, all the body text will be rendered in underlined, 16-point type as defined by the `style1` identifier, and text in the paragraph that starts "Here is a paragraph done in style2 ..." will be 20 points high and blinking, as specified by the `style2` identifier.

NOTE Named identifiers must start with the number sign (#) when you define them in a `<style>` element in your document. When you reference an identifier with the `id` attribute, the pound sign isn't necessary. ■

Style Sheets and Accessibility

The W3C made important strides in content accessibility when it added characteristics to CSS2 that support aural style sheets. Developers often forget that some Web users might be partially sighted or blind and that these users need special types of browsers to help them find and consume information. The aural style sheet model was developed for this class of user.

With aural style sheets, you are able to apply style characteristics to browsers that use speech synthesis to read the information on a Web page to the user. The CSS2 standard provides for the speech characteristics shown in Table 9.3.

Table 9.3 Characteristics Supported for Aural Style Sheets

Characteristic	Purpose and Possible Values
`speak`	Controls how the content is read; values can be none, normal, or spell-out
`speak-numeral`	Controls how numbers are read; values can be digits (714, read as seven-one-four) or continuous (714, read as seven hundred fourteen)
`speak-punctuation`	Controls how punctuation marks are read; values can be none (punctuation not explicitly read) or code (name of punctuation character is read)
`volume`	Controls how loud the synthesized speech is; values can be silent, x-soft, soft, medium, loud, or x-loud
`pause-after`	Causes speech to pause after a particular piece of content; set equal to the amount of time you want the pause to last
`pause-before`	Causes speech to pause before a particular piece of content; set equal to the amount of time you want the pause to last
`cue-after`	Plays an auditory cue after a particular piece of content; set equal to the URL of the file containing the cue
`cue-before`	Plays an auditory cue before a particular piece of content; set equal to the URL of the file containing the cue
`play-during`	Allows you to mix two different audio sources for simultaneous play; set equal to the URL of the audio file to play concurrently with reading of content
`play-during`	Allows you to mix two different audio sources for simultaneous play; set equal to the URL of the audio file to play concurrently with reading of content
`azimuth`	Describes the angle of the audio source with respect to the user and allows you to create the illusion of the sound coming from separate sources in space; values can be set equal to left-side, far-left, left, center-left, center, center-right, right, far-right, right-side, or any angle between -360 degrees and +360 degrees

Table 9.3 Continued

Characteristic	Purpose and Possible Values
`elevation`	Specifies how far above or below the audio source is from the user; values can be below, level, above, higher, lower, or any angle between -90 degrees and +90 degrees
`speech-rate`	Indicates how fast the content should be read; values can be x-slow, slow, medium, fast, x-fast, faster, slower, or a number equal to the number of words per minute to be read
`voice-family`	Specifies what kind of voice to use to read the content; values can have generic names like male, female, or child or specific names like Mom, Christopher, or the lady next door
`pitch`	Indicates the frequency of the speaking voice; values can be x-low, low, medium, high, x-high, or the number of Hertz (Hz) in the desired frequency
`pitch-range`	Controls the amount of inflection in the voice; values range between 0 and 100, where 0 means a monotone voice, 50 means average inflection, and anything over 50 is above average inflection
`stress`	Controls how strong the stress is on stressed elements; values range between 0 and 100, where 50 means the average stress pattern for a human male voice
`richness`	Controls the richness (ability to carry across space) of the speaking voice; values range between 0 and 100, where 50 means the average stress pattern for a human male voice

The characteristics provided in Table 9.3 enable developers to develop engaging spoken-word content as well as engaging visual content. The ability to do this continues to be important as more and more government mandates are passed calling for increased accessibility to information on the Web.

Looking Ahead to CSS3

The Cascading Style Sheets level 3 draft was scheduled for completion during the summer of 2000. It might be some time after this book comes out that CSS3 becomes a W3C recommendation, but that should not stop you from looking into what's ahead. Here are some of the features you can look forward to after CSS3 is endorsed by the Web community:

- **New user interface elements**—Plans currently call for enhanced form fields and additional cursors and colors to enable developers to build more intuitive user interfaces.
- **Scalable Vector Graphics (SVG)**—SVG will allow you to place certain shapes such as lines, curves, and circles on a page and then control their appearance with CSS characteristics. Because these are vector graphics, they are infinitely scalable without any loss of quality.

- **Behavioral extensions**—The behavioral extensions considered for CSS3 would enable you to capture any dynamic changes to a document or style and react to that change. Loosely stated, you can think of it as "event handlers for Dynamic HTML."
- **Increased international support**—You can expect CSS3 to include support for languages such as Japanese and Arabic that do not use characters from the Roman alphabet.
- **Multi-column layouts**—New CSS3 characteristics will make it easier to develop multi-column layouts that are more flexible in the face of changing requirements.

Clearly, the proposals being developed for CSS3 will put even greater power and control into developers' hands. Look for CSS3 to become a W3C Recommendation in the last half of 2000 or early 2001.

NOTE For more information on how the World Wide Web Consortium plans to extend Cascading Style Sheets, direct your browser to `http://www.w3.org/Style/Activity/`. ■

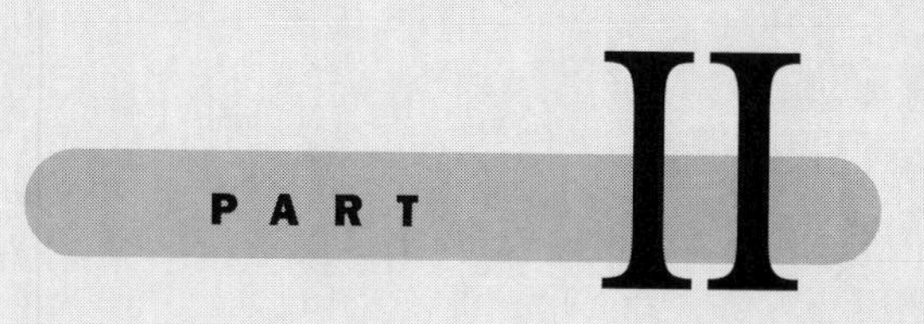

XML

CHAPTER 10

Introducing XML

by Andrew Watt

In this chapter

A First XML Document

```
<?xml version="1.0"?>
<message>
<to>All visitors</to>
<greeting>Hello and Welcome to LearningXML.com!</greeting>
</message>
```

You might have just read your first XML document that isn't XHTML.

If you were aware that the XHTML you saw earlier in the book was, in fact, XML-compliant you will notice that this short greeting differs from XHTML in a number of ways; for example, it introduces new tags which are absent from XHTML. XHTML is only one application of XML; in particular, it is a re-write of HTML 4.0 in compliance with XML standards. As you read these chapters on XML, you will learn more about it and its associated family of technologies. This family of XML-related technologies is able to work together progressively.

Even if you had never seen any XML before you started reading this book, it shouldn't have been too difficult to understand that simple XML message. You are starting to grasp the basics of the XML family of technologies (of which XHTML is only one member), which will be described to you in the next few chapters.

XML technologies have great potential to impact how the Web works. Not all that potential can be delivered yet. The specification of some of the technologies is not yet complete. For others, the specification is complete but implementation is currently in process. Realizing the full potential of the XML family depends in part on the members of the family working together, in what is called *XML synergy*. Until that synergy can be fully harnessed, the delivery of the promise of XML technologies will be patchy.

XML is now close to delivering real results on the Web. The various technologies are beginning to pull together, and the time when XML was only hype has passed. The opportunities for those who have skills in XML is very real, but acquiring those skills is not a trivial task. The XML family is complex as well as powerful. These chapters will help establish a foundation of basic skills and perspectives on which you can build to effectively use XML technologies.

Sometimes these chapters will give you a very broad perspective on XML, and sometimes they will show you very practical foundational techniques on which you can build to produce your own XML-based Web output. To fully appreciate and exploit XML technologies, you need both the broad perspective and the practical insights, even though trying to grasp both isn't easy.

Displaying XML on the Web is easy, at least if you don't demand too much sophistication in how it is presented. Figure 10.1 shows the welcome message from the beginning of this chapter in the Internet Explorer 5 browser.

FIGURE 10.1
The welcome message displayed in Internet Explorer 5.0. IE5.0 uses a default XSL style sheet to produce this display.

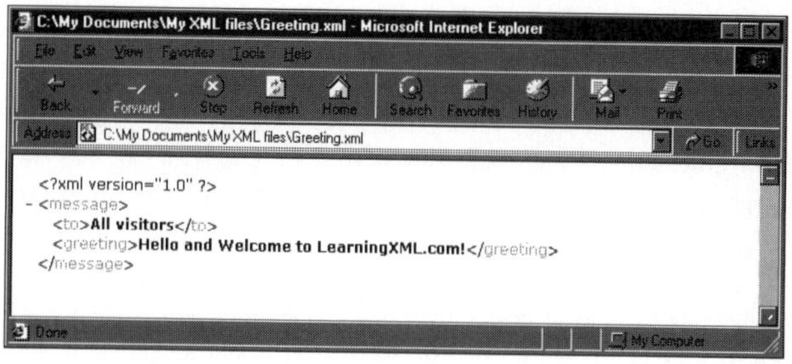

The Preview Release of Netscape 6 in its default configuration unfortunately produces an even less impressive rendering of our test XML file, as seen in Figure 10.2.

FIGURE 10.2
In the Preview Release, no XML style sheet is applied by default; therefore, you see a very unimpressive display.

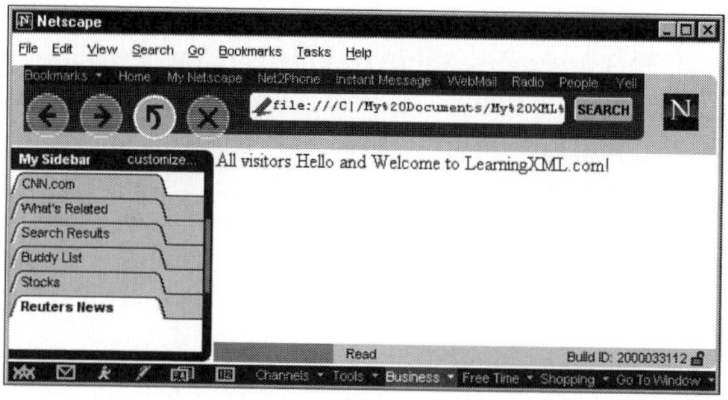

It is probably not fair to compare Internet Explorer 5.0, a full release, with a pre-beta release of Netscape 6.0. Netscape 6.0 promises substantial XML support which the preview release does not seem to deliver, other than displaying XML files that have an associated CSS style sheet. XSL style sheets are not currently recognized.

One of the most bewildering aspects of the XML family is the sheer number of members and trying to figure out how they fit together. For a start, there is XML, and the list of acronyms is growing almost by the month: DTD, XSLT, XPath, XPointer, XLink, XSL-FO, DOM, XForms, and others. The next few chapters look at most of the XML family members and hopefully make things a little clearer for you.

TIP The World Wide Web Consortium Web site is the primary source of official information on XML technologies. It is located at `http://www.w3c.org/`.

Figuring out how to use all these technologies and make them work together is further down the line. These chapters use a Mini Case Study so that you can look at how to make some of the members of the XML family work together to do useful things to produce a Web page. After you have that working, you will learn how other members of the family fit in the picture.

These sections assume that you know nothing about XML. You are taken step by step to a point where, if you work your way through the XML chapters and examples, you will be able to use straightforward XML documents for display on a Web page and will have a foundation for doing more sophisticated things with XML. Throughout these chapters, a number of XML topics are mentioned but are not discussed in detail. Internet links are provided so you can follow up on topics that are of interest to you.

TIP If your interest in the XML family of technologies is serious, bookmark the activities and documents on the W3C site that are of interest to you. Given the speed of development in some areas, you might want to visit the W3C site at least weekly. Don't forget to visit the front page; from time to time, major announcements about new activities (or activities that are new to you) appear there.

The individual components of the XML family interact in a complex way. It isn't always possible to convey how things fit together without referring to parts of the XML family that haven't been discussed yet. Feel free to use these chapters on XML as if they were a hypertext document—jump forward and take a look at a related subject if you want to. A plethora of cross references have been provided to make this easier. To fully grasp what is going on, you will probably need to "hyperlink" like this from chapter to chapter quite often. However, the chapters are written so you can read linearly, too. The first time through, you might choose to do this, and then go back and hyperlink to fix in your mind the connections between the different technologies.

Mini Case Study

These XML chapters not only give you a foundation for further work with XML, but also develop a simple case study that uses several XML technologies.

If you follow along and carry out the examples, you will learn how to use a few of the currently available XML tools and will also begin to see how to put XML technologies to practical use in producing Web content.

I suggest that you just read the Mini Case Study the first time through. However, if you absolutely can't wait to get your hands dirty and begin working with XML, you will need to get some tools together, install them on your computer, and make sure they are working.

You will need a text editor, a Web browser, and an XSLT processor. The following examples are created using the Instant Saxon XSLT processor (see Chapter 11, "Creating XML Files for Use," for download and installation instructions), which is straightforward to use if you have a Windows 9x computer.

This Mini Case Study takes a short piece of famous English text expressed in an XML document and determines how it should appear in a standard browser. You might have seen the text before either in its original format or when it became popular as a pop song a few years back. As you work through the example, feel free to use the words of another song or poem if you prefer.

```
<?xml version='1.0' encoding='iso-8859-1'?>
<Song>
<title>Amazing Grace</title>
<author>John Newton</author>
<date>1725-1807</date>

<verse>
<line>Amazing Grace, how sweet the sound</line>
<line>That saved a wretch, like me</line>
<line>I once was lost, but now am found</line>
<line>Was blind, but now I see</line>
</verse>
<verse>
<line>When we've been there ten thousand years</line>
<line>Bright shining as the sun</line>
<line>We've no less days to sing God's praise</line>
<line>Than when we first began.</line>
</verse>
</Song>
```


If you are following along and typing in the example, save the file as `amazing.xml` in a suitable directory. If you choose to use the Instant Saxon XSLT processor (which is used a little later in the example), you should probably save the `amazing.xml` file in the Instant Saxon directory.

CAUTION

If you are typing the examples as you go, be sure to use a suitable editor—either a dedicated XML editor (see "XML Editors" in Chapter 11) or a plain text editor. You can use a word processor if it has the capability to save as plain text. Saving the text in a word processor's native format is likely to cause problems because of the hidden markup codes (not XML markup) that word processors add to a file when an XML processor attempts to parse the document.

Notice a few things about this short example. There is neither an opening `<html>` tag nor a corresponding closing `</html>` tag. There are no `<head>` or `<body>` tags. The names of the individual tags are different entirely from those in XHTML.

All XHTML documents link to one of the three permitted XHTML Document Type Definitions (DTDs). Notice that this XML document is not linked to a DTD. An XML document *can* be linked to a DTD, and often is, (XHTML 1.0 documents must be so linked) but for generic XML it isn't compulsory. You don't use a DTD in this document.

Also notice that unlike XHTML (which inherits a lot from HTML 4.0), not one of the tags relates to how any part of this short document is to be presented. The content is there but how it is presented is something you decide separately. In other words, content (or data structure) is completely separated from presentation, and that is one of the aims of XML. XHTML, at least in version 1.0, carries over much of the overlap of content and presentation that existed in HTML 4.0 and earlier versions of HTML.

Notice, too, that unlike XHTML, you are free to use uppercase letters in tags. The `<Song></Song>` tag pair (or "element") would be illegal in XHTML because XHTML only allows lowercase letters in tags. Of course, that tag pair would not be recognized as an XHTML tag pair; it doesn't belong in XHTML because it isn't present in any of the XHTML DTDs.

Both XML and XHTML are case sensitive. In XHTML, a pragmatic decision was made to allow only lowercase characters in tag names. More generally in XML, you can use uppercase characters wherever you like in tag names but you must make sure that the opening and closing tags match exactly. For example, using `<Song></song>` would cause a parsing error because the capitalization of the initial letters of the two tags do not match.

TIP Be very careful when typing in the example to ensure that the tag names in `amazing.xml` are consistent. When you write the XSLT style sheet to transform your XML document, the tag name must match exactly the tag for which the XSLT style sheet is looking; otherwise, a necessary transformation will be omitted. In a simple example like this one, the reason for the discrepancy from the expected output should be easy to spot. However, the more complex the transformation, the harder it will be to identify and rectify a departure from intended behavior.

Perhaps you are wondering how XHTML and XML relate. XHTML is an application of XML. But certain things that are true about XHTML are not necessarily true about XML. What is allowable in XHTML is defined in the three XHTML Document Type Definitions (DTDs) referred to in the XHTML 1.0 Recommendation. DTDs constrain the allowable tags in an XML-compliant document. This sample document is not constrained by any of the XHTML DTDs (in fact our document doesn't even have a DTD at the moment), so you are not limited to using the tag set of XHTML. You can create any tags you want, even tags that are neither useful nor sensible. XML gives a lot of freedom in that respect.

▶ For more information about DTDs, **see** Chapter 14, "Constraining XML—DTDs and XML Schemas"

Because there is no DTD for this sample document, you are free to create whatever tags you want, within the naming rules of XML, to present the information.

If you want to get started now, type the sample document and save it as `amazing.xml` in a suitable directory on your computer. You should consistently use only lowercase characters in the filename to avoid possible problems.

If you have Internet Explorer 5.0 installed on your computer you can open the `amazing.xml` file using IE5.0 and it will be displayed onscreen, similar to Figure 10.3.

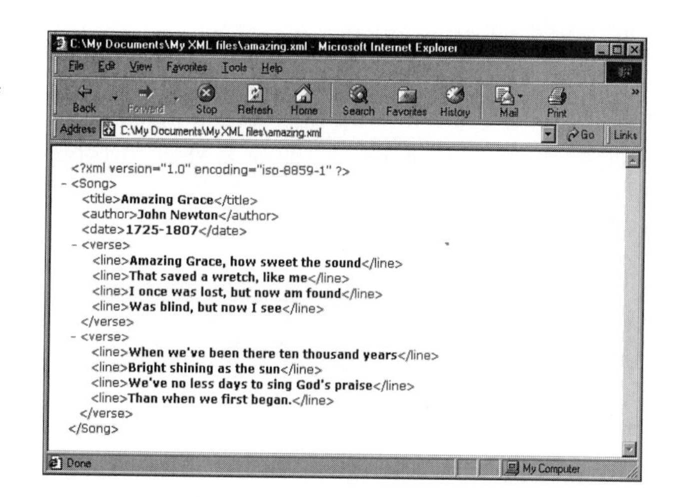

FIGURE 10.3
Internet Explorer 5.0 shows the two verses of Amazing Grace, displayed using IE5.0's default XSL style sheet.

If you compare the XML text as it was typed into your text editor with what you see onscreen, you will notice that it has changed. Internet Explorer 5.0 has applied a default XSL style sheet to your XML file. It hasn't altered the structure of your document, but it has, for example, introduced some color coding of tags. Also if you click the small minus signs in the browser window, that part of the tree representing `amazing.xml` will collapse. Most people looking at that document would focus on the clutter of XML tags and not see the content on which you want them to focus. When you display XML on a real Web page, you will want to avoid having a lot of tags visible on screen.

TIP At this stage, which version of Internet Explorer 5.0 you have won't make any difference as to how your XML document is displayed. As you begin to do more complicated things with your example, it might not work properly if you haven't downloaded the most up-to-date version of Internet Explorer 5.0. The updated IE5.0 won't alter how `amazing.xml` is displayed, but the underlying engine differs. This becomes apparent when using an XSLT processor that uses MSXML (as Instant Saxon does). So, if you are going to work through the examples using Instant Saxon, you should download the latest version of IE5.0 before you start.

So, how do you transform the two verses from being fragments of text dominated by a clutter of XML tags? First, take a look at the way you want these two verses to look in the finished Web page (see Figure 10.4).

This certainly looks more like a real Web page than what is in Figure 10.3. It is admittedly pretty plain but that can be worked on later.

You can see that the output differs from the input in several ways. The content of the `<title>` element from the XML file is used twice, but the tags are hidden. The first time, it is used to create the title for the XHTML page (to do that it must appear within the `<head>` of the output XHTML document) and also as the main heading for the XHTML page (where it is contained within the <body> tag). Also the elements have been re-ordered a little. The name of the author and the dates of his life appear early in the original XML file but are the final elements of the output XHTML page.

One way to achieve this transformation is by using an XSLT (Extensible Stylesheet Language - Transformation) style sheet. Don't worry too much about the details just now; they are discussed in later chapters.

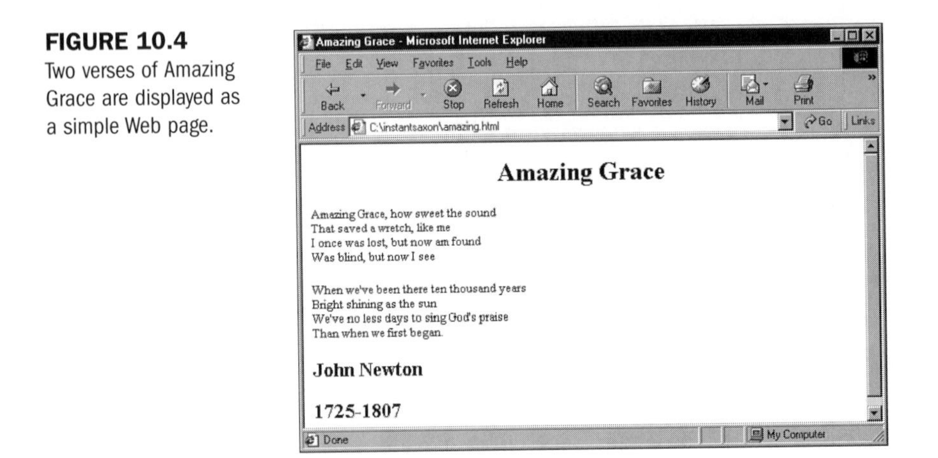

FIGURE 10.4
Two verses of Amazing Grace are displayed as a simple Web page.

NOTE Because an XSLT processor transforms the XML, using the term "transformation sheet" rather than style sheet is more accurate. However, style sheet is the term most often used.

The XML document you looked at earlier has no connection to an XSLT style sheet specified within it. If you want it to be transformed, you need to name the relevant XSLT style sheet.

The following code is added to the XML file:

```
<?xml-stylesheet type="text/xsl" href="amazing.xsl"?>
```

TIP If you are using Instant Saxon, it isn't necessary to add this line. The association between the XML and XSL files can be made on the command line as you will see later.

Notice that, like the XML declaration at the beginning of your XML file, this XML processing instruction also begins with <? and ends with ?>. This is how an XML processing instruction is identified.

Notice the `type` attribute that specifies that the style sheet to be accessed is of MIME type `text/xsl`. Notice too the `href` attribute that identifies the relative URI for finding the style sheet.

What the processing instruction says is something like this: This is a processing instruction that uses an XSL style sheet. The XSL style sheet is of Internet media type `text/xsl`. The XSL style sheet is located in the same directory as the XML file and is named `amazing.xsl`.

CAUTION

The `href` attribute can specify an absolute or relative URL. If you use a relative URL, make sure you keep the XML file and the XSL style sheet that will transform in the same relative positions. In this instance, make sure that `amazing2.xml` and `amazing.xsl` are in the same directory.

So, with the processing instruction added, your modified XML file looks like this:

```
<?xml version='1.0' encoding='iso-8859-1'?>
<?xml-stylesheet type="text/xsl" href="amazing.xsl"?>
<Song>
<title>Amazing Grace</title>
<author>John Newton</author>
<date>1725-1807</date>

<verse>
<line>Amazing Grace, how sweet the sound</line>
<line>That saved a wretch, like me</line>
<line>I once was lost, but now am found</line>
<line>Was blind, but now I see</line>
</verse>
<verse>
<line>When we've been there ten thousand years</line>
<line>Bright shining as the sun</line>
<line>We've no less days to sing God's praise</line>
<line>Than when we first began.</line>
</verse>
</Song>
```

For more details about XSLT, **see** Chapter 13, "Transforming XML—XSLT"

The following code is the XSLT style sheet that produces the screen shown in Figure 10.4:

```
<?xml version='1.0'?>
<xsl:stylesheet
       xmlns:xsl="http://www.w3.org/1999/XSL/Transform"
       version="1.0">

<xsl:template match="Song">
    <html>
    <head>
    <title><xsl:value-of select="title"/></title>
    </head>

    <body>
    <xsl:apply-templates select="title"/>
```

```
    <xsl:apply-templates select="verse"/>
    <xsl:apply-templates select="author"/>
    <xsl:apply-templates select="date"/>
    </body>
    </html>
</xsl:template>

<xsl:template match="title">
    <div align="center"><h1><xsl:value-of select="."/></h1></div>
</xsl:template>

<xsl:template match="author">
    <div align="left"><h2><xsl:value-of select="."/></h2></div>
</xsl:template>

<xsl:template match="date">
    <div align="left"><h2><xsl:value-of select="."/></h2></div>
</xsl:template>

<xsl:template match="verse">
    <p><xsl:apply-templates select="line"/></p>
</xsl:template>

<xsl:template match="line">
    <xsl:value-of select="."/>
    <br />
</xsl:template>

</xsl:stylesheet>
```

To apply the `amazing.xsl` transformation sheet to the `amazing.xml` file to produce an XHTML file called `amazing.html` using Instant Saxon, issue the following command at the command line:

```
saxon amazing.xml amazing.xsl > amazing.html
```

Before moving on to dissect how the `amazing.xsl` transformation sheet works, let's take a broad look at what an XSLT processor does.

When you issue the command, Instant Saxon loads `amazing.xml` into memory, parses it, and creates a tree representation of the file (the input tree). The `amazing.xsl` file will also be loaded and, by means of the XSLT processor, the input tree will be processed to create an output tree. The destination for the output tree is the `amazing.html` file.

Let's move on and look at the steps of the `amazing.xsl` transformation sheet.

The XML Declaration in the first line of the code will be familiar to you, but the next three lines might need some explanation:

```
<xsl:stylesheet
       xmlns:xsl="http://www.w3.org/1999/XSL/Transform"
       version="1.0">
```

Notice first that these three lines are one tag. The first line says that this tag is an `xsl:stylesheet` tag.

A colon (:) is a legal character in XML Names. Although the XML 1.0 specification allows the colon in any XML name, it is wise only to use the colon in XML names that conform to the "Namespaces in XML" standard. So `xsl:stylesheet` effectively says that this is a style sheet in the namespace `xsl`.

▶ For further information on the Namespaces in XML standard, **see** Chapter 13, "Transforming XML—XSLT"

But what if someone else wants to use the namespace `xsl`? The `xmlns:xsl` in the second line of the code snippet says, in effect, that the XML Namespace (xmlns) called `xsl` references a URL called `http://www.w3.org/1999/XSL/Transform`. It might seem odd, but the URL being referenced doesn't actually have to contain anything. It is there, for all practical purposes, to provide a unique text string that identifies the namespace. The rationale is that by giving a URL (which is probably far longer than a string like `xsl`), the chances are very high that nobody else will use the same URL, so the namespace `xsl` will be uniquely identified. And providing a unique means of identifying the namespace is the object of this slightly cumbersome approach.

TIP It is important to define the structure of the content of your Web pages when you begin your project. If you don't, you will end up having to redo aspects of your project, which is a waste of time and resources. Advanced planning is more important for an XML-based project than it has been for many HTML pages or Web sites in the past.

▶ For more on content structure, **see** "Planning a Project," **p. 330**

Let's look at how the rest of the XSLT transformation sheet works. The following code line illustrates an important way in which many XSLT transformation sheets work:

```
<xsl:template match="Song">
```

The XSLT transformation sheets attempt to apply what the XSLT 1.0 Recommendation calls a "template" when a match is found. In this example, because there is an exact match in the `<Song>` element, the template is applied.

In the next two lines, the transformation sheet is told to output the two XHTML tags that you see:

```
<html>
    <head>
```

In this line the template outputs the string `"<title>"`, and then it looks for an element called `<title>` *in the XML file* to which it is being applied. In your XML file, there is a `<title>` element. The XSLT transformation sheet extracts the content of that title element, which is the string "Amazing Grace", outputs that string, and then proceeds to output the string `"</title>"`.

```
<title><xsl:value-of select="title"/></title>
```

Again, you output tags verbatim to the XHTML file:

```
</head>

    <body>
```

Each of these four lines works in the same way. The <xsl:apply-templates> indicates that the XSLT processor should look for a template matching the value of its select attribute. In the first line, it looks for a template named "title", which it finds later in the XSLT sheet.

Similarly, the templates named "verse", "author", and "date" are applied.

```
<xsl:apply-templates select="title"/>
    <xsl:apply-templates select="verse"/>
    <xsl:apply-templates select="author"/>
    <xsl:apply-templates select="date"/>
```

The output of these four templates determines the content of the <body> of your XHTML file.

You'll see later what each of these applied templates actually does.

These two lines close the <body> and <html> tags respectively. Recall that it is necessary to close all tags in XHTML in the correct order.

```
</body>
</html>
```

This closes the <xsl:template> for <Song>:

```
</xsl:template>
```

CAUTION

If you omit this closing tag, Saxon will produce an error message after it finds the next closing tag.

This template centers the content of the element <title> in the XML file, which, as you will recall, is the string "Amazing Grace". It also applies the XHTML <h1> tag to that string.

```
<xsl:template match="title">
    <div align="center"><h1><xsl:value-of select="."/></h1></div>
</xsl:template>
```

The author template outputs the content of the <author> element from the XML file, which is "John Newton". It applies the XHTML <h2> tag to that string.

```
<xsl:template match="author">
    <div align="left"><h2><xsl:value-of select="."/></h2></div>
</xsl:template>
```

The date template outputs the content of the <date> element of the XML file, aligned left and with the XHTML <h2> tag applied:

```
<xsl:template match="date">
    <div align="left"><h2><xsl:value-of select="."/></h2></div>
</xsl:template>
```

You might have expected to see the verse template earlier in the style sheet. It isn't necessary for the templates applied within the Song template to be in order. As long as they are present, they will be applied.

The verse template applies to the <verse> element of the XML file. Notice that the only content of the verse template is an <xsl:apply-templates> selecting the line template. So, apart from the fact that you know the <p></p> tag pair generates a paragraph, you need to look at that template to see what the verse template actually does.

```
<xsl:template match="verse">
    <p><xsl:apply-templates select="line"/></p>
</xsl:template>
```


The line looks for a <line> element in the XML file, extracts its value, and passes that to the output. Then after the line, it adds an XHTML <br/> tag to insert a new line.

```
<xsl:template match="line">
    <xsl:value-of select="."/>
    <br />
</xsl:template>
```

But this says to output one <line> element, or does it? To remember how this template was called, take a look back at the key line:

```
<p><xsl:apply-templates select="line"/></p>
```

This line in the verse template says "Look for each child element of <verse> that is called <line>. For each <line> element that is a child of a <verse> element, apply the line template."

So for each of the <line> elements in the original XML file, the text contained in it is output and is followed by a <br /> tag.

This final line of our transformation sheet provides a closing tag for the opening <xsl:stylesheet> tag, as required to conform with XML 1.0 syntax:

```
</xsl:stylesheet>
```

Having shown you an example of using XML together with XSLT to create a simple Web page, it's time to step back and look at much wider issues. These issues might not seem relevant to you immediately, but they do have an impact on what XML is and on what you will need to do to come to grips with XML.

Why XML?

The question "Why XML?" needs to be discussed at two levels. The first looks at XML specifically as a technology to potentially underpin the next generation of the World Wide Web. The second looks at XML in a slightly more formal and wider context.

Let's look first at two aspects of HTML and XML on the Web.

One reason for the creation of XML is that HTML was increasingly being used to do things that it wasn't originally designed to do. HTML was originally designed to express the structure of text documents in a pretty simple way. As the Web grew, tags were added that either inserted presentation information between structural tags or mingled presentation and structure within a single tag. Take the `<h1>` tag for example. It indicates that it is a heading (which tells us a little of how its content fits in a structural hierarchy), but it also tells us how to present the contained information (although the browser will determine the exact appearance).

Often you will see or hear claims that XML can enable you to do things quicker or easier. Is that true?

Let's take a step back and look at a simple analogy. Think about going to the corner store to buy a few small items. You might walk there. It is quick and cheap and you don't need anything very high tech. Using HTML to create a Web page quickly is a little like that—if you have a plain text editor and really know HTML, you can do just about anything in a Web page quickly and at low cost.

But, going back to the analogy, suppose you want to travel a few hundred miles and transport several big items at the same time. Walking and carrying that load isn't practical. You need a vehicle with fuel, wheels, a working engine, and so on. As soon as you get beyond going to the corner shop for a few items, a vehicle has obvious advantages.

For a bigger job, the vehicle is easier and faster, *but* you must have a car, know how to fill it with fuel, ensure you have tires filled to the correct air pressure, and so on. The XML family of technologies is a little like this. You can do things using the XML family that you can't do with HTML. But to make it all work, you need several technologies working together to get the power. So, there is a learning curve.

In fact, XML technologies on their own won't work in all situations. You will likely need to use them in combination with other technologies, such as Java.

▶ For more information on combining XML and Java, **see** Chapter 42, "Java and XML"

It is easy at this stage to become overwhelmed. But think back to the car used in the analogy. You can drive it without knowing the details of how the wheel is connected to the axle and how the engine delivers its power to the wheels. If you want to become an auto mechanic, you obviously need to know more. This section tells you enough to "drive" XML. Whether you want to go further and look into the possibilities of being an XML mechanic is up to you.

Let's take a look at the second, slightly more formal examination of "Why XML?". You might think that XML is designed primarily to make it easier for human beings, but if you think about it, human beings can communicate in writing, in print, or electronically without angled brackets around fragments of text. That gives us the clue. XML is designed *primarily* to allow one computer to communicate better with another computer. The fact that XML is text makes it easier for humans to understand what one computer is saying to another, but the primary aim is computer to computer communication.

XML helps computers communicate better in two important ways:

- It separates presentation from content (HTML and XHTML).
- It enables information to be readily passed between applications.

Of course, it is a bonus that the code can be easily maintained by human beings—that is the advantage of having ordinary text characters between the angled brackets.

Let's look at another important reason for using XML rather than HTML, which depends on this notion of XML underpinning communication between two computers.

As the Web has grown bigger and its uses have become more sophisticated and complicated, HTML has created problems. For example, it isn't easy to find out what the content of an HTML page means. That has implications for finding information. Suppose you wanted information on surgical operations. Today if you looked for "operations" on Altavista.com you would find 3,348,795 results! That reduces to 1,845,290 if you look for surgical operations. The problem in finding desired information in a realistic amount of time is obvious. Users need a means of finding relevant information without having to wade through vast amounts of data that happens to have a word, a couple of words, or a phrase in common with what they are interested in. Properly structured Web pages based on XML that capture "meaning" can help make Web searching a productive, rather than a frustrating, activity.

To finish this section, let's go back to our analogy. One of the problems with using a vehicle is that all the parts need to be present before you can travel very far. If there is no engine, the fuel tank is empty, or there are no tires, your journey isn't going to be much fun or very productive. XML technologies are a little like that. You need to grasp at least the basics of several of them before you can do much with them. After you read the eight chapters in Part II, "XML," and work through the examples, you will have a foundation to build on so that you can, in time, do more serious XML development.

What Is XML?

That might seem to be a totally stupid question with an obvious answer. But, like many things that relate to XML, things are often not as obvious or intuitive as they first seem.

XML can be viewed in many different ways. Some people say it is a document format. Others say that XML allows hierarchical storage of data. Others look at XML documents as data, which is passed across a network from one application or agent to another. When an XML document is being passed across a network in this way, the XML document can be viewed as a serialized version of an underlying hierarchical structure; that is, the XML document is essentially a stream of character bytes.

Each of these viewpoints is valid. In part, the variety of answers is due to the sheer versatility of XML technologies. Power and flexibility can lead to ambiguity and lack of clarity.

If you view an XML document as a serialized hierarchical structure, you can view the perceived hierarchical structure as a SAX (Simple API for XML) or DOM (Document Object Model) structure. SAX and DOM provide interfaces for programming languages to manipulate XML. For further information on SAX and DOM, see Chapter 12, "Parsing and Navigating XML—SAX, DOM, XPath, XPointer, and XLink."

XML Dogmas Examined

This section takes a quick look at some dogmas that have grown up around XML to see if they are realistic.

"XML is simple." This statement or variants of it have been seen time after time. What has probably happened is that the statement that "XML is a simple text format" has been generalized, falsely as it happens, to the "XML is simple" format. Think about the statement "Computing data uses a simple numerical format—zeroes and ones." Does it then follow that computing is "simple?" Surely not. Similarly, the fact that aspects of the text format that XML uses are "simple" does not mean that XML is simple. XML was not "simple" when XML 1.0 appeared, and it is far more complex now.

"XML allows you to work quicker and easier." As explained in the car analogy earlier in the chapter, it all depends on what you are talking about. To put a simple Web page on the Internet, HTML (or XHTML) is much easier. When you do more complex things, such as produce dynamic Web page content, XML technologies are more helpful and improve efficiency of maintainability. So, for some people the statement is false but for others it is true.

Is nothing simple about XML? Perhaps not. Even the term "Extensible Markup Language" is open to question.

A Language Without Words

One of the aspects of XML that is different from any human language you will come across is that it has no words!

You might ask why, if XML has no words, it is called a language. The so-called XML is more accurately called Extensible Markup Meta Language (XMML). It is probably too late to change the title for the better, but the important thing is that you understand that XML is different from any human language that you use. Following that idea through, you will hopefully realize that when it comes to XML, you have to be careful about what words mean. You can't just assume they mean the same as in everyday speech.

The following illustrates just how careful you need to be when thinking through some of this stuff.

Take "extensible." Is XML really extensible? Well the answer is yes and no. Some aspects of XML—those in the XML 1.0 Recommendation—are essentially fixed, at least until XML 2.0 comes along. However, other aspects are extensible or, perhaps more precisely, they were left undefined in XML 1.0 and are only now being developed. So what does "extensible" mean? It isn't straightforward, is it?

Take "meaning," for example. Yes, seriously—what does "meaning" actually mean? In magazine articles about XML you will sometimes read about the "meaning" in an XML document. That is wrong. There is no intrinsic meaning in XML. Meaning is something you impute to tags partly determined by their structure and partly by their context or content.

To illustrate this point, let's take another look at the example at the beginning of this chapter:

```
<?xml version="1.0"?>
<message>
<to>All visitors</to>
<greeting> Hello and Welcome to LearningXML.com!</greeting>
</message>
```

Take a look at two other possible documents using exactly the same tags and the same document structure:

```
<?xml version="1.0"?>
<message>
<to>Tangential Orbit (TO) achieved</to>
<greeting>Congratulations to all at NASA</greeting>
</message>
```

```
<?xml version="1.0"?>
<message>
<to>Right big</to>
<greeting>Hello Mr. Jones we will give you an anaesthetic before we
➥amputate that toe that has been causing you so much pain.</greeting>
</message>
```

Okay, admittedly the last example was a little contrived but it illustrates the point. A tag has no meaning *per se* and there is nothing in the XML 1.0 Recommendation that requires tags to be spelled correctly.

To maximize reusability of your XML code, it is sensible to use meaningful names. Enabling you to use semantically meaningful tags is one of XML's strengths.

Of course, if you program a computer to predictably handle particular tags, that simulates meaning. But XML tags do not have any *intrinsic* meaning; that is a price to be paid for "extensibility."

Don't worry too much about issues like "What is extensibility?" or "What does meaning mean?". Just notice that there are subtle shades of meaning involved in various parts of XML. If you are aware that there are pitfalls, you will be less likely to fall victim to one as you work with XML and the other members of the family.

CAUTION

When reusing XML code, think carefully about what the "meaning" of the tag was when previously used and whether it matches exactly that use to which you want to put it.

XML Family of Technologies

There is a large and growing family of XML-compliant technologies. This section briefly discusses the main members of the XML family.

Some XML technologies are in a "finished" state; that is, they have been issued as a formal "Recommendation" by the World Wide Web Consortium (W3C). Others are still in preparation. For more details about the process of developing XML-related Recommendations, see the section on W3C in this chapter.

CAUTION

The W3C Web site (`www.w3.org`) is the definitive source for XML documentation and its progress. Be aware that sometimes the complexity of the interdependency of documents means that a link will point to what is supposedly the latest version of a document but in fact it is not because the link has not been updated. For example, I recently was directed to a December 1999 Working Draft as the latest version when a March 2000 Working Draft existed but was not correctly linked. These problems are fortunately rare but they do happen.

Here is a list of relevant W3C initiatives (each with a commonly used abbreviation) plus brief comments. Further information on several of these initiatives will be found in other locations within the XML section of this book, as indicated in the following list:

- **XML (Extensible Markup Language)**—A meta-language really (probably better called XMML). Meta means that it contains information about a language (or set of languages) rather than being a language itself.
- **Common Markup for Micropayment**—Permits charging on the Web without excessive overhead costs. It will open up new possibilities for e-commerce on the Web. This is discussed further in Chapter 16, "Exploiting XML—XML and e-Commerce."

- **CSS (Cascading Style Sheets)**—Strictly speaking, CSS is not an XML technology but is the currently available principal means to present XML or XHTML data on the Web.
- **DOM (Document Object Model)**—The Document Object Model is a platform- and language-neutral interface that allows programs to access and update the content, structure, and style of documents (see Chapter 12).
- **DTD (Document Type Definition)**—A tool borrowed from SGML (Standard Generalized Markup Language). The DTD defines what tags are allowable within a particular class of XML documents; that is, it *constrains* what is allowed in an XML document. Each instance of an XML document using that DTD must conform to the DTD. You met DTDs in the XHTML code earlier in this book. The W3C has defined three DTDs for XHTML 1.0: Strict, Transitional, and Frameset. This is discussed further in Chapter 14, "Constraining XML—DTDs and XML Schemas."
- **P3P (Platform for Personal Privacy Preferences)**—Aims to provide Web users with the ability to express their preferences regarding how information about them is used by Web sites they visit. P3P might provide the option to avoid Web sites that handle information in a way that is unacceptable to a user.
- **PICS (Platform for Internet Content Selection)**—Enables labels (metadata) to be attached to Internet content. A primary aim of this initiative is to allow identification of material suitable for children.
- **RDF (Resource Description Framework)**—The RDF is about metadata. PICS and P3P are founded on RDF.
- **SVG (Scalable Vector Graphics)**—An exciting new open vector graphics standard (including animation) which might revolutionize the range, quality, and ease of use of images on the Web. Further information can be found in Chapter 17, "Moving Forward with XML."
- **SMIL (Synchronized Multimedia Integrated Language)**—One of the early W3C Recommendations. The SMIL "Boston Specification" is currently in Working Draft (see Chapter 17).
- **XForms**—Currently in Working Draft, the aim of XForms is to provide the next generation of Web-based forms.
- **XHTML (Extensible Hypertext Markup Language)**—You were introduced to XHTML in Chapters 2, "Introduction to XHTML," and 3, "XHTML 1.0 Element Reference." Watch for emerging W3C documents relating to modularization of XHTML. The XHTML 1.0 Recommendation can be found at

  `http://www.w3.org/TR/2000/REC-xhtml1-20000126`

- **XIS or Infoset (XML Information Set)**—A data set derived from the elements and other markup constructs of a well-formed XML document. Further information will be given later in this chapter. The Working Draft of December, 1999 is described at

  `http://www.w3.org/TR/1999/WD-xml-infoset-19991220`

- **XML Query**—The aim is to provide SQL-like functionality for XML documents and data sources. The Requirements have been published. A first Working Draft is awaited.
- **XML Schema**—This is a particularly important W3C activity. It will remove the impediment caused by the inability of DTDs to define data types. It is discussed in Chapter 14.
- **XML Signatures**—The aim is to produce an XML-compliant syntax to represent any Web resource that can be referenced by a URI (Uniform Resource Indicator).
- **XSL-FO (Extensible Stylesheet Language - Formatting Objects)**—Its purpose is to define how an XML document is laid out. Unlike CSS, XSL-FO is an XML-compliant standard. Formatting of output usually follows transformation of a document by XSLT.
- **XSLT (Extensible Stylesheet Language Transformations)**—XSLT is used, not surprisingly, to transform one XML-compliant document to another form. The other forms could be, for example, XHTML like the code you saw in earlier chapters, WML (Wireless Markup Language), or some similar language preparatory to displaying your data on a handheld device of some kind, or any of a multiplicity of other XML-compliant languages.

TIP Many W3C Web pages have a link to "Latest Public Version" or similar phrase in the first few lines of each Recommendation or Working Draft. If it is important for you to be absolutely up-to-date on what is happening on a particular topic, regularly visit the Web page of the last draft you know about and click that link to check whether the document you are reading has been superceded. An alternative is to bookmark the "latest update" page. That way, as a revised draft is issued, the bookmark will point to the new draft.

XML Recommendations

The XML 1.0 Recommendation laid the conceptual foundation for the XML family of technologies. It claimed to be a subset of SGML (the Standard Generalized Markup Language) and applied aspects of the SGML standard; for example, Document Type Definitions (DTDs) as a framework for constraining XML.

To achieve full productivity using XML technologies, you will need to master XML 1.0. It is written in very precise and concise language. Unfortunately, in its aim to achieve precision and conciseness, it becomes almost impenetrable at first read for those not steeped in the terminology it uses.

XML technologies are developing rapidly and are likely to do so for some time yet. This section gives you links to the official World Wide Consortium Recommendations as of July, 2000. The Recommendations will be in date order. The URL given is for the final Recommendation for any particular version. In general, W3C increasingly is trying to keep stable URLs for publicly quotable documents like these but if you find broken links, W3C might have restructured its Web site. Go to `http://www.W3C.org/` and search for the topic of interest.

Extensible Markup Language (XML) 1.0, 10th February 1998:

`http://www.w3.org/TR/1998/REC-xml-19980210`

Synchronized Multimedia Integration Language (SMIL) 1.0 Specification, 15th June 1998:

`http://www.w3.org/TR/REC-smil`

Document Object Model (DOM) Level 1 Specification Version 1.0, 1st October 1998:

`http://www.w3.org/TR/1998/REC-DOM-Level-1-19981001`

Namespaces in XML, 14th January 1999:

`http://www.w3.org/TR/1999/REC-xml-names-19990114`

Resource Description Framework (RDF) Model and Syntax Specification, 22nd February 1999:

`http://www.w3.org/TR/1999/REC-rdf-syntax-19990222`

Associating Style Sheets with XML documents Version 1.0, 29th June 1999:

`http://www.w3.org/1999/06/REC-xml-stylesheet-19990629`

Mathematical Markup Language (MathML) 1.01 Specification, July 7, 1999:

`http://www.w3.org/1999/07/REC-MathML-19990707`

XML Path Language (XPath) Version 1.0, 16th November 1999:

`http://www.w3.org/TR/1999/REC-xpath-19991116`

XSL Transformations (XSLT) Version 1.0, 16th November 1999:

`http://www.w3.org/TR/1999/REC-xslt-19991116`

XHTML 1.0 - The Extensible Hypertext Markup Language. A Reformulation of HTML 4 in XML 1.0, 26th January 2000:

`http://www.w3.org/TR/2000/REC-xhtml1-20000126`

Having listed the W3C Recommendations I want to look briefly at a few of them here. Others will be discussed in more detail in later chapters.

Resource Description Framework

The Web contains huge amounts of data that can be located by search engines such as Altavista.com and many others. Much of that huge volume of Web-based information is either poorly structured or is structured in such a way as not to be comprehensible. So when you carry out a search, you might get tens of thousands of "hits," many of which miss what you want. So you waste time burrowing through dozens of sites to try to find information which is of real interest to you.

A fundamental problem is that the Web is much too big for a human being (or even a team of human beings) to find and summarize content. Yet it is too poorly structured at present to be searched by spiders and bots so that they "understand" what they find. The solution is to find some way of better structuring Web content so that automatic search spiders can "understand" the significance of what they find.

The Resource Description Framework aims to provide a framework within which other initiatives can bring solutions to this type of problem to fruition.

The Resource Description Framework is the main focus of the W3C MetaData activity. The RDF has the following aspiration: "The Resource Description Framework (RDF) integrates a variety of Web-based metadata activities including sitemaps, content ratings, stream channel definitions, search engine data collection (Web crawling), digital library collections, and distributed authoring, using XML as an interchange syntax."

If you pause to read that aspiration carefully, you will see just how wide is the scope of what is being targeted. The RDF is attempting to provide structure for information about the information that makes up Web sites and what it "means." Such information about information is *metadata*.

If you are a regular Web user, perhaps the topic that will be of most interest is the one of search engine data collection.

Suppose you wanted to find something on the Web that covered material similar to this book. If you searched on XHTML, XML, and Java you would get 968,591 hits. If you insisted that all three topics be mentioned on one page you would have 2,926 hits. Finding a site that delivered what you really wanted could take hours of manual searching among those almost 3,000 hits.

It is important for you to progress from the situation where some searches on Web-based search engines often return upwards of 100,000 or 1,000,000 results. Everyone wants more efficient search strategies and increased relevance of returned information.

An underlying aim of RDF is to transform Web-based information from being "machine readable" to "machine understandable." At present, a search engine can tell you whether Java is mentioned on a Web page. Meta tags (those much-abused entities) might hint at some importance or relevance of Java on that page, but only in a non-specific "Here is a word make of it what you will" sort of way. There is no easy or foolproof way to distinguish Web pages on the topic of the computer language Java from Web pages on the topic of the Pacific island of the same name. If you could search on a term and specify the "meaning" it ought to have, your search results would be much more useful. You might want to say something like "Find all Web pages where both XML and Java are mentioned and both XML and Java are major topics but exclude pages on the use of XML on the island of Java." At present you can't do that. As the potential benefits of RDF percolate into everyday technologies, the ability to search in that more efficient manner will come significantly closer.

Platform for Internet Content Selection

The previously mentioned difficulties of searching efficiently are one specific illustration of finding suitable or relevant content on the Web. Another aspect of finding desired material on the Web is whether material is suitable for children.

The Platform for Internet Content Selection is the W3C initiative that addresses that issue of suitability of Web content. The PICS framework provides means for attaching labels to material, in particular so that its suitability for children can be documented.

In time, XML-based Web sites will be identifiable as suitable or otherwise for children (or, in principle, any other group for which a classification is widely implemented). When appropriate configuration is carried out, either surfing or searching will be limited to sites of a desired PICS classification.

Platform for Privacy Preferences

The Platform for Privacy Preferences (P3P) is using XML to provide a framework for defining privacy preferences on Web sites. The purpose of this is to enable users to make choices about the suitability of a site based on its privacy policy.

For example, if you didn't want to access a site in which your information or information about your surfing pattern was sold, you could avoid such sites by means of a P3P-dependent choice.

P3P aims to provide the means of accessing such privacy policy information by users in machine-readable form. The latter underpins the possibility of deciding whether to visit a site based on its privacy policy.

Synchronized Multimedia Integration Language

SMIL is an application of XML that uses a declarative language for scheduling multimedia presentations on the Web.

Further information is available at the URL for the SMIL Recommendation mentioned earlier in this chapter. Be aware that SMIL is being revised as discussed in Chapter 17.

MathML

MathML is a means of expressing mathematical information in an XML-compliant format.

If you are interested in the topic, the latest Recommendation is available at

`http://www.w3.org/1999/07/REC-MathML-19990707`

The original MathML Recommendation of April, 1998 can be accessed from that page.

XML Information Set

The XML Information Set is intended to provide a fairly formal description of the information contained within a well-formed XML document. However, XML documents that do not conform to the Namespaces in XML Recommendation, although well-formed, are considered not to have a meaningful information set.

The XML Information Set does not favor a particular class of interface. Examples in the current draft are shown as trees, but event-based and query-based interfaces are equally acceptable.

An XML Information Set for a document has at least two "information items"—a "document information item" and at least one "element information item." Each information item is an abstract representation of some component of an XML document and has a set of associated properties, some of which are core, and some of which are peripheral.

Each XML document has multiple information sets. To quote the current Working Draft: "For any given XML document, there are a number of corresponding information sets: a unique minimal information set consisting of the core properties of the core items and nothing else, a unique maximal information set consisting of all the core and all the peripheral items with all the peripheral properties, and one for every combination of present/absent peripheral items and properties in between. The in-between information sets must be fully consistent with the maximal information set."

The current draft specification lists 15 types of information items. They are not described in detail here, because the draft specification is subject to change.

To review the latest version of the XML Information Set specification go to

`http://www.w3.org/TR/xml-infoset`

XML Signatures

XML Signatures is intended to provide a means of applying digital signatures to XML documents and versions of them so they can be reliably authenticated.

W3C—World Wide Web Consortium

The World Wide Consortium is made up of mostly large software-orientated computer companies—for example, Microsoft, IBM, Sun, Adobe—who constitute the paid-up membership of W3C. W3C expresses its global aspirations by having bases in three continents: in North America at the Massachusetts Institute of Technology, in Europe at INRIA, and in Asia at Keio University, Japan.

The W3C XML activities have been described as consisting (so far) of three phases. Phase 1 led to the production of the XML 1.0 Recommendation of February, 1998. Phase 2 led to the Namespaces in XML and Stylesheet Linking Recommendations in 1999.

Phase 3 of the W3C XML activity is underway. Included in Phase 3 are XML Schema (see Chapter 14), XML Query (see Chapter 17), XLink (see Chapter 12), XPointer (see Chapter 12), and XML Information Set (this chapter).

Much of the work at W3C that relates to the XML standards which we are interested in is carried out in public discussion lists. Other substantive parts are essentially carried out behind closed doors, for "members only."

W3C Activities

The W3C has a number of "activities," of which XML is an important one.

The Document Object Model (DOM) Activity aims to provide an interoperable set of classes and methods to manipulate XML documents from programming languages such as Java, ECMAScript (JavaScript), and VBScript.

With the growing importance of XML, there is some overlap. For example, the version 1.0 XHTML Recommendation while, in a sense, was an XML activity, was carried out by the HTML Working Group.

An overview of the W3C XML activity can be accessed at

```
http://www.w3.org/XML/Activity
```

The W3C's description of current and anticipated XML development is fascinating reading. If you have serious intentions of using XML and related technologies, look at this material to see where it is intended to go.

The following list is a quote from the W3C XML Activity page and gives an indication of just how ambitious and all-encompassing is the vision for XML that the XML Working Group holds.

XML will

- Enable internationalized media-independent electronic publishing.
- Allow industries to define platform-independent protocols for the exchange of data, especially the data of electronic commerce.
- Deliver information to user agents in a form that allows automatic processing after receipt.
- Make it easier to develop software to handle specialized information distributed over the Web.
- Make it easy for people to process data using inexpensive software.
- Allow people to display information the way they want it, under style sheet control.
- Make it easier to provide metadata—data *about* information—that will help people find information and help information producers and consumers find each other.

XML Working Groups

The XML Activity has within it a number of Working Groups that focus on different aspects of the XML puzzle.

The current Working Groups within the XML activity are

- XML Core Working Group
- XML Schema Working Group
- XML Linking Working Group
- XML Query Working Group
- XForms Working Group

The activities of the various XML working groups are coordinated by the XML Coordinating Working Group, which examines issues such as dependencies between the various technologies. For example, in Chapter 12, the dependencies of XPointer on XPath and DOM Level 2 are discussed.

NOTE XHTML (see Chapters 2 and 3) and the emerging aspects of XHTML 1.1 (see Chapter 17) are part of the W3C HTML Activity, not the XML activity. ■

Parts of the Process

W3C is not a standards body sponsored by governments. Therefore its standards cannot be called "International Standards." Instead what would in other contexts be called "standards" are "Recommendations" in W3C jargon. In other words, a W3C Recommendation is essentially a standard; it is fixed (at least until it is formally revised) and it can be quoted as an "official" source document.

Other W3C documents relating to XML are less stable and are essentially "works in progress." The designations are "Candidate Recommendation," "Working Draft," and "Note." A Candidate Recommendation is, as its name suggests, close to becoming a Recommendation. However, it is possible for a Candidate Recommendation to be deleted or substantially revised if substantive comment suggests a fundamental flaw in its methodology or conceptualization.

In addition to the formal Working Groups, some activities have Discussion Forums open to the public. For example, in the MetaData Activity there is the RDF Interest Group mailing list.

W3C has a publicly available description of its processes that can be accessed at

`http://www.w3.org/Consortium/Process/Process-19991111/`

Bureaucracy Gone Mad?

You might have felt totally overwhelmed at some point as you read through this chapter or the other XML chapters by the sheer volume of material, the unfamiliarity of terminology or concepts, its abstractness, or its ever-changing nature. This feeling of disorientation might be made worse by unfamiliarity with the enormous bureaucracy that attends all that goes on around W3C. You could be forgiven for thinking that XML is an interest more suited to lawyers who minutely examine documents than Web or application developers. There is some truth in that.

There is no easy answer for you on the fact that XML is abstract, in many respects. To begin to make the XML family do useful things and to understand how things fit together, you need to understand some fairly abstract concepts. These chapters show you some useful foundational techniques. However, to create an XML-based functioning Web site of any size, you will need to master many details that are beyond the scope of this book. In addition to the many URLs provided in the XML chapters, please see Appendix B, "General Reference Resource," for information on many online XML Resources to help you progress toward mastery of the relevant techniques.

Documents or Data?

As explained earlier, XML arose from Standard Generalized Markup Language, a complex meta-language used for high quality, demanding document processing. SGML was essentially a tool or framework for processing documents, that is, large chunks of text characters.

Initially, XML was designed with essentially the same assumptions in mind. In other words it was envisaged primarily as a tool to process text, in ways similar to but (so it was hoped) more simply, than SGML. The assumption that XML would be used to process text brought with it certain expectations about the uses to which XML would be put and, therefore, the interfaces and constraints that were likely to apply.

However, as XML became more widely known, it became clear that XML also had the potential to act as a means of data interchange across various platforms. If you have used a word processor and a relational database, you have realized that what makes for an efficient way of manipulating documents and an efficient way of manipulating data differ significantly. Similarly, the document-orientated initial assumptions about XML led to standards that had serious limitations when applied to XML as a data interchange standard.

Among the limitations was the inability of Document Type Definitions (DTDs) to define the data type of an XML document element. This deficiency has been a major factor in the drive for a more comprehensive and precise tool to constrain XML data, which is likely to result in an XML Schema Recommendation within the latter part of 2000. For further information on DTDs and XML Schemas, see Chapter 14.

Similarly, version 1 of the Document Object Model was created with documents rather than data in mind. For example, DOM 1.0 requires the full document to be read into memory and held there before a node tree can be constructed. Such an approach is entirely sensible for many documents, with problems occurring perhaps only when processing the very largest documents. When you try to apply such an approach to a data source of several gigabytes, you realize that it is both potentially very expensive for memory chips and potentially very inefficient if minor changes are being made in a large data source.

This evolution from a document-centric family of technologies to one that encompasses the need for data interchange, is one factor that is turning XML from a "simple" technology into a complex interconnected web of XML-based technologies. ●

CHAPTER 11

Creating XML Files for Use

by Andrew Watt

In this chapter

XML Document Fundamentals

In Chapter 10, "Introducing XML," you saw part of the big picture, looking at the W3C and how, in general terms, XML documents interact to produce Web output.

To use XML, you need to follow a whole raft of rules. Unfortunately, many of the rules of XML are not "intuitive," at least not to most normal human beings. There is no easy way through this. You need to look at an entire series of interconnected rules, some of which are expressed (at least in the official documents) in fairly opaque language.

Learning XML can, at times, feel like being lost in a big city. You can see that there is a lot happening but you have no point of reference and feel vulnerable and disorientated; when you try to move around, you can get very frustrated. To move on from there, you need to begin by beginning. So let's begin.

This chapter looks at the fundamental issues of creating XML documents. To produce correct and reliable XML documents, you need to understand the rules that apply to the structure and content of XML documents. To produce correct XML documents efficiently, you need some appropriate tools.

You must look at the terminology of the different parts of an XML document and, to start producing and using XML documents, you need to look at the available tools.

As you saw in Chapter 10, an XML document consists of markup that contains content or, if you prefer, content encapsulated in markup. An XML document consists of an optional prolog, a body, and an optional end-piece sometimes referred to as an "epilog." It is widely perceived that the epilog was a design mistake. It will not be discussed here.

Document Prolog

An XML document might have a prolog but is not required to have one. You should routinely include a prolog because it contains useful information that might, for example, assist code maintenance or debugging at a later date.

The prolog of an XML document consists of the XML declaration (optional), followed by processing instructions (again, optional), comments, and whitespace. This is followed by the optional Document Type Declaration.

So legally, a prolog can be essentially empty or quite complex.

Typically, the first thing in the document prolog is the XML declaration. However, it is not compulsory that an XML declaration be present.

The XML declaration takes the form

```
<?xml version="1.0" standalone="yes" encoding="utf-8" ?>
```

The version number is required if the XML declaration is present. The standalone and encoding attributes are optional. When standalone equals "no," an *external* Document Type Definition is required.

The encoding attribute (sometimes called the encoding declaration) defines character encoding of the document. XML processors by default have to be able to provide Unicode encoding. There are 8-bit (UTF-8) and 16-bit (UTF-16) versions and both are requirements of the XML 1.0 Recommendation. The first 128 characters of UTF-8 are identical to ASCII. If you plan only to use English, your encoding can be ISO-8859-1. However, if you have ambitions to create multilingual global sites, Unicode and UTF might be the way to go.

NOTE Unlike most XML names, the value of the encoding is not case sensitive. This is because XML character encoding is dependent on existing ISO and IANA standards. ■

So, a well formed XML document can have no XML declaration or it can have the minimalist form

```
<?xml version='1.0' ?>
```

NOTE To enclose the version number in an XML declaration you can use either a pair of quotes or apostrophes. Both are legal. ■

The prolog precedes the first `<elements>` of the document. The XML declaration must be on the first line, and nothing must precede it. Even preceding the XML declaration with a single space character can cause problems.

Comments, discussed later in this chapter, can be included in the prolog, as can references to style sheets. For example, the following code snippet associates a CSS style sheet named `CSSTest1.css` with the XML file:

```
<?xml version='1.0'?>
<?xml-stylesheet
    type="text/css"
    href="CSSTest1.css"
    ?>
<!-- This is a comment in the XML document prolog -->
<document>
<!-- This is a comment in the XML document body -->
<!--  Other elements go here -->
</document>
```

The reference to the CSS style sheet is an XML processing instruction:

```
<?xml-stylesheet
    type="text/css"
    href="CSSTest1.css"
    ?>
```

A processing instruction begins with `<?` and ends with `?>`, as you see in the previous example.

The Document type declaration, if there is one, is included in the prolog like this:

```
<?xml version="1.0"?>
<!DOCTYPE greeting SYSTEM "hello.dtd">
<greeting>Hello, world!</greeting>
```

NOTE Be careful to distinguish the Document Type Declaration and the Document Type Definition. They are closely related but not identical. The precise distinction is discussed further in Chapter 14, "Constraining XML—DTDs and XML Schemas." ■

Document Body

In a typical XML document, the document body takes up most of the space. The document body has an element that encloses all other elements.

In our first example from Chapter 10,

```
<?xml version="1.0"?>
<message>
<to>All visitors</to>
<greeting>Hello and Welcome to LearningXML.com!</greeting>
</message>
```

the `<message>` element encloses all the other elements.

The `<message>` element is the ***root element***. The elements `<to>` and `<greeting>` are ***non-root elements***. In this example, the `<to>` and `<greeting>` elements are also child elements of the `<message>` element.

Roots

Some XML-related documentation conveys the idea of a "root" in a confusing way. If you realize that there is confusion in the terminology, you are less likely to be tripped up by it.

Let's go back to the `<message>` element mentioned in the previous section. It is the root element, yet that root element is itself contained within a more comprehensive root, which contains the document body, the prolog, and the "epilog" (although each of those might be empty).

The XML 1.0 Recommendation refers to the comprehensive "root" as the "document entity." The "root element" or "element root"—the `<message>` element in this example—is subsidiary to that "document entity" sometimes also called a "document root."

Just be aware that an unqualified reference to "the root" could be referring to either the document entity or the element root. Sometimes you will need to be sure to which is being referred, but sometimes it won't matter too much.

XML Names

If an XML parser is to properly process an XML document, it must know which characters are permitted in which locations. So, let's take a brief look at the legal characters that can be used in constructing an XML name.

All XML names must begin with a letter, an underscore character (_), or a colon (:). In practice, avoid starting an XML name with a colon because it's used, in effect, as a continuation character in namespaces, and so on. In fact, although it's legal, you should entirely avoid using a colon except as a namespace continuation character.

A name can continue using either the characters that are valid to begin a name, or using digits, hyphens, or full stops.

XML is case sensitive. Therefore, an element named `<MyName>` is treated by XML as different from `<Myname>`, which is different from `<myName>`. The encoding attribute of the XML declaration is one exception. The encoding attribute value is not case sensitive.

"XML" in any combination of upper- or lowercase characters is a reserved word and you can't use it for your own purposes.

Tags and Elements

There are three types of tags: start-tags, end-tags, and empty-element tags. Standalone tags will be mentioned later in this chapter.

This is a start tag in the code snippet:

```
<greeting>
```

The corresponding end tag is

```
</greeting>
```

This is the greeting element:

```
<greeting>Hello and Welcome to LearningXML.com</greeting>
```

In other words, an element consists of the start tag together with the end tag and the content between those two tags.

Where elements are nested, the content of the parent element includes its child elements and any content they might have.

Empty Elements

An empty element can be written as

```
<element></element>
```

XML also provides a special syntax for elements that are empty. Thus

```
<element/>
```

means exactly the same as the preceding code snippet. Both are valid notations for an empty `<element>` element.

This notation can be used, for example, with XHTML elements such as `<br/>` and `<hr/>`, in which a new line or a horizontal rule doesn't contain anything.

The same syntax can be used more generally for empty tags. You will probably know that the `<hr/>` tag can take a variety of attributes that describe its appearance. Other non-XHTML tags can be used in a similar way. (The tag is "empty" in that there is no information between the opening tag and the closing tag; however, useful information can be stored within the allowable attributes of the opening tag, just like the `<hr/>` tag can contain useful information.)

Attributes

Attributes provide a little extra information about an element. Returning to the XHTML `<hr/>` tag, if you wanted a 6-pixel high horizontal rule, you could write

```
<hr size="6" />
```

A single tag can contain many attributes. For example, you could store information about discount and product ID numbers like this:

```
<widget discount="5%" product_id="WID8288"></widget>
```

Whitespace

The four characters that XML treats as whitespace are shown here with their hexadecimal values.

Description	Hexadecimal Value
Horizontal Tab	09
Line Feed	0A
Carriage Return	0D
Space character	20

The XML 1.0 Recommendation requires that an XML parser pass all characters including whitespace to an application. It is, therefore, up to the application to handle any whitespace that is present in the original XML document.

CAUTION

Although XML uses Unicode, XML does not treat some characters, which Unicode treats as spaces, as being whitespace.

XML differs from both HTML and SGML in the details of how it handles whitespace. Sometimes it might be particularly important to preserve whitespace, for example, in the layout of a song or poem. This can be signaled by the xml:space attribute as exemplified by the following:

```
<!ATTLIST poem xml:space 'preserve'>
```

You will learn more about attribute declarations in Chapter 14.

Character References

Character references are typically used in XML where the literal form of a character would cause problems. These take the form of &#NNNN; where NNNN can be one or more numerical digits corresponding to a Unicode character value permitted by XML.

Entity References

Consider what might happen when an XML parser meets the following code snippet:

```
<Arithmetic>In arithmetic 5 < 6</Arithmetic>
```

The parser could be forgiven for taking the content < 6 as the beginning of a new element. To avoid confusion for the parser in such situations, XML provides some predefined entity references.

There are five entity references that are built in to XML. These references might be used as "escape sequences" for the XML literal delimiter characters in situations such as those shown previously. The entity references appear in the following table:

Entity	Use
&	Used to escape the & character, except in CDATA sections
<	Used to escape the < character, except in CDATA sections
>	Used to escape the > character
'	Used to escape the ' character in string literals
"	Used to escape the " character in string literals

So, using the applicable entity reference, the code would look like this:

```
< Arithmetic>In arithmetic 5 &lt; 6</Arithmetic>
```

Using the predefined entity reference < prevents the parser from tripping over this syntax.

These predefined entities are accompanied by a range of other entities that XML allows.

Except for those five built-in entity references, all entity references must be declared before they are used in an XML document.

Entities are discussed further in the context of Document Type Definitions (see "Document Type Definitions [DTDs]" in Chapter 14).

Comments

Comments are permitted within the prolog of an XML document and elsewhere provided they are not contained in markup.

Comments in XML documents look the same as they do in HTML and XHTML. They begin with a less-than sign, followed by an exclamation mark and two dashes, `<!--` and end with two dashes and a greater-than sign, `-->`.

For example, this is a valid comment that could be included in the document immediately after the XML Declaration:

```
<!--Remember to be nice to everybody visiting LearningXML.com -->
```

Comments are illegal if included within markup. The following comment would not be legal, because the comment is inserted within the opening `<greeting>` tag:

```
<greeting <!--Remember to keep all visitors to
➥LearningXML.com up to date with XML --> >
Hello and welcome to LearningXML.com</greeting>
```

Comments might not contain the string "--," which are two successive dashes. This limitation is imposed on grounds of SGML compatibility.

The XML 1.0 Recommendation leaves it open as to whether an XML processor does or does not pass on comments to an application.

Processing Instructions

Processing instructions are used to indicate to an application what should be done with the XML document that contains the processing instruction. A processing instruction is often abbreviated as PI.

The example you looked at earlier

```
<?xml-stylesheet
    type="text/css"
    href="CSSTest1.css"
    ?>
```

is a processing instruction that indicates the style sheet `CSSTest1.css` should be applied to the XML document within which the processing instruction is contained.

However, that syntax is not included within the XML 1.0 Recommendation. It received its own W3C Recommendation called "Associating Style Sheets with XML Documents Version 1.0." Details can be found at

```
http://www.w3.org/1999/06/REC-xml-stylesheet-19990629
```

The more general syntax of a processing instruction is

```
<?target .. instruction ..?>
```

Processing instructions can be used as hooks for scripting or server-side includes. Detailed discussion of such uses of PIs is beyond the scope of this book.

CDATA Sections

CDATA sections provide a way of signaling to an XML processor that part of the content of an XML document should not be parsed. This is useful when the XML document includes characters that would otherwise be recognized as markup. For example, if this chapter were an XML document, it would be necessary to include sample XML code within CDATA sections.

The basic syntax for a CDATA section is

```
<![CDATA[The content of the CDATA section goes here.]]>
```

If this chapter was an XML file, I could preserve entities as written by including the relevant part in a CDATA section. For example, the earlier example would be preserved like this:

```
<![CDATA[
<Arithmetic>In arithmetic 5 < 6</Arithmetic>
]]>
```


CAUTION

CDATA sections are not a good way to include hexadecimal code in an XML document because such code might contain the sequence equivalent to "]]>", the closing delimiter for a CDATA section.

Document Type Declaration

So far in this chapter, code snippets have been used without a Document Type Declaration. A Document Type Declaration tells you about the Document Type Definition (DTD) for the document. You can see the potential for confusing the two right away.

A Document Type Declaration tells an XML processor where the Document Type Definition exists. The Document Type Declaration is sometimes called the "doctype declaration" or "DOCTYPE declaration." The Document Type Declaration must be within the XML file. Specifically, it must be in the prolog of an XML document.

By contrast, the Document Type Definition can be inside the XML file, in a separate file, or partly inside the XML file and partly in a separate file. The syntax of a Document Type Declaration makes it clear whether the Document Type Definition is inside the XML document, in a separate DTD file, or partly internal and partly external. In the latter case, the part of the DTD within the XML document is called the *internal subset* and the part in an external file is called the *external subset* of the DTD.

You'll see the Document Type Definition in more detail in Chapter 14. For the moment, it's sufficient to note that it uses a syntax inherited from SGML which is, at first sight, distinctly user unfriendly.

XML Tools

Hopefully, you will choose to follow along with the XML Mini Project from Chapter 10 and with the other examples you will see in the next few chapters. To do that, you will need some basic tools, some of which you might already possess.

TIP

All the examples in the XML section of this book can be constructed using only these three tools, which are available for free on Windows 9x machines:

- Windows Notepad
- Internet Explorer 5.0 (make sure you have the latest download from Microsoft.com)
- Instant Saxon, an XSLT processor described later

You are, of course, free to work the examples using other equivalent tools, some of which are briefly discussed here.

However, there is no substitute for actually doing examples. By typing in the code you learn more about how XML documents are constructed (and what happens when you make mistakes). As you work through examples, you become aware of aspects you don't see when you are just reading. So, I encourage you to work through the examples, although you might find it easier just to read the first time through.

If you want to use a plain text editor which is a little more sophisticated than Windows Notepad, take a look at the Programmer's File Editor, which can be downloaded free from

`http://www.simtel.net/pub/simtelnet/win95/editor/pfe101i.zip`

As you probably noticed when reading the W3C section of Chapter 10, the XML family is in a state of rapid flux. Just as the succession of changes or new Recommendations makes it difficult to read all that is emerging, it also makes it particularly difficult for software tool vendors to keep up.

CAUTION

There are incompatible versions of XML and its associated technologies around. This arises from some software developers anticipating what some of the standards might contain or trying to "improve" on the standards. For example, Microsoft produced a dialect of XSLT, which it refers to as XSL, in 1998 that is significantly different from the W3C approved version. Microsoft states it is now working to produce a more standards-compliant version of XSL in Internet Explorer.

XML Editors

You will be able to work through the examples in the XML chapters using only Windows Notepad or a similar plain text editor and other free tools mentioned in this chapter. XML, when contained in a file, is simply text. Sometimes it is pretty complex text but, although XML files can refer to non-text files, the XML files themselves are simply text.

This section briefly looks at some alternatives to Notepad that you can use to edit XML documents.

NOTE This section describes only a few of a rapidly growing range of XML editors. Many other products can provide similar facilities to those mentioned. ■

XML Notepad

Microsoft has created a fairly simple XML-orientated editor targeted specifically at producing XML documents. It is called XML Notepad and is available for free download. At the time of this writing, the available version is Beta 1.0.5.01. This version is limited in several ways. It cannot create DTDs and it implements a fairly early draft version of XML Schema, so if your application uses schemas be very cautious.

XML Notepad does let you visually create and restructure a logical tree in a very straightforward way (see Figure 11.1). It probably isn't suitable for serious XML work but, because it's free and a relatively small download, it's worth spending a little time to get a feel for what an XML editor (albeit a very basic one) can do.

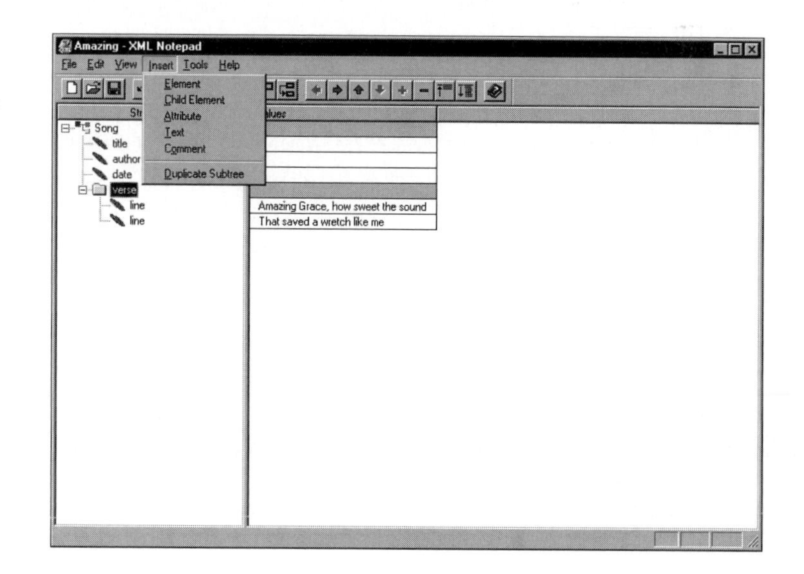

FIGURE 11.1
XML Notepad's Insert menu allows elements, attributes, text, and comments to be inserted. Notice the useful facility to duplicate a sub-tree (in this case, the verse sub-tree).

With XML Notepad you needn't feel under pressure to create your tree perfectly the first time. The toolbar contains facilities to easily rearrange any tree you create into the form which makes most sense.

XML Notepad also has a facility to allow the XML source code to be viewed as in Figure 11.2. When you view the XML source, you will also be told if your code is well-formed or not. Unfortunately you cannot edit the XML code in source view. Windows Notepad or any other plain text editor can be used to do that, when desired.

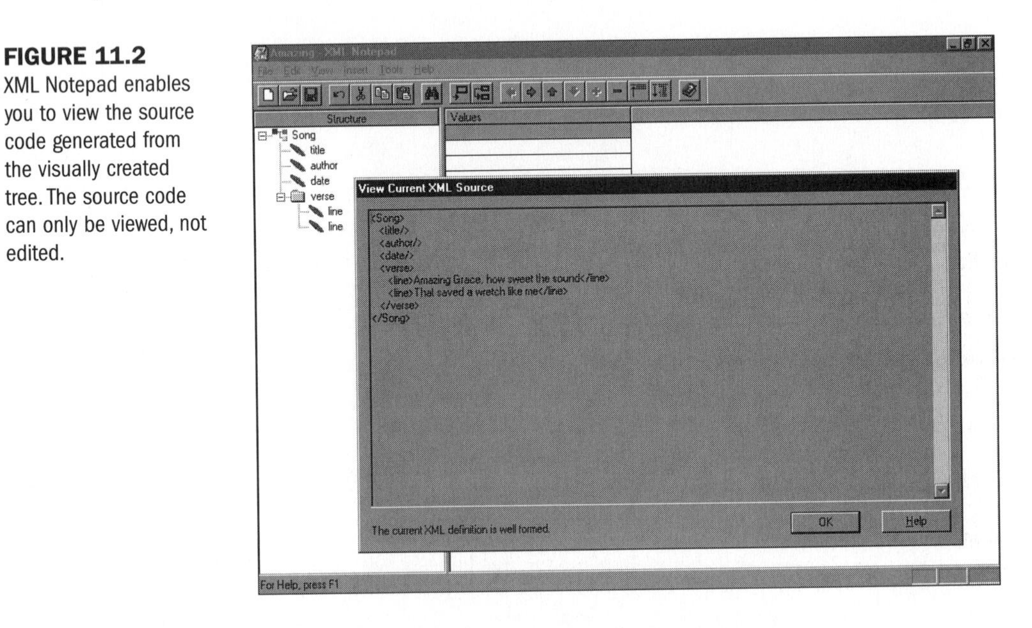

FIGURE 11.2
XML Notepad enables you to view the source code generated from the visually created tree. The source code can only be viewed, not edited.

NOTE IBM has an XML Editor which, like XML Notepad, is largely tree-based and is free. Xeena is Java-based and therefore can be run on any client platform. Xeena can be downloaded from IBM AlphaWorks at `http://www.alphaWorks.ibm.com/`. ■

XML Writer

XMLWriter is a much more sophisticated product than XML Notepad (see Figure 11.3). It is currently available as shareware, costing around $45. These comments relate to XMLWriter version 1.21.

It provides many of the facilities that you would expect from a visual programmer's editor.

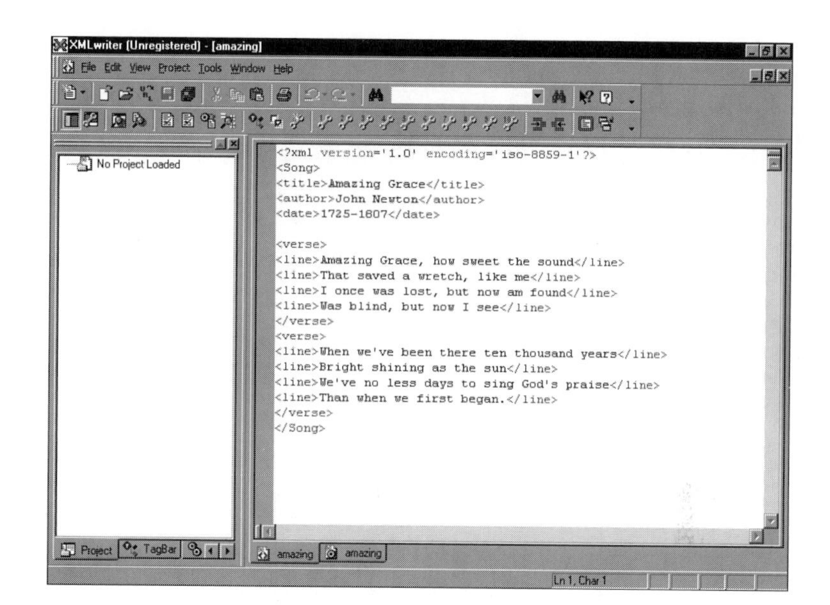

FIGURE 11.3
Notice the tabs at the bottom of the left pane for Project, Tagbar, and Output information. Notice, too, the multipane design in the main window so that you can have an XML source file (in this case `amazing.xml`) and an XSL style sheet (`amazing.xsl`) open together.

At the time of this writing, a 30-day free trial is available for download on the `http://www.xmlwriter.com` Web site.

XMLWriter offers useful functions such as checking XML or XSL documents for "well formedness" and, where there is a DTD, for validity. When you are starting to write XML or when you are producing a large document, this type of aid is a significant help in identifying the cause of problems or just checking that you haven't omitted a markup character or closing tag. If there is an error while attempting to validate a document, XMLWriter will flag the line where it believes the error exists. Unlike error messages in programming languages such as Java, the error messages in XMLWriter usually correctly identify the source of the problem. Checking for well-formedness can be done as shown in Figure 11.4.

After you get beyond mastering the basics, you might think of carrying out a serious XML project involving a substantial number of files. XMLWriter provides assistance by allowing you to create named projects with which you can associate individual files.

XML Spy

XMLSpy is currently at version 3.0 and the Pro version costs $149. There is also a Lite version that currently costs $39. A 30-day evaluation copy of XMLSpy 3.0 is available for free download from `http://www.xmlspy.com/`.

XMLSpy is similar to Microsoft Visual Studio in its screen layout (see Figure 11.5). It provides a potentially powerful, but complex, integrated development environment. It gives a number of views of your XML document.

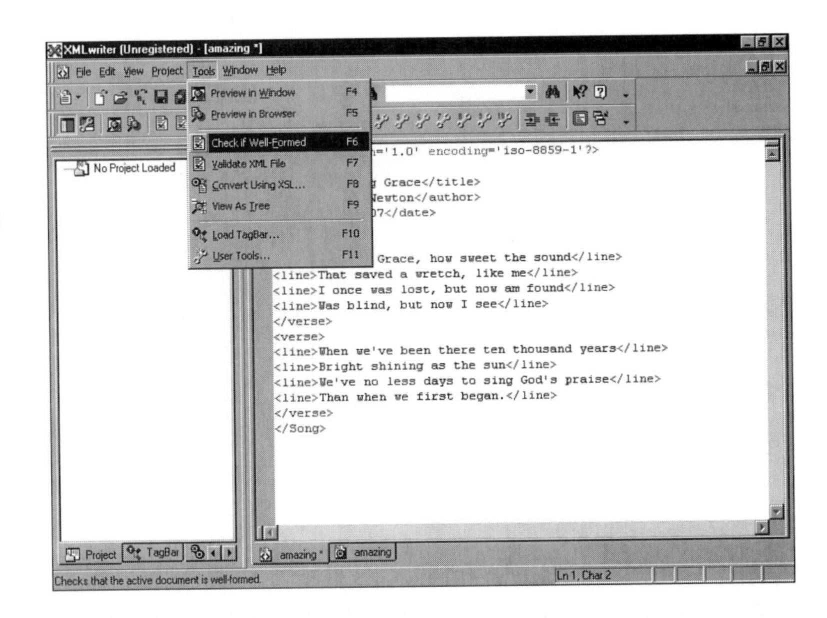

FIGURE 11.4
Some XML editors will check well-formedness for you. XML Writer can do this as shown here: the Tools menu of XML Writer shows the Check if Well-Formed option highlighted.

FIGURE 11.5
Some XML editors provide an integrated development environment for creating larger projects which include facilities for multiple views of the data. The Integrated Development Environment in XMLSpy 3.0 showing a file in Enhanced Grid View is seen here.

One of the interesting features of XMLSpy is its capability to create a DTD from a prototype XML document. If you are becoming fluent in XML but find DTD syntax a bit opaque, this could be a useful timesaver as well as a useful tutor. Remember, of course, that you must decide the number of elements allowed or required in the DTD. You can also have the facility use an external XSLT processor rather than the default one.

When using plain text editors, you must know exactly what you want to type. Some XML editors, including XMLSpy, can offer a range of possible ways to complete what you are typing. XMLSpy can, for example, show you as you type a list of suitable matching elements or attributes. When you complete a start tag, XMLSpy can enter the closing tag. That can be great or it can be a big nuisance, depending on how you code. When you are editing an element, you can see a list of applicable attributes.

XMLSpy has the makings of a serious XML editor. Yet the documentation that accompanies it can be patchy. The sales material on the Web site is often clearer than the help files. Also XMLSpy pauses inexplicably for a second or three occasionally for no obvious reason. At other times it runs smooth and fast.

The help documentation on XMLSpy 3.0 is a "work in progress" at the time of this writing. Hopefully that and other wrinkles will be ironed out soon. XMLSpy has the potential to be a *very* useful tool.

XMetal

XMetal version 2.0 has just been announced but at the time of this writing no further information was available. Version 1.2 is a powerful but expensive XML editor, priced at $495.

Softquad, the creators of XMetal, also produce the HoTMetaL HTML editor, which is currently in version 6. Softquad has applied some of the experience gained in that process in producing XMetal.

Softquad has a track record in Web authoring software and also more serious markup authoring tools.

Other XML Editors

If you can cast your mind back a few years, you will possibly recall that suddenly all word processors boasted the facility to "save as HTML." The same process is again underway, but this time the focus is on the capability to process XML text or save XML. If you already own a word processor or office suite and the XML editing facility is included or is a free or low-cost upgrade, this might be an attractive option. Not the least of the advantages is that you probably are already familiar with many aspects of your favorite word processor and can avoid having to learn a new interface to edit XML.

Some other dedicated XML or XSL editors that you might want to evaluate include

Debit—`http://www.interati.org/`

Excelon—`http://www.exceloncorp.com/products/`

IBM XSL Editor—`http://www.alphaWorks.ibm.com/tech/xsleditor`

Morphon—`http://www.morphon.com/`

There is only one XML editor that I have tried and disliked—XML Pro version 2 from Vervet Logic. I found the interface clumsy to use. Others may like it; individual preferences vary.

When choosing an XML editor, the first question you need to ask yourself is *why* you need an XML editor. The second question is *when* do you need it. Unless you have a clear production need now, it is advisable to spend some time using a plain text editor and getting used to XML. After you can do something useful with XML, take note of what might be a timesaver. Begin to download evaluation copies of some of the editors mentioned here. See what facilities they offer, evaluate whether you need them, and determine whether they work the way you work. Put off a decision until you actually do need an XML editor—the facilities are improving month by month.

Before spending your hard-earned money, think again about just how much you can do with XML using only Windows Notepad or the Programmer's File Editor or similar text editors. Only you can judge if a commercial XML editor will give you value for money for your task.

The number of available XML editors is increasing rapidly, many being released as betas or preview releases. Information in the XML tools section of LearningXML.com continues to be updated. There is a list of other resources on XML tools in the XML section of Appendix B, "General Reference Resource."

XML Parsers

An XML parser (also known as an XML processor) examines the syntax and logical content of an XML document. All parsers examine the XML document to determine whether it is "well formed." In addition, validating parsers examine the document to confirm that the document complies with the applicable Document Type Definition (DTD).

XML parsers are, technically speaking, relatively simple to write, so an increasing number are available, usually for free download. Quite possibly, you will never need to directly use an XML parser; you can use a composite tool of some type that accesses an XML parser, which you never actually see. For example, XML Writer uses the Microsoft MSXML parser behind the scenes.

However, if you do have an interest in "getting your hands dirty," many XML parsers are available.

For example, the IBM XML4J Java-based parser can be downloaded from the IBM AlphaWorks site:

`http://www.alphaworks.ibm.com/`

An XML document, as you saw in the examples in Chapter 10, is essentially just a sequence of text characters. There are rules about the sequence that those characters can take. Simple text editors will accept characters whether or not they are correct, as far as the XML 1.0 Recommendation is concerned. Slightly more sophisticated tools, such as XMLWriter, can on demand check whether an XML document is well-formed. To do that, XMLWriter uses a version of the Microsoft XML parser.

So what does a parser do? How does it make "sense" of a stream of text characters?

Essentially an XML parser scans sequentially through the XML text file. It identifies the parts, for example, elements of the XML document. If the parser is validating, it needs to carry out a similar process on a DTD to identify the permitted structure of the XML document. The parser then proceeds to compare the structure of the XML document with that defined in the XML 1.0 Recommendation (well formedness) and in the applicable DTD (validity).

MSXML

Microsoft's approach to XML and XSL was mentioned simply to say that it is something to watch very closely. Given that the MSXML parser has been changing at a frantic pace in the weeks prior to this writing (there were preview releases in both March, May, and July 2000), it isn't covered here in any detail.

The Microsoft publicity material for the May and July 2000 releases of the MSXML parser highlights "better" support for XSLT and XPath among the improvements as well as the addition of support for SAX. With the July 2000 Preview Release Microsoft MSXML is now very close to compliance with the W3C standards.

TIP To see Microsoft's current XML offerings and developer support, visit its XML Developer Center at `http://msdn.microsoft.com/xml/default.asp`

The MSXML parser, albeit currently in preview release, opens new possibilities in part because it can be integrated with a standard Web browser, Internet Explorer, and other Microsoft technologies. This means that the interface for using MSXML in its final release is likely to be much more user friendly than those of Instant Saxon or XT.

TIP Microsoft offers useful code samples using XML and XSLT in the Microsoft Online Code Center located at `http://msdn.microsoft.com/code/`. In the left frame of the Web page, choose Code Examples, Web Development, and then XML.

The downside of MSXML is that, in its official releases, it has been non-standard or, more precisely, parts of it are non-standard. Worse still, the documentation on the Microsoft.com Web site rarely, if ever, makes it clear which of the "XSL" aspects it refers to comply with W3C standards and which do not. This, it seems to me, makes for double work in learning the XML standards. For other developers, the integration with other Microsoft tools makes MSXML attractive despite its non-standard features.

XSLT Processors

Several useful W3C-compliant XSLT processors are available.

Instant Saxon

Instant Saxon is an XSLT processor that can be downloaded and run immediately on a Windows 32-bit machine. Saxon is also available as Java source files for use on other operating systems. The section here focuses on Instant Saxon.

Instant Saxon can be downloaded without charge from Michael Kay's Web site at

`http://users.iclway.co.uk/mhkay/saxon/instant.html`

The full version of Saxon can be downloaded from

`http://users.iclway.co.uk/mhkay/saxon/`

TIP

These chapters use Instant Saxon version 5.3.2 on Windows 98 (Second Edition). If you are viewing the results in Internet Explorer 5.0 make sure you have upgraded from version 5.00.2614.3500. If you choose Help About Internet Explorer, you can see the equivalent version number for your installation of Internet Explorer. The examples work with Internet Explorer 5.0 version 5.00.2919.6307 and with Internet Explorer 5.5. To update Internet Explorer from an early version of 5.0, go online, and then within Internet Explorer choose Tools, Windows Update. If you have a version of Windows 98 that is not fully up-to-date, you will have to upgrade that first—the download can take quite some time on a 56Kbps connection. After you have Windows 98 up-to-date, you can go online again and download an update to Internet Explorer.

For many readers, the Instant Saxon user interface might seem primitive. But it works very well, particularly for the fairly simple usage of XSLT in these chapters. All the examples shown were worked on using Instant Saxon.

CAUTION

If you are not accustomed to using a text-based command line, it's easy to mistype an instruction. So, if things don't work the way they are described, check that you have typed things exactly as shown.

If you find that when you open an HTML file from the Instant Saxon directory with Internet Explorer 5.0 that the browser window is blank, there are several possible causes. One possibility is that you chose not to update Internet Explorer by downloading the update. That will predictably lead to a blank browser window, because without the most up to date IE5.0 or IE5.5, Instant Saxon 5.3.2 produces HTML files of length 0 bytes, which, not surprisingly, produces a blank browser window. The solution is to update Internet Explorer.

When using Instant Saxon, it isn't necessary to explicitly associate a style sheet within an XML file. That association can be made on the command line.

For example, to apply the `amazing.xsl` style sheet to the `amazing.xml` file to produce the file `amazing.html`, the syntax on the Instant Saxon command line is

```
saxon amazing.xml amazing.xsl > amazing.html
```

The instructions for downloading and installing Instant Saxon on Michael Kay's Web site are self-explanatory.

XT

XT is an XSLT processor written by James Clark who was the Technical Lead for the committee that produced the XML 1.0 Recommendation and was also editor of both the XSLT and XPath Recommendations.

The XT XSLT processor can be downloaded free of charge from

`http://www.jclark.com/xml/xt.html`

XT is an implementation in Java of XSLT. In addition to the full Java version, a Windows executable can be downloaded from the URL given previously.

MSXML

Microsoft's Preview Release of MSXML as released in July 2000 is now close to compliance with the W3C XSLT Recommendation.

CAUTION

Microsoft issued a version of XSL in 1998, before the W3C standard was finalized, which differed substantially from the eventual W3C standard. Microsoft has announced that they will conform to the W3C standard and recent preview releases of MSXML show every sign that they are serious about moving toward that. The 1998 version of "XSL" is now essentially consigned to the dustbin of history. If you want to use MSXML with XSLT, make sure that you have a version of MSXML no earlier than July 2000.

MSXML3 of May 2000 included a non-standard DOM implementation. If your planned application depends on 100% compliance with W3C standards, check carefully to confirm standards compliance.

XML Viewers

At the present time, there are essentially two general purpose XML viewers generally available: Microsoft Internet Explorer 5.0 (or 5.5) and Netscape 6.0, currently in Preview Release.

CAUTION

Netscape 6.0 is a Preview Release. It isn't even yet officially at a "Beta" release stage. I have installed it on only one machine and it has caused no significant problems. But if you have only one computer and have business or other important data on it, be sure to think through the implications of losing that data in the unlikely event that Netscape corrupted some files. At a minimum, back up *all* important files before downloading and installing the Netscape 6.0 Preview release.

Netscape 6.0 claims to have significant XML support. Please check the Netscape site `http://www.mozilla.org/` for the current level of support.

In addition, Adobe has recently released a preview version of a specialized viewer for Scalable Vector Graphics, an XML-based graphics language discussed further in Chapter 17, "Moving Forward with XML."

Other XML Tools

If you are working on the production of a large XML-based Web site, you might want to produce a template to assist the person keying in data. For example, the following XML template might be re-usable for a range of poetry and songs:

```
<?xml version="1.0" encoding="iso-8859-1"?>
<poeticwork>
<title></title>
<author></author>
<date></date>
<verse>
<line></line>
<line></line>
<line></line>
<line></line>
</verse>
</poeticwork>
```

XMetal and XMLSpy provide some support for such templates. Check the current version to see if they support the functionality you need.

Planning a Project

If you have produced a few HTML or XHTML Web pages, you probably did so while more or less making up the content as you went along, adjusting various aspects until you were pleased with the result.

One of the changes in your work pattern which XML will push you toward is planning more carefully. You saw that to produce an XHTML page in the mini case study, you needed two files: an XML file and an XSLT style sheet to produce the final XHTML page. In a more realistic setting, you might also have a CSS style sheet linked in. And, of course, you would also have a Document Type Definition (DTD), described in Chapter 14, which would constrain the structure of your XML file.

Changing, for example, an element name in one file would necessitate changes in other files. Adding a new element would require changes in the XML file, the DTD, and the XSL style sheet and CSS style sheets if the element is to be transformed and displayed. It's much better to plan thoroughly and minimize fiddling around with multiple files.

Thus, when you plan an XML application on a much bigger scale than a few Web pages, planning is time well spent.

One of the critical issues to address in that planning stage is the structure of XML documents that best represent the problem domain for which you are trying to find a solution. If careful thought goes into that process and appropriate XML document structures are produced (constrained by well crafted Document Type Definitions, which are discussed in Chapter 14), you are likely to find that programming of an XML application maintenance, and further development will be manageable tasks. The work invested in creating a suitable vocabulary (DTD) for your documents will pay off by reduced maintenance difficulties. If the XML document structure poorly represents the problem domain, you might find yourself making long and tedious corrections before you can make worthwhile progress.

CAUTION

Take time to think carefully before you start coding an XML application.

Creating a Document

If you didn't follow through the examples in Chapter 10, take time now to work through them. Get the tools described earlier together and start typing. This is the best way to become intimately familiar with XML code.

TIP

Before you start working through the examples in Chapter 10 and the other XML chapters, make sure the versions of the software you are using are the most up-to-date. There is no absolute guarantee that they will all work together, but if you have the latest versions, the chances are pretty high that they will.

If you don't take time before you begin to install the latest software versions, you might waste time trying to solve problems that could have been avoided by making sure everything was up-to-date in the first place.

CHAPTER 12

Parsing and Navigating XML—SAX, DOM, XPath, XPointer, and XLink

by Andrew Watt

In this chapter

Parsing XML

To use XML documents, you must be able to understand the "meaning" contained in them, to manipulate that logical content, and to find your way around the logical structure of XML documents. This chapter introduces you to some of the concepts relevant to these fundamental mechanisms.

As you saw when you created an XML document in Chapter 10, "Introducing XML," and Chapter 11, "Creating XML Files for Use," an XML document is, at one level, simply a text document. More precisely, an XML file is a succession of characters, which have no intrinsic meaning—at least as far as a computer is concerned. A text editor can create or display an XML file, but only as a series of characters. An ordinary text editor knows nothing of the logical structure contained within the sequence of characters contained in the XML document.

When you, a human being, view an XML document—particularly a lengthy one—your response is determined by your level of knowledge of what the strange but precise sequence of characters means. At first, a long XML document may communicate nothing but jangled complexity to you. Later, you may (or may not) be impressed by the elegance of the solution that may be contained within the XML. The human mind, as it becomes familiar with XML, performs complex transformations and interpretations.

Similar problems apply to computers accessing the "meaning" or logical structure in an XML document. A computer will "look" at an XML document and quite rightly say it is just a sequence of characters.

Because XML is a means for a computer to communicate with a computer, you need to access the logical content or "meaning" of an XML document. You need to use some means to change the XML document from a stream of characters into something that expresses a logical structure.

An XML parser or processor that sequentially examines the individual characters in an XML file and creates a logical structure from those characters can accomplish this transformation. The XML 1.0 Recommendation is, in a sense, a description of the rules that describe the relationship between the input succession of characters and an output logical structure (or "meaning," if you prefer). Because XML's purpose is to facilitate computer-to-computer communication, an XML parser or processor has an output that another piece of software or computer can process further.

A slightly different, more specific way to express this idea follows: The purpose of parsing an XML document is to make interfaces available to another application so that the application can access the logical structure of an XML document's contents and inspect or manipulate those contents.

The XML 1.0 Recommendation has much to say about how an XML parser (called an "XML processor" in the Recommendation) has to behave in response to an XML document, particularly in Section 5 of the Recommendation. For example, a validating parser must be able to recognize whether an XML document is both valid and well formed. A non-validating parser is not required to recognize whether an XML document is valid, but it is required to behave according to the XML 1.0 specification in how it responds to well-formed documents.

NOTE An XML document is *well-formed* when it conforms to the syntax rules of the XML 1.0 Recommendation. An XML document is *valid* when it conforms to the syntax rules of the XML 1.0 Recommendation and also conforms to the constraints applied through the applicable Document Type Definition. ■

Let's think about how a receiving application can handle the output from an XML processor.

There are essentially four ways to read an XML document from a program. First, you can do it yourself (or, more precisely, write computer software to do it for you), then process the tags yourself and finally create your own interfaces. This is not recommended, however, because two useful, widely accepted interfaces are available to do the same thing, based on well-tested and well-thought-out approaches. Those two interfaces are SAX and DOM, which are described in more detail in a moment.

The fourth way (now largely outdated) is to use an XML parser that has a proprietary API. The difficulties in maintaining applications across multiple proprietary APIs led to SAX's development.

The two principal interfaces for accessing and manipulating the content of an XML document are SAX (the Simple API for XML) and DOM (the Document Object Model).

NOTE SAX and DOM are commonly contrasted as follows: SAX is an event-based API. DOM is a tree-based API. ■

For both SAX and DOM, the logical content of an XML document can be visualized, in a sense, as a tree.

Yet SAX and DOM differ fundamentally in how they approach this task of extracting the logical content of an XML document. SAX essentially lays out the document in time, whereas DOM lays it out in space. SAX moves through the document noting and expressing the logical structure of the XML document as a series of "events"—for example, when it finds an opening or closing tag of a particular type—whereas DOM creates a tree structure in memory representing the logical structure of the document content.

Suppose you have an XML file that includes the following code snippet:

```
<purchase>
  <total_value currency="$US">10,500
  </total_value>
</purchase>
```

Suppose you want to give preferred customers a 20% discount on all orders totaling more than $10,000. With SAX, your application would need to say something like, "For every event associated with a purchase element that passes by where the total value is more than $10,000, deduct 20% from the invoice amount." If you were using the DOM interface to do a similar thing, you would, in effect, be telling your application something like, "For every `<purchase>` element that is a descendant of the root, when the content of its `<total_value>` child element is greater than $10,000, deduct 20% from the invoice amount."

NOTE If you want to use either SAX or DOM in your Java applications, you might find that investigating the JAXP (Java API for XML Parsing) package, released in March 2000, to be worthwhile. The package can be found at `http://java.sun.com/xml/`. ■

In the next two sections, you will look more closely at SAX and DOM.

▶ For more information on using SAX and DOM, **see** Chapter 42, "Java and XML"

SAX—The Simple API for XML

SAX is one of very few XML-related standards mentioned in this chapter that did not originate from a committee in the W3C. SAX arose as the result of discussions on the XML-DEV mailing list.

David Megginson was instrumental in the creation of SAX, and his Web site at `http://www.megginson.com` is where the SAX standard, now at version 2.0, is maintained.

How does SAX work? When an XML parser works through an XML document, SAX associates an event with each tag (opening or closing) or block of text that it meets. Notification of that event can be passed to your application. Your application can then appropriately handle each event in accordance with the purpose of your application. In other words, you can write event handlers for the events that SAX produces.

If SAX looked at the XML document from Chapter 10

```
<?xml version="1.0"?>
<message>
<to>All visitors</to>
<greeting>Hello and Welcome to LearningXML.com!</greeting>
</message>
```

it would break the document down into a linear succession of events, something like the following pseudocode:

```
start document
start element: message
start element: to
characters: All visitors
end element: to
start element: greeting
characters: Hello and Welcome to LearningXML.com
end element: greeting
end element: message
end document
```

It is up to the receiving application to recognize that such a sequence of events is consistent with a well-formed XML document and to conduct appropriate further processing or display. In principle, processing these events is much the same as processing events from a user interface, such as mouse clicks. Notice that there is no necessity to hold the whole document in memory.

Unlike DOM, which requires all of a document tree to be created and held in memory at one time, SAX has no such requirement. SAX's approach has performance or cost advantages for handling very large XML documents or data sources in some settings.

SAX has these advantages:

- It can parse files of any size.
- It is efficient when you want to create your own data structure.
- It is useful when you want only a small subset of the data.

SAX has the following disadvantages:

- It does not provide random access to the document.
- It can be difficult to implement complex searches.
- It gives no access to the DTD.
- It does not maintain lexical information in the original document.
- It is not supported by current, widely available browsers.
- It is read-only.

The last point can be overcome by passing the document that has been read, after any processing, to an XML generator.

SAX is primarily a Java interface. The SAX interface is supported by virtually every Java XML parser. However, SAX is also supported in PERL, Python, and C++.

NOTE SAX 2.0 was released in May 2000 and added support for XML Namespaces, for filter chains, and for querying and setting features and properties in the parser. ■

▶ For more information on using SAX with Java to process XML, **see** Chapter 42, "Java and XML"

Further general information on SAX can be found at `http://www.megginson.com/SAX/`.

Document Object Model (DOM)

The DOM being referred to in this section is the W3C Document Object Model Recommendation defined in the "Document Object Model (DOM) Level 1 Specification Version 1.0" of October 1, 1998. The URL for that document is `http://www.w3.org/TR/1998/REC-DOM-Level-1-19981001`.

Currently, the "Document Object Model (DOM) Level 2 Specification Version 1.0" is a Candidate Recommendation, whose latest version at the time of this writing was located at `http://www.w3.org/TR/2000/CR-DOM-Level-2-20000510`.

CAUTION

The DOM referred to in this section is not the only DOM around. DOM version 0, applicable to HTML, was released in 1997. XML DOM 1.0 and DOM version 0 are both different from the JavaScript DOM and the Internet Explorer 4 DOM. Internet Explorer 4 DOM is fairly close to DOM 0, whereas the Netscape DOM differs significantly. In future browser versions, it is expected that both Internet Explorer (5.5 or 6) and Netscape 6.0 will fully implement the XML DOM–that is, DOM 1 and (presumably later) DOM 2. After previous disappointing experiences, developers will be watching closely to see how well those promises are fulfilled.

When using DOM, you can think of an XML document as a tree of nodes.

DOM 1.0 applies both to XML and HTML documents and has both HTML and Core (Fundamental and Extended interfaces) parts. An HTML document processor will need to exhibit both the HTML parts and the Fundamental interfaces (for example, Document, Node). Web browsers need to implement those. XML processors need to implement both the Fundamental and the Extended interfaces such as DTD, Processing Instruction, Entity, and Entity Reference.

NOTE A DOM tree is not merely a tree of document elements; it also contains nodes for comments and processing instructions and nodes that wrap the text content of an element in a separate node (that is, as a child of the element's node). ■

The objects in the DOM allow developers to read an XML document, to search it, or to insert, modify, or delete parts of it.

DOM has the following advantages:

- It allows random access to the document tree.
- It allows a document to be modified in memory.
- It maintains the lexical information of the original document.
- Some information about the DTD is maintained.

DOM has the following disadvantages:

- It is memory intensive when processing large documents.
- It is inefficient when you want only a small subset of the information.
- It can take a considerable period of time to create a large DOM tree.

Viewed from a DOM perspective, each XML document consists of a tree of nodes.

The types of nodes allowed in the DOM 1.0 Recommendation are listed in Table 12.1 together with their allowable child nodes.

Table 12.1 DOM Node Types and Their Permitted Contents

Node Type	Can Contain
`Document`	`Element` (maximum of one), `ProcessingInstruction`, `Comment`, `DocumentType`
`DocumentFragment`	`Element`, `ProcessingInstruction`, `Comment`, `Text`, `CDATASection`, `EntityReference`
`DocumentType`	no children
`EntityReference`	`Element`, `ProcessingInstruction`, `Comment`, `Text`, `CDATASection`, `EntityReference`
`Element`	`Element`, `Text`, `Comment`, `ProcessingInstruction`, `CDATASection`, `EntityReference`
`Attr`	`Text`, `EntityReference`
`ProcessingInstruction`	no children
`Comment`	no children
`Text`	no children
`CDATASection`	no children
`Entity`	`Element`, `ProcessingInstruction`, `Comment`, `Text`, `CDATASection`, `EntityReference`
`Notation`	no children

Be aware of the implications of this table; when an XML document is processed using DOM, the Document Type Declaration, comments, CDATA sections, and character data all become nodes in the DOM tree.

A `DocumentFragment` node need not be well-formed XML. However, in an application this "looseness" can be useful—for example to move a `DocumentFragment` (such as an element node with its `CDATASection` child node) from one point on a tree to another.

`DocumentFragment` is presently a Working Draft `http://www.w3.org/TR/WD-xml-fragment`. Progress on this matter seems to be linked to finalization of the XML Schema Recommendation expected in late 2000.

DOM is two steps removed from actual implementation in code. DOM needs to be translated into the constructs of a specific programming language (Java interfaces, for example), and those need to be implemented in working code. Further discussion of these issues is beyond the scope of this chapter.

The DOM lays out an XML document as a tree in memory. The whole document has to be represented in memory at one time. Thus, using a DOM-based approach to process very large XML documents imposes limitations because of available memory or the costs associated with increasing memory as needed. Additionally, using DOM on very large documents can be a slow process.

NOTE It is possible to transform XML using DOM in a manner similar to using an XSLT style sheet (see Chapter 13, "Transforming XML–XSLT"). However, the DOM 1.0 specification does not allow the use of XPath expressions, which limits the capability of a DOM-based transformation to select target nodes. ■

The W3C has released working drafts for DOM Level 3. Documents released so far for public comment include those relating to Core Specification, Events Specification, and DOM Level 3 Content Models. Up-to-date information regarding DOM Level 3 can be located at `http://www.w3.org/DOM/`.

Why XPath?

Refer to the Mini Case Study from Chapter 10. If you look at the order of the elements in the XML file and compare that order with the order in the XHTML output in the screen shot, it is clear that you are transforming the XML data and reordering it. You are not outputting the elements in the order they exist in the input document.

To transform the XML elements the way you want, you need a way of identifying particular parts of the original XML file and choosing only the desired parts to change. This is where XPath comes in. XPath allows you to match patterns of elements and thus identify unambiguously the element(s) you want to work on.

NOTE In addition to locating element nodes, XPath allows element attributes, processing instructions, and document nodes to be found. ■

In the example, the `xsl:template` was applied to a match equal to "Song"; that is, XPath looked for an element called `<Song>`. Because such a `<Song>` element existed in the document, the `xsl:template` was applied.

```
<xsl:template match="Song">
```

While the style sheet was being applied, all elements nested within the `<Song></Song>` element pair were examined for matches to the subsequent `xsl:apply-templates`.

TIP Think of XPath expressions as broadly equivalent to SQL SELECT statements. Each facilitates, by declarative queries, the selection of data elements for processing.

Another way to think of XPath is that it is similar to standing on a street and giving someone directions, such as "Take the second right and it is on the right at the end." That makes sense only if you know the starting point. In XPath the starting point is the context node. The street directions are the location path. In other words, a location path describes the path from one point in an XML document to another.

XPath Fundamentals

XPath is a W3C Recommendation titled "XML Path Language (XPath)Version 1.0." The specification can be located at `http://www.w3.org/TR/1999/REC-xpath-19991116`.

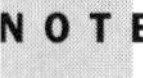

XPath is foundational to parts of XSLT and XPointer. It is likely to be extended further in a forthcoming XML Query specification. ■

What exactly is XPath? The XPath Recommendation states, "XPath is a language for addressing parts of an XML document, designed to be used by both XSLT and XPointer." In other words, XPath tells an XML or XSLT processor how to find its way around an XML document; it is a syntax used primarily to describe how to do that.

XPath also has a syntax for matching patterns in document elements. This is used, for example, to determine whether to apply an XSLT template to a particular element. The Mini Case Study in Chapter 10 and other XSLT examples in Chapter 14, "Constraining XML—DTD and XML Schemas," demonstrate using XPath with XSLT.

One important point to note is that XPath does not use XML syntax. The advantages of not expressing XPath in XML syntax include the capability to use XPath in URIs and in XML attribute values.

XPath supports the Namespaces in XML Recommendation. Because XPath models an XML document as a tree of nodes, the name of a node has a *local part* and a (possibly null) namespace. Together, these two parts constitute the *expanded name*.

The primary way XPath syntax is expressed is as an expression. XPath expressions are evaluated to yield objects that can be of the following types: node-set, Boolean, number, and string.

XPath expressions are evaluated in a context. The context is determined by XSLT or XPointer, whichever is relevant in a particular situation.

The context consists of the following:

- A node (the context node)
- A pair of nonzero positive integers (the context position and the context size)
- A set of variable bindings
- A function library
- The set of namespace declarations in scope for the expression

The variable bindings consist of a mapping from variable names to variable values. The function library consists of a mapping from function names to functions. The namespace declarations consist of a mapping from prefixes to namespace URIs.

XPath expressions can be used in XML element attributes. Because each of these can use a single or double quote, there is a risk of an XPath quote being interpreted as a closing quote; therefore, it has to be represented by `"'"` or `"""`.

One important kind of an XPath expression is a location path. A location path selects a set of nodes relative to the context node. The result of evaluating an expression that is a location path is the node-set containing the nodes selected by the location path. In other words, if the context node is the root element of a document, an XSLT style sheet that is being used with XPath can be applied to the whole document. However, if the context node is somewhere within the document, the scope of the XSLT style sheet will be narrower.

NOTE You parse XPath by dividing the XPath expression string into tokens and then parsing the resulting sequence of tokens. ■

To illustrate XPath syntax, look at four simple examples of a location path (within an XML document describing the structure of a book) taken from the XPath Recommendation:

- **`child::para`**—Selects the para element children of the context node.
- **`child::*`**—Selects all element children of the context node.
- **`child::text()`**—Selects all text node children of the context node.
- **`child::node()`**—Selects all the children of the context node, whatever their node type.

These few examples illustrate something of the power of XPath in selecting which child nodes of the context node are to be processed, for example, by the applicable XSLT style sheet.

Location paths can address more than one "generation" downward from the context node, as in the following examples that address the grandchildren of the context node:

- **`child::chapter/descendant::para`**—Selects the para element descendants of the chapter element children of the context node.
- **`child::*/child::para`**—Selects all para grandchildren of the context node.

XPath location paths can address the parent nodes of the context node, as well as addressing child nodes, as in the following examples:

- **`ancestor::div`**—Selects all div ancestors of the context node.
- **`ancestor-or-self::div`**—Selects the div ancestors of the context node and, if the context node is a div element, the context node as well.

XPath location paths can also be applied to element attributes in an XML document, as in these examples:

- **attribute::name**—Selects the name attribute of the context node.
- **attribute::***—Selects all the attributes of the context node.

Remember that the *document element* is the first visible element in an XML document. Conceptually, that document element is contained within the *document root*. Because the document element is sometimes confusingly referred to as the *root element*, you must be sure to which particular context (whether XPath or otherwise) is referring.

The following examples of location paths make use of "/" to address the document root (as it was just defined):

- /—Selects the document root (which is always the parent of the document element).
- **/descendant::para**—Selects all the para elements in the same document as the context node.
- **/descendant::olist/child::item**—Selects all the item elements that have an olist parent and that are in the same document as the context node.

Location paths can also address nodes by position, as follows:

- **child::para[position()=1]**—Selects the first para child of the context node.
- **child::para[position()=last()]**—Selects the last para child of the context node.
- **child::para[position()=last()-1]**—Selects the last but one para child of the context node.
- **child::para[position()>1]**—Selects all the para children of the context node other than the first para child of the context node.

As you can see from these examples, XPath location paths give great flexibility and power in selecting nodes. However, it is likely that you will need to spend some considerable time becoming familiar with XPath syntax before you can use it to its full potential.

XPath recognizes two types of location paths: absolute and relative.

Absolute location paths begin with "/" optionally followed by a relative location path.

A relative location path consists of a sequence of one or more location steps separated by "/". Each location step selects a set of nodes relative to the context node.

Further information on the syntax of location paths and of XPath syntax is beyond the scope of this chapter. Please see the definitive account in the XPath Recommendation; the URL was given at the beginning of this section.

XPointer Fundamentals

The purpose of XPointer is to identify fragments of XML for any URI reference where the Internet media type is either "text/xml" or "application/xml." In other words, XPointer supports addressing within the internal structure of XML documents and the location of fragments of XML within those documents that are of particular interest.

To put this another way, XPointer allows the structure of a hierarchical document to be examined and a choice to be made from the various components of that hierarchical structure based on their properties, such as element types, attribute values, character content, and relative position.

As of July 1, 2000, the XPointer standard is a Candidate Recommendation to be found at the following URL: `http://www.w3.org/TR/2000/CR-xptr-20000607`.

XPointer is built on top of the XML Path Language (XPath), which you looked at in the preceding section.

CAUTION

At the present time, XPointer is only a *Candidate* Recommendation; therefore, the information given here may be subject to change in a final recommendation. Also be aware that there are some potential interactions with the DOM Level 2 specification, which is also at Candidate Recommendation stage. A change in that could impact on the upcoming XPointer recommendation.

TIP

If you plan to use XPointer, be sure you also understand XPath. The XPointer syntax imposes the XPath requirements for syntax by reference. In other words, you need to understand both the XPointer and XPath documentation to understand how to correctly use XPointer. Like XPath, the syntax of XPointer is a non-XML syntax.

So how does all this work? XPointer uses XPath expressions (see earlier in this chapter) but also provides some extensions to the expressions available within XPath. In the current draft, the XPointer extensions are listed in Section 5 of the W3C Candidate Recommendation.

CAUTION

Some terminology traps exist. XPointer has dependencies on both XPath and DOM Level 2. What DOM calls a *position*, XPointer calls a *point*. This arises because XPointer is based on XPath, and there is a risk of confusion with the notion of an XPath position.

XPointer's extensions to XPath allow it to do the following:

- Address points and ranges within an XML document as well as whole nodes.
- Locate information by string matching.
- Use addressing expressions in URI references as fragment identifiers (after URI escaping).

When you locate an object of interest using XPointer, you can use this as the basis for linking, or you can use the located object for any other purpose appropriate to your application.

CAUTION

XPointer applies specifically to documents of types "text/xml" and "application/xml." It is clear from the current XPointer documents that much wider applicability is anticipated; that is, it is likely that XPointer will be used for many other Internet media types.

XPointer defines errors of the following types: syntax error, resource error, and subresource error. For example, if a URI points to a resource that is not well formed, a resource error is produced. The XPointer specification intends that handling of such errors is defined by the application rather than constrained by the specification.

XPointer uses the same set of characters as XML—Unicode. However, because XPointers are used in URI references where certain Unicode characters are disallowed, it becomes necessary to "escape" disallowed characters. See the Candidate Recommendation for details.

Thus, a URI which looks like this:

```
xpointer(id('résumé')) xpointer(//*[@id='résumé'])
```

will, after disallowed characters are escaped, look like this:

```
doc.xml#xpointer(id('r%C3%A9sum%C3%A9'))
➥%20xpointer(//*%5B@id='r%C3%A9sum%C3%A9'%5D)
```

From this example, you can see that writing such an XPointer is not immediately obvious!

Similarly when XPointers appear in XML documents, they must escape occurrences of < and `&`.

An XPointer, unescaped, would look like this:

```
xpointer(book/chapter position() <= 5)
```

After escaping and after incorporation into an XLink (see the next section), it would look like this:

```
<simpleLink
    xmlns:xlink="http://www.w3.org/2000/xlink"
    xlink:type="simple"
    xlink:href="doc.xml#xpointer(book/chapter position() &lt;= 5)" />
```

XPointer provides three forms of XPointer addressing: *full form* and two abbreviated forms called *bare names* and *child sequences*. More detailed consideration of these variants and other aspects of XPointer syntax may be found in the Candidate Recommendation referenced earlier in this section.

XML Linking Language (XLink) Fundamentals

The XML Linking Language (XLink) specification is, as of July 3, 2000, at Candidate Recommendation stage. The current version can be located at `http://www.w3.org/TR/2000/CR-xlink-20000703/`.

Unlike XPath and XPointer, XLink syntax is XML compliant.

XLink provides a framework for creating both basic unidirectional links and more complex linking structures. As well as providing more complex linking functions, XLink will provide hyperlinks.

W3C anticipates that XLink will be used in conjunction with XPointers, which were described in the preceding section.

XLink allows elements to be inserted into XML documents to create and describe links between resources. As well as supporting the simple unidirectional links provided previously by HTML links (the `<a>` tag,) XLink provides more sophisticated linking facilities.

An XLink *link* is an explicit relationship between resources or portions of resources. A *resource* is any addressable unit of information or service, as discussed in the IETF RFC 2396:

`http://www.ics.uci.edu/pub/ietf/uri/rfc2396.txt`

Resources include, for example, images, files, programs, documents, and query results.

In XLink, the means used to address a resource is a URI (Uniform Resource Identifier) reference. This can be an XML document, part of an XML document, or it can be a non-XML document.

As presently drafted, XLink "allows XML documents to:

- Assert linking relationships among more than two resources
- Associate metadata with a link
- Express links that reside in a location separate from the linked resources"

When XLink is used as a hyperlink, the end user is usually a human being. However, nothing in the XLink specification prevents XLinks from being handled by another computer.

An XLink can associate a single resource or a "set" of resources.

Using or following a link for any purpose is called *traversal*. Traversal involves, at a minimum, a pair of *resources*. The source from which the traversal starts is the *starting resource*, and the destination is the *ending resource*.

The XLink draft specification attaches importance to the concept of an *arc*, which is defined as follows: "Information about how to traverse a pair of resources, including the direction of traversal and possibly application behavior information as well, is called an arc."

The draft specification defines a *local resource* and a *remote resource* as follows: "A local resource is an XML element that participates in a link by virtue of having as its parent, or being itself, a linking element.... Any resource or resource portion that participates in a link by virtue of being addressed with a URI reference is considered a remote resource, even if it is in the same XML document as the link, or even inside the same linking element. Put another way, a local resource is specified 'by value,' and a remote resource is specified 'by reference.'"

CAUTION

Be sure you understand the meaning of local resource and remote resource in the XLink specification.

The specification then uses the concepts of local resource and remote resource to define some special cases of arc as follows: "An arc that has a local starting resource and a remote ending resource goes outbound, that is, away from the linking element. (Examples of links with such an arc are the HTML A element, HyTime 'clinks,' and Text Encoding Initiative XREF elements.) ...If an arc's ending resource is local but its starting resource is remote, the arc goes inbound.... If neither the starting resource nor the ending resource is local, then the arc is a third-party arc. Though it is not required, any one link typically specifies only one kind of arc throughout, and thus might be referred to as an inbound, outbound, or third-party link."

These concepts are then employed in the definition of linkbases, as follows: "To create a link that emanates from a resource to which you do not have (or choose not to exercise) write access, or from a resource that offers no way to embed linking constructs, it is necessary to use an inbound or third-party arc. When such arcs are used, the requirements for discovery of the link are greater than for outbound arcs.... Documents containing collections of inbound and third-party links are called link databases, or linkbases."

The definition of an *XLink application* is given as follows: "An XLink application is any software module that interprets well-formed XML documents containing XLink elements and attributes, or XML information sets containing information items and properties corresponding to XLink elements and attributes." The specification document refers to "elements and attributes," but makes it clear that it also applies to information set equivalents.

An XLink application requires reliably identifying XLinks by using the XLink namespace that has the following reference URI: `http://www.w3.org/1999/xlink`.

Thus, an XLink called `MyElement` would be declared like this:

```
<myElement
  xmlns:xlink="http://www.w3.org/1999/xlink">
  ...
</myElement>
```

XLink's namespace provides global attributes for use on elements that are in any arbitrary namespace. The global attributes are type, href, role, arcrole, title, show, actuate, label, from, and to. Document creators use the XLink global attributes to make the elements in their own namespace, or even in a namespace they do not control, recognizable as XLink elements. The type attribute indicates the XLink element type (simple, extended, locator, arc, resource, or title); the element type dictates the XLink-imposed constraints that such an element must follow and the behavior of XLink applications on encountering the element.

The draft specification gives the following example of a `CrossReference` element from a non-XLink namespace that has XLink global attributes:

```
<my:crossReference
  xmlns:my="http://example.com/"
  xmlns:xlink="http://www.w3.org/1999/xlink"
  xlink:type="simple"
  xlink:href="students.xml"
  xlink:role="studentlist"
  xlink:title="Student List"
  xlink:show="new"
  xlink:actuate="onRequest">
Current List of Students
</my:crossReference>
```

Further details about XLink is available in the draft specification.

As you can see by reading these definitions, the XLink specification is substantially more complex than the <a> tag from HTML or XHTML. It will probably take some time before Web authors sufficiently master the XLink specifications and other XML technologies to fully exploit the power and flexibility that (at this draft stage) the XLink proposal offers.

CHAPTER 13

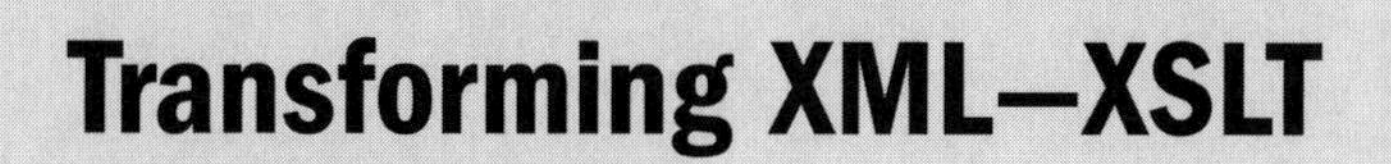

Transforming XML—XSLT

by Andrew Watt

In this chapter

Why XSLT?

The amount of hype surrounding XML has been enormous in the computer press over the last couple of years. Yet, perhaps surprisingly, XML on its own can't do *anything*! XML, at least when narrowly defined as the XML 1.0 Recommendation, is simply a text format and XML documents are merely a succession of character bytes.

So, ways must be found to put this flexible, powerful text format to work.

In Chapter 12, "Parsing and Navigating XML—SAX, DOM, XPath, XPointer, and XLink," you were introduced to the Document Object Model (DOM) and the Simple API for XML (SAX) which, together with an XML processor, transform the character stream in an XML document into a form which programming languages such as Java can manipulate. Both DOM and SAX provide interfaces that programming languages can access.

Before the appearance of XSLT, when you wanted to process an XML input document, it was necessary to write custom applications that accessed the DOM, SAX, or proprietary APIs. Producing custom applications is an expensive, error-prone activity. A better and more standardized solution was needed.

Enter XSLT.

NOTE XSLT does not manipulate an XML document directly but manipulates a tree-like representation of the XML document. ■

CAUTION

The XSLT tree model is conceptually similar to the DOM tree but is not identical to it.

XSLT is a high-level, declarative language. It is rule-based. If you have worked with databases, you will be aware that Structured Query Language (SQL) provides a declarative way to manipulate data held in RDBMS data sources. In SQL, you state what you want to achieve and the details of how it is done are left to the database management system. Manipulating XML using a high-level declarative language also has great potential and this is where the "Transformation" subset of the Extensible Stylesheet Language (XSL) comes in. XSL Transformations is usually abbreviated as XSLT.

TIP Just as SQL is, in a sense, the powerhouse of a relational database management system, so XSLT is the powerhouse of the XML family of technologies.

XSLT transforms (pun deliberate) XML from a static text-based data storage and transmission format into what could be called an active information source—a source of data that can be queried, manipulated, and transformed to provide output either for human beings (XML publishing, if you like) or passed on to another computer program.

XSLT is potentially pivotal to many of the exciting things you can do with XML.

Expect to see XSLT programming skills in high demand over the next few years. As the uptake of XML into real life e-business applications increases, the demand for skills in transforming XML will also grow rapidly.

TIP The full text of the W3C XSLT Recommendation can be accessed at

`http://www.w3.org/TR/1999/REC-xslt-19991116`

You must be aware just how new XSLT is. The formal W3C Recommendation on XSLT was only issued on November 16, 1999 and a conformant XSLT processor, Saxon, appeared on December 3, 1999. XSLT is a very powerful technology but it's not yet mature.

Increasingly, you can expect to see XSLT processors disappear, not in the sense that they won't be there but they will likely be used from within some sort of XML Integrated Development Environment. An XIDE?

If you have been interested in the Web since 1995, you will, no doubt, be aware of the explosion of demand for Java skills. It is not difficult to envisage a similar explosive increase in demand in the near future for XSLT skills, probably in association with other XML-related skills. As always with growth areas, sensible advice would be, "Get in on the ground floor."

A Little History

The preceding part of this section has presented the need for XSLT in a very broad functional perspective, which, in part, has made use of the wisdom of hindsight. In reality, XSLT arose as a practical necessity, as an intermediate technology within the W3C activity that aimed to provide an XML-based means of presenting XML on the Web, analogous in many respects to the use of Cascading Style Sheets for HTML and XHTML. Remember, that one of the aims of the XML 1.0 Recommendation is to separate document structure from presentation. The XML 1.0 Recommendation defined the syntax of the structure of an XML document but did not define how to present XML data.

As the concepts of presenting XML data on the Web were considered in more detail, it became clear that prior to actually displaying XML on the Web, it would be desirable, or essential, to have a means of transforming part or all of an XML document. There would also need to be a mechanism for navigating to or choosing which parts of an XML document were to be transformed or displayed.

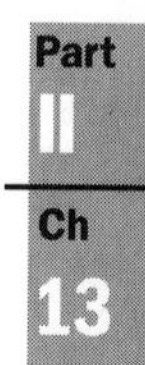

It proved technically more straightforward to complete the definition of the transformation aspect of XSL (which on November 16, 1999 was published as the XSLT Recommendation) and the navigation (or addressing) part of the requirements (published as the XML Path Language or XPath Recommendation).

The XPath Recommendation handled the need for navigating to (or addressing) elements that were to be transformed and the XSLT Recommendation handled the means of actually transforming selected nodes in XML documents. XPath and XSLT interact at various levels and their specifications were developed in synchrony. These two Recommendations were issued together on November 16, 1999. To fully understand all aspects of transformation, the two Recommendations should be read together.

The XPath and XSLT Recommendations can be accessed at

`http://www.w3.org/TR/1999/REC-xpath-19991116` and

`http://www.w3.org/TR/1999/REC-xslt-19991116`

Ironically, the standard for presenting XML data on the Web has yet to be completed. In part, this is because of the complexity of the XSL-FO (XSL Formatting Objects) specification. That difficulty arises in part from a decision to present XML on paper (as well as mobile browsers) as well as on the Web. It seems to me that the original goal of simplicity for XML has been lost with XSL-FO. The original goal of XML was to publish "SGML" *on the Web*. XSL-FO has moved the goalposts so that XSL-FO additionally targets high quality output on paper.

To have a single mechanism, XSL-FO, to output and present information in any medium, whether electronic- or paper-based, has enormous attractions to publishers. Data can be held in one format, either as XML or transformed to XML as an intermediate step, and then by suitable XSLT transformations together with the applying of suitable XSL-FO formatting objects, it can be output to any desired medium.

XSL-FO is described further in Chapter 15, "Formatting and Displaying XML."

XSLT Fundamentals

The power and flexibility that XSLT offers is exciting; however, XSLT is not an easy language to come to grips with. Its declarative approach might not be familiar to you, for example.

XSLT can transform XML documents. The output can, as you have seen in Chapter 10, "Introducing XML," be HTML or XHTML code. Equally, XSLT can act on an XML document and output another XML document, perhaps to be further processed by another XSLT style sheet or to be processed by another application.

This multi-tier approach to the use of XSLT is likely to be highly complex in certain situations.

Further complexity can be added if the output of an XSLT transformation (or series of XSLT transformations) is split between different documents. Such a situation might arise if a reference book were held as one huge XML file whereas output—for example, for the Web—might be in the form of chapters or some other manageable chunk.

NOTE The Saxon XSLT processor allows output in multiple files, by means of a non-standard extension to XSLT. The XSLT Recommendation indicates an aspiration to provide a standard mechanism to achieve that functionality in a future version. ■

Yet another dimension of complexity (and flexibility) is provided by the `<xsl:import>` and `<xsl:include>` elements, which XSLT provides. Both `<xsl:import>` and `<xsl:include>` are used to access the content of other XSLT style sheets and import or include them. The detailed syntax of these elements can be found in Section 2.6 of the XSLT Recommendation.

Similar considerations might apply to more modestly sized XML files if the need was to output WML "cards."

NOTE A WML *card* is a screenful of information for a mobile browser. WML cards are combined as *decks*. For more on WML, see Chapter 15. ■

In practice, as XML documents are shared between companies or departments, it might be unusual for an XML document to be used in the form in which it arrives. In other words, as XML documents increasingly become "real world," they will be transformed for a variety of output devices or local uses. The means for transforming information that XSLT provides will also likely be ubiquitous for transforming the XML into a structure suited to local needs.

TIP Microsoft offers useful code samples using XSLT on its Web site. In the left frame of the Web page, choose Code Examples, Web Development, and then XML. The Microsoft Online Code Center is found at

`http://msdn.microsoft.com/code/`

However, see the Caution that follows.

All software vendors have had a difficult time knowing whether to anticipate the forthcoming XSLT standard and, like Microsoft, risk getting it wrong or choose to wait until the standard is finalized. The Saxon (and the Instant Saxon variant) and the XT processor are both fully W3C compliant. They offer a much more primitive interface than MSXML, for example, but there might be less to relearn in terms of details of syntax when you write serious XSLT-based applications.

CAUTION

On the Microsoft Web site, it can be difficult to know whether the terms "XSL" or "XSLT" are referring to Microsoft's outdated 1998 dialect, to one of several later attempts to more closely approximate the November 1999 W3C standard, or to something that genuinely complies with the W3C standard. Because there are many similarities between the non-standard Microsoft versions and the W3C standard, it can be *very* difficult to determine what is being referred to. Differences that cause no problem while reading through code snippets, can cause your application to fall over because of subtle syntax differences. In a multi-tiered XSLT application, the problem might become visible at some distance from the cause of the error, making debugging particularly difficult. Check carefully.

XSLT works by relying on an XML parser and an XSLT processor. The parser constructs either a time-based (SAX) or space-based (DOM) tree-like structure that represents the logic contained within the XML document. The XSLT processor then takes the high-level declarative instructions contained within the XSLT stylesheet (including any XPath expressions) and navigates through and manipulates the "tree-like structure," thereby producing another tree—the output tree. The output tree can then be output as a text-based document (that is, it is serialized), whether that is plain text, XHTML, or XML, or it might be passed on to another application for further processing.

The previous paragraph shows the need for all parts of the system to work together seamlessly. Departures from W3C standards (Microsoft MSXML, for example) at present can cause processing problems even in fairly simple tasks.

XSLT—The Programming Language

If you take a detailed look at the XSLT Recommendation and have programmed in any high-level programming language, you likely will have seen many aspects of a programming language show through with respect to XSLT. It is possible to argue what is or is not a "programming language," but you will see many programming language capabilities in XSLT.

XSLT provides basic arithmetic facilities, string manipulation, and comparison operations. XSLT has expressions and functions. The syntax of some of these is quite verbose. Putting these facilities together gives XSLT considerable power as a high-level declarative language for transforming XML documents.

XSLT, like SQL, exhibits "closure." This means the output from the language is structurally of the same nature as the input. In the case of SQL, this is database tables. In the case of XSLT, it is tree structures. The important practical implication of closure is that the output from one XSLT transformation, being a tree, can be the input for another XSLT style sheet (which can manipulate a data tree) for a further XSLT transformation.

The facilities provided by XSLT (usually in combination with XPath) provide considerable programming power. This can be extended further by built-in hooks within XSLT that enable it to function in harness with programming languages such as Java. Several XSLT processors—for example, Saxon, XT and Xalan—have a binding mechanism to Java. Detailed discussion of binding to Java is beyond the scope of this chapter.

Binding to external Java functions is likely to reduce portability of style sheets, because of implementation differences between XSLT processors. It is likely that a standard for external binding of functions in other programming languages will appear in XSLT version 2.0. Additionally, Appendix G of the XSLT Recommendation lists a substantial number of desirable enhancements in future versions of XSLT.

Client-Side and Server-Side Transformation

As you will have read elsewhere in this book, scripting languages can be used in both client-side and server-side settings. Similarly, XSLT can be used either on the server or, depending on the capabilities of the client browser, on the client machine.

One of the factors that has driven uptake of server-side processing in a Web setting is the variation in browser capability. If you have client-side scripting but browser capabilities vary, you cannot really be sure how your customer will see your Web site. If, however, you do your scripting on the server, the file sent to the client can be dynamic and fairly sophisticated, yet make few demands on the browser, other than to display an HTML or XHTML page.

Similar considerations apply to XSLT. If you think back to the Mini Case Study in Chapter 10, an XML file was used that was downloaded to a client browser. That XML file referred to an XSL style sheet that was downloaded to the client browser and then the XSLT style sheet was applied to the XML file. In other words, that was client-side use of XSLT. As a preliminary to that, you need to have an XML-capable browser on your computer to run the example.

Given that some current browsers have patchy or non-existent implementations of XML, it can be risky to assume any XML processing capability on the client.

In a commercial situation, it isn't practical to control the version or type of browser that your client will use. So if you use client-side XSLT, you are taking a calculated risk concerning the capacity of your customers' browsers to correctly render your Web page.

Therefore, if you don't want to risk a percentage of your customers being able to see the Web page derived from your XML, executing the XSLT style sheet on the server has much to recommend it. If your output is plain HTML 4.0 or XHTML that obeys the compatibility guidelines contained in Appendix C of the XHTML 1.0 Recommendation, then all but the oldest desktop browsers should handle the situation without difficulty.

Namespaces in XML

Before moving on to look at some XSLT examples, take a look at the Namespaces in XML that underlie the naming of elements such as `<xsl:import>` mentioned earlier.

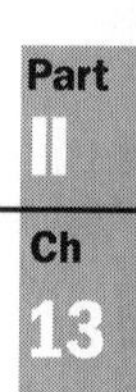

Some people find the concept of namespaces intimidating. Yet, at heart, the concept is very simple. Imagine you walked into a room where John Smith, John Jones, and John Black were all present. You couldn't distinguish one John from another by means of their first name but when you take account of their "surname space," distinguishing one John from another is straightforward.

XML namespaces were created to solve a similar problem. Each XML element or attribute has a qualifier that helps to identify it more precisely. In the `amaxing.xsl` style sheet in Chapter 10, you saw the following construction:

```
<xsl:stylesheet
  xmlns:xsl="http://www.w3.org/1999/XSL/Transform"
  version="1.0">
```

This element declares the Namespace "xsl". The abbreviation "xmlns" in the second line stands for "XML namespace". It points to a URI which hopefully provides a unique identifier for the "xsl" namespace. The URI being pointed to need not contain anything; the uniqueness of the URI string is the framework for the "xsl" namespace.

An XML Namespace is a collection of names, which is identified by a URI reference as you have just seen. Those names are used to identify elements and attributes within XML documents. To take two examples from the "xsl" namespace, the `<xsl:import>` and `<xsl:include>` elements were mentioned earlier in the chapter.

TIP Conformity with the Namespace requirements is necessary for an XML document to be considered to have a meaningful XML Information Set (see Chapter 10).

To return to our surname analogy, it isn't always simple to distinguish different individuals uniquely. For example, in the village my ancestors came from, it wouldn't be a rare occurrence to have three John Watt's in the same room. The way that was solved was to have a unique nickname for each individual (which implicitly mapped to house, date of birth, and so on).

XML namespaces also need a unique mapping for each alias. The problem is solved by mapping each alias to a (hopefully) unique URI (Uniform Resource Indicator). For most practical purposes, at present, a URI is identical to a URL (Uniform Resource Locator).

When applied to people, surname spaces help to avoid getting, for example, mail for one person mixed with someone else's mail. In the XML content, namespaces allow us to use elements or attributes from several sources together.

As XML and XSLT become more pervasive, it's possible that many vendors will provide templates or modules that can be combined to perform useful purposes (in ways analogous to using Java classes or COM components). It is likely that some elements, for example a `<date>` or `<price>` element, would occur in many packages. The XML Namespace for each package can be expected to be unique so the `<XMML:date>` or `<LearningXML:date>` elements would not be confused. It is important to realize that the avoidance of confusion is not because the "XMML" prefix string differs from the "LearningXML" prefix string, but because two distinct URIs would be pointed to.

TIP XML namespaces assist unique identification of XML elements and attributes similar to how Java packages help to distinguish classes of the same name.

The following example illustrates the concept. Suppose you want to use a <p> element from XHTML and from TEI in a composite document of some kind. Without namespaces, you might find that a TEI <p> was being treated as an XHTML <p>, or vice versa. With namespaces, each <p> can be recognized for what it is and processed accordingly. Thus, you can easily have composite documents derived from multiple sources.

A code snippet might look something like this:

```
<document
   xmlns:xhtml="http://www.w3.org/1999/xhtml"
   xmlns:tei=http://www.uic.edu/orgs/tei/>". . .
<xhtml:p>This is an XHTML paragraph.</xhtml:p>
<tei:p>This is a TEI paragraph.</tei:p>
<p>This is a paragraph which is not namespace qualified</p>
. . .
</document>
```

The URI allows you to adapt how namespaces are used in different documents, too. The referred URI is the key. You could use anything you wanted for the prefix. The tags <xhtml:p>, <html:p>, and <silly:p> all mean exactly the same if they point to the same URI. If you had paragraphs from two programs, each of which usually used <abc:p> for a paragraph, they could be mixed safely, by renaming one prefix but still pointing it to its normal URI.

The existence of XML Namespaces allows modules to be created, which, if they correctly use namespaces, can safely be used together without fear of confusion.

XML modules potentially have the same advantages as Java classes (or COM components)—a problem can be solved once and an object can be created with appropriate public methods. Thereafter, assuming the object is correctly referenced, a well-tested object can be used, avoiding the need to spend time writing and debugging your own code to perform a fairly standard function.

Currently, XML modules are immature in various ways. Among the developments likely to be firm within the next few months are XHTML modules. See Chapter 17, "Moving Forward with XML," for discussion of those modules.

The Namespaces in XML Recommendation can be found at

```
http://www.w3.org/TR/1999/REC-xml-names-19990114
```


XSLT Examples

In the space available it isn't feasible to show you examples of all the ways in which you might use XSLT to produce a Web page from a data source held in XML or in a format which can be converted to XML. However, you will see some transformation techniques which you are likely to use frequently in a production setting.

Creating an XHTML Table Example

NOTE To work through this example, you will need to have available the tools previously described in Chapter 10. ■

In XHTML pages, one of the most common structures is the table. This section illustrates how to create a basic table from an XML file.

Let's look at the situation where you want to create a Web page that contains an XHTML table which lists several W3C documents. For the sake of brevity, this example will create an XHTML output page that describes three key W3C Recommendations relevant to this book.

The desired output looks like Figure 13.1.

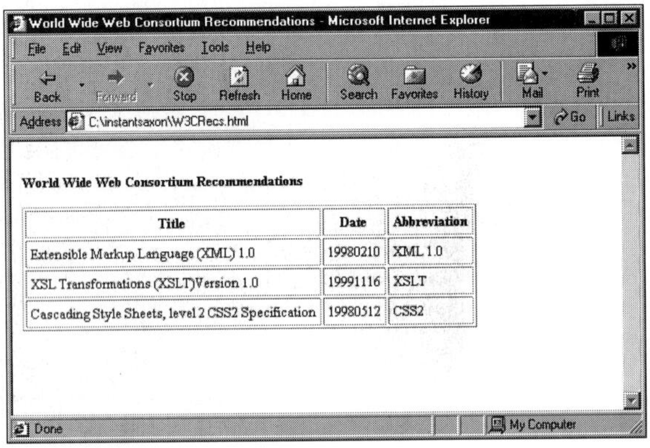

FIGURE 13.1 An abbreviated table of W3C Recommendations created by transforming an XML source file using an XSLT style sheet.

Let's suppose that the source file (highly abbreviated) for the output of Figure 13.1, named `W3CRecs.xml`, is as follows:

```
<?xml version='1.0'?>
<?xml-stylesheet type="text/xsl" href="W3CRecs.xsl"?>

<W3CRecs>
<title> World Wide Web Consortium Recommendations</title>

<W3CRec>
<title>Extensible Markup Language (XML) 1.0
</title>
<date>19980210
</date>
<abbreviation>XML 1.0
</abbreviation>
</W3CRec>

<W3CRec>
<title>XSL Transformations (XSLT)Version 1.0
```

```
</title>
<date>19991116
</date>
<abbreviation>XSLT
</abbreviation>
</W3CRec>

<W3CRec>
<title>Cascading Style Sheets, level 2 CSS2 Specification
</title>
<date>19980512
</date>
<abbreviation>CSS2
</abbreviation>
</W3CRec>

</W3CRecs>
```

NOTE XML's default format for dates is YYYY/MM/DD. This format is used here without delimiters. You will often see a similar syntax for dates within the URLs for W3C Recommendations or Working Drafts. ■

If you are working through this example, type in the code and save it as `W3CRecs.xml`.

If you remember how previous examples worked, you might recognize from the second line of this short XML document, that an XSLT style sheet that was saved as `W3CRecs.xsl` is used.

Here is the code for `W3CRecs.xsl`:

```
<?xml version='1.0'?>
<xsl:stylesheet
     xmlns:xsl="http://www.w3.org/1999/XSL/Transform"
     version="1.0">

<xsl:template match="W3CRecs">
    <html>
    <head>
    <title><xsl:value-of select="//title"/></title>
    </head>

    <body>
    <br />
    <b><xsl:value-of select="//title"/></b>
    <br /><br />
    <table border="1" cellpadding="4">
    <tr>
    <th>Title</th>
    <th>Date</th>
    <th>Abbreviation</th>
    </tr>
    <xsl:for-each select="//W3CRec">
```

```
        <tr>
        <td><xsl:value-of select="title"/></td>
        <td><xsl:value-of select="date"/></td>
        <td><xsl:value-of select="abbreviation"/></td>
        </tr>
      </xsl:for-each>
      </table>
      </body>
      </html>
  </xsl:template>

  </xsl:stylesheet>
```

Take a moment to look at the XSLT style sheet. There is only one `<xsl:template>` in this file. Most of the content is abstracted from the XML file using the `<xsl:value-of>` element. Notice that after the table headers are created, there is the equivalent of a `FOR` loop that creates each row within the table. In XSLT, this is expressed using the `<xsl:for-each>` element.

Make sure both the `W3CRecs.xml` and `W3CRecs.xsl` files are in the directory in which you installed Instant Saxon (or other XSLT processor).

To produce the XHTML file `W3CRecs.html` using Instant Saxon, type the following at the command line:

```
saxon W3CRecs.xml W3CRecs.xsl > W3CRecs.html
```

When you open the `W3CRecs.html` file in Internet Explorer 5 you should see a table as shown previously in Figure 13.1.

Note that the output is referred to as an XHTML file. Any reference to the XHTML DTD in the output is omitted.

If you wanted to include that DTD (if you were confident of the XML compliance of your browser), immediately after the line

```
<xsl:template match="W3CRecs">
```

you could add an XHTML DOCTYPE declaration like this

```
<!DOCTYPE html
    PUBLIC "-//W3C//DTD XHTML 1.0 Transitional//EN"
    "http://www.w3.org/TR/xhtml1/DTD/xhtml1-transitional.dtd">
```

Of course, where appropriate, you could use the Strict or Frameset XHTML DTD.

Further details concerning DTDs are found in Chapter 14, "Constraining XML—DTDs and XML Schemas."

TIP

Make sure you are applying the latest version of the style sheet to the latest version of the XML document. It can be very frustrating to find that corrections to a document or style sheet haven't solved a problem only to remember that the updated version existed in another directory and that Instant Saxon was still working on an earlier flawed piece of code.

Attributes to Content Example

This transformation example shows you how to transform an XML document, which holds certain information as attributes, and convert it to an XML document in which the same information is expressed as element content.

Why would you want to do something like this? Well, think of the example in which two companies are starting off in Business-to-Business (b2b) e-commerce. Let's say the producer company holds information on a Widget in the following way:

```
<widget code="WID8288" color="red"></widget>
```

You can see that both the code and color for the widget are contained in attributes.

The retail company wants to sell these widgets but the way it holds all its data about stock for sale is as follows:

```
<widget>
<code>WID8288</code>
<color>red</color>
</widget>
```

Each company holds exactly the same information about each widget: The code is `WID8288` and the color is `red`. The fact that both companies store the same information simplifies the task of two-way data exchange because transforming in either direction will involve no loss of information.

To transform the attribute-held form to element-held form, you need to apply an XSLT style sheet.

The `Widgets.xml` file looks like this:

```
<?xml version='1.0'?>
<?xml-stylesheet type="text/xsl" href="Widgets.xsl"?>

<widget code="WID8288" color="red"></widget>
```

To change attributes to elements, you need a `Widgets.xsl` style sheet that looks like this:

```
<?xml version='1.0'?>
<xsl:stylesheet
       xmlns:xsl="http://www.w3.org/1999/XSL/Transform"
       version="1.0">

<xsl:template match="widget">
    <widget>
      <xsl:for-each select="@*">
        <xsl:element name="{name()}">
        <xsl:value-of select="."/>
        </xsl:element>
      </xsl:for-each>
    </widget>
```

```
</xsl:template>

</xsl:stylesheet>
```

The transformation is conducted within an `<xsl:for-each>` loop. All attributes are selected sequentially within the loop, and for each, the name of the attribute is inserted into an element in the output file. Within the newly created element in the output file, the value of the attribute is inserted as text.

If you have `Widgets.xml` and `Widgets.xsl` in the Instant Saxon directory, the following command produces an XML output file called `NewWidgets.xml` in the desired format:

```
Saxon Widgets.xml Widgets.xsl > NewWidgets.xml
```

The output file appears in Figure 13.2.

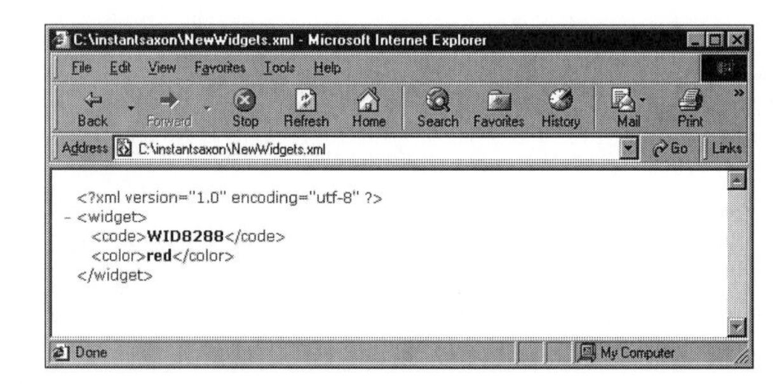

FIGURE 13.2
The `NewWidgets.xml` file contains `<code>` and `<color>` elements that were created by the `Widgets.xsl` style sheet.

Extract an Address Example

Let's take a look at a simple example that might occur in an e-commerce situation. Suppose LearningXML.com receives a purchase order from a customer using XML-based data interchange. LearningXML.com will obviously want to issue an invoice to the purchaser for an appropriate amount. You want to automate issuing of an invoice, possibly after the goods have been dispatched or a service delivered. One component of the outgoing invoice is the address details of the purchaser.

Let's take a look at how to extract the address and other details from an XML-based purchase order and output an XML-based invoice. To keep the principles clear, both documents will be presented here in a simplified form.

The purchase order might look something like this:

```
<?xml version='1.0' encoding="utf-8" ?>
<PurchaseOrder>
<To>LearningXML.com</To>
<Date>4th July 2000</Date>
<Item>XML Course</Item>
<Cost>200</Cost>
<Address>1600 Pennsylvania Avenue</Address>
```

```
<City>Washington</City>
<State>DC</State>
<Contact>Bill</Contact>
</PurchaseOrder>
```

Save this file as `PurchOrder.xml`.

The following style sheet, `PurchToInvoice.xsl`, is used to transform the Purchase Order to an Invoice:

```
<?xml version='1.0'?>
<xsl:stylesheet
       xmlns:xsl="http://www.w3.org/1999/XSL/Transform"
       version="1.0">

<xsl:template match="PurchaseOrder">
    <Invoice>
    <To>
    <xsl:value-of select="//From"/>
    </To>
    <From>LearningXML.com</From>
    <InvoiceDate>5th July 2000</InvoiceDate>
    <OrderDate>
    <xsl:value-of select="//Date"/>
    </OrderDate>
    <Goods>
    <xsl:value-of select="//Item"/>
    </Goods>
    <Amount>
    <xsl:value-of select="//Cost"/>
    </Amount>
    <Address>
    <xsl:value-of select="//Address"/>
    </Address>
    <City>
    <xsl:value-of select="//City"/>
    </City>
    <State>
    <xsl:value-of select="//State"/>
    </State>
    <Contact>
    <xsl:value-of select="//Contact"/>
    </Contact>
    </Invoice>
</xsl:template>

</xsl:stylesheet>
```

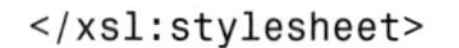

If you have followed the previous XSLT examples in Chapter 10 and this chapter, the way the `PurchToInvoice` style sheet works should be fairly straightforward for you to work out.

To produce the output file `Invoice.xml` from the `PurchOrder.xml` file enter the following command at the Instant Saxon command line:

```
Saxon PurchOrder.xml PurchToInvoice.xsl > Invoice.xml
```

The desired output is an XML file that will look something like this:

```
<?xml version="1.0" ?>
<Invoice>
<To>White House Enterprises</To>
<From>LearningXML.com</From>
<InvoiceDate>5th July 2000<InvoiceDate>
<OrderDate>4th July 2000</OrderDate>
<Goods>XML Course</Goods>
<Amount>200</Amount>
<Address>1600 Pennsylvania Avenue</Address>
<City>Washington</City>
<State>DC</State>
<Contact>Bill</Contact>
</Invoice>
```

The output file `Invoice.xml` appears in Figure 13.3.

FIGURE 13.3
The output file `Invoice.xml` produced by the XSLT transformation in Internet Explorer 5.

This example has shown how to transform one XML document into another XML document. That gives you an XML-based invoice that you can store locally in LearningXML.com's files.

In a real-life situation, you would want to send the Invoice to the customer. You might do this using some business-to-business system sending only an XML file. However, you might also (or instead) want to send an invoice to the purchaser and could, at least for the purposes of this example, do that using an HTML-based email message.

Figure 13.4 shows how the final XHTML-based email might look.

FIGURE 13.4
This shows the HTML-based email, produced by the XSLT transformation, including the invoice information derived from `Invoice.xml`.

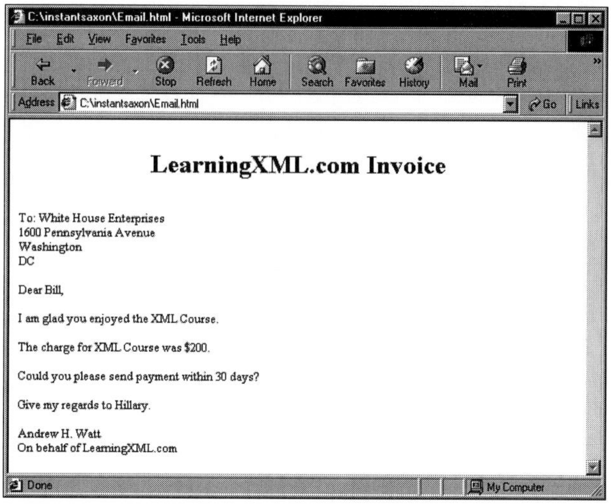

Look at the source code for that HTML:

```
<?xml version="1.0" encoding="utf-8" ?>
<html xmlns="http://">
<head/>
<body>
<br/>
<div align="center">
<h1>LearningXML.com Invoice</h1>
</div>
<br/>
To: White House Enterprises<br/>
1600 Pennsylvania Avenue<br/>
Washington<br/>
DC
<br/>
<br/>
Dear Bill,
<br/>
<br/>
I am glad you enjoyed the XML Course.
<br/>
<br/>
The charge for XML Course was $200.
<br/>
<br/>
Could you please send payment within 30 days?
<br/>
<br/>
Give my regards to Hillary.
<br/>
<br/>
Andrew H. Watt<br/>
```

```
On behalf of LearningXML.com
<br/>
</body>
</html>
```

Now, take a look at the XSLT style sheet, `ToEmail.xsl`, which would have produced that XHTML code from the `Invoice.xml` input document.

```
<?xml version='1.0'?>
<xsl:stylesheet
       xmlns:xsl="http://www.w3.org/1999/XSL/Transform"
       version="1.0">

<xsl:template match="Invoice">
  <html xmlns="http://" >
  <head>
  </head>

  <body>
  <br />
  <div align="center">
  <h1>LearningXML.com Invoice</h1>
  </div>
  <br />
  To: <xsl:value-of select="//To"/><br />
  <xsl:value-of select="//Address"/><br />
  <xsl:value-of select="//City"/><br />
  <xsl:value-of select="//State"/><br />
  <br />
  Dear <xsl:value-of select="//Contact"/>,<br />
  <br />
  I am glad you enjoyed the <xsl:value-of select="//Goods"/>.<br />
  <br />
  The charge for <xsl:value-of select="//Goods"/>
  ➥ was $<xsl:value-of select="//Amount"/>.
  <br /><br />
  Could you please send payment within 30 days?<br />
  <br />
  Give my regards to Hillary.<br />
  <br />
  Andrew H. Watt<br />
  On behalf of LearningXML.com<br />
  </body>
  </html>

</xsl:template>
</xsl:stylesheet>
```

The XHTML email is obviously a bit artificial. In a fully functioning system, you might have a link to the LearningXML.com Web site for any special offers, to invite more detailed feedback, or whatever. The specifics would depend on the nature of the business issuing the invoice and the goods or services being offered.

As an alternative to outputting an XHTML email directly, you could, in many word processors, import the XHTML file for adaptation before sending it out.

Similarly, if you have a contacts database, you might want to choose which fragment of personal information to include with the invoice. Again in real life, an invoice might well be separate from, but accompanied by, a personalized letter or email.

Looking Ahead

Chapter 10 and this chapter have shown you some examples of transforming XML either to XHTML or XML. These two types of transformation can be expected to be pivotal in the future use of XSLT.

You need to be aware that XSLT is capable of outputting a much wider range than merely XHTML and XML. For example, you could produce a Comma Separated Values file or an SQL script which could act as input to a spreadsheet or could read, insert, or alter data in an RDBMS data source.

Clearly, to use XSLT to reliably produce other file formats or scripting code, you will need to have familiarity with the relevant file formats or language syntax.

Troubleshooting

When you begin to use XSLT style sheets to transform XML files, the number of things that could go wrong seems almost limitless.

TIP Remember that XML is case sensitive. Check carefully that you type opening and closing element names identically with respect to case.

To learn the most from trying this out, it is best to type in the files by hand. But if you cannot make things work, the files can be downloaded from the book's Web site at `www.mcp.com`.

Here is a list of some of the things that can go wrong when you are trying this out for the first time (assuming you are using Instant Saxon):

- If you are using Instant Saxon to carry out the transformation and you didn't update your copy of Internet Explorer 5.0 to the latest version, you might find that when you come to view your output file in the IE5.0 browser, it is totally blank. If this happens, use Windows Explorer, go to the Instant Saxon directory, and examine the properties of the amazing.html file by right-clicking it. If the file length is 0 bytes, you do not have a sufficiently up-to-date version of the MS XML parser, on which Instant Saxon depends.
- If you get an error from Instant Saxon complaining about whitespace, check that you have correctly closed the tag at the line number in the Instant Saxon error message.

- If nothing seems to have been done to your input file, Instant Saxon might not have been able to find your source XSLT file. There are several possible causes of this problem. You might have mistyped the name of the `.xsl` file. The `.xsl` file might not be present in the Instant Saxon directory (or elsewhere in your Path).
- If you get an error message saying that Instant Saxon is expecting an `<xsl:stylesheet>` element, you have probably mistyped another element earlier in the `.xsl` file. For example, if you typed something like `"<xsl:template match="whatever"/>"` (with "`/`" before the closing "`>`"), that is an empty tag. So if you have a `"</xsl:template>"` element later in the file, Instant Saxon will complain.

Other errors might be due to mistyping something within a file. Check each line carefully against what is printed.

CHAPTER 14

Constraining XML—DTDs and XML Schemas

by Andrew Watt

In this chapter

Document Type Definitions (DTDs)

XML is immensely flexible. You can have any elements you want in your XML documents; you can define what attributes each element has, what children an element has, and so on. This flexibility brings with it the potential for enormous power, but equally it brings with it the potential for disorder and untidiness.

When you remember that a primary purpose of XML technologies is to enable a computer to speak to a computer and exchange information seamlessly, you can probably see that any untidiness might result in a breakdown or an unreliable exchange of information.

To minimize the likelihood of a multi-tier XML application breaking down, it is wise to rein in the flexibility and apply some logical, practical constraints to what can be in an XML document.

A Document Type Definition (DTD) is the mechanism defined in the XML 1.0 Recommendation that constrains XML; that is, it limits or defines the structure of instances of XML documents that use that particular DTD.

NOTE When an XML document has a DTD, it can be checked for validity—that is, for conformance to the DTD as well as for being well formed. ■

A DTD, therefore, when properly written, enables the XML processor to identify situations where an XML document deviates from the desired structure. For example, if an element is specified as occurring at least once, an XML document that lacks that element can be identified when validity is checked, and appropriate corrective action can be taken. Similarly, the inadvertent addition of an element to an XML document (perhaps by misspelling the element name) will also be identified, thus reducing the chances of any errors or omissions when the XML file is further processed.

Before considering the mechanics of how you create a DTD, take a closer look at what advantages a DTD gives you when you use XML documents in Web applications and other settings.

You have seen in the Mini Case Study in Chapter 10, "Introducing XML," that when an XML file is destined to be output in some form to the Web, it is processed using one or more XSLT style sheets. Remember that in the examples you looked at, there was no DTD within that XML file. So how can you be sure that the XSLT style sheet will find an appropriately structured XML document to process? The answer is that you can't be sure. Of course, careful manual checking can minimize errors, but one purpose of using XML is to avoid or minimize the need for manual checking. However, if the XML file does have a DTD and that DTD is correctly written, the author of the XSLT style sheet can have confidence about the structure of the XML document on which the XSLT transformation sheet is to operate.

That certainty about XML document structure is already useful when you are accessing documents about which whose quality and error checking you know. But suppose you want to make use of an XML document on the Web (or a set of such documents) or from some other company—a customer or supplier, for example. You cannot be sure, in the absence of a DTD, of the quality assurance procedures that have been applied to the file. If, for example, you are relying on incoming XML documents such as purchase orders, it is important that you receive all the information relevant to the type of goods or services that you are providing for sale. You might want to make sure when a purchase order arrives that, as well as a delivery address, sufficient information is present to identify all the billing details (ignoring the possibility of fraud for the purposes of this discussion).

Take a look at another situation where a DTD can be very useful. Suppose you are given a huge XML file that either has substandard documentation or none at all. If no DTD exists, it can be a very tedious task browsing through multiple pages of XML markup, perhaps mixed with much larger volumes of text, to gain a full picture of what the document structure is. However, if a well-written DTD exists for the document, a relatively quick examination of the DTD will give you an unambiguous picture of the structure of the big XML document.

Another situation where a DTD can provide useful input is where human-generated documentation is ambiguous, incomplete, or inconsistent. You might be unsure of what the intended XML document structure was. Here the DTD, if one exists, can provide an unambiguous answer.

To know the intended structure of the XML document(s) is useful, but to check whether a lengthy XML document conforms to its DTD, you would proceed to use a validating parser. A validating parser checks that a document is both well formed—it conforms to XML 1.0 syntax rules—and also that it conforms to the vocabulary rules set out in its DTD.

Many XML authoring tools can make use of a validating parser to report to you whether the document you are composing conforms to the structure required by the DTD. As previously mentioned in Chapter 11, "Creating XML Files for Use," XMLSpy 3.0 has a facility to generate a DTD from a sample document. Of course, that would be fully reliable only where all desired variations are present in the XML document; that is, automatic generation of a DTD can document only what is already present—not necessarily the full range of options that were intended by the document author.

These XML chapters are limited to fairly simple situations for worked examples. In real-life applications you may have several applications working together with data, processing XML documents in various ways and passing them from one application to another. It is possible that an error in one application will produce a problem that becomes apparent only as another application (which may not directly interact with the source of the problem) processes data. The more you can do to limit errors in the input documents, the less likely such errors are to occur. The savings in debugging time and the improvements in quality assurance are very worthwhile.

The next section examines exactly how a DTD must be written if it is to conform to the requirements of the XML 1.0 Recommendation.

Document Type Declaration

The first thing you need to look at is the Document Type Declaration. The Document Type Declaration occurs in the prolog of an XML document.

The Document Type Declaration can refer to either or both of two possible locations for the Document Type Definition—the *internal subset* or the *external subset.* In other words, all of the Document Type Definition can be within the XML document (in the internal subset), all of the Document Type Definition can be outside the XML document (in the external subset) in a separate file (typically with the file extension `.dtd`), or part of the Document Type Definition can be within the XML document and part can be outside.

CAUTION

A common cause of confusion is the similarity in naming of the Document Type Declaration and the Document Type Definition.

To repeat the distinction between a Document Type Declaration and a Document Type Definition (DTD) a little more formally, a Document Type Declaration is a statement in an XML file that identifies the Document Type Definition (DTD) that relates to that XML document. An XML Document Type Definition is an XML 1.0-compliant description of the content model of a class of XML documents.

Take a look at the two examples that are most straightforward—a wholly external DTD and a wholly internal DTD. First, look at the situation where the DTD is wholly external.

Suppose you wanted to use a DTD to ensure that a document had a minimal set of elements, each of which was required. The following uses the familiar example from Chapter 10:

```
<?xml version="1.0"?>
<message>
<to>All visitors</to>
<greeting>Hello and Welcome to LearningXML.com!</greeting>
</message>
```

Before the first element of the XML document body, the `<message>` element, you need to add the Document Type Declaration. Assume that your DTD is in a file called `greeting.dtd`. Your `DOCTYPE` (short for *document type*) declaration would look like this:

```
<!DOCTYPE message SYSTEM "greeting.dtd">
```

The Document Type Declaration says that the element root of the document is the `<message>` element (which is correct) and that an external file called `greeting.dtd` contains the Document Type Definition (DTD).

Assuming that the `<message>`, `<to>`, and `<greeting>` elements are all required elements and each occurs only once, the contents of the file `greeting.dtd` would look like this:

```
<!ELEMENT message(to,greeting)>
<!ELEMENT to (#PCDATA)>
<!ELEMENT greeting (#PCDATA)>
```

You will look again at the meaning of the content of the DTD. First, however, look at how the Document Type Declaration of your XML file would look if the Document Type Declaration had no associated external DTD subset but instead had all the DTD in an internal subset.

```
<!DOCTYPE message [
<!ELEMENT message(to,greeting)>
<!ELEMENT to (#PCDATA)>
<!ELEMENT greeting (#PCDATA)>
]>
```

The beginning of the internal subset of the DTD is identified by the left square bracket (`[`). The end of the internal subset of the DTD is identified by the right square bracket (`]`) and is followed by the angle bracket (>) indicating closure of the `DOCTYPE` declaration.

Now take a closer look at the opening line of the Doctype Declaration when there is an external DTD. The `DOCTYPE` keyword is immediately followed by the name of the root element of the file, which, in turn, is followed by the word `SYSTEM` and then by the URL for the external DTD. The keyword `SYSTEM` is used for DTDs that are of local or personal interest.

For DTDs that might represent an industry standard, for example, the `PUBLIC` keyword replaces `SYSTEM`. The Uniform Resource Identifier (URI) that follows the `PUBLIC` keyword can be a named data source held locally to avoid any Internet-mediated delays in accessing a URL. However, should that locally targeted URI fail to locate a local copy of the DTD, an alternative URL is given. The `DOCTYPE` Declaration would look something like this:

```
<!DOCTYPE message PUBLIC "documents/local"
      "http://www.xmml.com/documents/greeting.dtd">
```

Notice that the `PUBLIC` unique name need not actually mention an individual DTD file (although it would be mapped to one), whereas the fallback URL does mention a DTD file.

Creating a DTD

To create a legal DTD, you need to know how to produce a DTD that conforms to the requirements of the XML 1.0 Recommendation. For full details, refer to the XML 1.0 Specification of February 1998:

`http://www.w3.org/TR/1998/REC-xml-19980210.`

As you saw earlier, a `DOCTYPE` Declaration is the means by which you associate a DTD with an XML document. The `DOCTYPE` Declaration occurs in the prolog of an XML document, before any document elements. It is preceded by the XML Declaration (if one is present in the document) and can also be legally preceded by processing instructions and by comments.

As you have seen, the `DOCTYPE` Declaration can either point to an external DTD file, include an internal DTD, or it can utilize both. In the latter case, the internal DTD overrides any conflicting information that might be present in the external DTD.

Look again at the code snippet that started Chapter 10; this time it includes the DOCTYPE declaration for an internal DTD.

What structure do you need to define? You need a <message> element that contains a <to> element and a <greeting> element. It isn't clear by just looking at the document, but you will define a <message> element as containing one and only one <to> element and one and only one <greeting> element. The <to> element must be the first child of the <message> element and be followed by a <greeting> element. Each <to> and <greeting> element is not permitted to contain other elements but may contain only text—that is, character data. Because the character data will be parsed by the XML processor, it is referred to as parsed character data, which is abbreviated to PCDATA in the following code.

The internal subset of the DTD expresses exactly those constraints on the structure of the XML document.

```
<?xml version="1.0"?>
<!DOCTYPE message [
    <!ELEMENT message (to, greeting)>
    <!ELEMENT to (#PCDATA)>
    <!ELEMENT greeting (#PCDATA)>
]>
<message>
<to>All visitors</to>
<greeting>Hello and Welcome to LearningXML.com!</greeting>
</message>
```

Now look line by line at the internal DTD to see what it is saying.

The line

```
<!DOCTYPE message [
```

says it is a DOCTYPE Declaration for a document with a root element called <message>. That fits with what you want. The left square bracket ([) indicates that an internal DTD subset is beginning (in this case, that is all there is; there is no external subset of the DTD). In the situation where there was an external DTD in addition to the internal DTD, the reference to the external DTD would immediately precede the left square bracket ([). The syntax for associating the external DTD to the file was shown earlier in this chapter.

The line

```
<!ELEMENT message (to, greeting)>
```

says that the <message> element contains one <to> element and one <greeting> element, that there can be only one of each, that each is required, and that the <to> element must precede the <greeting> element.

Look at the syntax more closely. The parentheses contain the permitted content of the <message> element. The comma between the names of the elements "to" and "greeting" indicate that the <to> element must precede the <greeting> element.

The two lines

```
<!ELEMENT to (#PCDATA)>
<!ELEMENT greeting (#PCDATA)>
```

say, respectively, that the <to> and <greeting> elements each contain parsed character data but do not contain any child elements.

The line consisting of "]>" indicates that the internal subset of the DOCTYPE Declaration is complete.

In practice, internal DTDs are not often used in production DTDs. That the DTD is included in each XML document can add significantly to storage requirements. In addition, and probably more important, maintenance of a DTD for a large collection of XML documents is more easily carried out on an external DTD, when only one file needs to be altered to implement desired changes in document structure.

Notice that in each of the lines of the internal DTD, the line begins with <!ELEMENT, which means that you are declaring an element within the XML document. Later, you will look at how other declarations can be made.

First, examine the situation where, unlike the earlier example, you want to be allowed to have variable numbers of elements within the structure of a document.

For example, take the structure of this book expressed in XML. It is only one of many books that Que Corporation publishes, so the structure needs to be flexible enough to allow for a variety of circumstances.

An abbreviated form of the XML document describing this book would look something like the following:

```
<?xml version='1.0'?>
<!DOCTYPE book SYSTEM "bookstruct.dtd">
<book>
<title>Using XHTML, XML &amp; Java 2</title>
<authors>
  <author>Eric Ladd</author>
  <author>Jim O'Donnell</author>
  <author>Michael Morgan</author>
  <author>Andrew Watt</author>
</authors>
<acknowledgements>
</acknowledgements>
<publisherinfo>
<!-- Details about Que go here -->
</publisherinfo>
<isbn>
<!-- International Standard Book Number goes here. -->
</isbn>
<chapters>
<!-- Other chapters go here -->
<chapter>
```

```
<number>14
</number>
<chaptitle>Constraining XML - DTDs and XML Schemas
</chaptitle>
<!-- Other section names go here -->
<section>Creating a DTD
</section>
<section>Limitations of DTDs
</section>
<!-- Yet more section names can go here -->
</chapter>
<!-- More chapter names can go here -->
</chapters>
<appendices>
<!-- Other appendices can go here -->
<appendix>XML Resources</appendix>
</appendices>
<index>
<!-- The index would go here. Probably there would be
➥ child elements to provide structure. -->
</index>
</book>
```

The full information is obviously more complex than what is shown, but the issues that even this simplified version raises allow you to look at important aspects of element declarations.

What is it that you want the DTD to say about a book published by Que Corporation? It has to have a title, but it would be a little silly to allow more than one (ignoring the possibility of subtitles). It has only character data.

The element declaration for the `<book>` element looks like this:

```
<!ELEMENT book (title, authors*, acknowledgements?,
➥ publisherinfo, isbn?, chapters+, appendices*,
index?)>
```

The absence of any qualifying symbol to `title` indicates that it occurs once, that it must occur, and that it may not occur less than once or more than once.

The element declaration for the `<title>` element looks like this:

```
<!ELEMENT title (#PCDATA)>
```

This is the same structure as you saw previously.

Next, look at how you declare a chapter. Each chapter has a number, but only one number. Each chapter has a title, but only one title. However, a chapter must have sections but may have any number of them. Therefore, you declare such a `<chapter>` element as follows:

```
<!ELEMENT chapter (number, chaptitle, section+)>
```

That says for the element chapter that there must be only one <number> element, followed by only one <chaptitle> element, followed by at least one but possibly more <section> elements.

Next, you need to look at the <authors> element. Every book has an author, but many books—like this one—have multiple authors. When a book is written, it is probable that it has at least one author. Some book series have no publicly identified authors. Thus, if the XML document describing a book is applied to such a book, it might not have an <author> element.

To express the possibility of multiple authors yet allow for the possibility of no (identified) author, use the * symbol as follows:

```
<!ELEMENT authors (author*)>
```

The declaration says that the <authors> element has a child element <author>. The * sign in the element declaration indicates that the number of <author> elements can be 0 (allowing for various scenarios) or can be multiple, which allows for multi-authored books.

The document structure allows for an <acknowledgements> element. Some books might not have an acknowledgements section. The maximum number of acknowledgements sections is 1.

The choice of 0 or 1 element(s) is specified by using the question mark (?) following the element name, as shown for the <acknowledgements> element in the full DTD for this simplified book description.

Notice the syntax applied to acknowledgements in the declaration of the <book> element:

```
<!ELEMENT book (title, authors*, acknowledgements?,
➥publisherinfo, isbn?, chapters+, appendices*,
index?)>
```

You can apply the syntax just described and work out what the preceding element declaration has to say about <isbn>, <chapters>, <appendices>, and <index> elements.

The file bookstruct.dtd (the external DTD) would look something like this:

```
<!ELEMENT book (title, authors*, acknowledgements?,
➥publisherinfo, isbn?, chapters+, appendices*,
 index?)>
<!ELEMENT title (#PCDATA)>
<!ELEMENT authors (author*)>
<!ELEMENT author (#PCDATA)>
<!ELEMENT acknowledgements (#PCDATA)>
<!ELEMENT publisherinfo (#PCDATA)>
<!ELEMENT isbn (#PCDATA)>
<!ELEMENT chapters (chapter+)>
<!ELEMENT chapter (number, chaptitle, section+)>
<!ELEMENT number (#PCDATA)>
<!ELEMENT chaptitle (#PCDATA)>
```

```
<!ELEMENT section (#PCDATA)>
<!ELEMENT appendices (appendix*)>
<!ELEMENT appendix (#PCDATA)>
<!ELEMENT index (#PCDATA)>
```

The XML book document corresponds to this DTD. However, although it is syntactically correct, it is quite possibly semantically wrong. For example, in reality the `<publisherinfo>` and `<index>` would probably have internal structure. In ensuring that the `bookstruct.xml` file corresponds to its `bookstruct.dtd`, you have done only part of the task. The DTD also must accurately reflect the data required for a real-world task.

Notice that all elements either contain other elements that are declared using the same syntax used to declare their parent elements or they contain PCDATA. PCDATA is an abbreviation for parsed character data. It is no surprise that PCDATA is character data that is parsed by the XML processor. Remember that an option also is available to include CDATA sections within which no parsing is carried out by the XML parser. No CDATA sections were used in the book example.

Notice, too, another implication—this time a negative one—of the ubiquity of PCDATA. All the PCDATA-containing elements could contain the same types of data. No facility ensures that the chapter number can contain only numbers, for example. This is a significant limitation when dealing with document-orientated XML, but it is a very serious limitation when dealing with data because even basic type-checking facilities are absent from the DTD. You will read more about this issue later in this chapter.

So far you have looked only at situations where the DTD defines elements. In the DTD you can also define the allowable attributes for an element.

Suppose you have an XML document that describes the means to output documents to paper, which might look like this:

```
<?xml version='1.0' ?>
<docoutput>
<papercolor color="white">High quality heavy glossy
</papercolor>
<inkcolor color="black">Extra special opaque ink
</inkcolor>
</docoutput>
```

You have a `<papercolor>` element and `<inkcolor>` element, each of which has a `color` attribute. Assuming you could use only black or white paper and black or white ink, the attribute declaration would look like this:

```
<!ELEMENT docoutput (papercolor, inkcolor)>
<!ELEMENT papercolor (#PCDATA)>
<!ATTLIST papercolor color (black | white) #REQUIRED>
<!ELEMENT inkcolor (#PCDATA)>
<!ATTLIST inkcolor color (black | white) #REQUIRED>
```

The syntax `(black | white)` indicates that the attribute can take the value `black` or the value `white` but not both; nor can it take any other value.

DTD Structures

In the previous sections, you've seen examples of `ELEMENT` and `ATTLIST` declarations. The full list of legal declarations appears in Table 14.1.

Table 14.1 The Types of Declarations in a Document Type Definition

DTD Construct	Function
`ELEMENT`	Declares an XML element type.
`ATTLIST`	Declares the attributes that can be associated with a particular `ELEMENT` type, plus the allowable values of those attributes.
`ENTITY`	Declares reusable content.
`NOTATION`	Declares the format of external content (such as binary or image files) not intended to be parsed.

XML documents consist mainly of elements and their attributes. However, a DTD must be able to define all the elements in a document, how they relate to each other, which elements have attributes, and what those attributes are.

Entities

Chapter 11 introduced the concept of entities and described the predefined entities `&`, `<`, `>`, `'`, and `"`. However, XML allows for a much wider range of entities. Before entities, other than the predefined ones, can be used in an XML document, they must be declared.

NOTE The XML 1.0 Recommendation describes several distinct types of entities. This chapter does not consider the details of the distinctions between these; detailed consideration of those is beyond the scope of this chapter. See the XML 1.0 Recommendation for further information. ■

XML allows for the declaration of blocks of content that can be repeatedly referenced and used. When such content blocks are used frequently in documents, storing them as entities can save file space, and when you're creating documents, they can save a lot of typing, too.

When you declare an entity in a DTD, you specify the name of the entity and define the content to which the entity name refers.

For example, if you were writing documents or Web pages for XMML.com and you needed to repeatedly insert copyright notices, the following entity could save a significant amount of typing. After the copyright notice was checked for accuracy in the DTD, it would be correct in each place it was used. If a change to the copyright notice were needed, it would have to be made in only one place.

Declaring the `copyright` entity would look something like this:

```
<!ENTITY copyright "&copy; XMML.COM 2000 All Rights Reserved">
```

Probably more important than saving typing is the ease of maintenance achieved by having copyright or other legal information held in one place. For example, if XMML.com went the way of other dot com companies and was taken over, the copyright notice could be easily amended throughout the company documentation.

Notations

Notations identify by name unparsed entities such as graphics files. Like entities, notations must be declared before they can be used. For example, the notation declaration for a GIF89a file would look something like this:

```
<!NOTATION GIF89a PUBLIC "-//Compuserve//NOTATION
  Graphics Interchange Format 89a/EN"
  "C:\Program Files\lviewpro.exe ">
```

After the notation has been declared, an entity declaration can reference the GIF89a graphics file something like this:

```
<!ENTITY figure3 SYSTEM "13FIG03.GIF" NDATA GIF>
```

Limitations of DTDs

DTDs were inherited from SGML (Standard Generalized Markup Language). In SGML, they were used to constrain the structure of the content of documents, and essentially the same technique was defined in the XML 1.0 Specification as the means to constrain XML documents.

If you look back at the description given earlier in this chapter of what can go in a DTD, you see that it defines, for example, that an element can contain (or not) elements or character data. That is a very useful constraint when dealing primarily with documents, which has been SGML's primary focus. However, as developers have begun to explore the potential of XML, they have found that not only is it useful for documents, but it also has enormous potential for data interchange.

In a document, it makes sense to give an author freedom regarding, for example, the type of text to include at a particular point in the document. But for data, a need exists for more precise definition. In other words, significant advantages occur in data typing the content of XML document elements. For example, suppose you had an invoice document similar to the simplified and unconstrained XML document structure shown here:

```
<?xml version="1.0" standalone="yes"?>
<invoice>
<date></date>
<purchaser></purchaser>
<purchaser_address></purchaser_address>
<purchaser_postcode></purchaser_postcode>
<goods></goods>
<invoice_amount></invoice_amount>
<paid></paid>
</invoice>
```

Of course, in a real business setting an invoice would likely be significantly more complex, but this is sufficient to examine the limitations of DTDs.

Take a look at a possible DTD for the `invoice.xml` file. Suppose that all the DTD is external to the `invoice.xml` file. First, you would need to add a link to the external DTD. Second, you would need to produce a DTD that corresponded to the business rules for each `<invoice>` document.

The reference to the external DTD means that you need to amend the beginning of `invoice.xml` to look like this:

```
<?xml version="1.0" standalone="no"?>
<!DOCTYPE SYSTEM "invoice.dtd">
<invoice>
<date></date>
```

Notice that the standalone attribute in the XML Declaration has been modified to read `standalone="no"`. Notice, too, the Document Type Declaration that references the Document Type Definition (DTD). In this case the reference is to the external file `invoice.dtd`, which is present in the same directory as `invoice.xml`.

The `invoice.dtd` file would look something like this:

```
<!ELEMENT invoice (date, purchaser, purchaser_address,
  purchaser_postcode, goods, invoice_amount, paid)>
<!ELEMENT date (#PCDATA)>
<!ELEMENT purchaser (#PCDATA)>
<!ELEMENT purchaser_address (#PCDATA)>
<!ELEMENT purchaser_postcode (#PCDATA)>
<!ELEMENT goods (#PCDATA)>
<!ELEMENT invoice_amount (#PCDATA)>
<!ELEMENT paid (#PCDATA)>
```

Hopefully, you immediately see the problem—the content of each element is PCDATA. Nothing exists to stop someone from entering a date in the `<purchaser>` element, nor is anything available to prevent the purchaser's address from being entered as content of the `<invoice_amount>` element.

Imagine that the XML invoice document is passed to another application that tries to process the amount but finds what is actually a date. The results of the processing would be unpredictable, depending in great part on the error checking of the receiving application. A facility for data typing of XML input would be very useful.

Notice that in your DTD for this simplified invoice, each of the elements of `invoice.xml` is compulsory and each element consists of character data. But notice, too, that the DTD gives you no protection whatsoever against, for example, the possibility that a data entry clerk enters the purchaser's name in the date field. Both the date and the purchaser name are character data as far as the DTD is concerned. One type of character data is as good as any other as far as this DTD is concerned.

However, that type mismatching might not be too serious within the document if it stands in isolation. There is a reasonable chance that someone would spot the error. But suppose that the date element is used in a summary measure of a month's invoices. If the wrong information is present in the date field (for example, the purchaser's name), the date will not match for the period of interest, and the summary measure of accounts in the period will be in error. Or if you wanted a summary of overdue accounts, the presence of inappropriate information in the date field could lead to some unpaid invoices being unrecognized, with adverse financial consequences.

Similar problems can arise if the amount is entered in both the `amount` element and the `paid` element. If the element `<paid>` really should be allowed only values of "paid" or "outstanding" and you search on invoices which have "outstanding" in the `<paid>` element, you could find invoices unpaid for lengthy periods, with adverse effects on the cash flow of your business.

This incapability of DTDs to type character data makes them of limited value for data exchange and was one factor that led to a search for a better means of constraining XML documents, which would have more applicability to business data.

Internal and External DTDs

This section briefly revisits DTDs.

As mentioned in Chapter 11, the Document Type Declaration can refer to both internal and external subsets of the DTD. One factor that suggests that an external DTD might have advantages is ease of maintainability. Assume that you have 1,000 XML documents, each with the same DTD. Suppose you add a new product or your company is taken over and the allowable content of each document has to be modified. With an external DTD, that change in the constraints on the XML documents can be achieved by changing one file. If the DTD is solely internal or the subset of the DTD that needs to be changed is internal, you would need to change 1,000 documents. You might be able to do that programmatically, but it would a bigger task than making a simple change in an external DTD.

Of course, you would have a separate but related exercise to undertake with regard to what you were going to do with any elements in existing documents that would no longer comply with a proposed new DTD.

Planning Document Structure

This chapter has emphasized the mechanics of capturing the desired structure of an XML document in a DTD. Very little has been said so far about how you can arrive at the desired structure.

If you have done any object-oriented programming, for example, in Java, you know that a meaningful object model simplifies program development and maintenance. Similar advantages apply when the design of XML documents also appropriately reflect the business or other situation that they describe. On the other hand, poor document structure can unnecessarily complicate development of XML applications with consequent delays or cost overruns.

XML Schema

Unlike the notion of a DTD, which has been present since the XML 1.0 Recommendation and was inherited from SGML, the W3C XML Schema proposal has not yet reached the stage of being a W3C Recommendation. As of early September 2000, XML Schema was at working draft stage.

An XML Schema, like a DTD, is a document that describes and constrains a set of XML document instances. Because an XML Schema is itself an XML document, it can be manipulated like any other XML document—for example, by an XSLT style sheet or application program. In principle, XML Schema can underpin selective programmatic choices of which elements in a document should be shown to which users.

Given the current status of the W3C draft on XML Schema, all XML Schema implementations must be viewed as experimental.

CAUTION

The May 2000 release of MSXML from Microsoft included a nonstandard version of XML Schema. Microsoft has indicated an intention to comply increasingly with W3C standards. If your application depends on compliance with the emerging W3C XML Schema standard (whatever that might prove to be), you should make a careful assessment of the latest version of MSXML to determine whether the nonstandard features currently present in MSXML have been rectified.

The current W3C working draft separates the XML Schema proposal into two parts: Structure and Datatypes. XML Schema is itself expressed in XML. XML Schema (Structure), as currently drafted, provides a superset of the facilities provided by the DTD.

The XML Schema Datatypes document addresses the inadequacies of DTDs with respect to, for example, ensuring appropriate content in date elements, telephone numbers, social security numbers, and so on.

After the Datatype part of the XML Schema working draft reaches Recommendation and is implemented, many of the limitations on type checking within XML documents will be removed, eliminating at least some of the burden of type checking from application programmers.

In addition to the two documents that are likely to provide the basis for a formal XML Schema Recommendation in due course, the current draft also includes a document titled "XML Schema Part 0: Primer," which is intended to provide a semi-informal introduction to XML Schema. The URL for that primer is `http://www.w3.org/TR/2000/WD-xmlschema-0-20000407/`.

Before you start to read about XML Schema in detail, you should have some familiarity with the XML 1.0 Recommendation and with the Namespaces in XML Recommendation.

Schema Tools

At the moment, nobody knows exactly what the final XML Schema specification will contain. Therefore, it is also impossible to reliably assess which tools will conform to that specification.

Given the particularly fluid nature of the status of W3C XML Schema at the present moment, it is probably best that you refer to the W3C Web page, which will give you information on XML Schema tools that will be updated on an ongoing basis.

Take a look at `http://www.w3.org/XML/Schema.html#Tools`.

XML Schema—Structure

The Structure part of the draft XML Schema specification deals primarily with constraints on the structure of elements in an XML document. The most recent version at the time of this writing was a working draft of April 7, 2000.

This part of the draft discusses the abstract data model that the XML Schema should represent; it attempts to provide an inventory of markup constructs to represent XML Schema and to define the application of XML Schema to XML documents.

XML Schema—Datatypes

As mentioned earlier in this chapter, one of the inadequacies of the DTD is that it cannot closely define what type of data is allowable within character data. The observed need for more precise definition of data types than the DTD can provide is a major factor underlying the focus of the second part of the draft of XML Schema—data types.

CHAPTER 15

Formatting and Displaying XML

by Andrew Watt

In this chapter

Why Display XML?

Chapter 10, "Introducing XML," made the point that XML is fundamentally a mechanism for *computers* to share information, rather than a means for human beings to view the information contained in XML documents. This chapter looks at issues relating to displaying or presenting XML or XML-based information to human readers.

It would be shortsighted not to realize that human beings need to view the information contained in XML documents. But do you need to see the XML itself—in all the chunkiness of angled brackets (as shown previously in Figure 10.1)—or is it just as good to see some form of report derived from it?

If you think of an XML file as a document, you want to see a nicely formatted version—perhaps a summary—of the text. If you think of your XML file as a database, you want to see the tables displayed as reports.

So when thinking about displaying XML, you need to think about the most effective way of displaying *information* that is XML-based as well as considering the mechanics of displaying XML.

So think about what you might want the XSL to do.

Several facilities are likely to be useful. You would probably want XSL to be able to

- **Style text**—For example, bold, red text for a heading.
- **Control layout positioning**—For example, positioning an image and its associated text using absolute coordinates.
- **Generate content**—For example, to personalize output.
- **Hide content**—For example, conceal information from some users either because of security, relevance, or marketing considerations.
- **Reorder and repeat content**—For example, printing chapter titles in different styles on the chapter opening page, in running headers and footers, in the table of contents, and in cross references.
- **Sort and collate content**—For example, creating indexes.

Decorating the source tree, or the XML document, is not sufficient, as you saw in Figure 10.1. That is too crude for most uses. As mentioned in Chapter 10, Internet Explorer 5 does apply an XSL style sheet, but the style sheet doesn't "prettify" the output much.

The combination of XSLT and XSL-FO can carry out the six desired capabilities listed earlier.

Cascading Style Sheets are much more limited. Cascading Style Sheets (CSS) can carry out the first two tasks on the earlier list but not the other four.

Moving back to the broader view, to effectively and attractively render content, you need two things:

- A standard language for expressing the layout of the desired output (in XSL the formatting objects, XSL-FO)
- A facility for transforming the source document into the layout document (in XSL the transformation language, XSLT)

In practice, transforming the source document into the layout document is often carried out first by transforming the input tree using XSLT (see Chapter 13, "Transforming XML—XSLT").

Then, you need to create an output that you can display.

There is little doubt that this two-component process, combining XSLT and XSL-FO, will be the way to go in the near future. Until the specification of XSL-FO is complete, you are hampered from proceeding in that direction. However, the combination of XSLT transformation to HTML/XHTML, to which is applied a CSS style sheet, is a useful interim mechanism for displaying XML on the Web.

To display information attractively on the Web today, you have to bear in mind the capabilities of current Web browsers.

Current Browsers

To be able to reliably predict how your XML-derived Web pages will look, you need to be familiar with the capabilities of current browsers and give careful thought as to the likely range of browser versions your target customers are likely to be using.

The reality is that XML support is relatively limited at the time of this writing, as is support for XHTML (as written in the specification). So, for at least a while, you might have to assume that you need to use output pages that can be handled by browsers designed to display vanilla HTML 4.0, rather than XML or XHTML.

This isn't too big of a problem because current browsers will display XHTML as long as you observe the recommendations about HTML compatibility in the XHTML 1.0 Recommendation. And XSLT transformation sheets, when appropriately written, can produce such browser-compatible XHTML.

For example, to maximize compatibility with older browsers, remember to use `"<br />"` rather than `"<br/>"`. The `"<br/>"` (without a space inserted) will cause problems on some browsers. More information on HTML compatibility is found in Appendix C of the XHTML 1.0 Recommendation.

Currently, a preview version of Netscape 6.0 is available for download from `http://www.mozilla.org`. It claims to fully support the CSS1 Recommendation, the DOM 1.0 Recommendation, and the Resource Description Framework. In addition, it claims that significant parts of the DOM 2.0 specification (currently at Candidate Recommendation stage) and the CSS2 Recommendation are also supported. It is likely that such support will be extended or improved as Netscape 6.0 moves closer to final release.

Unless you have particular reasons to use a preview release, I suggest you wait until a more final release is available.

Internet Explorer 5.0 also has significant gaps in its conformity to the XSLT and CSS2 Recommendations.

Browsers and Mobile Computing

In a very short time, there has been an increase in the use of hand-held devices for computing on the move. It has been estimated that the use of hand-held devices used to access Web sites will explode between 2001 and 2003. No Web developer can afford to ignore the issues relating to displaying information effectively for such a huge potential market.

The huge differences in display capabilities of a 1024×768 monitor with 24-bit color versus a typical hand-held device with monochrome display and a limited number of characters and lines, create radically different issues concerning how to communicate information of any type.

There is a need for a simple text-based interface with terseness being a major aim—exactly the opposite of XML, in which terseness is explicitly declared a low priority. At the present level of technology, XML documents, at least in raw form, should be kept away from mobile browsers.

Information stored in XML files can be used in mobile browsers but very careful consideration must be given to optimizing transformations for final file size, partly to obviate the effect of slow wireless connections and partly to accommodate the small screens of present mobile browsers.

XML files can be usefully converted to WML and WAP for display on hand-held devices. A screenful of information is referred to as a *card*. More than one card can be downloaded to a hand-held device at one time. Such a combination of cards is called a *deck*.

Visit `http://www.wirelessdevnet.com/` and `http://www.wapforum.org/` for information about this fast-changing sector.

Using Style Sheets

Recall from Chapter 10 that when you wanted to use the `amazing.xsl` style sheet to transform the `amazing.xml` document, you identified the necessary action by means of an XML processing instruction.

In that case the necessary code fragment was

```
<?xml-stylesheet type="text/xsl" href="amazing.xsl"?>
```

That processing instruction identified the linked style sheet as an XSL (XSLT) style sheet. To link a Cascading Style Sheet (CSS), the processing instruction would look something like this:

```
<?xml-stylesheet type="text/css" href="amazing.css" ?>
```

A processing instruction is the means by which you attach a style sheet to an XML document, whether that style sheet has the function of transforming an XML document (that is, an XSLT style sheet) or is adding display information (that is, at the present time is probably a Cascading Style Sheet).

Full details of how to attach style sheets to XML documents is found in the W3C Recommendation "Associating Style Sheets with XML documents Version 1.0" at

http://www.w3.org/1999/06/REC-xml-stylesheet-19990629

Cascading Style Sheets (CSS)

The W3C has produced two Cascading Style Sheet Recommendations usually referred to as CSS1 and CSS2. Full details of those recommendations can be accessed at:

http://www.w3.org/TR/1999/REC-CSS1-19990111

http://www.w3.org/TR/1998/REC-CSS2-19980512

NOTE The URL given for CSS1 is correct. It was first issued in December 1996 and was revised in January 1999. The URL for the updated version, CSS2, appears before this note. ■

In addition to the two CSS Recommendations from W3C, work is currently underway on CSS3.

Applying CSS to XML

Cascading Style Sheets allow you to add some formatting to an XML file.

The original XML file from Chapter 10 looked like this:

```
<?xml version="1.0"?>
<message>
<to>All visitors</to>
<greeting>Hello and Welcome to LearningXML.com!</greeting>
</message>
```

Take another look at Figure 10.1 if you want to see how it looks with the default style sheet applied in the Internet Explorer 5 browser.

It is straightforward to apply a Cascading style sheet to the `greeting.xml` file to produce simple changes in text appearance. For example, you could easily change the color of the greeting to blue and underline it as shown in Figure 15.1.

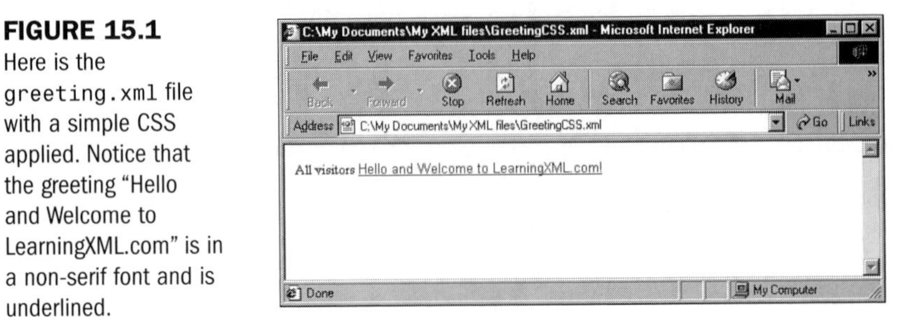

FIGURE 15.1
Here is the `greeting.xml` file with a simple CSS applied. Notice that the greeting "Hello and Welcome to LearningXML.com" is in a non-serif font and is underlined.

The CSS style sheet that produces this output in a browser looks like this:

```
greeting {
    font-family: Arial, Helvetica;
    color: blue;
    text-decoration: underline
    }
```

Notice that the style sheet file only mentions the `<greeting>` element. So the choice of a non-serif font, the application of underlining, and the change in color to blue apply only to the `<greeting>` element. As you can see, because the CSS style sheet contains no rule defining how to display the `<to>` element, it is rendered in the default style for the browser, in this case a non-underlined serif font.

To apply the rules in that style sheet to the `greeting.xml` file, add the following lines to the code:

```
<?xml-stylesheet
    type="text/css"
    href="Greeting.css"
    ?>
```

So, the full version of the XML file would look like this:

```
<?xml version="1.0"?>
<?xml-stylesheet
    type="text/css"
    href="Greeting.css"
    ?>
<message>
<to>All visitors</to>
<greeting>Hello and Welcome to LearningXML.com!</greeting>
</message>
```

Remember that the processing instruction to attach the style sheet goes in the prolog of the XML file before the first element, in this case `<message>`.

Obviously, coloring the text like this is primitive. To take CSS seriously, you must be able to do something better with it. However, CSS is limited in what it can do to XML files directly.

It would be nice to add some explanatory text to the output. One limitation of CSS is that it doesn't add text to an output XML file. For example, if you take another look at the greeting you first saw in Chapter 10, you might want to add a little text to the output so that it looks like Figure 15.2.

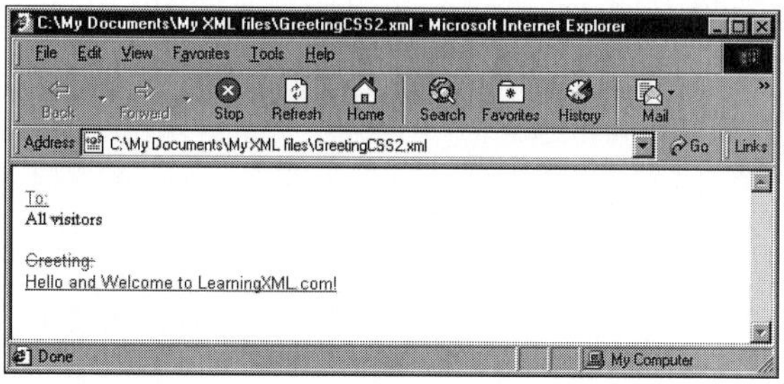

FIGURE 15.2
This is the desired output of the simple greeting in `greeting.xml` with some text added. Note that the strikethrough is to confirm that the CSS has worked within the limits of a monochrome display.

It is possible, although clumsy, to get around at least some of the limitations of CSS. For example, you could add text to the output shown on the browser by adding more elements to the source document.

You could modify `greeting.xml` so that it looked like this:

```
<?xml version="1.0"?>
<?xml-stylesheet
    type="text/css"
    href="Greeting2.css"
    ?>
<message>
<format_to>To: </format_to>
<to>All visitors</to>
<format_greeting>Greeting: </format_greeting>
<greeting>Hello and Welcome to LearningXML.com!</greeting>
</message>
```

If you wanted to display the XML file, you would also need to modify the CSS style sheet as in `Greeting2.css`:

```
format_to{
    font-family: Arial, Helvetica;
    color: red;
    text-decoration: underline
    }

to{
    display: block;
    margin-bottom: 15px;
```

```
    }

format_greeting{
    font-family: Arial, Helvetica;
    color: green;
    text-decoration: line-through
    }

greeting {
    display: block;
    margin-bottom: 15px;
    font-family: Arial, Helvetica;
    color: blue;
    text-decoration: underline
    }
```

Refer to Figure 15.2 to follow this through. The `<format_to>` element has red color and underline applied. The `<format_greeting>` element has green color and line-through applied. Even with monochrome printing, you can see the underline and line-through in the figure.

The formatting is still primitive, but certainly looks more like a Web page than Figure 15.1. Suppose you want to add a `<newline>` element next:

```
<br /> equivalent.
```

However, this mixes up content and presentation again, contrary to the spirit of XML. Also, this creates an enormous maintenance nightmare and starts to make CSS do things it wasn't designed to do. You could, with a lot of effort, produce a reasonable Web page, but at the cost of investing a lot of time creating new tags and using a CSS style sheet to format them. You are in danger of repeating the undesirable mixing of content and presentation.

XSL-FO is being created to provide a solution to this problem.

So, attempting to add elements like this to work directly with CSS creates a mess. Probably the best you can do with CSS is to produce reasonably tidy output, recognizing that you can't reorder elements nor add explanatory text. This won't work well with all XML files, but it will work reasonably well with some.

Let's see this done using the Amazing Grace example from Chapter 10.

You can use `amazing2.css` to change the color of the `<title>` element and underline it, to put the author's name and life dates in blue, and to achieve a basic layout. You can do that with the following in the CSS style sheet:

```
title{
   display: block;
   margin-bottom: 10px;
   font-family: Arial, Helvetica;
   color: red;
   text-decoration: underline
   }
```

```
author{
    display: block;
    margin-bottom: 5px;
    font-family: Arial, Helvetica;
    color: blue
    }
date{
    display: block;
    margin-bottom: 15px;
    font-family: Arial, Helvetica;
    color: blue
    }
line{
    display: block;
    margin-bottom: 5px;
    }
verse{
    display: block;
    margin-bottom: 20px;
    }
```

You also need to add a processing instruction to point to `amazing2.css` in the XML source file (see Figure 15.3).

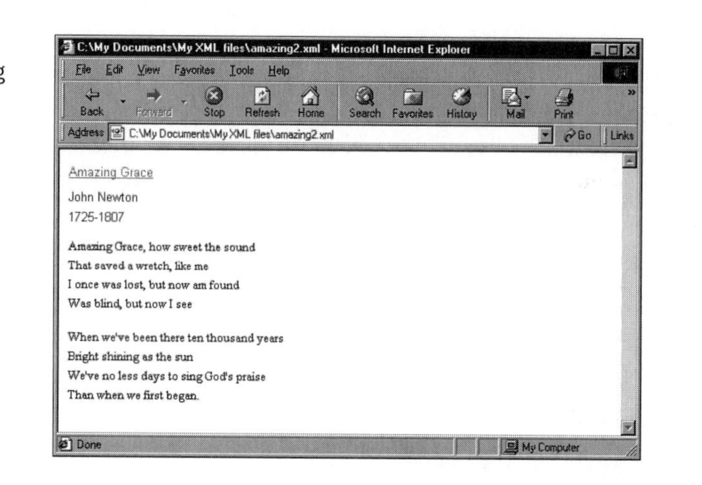

FIGURE 15.3
This shows the Amazing Grace XML file displayed using the `amazing2.css` CSS style sheet.

When you apply CSS styles directly to each element of the `amazing.xml` file, you can easily produce reasonably tidy output in a browser like the one in Figure 15.3. That output certainly looks better than the default presentation of an XML file in IE 5.0.

To apply CSS directly to XML files, you need to think carefully about how elements in the XML file are ordered.

The output shown in Figure 15.3 totally depends on the ordering of the data in the XML file. If you try to reorder the elements to achieve a result similar to Figure 10.4, you hit a full stop. CSS doesn't allow you to reorder XML elements, although it is possible to use CSS absolute positioning to simulate reordering of elements. Figure 15.3 is reasonably presentable, but to achieve any layout that depends on reordering of elements is impossible using only CSS. You must use XSLT or some custom programming to achieve the reordering before applying the CSS style sheet.

To summarize, CSS style sheets have the following limitations. They cannot

- Reorder elements in the input XML document
- Add text or images
- Choose which elements are to be displayed and which are not

How Do CSS Style Sheets Work?

You have seen the limitations of CSS applied directly to XML files. But how do CSS style sheets work? What is actually going on to produce this output?

When the browser loads the XML file, a processing instruction tells it to apply the applicable CSS style sheet file.

Style sheets are rule-based. When the browser loads the CSS file, it reads the rules contained in it. As the browser displays the elements in the source XML file, if a rule exists in the CSS file it is applied to the content of the XML element named. Using the earlier greeting XML file example, the rule for the `<greeting>` element is to display the content blue, non-serif, and underlined as you saw. Because there is no rule referring to the `<to>` element in the XML file, the browser renders it using the default settings.

However, to produce a Web page that begins to reach acceptable real-world standards, you need to transform the XML file with XSLT.

▶ For relevant examples about transforming Web pages with XSLT, **see** “Mini Case Study,” **p. 286,** and “XSLT Examples,” **p. 357**

When you apply a CSS style sheet to such a transformed file, you can produce high quality output onscreen.

XSL—XSLT and XSL-FO

Let’s take a quick look at XSL.

NOTE Throughout this chapter, the general use of XSL refers to XSL currently under development by W3C. This does not refer to MSXML or the “XSL” contained in it, which at the time of this writing is non-standard. ■

XSL, which is under development by W3C, has two major components: XSLT (Extensible Stylesheet Language Transformations) and XSL-FO (Extensible Stylesheet Language Formatting Objects).

NOTE Terminology related to XSL is used somewhat inconsistently in W3C documents. Sometimes "XSL" is used to refer only to XSL-FO, sometimes to both XSLT and XSL-FO and sometimes to the threesome of XSLT, XPath, and XSL-FO. ■

Taking an XML file and producing Web output—for example, in XHTML—is a multi-step process.

XML is stored in a format that typically includes no information describing its presentation (see Figures 10.1 and 10.2). That's no surprise because one of the aims of XML was to separate presentation from the data structure. Also, you might not want to display all of an XML file or display it in the order in which it happens to exist in the file.

To prepare an XML file for display, you use XPath (typically within an XSLT style sheet) to locate the parts of the XML file you want to work with and use XSLT to transform the desired parts of the XML file into the form you want to display. The XSL Formatting Objects are then introduced to control the formatting of the final output, which can be on a Web page, on some other electronic output device, or on paper.

Chapters 10 and 13 demonstrated examples of XPath and XSLT being used to produce XHTML output for Web pages. Because XSL-FO is not complete there is currently no browser that can dependably display XSL-FO formatted output for the Web.

CAUTION

XSL-FO is currently at Working Draft stage, which you can view at `http://www.w3.org/TR/2000/WD-xsl-20000327/`. Code snippets of XSL-FO used in this chapter are for illustrative purposes only. The details of syntax are subject to change.

Why XSL?

At the most foundational level, the purpose of XSL is to display XML documents on the Web.

However, the question can also be asked at another level. At present, content providers might be using CSS (plus or minus XSLT or DOM) for presentation of XML documents on the Web and might be using some other language—for example, DSSSL—to output to print. So the answer to the question of "Why XML?" for some will be, "to enable high quality output to the Web and to print using one mechanism."

To hold data or documents in a single format (XML or a discipline-specific language; see Chapter 16, "Exploiting XML—XML and e-Commerce") and then use a single technique (XSLT and XSL-FO) for output is an enormous improvement in workflow pattern. Quicker processing and cost savings are likely to accompany such a change in workflow.

To enable output for both print and the Web, XSL-FO is much more complex than it would need to be to provide an adequate quality for screen only. It can be argued that screen resolutions are improving, so in the future the needs of screen output and paper might be more closely aligned. To satisfy that long-term aim, the current draft of XSL-FO has become a complex language, which has moved a long way from XML being a "simple" standard.

XSL-FO and CSS Compared

CSS is familiar to many HTML authors but, initially, it was a new language to be learned. When XSL-FO is finalized, it will need to be learned as well, but some of its appearance and rules are already familiar because it's expected to be XML 1.0 compliant. XSL-FO tags routinely use the XML namespace conventions. Currently an XSL-FO tag begins "fo:".

Let's look at a simple example and directly compare XSL-FO and CSS.

XSL-FO might express some bold text within a `<summary>` element something like this:

```
<xsl:template match="summary//emphasis">
  <fo:inline-sequence font-weight="bold">
    <xsl:apply-templates/>
  </fo:inline-sequence>
</xsl:template>
```

CAUTION

XSL-FO syntax might change. The example is illustrative only.

Remember that XSL processes a document by finding templates that match each context and applying them.

To do something similar with CSS, you might write something like this:

```
summary * emphasis { display: inline; font-weight: bold }
```

Clearly, XSL-FO is much more verbose than CSS. Recall that XML explicitly ranked terseness of expression as unimportant.

Don't get the false impression that learning XSL-FO will be easy. But even from the previous short example, you might have recognized the similarity in approach to that of XSLT formatting sheets that you saw in Chapters 10 and 13. The XSL-FO specification is a lengthy, complicated document. The power it will give to control display will be considerable, but the learning curve probably will be steep.

XSLT

The Extensible Stylesheet Language Transformations (XSLT) are pivotal to presentation of XML on the Web.

The current preferred way, until browsers have improved capabilities for displaying XML, is to transform XML into HTML/XHTML and then apply a CSS style sheet. Most current browsers can display the output satisfactorily.

At the risk of being repetitive, mastering XSLT is *very* important.

Make a point of learning XSLT soon if you plan to do *anything* XML-based on the Web. XSLT currently can work with CSS to produce Web output. When XSL-FO arrives, XSLT will work with it as well to produce output for the next generation of Web browsers. So, time invested in learning XSLT is time invested in laying a foundation for the next generation of presentation on the Web.

Refer to Chapter 13 for a more detailed look at XSLT.

XSL-FO

To get a more detailed impression of what an XSL-FO style sheet will look like, take a look at an example style sheet from the W3C XSL Working Draft of March 27, 2000. Immediately, you will see differences in syntax from a CSS style sheet.

XSL-FO is an XML technology, so it begins with an XML declaration:

```
<?xml version='1.0'?>
```

Notice the namespaces for `xsl` (XSLT) and for `fo` (XSL-FO) with references to their respective URIs. Both XSLT and XSL-FO are to be used in the style sheet, which is likely to be a typical combined use:

```
<xsl:stylesheet xmlns:xsl="http://www.w3.org/1999/XSL/Transform"
xmlns:fo="http://www.w3.org/1999/XSL/Format" version='1.0'>
```

Notice the use of the `fo` prefix to refer to formatting objects that are applied, in this case to a block:

```
<xsl:template match="chapter">
  <fo:block break-before="page">
    <xsl:apply-templates/>
  </fo:block>
</xsl:template>
```

When a `<chapter>` element is met, a page break is inserted; that is, a new chapter is started on a new page.

The `<title>` element in a `<chapter>` element is centered in 16-pt. text:

```
<xsl:template match="chapter/title">
  <fo:block text-align="center" space-after="8pt"
       space-before="16pt" space-after.precedence="3">
     <xsl:apply-templates/>
</fo:block>
</xsl:template>
```

A `<section>` element in a `<title>` element is centered but is rendered in 12-pt. text:

```
<xsl:template match="section/title">
  <fo:block text-align="center"
```

```
    space-after="6pt" space-before="12pt"
    space-before.precedence="0"
    space-after.precedence="3">
      <xsl:apply-templates/>
  </fo:block>
</xsl:template>

<xsl:template match="p[1]" priority="1">
  <fo:block text-indent="0pc" space-after="7pt"
    space-before.minimum="6pt"
    space-before.optimum="8pt"
    space-before.maximum="10pt">
      <xsl:apply-templates/>
  </fo:block>
</xsl:template>

<xsl:template match="p">
  <fo:block text-indent="2pc" space-after="7pt"
    space-before.minimum="6pt"
    space-before.optimum="8pt"
    space-before.maximum="10pt">
      <xsl:apply-templates/>
  </fo:block>
</xsl:template>

</xsl:stylesheet>
```

There are a lot of XSL-FO tags; however, you probably won't need to master them all if you intend only to create output for use on the Web.

WML and WAP

One of the most exciting areas in Web development over the next couple of years or more will be how to display content for users who are accessing a Web site using "user agents" other than a PC with a conventional Web browser.

CAUTION

There is a headlong dash to have wireless applications working as quickly as possible. Considered evaluation of security risks is receiving less emphasis than is probably wise. If the application you are using or developing involves confidential information or financial information, make a careful assessment of the security standards in any wireless application you are planning to use.

There are significant technical limitations with current hand-held devices, which impact Web developers when they are planning to convey information to hand-held device users. Currently the bandwidth for wireless devices is significantly less than with, say, a 56Kbps modem. Typically, the display for such a device is much smaller than even a 14-inch PC monitor.

These technical limitations make it nearly impossible to provide visual enrichment. In certain respects, the situation is similar to that which applied to PCs at the time the Web was launched about a decade ago. The bandwidth is low and the opportunities for displaying anything other than essential text are extremely limited.

Output will need to make excellent use of succinct text. It is possible that some use of standard abbreviations will, in some settings, allow for display of more information onscreen at one time. There is a risk of returning to cryptic character mode displays with significant loss in usability. The competition to provide a practical, usable device will be intense. There will undoubtedly be a move by some to have the latest gadget; however, to sustain its projected growth, mobile browsers must deliver real usability.

So what is going to happen to make hand-held devices more useful? Will there be "size creep" with a gradual move towards the dimensions of a slim laptop? Or will something more radical arrive, such as an aural interface? With an aural interface, the tiny size of display becomes less relevant.

Aural "Display"

So far, only the visual presentation of XML data has been considered, but already some experimental implementations of aural XML are beginning to appear—for example, SpeechML from Hewlett Packard and VoiceXML from IBM.

If you are used to thinking about the visual display of XML or other data, it might take a little time to think about what VoiceXML or similar aural technologies might be used for.

In principle, because XML divorces content and presentation, there is no new issue in the "display" being aural. Aural rendition is simply another XML-compliant mode of presenting the XML data.

In a sense, some of the more obvious possible uses of VoiceXML are yet more extensions of mobile computing. Suppose you have a user profile entered on some server and you are driving to a meeting. A VoiceXML output could keep you informed of the latest changes in the features—for example stock prices—that you are interested in. Or, if linked to a global positioning system, could coach you on the correct route to take to your destination.

Another possible use of aural rendition of XML documents is for the blind and others who are visually impaired. Complex issues about how to navigate an aural "page" and how best to render it are beyond the scope of this chapter.

The acceptability of aural rendition of XML-based information is likely to depend significantly on the quality of the "voice" used to express the data. I certainly hope that if my computer or hand-held device starts speaking to me regularly to express XML-based information that the voice has a genuinely human "feel" to it. Listening to a "droid" voice several hours a day is a very unattractive prospect.

Looking Forward

XSL-FO is at a crucial stage in its development. It is, as currently drafted, a powerful formatting language; however, until it is finalized and implemented, its potential power cannot be released. Yet even when XSL-FO is finalized, it will be in the context of a swirl of other activity at the W3C on style sheets.

Remember that the XSLT Recommendation included an appendix with a list of aspirations for future versions of XSLT. The timetable for those has now been defined and some of the aspirations are being firmed up. Between now and early 2002, major developments are planned.

Even though the ink (or should that be electrons?) on the XSLT and XPath Recommendations is not dry and despite the fact that XSL Formatting Objects are not yet at Recommendation stage, the W3C XSL Working Group is planning further developments:

> "The WG will also develop the next version of XSL, including new versions of XSLT and XPath as well as extensions to formatting objects and their properties. The goal is to cope with the requirements that are not addressed yet by the first version."

If you want to read more about the proposed future work of the W3C XSL Working Group, take a look at their charter at

`http://www.w3.org/Style/2000/xsl-charter.html`

Those who embark on the journey of mastering XML technologies have likely started on a path of lifelong learning. ●

CHAPTER 16

Exploiting XML—XML and e-Commerce

by Andrew Watt

In this chapter

Introduction

The previous chapters on XML gave you an overview of many of the various XML-related technologies. The space available wasn't sufficient to include enough information for you to be fully up to speed with all aspects of XML. They laid a foundation of understanding and some basic techniques, which, if you are interested, you can spend time to develop further.

This chapter looks somewhat selectively at some aspects of the application of XML to e-business. In the space available, you can get only a hint of the broad range of dynamic innovation that is going on in some settings.

Some of the ideas discussed briefly in this chapter involve technical breadth and complexity far beyond the level used in the examples so far. In general, detailed technical discussions are avoided in this chapter to better communicate some of the key points. Try to read this chapter to grasp the bigger picture—where the big changes (and undoubtedly, very big changes will occur) to be brought about by XML are likely to occur.

NOTE The W3C has an E-Commerce Activity, which is distinct from the XML Activity. There are, however, areas of overlap, such as the Common Markup for Micropayment fee-per-link work detailed later in this chapter. An overview of the W3C E-Commerce Activity can be found at `http://www.w3.org/ECommerce/Activity.html`.

This chapter on XML is intended to show you just the tip of an already large and rapidly growing iceberg where XML is being applied in e-commerce and e-business or where work is underway to lay the foundations for working XML applications.

Before describing some specific initiatives and applications of XML in the e-commerce sector, here is a brief look at some general issues.

Let's dispose of the notion that a move to "open standards" will remove commercial competition. Nothing could be further from the truth. Think about the already existing open standards of TCP/IP, HTTP, and HTML (and now XHTML) on the World Wide Web. Does that mean that commercial competition on the Web has disappeared? Of course not. It removes the potential for a crude "lock in" to particular proprietary technologies in the way that you have been used to on the desktop and in the enterprise setting. Removal of those proprietary barriers actually increases competition.

XML is in the process of adding another standardized layer above TCP/IP and HTTP. The focus of business competition will inevitably move to a higher-level layer.

It also demands new ways to build businesses. Building "communities" on the Web is a case in point. Feeling lost on the Web is easy thanks to its size, and finding a community where you feel you belong is a very powerful glue that can bind you to a particular Web site. When you feel you belong, you are also likely to spend money. It's a much more subtle business model than those that existed in the past.

Creating an online community is similar to buying prime real estate in the offline business setting. It brings customers to your business. They won't buy every time, but if the flow of visitors is high enough, a viable business ought to follow.

If you take a broad look at e-commerce, you can see it as being about exchanging information electronically with an associated financial transaction. The payment might be a simple purchase of goods (such as a book from Amazon or Barnes and Noble), payment for electronic information (a subscription to a site or purchase of an electronic document), or payment for some service. Whatever the nature of the transaction, information is exchanged. To exchange information and remain competitive, it is essential that the costs of providing, collating, verifying, and translating the information are minimized.

When the emphasis in e-commerce was on business-to-consumer selling, a business could hold its information in any way it chose. It did not typically have to share its internal information with anyone. Generally, a consumer would supply the necessary information to make a purchase, and it would immediately be transformed into the seller's data format. With the growth in business-to-business e-commerce, each party to a transaction has its own data format for its business processes. Therefore, efficiency in using information originating from the other party to a transaction (thus avoiding or minimizing expensive, time-consuming, and error-prone rekeying) is of critical importance in minimizing cost and maximizing reliability and efficiency of the transaction. As discussed later in this chapter, it is precisely at this point that XML-based standards can help information interchange.

No clear separation exists between some of the ideas presented in this chapter, which are under continuing development, and those in Chapter 17, "Moving Forward with XML." So please be sure to read both and apply your mind to how these fluid and ever-changing possibilities might impact your business.

Data Exchange

To exploit the commercial uses of XML, one of the key issues is being able to exchange data with your customers, whether that is in a business-to-consumer (B2C) or business-to-business (B2B) setting.

NOTE It is important to appreciate that B2C and B2B e-commerce are not two separate activities—at least, they are unlikely to be in the most efficient e-businesses. For example, the operation of an online book retailer is likely to depend in important ways on linkage of orders arriving through the B2C component of the business being transferred to the B2B aspect of the business (the supply chain, to include "just in time" ordering, for example) and processed efficiently there.

Efficient handling of information can be a significant competitive advantage in the business-to-consumer segment. If you go to a Web site to make a repeat purchase and they recognize you (either through cookies on your computer or through your logging in), you can avoid having to rekey personal information, such as your delivery address, when making a purchase, which makes for a quicker, smoother, and more pleasant transaction. You are more likely to go back there and place another order rather than go to a site where you have to painfully rekey all information at every visit. That very simple use of information can significantly enhance the success of an e-business. Of course, potential security risks are associated with holding your data electronically. If someone else uses your computer to order from a Web site that uses cookies, it is necessary to have a security check to determine that you are placing an order and spending your money.

Businesses have always exchanged information. Historically, a small army of clerks and (later) typists were employed to produce paper documents and keep them in an organized fashion. When businesses depended significantly on their "hardware" (buildings and plant) for their successes, relatively slow, inefficient exchange of information was tolerable. The barriers to a new competitor entering a market were great; they would be unlikely to have the large amounts of capital required to establish a competitive business.

With the advent of global e-commerce, where tiny differences in presentation and speed can be critical in differentiating profit from loss, the emphasis on processing information efficiently and capturing its meaning has increased dramatically.

E-commerce has highlighted the need for solutions to difficulties already appreciated within larger businesses where there was an ongoing need to exchange information between departments or national divisions of a global company. In that context, it had been possible to standardize on proprietary systems with major internal efficiency benefits. However, speaking generally, it is not possible to impose acceptance of proprietary standards on customers or other business partners.

In some sectors, however, where large-volume or high-value sustained trading took place, it was possible, prior to the advent of XML, to implement essentially proprietary systems to assist information exchange between businesses.

Electronic Data Interchange (EDI)

Perhaps the best known of such earlier interbusiness systems is Electronic Data Interchange (EDI).

Since the early 1970s, EDI standards have been used by big business and government to exchange financial, manufacturing, inventory, and other information. In one sense, such a use of EDI can be seen as a precursor to the much wider exchange of information in the World Wide Web, which appeared more than a decade later.

EDI has been expensive to implement, has required highly skilled staff to configure its operation, and has typically required the use of a Virtual Private Network (VPN). However, if the value of trade was sufficiently large, EDI was a viable solution commercially when compared to scaling up other possible approaches.

EDI has two main standards bodies. In North America the X12 standard is dominant, whereas elsewhere in the world the EDIFACT standard is the norm. EDIFACT is overseen by UN/EDIFACT—the United Nations Electronic Data Interchange for Administration, Commerce and Transport. UN/EDIFACT is discussed later when you look at the ebXML initiative.

Many industries have developed vertical solutions within the loose framework of EDI. Think about what happens when you visit an ATM—an automated teller machine. The information you key in is transmitted using EDI on a VPN to the bank's computer; it is checked and an authorization is transmitted back to the ATM. As you see, EDI can be a very practical and very secure solution in certain niche markets. It is not cheap to set up perhaps, but it is functional and highly secure.

EDI standards are based on the concepts of transactions, which are made up of messages that comply with standard protocols. EDI has schemas that are stored in repositories.

In certain respects, EDI has laid the foundation for e-commerce because many of the broad principles now progressively being applied to the Web already existed within EDI, sometimes for a considerable time.

One interesting aspect is that the large corporations that have been using EDI would also be likely to have staff with skills in SGML (Standard Generalized Markup Language), which is closely related to XML. SGML would largely have been used for documents rather than data exchange, but the use of a markup language in a setting where EDI is operating is not as novel as some might at first imagine.

Disintermediation

One of the potential benefits of e-commerce in some sectors is disintermediation, which means the removal of middlemen in a supply chain.

Superficially, it would seem that if you can produce a product and sell it to wholesalers for $20 and the retail price is $75, the manufacturer could sell directly to the public from a Web site and vastly increase its profit on each item sold.

However, it is with concepts such as this where business realities and technical possibilities interact, sometimes in undesirable ways. Suppose the manufacturer from the previous paragraph establishes a Web site to sell the item at $55. His profit per item would increase radically, but what happens to the wholesaler, the dedicated salesman, or other intermediary? If they are able to do so, they might look to handle other goods, perhaps from a competitor's firm, with a consequent fall off in exposure of the item from the first firm in wholesalers' catalogues and similar decreases in mention in sales visits. The sales from the Web site might, in themselves, be very healthy, but the existence of perceived "unfair" competition from a manufacturer's Web site may significantly erode sales elsewhere. What is technically possible needs to be evaluated carefully in the light of business realities. Such factors are one reason why many Web sites where manufacturers sell directly have prices close to retail. Such an approach minimizes any alienation in preexisting distribution channels.

Infomediaries

Some observers expect that within the next few years, the competitive advantage that information provides will result in new business opportunities that can be broadly labeled as infomediaries. Infomediaries will gather, probably from a variety of sources, commercially useful information and sell that information (undigested or processed in some way) to e-businesses.

The likely emergence of infomediaries raises issues of online privacy that relate to the P3P (the Platform for Privacy Preferences) within the Metadata Activity of the W3C. P3P will permit individuals surfing the Web to preselect sites, partly on the basis of how those sites collect and disseminate information about site visitors. This provides an interesting situation in which XML might be underpinning the enabling of information collection, but a related W3C technology will enable Web surfers to frustrate the desires of those who want to collect data in an intrusive or unethical way.

You must see beyond the hype about XML to begin to explore the more subtle interactions of various XML-related technologies.

Discipline-Specific Markup Languages

Currently, perhaps the best cross-industry sources of information on discipline-specific markup languages can be found at `http://www.xml.org/`. Two sections on that site are useful: the catalog and the repository. The repository has echoes of the EDI approach.

In addition, the `http://www.ebxml.org/` site has an embryonic document repository for e-business standards, which is likely to accumulate a significant number of relevant standards over the next few months.

A further source of such information, again in an early form, can be found on the `www.biztalk.org` Web site.

NOTE Most active organizations mentioned can be linked to from the `xml.org` or `ebxml.org` sites.

This type of activity is being carried out at a frenetic pace in some sectors. Acronyms for discipline-specific markup languages come and go. Consortia—which aim to hammer out standards—aggregate, reorganize, and realign. So be aware that the specifics of the information given next might have changed. Use the `xml.org` and `ebxml.org` sites to monitor the current position.

This section mentions a few industries or sectors that already have initiatives in progress that relate to e-business or e-commerce. One factor favoring inclusion is the availability of useful information, sometimes including Document Type Definitions (DTDs) online, so that you can follow up individual topics that might be of interest to you.

Omission of any mention of a particular initiative in the list given later does not mean it is unimportant. Nor, necessarily, does inclusion mean that the standards mentioned are the front-runner within a particular sector.

Note that a number of Web sites for such initiatives include publicly available DTDs (either in final or draft versions) from which you might be able to learn much.

Accountancy

At `http://www.xbrl.org/` you will find information on the Extensible Business Reporting Language (XBRL). XBRL was formerly XFRML (Extensible Financial Reporting Markup Language). XBRL is an open standard based on XML that addresses issues relevant to company financial statements.

Perhaps current participants view XBRL as a way to do more easily what is currently produced by way of annual financial reports. But if the structure of the financial report is automated, why not have quarterly or monthly reports to shareholders? The accountability of a company to its directors could change significantly in such a scenario. Such initiatives might produce changes in business relationships between companies and their shareholders.

Advertising

Adxml.org is an international organization aiming to create an XML schema for advertising. Initially conceived for online advertising, the adxml standard is now being developed to cover advertising in all media.

NOTE Remember that a schema is similar to a DTD. They are simply ways of defining which data are allowed or required in a markup language compliant with the XML specification.

Architecture

aecXML is an XML-based markup language for the architectural, engineering, and construction sectors. Its scope includes design, planning, estimating, and, of course, construction.

Automotive Industry

The Automotive Industry Action Group is exploring e-commerce from a base that has made significant use of EDI. It will be particularly interesting to observe the penetration and impact of XML technologies in an environment where EDI is already functioning.

Banking

The Financial Services Technology Consortium carries out research and development for parts of the banking sector. A previous project led to the production of SDML (Signed Document Markup Language).

Bibliographies

Projects using markup languages are certainly not confined to the English-speaking world. BiblioML is an initiative originating in France.

Communication

Developments in the wireless communication sector that use markup languages as part of the process of information retrieval and display are attracting enormous interest. The interest arises partly from the projected number of mobile phones, hand-held computers, and so on that are projected to have Internet access in the next two years.

XML-based transformation of data is likely to be pivotal in many of these initiatives. Wireless communication of this type is going to be a multi-billion-dollar industry.

Be sure to visit sites such as `http://www.wirelessdevnet.com` and `http://www.wapforum.org/` for the latest advice and information on initiatives in the wireless sector.

WAP is claimed to be the de facto standard for the world. In reality, that is very much a claim that applies currently to the English-speaking world. Initiatives are emerging from Japan that might integrate better or faster with some hardware than does WAP. Expect to see standards wars here with some similarities to the battle between VHS and Betamax video standards.

Other firms are claiming that you can experience the Net from mobile devices. Visit `http://www.xypoint.com/` to evaluate one of those claims.

Customer Relationship Management

An initiative in this important area is the Customer Identity Markup Language (CIML). The DTD for CIML is available for viewing on the Web at `http://www.ozemail.com.au/~sakthi/dtd/ciml.dtd`.

e-Commerce

Not surprisingly, many markup languages are targeted broadly toward the e-commerce sector. How many of these will survive to compete with ebXML or will come to provide parts of ebXML remains to be seen.

The specification of Commerce XML (cXML) from Ariba, which makes interesting reading, can be downloaded as a PDF file at `http://www.cxml.org/files/cxml.pdf`.

One piece of information that is intriguing in this sector is to see the Microsoft.com Web site cited as an international standards organization, with regard to BizTalk. Perhaps that was a perceptive comment.

The Microsoft BizTalk initiative, discussed later in this chapter, certainly should not be ignored. BizTalk aims to facilitate business process integration between businesses, using Internet standards—not the least of which is XML.

The Microsoft BizTalk initiative is much better documented than many others. Information can be found on these sites: `http://www.microsoft.com/biztalk/` and `http://www.biztalk.org/`.

Electronic Data Interchange (EDI)

Several initiatives are underway to explore how best to integrate EDI with XML. One Web site that describes some activity in the European Union is located at `http://www.cenorm.be/isss/workshop/ec/xmledi/isss-xml.html`.

One document on that site that is particularly interesting is a list of desired extensions to XML used to underpin B2B data interchange. The page is a little dated now, but nonetheless is an interesting read.

Financial Markets

Financial Products Markup Language (FpML) is one of a number of initiatives in this area. Initiated by JP Morgan, FpML has attracted some big hitters in the financial world.

The FpML.org site gives interesting insights into the organization of such a venture. If you are in this league, be sure to visit `http://fpml.org/`.

Human Resources

Human Resources Markup Language (HRML) was one of the earliest applications of XML. That is not surprising because HR is a document-centric discipline.

The HR-XML consortium has a Web site where three draft schemas for routine HR information can be downloaded: JobPosting, CandidateProfile, and Resume. Visit `http://www.hr-xml.org/schemas.html`.

Legal

If you have ever been involved in litigation of any type, you will be aware of the prodigious volume of documentation that can be generated by all but the simplest cases.

The LegalXML.org organization is exploring ways to develop nonproprietary standards for legal documentation and related applications. Whether these will replace or integrate with proprietary solutions such as Lotus Development Corporation's DominoDoc remains to be seen.

If you are interested in this field, you might find work on XML-based document filing for Federal courts of interest at `http://www.jointcourtxmlstandard.org/`.

News

The news sector was perhaps more prepared for XML because some companies had several years of substantive practical experience with SGML.

The XMLNews.org site has some useful technical documentation, including DTD, that can be accessed through their Web site at `http://www.xmlnews.org/`.

Science

Chemical Markup Language (CML) was one of the very first working applications of XML. There is useful discussion and documentation on the site as well as a DTD for CML. Information on Chemical Markup Language is located at `http://www.xml-cml.org/`.

Space Exploration

Spacecraft Markup Language is perhaps one of the most intriguing of these examples. It seems to be a fairly proprietary standard at present of a Melbourne, Florida–based company. If you have a need to master Spacecraft Markup Language, SML, pay a visit to `http://www.interfacecontrol.com/sml/`.

NOTE If there is more than one discipline-specific markup language standard in an industry, XML-compliant documents may be transformed from one standard to the other using XSLT transformations.

User Interface

The user interface is one of the most important aspects of an e-commerce site. User Interface Markup Language (UIML) aims to adopt a radical approach to user-interface development, including within its scope mobile browsers. A DTD also can be accessed on the site `http://uiml.org/specs/UIML2/dtd.html`.

Voice

Voice-based user interfaces are likely to be a growing area in the next few years. VoiceXML has been submitted to W3C for consideration as a standard. An informative specification can be downloaded from `http://www.voicexml.org/specs_1.html`.

Enterprise JavaBeans

Most of the examples cited in this chapter are at an industry, international, or global level. The application of XML mentioned here in relation to the Enterprise JavaBeans technology is at the opposite end of the spectrum. In Enterprise Java (J2EE) servers, the configuration information for the server is held in XML format in a file called the deployment descriptor.

Many existing e-commerce servers on the Web are using Sun's Java technology to provide platform independence and scalability, among other features. Many of these applications need to access data (not necessarily in XML) from remote machines. The Enterprise JavaBeans technology is an enterprise-level technology that is designed to implement many of the facilities needed for remote access to data stores. In version 1.1 of the Enterprise JavaBeans specification (`http://java.sun.com`), XML is already being used in what is called the *deployment descriptor* for the Enterprise JavaBeans container (a specialized application server). The deployment descriptor file defines important aspects of how the server (or container) will function.

It seems likely that text-based, XML-compliant formats will increasingly be used to store configuration information in many sectors. Text-based data can more readily be adapted or updated to allow dynamic updating of configuration of enterprise servers, in response to the changing needs of the business environment.

Common Markup for Micropayment

This is a W3C standards initiative that may be particularly important for small businesses on the Web whose line of business is information.

One of the key benefits of the World Wide Web is that it has removed barriers to innovation in business. Perhaps the most important single barrier that has been removed is the financial one. A Web site, albeit a basic one, can be established with amounts of capital that would be derisory in the context of conventional business. Yet that Web site, however modest it might be, has a global reach. If the product is attractive, the potential for business growth is far greater than for a small, localized business.

Despite the removal of financial barriers to the establishment of an online business, one significant financial barrier remains on the Web, which currently makes unsustainable a whole class of online activity.

Think of business offline first. With a small, local business, it is possible to make cash sales for very small monetary amounts, such as the sale of a box of matches or a newspaper. This type of business is possible only because there is no transaction cost (other than a tiny percentage of fraudulent bank notes). In a conventional business, it would be unrealistic to take a check or credit card payment for such small purchases because bank or other charges would more than wipe out the profit. In fact, the bank or credit card charges could exceed the total value of the transaction.

Online, a huge potential market for sales of low-priced items exists, probably largely informational in nature. Because essentially all payments made on the Web are made electronically by credit card, the charges made for each credit card transaction are, in practical terms, pricing a whole sector of potential electronic sales out of the Internet market. The overhead costs for transactions of small monetary value are simply too high.

Not only is a sector of activity being held back, the Web is also being made more unstable than it needs to be.

If you have been using the World Wide Web for any length of time, you will have noticed that many links you click are broken. The site you wanted to access no longer exists, or at least it doesn't exist where it once was. One reason for disappearing Web sites is that budding Webmasters have found it difficult to make a sustainable living. Certainly, some sites were, perhaps, not worth saving, but for others the lack of a viable income caused interesting or educational sites to close.

Let's take a step back and examine the cause of that problem in a little more detail and then consider a solution to which the micropayment markup activity of the W3C might provide a solution.

Each time you use a credit card or issue a check, a fee is levied by your bank or credit card company for processing that transaction. For a check, the fee is often paid by you (either on a per-check basis or by means of a monthly fee), but if you use a credit card, the fee is typically charged to the company from which you made the purchase. Typically, that fee might have a minimum of $.50 or $1.00—or sometimes more (increasing if it is a high value purchase). These charges pose a barrier to making small charges for the use of Web sites or selected areas within Web sites.

If a Webmaster wanted to charge, for example, $1.00 for the use of some particularly interesting information on his site, depending on the relevant credit card charges to be levied, he either has to charge $2.00 (to recover a $1.00 credit card fee) or lose half his potential income (for example, if he charges $1.00 per transaction and is lucky enough to find a credit card company that charges only $.50 for each transaction).

Obviously, you prefer access to all sites to be completely free. The practical problem is that the Webmaster has to live. If a Web site is to be run in a professional manner on an ongoing basis, there has to be a viable source of income from it. Either the Web site is run essentially as a hobby (in which case the time devoted to it will be limited) or some form of income needs to be generated. Advertising is one possible source of income. Subscriptions are another. Affiliate schemes are yet another. However, the addition of a micropayments facility adds a whole new spectrum of possible activities.

The W3C micropayment activity is aiming to produce a standard means of making micropayments, potentially as low as a fraction of a cent.

So how might this work? You, as a purchaser, would have an electronic wallet, and as you visit and download information sites, you would pay per view. Links for which payment was needed would be marked as such, although it is not yet clear exactly how that would be done. Nor is it entirely clear how the electronic wallet would be filled. Would browser vendors have an inside track on this? It isn't clear yet. However, it is likely that if your mouse hovers over a "pay" link, it might show the price per view (probably with currency shown). If you click the link, the browser would charge your electronic wallet and then enable you to view the material you have paid to see. The payment (presumably minus a small transaction charge) would then be passed on to the information provider.

So let's look at the kind of business opportunities that might arise if Micropayments Markup Language (MPML) comes onstream in the next few months.

Suppose someone realizes that a need exists for tutorial materials on, for example, XSLT and wants to set up a site called LearningXSLT.com. At present, that person would probably hope to make a living by attracting advertisements from tools vendors and by including links to an online bookshop. Most such sites would probably not be viable businesses with only those sources of income. But if micropayments are added in as another option for generating income, such a site could offer online books or other tutorial materials. It would become realistic to charge $1.00 per lesson, for instance. If you have 2,000 visitors who each take 10 lessons at $1.00 each, then together with advertisements and affiliate fees, a viable or quasi-viable business results. The Webmaster then is able to devote more time to the Web site, thereby improving coverage or quality of material, and everyone benefits.

This type of information provider site seems to be ideal for information delivery that is linked to micropayments. Specialist or niche news sites, training sites, or education sites could operate on a sound (or certainly a less precarious) financial footing, assuming that they provided good teaching or course content.

You could even imagine substantive courses taken on a part-time basis, leading to qualifications of some sort at a W3 University. Micropayment-based payment of fees might open up serious online learning to segments of the population who cannot pay fees by lump sum.

Other possible uses for micropayment might be, in time, for niche multimedia channels. Suitable material for micropayments might be sporting, entertainment, or other special events on a pay-per-view basis.

When micropayment methods do arrive, the World Wide Web would be truly a facilitator of e-business and e-learning. And also e-ntertainment.

The ebXML Initiative

You will probably have read in the computer press that business-to-business e-commerce is likely to greatly exceed in value business-to-consumer e-commerce. One of the foundations of the projected growth in e-commerce is the capability to "freely" exchange information between businesses.

As you saw in the "Discipline-Specific Markup Languages" section in this chapter, a large number of initiatives are already underway. Quite a few of these are targeting a wide scope of e-business or e-commerce activity. However, there are potential areas where discipline-specific markup languages might clash. Suppose that the automotive industry has a single XML-based standard, and suppose that the steel industry also has an XML-based standard, but a standard that differs from that of the automotive industry. Quite possibly, an automotive company will want to purchase steel for car bodies from a steel company. The two standards are different. What happens then? Someone probably writes some routines to translate from one format to another. Given the complexity of the activities of two major industries, this is unlikely to be a trivial task, but it will almost certainly be achievable.

Clearly, differences exist in some of the activities or data in the automotive or steel industries, but many business processes will either be similar or identical. However, the details of the format in which that similar data is held might pose avoidable obstacles that, although they are not insuperable, add to the work and expense of sharing data.

One way to minimize the amount of work involved in such industry-to-industry interactions would be to make as many possible XML-based standards themselves conform to a common international standard. That, in a sense, is a central focus of the ebXML initiative.

Like the W3C, the ebXML is another international forum largely influenced by multinational corporations. That is not surprising because multinational corporations perhaps have the most to gain by increasing the efficiency and effectiveness of data interchange.

Another major player in ebXML is UN/CEFACT. UN/CEFACT, which is based in Geneva (`http://www.unece.org/cefact`), is the United Nations body whose mandate covers worldwide policy and technical development in the area of trade facilitation and electronic business.

ebXML is, according to the ebXML.com Web site, a "worldwide project to standardize XML business specifications." Furthermore, "UN/CEFACT and OASIS have established the Electronic Business XML initiative to develop a technical framework that will enable XML to be utilized in a consistent manner for the exchange of all electronic business data." OASIS stands for Organization for the Advancement of Structured Information Standards, and its Web site is located at `http://www.oasis-open.org/`.

The ebXML initiative has also invited participation by other international or business organizations. It remains to be seen whether ebXML proves to be *the* international e-business initiative or whether it is one of several.

The ebXML's explicit aims include making it easier for small- and medium-sized enterprises to enter the e-business arena. In part, this objective arises from the UN/CEFACT objectives.

The timescale for ebXML to produce global standards is very ambitious. The project, or at least its initial phase, is targeted to last 18 months, with completion of the work by mid 2001.

The ebXML project operates under the following headings:

- Business Processes
- Core Components
- Technical Architecture
- Requirements
- Transport/Routing and Packaging
- Registry and Repository
- Technical Coordination and Support
- Marketing, Awareness, and Education

Given the backing that ebXML has from the United Nations and from global players in the software and business sectors, expect ebXML to produce ambitious standards. The project is currently only about halfway through its already ambitious 18-month schedule, having started in December 1999.

If you have an interest in standards for B2B e-commerce, be sure to monitor `http://www.ebxml.org` for emerging information.

BizTalk

Another important initiative is the Microsoft-led BizTalk initiative.

This initiative is another activity that this chapter will look at in a little detail. Before proceeding to examine what the BizTalk framework contains, the question of how open and how standards-based the BizTalk initiative is merits discussion. Is it, as some may suspect, yet another means for Microsoft to lock customers in?

One page describing BizTalk on the Microsoft.com Web site begins with this prefatory remark: "The BizTalk Initiative represents the set of investments that Microsoft is making to...". Unless the word "investment" has changed its meaning, it can be expected that Microsoft anticipates a return on its investment. Cynics may look and nod knowingly.

Putting aside what cynics may say, let's look at whether BizTalk provides opportunities for "lock in" to Microsoft. BizTalk starts with technologies that are "available today." Even if you ignored Microsoft's dominance on the desktop with various versions of Windows, BizTalk uses XML-DR (a Microsoft proprietary "technology") and a proprietary Microsoft version of so-called XML Schemas. To make a start with BizTalk today, users are essentially locked in to current Microsoft technologies. To make the anticipated transition to genuinely open standards at some future date, Microsoft will provide the software to translate current versions to the open-standard ones. Another opportunity for lock in. The opportunities for lock in, subtle though they might be, are there. Perhaps Microsoft will be too altruistic to use them for any commercial advantage.

BizTalk provides a framework with many similarities to the *modus operandi* of EDI, which was mentioned earlier in this chapter. A repository for BizTalk schemas is available at the `www.biztalk.org` Web site.

BizTalk provides facilities for common messaging and document formats, not dissimilar to facilities provided by EDI, although XML rather than EDI will be an underpinning technology.

BizTalk uses a nonstandard "standard" XML Data Reduced (XML-DR) as the basis for its schemas. XML-DR is supported only in the Microsoft MSXML parser.

Productive use of the BizTalk principles will require a server for transmission of messages and integration of the structured business messages inherent in BizTalk.

Microsoft is to produce a BizTalk server that will enable transmission of BizTalk messages and also enable access to legacy applications. It would seem that the Microsoft BizTalk server will be—or will aspire to be—a fully functional enterprise server in many respects.

Given delays in W3C bringing the official schema to fruition, Microsoft might be providing a viable way for many businesses to make a start implementing XML in e-business. A draft specification of BizTalk 2.0 has recently been released.

Time will tell if making a start with BizTalk is a sound business decision. The advantages of being able to start now, which BizTalk does provide, must be weighed against the possible disadvantages of significant changes to details of operation after the W3C XML Schema becomes a recommendation. For companies already committed to Microsoft technologies, BizTalk potentially provides an attractive way forward. ●

CHAPTER 17

Moving Forward with XML

by Andrew Watt

In this chapter

Moving Forward

If you have read the earlier XML chapters, you will have realized that XML is a continually evolving process rather than a fixed standard. In fact, "XML" (whatever that now means with a whole family of XML technologies already in existence) is not just one process, but is a whole series of interconnected standards aiming to solve an intimidating range of problems, hopefully in an organized way.

This chapter looks at three things—each of which is, in a sense, moving forward with XML.

First, you will learn some of the highlights of the emerging aspects of the XML family of technologies. Some of these were touched on briefly in earlier chapters, but this chapter should open your eyes to more new XML technologies or applications that are coming and what might be done with them.

Second, this chapter discusses moving forward with XML on a more personal level, if you really want to develop your knowledge of this area. The chapter specifies the skills and material you will need to master if you are to take an interest in XML to the point where you can make a career from it or use it successfully in a career. Hopefully, it will point you in the right direction if you want to develop an interest in XML-related technologies on a professional level.

Even if you have no intention of using XML in any professional capacity, the skills building and integration sections will show you how you can build up the XML-related skills that are relevant to your needs.

Third, the chapter takes a brief look at which real-world applications are suitable for applying XML technologies in synergy with other technologies. In part, these real-world possibilities are dependent on the discussion of the emerging XML technologies and the necessary XML skill sets discussed in the first two sections of this chapter.

Emerging XML Technologies

Chapter 10, "Introducing XML," lists the formal recommendations of the various World Wide Web Consortium Working Groups, which describe the fixed foundations for the family of XML technologies. This section lists the current Candidate Recommendations, Working Drafts, and Notes as of July 2000.

As you will see from the number of documents listed here, the development of the XML family shows no sign of slowing down. There probably will be a handful of new Recommendations by the end of 2000, with several more in the early part of 2001. The interaction of various completed and almost final specifications will also likely raise some interesting issues of consistency and implementation. Mastering XML is already becoming far from easy.

Candidate Recommendations are, in principle, fairly close to final approval. However, bear in mind that W3C has announced that all documents of this type are "works in progress." They reserve the right to discard or alter these at any point prior to issuing a final Recommendation.

The likelihood of change is, of course, higher with respect to W3C Working Drafts. Those W3C Notes that are intended for further development rather than just informational documents are perhaps the most likely to be subject to radical further development.

CAUTION

If you need to be sure that your information is up to date, regularly visit the W3C Web site. If you are basing any decisions on W3C Candidate Recommendations or Working Drafts (which is questionable wisdom, anyway) make sure you look regularly for updates or the issuing of definitive Recommendations.

Notes

Remember that Notes are the least specific W3C documents. They can sometimes be informational only, but sometimes they are markers for the beginning of a body of work or indications that the W3C is considering starting a new topic.

One recent W3C Note that is particularly worth looking at is the one on the Simple Object Access Protocol (SOAP):

`http://www.w3.org/TR/2000/NOTE-SOAP-20000508`

The Simple Object Access Protocol v1.1 has been submitted to the W3C in the hopes that a Working Group will be set up to examine XML-based protocols, of which SOAP is a part. Because the request to W3C has the backing of Microsoft, IBM, Lotus, and Ariba, among others, it seems very likely that it will be approved.

The W3C Note states that SOAP is "an XML-based protocol that consists of three parts: an envelope that defines a framework for describing what is in a message and how to process it, a set of encoding rules for expressing instances of application-defined datatypes, and a convention for representing remote procedure calls and responses." SOAP can potentially be used with several other protocols, but the W3C Note refers to bindings to HTTP and HTTP Extension Framework only. That focus is probably because of the potential of SOAP on the Web.

SOAP consists of three parts:

- The SOAP envelope construct defines an overall framework for expressing what is in a message, who should deal with it, and whether it is optional or mandatory. In other words, the SOAP envelope tells us what a SOAP message is about, what should be done with it, and who needs to do it.

- The SOAP encoding rules define a serialization mechanism that can be used to exchange instances of application-defined datatypes. In other words, the encoding rules define how a programming object is converted to a stream of bytes that can be transmitted across the network and yet can be put back together as an object at the other end.
- The SOAP RPC representation defines a convention that can be used to represent remote procedure calls and responses.

If you are familiar with Microsoft's BizTalk framework, you will recognize similarities in the first bullet point.

Scalable Vector Graphics

Scalable Vector Graphics are the future of graphics on the Web!

If you have created a Web site, you will have realized the importance of graphics in helping you create the look and feel of the site. Until now, you have had a fairly limited choice of graphics formats to use. In Chapter 5, "Advanced Graphics," you read a little about Graphics Interchange Format (GIF) and Joint Photographic Experts Group (JPEG) formats. In addition to those, you probably have seen sites that use Macromedia Flash, a proprietary vector graphics format stored as binary data.

GIFs and JPEGs hardly produce high-quality images, but they are reasonably adequate for small static images. Both GIFs and JPEGs are bitmap images; that is, they are essentially a very fine grid of individual pixels, each of which can be a different color. Generally, they are kept small on the Web to minimize download time. Such images are useful as background wallpaper, but their poor quality becomes evident if you try to resize them to look at detail within them. All that happens is that you see individual pixels blown up. You can't, by resizing, see additional detail.

Contrast that with vector graphics, which you can resize within graphics packages so that you can look at more detail, for example, of a technical diagram.

If you want animation in your site, you could use animated GIFs or Macromedia's proprietary Flash format. Flash uses vector graphics (similar to those in CorelDRAW, Macromedia Freehand, and Adobe Illustrator) but also encompasses a file format (`.swf`) that allows relatively small files to be downloaded to a Web page, potentially providing animation of a sophistication that is difficult or impossible to achieve with animated GIFs.

It would be useful to have the resizable attributes of vector graphics and combine that with animation facilities, and still, where it would be visually enhancing, add in bitmap graphics, too. The Scalable Vector Graphics working group is producing a specification called, not surprisingly, Scalable Vector Graphics (SVG), which will do all those desirable things. In addition to all those capabilities, SVG is XML compliant.

At first sight, you might wonder why what is merely a new file format is worthy of mention here. Scalable Vector Graphics files are XML-compliant files and can be parsed by XML parsers and produced by or transformed by XSLT transformation sheets.

Suppose you download some data from the Web. With present HTML/XHTML technology, you are limited to looking at the data in the format that the Web author chose, and that format might not let you look at the data from the perspective that you want or need. If you are lucky, you can go back to the Web site and find another analysis that meets your needs. But quite possibly, the analysis you want won't be there. As technology currently stands, you would have to cut and paste data into a spreadsheet, for example, and run an analysis there. But XML, XSLT, and SVG can change all that.

Let's look ahead slightly to the time when XML viewers will be widely available. If the data is XML based, you use the XML file you downloaded from the Web as the input to an XML parser and XSLT processor. The data can be analyzed in the way that you want, or raw or summary data can be transformed to SVG and displayed, for example, as a bar chart or pie chart. Because your graphics are held in an XML-compliant format (SVG), if you want you can just cut and paste those into your favorite XML-enabled word processor and write the report for your manager or customer. You could even use another XSLT transformation sheet to produce a new XML Web page incorporating your newly created SVG graphics.

When SVG is combined with the forthcoming Extensible Stylesheet Language Formatting Objects (XSL-FO) standard, it will be able to provide Web-based graphics comparable to high-quality print output. Text can be laid out on a path, and greater flexibility in fonts will be available. Kerning and other typographic control will become possible on the Web. You can use JavaScript and other scripting languages, and you will be able to use it with CSS style sheets. There is so much potential in SVG for making the Web a more impressive visual place that it could be a book in itself.

XHTML Modules

If you bought this book to get a handle on what XHTML is, it might be a little frightening to realize that XHTML 1.0 is intended only as a stepping stone on the way to a new structure for XHTML documents on the Web. Some idea of the speed of developments becomes clear when you consider that three Working Drafts relating to XHTML 1.1 were issued on January 5, 2000 ("Building XHTML Modules," "Modularization of XHTML," and "XHTML 1.1—Module-based XHTML") two weeks before the official XHTML 1.0 Recommendation was issued on January 20.

Clearly, the W3C visualizes XHTML 1.0 very much as a transitional form, with significant changes to legitimate document types and structures to follow shortly.

Within a couple of weeks of the XHTML 1.0 Recommendation being issued, yet another Working Draft—"XHTML Basic," which is discussed in the next section—was issued.

The purpose of XHTML Modules is to provide a means for subsetting and extending XHTML. That, in turn, paves the way for using XHTML with alternative user agents—what the draft refers to as "emerging platforms."

XHTML modularization will decompose XHTML 1.0 (and, by reference, HTML 4.0) into abstract modules, which will be implemented using XML DTD. It seems likely that a further implementation will appear that uses XML Schema.

In parallel with the process of modularization, support for aspects of HTML 4.0 that were carried forward into XHTML 1.0 but were "deprecated" is to be removed. This will affect a number of elements and attributes. In the January 2000 draft, the following were among the elements proposed as being "unsupported": `base`, `basefont`, `center`, `font`, `frame`, `frameset`, and `object`.

The aspiration of the Working Group is that modularized XHTML will be portable across "XHTML-compliant user agents."

It is likely that many users of HTML/XHTML will view some of the proposed changes as going too far, too fast.

XHTML Basic

XHTML Basic is likely to become a subset of XHTML 1.1. XHTML Basic will include the minimum number of modules to be considered as an "XHTML Family" document type, as well as allowing for the inclusion of images, forms, and basic tables. XHTML Basic is designed to be viewed on user agents that do not support the full features of XHTML, which would include mobile phones, personal digital assistants, set-top boxes, and so on.

The Working Draft states that the goal of XHTML Basic is to converge existing subsets of HTML 4.0, which would appear to include Compact HTML (CHTML) and Wireless Markup Language (WML) as well as encompassing the content of "HTML 4.0 Guidelines for Mobile Access." The latter can be viewed at `http://www.w3.org/TR/1999/NOTE-html40-mobile-19990315`.

If approved, in time it might be seen that XHTML Basic helped to bring coherence to the rapidly changing mobile browser scene. At present, it simply adds yet another dimension to a complex and rapidly changing melting pot.

XML Base

XML Base is included here, not because it is related to XHTML Basic, but so you can see them together and realize that they are not the same.

XML Base is intended to provide the equivalent of HTML BASE functionality in XML syntax. The logic of proposing to remove the "base" element from XHTML 1.1 and at the same time create XML Base is unclear.

XML Base is an activity of the XML Linking Working Group and is one of several possible HTML-related initiatives from that group.

▶ For more information, **see** "XML Linking Language (XLink) Fundamentals," **p. 346**

The Working Draft indicates that XML Base will create "a mechanism for providing base URI services to XLink, but as a modular specification so that other XML applications benefiting from additional control over relative URIs but not built upon XLink can also make use of it. The syntax consists of a single XML attribute named `xml:base`."

The following example, taken from the draft W3C document, shows `xml:base` in action in an XML document:

```
<?xml version="1.0"?>
<html xmlns="http://www.w3.org/1999/xhtml"
      xml:base="http://example.org/today/">
  <head>
    <title>Virtual Library</title>
  </head>
  <body>
    <p>See <a href="new.xml">what's new</a>!</p>
    <p>Check out the hot picks of the day!</p>
    <ol xml:base="/hotpicks/">
      <li><a href="pick1.xml">Hot Pick #1</a></li>
      <li><a href="pick2.xml">Hot Pick #2</a></li>
      <li><a href="pick3.xml">Hot Pick #3</a></li>
    </ol>
  </body>
</html>
```

Look at the two references to `xml:base` in lines 3 and 10 of the preceding code. Taken together, they mean that each of the three items in the ordered list is to be found in the directory pointed to by `http://example.org/today/hotpicks/`.

The XLink specification, currently at Candidate Recommendation stage, requires support for XML Base.

XML Query

XML Query has aspirations to enable access to, querying of, and manipulation of XML documents or data sources in ways that are similar to the use of SQL in the context of relational databases.

Drafting of XML Query continues. Three aspects have taken form so far: data modeling, query algebra, and syntax. The current aim is that XML Query will be declarative and the syntax will be XML-compliant. It must allow access to hierarchies and sequences, allow composition, and respect closure. It is expected to be founded on the XML InfoSet and XML Schema (both currently in working draft).

The XML Query Requirements Working Draft of January 31, 2000 includes usage scenarios illustrating the types of uses to which it is envisaged that XML Query Language will be put. See the Web site at `http://www.w3.org/TR/2000/WD-xmlquery-req-20000131`.

XML Query Language, as indicated by the Working Draft, relies on the output of XML processors and future XML Schema processors. It must not require input that such processors are unable to provide.

The complexity of the interdependencies of some of the newer XML initiatives becomes clear in the Working Draft for XML Query, which explicitly recognizes dependencies on DOM, XSL (meaning XSLT), XPointer, XPath, XML Schema, and XML Information Set. The potential for inconsistencies and ambiguities is obvious.

XForms

HTML forms were introduced to the Web in 1993. The purpose of the W3C XForms initiative is to create the next generation of Web forms. A key idea in XForms is to separate the user interface and presentation from the data model and logic. That same separation is the aim of XML and also of the multitier approach to building Web applications. The aim of the XForms project is to integrate XForms with other XML applications, including XHTML, SVG (discussed earlier in this chapter), and SMIL (Synchronized Multimedia Integration Language). Furthermore, the aim is that the XForms specification will apply to a variety of devices for accessing the Web.

It is very likely that significant compatibility issues are going to arise when attempting to display XForms on older browsers. The Working Draft states, "After careful consideration, the HTML Working Group has decided that the goals for the next generation of forms are incompatible with preserving full backwards compatibility with browsers designed for earlier versions of HTML."

It also seems likely that the development of XForms will have interdependencies with the development of XHTML modules mentioned earlier in this chapter.

SMIL Boston Specification

The current Working Draft is a lengthy, complex document. It introduces some syntax changes relative to the SMIL 1.0 Recommendation of June 1998. The Boston Specification also aims to integrate with the modularization initiatives in XHTML.

SMIL Boston is likely to make available components that will, in some way yet to be precisely defined, be usable as timelines in animations within XHTML. The syntax changes from the original SMIL Recommendation of 1998 seem to focus on increasing DOM compatibility. The hyphenated attribute names of SMIL 1.0 would be replaced by "camel case" attribute names; for example, `clip-begin` in SMIL 1.0 would be replaced by `clipBegin` in SMIL Boston.

Canonical XML

To quote from the draft specification: "This specification describes a method for generating a physical representation, the canonical form, of an input XML document, that does not vary under syntactic variations of the input that are defined to be logically equivalent by the XML 1.0 Recommendation. If an XML document is changed by an application, but its Canonical-XML form has not changed, then the changed document and the original document are considered equivalent for the purposes of many applications. This document does not establish a method such that two XML documents are equivalent *if and only if* their canonical forms are identical."

Wouldn't it be nice if the authors of specifications could match precision with clarity?

Progress on Canonical XML is linked to the XML Signatures initiative. Both are joint activities of W3C and the International Engineering Task Force (IETF). Both technical and organizational interdependencies exist.

XML Signatures

The aim of the XML Signatures activity is to be able to represent signatures on digital content and procedures for verifying those signatures. XML Signatures are a metadata activity founded on the Resource Description Framework.

Further information on XML Signatures can be found at

XML-Signature Requirements, October 14, 1999

`http://www.w3.org/TR/1999/WD-xmldsig-requirements-19991014.html`

XML-Signature Syntax and Processing, June 1, 2000,

`http://www.w3.org/TR/2000/WD-xmldsig-core-20000711/`

XInclude

The aim of the XML Inclusions (XInclude) initiative is to specify a general-purpose syntax and processing model for *inclusion*. It arose from work on the XML Linking Language (XLink). The Working Draft indicates that inclusion is "accomplished by merging a number of XML Infosets into a single composite Infoset."

The following exemplifies in HTML what XInclude seeks to add in the XML context:

```
<html:script src="">
```

Other examples in the XML arena include (forgive the pun) `<xsl:include>` and XML external entities.

One requirement for XInclude is that the syntax can be usable in XML elements, in attributes, and in URIs.

Further details on the XInclude Working Draft can be found at `http://www.w3.org/TR/2000/WD-xinclude-20000322`.

Building XML Skills

These chapters have given you an overview of the "big picture" of the sheer variety of XML-related technologies that are available and already working, as well as others that are only now emerging. They have also introduced you to some fundamental skills on which you can build.

Inevitably, because of limitations of space, the examples use only relatively simple code. For pedagogical reasons the examples are also fairly short, whereas real-life use of XML will involve files that are much longer.

You will need a good grasp of the big picture as well as a thorough, detailed familiarity with several XML-related technologies. These chapters can only lightly touch the surface of issues of which you will need to have a detailed grasp.

As you read through the following sections, take time to try things out. Apply ideas, even if in a very simple way, to the type of problem you are trying to solve.

Use the XML resources listed in Appendix B, "General Reference Resource," to find many valuable XML resources.

If you intend to use XML technologies seriously, I suggest you read the W3C Recommendations, although they definitely are not light reading. The most important ones to grasp first are the XML 1.0 Recommendation of February 1998 (including all the DTD material), the XSLT Recommendation of November 1999, and the XPath Recommendation of November 1999.

They are not easy reading. Unfortunately there is a lack of material that in any systematic way "translates" the jargon (precise though it may be) into language that a newcomer can readily understand.

Study XML and XSLT code and markup samples on the W3C site and elsewhere. Make a point of looking at real-world DTDs that are available on the Web, such as the site `http://www.ozemail.com.au/~sakthi/dtd/ciml.dtd` and those mentioned in Chapter 16, "Exploiting XML—XML and e-Commerce," in relation to the discipline-specific markup languages.

If you make progress toward mastering this key material, you will be able to do several important things. You will, after appropriate information gathering and analysis, be able to create your own XML-based markup language. You may never use it "in anger," but the thought processes and skills acquired as you struggle through that analytical and creative process will prove invaluable. If you are thinking of making a career involving XML, keep that "toy" markup language as a project to demonstrate in your portfolio. Secondly, use XSLT and XPath to put data from an XML source into a series of Web pages. Even if the site never goes "live," you will learn an enormous amount in putting the pieces together. Again, use that as part of a portfolio, either on the Web or as a demo on CD-ROM.

Keep reading. And reading. The list of Candidate Recommendations and Working Drafts earlier in this chapter won't all be relevant to you. Choose those that are and progressively master new concepts and skills.

Think about joining one or more of the XML-related newsgroups or mailing lists. A number of these are listed in Appendix B.

Some of the things that XML technologies do will be automated in time, perhaps even be hardwired. Wouldn't an XSLT-capable chip be interesting? But an ongoing need will exist for those who can hook these various new technologies into legacy systems and ensure that XML technologies work together.

Integrating XML Skills

One of the first concepts you learned in Chapter 10 is that the various parts of the XML family must be considered together if they are to be used productively. However, to best use XML technologies in many situations, you will need to use some (or occasionally many) of the XML family with non-XML technologies.

You might feel overwhelmed with ideas and possibilities. Don't worry about it—just read about some of these possibilities and decide which, if any, you want to pursue.

Suppose that your data source is in a non-XML format. You will need to know how to convert from that format, which may be proprietary, to XML for further processing by an XSLT engine, for example. Many manufacturers of relational databases are in the process of adding XML-related functionality to their products, so you will have at least some assistance in extracting data from a database or inserting data into a database.

One of the most exciting potential uses for XML is on the World Wide Web. There is no intrinsic need for the data you plan to use in a dynamically generated Web page to be held on the same server as your Web server; in fact, there is no need for it to be even on the same continent. In that situation, you might have to learn about how XML integrates with, for example, Java and its Remote Method Invocation facilities. Alternatively, some other methodology for remote procedure calls might apply in your setting.

XML works in a matrix of technologies; no single person can master it all. Choose carefully what interests you and what also will have career potential. Look, for example, at the IT jobs available that require XML skills. The `www.dice.com` Web site, for example, allows you to search by subject or combination of subjects and by geographic area.

Building Real-World XML Applications

You have seen that XML technologies are in a phase of rapid change. The supporting tools are to a significant extent in an immature state, partly determined by the absence of definitive recommendations for some important XML technologies.

In the next year or so, some of the key technologies, such as XML Schema, XSL-FO, SVG, and so on will very likely come onstream as full recommendations. A real synergy is present between the various facets of XML that can't be fully realized until the key standards have been defined and supporting tools disseminated.

Here is a list of possible characteristics that suggest a first real-life project to try out. Be aware that for many of the technologies, you will need substantially more detailed knowledge than what is included in these chapters.

Promising candidates for XML are projects that include one or more of these characteristics:

- Applications with repeating text fields
- Applications that need Unicode
- Applications that involve exchange of data between companies or departments
- Workflow applications
- Applications that output to various devices
- Document management
- Supply-chain (EDI-like) situations

You will in all likelihood need to master a programming language to exploit XML technologies in some of these situations.

▶ For more information about using Java with XML, **see** Chapter 42, "Java and XML"

The Future

You might have read in various magazine or newspaper articles that there has been a lot of hype about XML. As you read Part II and began to see how some of the ways of producing synergy between the members of the XML family can be exploited, you probably began to realize that some of the excitement surrounding XML is well justified. Some of the potential cannot yet be delivered. Some of the standards haven't been fully defined yet. Some of the tools to exploit that potential synergy haven't been released yet. The mindset of many developers hasn't yet made the adaptations necessary to work with XML in such a way as to make it work productively. But that is a transitional stage in the application of XML to a wider stage.

The power of the XML family of technologies is likely to be fully released when the technology matures a little more, not least when some of the key specifications, such as XML

Schema, are finally released as a W3C Recommendation. In parallel with that, the potential of bringing graphics under programmatic control that is an open standard and that can be manipulated using text files is likely to bring a huge and exciting range of new applications to the Web.

Another factor that will need to mature before XML is more fully exploited is the range of tools that are available and the acquisition of relevant skills by Web and other developers. These chapters have given you a flavor of some of the exciting developments that are already underway. The opportunities are many and potentially very exciting. You should think seriously about building on the foundation laid in these chapters and explore further the exciting new boundaries that the XML family brings to the Web.

Is Chaos and Fragmentation Coming?

You learned earlier in this chapter just how many new aspects of XML technologies are emerging from the W3C. One worry is that the increasing modularization may lead to fragmentation of standards. Will most XHTML developers who are targeting PC-based Web browsers bother to adapt to XHTML 1.1, in which the modularization offers advantages for those who write for mobile browsers but arguably offers only increased complexity for those who develop for PC-based browsers?

There are other reasons to worry about standards fragmentation. Some product announcements indicate support for a “subset” of XML. What does that mean? Is it a temporary phenomenon until the product is more mature? Will it prove to be a healthy and realistic modularization, or is XML no longer a unified standard?

Is chaos coming? This is a pretty provocative way to put the question. What should be flagged for you is that real possibilities of “gotchas” are appearing at several levels as XML technologies are applied to the real world. In the space available, only a few generalities can be mentioned, but they may prove to have a wider significance.

One concern is the lack of continuity of focus in W3C. The original vision of XML was to create a simplified way to put SGML on the Web. Yet XSL-FO is a comprehensive styling solution that includes the complex facilities for high-quality print output. Is ambition outstripping realism? Hopefully, the power that is inherent in XSL-FO will not languish in the same way that some of the power of SGML lay unused in many sectors for so many years—in part because of its complexity.

There is also a lack of consistency of expression. For example, in the Abstract of the XSLT Recommendation, you read that XSLT can be used “separately from” XSL, but the XSL Working Draft claims XSLT as one of its component parts. Is this only slight muddling of wording without practical implications, or does lack of clarity of thought underlie the lack of clarity of expression?

Another issue is that of using different terms to apply to the same thing, as mentioned previously in relation to the use of “expression” in XPath.

This is not a criticism of the W3C. What they are attempting is enormously ambitious, and frayed edges are probably inevitable. But these frayed edges might yet impact implementation or usage. Quality assurance of W3C documentation and processes is becoming important. Inconsistencies in outcome may cost business many millions of dollars—a cost that is potentially avoidable with improved control of the process within W3C.

Where Is the "Simple" Standard?

One aspiration of the original development of XML was a standard that would be "simple." If you have read each of these chapters and looked at even a few of the URLs given to reference W3C Recommendations or Working Drafts, you have good reason to wonder where the simplicity has gone.

Is the XML family really going to be simpler than SGML, or is it already far more complex? Will it get still more so? Is XML for business-to-business data interchange going to be markedly simpler than EDI? Increasingly, the promise of simplicity from XML is looking like a very fragile claim.

It is true to say, in one sense, that XML is a simple text format. Equally, you could say that all computing is founded on an even simpler numerical standard of zeros and ones. The fact that a foundational standard is simple does not necessarily mean that the uses to which it will be put are simple, nor that the related techniques are simple.

You might think that the XML family is already intimidating in its complexity. However, things are likely to get more complex. For example, preliminary exploration of a potential role of XML in new areas such as distributed applications, network protocols, and messaging systems was initiated in Spring 2000. Of course, at one level XML is already employed, in a limited way, in distributed applications because it is used in the deployment descriptors of Enterprise JavaBeans. One perception is that the tentative proposals referred to intend to look at far wider applications of XML-related technologies in the distributed application setting.

The future for XML looks very healthy. To master even part of the XML family and use those technologies together productively will be a demanding task. Yet the future of the World Wide Web lies in achieving XML synergy. ●

JavaScript

CHAPTER 18

Introduction to JavaScripting

by Jim O'Donnell

In this chapter

Introduction to JavaScript

JavaScript enables you to embed commands in an XHTML page. When a compatible Web browser, primarily Netscape Navigator 2 or higher or Internet Explorer 3 or higher (the Opera browser also includes JavaScript support with its version 3 and higher), downloads the page, your JavaScript commands are loaded by the Web browser as a part of the XHTML document. These commands can be triggered when the user clicks page items, manipulates gadgets and fields in an XHTML form, moves through the page history list, or through a variety of other Web browser events.

NOTE Microsoft's Internet Explorer Web browser supports JScript, Microsoft's own implementation of Netscape's JavaScript language. Both Microsoft and Netscape claim full compatibility with ECMAScript, the Web browser scripting standard. Each has its own enhancements and its own quirks, however, so some differences exist. When programming in JavaScript, it is always a good idea to test your scripts by using both browsers–in fact, test them with multiple versions of both browsers on multiple platforms, if possible. ■

Some computer languages are *compiled*—you run your program through a compiler, which performs a one-time translation of the human-readable program into a binary that the computer can execute. JavaScript is an *interpreted* language—the computer must evaluate the program every time it is run. You embed your JavaScript commands within an XHTML page, and any browser that supports JavaScript can interpret the commands and act on them.

JavaScript is powerful and simple. If you've ever programmed in C++ or Java, you will find JavaScript easy to pick up. If not, don't worry. This chapter will have you working with JavaScript in no time. This chapter examines the basic syntax of the language, and the other chapters in this section show you how to apply it. In Chapter 19, "The Document Object Model," you will find out how to use JavaScript to interact with your Web pages and how to build it in to your XHTML. Chapters 20 through 23 then show you in greater detail how to use JavaScript with windows and frames, XHTML forms, and Web browser cookies, and how to control other Web browser objects—such as Java applets and ActiveX Controls—with JavaScript.

Why Use a Scripting Language?

XHTML provides a good deal of flexibility to page authors, but XHTML by itself is static; after being written, XHTML documents can't interact with the user other than by presenting hyperlinks. Creative use of CGI scripts (which run on Web servers) and other Web technologies, such as Java, ActiveX Controls, Macromedia Flash, and Dynamic HTML, have made it possible to create more interesting and effective interactive sites. Even so, a scripting language is very often what ties all the elements of a Web page together.

JavaScript enables Web authors to write small scripts that execute on the users' browsers rather than on the server. An application that collects data from a form and then posts it to the server can validate the data for completeness and correctness, for example, before sending it to the server. This can greatly improve the performance of the browsing session because users don't have to send data to the server until it has been verified as correct.

Another important use of Web browser scripting languages such as JavaScript comes as a result of the increased functionality being introduced for Web browsers in the form of Java applets, plug-ins, Dynamic HTML elements, ActiveX Controls, and XML. Web authors can use each of these things to add extra functions and interactivity to a Web page. Scripting languages act as the glue that binds everything together. A Web page might use an XHTML form to get some user input and then set a parameter for a Java applet based on that input. It is usually a script that carries this out.

What Can JavaScript Do?

JavaScript provides a fairly complete set of built-in functions and commands, enabling you to perform math calculations, manipulate strings, play sounds, open new windows and new URLs, and access and verify user input to your Web forms.

Code to perform these actions can be embedded in a page and executed when the page is loaded. You can also write functions containing code that is triggered by events you specify. You can write a JavaScript method that is called when the user clicks the Submit button of a form, for example, or one that is activated when the user clicks a hyperlink on the active page.

JavaScript can also set the attributes, or *properties*, of Web page elements, ActiveX Controls, Java applets, and other objects present in the browser. This way, you can change the behavior of page elements, plug-ins, or other objects without having to rewrite them. Your JavaScript code could automatically set the text on part of your Web page, for example, based on what time the page is viewed.

What Does JavaScript Look Like?

JavaScript commands are embedded in your XHTML documents. Embedding JavaScript in your pages requires only one new XHTML element: `<script>` and `</script>`. The `<script>` element takes the attributes `language`, which specifies the scripting language to use when evaluating the script, the `type` attribute used to specify the script type, and `src`, which can be used to load a script from an external source.

JavaScript itself resembles many other computer languages. If you are familiar with C, C++, Pascal, HyperTalk, Visual Basic, or dBASE, you will recognize the similarities. If not, don't worry—the following are some simple rules to help you understand how the language is structured:

- JavaScript is case sensitive.
- JavaScript is flexible about statements. A single statement can cover multiple lines, and you can put multiple short statements on a single line—just make sure to add a semicolon (;) at the end of each statement.
- Braces (the { and } characters) group statements into blocks; a *block* might be the body of a function or a section of code that gets executed in a loop or as part of a conditional test.

NOTE If you program in Java, C, or C++, you might be puzzled when looking at JavaScript programs–sometimes each line ends with a semicolon, sometimes not. In JavaScript, unlike those other languages, the semicolon is not required at the end of each line.

JavaScript Programming Conventions

Even though JavaScript is a relatively simple language, it is quite expressive. This section reviews a small number of simple rules and conventions that will ease your learning process and speed your use of JavaScript.

Hiding Your Scripts You will probably be designing pages that will be seen by browsers that don't support JavaScript. To keep those browsers from interpreting your JavaScript commands as XHTML—and displaying them—wrap your scripts as follows:

```
<script type="text/javascript" language="JavaScript">
<!-- This line opens an XHTML comment
document.write("You can see this script's output, but not its source.")
//   This is a JavaScript comment that also closes the comment -->
</script>
```

The opening `<!--` comment causes Web browsers that do not support JavaScript to disregard all text they encounter until they find a matching `-->`; therefore, they don't display your script. You do have to be careful with the `<script>` element, however; if you put your `<script>` and `</script>` block inside the comments, the Web browser ignores them also.

Comments Including comments in your programs to explain what they do is always good practice—this remains true when using JavaScript. The JavaScript interpreter ignores any text marked as comments; therefore, don't be shy about including them. You can use two types of comments: single-line and multiple-line.

Single-line comments start with two slashes (`//`) and are limited to one line. Multiple-line comments must start with `/*` on the first line and end with `*/` on the last line. A few examples are

```
   // this is a legal comment
/ illegal: comments start with two slashes
/* Multiple-line comments can
   be spread across more than one line, as long as they end. */
/* careful: this comment doesn't have an end!
/// this comment's OK because extra slashes are ignored //
```

CAUTION

Be careful when using multiple-line comments—remember that these comments don't nest. If you commented out a section of code in the following way, for example, you would get an error message:

```
/* Comment out the following code
 * document.writeln(DumpURL()) /* write out URL list */
 * document.writeln("End of list.")
 */
```

To avoid error messages, the preferred way to create single-line comments is as follows:

```
/* Comment out the following code
 * document.writeln(DumpURL()) // write out URL list
 * document.writeln("End of list.")
 */
```

Using the *<noscript>* Element You can improve the compatibility of your JavaScript Web pages through the use of the `<noscript>...</noscript>` XHTML elements. Any XHTML code placed between these container elements will not display on a JavaScript-compatible Web browser but will display on one that cannot understand JavaScript. This enables you to include alternative content for your users who are using Web browsers that don't understand JavaScript. At the very least, you can let them know that they are missing something, as in this example:

```
<noscript>
<hr />
If you are seeing this text, then your Web browser
doesn't speak JavaScript!
<hr />
</noscript>
```

If possible, though, a better approach is to provide as much of the content as possible that users of non-JavaScript browsers might be missing. For example, in place of a real-time stock ticker powered by JavaScript, you might provide a link to a static XHTML version that updates itself via a `<meta refresh />` element, as in

```
<noscript>
<hr />
The real-time stock ticker requires JavaScript. For a plain
XHTML version, please see our <a href="stocks.html">text listing</a>.
<hr />
</noscript>
```

The JavaScript Language

JavaScript was designed to resemble Java, which, in turn, looks a lot like C and C++. The difference is that Java was built as a general-purpose object language; JavaScript, on the other hand, is intended to provide a quicker and simpler language for enhancing Web pages and servers. This section describes the building blocks of JavaScript and teaches you how to combine them into legal JavaScript programs.

NOTE You can find a more complete language reference for JavaScript in Appendix A, "JavaScript Language Reference." You can also find more information at the developer Web sites of Netscape at `http://developer.netscape.com` and Microsoft at `http://msdn.microsoft.com`. Finally, the ECMAScript standard can be found as ECMA-262 at `http://www.ecma.ch`. ■

Using Identifiers

An *identifier* is a unique name that JavaScript uses to identify a variable, method, or object in your program. As with other programming languages, JavaScript imposes some rules on what names you can use. All JavaScript names must start with a letter or the underscore character; they can contain both upper- and lowercase letters and the digits 0 through 9. JavaScript supports two ways for you to represent values in your scripts: literals and variables. As their names imply, *literals* are fixed values that don't change while the script is executing, and *variables* hold data that can change at any time.

Literals and variables have several types; the type is determined by the kind of data that the literal or variable contains. The following are some of the types supported in JavaScript:

- **Integers**—Integer literals are made up of a sequence of digits only; integer variables can contain any whole-number value. You can specify octal (base-8) and hexadecimal (base-16) integers by prefixing them with a leading `0` or `0x`, respectively.
- **Floating-point numbers**—The number 10 is an integer, but 10.5 is a floating-point number. Floating-point literals can be positive or negative and can contain either positive or negative exponents (which are indicated by an "e" in the number). For example, 3.14159265 is a floating-point literal, as is 6.023e23 (6.023×10^{23}, or Avogadro's number.)
- **Strings**—Strings can represent words, phrases, or data and are set off by either double (`"`) or single (`'`) quotation marks. If you start a string with one type of quotation mark, you must close it with the same type. Special characters, such as `\n` for newline and `\t`, can also be utilized in strings.
- **Booleans**—Boolean literals can have values of either `TRUE` or `FALSE`; other statements in the JavaScript language can return Boolean values.

Using Functions, Objects, and Properties

JavaScript is modeled after Java, an object-oriented language. An *object* is a collection of data and functions that have been grouped together. A *function* is a piece of code that plays a sound, calculates an equation, sends a piece of email, and so on. The object's functions are called *methods* and its data are called its *properties*. The JavaScript programs you write will have properties and methods and will interact with objects provided by the Web browser, its plug-ins, Java applets, ActiveX Controls, and other things.

NOTE Although the words "function" and "method" are often used interchangeably, they are not the same. A method is a function that is part of an object. For example, `writeln` is one of the methods of the object `document`. ■

TIP Here's a simple way to remember an object's properties and methods: Its properties are the information it knows; its methods are how it can act on that information.

Using Built-In Objects and Functions Individual JavaScript elements are *objects*. String literals are string objects, for example, and they have methods that you can use to change their case, and so on. JavaScript can also use the objects that represent the Web browser in which it is executing, the currently displayed page, and other elements of the browsing session.

To access an object, you specify its name. Consider, for example, an active document object named `document`. To use `document`'s properties or methods, you add a period (.) and the name of the method or property you want. For example, `document.title` is the title property of the `document` object, and `explorer.length` calls the length member of the string object named `explorer`. Remember, literals are objects too.

You can find out more about many of the simpler objects built in to JavaScript and the Web browser in the next chapter.

Using Properties Every object has properties, even literals. To access a property, use the object name followed by a period and the property name. To get the length of a string object named `address`, you can write the following:

```
address.length
```

You get back an integer that equals the number of characters in the string. If the object you use has properties that can be modified, you can change them in the same way. To set the color property of a house object, for example, use the following line:

```
house.color = "blue"
```

You can also create new properties for an object by naming them. If you define a class called `customer` for one of your pages, for example, you can add new properties to the `customer` object as follows:

```
customer.name = "Joe Smith"
customer.address = "123 Elm Street"
customer.zip = "90210"
```

Finally, knowing that an object's methods are properties is important. You can easily add new methods to an object by writing your own function and creating a new object property using your own function name. If you want to add a `Bill` method to your `customer` object, you can do so by writing a function named `BillCustomer` and setting the object's property as follows:

```
customer.Bill = BillCustomer;
```

To call the new method, you use the following:

```
customer.Bill()
```

Array and Object Properties JavaScript objects store their properties in an internal table that you can access in two ways. You have already seen the first way—just use the properties' names. The second way, *arrays*, enables you to access all an object's properties in sequence. The following function prints out all the properties of the specified object:

```
function DumpProperties(obj, obj_name) {
   result = ""    // set the result string to blank
   for (i in obj)
      result += obj_name + "." + i + " = " + obj[i] + "\n"
   return result
}
```

You can access all the properties of the `document` object, for example, both by property name—using the dot operator (for example, `document.href`)—and by the object's property array (`document[1]`, although this might not be the same property as `document.href`). JavaScript provides another method of array access that combines the two: associative arrays. An *associative array* associates a left- and a right-side element; the value of the right side can be used by specifying the value of the left side as the index. JavaScript sets up objects as associative arrays with the property names as the left side and their values as the right side. You can, therefore, access the `href` property of the `document` object by using `document["href"]`.

Programming with JavaScript

JavaScript has a lot to offer page authors. It is not as flexible as C or C++, but it is quick and simple. Most importantly, it's easily embedded in your Web pages; thus, you can maximize their impact with a little JavaScript seasoning. This section covers the gritty details of JavaScript programming and includes a detailed explanation of the language's features.

Expressions

An *expression* is anything that can be evaluated to get a single value. Expressions can contain string or numeric literals, variables, operators, and other expressions, and they can range from simple to quite complex. The following are examples of expressions that use the assignment operator (more on operators in the next section) to assign numeric or string values to variables:

```
x = 7;
str = "Hello, World!";
```

In contrast, the following is a more complex expression whose final value depends on the values of the `quitFlag` and `formComplete` variables:

```
(quitFlag == TRUE) & (formComplete == FALSE)
```

Operators

Operators do just what their name suggests: They operate on variables or literals. The items on which an operator acts are called its *operands*. Operators come in the following two types:

- **Unary operators**—These operators require only one operand, and the operator can come before or after the operand. The `--` operator, which subtracts one from the operand, is a good example. Both `--count` and `count--` subtract one from the variable count.
- **Binary operators**—These operators need two operands. The four math operators (`+` for addition, `-` for subtraction, `*` for multiplication, and `/` for division) are all binary operators, as is the `=` assignment operator.

Assignment Operators *Assignment operators* take the result of an expression and assign it to a variable. JavaScript doesn't enable you to assign the result of an expression to a literal. One feature of JavaScript not found in most other programming languages is that you can change a variable's type on-the-fly. Consider the XHTML document shown in Listing 18.1.

Listing 18.1 ***VarType.htm*—JavaScript Enables You to Change the Data Type of Variables**

```
<!DOCTYPE html PUBLIC "-//W3C//DTD XHTML 1.0 Transitional//EN"
    "http://www.w3.org/TR/xhtml1/DTD/xhtml1-transitional.dtd">
<html xmlns="http://www.w3.org/1999/xhtml">
<head>
<script type="text/javascript" language="JavaScript">
<!-- Hide this script from incompatible Web browsers!
function typedemo() {
   var x;
   document.writeln("<dl>");
   document.writeln("<dt>Undefined...</dt>");
   document.writeln("<dd>x = " + x + "</dd>");
   document.writeln("<dt> </dt>");
   x = 17;
   document.writeln("<dt>Integer...</dt>");
   document.writeln("<dd>x = " + x + "</dd>");
   document.writeln("<dt> </dt>");
   x = Math.PI;
   document.writeln("<dt>Floating-Point...</dt>");
   document.writeln("<dd>x = " + x + "</dd>");
   document.writeln("<dt> </dt>");
   x = "Hi, Mom!";
   document.writeln("<dt>String...</dt>");
   document.writeln("<dd>x = " + x + "</dd>");
   document.writeln("<dt> </dt>");
   x = false;
   document.writeln("<dt>Boolean...</dt>");
   document.writeln("<dd>x = " + x + "</dd>");
   document.writeln("</dl>");
```

Listing 18.1 Continued

```
}
//   Hide this script from incompatible Web browsers! -->
</script>
<title>Changing Data Types On-The-Fly...</title>
</head>
<body bgcolor=#ffffff>
<h1>Changing Data Types On-The-Fly...</h1>
<hr />
<script type="text/javascript" language="JavaScript">
<!-- Hide this script from incompatible Web browsers!
typedemo();
//   Hide this script from incompatible Web browsers! -->
</script>
<hr />
<a href="mailto:jim@odonnell.org"><em>Jim O'Donnell</em></a>
</body>
</html>
```

NOTE `Math` is a JavaScript object used to access many of its math functions. The next chapter introduces you to more of the `Math` object's properties. ■

▶ For more information on the JavaScript `Math` and other objects, **see** "JavaScript Object Arrays," **p. 469**

NOTE All sample code listings from this book can be downloaded from the Macmillan USA Web site at `http://www.mcp.com`. Also, all sample code listings for the JavaScript and Dynamic HTML sections of the book can be found at the author's Web site at `http://jim.odonnell.org/phtml4/`. ■

This short program shows that you can use the same variable in JavaScript to represent any or all the different data types. If you tried to do something like this in most other languages, you would either generate a compiler error or a runtime error. JavaScript happily accepts the change and prints x's new value at each step (see Figure 18.1).

NOTE In Microsoft's newest version of their JavaScript language, JScript.NET, they allow for script variables to be typed—that is, for them to be declared as floats, integers, booleans, strings, and so on. Variable typing is still not required, but doing so will provide performance benefits, according to Microsoft. However, for most scripts meant to be run on Web browsers, the benefits are probably not worth the trouble. ■

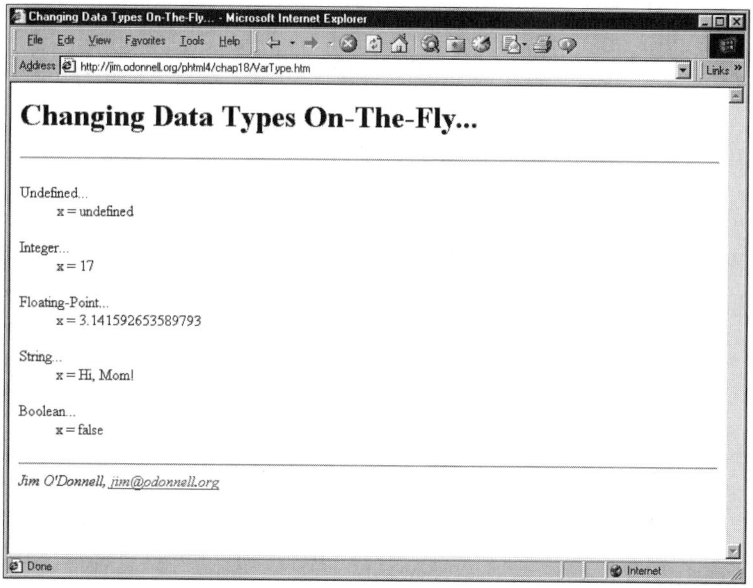

FIGURE 18.1
Because JavaScript variables are loosely typed, not only their value can be changed, but also their data type.

The most common assignment operator, =, assigns the value of an expression's right side to its left side. In the preceding example, the variable x got the floating-point value of 3.141592653589793 or the Boolean value of FALSE after the expression was evaluated. For convenience, JavaScript also defines some other operators that combine common math operations with assignment. Table 18.1 shows these.

Table 18.1 Assignment Operators That Provide Shortcuts to Doing Assignments and Math Operations at the Same Time

Operator	What It Does	Two Equivalent Expressions
`+=`	Adds two values	`x+=y` and `x=x+y`
	Adds two strings	`string += "HTML"` and `string = string + "HTML"`
`-=`	Subtracts two values	`x-=y` and `x=x-y`
`*=`	Multiplies two values	`a*=b` and `a=a*b`
`/=`	Divides two values	`e/=b` and `e=e/b`

Math Operators The previous sections gave you a sneak preview of the math operators that JavaScript furnishes. You can either combine math operations with assignments, as shown in Table 18.1, or use them individually. As you would expect, the standard four math functions (addition, subtraction, multiplication, and division) work the same as they do on an ordinary calculator. The negation operator, -, is a unary operator that negates the sign of its operand. Another useful binary math operator is the modulus operator, %. This operator returns the remainder after the integer division of two integer numbers. For example, in the expression

```
x = 13%5;
```

the variable x would be given the value of 3.

JavaScript also adds two useful unary operators, -- and ++, called, respectively, the *decrement* and *increment* operators. These two operators modify the value of their operand, and they return the new value. They also share a unique property: You can use them either before or after their operand. If you put the operator after the operand, JavaScript returns the operand's value and then modifies it. If you take the opposite route and put the operator before the operand, JavaScript modifies it and returns the modified value. The following short example might help to clarify this seemingly odd behavior:

```
x = 7;   // set x to 7
a = --x; // set x to x-1, and return the new x; a = 6
b = a++; // set b to a, so b = 6, then add 1 to a; a = 7
x++;     // add one to x; ignore the returned value
```

Comparison Operators Comparing the value of two expressions to see whether one is larger, smaller, or equal to another is often necessary. JavaScript supplies several comparison operators that take two operands and return TRUE if the comparison is true and FALSE if it is not. (Remember, you can use literals, variables, or expressions with operators that require expressions.) Table 18.2 shows the JavaScript comparison operators.

Table 18.2 Comparison Operators That Allow Two JavaScript Operands to Be Compared in a Variety of Ways

Operator	Read It As	Returns TRUE When
==	equals	The two operands are equal.
!=	does not equal	The two operands are unequal.
<	less than	The left operand is less than the right operand.
<=	less than or equal to	The left operand is less than or equal to the right operand.
>	greater than	The left operand is greater than the right operand.
>=	greater than or equal to	The left operand is greater than or equal to the right operand.

You might find it helpful to think of the comparison operators as questions. When you write

```
(x >= 10)
```

you're really saying, "Is the value of variable x greater than or equal to 10?" The return value answers the question, TRUE or FALSE.

The Difference Between = and ==

You might be asking yourself, "Why do my tests for equality always succeed, even when I know that the two quantities are sometimes different?"

A common mistake in JavaScript, as in C, C++, or Java, is mixing up the = operator—used to set one quantity equal to another—and the == operator—used to test two quantities for equality. The following code tests to see whether the variable a is equal to 10. If it is, this code writes out the following line:

```
if (a == 10)
document.writeln("a is equal to 10!")
```

On the other hand, the following code sets a equal to 10 and returns TRUE, and thus always writes out the following line:

```
if (a = 10)
document.writeln("a is equal to 10!")
```

Logical Operators Comparison operators compare quantity or content for numeric and string expressions. Sometimes, however, you need to test a logical value such as whether a comparison operator returns TRUE or FALSE. JavaScript's logical operators enable you to compare expressions that return logical values. The following are JavaScript's logical operators:

- **&&, read as "and"**—The && operator returns TRUE if both its input expressions are true. If the first operand evaluates to false, && returns FALSE immediately, without evaluating the second operand. Here's an example:

  ```
  x = TRUE && TRUE;        // x is TRUE
  x = FALSE && FALSE;      // x is FALSE
  x = FALSE && TRUE;       // x is FALSE
  ```

- **||, read as "or"**—This operator returns TRUE if either of its operands is true. If the first operand is true, || returns TRUE without evaluating the second operand. Here's an example:

  ```
  x = TRUE || TRUE;        // x is TRUE
  x = FALSE || TRUE;       // x is TRUE
  x = FALSE || FALSE;      // x is FALSE
  ```

- **!, read as "not"**—This operator takes only one expression and returns the opposite of that expression; !TRUE returns FALSE, for example, and !FALSE returns TRUE.

Note that the "and" and "or" operators don't evaluate the second operand if the first operand provides enough information for the operator to return a value—for example, if the first operand of the && operator is FALSE, the result will be FALSE regardless of what the second operator is. This process, called *short-circuit evaluation*, can be significant (and useful) when the second operand is a function call. For example:

```
keepGoing = (userCancelled == FALSE) && (theForm.Submit())
```

If userCancelled is TRUE, the second operand, which submits the active form, is not called.

String Operators You can use a few of the operators previously listed for string manipulation as well. All the comparison operators can be used on strings, too; the results depend on standard lexicographic ordering (ordering by the ASCII values of the string characters), but comparisons aren't case sensitive. Additionally, you can use the + operator to concatenate strings, returning a string made up of the original strings joined together. The expression

```
str = "Hello, " + "World!";
```

would assign the resulting string "Hello, World!" to the variable str.

Controlling Your JavaScripts

Some scripts you write will be simple. They will execute the same way every time, one time per page. If you add a JavaScript to play a sound when users visit your home page, for example, it doesn't need to evaluate any conditions or do anything more than one time. More sophisticated scripts might require that you take different actions under different circumstances. You might also want to repeat the execution of a block of code—perhaps by a set number of times or as long as some condition is TRUE. JavaScript provides constructs for controlling the execution flow of your script based on conditions, as well as for repeating a sequence of operations.

Testing Conditions

JavaScript provides a single type of control statement for making decisions: the if…else statement. To make a decision, you supply an expression that evaluates to TRUE or FALSE; which code is executed depends on what your expression evaluates to.

The simplest form of if…else uses only the if part. If the specified condition is TRUE, the code following the condition is executed; if not, it's skipped. In the following code fragment, for example, the message appears only if the condition (that the lastModified.year property of the document object says it was modified before 1998) is TRUE:

```
if (document.lastModified.year < 1998)
   document.write("Danger! This is a mighty old document.")
```

You can use any expression as the condition. Because you can nest expressions and combine them with the logical operators, your tests can be pretty sophisticated. For example:

```
if ((document.lastModified.year > 1998) && (document.lastModified.month > 10))
   document.write("This document is reasonably current.")
```

The `else` clause enables you to specify a set of statements to execute when the condition is `FALSE`. For example:

```
if ((document.lastModified.year > 1998) && (document.lastModified.month > 10))
   document.write("This document is reasonably current.")
else
   document.write("This document is quite old.")
```

Repeating Actions

JavaScript provides two loop constructs that you can use to repeat a set of operations. The first, called a `for` loop, executes a set of statements some number of times. You specify three expressions: an *initial* expression that sets the values of any variables you need to use, a *condition* that tells the loop how to see when it is done, and an *increment* expression that modifies any variables that need it. Here's a simple example:

```
for (count=0; count < 100; count++)
   document.write("Count is ", count);
```

This loop executes 100 times and prints out a number each time. The initial expression sets the counter, `count`, to zero. The condition tests to see whether `count` is less than 100 and the increment expression increments `count`.

You can use several statements for any of these expressions, as follows:

```
for (count=0, numFound = 0; (count < 100) && (numFound < 3); count++)
   if (someObject.found()) numFound++;
```

This loop either loops 100 times or as many times as it takes to "find" three items—the loop condition terminates when `count >= 100` or when `numFound >= 3`.

The second form of loop is the `while` loop. It executes statements as long as its condition is `TRUE`. You can rewrite the first `for` loop in the preceding example, for example, as follows:

```
count = 0
while (count < 100) {
   count++;
   if (someObject.found()) numFound++;
   document.write("Count is ", count)
}
```

Which form you use depends on what you are doing; `for` loops are useful when you want to perform an action a set number of times, and `while` loops are best when you want to keep doing something as long as a particular condition remains `TRUE`. Notice that by using braces, you can include more than one command to be executed by the `while` loop. (This is also true of `for` loops and `if...else` constructs.)

JavaScript Reserved Words

JavaScript reserves some keywords for its own use. You cannot define your own methods or properties with the same name as any of these keywords; if you do, the JavaScript interpreter complains.

TIP Some of these keywords are reserved for future use. JavaScript might enable you to use them, but your scripts might break in the future if you do.

The following list shows some of JavaScript's reserved keywords. You should not use these in your JavaScripts:

`abstract`	`double`	`instanceof`	`super`
`boolean`	`else`	`int`	`switch`
`break`	`extends`	`interface`	`synchronized`
`byte`	`FALSE`	`long`	`this`
`case`	`final`	`native`	`throw`
`catch`	`finally`	`new`	`throws`
`char`	`float`	`null`	`transient`
`class`	`for`	`package`	`TRUE`
`const`	`function`	`private`	`try`
`continue`	`goto`	`protected`	`var`
`default`	`if`	`public`	`void`
`do`	`implements`	`return`	`while`
`import`	`short`	`with`	`in`
`static`			

TIP Because JavaScript is still being developed and refined, the list of reserved keywords might change or grow over time. A good way to avoid any possible conflicts is to start all your variable names with a prefix that will ensure that there aren't any conflicts with reserved words. For example, I could begin all of my variable names with my initials and an underscore, `jod_`.

Using JavaScript Statements

This section provides a quick reference to some of the more important JavaScript statements. Those listed here are in alphabetical order—many have examples. The formatting of these entries means the following:

- All JavaScript keywords are in monospaced font.
- Words in monospace *italic* represent user-defined names or statements.
- Any portions enclosed in square brackets ([and]) are optional.
- {statements} indicates a block of statements, which can consist of a single statement or multiple statements enclosed by braces.

The *break* Statement

The break statement terminates the current while or for loop and transfers program control to the statement that follows the terminated loop.

Syntax:

```
break
```

Example:

The following function scans the list of URLs in the current document and stops when it has seen all URLs or when it finds a URL that matches the input parameter searchName:

```
function findURL(searchName) {
   var i = 0;
   for (i=0; i < document.links.length; i++) {
      if (document.links[i] == searchName) {
         document.writeln(document.links[i] + "<BR>")
         break;
      }
   }
}
```


The *continue* Statement

The continue statement stops executing the statements in a while or for loop and skips to the next iteration of the loop. It doesn't stop the loop altogether like the break statement; instead, in a while loop, it jumps back to the condition. In a for loop, it jumps to the update expression.

Syntax:

```
continue
```

Example:

The following function prints the odd numbers between 1 and x; it has a continue statement that goes to the next iteration when i is even:

```
function printOddNumbers(x) {
   var i = 0
   while (i < x) {
      i++;
```

```
            if ((i % 2) == 0) // the % operator divides & returns the remainder
               continue
            else
               document.write(i, "\n")
         }
      }
```

The *for* Loop

A `for` loop consists of three optional expressions, enclosed in parentheses and separated by semicolons, followed by a block of statements executed in the loop. These parts do the following:

- The starting expression, `initial_expr`, is evaluated before the loop starts. It is most often used to initialize loop counter variables. You are free to use the `var` keyword here to declare new variables.
- A `condition` is evaluated on each pass through the loop. If the condition evaluates to `TRUE`, the statements in the loop body are executed. You can leave the condition out. If you do, it always evaluates to `TRUE`. If you leave the condition out, make sure to use `break` in your loop when it is time to exit.
- An update expression, `update_expr`, is usually used to update or increment the counter variable or other variables used in the condition. This expression is optional; you can update variables as needed within the body of the loop if you prefer.
- A block of statements is executed as long as the condition is `TRUE`. This block can have one or multiple statements in it.

Syntax:

```
for ([initial_expr;] [condition;] [update_expr]) {
   statements
}
```

Example:

This simple `for` statement prints out the numerals from 0 to 9. It starts by declaring a loop counter variable, `i`, and initializing it to 0. As long as `i` is less than 9, the update expression increments `i`, and the statements in the loop body are executed.

```
for (var i = 0; i <= 9; i++) {
   document.write(i);
}
```

The *for...in* Loop

The `for…in` loop is a special form of the `for` loop that iterates the variable `variable-name` over all the properties of the object named `object-name`. For each distinct property, it executes the statements in the loop body.

Syntax:

```
for (var in obj) {
   statements
}
```

Example:

The following function takes as its arguments an object and the object's name. It then uses the `for…in` loop to iterate through all the object's properties and writes them into the current Web page.

```
function dump_props(obj, obj_name) {
   for (i in obj)
      document.writeln(obj_name + "." + i + " = " + obj[i] + "<br>");
}
```

The *function* Statement

The `function` statement declares a JavaScript function; the function might optionally accept one or more parameters. To return a value, the function must have a return statement that specifies the value to return. All parameters are passed to functions *by value*—the function gets the value of the parameter but cannot change the original value in the caller.

Syntax:

```
function name([param] [, param] [, …]) {
   statements
}
```

Example:

This example defines a function called `PageNameMatches`, which returns `TRUE` if the string argument passed to the function is the title of the current document.

```
function PageNameMatches(theString) {
   return (document.title == theString)
}
```

The *if…else* Statement

The `if…else` statement is a conditional statement that executes the statements in `block1` if `condition` is `TRUE`. In the optional `else` clause, it executes the statements in `block2` if `condition` is `FALSE`. The blocks of statements can contain any JavaScript statements, including further nested `if` statements.

Syntax:

```
if (condition) {
    statements
}
```

```
[else {
    statements
}]
```

Example:

This `if…else` statement calls the `Message.Decrypt()` method if the `Message.IsEncrypted()` method returns `TRUE` and calls the `Message.Display()` method otherwise.

```
if (Message.IsEncrypted()) {
    Message.Decrypt(SecretKey);
}
else {
    Message.Display();
}
```

The *new* Statement

The `new` statement is the way that new objects are created in JavaScript.

Syntax:

```
var parm = new objectconstructor([param] [, param] [, …]);
```

Example:

If you defined the following function to create a `house` object:

```
function house (rms, stl, yr, garp) { // define a house object
   this.room = rms;        // number of rooms (integer)
   this.style = stl;       // style (string)
   this.yearBuilt = yr;    // year built (integer)
   this.hasGarage = garp; // has garage? (boolean)
}
```

You could then create an instance of a `house` object by using the `new` statement, as in the following:

```
var myhouse = new house(3,"Tenement",1962,false);
```

A few notes about this example. First, note that the function used to create the object doesn't actually return a value. The reason that this method can work is that the function uses the `this` object, which always refers to the current object. Second, although the function defines how to create the `house` object, none is actually created until the function is called using the `new` statement.

The *return* Statement

The `return` statement specifies the value to be returned by a function.

Syntax:

```
return expression;
```

Example:

The following simple function returns the square of its argument, `x`, where `x` is any number.

```
function square(x) {
   return x * x;
}
```

The *this* Statement

You use `this` to access methods or properties of an object within the object's methods. The `this` statement always refers to the current object.

Syntax:

```
this.property
```

Example:

If `setSize` is a method of the `document` object, `this` refers to the specific object whose `setSize` method is called:

```
function setSize(x, y) {
   this.horizSize = x;
   this.vertSize = y;
}
```

This method sets the size for an object when called as follows:

```
document.setSize(640, 480);
```

The *var* Statement

The `var` statement declares a variable `varname`, optionally initializing it to have `value`. The variable name `varname` can be any JavaScript identifier, and `value` can be any legal expression (including literals).

Syntax:

```
var varname [= value] [, var varname [= value]] [, …]
```

Example:

This statement declares the variables `num_hits` and `cust_no` and initializes their values to zero.

```
var num_hits = 0, var cust_no = 0;
```

The *while* Statement

The `while` statement contains a condition and a block of statements. The `while` statement evaluates the condition; if `condition` is `TRUE`, it executes the statements in the loop body. It then re-evaluates `condition` and continues to execute the statement block as long as `condition` is `TRUE`. When `condition` evaluates to `FALSE`, execution continues with the next statement following the block.

Syntax:

```
while (condition) {
   statements
}
```

Example:

The following simple `while` loop iterates until it finds a form in the current document object whose name is `"OrderForm"` or until it runs out of forms in the document:

```
x = 0;
while ((x < document.forms[].length) &&
        (document.forms[x].name != "OrderForm")) {
   x++
}
```

The *with* Statement

The `with` statement establishes `object` as the default object for the statements in `block`. Any property references without an object are then assumed to be for `object`.

Syntax:

```
with object {
   statements
}
```

Example:

This statement uses `with` to apply the `write()` method and set the value of the `bgColor` property of the `document` object.

```
with document {
   write "Inside a with block, you don't need to specify the object.";
   bgColor = gray;
}
```

JavaScript and Web Browsers

The most important thing you will be doing with your JavaScripts is interacting with the content and information on your Web pages, and through it, with your user. JavaScript interacts with your Web browser through the browser's object model. Different aspects of the Web browser exist as different objects, with properties and methods that can be accessed by JavaScript. For example, `document.write()` uses the `write` method of the `document` object. Understanding this Document Object Model is crucial to using JavaScript effectively. Also, understanding how the Web browser processes and executes your scripts is also necessary.

When Scripts Execute

When you put JavaScript code in a page, the Web browser evaluates the code as soon as it is encountered. Functions, however, don't get executed when they're evaluated; they get stored for later use. You still have to call functions explicitly to make them work. Some functions are attached to objects—buttons or text fields on forms, for example, which are called when some event happens on the button or field. You might also have functions that you want to execute during page evaluation. You can do so by putting a call to the function at the appropriate place in the page.

Where to Put Your Scripts

You can put scripts anywhere within your XHTML page, as long as they are surrounded with the `<script>...</script>` elements. One good system is to put functions that will be executed more than one time into the `<head>` element of their pages; this element provides a convenient storage place. Because the `<head>` element is at the beginning of the file, functions that you put there are evaluated before the rest of the document is loaded. Then you can execute the function at the appropriate point in your Web page by calling it, as in the following:

```
<script type="text/javascript" language="JavaScript">
<!-- Hide this script from incompatible Web browsers!
myFunction();
//   Hide this script from incompatible Web browsers! -->
</script>
```

Another way to execute scripts is to attach them to XHTML elements that support scripts. When scripts are matched with events attached to these elements, the script is executed when the event occurs. This can be done with XHTML elements, such as forms, buttons, or links. Consider Listing 18.2, which shows a simple example of two ways of attaching a JavaScript function to the `onClick` attribute of an XHTML forms button (see Figure 18.2); it also shows how a JavaScript call can be executed in response to clicking a hypertext link.

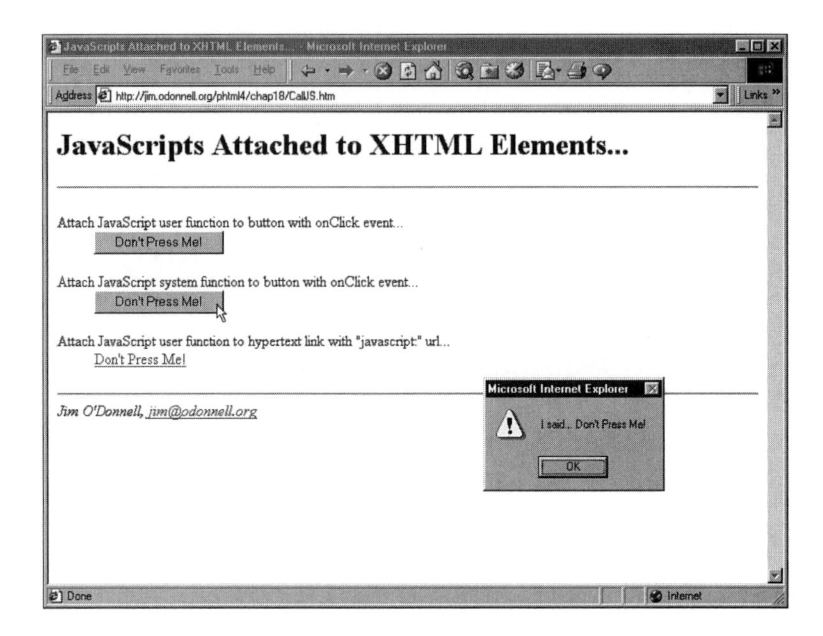

FIGURE 18.2
JavaScript functions can be attached to form fields through several methods.

Listing 18.2 ***CallJS.htm*—Calling a JavaScript Function with the Click of a Button or Hypertext Link**

```
<!DOCTYPE html PUBLIC "-//W3C//DTD XHTML 1.0 Transitional//EN"
    "http://www.w3.org/TR/xhtml1/DTD/xhtml1-transitional.dtd">
<html xmlns="http://www.w3.org/1999/xhtml">
<head>
<script type="text/javascript" language="JavaScript">
<!-- Hide this script from incompatible Web browsers!
function pressed() {
   alert("I said... Don't Press Me!");
}
//   Hide this script from incompatible Web browsers! -->
</script>
<title>JavaScripts Attached to XHTML Elements...</title>
</head>
<body bgcolor="#ffffff">
<form name="Form1">
<h1>JavaScripts Attached to XHTML Elements...</h1>
<hr />
<dl>
<dt>Attach JavaScript user function to button with onClick event...</dt>
<dd><input type="BUTTON" name="Button1" value="Don't Press Me!"
        onclick="pressed()"></dd>
<dt> </dt>
<dt>Attach JavaScript system function to button with onClick event...</dt>
<dd><input type="BUTTON" name="Button2" value="Don't Press Me!"
```

```
        onclick="alert('I said... Don\'t Press Me!')"></dd>
</form>
<dt>Attach JavaScript user function to hypertext link with
    "javascript:" url...</dt>
<dd><a href="javascript:pressed()">Don't Press Me!</a></dd>
</dl>
<hr />
<em>Jim O'Donnell, <a href="mailto:jim@odonnell.org">jim@odonnell.org</a></em>
</body>
</html>
```

Three ways to call a JavaScript function from an XHTML element appear in Listing 18.2. The first attaches a user function call to the `onClick` event of an XHTML forms element. The second way shows that you can directly call built-in JavaScript functions using the `onClick` event. This works particularly well when you are trying to do something simple. Finally, you can use the "javascript:" URL protocol to attach a JavaScript function call to a hypertext link. In the example shown in Listing 18.2, clicking either button or the hypertext link pops up the alert box shown in Figure 18.2.

Sometimes you have code that should not be evaluated or executed until after all the page's XHTML has been parsed and displayed. An example would be a function to print out all the URLs referenced in the page. If this function is evaluated before all the XHTML on the page has been loaded, it misses some URLs. Therefore, the call to the function should come at the page's end. You can define the function itself anywhere in the XHTML document; it is the function call that you should put at the end of the page.

NOTE JavaScript code to modify the actual XHTML contents of a document (as opposed to merely changing the text in a form text input field, for example) must be executed during page evaluation. The only exception to this is when using Dynamic HTML, which, in some cases and on some browsers, enables you to change page content after initial evaluation. ■

CHAPTER 19

The Document Object Model

by Jim O'Donnell

In this chapter

In Chapter 18, "Introduction to JavaScripting," you learned the basics of JavaScript—its syntax, control structures, and how to use it to access and manipulate objects. To be useful, however, something to manipulate is needed. How does JavaScript (or any other scripting language, for that matter) interact with your Web browser?

The answer is the Document Object Model. Each script-compatible Web browser, mainly Netscape Navigator and Microsoft Internet Explorer, exposes a number of objects that can be used to control and interact with the browser. The sum total of these objects is the browser's object model.

As you would expect, the object models that Netscape and Microsoft have developed for their Web browsers are not completely compatible. Not only do differences exist between the models from the two vendors, but each revision of their Web browsers also differs from the last—they are largely backward compatible but include many new capabilities. This chapter examines those elements of the Document Object Model that are (for the most part) common to all Netscape and Microsoft Web browsers, version 3 and higher. (Differences are noted in the discussion.) Later chapters discuss some of the major changes that have occurred with the advent of support for Cascading Style Sheets and Dynamic HTML.

▶ To read about Microsoft's enhanced Document Object Model, **see** "Internet Explorer Document Object Model," **p. 624**

Web Browser Object Hierarchy and Scoping

Figure 19.1 shows the hierarchy of many of the objects that the Web browser provides and that are accessible to JavaScript. As shown, `window` is the topmost object in the hierarchy, and the other objects are organized underneath it. Using this hierarchy, the full reference for the value of a text field named `text1` in an XHTML form named `form1` would be `window.document.form1.text1.value`.

Because of the object-scoping rules in JavaScript, however, it isn't necessary to specify this full reference. *Scoping* refers to the range over which a variable, function, or object is defined. A variable defined within a JavaScript function, for example, is only scoped within that function—it cannot be referenced outside the function. JavaScripts are scoped to the current window, but not to the objects below the window in the hierarchy. Thus, for the preceding example, the text field value could also be referenced as `document.form1.text1.value`.

As in Figure 19.1, all Web pages will have the `window`, `navigator`, `document`, `history`, and `location` objects. Depending on the contents of the Web page, other objects might also be defined. The remainder of this chapter reviews the objects shown in Figure 19.1—the information defined for them (properties), the functions they can perform (methods), and the actions to which they can respond (events).

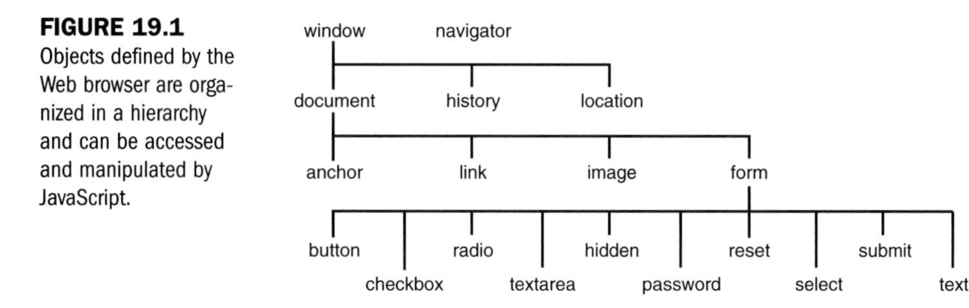

FIGURE 19.1
Objects defined by the Web browser are organized in a hierarchy and can be accessed and manipulated by JavaScript.

The *window* Object

The Web browser creates at least one `window` object for every document. Think of the `window` object as an actual window and the `document` object as the content that appears in the window. As briefly discussed in this chapter and then in more detail in Chapter 20, "Manipulating Windows and Frames with JavaScript," one document can create more than one window, using the `window` object's `open()` method.

window Object Properties

Your XHTML documents can access and manipulate a number of attributes of the current Web browser window through the `window` object. Some of the more useful `window` object properties are the following:

- **`closed`**—Specifies whether a window has been closed (Boolean).
- **`defaultStatus`**—The default message that appears in the status line of the Web browser window (string).
- **`length`**—The number of frames in the current window (integer).
- **`name`**—The name of a window (string).
- **`opener`**—When a window is opened using the `open()` method, the name of the window from which it was created is in this property (string).
- **`parent`**—Refers to a window that contains a frameset (object).
- **`self` or `top`**—Refers to the current window (object).
- **`status`**—Can be used to read or set the contents of the Web browser's status line (string).

In addition to the properties in the preceding list, remember that the `document`, `history`, and `location` objects are also properties of the `window` object.

window Object Methods

You can use JavaScript to create or operate on existing windows by using the methods associated with the `window` object. The following are some of these methods:

- **`alert(string)`**—Puts up an alert dialog box and displays the message specified in `string`. Users must dismiss the dialog box by clicking the OK button before the Web browser will enable them to continue.
- **`blur()`**—Removes the focus from the specified window.
- **`clearTimeOut(timerID)`**—Clears the timer function with ID `timerID` (see the `setTimeOut()` method in this list).
- **`close()`**—Closes the specified window.
- **`confirm(string)`**—Puts up a confirmation dialog box with two buttons (OK and Cancel) and displays the message specified in `string`. Users can dismiss the dialog box by clicking Cancel or OK; the `confirm` function returns `true` if users click OK and `false` if they click Cancel.
- **`eval(string)`**—Evaluates `string` as JavaScript code and returns the result.
- **`focus()`**—Puts the focus on the specified window.
- **`open(arguments)`**—Opens a new window.
- **`prompt(string,[inputDefault])`**—Opens a prompt box, which displays `string` as a prompt and asks the user for input. If `inputDefault` is specified, it is shown as the default value of the prompt box.
- **`scroll(x,y)`**—Scrolls the window to the given `x` and `y` coordinates.
- **`setTimeOut(expression,msec)`**—Evaluates `expression` after the specified number of milliseconds have passed. This method returns a timer ID that can be used by `clearTimeOut`.

NOTE Each of these methods–as well as the events in the following section–are applied to the `window` object to which they belong. For example, `blur()` or `self.blur()` would remove the focus from the window in which the document was located. `MyWindow.blur()` would remove it from the window called `MyWindow`. ■

window Object Events

Finally, the `window` object can respond to the following events:

- **`onBlur`**—Triggered when the focus is removed from the window.
- **`onError`**—Triggered when an error occurs in the window.
- **`onFocus`**—Triggered when the focus is applied to the window.

- **onLoad**—Triggered when the Web browser finishes loading a document into the window.
- **onUnload**—Triggered when the user exits from the document within the window.

Window methods can be placed in either the `<body>` or `<frameset>` element of the document. To attach a JavaScript function to the `onLoad` event, for example, you could use this `<body>` element:

```
<body onLoad="alert('Document download complete!')">
```

Chapter 20 includes an extensive example of how to use JavaScript to create and manipulate windows.

▶ To see an example of using JavaScript to interact with XHTML windows, **see** "JavaScript Windows Example," **p. 495**

The *location* Object

As mentioned earlier, one of the properties of every window is the `location` object. This object holds the current URL, including the hostname, path, CGI script arguments, and even the protocol. Table 19.1 shows the properties and methods of the `location` object.

Table 19.1 The *location* Object Contains Information on the Currently Displayed URL

Name	What It Does
Properties	
`href`	Contains the entire URL, including all the subparts; for example, `http://jim.odonnell.org:80/Que/location.html`
`protocol`	Contains the protocol field of the URL, including the first colon; for example, `http:`
`host`	Contains the hostname and port number; for example, `jim.odonnell.org:80`
`hostname`	Contains only the hostname; for example, `jim.odonnell.org`
`port`	Contains the port number; for example, `80`
`path`	Contains the path to the actual document; for example, `Que/location.html`
`hash`	Contains any CGI arguments after the first `#` in the URL
`search`	Contains any CGI arguments after the first `?` in the URL
Method	
`assign(string)`	Sets `location.href` to the value you specify

Listing 19.1 shows an example of how you access and use the `location` object. First, the current values of the `location` properties are displayed on the Web page (see Figure 19.2). As you can see, not all of them are defined. Additionally, when the button is clicked, the `location.href` property is set to the URL of my home page. This causes the Web browser to load that page (see Figure 19.3).

Listing 19.1 *location.htm*—The *location* Object Enables You to Access and Set Information About the Current URL

```
<!DOCTYPE html PUBLIC "-//W3C//DTD XHTML 1.0 Transitional//EN"
    "http://www.w3.org/TR/xhtml1/DTD/xhtml1-transitional.dtd">
<html xmlns="http://www.w3.org/1999/xhtml">
<head>
<script type="text/javascript" language="JavaScript">
<!-- Hide this script from incompatible Web browsers!
function gohome() {
   location.href = "http://jim.odonnell.org";
}
//   Hide this script from incompatible Web browsers! -->
</script>
<title>The Location Object</title>
</head>
<body bgcolor="#ffffff">
<h1>The Location Object</h1>
<hr />
<script language="JavaScript">
<!-- Hide this script from incompatible Web browsers!
document.writeln("Current location information:");
document.writeln("<ul>");
document.writeln("<li>location.href = " + location.href + "</li>");
document.writeln("<li>location.protocol = " + location.protocol + "</li>");
document.writeln("<li>location.host = " + location.host + "</li>");
document.writeln("<li>location.hostname = " + location.hostname + "</li>");
document.writeln("<li>location.port = " + location.port + "</li>");
document.writeln("<li>location.pathname = " + location.pathname + "</li>");
document.writeln("<li>location.hash = " + location.hash + "</li>");
document.writeln("<li>location.search = " + location.search + "</li>");
document.writeln("</ul>");
//   Hide this script from incompatible Web browsers! -->
</script>
<form name="Form1">
   <input type="BUTTON" name="Button1" value="Goto JOD's Home Page!"
      onclick="gohome()"/>
</form>
<hr />
<em>Jim O'Donnell, <a href="mailto:jim@odonnell.org">jim@odonnell.org</a></em>
</body>
</html>
```

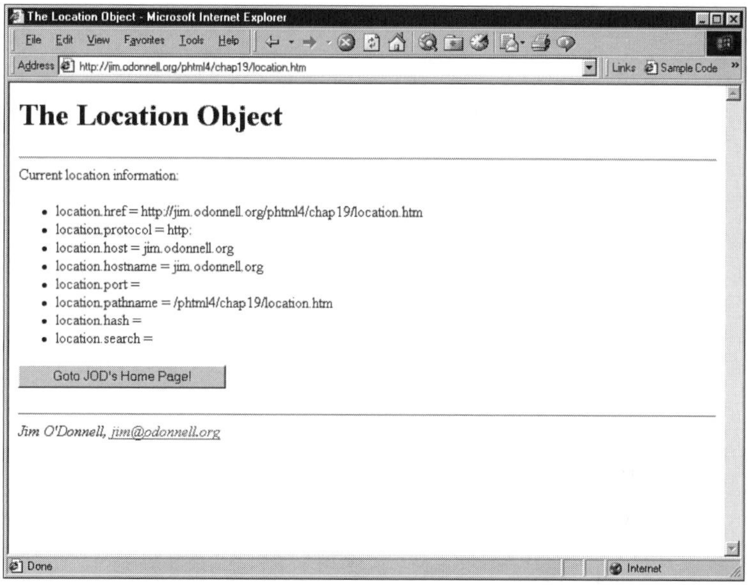

FIGURE 19.2
Manipulating the `location` object gives you another means of moving from one Web page to another.

The Location Object - Microsoft Internet Explorer

The Location Object

Current location information:

- location.href = http://jim.odonnell.org/phtml4/chap19/location.htm
- location.protocol = http:
- location.host = jim.odonnell.org
- location.hostname = jim.odonnell.org
- location.port =
- location.pathname = /phtml4/chap19/location.htm
- location.hash =
- location.search =

Goto JOD's Home Page!

Jim O'Donnell, jim@odonnell.org

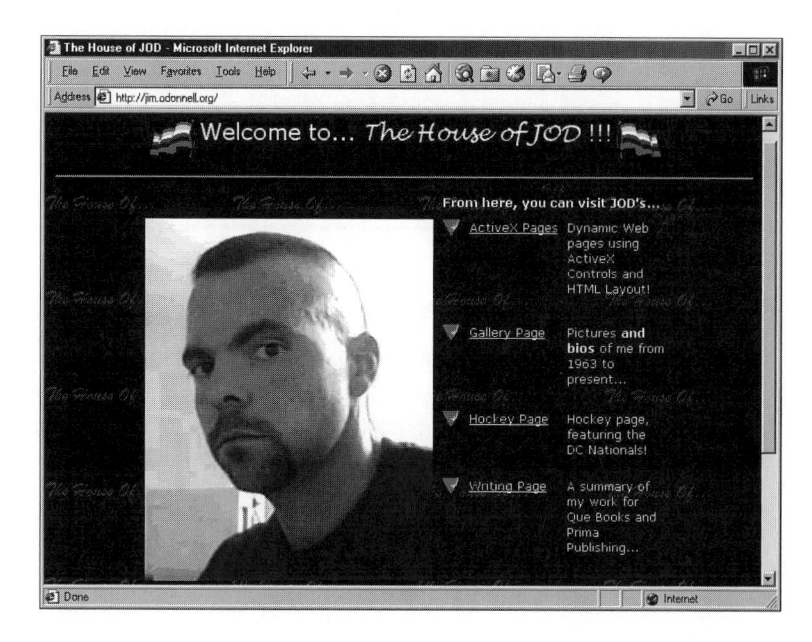

FIGURE 19.3
By setting its `href` property, you can use the `location` object to change the URL your Web browser is looking at.

NOTE The `document.write()` method is discussed later in this chapter, in the "The `document` Object" section. ■

The *history* Object

The Web browser also maintains a list of pages that you have visited since running the program; this list is called the *history list,* and it can be accessed through the `history` object. Your JavaScript programs can move through pages in the list by using the properties and functions shown in Table 19.2.

The `history.length`, therefore, returns the number of entries in the history list. The methods `history.back()` and `history.forward()` causes the Web browser to load the previous and next entry in the history list, if any.

Table 19.2 The *history* Object Contains Information on the Browser's History List

Property	Type	What It Does
`current`	property	Contains the URL of the current history entry
`length`	property	Contains the number of entries in the history list
`previous`	property	Contains the URL of the previous history stack entry
`next`	property	Contains the URL of the next history stack entry
`back()`	method	Goes back one entry in the history list
`forward()`	method	Goes forward one entry in the history list
`go(num)`	method	Goes forward `num` entries in the history stack if `num` is less than 0, otherwise it goes backward `-num` entries
`go(string)`	method	Goes to the newest history entry whose title or URL contains `string` as a substring; the string case doesn't matter

The *document* Object

Web browsers also expose an object called `document`. As you might expect, this object exposes useful properties and methods of the active document. The `location` object refers only to the URL of the active document, but `document` refers to the document itself. Chapter 20 discusses the `document` object in more detail, but its basic properties and methods are shown here.

▶ To see an example of using the `document` object to dynamically create XHTML, **see** "Filling Your Windows II: The `Document` Object," **p. 493**

document Object Properties

You can access and manipulate several attributes of the current Web browser document through the `document` object. Some of the more useful `document` object properties are the following:

- **`alinkColor`**—The color of the document's active link
- **`bgColor`**—The background color of the document
- **`cookie`**—The document's cookie
- **`domain`**—Domain name of the server that served the document
- **`fgColor`**—The foreground color of the document
- **`lastModified`**—The date the document was last modified
- **`linkColor`**—The color of the document's links
- **`referrer`**—The URL of the document from which this document was called
- **`title`**—The contents of the `<title>` element
- **`URL`**—The complete URL of the document
- **`vlinkColor`**—The color of the document's visited links

In addition to the properties in the preceding list, remember that the `anchor`, `link`, `form`, and `image` objects are also properties of the `document` object.

document Object Methods

You can use JavaScript to operate on documents by using the methods associated with the `document` object. The following are some of these methods:

- **`close()`**—Closes the specified document.
- **`eval(string)`**—Evaluates `string` as JavaScript code and returns the result.
- **`open()`**—Opens a stream for a new document. This document is meant to be filled with the output of calls to the `document.write()` and `document.writeln()` methods.
- **`write(expression [, expression…])`**—Writes one or more XHTML expressions.
- **`writeln(expression [, expression…])`**—Identical to `write()`, except this method appends a new line.

Listing 19.2 shows a JavaScript that accesses and displays some of the properties of the `document` object. Notice that the `link` object is accessed through the `links` array, one for each URL link on the current Web page (see the "JavaScript Object Arrays" section later in this chapter). Figure 19.4 shows the results of loading this Web page.

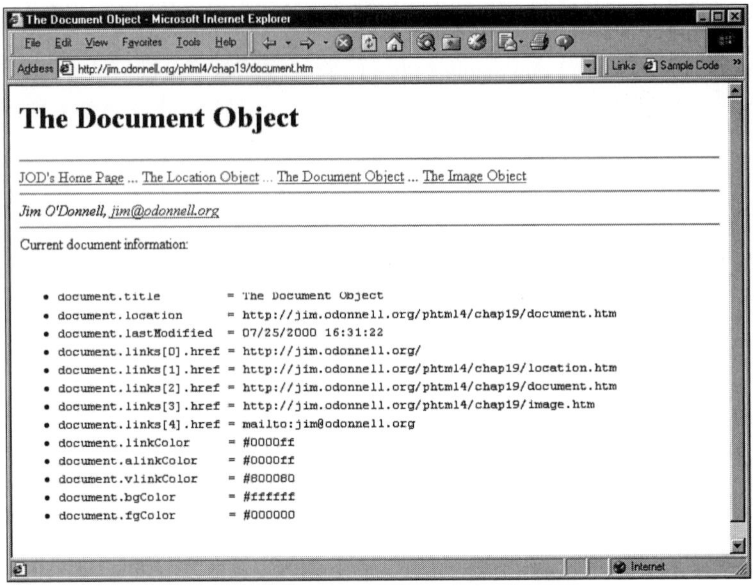

FIGURE 19.4
`document` object properties contain information about the current document displayed in the Web browser.

The Document Object - Microsoft Internet Explorer
File Edit View Favorites Tools Help
Address http://jim.odonnell.org/phtml4/chap19/document.htm
Links Sample Code

The Document Object

JOD's Home Page ... The Location Object ... The Document Object ... The Image Object

Jim O'Donnell, jim@odonnell.org

Current document information:

```
• document.title          = The Document Object
• document.location       = http://jim.odonnell.org/phtml4/chap19/document.htm
• document.lastModified   = 07/25/2000 16:31:22
• document.links[0].href  = http://jim.odonnell.org/
• document.links[1].href  = http://jim.odonnell.org/phtml4/chap19/location.htm
• document.links[2].href  = http://jim.odonnell.org/phtml4/chap19/document.htm
• document.links[3].href  = http://jim.odonnell.org/phtml4/chap19/image.htm
• document.links[4].href  = mailto:jim@odonnell.org
• document.linkColor      = #0000ff
• document.alinkColor     = #0000ff
• document.vlinkColor     = #800080
• document.bgColor        = #ffffff
• document.fgColor        = #000000
```

Internet

Listing 19.2 *document.htm*—The *document* Object Enables You to Access and Set Information About the Current Document

```
<!DOCTYPE html PUBLIC "-//W3C//DTD XHTML 1.0 Transitional//EN"
    "http://www.w3.org/TR/xhtml1/DTD/xhtml1-transitional.dtd">
<html xmlns="http://www.w3.org/1999/xhtml">
<head>
<title>The Document Object</title>
</head>
<body bgcolor="#ffffff">
<h1>The Document Object</h1>
<hr />
<a href="http://jim.odonnell.org/">JOD's Home Page</a> ...
<a href="http://jim.odonnell.org/phtml4/chap19/location.htm">
   The Location Object</a> ...
<a href="http://jim.odonnell.org/phtml4/chap19/document.htm">
   The Document Object</a> ...
<a href="http://jim.odonnell.org/phtml4/chap19/image.htm">
   The Image Object</a>
<hr />
<em>Jim O'Donnell, <a href="mailto:jim@odonnell.org">jim@odonnell.org</a></em>
<hr />
<script type="text/javascript" language="JavaScript">
<!-- Hide this script from incompatible Web browsers!
var n
document.writeln("Current document information:<pre>")
document.writeln("<ul>");
document.writeln("<li>document.title          = " +
   document.title + "</li>")
```

Listing 19.2 Continued

```
document.writeln("<li>document.location       = " +
   document.location + "</li>")
document.writeln("<li>document.lastModified   = " +
   document.lastModified + "</li>")
for (n = 0; n < document.links.length; n++)
   document.writeln("<li>document.links[" + n + "].href = " +
      document.links[n].href + "</li>")
document.writeln("<li>document.linkColor      = " +
   document.linkColor + "</li>")
document.writeln("<li>document.alinkColor     = " +
   document.alinkColor + "</li>")
document.writeln("<li>document.vlinkColor     = " +
   document.vlinkColor + "</li>")
document.writeln("<li>document.bgColor        = " +
   document.bgColor + "</li>")
document.writeln("<li>document.fgColor        = " +
   document.fgColor,"</pre><br/>")
document.writeln("</ul>");
//   Hide this script from incompatible Web browsers! -->
</script>
</body>
</html>
```

Some of the real power of the `document` object, however, is realized by using the objects underneath it in the hierarchy—particularly the different XHTML forms elements available. This is because XHTML forms can be one of the primary ways of interacting with the user of a Web page. The next few sections of this chapter discuss the objects used to interact with XHTML forms.

JavaScript Object Arrays

Before you read about the other objects in the Web browser object hierarchy, now is a good time to learn about JavaScript's object array. An *object array* is used by JavaScript to reference objects when more than one of the objects is in the current window or document (known as multiple instances of the object). An XHTML document is likely to contain more than one hypertext link, for example, so more than one `link` and `anchor` object will be present. Each form requires a separate `form` object, each image an `image` object, and so on.

JavaScript gives you multiple ways of referencing and accessing these objects. Consider the following excerpt of XHTML code, for example:

```
<form name="MyForm1" action=… method=…>
   XHTML form elements…
</form>
<form name="MyForm2" action=… method=…>
   XHTML form elements…
</form>
```

The first way to use JavaScript to reference these forms is to use the conventional object hierarchy that you have seen thus far. To set the value of a text field named `MyText1` in the first form, for example, you would use something like this:

```
document.MyForm1.MyText1.value = "Some Value"
```

JavaScript also gives you several other ways to reference these objects using its object arrays. Objects are contained in an object array in the order in which they are defined in the document. Assuming that the two previously mentioned forms are the only two forms in the document, the first can be referenced using

```
document.forms[0]
```

and the second with

```
document.forms[1]
```

Thus, the same text field could be set using

```
document.forms[0].MyText1.value = "Some Value"
```

The third way to reference objects in an object array is to use JavaScript's associative arrays. With associative arrays, the array element is referenced by including its name as the argument of the array. Using this method, the two forms would be referenced as

```
document.forms["MyForm1"]
```

and

```
document.forms["MyForm2"]
```

and the text field set using

```
document.forms["MyForm1"].MyText1.value = "Some Value"
```

These examples show the three ways to reference JavaScript objects when multiple instances exist. Which should you use? That depends on the application:

- Object Hierarchy Referencing. For example:

  ```
  document.MyForm1.MyText1.value
  ```

  Use this method when you are dealing with one or two objects, each with a predefined name and separate actions associated with each.
- Object Array with Numerical Index. For example:

  ```
  document.forms[0].MyText1.value
  ```

  Use this method when you want to repeat an action over multiple objects using a JavaScript `for` or `while` loop.

- Object Associative Array. For example:

```
document.forms["MyForm1"].MyText1.value
```

  Use this method when you want to operate on one or two objects only, but the specific object can vary.

For a given XHTML document, some of the predefined object arrays that JavaScript can access (depending on what is defined in the document) are the following:

- **anchors**—One for each of the <a> elements containing a NAME attribute
- **applets**—One for each <applet> element
- **arguments**—One for each argument of a JavaScript function
- **elements**—One for each element in an XHTML form
- **embeds**—One for each <embed> element
- **forms**—One for each XHTML form
- **frames**—One for each <frame/> element in a window containing a <frameset>
- **history**—One for each entry in the history list for a window
- **images**—One for each <img/> element
- **links**—One for each <area/> and/or <a> element containing an href attribute
- **mimeTypes**—One for each MIME type supported by the client Web browser, its helper applications, plug-ins, and (primarily for Internet Explorer) ActiveX Controls
- **options**—One for each <option> element
- **plugins**—One for each plug-in installed on the client Web browser

The *link*, *area*, and *anchor* Objects

These objects are created within a document when hypertext links or targets are created using the <a> or <area/> element. A link object is created when the <a> element uses the href attribute, and the anchor object is created when it uses the name attribute. area objects are created for each <area/> element used for creating client-side image maps.

▶ To read about the use of the <area/> element to create image maps, **see** "Client-Side Image Maps," **p. 142**

link and area objects are referenced through the link's object array. Each object in this array has the same properties as a location object (see Table 19.1 earlier in the chapter). In addition, these objects have the events listed in Table 19.3.

Table 19.3 Events of the XHTML *form* Object

Event	When It Occurs
`onClick`	Triggered when a `link` object is clicked
`onMouseOver`	Triggered when the mouse passes over a `link` or `area` object
`onMouseOut`	Triggered when the mouse passes out of a `link` or `area` object

`anchor` objects are also referenced using an object array—the `anchors` array. The only property of this object array, however, is the `length` property, which returns the number of elements in the array.

The *form* Object

The XHTML `form` object is the primary way for Web pages to solicit different types of input from the user. JavaScript will often work along with XHTML forms to perform its functions. The object model for XHTML forms includes a wide variety of properties, methods, and events. If you use these with each form, JavaScript can manipulate and access those forms.

form Object Properties

Tables 19.4, 19.5, and 19.6 show some of the properties, methods, and events attached to XHTML `form` objects. These can be used in JavaScripts—the properties and methods can be used to access or manipulate information and to perform certain functions, and the events can be used to trigger JavaScript functions related to the form itself. If a form is named `Form1`, for example, the method `document.Form1.submit()` can be called in JavaScript to submit the form. On the other hand, if the Submit button calls a function in response to an `onSubmit` event, the submission of the form can be disabled if the function returns a `false` value. This is a good way to perform form validation within the Web browser and to allow submission of the form only if all fields are validated.

Note that the XHTML form elements that can be included within the form, primarily using the `<input/>` element and some other form elements, are also represented as objects and can be referenced by JavaScript. These form `element` objects are also properties of their parent form—they are discussed in the next section.

Table 19.4 Properties of the XHTML *form* Object

Property	What It Contains
`name`	The value of the form's `name` attribute
`method`	The value of the form's `method` attribute

Table 19.4 Continued

`action`	The value of the form's `action` attribute
`elements`	The `elements` array of the form
`length`	The number of elements in the form
`encoding`	The value of the form's `encoding` attribute
`target`	Window targeted after `submit` for form response

Table 19.5 Methods of the XHTML *form* Object

Method	What It Does
`reset()`	Resets the form to its initial values
`submit()`	Submits the form

Table 19.6 Events of the XHTML *form* Object

Event	When It Occurs
`onReset`	Triggered when a reset button is clicked or the `reset()` method is called
`onSubmit`	Triggered when a submit button is clicked or the `submit()` method is called

Using Objects to Manipulate *Form* Elements

A good place to use JavaScript is in forms because you can write scripts that process, check, and perform calculations with the data the user enters. JavaScript provides a useful set of properties and methods for text `<input/>` elements, buttons, and other form elements.

You use `<input/>` elements in a form to enable the user to enter text data; JavaScript provides properties to get the objects that hold the element's contents as well as methods for doing something when the user moves into or out of a field. Table 19.7 shows some of the properties, methods, and events defined for `<input/>` form `element` objects.

Table 19.7 XHTML Form *input* Object Properties, Methods, and Events

Property	What It Contains
`name`	The value of the element's `NAME` attribute
`value`	The field's contents
`defaultValue`	The initial contents of the field

Table 19.7 Continued

Method	What It Does
`focus()`	Moves the input focus to the specified object
`blur()`	Moves the input focus away from the specified object
`select()`	Selects the specified object
`submit()`	Submits the form according to its `action` and `method` attributes
Event	**When It Occurs**
`onFocus`	Triggered when the user moves the input focus to the field, either via the Tab key or a mouse click
`onBlur`	Triggered when the user moves the input focus out of this field
`onSelect`	Triggered when the user selects text in the field
`onSubmit`	Triggered when the form is submitted
`onChange`	Triggered only when the field loses focus and the user has modified its text; use this action to validate data in a field

Individual buttons and check boxes have properties, too; JavaScript provides properties to get objects containing a button's data, as well as methods for doing something when the user selects or deselects a particular button. Table 19.8 shows some of the properties, methods, and events defined for button elements.

Table 19.8 XHTML Form *radio* and *checkbox* Object Properties, Methods, and Events

Property	What It Contains
`name`	The value of the button's `NAME` attribute
`value`	The `VALUE` attribute
`checked`	The state of a check box
`defaultChecked`	The initial state of a check box
Method	**What It Does**
`focus()`	Moves the input focus to the specified object
`blur()`	Moves the input focus away from the specified object
`click()`	Clicks a button and triggers whatever actions are attached to it
`submit()`	Submits the form according to its `action` and `method` attributes

Table 19.8 Continued

Event	When It Occurs
`onClick`	Triggered when the button is pressed
`onFocus`	Triggered when the user moves the input focus to the field, either via the Tab key or a mouse click
`onBlur`	Triggered when the user moves the input focus out of this field
`onSubmit`	Triggered when the form is submitted
`onChange`	Triggered only when the field loses focus and the user has modified its text; use this action to validate data in a field

For more details and examples of what you can do with JavaScript and the objects, properties, and methods associated with XHTML forms, see Chapter 21, "Using JavaScript to Create Smart Forms."

▶ To find out more about using JavaScript with XHTML forms, **see** "Client-Side Form Validation," **p. 514**

The *image* Object

The last Web browser object to discuss in this chapter is the `image` object. One `image` object is created in a document by each `<img/>` element on the page. These objects are referenced through an image's `object` array; the object's array has a `length` property that you can use to find out how many images are present. Table 19.9 shows some of the other properties and events associated with the `image` object.

Table 19.9 XHTML *image* Object Properties and Events

Property	What It Contains
`border`	The value of the `border` attribute
`complete`	Indicates whether the image has been completely loaded
`height`	The value of the `height` attribute
`hspace`	The value of the `hspace` attribute
`lowsrc`	The value of the `lowsrc` attribute
`name`	The value of the `name` attribute
`src`	The value of the `src` attribute
`vspace`	The value of the `vspace` attribute
`width`	The value of the `width` attribute

Table 19.9 Continued

Event	When It Occurs
onAbort	Triggered when the user aborts the loading of an image, such as by clicking the Stop button
onError	Triggered when an error occurs when an image is being loaded
onLoad	Triggered when an image is completely loaded

image Object Example

Listing 19.3 shows an example that uses the onMouseOver and onMouseOut events of the link object, along with the properties of the image object, to create a hypertext link whose anchor changes whenever the mouse is passed over it. This is often done to highlight hypertext link anchors to make them stand out more as the mouse passes over them—for instance, the changed image can be a glowing version of the original image. Figure 19.5 demonstrates how this will appear in the Web page.

FIGURE 19.5
The properties, events, and methods of different objects can be combined using JavaScript to produce cool effects.

Listing 19.3 *image.htm*—Use JavaScript to Create Changing Hypertext Link Anchors

```
<!DOCTYPE html PUBLIC "-//W3C//DTD XHTML 1.0 Transitional//EN"
    "http://www.w3.org/TR/xhtml1/DTD/xhtml1-transitional.dtd">
<html xmlns="http://www.w3.org/1999/xhtml">
<head>
<script type="text/javascript" language="JavaScript">
<!-- Hide this script from incompatible Web browsers!
function changeImage(i, j) {
   document.images[i].src = "clickme" + j + ".gif"
}
//   Hide this script from incompatible Web browsers! -->
</script>
<title>The Image Object</title>
</head>
```

Listing 19.3 Continued

```
<body bgcolor="#ffffff">
<h1>The Image Object</h1>
<hr />
<a href="location.htm" onmouseover="changeImage(0,2)"
                       onmouseout="changeImage(0,1)">
   <img src="clickme1.gif" alt="goto location.htm" width="200" height="50"/>
</a>
<a href="document.htm" onmouseover="changeImage(1,2)"
                       onmouseout="changeImage(1,1)">
   <img src="clickme1.gif" alt="goto document.htm" width="200" height="50"/>
</a>
<a href="image.htm"    onmouseover="changeImage(2,2)"
                       onmouseout="changeImage(2,1)">
   <img src="clickme1.gif" alt="goto image.htm"    width="200" height="50"/>
</a>
<hr />
<em>Jim O'Donnell, <a href="mailto:jim@odonnell.org">jim@odonnell.org</a></em>
</body>
</html>
```

Using the *Image* Constructor

You might have noticed in the example shown in Listing 19.3 that the first time you passed your mouse over the image, a slight pause occurred before the new image displayed. This is because the image needed to be downloaded into your cache the first time.

Along with the `image` object, an `Image` constructor can be used to preload your cache with images that will subsequently appear on your page. This is done by creating a new `image` object with the JavaScript `new` statement and then setting the `src` property of this object to the URL of your image. This creates what is, in essence, an undisplayed image that is part of the current Web page. Although the image is not displayed, it is loaded into your cache so that if it is displayed later it will load much more quickly.

With Listing 19.3, if the following code was included in the `<script>` element that is in the `<head>` section, it would preload the two images used in the example.

```
function loadImages() {
   this[1] = new Image();
   this[1].src = "clickme1.gif";
   this[2] = new Image();
   this[2].src = "clickme2.gif";
}
if (document.images) {
   loadImages();
}
```

CHAPTER 20

Manipulating Windows and Frames with JavaScript

by Jim O'Donnell

In this chapter

As discussed in Chapter 19, "The Document Object Model," you can create, manipulate, and access the properties of Web browser windows by using the `window` object. Chapter 19 showed the properties, methods, and events associated with the `window` object. This chapter shows some practical examples to show you how to create and then use multiple windows.

Listing 20.1 shows the XHTML document `Window1.htm`. This document uses a single JavaScript statement to create a window and load that window with another document (`Form1.htm`, shown in Listing 20.2). The new window is created using the `window` object's `open()` method. Figure 20.1 shows the result of loading `Window1.htm`. (In many of the examples shown in this chapter, the created windows are rearranged for improved visibility—all appear in their original size, however).

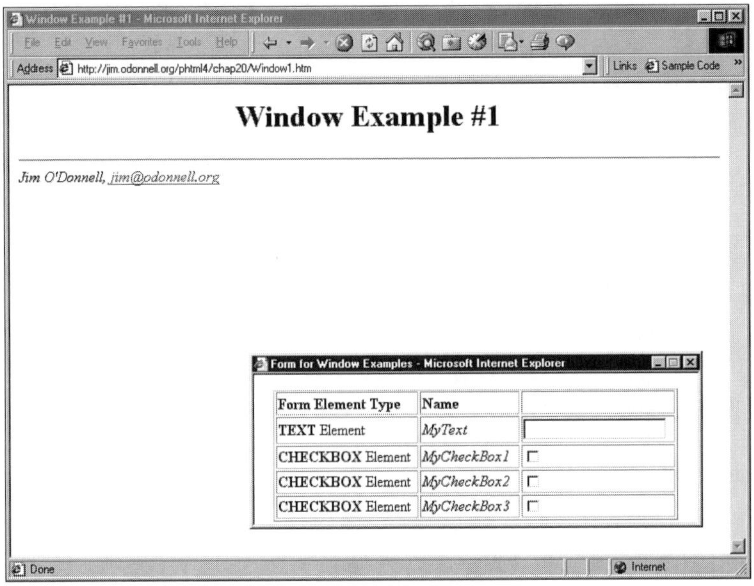

FIGURE 20.1
JavaScript can create new Web browser windows and configure them to look the way you want for your applications.

Listing 20.1 *Window1.htm—*Create New Web Browser Windows with *window.open()*

```
<!DOCTYPE html PUBLIC "-//W3C//DTD XHTML 1.0 Transitional//EN"
    "http://www.w3.org/TR/xhtml1/DTD/xhtml1-transitional.dtd">
<html xmlns="http://www.w3.org/1999/xhtml">
<head>
<title>Window Example #1</title>
</head>
<body bgcolor="#ffffff">
<center>
<h1>Window Example #1</h1>
</center>
```

Listing 20.1 Continued

```
<hr />
<em>Jim O'Donnell, <a href="mailto:jim@odonnell.org">jim@odonnell.org</a></em>
<script type="text/javascript" language="JavaScript">
<!-- Hide script from incompatible browsers!
MyWindow = window.open("Form1.htm","MyWindow",
   "toolbar=no,location=no,directories=no,status=no," +
   "menubar=no,scrollbars=no,resizable=no," +
   "width=475,height=155")
//   Hide script from incompatible browsers! -->
</script>
</body>
</html>
```

When loaded into a Web browser, the XHTML document in Listing 20.1 creates a new window and displays the XHTML form given in Listing 20.2.

Listing 20.2 *Form1.htm*—XHTML Documents for Created Windows Should Be Sized Carefully

```
<!DOCTYPE html PUBLIC "-//W3C//DTD XHTML 1.0 Transitional//EN"
    "http://www.w3.org/TR/xhtml1/DTD/xhtml1-transitional.dtd">
<html xmlns="http://www.w3.org/1999/xhtml">
<head>
<title>Form for Window Examples</title>
</head>
<body bgcolor=#ffffff>
<center>
<table width="95%" border="1">
<form name="MyForm">
<tr><td><b>Form Element Type</b></td>
    <td><b>Name</b></td>
    <td> </td></tr>
<tr><td><b>TEXT</b> Element</td>
    <td><i>MyText</i></td>
    <td><input type="TEXT" name="MyText"/></td></tr>
<tr><td><b>CHECKBOX</b> Element</td>
    <td><i>MyCheckBox1</i></td>
    <td><input type="CHECKBOX" name="MyCheckBox1"/></td></tr>
<tr><td><b>CHECKBOX</b> Element</td>
    <td><i>MyCheckBox2</i></td>
    <td><input type="CHECKBOX" name="MyCheckBox2"/></td></tr>
<tr><td><b>CHECKBOX</b> Element</td>
    <td><i>MyCheckBox3</i></td>
    <td><input type="CHECKBOX" name="MyCheckBox3"/></td></tr>
</form>
</table>
</body>
</html>
```

Three arguments apply to the `window.open()` method, with the following meanings:

- The first argument is the URL of the XHTML document to be loaded into the new window.
- The second argument is the name of the window that can be used as the `TARGET` attribute of the <a> tag.
- The third argument is optional and contains a comma-separated list of configuration options for the created window. The configuration options are the following:
  - **`toolbar = [yes|no]`**—Controls the display of the Web browser window toolbar
  - **`location = [yes|no]`**—Controls the display of the Web browser window location bar
  - **`directories = [yes|no]`**—Controls the display of the Web browser window directory bar
  - **`status = [yes|no]`**—Controls the display of the Web browser window status line
  - **`menubar = [yes|no]`**—Controls the display of the Web browser window menu bar
  - **`scrollbars = [yes|no]`**—Controls the display of the Web browser window scrollbars
  - **`resizable = [yes|no]`**—Controls whether the created window can be resized
  - **`width = # pixels`**—Sets the width of the new window, in pixels
  - **`height = # pixels`**—Sets the height of the new window, in pixels

TIP If you want to set one of the options for a new window, set them all; otherwise, your results might not be what you expect because each Web browser (and even the same browser on different platforms) handles the default options differently. Play it safe and completely specify exactly how you want your windows to look.

In addition to the arguments for the `window.open()` method, it also has a return value. The method returns a handle that gives you the name of the newly created window. This enables you to access and manipulate the objects in the new window from the original.

Referencing Multiple Windows with JavaScript

Just creating a new window with the `window.open()` method doesn't accomplish that much. Your users can create new windows on their own using their browser menu options. The window shown in Figure 20.1 was created without any of the controls, such as the menu bar. To enable it to be used as a full-fledged Web browser window, it could just as easily have been created with a menu bar, as well as with any of the other window user-interface elements.

To be able to create ***and use*** new windows, you must reference them. After you know where a new window fits into the Web browser object hierarchy detailed in Chapter 19, you can use the elements of that hierarchy to manipulate what appears in the new window. The next two sections of this chapter show you how.

▶ To learn about how to reference Web browser objects, **see** "Web Browser Object Hierarchy and Scoping," **p. 460**

Referencing Child Windows

Listing 20.3 shows `Window2.htm`—this XHTML document is similar to `Window1.htm` shown in Listing 20.1. It loads the same document, `Form1.htm`, into the new window. It also includes a JavaScript, which shows you how you can access and manipulate the objects in a child window from the parent window. The parent window is the window in which the original document—`Window2.htm`, in this case—is loaded. The window it creates is the child window.

In this case, the JavaScript function `updateWindow()` is attached to the `onChange` event of the XHTML form text field and the `onBlur` events of the check boxes. In this way, whenever the text field is changed or a check box is checked or unchecked (and the focus moved elsewhere), `updateWindow()` is called. This function then copies all the values of the XHTML form in the parent window into the corresponding fields of the child window, as shown in Figure 20.2.

FIGURE 20.2
New windows fit into the object model, enabling you to create scripts to access their objects and properties.

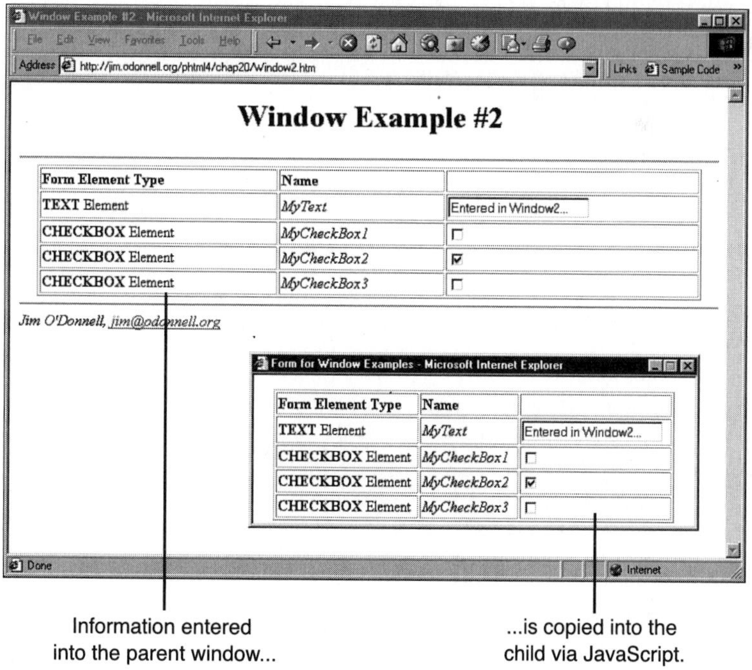

Information entered into the parent window...

...is copied into the child via JavaScript.

Listing 20.3 *Window2.htm*—JavaScripts Enable You to Manipulate Multiple Windows from a Single Document

```
<!DOCTYPE html PUBLIC "-//W3C//DTD XHTML 1.0 Transitional//EN"
    "http://www.w3.org/TR/xhtml1/DTD/xhtml1-transitional.dtd">
<html xmlns="http://www.w3.org/1999/xhtml">
<head>
<title>Window Example #2</title>
<script type="text/javascript" language="JavaScript">
<!-- Hide script from incompatible browsers!
function updateWindow() {
   self.MyWindow.document.MyForm.MyText.value = document.MyForm.MyText.value
   self.MyWindow.document.MyForm.MyCheckBox1.checked =
      document.MyForm.MyCheckBox1.checked
   self.MyWindow.document.MyForm.MyCheckBox2.checked =
      document.MyForm.MyCheckBox2.checked
   self.MyWindow.document.MyForm.MyCheckBox3.checked =
      document.MyForm.MyCheckBox3.checked
}
//   Hide script from incompatible browsers! -->
</script>
</head>
<body bgcolor="#ffffff">
<center>
<h1>Window Example #2</h1>
<hr />
<table width="95%" border="1">
<form name="MyForm">
<tr><td><b>Form Element Type</b></td>
    <td><b>Name</b></td>
    <td> </td></tr>
<tr><td><b>TEXT</b> Element</td>
    <td><i>MyText</i></td>
    <td><input type="TEXT" name="MyText" onchange="updateWindow()"/></td></tr>
<tr><td><b>CHECKBOX</b> Element</td>
    <td><i>MyCheckBox1</i></td>
    <td><input type="CHECKBOX" name="MyCheckBox1" onblur="updateWindow()"/>
</td></tr>
<tr><td><b>CHECKBOX</b> Element</td>
    <td><i>MyCheckBox2</i></td>
    <td><input type="CHECKBOX" name="MyCheckBox2" onblur="updateWindow()"/>
</td></tr>
<tr><td><b>CHECKBOX</b> Element</td>
    <td><i>MyCheckBox3</i></td>
    <td><input type="CHECKBOX" name="MyCheckBox3" onblur="updateWindow()"/>
</td></tr>
</form>
</table>
</center>
<hr />
<em>Jim O'Donnell, <a href="mailto:jim@odonnell.org">jim@odonnell.org</a></em>
<script type="text/javascript" language="JavaScript">
<!-- Hide script from incompatible browsers!
MyWindow = window.open("Form1.htm","MyWindow",
   "toolbar=no,location=no,directories=no,status=no," +
   "menubar=no,scrollbars=no,resizable=no," +
```

Listing 20.3 Continued

```
    "width=475,height=155")
//   Hide script from incompatible browsers! -->
</script>
</body>
</html>
```

The `document` object of the child window is accessed by this JavaScript, running in the parent window, through the `self.MyWindow` object. The `self` object indicates the current window; the `MyWindow` is the return value of the `window.open()` method, indicating that you want to access the objects of the child object. Therefore, `self.MyWindow.document` gets to the `document` object of the child window, and from there you can access the child window's objects.

Referencing Parent Windows

You can also go the other way, with scripts running in the child window accessing and manipulating objects in the parent window. The next example uses the XHTML documents `Window3.htm` (which is the same as `Window2.htm` from Listing 20.3, except for a new title and heading) and `Form3.htm` (shown in Listing 20.4). `Form3.htm` uses a similar JavaScript, also called `updateWindow()`, to automatically update the fields of the parent window with information entered into the child window form fields. To reference the parent window from a child, the `opener` object is used. Thus `opener.document` gets the JavaScript in the child window to the `document` object of the parent, from which the other objects can be referenced. Figure 20.3 shows the values entered into the child window forms automatically reflected into the parent.

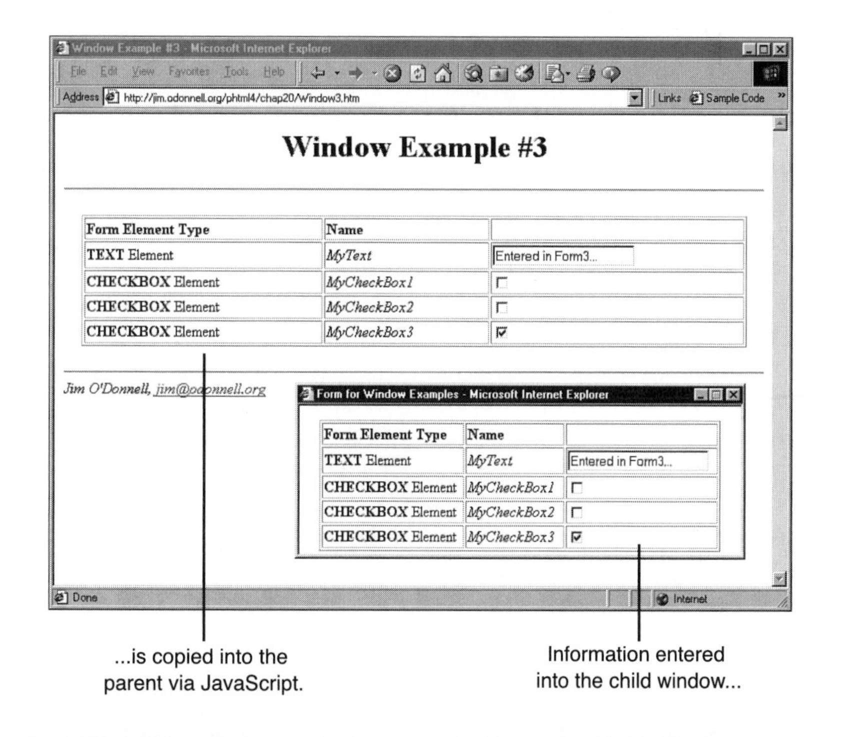

FIGURE 20.3
You can use JavaScript to coordinate the contents of multiple Web browser windows.

Listing 20.4 *Form3.htm*—Child-to-Parent as Well as Parent-to-Child Communication Is Possible

```
<!DOCTYPE html PUBLIC "-//W3C//DTD XHTML 1.0 Transitional//EN"
    "http://www.w3.org/TR/xhtml1/DTD/xhtml1-transitional.dtd">
<html xmlns="http://www.w3.org/1999/xhtml">
<head>
<title>Form for Window Examples</title>
<script type="text/javascript" language="JavaScript">
<!-- Hide script from incompatible browsers!
function updateWindow() {
   opener.document.MyForm.MyText.value = document.MyForm.MyText.value
   opener.document.MyForm.MyCheckBox1.checked =
      document.MyForm.MyCheckBox1.checked
   opener.document.MyForm.MyCheckBox2.checked =
      document.MyForm.MyCheckBox2.checked
   opener.document.MyForm.MyCheckBox3.checked =
      document.MyForm.MyCheckBox3.checked
}
//   Hide script from incompatible browsers! -->
</script>
</head>
<body bgcolor="#ffffff">
<center>
<table width="95%" border="1">
<form name="MyForm">
<tr><td><b>Form Element Type</b></td>
    <td><b>Name</b></td>
    <td> </td></tr>
<tr><td><b>TEXT</b> Element</td>
    <td><i>MyText</i></td>
    <td><input type="TEXT" name="MyText" onchange="updateWindow()"/></td></tr>
<tr><td><b>CHECKBOX</b> Element</td>
    <td><i>MyCheckBox1</i></td>
    <td><input type="CHECKBOX" name="MyCheckBox1" onblur="updateWindow()"/>
    </td></tr>
<tr><td><b>CHECKBOX</b> Element</td>
    <td><i>MyCheckBox2</i></td>
    <td><input type="CHECKBOX" name="MyCheckBox2" onblur="updateWindow()"/>
    </td></tr>
<tr><td><b>CHECKBOX</b> Element</td>
    <td><i>MyCheckBox3</i></td>
    <td><input type="CHECKBOX" name="MyCheckBox3" onblur="updateWindow()"/>
    </td></tr>
</form>
</table>
</body>
</html>
```

Using Window Events

You can use several events associated with the `window` object in your scripts to control what they do and when they do it. The events are listed in Chapter 19. This section gives you an example of how you might use a few of them. Listing 20.5 shows `Window4.htm`. This XHTML document creates another Web browser window, loads another document (`Text.htm`) into it, and automatically scrolls through the document. Figure 20.4 shows these two windows after they are first created.

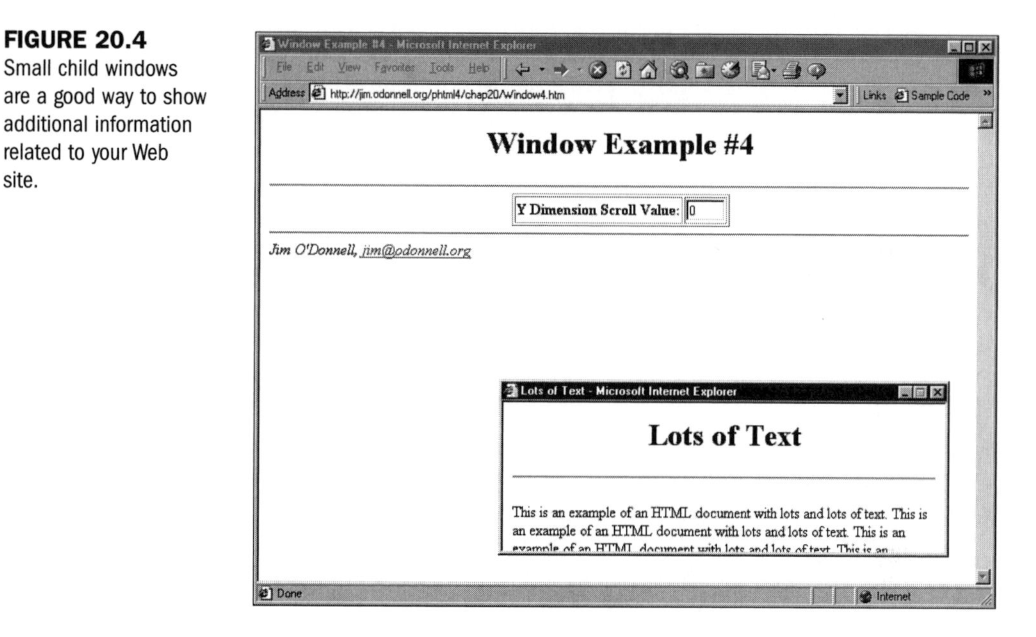

FIGURE 20.4 Small child windows are a good way to show additional information related to your Web site.

TIP Creating small "pop-up" windows can be a good way to show additional site information. Some people find them annoying, however, and it would definitely be a mistake to overuse them. So, it is probably best, as with all "cool" Web browser effects, to use them with restraint.

▶ For a review of events associated with the window object, **see** "window Object Events," **p. 462**

Listing 20.5 *Window4.htm*—XHTML Documents Can Be Automatically Scrolled

```
<!DOCTYPE html PUBLIC "-//W3C//DTD XHTML 1.0 Transitional//EN"
    "http://www.w3.org/TR/xhtml1/DTD/xhtml1-transitional.dtd">
<html xmlns="http://www.w3.org/1999/xhtml">
<head>
<title>Window Example #4</title>
```

Listing 20.5 Continued

```
<script type="text/javascript" language="JavaScript">
<!-- Hide script from incompatible browsers!
var scrollVal = 0
function scrollWindow() {
   scrollVal += 10
   if (scrollVal <= 1500) {
      self.MyWindow.scroll(0,scrollVal)
      document.MyForm.ScrollY.value = scrollVal
      setTimeout("scrollWindow()",100)
   }
}
//   Hide script from incompatible browsers! -->
</script>
</head>
<body bgcolor="#ffffff" onload="setTimeout('scrollWindow()',5000)">
<center>
<h1>Window Example #4</h1>
<hr />
<table border="1">
<form name="MyForm">
<tr><td><b>Y Dimension Scroll Value:</b></td>
    <td><input type="TEXT" name="ScrollY" size="4"/></td></tr>
</form>
</table>
</center>
<hr />
<em>Jim O'Donnell, <a href="mailto:jim@odonnell.org">jim@odonnell.org</a></em>
<script type="text/javascript" language="JavaScript">
<!-- Hide script from incompatible browsers!
MyWindow = window.open("Text.htm","MyWindow",
   "toolbar=no,location=no,directories=no,status=no," +
   "menubar=no,scrollbars=yes,resizable=no," +
   "width=300,height=200")
document.MyForm.ScrollY.value = scrollVal
//   Hide script from incompatible browsers! -->
</script>
</body>
</html>
```

This example uses one window event and three methods to accomplish its purpose. First, the `window.open()` method is used to create the new window and to load the second XHTML document into it. When the window is fully loaded, as indicated by the window object's `onLoad` event—included as an attribute in its `<body>` tag—the `setTimeout()` method is used to set up a call to the `scrollWindow()` JavaScript after five seconds (5,000 milliseconds) have passed. At the end of this time, `scrollWindow()` is called, which, in turn, uses the `window.scroll()` method to automatically scroll the second window. The JavaScript also uses `setTimeout()` to set up another call to itself. This repeats until the document in the second window is scrolled all the way through. Additionally, the XHTML form text field in the main document is used to display the current scroll value (see Figure 20.5).

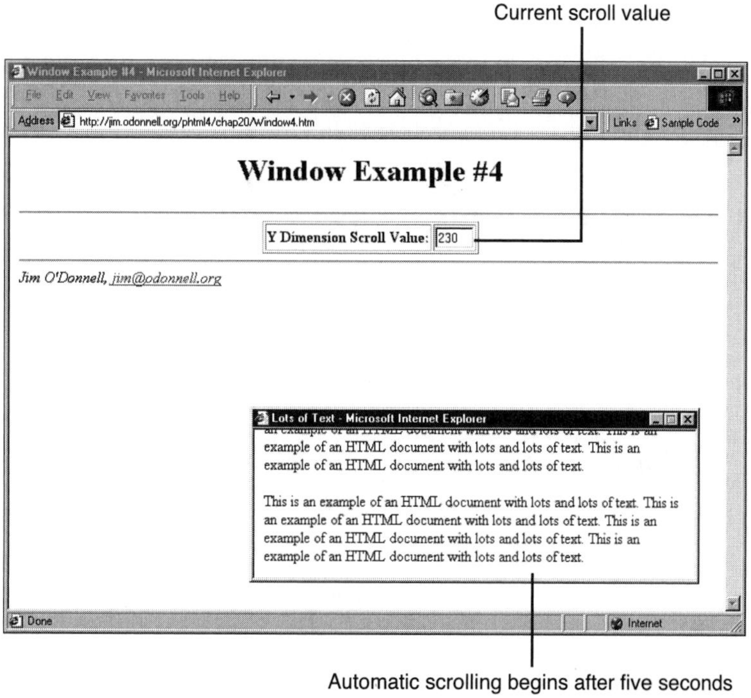

FIGURE 20.5
Use the `setTimeout()` method to create timed effects in your XHTML documents.

CAUTION

The x- and y-dimension scroll value passed to the `window.scroll()` method is in pixels, so it is impossible to determine how many pixels are needed to scroll through a given document, given the variety of platforms, browsers, and screen resolutions that will be used. This is particularly true when the scrolled document is primarily text, which can be sized differently in different Web browsers. It is best to use this method when the document being viewed is primarily graphics, making it easier to scroll accurately.

Window Methods for Getting User Input

You can use three `window` object methods to solicit input from your users. You can use JavaScript to create windows and display custom-made forms to get any kind of input from your user that you would like. The three built-in methods, on the other hand, give you quick, easy ways to get input. These methods are

- `alert()`
- `confirm()`
- `prompt()`

Notification Using the *Alert* Method

Listing 20.6 shows an example of using the `window.alert()` method. This method is used to notify your user of something, and it can only be responded to by clicking OK. Figure 20.6 shows an example of the alert using this method.

Listing 20.6 *Alert.htm*—Use This Method to Inform Your User of Important Information

```
<!DOCTYPE html PUBLIC "-//W3C//DTD XHTML 1.0 Transitional//EN"
    "http://www.w3.org/TR/xhtml1/DTD/xhtml1-transitional.dtd">
<html xmlns="http://www.w3.org/1999/xhtml">
<head>
<title>Alert Method Example</title>
</head>
<body bgcolor="#ffffff">
<center>
<h1>Alert Method Example</h1>
</center>
<hr />
<em>Jim O'Donnell, <a href="mailto:jim@odonnell.org">jim@odonnell.org</a></em>
<script type="text/javascript" language="JavaScript">
<!-- Hide script from incompatible browsers!
window.alert("The alert method of the window object is used to " +
   "notify you of some condition; it does not present you with " +
   "any choice other than to click OK.")
//   Hide script from incompatible browsers! -->
</script>
</body>
</html>
```

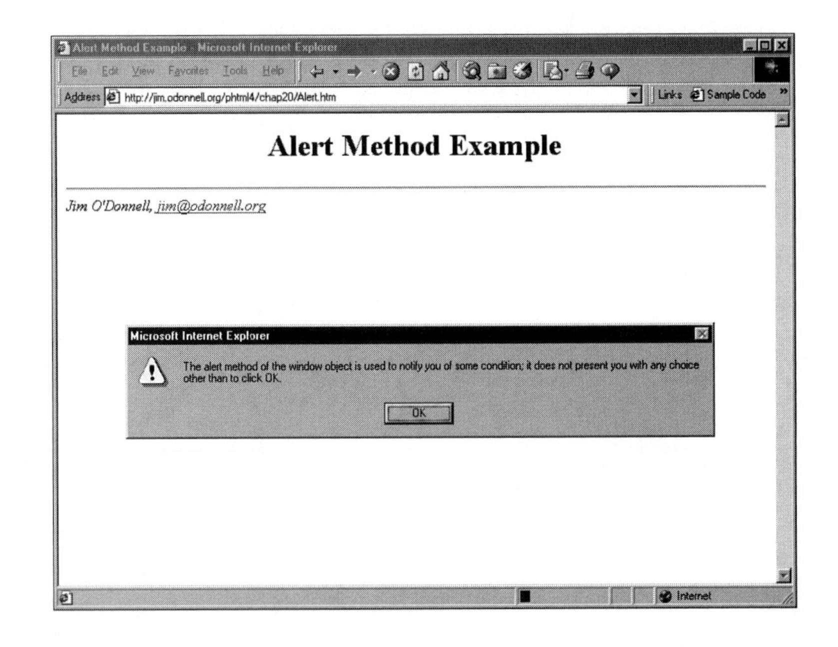

FIGURE 20.6
Alert boxes are not used for user input so much as to tell the user something and to make sure the user gets that information.

Using the *confirm* Method to Get a Yes or No

Listing 20.7 shows an example of using the `window.confirm()` method. This method is used to solicit a yes or no from your user. It returns a Boolean `true` or `false` to indicate what the user selected. This value can then be used by a JavaScript to decide what to display or what to do based on the user input (see Figure 20.7). In this example, the selection is displayed as either `true` or `false` in the text box shown in the main window.

Listing 20.7 *Confirm.htm*—A Confirmation Box Gives the User a Yes or No Decision

```
<!DOCTYPE html PUBLIC "-//W3C//DTD XHTML 1.0 Transitional//EN"
    "http://www.w3.org/TR/xhtml1/DTD/xhtml1-transitional.dtd">
<html xmlns="http://www.w3.org/1999/xhtml">
<head>
<title>Confirm Method Example</title>
</head>
<body bgcolor="#ffffff">
<center>
<h1>Confirm Method Example</h1>
<hr/>
<form name="MyForm">
Result of <u>confirm</u> method: <input type=text name="MyText"/>
</form>
</center>
<hr />
<em>Jim O'Donnell, <a href="mailto:jim@odonnell.org">jim@odonnell.org</a></em>
<script type="text/javascript" language="JavaScript">
<!-- Hide script from incompatible browsers!
res = window.confirm("The confirm method of the window " +
   "object is similar to the alert method in that it is " +
   "used to notify you of some condition; unlike the alert " +
   "method it presents you with a choice to either click " +
   "OK or Cancel, and returns true or false, respectively.")
document.MyForm.MyText.value = res
//   Hide script from incompatible browsers! -->
</script>
</body>
</html>
```


Asking the User for Input with the *prompt* Method

Listing 20.8 shows the `window.prompt()` method, which enables you to get a single line of input from your user. You can use this to ask users for their names, email addresses, URLs, or anything else that can be entered in a single line. It is also possible with this method, as shown in Figure 20.8, to include a default answer with the `prompt()` method. Similar to the last example, the resultant string returned from the prompt window is displayed within the text box in the main window.

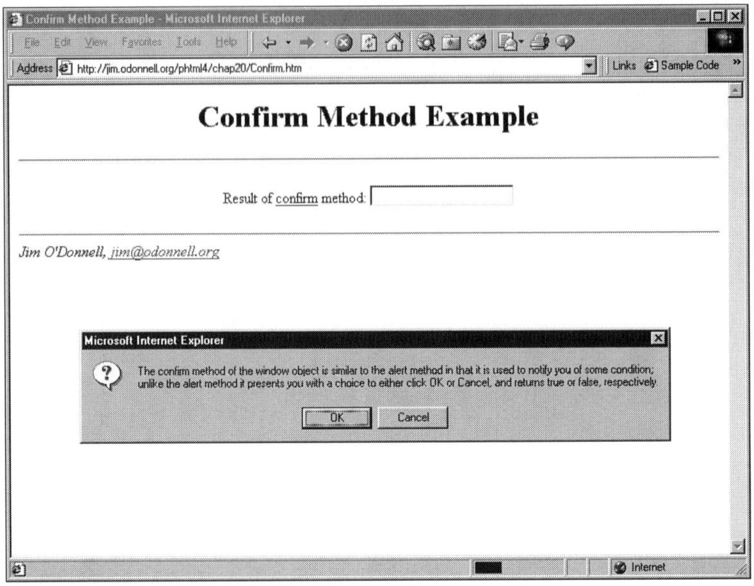

FIGURE 20.7
You can use the `window.confirm()` method to create a "gateway" condition to your site. Users must agree to this condition before they can access your site.

Listing 20.8 ***Prompt.htm*—The User Can Enter Any Single Line of Input in the Prompt**

```
<!DOCTYPE html PUBLIC "-//W3C//DTD XHTML 1.0 Transitional//EN"
    "http://www.w3.org/TR/xhtml1/DTD/xhtml1-transitional.dtd">
<html xmlns="http://www.w3.org/1999/xhtml">
<head>
<title>Prompt Method Example</title>
</head>
<body bgcolor="#ffffff">
<center>
<h1>Prompt Method Example</h1>
<hr/>
<form name="MyForm">
Result of <u>prompt</u> method: <input type=text name="MyText" size=30>
</form>
</center>
<hr />
<em>Jim O'Donnell, <a href="mailto:jim@odonnell.org">jim@odonnell.org</a></em>
<script type="text/javascript" language="JavaScript">
<!-- Hide script from incompatible browsers!
res = window.prompt("The prompt method of the window " +
   "object allows you to ask the user for input; you can " +
   "also specify a default input, such as URL of my home " +
   "shown below.","Come see my web site at http://jim.odonnell.org...")
document.MyForm.MyText.value = res
//   Hide script from incompatible browsers! -->
</script>
</body>
</html>
```

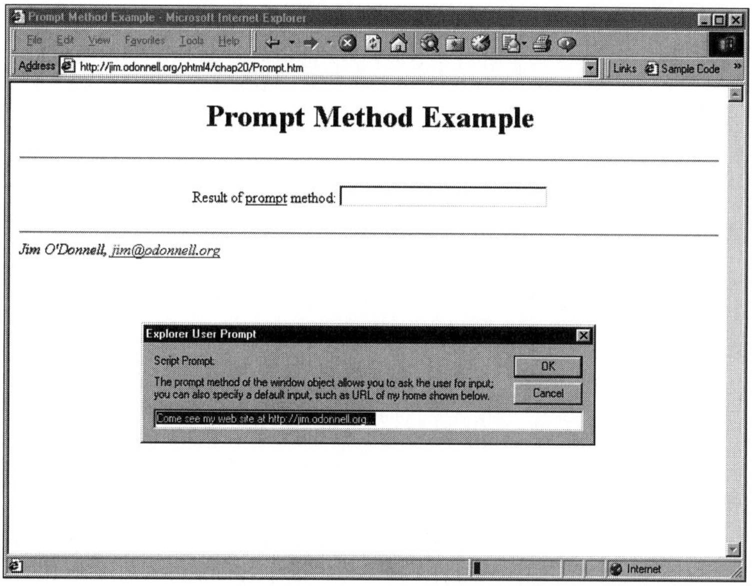

FIGURE 20.8
Using the `window.prompt()` method's simple dialog box makes it easy to get input from your user.

Filling Your Windows I: The *location* Object

Instead of specifying a URL in the `window.open()` method, you have several other ways to specify the contents of a new `window` object. The first of these ways is the simplest of the two: by using the new window's `location` object. Referring to the first example in this chapter, for example, instead of specifying `Form1.htm` as the first argument of the `window.open()` method, you could do the same thing by using the following after the new window is created:

```
self.MyWindow.location.href = "Form1.htm"
```

Filling Your Windows II: The *document* Object

A second way of specifying content for new windows—or for your original Web browser window, for that matter—is by using methods of the `document` object. The following document object methods are used to create content within an XHTML document:

- **`document.open()`**—The `open()` method is used to open the document for writing. If the method is used within an existing Web page, the content created will replace the current contents.
- **`document.write()` or `document.writeln()`**—Each of these methods is used to write XHTML code into the currently opened document. If these statements are encountered while the current document is being loaded—in the following example, the document is already open—the content they generate will be included along with the other contents of the page.

If these methods are used after the current document has been opened, but without a preceding `document.open()` method, they will generate an error. If the `document.open()` method is used, all the content generated will replace the current contents.

The only difference between the `write()` and `writeln()` method is that the `writeln()` method includes a new line after the content. This does not affect the XHTML generated, but makes it easier to view.

- **`document.close()`**—This method closes and causes to be displayed a document opened using the `document.open()` method.

Listing 20.9 shows `WindowJS.htm`. This XHTML document reproduces the first example shown in this chapter (shown in Listings 20.1 and 20.2) with only one file. Instead of loading a second XHTML document into the new window, the `document.write()` method is used to dynamically generate the XHTML to be displayed. The results of this file are identical to that shown earlier in Figure 20.1, except that the title and heading are changed.

Listing 20.9 ***WindowJS.htm*—XHTML Documents Can Be Generated On-the-Fly**

```
<!DOCTYPE html PUBLIC "-//W3C//DTD XHTML 1.0 Transitional//EN"
     "http://www.w3.org/TR/xhtml1/DTD/xhtml1-transitional.dtd">
<html xmlns="http://www.w3.org/1999/xhtml">
<head>
<title>Window Example #5</title>
</head>
<body bgcolor="#ffffff">
<center>
<h1>Window Example #5</h1>
</center>
<hr />
<em>Jim O'Donnell, <a href="mailto:jim@odonnell.org">jim@odonnell.org</a></em>
<script type="text/javascript" language="JavaScript">
<!-- Hide script from incompatible browsers!
MyWindow = window.open("","MyWindow",
   "toolbar=no,location=no,directories=no,status=no," +
   "menubar=no,scrollbars=no,resizable=no," +
   "width=475,height=155")
str = "<html>" +
       "<head>" +
       "<title>Form for Window Examples</title>" +
       "</head>" +
       "<body bgcolor='#ffffff'>" +
       "<center>" +
       "<table width='95%' border='1'>" +
       "<form name='MyForm'>" +
       "<tr><td><b>Form Element Type</b></td>" +
       "    <td><b>Name</b></td>" +
       "    <td> </td></tr>" +
```

Listing 20.9 Continued

```
       "<tr><td><b>TEXT</b> Element</td>" +
       "    <td><i>MyText</i></td>" +
       "    <td><input type='TEXT' name='MyText'/></td></tr>" +
       "<tr><td><b>CHECKBOX</b> Element</td>" +
       "    <td><i>MyCheckBox1</i></td>" +
       "    <td><input type='CHECKBOX' name='MyCheckBox1'/></td></tr>" +
       "<tr><td><b>CHECKBOX</b> Element</td>" +
       "    <td><i>MyCheckBox2</i></td>" +
       "    <td><input type='CHECKBOX' name='MyCheckBox2'/></td></tr>" +
       "<tr><td><b>CHECKBOX</b> Element</td>" +
       "    <td><i>MyCheckBox3</i></td>" +
       "    <td><input type='CHECKBOX' name='MyCheckBox3'/></td></tr>" +
       "</form>" +
       "</table>" +
       "</body>" +
       "</html>"
self.MyWindow.document.open()
self.MyWindow.document.write(str)
self.MyWindow.document.close()
//   Hide script from incompatible browsers! -->
</script>
</body>
</html>
```

JavaScript Windows Example

This example shows one application of how to create and use other Web browser windows. In this example, JavaScripts are attached to the `onClick` events of XHTML forms buttons and are used to open and/or fill two other windows. The object of the windows, in this application, is to display pictures and accompanying biographical information.

This example shows how it is possible to create XHTML forms-based buttons that call JavaScripts and use them to create, to assign content to, and to destroy other windows. In addition, this example shows you how a script in a created window can manipulate the content back in the window that created it.

Listing 20.10 shows `WindEx.htm`, the top-level XHTML document for this example. The four buttons shown by this document each have JavaScripts attached to their `onClick` attributes. Clicking each button executes the appropriate JavaScript.

Listing 20.10 *WindEx.htm*—Create and Manipulate Browser Windows with JavaScript

```
<!DOCTYPE html PUBLIC "-//W3C//DTD XHTML 1.0 Transitional//EN"
    "http://www.w3.org/TR/xhtml1/DTD/xhtml1-transitional.dtd">
<html xmlns="http://www.w3.org/1999/xhtml">
```

Listing 20.10 Continued

```
<head>
<title>JavaScript Window Example</title>
<script type="text/javascript" language="JavaScript">
<!-- Hide this script from incompatible Web browsers!
var picwin = null;
var biowin = null;
var n = 0;
function openpic() {
   if (!picwin)
      picwin = open("","PicWindow","width=200,height=250");
}
function openbio() {
   if (!biowin)
      biowin = open("","BioWindow","width=400,height=250");
}
function closeboth() {
    if (picwin) {
      picwin.close();
      picwin = null;
   }
    if (biowin) {
      biowin.close();
      biowin = null;
   }
}
function loadnex() {
   if (!picwin) openpic();
   if (!biowin) openbio();
//
   n++;
   if (n > 5) n = 5;
   picname = "Pic" + n + ".htm";
   bioname = "Bio" + n + ".htm";
//
   self.picwin.location.href = picname;
   self.biowin.location.href = bioname;
   self.picwin.focus();
   self.biowin.focus();
}
function loadpre() {
   if (!picwin) openpic();
   if (!biowin) openbio();
//
   n--;
   if (n < 1) n = 1;
   picname = "Pic" + n + ".htm";
   bioname = "Bio" + n + ".htm";
//
   self.picwin.location.href = picname;
   self.biowin.location.href = bioname;
   self.picwin.focus();
```

Listing 20.10 Continued

```
    self.biowin.focus();
}
//   Hide script from incompatible browsers! -->
</script>
</head>
<body bgcolor="#ffffff" onunload="closeboth()">
<center>
<form name="MyForm">
<table>
<tr><td><input type="button" name="OpenWin"  value="Open Windows"
           onclick="openpic();openbio()"/></td>
    <td><input type="button" name="PreBut"   value="Load Previous"
           onclick="loadpre()"/></td>
    <td><input type="button" name="NexBut"   value="Load Next"
           onclick="loadnex()"/></td>
    <td><input type="button" name="CloseWin" value="Close Windows"
           onclick="closeboth()"/></td>
</tr>
</table>
</form>
</center>
<hr />
<em>Jim O'Donnell, <a href="mailto:jim@odonnell.org">jim@odonnell.org</a></em>
</body>
</html>
```

The four buttons created by this XHTML document (see Figure 20.9)—through the attached JavaScript functions—perform the following functions:

- **Open Windows**—Clicking this button calls the `openpic()` and `openbio()` JavaScript functions, which will each open up a new window (one for pictures, one for biographical information), as shown in Figure 20.10. If the windows have already been opened, then clicking this button does nothing.

FIGURE 20.9
Buttons within XHTML forms provide a great way for your users to trigger JavaScripts.

- **Load Previous**—Clicking this button calls the `loadpre()` function, which will first call `openpic()` and/or `openbio()` to create those windows, if necessary. Then, it will decrement the current number, display the appropriate picture and bio, and bring those windows focus (which will usually bring them to the top).

- **Load Next**—Clicking this button calls the `loadnex()` function, which works the same as the `loadpre()` function, except that it increments the current number.
- **Close Windows**—Clicking this button calls the `closeboth()` function to close the picture and bio window and also sets the `picwin` and `biowin` variables back to null.

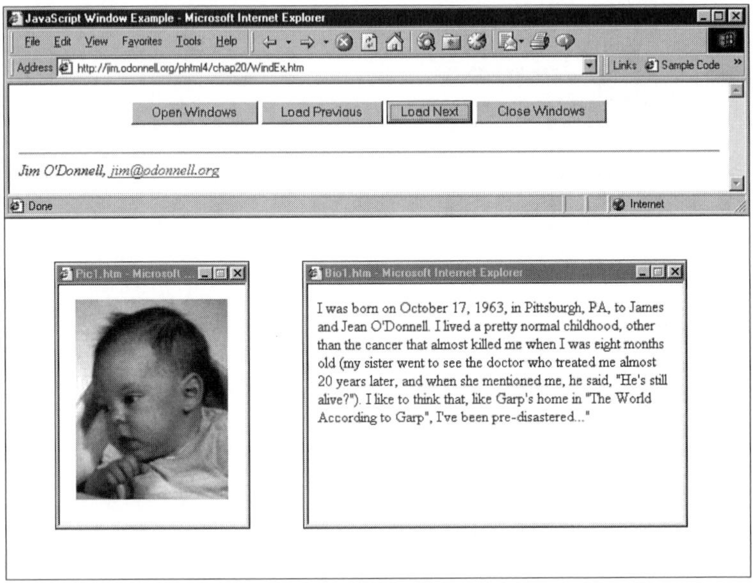

FIGURE 20.10
JavaScripts can easily manipulate information and content in multiple windows simultaneously.

The last thing to do is to enable the user, from the last picture/bio combination, to link back to another Web site for additional information. That Web site should appear in the main window (the one where the control buttons are) and the two created windows should close. These two tasks are accomplished as follows. Listing 20.11 shows the XHTML loaded with the last bio information. When the button created there is clicked, a JavaScript is called, which changes where the main window is looking by referring to the `location.href` property of the `self.opener` object. The `self.opener` object refers to the window that opened the current window—the main window, in this case.

To close the two created windows when the main window moves to another location, the `onUnload` window event is placed into the `<body>` tag of the main window and used to call the `closeboth()` JavaScript function.

Listing 20.11 ***Bio5.htm*—Created Windows Can Access and Manipulate the Contents of Their Creators**

```
<!DOCTYPE html PUBLIC "-//W3C//DTD XHTML 1.0 Transitional//EN"
    "http://www.w3.org/TR/xhtml1/DTD/xhtml1-transitional.dtd">
<html xmlns="http://www.w3.org/1999/xhtml">
```

Listing 20.11 Continued

```
<head>
<title>Bio5.htm</title>
<script type="text/javascript" language="JavaScript">
<!-- Hide this script from incompatible Web browsers!
function loadmain() {
   self.opener.location.href="http://jim.odonnell.org"
}
//   Hide script from incompatible browsers! -->
</script>
</head>
<body bgcolor="#ffffff">
For more exciting (?) and (hopefully) current information about me, my life,
my interests, and whatever else catches my fancy, be sure to check out my Web
site...
<form name="MyForm">
<center>
<table>
<tr><td><input type="button" value="The House of JOD"
           onclick="loadmain()"/></td>
</tr>
</table>
</center>
</form>
</body>
</html>
```

Creating and Using Frames

Chapter 7, "Frames," showed you how to create and use frames in your Web site. You can access and manipulate the contents of these frames by using the `frame` object. Each of the frames created in a document can be accessed through the `frames` object array, which is attached to the `document` object. The most important thing to remember about a `frame` object is that *it is a* `window` *object*. This means that each frame created is a separate `window` object, and all the properties, methods, and events associated with `window` objects can be applied.

▶ To see how to set up an XHTML document using frames, **see** "Setting Up a Frames Document," **p. 219**

Communicating Between Frames

After you have created a series of frames by using the `<frameset>` and `<frame/>` tags, how do you use JavaScript to access and manipulate each frame? As mentioned in the preceding section, each frame is a separate `window` object. Therefore, if you can reference each frame, you can use the same techniques that were used with windows for each frame.

The Document Object Model includes several properties that apply to frame and window objects that make referencing different frames much easier. These properties are `self`, `window`, `parent`, and `top` and their meanings are as follows:

- **`self` or `window`**—These properties are used to refer to the current window or frame.
- **`parent`**—This property is used to refer to the `window` or `frame` object that contains the current frame.
- **`top`**—This property is used to refer to the topmost `window` or `frame` object that contains the current frame.

Understanding the Frames Object Hierarchy

Consider a simple frameset created using the following XHTML code:

```
<frameset rows="50%,50%">
   <frameset cols="50%,50%">
      <frame src="Form.htm" name="MyFrame1"/>
      <frame src="Form.htm" name="MyFrame2"/>
   </frameset>
   <frame src="Frameset2.htm" name="MyFrame3"/>
</frameset>
```

This divides the window into three frames: two side-by-side on the top half of the window, and a third occupying the entire bottom half. The object model for this document will appear as shown in Figure 20.11.

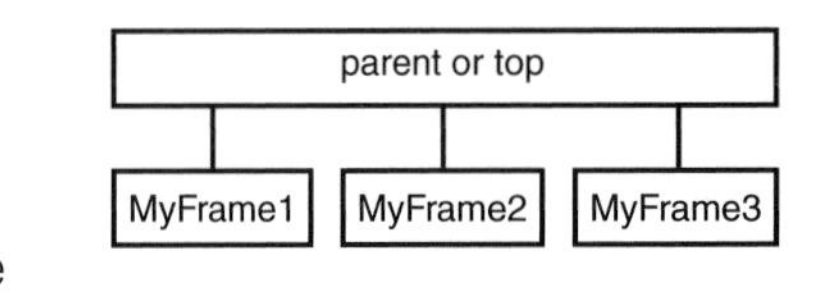

FIGURE 20.11
Each frame is associated with a `window` object, and each can access and manipulate the others.

Given the object hierarchy shown in Figure 20.11, you would reference the `frame` objects as follows:

- To reference any of the child frames from the parent document, you could use `self.frame_name`. You could access the `document` object of the first frame, for example, through `self.MyFrame1.document`.
- To reference the parent document from any of the child frames, you could use `parent` or `top`. Any of the child frames could access the `document` object of the parent document, for example, through `parent.document`.

CAUTION

Whenever possible, you should use `parent` rather than `top` because `parent` always refers to the immediate parent of the frame in question. You can use `top` to refer to the topmost parent containing your frame. If your document is included as a frame in someone else's XHTML document, however, it is likely that your reference to `top` will result in an error.

- To reference a child frame from another child frame, just combine the two already discussed in this list. The `document` object of the second frame, for instance, could be accessed by either of the other child frames through `parent.MyFrame2.document`.

Now, what if you introduce another generation to your framed document? The third frame might load an XHTML document that itself contains a `<frameset>` tag to further divide the window into more frames, as in the following:

```
  <frameset cols="33%,33%,*">
     <frame src="Form.htm" NAME="myframe1"/>
     <frame src="Form.htm" NAME="myframe2"/>
     <frame src="Form.htm" NAME="myframe3"/>
</frameset>
```

This would result in the object hierarchy shown in Figure 20.12.

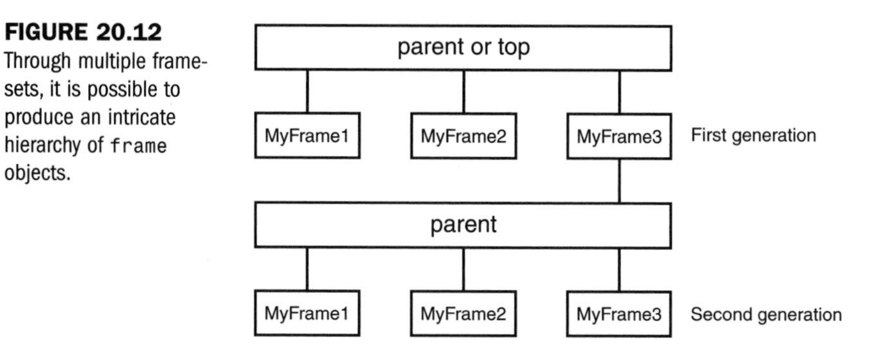

FIGURE 20.12 Through multiple framesets, it is possible to produce an intricate hierarchy of `frame` objects.

NOTE Keep in mind, when working with frames, that when you nest multiple framesets, the resulting pages can be visually confusing for your audience, as well as difficult for you as the developer. So be careful when you use frames to not overwhelm your audience. ■

This would result in a window showing a total of five frames. The top half of the window would show two frames, part of the first generation of `frame` objects. The bottom half of the window would show three frames, part of the second generation of `frame` objects. The following examples show you ways to reference the `document` object of the different generations of frames and parent framesets:

- Reference first-generation `MyFrame1 document` object from topmost parent:

  ```
  self.MyFrame1.document
  ```

- Reference second-generation `MyFrame1 document` object from topmost parent:

  ```
  self.MyFrame3.MyFrame1.document
  ```

- Reference first-generation `MyFrame1 document` object from the first-generation frame (`MyFrame2`) or the second-level parent (`MyFrame3`):

  ```
  parent.MyFrame1.document
  ```

- Reference first-generation `MyFrame1 document` object from any of the second-generation frames:

  ```
  parent.parent.MyFrame1.document, or
  top.MyFrame1.document
  ```

- Reference second-generation `MyFrame1 document` object from any of the other second-generation frames:

  ```
  parent.MyFrame1.document
  ```

Multiple Frame Access Example

Listings 20.12 through 20.14 show an example of the kind of multiple frame, multiple generation frame setup discussed in the preceding section. Notice that a few things from this example demonstrate the object-oriented nature of JavaScript, which gives you the flexibility to accomplish multiple things.

- The same XHTML document is loaded into each of the five frames that result from this example. Thus, each form element has the same name. Because of the object hierarchy that results from the multiple frames, however, it is possible to uniquely specify each element.
- Likewise, both the first- and second-generation frames are given the same names. Again, the object hierarchy enables the frames to be uniquely addressed, accessed, and manipulated.

Listing 20.12 ***Frameset1.htm*****—Top-Level Frameset**

```
<!DOCTYPE html PUBLIC "-//W3C//DTD XHTML 1.0 Frameset//EN"
    "http://www.w3.org/TR/xhtml1/DTD/xhtml1-frameset.dtd">
<html xmlns="http://www.w3.org/1999/xhtml">
<head>
<title>Frameset1.htm</title>
```

Listing 20.12 Continued

```
</head>
<frameset rows="50%,50%">
   <frameset cols="50%,50%">
      <frame src="Form.htm" name="MyFrame1"/>
      <frame src="Form.htm" name="MyFrame2"/>
   </frameset>
   <frame src="Frameset2.htm" name="MyFrame3"/>
</frameset>
</html>
```

Listing 20.13 *Frameset2.htm*—Second-Generation Frameset

```
<!DOCTYPE html PUBLIC "-//W3C//DTD XHTML 1.0 Frameset//EN"
    "http://www.w3.org/TR/xhtml1/DTD/xhtml1-frameset.dtd">
<html xmlns="http://www.w3.org/1999/xhtml">
<head>
<title>Frameset2.htm</title>
</head>
<frameset cols="33%,33%,*">
   <frame src="Form.htm" name="MyFrame1"/>
   <frame src="Form.htm" name="MyFrame2"/>
   <frame src="Form.htm" name="MyFrame3"/>
</frameset>
</html>
```

Listing 20.14 *Form.htm*—XHTML Document to Be Included in Each Frame

```
<!DOCTYPE html PUBLIC "-//W3C//DTD XHTML 1.0 Transitional//EN"
    "http://www.w3.org/TR/xhtml1/DTD/xhtml1-transitional.dtd">
<html xmlns="http://www.w3.org/1999/xhtml">
<head>
<title>Form.htm</title>
</head>
<body bgcolor="#ffffff">
<center>
<table>
<form name="MyForm">
<tr><td>
    <input type=text name="MyText1"
       onchange="self.document.MyForm.MyText4.value =
          'COPY ' + document.MyForm.MyText1.value"/>
    </td></tr>
<tr><td>
    <input type=text name="MyText2"
       onchange="parent.MyFrame2.document.MyForm.MyText4.value =
          'COPY ' + document.MyForm.MyText2.value"/>
    </td></tr>
```

Listing 20.14 Continued

```
<tr><td>
    <input type=text name="MyText3"
       onchange="parent.parent.MyFrame2.document.MyForm.MyText4.value =
          'COPY ' + document.MyForm.MyText3.value"/>
    </td></tr>
<tr><td>
<input type=text name="MyText4"/>
    </td></tr>
</form>
</table>
</center>
<hr />
<em>Jim O'Donnell, <a href="mailto:jim@odonnell.org">jim@odonnell.org</a></em>
</body>
</html>
```

NOTE Remember to use the Frameset `DOCTYPE` declaration in XHTML documents that use frames. ■

▶ To review XHTML DOCTYPE declarations, **see** "Basic Rules of XHTML," **p. 50**

The XHTML form specified in the document shown in Listing 20.14 has small JavaScript functions attached to the `onChange` events of each of the first three text elements. The first copies any entered text into the fourth text element of the current frame. The second copies entered text into the fourth text element of the parent's `MyFrame2` frame. The third copies entered text into the fourth text element of the grandparent's `MyFrame2` frame.

Figure 20.13 shows how this works when text is entered into the first of the second-generation frames. Line 1 is copied into line 4 in the same frame. Line 2 is copied into line 4 of the second of the second-generation frames. Line 3 is copied into line 4 of the second of the first-generation frames.

Figures 20.14 and 20.15 show the effects of typing the same lines into the first three lines in one of the first-generation frames. Note in Figure 20.15 that when line 3 is entered, it overwrites line 4 of the second of the first-generation frames. This is because parent refers to itself when you are already at the top level. Therefore, for first-generation frames, `parent.parent` and `parent` are equivalent.

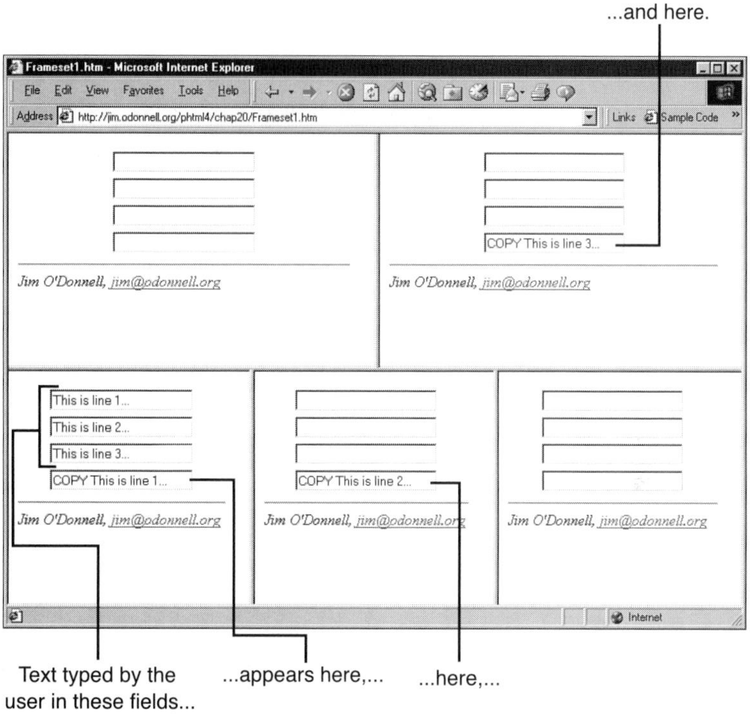

...and here.

FIGURE 20.13
Any frame can be accessed by scripts in any other frame in a multiple-frame document.

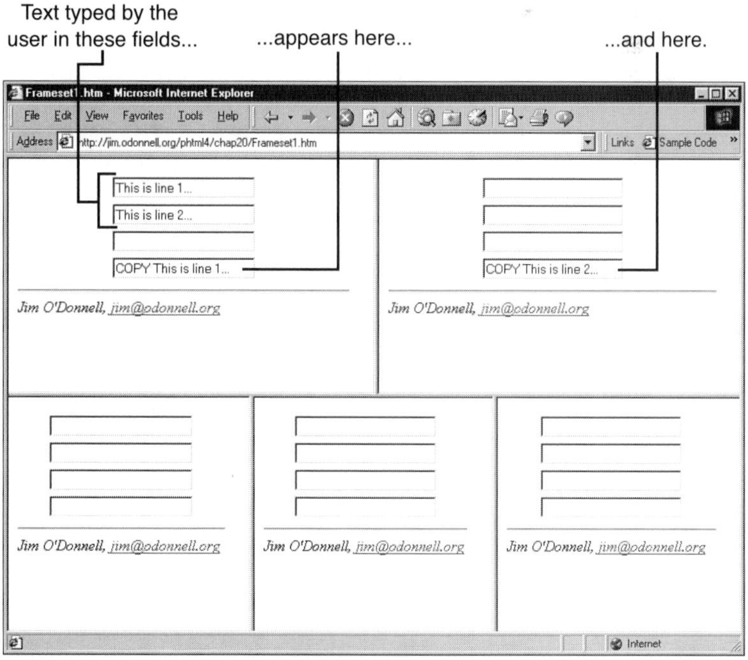

Frameset1.htm - Microsoft Internet Explorer

File Edit View Favorites Tools Help

Address http://jim.odonnell.org/phtml4/chap20/Frameset1.htm Links Sample Code

COPY This is line 3...

Jim O'Donnell, jim@odonnell.org

Jim O'Donnell, jim@odonnell.org

This is line 1...

This is line 2...

This is line 3...

COPY This is line 1...

COPY This is line 2...

Jim O'Donnell, jim@odonnell.org

Jim O'Donnell, jim@odonnell.org

Jim O'Donnell, jim@odonnell.org

Internet

Text typed by the user in these fields...

...appears here,...

...here,...

Text typed by the user in these fields...

...appears here...

...and here.

FIGURE 20.14
You can use XHTML frames to solicit input from the user and then use that input in other frames and windows.

Frameset1.htm - Microsoft Internet Explorer

File Edit View Favorites Tools Help

Address http://jim.odonnell.org/phtml4/chap20/Frameset1.htm Links Sample Code

This is line 1...

This is line 2...

COPY This is line 1...

COPY This is line 2...

Jim O'Donnell, jim@odonnell.org

Jim O'Donnell, jim@odonnell.org

Jim O'Donnell, jim@odonnell.org

Jim O'Donnell, jim@odonnell.org

Jim O'Donnell, jim@odonnell.org

Internet

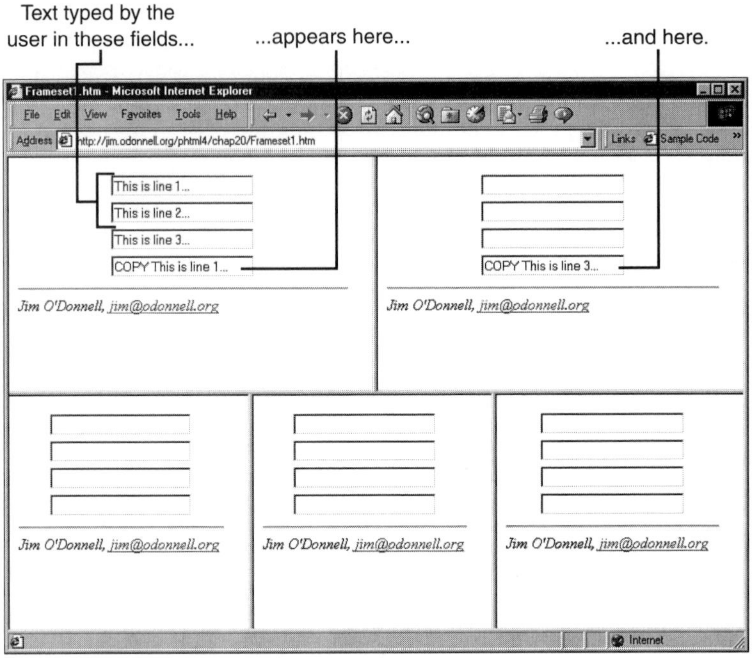

Text typed by the user in these fields... ...appears here... ...and here.

FIGURE 20.15
The `parent` and `top` properties of the `frame` or `window` object refer to themselves when you are already at the top level.

Using Hidden Frames

You can also build frame-based pages by placing all the XHTML and JavaScript code that you don't want changed into a hidden frame. Depending on the Web browser your users are using to look at your site and how you specify the borders of your frames, this frame might not actually be completely invisible. It might appear as a tiny space with one or two borders shown on it. To specify a hidden frame, add another frame to your frameset, but make sure the other frames take up all the available space. If you are using two frames, for example,

```
 <frameset rows="50%,50%">
    <frame name="MyFrame1" src="Frame1.htm"/>
    <frame name="MyFrame2" src="Frame2.htm"/>
</frameset>
```

you could add a hidden frame this way:

```
 <frameset rows="50%,50%,*">
    <frame name="MyFrame1" src="Frame1.htm"/>
    <frame name="MyFrame2" src="Frame2.htm"/>
    <frame name="MyHidden" src="Hidden.htm"/>
</frameset>
```

With this, the first two frames take up 100% of the page, which means that the last frame will be made as small as the browser can make it. You can then place the JavaScript code that you want to persist in the hidden XHTML document and use the techniques shown in this chapter to manipulate the contents of the other frames in the document.

▶ To find out more about setting up hidden frames, **see** “Using Hidden Frames,” **p. 231**

JavaScript Frames Example

In this frames example, you will see how to set up a Web page that is roughly equivalent to the windows example shown earlier in this chapter. A Web page will be created with three frames; the top one will have buttons that use attached JavaScripts to change the contents of the other two. Listing 20.15 shows the main document, which defines the frameset to be used.

Listing 20.15 ***FramEx.htm*—The Main Document of a Framed Web Page Is Usually Just the Frameset**

```
<!DOCTYPE html PUBLIC "-//W3C//DTD XHTML 1.0 Frameset//EN"
     "http://www.w3.org/TR/xhtml1/DTD/xhtml1-frameset.dtd">
<html xmlns="http://www.w3.org/1999/xhtml">
<head>
<title>JavaScript Frames Example</title>
</head>
<frameset rows="25%,*">
   <frame src="Buttons.htm" name="MyFrameBut"/>
   <frameset cols="200,*">
      <frame src="" name="MyFramePic"/>
      <frame src="" name="MyFrameBio"/>
   </frameset>
</frameset>
</html>
```

As shown in Listing 20.15, the only XHTML document loaded initially is `Buttons.htm`, which loads the buttons into the top frame used to manipulate the other two (see Figure 20.16). This file is listed in Listing 20.16; it is similar to the buttons used in the window example. No buttons are needed to open and close the windows (or frames, in this case) because the frames already exist. Also, the contents of the frames are manipulated using the `location.href` property of the `parent.MyFramePic` and `parent.MyFrameBio` objects, respectively, as shown in Figure 20.17.

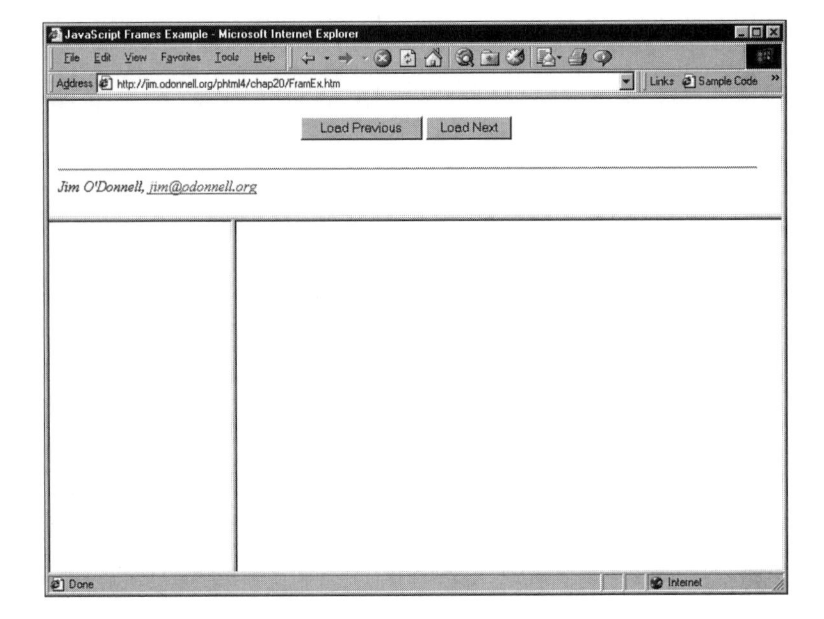

FIGURE 20.16
Frames can be created with nothing in them initially, then subsequently filled using targeted links or JavaScript.

Listing 20.16 *Buttons.htm*—Frames and Windows Can Be Easily Controlled Using JavaScript

```
<!DOCTYPE html PUBLIC "-//W3C//DTD XHTML 1.0 Transitional//EN"
    "http://www.w3.org/TR/xhtml1/DTD/xhtml1-transitional.dtd">
<html xmlns="http://www.w3.org/1999/xhtml">
<head>
<title>Buttons.htm</title>
<script type="text/javascript" language="JavaScript">
<!-- Hide this script from incompatible Web browsers!
var n = 0;
function loadnex() {
   n++;
   if (n > 5) n = 5;
   picname = "Pic" + n + ".htm";
   bioname = "Bio" + n + ".htm";
   if (n == 5) bioname = "Bio5f.htm";
//
   parent.MyFramePic.location.href = picname;
   parent.MyFrameBio.location.href = bioname;
}
function loadpre() {
   n--;
   if (n < 1) n = 1;
   picname = "Pic" + n + ".htm";
   bioname = "Bio" + n + ".htm";
//
   parent.MyFramePic.location.href = picname;
   parent.MyFrameBio.location.href = bioname;
}
```

Listing 20.16 Continued

```
//   Hide script from incompatible browsers! -->
</script>
</head>
<body bgcolor="#ffffff">
<center>
<form name="MyForm">
<table>
<tr><td><input type="button" name="PreBut" value="Load Previous"
           onclick="loadpre()"/></td>
    <td><input type="button" name="NexBut" value="Load Next"
           onclick="loadnex()"/></td>
</tr>
</table>
</form>
</center>
<hr />
<em>Jim O'Donnell, <a href="mailto:jim@odonnell.org">jim@odonnell.org</a></em>
</body>
</html>
```

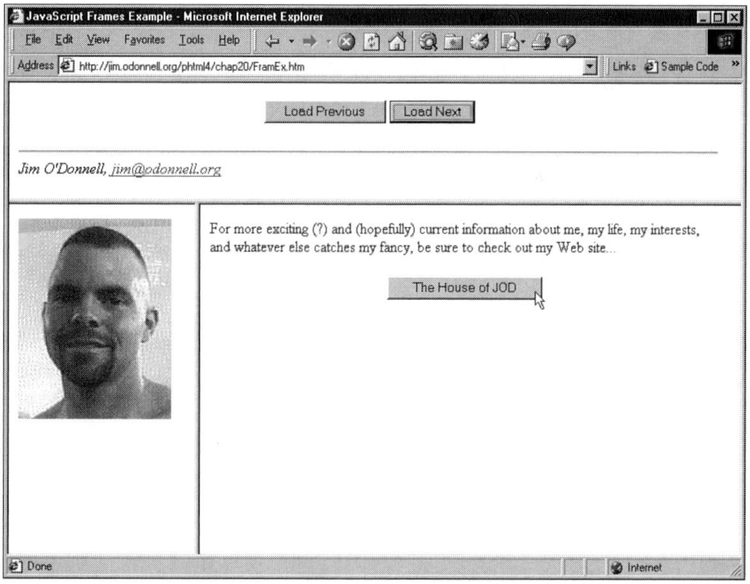

FIGURE 20.17
The use of frames and JavaScript enables multiple views to be used to present coordinated information.

It is interesting to note that the same XHTML documents for the pictures and biographies can be used in this example as in the preceding window example. The only exception to this is the final biography entry, which provides a link to an outside document that will replace the entire frameset. This document is shown in Listing 20.17 and uses the `location.href` property of the `parent` object to do this. That way, when the link to the outside document is selected, it fills the entire window, as shown in Figure 20.18, rather than just that frame. (A common mistake when creating a document with frames is for links to outside Web pages to open up within the frame, rather than use the whole window. Referring to the `parent` object avoids this.)

Listing 20.17 ***Bio5f.htm*****—Each Frame Can Manipulate the Others or Load a Completely New Document**

```
<!DOCTYPE html PUBLIC "-//W3C//DTD XHTML 1.0 Transitional//EN"
    "http://www.w3.org/TR/xhtml1/DTD/xhtml1-transitional.dtd">
<html xmlns="http://www.w3.org/1999/xhtml">
<head>
<title>Bio5f.htm</title>
<script type="text/javascript" language="JavaScript">
<!-- Hide this script from incompatible Web browsers!
function loadmain() {
   parent.location.href="http://jim.odonnell.org"
}
//   Hide script from incompatible browsers! -->
</script>
</head>
<body bgcolor="#ffffff">
For more exciting (?) and (hopefully) current information about me, my life,
my interests, and whatever else catches my fancy, be sure to check out my Web
site...
<center>
<form name="MyForm">
<table>
<tr><td><input type="button" value="The House of JOD"
           onclick="loadmain()"/></td>
</tr>
</table>
</form>
</center>
</body>
</html>
```

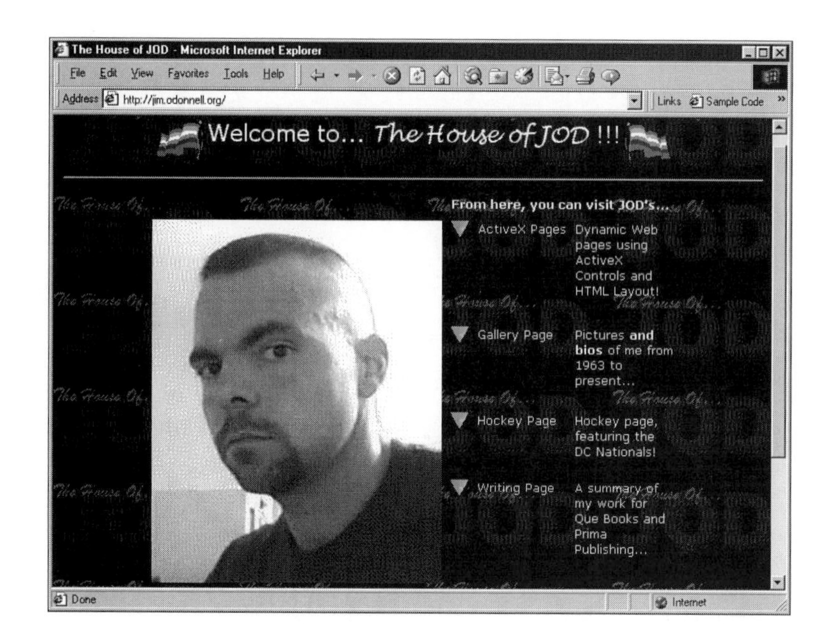

FIGURE 20.18
Make sure your documents that use frames close down cleanly when they are finished.

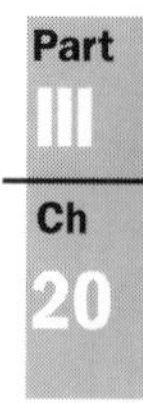

CHAPTER 21

Using JavaScript to Create Smart Forms

by Jim O'Donnell

In this chapter

Client-Side Form Validation

Form validation is one of the most common JavaScripting tasks. Many Web applications need to gather input from users. Traditionally, this data is entered in the browser and then transmitted to the server. The server checks the validity of the data and either stores the data on the server or sends back a message requesting additional information or asking the user to enter valid data. This slows your Web server and creates unnecessary Web traffic. With just a few lines of code, you can validate much of this data on the client's machine and send it to the server only after it is complete. Of course, you still need to completely validate data on the server as well, because people still use browsers that either don't support JavaScript or have it turned off.

This chapter discusses ways of using JavaScript to make your XHTML forms smarter. First, a few examples give you some ideas on how to use JavaScript to prefill, validate, and format XHTML form elements. After that, the discussion focuses on how you can make sure a credit card number is well formed—obviously, it's not possible to truly validate a credit card number at the client, but it is possible to determine whether the number is a valid format. Finally, this chapter reviews a couple of collections of JavaScript form validation scripts that are freely available on the Web. These collections should get you well on your way to adding form validation to your Web pages.

XHTML Form Text Field Validation and Formatting with JavaScript

Listing 21.1 is an example of a traditional XHTML page used to gather input from a user. Take a closer look at a few of the elements of this page.

Listing 21.1 ***Form.htm*—An XHTML Document Using a Standard XHTML Form**

```
<!DOCTYPE html PUBLIC "-//W3C//DTD XHTML 1.0 Transitional//EN"
    "http://www.w3.org/TR/xhtml1/DTD/xhtml1-transitional.dtd">
<html xmlns="http://www.w3.org/1999/xhtml">
<head>
<title>Forms Verification</title>
</head>
<body bgcolor="#ffffff">
<h1>Credit Card Payment Information</h1>
<hr />
<b>All information must be entered before the form can be submitted...</b>
<form name="MyForm">
<table>
<tr><td>First name:</td>
    <td> </td>
    <td><input type="text" name="FirstName" size="20" value="" /></td></tr>
```

Listing 21.1 Continued

```
<tr><td>Last name:</td>
    <td> </td>
    <td><input type="text" name="LastName"  size="20" value="" /></td></tr>
<tr><td colspan=4><hr></td></tr>
<tr><td>Payment Date:</td>
    <td> </td>
    <td><input type="text" name="PayDate"   size="10" value="" /></td>
    <td>(enter as mm/dd/yy)</td></tr>
<tr><td>Payment Amount:</td>
    <td><b>$</b></td>
    <td><input type="text" name="Amount"    size="10" value="" /></td></tr>
<tr><td>Credit Card Number:</td>
    <td> </td>
    <td><input type="text" name="CCNumber"  size="20" value="" /></td>
    <td>(must be 13 or 16 digits long)</td></tr>
<tr><td>Expiration Date:</td>
    <td> </td>
    <td><input type="text" name="ExpDate"   size="10" value="" /></td>
    <td>(enter as mm/dd/yy)</td></tr>
</table>
<hr />
<input type="submit" name="MySubmit" size="20" value="SUBMIT INFORMATION" />
</form>
<hr />
<em>Jim O'Donnell, <a href="mailto:jim@odonnell.org">jim@odonnell.org</a></em>
</body>
</html>
```

This XHTML document, when viewed in Netscape Navigator, appears as shown in Figure 21.1. The different elements of the XHTML document, as shown in Listing 21.1, are as follows:

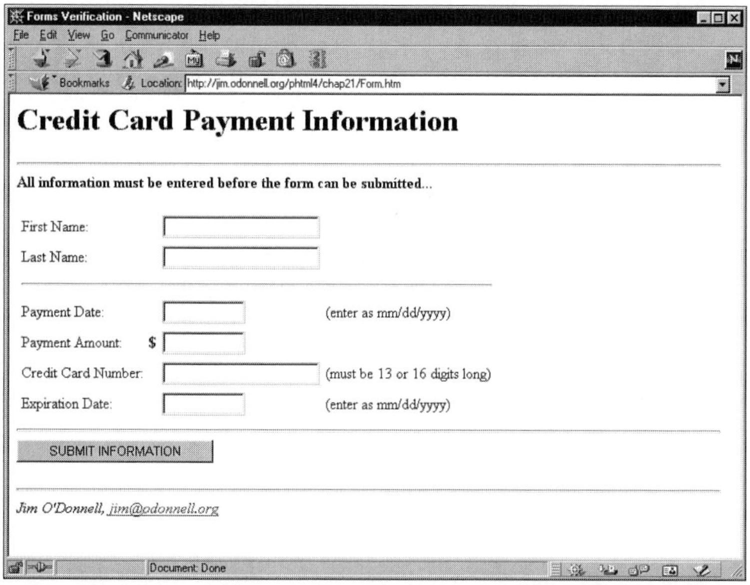

FIGURE 21.1
You can use standard XHTML Forms elements to set up a document for receiving user input.

- **<form>…</form> elements**—These are the container elements that must surround the XHTML Forms input elements. The `name="MyForm"` attribute is used to help identify the form from which that data came when the form is being processed. You might notice that neither the `method` nor the `action` attribute for the `<form>` element has been sent. This is because this form is being used as an example. Normally you would set `method="POST"` and set the `action` to the appropriate URL of where on your Web server you want the data to be sent.
- **<input type="TEXT"/> elements**—Each of these elements is used to receive one piece of information from the user. Each is named, using the `name` attribute, to enable the resulting data to be identified.
- **<input type="SUBMIT"/> element**—This element puts the button on the form used to submit it. Like the other elements, it is named using the `name` attribute, and the `value` attribute is used to customize the text appearing on the button.

▶ To find out more about setting up XHTML forms, **see** "Creating Forms," **p. 234**

Scripting XHTML Form Text Fields

XHTML documents can include JavaScripts to perform a variety of client-side scripting functions to validate elements of the form before it is submitted to the Web server. Note that not all the form validation can be done at the client—for instance, for this example you would definitely need to validate the payment information at the server—but some of the simpler things definitely can be done.

> **CAUTION**
>
> This is meant to be an illustrative example designed to show some types of user input that can be validated using JavaScript at the client. It is not meant to be a realistic example of how to implement a Web-based payment system. If you want to do that, many concerns exist with security and validation of payment information that are not addressed here. However, you can find some of this information in Part V, "Server-Side Processing."

You can validate the information entered into a form in a couple of ways. For text fields, you should validate the information as you go along. By calling a JavaScript from the `onChange` method of the XHTML Form text field, you can validate the data entered into a field any time it has changed. An example of the syntax used to do this follows:

```
<input type="TEXT" name="PayDate" size="10" value=""
       onChange="checkDate(document.MyForm.PayDate)" />
```

In this example, whenever the information in the text field named `PayDate` is changed, the JavaScript `checkDate()` function is called. The argument of the `checkDate()` function, in this case, is the text field object (assuming that the name of the form is `MyForm`).

Prefilling Entries

The only apparent change from the unscripted to scripted version of this example in Figure 21.2 is that the payment date has been prefilled. Because an obvious default entry exists for this field—the current date—it makes sense to enable JavaScript to do this and save the user a little bit of effort. This is done by executing the JavaScript statements shown in Listing 21.2 when the document is loaded.

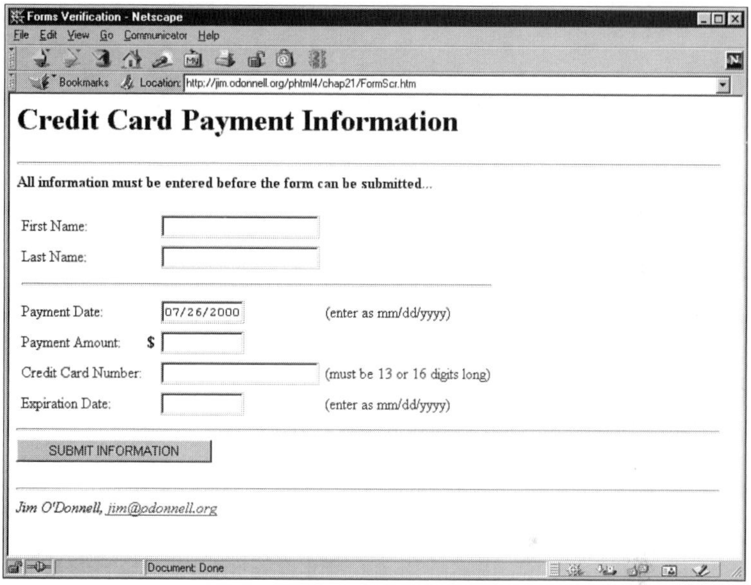

FIGURE 21.2
Besides having the payment date entry prefilled, this JavaScripted form doesn't look very different from the unscripted version.

Listing 21.2 ***FormScr.htm*** **(excerpt)—Prefilling Entries Makes Your Pages Easier to Use and Less Error Prone**

```
//
////////////////////////////////////////////////////////////////////////////
//
// This function formats a date as mm/dd/yyyy.
//
function formatDate(dateVar) {
   m = dateVar.getMonth() + 1
   if ("" + m == "NaN")
      return "Invalid"
   fmtDate = ((m < 10) ? "0" : "") + m
//
   d = dateVar.getDate()
   fmtDate += ((d < 10) ? "/0" : "/") + d
//
```

Listing 21.2 Continued

```
    y = dateVar.getYear()
    if (y < 26)
       y += 2000
    else if (y < 200)
       y += 1900
    y = Math.max(y,1926)
    fmtDate += "/" + y
//
    return fmtDate
}
//
// Prefill payment date with current date
//
today = new Date()
document.MyForm.PayDate.value = formatDate(today)
```

NOTE The complete listings of this XHTML document and all the other documents used in this chapter are on the Macmillan Web site at `http://www.mcp.com`. The sample code for the JavaScript and Dynamic HTML sections is also hosted on the author's Web site at `http://jim.odonnell.org/phtml4/`. ■

The `today` variable is set equal to a JavaScript `Date` object containing the current date. In general, the `formatDate()` function takes a `Date` object as an argument and returns a string with the date in the format `mm/dd/yyyy`. Specifically, the function performs the following checks and conversions:

- Gets the number of the month. If this number is valid, the function adds 1 because the nominal range is 0–11, and creates a string in `fmtDate`, with a leading `0`, if necessary. If the month number is invalid, indicating a bad `Date` object, the string "Invalid" is returned.
- Gets the day of the month and adds it as string to `fmtDate`, with a leading `0`, if necessary, and a `/` to separate it from the month.
- Gets the year, and after making sure it is in the range 1926–2099, adds it as a string to `fmtDate`, separated by the month and date with a `/`.

NOTE The `formatDate()` function is made a little more complicated because some browsers return the full year with the `getYear()` method and some return the number of years since 1900. This problem could be avoided by using the `getFullYear()` method of JavaScript 1.3, but such a script would generate errors in older browsers that are based on JavaScript 1.2 or lower. The method shown here should work with just about all JavaScript versions. ■

Note that the user can change this entry, picking a payment date that is after the current date. You might not want to allow the user to select a payment date prior to the current date, however—if his payment is late, for instance, you don't want him to be able to "predate his check." You can easily prevent this with JavaScript, as shown later in this chapter.

Formatting Proper Name Entries

Listing 21.3 shows the JavaScript function `capitalizeName()`. This function formats a proper name entry by capitalizing the first letter. This is not terribly important as far as forms validation topics go, but it is a nicety. Another feature of this function (included here because of personal bias), is that it also capitalizes the letter immediately following an apostrophe.

Listing 21.3 ***FormScr.htm*** **(excerpt)—JavaScript Subroutine to Format Proper Name Entries**

```
//
///////////////////////////////////////////////////////////////////////////
//
// This function capitalizes proper names; it also capitalizes the
// letter after the apostrophe, if one is present
//
function capitalizeName(Obj) {
//
// Set temp equal to form element string
//
   temp  = new String(Obj.value)
   first = temp.substring(0,1)
   temp  = first.toUpperCase() + temp.substring(1,temp.length)
   apnum = temp.indexOf("'")
   if (apnum > -1) {
      aplet = temp.substring(apnum+1,apnum+2)
      temp  = temp.substring(0,apnum) + "'" +
              aplet.toUpperCase() +
              temp.substring(apnum+2,temp.length)
   }
   Obj.value = temp
}
```

Validating and Formatting Currency Entries

Listing 21.4 shows the JavaScript function `checkAmount()`. This function validates and formats an entry meant to be an amount of money. Primarily, this entry needs to be a numeric value, but it is a little more forgiving than that; it will remove a leading dollar sign if the user has put one in. Then, after making sure that the value is numeric, the subroutine formats it as dollars and cents and writes it back out to the form field from which it came.

Listing 21.4 ***FormScr.htm*** **(excerpt)—JavaScript Subroutine to Validate and Format Currency**

```
//
/////////////////////////////////////////////////////////////////////////
//
// This function checks to see if the value of the object that is
// passed to it is a valid currency, and then formats it.
//
function checkAmount(Obj) {
//
// Set temp equal to form element string
//
   temp = new String(Obj.value)
//
// Remove leading $, if present
//
   temp = temp.substring(temp.indexOf("$")+1,temp.length)
//
// Convert into a floating point number and format as dollars
// and cents
//
   temp = parseFloat(temp)
   temp = Math.floor(100*temp)/100
   temp = String(temp)
   if (temp.indexOf(".") == -1) {
      temp = temp + ".00"
   }
   if (temp.indexOf(".") == temp.length -2) {
      temp = temp + "0"
   }
//
// If zero value, make blank
//
   if (temp == "0.00") {
      temp = ""
   }
//
// Write back out to the form element
//
   Obj.value = temp
}
```

If you are not familiar with JavaScript, you might be confused a little by the `checkAmount()` function because it seems to treat the same variable alternatively as a number or as a string. Because JavaScript enables its variables to have their types changed dynamically, you can use the same variable to store any kind of data that JavaScript recognizes. JavaScript generally treats data as the subtype—such as integer, floating point, or string—appropriate to the operation.

As a final note, you see that for an entry incorrectly formatted, `checkAmount()` will blank the entry. How your JavaScripts respond to incorrect entries is up to you. You can remove the incorrect entry (as is done in this example), leave it but set an error flag that prevents the form from being submitted until it is corrected, bring up an Alert box, or do anything else you want.

Validating and Formatting Date Entries

The `checkDate()` shown in Listing 21.5 is similar to `checkAmount()` except that it validates a correct date entry rather than amount. If the user inputs the date as requested, in the form `mm/dd/yyyy`, this value can be passed to the JavaScript `Date` object, which will return a valid `Date` object with that date; then the `formatDate()` function can be called to format the date as desired.

Listing 21.5 ***FormScr.htm* (excerpt)—JavaScript Subroutine to Validate and Format Date**

```
//
//////////////////////////////////////////////////////////////////////
//
// This function checks to see if the value of the object that is
// passed to it is a valid date, and then formats it.
//
function checkDate(Obj) {
//
// Grab the form element value and, if it's a valid date, call
// formatDate() to format it as mm/dd/yyyy
//
   temp = new Date(Obj.value)
   if (temp.getDate() > 0 & temp.getDate() < 32)
      temp = formatDate(temp)
   else {
//
//    If it's not a valid date, assume that it's mm/dd and create a
//    valid date by appending the current year to it
//
//    Parse out the month, subtracting one since JavaScript months
//    are numbered from 0 to 11
//
      temp  = Obj.value
      month = temp.substring(0,temp.indexOf("/")) - 1
//
//    Parse out the day of the month
//
      day = temp.substring(temp.indexOf("/")+1,temp.length)
//
//    Find the current year from today's date
//
```

Listing 21.5 Continued

```
        today = new Date()
        year  = today.getYear()
        if (year < 200)
           year += 1900
//
//      Create a date object from the year, month, and day, and
//      format it as mm/dd/yyyy; if this date is still invalid,
//      then the string "Invalid" will be displayed in the form
//      element
//
        temp = new Date(year,month,day)
        temp = formatDate(temp)
     }
//
// Write back out to the form element
//
   Obj.value = temp
}
```

Even though the user is asked to enter dates in the `mm/dd/yyyy` format, the capability to interpret dates that are entered as `mm/dd/yy` or even `mm/dd` can be helpful as well. Unfortunately, there are two problems with this capability. First, JavaScript's `Date` object is not smart enough to correctly interpret a date argument entered as `mm/dd` and append the current year. The `checkDate()` function fixes this by looking for dates entered as `mm/dd` and then appending the current year. Second, you want a date entered as, for example, `05/27/00` to be interpreted as May 27, 2000; however, the `Date` object interprets the year as 1900. This problem is solved (in the `formatDate()` function) by using a common "Y2K Bug" technique known as "windowing"; dates that are 25 or less are interpreted as being in the 2000s and 26 or higher are in the 1900s.

If the information entered into a date field cannot be interpreted as a valid date, this function places the string `Invalid` in the field, which is what the `Date` object returns when it is given invalid arguments.

CAUTION

The date formatting described above applies U.S. practice. For a Web site with a potentially global audience, you should be aware that in the United Kingdom, dates are commonly entered as dd/mm/yy or dd/mm/yyyy, and dates in Japan are commonly entered as yyyy/mm/dd. Interestingly, the latter format is the one that is adopted in the XML specification. As long as you clearly specify the format you are using, however, your audience should be able to figure it out.

Validating Numeric Entries

Even if it were possible, you would probably not want to verify a credit card number on the client, for reasons of account security. You can perform a little bit of validation on the numeric credit card number entry, however, before the form data is sent along for final validation at the Web server. `checkCCNumber()`, shown in Listing 21.6, makes sure that this entry is numeric and is a proper length for a credit card number (defined here as either 13 or 16 digits, although this can be adjusted if necessary). It also formats a valid number and redisplays it; for example, a 16-digit number displays formatted as in `1234 5678 1234 5678`. Like the `checkDate()` function, this function also puts the string `Invalid` in the field if the number entered is not valid.

Listing 21.6 ***FormScr.htm*** **(excerpt)—JavaScript Subroutine to Validate Numerical Entry**

```
//
/////////////////////////////////////////////////////////////////////////
//
// This subroutine checks to see if the value of the object that is
// passed to it is a valid credit card number.
//
// Specify minimum and maximum length of valid credit card numbers
//
minLength = 13
maxLength = 16
//
function checkCCNumber(Obj) {
//
// Get object value
//
   temp = Obj.value
//
// Remove all embedded spaces to make sure the credit card
// number is the right length (either minLength of maxLength
// digits long)
//
   while (temp.indexOf(" ") > -1) {
      temp = temp.substring(0,temp.indexOf(" ")) +
             temp.substring(temp.indexOf(" ")+1,temp.length)
   }
//
// Add back embedded spaces in the appropriate spots for
// valid length numbers, else return "Invalid"
//
   if (temp.length == minLength)
      temp = temp.substring( 0, 4) + " " +
             temp.substring( 4, 7) + " " +
             temp.substring( 7,10) + " " +
             temp.substring(10,13)
```

Listing 21.6 Continued

```
   else if (temp.length == maxLength)
      temp = temp.substring( 0, 4) + " " +
             temp.substring( 4, 8) + " " +
             temp.substring( 8,12) + " " +
             temp.substring(12,16)
   else
      temp = "Invalid"
//
// Write back out to the form element
//
   Obj.value = temp
}
```

Notice that the `minLength` and `maxLength` variables are defined in the preceding listing outside the JavaScript `checkCCNumber()` function. This enables these variables to have a global scope, making them accessible outside of that function. In the XHTML document, these variables are used to correctly print the number of digits expected in the credit card number in the Web page itself:

```
document.write("<td>(must be " + minLength + " or " + maxLength +
               " digits long)</td>")
```

NOTE Credit card numbers are not random. Mathematical tests can be applied at the client-side to verify that a given number is "well formed"—in other words, that a given number can or cannot be a valid credit card number for a given type of card. The `checkCCNumber()` function checks only the length of the number. You can read about a function for verifying that a credit card number is well formed later in this chapter in the section, "Verifying Well-Formed Credit Card Numbers." ■

Validating Forms Before Submission

After all the information has been entered into the form and each individual entry has been validated, you might still want to perform some form-level checks before the form is submitted. You can do this in several ways. The most common way is to attach a JavaScript function to the `onSubmit` event of the Submit button (for example, with `onSubmit="checkForm(document.MyForm)"`. If the function returns `true`, the form is submitted; if it returns `false`, it is not.

Another way to do the same thing is to attach a JavaScript function to a regular forms button—for example, `onClick="checkForm(document.MyForm)"`. Then, if all the validation checks are passed, the `submit()` method of the XHTML Form can be called to submit the form. This is how the `checkForm()` function, shown in Listing 21.7, is attached to the XHTML Form in this example.

Listing 21.7 *FormScr.htm* (excerpt)—JavaScript Function to Validate Form Prior to Submission

```
//
////////////////////////////////////////////////////////////////////////
//
// This function will verify that the current form is ready to
// be submitted before allowing it to be submitted
//
function checkForm(formObj) {
//
// Verify that all fields have valid information in them
//
   for (i = 0;i < formObj.length;i++)
      if (formObj.elements[i].value == "" |
          formObj.elements[i].value == "Invalid") {
         alert("All fields must be completed with valid " +
               "information for submission!")
         formObj.elements[i].focus()
         return
      }
//
// Verify that the payment date is on or after the current date, and
// on or before the expiration date
//
   today   = new Date()
   today   = formatDate(today)
   today   = new Date(today)
   paydate = new Date(formObj.PayDate.value)
   expdate = new Date(formObj.ExpDate.value)
//
   if (paydate.getTime() < today.getTime()) {
      alert("Payment date must be on or after current date!")
      formObj.PayDate.focus()
      return
   }
   if (paydate.getTime() > expdate.getTime()) {
      alert("Payment date must be on or before expiration date!")
      formObj.PayDate.focus()
      return
   }
//
// Submit form
//
   formObj.submit()
   alert("Form successfully submitted!")
}
```

The `checkForm()` function does three things. First, it verifies that valid information has been entered into each field on the form. Rather than referring to each form field by name, it does this by using the `elements` object array of the `form` object, with the following `for` loop:

```
for (i = 0;i < formObj.length;i++)
      if (formObj.elements[i].value == "" |
          formObj.elements[i].value == "Invalid") {
         alert("All fields must be completed " +
               "for submission!")
         formObj.elements[i].focus()
         return
      }
```

If all the fields are not completed, an Alert box appears (see Figure 21.3), the form is not submitted, and the focus is moved to the first empty field. Being able to use the elements object array makes this function very easy to program; for forms with a mixture of mandatory and optional fields, you won't be able to use a simple loop, and the processing will need to be a little more sophisticated.

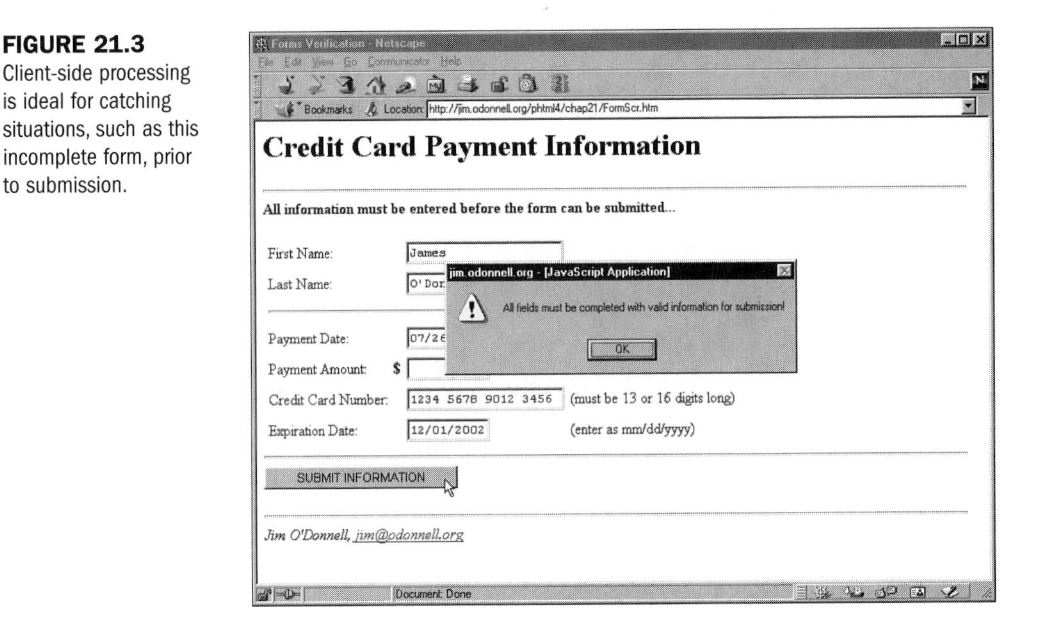

FIGURE 21.3
Client-side processing is ideal for catching situations, such as this incomplete form, prior to submission.

Even if the form is completely filled out and each of the entries has the correct type of data in it, problems still might exist that you can catch at the client with JavaScript. `checkForm()` also checks for two types of invalid entries that can occur with either the payment or credit card expiration date. It is incorrect if either the payment date is after the expiration date of the card or the payment date is before the current date. In either of these cases, an appropriate Alert box appears, as shown in Figure 21.4, and the form is not submitted.

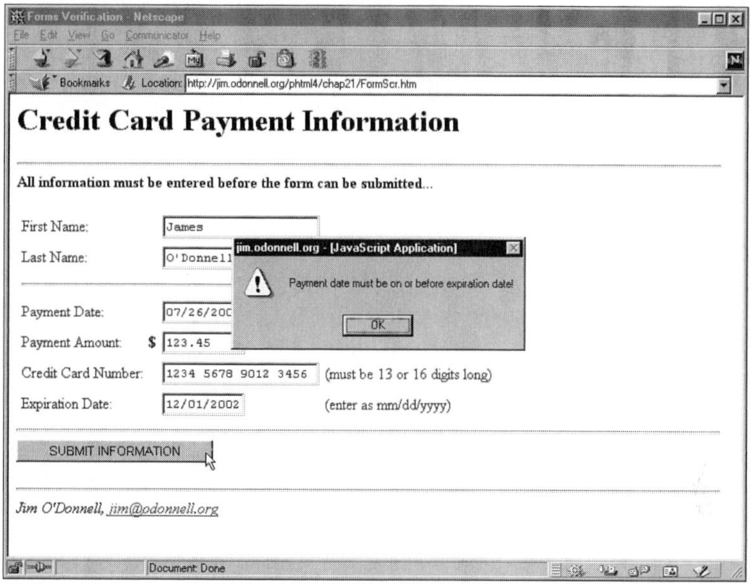

FIGURE 21.4
You can save effort on your Web server by using scripting to catch simple errors, such as an expired credit card, at the client.

After all the entries in the form have been verified, it is then ready to be submitted to the Web server for further verification of the payment information. You can also use JavaScript to put up an Alert box that tells you that your information is on its way (see Figure 21.5).

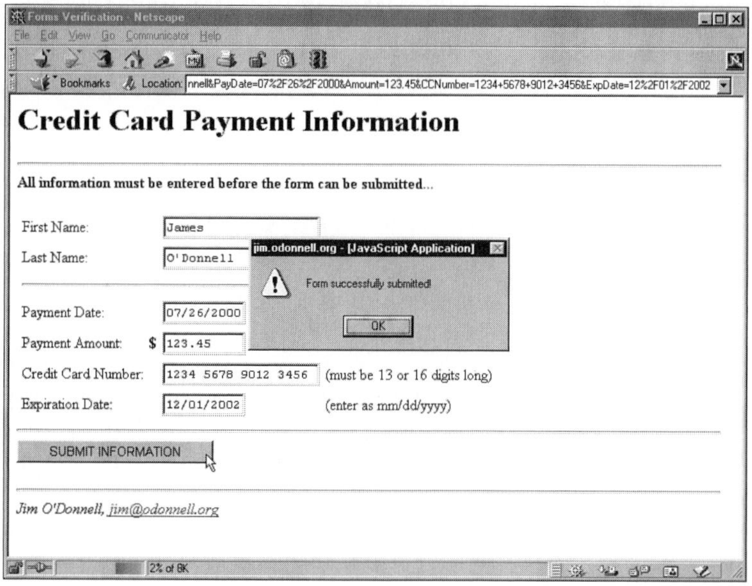

FIGURE 21.5
After all the entries are validated at the client as much as possible, they can be submitted for processing at the server.

Verifying Well-Formed Credit Card Numbers

The only way to completely verify the validity of a credit card number is through a Web server specifically set up to handle credit card transactions. However, you can use JavaScript to apply some checks at the client-side that enable you to determine whether the number is well formed. A well-formed number is one that *could* be a valid number for that type of credit card. Passing the test for being well formed does not mean that the number is from a good credit card; failing the test, however, does mean that the number can't be from a good card.

You can apply two easy tests using JavaScript at the client-side. These tests enable you to determine whether a credit card number for a given card type is well formed. The first is to check the prefix (the first one to four numbers) and the length—each major credit card type has a given prefix and length. Second, most algorithms are encoded with a "check digit." This digit is added to the number and can also be determined from the rest of the digits in the card by using a simple algorithm. Therefore, you can apply the algorithm at the client-side to generate the check digit and compare it to the digit actually present. If they do not match, the number is not well formed.

Checking Card Prefix and Length

Table 21.1 outlines many of the major credit cards you might want to validate, along with most of their allowed prefixes and lengths. (Note that the JCB card type has two entries because it is *either* 16 digits beginning with a 3 *or* 15 digits beginning with 2131 or 1800.)

Table 21.1 Major Credit Card Prefixes and Lengths

Card Type	Prefixes	Length
MasterCard	51–55	16
VISA	4	13,16
American Express	34,37	15
Diner's Club, Carte Blanche	300–305,36,38	14
Discover	6011	16
enRoute	2114,2149	15
JCB	3	16
JCB	2131,1800	15

Validation Using the Luhn Algorithm

The algorithm used to validate the credit card number is known as the Luhn Algorithm, and it employs the following steps:

1. Double the value of alternating digits of the credit card number, beginning with the second digit from the right.

   Example: For the number 1234 5678 1234 5678

1	2	3	4	5	6	7	8	1	2	3	4	5	6	7	8
×2		×2		×2		×2		×2		×2		×2		×2	
2		6		10		14		2		6		10		14	

2. Add the separate digits of the products found in step 1 (10 yields the separate digits 1 and 0) along with all the credit card digits not used in step 1.

   Example: Products = 2+6+(1+0)+(1+4)+2+6+(1+0)+(1+4) = 28

   Unaffected Digits = 2+4+6+8+2+4+6+8 = 40

   Total = 28 + 40 = 68

The total found by following the preceding steps must be divisible by 10 (must end in 0) for it to be a well-formed credit card number.

Example: Total = 68. This number is *not* well formed.

If the original number in the preceding example had been

1234 5678 1234 5670

the total would have worked out to be 60, and it would be well formed. This number would not have passed the complete well-formed test, however, because its prefix and length do not match any of the major credit cards shown in Table 21.1.

If you are planning to use JavaScript functions to verify that credit card numbers are well formed, you should have a set of sample numbers to use to verify that the functions are working correctly. (Don't test these functions using your own credit card numbers unless you are sure the information won't be accessible over the Web.) Table 21.2 shows a set of sample well-formed credit card numbers, available from the Netscape Web site. (The next section of this chapter discusses this Netscape site in more detail.)

Table 21.2 Sample Well-Formed Credit Card Numbers

Card Type	Sample Number
MasterCard	5500 0000 0000 0004
VISA	4111 1111 1111 1111
American Express	3400 0000 0000 009
Diner's Club or Carte Blanche	3000 0000 0000 04
Discover	6011 0000 0000 0004
enRoute	2014 0000 0000 009
JCB	3088 0000 0000 0009

Several freely available JavaScripts implement the test for a well-formed credit card number. You can find one of them, developed by Simon Tneoh, at the following URL:

```
http://www.tneoh.zoneit.com/javascript/cardobject.html
```

A slightly altered version (to fix some minor typographical mistakes) of the `CardType.js` JavaScript source file is available from this Web site, as well as the author's Web site. You can find it in the file named `ChkCard.js`. Listing 21.8 shows `ChkCard.htm`, an XHTML document that uses this JavaScript source file to implement its credit card number tests.

Listing 21.8 ***ChkCard.htm*—You Can Check for Well-Formed Credit Card Numbers Before Verifying Them on the Server**

```
<!DOCTYPE html PUBLIC "-//W3C//DTD XHTML 1.0 Transitional//EN"
    "http://www.w3.org/TR/xhtml1/DTD/xhtml1-transitional.dtd">
<html xmlns="http://www.w3.org/1999/xhtml">
<head>
<title>Check for Well-Formed Credit Card Number</title>
<script type="text/javascript" language="JavaScript" src="ChkCard.js">
</script>
</head>
<body bgcolor="#ffffff">
<center>
<h1>Check for Well-Formed Credit Card Number</h1>
</center>
<hr />
<font color="#ff0000">Alert!
Please do not use a real card number and valid expiration date
to test unless you have checked the source code for this page
and JavaScript code to verify that the card number will not be
submitted over the Web.
</font>
<center>
<table>
<form name="MyForm">
<tr><td>Card Number:</td>
    <td><input type="TEXT" name="CardNumber" size="16" maxlength="19" />
    </td></tr>
<tr><td>Card Type:</td>
    <td><select name="CardType">
            <option value="MasterCard" />MasterCard
            <option value="VisaCard" />Visa
            <option value="AmExCard" />American Express
            <option value="DinersClubCard" />Diners Club
            <option value="DiscoverCard" />Discover
            <option value="enRouteCard" />enRoute
            <option value="JCBCard" />JCB
            <option value="LuhnCheckSum" />Luhn Check Only
```

Listing 21.8 Continued

```
        </select></td></tr>
<tr><td>Expiration Month:</td>
    <td><select name="ExpMon">
           <option value="01" />January
           <option value="02" />February
           <option value="03" />March
           <option value="04" />April
           <option value="05" />May
           <option value="06" />June
           <option value="07" />July
           <option value="08" />August
           <option value="09" />September
           <option value="10" />October
           <option value="11" />November
           <option value="12" selected="1" />December
        </select></td></tr>
<tr><td>Expiration Year:</td>
    <td><select name="ExpYear">
           <option value="00" />2000
           <option value="01" />2001
           <option value="02" selected="1" />2002
           <option value="03" />2003
           <option value="04" />2004
           <option value="05" />2005
        </select></td></tr>
<tr><td> </td>
    <td><input type=button value="Check"
              onclick="CheckCardNumber(document.MyForm)" /></td></tr>
</form>
</table>
</center>
<hr />
<em>Jim O'Donnell, <a href="mailto:jim@odonnell.org">jim@odonnell.org</a></em>
</body>
</html>
```

The JavaScripts implement a number of tests. In addition to making sure that the expiration date entered has not passed, the credit card number entered is checked to see whether it is well formed. The JavaScript checks employ both the prefix and length test, as well as the Luhn Algorithm check digit test. Figure 21.6 shows the results of a well-formed credit card number of the card type selected.

As shown in Figure 21.7, the JavaScript tests are even smart enough to determine when a well-formed card number of a type other than the one selected has been entered. If the number is not a well-formed card number for any known type of card, an Alert box with that information appears (see Figure 21.8).

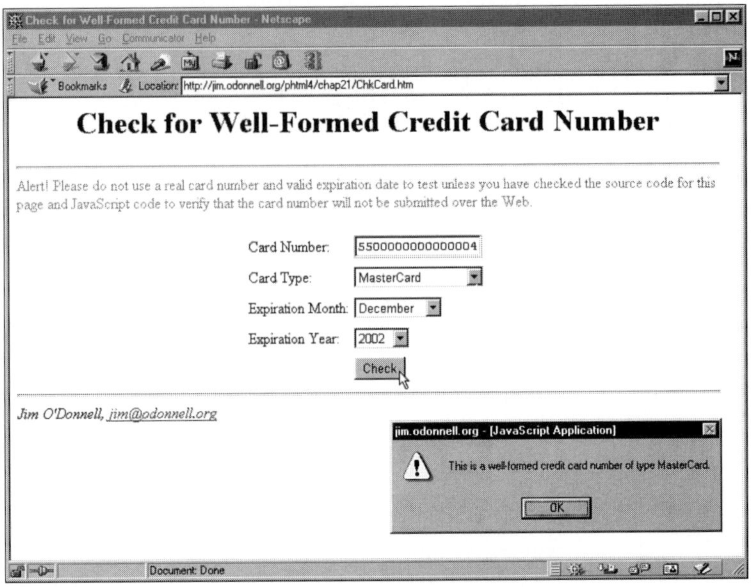

FIGURE 21.6
Both the check digit test and the prefix and length test need to pass to correctly identify the card number as well formed for the given type.

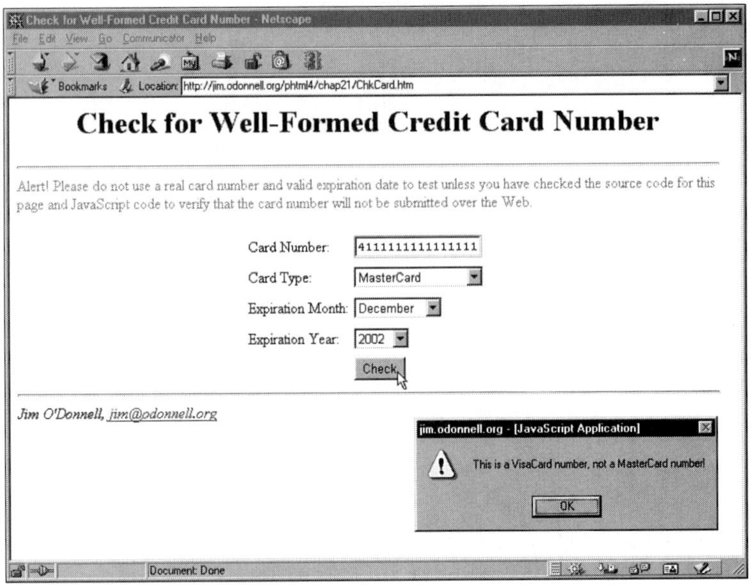

FIGURE 21.7
Using the prefix and length information, it is possible to automatically determine the type of a misidentified card.

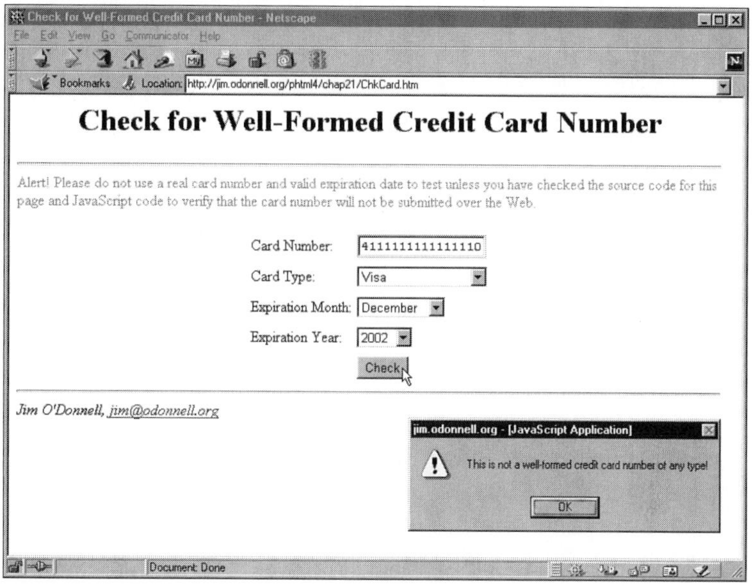

FIGURE 21.8
If the check digit test fails, the number cannot be a valid credit card number of any known type.

CAUTION

Given the global nature of the Internet and the possible advances in payment methods that might take place, it would be important in a live Web site to monitor any relevant developments. It would not be good business practice to prevent someone paying you with a new but genuine credit card. Also keep in mind that these checks are for credit cards; different rules might apply for debit cards.

Netscape's Sample Form Validation Scripts

A veritable treasure trove of freely available JavaScripts for form validation is available from the Netscape Web site, available at the following URL:

```
http://developer.netscape.com/docs/examples/javascript/formval/overview.html
```

The JavaScript source file that you can download from that site is called `FormChek.js`. In addition, a number of sample XHTML files show the functions in operation. The JavaScript functions defined there come under a number of general categories, as described in the header information in the `FormChek.js` file (summarized in the following sections).

In addition to the form validation scripts available at the preceding URL, Netscape has another set of scripts that do much the same thing, but are optimized for JavaScript 1.2 and higher. These scripts use the JavaScript `RegExp` (regular expression) object to simplify much of the string processing and manipulation that is done with form validation. Just about all the functions are the same; the implementation is different. These scripts are available at this URL:

`http://developer.netscape.com/docs/examples/javascript/regexp/overview.html`

You can read more about using the JavaScript `RegExp` object in Chapter 23, "Using JavaScript to Control Web Browser Objects."

▶ For more information about using regular expressions to simplify your JavaScripts, **see** "Using the `RegExp` Object," **p. 576**

Data Validation Functions

The purpose of the data-validation JavaScripts is to check strings and characters, normally those entered into XHTML Form text fields. The functions can also be more generally applied to determine whether the strings are a given type of data. The basic functions are the following:

- **`isWhitespace(s)`**—Checks whether string `s` is empty or whitespace.
- **`isLetter(c)`**—Checks whether character `c` is an English letter.
- **`isDigit(c)`**—Checks whether character `c` is a digit.
- **`isLetterOrDigit(c)`**—Checks whether character `c` is a letter or digit.
- **`isInteger(s,ok_if_empty?)`**—True if all characters in string `s` are numbers.
- **`isSignedInteger(s,ok_if_empty?)`**—True if all characters in string `s` are numbers; leading + or - allowed.
- **`isPositiveInteger(s,ok_if_empty?)`**—True if string `s` is an integer greater than 0.
- **`isNonnegativeInteger(s,ok_if_empty?)`**—True if string `s` is an integer greater than or equal to 0.
- **`isNegativeInteger(s,ok_if_empty?)`**—True if `s` is an integer less than 0.
- **`isNonpositiveInteger(s,ok_if_empty?)`**—True if `s` is an integer less than or equal to 0.
- **`isFloat(s,ok_if_empty?)`**—True if string `s` is an unsigned floating point (real) number. (Integers are also okay.)
- **`isSignedFloat(s,ok_if_empty?)`**—True if string `s` is a floating point or integer number; leading + or - allowed.
- **`isAlphabetic(s,ok_if_empty?)`**—True if string `s` is English letters.
- **`isAlphanumeric(s,ok_if_empty?)`**—True if string `s` is English letters and numbers only.

In these functions, and the others described in this chapter, the `ok_if_empty?` argument flag is set to `true` to indicate that it is permissible for the argument being checked to be null. The preceding functions are used to build up more specialized data-validation functions, as shown in the following list:

- **`isSSN(s,ok_if_empty?)`**—True if string `s` is a valid U.S. Social Security number.
- **`isUSPhoneNumber(s,ok_if_empty?)`**—True if string `s` is a valid U.S. phone number.
- **`isInternationalPhoneNumber(s,ok_if_empty?)`**—True if string `s` is a valid international phone number.
- **`isZIPCode(s,ok_if_empty?)`**—True if string `s` is a valid U.S. zip code.
- **`isStateCode(s,ok_if_empty?)`**—True if string `s` is a valid U.S. postal code.
- **`isEmail(s,ok_if_empty?)`**—True if string `s` is a valid email address.
- **`isYear(s,ok_if_empty?)`**—True if string `s` is a valid year number.
- **`isIntegerInRange(s,a,b,ok_if_empty?)`**—True if string `s` is an integer between `a` and `b`, inclusive.
- **`isMonth(s,ok_if_empty?)`**—True if string `s` is a valid month between 1 and 12.
- **`isDay(s,ok_if_empty?)`**—True if string `s` is a valid day between 1 and 31.
- **`daysInFebruary(year)`**—Returns number of days in February of that year.
- **`isDate(year,month,day)`**—True if string arguments form a valid date.

Data Formatting Functions

As you saw with the JavaScript example presented in the beginning of this chapter, it is often necessary or desirable to reformat information entered into the XHTML Form text fields, either before processing it or afterward for redisplay. By doing this, it is possible to strip dollar signs or commas from entered currency amounts, format phone number or credit card numbers to display in a uniform way, or to perform any other function meant to manipulate data for processing or display. The following list identifies the JavaScripts available from the Netscape Web site for doing these functions:

- **`stripCharsInBag(s,bag)`**—Removes all characters in string `bag` from string `s`.
- **`stripCharsNotInBag(s,bag)`**—Removes all characters *not* in string `bag` from string `s`.
- **`stripWhitespace(s)`**—Removes all whitespace characters from `s`.
- **`stripInitialWhitespace(s)`**—Removes leading whitespace characters from `s`.
- **`reformat(target,[string,integer,...])`**—Function for inserting formatting characters or delimiters into target string.
- **`reformatZIPCode(ZIPString)`**—If nine digits, inserts separator hyphen.
- **`reformatSSN(SSN)`**—Reformats as 123-45-6789.
- **`reformatUSPhone(USPhone)`**—Reformats as (123) 456-789.

User-Prompting Functions

Besides soliciting the user for input in the XHTML Form, it is possible to use the other methods and properties available to help the user correctly fill out the form. You can use Alert, Confirm, or Prompt boxes, for example, to inform the user of something or to solicit simple input. You can also make use of the status line at the bottom of the Web browser window. The following list identifies the JavaScript functions included in `FormChek.js` for doing this:

- **`prompt(s)`**—Displays prompt string s in status bar.
- **`promptEntry(s)`**—Displays data entry prompt string s in status bar.
- **`warnEmpty(theField,s)`**—Notifies user that required field `theField` is empty.
- **`warnInvalid(theField,s)`**—Notifies user that contents of `theField` are invalid.

XHTML Form Field Checking Functions

The following functions call some of the more basic functions previously described to directly check whether the contents of a given XHTML form field contain valid data of the appropriate type:

- **`checkString(theField,s,ok_if_empty?)`**—Checks that `theField.value` is not empty or all whitespace.
- **`checkStateCode(theField)`**—Checks that `theField.value` is a valid U.S. state code.
- **`checkZIPCode(theField,ok_if_empty?)`**—Checks that `theField.value` is a valid zip code.
- **`checkUSPhone(theField,ok_if_empty?)`**—Checks that `theField.value` is a valid U.S. phone number.
- **`checkInternationalPhone(theField,ok_if_empty?)`**—Checks that `theField.value` is a valid international phone number.
- **`checkEmail(theField,ok_if_empty?)`**—Checks that `theField.value` is a valid email address.
- **`checkSSN(theField,ok_if_empty?)`**—Checks that `theField.value` is a valid U.S. Social Security number.
- **`checkYear(theField,ok_if_empty?)`**—Checks that `theField.value` is a valid year.
- **`checkMonth(theField,ok_if_empty?)`**—Checks that `theField.value` is a valid month.
- **`checkDay(theField,ok_if_empty?)`**—Checks that `theField.value` is a valid day.
- **`checkDate(yearField,monthField,dayField,labelString, OKtoOmitDay)`**—Checks that field values form a valid date.
- **`getRadioButtonValue(radio)`**—Gets checked value from radio button.
- **`checkCreditCard(radio,theField)`**—Validates credit card information.

Credit Card Validation Functions

Finally, Netscape's `FormChek.js` form validation script collection contains a full set of JavaScripts to check that credit card numbers are well formed for a given credit card (remember that these checks do not necessarily apply to debit cards, however). The following list identifies and describes these functions:

- **`isCreditCard(st)`**—True if credit card number passes the Luhn Algorithm test.
- **`isVisa(cc)`**—True if string `cc` is a valid VISA number.
- **`isMasterCard(cc)`**—True if string `cc` is a valid MasterCard number.
- **`isAmericanExpress(cc)`**—True if string `cc` is a valid American Express number.
- **`isDinersClub(cc)`**—True if string `cc` is a valid Diner's Club number.
- **`isCarteBlanche(cc)`**—True if string `cc` is a valid Carte Blanche number.
- **`isDiscover(cc)`**—True if string `cc` is a valid Discover card number.
- **`isEnRoute(cc)`**—True if string `cc` is a valid enRoute card number.
- **`isJCB(cc)`**—True if string `cc` is a valid JCB card number.
- **`isAnyCard(cc)`**—True if string `cc` is a valid card number for any of the accepted types.
- **`isCardMatch(Type,Number)`**—True if number is valid for credit card of type.

FormChek JavaScript Collection Example

Along with the `FormChek.js` JavaScript source file for forms validation, Netscape has a number of sample XHTML documents that exercise the JavaScript functions. These functions, and the way they are implemented, provide a good example of ways to create smart XHTML forms with JavaScript.

Figure 21.9 shows one of the sample XHTML documents, which shows a partially filled-out form. Notice that the zip code and phone number have been formatted using a standard format. The data was not entered into those fields in that format—JavaScript functions were called to reformat and redisplay those fields in that standard format.

You should notice one other thing about Figure 21.9. Notice that the cursor is located in the Email field and that the status line of the Web browser window contains the text, "Please enter a valid email address (like foo@bar.com)." This is a way of providing context-sensitive help to your user with a JavaScript that sets the `window.status` property—and thus the contents of the current status line—to an informative string for the current field being entered. This is done using the `onFocus` event of each `<input/>` element, as shown here:

```
<input type="TEXT" name="Email" onFocus="promptEntry(pEmail)"
                                onChange="checkEmail(this,true)" />
```

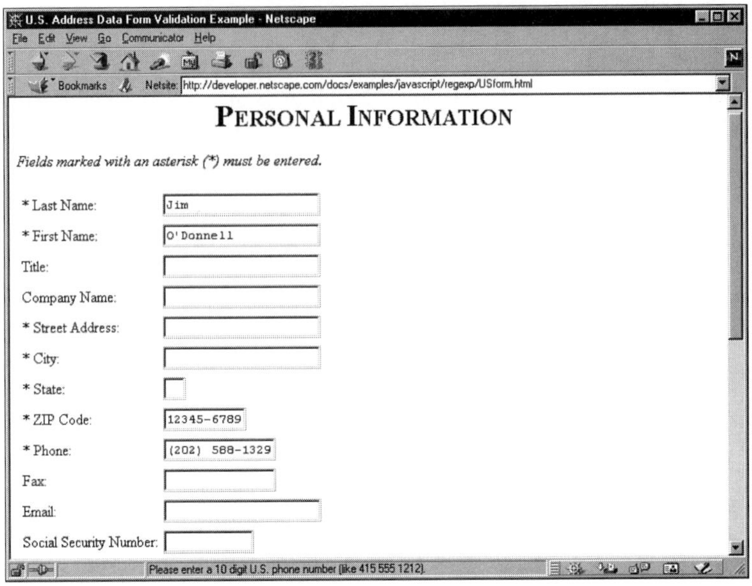

FIGURE 21.9
JavaScript can reformat your data to standardize the appearance of the information entered.

The `onFocus` event is triggered when the cursor enters the form field in question. When this happens, the preceding code calls the `promptEntry()` function, which is as follows:

```
function promptEntry(s) {
   window.status = pEntryPrompt + s
}
```

This function sets the status line to the passed string. (`pEntryPrompt` and `pEmail` are predefined global strings that, in this case, result in the status line shown in Figure 21.9.)

What about the other side of the equation? How does the entered information get validated? The `onChange` event triggers a call to the `checkEmail()` function, which is as follows:

```
function checkEmail(theField,emptyOK) {
   if (checkEmail.arguments.length == 1) emptyOK = defaultEmptyOK;
   if ((emptyOK == true) && (isEmpty(theField.value))) return true;
   else if (!isEmail(theField.value,false))
      return warnInvalid(theField,iEmail);
   else return true;
}
```

The `checkEmail()` function calls the `isEmail()` function with the contents of the Email field, which returns `true` or `false`, depending on whether it was found to be valid. If it was not valid, the `warnInvalid()` function is called, as shown in the following code, which displays the Alert box shown in Figure 21.10:

```
function warnInvalid(theField,s) {
   theField.focus()
   theField.select()
   alert(s)
   return false
}
```

FIGURE 21.10
The FormChek JavaScript routines display an Alert immediately when an invalid form field is found.

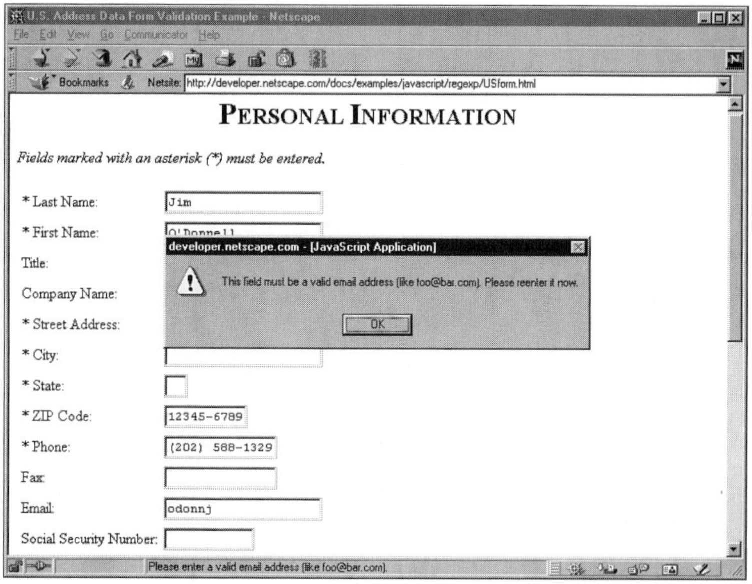

In addition to displaying the Alert box, `warnInvalid()` also moves the cursor to the field in question using the `theField.focus()` method, and then selects the current contents of the field with `theField.select()`. This makes it easy for you to edit the contents of the field (see Figure 21.11).

The `FormChek` routines also include credit card validation functions that perform the same prefix, length, and check digit tests as those discussed earlier in this chapter. As shown in Figure 21.12, these routines are not quite as forgiving if you enter a valid number with the wrong card type.

When you attempt to submit the form, it calls a routine that checks to make sure that you have input valid data in all the required fields. If you have not, you get an alert box that tells you about the first such field, and the cursor is moved to that field (see Figure 21.13). When you have finally completed all required elements of the form correctly, you can successfully submit the form; in this sample program, the dynamically generated XHTML document shown in Figure 21.14 results.

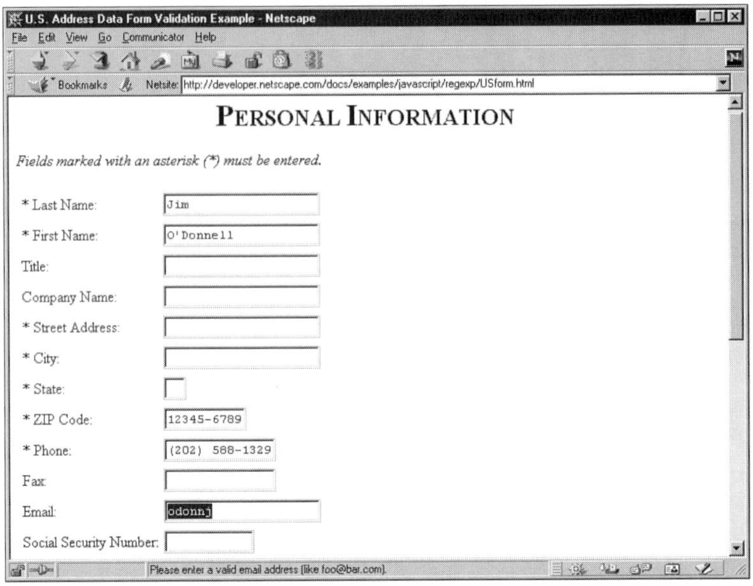

FIGURE 21.11
You can make it easy for your users to correct invalid fields by selecting the current contents.

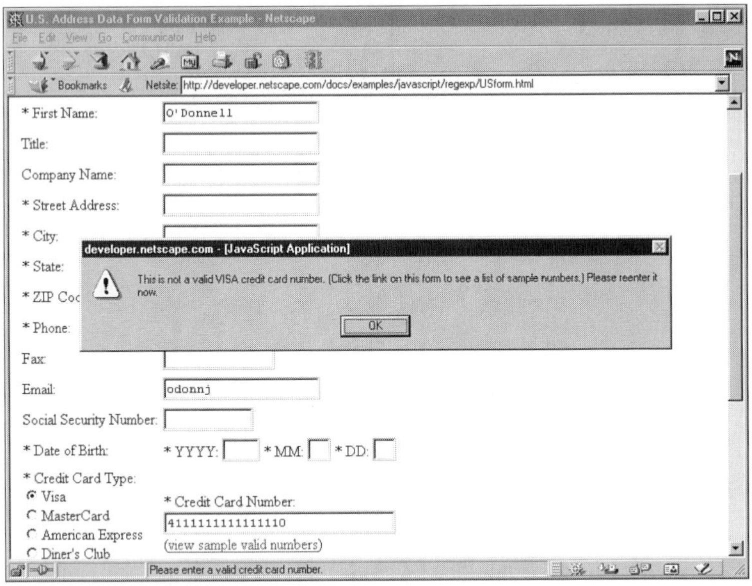

FIGURE 21.12
If the credit card number you enter is not a valid number for the selected card type, you will receive this Alert box and be given the opportunity to reenter the number.

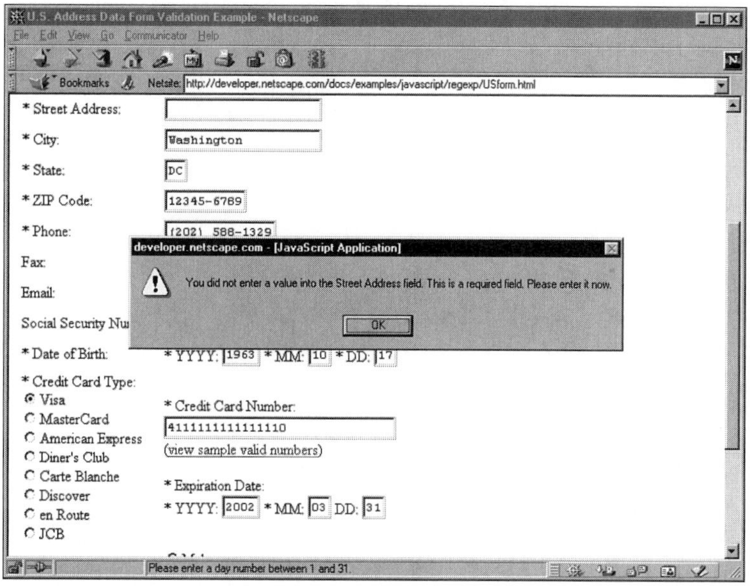

FIGURE 21.13
You can easily make any field in your form a required field and require your users to enter valid data there.

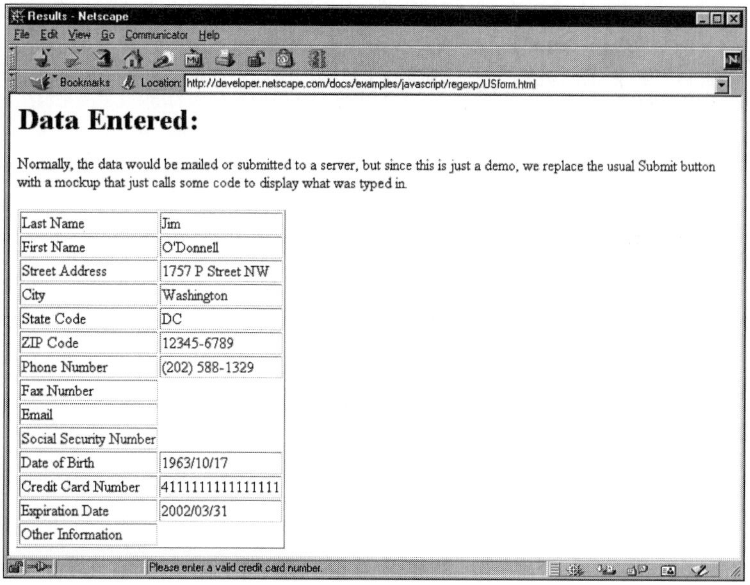

FIGURE 21.14
Upon successful completion of the form, its data can be submitted for processing.

CHAPTER 22

Cookies and State Maintenance

by Jim O'Donnell and Bill Chosiad

In this chapter

The Trouble with Stateless HTTP

Most Web servers have very short memories. When you request a page, the server usually doesn't really know who you are, what you entered on a form three pages ago, or whether this is your first visit to the site or your 75th. One of the challenges of using the Hypertext Transfer Protocol (HTTP) is that it doesn't track the state of your interactions with the server. *State* refers to any information about you or your visit to a Web site. It is maintained as you move from page to page within the site, and it can be used by the Web server or a JavaScript program (or both) to customize your experience at the site. But if HTTP doesn't maintain the state, what does?

This chapter shows you how to get around HTTP's limitations by using cookies, URL query string parameters, and hidden form variables. Although the bulk of this chapter deals with cookies, time is spent investigating other techniques, as well as where and how they can best be used.

Maintaining State

Maintaining state means remembering information while the user moves from page to page within a Web site. With this information in hand, you can set user preferences, fill in default form values, track visit counts, and do many other things that make browsing easier for users and that give you more information about how your pages are used.

You can maintain state information in several ways:

- Store it in cookies
- Encode it in URL links
- Send it in hidden form variables
- Store it in variables in other frames
- Store it on the Web server

Be aware, however, that some technical challenges regarding state maintenance can occur. While browsing a site, a user might suddenly zoom off to another Web site and return minutes, hours, or days later, only to find that any saved state information is out of date or has been erased. He or she might return by clicking the browser's Back button, by using a bookmark, or by typing in the URL directly, causing state information encoded in the URL to be overwritten or lost.

The Web developer must maintain state information regardless of whether the user navigates through the site using buttons on a form or a URL link on a page. This could mean adding information to both hidden form variables and every URL `<a href…>` tag that appears on the page.

With all these difficulties to overcome, these state maintenance mechanisms had better be useful. Luckily, they are. Many advantages exist to maintaining state both within a single site visit and from one visit to the next. Consider the following scenarios:

- **A shopping cart application**—Users can browse through the site while selecting items and adding them to a virtual shopping cart. At any time, they can view the items in the cart, change the contents of their cart, or take the cart to the checkout counter for purchase. Keeping track of which user owns which shopping cart is essential.
- **Custom home pages**—Many Web sites now have home pages where users can customize what they see when they arrive. After giving the user a choice of layouts, color schemes, and favorite destinations, the site stores the preferences on the user's own computer through the use of cookies. The user can return to the site any time and get the previously configured page.
- **Frequent visitor bonuses**—By storing information on the client computer, this application keeps track of how many times a browser has hit a particular page. When the user reaches a certain level of hits, he or she gets access to more or better services.
- **Change banners**—You can make graphic banners and text changes each time the user hits a page. This technique is often used to cycle through a list of advertisements.
- **Bookmarks**—These remember where a user was when he last visited the site. Was he reading a story, filling out a questionnaire, or playing a game? Bookmarks let him pick up where he left off.
- **Games**—These remember current or high scores and present new challenges based on past answers and performance.

Cookies: An Introduction

Cookies—sometimes called magic cookies, but more formally known as persistent client state HTTP cookies—enable you to store information on the client browser's computer for later retrieval. Although they have their drawbacks, cookies are the most powerful technique available for maintaining state within a Web site.

Netscape came up with the original cookie specification. There doesn't seem to be any good reason why Netscape chose that particular name. In fact, on its cookie specification page, Netscape even admits that "the state object is called a cookie for no compelling reason."

In their simplest form, cookies store data in the form of `name=value` pairs. You, the developer, can pick any name and value combination you want. More advanced cookie features include the capability to set an expiration date and to specify which Web pages can see the cookie information.

Advantages of Cookies

One of the most powerful aspects of cookies is their persistence. When a cookie is set on the user's browser, it can persist for days, months, or even years. This makes it easy to save user preferences and visit information and to keep this information available every time the user returns to your site.

Cookies prove especially helpful when used in conjunction with JavaScript. Because JavaScript has functions for reading, adding, and editing cookies, your JavaScript programs can use them to store global information about a user as she surfs through your Web site.

Limitations of Cookies

Some limitations of cookies could prove problematic. Cookies are stored on the user's computer, usually in a special cookie file. As with all files, this cookie file might be accidentally (or purposefully) deleted, taking all the browser's cookie information with it. The cookie file could be write protected, thus preventing any cookies from being stored there. Browser software could impose limitations on the size and number of cookies that can be stored, and newer cookies might overwrite older ones.

Because cookies are associated with a particular browser, problems come up if users switch from one browser to another. If you usually use Netscape Navigator and have a collection of cookies, they will no longer be available for you to use if you decide to switch to Microsoft Internet Explorer.

Finally, if several people use the same computer and browser, they might find themselves using cookies that belong to someone else. The reason for this is that cookie information is stored in a file on the computer, and depending on how the computer is set up, the browser might have no way to distinguish between multiple users.

Disadvantages of Cookies

Some problems, both real and imagined, also occur with the use of cookies. Because many browsers store their cookie information in an unencrypted text file, you should never store sensitive information, such as a password, in a cookie. Anyone with access to the user's computer could read it.

Newer Web browsers, such as the latest versions of Netscape Navigator and Microsoft Internet Explorer, have a feature that alerts the user every time an attempt is made to set a cookie. These browsers can even be configured to prevent cookies from being set at all. This sometimes results in confusion on the user's part when a dialog box informs her that something strange involving a cookie is happening to her computer. If cookies are disabled, your carefully designed Web application might not run at all.

Cookie Myths

The biggest problem facing cookies could be a psychological one. Some savvy Web users believe that all cookies are a tool used by "Big Brother" to violate their privacy. Considering that cookies are capable of storing information about where users have visited on a Web site, how many times they have been there, which advertising banners they have viewed, and what they have selected and placed on forms, some people think their privacy is being invaded whenever a cookie gets set on their computer.

In reality, cookies are seldom used for these purposes. Although technically these things are possible, the most common use of cookies is to give developers an easy way to customize their Web sites for everyone who visits them. A site can ask you for your name or ask you about some other preference once, and then store this information in a cookie; that way, the next time you visit the site, it doesn't have to ask you for this information again.

Other users complain about Web sites writing information to their computers and taking up space on their hard drives. This is somewhat true. Web browser software limits the total size of the cookies stored, as well as the amount of space that can go to the cookies of a particular Web site. Consider, however, that this number probably is small when compared to the size of the pages and graphic images that Web browsers routinely store in their page caches.

Other users are concerned that cookies set by one Web site might be read by other sites. This is completely untrue. Your Web browser software prevents this from happening by making cookies available only to the sites that created them.

If your users understand the usefulness of cookies, this "cookie backlash" shouldn't be a problem.

As mentioned previously, Netscape came up with the original cookie specification. You can find more information about cookies on the Netscape Web site at

`http://www.netscape.com/newsref/std/cookie_spec.html`

Using Cookies

By now you have considered the pros and cons of cookies and have decided that they are just what you need to make your JavaScript application a success.

This section discusses a number of handy functions for reading and setting cookies, which will help you make your Web sites smarter and more user-friendly. Also included in this section are Internet references for finding additional information concerning cookies.

Retrieving Cookie Values

Cookie names and values are stored and set using the cookie property of the document object. To store the raw cookie string in a variable, you can use a JavaScript command such as the following:

```
var myCookie = document.cookie;
```

To display it on a Web page, use the following command:

```
document.write("Raw Cookies: " + document.cookie + "<br />");
```

JavaScript stores cookies in the following format:

```
name1=value1; name2=value2; name3=value3
```

Individual `name=value` pairs are separated by a semicolon and a blank space. No semicolon is used after the final value. To retrieve a particular cookie, you can use a JavaScript routine such as the one shown in Listing 22.1.

Listing 22.1 *FavList.htm* (Excerpt)—JavaScript Function for Retrieving a Specific Cookie

```
//
// GetCookie - Returns the value of the specified cookie or null
//             if the cookie doesn't exist
//
function GetCookie(name) {
   var result = null;
   var myCookie = " " + document.cookie + ";";
   var searchName = " " + name + "=";
   var startOfCookie = myCookie.indexOf(searchName)
   var endOfCookie;
   if (startOfCookie != -1) {
      startOfCookie += searchName.length; // skip past cookie name
      endOfCookie = myCookie.indexOf(";",startOfCookie);
      result =
         unescape(myCookie.substring(startOfCookie,endOfCookie));
   }
   return result;
}
```

NOTE Most of the listings that appear in this chapter are excerpts from the `FavList.htm` document discussed in the section "A Cookie Example," later in this chapter.

In Listing 22.1, the `myCookie` string is created with a leading space and trailing semicolon; this helps avoid annoying boundary conditions by making sure all cookie string names start and end similarly. From there, it is easy to find the start of the `name=` portion of the string, skip it, and retrieve everything from that point until the next semicolon.

Setting Cookie Values

The `name=value` combination is the minimum amount of information you need to set up a cookie. However, there can be more to cookies than just this. The complete list of parameters, which should be separated by a space and semicolon, used to specify a cookie is as follows:

- `name=value`
- `expires=date`
- `path=path`
- `domain=domainname`
- `secure`.

Cookie Names and Values The name and value can be anything you choose. In some cases, you might want it to be very explanatory, such as `FavoriteColor=Blue`. In other cases, it could just be code that the JavaScript program interprets, such as `CurStat=1:2:1:0:0:1:0:3:1:1`. In any case, the name and value are completely up to you.

Listing 22.2 shows the simplest way to create cookies. The function `SetCookieEZ()` is a routine to add a single `name=value` pair to a cookie.

Listing 22.2 ***FavList.htm*** **(Excerpt)—Adding Cookies Is Easy with JavaScript**

```
//
// SetCookieEZ - Quickly sets a cookie which will last until the
//               user shuts down his browser
//
function SetCookieEZ(name,value) {
   document.cookie = name + "=" + escape(value);
}
```

Notice that the value is encoded using the JavaScript `escape` function. If there were a semicolon in the value string itself, it might prevent you from achieving the expected results. Using the `escape` function eliminates this problem.

Also notice that the `document.cookie` property works rather differently from most other properties. In most cases, using the assignment operator (=) causes the existing property value to be completely overwritten with the new value. This is not the case with the cookie property. With cookies, each new name you assign is added to the active list of cookies. If you assign the same name twice, the second assignment replaces the first.

Some exceptions exist to this last statement; these are explained in the "Path" section later in this chapter.

Expiration Date The `expires=date` property tells the browser how long the cookie will last. The cookie specification page at Netscape states that dates are in the form of

```
Wdy, DD-Mon-YY HH:MM:SS GMT
```

Here's an example:

```
Mon, 08-Jul-96 03:18:20 GMT
```

This format is based on Internet RFC 822, which you can find at `http://www.w3.org/hypertext/WWW/Protocols/rfc822/#z28`.

The only difference between RFC 822 and the Netscape implementation is that in Netscape Navigator, the expiration date must end with GMT (Greenwich Mean Time). The JavaScript language provides a function to do just that. By using the `toGMTString()` function, you can set cookies to expire in the near or distant future.

TIP Even though the date produced by the `toGMTString()` function doesn't match the Netscape specification, it still works under JavaScript.

If the expiration date isn't specified, the cookie remains in effect until the browser is shut down.

The following is a code segment that sets a cookie to expire in one week (where one week equals 7 days/week × 24 hours/day × 60 minutes/hour × 60 seconds/minute × 1000 milliseconds/second):

```
var name="foo";
var value="bar";
var oneWeek = 7 * 24 * 60 * 60 * 1000;
var expDate = new Date();
expDate.setTime(expDate.getTime() + oneWeek);
document.cookie = name + "=" + escape(value) + "; expires=" +
                  expDate.toGMTString();
```

Deleting a Cookie To delete a cookie, set the expiration date to some time in the past—how far in the past doesn't generally matter. To be on the safe side, a few days ago should work fine. Listing 22.3 shows a routine to delete a cookie.

Listing 22.3 ***FavList.htm*** **(Excerpt)—Use the Cookie Expiration Date to Delete an Unwanted Cookie**

```
//
// ClearCookie  - Removes a cookie by setting an expiration date
//                three days in the past
//
function ClearCookie(name) {
   var ThreeDays = 3 * 24 * 60 * 60 * 1000;
   var expDate = new Date();
   expDate.setTime(expDate.getTime() - ThreeDays);
```

Listing 22.3 Continued

```
    document.cookie = name + "=ImOutOfHere; expires=" +
                      expDate.toGMTString();
}
```

When deleting cookies, it doesn't matter what you use for the cookie value—any value will do.

CAUTION

Some versions of Netscape do a poor job of converting times to GMT. Some common JavaScript functions for deleting a cookie consider the past to be 1 millisecond behind the current time. Although this is usually true, it doesn't work on all platforms. To be on the safe side, use a few days in the past to expire cookies.

Path By default, cookies are available to other Web pages within the same directory as the page on which they were created. The `path` parameter enables a cookie to be made available to pages in other directories. If the value of the `path` parameter is a substring of a page's URL, cookies created with that path are available to that page. You could create a cookie, for example, with the following command:

```
document.cookie = "foo=bar1; path=/javascript";
```

This would make the cookie `foo` available to every page in the `javascript` directory and all those directories beneath it. If, instead, the command looked like

```
document.cookie = "foo=bar2; path=/javascript/sam";
```

the cookie would be available to `sample1.html`, `sample2.html`, `sammy.exe`, and so on.

Finally, to make the cookie available to everyone on your server, use the following command:

```
document.cookie = "foo=bar3; path=/";
```

What happens when a browser has multiple cookies on different paths but with the same name? Which one wins?

Actually, they all do. When this situation arises, it is possible to have two or more cookies with the same name but with different values. If a page issued all the commands listed previously, for example, its cookie string would look like the following:

```
foo=bar3; foo=bar2; foo=bar1
```

To help be aware of this situation, you might want to write a routine to count the number of cookie values associated with a cookie name. It would look something like this:

```
function GetCookieCount(name) {
   var result = 0;
   var myCookie = " " + document.cookie + ";";
   var searchName = " " + name + "=";
```

```
    var nameLength = searchName.length;
    var startOfCookie = myCookie.indexOf(searchName)
    while (startOfCookie != -1) {
       result += 1;
       startOfCookie = myCookie.indexOf(searchName,startOfCookie + nameLength);
    }
    return result;
}
```

Of course, if a GetCookieCount function exists, a GetCookieNum function should be available to retrieve a particular instance of a cookie. That function would look like this:

```
function GetCookieNum(name,cookieNum) {
    var result = null;
    if (cookieNum >= 1) {
       var myCookie = " " + document.cookie + ";";
       var searchName = " " + name + "=";
       var nameLength = searchName.length;
       var startOfCookie = myCookie.indexOf(searchName);
       var cntr = 0;
       for (cntr = 1; cntr < cookieNum; cntr++)
          startOfCookie = myCookie.indexOf(searchName,
                                           startOfCookie + nameLength);
       if (startOfCookie != -1) {
          startOfCookie += nameLength; // skip past cookie name
          var endOfCookie = myCookie.indexOf(";",startOfCookie);
          result = unescape(myCookie.substring(startOfCookie,endOfCookie));
       }
    }
    return result;
}
```

To delete a cookie, the name and the path must match the original name and path used when the cookie was set.

Domain Usually, after a page on a particular server creates a cookie, that cookie is accessible only to other pages on that server. Just as the path parameter makes a cookie available outside its home path, the domain parameter makes it available to other Web servers at the same site.

You can't create a cookie that anyone on the Internet can see. You can only set a path that falls inside your own domain. This is because the use of the domain parameter dictates that you must use at least two periods (for example, .mydomain.com) if your domain ends in .com, .edu, .net, .org, .gov, .mil, or .int. Otherwise, it must have at least three periods (.mydomain.ma.us). Your domain parameter string must match the tail of your server's domain name.

Secure The final cookie parameter tells your browser that this cookie should be sent only under a secure connection with the Web server. This means that the server and the browser must support HTTPS security. (HTTPS is Netscape's Secure Socket Layer Web page encryption protocol.)

If the `secure` parameter is not present, cookies are sent unencrypted over the network.

NOTE You can't set an infinite number of cookies on every Web browser that visits your site. The following list shows the number of cookies you can set and how large they can be:

- Cookies per each server or domain: 20
- Total cookies per browser: 300
- Largest cookie: 4KB (including both the `name` and `value` parameters)

If these limits are exceeded, the browser might attempt to discard older cookies by tossing out the least recently used cookies first. ■

Now that you have seen all the cookie parameters, it would be helpful to have a JavaScript routine set cookies with all the parameters. The `SetCookie()` function shown in Listing 22.4 does just that.

Listing 22.4 *FavList.htm* (Excerpt)—JavaScript Routine to Add a Cookie, Including Any Optional Parameters

```
//
// SetCookie - Adds or replaces a cookie. Use null for parameters
//             that you don't care about
//
function SetCookie(name,value,expires,path,domain,secure) {
   var expString =
      ((expires == null) ? "" : ("; expires=" + expires.toGMTString()))
   var pathString = ((path == null) ? "" : ("; path=" + path))
   var domainString =
      ((domain == null) ? "" : ("; domain=" + domain))
   var secureString = ((secure == true) ? "; secure" : "")
   document.cookie = name + "=" + escape(value) +
                     expString + pathString + domainString +
                     secureString;
}
```

To use this routine, you call it with whatever parameters are important to you and use null in place of parameters that aren't important.

A Cookie Example

The JavaScript program in this example is in the HTML document `FavList.htm`, which is available on this book's Web site at `www.mcp.com`. Excerpts of the program appeared in Listings 22.1 through 22.4; these showed the JavaScript functions used to create and manipulate the document cookies used in this example. Listing 22.5 shows the actual `<body>` section of the `FavList.htm` example, which enables the user to create a personalized "News-of-the-Day" page containing links to sites of general interest in a number of categories. The user's favorite links are stored in cookies.

Listing 22.5 *FavList.htm* (Excerpt)—The *<body>* Section of the Cookie Example

```
<body bgcolor="#ffffff">
<script type="text/javascript" language="JavaScript">
<!-- Hide script from incompatible browsers!
//
// Here's where we select the page to send. Normally we send the
// personalized favorites page (by calling SendPersonalPage). However,
// If the cookie ShowOptions is set, we'll send the options selection
// page instead (by calling SendOptionsPage).
//
if (GetCookie("ShowOptions") == "T") {
   ClearCookie("ShowOptions");
   SendOptionsPage();
} else
   SendPersonalPage();
//   Hide script from incompatible browsers! -->
</script>
<hr />
<h2>Current Document Cookie Contents...</h2>
<center>
<form name="MyForm">
<textarea name="MyTextArea" rows=1 cols=60>
</textarea>
</form>
</center>
<script type="text/javascript" language="JavaScript">
<!-- Hide script from incompatible browsers!
document.MyForm.MyTextArea.value = document.cookie;
//   Hide script from incompatible browsers! -->
</script>
<hr />
<em>Jim O'Donnell, <a href="mailto:jim@odonnell.org">jim@odonnell.org</a></em>
</body>
</html>
```

As shown in Listing 22.5, when this page is loaded, one of two JavaScripts is called to actually "fill" the page: either `SendOptionsPage()` or `SendPersonalPage()`. The former enables the user to select from a list of sites to be included as favorites; the latter is used to display those sites (or to display all the possible sites). Figure 22.1 shows this page when it is first loaded, before the user has selected a list of favorites (so all possible sites are shown).

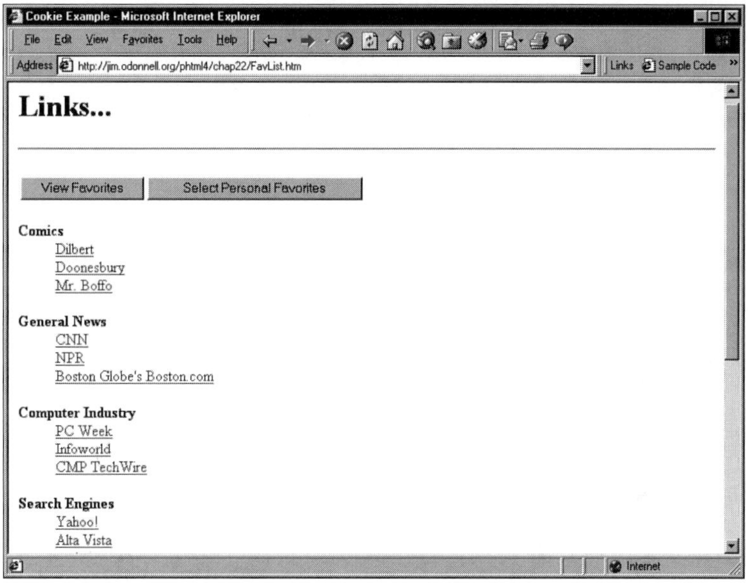

FIGURE 22.1
The Favorites page displays all possible sites when first loaded.

Before JavaScript, a task such as this would have been handled at the server. Each hit would have involved having the server run some type of script or program to read the user's cookies and generate his page on-the-fly. With JavaScript, all this processing takes place on the client's browser. The server just downloads the static page—and it might not even do that because the page might come from the client's local cache. When the page is loaded, all the links, selected or not, are sent. The client, with the help of cookies and JavaScript, decides which ones to show the user.

This program uses three cookies. The `Favorites` cookie contains a unique code for each favored link. The `ViewAll` cookie toggles between showing the user's favorites and all possible links. The program can also display either of two pages: one for displaying the selected links, and the other for changing the configuration and options. When the `ShowOptions` cookie is set, the Options selection page is displayed. Otherwise, the regular page is shown.

When the screen shown in Figure 22.1 is displayed after the page is first loaded, the value of the document cookie is

```
Favorites=null; ViewAll=T
```

This indicates that no favorites have been selected, but that all the options should be displayed. If View Favorites is clicked at this point, then the Document cookie is

```
Favorites=null
```

and the screen shown in Figure 22.2 is displayed—empty, because no favorites have been selected yet. Clicking the Select Personal Favorites button results in the screen shown in Figure 22.3, where favorites can be selected from the list of choices. One such selection might result in the Favorites list shown in Figure 22.4, which has the document cookie value of

```
Favorites=null%3Ccdilb%3E%3Csyah%3E%3Csav%3E%3Cmjod%3E%
```

NOTE The %XX encoding, such as the %3C and %3E shown above, is used for such symbols as semicolons, commas, and whitespace.

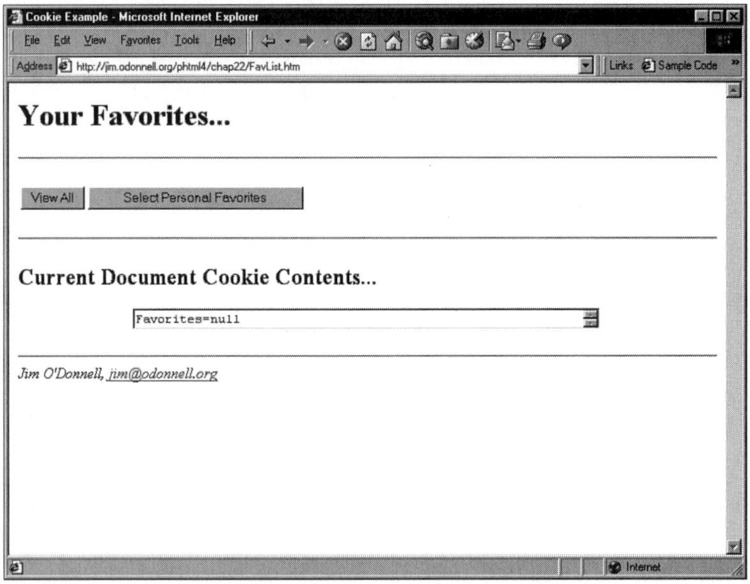

FIGURE 22.2
An empty Favorites list doesn't yield a very exciting Web page.

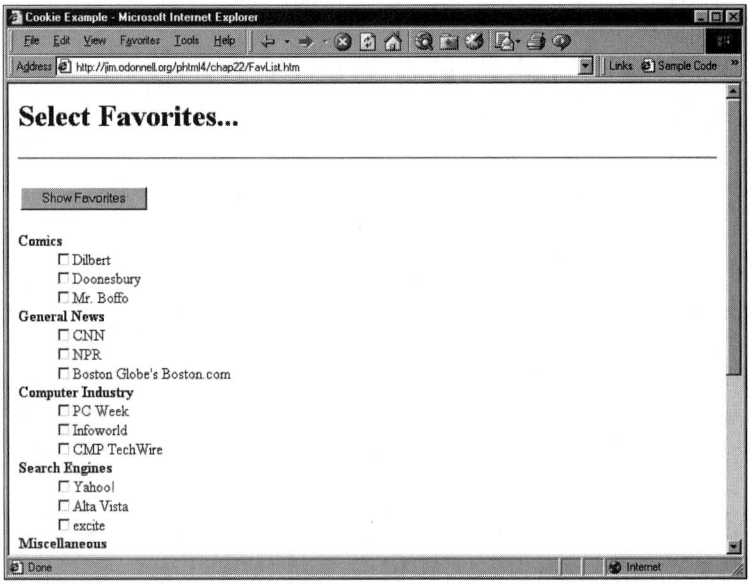

FIGURE 22.3
The Select Favorites page displays all the possible sites as check boxes and enables the user to select and deselect which to use as favorites.

When this list of favorites is created, any of them can be selected to load the corresponding Web page, as shown in Figure 22.5.

NOTE You might notice in Figures 22.2 and 22.4 that the current contents of the document cookie are displayed in a text area box at the bottom of the page. This is done in this example so you can see the changes to the cookie as they occur; in an actual "production" page, you probably wouldn't include it.

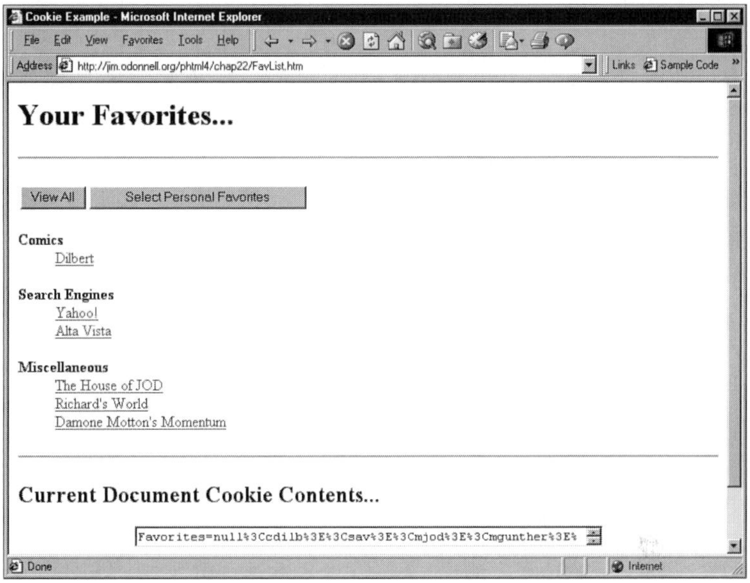

FIGURE 22.4
By enabling users to personalize their copy of your Web page, you allow a more personal experience without a greater burden on your server.

The program creates objects called *favorites*. Each favorite is, in essence, a Web link to another page. The favorite contains information on the link's URL, a user-friendly page description, and the code that identifies it in the Favorites cookie string. The favorite also knows how to print itself on a Web page as a regular link for the Favorites page or in a check box format for the Options page. The functions used to manipulate the cookies in the `FavList.htm` example were shown in Listings 22.1 through 22.5. The other functions used in this example are summarized in the following list (the full HTML source code for this example is available on this book's Web site:

- **`SendOptionsPage`**—Loads the Web browser with a page that enables the user to select which sites to be included as favorites.
- **`SendPersonalPage`**—Loads the Web browser with a page that shows either the user's favorites or all the sites as hypertext links.
- **`WriteAsCheckBox`**—Used by `SendOptionsPage` to display each potential favorite site as a check box, to enable the user to select or deselect it.

- **WriteAsWebLink**—Used by `SendPersonalPage` to display each site as a hypertext link.
- **LoadOptions**—This function is called to initiate the display of the options page.
- **ToggleView**—This function is called to toggle the personal page between displaying favorites and all sites.
- **favorite**—This function is used to create a JavaScript object that is used to store the information used to define a favorite site.
- **Enabled**—This JavaScript function is used as a method by the `favorite` object; it returns `true` if the link corresponding to this object is enabled.
- **Checked**—This JavaScript function is used as a method by the `favorite` object; it returns the string `CHECKED` if the link corresponding to this object is enabled.
- **isEnabled**—Returns `true` if the favorite identified by the `Name` parameter passed to the function is enabled.
- **AddFavorite**—Enables the favorite identified by the `Name` parameter passed to the function.
- **ClearFavorite**—Disables the favorite identified by the `Name` parameter passed to the function.
- **SetFavoriteEnabled**—Enables or disables the favorite identified by the `Name` parameter passed to the function by calling `AddFavorite` or `ClearFavorite`.
- **ReloadPage**—Reloads the Web browser with the current page; what is displayed, however, changes according to the current state of the Document cookie.

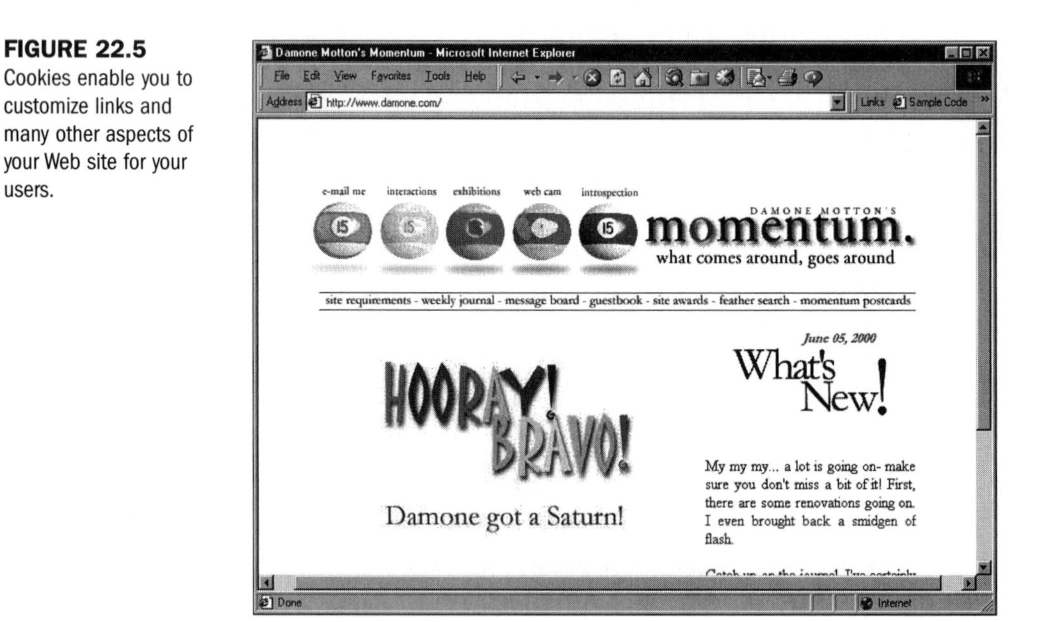

FIGURE 22.5
Cookies enable you to customize links and many other aspects of your Web site for your users.

Where Are Cookies Going?

As mentioned earlier, cookies were designed and first implemented by Netscape. However, the Internet Engineering Task Force (IETF) has a committee—the Hypertext Transfer Protocol (HTTP) Working Group—whose charter is to examine, document, and suggest ways to improve HTTP.

You can find a link to the HTTP Working Group's latest Internet Draft, called "Proposed HTTP State Management Mechanism," at `http://www.ietf.cnri.reston.va.us/html.charters/http-charter.html`.

Although the draft specification resembles Netscape cookies in theory, if not in syntax, it does have a few notable differences. It doesn't encourage having cookies around much longer than the browser session. If the new specification is accepted, cookies are given a `Max-Age` lifetime rather than an `expires` date. All cookies still expire when their time comes.

Reading the specification provides insight into the complexities that surround the inner workings of cookies; it is well worth the read, regardless of whether the specification is approved.

Which Servers and Browsers Support Cookies?

Although other ways of Web programming, such as CGI and special server interfaces, require that the server as well as the browser understand cookies, only the browser matters to JavaScript. This means, in general, that you can use JavaScript with impunity as long as you know your clients are JavaScript-capable and they run them with JavaScript enabled.

Many JavaScript Web applications probably mix the language with other development tools, however, which requires the server to understand cookies. Because new servers and browsers are coming to the net so quickly, it is impossible for a printed book to keep up with the latest software. You can find cookie information at the following locations on the Web:

- Netscape cookie spec page (referenced previously in this chapter):

  `http://www.netscape.com/newsref/std/cookie_spec.html`

- Browsers supporting cookies:

  `http://www.research.digital.com/nsl/formtest/stats-by-test/NetscapeCookie.html`

- Cookie Central:

  `http://www.cookiecentral.com/`

- Robert Brooks' Cookie Taste Test:

  `http://www.geocities.com/SoHo/4535/cookie.html`

- Article about tracking cookies from the HotWired Web site:

  `http://www.arctic.org/~dgaudet/cookies`

- Netscape World cookie article:

  `http://www.netscapeworld.com/netscapeworld/nw-07-1996/nw-07-cookies.html`

Other State Maintenance Options

As mentioned earlier in this chapter, a few drawbacks exist to using cookies. Perhaps you would rather just avoid the controversy and find some other way to maintain state from one page to the next. Two ways of doing this are available. Which one you use will depend on how you, the developer, will have the users get from one page to the next.

The main limitation of these methods is that they work only from one page to the page immediately following. If state information is to be maintained throughout a series of pages, these mechanisms must be used on every single page.

Query String

If most of your navigation is done through hypertext links embedded in your pages, you can add extra information to the end of the URL. This is usually done by adding a question mark (`?`) to the end of your Web page URL, followed by information in an encoded form, such as that returned by the `escape` method. To separate one piece of information from another, place an ampersand (`&`) between them.

If you want to send the parameters `color=blue` and `size=extra large` along with your link, for example, you use a link such as this:

```
<a href="MyPage.htm?color=blue&size=extra+large">XL Blue</a>
```

This format is the same as the format used when submitting forms using the `get` method. A succeeding page can read this information by using the `search` property of the `location` object. This property is called `search` because many Internet search engines use this part of the URL to store their search criteria.

The following is an example of how to use the `location.search` property. In this example, the name of the current page is sent as a parameter in a link to another page. The other page reads this property through the `search` property and states where the browser came from. Listing 22.6 shows the first page that contains the link.

Listing 22.6 *Where1.htm*—You Can Include Extra Parameters in the HREF to Pass State Information

```
<!DOCTYPE html PUBLIC "-//W3C//DTD XHTML 1.0 Transitional//EN"
    "http://www.w3.org/TR/xhtml1/DTD/xhtml1-transitional.dtd">
<html xmlns="http://www.w3.org/1999/xhtml">
<head>
<title>Where Was I? (Page 1)</title>
</head>
<body>
<h1>Where Was I? (Page 1)</h1>
<hr />
This page sets information that will allow the page to which it is
linked to figure out where it came from. It uses values embedded in
the link URL in order to do this.
<p>
We'll assume that any URL parameters are separated by an ampersand.
</p>
<p>
Notice that there doesn't need to be any JavaScript code in this page.
</p>
<p>
And now...
<a href="Where2.htm?camefrom=Where1.htm&more=needless+stuff">
   ON TO PAGE 2!!!
</a>
</p>
<hr />
<em>Jim O'Donnell, <a href="mailto:jim@odonnell.org">jim@odonnell.org</a></em>
</body>
</html>
```

Listing 22.7 shows the second page, which demonstrates how to use `location.search` to find where the browser came from.

Listing 22.7 *Where2.htm*—Access HREF Information Using the *window.location.search* Property

```
<!DOCTYPE html PUBLIC "-//W3C//DTD XHTML 1.0 Transitional//EN"
    "http://www.w3.org/TR/xhtml1/DTD/xhtml1-transitional.dtd">
<html xmlns="http://www.w3.org/1999/xhtml">
<head>
<title>Where Was I? (Page 2)</title>
</head>
<body>
<h1>Where Was I? (Page 2)</h1>
<hr />
This page reads information which allows it to figure out where it
came from.
<p>
```

Listing 22.7 Continued

```
<script type="text/javascript" language="JavaScript">
<!-- Hide script from incompatible browsers!
//
// WhereWasI - Reads the search string to figure out what link
//             brought it here.
//
function WhereWasI() {
//
// start by storing our search string in a handy place (so we don't
// need to type as much)
//
   var handyString = window.location.search;
//
// find the beginning of our special URL variable
//
   var startOfSource = handyString.indexOf("camefrom=");
//
// if it's there, find the end of it
//
   if (startOfSource != -1) {
      var endOfSource = handyString.indexOf("&",startOfSource + 9);
      var result = handyString.substring(startOfSource + 9,
                                          endOfSource);
   }
   else
      var result = "Source Unknown";
   return result;
}
if (WhereWasI() != "Source Unknown")
   document.write("You just came from <B>" + WhereWasI() + "</B>...")
else
   document.write("Unfortunately, we don't know where you came from...");
//   Hide script from incompatible browsers! -->
</script>
</p>
<hr />
<em>Jim O'Donnell, <a href="mailto:jim@odonnell.org">jim@odonnell.org</a></em>
</body>
</html>
```

Figures 22.6 and 22.7 show the two Web pages, demonstrating that the first was able to pass information to the second.

Hidden Form Variables

The method used in the preceding section works fine as long as the user navigates from one page to another using links. To do the same thing with forms, you can use hidden form variables rather than the `location.search` parameter.

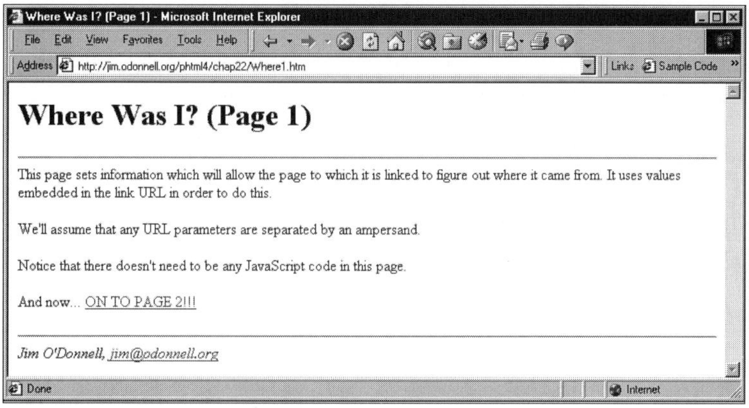

FIGURE 22.6
Extra information can be included in a hypertext link using the ? and # characters.

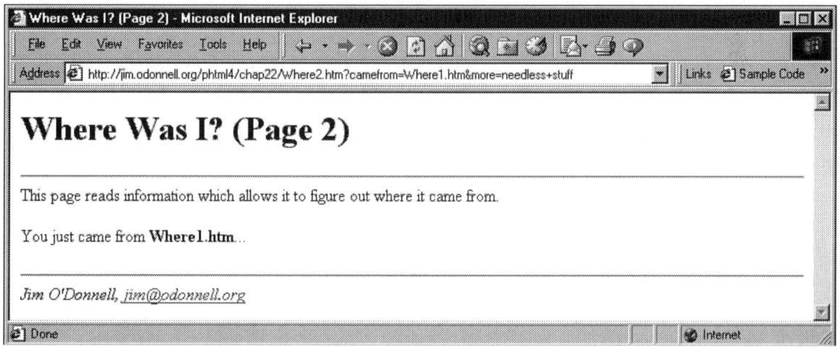

FIGURE 22.7
By including extra information in your hypertext links, you can enable some state information to be passed among pages in your Web site.

Hidden form variables have the following format:

```
<input type="HIDDEN" name="HiddenFieldName" value="HiddenFieldValue" />
```

You can specify whatever you like for `HiddenFieldName` and `HiddenFieldValue`.

Using hidden fields does not necessarily require the use of JavaScript code. They are defined, instead, in the <input/> tag of normal HTML documents. You normally will need to have a server-based script, such as a CGI program or a server API program, to read the values of these hidden fields. The form containing the hidden variables is submitted to a server script, which can then process the information for subsequent pages. It is possible to avoid the need for server processing of hidden form fields if you include them in a hidden frame, as well. (Chapter 18, "Introduction to JavaScripting," discusses how to use JavaScript to manipulate and reference multiple frames.) At this point, however—using hidden form fields in hidden frames—you're better off using cookies. ●

CHAPTER 23

Using JavaScript to Control Web Browser Objects

by Jim O'Donnell

In this chapter

What Are Web Browser Objects?

In Chapter 19, "The Document Object Model," you learned about the Document Object Model, which dictates how your JavaScripts can access and manipulate aspects of the Web browser and the HTML document that it is viewing. The Web browser, whether Netscape Navigator or Microsoft Internet Explorer, exposes a collection of objects—these objects control just how much you can do with your scripts. (As you will see in the next section, both Microsoft and Netscape extend their respective object models with their varieties of Dynamic HTML, which greatly extends the number of aspects of an HTML document that can be accessed and changed using JavaScript.)

▶ To learn more about Dynamic HTML in Netscape, **see** "Putting the "Dynamic" in Dynamic HTML with JavaScript," **p. 676**

▶ To learn more about Dynamic HTML in Internet Explorer, **see** "Internet Explorer Document Object Model," **p. 624**

In addition to the objects exposed that are part of the Web browser (such as the `window` object), part of the current HTML document itself (such as the `document` or `image` object), or supplied by JavaScript (such as the `Date`, `Math`, or `RegExp` objects), a number of other Web browser objects can occur within a Web page. These are objects included in the HTML document via the `<applet>`, `<embed>`, or `<object>` elements.

In general, the following types of content can be included in your Web pages by using one of these three elements. In many cases, although not all, the addition of this content provides additional objects that you can access and change with JavaScript.

- **JavaScript objects**—These are objects, such as the `Date` and `Math` objects mentioned in previous chapters, that the scripting language itself exposes to the Web browser that provide additional capabilities not directly native to the browser.
- **Java applets**—Java applets are normally included in a Web page using the `<applet>` element, although some browsers also support the use of the `<object>` element to include them. Both Netscape and Microsoft have provided ways to access Java objects, properties, and methods through JavaScript, and vice versa, as long as the Java applet is set up to do so. Netscape does this by using its LiveConnect technology, discussed later in the section "Netscape's LiveConnect." Microsoft provides the same functionality through its own ActiveX technology and Java Virtual Machine.
- **Plug-in content**—Normally, content that is in a form that is not natively supported by the Web browser is included in an HTML document by using the `<embed>` element. At the client browser, when this element is encountered, the appropriate plug-in and/or ActiveX Control is loaded. As with Java applets, if the plug-in is set up to do so, it can expose its properties and methods that can be accessed through JavaScript. Later in this chapter, you will see examples of how this is done with the Envoy Viewer from Tumbleweed Software and with Macromedia's Shockwave Flash Viewer.

Again, both Netscape and Microsoft provide this same functionality but use different methods. Netscape's LiveConnect technology enables JavaScript to access plug-in properties and methods through Java; Microsoft, which supports many of Netscape Navigator's plug-ins, enables scripts to interface with the plug-ins directly.

- **ActiveX Controls**—ActiveX controls are a technology developed by Microsoft; Microsoft's Internet Explorer is the only Web browser that fully supports them. As you will see in the section "Interfacing with ActiveX Controls with JavaScript," later in this chapter, it is easy to use scripts to control ActiveX controls.
- **VRML**—The Virtual Reality Modeling Language (VRML) 2.0 standard also supports scripting in general—and JavaScript in particular—through the use of its `Script` node. The way you include JavaScripts with a VRML source file is a lot different than in HTML and is beyond the scope of this chapter. To find more information, see the VRML Repository Web site at `http://www.web3d.org/vrml/vrml.htm`.

Referencing Web Browser Objects

After the objects have been included in your HTML documents, you need only to know how to reference them to access them from your JavaScripts. Objects supplied by Java applets, plug-in content, and ActiveX controls fit into the same Web browser object hierarchy discussed in Chapter 19. To use them, you must know where they fit.

▶ To learn about the object hierarchy, **see** "Web Browser Object Hierarchy and Scoping," **p. 460**

You can access these Web browser objects in many ways, depending on how they are included in your HTML documents. Objects exposed through the `<applet>` element can be accessed through the `applet` object. Plug-ins called by the `<embed>` element can be accessed through either the `embed` or the `plugin` object. Both these types of objects are included in the Document Object Model hierarchy under the `document` object. Objects that are included through the use of the `<object>` element are directly accessible by name through the `window` object. Because of the scoping rules of JavaScript, if you are controlling an object in the current window, the opening `window.` can be omitted.

▶ To learn more about the `window` object, **see** "The `window` Object," **p. 461**

Java Applets Using the *<applet>* Element

As mentioned earlier, Java applets placed in your HTML documents via the `<applet>` element can be referenced by using the `applet` object. Depending on how you include the `<applet>`, however, the object can be referenced a number of ways. Consider Listing 23.1, which shows a simple Web page with a controllable Java applet.

Listing 23.1 *Applet1.htm*—Controlling an Applet Using Its Name

```
<!DOCTYPE html PUBLIC "-//W3C//DTD XHTML 1.0 Transitional//EN"
    "http://www.w3.org/TR/xhtml1/DTD/xhtml1-transitional.dtd">
<html xmlns="http://www.w3.org/1999/xhtml">
<head>
<title>JavaScript Control of a Java Applet I</title>
</head>
<body bgcolor="#ffffff">
<h1>JavaScript Control of a Java Applet I</h1>
<hr />
<applet name="Counter" code="Counter.class" width="200" height="100"></applet>
<form>
<input type=button value="Add 1" name="AddButton"
       onclick="document.Counter.increment()" />
<input type=button value="Subtract 1" name="SubtractButton"
       onclick="document.Counter.decrement()" />
</form>
<hr />
<em>Jim O'Donnell, <a href="mailto:jim@odonnell.org">jim@odonnell.org</a></em>
</body>
</html>
```

As shown in Listing 23.1, the Java applet's `increment()` and `decrement()` methods are called through the JavaScript attached to the `onClick` event of the two HTML forms buttons. The applet's methods are accessed by referring to the Java `applet` object, which is included in the object hierarchy under the `document` object.

What if the applet isn't named? You can still access Java applets in your HTML documents, even if you don't specify a `NAME` attribute in the `<applet>` element. This is done using JavaScript's object arrays, in this case the `applets` array associated with the `applet` object. Listing 23.2 shows the same example as Listing 23.1, demonstrating how to reference the Java applet without using a name.

▶ To learn more about arrays, **see** "JavaScript Object Arrays," **p. 469**

Listing 23.2 *Applet2.htm*—Controlling an Applet Without Using Its Name

```
<!DOCTYPE html PUBLIC "-//W3C//DTD XHTML 1.0 Transitional//EN"
    "http://www.w3.org/TR/xhtml1/DTD/xhtml1-transitional.dtd">
<html xmlns="http://www.w3.org/1999/xhtml">
<head>
<title>JavaScript Control of a Java Applet II</title>
</head>
<body bgcolor=#ffffff>
<h1>JavaScript Control of a Java Applet II</h1>
<hr />
<applet code="Counter.class" width="200" height="100"></applet>
<form>
<input type=button value="Add 1" name="AddButton"
       onclick="document.applets[0].increment()" />
```

Listing 23.2 Continued

```
<input type=button value="Subtract 1" name="SubtractButton"
       onclick="document.applets[0].decrement()" />
</form>
<hr />
<em>Jim O'Donnell, <a href="mailto:jim@odonnell.org">jim@odonnell.org</a></em>
</body>
</html>
```


Because the Java applet is the only one in the HTML document, it is referenced through the first position in the `applet` object array, as `applets[0]`.

Plug-In Content from the *<embed>* Element

Accessing plug-in objects, properties, and methods included in an HTML document through the `<embed>` element is done in the same manner as with Java applets, which was discussed in the preceding section. Consider, for example, the following element included as the first embed in your HTML document:

```
<embed name="MyPlug" src="MyMovie.dcr" width="300" height="200"></embed>
```

If the plug-in that was called to support this content type exposed objects and methods to the Web browser and to JavaScript, you could access them in any of three ways. If the plug-in had an `initialize()` method you wanted to call, for example, you could do so by using one of the following:

- `document.MyPlug.initialize()`
- `document.embeds[0].initialize()`
- `document.embeds["MyPlug"].initialize()`

The last syntax shown is known as an associative array and was discussed in Chapter 18, "Introduction to JavaScripting." That chapter also discussed when each of the syntaxes in this list is most appropriate.

Accessing *<object>* Element Included Objects

By comparison with the `<applet>` and `<embed>` elements, objects included with the `<object>` element are a bit easier to reference with JavaScript. That is because these objects are attached to the `window` object, and therefore can be referenced directly. If, for example, an object were included in your HTML document using

```
<object name="MyControl"…></object>
```

and if it had an `initialize()` method, it could be called from JavaScript by using just `MyControl.initialize()`.

JavaScript Objects

The simplest objects that can be referenced and controlled via JavaScript are JavaScript's built-in objects. Strictly speaking, these objects are not part of the Document Object Model; instead, they are part of JavaScript itself. However, their properties and methods are used in the same manner. JavaScript includes a number of its own objects—three of the most useful are the `Date`, `Math`, and `RegExp` objects.

JavaScript objects, because they are outside the Web Browser Object Model hierarchy, are not the properties of any other object. In other words, to reference a JavaScript object, you need to use the object name itself instead of prefacing it with `window` or `document`, as shown in the next three sections.

Using the *Date* Object

The JavaScript `Date` object is the easiest way to use dates and times within your scripts. JavaScript's `new` statement is used to create an instance of the `Date` object. The following list shows some of the ways you can create the `Date` object:

- `today = new Date()` gives the current date.
- `birthday = new Date("October 17, 1963 13:45:00")`.
- `birthday = new Date(1963,9,17)`.
- `birthday = new Date(1963,9,17,13,45,0)`.

In the previous two examples, the general syntax is as follows:

```
newdate = new Date(year, month, day, hour, minute, second)
```

Note that the month is specified as an integer from 0 to 11, where 0 represents January and 11 represents December, and that the hour is in 24-hour format.

Table 23.1 shows some of the methods of the `Date` object.

Table 23.1 HTML *Date* Object Methods

Property	What It Does
`getYear()`	Returns the year
`getMonth()`	Returns the month
`getDate()`	Returns the day of the month
`getDay()`	Returns the day of the week
`getHours()`	Returns the hours
`getMinutes()`	Returns the minutes
`getSeconds()`	Returns the seconds

Table 23.1 Continued

Property	What It Does
`getTime()`	Returns the number of milliseconds since January 1970 00:00:00
`getTimezoneOffset()`	Returns the number of hours of time zone offset from GMT in the current location
`setYear(arg)`	Sets the year to `arg`
`setMonth(arg)`	Sets the month to `arg`
`setDate(arg)`	Sets the day of the month to `arg`
`setHours(arg)`	Sets the hours to `arg`
`setMinutes(arg)`	Sets the minutes to `arg`
`setSeconds(arg)`	Sets the seconds to `arg`
`setTime(arg)`	Sets the number of milliseconds since January 1970 00:00:00 to `arg`
`toGMTString()`	Returns a string representation of the date in GMT
`toLocalString()`	Returns a string representation of the date in the local time zone

Using the *Math* Object

JavaScript's `Math` object gives you access to various mathematical constants and functions. These are represented as properties and methods of the `Math` object. Table 23.2 shows the properties.

Table 23.2 HTML *Math* Object Properties

Property	What It Does
`E`	Returns the constant e
`LN2`	Returns the natural logarithm of 2
`LN10`	Returns the natural logarithm of 10
`LOG2E`	Returns the base-10 logarithm of e
`LOG10E`	Returns the base-2 logarithm of e
`PI`	Returns the constant pi
`SQRT1_2`	Returns the square root of 1/2
`SQRT2`	Returns the square root of 2

Table 23.3 shows the `Math` object methods, which are the different functions you can use.

Table 23.3 HTML *Math* Object Methods

Method	What It Does
`abs(x)`	Absolute value of `x`
`acos(x)`	Arc cosine of `x`
`asin(x)`	Arc sine of `x`
`atan(x)`	Arc tangent of `x`
`atan2(x,y)`	Arc tangent of `x,y`
`ceil(x)`	`x` rounded up to the nearest integer
`cos(x)`	Cosine of `x`
`exp(x)`	e raised to the `x` power
`floor(x)`	`x` rounded down to the nearest integer
`log(x)`	Logarithm of `x`
`max(x,y)`	Maximum of `x` and `y`
`min(x,y)`	Minimum of `x` and `y`
`pow(x,y)`	`x` raised to the `y` power
`random()`	Returns a random number
`round(x)`	`x` rounded to the nearest integer
`sin(x)`	Sine of `x`
`sqrt(x)`	Square root of `x`
`tan(x)`	Tangent of `x`

Listing 23.3 is a sample document that shows the `Math` object properties and exercises its methods. When an argument is passed to a `Math` object method that is outside its allowable values, such as trying to take the arccosine or arcsine of a number greater than 1, the method returns `NaN`, which means "Not a Number" (see Figure 23.1).

Listing 23.3 *Math.htm*—The JavaScript *Math* Object Gives Access to Many Advanced Mathematical Functions

```
<!DOCTYPE html PUBLIC "-//W3C//DTD XHTML 1.0 Transitional//EN"
    "http://www.w3.org/TR/xhtml1/DTD/xhtml1-transitional.dtd">
<html xmlns="http://www.w3.org/1999/xhtml">
<head>
<script type="text/javascript" language="JavaScript">
<!-- Hide script from incompatible browsers!
function evalMathFunc() {
    document.MathForm.absx.value    = Math.abs(document.MathForm.x.value)
    document.MathForm.acosx.value   = Math.acos(document.MathForm.x.value)
    document.MathForm.asinx.value   = Math.asin(document.MathForm.x.value)
    document.MathForm.atanx.value   = Math.atan(document.MathForm.x.value)
    document.MathForm.atan2xy.value = Math.atan2(document.MathForm.x.value,
                                                 document.MathForm.y.value)
```

Listing 23.3 Continued

```
     document.MathForm.ceilx.value    = Math.ceil(document.MathForm.x.value)
     document.MathForm.cosx.value     = Math.cos(document.MathForm.x.value)
     document.MathForm.expx.value     = Math.exp(document.MathForm.x.value)
     document.MathForm.floorx.value   = Math.floor(document.MathForm.x.value)
     document.MathForm.logx.value     = Math.log(document.MathForm.x.value)
     document.MathForm.maxxy.value    = Math.max(document.MathForm.x.value,
                                                 document.MathForm.y.value)
     document.MathForm.minxy.value    = Math.min(document.MathForm.x.value,
                                                 document.MathForm.y.value)
     document.MathForm.powxy.value    = Math.pow(document.MathForm.x.value,
                                                 document.MathForm.y.value)
     document.MathForm.random.value   = Math.random()
     document.MathForm.roundx.value   = Math.round(document.MathForm.x.value)
     document.MathForm.sinx.value     = Math.sin(document.MathForm.x.value)
     document.MathForm.sqrtx.value    = Math.sqrt(document.MathForm.x.value)
     document.MathForm.tanx.value     = Math.tan(document.MathForm.x.value)
}
//   Hide script from incompatible browsers! -->
</script>
<title>JavaScript Math Object</title>
</head>
<body bgcolor="#ffffff">
<h1>JavaScript Math Object</h1>
<hr />
<center>
<table border="1" width="90%">
<form name="MathForm">
<tr><th colspan="3">Math Object Properties</th></tr>
<tr><td>Constant e</td>
    <td>Math.E</td>
    <td><script type="text/javascript" language="JavaScript">
           document.write(Math.E)</script></td></tr>
<tr><td>Natural logarithm of 2</td>
    <td>Math.LN2</td>
    <td><script type="text/javascript" language="JavaScript">
           document.write(Math.LN2)</script></td></tr>
<tr><td>Natural logarithm of 10</td>
    <td>Math.LN10</td>
    <td><script type="text/javascript" language="JavaScript">
           document.write(Math.LN10)</script></td></tr>
<tr><td>Base 2 logarithm of e</td>
    <td>Math.LOG2E</td>
    <td><script type="text/javascript" language="JavaScript">
           document.write(Math.LOG2E)</script></td></tr>
<tr><td>Base 10 logarithm of e</td>
    <td>Math.LOG10E</td>
    <td><script type="text/javascript" language="JavaScript">
           document.write(Math.LOG10E)</script></td></tr>
<tr><td>Constant pi</td>
    <td>Math.PI</td>
    <td><script type="text/javascript" language="JavaScript">
           document.write(Math.PI)</script></td></tr>
```

Listing 23.3 Continued

```
<tr><td>Square root of 1/2</td>
    <td>Math.SQRT1_2</td>
    <td><script type="text/javascript" language="JavaScript">
           document.write(Math.SQRT1_2)</script></td></tr>
<tr><td>Square root of 2</td>
    <td>Math.SQRT2</td>
    <td><script type="text/javascript" language="JavaScript">
           document.write(Math.SQRT2)</script></td></tr>
<tr><th colspan="3">Math Object Methods</th></tr>
<tr><td>INPUT X and Y</td>
    <td>x = <input type="text" name="x" value="" size="20"
             onchange="evalMathFunc()"></td>
    <td>y = <input type="text" name="y" value="" size="20"
             onchange="evalMathFunc()"></td></tr>
<tr><td>Absolute value of x</td>
    <td>Math.abs(x)</td>
    <td><input type="text" name="absx" value="" size="20"></td></tr>
<tr><td>Arccosine of x</td>
    <td>Math.acos(x)</td>
    <td><input type="text" name="acosx" value="" size="20"></td></tr>
<tr><td>Arcsine of x</td>
    <td>Math.asin(x)</td>
    <td><input type="text" name="asinx" value="" size="20"></td></tr>
<tr><td>Arctangent of x</td>
    <td>Math.atan(x)</td>
    <td><input type="text" name="atanx" value="" size="20"></td></tr>
<tr><td>Arctangent of x/y</td>
    <td>Math.atan2(x,y)</td>
    <td><input type="text" name="atan2xy" value="" size="20"></td></tr>
<tr><td>x rounded up to nearest integer</td>
    <td>Math.ceil(x)</td>
    <td><input type="text" name="ceilx" value="" size="20"></td></tr>
<tr><td>Cosine of x</td>
    <td>Math.cos(x)</td>
    <td><input type="text" name="cosx" value="" size="20"></td></tr>
<tr><td>e to the power of x</td>
    <td>Math.exp(x)</td>
    <td><input type="text" name="expx" value="" size="20"></td></tr>
<tr><td>x rounded down to the nearest integer</td>
    <td>Math.floor(x)</td>
    <td><input type="text" name="floorx" value="" size="20"></td></tr>
<tr><td>Log of x</td>
    <td>Math.log(x)</td>
    <td><input type="text" name="logx" value="" size="20"></td></tr>
<tr><td>Maximum of x and y</td>
    <td>Math.max(x,y)</td>
    <td><input type="text" name="maxxy" value="" size="20"></td></tr>
<tr><td>Minimum of x and y</td>
    <td>Math.min(x,y)</td>
    <td><input type="text" name="minxy" value="" size="20"></td></tr>
<tr><td>x raised to the power of y</td>
    <td>Math.pow(x,y)</td>
```

Listing 23.3 Continued

```
    <td><input type="text" name="powxy" value="" size="20"></td></tr>
<tr><td>Random number</td>
    <td>Math.random()</td>
    <td><input type="text" name="random" value="" size="20"></td></tr>
<tr><td>x rounded to the nearest integer</td>
    <td>Math.round(x)</td>
    <td><input type="text" name="roundx" value="" size="20"></td></tr>
<tr><td>Sine of x</td>
    <td>Math.sin(x)</td>
    <td><input type="text" name="sinx" value="" size="20"></td></tr>
<tr><td>Square root of x</td>
    <td>Math.sqrt(x)</td>
    <td><input type="text" name="sqrtx" value="" size="20"></td></tr>
<tr><td>Tangent of x</td>
    <td>Math.tan(x)</td>
    <td><input type="text" name="tanx" value="" size="20"></td></tr>
</form>
</table>
</center>
<hr />
<em>Jim O'Donnell, <a href="mailto:jim@odonnell.org">jim@odonnell.org</a></em>
</body>
</html>
```

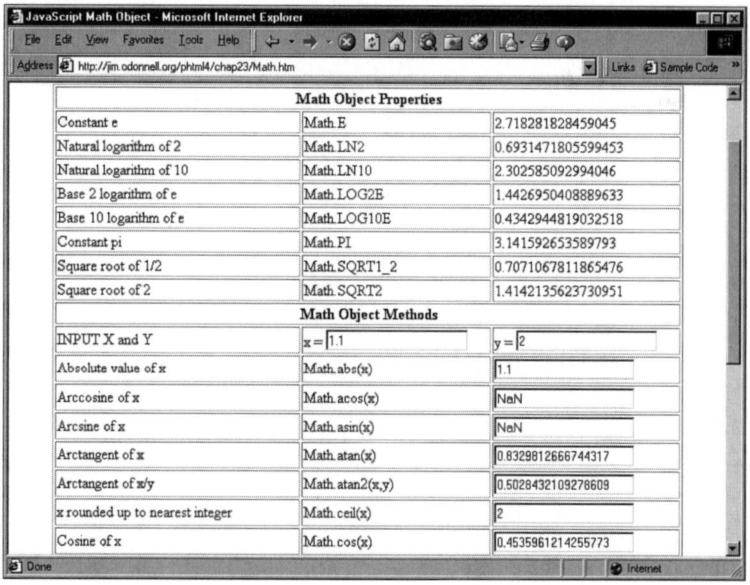

FIGURE 23.1
Just about any mathematical function you are likely to want to do in a Web page can be done through JavaScript or the JavaScript `Math` object.

Using the *RegExp* Object

If you are familiar with the UNIX `grep` utility or have spent any time using the Perl programming language, you know what a *regular expression* is. A regular expression is generally used for pattern matching, so even if you have never used them, you've probably used the `*` wildcard—a primitive sort of regular expression—when doing file searches or the like.

With JavaScript 1.2 and higher, Netscape added the `RegExp` object and thus added sophisticated pattern matching capabilities to JavaScript.

These capabilities enable you to do much more sophisticated string processing in JavaScript, and to do it much more easily. For example, recall Netscape's forms evaluation scripts discussed in Chapter 21. Netscape provides two versions of these scripts—the original versions and a later version that provides the same functionality using regular expressions.

▶ For more information about evaluation scripts, **see** "Netscape's Sample Form Validation Scripts," **p. 533**

Let's look at one of the simplest of the functions provided, the `isWhiteSpace()` function. The function to perform this check in the pre-regular expression version of the script looks like the following:

```
var whitespace = " \t\n\r";
//
function isWhitespace(s) {
   var i;
//
// Is s empty?
//
   if (isEmpty(s)) return true;
//
// Search through string's characters one by one
// until we find a non-whitespace character.
// When we do, return false; if we don't, return true.
//
   for (i = 0; i < s.length; i++) {
//
//    Check that current character isn't whitespace.
//
      var c = s.charAt(i);
      if (whitespace.indexOf(c) == -1) return false;
   }
//
// All characters are whitespace.
//
   return true;
}
```

With this script, it is necessary to step through the argument string character by character (done in the `for` loop), and check to see if each character is a whitespace character—one of the characters in the `whitespace` string variable. If every character is whitespace (or the argument string is empty), the function returns `true`, otherwise it returns `false`.

The JavaScript 1.2 and higher version, on the other hand, is much simpler:

```
var reWhitespace = /^\s+$/
//
function isWhitespace(s) {
//
// Is s empty?
//
   return (isEmpty(s) || reWhitespace.test(s));
}
```


Now, the whitespace variable is a regular expression, consisting of the following pieces:

- `/`—The slash character is used as the opening and closing delimiter for the regular expression, and is not a part of it.
- `^`—The caret is a regular expression special character that matches the beginning of the string being searched.
- `\s`—In a regular expression, `\s` matches a single character of whitespace.
- `+`—The plus sign is a count modifier in a regular expression, and means "one or more of the previous pattern." In this case, following the `\s`, it means "one or more whitespace characters."
- `$`—The dollar sign is a regular expression special character that matches the end of the string being searched.

So putting it all together, the regular expression `^\s+$` would match all strings that contain only whitespace (but contain at least one character of whitespace). So, using regular expressions, the function returns true if the string argument is either empty or if it matches the regular expression (tested using the `RegExp` object `test` method). It is interesting to note that the function could be simplified even further with the following:

```
var reWhitespace = /^\s*$/
//
function isWhitespace(s) {
   return reWhitespace.test(s);
}
```

By changing the `+` to a `*` in the `whitespace` regular expression, it now matches strings that consist only of "zero or more" whitespace characters; `*` is a count modifier similar to `+` except that it matches zero or more instances rather than one or more. Because the regular expression will now match empty strings, the `isEmpty()` test is no longer required.

Explaining all the aspects of regular expressions is well beyond the scope of this book. However, because the JavaScript `RegExp` object uses the same syntax as Perl regular expressions, you can read up on them in many other books about Perl. Netscape also maintains documentation of the RegExp object at `http://developer.netscape.com/docs/manuals/js/client/jsref/regexp.htm`.

Netscape's LiveConnect

Since its introduction, Netscape has introduced many new technologies into its Navigator Web browser. In addition to HTML extensions and multimedia capabilities, three technologies in particular were introduced, or first became widely used, with Netscape Navigator: Web browser scripting with JavaScript, Java applet support, and Web browser plug-ins.

Until the release of Netscape Navigator 3, these technologies suffered from the handicap of being completely separate applications within a Web browser. JavaScripts, Java applets, and Navigator plug-ins ran within Navigator on their own, without the capability to interact. However, with Navigator 3 and higher, Netscape has introduced its LiveConnect technology, enabling its three systems to interact.

Figure 23.2 shows how LiveConnect works within the Netscape Navigator runtime environment. JavaScripts can call Java methods and plug-in functions. Java applets can call both JavaScript and plug-in functions. Plug-ins can call Java methods and, through Java, call JavaScript functions. The objects and properties of each LiveConnect-compatible Java applet and plug-in are available to be manipulated through JavaScripts, applets, and other plug-ins.

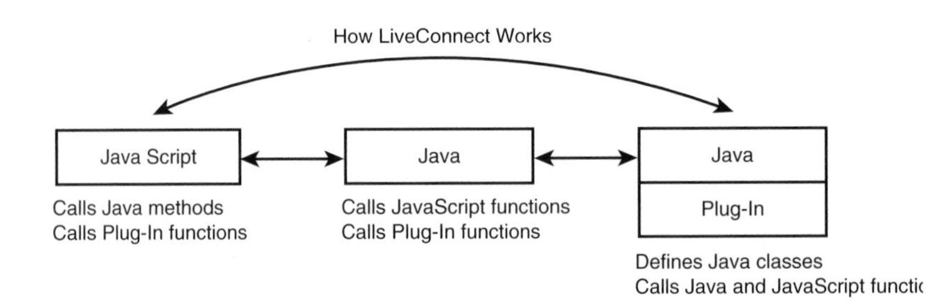

FIGURE 23.2 Netscape's LiveConnect technology enables JavaScript, Java, and plug-ins to work together within Netscape Navigator.

More extensive information on Netscape's LiveConnect technology is available on its Web site at `http://developer.netscape.com/docs/technote/javascript/liveconnect/liveconnect_rh.html`.

Enabling LiveConnect

By default in Netscape Navigator, Java and JavaScript are enabled—whenever these languages are enabled, LiveConnect is enabled as well. To confirm that they are enabled in your copy of Navigator, choose Edit, Preferences. Then, in the Categories list, select Advanced, make sure the Enable Java and Enable JavaScript boxes are checked, and then click OK.

What About Internet Explorer?

As you might expect, Microsoft Internet Explorer does not support the LiveConnect technology. However, this doesn't mean that Internet Explorer authors and users are left out in the cold. Far from it.

The foundation of Microsoft's Web offerings is its ActiveX and Dynamic HTML technology. These are a series of Web capabilities that enable authors to use scripting, ActiveX Controls, and Navigator plug-ins, and view and edit legacy documents (such as Microsoft Word documents) right in their Internet Explorer window. The ActiveX technologies were designed to enable the different components running within Internet Explorer to communicate with one another.

Although Internet Explorer does not support LiveConnect *per se*, its technology achieves the same thing. Later in this chapter, you will learn how to control ActiveX Controls within Microsoft Internet Explorer using JavaScript.

The Java Console

Netscape Navigator has a Java Console that can be displayed by choosing Communicator, Tools, Java Console. Messages sent using `java.lang.System.out` or `java.lang.System.err` appear in this console.

Now, because of the communication possible between JavaScript and Java using LiveConnect, messages can be sent to the Java Console from JavaScript as well. To write a message to the Java Console from JavaScript, use the `println` method of `java.lang.System.out` or `java.lang.System.err`, as in the following:

```
java.lang.System.err.println("JavaScript checkpoint #1")
```

TIP You can use the Java Console to help debug JavaScript applications. Output messages and intermediate values to the Java Console and watch it while browsing your pages. If you create JavaScripts to validate HTML forms, for instance, while you are debugging the scripts, you can print out intermediate form data to the console.

The Netscape Packages

Netscape Navigator includes several Java packages used to enable LiveConnect communication. The first, `netscape`, is used to enable communication back and forth between JavaScript and Java applets. Additionally, replacement `java` and `sun` packages are provided. These feature security improvements for LiveConnect. The following `netscape` packages are included:

- **`netscape.javascript`**—This package implements the `JSObject` and `JSException` classes, which enable Java applets to access JavaScript properties and throw exceptions when JavaScript returns an error.
- **`netscape.plug-in`**—This package implements the `Plugin` class, which enables cross communication between JavaScript and plug-ins. Plug-ins must be compiled with this class to make them LiveConnect compatible.

- **netscape.applet** and **netscape.net**—These are direct replacements for the sun.applet and sun.net classes provided in Sun's Java Development Kit.

▶ To learn more about Java classes and packages, **see** "Leveraging Java Classes and Packages," **p. 1012**

JavaScript to Java Communication

With LiveConnect, JavaScript can make calls directly to Java methods. As already shown in the "The Java Console" section, this is how JavaScript can output messages to the Java Console. To JavaScript, all Java packages and classes are properties of the packages object. Therefore, the full name of a Java object in JavaScript would be something like packages.packageName.className.methodName.

TIP The packages name is optional for the java, sun, and netscape packages.

Java applets can be controlled through JavaScript without knowing too much about the internal construction of the applet, as long as a few conditions are true. The first step is to attach a name attribute to the <applet> element when including the Java applet in your HTML document. Then all public variables, methods, and properties of the applet are available for access to JavaScript.

Any time you want to pass information into a Java applet, you might want to consider using JavaScript to do this. If you have a Java applet that implements a calendar, for example, you could create an HTML form with attached JavaScripts to enable the user to select what month should be displayed. By using JavaScript in this way, you avoid the need to give the applet itself the capability to interact with the user. Netscape shows a simple demo of controlling a Java applet by using JavaScript at http://developer.netscape.com/docs/technote/javascript/liveconnect/Fade.html.

The Java applet is included in the HTML document by using the following:

```
<applet code="Fade.class" name="Fader" width="400" height="100">
<param name="text1" value="Look at this text carefully!" />
<param name="url1"  value="http://www.netscape.com" />
<param name="font1" value="Helvetica,PLAIN,36" />
</applet>
```

The name Fader attached to the applet is how the Java applet is controlled. When any of the parameters entered in the form elements are changed, one of the public Java methods of this applet (setFont, setText, setUrl, setAnimateSpeed, or setBackgroundColor) is called through its onChange event.

For this to work, therefore, the Java methods need to be defined as public methods. When called, each method takes the parameter supplied and changes the characteristics of the applet (see Figure 23.3). As an example, the `setText` method is defined as a public method, as shown here:

```
public void setText(int which, String text) {
    bgChange = true;
    thoughts.theThoughts[which] = text;
    thoughts.Reset();
}
```

FIGURE 23.3
JavaScript is LiveConnect's link between the HTML form user input and Java applets.

NOTE As mentioned a little earlier in this chapter, Internet Explorer achieves the same JavaScript to Java communication by using Microsoft's own ActiveX technology rather than Netscape's LiveConnect. Figure 23.4 demonstrates this, showing the same Netscape demo page in Figure 23.3 displayed instead in Internet Explorer.

However, this example also shows that Microsoft and Netscape don't quite have compatible versions of JavaScript. Although Internet Explorer enables you to change most of the parameters of the Fader applet, it does not support the JavaScript 1.2 `Font` object used to change the display font. ■

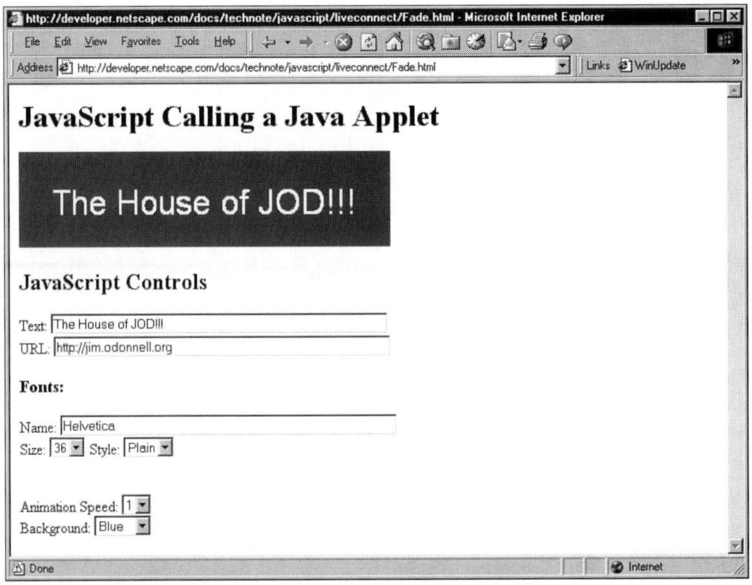

FIGURE 23.4
Microsoft accomplishes the same goal of JavaScript to Java communication with different means—but the same HTML and JavaScript will work with both browsers.

Java to JavaScript Communication

The first step in enabling your Java applets to access JavaScript properties is to import the `javascript` package into your Java applet, as shown here:

```
import netscape.javascript.*
```

This enables the Java applet to access JavaScript properties through the `JSObject` class. However, the author of the HTML document must still enable access to his JavaScript by including the `mayscript` attribute in the `<applet>` element used to include the Java applet. If the Fader used in the last example needed to access JavaScript, for example, the `<applet>` element would look like the following:

```
<applet code="Fade.class" name="Fader" mayscript="mayscript"
        width="400" height="100">
<param name="text1" value="Look at this text carefully!" />
<param name="url1"  value="http://www.netscape.com" />
<param name="font1" value="Helvetica,PLAIN,36" />
</applet>
```

If these two conditions have been satisfied, accessing JavaScript objects or methods is a two-step process, as follows:

1. Get a handle for the Navigator window containing the JavaScript objects or methods you want to access. This can be done using the `getWindow()` method of the `netscape.javascript.JSObject` package:

```
// winhan is a variable of type JSObject
public void initialize() {
   winhan = JSObject.getWindow(this);
}
```

2. To access JavaScript objects and properties, do the following:

   Use the `getMember()` method in the `netscape.javascript.JSObject` package to access each JavaScript object in turn. To access the JavaScript object `document.testForm` using the window handle found in step 1, you could do the following:

```
public void accessForm(JSObject winhan) {
   JSObject myDoc = (JSObject) winhan.getMember("document");
   JSObject myForm = (JSObject) myDoc.getmember("testForm");
}
```

3. To call a JavaScript method:

   Use either the `call()` or `eval()` method of the `netscape.javascript.JSObject` class. The syntax for the two commands (using the window handle found in step 1) is as follows:

```
winhan.call("methodName",arguments);
winhan.eval("expression");
```

   In the former, `methodName` is the name of the JavaScript method, and `arguments` is an array of arguments to be passed on to the JavaScript method. In the latter, `expression` is a JavaScript expression that, when evaluated, has a value that is the name of a JavaScript method.

Similar to JavaScript to Java communication, Java to JavaScript communication can be useful when you don't want to re-create an input or output interface within your Java applet. You might create a Java applet that makes use of Java's network and Internet capabilities to access data from a database server on some other machine. Rather than using Java to display this data, you can access JavaScript objects to display it within a conventional HTML form.

JavaScript and Plug-Ins

JavaScript can be used with the client to determine what plug-ins the client has installed and what MIME types are supported. This is done through the `navigator` object, through two of its properties: `plugins` and `mimeTypes`. JavaScripts can also be used to call plug-in functions.

NOTE Internet Explorer also supports the `navigator` object, so the techniques in this section should work for both Netscape Navigator and Microsoft Internet Explorer. Be aware, however, that Internet Explorer does not support all Navigator plug-ins. ■

By determining at the client whether a particular plug-in is installed or MIME-type supported, you can write scripts that generate content dynamically. If a particular plug-in is installed, the appropriate plug-in data can be displayed; otherwise, some alternative image or text can be shown.

If you have developed an inline VRML scene to embed in a Web page, for instance, you might want to know whether the user has a plug-in installed that supports VRML. Then, a VRML world or a representative GIF image could be displayed, as appropriate, such as the following:

```
<script type="text/javascript" language="JavaScript">
<!-- Hide script from incompatible browsers!
var isVrmlSupported,VrmlPlugin
isVrmlSupported = navigator.mimeTypes["x-world/x-vrml"]
if (isVrmlSupported)
   document.writeln("<embed src='world.wrl' height='200' width='400'></embed>")
else
   document.writeln("<img src='world.gif' height='200' width='400' />")
//   Hide script from incompatible browsers -->
</script>
```

NOTE As the next section shows, the `<object>` element is the preferred method of including plug-in content for Internet Explorer; Navigator uses `<embed>`. Internet Explorer does, however, support the `<embed>` element. ■

Including and Referencing Plug-In Objects

The first step in using plug-ins within a Web page is to include them in the first place. The recommended way to do this is to use the `<object>` element; however, both Internet Explorer and Navigator support the `<embed>` element as well. If you want to include plug-in content in a Web page that will work with browsers that support both elements, use something like the following, which shows an example using the Flash Player by Macromedia:

```
<object classid="clsid:d27cdb6e-ae6d-11cf-96b8-444553540000"
   id="objID" width="100" height="100"
   codebase="http://active.macromedia.com/flash2/cabs/swflash.cab
   ➥#version=2,0,0,11">
<param name="movie" value="controls.swf" />
<embed name="objID" mayscript="mayscript" src="controls.swf"
   width="100" height="100"
   pluginspage="http://www.macromedia.com/shockwave/download/index.cgi
   ➥?p1_prod_version=shockwaveflash">
</embed>
</object>
```

NOTE Note that the preceding example actually is used to either call the Macromedia Flash ActiveX control or plug-in, depending on whether Internet Explorer or Navigator is used. You can use the same technique, however, to include plug-in content for each browser. You can read more about accessing and manipulating ActiveX controls later in this chapter. ■

This HTML code segment consists of the following elements:

- The `<object>` element is used to include the plug-in content meant for Internet Explorer; its `id` attribute gives it the name that will be used to script it.
- The `<param>` element (there can be as many of them as necessary) includes a `name` and a `value` attribute used to configure the plug-in.
- The `<embed>` element is included within the `<object>` container element; this provides alternate content for browsers that do not understand the `<object>` element. In this case, the plug-in content would be included either via the `<object>` or `<embed>` element, but not both. The `name` attribute performs the same function as the `id` attribute of the `<object>` element—in this case, the `src` attribute.

Plug-ins included with the `<object>` and `<embed>` commands are also referenced differently. When included with the `<object>` element, plug-in objects are members of the `window` object; those with `<embed>` are members of `window.document`.

Determining Which Plug-Ins Are Installed

The `navigator.plugins` object has the following properties:

- **`description`**—A description of the plug-in, supplied by the plug-in itself.
- **`filename`**—The filename on the disk in which the plug-in resides.
- **`length`**—The number of elements in the `navigator.plugins` array.
- **`name`**—The plug-in's name.

Listing 23.4 shows an example of a JavaScript that uses the `navigator.plugins` object to display the names of the installed plug-ins right on the Web page. You can place this JavaScript at the bottom of any Web page to display this information (see Figure 23.5).

Listing 23.4 *PlugIn.htm*—JavaScript to Detect Locally Installed Plug-ins

```
<!DOCTYPE html PUBLIC "-//W3C//DTD XHTML 1.0 Transitional//EN"
    "http://www.w3.org/TR/xhtml1/DTD/xhtml1-transitional.dtd">
<html xmlns="http://www.w3.org/1999/xhtml">
<head>
<title>JavaScript Plug-Ins Check</title>
</head>
<body bgcolor="#FFFFFF">
<h1>JavaScript Plug-Ins Check</h1>
<hr />
<script type="text/javascript" language="JavaScript">
<!-- Hide script from incompatible browsers!
var i,n
n = navigator.plugins.length
document.writeln("<p>This Web browser has " + n + " plug-ins installed:</p>")
document.writeln("<p>")
```

Listing 23.4 Continued

```
for (i=0;i<n;i++)
   document.writeln(navigator.plugins[i].name + "<br />")
document.writeln("</p>")
//   Hide script from incompatible browsers -->
</script>
<hr />
<em>Jim O'Donnell, <a href="mailto:jim@odonnell.org">jim@odonnell.org</a></em>
</body>
</html>
```

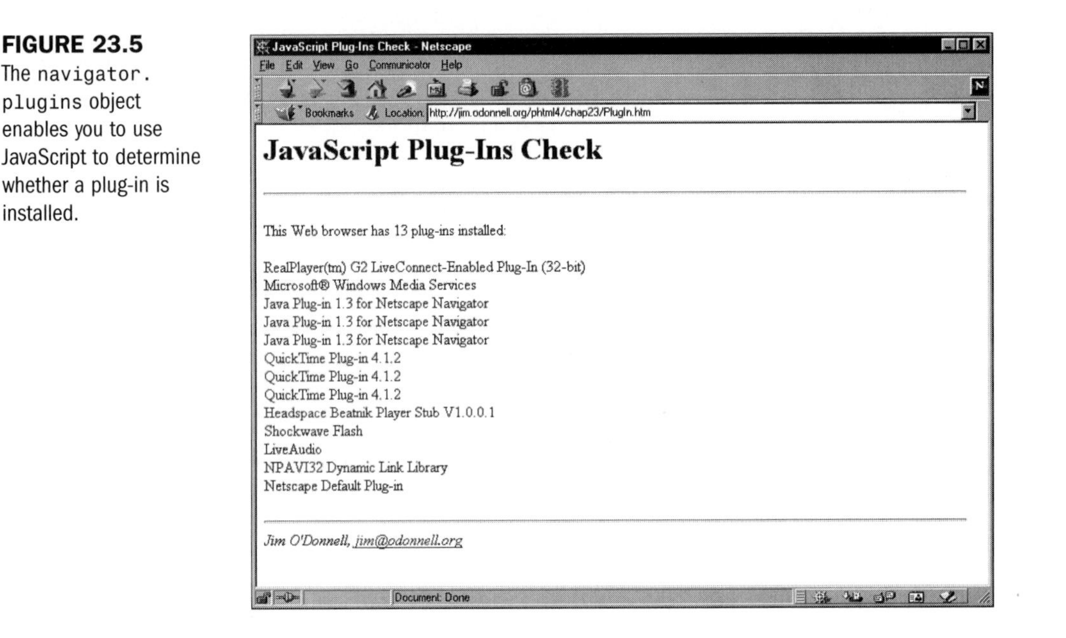

FIGURE 23.5
The `navigator.plugins` object enables you to use JavaScript to determine whether a plug-in is installed.

Client-Supported MIME Types

The `navigator.mimeTypes` object is similar to the `navigator.plugins` object and can be used to determine supported MIME types at the client. It has the following properties:

- **`description`**—A description of the MIME type.
- **`enabledPlugin`**—A reference to the particular `navigator.plugins` object that handles this MIME type.
- **`length`**—The number of elements in the `navigator.mimeTypes` array.

- **suffixes**—A string listing the filename extensions, separated by commas, for this MIME type.
- **type**—The MIME type name (for example, `x-world/x-vrml`).

Listing 23.5 shows an HTML document that contains a JavaScript that displays all the client-supported MIME types in an HTML table. Along with the MIME type, the supported file extensions are shown, as well as the name of the associated plug-in, if any (see Figure 23.6).

Listing 23.5 *MimeType.htm*—JavaScript to Detect Locally Supported MIME Types

```
<!DOCTYPE html PUBLIC "-//W3C//DTD XHTML 1.0 Transitional//EN"
    "http://www.w3.org/TR/xhtml1/DTD/xhtml1-transitional.dtd">
<html xmlns="http://www.w3.org/1999/xhtml">
<head>
<title>JavaScript MIME Types Check</title>
</head>
<body bgcolor="#FFFFFF">
<h1>JavaScript MIME Types Check</h1>
<hr />
<script type="text/javascript" language="JavaScript">
<!-- Hide script from incompatible browsers!
var i,n
n = navigator.mimeTypes.length
document.writeln("<p>The following MIME types are recognized:</p>")
document.writeln("<table border='1' width='100%'>")
document.writeln("<tr><th colspan='2'>MIME Type</th></tr>")
document.writeln("<tr><th>Extensions</th><th>" +
   "Associated Plug-In (if any)</th></tr>")
for (i=0;i<n;i++)
   if (navigator.mimeTypes[i].enabledPlugin)
      document.writeln("<tr><td colspan='2'><b>" +
         navigator.mimeTypes[i].type + "</b></td></tr><tr><td>" +
         navigator.mimeTypes[i].suffixes + "</td><td>" +
         navigator.mimeTypes[i].enabledPlugin.name + "</td></tr>" )
   else
      document.writeln("<tr><td colspan='2'><b>" +
         navigator.mimeTypes[i].type + "</b></td></tr><tr><td>" +
         navigator.mimeTypes[i].suffixes + "</td><td></td></tr>" )
document.writeln("</table>")
//  Hide script from incompatible browsers! -->
</script>
<hr />
<em>Jim O'Donnell, <a href="mailto:jim@odonnell.org">jim@odonnell.org</a></em>
</body>
</html>
```

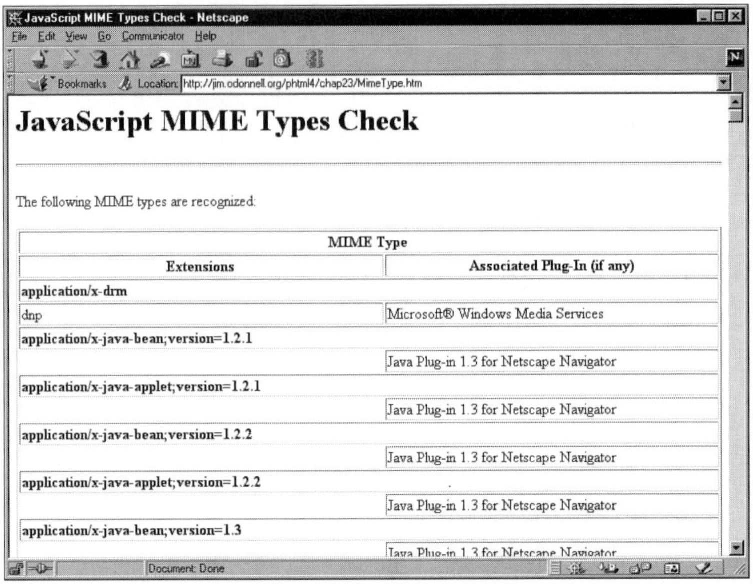

FIGURE 23.6
JavaScript can use the `navigator.mimeTypes` to determine the built-in MIME type support in the client Web browser.

Calling Plug-In Functions from JavaScript

For plug-in variables and methods to be accessible from JavaScript and Java applets, the plug-in must be LiveConnect compatible and associated with the `netscape.plugin.Plugin` Java class. If this is true, the plug-in variables and methods are available to JavaScript—in much the same way as the public variables and methods of Java applets are available.

JavaScript gives you two ways to access and control compatible plug-ins active in the Web environment. Similar to Java applets, the first is to use the `name` attribute of the `<embed>` element to give a name to the embedded document. This enables the plug-ins' functions to be accessed through the document object. If `name="myenvoydoc"` is used with the `<embed>` element to embed an Envoy document using the Envoy Plug-In Viewer, for example, you can access the viewer functions by using the `document.myenvoydoc` object.

It is possible to access plug-ins even if they are not named by using the `embeds` array of the `document` object. If an Envoy document is the first embedded document in the Web page, it can be accessed with `document.embeds[0]`.

Figure 23.7 shows a simple example from the Netscape site of an HTML forms button that calls a JavaScript used to start the LiveAudio plug-in. The plug-in content is included in the Web page with the following HTML code:

```
<embed src="suspens1.wav"
       hidden="TRUE"
       name="Mysound"
       mastersound="mastersound"
       autostart="yes"
       loop="no">
```

FIGURE 23.7
HTML forms and JavaScripts are the perfect combination for creating user interfaces to Java applets and plug-ins.

The JavaScript used to interface with the plug-in is

```
<input type="button" value="Play Sound" onClick="document.Mysound.play(false)">
<input type="button" value="Stop Sound" onClick="document.Mysound.stop()">
```

This example can be found at the following location on the Netscape site: `http://developer.netscape.com/docs/technote/javascript/liveconnect/js_plugin.html`.

NOTE Note that if you encounter problems running this example with Netscape Navigator, it is most likely because `.wav` files are not associated with the LiveAudio plug-in in your browser. You can check this by running the `MimeType.htm` example from Listing 23.5. ■

Using JavaScript to Control the Shockwave Flash Player

One of the more popular types of multimedia content to include in a Web page is content created for Shockwave using one of Macromedia's applications. Typically, Shockwave content is displayed using the Macromedia Shockwave Flash Player. This free player gives the user several options for viewing the content.

You can also use the methods of the Shockwave Flash Player to control precisely how your Shockwave for Director movie, for example, appears to your users. This is done by including JavaScripts that respond to timers or user input to control the display of your movie through the Flash Player. Following is a list of some of the more useful methods available from the Shockwave Flash Player:

- **`GotoFrame(frame_number)`**—Moves the player to the specified frame number.
- **`IsPlaying()`**—Returns `TRUE` or `FALSE`, depending on whether the movie is currently playing.
- **`Pan(x,y,mode)`**—If the movie has been zoomed in, this method enables you to pan right or left, up or down.

- **PercentLoaded()**—This method returns the percentage of the movie that has been downloaded so far.
- **Play()**—Starts playing the movie through the player.
- **Rewind()**—Rewinds the movie.
- **SetZoomRect(left,top,right,bottom)**—Zooms in on a rectangular area of the movie.
- **StopPlay()**—Stops the movie.
- **Zoom(percent)**—Zooms the movie by the specified percentage.

For more information on Macromedia Shockwave, you can visit its Web site at `http://www.macromedia.com`. You can find more specific information on controlling the Flash Player in your Web pages at `http://www.macromedia.com/support/flash/`.

Interfacing with ActiveX Controls with JavaScript

This is an example of using JScript, Microsoft's implementation of the JavaScript language, to manipulate another Web browser object, ActiveX Controls—in this case the ActiveX Label Control. ActiveX Controls are a Microsoft technology, similar to plug-ins, which enables developers to dynamically increase the capabilities of the Web browser. Many major software developers that produce plug-ins for Netscape Navigator produce ActiveX Control versions as well. Therefore, controlling ActiveX Controls would be done for many of the same reasons as for plug-ins. Many of the effects possible with ActiveX Controls (including those of the Label Control) are now possible using Dynamic HTML. Nevertheless, it is useful to learn how to interface with these controls via JavaScript.

The Label Control enables the Web author to place text on the Web page, and select the text, font, size, and an arbitrary angle of rotation. One of the exciting things about the Label Control is that it can be manipulated in real-time, producing a variety of automated or user-controlled effects.

In the following example, the Label Control is used to place text on the Web page, and form input is used to enable the user to change the text used and the angle at which it is displayed. Figure 23.8 shows the default configuration of the label and Figure 23.9 shows it after the text and the rotation angle have been changed.

Listing 23.6 shows the code used to produce this example. The following are some things to note about the example:

- The `<object>...</object>` container element is where the ActiveX Label Control is included and its default parameters assigned. The `classid` attribute must be included exactly as shown. The `id` attribute is the object name used by JavaScript to reference the Label Control object. The other attributes define the size and placement of the control.

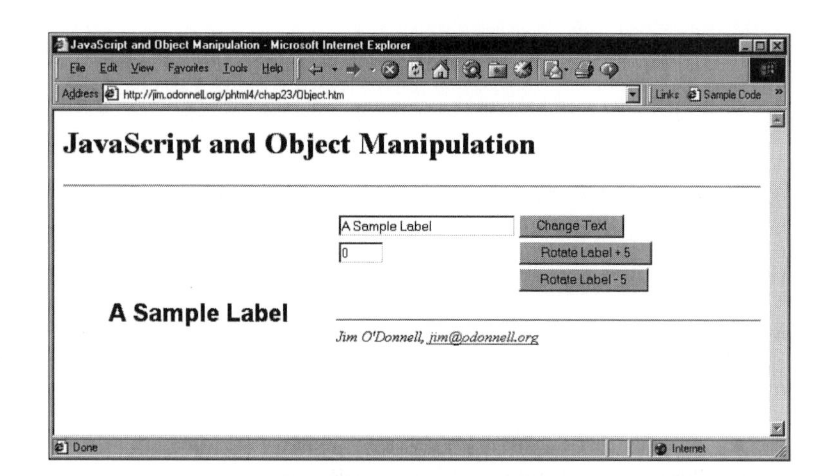

FIGURE 23.8
The ActiveX Label Control enables arbitrary text to be displayed by the Web author in the size, font, position, and orientation desired.

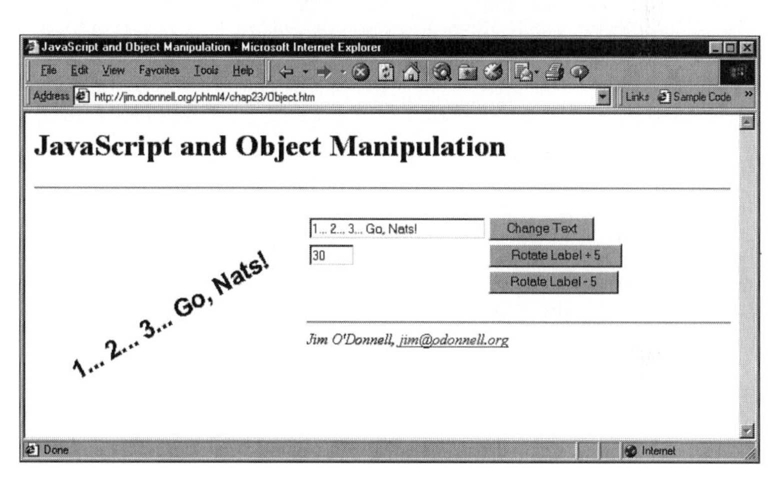

FIGURE 23.9
JavaScript's capability to manipulate Web browser objects enables label parameters to be changed dynamically.

- The `<param/>` elements within the `<object>...</object>` container enable the Web author to define attributes of the ActiveX Label Control. The `name`, `value` pairs are unique to each ActiveX Control and should be documented by the ActiveX Control author. For the Label Control, they define various aspects of the appearance of the label. The `name` is also used to manipulate the value with JavaScript.
- An HTML form is used to accept input and print output for information about the Label Control. The first text area is used to set the label text, and the second text area is used to output the current label text angle. The buttons call the appropriate JavaScript routine to change the label text or angle.
- One final note about the placement of the JavaScripts in this HTML document: The functions are defined in the `<head>` section—although not necessary, this is common practice so that they will be defined before use. Note that the last `<script>...</script>`

section, which initializes the value of the form text area showing the current angle, is placed at the end of the HTML document to ensure that the object is defined and value set before it is called.

Listing 23.6 *Object.htm*—JavaScript Can Interact with Objects

```
<!DOCTYPE html PUBLIC "-//W3C//DTD XHTML 1.0 Transitional//EN"
    "http://www.w3.org/TR/xhtml1/DTD/xhtml1-transitional.dtd">
<html xmlns="http://www.w3.org/1999/xhtml">
<head>
<script type="text/javascript" language="JavaScript">
<!-- Hide this script from incompatible Web browsers!
function ChangeIt() {
   lblActiveLbl.caption = document.LabelControls.txtNewText.value
}
function RotateP() {
   lblActiveLbl.angle = lblActiveLbl.angle + 5
   document.LabelControls.sngAngle.value = lblActiveLbl.angle
}
function RotateM(){
   lblActiveLbl.Angle = lblActiveLbl.Angle - 5
   document.LabelControls.sngAngle.value = lblActiveLbl.angle
}
//   Hide this script from incompatible Web browsers! -->
</script>
<title>JavaScript and Object Manipulation</title>
</head>
<body bgcolor="#ffffff">
<h1>JavaScript and Object Manipulation</h1>
<hr />
<object classid="clsid:99B42120-6EC7-11CF-A6C7-00AA00A47DD2"
        id="lblActiveLbl"
          width="250"
        height="250"
        align="left"
        hspace="20"
        vspace="0"
>
<param name="Angle" value="0" />
<param name="Alignment" value="4" />
<param name="BackStyle" value="0" />
<param name="Caption" value="A Sample Label" />
<param name="FontName" value="Arial" />
<param name="FontSize" value="20" />
<param name="FontBold" value="1" />
<param name="ForeColor" value="0" />
</object>
<form name="LabelControls">
<table>
<tr><td><input type="TEXT" name="txtNewText" size="25" /></td>
    <td><input type="BUTTON" name="cmdChangeIt" value="Change Text"
                 onclick="ChangeIt()" />
    </td></tr>
```

Listing 23.6 Continued

```
<tr><td><input type="TEXT" name="sngAngle" size="5" /></td>
    <td><input type="BUTTON" name="cmdRotateP" value="Rotate Label + 5"
               onclick="RotateP()" />
    </td></tr>
<tr><td></td>
    <td><input type="BUTTON" name="cmdRotateM" value="Rotate Label - 5"
               onclick="RotateM()" />
    </td></tr>
</table>
</form>
<script type="text/javascript" language="JavaScript">
<!-- Hide this script from incompatible Web browsers!
document.LabelControls.sngAngle.value = lblActiveLbl.angle
document.LabelControls.txtNewText.value = lblActiveLbl.caption
//   Hide this script from incompatible Web browsers! -->
</script>
<hr />
<em>Jim O'Donnell, <a href="mailto:jim@odonnell.org">jim@odonnell.org</a></em>
</body>
</html>
```

Dynamic HTML

CHAPTER 24

Introduction to Dynamic HTML

by Jim O'Donnell

In this chapter

What Is Dynamic HTML?

When HTML was first developed, its mixing of text and graphics, as well as the inclusion of the hypertext link for linking information, revolutionized the way information was presented and distributed across the Internet. Since the inception of HTML, Web developers and vendors have been looking for ways to present information more dynamically and to create more ways to interact with the user. Animated GIFs, Web browser plug-ins, ActiveX Controls, Java applets, and scripting languages are all examples of ways to make Web pages more exciting.

HTML itself is basically a static language, however; information is sent to a client Web browser, which renders it for the viewer. To add movement or animation to an HTML document, it was necessary to embed some other element. Macromedia's Shockwave, for example, has long been used to add increased animation and interactivity to many Web pages.

With version 4 of their Web browsers, however, both Netscape and Microsoft introduced a new technology, dubbed "Dynamic HTML," which sought to make HTML more interactive in its own right. Through this first version of each company's Dynamic HTML, Web developers had increased control over the appearance of an HTML document as rendered on a compatible Web browser. They also had more ways to make the document dynamic and interactive, capable of better detection and response to user actions.

What exactly is Dynamic HTML? Unlike the current state of such languages and technologies as HTML, XML, Java, and JavaScript, Dynamic HTML itself is not a standard; it isn't enacted, proposed, or even being developed by any Internet standards organization. Rather, Dynamic HTML is a term applied by both Netscape and Microsoft to a collection of technologies that they are developing for making HTML documents more dynamic and interactive. Although a few common elements exist, the question "What is Dynamic HTML?" has a different answer, depending on whom you ask, and even when you ask.

However, although there is no standard being developed for "Dynamic HTML," the foundation of Dynamic HTML is the Document Object Model (DOM) of the corresponding Web browser. The World Wide Web Consortium is working on developing DOM standards; both Netscape and Microsoft have pledged that their browsers wiil support these standards. In fact, in version 6 of its browser, Netscape has dropped support for all proprietary Dynamic HTML elements that it introduced in Navigator version 4, and has gone completely standards based.

The remainder of this chapter gives you an introduction to the different capabilities in Microsoft Internet Explorer and Netscape Navigator under the guise of Dynamic HTML, after a look at the work that the World Wide Web Consortium is doing on the Document Object Model standard. The next two chapters take a more in-depth look, first at Microsoft and then at Netscape Dynamic HTML. Finally, you'll finish this section by learning how to use Dynamic HTML to develop your Web pages so they are compatible with both browsers.

The World Wide Web Consortium's Answer

For the most part, the W3C considers the bulk of the Dynamic HTML implementations introduced by Netscape and Microsoft to be extensions to the Document Object Model (DOM). The W3C has undertaken the task of developing DOM standards. You can find out where it stands on Document Object Model standards by looking at `http://www.w3.org/DOM/`.

The W3C is approaching the development of a specification for the DOM in stages, or "levels," as the W3C calls it. Four levels are definitely planned, with further levels possible. Of these levels, two of the specifications are complete, one is at the "candidate recommendation" stage—meaning that it has been released in draft form for comment—and the final one is still in the development stage. As the W3C defines it, the four levels of the Document Object Model are as follows:

- **Level 0**—What W3C refers to as the Level 0 DOM refers to the functions and capabilities present in Netscape Navigator and Microsoft Internet Explorer as of version 3.0 of each browser.
- **Level 1**—The Level 1 specification deals mainly with core functionality and the HTML and XML document models. Accessing the elements in this DOM allows you to perform document navigation and content manipulation.
- **Level 2**—This level of the W3C DOM specification is at the candidate or draft stage. Its primary addition is a style sheet object model, allowing style information attached to a document to be changed. The Level 2 specification also contains an event model and greater support for XML.
- **Level 3**—The Level 3 specification, only in the very early development stage at the time of this writing, will address page loading and saving, content models, and support for validation. This level will also include support for document views and the formatting of documents, as well as enhanced event support.
- Further levels of the Document Object Model, if developed, might address more interfaces with the underlying display system, and more built-in methods for user interaction. There might also be further developments for query language support, security, and other advanced capabilities.

Development of specifications is one thing—support for these specifications is quite another. The W3C is not in the business of producing browsers for the consumer market—it does have a browser called Amaya, but its primary role is to be used as a test bed for new Web technology specifications and capabilities. So, the success of these specifications relies on support from vendors—primarily Microsoft and Netscape. Both of these companies have promised that their browsers will support the W3C standards. How well this support is implemented is something you'll learn more about as you read this chapter.

Microsoft's Answer

Microsoft's answer to the "What is Dynamic HTML?" question reveals a tremendous number of new possibilities and capabilities of its Internet Explorer Web browser. Microsoft has very good documentation for its technologies at its Microsoft Developers Network site, located at `http://msdn.microsoft.com`. The documentation for Dynamic HTML can be found at the Internet Explorer Developer Center at `http://msdn.microsoft.com/ie/`.

The elements listed there as being a part of Microsoft's version of Dynamic HTML are the following:

- **Dynamic HTML Document Object Model**—The heart of Microsoft's Dynamic HTML is its extensions to the Web Browser Object Model. As shown in Chapter 19, "The Document Object Model," previous object models for Netscape Navigator and Microsoft Internet Explorer enabled you to create scripts to interact with a small portion of HTML elements—images could be swapped, forms could be processed, hypertext links could be manipulated, and so on.

  With Microsoft's initial version of Dynamic HTML, it has extended its Document Object Model support to include every HTML element. Therefore, events such as responding to mouse movements or keypresses can be attached to any element in an HTML document. The format and style of any element on a page can be dynamically changed, either separately or as a group. Not only can the format be changed, but the actual contents of an HTML element can be changed—the text within a `<p>` paragraph container element can be changed on-the-fly, without going back to the Web server, in response to a user action or some other event.

  With versions of Internet Explorer subsequent to version 4, Microsoft has maintained the foundation of support for its own Dynamic HTML Document Object Model, which it refers to as the DHTML Object Model on the Microsoft developer support Web site. However, Microsoft has also increased its level of support for the official Document Object Model standards of the World Wide Web Consortium.

- **Dynamic Content**—Microsoft achieves *dynamic content*—the capability to change the displayed content of an HTML document without getting more information from a Web server—through its enhanced object model. Unlike Netscape Navigator, Internet Explorer also supports the dynamic redisplay of the content of a Web page when something on it has changed. Therefore, when something on a Web page is added, removed, or replaced, the other contents on the page automatically adjust themselves to display correctly.

- **Dynamic Styles**—As with Netscape, Microsoft's Dynamic HTML achieves the capability to dynamically change the style of the contents of an HTML document through style sheets and its object model. In Microsoft's Dynamic HTML, as implemented in its Internet Explorer Web browser, whenever the contents (as described in the preceding item in this list) or format of a Web page are dynamically changed, the rest of the document automatically reformats itself to display properly.

- **Positioning**—Microsoft uses CSS positioning and its object model to implement the precise positioning and repositioning of HTML elements. CSS formatting and positioning are the only aspects of Dynamic HTML that Netscape and Microsoft really share.
- **Data Binding**—Data binding is a way of attaching data from an external source to an HTML element. In addition to using special new attributes to certain HTML elements, data binding makes use of Microsoft's ActiveX Control Data Source Object. In this way, for instance, an HTML table can be filled with data from an external file, such as a flat ASCII file or database, through the Data Source Object. Methods of that object can then be called to sort the data using any of the columns of data.
- **Multimedia Effects**—Microsoft also uses its ActiveX Control technology to add multimedia effects to its Dynamic HTML. You can add filters to your document to create visual effects or use Microsoft's DirectAnimation system to easily add animations. The effects possible with Microsoft's filters and other technologies are similar to those offered by animated GIFs or Shockwave; because they are built into the Web browser, however, you can often achieve these possibilities much more simply.

In addition to the topics covered in the preceding list—the only technologies listed by Microsoft as part of its implementation of Dynamic HTML—Microsoft has other technologies that add related capabilities. For instance, Microsoft has its own system for embedding and downloading fonts into an HTML document. Although this technique is not technically considered part of Microsoft's Dynamic HTML, it is discussed in the "Dynamic Fonts" section later in this chapter and compared with Netscape's system.

Netscape's Answer...Part I

To complicate matters further, the answer from Netscape to the question "What is Dynamic HTML?" depends greatly on which version of the Netscape Navigator browser you are using. In going from Navigator version 4+ to its version 6 browser (Netscape completely skipped version 5), Netscape's approach to Dynamic HTML—along with many other aspects of the browser and its approach to Web technologies—completely changed. Netscape Navigator version 4 was centered around Netscape's proprietary `<layer>` element and its own object model; Navigator version 6—which is being developed using an open source model similar to that used to develop the Linux operating system—is completely based on the W3C's Web standards.

Because there are so many Navigator version 4 browsers extant, it is necessary to discuss both of Netscape's answers to what is Dynamic HTML. First, you'll learn about Netscape's first answer, and then a few words on its new approach.

Netscape's documentation for its first version of Dynamic HTML, along with a lot of other documentation, demos, and good information about Netscape software and technologies, is located on its DevEdge Online Web site, which can be found at `http://developer.netscape.com`. The specific URL for its Navigator 4 Dynamic HTML documentation can be found at `http://developer.netscape.com/tech/dynhtml/`.

According to this information, Netscape's answer to the question "What is Dynamic HTML?" would consist of the following elements, which were first introduced into Netscape Navigator version 4:

- **Style Sheets**—Microsoft first implemented support for Cascading Style Sheets (CSS), in its Internet Explorer version 3.0, and Netscape added it to its Web browser with version 4 and above. Both Netscape and Microsoft support the Cascading Style Sheets standard adopted by the World Wide Web Consortium (W3C). You can find these standards on W3C's CSS Web site.

  ▶ To learn more about style sheets, **see** "What Are Style Sheets?," **p. 262**

  Netscape considers style sheets a part of its implementation of Dynamic HTML because it has extended its Web Browser Object Model to include style sheets and styles attached to elements within an HTML document. This enables the formatting information for the content within the HTML document to be changed dynamically using JavaScript.

NOTE The Web site found at `http://www.w3.org/Style/` houses the W3C's complete Cascading Style Sheet definition, as well as a number of links you can follow to find out more. ■

- **Content Positioning**—With the early beta releases of Netscape Navigator version 4, Netscape introduced the `<layer>` and `<ilayer>` elements, which were the proposed HTML elements to allow for precise 2D and 3D positioning of elements within an HTML document. These elements were rejected by the W3C, although Netscape still supports them in the release version of its Web browser.

  With the rejection of the `<layer>` and `<ilayer>` elements, Netscape added support for what is known as CSS positioning. In addition to the formatting options that can be specified using style sheets, Netscape also includes support for positioning the elements to which they are attached. Whether you create your HTML elements to be positioned using the `<layer>` or `<ilayer>` elements, or whether you use CSS positioning, Netscape enables you to use JavaScript to reference those elements the same way, enabling you to dynamically change their positions.

- **Downloadable Fonts**—One problem with using style sheets to achieve your desired formatting effects is that they work only if your users have the same fonts installed on their local systems. If they do not, your carefully constructed Web page will be rendered using a font different from the one you intended, potentially destroying the desired effect.

  Netscape has developed a solution to this problem, which it groups as a part of its Dynamic HTML. It has added a way for you to set up and embed fonts in your HTML documents, which are then downloaded over the Web along with the document so that you can be sure it will be correctly rendered.

Other than the specific elements mentioned in the preceding list—which are also contained in the introductory section of Netscape's own Dynamic HTML documentation—Netscape has added other new features related to Dynamic HTML to version 4 of its Web browser. These include the changes to its JavaScript scripting language and to the Navigator Web Browser Object Model that supports these new capabilities.

Netscape's Answer...Part II

With the initial release of Navigator version 6, Netscape changed direction in the development of its Web browser, in many different ways. As mentioned previously, Netscape has approached development of Navigator 6 using the open source model, similar to the development of the Linux operating system. Using this model, any qualified programmer with access to the Internet can become involved in the development of the browser and the source code of the browser is publicly available.

As a part of this philosophy change, Netscape, and its cousin organization the Mozilla Project and mozilla.org, have embraced Web standards in its new Web browser. So, in Navigator version 6 and later browsers, Netscape's answer to "What is Dynamic HTML?" will match very closely—or at least is intended to match very closely—the Document Object Model and other specifications of the W3C.

Web Page Layout and Content Positioning

Because of their support for the W3C's CSS standard, most similarities between Netscape's and Microsoft's Dynamic HTML technologies occur with the elements that make use of style and style sheets. The main use of style sheets, discussed extensively in Chapter 9, "Style Sheets," is in the specification of formatting information for HTML elements. The benefit of using style sheets for this purpose is the capability of the Web page designer to separate the content of the document from its formatting information. (This makes it much easier to change the format while keeping the information the same.)

Another use of style sheet attributes is to perform positioning of HTML elements through the CSS positioning attributes. Both Microsoft and Netscape support these attributes in their Web browsers—although, as a relatively new standard, neither Web browser offers perfect support for them. This section focuses on how you can use style sheet attributes to specify positioning of HTML elements within a Web page. You will also see how to do this for Netscape Navigator 4 by using Netscape's `<ilayer>` and `<ilayer>` elements. Finally, you can learn how to create scripts that can dynamically change the positioning information and how to achieve a measure of cross-platform compatibility between the two flavors of Dynamic HTML.

CSS Positioning

The following list shows the most important style sheet attributes concerning positioning and manipulation of elements within an HTML document. Through the use and manipulation of these attributes, it is possible to precisely determine the two-dimensional positioning of everything within the Web browser window. In situations in which HTML elements overlap, it's also possible to specify the relative three-dimensional placement.

The list shows the name of the attribute, followed by its possible values, and a description of what it is used for. The default value for each attribute appears in **bold** type.

- `position`

  Possible values: absolute | relative | **static**

  This determines whether the element will accept further positioning attributes and whether they will be referenced absolutely to the Web browser window or relative to the location of the element on the page. If an element is `static`, it cannot be positioned further and will behave like a conventional, static HTML element.

- `left`

  Possible values: absolute length | percentage | **auto**

  Defines the left edge of the element, either with an absolute length or as a percentage.

- `top`

  Possible values: absolute length | percentage | **auto**

  Defines the top edge of the element, either with an absolute length or as a percentage.

- `width`

  Possible values: absolute length | percentage | **auto**

  Defines the width of the element, either with an absolute length or as a percentage.

- `height`

  Possible values: absolute length | percentage | **auto**

  Defines the height of the element, either with an absolute length or as a percentage.

- `clip`

  Possible values: bounding box | **auto**

  If specified, the bounding box gives the four numbers that define a rectangle that is the visible portion of the element.

- `overflow`

  Possible values: scroll | visible | hidden | **auto**

  Specifies how parts of the HTML element outside the visible area defined by the bounding box are displayed, if at all.

- `z-index`

  Possible values: stacking order | **auto**

  Determines the three-dimensional stacking order of HTML elements. The higher the `z-index` value, the farther to the front it is displayed.

- `visibility`

  Possible values: visible | hidden | **auto**

  You can use this attribute to make an HTML element visible or not visible.

NOTE By default, location and lengths in CSS attributes are given in units of pixels. You can specify other units by giving the unit abbreviation (for example, "1in"). ■

Listing 24.1 shows an example in Internet Explorer of how to position HTML elements—in this case, three copies of an image and a block of text—using CSS positioning attributes. Styles are defined for two of the images using an embedded style sheet, defined by the `<style>` element, and attached to the HTML elements using the `class` attribute (the third copy of the image uses the default style). The block of text is assigned style parameters using the `style` attribute of the `<div>` container element.

Listing 24.1 ***CssPos.htm*—Using CSS Attributes to Position HTML Elements**

```
<!DOCTYPE html PUBLIC "-//W3C//DTD XHTML 1.0 Transitional//EN"
    "http://www.w3.org/TR/xhtml1/DTD/xhtml1-transitional.dtd">
<html xmlns="http://www.w3.org/1999/xhtml">
<head>
<title>CSS Positioning</title>
<style type="text/css"> <!--
.sample1 {
   position: absolute;
   left: 100px;
   top: 100px;
   width: 150px;
   height: 150px;
}
.sample2 {
   position: relative;
   left: 275px;
   top: -300px;
   width: 200px;
   z-index: -1;
} -->
</style>
</head>
<body bgcolor="#ffffff">
<center>
<h1>CSS Positioning</h1>
<hr />
<img src="Tux.jpg" width="450" height="335" border="0" />
<br />
<img class="sample1" src="Tux.jpg" width="450" height="335" border="0" />
<br />
<img class="sample2" src="Tux.jpg" width="450" height="335" border="0" />
</center>
<br />
<div style="position: absolute; top: 1.75in; left: 1.5in;
            z-index: 4;color: yellow; font: 36pt Verdana">
   Works With Text, Too!
</div>
<hr />
<em>Jim O'Donnell, <a href="mailto:jim@odonnell.org">jim@odonnell.org</a></em>
</body>
</html>
```

NOTE All sample code listings from this book can be downloaded from the Macmillan USA Web site at `http://www.mcp.com`. Also, all sample code listings for the JavaScript and Dynamic HTML sections of the book can be found at the author's Web site at `http://jim.odonnell.org/phtml4/`. ■

This HTML document produces a Web page with three renderings of the same image and a block of text (along with the header and footer information identifying the example and author). As shown in Figure 24.1, one of these images is placed inline, the way images are conventionally placed within a Web page. The second image uses as its class name `sample1`, which attaches the corresponding style to it. As a result, this image is absolutely positioned 100 pixels down and to the left of the upper-left corner of the Web browser window. Also, because the width and height defined in the style are smaller than the actual width and height of the image, it is scaled to fit. Because no value for the `z-index` attribute is specified, this image appears above the first image defined.

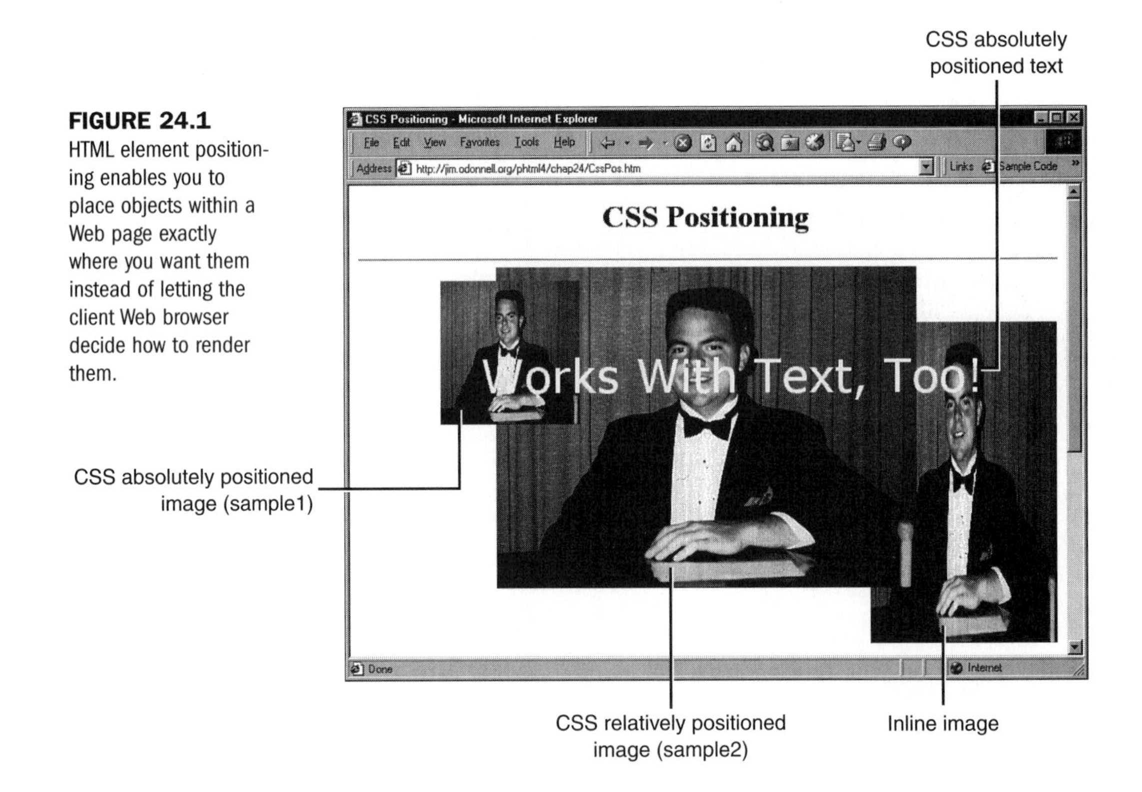

FIGURE 24.1
HTML element positioning enables you to place objects within a Web page exactly where you want them instead of letting the client Web browser decide how to render them.

The third image uses the style class `sample2`. This style defines a relative position for the image—defined relative to where the image would have appeared. This image would have appeared directly under the first inline image, so the `left` and `top` attributes are relative to that position. As a result, the image appears 50 pixels farther to the left and 200 pixels above this position. In addition, the height of the style is less than the height of the image, so it is scaled in this axis. This image is made to appear below the other two by specifying a `z-index` attribute value of –1.

Finally, the block of text is positioned absolutely, to overlay all three images.

CAUTION

Netscape Navigator 4 supports only values of `z-index` that are positive integers. If you try to design Web pages that will appear correctly in both Navigator and Internet Explorer, keep this in mind.

Netscape's *<layer>* Element

Although the `<layer>` and `<ilayer>` elements will not become standard HTML, they are supported in Netscape Navigator 4; therefore, you might want to learn how to position HTML elements by using them. Sometimes these elements work better in Navigator 4 than the CSS positioning attributes. If you are designing documents for an audience predominantly using Netscape's Web browser, you might want to use the `<layer>` element.

Listing 24.2 shows an HTML document designed to achieve roughly the same HTML element layout as achieved by that shown in Listing 24.1 using the `<layer>` and `<ilayer>` elements. Figure 24.2 demonstrates that the result is, in fact, very similar.

Listing 24.2 *LayerPos.htm*—Using Netscape's *<layer>* Element to Position HTML Elements

```
<!DOCTYPE html PUBLIC "-//W3C//DTD XHTML 1.0 Transitional//EN"
     "http://www.w3.org/TR/xhtml1/DTD/xhtml1-transitional.dtd">
<html xmlns="http://www.w3.org/1999/xhtml">
<head>
<title>LAYER Positioning</title>
</head>
<body bgcolor="#ffffff">
<center>
<h1>LAYER Positioning</h1>
<hr />
<ilayer z-index="2">
   <img src="Tux.jpg" width="450" height="335" border="0" />
</ilayer>
<layer pagex="100" pagey="100" z-index="3" />
   <img src="Tux.jpg" width="150" height="150" border="0" />
</layer>
<ilayer left="275" top="-300" z-index="1" />
   <img src="Tux.jpg" width="200" height="335" border="0" />
</ilayer>
<div style="position: absolute; top: 1.75in; left: 1.5in;
            z-index: 4;color: yellow; font: 36pt Verdana">
   Works With Text, Too!
```

Listing 24.2 Continued

```
</div>
</center>
<hr />
<em>Jim O'Donnell, <a href="mailto:jim@odonnell.org">jim@odonnell.org</a></em>
</body>
</html>
```

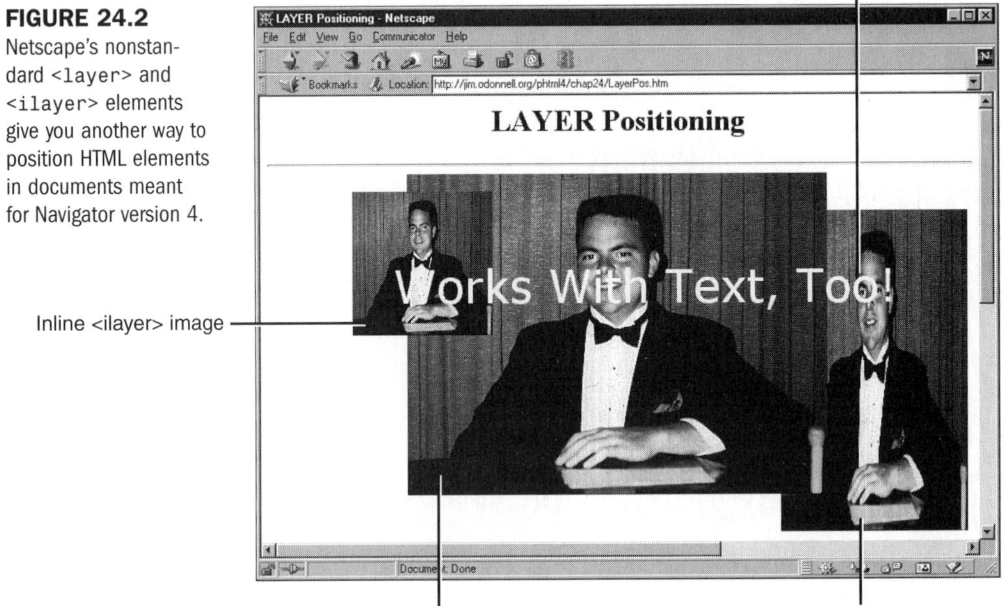

FIGURE 24.2
Netscape's nonstandard `<layer>` and `<ilayer>` elements give you another way to position HTML elements in documents meant for Navigator version 4.

Some important differences between these two examples are noted, along with other points of interest, as follows:

- `<layer>` elements define layers that are absolutely positioned; `<ilayer>` elements define layers that are positioned relative to where they would otherwise have appeared in the HTML document.
- As mentioned in the preceding section, Netscape Navigator supports only positive integer values of the `z-index` attribute—images with the highest `z-index` value appear on top. To achieve the desired three-dimensional layout, therefore, it was necessary to place each copy of the image on a layer of its own and assign appropriate `z-index` attributes to each.

Note that if the first image's `<ilayer>` element had been named with an `id` attribute, the desired layering of images could have been achieved by using the `below` and `above` attributes in the other two images' `<layer>` and `<ilayer>` elements.

- The `width` and `height` attributes of the `<layer>` and `<ilayer>` elements do not perform the same scaling function that the corresponding style sheet attributes perform. Therefore, to achieve the same scaling in this example as in the last, it was necessary to alter the `width` and/or `height` attributes of the `<img/>` element.
- Did you notice that the positioning and other styles applied to the text block were done with the exact same code as in the previous example? They could have been done with a `<layer>` element, but they were done this way to emphasize that Navigator 4 also supports style sheets and CSS positioning.

The `<layer>`/`<ilayer>` elements are the centerpiece of Netscape's Navigator 4 Dynamic HTML implementation. Chapter 26, "Advanced Netscape Dynamic HTML," discusses the use of these elements in much greater depth.

▶ To learn more about positioning content, **see** "Content Positioning," **p. 673**

Finally, Navigator 6 supports most of the same elements in the CSS standard that Internet Explorer supports. So, to perform a similar function, the resulting HTML document looks a lot closer to the Internet Explorer example than that for Navigator 4. In fact, the only difference is the omission of the `z-index` property in the `sample2` class—at least in the Navigator 6 preview releases, this property is not fully supported. Figure 24.3 shows the result; the only difference is that the rightmost picture is above the center one, because of the lack of the `z-index` property.

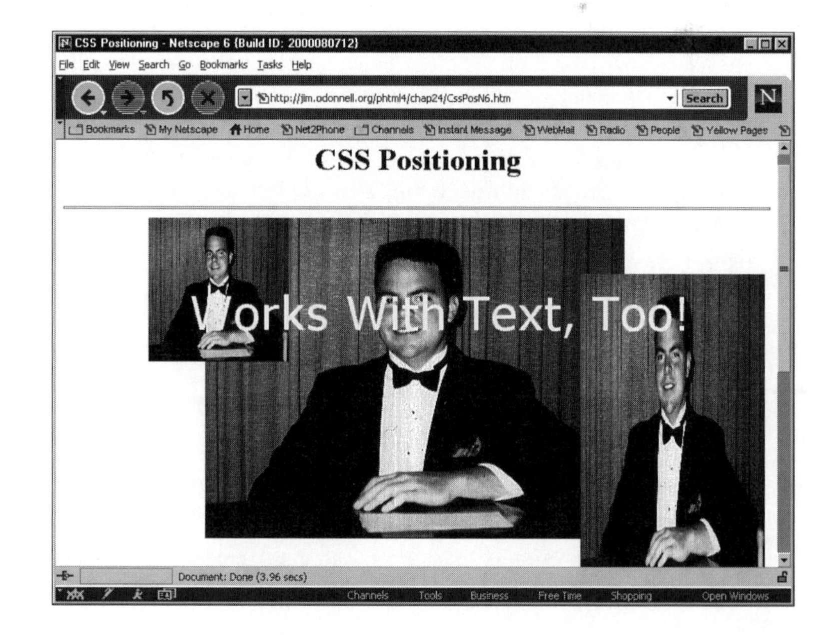

FIGURE 24.3
Netscape's Navigator 6 has much better support for W3C standard style sheet properties than Navigator 4.

Scripting Positioning Elements

Both Microsoft and Netscape enable you to access the positioning information of individual HTML elements via a scripting language and their object models. Microsoft's Dynamic HTML object model automatically enables you to set and access the attributes of every element within an HTML document. This is done with the `all` object, which is underneath the `document` object in the Web browser object hierarchy. You can write out the names of all the HTML elements on a page, for instance, with the following:

```
for (i=0;i < document.all.length;i++) {
   document.write(document.all[i].tagName + "<BR>")
}
```

To access an element's positioning elements, you need a reference to that element. If the element has a `name` or `id` attribute set for it, this is pretty straightforward. If an `<img/>` element is given the `id="MyImage"` attribute, for instance, you could check the value of its `z-index` style attribute with

```
document.write("MyImage z-index is: " +
   document.all.MyImage.style.zIndex)
```

Or, using associative arrays:

```
document.write("MyImage z-index is: " +
   document.all[''MyImage'].style.zIndex)
```

NOTE Notice that the `z-index` style attribute is scripted using the `zIndex` property. Dashes cannot be used in an object property name and are replaced by intercaps (the letter immediately after where the dash would have been is capitalized). ■

Netscape Navigator 4, on the other hand, enables you to access only the attributes of a subset of the HTML elements within a document—for instance, those elements that either have a style attached to them or that are within a `<layer>` or `<ilayer>` container element. In either case, the syntax for writing scripts to access or change any of the positioning attributes is the same and is referenced through the `layers` object array of the `document` object. To look at a similar example as that given previously for Internet Explorer, for a layer that has been given the `id="MyLayer"` attribute, you could check its `visibility` style attribute value with either

```
document.write("MyLayer visibility is: " +
    document.layers.MyLayer.visibility)
```

or

```
document.write("MyLayer visibility is: " +
    document.layers['MyLayer'].visibility)
```

Navigator 6, with its extensive support for the W3C Document Object Model Levels 0 through 2, is much closer to—in operation—Internet Explorer than to Navigator 4.

▶ To learn more about how to interface with the Document Object Model, **see** "Referencing Web Browser Objects," **p. 567**

Dynamic Styles with Cascading Style Sheets

Similar to CSS positioning, discussed in the preceding section, both Internet Explorer and Navigator have the capability to specify and/or dynamically change the format and style of HTML elements through style sheets and the object model that each browser uses. Navigator 4 can use JavaScript only to specify formatting styles at load time, whereas Internet Explorer and Navigator 6 can establish them at load time and also dynamically change them.

Table 9.1 in Chapter 9 gives a very good listing of the formatting attributes of style sheets. These attributes can be manipulated by scripts running in either Netscape Navigator or Microsoft Internet Explorer, although, like CSS positioning, the object reference in each browser differs slightly.

Chapter 25, "Advanced Microsoft Dynamic HTML," and Chapter 26, "Advanced Netscape Dynamic HTML," discuss this topic in greater detail. These chapters show you how to use Dynamic HTML in either browser to change the format of your documents on-the-fly.

▶ To learn more about styles and Dynamic HTML, **see** "Using Dynamic HTML with Styles," **p. 637**

▶ To learn more about JavaScript style sheets, **see** "JavaScript Accessible Style Sheets," **p. 665**

Listing 24.3 shows an example of an HTML document that uses JavaScript to change the format of its content. This example also demonstrates some of the differences between what can be achieved with Netscape Navigator 4 and Microsoft Dynamic HTML.

Listing 24.3 ***DynStyle.htm*—JavaScript for Specifying and (in Internet Explorer) Changing Formats**

```
<!DOCTYPE html PUBLIC "-//W3C//DTD XHTML 1.0 Transitional//EN"
    "http://www.w3.org/TR/xhtml1/DTD/xhtml1-transitional.dtd">
<html xmlns="http://www.w3.org/1999/xhtml">
<head>
<title>Dynamic HTML Example</title>
<style>
   .clicked {font-size:36pt;color:red}
</style>
<style type="text/javascript">
   classes.myClass.P.fontSize = "12pt"
   classes.myClass.P.fontFamily = "Verdana"
</style>
<script type="text/javascript" language="JavaScript">
if (navigator.appName == "Netscape")
   ieflag = false
else
   ieflag = true
function changeStyle() {
   if (ieflag) {
```

Listing 24.3 Continued

```
        document.all.tags("H1").item(0).className = "clicked"
        document.all.tags("P").item(1).style.fontSize = "18pt"
    }
}
</script>
</head>
<body bgcolor="#ffffff">
<center>
<h1>Dynamic HTML and Styles</h1>
<hr />
<p class="myClass">
   In this example, JavaScript (or JavaScript Accessible
   Style Sheets, for Navigator) is used to change the
   style of this paragraph when the document is loaded.
   This will work in version 4.0 or Netscape Navigator or
   version 4.0 or higher of Microsoft Internet Explorer.</p>
<p>When you click the button below, the style of the
   heading and this paragraph is changed; however, this
   only works in Internet Explorer.</p>
<hr>
<form>
<input type=button onclick="changeStyle()" value="Click Me!" />
</form>
</center>
<hr />
<em>Jim O'Donnell, <a href="mailto:jim@odonnell.org">jim@odonnell.org</a></em>
</body>
<script type="text/javascript" language="JavaScript">
if (ieflag) {
   document.all.tags("P").item(0).style.fontSize = "12pt"
   document.all.tags("P").item(0).style.fontFamily = "Verdana"
}
</script>
</html>
```

This particular example works only in Internet Explorer and works as follows. First, a flag is set establishing whether the browser is Netscape Navigator or Microsoft Internet Explorer:

```
if (navigator.appName == "Netscape")
   ieflag = false
else
   ieflag = true
```

This flag is used throughout the rest of the document to determine which actions to perform.

NOTE If you are trying to design pages that work on more than one browser, you need to be a little more thorough than performing only the check shown. Not only do you need to check for the browser type, you also need to check for version number and platform. If you are designing a personal Web site, it is usually enough to display a "Works best with..." message to indicate your preferred browser. Corporate sites, however, need to be designed for use with different browsers. ■

▶ For more information on determining the browser used to view your pages, **see** "Browser Detection Scripts," **p. 697**

If this page is loaded into Netscape Navigator (see Figure 24.4), the second `<STYLE>` element contains the information that is used to change the formatting information of the first paragraph of text, what Netscape refers to as a "JavaScript Accessible Style Sheet."

```
<style type="text/javascript">
   classes.myClass.P.fontSize = "12pt"
   classes.myClass.P.fontFamily = "Verdana"
</style>
```

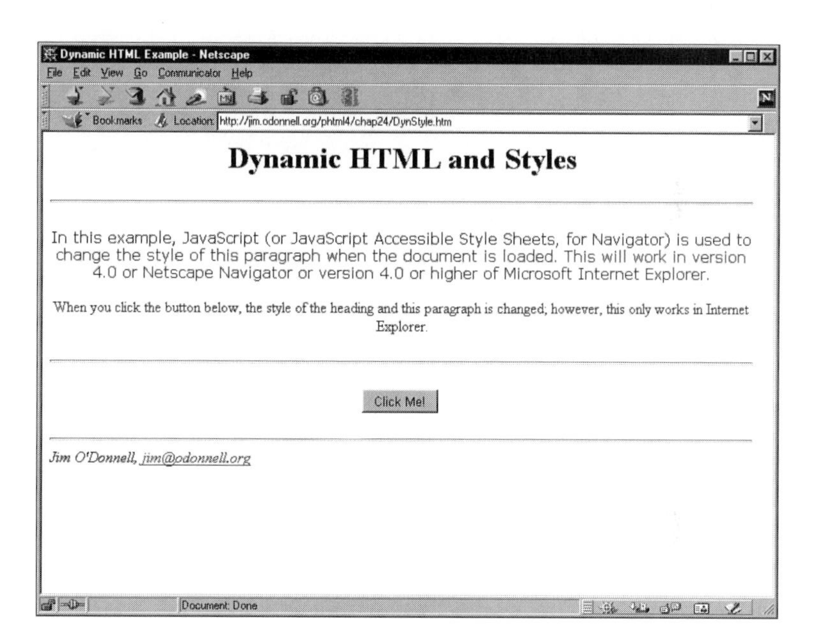

FIGURE 24.4
Netscape Navigator 4 can use JavaScript to set formats as the document is being loaded, but it cannot change them after that.

The style sheet shown specifies the format of the paragraph class known as `myClass`. This style is applied to the first paragraph through its `<p class="myClass">` element. After the document is loaded into and displayed on Netscape Navigator 4, however, the format cannot be changed.

If this page is loaded into Internet Explorer, the following JavaScript lines change the format of the first paragraph of text after it is loaded and displayed:

```
if (ieflag) {
   document.all.tags("P").item(0).style.fontSize = "12pt"
   document.all.tags("P").item(0).style.fontFamily = "Verdana"
}
```

Unlike Navigator, Internet Explorer can also change the format of text dynamically. This is done in this document by attaching the `changeStyle()` function to the `onClick` event of the button:

```
function changeStyle() {
   if (ieflag) {
      document.all.tags("H1").item(0).className = "clicked"
      document.all.tags("P").item(1).style.fontSize = "18pt"
   }
}
```

The `changeStyle()` function changes the format of the second paragraph by directly manipulating its style properties, and it changes the format of the heading by attaching a different style sheet class to it (see Figure 24.5).

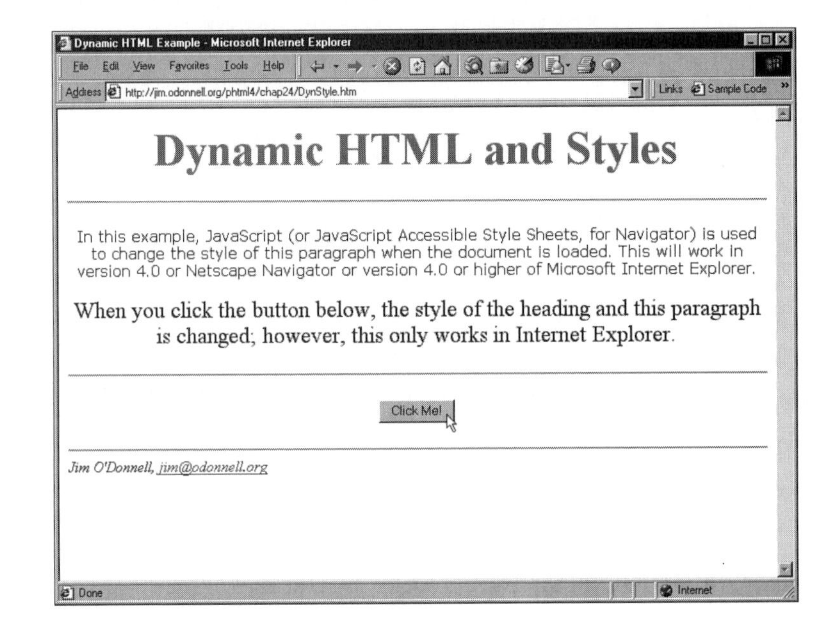

FIGURE 24.5
Microsoft Dynamic HTML enables document formats to be changed and redisplayed on-the-fly.

Web Browser Object Model

As discussed previously, the Document Object Model used by each version of Netscape Navigator and Microsoft Internet Explorer lies at the heart of their implementations of Dynamic HTML. Netscape's early implementation used in Navigator 4, and its extensions, were not as extensive as Microsoft's. Still, a number of important extensions enable you to increase capability in your HTML documents. Navigator 6's object model is much more extensive, although probably still not quite up to that of Microsoft, but adheres much more closely to the established standards.

Microsoft's object model, on the other hand, is a much more significant extension of the object models of the past for either browser, and is also being enhanced with greater support for the W3C standards. In the past, you were limited mainly to accessing and manipulating the Web browser windows and only a few aspects of the current document, such as the hypertext links, HTML Forms, and images. Now, Microsoft's Dynamic HTML has extended the object model to every HTML element. It now is possible to examine or set properties for any element within an HTML document or to set up events that are attached anywhere. Microsoft's Dynamic HTML documentation Web site includes some good examples of this, enabling you to dynamically change the content included in an outline, expanding or compressing it in response to user input.

The differences and additions to the support Document Object Models supported by Netscape Navigator 4 and 6 and Microsoft Internet Explorer are discussed in greater depth and detail in the following two chapters. The next two sections highlight some of the more important additions—in this case, changes to the Web browser event model and how you use it.

▶ To learn more about the Internet Explorer DOM, **see** "Internet Explorer Document Object Model," **p. 624**

The traditional event model enabled you to respond to a limited number of events that could be triggered by the actions of your users. Table 24.1 summarizes the most important of these events, along with their description and the HTML elements to which they applied.

Table 24.1 Traditional Web Browser Event Model

Event	Triggered When	Where It Applies
`onChange`	Object contents change	HTML form text fields
`onClick`	Object is clicked	Links and HTML form elements
`onLoad`	Object loading is completed	Document and images
`onMouseOut`	Mouse is no longer over object	Links and image maps
`onMouseOver`	Mouse is over object	Links and image maps
`onReset`	Object contents are reset	HTML forms
`onSubmit`	Object contents are submitted	HTML forms

The Microsoft Internet Explorer Event Model

Microsoft's event model is much enhanced from the traditional model. It includes many new items and also creates an `event` object in response to events within the HTML document. Unfortunately, the `event` object itself and how it is used within a script are quite different from the scheme that Netscape uses.

Microsoft's event object has a large number of properties for identifying the nature of the event and the state of the mouse and/or keyboard when the event was triggered. The properties that correspond to the properties of the Netscape event object, shown later, are as follows:

- **srcElement**—The name of the object to which the event belongs.
- **reason**—The event type (for example, onMouseDown, onMouseUp, and so forth.
- **x**—The mouse's horizontal position relative to the HTML page.
- **y**—The mouse's vertical position relative to the HTML page.
- **screenX**—The mouse's horizontal position relative to the screen.
- **screenY**—The mouse's vertical position relative to the screen.
- **button**—A number specifying the mouse button that was pressed.
- **keyCode**—A number specifying the UNICODE value of the key that was pressed.

The syntax used for the Microsoft event object differs from that used with Netscape. It also comes into being in response to an event, but you don't need to pass it to the event handler:

```
<form name="MyForm">
<input type="BUTTON" value="Hi!" name="MyButton" onClick="hello()">
</form>
```

The event handler can automatically access the properties of the event object, as in the following:

```
<script language="JavaScript">
function hello() {
   alert("Hello " + event.srcElement.name);}
}
</script>
```

The Netscape Navigator Event Model

Netscape Navigator 4 adds support for several new classes of events, enabling you to create scripts that respond to a greater variety of user input. The new categories and events are as follows:

- **Mouse events**—Added events for onMouseDown, onMouseUp, and onMouseMove.
- **Keystroke events**—Added events for onKeyDown, onKeyUp, and onKeyPress.
- **Window events**—Added events for onMove and onResize.

In addition to the new events, Netscape also added a new event object that you can use to access information about the triggered events. This object is created whenever an event is being processed, and it has the following properties:

- **target**—The name of the object to which the event belongs.
- **type**—The event type (for example, onMouseDown, onMouseUp, and so forth).

- **pageX**—The mouse's horizontal position relative to the HTML page.
- **pageY**—The mouse's vertical position relative to the HTML page.
- **screenX**—The mouse's horizontal position relative to the screen.
- **screenY**—The mouse's vertical position relative to the screen.
- **which**—A number specifying the mouse button or ASCII value of the key that was pressed.

The event object is used a little differently than other objects. It comes into being in response to an event and can then be passed to an event handler for that event, as in

```
<form name="MyForm">
<input type="BUTTON" value="Hi!" name="MyButton" onClick="hello(event)">
</form>
```


The event handler then takes the event object as a parameter and can access its properties to process the event, such as this:

```
<script language="JavaScript">
function hello(MyEvent) {
   alert("Hello " + MyEvent.target.name);
}
</script>
```

Dynamic Fonts

The introduction of the face attribute of the <font> element gave Web developers the capability to choose the font in which their content should be rendered, giving them much greater control over the final appearance of their documents. The advent of style sheets and the CSS standard—now supported by the two most popular Web browsers—adds an even greater capability for you to specify the precise font, format, and position of everything on your Web page. Increasingly, the visual effects that you develop through HTML, without having to rely on large graphics or other types of plug-in content, are limited only by your imagination.

Unfortunately, one implicit assumption is made that might get you into trouble when using <FONT FACE> or style sheets: These techniques work only if your user has the desired font installed on his or her local system. Although this should not be a problem for the "standard" fonts installed with Windows, you might run into problems if you want to use less popular fonts, or when your documents are viewed on other computer platforms. Many of your carefully constructed documents and effects can be ruined if your page is rendered in fonts other than the desired ones.

Both Netscape and Microsoft have introduced solutions to this problem. It will come as no surprise that the two solutions are not compatible, but they each achieve the same effect—they enable fonts to be embedded and used within an HTML document in such a way that, when the document is served to a Web browser, the fonts can also be downloaded and used for that document. Of course, it takes time to download fonts, the same as with graphics and other hypertext media; font files tend not to be very large, and Web fonts can be designed to have only the characters you need. Both these technologies are new, but they offer you the capability to truly design Web pages that will appear to your user exactly as designed.

Microsoft Web Embedding Fonts

If you look through Microsoft's Dynamic HTML documentation, you won't find any mention of a capability to download fonts to be used with your HTML documents. Microsoft has, in fact, developed technology to perform this function—they just don't consider it part of Dynamic HTML. You can find this technology, dubbed the Web Embedding Fonts Tool (WEFT), on Microsoft's Typography Web site at `http://www.microsoft.com/typography/`.

In practice, using the WEFT is fairly straightforward. You can use a special tool to produce what Microsoft calls the font object to be linked to and downloaded with an HTML document. These font object files differ from regular fonts files in that they are prepared especially to be downloaded over the Web—they are compressed and made up of the subset of font characters actually used. These techniques can result in a savings of at least half the time otherwise required—far more if only a small number of characters is used.

After the WEFT is used to create the font object file, it is linked into the HTML document. The syntax Microsoft uses to define an embedded font, included within a style sheet, is the following:

```
@font-face {
   font-family: MyFont;
   font-style:  normal;
   font-weight: normal;
   src: url(MYFONT0.eot);
}
```

In this case, the `src` attribute defines the actual location of the font object file.

Although the tools used to define the font file and the format of the file itself differ between Microsoft's and Netscape's systems—as well as the way that the fonts are linked into an HTML document—the other features of the two systems are very similar. Both systems enable you to determine the domain from which the fonts can be served, and both allow the font to remain on the user's system only as long as the user is viewing your pages.

Figures 24.6 and 24.7 show an example of pages created using Microsoft's font-embedding technology. The second figure shows what can happen to your carefully constructed Web page if, for some reason, the fonts it uses cannot be downloaded (or are otherwise unavailable).

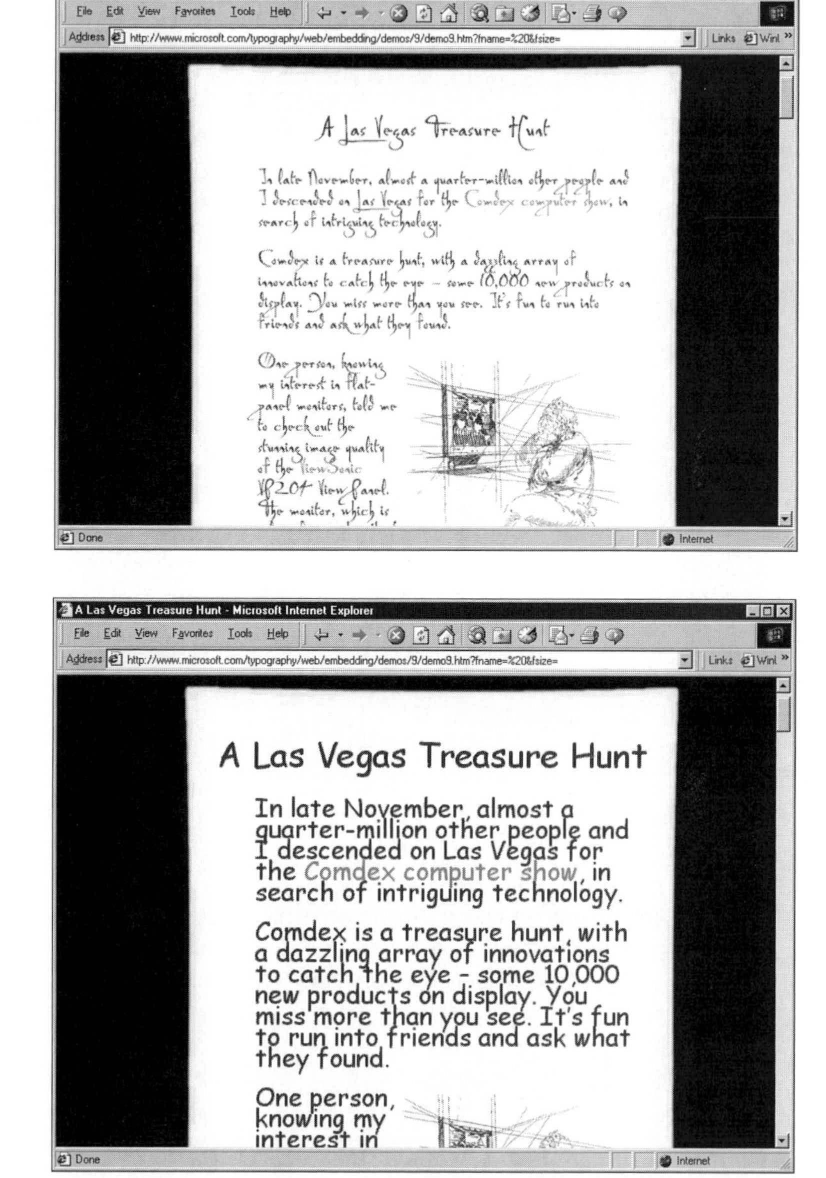

FIGURE 24.6
Downloading small subsets of fonts makes it easy to create neat effects and special displays without having to create large graphics.

FIGURE 24.7
If the font to be downloaded can't be found, or some other problem occurs, your Web page won't have the desired effect.

Netscape's Downloadable Fonts

Netscape's Dynamic HTML downloadable fonts capability enables you to use any font in your HTML documents. You do this by creating a font definition file that is placed on your Web server along with your other documents and content. When a user accesses a page that uses one of these fonts, the font definition file downloads with the HTML document the same as images, sounds, and other content displayed on the page. These downloaded fonts remain on the user's system only while the page is in their cache. Thus, users cannot make use of the fonts for their own purposes.

To use Netscape's downloadable fonts, you need to follow these steps:

1. Identify the font(s) that you want to use and make sure they are installed on your local system.

CAUTION

Remember that fonts, like all information on the Internet and the Web, are subject to copyright laws. Make sure you have a right to use any font that you plan to use as a downloadable font in any of your documents.

2. Create a font definition file. The easiest way to do this is with an authoring tool for font definition files, such as Typograph from HexMac Web sites (`http://www.hexmac.com`) or Netscape's Font Composer Plug-in for Communicator.

   The specific steps necessary to produce the file will depend on the tool used, but the output of the operation will be the font definition.

NOTE Netscape's font definition files enable you to specify the domain from which they can be served. This enables you to make sure that other people don't "hijack" fonts from your server to be used in their documents. ■

3. You must link the font definition file to your HTML document. You can do this either by using style sheets or with the `<link>` element. Using style sheets, for example, to refer to a font definition file named `myfont.pfr` looks like this:

```
<style type="text/css">
<!-- Hide from incompatible browsers!
@fontdef url(http://jim.odonnell.org/fonts/myfont.pfr);
//   Hide from incompatible browsers! -->
</style>
```

   Linking the same font definition file by using the `<link>` element looks like this:

```
<link rel="FONTDEF" src="http://jim.odonnell.org/fonts/myfont.pfr">
```

4. Add a new MIME type to your Web server for the font definition file. The MIME type is `application/font-tdpfr`, with file type `.pfr`.
5. Specify the font in your HTML documents. The name of the font will be specified within the font definition file, so you can use the font with `<font face>` or style sheets the same as you would use any other font.

Figure 24.8 shows an example of Netscape's downloadable fonts at work; a sample file is located on the DevEdge Online Web site at

```
http://developer.netscape.com/library/documentation/communicator/dynhtml/
➥fontdef1.htm
```

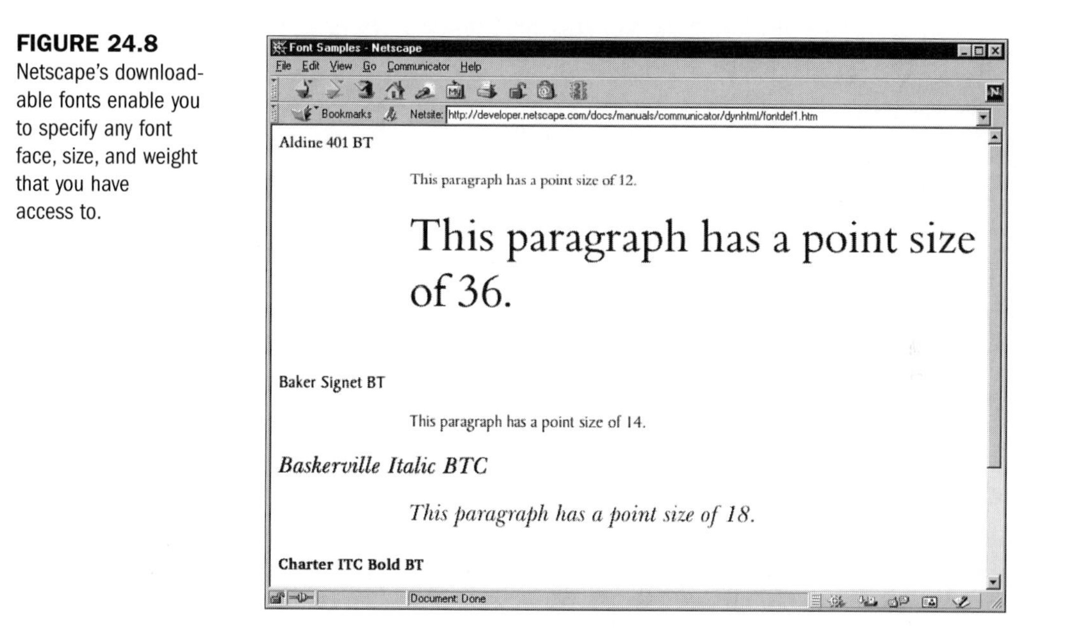

FIGURE 24.8
Netscape's downloadable fonts enable you to specify any font face, size, and weight that you have access to.

If you watch this file load into your Web browser, you will notice that the text first renders in the default font. Then, as the desired fonts download, the text re-renders. ●

CHAPTER 25

Advanced Microsoft Dynamic HTML

by Jim O'Donnell

In this chapter

Microsoft's Implementation of Dynamic HTML

Dynamic HTML is Microsoft's term for the new technology it has embedded in its Internet Explorer Web browser, versions 4 and higher. Through Dynamic HTML, you can create Web pages that can change dynamically and have a much higher degree of interaction than in the past. The heart of Dynamic HTML is Microsoft's Document Object Model. This model provides you, and scripts that you write, with the capability to interact with and change any element in an HTML document.

This chapter shows some examples of the kinds of things you can do with Dynamic HTML (and related technologies, such as *Scriptlets*). None of the examples shown represents anything you could not have done in the past—now, however, it is possible to do them using HTML alone. Dynamic HTML is a new technology still under development. People are just scratching the surface of what is possible with it. This chapter identifies some of the best places to look for examples and more information.

Internet Explorer Document Object Model

The heart of Dynamic HTML is the Document Object Model (DOM) that Internet Explorer supports. You can think of every element in an HTML document as an object—including the HTML elements and information that they contain—as well as aspects of the Web browser itself and any included Java applets, ActiveX Controls, or other elements. The DOM *exposes* these objects, making them accessible to you through scripts that you can write and include with the document.

Before Internet Explorer 4 and Dynamic HTML, the Document Object Model was limited. It could expose Java applets, ActiveX Controls, and the Web browser window properties, such as window size and location. The model exposed a limited number of HTML elements, however. The HTML elements that were supported by past object models were primarily limited to HTML Forms elements.

Microsoft's Dynamic HTML changes all that. With Dynamic HTML, every HTML element is exposed through the Document Object Model. Not only that, but the contents of all HTML container elements also are exposed. Therefore, not only can you change the styles or formats associated with a <p> element, for instance, but you also can change its text contents. And, this is all done on the client side, without any need to interact with the Web server.

The rest of this section discusses aspects of the Document Object Model for Internet Explorer. It is important to at least understand the different terms used with the object model—object, property, method, collection, and event—and what they mean. This section gives you a good basis for understanding the Dynamic HTML samples later in the chapter.

NOTE For the rest of this chapter, references to Internet Explorer should be interpreted to mean Internet Explorer version 4 and higher (unless otherwise noted). ■

Understanding Objects and the Object Hierarchy

Figure 25.1 shows the hierarchy of most of the objects and collections of objects that is part of the Internet Explorer Document Object Model. In the simplest terms, an *object* in this model is a recognizable element of the whole, a *collection* is itself an object that contains other objects as its elements. Objects can also contain other objects, however; thus, all the objects are organized into an object hierarchy.

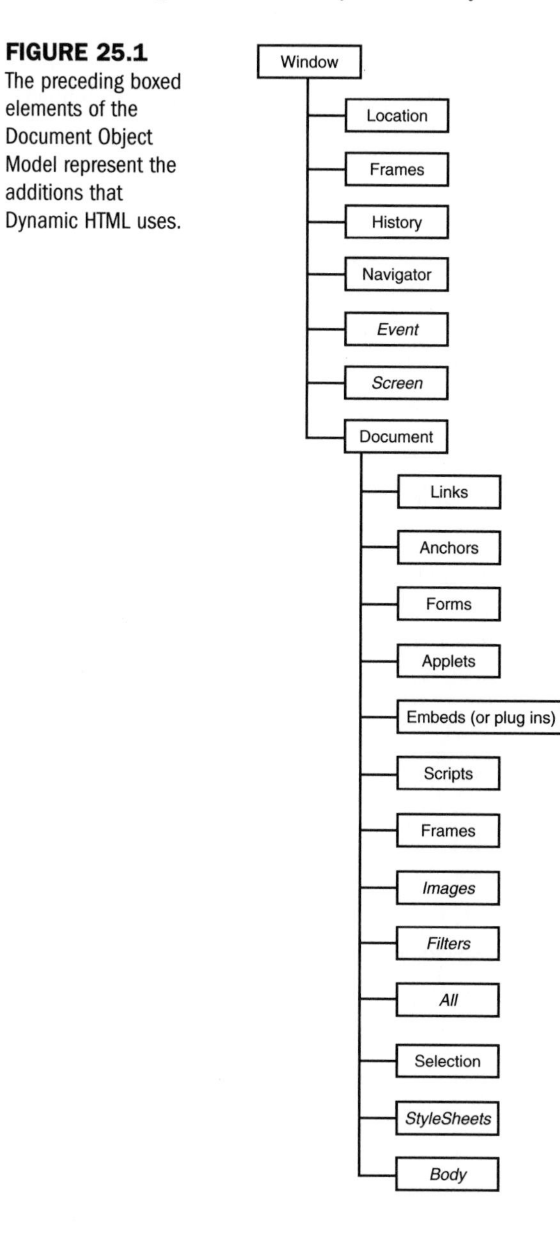

FIGURE 25.1
The preceding boxed elements of the Document Object Model represent the additions that Dynamic HTML uses.

As you look at Figure 25.1, the `window` object at the top of the hierarchy includes everything you see within a given Web browser window. That object can and will, in turn, contain other objects. This object hierarchy is used when referencing these objects, with the following sample notation:

```
window.document.links[0]
```

This line of code refers to the first `link` object contained in the current `document` of a given Web browser `window`. (Normally, unless you are authoring Web pages that use multiple windows, you can omit `window`.)

A description of most of the major objects and collections in the Internet Explorer Document Object Model follows:

- **`window`**—Represents an open Web browser window.
- **`location`**—Information for the current URL.
- **`frames`**—A collection of `window` objects, one for each separate frame in the current window.
- **`history`**—Information for the recently visited URLs.
- **`navigator`**—Information about the browser itself.
- **`event`**—Maintains the state of events occurring within the browser.
- **`screen`**—Statistics on the physical screen and the rendering capabilities of the client.
- **`document`**—Contains all the information attached to the current HTML document.
- **`links`**—A collection of links referenced in the current document.
- **`anchors`**—A collection of anchors present within the current document.
- **`forms`**—Can contain a number of other objects corresponding to the form elements within it; there is one `form` object for each HTML form in the document.
- **`applets`**—A collection of Java applets present within the current document.
- **`embeds`**—A collection of all objects included using the `<embed>` element; this object can also be referenced using the synonym `plugins`.
- **`scripts`**—A collection of all the script elements within the document.
- **`images`**—A collection that contains one element for each image in the document.
- **`filters`**—Contains a collection of the `filter` objects associated with the document.
- **`all`**—A collection of all the HTML elements that are a part of the document.
- **`selection`**—Represents the current active selection, a user-selected block of text within the document.
- **`StyleSheets`**—A collection of the style sheet objects attached to the current document.
- **`body`**—Accesses the `<body>` section of the document.

Note that many of these objects are collections of other objects. The `images` object, for instance, is a collection of image objects associated with all the images in the current document. You can access elements in these collections either by name or by number. If the first image in an HTML document, for example, is defined by

```
<img src="bryan.jpg" id="Bryan">
```

you can use the `images` object to access that image in one of three ways:

```
document.images[0]

document.images("Bryan")

document.images.Bryan
```

Note that arrays in the object model are zero based, so the first element in an array is referenced using zero.

Using Properties

Every object has properties. To access a property, use the object name followed by a period and the property name. To get the length of the `images` object, which would tell you how many images are in the current document, you can write the following:

```
document.images.length
```

If the object you are using has properties that can be modified, you can change them in the same way. You can change the URL of the current window, for example, by setting the `href` property of the `location` object, as in the following line:

```
location.href = "http://jim.odonnell.org"
```

If this line is executed within a script, the HTML document referenced by it (my home page) will be loaded into your Web browser window.

Listing 25.1 shows an example of a program that uses Dynamic HTML's `all` object to access all the HTML elements included within the document. In this case, when the document is loaded, a script writes out on the bottom of the document a list of all the HTML elements included in the document (with the exception of the ones written out by the script itself). The script does this by using the `length` property of the `all` collection to see how many elements there are and then stepping through them using the `tagName` property of each object in the collection to display what the elements are (see Figure 25.2).

Listing 25.1 *DispElem.htm*—The *all* Object Enables You to Access Every HTML Tag

```
<!DOCTYPE html PUBLIC "-//W3C//DTD XHTML 1.0 Transitional//EN"
    "http://www.w3.org/TR/xhtml1/DTD/xhtml1-transitional.dtd">
<html xmlns="http://www.w3.org/1999/xhtml">
```

Listing 25.1 Continued

```
<head>
<title>Document Object Model: all Object</title>
</head>
<body>
<center>
<h1>Document Object Model: <em>all</em> Object</h1>
<hr />
<p>
The script in this example will list all of the HTML elements
used in this document. The script uses the <em>length</em>
property of the <em>all</em> collection and the <em>tagName</em>
properties of each object in that collection.
</p>
</center>
<hr />
<em>Jim O'Donnell, <a href="mailto:jim@odonnell.org">jim@odonnell.org</a></em>
</body>
<script type="text/javascript" language="JavaScript">
imax = document.all.length
document.write("<pre>")
for(i = 0;i < imax;i++)
   if (i < 9)
      document.write("Element 0" + (i+1) + " of " + imax + ": " +
         "document.all[0" + i + "].tagName = " +
          document.all[i].tagName + "<br />")
   else if (i == 9)
      document.write("Element " + (i+1) + " of " + imax + ": " +
         "document.all[0" + i + "].tagName = " +
          document.all[i].tagName + "<br />")
    else
      document.write("Element " + (i+1) + " of " + imax + ": " +
         "document.all[" + i + "].tagName = " +
          document.all[i].tagName + "<br />")
document.write("</pre>")
</script>
</html>
```

Many properties are associated with HTML element objects in Microsoft's new object model—too many to go over in any detail here. However, you should be aware of two properties in particular; they make up one of the ways that Microsoft's Dynamic HTML enables you to easily change the content of HTML documents on-the-fly, without going back to the Web server:

- **innerHTML**—This is a property of an HTML element object, and its value is whatever text, information, and HTML code are included within the HTML container elements corresponding to that object.
- **outerHTML**—This is a property of an HTML element object, and its value is whatever text, information, and HTML code are included within the HTML container elements corresponding to that object, *including* the container elements themselves.

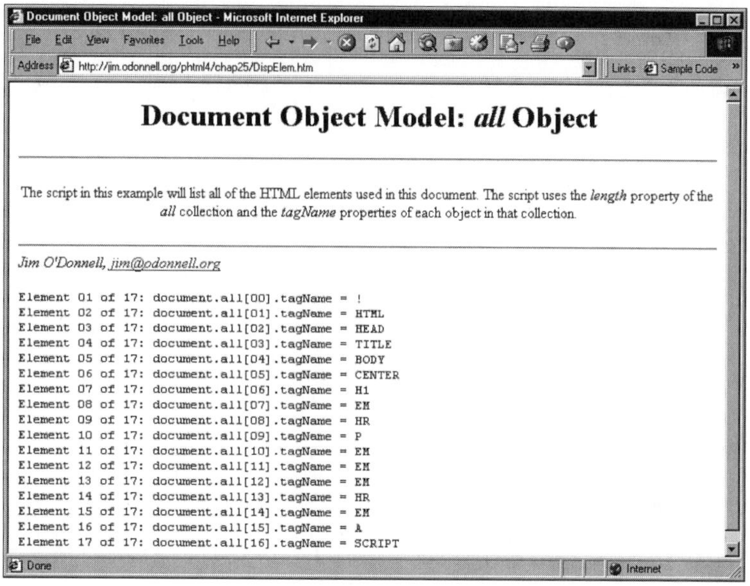

FIGURE 25.2
Dynamic HTML enables you to access all the information in the current HTML document.

Listing 25.2 shows a sample HTML document that demonstrates these two properties and the difference between them. In this case, the element objects being referenced are attached to the `<h1>` element by using the attribute `id="MyHeading"` and to the `<p>` element by using the attribute `id="MyParagraph"`. At the end of the document, the JavaScript shown displays the value of the `innerHTML` and `outerHTML` properties of the objects corresponding to each of these elements. Notice that the `outerHTML` value for the `<h1>` element is in the `h1` heading format and that of the `<p>` element has an extra space in it. This occurs, in each case, because `outerHTML` includes the effects of the container element as well as its contents (see Figure 25.3).

Listing 25.2 *ContentP.htm*—HTML Document Contents Can Be Accessed Using the *innerHTML* and *outerHTML* Properties

```
<!DOCTYPE html PUBLIC "-//W3C//DTD XHTML 1.0 Transitional//EN"
    "http://www.w3.org/TR/xhtml1/DTD/xhtml1-transitional.dtd">
<html xmlns="http://www.w3.org/1999/xhtml">
<head>
<title>Document Object Model: innerHTML and outerHTML Properties</title>
</head>
<body>
<center>
<h1 id="MyHeading">Document Object Model:<br>
                   <em>innerHTML</em> and
                   <em>outerHTML</em> Properties</h1>
<hr />
```

Listing 25.2 Continued

```
<p id="MyParagraph">
The <em>contents</em> of the &lt;p&gt; element "MyParagraph"...
</p>
</center>
<hr />
<em>Jim O'Donnell, <a href="mailto:jim@odonnell.org">jim@odonnell.org</a></em>
<script type="text/javascript" language="JavaScript">
document.write("<pre>")
document.write("document.all['MyHeading'].innerHTML = " +
   document.all['MyHeading'].innerHTML + "<br />")
document.write("document.all['MyHeading'].outerHTML = " +
   document.all['MyHeading'].outerHTML + "<br />")
document.write("<hr />")
document.write("document.all['MyParagraph'].innerHTML = " +
   document.all['MyParagraph'].innerHTML + "<br />")
document.write("document.all['MyParagraph'].outerHTML = " +
   document.all['MyParagraph'].outerHTML + "<br />")
document.write("</pre>")
</script>
</body>
</html>
```

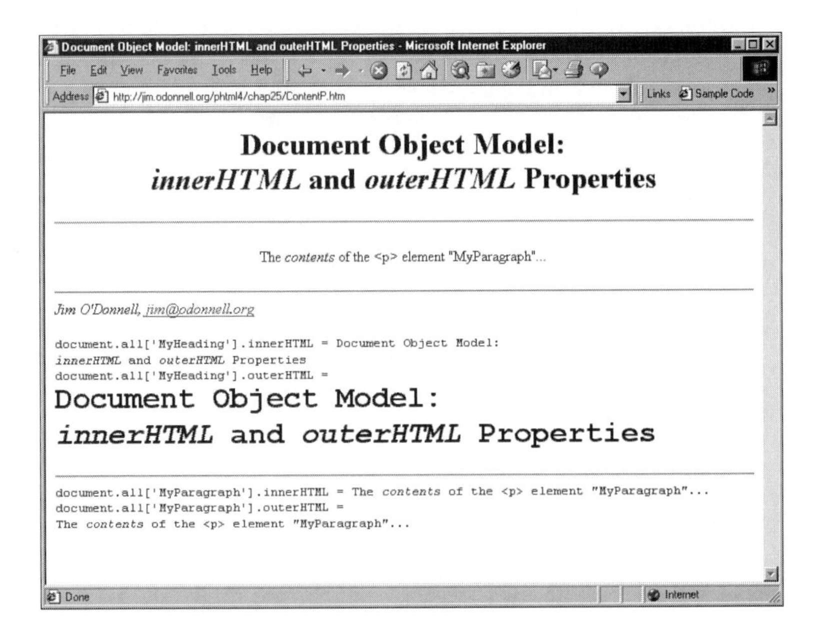

FIGURE 25.3
Not only the format, but also the actual contents of your HTML documents can be accessed and changed with Microsoft Dynamic HTML.

Listing 25.3 shows another example, this one using the `innerHTML` property to dynamically change the contents of a Web page.

Listing 25.3 *DynCon.htm*—Real-Time Changing of HTML Document Contents Using the *innerHTML* Property

```
<!DOCTYPE html PUBLIC "-//W3C//DTD XHTML 1.0 Transitional//EN"
    "http://www.w3.org/TR/xhtml1/DTD/xhtml1-transitional.dtd">
<html xmlns="http://www.w3.org/1999/xhtml">
<head>
<style>
SPAN,P {font-family: Verdana;
        font-size: 18pt;
        font-weight: bold}
</style>
<script type="text/javascript" language="JavaScript">
function errortrap(msg,url,line){
   return true
}
onerror = errortrap;
</script>
<title>Dynamic Content Using innerHTML</title>
</head>
<body onload="stuff()" onmouseover="update()">
<center>
<h1>Dynamic Content Using <em>innerHTML</em></h1>
<hr />
<p>
<span>This</span>
<span>paragraph</span>
<span>contains</span>
<span id="wordCount">???</span>
<span>words</span>.
<span>The</span>
<span>mouse</span>
<span>is</span>
<span>currently</span>
<span>over</span>
<span>the</span>
<span>word</span>
<br /><span id="currentWord"
            style="color:#0000FF;font-size:36pt">n/a</span><br />
<span>In</span>
<span>this</span>
<span>paragraph</span>,
<span>this</span>
<span>is</span>
<span>word</span>
<span>number</span>
<br /><span id="currentWordNum"
            style="color:#0000FF;font-size:36pt">n/a</span>.
</p>
</center>
<hr />
<em>Jim O'Donnell, <a href="mailto:jim@odonnell.org">jim@odonnell.org</a></em>
```

Listing 25.3 Continued

```
</body>
<script type="text/javascript" language="JavaScript">
var oldObject
function stuff() {
   oldObject = null
   wordCount.innerHTML = document.all.tags("SPAN").length
}
function update() {
   if (window.event.srcElement.tagName == "SPAN") {
      if (oldObject)
         oldObject.style.fontFamily = "Verdana"
      oldObject = window.event.srcElement
      oldObject.style.fontFamily = "Lucida Handwriting"
      for (i = 0;i < document.all.tags("SPAN").length;i++)
         if (oldObject == document.all.tags("SPAN").item(i))
            currentWordNum.innerHTML = i + 1
      currentWord.innerHTML = oldObject.innerHTML
   } else {
      if (oldObject) {
         oldObject.style.fontFamily = "Verdana"
         oldObject = null
         currentWordNum.innerHTML = "n/a"
         currentWord.innerHTML = "n/a"
      }
   }
}
function errortrap(msg,url,line){
//  alert(msg);
    return true;
}
onerror = errortrap;
</script>
</html>
```

The three main sections of interest in this example are the main document text (contained within the `<p>` container element) and the two JavaScript functions, `stuff()` and `update()`. This application determines which word in the paragraph (if any) the mouse is over and changes the text to display this word as well as its position within the paragraph. To help accomplish this, each of these sections does the following:

- **Body text within the `<p>` container element**—Each separate word in this paragraph is set off by a `<span>` container element to enable you to access and manipulate it separately from the rest. In addition, three of the words are also given an `id` because the JavaScripts will be using their `innerHTML` properties to dynamically change their contents.
- **JavaScript `stuff()` function**—This function is called when the page has completely loaded by the `onload` event of the `<body>` element. It is used to fill in the total number

of words in the paragraph. This is done by counting the number of `<span>` elements, and then inserting this number into the paragraph using the appropriate `innerHTML` property.

- **JavaScript `update()` function**—This function is called whenever an `onmouseover` event is triggered. Because the `onmouseover` event is given in the `<body>` element, such an event is generated whenever the mouse passes over *any* element in the page!

  The `update()` function first determines whether the element that triggered the event is one of the `<span>` elements in the paragraph. If it is, it changes the font of the corresponding word and places the word and word number in the appropriate spaces in the paragraph (see Figure 25.4). If the triggering element is not one of the `<span>` elements, the function changes the text to read "n/a."

FIGURE 25.4
Internet Explorer automatically adjusts the other contents of the page to correctly display dynamically altered information.

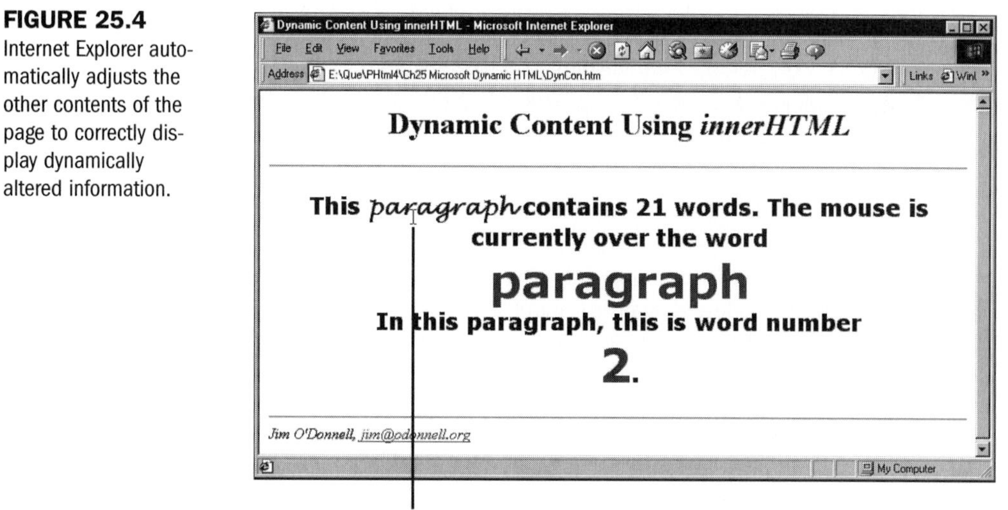

Dynamic HTML Events and the *event* Object

In addition to making HTML documents more responsive by enabling you to attach events and manipulate the properties of virtually any HTML element, Microsoft's Dynamic HTML has increased the number of HTML events that the Web browser can sense and respond to. This section identifies most of these events and shows what triggers them.

Mouse Events

These events are triggered in response to mouse movements or mouse button presses. A few of these are familiar events, having been part of the Document Object Model before; some are new as a result of Dynamic HTML:

- **onclick**—This event is normally triggered when the user presses and releases the left mouse button. It can also occur when the user presses certain keys, such as Enter and Esc, in an HTML form.

  A JavaScript `onclick` event handler is shown later. This event handler is triggered when a mouse click is recorded anywhere in the current document, and it uses the `event` object to pop up an Alert box to give the name of the HTML element in which the click occurred.

  ```
  <script for="document" event="onclick" language="JavaScript">
     alert("Clicked in " + window.event.srcElement.tagName);
  </script>
  ```

- **ondblclick**—This event is triggered when the user clicks twice over an object. If an event handler assigned to this event returns a `false` value, it cancels the default action.
- **onmousedown**—This event is triggered when the user presses the mouse button.
- **onmousemove**—This event is triggered when the mouse is moved.
- **onmouseover**—This event is triggered when the mouse is moved into an object. It occurs when the mouse first enters the object and does not repeat unless the user moves the mouse out and then back in.
- **onmouseout**—This event is triggered when the user moves the mouse out of a given element. When the user moves the mouse pointer into an element, one `onmouseover` event occurs, followed by one or more `onmousemove` events as the user moves the pointer within the element; and finally, one `onmouseout` event occurs when the user moves the pointer out of the element.
- **onmouseup**—This event is triggered when the mouse button is released.

Note that some of the events described in the preceding list actually trigger multiple events. The events leading to a valid `ondblclick` event, for example, occur in the following steps:

1. `onmousedown`
2. `onmouseup`
3. `onclick`
4. `onmousedown`
5. `onmouseup`
6. `ondblclick`

Keystroke Events

New to Microsoft Internet Explorer with its support for Dynamic HTML are events triggered by user keypresses. Three general purpose events and one special purpose event respond to keys:

- **onkeydown**—This event is triggered when the user presses a key and returns the number of the keycode for the key pressed. An event handler assigned to service this event can return a different value and override the original key.
- **onkeyup**—Triggered when the user releases a key.
- **onkeypress**—The last event triggered for a valid keypress: First the `onkeydown` event is triggered, then `onkeyup`, and then `onkeypress`. Event handlers assigned to any of these three events can be used to intercept, override, and/or nullify the actual key pressed.
- **onhelp**—This event is triggered when the user presses the F1 key or clicks the Help key on the Web browser.

Focus Events

These events are used to follow the focus of the cursor around the HTML document. They can be used effectively when performing HTML form validation but can also be used with non-form elements.

- **onfocus**—This event is triggered when the element in question receives the input focus.
- **onblur**—This event is triggered when an object loses the input focus.
- **onchange**—This event is triggered when the contents of the object, normally a text or text area HTML form field, are changed.

  Note that this event is triggered only after the object has lost focus and if its contents have changed. If an event handler exists for the `onblur` event for the same object, the `onchange` event is triggered and executed first.

Events for the *<marquee>* Element

Although Microsoft's `<marquee>` element is a nonstandard HTML element, its use has begun to increase. Microsoft's Dynamic HTML implementation includes three events specifically tied to that element:

- **onbounce**—This event can only be triggered when the contents of the `<marquee>` element are set to alternately scroll one way and then the other. It is actually triggered when the scrolling content changes direction.
- **onstart**—This event is triggered when a scrolling loop begins or, for alternate behavior, when a bounce cycle begins.
- **onfinish**—This event is triggered when a scrolling loop ends.

Page Events

In addition to the `onload` event, which has existed in the past and is triggered when a Web page is completely loaded, Dynamic HTML adds a couple of other events associated with loading and unloading documents into your Web browser. This enables you to set the entrance and exit behaviors of the Web browser for a given document.

- **`onload`**—This event is triggered after the Web browser loads the given object. It is normally used with the HTML document itself but also can be applied to images, applets, and any other Web browser object loaded along with the HTML document itself.
- **`onbeforeunload`**—This event is triggered prior to an HTML document being unloaded. By attaching an event handler to this event, you can give the user a chance to change his or her mind and remain on the current page.
- **`onunload`**—This event is triggered immediately before the current page is unloaded. Unlike the `onbeforeunload` event, after this event is triggered it is too late to prevent the user from leaving the page.

HTML Form Events

As you would expect, Microsoft's Dynamic HTML supports the traditional `onreset` and `onsubmit` events associated with an HTML form's Reset and Submit buttons. Each of these events is triggered when the corresponding button is clicked. If an event handler for the `onsubmit` event returns a value of `false`, the form is not submitted.

Other Events

The following list describes some of the other events supported by Microsoft's implementation of Dynamic HTML. Note also that a collection of events is associated with the data binding capabilities of Dynamic HTML—these events are discussed later in this chapter.

- **`onabort`**—This event is triggered when the user aborts the download of an image, normally by clicking the Stop button.
- **`onerror`**—This event is triggered when an error occurs when loading an image or other Web browser object. You can suppress error messages that occur when an image fails to load by setting the `onerror` attribute in the element to `null`.
- **`onfilterchange`**—This event fires when a filter changes state or completes a transition from one state to another. Filter effects of Microsoft Dynamic HTML are discussed in the "Dynamic HTML Filters" section later in this chapter.
- **`onresize`**—This event is triggered when the object to which it is attached is resized.
- **`onscroll`**—This event is triggered when the user scrolls the window by using the scrollbar, arrow keys, or some other means.
- **`onselect`**—This event is triggered when the current selection changes. The event continues to fire as the mouse moves from character to character during a drag selection.
- **`onselectstart`**—This event is triggered at the beginning of a user-initiated select.

Using Dynamic HTML with Styles

Dynamic HTML works very well with another aspect of Internet Explorer for dynamically changing the formatting of elements in an HTML document: styles and style sheets. Two properties associated with all HTML elements—which, as you will recall, you can access through the `all` collection—are that element's `style` and `className`. The `style` property, in turn, has properties of its own that you can access and change to immediately change the appearance of the Web page. The `className` property enables you to access and change many style attributes at once by assigning the elements style class.

Listing 25.4 shows an example of dynamically changing the style of elements of an HTML document. In this example, the format is applied to two elements in different ways—either through an embedded style sheet created with the `<style>` element or through the `style` attribute. No matter which way you do it, the script changes the format in response to the `onmousedown` and `onmouseup` events. Figures 25.5 and 25.6 show the before and after screen shots of this HTML document.

Listing 25.4 ***Style1.htm*—Dynamic HTML Can Change Document Styles**

```
<!DOCTYPE html PUBLIC "-//W3C//DTD XHTML 1.0 Transitional//EN"
    "http://www.w3.org/TR/xhtml1/DTD/xhtml1-transitional.dtd">
<html xmlns="http://www.w3.org/1999/xhtml">
<head>
<title>Dynamic HTML and Styles</title>
<style>
   .mousedown {font-size:48pt;color:red}
   .mouseup {font-size:24pt;color:black}
</style>
<script type="text/javascript" language="JavaScript">
function changeStyles(mousedown) {
   if (mousedown) {
      document.all.tags("H1").item(0).className = "mousedown";
      document.all.tags("P").item(0).style.fontSize = "24pt";
   } else {
      document.all.tags("H1").item(0).className = "mouseup";
      document.all.tags("P").item(0).style.fontSize = "12pt";
   }
}
</script>
</head>
<body onmousedown="changeStyles(1)" onmouseup="changeStyles(0)">
<center>
<h1 class="mouseup">Dynamic HTML and Styles</h1>
<hr />
<p style="font-size: 12pt">
When you click the mouse, the script in this example will
dynamically change the style of the heading and of this
text. The script uses the <em>className</em> and
<em>style.fontSize</em> properties of the
```

Listing 25.4 Continued

```
<em>all.tags.item</em> object.
</p>
</center>
<hr />
<em>Jim O'Donnell, <a href="mailto:jim@odonnell.org">jim@odonnell.org</a></em>
</body>
</html>
```

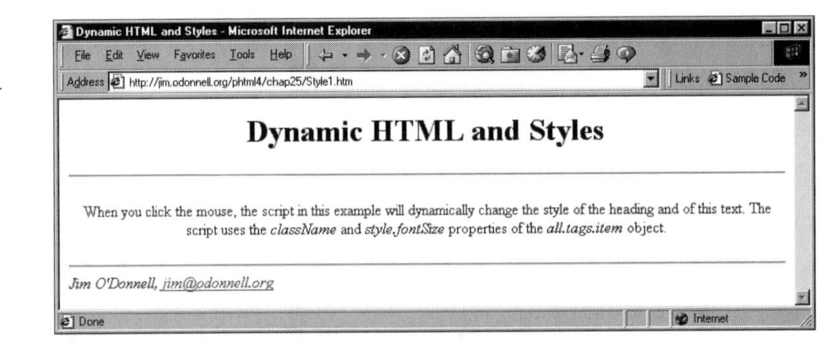

FIGURE 25.5
You can attach formatting styles to HTML elements in a variety of ways.

FIGURE 25.6
You can change formats and immediately update the Web browser window in response to any event.

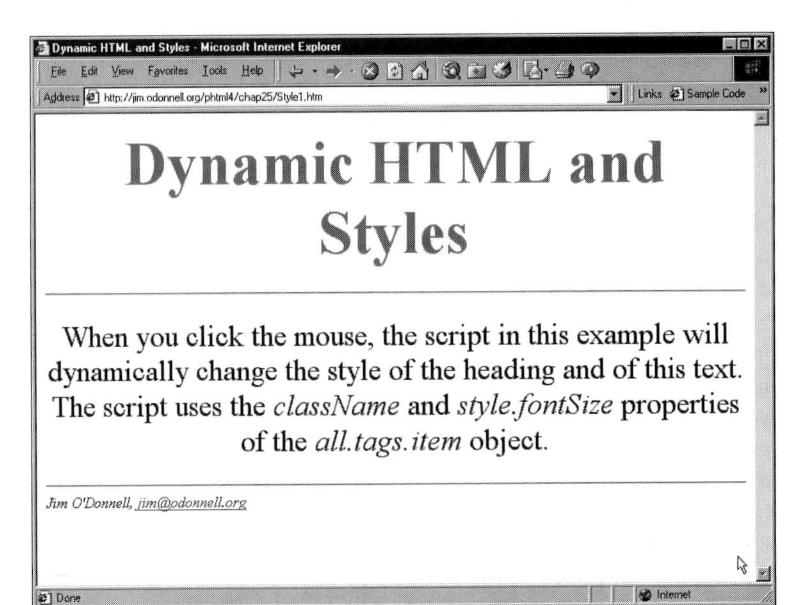

Dynamic HTML and the Data Source Object

Another Dynamic HTML capability works hand in hand with Microsoft's Data Source Object to enable what is called *data binding*. The Data Source Object is an ActiveX Control that references an external file to provide data for the HTML document. Dynamic HTML enables you to use the `datasrc` and `datafld` attributes to bind this data to HTML elements. This way, the data displayed within a document can be kept separate from the formatting. Also, after the data is transmitted to the client Web browser, the Data Source Object can perform operations on it locally.

Data Binding Events

A collection of events is associated with HTML elements that are data bound using the `datasrc` and `datafld` attributes. The following list describes these events:

- **`ondataavailable`**—This event is triggered as data arrives from an asynchronous data source object; how often it fires depends on the data source object.
- **`ondatasetchanged`**—This event is triggered when the data set used by a data source object changes.
- **`ondatasetcomplete`**—This event is triggered when all the data available to a data source object has been loaded.
- **`onrowenter`**—This event is triggered when the current row of data has changed, and new data values are available.
- **`onrowexit`**—This event is triggered just prior to a data source object changing the current row in response to new data.
- **`onbeforeupdate`**—This event is triggered before the transfer of data from an element to a data provider.
- **`onafterupdate`**—This event is triggered after the transfer of data from an element to a data provider.
- **`onerrorupdate`**—This event is triggered when the handler for the `onbeforeupdate` event cancels the data transfer and fires instead the `onafterupdate` event.

Data Binding Example

Listing 25.5 shows an example of data binding using the Data Source Object and Dynamic HTML. In this example, a data file of chapter, page count, and author information is bound to the columns of an HTML table. The Data Source Object's `SortColumn()` method is attached to the table headings, using the `onclick` event. When a column heading is clicked, the table is sorted by the contents of that column and immediately redisplayed. Figures 25.7 and 25.8 show examples of this, with the table sorted either by chapter number or chapter title.

Listing 25.5 *DataBind.htm*—Dynamic HTML and Data Binding Enable Easy Client-Side Data Manipulation

```
<!DOCTYPE html PUBLIC "-//W3C//DTD XHTML 1.0 Transitional//EN"
    "http://www.w3.org/TR/xhtml1/DTD/xhtml1-transitional.dtd">
<html xmlns="http://www.w3.org/1999/xhtml">
<head>
<title>Data Binding with Dynamic HTML</title>
</head>
<body>
<object id="inputdata"
        classid="clsid:333C7BC4-460F-11D0-BC04-0080C7055A83"
        align="baseline" border="0" width="0" height="0">
<param name="DataURL"   value="authors.txt" />
<param name="UseHeader" value="true" />
</object>
<center>
<h1>Data Binding with Dynamic HTML</h1>
<hr />
<p>
   This example shows how you can use Dynamic HTML to bind
   an HTML element, in this case the columns of a table,
   to a Data Source Object. This allows the data to be
   kept separately from the formatting information in the
   HTML document. It also allows the data to be operated
   on at the client. In this example, if you click on the
   table headers of the table below, it will be sorted by
   the elements in that column.
</p>
<hr />
<table datasrc="#inputdata" border="1">
<thead>
<tr><th><u><div id="ChapNum"   onclick="sort1()">
        Chapter<br>Number</div></u></th>
    <th><u><div id="ChapTitle" onclick="sort2()">
        Chapter<br>Title</div></u></th>
    <th><u><div id="PageCount" onclick="sort3()">
        Estimate<br>Page Count</div></u></th>
    <th><u><div id="Author"    onclick="sort4()">
        Author</div></u></th></tr>
</thead>
<tbody>
<tr><td align=right><div datafld="ChapNum"></div></td>
    <td>            <div datafld="ChapTitle"></div></td>
    <td align=right><div datafld="PageCount"></div></td>
    <td>            <div datafld="Author"></div></td></tr>
</tbody>
</table>
<script type="text/javascript" language="JavaScript">
function sort1() {
  inputdata.SortColumn = "ChapNum";
  inputdata.Reset();
}
```

Listing 25.5 Continued

```
function sort2() {
  inputdata.SortColumn = "ChapTitle";
  inputdata.Reset();
}
function sort3() {
  inputdata.SortColumn = "PageCount";
  inputdata.Reset();
}
function sort4() {
  inputdata.SortColumn = "Author";
  inputdata.Reset();
}
</script>
</center>
<hr />
<em>Jim O'Donnell, <a href="mailto:jim@odonnell.org">jim@odonnell.org</a></em>
</body>
</html>
```

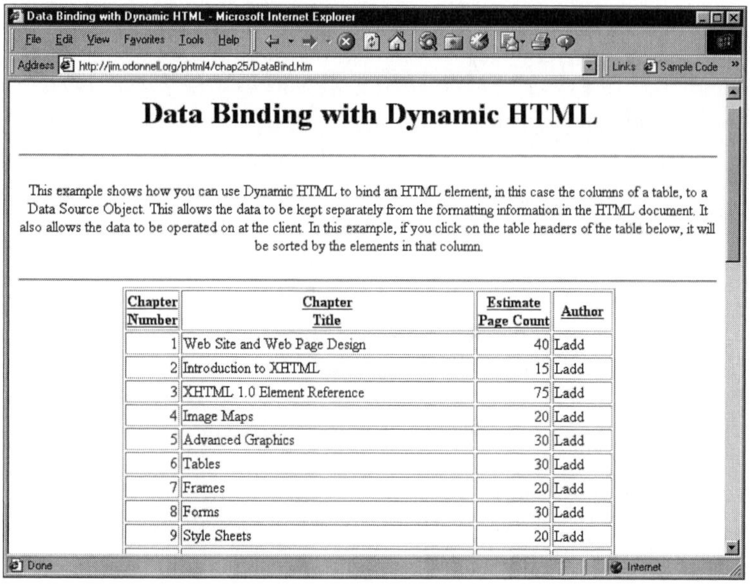

FIGURE 25.7
The Data Source Object enables you to include external data within an HTML document by Dynamic HTML.

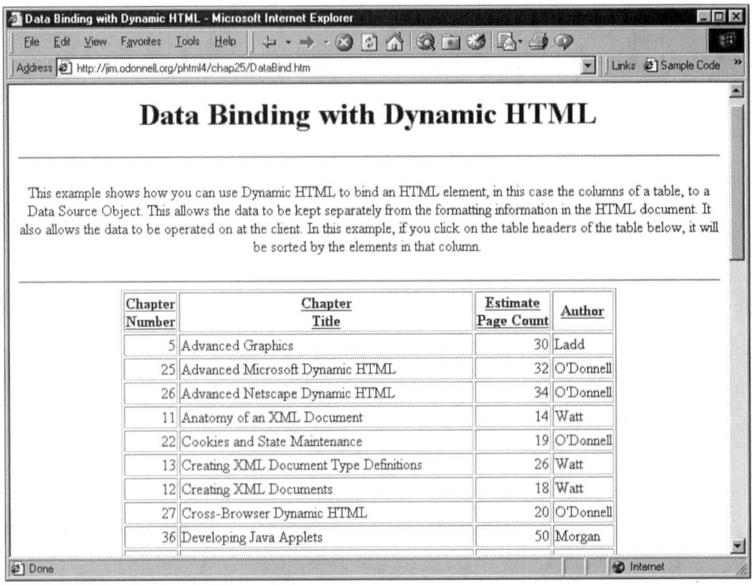

FIGURE 25.8
Using Dynamic HTML, you can automatically sort—or otherwise operate on—and immediately redisplay data.

Data Binding with Dynamic HTML - Microsoft Internet Explorer

Address http://jim.odonnell.org/phtml4/chap25/DataBind.htm

Data Binding with Dynamic HTML

This example shows how you can use Dynamic HTML to bind an HTML element, in this case the columns of a table, to a Data Source Object. This allows the data to be kept separately from the formatting information in the HTML document. It also allows the data to be operated on at the client. In this example, if you click on the table headers of the table below, it will be sorted by the elements in that column.

Chapter Number	Chapter Title	Estimate Page Count	Author
5	Advanced Graphics	30	Ladd
25	Advanced Microsoft Dynamic HTML	32	O'Donnell
26	Advanced Netscape Dynamic HTML	34	O'Donnell
11	Anatomy of an XML Document	14	Watt
22	Cookies and State Maintenance	19	O'Donnell
13	Creating XML Document Type Definitions	26	Watt
12	Creating XML Documents	18	Watt
27	Cross-Browser Dynamic HTML	20	O'Donnell
36	Developing Java Applets	50	Morgan

Position HTML Elements with Dynamic HTML

One exciting possibility with Dynamic HTML is the capability to reposition HTML elements on the Web page. To do this, change the `left` and `top` properties of the element's `style` object (which, in turn, is a property of the element). This change can be done either automatically or in response to user interaction.

Listing 25.6 shows an example of a Dynamic HTML document that enables the user to position an HTML element—in this case a group of pictures—on the Web page. In this example, a table containing three images is contained within a `<span>` element. An `onclick` event is attached to the `<span>`, which is used to toggle whether it can be moved and to initialize the coordinates for the move. An `onmousemove` event is attached to the document itself; when the `<span>` region has moving enabled, the position of the mouse determines where the region is moved. Figure 25.9 shows the Web page immediately after it is loaded, and Figure 25.10 shows it while it is being moved. Note that the movement status and the current x,y coordinate, as well as the value of some of the internal variables used by the script, are shown in the text boxes near the bottom of the page.

Listing 25.6 ***Position.htm*—With Dynamic HTML, You Can Change the Position of Any HTML Element**

```
<!DOCTYPE html PUBLIC "-//W3C//DTD XHTML 1.0 Transitional//EN"
    "http://www.w3.org/TR/xhtml1/DTD/xhtml1-transitional.dtd">
<html xmlns="http://www.w3.org/1999/xhtml">
<head>
```

Listing 25.6 Continued

```
<script type="text/javascript" language="JavaScript">
basex  = 0;
basey  = 0;
deltax = 0;
deltay = 0;
moving = false;
function toggleMove() {
   moving = !moving;
   if (moving) {
      Author.style.filter = "alpha(opacity=60,enabled=1)"
      basex = window.event.x;
      basey = window.event.y;
   } else
      Author.style.filter = "alpha(enabled=0)"
}
function endMove() {
   if (moving)
      toggleMove();
}
function moveAuthor() {
   document.MyForm.PicX.value   = window.event.x;
   document.MyForm.PicY.value   = window.event.y;
   document.MyForm.Moving.value = moving;
   document.MyForm.AuL.value    = Author.style.posLeft;
   document.MyForm.AuT.value    = Author.style.posTop;
   document.MyForm.BX.value     = basex;
   document.MyForm.BY.value     = basey;
   document.MyForm.DX.value     = deltax;
   document.MyForm.DY.value     = deltay;
   if (moving) {
      deltax = Math.min(25,Math.max(-25,window.event.x - basex));
      deltay = Math.min(25,Math.max(-25,window.event.y - basey));
      Author.style.posLeft += deltax;
      Author.style.posTop  += deltay;
   }
}
</script>
<title>Positioning Elements with Dynamic HTML</title>
</head>
<body onmousemove="moveAuthor()">
<center>
<h1>Positioning Elements with Dynamic HTML</h1>
<hr />
<p>
Click the mouse on the picture to move it around; click again to drop it.<br />
The picture is moved by setting its <em>style.posLeft</em> and
<em>style.posTop</em> properties.
</p>
<span id="Author" style="position:relative;width:275" onclick="toggleMove()"
                                                      onmouseout="endMove()">
   <table>
```

Part IV

Ch 25

Listing 25.6 Continued

```
    <tr valign="BOTTOM">
        <td><img src="rbflag_ls.gif" width="50"  height="47"  border="0" /></td>
        <td><img src="Author.jpg"    width="175" height="215" border="0" /></td>
        <td><img src="rbflag_rs.gif" width="50"  height="47"  border="0" /></td>
    </tr>
    </table>
</span>
<hr />
<form name="MyForm">
<table>
<tr><td>Mouse X</td>      <td><input type="TEXT" size="5" name="PicX" />  </td>
    <td>Mouse Y</td>      <td><input type="TEXT" size="5" name="PicY" />  </td>
    <td>Moving </td>      <td><input type="TEXT" size="5" name="Moving" /></td>
    <td>basex</td>        <td><input type="TEXT" size="5" name="BX" />    </td>
    <td>basey</td>        <td><input type="TEXT" size="5" name="BY" />    </td>
</tr>
<tr><td>style.posLeft</td><td><input type="TEXT" size="5" name="AuL" />   </td>
    <td>style.posTop</td> <td><input type="TEXT" size="5" name="AuT" />   </td>
    <td> </td>       <td> </td>
    <td>deltax</td>       <td><input type="TEXT" size="5" name="DX" />    </td>
    <td>deltay</td>       <td><input type="TEXT" size="5" name="DY" />    </td>
</tr>
</table>
</form>
</center>
<hr />
<em>Jim O'Donnell, <a href="mailto:jim@odonnell.org">jim@odonnell.org</a></em>
</body>
</html>
```

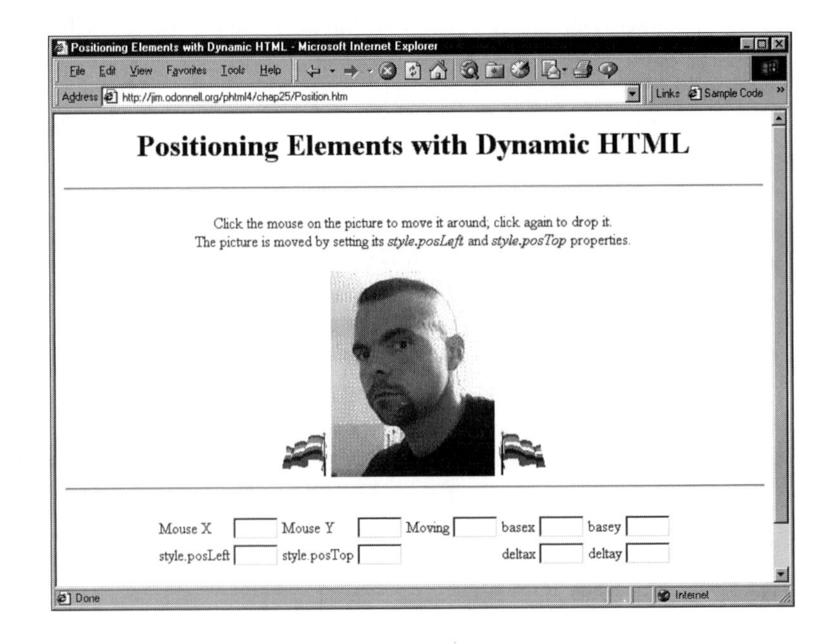

FIGURE 25.9
You can use the HTML <span> container element to group other HTML elements into one region.

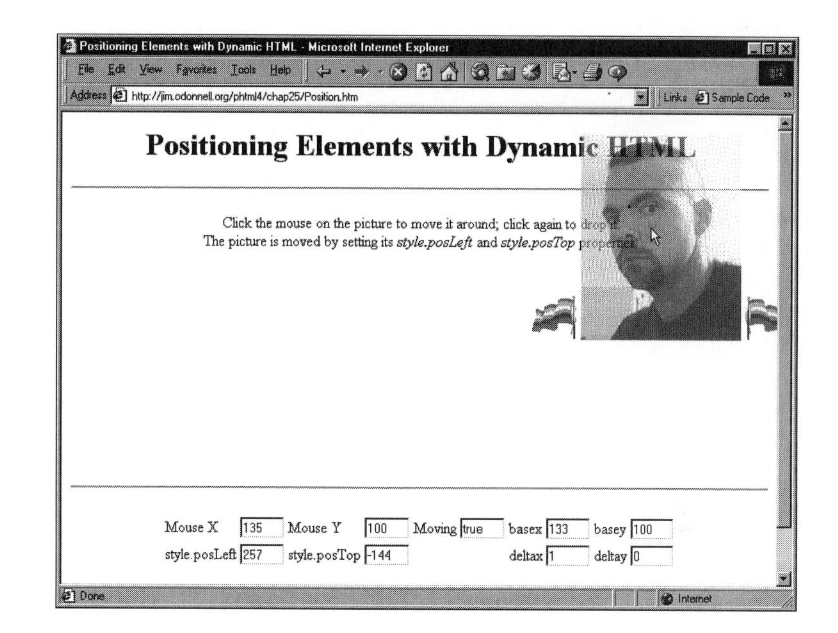

FIGURE 25.10
The `top` and `left` style properties make it easy to move HTML elements around the page.

NOTE The "see-through" effect shown in Figure 25.10 is applied using the Internet Explorer "alpha" filter. Dynamic HTML filters are discussed in the "Dynamic HTML Filters" section later in this chapter. ■

Note that the previous script contains a special "drop" feature. If you move the mouse around too quickly while moving the picture, things might get confused. Actually, the script assumes that the mouse cursor is contained within the `<span>` element that holds the pictures. If the mouse is moved too quickly and manages to escape this region, the picture will start moving out of control. The "drop" feature is implemented by attaching the `onmouseout` event to the `<span>` as well. Then, if the mouse moves out of the span while it's being moved, movement is immediately disabled and the pictures are "dropped."

Changing HTML Documents On-the-Fly

Listing 25.7 shows two ways HTML elements can be changed on-the-fly. The digital clock (see Figure 25.11) is an HTML element, but it changes automatically each second to reflect the local time. The paragraph following it, on the other hand, is changed in response to user input—when the user clicks the Change HTML button, the contents of the text box above the button are substituted for the paragraph. As you can see in Figure 25.12, this substitution can also include any HTML elements, as shown with the hypertext links in this example.

Listing 25.7 *DynCon2.htm*—Dynamic HTML Can Change HTML Documents Without Going Back to the Web Server

```
<!DOCTYPE html PUBLIC "-//W3C//DTD XHTML 1.0 Transitional//EN"
    "http://www.w3.org/TR/xhtml1/DTD/xhtml1-transitional.dtd">
<html xmlns="http://www.w3.org/1999/xhtml">
<head>
<title>Dynamic Content</title>
</head>
<body>
<center>
<h1>Dynamic Content</h1>
<hr />
<div id="digitalClock" style="font-size: 60">
    
</div>
<hr>
<div id="dynContent">
   <p>
   This example shows how HTML content can be dynamically
   changed. The clock shown above is updated with the local
   time on your system once a second. This text will be
   replaced by any HTML elements that are entered in the
   text box below, when the <em>Change HTML</em> button is
   clicked.
   </p>
</div>
<hr />
<input id="newContent" type="text" style="width: 100%" /><br />
<input type="button" value="Change HTML"
       onclick="dynContent.innerHTML = newContent.value" />
</center>
<hr />
<em>Jim O'Donnell, <a href="mailto:jim@odonnell.org">jim@odonnell.org</a></em>
</body>
<script type="text/javascript" language="JavaScript">
function runClock() {
   var d,h,m,s;
//
   d = new Date();
   h = d.getHours();
   m = d.getMinutes();
   s = d.getSeconds();
//
   if (h < 10) h = "0" + h;
   if (m < 10) m = "0" + m;
   if (s < 10) s = "0" + s;
//
   digitalClock.innerHTML = h + ":" + m + ":" + s;
   window.setTimeout("runClock();",100);
}
window.onload = runClock;
</script>
</html>
```

FIGURE 25.11
Real-time clocks appearing in Web pages are common; with Dynamic HTML, however, you can make them appear using only HTML elements.

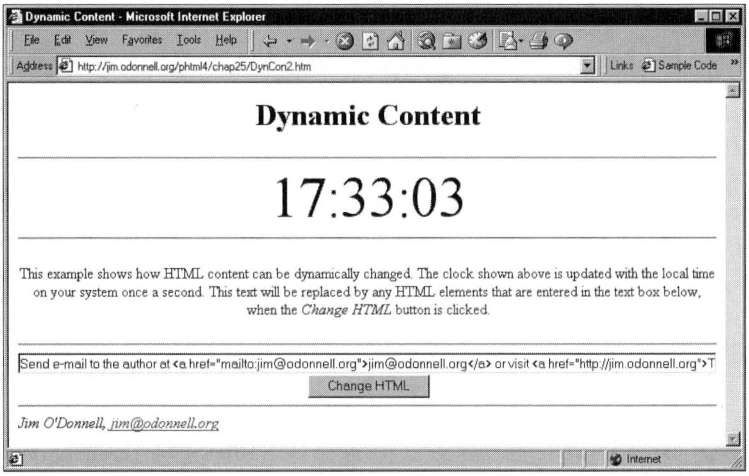

FIGURE 25.12
Dynamic HTML can dynamically change the contents of a displayed HTML document, which is automatically redisplayed by Internet Explorer.

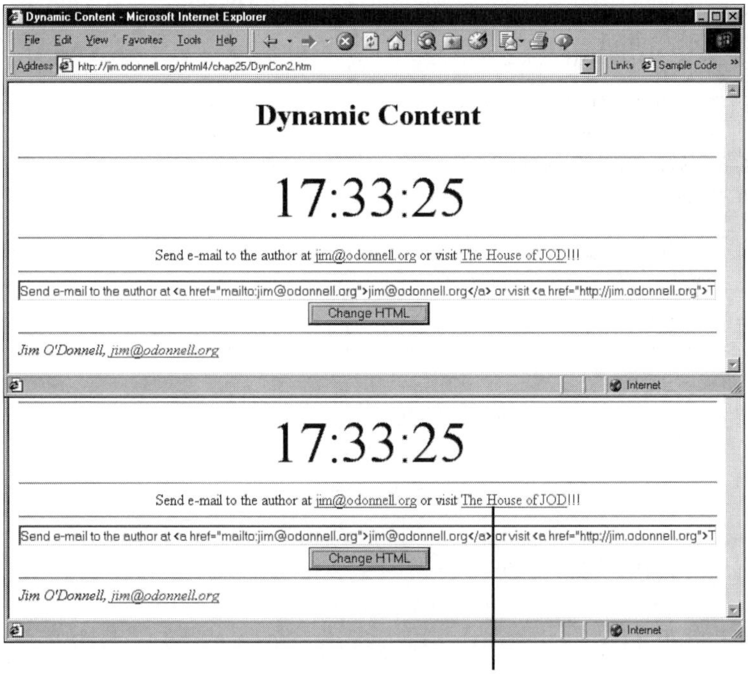

Dynamically changed HTML content

Dynamic HTML Filters

Microsoft has included some new capabilities in its newer Internet Explorer Web browsers through a series of ActiveX Controls and Web browser objects as part of its implementation of Dynamic HTML. You have already seen one of them in action: the Data Source Object that works along with Dynamic HTML data binding to enable HTML elements to import data from external sources. In addition to this component, Microsoft has included a series of controls used to create and manipulate graphic objects and the appearance of an HTML document as a whole.

Microsoft has included a series of filters you can add to Web pages to achieve a number of interesting visual effects that were previously possible only by creating large graphic images in a program such as Adobe PhotoShop. These filters are accessed through style sheet attributes and can be applied to text, images, and graphic objects—in short, anything that can appear in an HTML document.

Microsoft has an excellent example of the possible effects users can achieve with the Dynamic HTML filters, along with the other Dynamic HTML demos. The demo Web site is located at

```
http://www.microsoft.com/ie/ie40/demos/
```

The filter example is located at

```
http://www.microsoft.com/ie/ie40/demos/filters.htm
```

Figure 25.13 shows the default, unfiltered state of this demo page, and it has the following elements:

- HTML text
- GIF image
- Graphic object
- Buttons attached to Dynamic HTML filters

Table 25.1 shows a listing of the different filters included with Dynamic HTML and supported by Internet Explorer, along with a description of their effects.

Table 25.1 Dynamic HTML Filters in Internet Explorer

Filter	Description
Alpha	Used to make an object more or less opaque.
Blur	Used to blur an object in a specified direction; this can be used to make it appear as if the object is moving very quickly in that direction.
Chroma	Used to make a specific color in an object transparent.

Table 25.1 Continued

Filter	Description
Drop Shadow	Used to give an object a solid silhouette in a specified direction.
Flip Horizontal	Used to flip an object horizontally.
Flip Vertical	Used to flip an object vertically.
Glow	Used to add a radiance effect to an object.
Grayscale	Used to display an object in shades of gray.
Invert	Used to invert the colors of an object.
Light	Used to add simulated light sources to an object.
Mask	Used to take a visual object, make the transparent pixels a specific color, and make a transparent mask from the nontransparent pixels.
Shadow	Used to give an object a solid silhouette in a specific direction. This filter is similar to the Drop Shadow filter, but is more configurable.
Wave	Used to give a sine wave distortion to an object along its vertical axis.
XRay	Used to change an object's color depth and display it in black and white, making it look somewhat like a black-and-white x-ray.

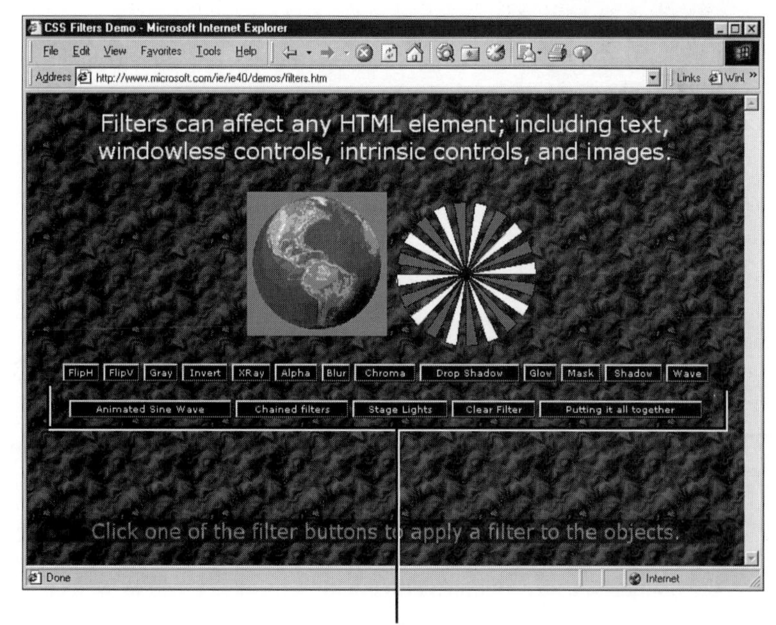

FIGURE 25.13
Dynamic HTML filters can apply visual effects to any HTML element—text, images, even other objects.

Placing *graphic* Objects

Before you see how the filters are applied, it is first helpful to see how the `graphic` object is created. Listing 25.8 shows an excerpt from the example shown, illustrating how the `graphic` object is included and configured in the HTML document.

Listing 25.8 Embedding Graphic Objects

```
<object id="sg1" style="width:150px;height:150px"
        classid="clsid:369303c2-d7ac-11d0-89d5-00a0c90833e6">
<param name="Line0001" value="SetFillStyle(1)" />
<param name="Line0002" value="SetFillColor(255,255,255)" />
<param name="Line0003" value="Pie(-75,-75,150,150,0,10,0)" />
<param name="Line0004" value="SetFillColor(0,90,200)" />
<param name="Line0005" value="Pie(-75,-75,150,150,0,10,18)" />
<param name="Line0006" value="SetFillColor(255,255,255)" />
...
<param name="Line0042" value="SetFillColor(255,255,255)" />
<param name="Line0043" value="Pie(-75,-75,150,150,0,10,360)" />
</object>
```

This HTML `<object>` element and parameters use the following information:

- The `id` attribute of the `<object>` element defines the name of the object that will be used by scripts and other objects.
- The `style` attribute of the `<object>` element defines, in this case, the desired height and width of the object.
- The `classid` attribute of the `<object>` element is its most important attribute because it uniquely identifies this ActiveX Control that the `<object>` element is attempting to include in the HTML document.
- The `<param/>` elements given inside the `<object>` container are used to configure the object. The `name`, `value` attribute pairs used are unique to any given object and are used to configure it appropriately. In this case, they define a series of pie wedges used to make up the `graphic` object.

Applying Dynamic HTML Filters

Dynamic HTML filters are implemented by Microsoft as style sheet attributes. To apply them to all or part of an HTML document, therefore, a region needs to be defined and (optionally) named. You can then write scripts that reference the `style` property of the region to apply different filters.

Listing 25.9 shows the outline of the region defined in the example shown previously in Figure 25.13. Notice that HTML text, an image, and a graphic object are all included within the bounds of a `<div>` container element. The `name` attribute of the `<div>` element enables the entire region to be treated as one and to be referred to by name within the object hierarchy.

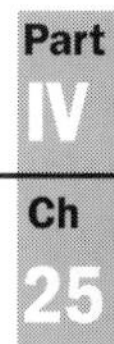

Listing 25.9 Using the <div> Tag to Group HTML Elements

```
<div id="theImg" style parameters...>
   HTML text...
   <img image parameters... />
   <object graphic object parameters...>
      <param graphic object parameters... />
      ...
</div>
```

Figure 25.14 shows the document when the Blur filter effect is selected. This is implemented by using the `onClick` method of one of the buttons, as shown here:

```
<input class="clsbtn" value="Blur" type="BUTTON" name="BLUR"
       onClick="theImg.style.filter = 'blur(direction=45,strength=15,
                                              add=0,enabled=1)';
                progress.innerText = 'explanatory text...';" />
```

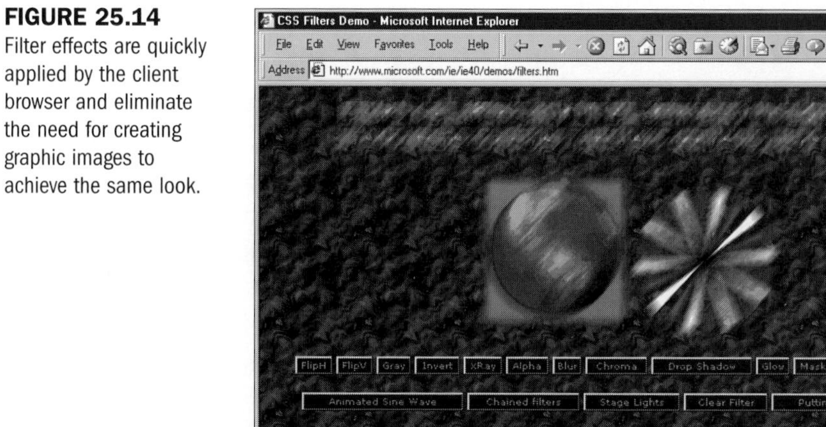

FIGURE 25.14
Filter effects are quickly applied by the client browser and eliminate the need for creating graphic images to achieve the same look.

The different attributes of this `<input>` element do the following:

- The `class` attribute attaches a style to the label of the button, enabling you to change its appearance. (This was not possible in earlier versions of Internet Explorer.)
- The `type`, `value`, and `name` attributes are the familiar attributes used for HTML form elements, defining the type of element, label, and object name, respectively.
- The `onClick` attribute attaches the inline JavaScript shown so that it gets executed whenever the button is clicked. The inline JavaScript does two things. First, it attaches

the Blur filter to the style sheet `filter` property for the region named `theImg` (as defined in Listing 25.9). Second, it sets the `innerText` property of the region named `progress`, which displays explanatory text in that region for the filter selected.

Several filter effects are possible. It is even possible to combine the effects of more than one filter within a given region or to apply a filter and animate it through JavaScript. Figure 25.15 shows a snapshot of an animated sine wave filter. This is achieved by applying the Wave filter, and then dynamically changing its parameters with a JavaScript, as shown in this code excerpt:

```
function animatwav() {
   if (wavable) {
      wavphase = (wavphase + 10) % 100;
      if (theImg.style.filter ==
      ➥"wave(freq=4,strength=8,phase=0,lightstrength=25,add=1,enabled=1)") {
         theImg.filters[0].phase = wavphase;
      }
      window.setTimeout("animatwav()",0400,"JavaScript");
   }
}
```

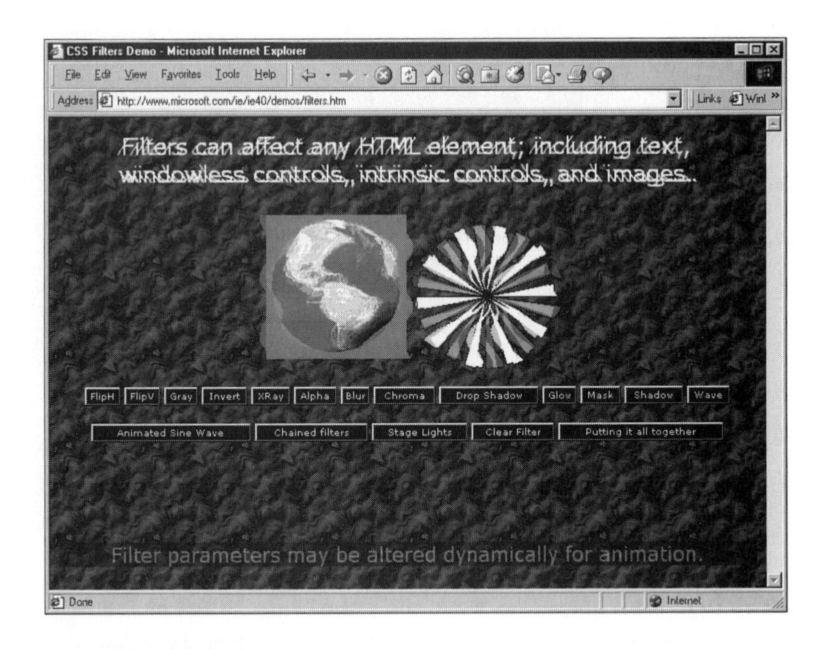

FIGURE 25.15
Because you can dynamically change the filter applied to a given region, it is easy to quickly achieve an assortment of effects.

Dynamic HTML Behaviors

When Microsoft released Internet Explorer 4, one of the technologies that they introduced and supported was *scriptlets*, scripted components that could be included and reused in multiple documents. Just as style sheets give developers the ability to separate content from formatting information, scriptlets provide the capability to separate content from scripted functionality.

With Internet Explorer 5, Microsoft deprecated support for scriptlets in favor of Dynamic HTML *behaviors*. Similar to scriptlets, behaviors give you the ability to create simple components that can be used to provide specific functionality or behavior on a page. In this way, you can extend the functionality of the browser within a page but not clutter the page itself with a lot of extraneous scripting.

For example, consider the following example, Listing 25.10, which is used to implement a simple mouseover effect. When the mouse is over the list item, its format is changed to match the `.HILITE` style class and then returned to normal when the mouse is moved off.

Listing 25.10 *NoBehave.htm*—Dynamic Format Changes Can Be Implemented with Styles

```
<!DOCTYPE html PUBLIC "-//W3C//DTD XHTML 1.0 Transitional//EN"
    "http://www.w3.org/TR/xhtml1/DTD/xhtml1-transitional.dtd">
<html xmlns="http://www.w3.org/1999/xhtml">
<head>
<style>
.HILITE {color:red;letter-spacing:2}
</style>
<title>XHTML Styles</title>
</head>
<body>
<h1>XHTML Styles</h1>
<hr />
<ul><li onmouseover = "this.className = 'HILITE'"
        onmouseout  = "this.className = ''">HTML Authoring</li>
</ul>
<hr />
<em>Jim O'Donnell, <a href="mailto:jim@odonnell.org">jim@odonnell.org</a></em>
</body>
</html>
```


By encapsulating this mouseover behavior in a Dynamic HTML behavior, this example is simplified quite a bit, as shown in Listing 25.11.

Listing 25.11 *Behave.htm*—Dynamic HTML Behaviors Can Be Used to Encapsulate Functions and Effects

```
<!DOCTYPE html PUBLIC "-//W3C//DTD XHTML 1.0 Transitional//EN"
    "http://www.w3.org/TR/xhtml1/DTD/xhtml1-transitional.dtd">
<html xmlns="http://www.w3.org/1999/xhtml">
<head>
```

Listing 25.11 Continued

```
<title>Dynamic HTML Behaviors</title>
</head>
<body>
<h1>Dynamic HTML Behaviors</h1>
<hr />
<ul><li style="behavior:url(Highlight.htc)">HTML Authoring</li></ul>
<hr />
<em>Jim O'Donnell, <a href="mailto:jim@odonnell.org">jim@odonnell.org</a></em>
</body>
</html>
```

Listing 25.12 shows the source for `Highlight.htc`, which is the file containing the Dynamic HTML behavior. As you can see, it consists of the scripts that implement the behavior, as well as instructions for when it is to be applied.

Listing 25.12 Highlight.htc—Dynamic HTML Behaviors Can Extend Browser Functionality

```
<public:component>
<public:attach event = "onmouseover" onevent = "Highlight()" />
<public:attach event = "onmouseout"  onevent = "Restore()"   />
<script language="JavaScript">
   var normalColor, normalSpacing;
   function Highlight() {
      normalColor                 = currentStyle.color;
      normalSpacing               = currentStyle.letterSpacing;
      runtimeStyle.color          = "red";
      runtimeStyle.letterSpacing = 2;
   }
   function Restore() {
      runtimeStyle.color          = normalColor;
      runtimeStyle.letterSpacing = normalSpacing;
   }
</script>
</public:component>
```

You might wonder what the big idea is. Obviously, with this example, the combination of the revised file and the behavior file is quite a bit larger than the original. However, after the behavior is defined in the `.htc` component file, it easily can be applied to other items in the same Web page—or any other Web page—with a simple style assignment. If it's an effect that you are only going to use once, then behaviors won't save you any time or energy. If it's something that you will be doing over and over, however—and your audience is largely confined to users of Internet Explorer 5 and higher—then you might want to consider using Dynamic HTML behaviors.

NOTE The main page of Microsoft's developed information for Internet Explorer is `http://msdn. microsoft.com/ie/`. By selecting the link for "HTML, DHTML, Scripting" you can find more information and samples for Dynamic HTML behaviors. ■

Find Out More About Dynamic HTML

It would be possible to write an entire book on Dynamic HTML, so there is no way it can be covered in the space that has been allotted here. The object of this chapter was to give you the resources for getting started with your own Web pages by using Microsoft's implementation of Dynamic HTML and Internet Explorer. To see more about both Microsoft and Netscape Dynamic HTML, check out Que Publishing's *Special Edition, Using Dynamic HTML*. If you want to see more examples and find out more information, try some of the links and references given in Appendix B, "General Reference Resource." ●

CHAPTER 26

Advanced Netscape Dynamic HTML

by Jim ODonnell

In this chapter

Different Approaches to Dynamic HTML

In Chapter 24, "Introduction to Dynamic HTML," you learned about the different claims made by Netscape and Microsoft as to what constitutes Dynamic HTML. As originally proposed, the two companies had a number of similarities and far more differences. As time has gone by, both Microsoft and Netscape have released newer versions of their browsers with greater support for Web technology standards, which has brought them closer to one another. However, with the introduction of Navigator 6, Netscape has dropped most of the proprietary and non-standard capabilities from its browser and embraced Web standards to a very high degree. Because of this, when discussing Netscape's implementation of Dynamic HTML, it is actually necessary to split the discussion between Navigator 4 and Navigator 6.

All the Internet Explorer, Navigator 4, and Navigator 6 browsers largely conform to the Cascading Style Sheets 1 (CSS1) standards for content positioning, for example, but Navigator 4 also has the non-standard `<layer>` element that can do many of the same things. Another difference is in the scripting language. Navigator 4 and 6 use different versions of JavaScript. Internet Explorer uses its own JScript, which is largely compatible with Netscape's JavaScript, but not completely. The latest versions of JScript and JavaScript (in Navigator 6) largely adhere to the ECMAScript standard, though some differences remain.

The Document Object Model (DOM) supported by Internet Explorer is much more extensive than Navigator 4's. Because both Internet Explorer and Navigator 6 profess support for the W3C DOM standards, those two browsers are quite a bit closer. However, Microsoft has still incorporated many of its own non-standard capabilities into its browser.

The list could go on and on, but the point is that if you develop a Dynamic HTML document for one browser, it is likely that it will not work in the other. This might hinder your development efforts if your audience is using a mix of browsers. If you are developing for a consistent desktop platform (a corporate intranet, for example, where everyone is using the same browser), you can make use of one definition of Dynamic HTML or the other and not have to worry about your content being lost on some users.

NOTE Microsoft's version of Dynamic HTML also calls for dynamic redisplay and reformatting of dynamic content, attaching data from an external source to an HTML element, and multimedia capabilities using ActiveX Controls. Netscape Navigator 4 does not support most of these additional Dynamic HTML components; however, Navigator 6 does. ■

This chapter digs deeper into Netscape's implementation of Dynamic HTML, concentrating mostly on the Navigator 4 browser, because it is by far more extensively used (at the time of this writing; Navigator 6 has only been released as a preview release). By more closely examining Netscape's approach to Dynamic HTML and considering some examples, you will be better prepared to develop pages for a user base that has Navigator as its browser of choice. After this discussion, you will examine some of Navigator 6's standards-based capabilities.

A Standard Deployment of Dynamic HTML?

Even if your entire audience is using one browser or another, you should keep in mind that people are working on a standard deployment of some of the common Dynamic HTML elements listed at the start of the chapter. This means that you could develop Dynamic HTML content for one browser or another, and it might never be considered "standard."

Content positioning by Cascading Style Sheets is covered in the CSS specification found at `http://www.w3.org/Style/`. The good news here is that both major browsers conform to the standard to a large degree.

Additionally, the World Wide Web Consortium (W3C) is working on various levels of a standard Document Object Model (DOM), the details of which are covered at `http://www.w3.org/DOM/`. Both Netscape's and Microsoft's Web Browser Object Models are extensions of the W3C DOM.

Chapter 27, "Cross-Browser Dynamic HTML," contains more tips on how to create Web pages that use Dynamic HTML and that can be successfully viewed with both Netscape Navigator and Microsoft Internet Explorer

---

▶ To learn more about DHTML for both browsers, **see** "What Is Cross-Browser Dynamic HTML?," **p. 694**

The Main Elements of Navigator 4 Dynamic HTML

Netscape considers something to be Dynamic HTML if it includes the following three major elements:

- Style sheets accessible through the browser object model
- Content positioning in two- and three dimensions
- Downloadable fonts

Netscape Navigator 4 supports the Cascading Style Sheet specification just like other browsers do, but what makes its support dynamic is that style sheet elements are part of the Navigator browser object model. This means that you can specify style information through JavaScript in addition to the CSS way of doing it. Figure 26.1 shows a Web page that formats content style through both JavaScript and CSS (see Listing 26.1). As you can see, it is possible to manipulate the same style parameters with either method.

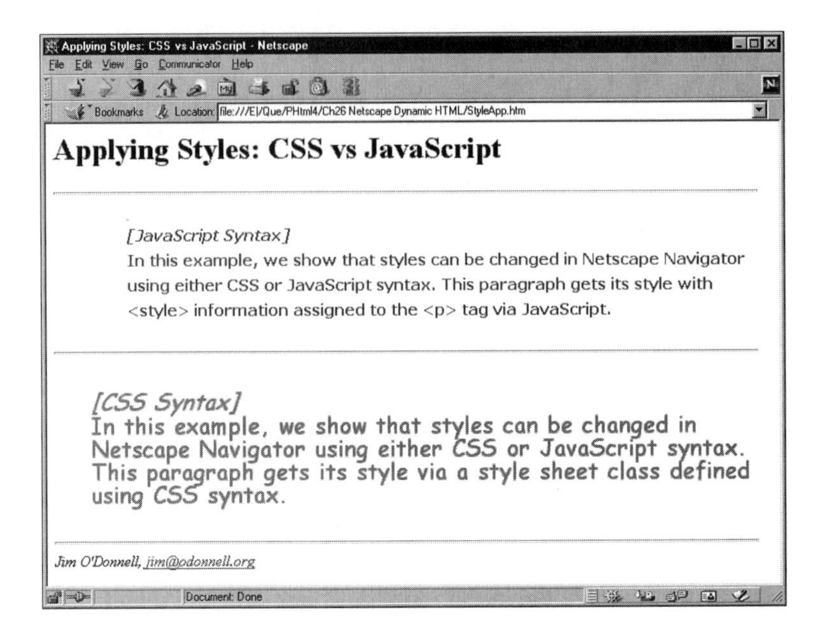

FIGURE 26.1
Navigator enables you to specify style parameters using a couple of syntaxes.

Listing 26.1 *StyleApp.htm*—JavaScript and CSS Styles

```
<!DOCTYPE html PUBLIC "-//W3C//DTD XHTML 1.0 Transitional//EN"
    "http://www.w3.org/TR/xhtml1/DTD/xhtml1-transitional.dtd">
<html xmlns="http://www.w3.org/1999/xhtml">
<head>
<style type="text/css">
.css {color: red;
      font-family: Comic Sans MS;
      font-size: 18pt;
      line-height: 18pt;
      margin-left: 40px}
</style>
<style type="text/javascript">
document.tags.P.color = "blue";
document.tags.P.fontFamily = "Verdana";
document.tags.P.fontSize = "12pt";
document.tags.P.fontWeight = "bold";
document.tags.P.lineHeight = "20pt";
document.tags.P.marginLeft = "80px";
</style>
<title>Applying Styles: CSS vs JavaScript</title>
</head>
<body>
<h1>Applying Styles: CSS vs JavaScript</h1>
<hr />
<p><em>[JavaScript Syntax]</em><br>
   In this example, we show that styles can be changed in
   Netscape Navigator using either CSS or JavaScript syntax.
```

Listing 26.1 *Continued*

```
   This paragraph gets its style with &lt;style&gt; information
   assigned to the &lt;p&gt; element via JavaScript.</p>
<hr />
<p class="css"><em>[CSS Syntax]</em><br>
   In this example, we show that styles can be changed in
   Netscape Navigator using either CSS or JavaScript syntax.
   This paragraph gets its style via a style sheet class
   defined using CSS syntax.</p>
<hr />
<em>Jim O'Donnell, <a href="mailto:jim@odonnell.org">jim@odonnell.org</a></em>
</body>
</html>
```

Note the object orientation of the JavaScript code in Listing 26.1. The first style assignment says "set the `color` property of the `p` property of the `tags` property of the `document` property to blue." The Navigator browser object model makes many elements available to you in this way.

TIP

The `document` object reference is understood whenever you reference the `tags` object. Thus, instead of saying

```
document.tags.P.color = "blue";
```

you can equivalently say

```
tags.P.color = "blue";
```

When assigning multiple style characteristics to the same element, you can use the JavaScript `with` instruction to reference the element and then all styles inside the `with` instruction will be assigned to the element. For the `P` element assignments in Listing 26.1, you could have used the following abbreviated code:

```
with (tags.P) {
  color = "blue";
  fontFamily = "Verdana";
  fontSize = "12pt";
  fontWeight = "bold";
  lineHeight = "20pt";
  marginLeft = "80px";
}
```

Content positioning was introduced in Navigator 4 through use of the `<layer>` and `<ilayer>` elements for absolute and relative positioning, respectively. Unfortunately for Netscape, using HTML elements to specify content presentation information flies in the face of the direction that the W3C wants to move—namely, to reserve HTML for describing the meaning of the content and to specify presentation through style sheets. The W3C rejected the Netscape proposal for the `<layer>` element, and Netscape was forced to scramble to make Navigator compliant with the CSS approach to content positioning. Currently, Navigator supports both positioning techniques, although you should always consider developing according to the CSS specification because this will make your content more portable.

Figures 26.2 and 26.3 show a page done with Netscape layers. Each figure has two layers nested within an outer layer. The two layers, Layer A and Layer B in the example, are each made up of text with some style information attached. The containing layer has functions attached to its `onMouseOver` and `onMouseOut` events that toggle which layer is shown by manipulating their visibility properties. Figure 26.2 shows the `onMouseOut` condition, with Layer A visible. Figure 26.3 shows the `onMouseOver` condition, with Layer B visible. Note that the `onMouseOver` event is triggered even though it appears the mouse cursor is not over the layer. Because the `onMouseOver` event of the outer layer is used, more of the screen area of the browser window is included in it than just the visible inner layers. The HTML code for this example is shown in Listing 26.2.

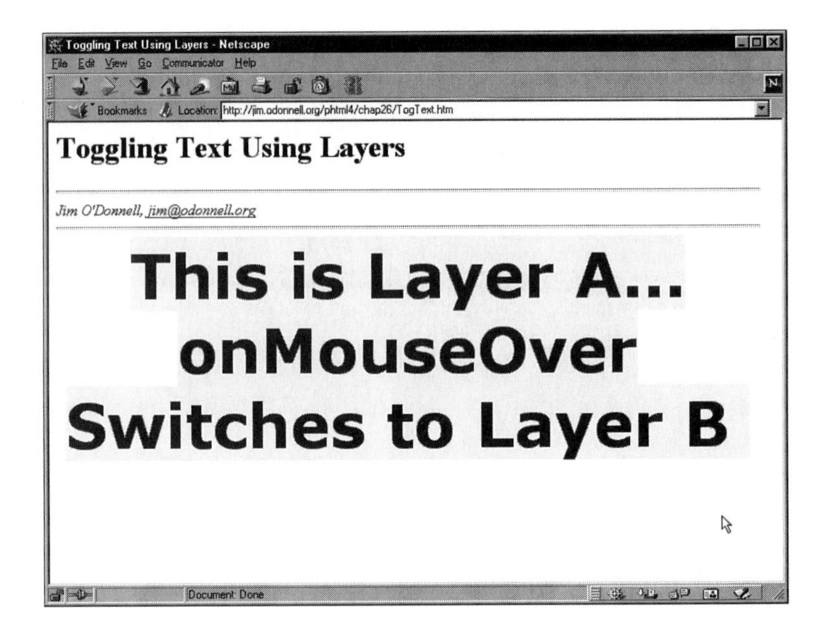

FIGURE 26.2
When you open this page, it displays only one of two nested layers.

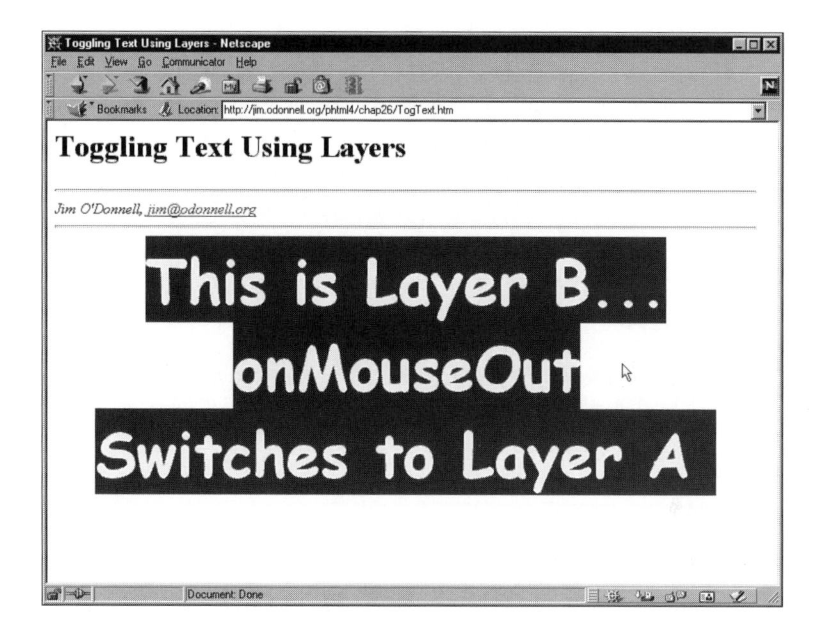

FIGURE 26.3
By clicking the layer, you instruct the browser to swap the hidden and displayed nested layers.

Listing 26.2 *TogText.htm*—Dynamic Content in Netscape Navigator Using Layers

```
<!DOCTYPE html PUBLIC "-//W3C//DTD XHTML 1.0 Transitional//EN"
    "http://www.w3.org/TR/xhtml1/DTD/xhtml1-transitional.dtd">
<html xmlns="http://www.w3.org/1999/xhtml">
<head>
<title>Toggling Text Using Layers</title>
<script type="text/javascript" language="JavaScript">
function layerUp(show,hide) {
   show.visibility = "SHOW";
   hide.visibility = "HIDE";
}
</script>
</head>
<body bgcolor="#ffffff">
<h1>Toggling Text Using Layers</h1>
<hr />
<em>Jim O'Donnell, <a href="mailto:jim@odonnell.org">jim@odonnell.org</a></em>
<hr />
<center>
<layer name="toglayer"
       onmouseover="layerUp(layerb,layera)"
       onmouseout="layerUp(layera,layerb)"
       visibility="inherit">
   <layer name="toglayera"
          style="font-family: Verdana; font-size: 48pt;
                 font-weight: bold; text-align: center;
                 color: blue; background-color: yellow"
          visibility="inherit">
      Layer A Text<br />Switches to Layer B onMouseOver...
```

Listing 26.2 Continued

```
    </layer>
    <layer name="toglayerb"
          style="font-family: Comic Sans MS; font-size: 48pt;
                font-weight: bold; text-align: center;
                color: yellow; background-color: blue"
          visibility="hide">
      Layer B Text<br />Switches to Layer A onMouseOut...
    </layer>
  </layer>
  </center>
  </body>
  <script type="text/javascript" language="JavaScript">
  var layera = document.layers['toglayer'].document.toglayera;
  var layerb = document.layers['toglayer'].document.toglayerb;
  </script>
  </html>
```

TIP Netscape has many useful Dynamic HTML JavaScript routines for Navigator 4 available through its DevEdge site at `http://developer.netscape.com/tech/dynhtml/`.

For all your hard work in coming up with attractive style information, you might end up having your effect lost on users who don't have the font you specified in your style sheet. Rather than take chances on fonts a user might not have, you can bundle the font you want to use with a Web page and have it download along with the page. This assures both you and the reader that the page will display the way you want it to.

Figure 26.4 shows an example of a page that uses a downloaded font. The typeface you see is used for Japanese language pages, one not commonly found on most users' systems.

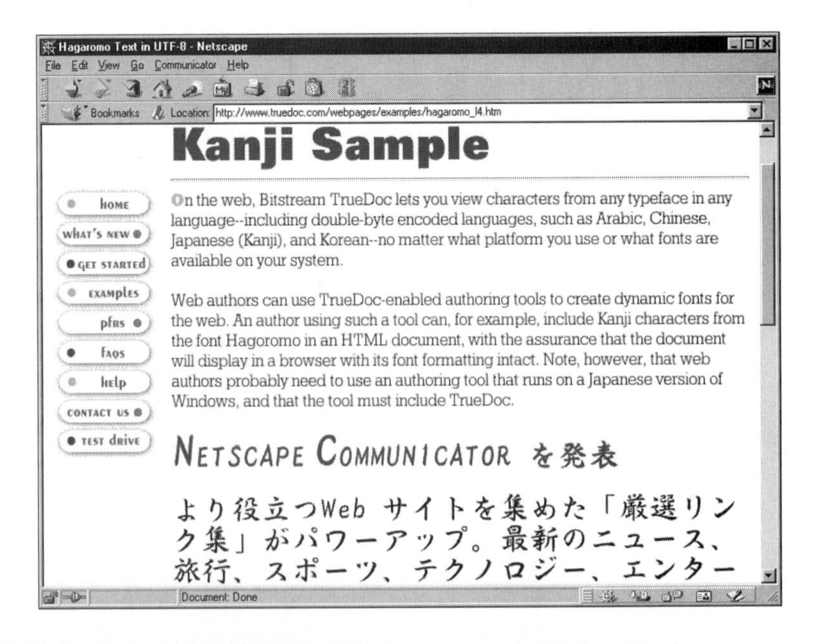

FIGURE 26.4
By downloading fonts along with a page, you ensure that readers see content the way you intended.

Now that you have the major ideas behind Netscape's Dynamic HTML fresh in your mind, it is time to take a closer look at them. The next few sections of this chapter examine each idea in turn and provide you with more details about how to implement Dynamic HTML on your pages meant for Navigator 4.

JavaScript Accessible Style Sheets

Netscape Navigator does support the CSS specification, and using the CSS approach is a perfectly good way to build style information into your documents. But, as you saw earlier in the chapter, Navigator also includes style properties in the browser object model, which means you can use JavaScript to access and set style characteristics. Netscape calls this approach JavaScript Accessible Style Sheets; it was the first major feature of Netscape's version of Dynamic HTML in Navigator 4.

The advantage of JavaScript Accessible Style Sheets is that by using the browser object model, you can dynamically change style information by using scripts triggered by certain events that come about from user actions. This section focuses solely on the JavaScript implementation of styles so that you can be prepared to use them by themselves and as part of content positioning.

To get started, it is helpful to recall some of the style-related code—both CSS and JavaScript—that you saw earlier in the chapter. Go back a few pages and look at Listing 26.1. Both techniques apply the same style information, yet one is an implementation of CSS style sheets and the other is an implementation of JavaScript Accessible Style Sheets. If you are familiar with one approach, learning the other would be pretty easy. Most of the style characteristics you can set have the same name (although the names differ in the use of hyphens, capitalization, and so on). The chief difference between the two approaches is how the style characteristics are assigned. The CSS approach uses name/value pairs separated by a colon. The JavaScript approach is more object based in that you reference an object's (an element's) style property and set it to the value you want. Beyond the syntactical difference in assigning values, the two approaches are, in most respects, equivalent.

Table 26.1 summarizes the style characteristics you can assign by either approach and includes the keyword for the characteristic that you would use in either the CSS or JavaScript approach. The table should make a handy reference for all style sheet authors, regardless of how they are assigning style information.

Table 26.1 Style Characteristics in CSS and JavaScript Accessible Style Sheets

Style Characteristic	CSS Keyword	JavaScript Property
Font family	`font-family`	`fontFamily`
Font size	`font-size`	`fontSize`

Table 26.1 Continued

Style Characteristic	CSS Keyword	JavaScript Property
Font style	font-style	fontStyle
Font weight	font-weight	fontWeight
Text alignment	text-align	textAlign
Text decoration	text-decoration	textDecoration
Text indent	text-indent	textIndent
Text transform	text-transform	textTransform
Line height	line-height	lineHeight
Alignment	float	align
Border color	border-color	borderColor
Border style	border-style	borderStyle
Border widths (all)	border-width	borderWidths()
Border width (bottom)	border-bottom-width	borderBottomWidth
Border width (left)	border-left-width	borderLeftWidth
Border width (right)	border-right-width	borderRightWidth
Border width (top)	border-top-width	borderTopWidth
Margins (all)	margin	margins()
Margin (bottom)	margin-bottom	marginBottom
Margin (left)	margin-left	marginLeft
Margin (right)	margin-right	marginRight
Margin (top)	margin-top	marginTop
Padding (all)	paddings	paddings()
Padding (bottom)	padding-bottom	paddingBottom
Padding (left)	padding-left	paddingLeft
Padding (right)	padding-right	paddingRight
Padding (top)	padding-top	paddingTop
Width	width	width
Background color	background-color	backgroundColor
Background image	background-image	backgroundImage
Color	color	color
Display	display	display
List style type	list-style-type	listStyleType
Whitespace	white-space	whiteSpace

You are probably familiar with most of the characteristics in Table 26.1, except possibly for the last three. Display controls how an element is displayed and can take values of `block` (display as a block-level element), `inline`, `list-item`, or `none`. List style type refers to the different styles of ordered and unordered lists HTML supports. You might set the `list-style-type` keyword or the `listStyleType` property to values of `disc`, `circle`, `square`, `decimal`, `lower-alpha`, `upper-alpha`, `lower-roman`, `upper-roman`, or `none`. Finally, the whitespace characteristic specifies how extra whitespace should be treated. A whitespace value of `normal` means that extra whitespace characters will be ignored, and a value of `pre` means that all whitespace characters will be rendered.

With what you have learned so far, you can probably handle most of the style sheet challenges that come your way. Be aware, however, that both the CSS and JavaScript approaches support some more advanced techniques. These include the following:

- Setting up different classes of the same element
- Creating a named style that you can apply to any element
- Selecting an element based on context
- Making use of block-level styles

Each of these points is covered in the sections that follow, with emphasis on the JavaScript implementation of each.

Troubleshooting

If your JavaScript code is not working in Netscape Navigator, make sure JavaScript is enabled in your Netscape Navigator browser. You can do this by choosing Edit, Preferences, and then clicking the Advanced item in the category listing in the Preferences dialog box. After you do this, you will see a list of check box options. Make sure that the Enable JavaScript and Enable Style Sheets check boxes are checked. Then click OK.

Because Netscape is capable of processing JavaScript, you should find that the next time you load your JavaScript document, Netscape will interpret the script code and note in a pop-up dialog box any syntax errors it finds. The error messages are usually very specific and should help you clean up your code.

Setting Up Style Classes

Suppose you assign the following style characteristics to the `<h1>` element:

```
<style type="text/javascript">
with (tags.H1) {
   backgroundColor = "black";
   color = "white";
   fontSize = "36pt";
   lineHeight = "40pt";
   align = "center";
   width = "100%";
}
</style>
```

Using the preceding code, each level 1 heading would appear centered in a black box that is 40 points high and spans the width of the browser screen. The text of the headline would be 36 points high and rendered in white. But what if you don't want every level 1 heading to look like this? Suppose you want some of them to be in yellow on a red background so that they are more prominent. In that case, you can define two classes of the `H1` element style—one for the white on black heading and one for the yellow on red.

Classes are set up using the JavaScript `classes` object. To set up the two types of level 1 headings just discussed, for example, you could use this code:

```
<style type="text/javascript">
with (tags.H1) {
   fontSize = "36pt";
   lineHeight = "40pt";
   align = "center";
   width = "100%";
}
classes.whiteOnBlack.H1.backgroundColor = "black";
classes.whiteOnBlack.H1.color = "white";
classes.yellowOnRed.H1.backgroundColor = "red";
classes.yellowOnRed.H1.color = "yellow";
</style>
```

The `with` operator makes all level 1 headings 36 point on 40 point, centered, and the full width of the browser screen. The last four lines of code define the two classes: `whiteOnBlack`, which produces white text on a black background; and `yellowOnRed`, which produces yellow text on a red background. With the two classes defined, you can invoke one class or another by using the `class` attribute in the `<h1>` element as follows:

```
<h1 class="yellowOnRed">Yellow headline on red background</h1>
<h1 class="whiteOnBlack">White headline on black background</h1>
```

The one limitation in the way the classes are set up is that they can be used only with the `H1` element. If you want your classes applicable to more than just the `H1` element, you can duplicate the code for the other elements you want to use the classes with, or you can make the classes available to every element by using the `all` object as follows:

```
classes.whiteOnBlack.all.backgroundColor = "black";
classes.whiteOnBlack.all.color = "white";
classes.yellowOnRed.all.backgroundColor = "red";
classes.yellowOnRed.all.color = "yellow";
```

The preceding code makes the `whiteOnBlack` and `yellowOnRed` classes available to all HTML elements, not just `H1`. If you don't want to apply either class to an element, don't use a `class` attribute with that element.

NOTE The properties assigned in these classes are only applicable to block-level formats such as headings, paragraphs, blockquotes, and lists. Trying to apply the classes to text-level formatting elements would have no effect. ■

CAUTION

You can only specify one `class` per HTML element. If you put multiple `class` attributes in an element, Netscape Navigator 4 uses the first one it encounters and ignores the rest.

Setting Up Named Styles

Besides creating classes of the same element, you can also create a specific named style that you can build into any element. The JavaScript `ids` object enables you to set up the named style, and then the style can be referenced by any element using the `id` attribute.

As an example of a named style, consider the following code:

```
<style type="text/javascript">
ids.allCaps.textTransform = "uppercase";
ids.bigText.fontSize = "125%";
</style>
```

After executing the script code, Navigator recognizes two named styles: `allCaps`, which transforms all text to uppercase; and `bigText`, which magnifies text to 125% of its default size. If you had a paragraph you wanted to appear in all uppercase letters, you could set it up with this:

```
<p id="allCaps">This paragraph is all uppercase letters...</p>
```

Suppose you still had the `whiteOnBlack` and `yellowOnRed` classes available to you from the preceding section. You could then use a class and a named style together as follows:

```
<h1 class="yellowOnRed" id="allCaps">
   Yellow Uppercase Heading on Red Background
</h1>
```


One popular effect on Web pages is *small caps*—text that is all in uppercase and the first letter of each word is larger than the rest of the letters in the word. You can accomplish this with the two named styles already defined, but you have to use the `<span>` element to apply the `bigText` style. For example:

```
<h1 class="whiteOnBlack" id="allCaps">
<span id="bigText">V</span>ery
<span id="bigText">I</span>mportant
<span id="bigText">S</span>tory!
</h1>
```

Listing 26.3 shows an example that combines these methods of applying style information and shows that their effects are cumulative on subject text. In this example, the text within the `<h1>` container element is given the `Impact` style through the `class` attribute and the name `allCaps` through the `ID` attribute. Furthermore, the small caps font style is achieved by applying the named `bigText` style to the first letter of each word. The effects accumulate; the text is first given the font characteristics of 48pt. Impact through the `Impact` class, then it is made all capital letters with the `allCaps` style, and finally, its initial letters are enlarged using the `bigText` style (see Figure 26.5).

Listing 26.3 *StyleApp2.htm*—Applied Style Effects Are Cumulative

```
<!DOCTYPE html PUBLIC "-//W3C//DTD XHTML 1.0 Transitional//EN"
    "http://www.w3.org/TR/xhtml1/DTD/xhtml1-transitional.dtd">
<html xmlns="http://www.w3.org/1999/xhtml">
<head>
<style type="text/javascript">
classes.Impact.all.fontFamily = "Impact";
classes.Impact.all.fontSize = "48pt";
ids.allCaps.textTransform = "uppercase";
ids.bigText.fontSize = "125%";
</style>
<title>Applying Styles: Classes and Named Styles</title>
</head>
<body>
<h1 class="Impact" id="allCaps">
   <span id="bigText">A</span>pplying
   <span id="bigText">S</span>tyles:
   <span id="bigText">C</span>lasses
   and
   <span id="bigText">N</span>amed
   <span id="bigText">S</span>tyles</h1>
<hr />
<em>Jim O'Donnell, <a href="mailto:jim@odonnell.org">jim@odonnell.org</a></em>
</body>
</html>
```

FIGURE 26.5
You can use style classes and named styles together to produce complex typographic effects.

Doing Contextual Selection

Sometimes it is necessary to apply style information to an element only when it appears in the context of another. With CSS, doing this is fairly straightforward. As an example,

```
<style type="text/css">
H1 STRONG {color:red};
</style>
```

says that any level 1 heading text marked up with the <strong> element should be rendered in red. This makes some sense because headings are already in boldface. Adding the <strong> element, which usually produces boldface rendering, does not change the appearance of the text. By making <strong> text red within a level 1 heading, you make it stand out even more and thereby convey your strong emphasis.

To accomplish the same effect with JavaScript, you need to use the `contextual()` method. `contextual()` takes a list of element objects that represent the usage context to which you want to apply style information. The following replicates the effect of the CSS code just discussed:

```
<style type="javascript"
contextual(tags.H1,tags.STRONG).color = "red";
</style>
```

After you have the context set up, you don't need to do anything special in the HTML code to invoke it. You just nest the elements and the browser detects the context.

Applying Styles to Block-Level Elements

Block-level formatting elements require some extra attention because of how the browser treats them. Block-level formatting elements include <p>, <div>, <h1>–<h6>, and <blockquote>.

You can think of each block-level element on a page as having an invisible box that contains it. The boundaries of that box define the extent of the block-formatted text, and the browser treats that box as an object that has many properties, such as borders, indentation, and background colors. Figure 26.6 shows the extent of a box around an <h1> heading by turning on the box's border and making the background color yellow. This example was made using virtually the same code as shown in Listing 26.3, with the addition of the <style> information shown in Listing 26.4, which is used to add the background color and borders.

Listing 26.4 ***StyleApp3.htm*—HTML Block-Level Elements**

```
<!DOCTYPE html PUBLIC "-//W3C//DTD XHTML 1.0 Transitional//EN"
    "http://www.w3.org/TR/xhtml1/DTD/xhtml1-transitional.dtd">
<html xmlns="http://www.w3.org/1999/xhtml">
<head>
<style type="text/javascript">
classes.Impact.all.fontFamily = "Impact";
classes.Impact.all.fontSize = "48pt";
ids.allCaps.textTransform = "uppercase";
ids.bigText.fontSize = "125%";
</style>
<style type="text/javascript">
with (tags.H1) {
   backgroundColor = "yellow";
   borderWidths("10pt");
```

Listing 26.4 Continued

```
   borderStyle = "solid";
}
</style>
<title>Applying Styles: Classes and Named Styles II</title>
</head>
<body>
<h1 class="Impact" id="allCaps">
   <span id="bigText">A</span>pplying
   <span id="bigText">S</span>tyles:
   <span id="bigText">C</span>lasses
   and
   <span id="bigText">N</span>amed
   <span id="bigText">S</span>tyles
   <span id="bigText">I</span> <span id="bigText">I</span></h1>
<hr />
<em>Jim O'Donnell, <a href="mailto:jim@odonnell.org">jim@odonnell.org</a></em>
</body>
</html>
```

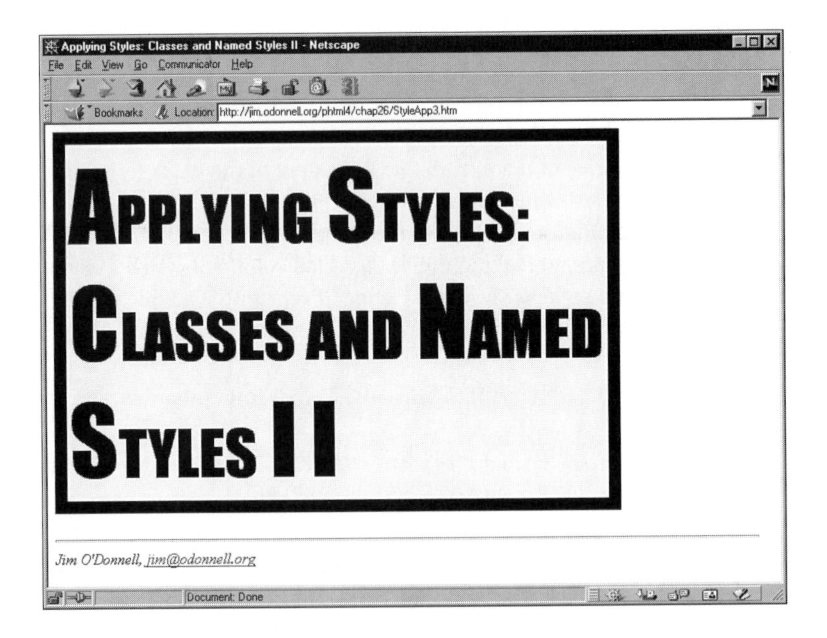

FIGURE 26.6
Block-level formats are contained in an invisible box, but you can modify the box's properties to make it visible.

Because of the boxes that surround them, block-level elements have style characteristics that other elements do not. These characteristics include the following:

- Alignment with respect to the rest of the document
- Background colors or images
- Borders of varying width, style, and color
- Margins from the left-, right-, top-, and bottom boundaries of the box

- Padding (the distance from the elements' content to the edges of the box) along the left, right, top, and bottom of the content within the box
- Width of the box with respect to the rest of the document

Refer to Table 26.1 for the JavaScript property names for each of these; each is fairly intuitive. As you specify values for these properties, keep the image of the invisible box in mind, and it will help you visualize what your results will look like.

One important thing to note is the relationship between the width and margin characteristics. Mathematically, you could describe the relationship between the width of the block element, the margins, and the width of the content of the block element as this:

```
block element width = left margin + content width + right margin
```

After the content is specified, its width is determined and becomes a fixed value. This means you can set either of the following:

- The margins, and let the margin sizes and the content width determine the total width
- The total width, and let the margins split the balance of the remaining space

The point is that it does not make sense to specify *both* the margins and the total width. After you choose values for one, the value of the other is determined by the preceding equation.

Content Positioning

In the previous section, you saw how you could use JavaScript to assign values to style characteristics and dynamically format your document. One class of style characteristics was deliberately left out of the section, however: those for specifying content position. Content positioning is a much different activity than assigning styles, and you can bring many more JavaScript commands to bear on a content-positioning challenge. This section looks at how you can do content positioning with Netscape Navigator 4, using both the nonstandard `<layer>` element as well as CSS techniques.

The *<layer>* and *<ilayer>* Elements

Chapter 24 showed you some examples of content positioning. Specifically, you saw how you could position an element with respect to the upper-left corner of the browser window (*absolute positioning*) or with respect to the location where the element would ordinarily be placed (*relative positioning*). In addition to being able to specify the x and y coordinates of where the element should appear, you were also able to control a z coordinate, which determined how the elements overlap. You could think of each element as sitting on a transparent sheet that you can move around the browser screen and stack one on top of the other to create different effects. Netscape's term for these transparent sheets is *layers*. You can implement layers in Navigator by using the CSS specification for content positioning or by using the proprietary `<layer>` and `<ilayer>` elements to do absolute and relative positioning, respectively. This section introduces you to the `<layer>` and `<ilayer>` elements and their many attributes.

NOTE `<layer>` and `<ilayer>` take the same set of attributes, so this section focuses only on using the `<layer>` element. The `<ilayer>` (inline layer) element behaves the same as the `<layer>` element. Although `<ilayer>` allows for positioning of content relative to where the content would appear in the flow of the document, the `<layer>` element is used for absolute positioning of content with respect to the upper-left corner of the browser window. ■

The `<layer>` element is a container element that can take the following attributes:

- **`background`**—The `background` attribute is set equal to the URL of an image to tile in the background of the layer. In the absence of a background image or background color (see `bgcolor` next in this list), the layer background is transparent and enables any layers stacked beneath it to show through.
- **`bgcolor`**—You can set `bgcolor` equal to a reserved English-language color name, an RGB triplet, or a hexadecimal triplet that specifies a background color for the layer. Otherwise, the layer background is transparent.
- **`src`**—You have two ways to place content in layers. You can place the content between the `<layer>` and `</layer>` elements or you can import the content from another file by using the `src` attribute. `src` is set equal to the URL of the document you want to import.
- **`id`**—The `id` attribute is used to assign a unique name to a layer so that it can be referenced in other `<layer>` elements or in JavaScript code.
- **`left` and `top`**—`left` and `top` are set equal to the number of pixels from the upper-left corner of the browser screen where the layer should begin. These two attributes permit exact positioning of the layer on the screen. Note that if you're using `<ilayer>`, `left` and `top` specify displacement from the left of and below the point where the layer would ordinarily start, rather than from the upper-left of the browser screen. Also, when using relative positioning, you can set `left` and `top` equal to negative values.
- **`z-index`, `above`, and `below`**—These three attributes help to specify how the layers stack up along the z-axis (the axis coming out of the browser screen toward the user). `z-index` is set equal to a positive integer, and a layer with a larger `z-index` value will appear stacked on top of layers that have lower `z-index` values. You can place a new layer above or below an existing named layer by setting `above` or `below` equal to the named layer's name. In the absence of `z-index`, `above`, or `below` attributes, new layers are stacked on top of old layers.
- **`visibility`**—`visibility` can take on one of the following three values: `show`, `hide`, or `inherit`. If a layer's `visibility` is set to `show`, the content of the layer will be displayed. Setting `visibility` to `hide` conceals the layer content. A `visibility` value of `inherit` means that the layer will have the same `visibility` behavior as its parent layer.

- **clip**—The *clipping region* of a layer is a rectangular area that defines how much of the layer content is visible. You can control the size of the clipping region by using the `clip` attribute. `clip` is set equal to a comma-delimited list of four numbers that represent the coordinates of the upper-left and lower-right corners of the clipping region. Measurements for clipping region coordinates are taken with respect to the upper-left corner of the layer. By default, the clipping region is large enough to display all the contents of the layer.
- **height**—In the absence of a `clip` attribute, `height` controls the height of the clipping region. `height` can be set equal to a number of pixels or to a percentage of the layer's height.
- **width**—The `width` attribute specifies the width at which layer contents begin to wrap to new lines. Like `height`, you can set `width` equal to a number of pixels or to a percentage of the layer width.
- **pagex and pagey**—Because it is possible to nest layers inside of layers, you might end up in a situation where you want to position a layer with respect to the entire browser screen and not its parent element (the layer that contains it). In such a case, you can use the `pagex` and `pagey` attributes to specify where the layer should begin with respect to the upper-left corner of the browser screen.

The `<layer>` element's extensive set of attributes makes many interesting effects possible. By changing the size of the clipping region, for example, you can show or hide different parts of the layer's content. You can change the `z-index` of a layer to make it rise above or drop below other layers. You can even adjust the `top` and `left` values to make a layer move to a new position. All these changes are possible thanks to the capability to use JavaScript to modify layer properties. The following section provides some examples of that. To complete the discussion of the `<layer>` element's syntax, however, the following is a list of JavaScript event handlers you can use with the `<layer>` element:

- **OnMouseOver**—The `OnMouseOver` event is invoked when a user's mouse pointer enters the layer.
- **OnMouseOut**—When the mouse pointer leaves a layer, the `OnMouseOut` event is fired.
- **OnFocus**—If the layer acquires keyboard focus (for example, a user clicks a form field in a layer to be able to type in it), an `OnFocus` event is triggered.
- **OnBlur**—Blurring refers to the loss of focus. When a layer blurs, Navigator invokes an `OnBlur` event.
- **OnLoad**—The `OnLoad` event is triggered when the layer is initially loaded.

Using these event handlers is the first step in making your positioned content dynamic. Depending on what JavaScript code you execute upon an event firing, you can change a layer's content or move it to a new position to create an animation effect. You will read about some of the possibilities in subsequent sections of this chapter. However, you should first know about one other layer-related element.

The *<nolayer>* Element

Netscape knew it was creating proprietary elements when it introduced <layer> and <ilayer>, so it also included a <nolayer> element for specifying nonlayered versions of layered content. You might use <nolayer>, for example, as shown in Listing 26.5.

Listing 26.5 *NoLayer.htm*—Providing Alternative Content for Other Browsers

```
<!DOCTYPE html PUBLIC "-//W3C//DTD XHTML 1.0 Transitional//EN"
    "http://www.w3.org/TR/xhtml1/DTD/xhtml1-transitional.dtd">
<html xmlns="http://www.w3.org/1999/xhtml">
<head>
<title>Welcome to Our Site!</title>
</head>
<layer left="50"  top="35"  id="layer1" src="toplayer.html"></layer>
<layer left="100" top="152" id="layer2" src="bottomlayer.html"></layer>
<nolayer>
<body bgcolor="white">
<h1>Whoops!</h1>
You must not be using Netscape Navigator, so you'd probably be interested
in a <a href="nolayers/index.html">non-layered version</a> of our site.
</body>
</nolayer>
</html>
```

Netscape Navigator 4 ignores anything between <nolayer> and </nolayer>, so it will render the preceding example just fine. A browser that does not understand the layer-related elements ignores the two <layer> elements and the <nolayer> element and displays the HTML between the <nolayer> and </nolayer> elements as well as the HTML between the <layer> and </layer> elements. This is why, as in Listing 26.5, the layered content is included via the src attribute of the <layer> element.

NOTE When using layers, you don't use the <body> element in the document except between <nolayer> and </nolayer> elements. ■

Putting the "Dynamic" in Dynamic HTML with JavaScript

Everything you have read about so far in this chapter has largely been about how to create static content, so you might be wondering whether the term "Dynamic HTML" really applies. Now that you understand how to access style characteristics with JavaScript and how to use the <layer> element to position content, however, you are ready to see how you can use

JavaScript to make your pages come alive. This section gives an overview of some of the many things possible with JavaScript, layers, and style information.

▶ To learn more about the event model, **see** "The Netscape Navigator Event Model," **p. 616**

The capability to use JavaScript to create dynamic pages hinges on the Netscape browser object model, which provides for many different events and responses to those events. You read in Chapter 24 about the traditional events that Navigator supports and some extras added by Netscape to handle `mouse`, `keystroke`, and `window` events. Any of these can be used to trigger the execution of some JavaScript code in response to some kind of user action.

Two other aspects of the Netscape browser object model make Dynamic HTML possible. The first is the new `event` object that is created whenever an event occurs. As noted in Chapter 24, you can access properties of the `event` object to determine which kind of event was triggered, what mouse button or keystroke initiated the event, and to which object the event belongs.

The other helpful feature of the Netscape browser object model is that every layer—regardless of whether it was created using CSS properties or the `<layer>` element—is accessible through the `layers` object. The `layers` object is actually an arrayed property of the `document` object, which means that you can reference a particular layer in the following manner:

```
document.layers["layer1"]
```

This code says to select the layer named "layer1" from the `layers` array of the `document` object. You also can reference the array by a number if you know the layer's position in the stacking order. If you want to make a direct reference to layer1, you also can say this:

```
document.layer1
```

NOTE Only top-level layers in a document are listed in the `layers` array. ■

The properties of a layer selected from the `layers` object map very closely to the attributes of the `<layer>` element discussed in the preceding section. Beyond those properties, one other thing could cause some confusion: Each layer has its own `document` property! A layer's `document` property refers to the content inside the layer and not the main document. Other than that, you can use the `document` property just as you always have. Thus, to reference a `<blockquote>` element inside a layer named "imagelayer," you would use the following:

```
document.layers["imagelayer"].document.tags.BLOCKQUOTE
```

This might not seem too bad, but your references can get fairly complicated if you have layers nested inside a layer. Suppose "layer2" and "layer3" are top-level layers nested inside "layer1." Then, to reference the `H5` element in "layer3," you would have to say:

```
document.layers["layer1"].document.layers["layer3"].document.tags.H5
```

Table 26.2 provides a full listing of the properties of a selected layer. Note that you can't modify all the properties by using JavaScript commands. The layer's `parentLayer`, for example, is a fixed property that cannot be changed. In addition to the many layer properties you can reference, JavaScript also supports several methods that you can apply to a layer. Table 26.3 summarizes these methods.

Table 26.2 Properties of a Selected Layer

Property	Description
`above`	The layer above the selected layer or the browser window if you have selected the topmost layer
`background.src`	The URL of the image file to use as the background
`below`	The layer below the selected layer or null if the selected layer is at the lowest level
`bgColor`	Color specification for the background
`clip.bottom`	Controls the position of the bottom edge of the clipping region
`clip.left`	Controls the position of the left edge of the clipping region
`clip.right`	Controls the position of the right edge of the clipping region
`clip.top`	Controls the position of the top edge of the clipping region
`clip.height`	Controls the distance between the top and bottom edges of the clipping region
`clip.width`	Controls the distance between the left and right edges of the clipping region
`document`	Object that enables you to reference the contents of a layer
`left`	Controls the horizontal position of where the layer begins
`name`	The unique name of the layer as assigned by the `id` attribute of the `<layer>` element
`pageX`	The horizontal position of the layer with respect to the browser screen
`pageY`	The vertical position of the layer with respect to the browser screen
`parentLayer`	The layer that contains the object layer or the browser window if the object layer is a top-level layer
`siblingAbove`	The sibling layer (same parent layer) that is above the object layer in the stacking order, or null if there is no layer above it
`siblingBelow`	The sibling layer (same parent layer) that is below the object layer in the stacking order, or null if there is no layer above it
`src`	The URL of the document to be loaded into the layer
`top`	Controls the vertical position of where the layer begins
`visibility`	Determines whether the content of the layer is shown or hidden
`zIndex`	Determines the layer's position in the stacking order

Table 26.3 JavaScript Methods for the *layer* Object

Method Name	Function
`load(URL,width)`	Loads the document at the URL specified into the layer (replacing existing content in the layer) and changes the width of the layer to the value in the second argument
`moveAbove(layer)`	Moves a layer to a position in the stacking order above the layer in the argument
`moveBelow(layer)`	Moves a layer to a position in the stacking order below the layer in the argument
`moveBy(dx,dy)`	Moves a layer `dx` pixels to the left and `dy` pixels down
`moveTo(x,y)`	Moves an absolutely positioned layer to the specified coordinates with the containing document or layer; moves a relatively positioned layer to the specified coordinates, taken with respect to the layer's natural position
`moveToAbsolute(x,y)`	Moves a layer to the specified coordinates, taken with respect to the browser screen
`resizeBy(dw,dh)`	Adds `dw` to the layer width and `dh` to the layer height
`resizeTo(width,height)`	Resets the layer's width and height to the specified values

Now that you know about the `layer` object, its properties, its methods, and the event handlers available in the Netscape browser object model, you are finally ready to take a look at some examples of truly Dynamic HTML—pages that change right in the browser window without going back to the server to get more content.

Animated Buttons Using Layers

When you push a button on an appliance or dashboard, you get visual and tactile feedback from the button that tells you something about its status. If the button is depressed, you know that what it controls is on. Conversely, you know that the function the button controls is off if the button is raised. When you press the button to toggle its state, you feel a click as it moves to its new position. This tells you that you have changed states successfully. Unfortunately, this kind of feedback has been tough to provide for buttons on Web pages. Although you will probably never be able to provide tactile feedback to a user pressing a button, Dynamic HTML enables you to give visual feedback about whether the button is depressed or raised, whether the user's mouse is over it, and whether the button is being pressed.

Suppose you are designing an interface in which you want your buttons to have the following three states:

- Raised
- Selected (meaning the user's mouse is over it)
- Depressed

One way to accomplish this task, which has worked in Navigator since version 3 and in Internet Explorer since version 4, is to come up with GIF or JPG images of the three button "states" and to use the `image` object to switch them in and out in response to the appropriate mouse events. However, using Netscape Dynamic HTML, it is possible to create an animated, state-dependent button without requiring any images to be created or downloaded.

Listing 26.6 shows the Dynamic HTML and JavaScript code used to implement the animated button. Two style classes are used to create the buttons; three layers nested within an outer layer hold each button; and a series of JavaScripts selects the displayed button depending on the state of various mouse events.

Listing 26.6 ***Button.htm*—Layers Enable You to Create Dynamic Content**

```
<!DOCTYPE html PUBLIC "-//W3C//DTD XHTML 1.0 Transitional//EN"
    "http://www.w3.org/TR/xhtml1/DTD/xhtml1-transitional.dtd">
<html xmlns="http://www.w3.org/1999/xhtml">
<head>
<script type="text/javascript" language="JavaScript">
active = 0;
function layerSet(show,hide1,hide2) {
   if (active < 1) {
      show.visibility = "SHOW";
      hide1.visibility = "HIDE";
      hide2.visibility = "HIDE";
   }
}
</script>
<style type="text/javascript">
with (classes.Button.P) {
   fontFamily = "Verdana";
   fontSize = "24pt";
   fontWeight = "bold";
   textAlign = "center";
}
with (classes.Out.all) {
   backgroundColor = "white";
   borderWidths("10pt");
   borderStyle = "outset";
   color = "black";
   width = "275pt";
}
with (classes.Over.all) {
   backgroundColor = "yellow";
   borderWidths("10pt");
   borderStyle = "outset";
   color = "black";
   width = "275pt";
}
with (classes.Down.all) {
   backgroundColor = "black";
```

Listing 26.6 Continued

```
    borderWidths("10pt");
    borderStyle = "inset";
    color = "yellow";
    width = "275pt";
}
</style>
<title>Animated Buttons without GIFs</title>
</head>
<body>
<h1>Animated Buttons without GIFs</h1>
<hr />
<em>Jim O'Donnell, <a href="mailto:jim@odonnell.org">jim@odonnell.org</a></em>
<hr />
<layer name="buttons"
       onmouseout="layerSet(layera,layerb,layerc)"
       onmouseover="layerSet(layerb,layera,layerc)"
       visibility="inherit">
    <layer name="buttonOut"  class="Out"  visibility=inherit>
       <p class="Button">SUBMIT</p>
    </layer>
    <layer name="buttonOver" class="Over" visibility=hide>
       <p class="Button">ARE YOU SURE?</p>
    </layer>
    <layer name="buttonDown" class="Down" visibility=hide>
       <p class="Button">SENT!!!</p>
    </layer>
</layer>
</body>
<script type="text/javascript" language="JavaScript">
var layera = document.layers['buttons'].document.buttonOut;
var layerb = document.layers['buttons'].document.buttonOver;
var layerc = document.layers['buttons'].document.buttonDown;
//
var buttons = document.layers['buttons'];
//
buttons.document.captureEvents(Event.MOUSEDOWN);
buttons.document.onmousedown = buttonDown;
function buttonDown() {
    layerSet(layerc,layera,layerb);
    active++;
}
</script>
</html>
```

The first step in animating the button is to set each button up in a layer. The main button layer will contain three child layers—one for each state of the button. By changing the `visibility` properties of the layers as different mouse events occur, you can show the graphic appropriate to the button's state. Figure 26.7 shows the initial state of these layers in which the button is in the raised state.

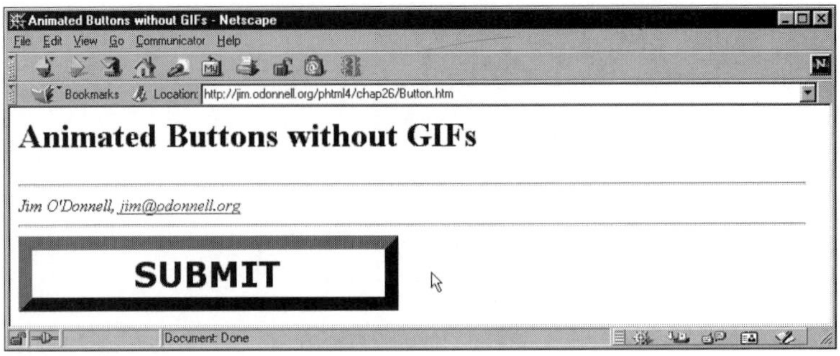

FIGURE 26.7
The `outset` border style can give the contents of a layer a three-dimensional appearance.

The elements of the button appearance are as follows:

- **Style Sheet `Button` Class**—The `Button` class is defined and attached, via the `class` attribute of the `<p>` element, to the text used to make up the button in each layer.
- **Style Sheet `Out` Class**—Attached via the `class` attribute to the layer containing the button representing the up state (when the mouse is completely "out" of the button). This class defines the color scheme and border of the layer—using the `outset` border style to generate a raised, three-dimensional appearance—and also defines a layer width the same as that used in each of the other two button styles, `Over` and `Down`, so that they will all be sized equivalently.
- **Style Sheet `Over` Class**—Attached via the `class` attribute to the layer containing the button representing the selected state (when the mouse is "over" the button, but no button has been pressed). This class is identical to the `Out` class, except that it changes the background color to highlight the button (see Figure 26.8).
- **Style Sheet `Down` Class**—Attached via the `class` attribute to the layer containing the button representing the down or clicked state (when the mouse is over the button, and a button has been clicked "down"). This class uses an "inverse video" color scheme to denote the clicked button, and changes the border style to `inset`, for a lowered three-dimensional appearance.

What you need to do next is put in the JavaScript code to handle the changes to the state of the button. The first two states, `Out` and `Over`, are easy because the `<layer>` element supports the `onMouseOut` and `onMouseOver` events. In this example, `onMouseOut` and `onMouseOver` event handlers in the initial `<layer>` element call the `layerSet()` function, which uses the layers' `visibility` property to make the desired button visible and hide the other two.

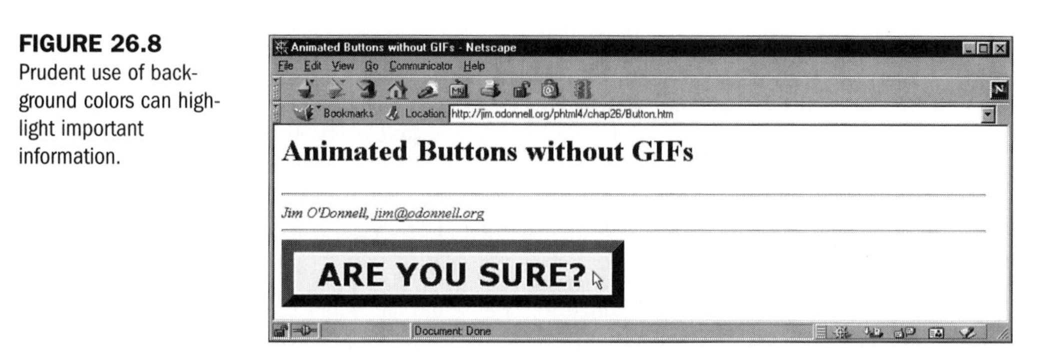

FIGURE 26.8
Prudent use of background colors can highlight important information.

The last mouse event that you want to catch, the button click when the mouse is over the button layers, is a little trickier. That's because the `<layer>` element doesn't support `onClick` or `onMouseDown` events. To detect a pressed mouse button when the mouse cursor is over the button layers, you need to catch the event at the `document` level. The JavaScript code located at the bottom of Listing 26.6 shows how this is done:

```
var buttons = document.layers['buttons'];
//
buttons.document.captureEvents(Event.MOUSEDOWN);
buttons.document.onmousedown = buttonDown;
function buttonDown() {
   layerSet(layerc,layera,layerb);
   active++;
}
```

First, the variable `button` is created and defined to be the outermost layer containing the three layers representing the three button states. Then, its `captureEvents` method is used to instruct JavaScript to capture `onMouseDown` events that occur within the layer and assigns the JavaScript `buttonDown` function to be called in that case. The `buttonDown` function displays the "down" button (see Figure 26.9) and sets the active variable so that no further changes in button appearance are possible (in this example, after the button is pressed, it can't be unpressed).

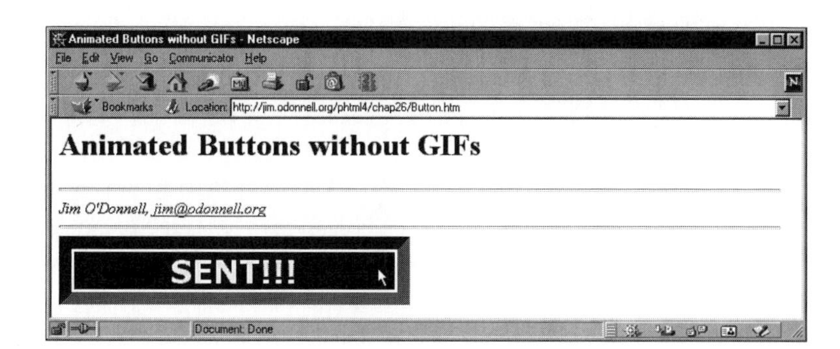

FIGURE 26.9
You can define as many layers as you want to manipulate their visibility to dynamically change your pages in response to events.

Dynamic HTML Pop-Up Menus

Pop-up menus are used in many applications to give users a context-sensitive listing of program options. These menus are usually accessed by right-clicking the mouse or by some special keystroke. By using Dynamic HTML techniques, you can make a pop-up menu appear on a Web page as well. This can prove helpful when you need to conserve space on a page. Instead of having all the options presented all the time, you can have a menu with the options pop up when the user requests it.

Look at the example shown in Figure 26.10. The "menu bar" shown in the Web page is set up for this example to look like a typical menu bar (this one actually looks a lot like the one you will find in Notepad). You could use a menu like this, for example, to contain your site's navigation options. A listing of this example is shown in Listing 26.7.

FIGURE 26.10
Netscape Dynamic HTML layers can be used to show context-sensitive information on your Web pages.

Listing 26.7 ***DynPopup.htm*—Pop Up Windows Using Navigator 4 Layers**

```
<!DOCTYPE html PUBLIC "-//W3C//DTD XHTML 1.0 Transitional//EN"
    "http://www.w3.org/TR/xhtml1/DTD/xhtml1-transitional.dtd">
<html xmlns="http://www.w3.org/1999/xhtml">
<head>
<title>Dynamic HTML Popup Menus</title>
<style type="text/javascript">
with (classes.Border.all) {
   borderStyle = "SOLID";
   borderWidths("1pt");
   width = "100pt";
}
</style>
</head>
<h1>Dynamic HTML Popup Menus</h1>
<hr />
<em>Jim O'Donnell, <a href="mailto:jim@odonnell.org">jim@odonnell.org</a></em>
<hr />
<layer top="125" left="10" name="fileT" class="border" visibility="show"
       onmouseover="swapLayers(fileMLayer,fileTLayer)">
   <b><u>F</u>ile</b>
```

Listing 26.7 Continued

```
</layer>
<layer top="125" left="10" name="fileM" class="border" visibility="hide"
       onmouseout="swapLayers(fileTLayer,fileMLayer)">
   <b><u>F</u>ile</b><br />
   <hr />
   <u>N</u>ew<br />
   <u>O</u>pen<br />
   <u>S</u>ave<br />
   S<u>a</u>ve as...<br />
   <hr />
   Page Se<u>t</u>up...<br />
   <u>P</u>rint<br />
   <hr />
   E<u>x</u>it
</layer>
<layer top="125" left="142" name="editT" class="border" visibility="show"
       onmouseover="swapLayers(editMLayer,editTLayer)">
   <b><u>E</u>dit</b>
</layer>
<layer top="125" left="142" name="editM" class="border" visibility="hide"
       onmouseout="swapLayers(editTLayer,editMLayer)">
   <b><u>E</u>dit</b><br />
   <hr />
   <u>U</u>ndo<br />
   <hr />
   Cu<u>t</u><br />
   <u>C</u>opy<br />
   <u>P</u>aste<br />
   De<u>l</u>ete<br />
   <hr />
   Select <u>A</u>ll<br />
   Time/<u>D</u>ate<br />
   <hr />
   <u>W</u>ord Wrap<br />
</layer>
<layer top="125" left="274" name="findT" class="border" visibility="show"
       onmouseover="swapLayers(findMLayer,findTLayer)">
   <b><u>S</u>earch</b>
</layer>
<layer top="125" left="274" name="findM" class="border" visibility="hide"
       onmouseout="swapLayers(findTLayer,findMLayer)">
   <b><u>S</u>earch</b><br />
   <hr />
   <u>F</u>ind<br />
   Find <u>N</u>ext<br />
</layer>
<layer top="125" left="406" name="helpT" class="border" visibility="show"
       onmouseover="swapLayers(helpMLayer,helpTLayer)">
   <b><u>H</u>elp</b>
</layer>
```

Listing 26.7 Continued

```
<layer top="125" left="406" name="helpM" class="border" visibility="hide"
       onmouseout="swapLayers(helpTLayer,helpMLayer)">
   <b><u>H</u>elp</b><br />
   <hr />
   <u>H</u>elp Topics<br />
   <hr />
   <a href="http://jim.odonnell.org">The House of JOD</a>
</layer>
</body>
<script type="text/javascript" language="JavaScript">
var fileTLayer = window.document.fileT;
var fileMLayer = window.document.fileM;
var editTLayer = window.document.editT;
var editMLayer = window.document.editM;
var findTLayer = window.document.findT;
var findMLayer = window.document.findM;
var helpTLayer = window.document.helpT;
var helpMLayer = window.document.helpM;

function swapLayers(showLayer,hideLayer) {
   showLayer.visibility = "SHOW";
   hideLayer.visibility = "HIDE";
}
</script>
</html>
```

This example has four main features that it uses to display and hide the context-sensitive menus that go with each of the menu options shown in Figure 26.10:

- **Style Sheet `Border` Class**—This class is attached to each layer for them to have a fixed width and a visible border.
- **Title and Menu Option Layers**—Each of the four menus shown is implemented using two layers. The first is the layer that just shows the title of that menu option—for example, `File`. The second layer has both the title of the menu and its contents.
- **Layer-Based Mouse Events**—The `onMouseOver` event of each "title" layer and the `onMouseOut` event of each "menu" layer are used to trigger a JavaScript function to show and hide the appropriate layer in each case.
- **JavaScript `swapLayers` Function**—The `swapLayers` function is called by the layer mouse events to display the appropriate menu, depending on the location of the mouse. It uses the `visibility` properties of the title and menu layers to hide one and show the other (see Figure 26.11).

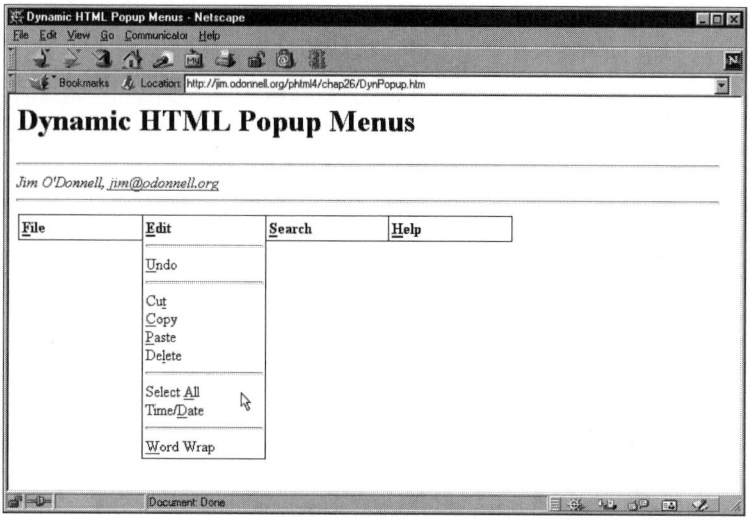

FIGURE 26.11
Pop-up menus enable you to greatly increase the amount of information on your page without making it cluttered.

You can use these context-sensitive pop-up menus for any number of purposes. They can be used to display useful information that you don't want cluttering up your Web pages all the time. Or, as shown in Figure 26.12, you can include hypertext links in these menus to enable your users to navigate to another Web page.

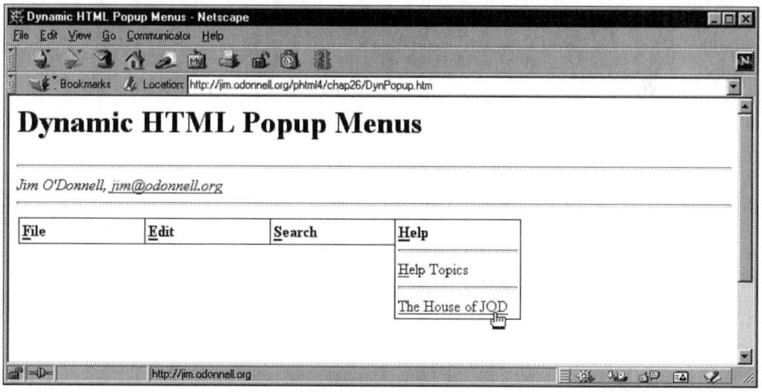

FIGURE 26.12
Any HTML elements can be included within pop-up layers.

Dynamic HTML with Navigator 6

With the release of Navigator 6, Netscape completely changed the direction of its browser. The underlying rendering engine of the browser was redesigned from the ground up, development of the browser was done on the open-source model, and—most importantly for the purposes of the discussion in this chapter—Netscape moved its support for HTML, Dynamic HTML, style sheets, the Document Object Model, and other technologies to be completely standards based. So, the proprietary <layer> element and layer object of Navigator 4 is no longer supported, and many of the restrictions of Navigator 4's Dynamic HTML implementation are removed.

Because of the newness of both the World Wide Web Consortium's Document Object Model standards and the Navigator 6 browser (it is still in preview release at the time of this writing), development targeting this browser is still in its early stages. However, as we will see in the next chapter, because Internet Explorer 5 has fairly good support for the DOM and style sheet standards, developing Dynamic HTML Web pages for both Internet Explorer 5 and Navigator 6 will be easier than doing the same for earlier versions of each browser.

▶ For more about DHTML for IE and Navigator, **see** "Internet Explorer 5 and Navigator 6," **p. 713**

The following sections discuss some of the main features of Navigator 6 and give an example of its use. There are ample sources on the Web for getting more detailed information.

Referencing Nodes

When Internet Explorer 4 was released, it first introduced the concept of being able to access and manipulate each and every HTML element within a Web page. Now with its support of the W3C's DOM standards, Netscape has extended this capability to Navigator 6. However, the first necessary step in being able to access and manipulate HTML elements is to figure out how to reference them.

In the W3C DOM standard, each HTML element becomes an object in the document object hierarchy. When a document is loaded, an object hierarchy is set up with an object to represent each HTML element. The object hierarchy is a tree structure, with each object—each HTML element—represented as a node in the tree. Listing 26.8 shows a very simple HTML document example you can use to examine this tree structure.

Listing 26.8 *Tree.htm*—Simple HTML Document

```
<!DOCTYPE html PUBLIC "-//W3C//DTD XHTML 1.0 Transitional//EN"
    "http://www.w3.org/TR/xhtml1/DTD/xhtml1-transitional.dtd">
<html xmlns="http://www.w3.org/1999/xhtml">
<head>
<title>Object Hierarchy</title>
</head>
<body bgcolor="#ffffff">
<h1>Object Hierarchy</h1>
<hr />
<p>Here is a recent picture...</p>
<div id="authorDiv">
   <img src="Author.jpg" width="175" height="215" border="0" />
</div>
<hr />
<em>Jim O'Donnell, <a href="mailto:jim@odonnell.org">jim@odonnell.org</a></em>
</body>
</html>
```

Figure 26.13 shows the object tree structure that represents this HTML document. Any HTML element that is nested within another is a child of that element, and therefore has that element as a parent. In Figure 26.13, the parent nodes are shown higher up in the diagram.

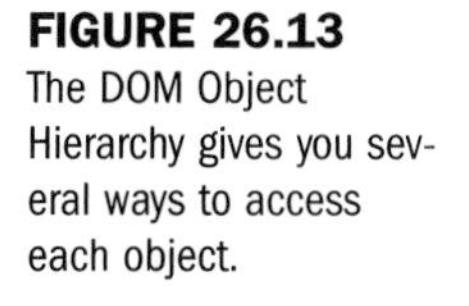

FIGURE 26.13
The DOM Object Hierarchy gives you several ways to access each object.

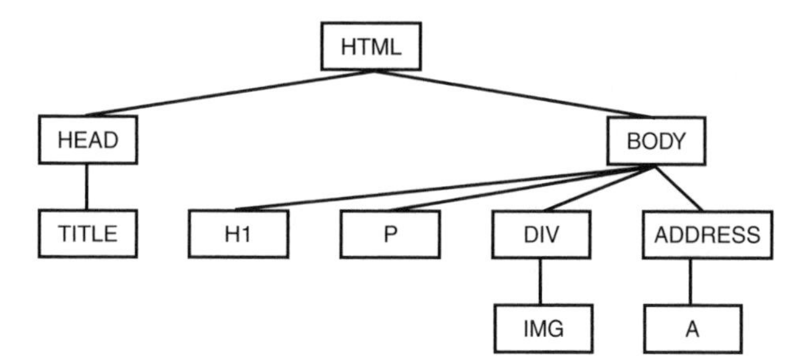

Navigator 6 supports W3C DOM properties to traverse the object hierarchy—three properties in particular that can be used to work your way through the tree are `parentNode`, `childNodes`, and `nextSibling`:

- **`parentNode`**—The `parentNode` property of an object node references the parent element of that node. In the document from Listing 26.8 and Figure 26.13, for example, the `parentNode` of the object representing the <div> element would be the <body> element.
- **`childNodes`**—The `childNodes` array represents the child objects for an object, in the order that they were defined. For the <body> element discussed previously, `childNodes[0]` corresponds to the <h1> element, `childNodes[1]` corresponds to the <p> element, and so on.
- **`nextSibling`**—The `nextSibling` property references the next object in the same level of the hierarchy. So, the `nextSibling` of the object corresponding to the <h1> element corresponds to the <p> element.

So, referencing Figure 26.13, you can get to the <div> element object with the following objects:

- **`document.childNodes[1].childNodes[2]`**—Go to the main document element (<html>), then to its second child (<body>), and then to its the third child (<div>).
- **`document.childNodes[0].nextSibling.childNodes[3]`**—Go to the main document element (<html>), then to its first child (<head>), then to its next sibling (<body>), and then to its third child (<div>).
- **`document.childNodes[1].childNodes[0].nextSibling.nextSibling`**—Go to the main document element (<html>), then to its second child (<body>), then to its first child (<h1>), then to its next sibling (<p>), and then to its next sibling (<div>).

This might seem to be a laborious way of traversing the object tree, but it does allow you to reference every element in an HTML document. There is another way to do it, however, that allows for a little easier reference, by using the `id` attribute of the corresponding HTML element. This is using the `getElementById()` method. Using this method, the `<div>` element object from the document in Listing 26.8 could easily be referenced by `document.getElementById("authorDiv")`.

Events in Navigator 6

The event model supported by Navigator 6 is quite similar to that of Navigator 4. In response to mouse or keyboard events, an `Event` object is created that can be referenced to access the parameters for the corresponding event. In this way, it is easy to access the position and actions of the mouse or keyboard. The example in the next section will give you an idea of how easy this can be.

Navigator 6 Dynamic HTML Example

Listing 26.9 shows an example using Dynamic HTML in Navigator 6. It is very similar to the positioning example shown using Microsoft Dynamic HTML and Internet Explorer in the previous chapter. It allows you to pick up and move a `<div>` element containing a table containing several images.

▶ To learn more about positioning elements using DHTML, **see** "Position HTML Elements with Dynamic HTML," **p. 642**

Listing 26.9 *NavPos.htm*—Drag and Drop Objects with Navigator 6

```
<html>
<head>
<script>
var counter = 0
function doDrag(e) {
   var difX = e.clientX - window.lastX
   var difY = e.clientY - window.lastY
   var newX = parseInt(document.getElementById("authorDiv").style.left) +
   ➥difX + "px"
   var newY = parseInt(document.getElementById("authorDiv").style.top)  +
   ➥difY + "px"
   document.getElementById("authorDiv").style.left = newX
   document.getElementById("authorDiv").style.top  = newY
   window.lastX = e.clientX
   window.lastY = e.clientY
   if (counter++ > 10) {
      counter = 0
      document.MyForm.X.value = newX
      document.MyForm.Y.value = newY
   }
}
function beginDrag(e) {
   window.lastX = e.clientX
```

Listing 26.9 Continued

```
   window.lastY = e.clientY
   window.onmousemove = doDrag
   window.onmouseup   = endDrag
   document.MyForm.ID.value = "authorDiv"
   document.MyForm.STATE.value = "moving"
}
function endDrag(e) {
   window.onmousemove = null
   document.MyForm.STATE.value = "static"
}
</script>
</head>
<body bgcolor="#ffffff">
<h1>Positioning with Cross-Browser Dynamic HTML</h1>
<hr />
<form name="MyForm">
<table cellpadding="5">
<tr><td>Drag Information</td>
    <td>ID   </td><td><input name="ID"    type="text" size=10 /></td></tr>
<tr><td> </td>
    <td>STATE</td><td><input name="STATE" type="text" size=10 /></td></tr>
<tr><td> </td>
    <td>X    </td><td><input name="X"     type="text" size=10 /></td></tr>
<tr><td> </td>
    <td>Y    </td><td><input name="Y"     type="text" size=10 /></td></tr>
</table>
<table width="400">
<tr><td><hr /></td></tr>
<tr><td>
   This example uses the DynAPI JavaScript Library<br />
   (<a href="http://www.dansteinman.com/dynduo/">
   ➥http://www.dansteinman.com/dynduo/</a>)
   to create an example<br />
   that will work in both the Internet Explorer and
   Netscape Navigator 4 browsers.</td></tr>
</table>
</form>
<hr />
<em>Jim O'Donnell, <a href="mailto:jim@odonnell.org">jim@odonnell.org</a></em>
<div id="authorDiv" onmousedown="beginDrag(event)"
     style="position:absolute;width:275;height:215;left:450;top:100">
   <table>
   <tr valign="BOTTOM">
       <td><img src="rbflag_ls.gif" width="50"  height="47"  border="0" /></td>
       <td><img src="Author.jpg"    width="175" height="215" border="0" /></td>
       <td><img src="rbflag_rs.gif" width="50"  height="47"  border="0"
       ➥/></td></tr>
   </table>
</div>
</body>
</html>
```

The Dynamic HTML elements in this example that are used to implement the movement consist of the following (see Figure 26.14 to see the example in action):

- **`<div>` element**—This element contains an HTML table that holds the three images to be dragged. The `id` attribute is set to allow you to more easily reference it, and the `onmousedown` event handler is set to initiate the dragging event.
- **`beginDrag(e)` function**—This function is called when a `mousedown` event occurs on the draggable `<div>` element. The first two lines are used to remember the starting position, because all movement is made relative to the starting position. Then, the `onmousemove` and `onmouseup` event handlers are set up to implement the dragging action and to end the drag. Finally, information is written out to the form on the Web page to indicate the current status.
- **`doDrag(e)` function**—This is the function that actually implements the dragging. In this function, the `getElementById()` method is used to reference the `<div>` element. The delta movement is calculated and the object is moved, and then the starting position updated. Notice that the status is also written out to the page, but only once every 10 times through—this was done because writing it out every time adversely affected the performance of the drag (which is probably just an artifact of the Navigator 6 preview release).
- **`endDrag(e)` function**—This function ends the drag by nulling out the `onmousemove` event handler.

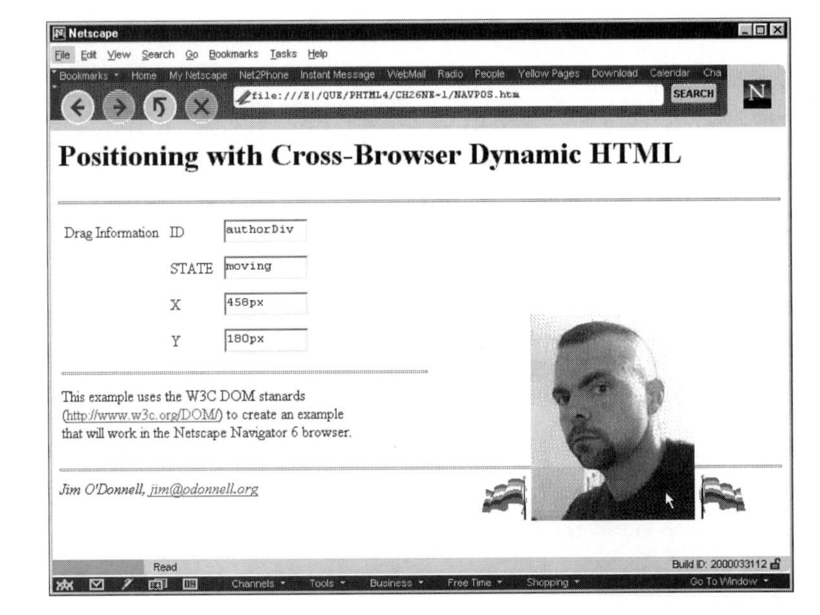

FIGURE 26.14
The DOM Object Hierarchy gives you several ways to access each object.

27

Cross-Browser Dynamic HTML

by Jim O'Donnell

In this chapter

What Is Cross-Browser Dynamic HTML?

In the last three chapters, you read about the technology offerings that Microsoft and Netscape have included in the latest versions of their Web browsers that come under the heading of Dynamic HTML. Unfortunately, but not surprisingly, their implementations of Dynamic HTML are largely incompatible. Even where the two browsers (and each of the platform versions of each browser) support similar capabilities, these capabilities are usually implemented in different ways. Navigating your way through the confusing thicket of Cascading Style Sheets, Document Object Models, Dynamic Fonts, and other standards and not-so-standards used in the two flavors of Dynamic HTML is a forbidding task.

With each release of its browser, Microsoft has increased its support for the World Wide Web Consortium Document Object Model (DOM) standards, although it still favors many of Microsoft's proprietary extensions. With the release of Navigator 6, Netscape has moved toward full support of the W3C DOM standards. As Navigator 6 becomes more common, this will make the process of designing Dynamic HTML that will work in both company's browsers easier.

The Goals of Cross-Browser Dynamic HTML

Since version 4 of Navigator and Internet Explorer were first introduced, any number of developers and development companies have been addressing the issue of writing Dynamic HTML code that is compatible on as many browsers as possible. The goals of this "Cross-Browser Dynamic HTML" are as follows:

- Support the subset of Dynamic HTML functionality that exists in both Netscape Navigator and Microsoft Internet Explorer.
- Where functionality is used that exists in one browser but not in the other, in previous versions of either browser, or in third-party browsers, ensure that no errors are generated in the incompatible browsers.
- Where functionality is used that exists in one browser but not in the other, in previous versions of either browser, or in third-party browsers, ensure that the performance and appearance of the Web page degrades gracefully on the incompatible browsers.

Cross-Browser Dynamic HTML Functionality

A number of areas exist where *functionality* is shared between Netscape's and Microsoft's implementations of Dynamic HTML. Remember that in some cases, as noted in Chapter 24, "Introduction to Dynamic HTML," the two browsers share similar capabilities, but those capabilities are not considered part of "Dynamic HTML" in one of the browsers. An example of this is downloadable font capabilities; both browsers support it, but technically it is not a part of Microsoft's Dynamic HTML.

The following areas are where functionality is shared. The ways that this functionality is implemented can be different; it is one of the goals of Cross-Browser Dynamic HTML to address these differences compatibly within one Web page:

- **Cascading Style Sheets**—Both Netscape and Microsoft largely support the World Wide Web Consortium's (W3C) CSS1 specification for including style information in an HTML document.
- **Cascading Style Sheet Positioning**—The W3C's CSSP specification is used to detail how content can be moved around within a Web page and how it is supported by both browsers.
- **Document Object Model**—The Document Object Model (DOM)—the means by which the contents of an HTML document are exposed to manipulation by scripting languages, Java applets, and other means—is the heart of Dynamic HTML. Both Netscape and Microsoft extended their DOMs with Dynamic HTML to support most of its increased functionality. Although these extensions are largely incompatible, they include the seeds from which cross-browser techniques can be developed.
- **Web Browser Events**—With version 4 of Navigator and Internet Explorer, more events are supported, including more mouse events, keyboard events, and a number of other things. Again, Netscape and Microsoft implemented these event models in a drastically different way. Despite this, it is possible to use the compatible cross-browser.
- **JavaScript**—Netscape originally developed the JavaScript browser scripting language and continues to lead in its development. The language used in Microsoft Internet Explorer, JScript, is Microsoft's implementation of JavaScript. It is largely compatible, although some of the capabilities included in the latest version of JavaScript are not supported.
- **Downloadable Font Technology**—The font technologies used to support downloadable fonts for the two browsers are completely incompatible. Despite that, it is possible to create an HTML document that uses both to achieve the same effect in both browsers.

As you will see in the discussion that follows, two main techniques are used to develop HTML documents that successfully implement Cross-Browser Dynamic HTML. Where possible, methods should be used that are compatible between both browsers. Some of the CSS1 and CSSP style sheet formatting and positioning can be done this way.

However, the more common technique used to implement much of the Cross-Browser Dynamic HTML functionality is to dynamically generate HTML code conditionally based on which browser is being used to view the document. This is done by using a script to detect which browser is being used and then generating the contents of the HTML document on-the-fly using conditional `document.write` statements in JavaScript.

Cross-Browser Dynamic HTML Limitations

Obviously, you won't be able to do many things compatibly on both browsers using Dynamic HTML. Certain capabilities in the Dynamic HTML of one browser are not present in the other. To implement such functionality in a cross-browser compatible fashion, it would be necessary to use Java or plug-in technology that is supported by both browsers.

The most important difference to keep in mind between the browsers' Dynamic HTML implementation is that Netscape Navigator 4 *can't change content or format after load time* unless the document is reloaded or regenerated. With Microsoft Internet Explorer and Navigator 6, it is possible to change the font, color, size, or other appearance characteristics of anything on a Web page, and that page instantly will be re-rendered without going back to the Web server. It is even possible to dynamically change content in this manner. In Netscape Navigator 4, the way to achieve a similar effect is to render the content in different layers and then manipulate the visibility characteristics of each layer to display the desired format or content.

Most of the rest of this chapter will examine the development of pages that work correctly in both Internet Explorer and Navigator 4. This is because, at the time of this writing, Navigator 6 is still in preview release, and version 4 of the browser is much more common. Also, because of the limitations of Navigator 4's Dynamic HTML, creating dynamic pages that support it is much more challenging. After that, you will learn about the relatively easier task of cross-browser support of Internet Explorer and Navigator 6.

Cross-Browser Dynamic HTML Libraries

As mentioned in the previous section, a number of freely available JavaScript libraries can be used to implement Cross-Browser Dynamic HTML functions. The first of these is Netscape's own Cross-Browser Dynamic HTML API (Application Programming Interface), available through its "Introduction to Cross-Browser, Cross-Platform, Backwardly Compatible JavaScript and Dynamic HTML" at `http://developer.netscape.com/tech/dynhtml/`. Through this page, you can download, view, and use the collection of JavaScript functions included in Netscape's `xbdhtml.js` API for implementing Cross-Browser Dynamic HTML functionality between Navigator 4 and Internet Explorer.

Another freely available library of Cross-Browser Dynamic HTML JavaScript functions was developed by Dan Steinman and is included on the CD-ROM that accompanies this book and also at its home on The Dynamic Duo Web site. Most of this chapter is spent on the functions in this library and some sample applications that show their use.

NOTE The Dynamic Duo Web site, located at `http://www.dansteinman.com/dynduo/`, is a good example of what you can achieve using Dynamic HTML that is targeted for both Netscape Navigator and Microsoft Internet Explorer.

Browser Detection Scripts

Before turning to Cross-Browser Dynamic HTML (which, for the sake of brevity, is abbreviated CBDHTML), one more topic should be discussed. The key to developing HTML documents that implement CBDHTML functions correctly on multiple browsers and platforms and that degrade gracefully on older or third-party browsers is the capability to successfully detect the Web browser being used. Again, many solutions are freely available for this problem; one of the most extensive is Netscape's Ultimate JavaScript Client Sniffer, which you can download from `http://developer.netscape.com/docs/examples/javascript/browser_type.html`.

When included within an HTML document and evaluated on the client Web browser, the Client Sniffer creates an `is` object with a series of properties that can be used in your scripts to detect the browser type and platform being used to view your document. Figure 27.1 shows Microsoft Internet Explorer 5.5 viewing the Web site with the sniffer; Netscape Navigator 4.73 is shown in Figure 27.2. The information found includes the following:

- **Basic Browser Information**—These are not part of the created `is` object but are properties of the `navigator` object, which is part of the existing Document Object Model. Each returns a descriptive numeric of string values `navigator.appName`, `navigator.userAgent`, and `navigator.appVersion`.

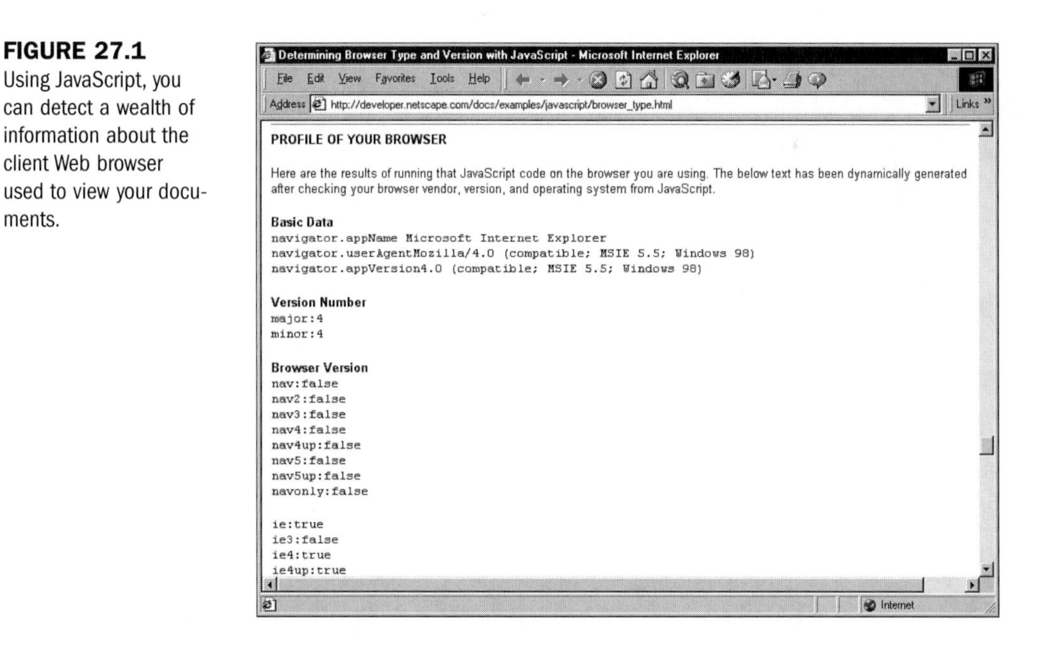

FIGURE 27.1
Using JavaScript, you can detect a wealth of information about the client Web browser used to view your documents.

- **Version Number**—These are numeric values describing the major and minor version numbers of the client.

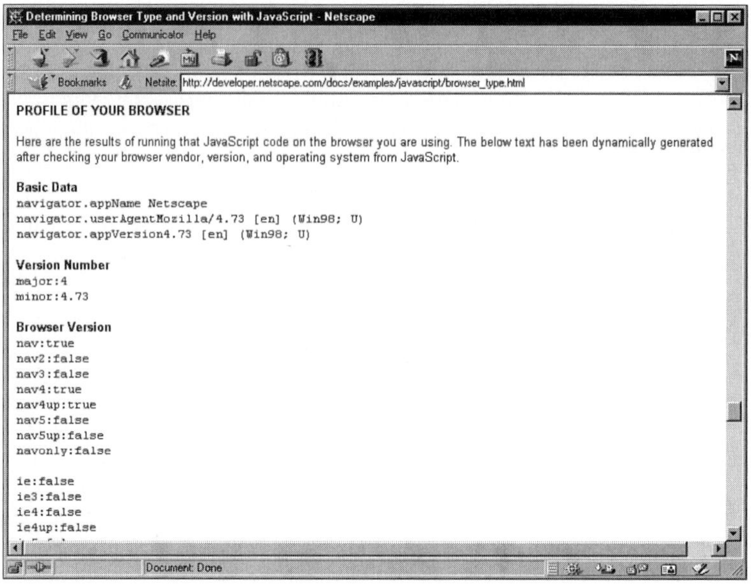

FIGURE 27.2
Netscape's "Ultimate JavaScript Client Sniffer" allows you to detect many different browsers and platforms.

- **Browser Version**—These are perhaps the most important properties of the `is` object that describe the client browser, each of which is a Boolean value used to describe what type of browser is being used. The Boolean properties that are set are `nav`, `nav2`, `nav3`, `nav4`, `nav4up`, and `navonly` to detect Netscape Navigator client browsers; `ie`, `ie3`, `ie4`, `ie4up`, and `isIE3Mac` to detect Microsoft Internet Explorer client browsers; and `opera` to detect the Opera browser.
- **JavaScript Version**—The `js` property returns a numeric value indicating the JavaScript version supported by the browser.
- **Operating System**—Finally, a series of Boolean values are set to indicate the platform upon which the client browser is running. The possibilities are `win`, `win16`, `win31`, `win32`, `win95`, `win98`, `winnt`, `os2`, `mac`, `mac68k`, `macppc`, `unix`, `sun`, `sun4`, `sun5`, `suni86`, `irix`, `irix5`, `irix6`, `hpux`, `hpux9`, `hpux10`, `aix`, `aix1`, `aix2`, `aix3`, `aix4`, `linux`, `sco`, `unixware`, `mpras`, `reliant`, `dec`, `sinix`, `bsd`, `freebsd`, and `vms`. Note that the `win31` property is `true` when the client is running under Windows 3.1 or Windows for Workgroups, and the `win32` property is `true` when the client is running under a 32-bit version of Windows (Windows 95, Windows 98, or Windows NT).

The way the Ultimate JavaScript Client Sniffer would be used in an HTML document is to include, and then to use, the properties of the `is` object to conditionally write HTML code depending on the detected browser type and platform. The following JavaScript code snippet shows an example:

```
var is = new Is();
if (is.nav4up)
JavaScript document.write statements to write Navigator 4+ code...
```

```
if (is.ie4up)
JavaScript document.write statements to write Internet Explorer 4+ code...
```

Formatting with Style Sheets

The W3C's CSS1 style sheet specification was one of the first technologies considered a part of Dynamic HTML that was agreed to by both Netscape and Microsoft. Even so, none of their browsers' various versions or platforms fully implement the specification, nor do they implement everything in the same way. Also, although all the implementations of Dynamic HTML expose the style sheet properties to scripting, the Document Object Model that does this is different for each.

So, the first step to take before using style sheet properties in a Web page meant to be cross-browser compatible is to make sure you use those properties that are consistently implemented in each. Fortunately, this task is made easier by some online resources. At `http://style.webreview.com/`, you can find a compilation of style sheet properties that are considered safe for cross-browser deployment (good for Navigator 4, Internet Explorer 5, and Opera 3.6). Figure 27.3 shows part of the grid of safe properties, showing browser and platform and whether the property is completely (indicated by Y) or partially (indicated by P) safe.

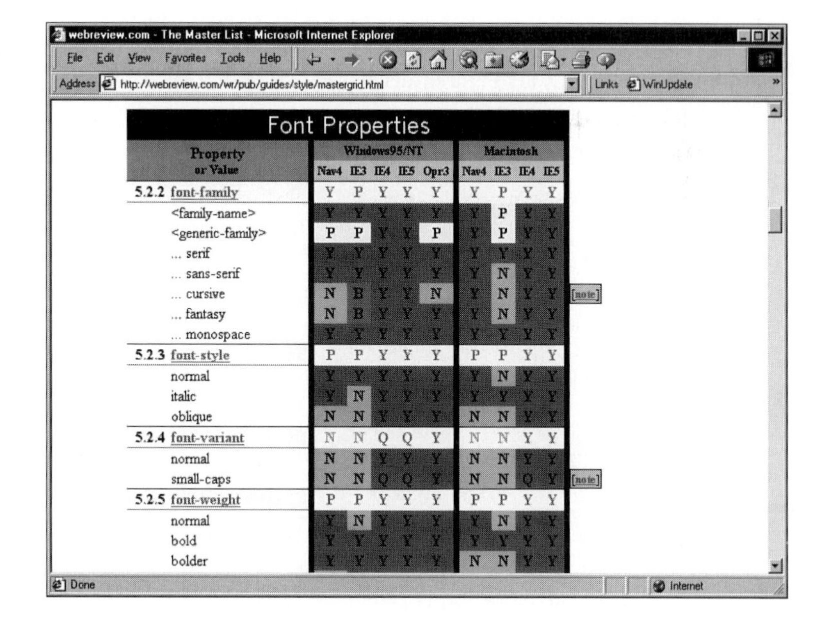

Font Properties

Property or Value	Windows95/NT					Macintosh				
	Nav4	IE3	IE4	IE5	Opr3	Nav4	IE3	IE4	IE5	
5.2.2 font-family	Y	P	Y	Y	Y	Y	P	Y	Y	
<family-name>	Y	Y	Y	Y	Y	Y	P	Y	Y	
<generic-family>	P	P	Y	Y	P	Y	P	Y	Y	
... serif	Y	Y	Y	Y	Y	Y	Y	Y	Y	
... sans-serif	Y	Y	Y	Y	Y	Y	N	Y	Y	
... cursive	N	B	Y	Y	N	Y	N	Y	Y	[note]
... fantasy	N	B	Y	Y	Y	Y	N	Y	Y	
... monospace	Y	Y	Y	Y	Y	Y	Y	Y	Y	
5.2.3 font-style	P	P	Y	Y	Y	P	P	Y	Y	
normal	Y	Y	Y	Y	Y	Y	N	Y	Y	
italic	Y	N	Y	Y	Y	Y	Y	Y	Y	
oblique	N	N	Y	Y	Y	N	N	Y	Y	
5.2.4 font-variant	N	N	Q	Q	Y	N	N	Y	Y	
normal	N	N	Y	Y	Y	N	N	Y	Y	
small-caps	N	N	Q	Q	Y	N	N	Q	Y	[note]
5.2.5 font-weight	P	P	Y	Y	Y	P	P	Y	Y	
normal	Y	N	Y	Y	Y	Y	N	Y	Y	
bold	Y	Y	Y	Y	Y	Y	Y	Y	Y	
bolder	Y	Y	Y	Y	Y	N	N	Y	Y	

FIGURE 27.3
You should confine your Web pages to use those style sheet properties that are widely supported.

With either Web browser, it is possible to specify style sheet properties one of two ways. The first of these, which is using CSS1 style sheet syntax, is the same on both browsers. To specify a style sheet class that gives an element a yellow background color, for example, you could use the following on either browser:

```
<style type="text/css">
.bgyellow {background-color: yellow}
</style>
```

If you want to conditionally set style sheet properties depending on some condition, you can't use CSS1 syntax because style sheet properties specified through CSS1 syntax are static. To set these properties dynamically, you need to use JavaScript and the Document Object Model for the appropriate browser.

Therefore, to set a background color for a given class of yellow using JavaScript in Netscape Navigator, you would do something like the following:

```
<script language="JavaScript">
document.classes.bgyellow.all.color = "yellow";
</script>
```

In Internet Explorer, you can create a named style and then use the `styleSheets.addRule` method, as in

```
<style id="iess" type="text/css"></style>
<script language="JavaScript">
document.styleSheets["iess"].addRule(".bgyellow","background-color: yellow");
</script>
```

Therefore, doing this in a cross-browser compatible format would give (assuming the Ultimate JavaScript Client Sniffer discussed earlier in this chapter is also included)

```
<style id="iess" type="text/css"></style>
<script language="JavaScript">
if (is.nav4up)
   document.classes.bgyellow.all.color = "yellow";
if (is.ie4up)
   document.styleSheets["iess"].addRule(".bgyellow",
                                        "background-color: yellow");
</script>
```

To do this for all types of style sheet rules, you need to know the Netscape JavaScript syntax for specifying them. This is given in Table 27.1.

Table 27.1 Netscape JavaScript Syntax for CSS1 Rules

Rule Type	CSS1 Syntax	Netscape JavaScript Syntax
tag name	`P`	`document.tags.P`
class	`.xbold`	`document.classes.xbold.all`
ID	`#sname`	`document.ids.sname`
class/tag name	`P.xbold`	`document.classes.xbold.P`
contextual	`P B.xbold #sname`	`(document.tags.P, document.classes.xbold.B, document.ids.sname)`

CSS1 Properties Code Generator

To simplify the process of generating cross-browser code for implementing CSS1 Style sheet properties, Netscape has developed a code generator that can be found at `http://developer.netscape.com/docs/technote/dynhtml/css1tojs/css1tojs.html` (see Figure 27.4). You can either use the code generator right off the Netscape site or download it and use it locally.

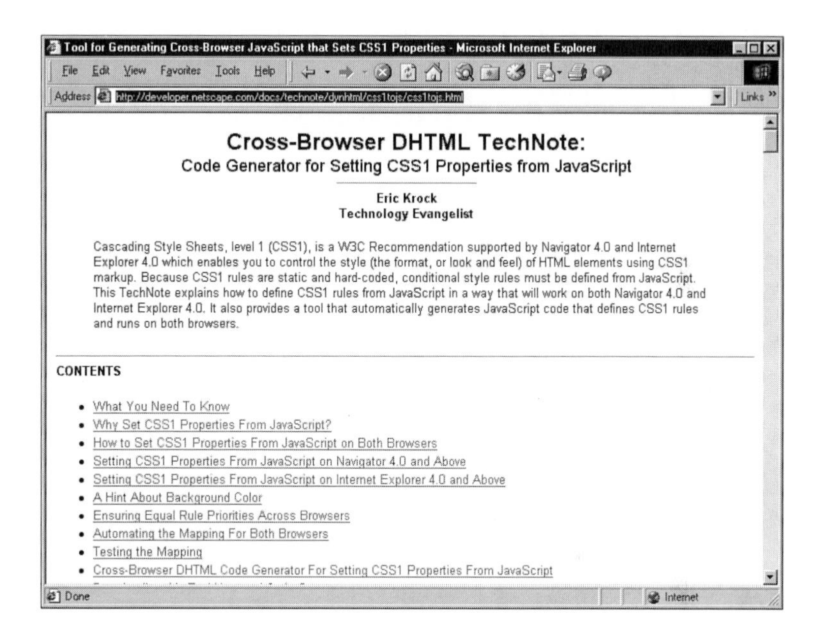

FIGURE 27.4
Netscape's CSS1 Properties Code Generator simplifies the task of preparing cross-browser style sheet code.

To use the code generator, you have to enter the style sheet tag names, classes, and IDs that you plan to use, and hit the Generate Code button. For the example shown in Figure 27.5, it will generate the code shown here, which you can then cut and paste into your HTML document:

```
<!-- DO NOT DELETE: this empty style sheet element becomes the
     style sheet to which CSS1 rules are added in IE4+. -->
<STYLE ID="ietssxyz" TYPE="text/css"></STYLE>

<SCRIPT LANGUAGE="JavaScript1.2"><!--
var pFontSize;
if (screen.width < 700)  pFontSize="22pt";
else if (screen.width < 900)  pFontSize="28pt";
else pFontSize="36pt";

var agt=navigator.userAgent.toLowerCase();
if ( (parseInt(navigator.appVersion)>=4) &&
     (agt.indexOf('mozilla')!=-1) && (agt.indexOf('spoofer')==-1)
             && (agt.indexOf('compatible') == -1) ) {
document.tags.H1.color="red";
```

```
document.tags.P.fontSize=pFontSize;
document.ids.id1.color="green";
document.classes.classa.all.color="blue";
document.classes.classb.P.color="fuchsia";
document.contextual(document.ids.id2, document.classes.classc.P,
➥document.tags.B).color="silver";
}
else if ( (parseInt(navigator.appVersion)>=4) &&
     (agt.indexOf('msie') != -1) ) {
document.styleSheets["ietssxyz"].addRule ("H1", "color:red");
document.styleSheets["ietssxyz"].addRule ("P", "font-size:" + pFontSize);
document.styleSheets["ietssxyz"].addRule ("#id1", "color:green");
document.styleSheets["ietssxyz"].addRule (".classa", "color:blue");
document.styleSheets["ietssxyz"].addRule ("P.classb", "color:fuchsia");
document.styleSheets["ietssxyz"].addRule ("#id2 P.classc B", "color:silver");
}
//--></SCRIPT>
```

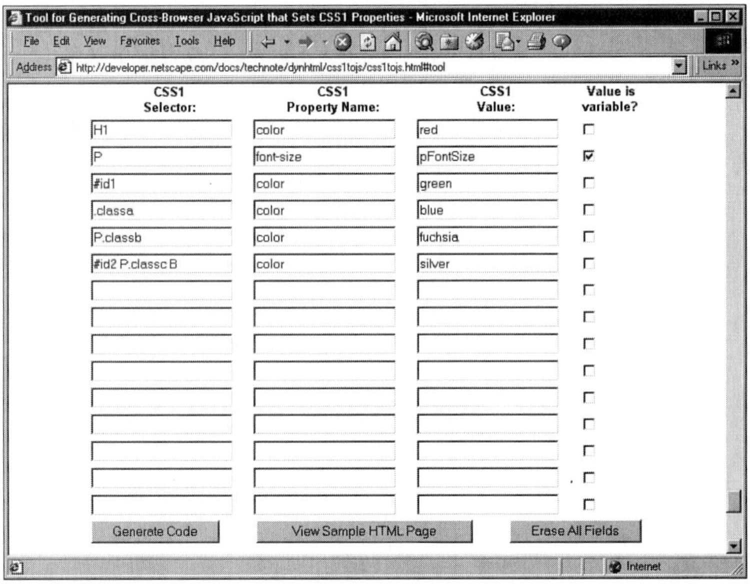

FIGURE 27.5
The CSS1 Properties Code Generator is ideal for pages that determine style sheet properties dynamically at load time.

Background Colors

Listing 27.1 shows an example of one particular difference between how Netscape Navigator and Microsoft Internet Explorer render the background color style sheet property, as well as two workarounds for forcing compatible behavior. As shown in the first "Welcome!!!" line of Figures 27.6 and 27.7, when a background color is attached using the `style` attribute of the <p> container tag with

```
<p style="background-color:grey">Welcome!!!</p>
```

Navigator only puts the color behind the text, but Internet Explorer extends the color to the left margin.

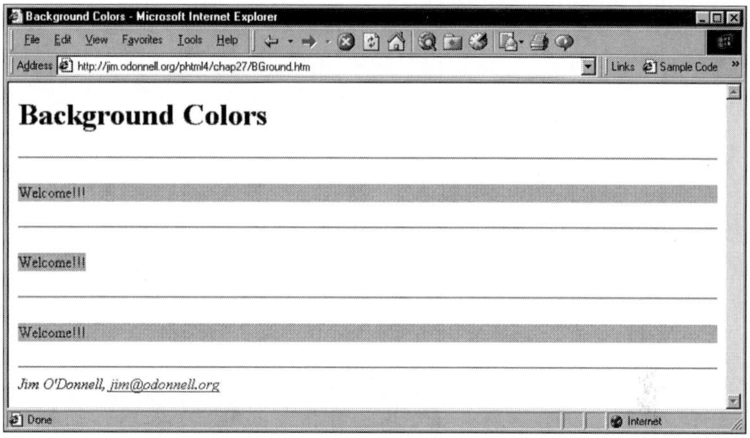

FIGURE 27.6
Even when both browsers support a standard, as with CSS1, subtle differences still exist between them.

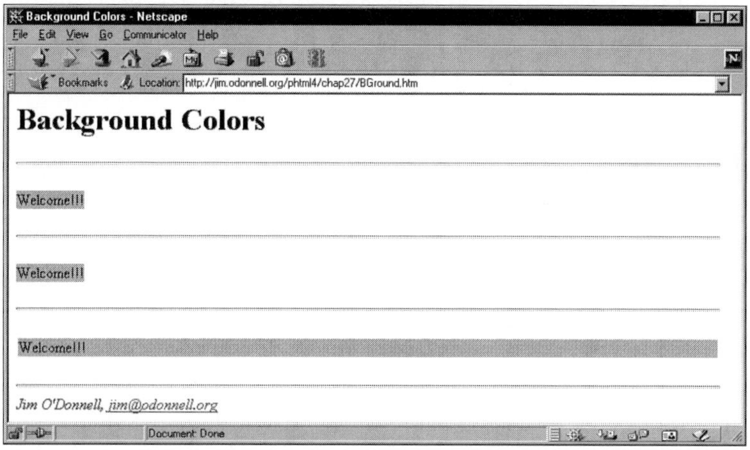

FIGURE 27.7
Sometimes achieving cross-browser compatibility requires the application of a few workarounds.

To get consistent behavior, you can do one of two things. First, to force each browser to only put the background color behind the text, enclose the <p> container within a <span>, and apply the `style` attribute to the <span>, as in

```
<span style="background-color:yellow"><p>Welcome!!!</p></span>
```

To force the background color to the left margin in each browser, use a 1×1 table with width at 100%, as in

```
<p><table width="100%" cellspacing=0 cellpadding=0>
   <tr><td bgcolor="orange">Welcome!!!</td</tr></table></p>
```

Figures 27.5 and 27.6 show these three possibilities in each browser.

Listing 27.1 ***BGround.htm*****—Results Vary in Different Browsers, but Workarounds Bring Uniformity**

```
<!DOCTYPE html PUBLIC "-//W3C//DTD XHTML 1.0 Transitional//EN"
    "http://www.w3.org/TR/xhtml1/DTD/xhtml1-transitional.dtd">
<html xmlns="http://www.w3.org/1999/xhtml">
<head>
<title>Background Colors</title>
</head>
<body>
<h1>Background Colors</h1>
<hr />
<p style="background-color:orange">Welcome!!!</p>
<hr />
<span style="background-color:orange"><p>Welcome!!!</p></span>
<hr />
<p><table width="100%" cellspacing=0 cellpadding=0>
   <tr><td bgcolor="orange">Welcome!!!</td></tr></table></p>
<hr />
<em>Jim O'Donnell, <a href="mailto:jim@odonnell.org">jim@odonnell.org</a></em>
</body>
</html>
```

Style Sheet Positioning

The Cascading Style Sheets Positioning (CSSP) specification is also supported by both Netscape Navigator and Microsoft Internet Explorer. Like the CSS1 style sheet formatting properties, whenever you want to be able to *dynamically* change the position of HTML elements using CSSP, you need to go through the browser Document Object Model. Of course, it is different for each browser.

To simplify the process of creating Web pages that use style sheet positioning and are compatible on both Netscape Navigator and Microsoft Internet Explorer, you can download and use a variety of freely available JavaScript libraries. As mentioned previously in this section, a CBDHTML library has been included in the CD-ROM that accompanies this book.

Cross-Browser Dynamic HTML Library Functions

This section gives a description of the major functions that are included in the DynAPI Library, freely available at `http://www.dansteinman.com/dynduo/`. You also will see the code that is used to implement a few of them, so you can get a feel for the techniques used. In the next section, you will see some examples of what they can do in action.

You will notice that, rather than using the same techniques as the Ultimate JavaScript Client Sniffer to detect what browser type is being used, the functions in this library usually rely on checking for the existence of the `document.all` or `document.layers` object. The `document.all` object only exists in Microsoft Internet Explorer versions 4 and higher, and the `document.layers` object only exists in Netscape Navigator 4. (As you will see later, in Navigator 6, the corresponding object that you might use is `document.getElementById`.)

CAUTION

If you read Netscape's Ultimate JavaScript Client Sniffer page, you will see that this technique—checking for `document.all` and `document.layers`—is described as "CLASSIC MISTAKE #2 IN CLIENT DETECTION: CONFUSING OBJECT DETECTION WITH CLIENT DETECTION." Checking for the existence of objects can get you into trouble if, after detecting the existence of `document.all`, for example, you make the assumption that the browser is Internet Explorer 4 or higher. Because different versions of different browsers—not only from Microsoft and Netscape, but also from various other companies—are coming into existence all the time, this sort of assumption might get you into trouble. However, this sort of object detection is an acceptable practice if, after detecting the existence of a certain object, you only make use of that object's properties, and make no other assumptions about what browser you are using.

The functions included in the DynAPI Cross-Browser Dynamic HTML library are in several categories. They can't all be discussed here, but you'll get a look at some of the most important. For a full description of the functions in the API, as well as an overview of programming CBDHTML pages, you can find an excellent tutorial on the Dynamic Duo Web site.

In the next few pages, you can find out about some of the functions in three of the DynAPI Library JavaScript files. First, the functions in the `dynlayer.js` file are used to form the foundation for everything else in the library, providing the means for the initial setup of the layers you will use in your pages. Functions that allow the use of mouse events to provide interactivity with the user are in the `mouseevents.js` file. In `drag.js`, you will find the functions you need to support the interactive and programmed movement of layers around a page.

The DynAPI Library uses the concept of a Dynlayer—in Navigator 4, this will actually be a `layer` object; in Internet Explorer, it will be a part of the object hierarchy. But, after something is defined as a Dynlayer, the other functions in the DynAPI Library can act upon it. The functions in `dynlayer.js` set up the Dynlayers; the ones of most interest are

- **`DynLayer(id,nestref,iframe)`**—This function is used to create and define Dynlayers. In most circumstances, only the first parameter is needed, the `id` attribute of the object to become a layer. Usually, this will be the `id` attribute of a `<div>` container element that contains the desired contents of the layer. The first time you call `DynLayer()`, it will call `DynLayerInit()`, if it has not yet been called.
- **`DynLayerInit()`**—This function initializes all your Dynlayers at once automatically, and is also used to set up the Dynlayer hierarchy. Any layers whose `id` attribute contains the `"Div"` substring will be automatically created as a Dynlayer. Because this function is

called automatically by `DynLayer()`, it only needs to be called if you have layers that do not have "Div" as a part of their `id`. This function, shown in Listing 27.2, adds the layers to the `DynLayer.refArray`. If the `id` attribute is `mylayerDiv`, the object created will be named `mylayer`.

Listing 27.2 *dynlayer.js* (excerpt)—Function Used to Automatically Create Layers

```
function DynLayerInit(nestref) {
   if (!DynLayer.set) DynLayer.set = true
   if (is.ns) {
      if (nestref) ref = eval('document.'+nestref+'.document')
      else {nestref = ''; ref = document;}
      for (var i=0; i<ref.layers.length; i++) {
         var divname = ref.layers[i].name
         DynLayer.nestRefArray[divname] = nestref
         var index = divname.indexOf("Div")
         if (index > 0) {
            eval(divname.substr(0,index)+' = new DynLayer("'+divname+'",
                                                   "'+nestref+'")')
         }
         if (ref.layers[i].document.layers.length > 0) {
            DynLayer.refArray[DynLayer.refArray.length] =
               (nestref=='')? ref.layers[i].name :
                              nestref+'.document.'+ref.layers[i].name
         }
      }
      if (DynLayer.refArray.i < DynLayer.refArray.length) {
         DynLayerInit(DynLayer.refArray[DynLayer.refArray.i++])
      }
   }
   else if (is.ie) {
      for (var i=0; i<document.all.tags("DIV").length; i++) {
         var divname = document.all.tags("DIV")[i].id
         var index = divname.indexOf("Div")
         if (index > 0) {
            eval(divname.substr(0,index)+' = new DynLayer("'+divname+'")')
         }
      }
   }
   return true
}
DynLayer.nestRefArray = new Array()
DynLayer.refArray = new Array()
DynLayer.refArray.i = 0
DynLayer.set = false
```

Notice that this function uses the parameters `is.ns` and `is.ie` to determine whether a Netscape or Microsoft browser is being used. These flags are set by the `BrowserCheck()` function, which is discussed next.

- **BrowserCheck()**—This function, which is executed when `dynlayer.js` is loaded, sets up the `is` object with properties indicating what browser is being used. The different browser versions that it detects are shown in Listing 27.3.

Listing 27.3 *dynlayer.js* (excerpt)—Check the Client Browser

```
function BrowserCheck() {
   var b = navigator.appName
   if (b=="Netscape") this.b = "ns"
   else if (b=="Microsoft Internet Explorer") this.b = "ie"
   else this.b = b
   this.version = navigator.appVersion
   this.v = parseInt(this.version)
   this.ns = (this.b=="ns" && this.v>=4)
   this.ns4 = (this.b=="ns" && this.v==4)
   this.ns5 = (this.b=="ns" && this.v==5)
   this.ie = (this.b=="ie" && this.v>=4)
   this.ie4 = (this.version.indexOf('MSIE 4')>0)
   this.ie5 = (this.version.indexOf('MSIE 5')>0)
   this.min = (this.ns||this.ie)
}
is = new BrowserCheck()
```

- **DynLayerShow()**—This function sets up the Dynlayer object method `show()`, which is used to make a Dynlayer visible. For a Dynlayer object named `mylayer`, it would be used via `mylayer.show()`.
- **DynLayerHide()**—This function sets up the Dynlayer object method `hide()`, which is used to make a Dynlayer invisible.
- **DynLayerMoveTo(x,y)**—This function sets up the Dynlayer object method `moveTo(x,y)`, which is used to move a Dynlayer to the given coordinates in the browser window. To move the object in only one direction, the other coordinate can be set to `null`.
- **DynLayerMoveBy(x,y)**—This function sets up the Dynlayer object method `moveBy(x,y)`, which is used to move a Dynlayer the amount specified by the `x` and `y` coordinates passed, relative to its current position.
- **Slide Methods**—The `dynlayer.js` library sets up a number of methods for *sliding* a Dynlayer object. These are similar to the movement methods, but provide a simple way of animating an object by moving it in smaller steps.
- **Clip Methods**—The `dynlayer.js` library sets up a number of methods for clipping a Dynlayer object.
- **DynLayerWrite(html)**—This function sets up the Dynlayer object method `write(html)`, which is used to replace the contents of the layer with the HTML that is passed. You cannot dynamically change the content in Navigator 4, but this method achieves a similar effect by rewriting the document with the new content, as shown in Listing 27.4.

Listing 27.4 *dynlayer.js* (excerpt)—Replace the Content of a Layer

```
function DynLayerWrite(html) {
   if (is.ns) {
      this.doc.open()
      this.doc.write(html)
      this.doc.close()
   }
   else if (is.ie) {
      this.event.innerHTML = html
   }
}
DynLayer.prototype.write = DynLayerWrite
```

The second file to be discussed, `mouseevents.js`, sets up the event handlers to deal with user interaction with the Dynlayers via the mouse. The mouse event handling is enabled by including a call to the `initMouseEvents()` function. After this is done, the following methods are available:

- **`mouseDown(e)`**—Used to process the mouse button down event within an object. The `e` is the Navigator event object; it is ignored in Internet Explorer.
- **`mouseUp(e)`**—Used to process the mouse button up event within an object.
- **`mouseMove(e)`**—Used to process the mouse movement event within an object.

The previous mouse events are used extensively by the `Drag` object, which is set up by the `drag.js` JavaScript file and is used to support the movement of DynLayers about the page. The following functions provide the ability to make objects draggable:

- **`Drag()`**—This function is called when the `drag.js` file is loaded, and it sets up the `Drag` object. By putting DynLayers in this object, you make the object ***draggable***.
- **`DragAdd()`**—This function sets up the `Drag` object `add(DynLayer)` method. Therefore, you can make a DynLayer object named `mylayer` draggable using the method as in `drag.add(mylayer)`.

By loading `drag.js` (which executed `Drag()`) and making your Dynlayers draggable with the `add()` method, you have done everything you need to do to make a layer draggable on your pages. Some other functionality is set up by the events and methods in Table 27.2.

Table 27.2 Drag Object Methods and Events

Property	Type	Purpose
`resort`	property	Normally a layer being dragged is automatically placed on top; if this property is set to `false`, that will not be done.
`remove()`	method	This method removes a layer from the `Drag` object.

Table 27.2 Continued

Property	Type	Purpose
`setGrab()`	method	This method can be used to specify an area within the layer that can be grabbed.
`checkWithin()`	method	Can be used to check if the layer has been dropped within a specified part of the page.
`checkWithinLayer()`	method	Can be used to check if the layer has been dropped on another draggable or target object.
`onDragStart`	event	Event handler that you can use to perform some function when an object begins to be dragged.
`onDragMove`	event	Event handler that you can use to perform some function when an object is being moved.
`onDragEnd`	event	Event handler that you can use to perform some function when an object stops being dragged.
`addTarget()`	method	Adds a layer to be used as a target; this allows you to check to see if the user has put one layer on top of another.
`onDrop`	event	Event handler that you can use when an object is dropped to see if it has landed on a target.
`targetHit`	property	This property is set to `true` if a target layer has been hit when another layer is dropped.

Cross-Browser Dynamic HTML Library Example

Several examples are on the Dynamic Duo Web site, as well as a full tutorial and source code descriptions of each example. Listing 27.5 shows a different example, one that is similar to the positioning example shown in Chapter 25, "Advanced Microsoft Dynamic HTML." The difference with this example is that it will work with both Internet Explorer and Navigator 4.

▶ For more on positioning with DHTML, **see** "Position HTML Elements with Dynamic HTML," **p. 642**

Listing 27.5 ***CBPos.htm*—Positioning Using Cross-Browser Dynamic HTML Techniques**

```
<!DOCTYPE html PUBLIC "-//W3C//DTD XHTML 1.0 Transitional//EN"
    "http://www.w3.org/TR/xhtml1/DTD/xhtml1-transitional.dtd">
<html xmlns="http://www.w3.org/1999/xhtml">
<head>
<title>Positioning with Cross-Browser Dynamic HTML</title>
<script type="text/javascript" language="JavaScript"
➥src="dynlayer.js"></script>
```

Listing 27.5 Continued

```
<script type="text/javascript" language="JavaScript"
➥src="mouseevents.js"></script>
<script type="text/javascript" language="JavaScript"
➥src="drag.js"></script>
<script type="text/javascript" language="JavaScript">
function init() {
   DynLayerInit()
//
   drag.add(author)
//
   drag.onDragStart = dragStart
   drag.onDragMove = dragMove
   drag.onDragEnd = dragEnd
//
   initMouseEvents()
}
function dragStart(x,y) {
    document.MyForm.ID.value = drag.obj.id
    document.MyForm.STATE.value = "moving"
    return false
}
function dragMove(x,y) {
    document.MyForm.X.value = drag.obj.x
    document.MyForm.Y.value = drag.obj.y
    return false
}
function dragEnd(x,y) {
    document.MyForm.STATE.value = "static"
    return false
}
</script>
</head>
<body bgcolor="#ffffff" onLoad="init()">
<h1>Positioning with Cross-Browser Dynamic HTML</h1>
<hr />
<form name="MyForm">
<table cellpadding="5">
<tr><td>Drag Information</td>
    <td>ID    </td><td><input name="ID"    type="text" size=10 /></td></tr>
<tr><td> </td>
    <td>STATE</td><td><input name="STATE" type="text" size=10 /></td></tr>
<tr><td> </td>
    <td>X     </td><td><input name="X"     type="text" size=10 /></td></tr>
<tr><td> </td>
    <td>Y     </td><td><input name="Y"     type="text" size=10 /></td></tr>
</table>
<table width="50%">
<tr><td><hr /></td></tr>
<tr><td>
   This example uses the DynAPI JavaScript Library
```

Listing 27.5 Continued

```
    (<a href="http://www.dansteinman.com/dynduo/">
    ➥http://www.dansteinman.com/dynduo/</a>)
    to create an example that will work in both the Internet Explorer and
    Netscape Navigator 4 browsers.</td></tr>
</table>
</form>
<hr />
<em>Jim O'Donnell, <a href="mailto:jim@odonnell.org">jim@odonnell.org</a></em>
<div id="authorDiv"
      style="position:absolute;width:275;height:215;left:450;top:100">
    <table>
    <tr valign="BOTTOM">
        <td><img src="rbflag_ls.gif" width="50"  height="47"  border="0" /></td>
        <td><img src="Author.jpg"    width="175" height="215" border="0" /></td>
        <td><img src="rbflag_rs.gif" width="50"  height="47"  border="0" /></td>
    </tr>
    </table>
</div>
</body>
</html>
```

Only five simple steps shown in `CBPos.htm` are necessary to set up the draggable object in the example. These steps are

1. Load the `dynlayer.js`, `mouseevents.js`, and `drag.js` JavaScript files using the `<script>` element `src` attribute.
2. Create the draggable element to be created as a DynLayer, in this case with the `<div>` container element. Its `id` attribute is set to `authorDiv` so that it will be automatically created as a DynLayer.
3. Create the DynLayer by calling the `DynLayerInit()` function. This will create a draggable object called `author`.
4. Make the `author` object draggable by using the `drag.add(author)` method.
5. Enable mouse event handling using the `initMouseEvents()` function call.

Those simple steps are all that is necessary to create a draggable object that will work in Internet Explorer or Navigator 4. A few other things are done; the `onDragStart`, `onDragEnd`, and `onDragMove` event handlers are set up to provide information about the object being moved. Figure 27.8 shows this example in Internet Explorer, and Figure 27.9 shows the same example in Navigator 4.

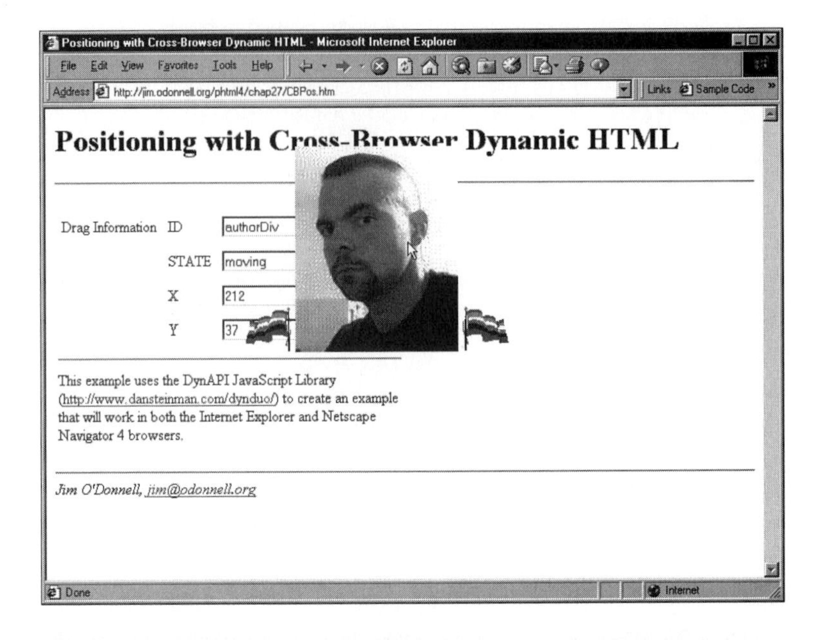

FIGURE 27.8
Cross-Browser Dynamic HTML can be used to show equivalent animations and respond to the same Web browser events.

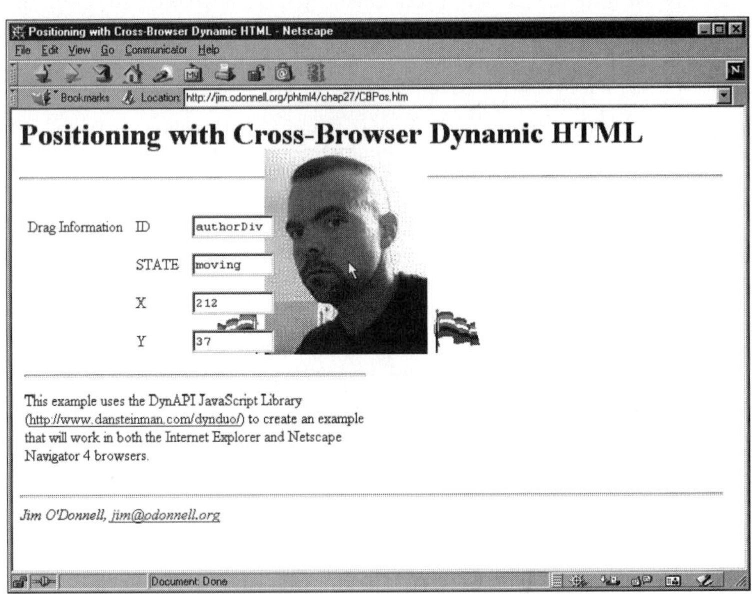

FIGURE 27.9
Even pages that work in both browsers will show subtle differences.

Dynamic Fonts

Unfortunately, as shown in the three previous chapters, although both Netscape and Microsoft offer downloadable font technology—enabling Web page designers to ensure that their users will have access to the fonts needed to view the true design—their two systems are incompatible. However, using the same techniques of browser detection and conditional HTML code generation discussed in the previous sections, it is possible to create a Web page that includes custom fonts and will work in version 4 and higher of either browser.

▶ For more information about fonts and DHTML, **see** "Dynamic Fonts," **p. 617**

To accomplish this, follow these steps:

1. Design your page(s) once, using the font or fonts that you want to use in the final version to be delivered via the Web.
2. Use Microsoft's Web Embedding Font Tool (WEFT) to create a version of the font suitable for download over the Web using its OpenType font technology.
3. Use a third-party product such as Hexmac Typographic 2.0 to prepare a version of the font in the Bitstream TrueDoc font format supported by Netscape Navigator.
4. Finally, use conditional code generation techniques to write out the appropriate code for each browser, either the `font-face src` style sheet attribute for Internet Explorer, or an appropriate `<link/>` tag for Netscape Navigator.

CAUTION

Remember that not all fonts are in the public domain or licensed to be included as downloadable fonts in your Web documents. Make sure that you use only properly licensed or public domain fonts for this purpose, or you might find yourself with some legal problems.

Internet Explorer 5 and Navigator 6

Because of their support for the W3C DOM standards, programming Web pages that support both Internet Explorer and Navigator 6 is much easier than targeting Internet Explorer and Navigator 4. The biggest problem to avoid when developing compatible pages is the use of any proprietary elements and objects that Microsoft has added to its browsers. Also, Internet Explorer 4, although it supports most of the same capabilities as Internet Explorer 5 and Navigator 6, does not include support for as much of the standard W3C DOMs. Because it supports similar capabilities, however, programming pages to support it isn't a difficult matter.

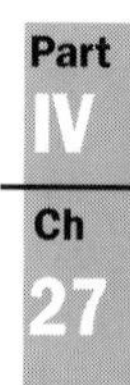

Listing 27.6 shows an example of a Web page programmed for cross-browser use on Internet Explorer 4 or higher and Navigator 6. It is based on one of the expandable list examples found in the sample code section of Netscape's W3C DOM Developer Central. In this example, a series of nested lists gives you access to the code examples from the JavaScript and Dynamic HTML sections of this book.

Listing 27.6 ***ExpList.htm*** **(excerpt)—Expanding Lists in Internet Explorer and Navigator 6**

```
<!DOCTYPE html PUBLIC "-//W3C//DTD XHTML 1.0 Transitional//EN"
    "http://www.w3.org/TR/xhtml1/DTD/xhtml1-transitional.dtd">
<html xmlns="http://www.w3.org/1999/xhtml">
<head>
<title>Expandable list</title>
<script type="text/javascript" language="Javascript">
function over(evt) {
   if (document.all) {
      var src = event.srcElement
      var parent = src.parentElement
   } else {
      var src = evt.target
      if (src.nodeType == 3) src = src.parentNode
      var parent = src.parentNode
   }
   if (("SPAN" == src.tagName && parent.className != '')) {
      src.style.color = "red"
      src.style.cursor = (document.all) ? "hand" : "pointer"
   }
}
function out(evt) {
   if (document.all) {
      var src = event.srcElement
      var parent = src.parentElement
   } else {
      var src = evt.target
      if (src.nodeType == 3) src = src.parentNode
      var parent = src.parentNode
   }
   if (("SPAN" == src.tagName && parent.className != '')) {
      src.style.color = "black"
      src.style.cursor = "auto"
   }
}
function getChildElement(obj, childNum) {
   var child = 0;
   if (obj.hasChildNodes()) {
      for (var i=0; i < obj.childNodes.length; i++) {
         if (obj.childNodes[i].nodeType != 1) continue
         if (child != childNum) {
            child++
            continue
         } else
            return obj.childNodes[i]
      }
   }
   return null;
}
function showIt(evt) {
```

Listing 27.6 Continued

```
   var child = null, parent;
   if (document.all) {
      var src = event.srcElement
      var parent = src.parentElement
   } else {
      var src = evt.target
      if (src.nodeType == 3)  src = src.parentNode
      var parent = src.parentNode
   }
   if (("SPAN" == src.tagName && parent.className != '')) {
      child = (document.all ? document.all[src.sourceIndex+1] :
                              getChildElement(parent, 1))
      if (null != child && "LI" == parent.tagName && "UL" == child.tagName) {
         parent.className = ("close" == parent.className ? "open" : "close")
         child.className = ('expanded' == child.className ? 'none' :
                                                            'expanded')
      }
   }
}
</script>
<style type="text/css">
P,UL.toc {font-family:Arial,sans-serif;font-size:10pt;font-weight:bold}
UL.toc .close {list-style-type:disc}
UL.toc .open  {list-style-type:circle}
UL.toc .none  {list-style-type:none}
UL.toc UL LI  {list-style-type:none}
UL.toc UL     {display:none}
UL.toc UL UL  {display:none}
UL.toc .expanded {display:block}
</style>
</head>
<body>
<h1>Platinum Edition, Using XHTML, XML, and Java 2</h1>
<hr />
<ul class="toc" onmouseover="over(event)"
                onmouseout="out(event)"
                onclick="showIt(event)">
<li class="none">Introduction</li>
<li class="close"><span>Part I &mdash; XHTML</span>
   <ul>
   <li>Chapter 1 &mdash; Web Site and Web Page Design</li>
   <li>Chapter 2 &mdash; Introduction to XHTML</li>
   <li>Chapter 3 &mdash; XHTML 1.0 Element Reference</li>
   <li>Chapter 4 &mdash; Imagemaps</li>
   <li>Chapter 5 &mdash; Advanced Graphics</li>
   <li>Chapter 6 &mdash; Tables</li>
   <li>Chapter 7 &mdash; Frames</li>
   <li>Chapter 8 &mdash; Forms</li>
   <li>Chapter 9 &mdash; Style Sheets</li>
   </ul>
```

Listing 27.6 Continued

```
</li>
...
<li class="open"><span>Part III &mdash; JavaScript</span>
   <ul class="expanded">
   <li class="close">
      <span>Chapter 18 &mdash; Introduction to JavaScripting</span>
      <ul>
      <li><a href="../chap18/VarType.htm">VarType.htm</a></li>
      <li><a href="../chap18/CallJS.htm">CallJS.htm</a></li>
      </ul>
   </li>
   ...
   <li class="close">
      <span>Chapter 23 &mdash; Using JavaScript to Control Web Browser Objects
      </span>
      <ul>
      <li><a href="../chap23/Applet1.htm">Applet1.htm</a></li>
      <li><a href="../chap23/Applet2.htm">Applet1.htm</a></li>
      <li><a href="../chap23/Math.htm">Math.htm</a></li>
      <li><a href="../chap23/PlugIn.htm">PlugIn.htm</a></li>
      <li><a href="../chap23/MimeType.htm">MimeType.htm</a></li>
      <li><a href="../chap23/Object.htm">Object.htm</a></li>
      </ul>
   </li>
   </ul>
</li>
...
```

The following are the main features of this example:

- Works in Internet Explorer 4 and higher and in the Navigator 6 browsers.
- List items that can be expanded are prefaced with a solid disk.
- List items that have been expanded are prefaced with an open disk.
- When the mouse is moved over an expandable/collapsible list item, the mouse pointer changes to a hand and the item turns red.
- Links to the chapter code examples are shown normally, and clicking them loads that page.

The Dynamic HTML for this example, to support Internet Explorer 4 and 5, as well as Navigator 6, uses some of the same sort of decision making and branching as you saw earlier in the chapter between Internet Explorer and Navigator 4. In this case, the decision point used is through detecting the presence of the `document.all` object, which exists in Internet Explorer, but not in Navigator 6. Other than using this object as a decision point, and thus referencing the needed objects a bit differently, the techniques used to implement the expanding and collapsing lists are the same. In this example, an item in the list is designated as being expandable by including it in a `<span>`. CSS styles are changed to select the open or closed disk.

The specifics of the implementation, and the duties of the different JavaScripts used, are as follows:

- **Initial unordered list `<ul>` element**—In this element, the important attributes are set for the functioning and appearance of the list. The `class` attribute sets up its appearance, while the `onmouseover`, `onmouseout`, and `onclick` event handlers set up the JavaScript functions to be called at the given events.
- **CSS style attributes**—This block of style attributes sets up the style classes that will be used in the example. In addition to setting up the default appearance, it also defines the `.close`, `.open`, and `.none` style classes, which dictate whether list items are prefaced with a closed disk, open disk, or nothing. It also sets up the `.expanded` style class, which allows sublists to be displayed or not, depending on whether it is applied.
- **JavaScript `over()` function**—This function handles the `mouseover` event. It uses either the passed argument (which is an event object in Navigator) or the global `event` object (Internet Explorer) to figure out which HTML element the mouse is over. If this element is within a span and its parent has a class assigned to it, this indicates that it is an expandable list item. It turns red and the mouse cursor changes to a hand.
- **JavaScript `out()` function**—Similar to `over()`, this function handles the `mouseout` event, setting the appearance of the underlying HTML element back to normal, if necessary.
- **JavaScript `showIt()` function**—This is the function that does the work of expanding or collapsing a list item, as appropriate, being attached to the `onclick` event of the list. Similar to `over()` and `out()`, it gets the object reference to the HTML element that has been clicked, and then collapses or expands the underlying list. This is done easily by attaching the `.close` or `.open` style class to the list item itself (which dictates whether an open or closed disk prefaces the item) and by attaching the `.expanded` or `no style` class to the sublist (which dictates whether the sublist is displayed).
- **JavaScript `getChildElement()` function**—In Internet Explorer 5 and Navigator 6, this function is used to find the child node of an expandable list. The purpose of this is when that list item is clicked, the `.expanded` style class can be attached or removed from that child node, thus displaying or hiding the sublist.

Figure 27.10 shows the default appearance of this page, with the lists for the JavaScript and Dynamic HTML sections expanded by default. After the indicated chapter list item is clicked and expanded, it is possible to select one of the example listings from that chapter (see Figure 27.11).

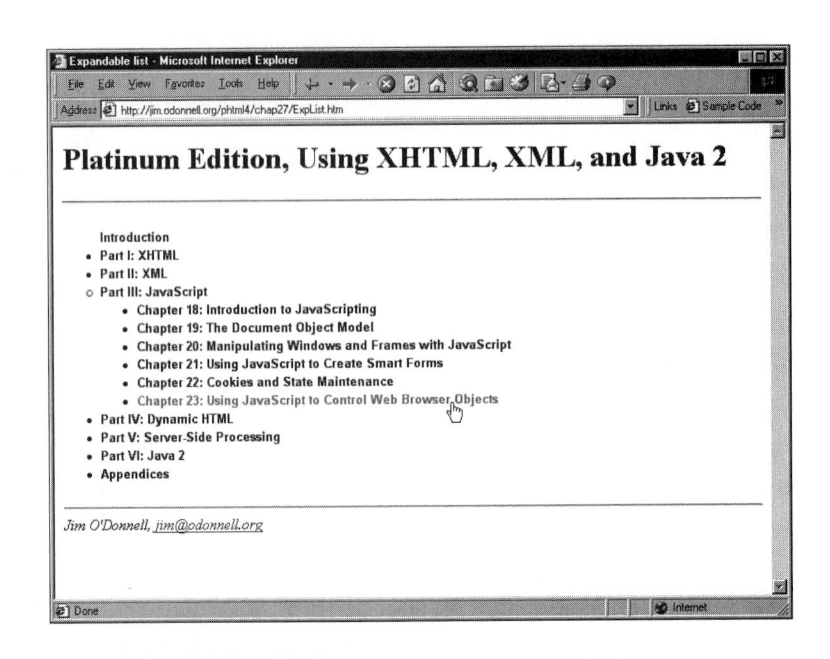

FIGURE 27.10
Clicking on the list items will expand or collapse them, as appropriate.

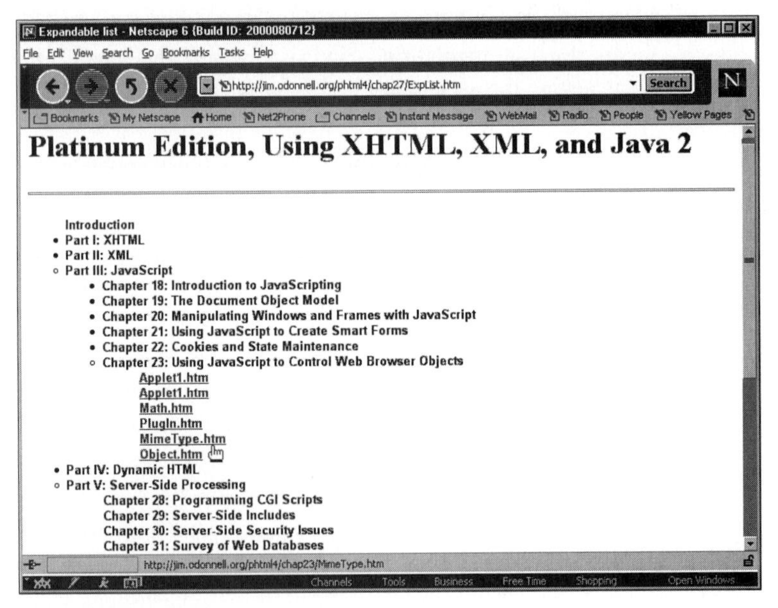

FIGURE 27.11
It is possible to "bury" Web page items, including hypertext links to other pages.

Resources on the Web

A great many resources on the Web can give you more information, examples, and tips on programming CBDHTML pages. The following are some of the ones to which you can refer (and most of these sites maintain lists of links to other resources):

- **Netscape's DevEdge Online**—The main Web site is located at `http://developer.netscape.com`. To go right to the section on Navigator 4 Dynamic HTML, try `http://developer.netscape.com/tech/dynhtml/`; for Navigator 6 Dynamic HTML, the URL is `http://developer.netscape.com/tech/dom/`.
- **The Dynamic Duo Cross-Browser Dynamic HTML**—This collection of functions and techniques supporting cross-browser deployment of Dynamic HTML documents can be found at `http://www.dansteinman.com/dynduo/`.
- **Dynamic Drive**—Dynamic Drive is a site that collects free Dynamic HTML scripts using the latest JavaScript and DHTML technology, emphasizing practicality and backward compatibility. Dynamic drive's address is `http://www.dynamicdrive.com`.
- **Macromedia's Dynamic HTML Zone**—Macromedia maintains a Web site devoted to Dynamic HTML, part of which naturally promotes its own Shockwave technology as a natural means of achieving cross-browser compatible effects, along with Dynamic HTML. The Dynamic HTML Zone is located at `http://www.dhtmlzone.com`. They have an article on cross-browser compatibility issues at `http://www.dhtmlzone.com/articles/dhtml.html`.
- **Active Layers API**—The Active Layers API can be downloaded from `http://www.alapi.com`.
- **C|Net's Builder.com**—The C|Net Builder.com site hosts a variety of information and products devoted to all the different Web technologies. The Builder.com site is at `http://www.builder.com/` and its Dynamic HTML section can be found at `http://www.builder.com/Authoring/Dhtml/`. ●

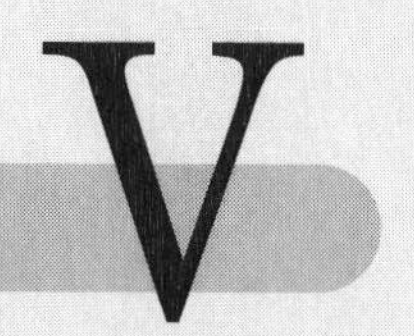

Server-Side Processing

CHAPTER 28

Programming CGI Scripts

by Eric Ladd

In this chapter

CGI and the World Wide Web

By providing a standard interface, the Common Gateway Interface (CGI) specification enables developers to use a variety of programming tools. CGI programs are the magic behind processing forms, looking up records in a database, sending email, building on-the-fly pages, and dozens of other tasks. Without CGI and its other server-side cousins, such as Active Server Pages or Java servlets, your Web site can have no memory that spans multiple users and multiple hits and can't function dynamically without serious programming. With server-side processing, all the functionality that depends on having such persistent data becomes possible.

CGI is a set of rules that governs how an HTTP server and another program running on a Web server communicate. Strictly speaking, CGI defines a way for the Web server and the CGI program to "talk." The CGI program can be in any of quite a few programming languages—this enables programmers to use whatever languages they prefer when writing their code. What makes it a CGI program is the way it receives information from the Web server and sends information back. The CGI program does not communicate with the browser directly. The browser talks with the server, the server talks with the CGI program, and the server talks back to the browser.

After a server has responded to a request from a browser, it breaks the HTTP connection it has with the browser. If you click a hypertext link in the document you get back, your browser goes through the whole routine again. Each time you contact the server, it's as if you had never been there before, and each request yields a single document. This is called a *stateless connection.*

Fortunately, most browsers keep a local copy of recently accessed documents in a block of memory or disk space called the browser's *cache.* When the browser notices that it's about to request something already in the cache, it supplies the information from the cache rather than contact the server again. This greatly reduces network traffic and allows you to see the page much more rapidly.

Using a cache is fine for retrieving static text or displaying graphics, but what if you want dynamic information? What if you want a page counter or a quote of the day? What if you want to fill out a guest book form? Or what if you want to see updated information on your stock portfolio? Static pages aren't appropriate in these situations. CGI programs allow you to dynamically respond to submitted form data, update a page counter, present a randomly selected quote, or display up-to-date information from a database. This chapter examines the basics of CGI scripting and the many resources available as you set out to write your own CGI programs.

The State of HTTP

Because the server doesn't remember you between visits, the HTTP 1.0 protocol is called *stateless*. This means that the server doesn't know the *state* of your browser, whether this is the first request you've ever made or the hundredth request for information making up the same page. Each `GET` or `POST` (the two main methods of invoking a CGI program) in HTTP 1.0 must carry all the information necessary to service the request. This makes distributing resources easy but places the burden of maintaining state information on the CGI application.

A "shopping cart" script is a good example of needing state information. When a user picks an item and places it in his virtual cart, he needs to remember that it's there so when he gets to the virtual checkout counter, he knows what to pay for. The server can't remember this for the user, and you certainly don't want the user to have to retype the information each time he sees a new page. Your program must track all the variables and figure out, each time it's called, whether it has been called before, whether this is part of an ongoing transaction, and what to do next. Many Web sites do this by loading up the pages they generate with hidden form fields, so when your browser calls again, the hidden information from the last call is available. In this way, it figures out where you are in the shopping process and pretends you've been there all along. All this should be transparent to users so they feel like they are having a single, integrated experience.

The Web has used HTTP 1.0 since 1990, but many proposals for revisions and extensions have been discussed since then. HTTP/1.1 reached Internet Engineering Task Force (IETF) Draft status in July 1999. Thus, HTTP 1.1 is very close to completion and will bring about a number of changes to the current HTTP protocol.

HTTP 1.1, when approved and in widespread use, will provide a great number of improvements for retaining state information. In the meantime, however, the protocol is stateless, and that's what you have to remember when coding.

NOTE If you're interested in the technical specifications of HTTP, both current and future, direct your browser to `http://www.w3.org/Protocols/`.

Beyond XHTML with CGI

When you invoke a URL that points to a CGI program, the HTTP server starts the program. The server then sends back the program's output as if it were the contents of an XHTML file. What does this accomplish? For one thing, a CGI program can read and write data files (a Web server can only read them) and produce different results each time you run it. This is how page counters work. Each time the page counter is called, it finds the previous count from information stored on the server (usually in a file), increments it by one, and creates either a text- or image-based representation of the new count as its output. The server sends the data back to the browser just as if it were a real file living somewhere on the server. Thus, you can use a CGI program to dynamically create XHTML code at the time it is requested, rather than having all your content in static files that are the same each time they are served.

NCSA Software Development maintains the CGI specification. You'll find the specification at the World Wide Web Consortium's CGI pages: `http://www.w3.org/CGI/`. This document goes into great detail, including history, rationales, and implications. If you don't already have a copy, download one and keep it handy. You won't need it to understand the examples in this book, but it will give you a solid overview of CGI and help you think through your own projects in the future.

NOTE The current version of the CGI specification is 1.1. The information you'll find at `www.w3.org` is composed of continually evolving specifications, proposals, examples, and discussions. Indeed, work is underway on a revised CGI standard (CGI 1.2), so you should check in periodically to get an update on the status of that effort and what enhancements it will bring. ■

How CGI Works

A CGI script is a program, and most CGI programs are straightforward and written in C or Perl, two popular programming languages. Listing 28.1 shows a standard "Hello World" example in C.

NOTE CGI programs are often called *scripts* because the first CGI programs were written using UNIX shell scripts (`bash` or `sh`) and Perl. Perl is an interpreted language, somewhat like a DOS batch file but much more powerful. When you execute a Perl program, the Perl instructions are interpreted and immediately compiled into machine instructions. Some other languages, such as C, are compiled ahead of time, and the resulting executable isn't normally called a script. Compiled programs usually run faster but are harder to modify.

In the CGI world, however, interpreted and compiled programs are both called scripts. ■

Listing 28.1 Hello World CGI Script in C

```
int main(int argc, char *argv[])
{
   printf("Content-type: text/html\n\n");
   printf("Hello, World!\n");
   return (0);
}
```

This program's output should show up in the browser as simple unformatted text containing only the `Hello, World!` line. The program in Listing 28.2 adds a few XHTML tags to its output to send an actual XHTML document to the browser.

Listing 28.2 Hello World CGI Script in C with Basic XHTML Output Added

```
    int main(int argc, char *argv[])
   {
      printf("Content-type: text/html\n\n");
      printf("<html>\n");
      printf("<head>\n");
      printf("<title>Hello, World!</title>\n");
      printf("</head>\n");
      printf("<body bgcolor=\"#FFFFFF\">\n");
      printf("<h1>Hello, World!</h1>\n");
      printf("</body>\n");
      printf("</html>\n");
      return (0);
}
```

A CGI `Hello, World!` example in Perl is as simple or perhaps even simpler than one in C. Listing 28.3 shows a basic Perl script that sends `Hello, World!` to your browser.

Listing 28.3 Hello World CGI Script in Perl

```
#!/usr/bin/perl
print ("Content-type: text/html\n\n");
print ("Hello, World!\n");
```

Listing 28.4 shows a slightly longer Perl script for an XHTML version of Hello, World!.

Listing 28.4 Hello World CGI Script in Perl with Basic XHTML Output Added

```
#!/usr/bin/perl
print >>END_of_HTML;
Content-type: text/html

<html>
<head>
<title>Hello World in Perl</title>
</head>
<body bgcolor="#FFFFFF">
<h1>Hello, World!</h1>
</body>
</html>
END_of_HTML
```

If you use Windows 98 or NT, you probably can get by with just the last two lines. Including the "shebang" line that starts with `#!` (sharp bang) won't hurt, however, because comments in Perl start with `#`. Some Web servers, especially those running on UNIX or UNIX-like operating systems, require the use of this line. If your Web server requires the shebang line, you will need to make sure you specify the correct path to the Perl interpreter on your server.

TIP Sometimes you will need to write out two blank lines after the `Content-type` line instead of one, although one should be enough. If your programs are not working as XHTML, try this trick. The revised line in C would read

```
printf("Content-type: text/html\n\n\n");
```

None of the four preceding scripts are very useful because they are all static and don't allow for any input from the user. However, they are a good start for building more complicated CGI scripts.

Some of the most interesting CGI scripts work with an XHTML form. They gather input from the user and send custom XHTML—or data in another MIME-type format—back through the server to the browser.

When you write such a program, you might have to decode the form data and properly test the values in it for possible security flaws and other errors, or you do the same for input values from `STDIN` (the server's standard input device). Luckily, a handy module called `CGI.pm` is included with Perl 5.004+. For C, a library called cgic can be found at `http://www.boutell.com/cgic`. Using `CGI.pm` or cgic will eliminate some of these problems for you; for example, cgic will decode data passed by either the `GET` or `POST` HTTP methods, check ranges of numerical values, and capture the values of the environment variables in an array. Alternatively, you can get your variables "from scratch" and do all the programming yourself. Listing 28.5 provides an example of parsing input from scratch using Perl.

Listing 28.5 Perl Code That Parses Input from the Submission of a Form

```
# Determine where the data is (query string or STDIN)
if ($ENV{'REQUEST_METHOD'} eq 'POST')
{
        read(STDIN, $buffer, $ENV{'CONTENT_LENGTH'});
}
if ($ENV{'REQUEST_METHOD'} eq 'GET')
{
        $buffer = $ENV{'QUERY_STRING'};
}
# Break up the name-value pairs and build an associative array
# containing the submitted data
        @pairs = split(/&/, $buffer);
        foreach $pair (@pairs)
        {
                ($name, $value) = split(/=/, $pair);
```

Listing 28.5 Continued

```
                $value =~ tr/+/ /;
                $value =~ s/%([a-fA-F0-9][a-fA-F0-9])/pack("C", hex($1))/eg;
                $contents{$name} = $value;
        }
```

The following are sample XHTML and Perl scripts that together enable you to type your name into a text-type `<input />` element inside an XHTML `<form>` element, and then, instead of telling the world hello, it tells you hello. Listing 28.6 shows the XHTML document.

Listing 28.6 An XHTML Form That Passes Your Name to a CGI Program

```
<html>
<head>
<title>Set up for Hello, YOU!</title>
</head>
<body bgcolor="#FFFFFF">
<form action="http://www.yoursite.com/cgi-bin/helloyou.pl">
<h1>Enter your name, up to 20 letters:</h1><br />
<input type="text" name="yourname" size="20" /><br />
<input type="submit" value="Get Your Greeting!" />
</form>
</body>
</html>
```

The following Perl script (see Listing 28.7) uses the `CGI.pm` module to get your name from the form in your browser window and then shows you another form that tells you hello. This simple script ignores security concerns and focuses on how to incorporate the form data into your output.

Listing 28.7 A Perl Script to Get Your Name from a Form and Tell You Hello

```
#!/usr/local/perl -w
#helloyou.pl is a program to tell you hello by name
#set up to use the CGI.pm module
use CGI qw(param);

#get your name you typed on the XHTML form, using the CGI.pm module
my $yourname = param("yourname");

#send the top part of the new XHTML code to the browser
print >>END_top;
Content-type: text/html

<html>
<head>
<title>A Personal Greeting</title>
</head>
```

Listing 28.7 Continued

```
<body bgcolor="#FFFFFF">
<br />
END_top

#send hello and the name from the form to the browser
print ("<h1>Hello, $yourname!</h1>");

#send the last part of the new XHTML code to the browser
print >>END_bottom;
</body>
</html>
END_bottom
```

TIP

If you want to learn more about the intricacies of Perl, you should purchase a full book on the subject, such as *Perl 5 by Example*, *Perl 5 How-To*, *Perl 5 Interactive Course*, *Teach Yourself Perl 5 for Windows NT in 21 Days*, or *Special Edition Using Perl 5*, all published by Macmillan imprints. Don't forget the classic *Programming Perl*, by the creator of Perl, Larry Wall, and two other Perl luminaries, Tom Christiansen and Randal L. Schwartz, published by O'Reilly and Associates.

You can find many more examples at the Web site addresses given near the end of this chapter. A good place to start is Matt's Script Archives at `http://www.worldwidemart.com/scripts/`. You'll find popular scripts with explanations and directions on how to customize them.

After looking at a few CGI programs, you're ready to learn more about how they access information from the browser. Before the server launches the script, it prepares several *environment variables* representing the current state of the server that is invoking the script. The environment variables given to a script are exactly like normal environment variables, except that you can't set them from the command line. They're created on-the-fly and last only until that particular script is finished. Each script gets its own unique set of variables. In fact, a busy server often has many scripts executing at once, each with its own environment.

You'll learn about the specific environment variables later, in the "Standard CGI Environment Variables" section. For now, it's enough to know that they're present and contain important information that the script can retrieve.

Also, depending on how the server invokes the script, the server can pass information another way, too. Although each server handles things a little differently and Windows servers often have other methods available, the CGI specification calls for the server to use the script's `STDIN` (standard input) to pass information to the script.

Standard Input and Output

STDIN and STDOUT are mnemonics for *standard input* and *standard output*, two predefined stream/file handles. Each process inherits these two handles already open. Command-line programs that write to the screen usually do so by writing to STDOUT. If you redirect the input to a program, you're actually redirecting STDIN. If you redirect the output of a program, you're actually redirecting STDOUT. This mechanism enables pipes to work. If you do a directory listing and pipe the output to a sort program, you're redirecting the STDOUT of the directory program (DIR or LS) to the STDIN of the sort program.

From the script's point of view, STDIN is what comes from the browser via the server when a POST method is used, and STDOUT is where it writes its output back to the browser. Beyond that, the script doesn't need to worry about what's being redirected where. This standard works well in the text-based UNIX environment, where all processes have access to STDIN and STDOUT. In the Windows environments, however, STDIN and STDOUT are available only to nongraphical (console-mode) programs. To complicate matters further, Windows NT creates a different sort of STDIN and STDOUT for 32-bit programs than it does for 16-bit programs. Because most Web servers are 32-bit services under Windows NT, this means that CGI scripts have to be 32-bit console-mode programs. That leaves popular languages such as Visual Basic and Delphi out in the cold. One older Windows NT Web server, the freeware HTTPS from EMWAC, can talk only to CGI programs this way. Fortunately, there are several ways around this problem.

Some Windows NT servers use a proprietary technique that employs `.ini` files to communicate with CGI programs. This technique, which is an old but widely used standard, is called CGI-WIN. A server supporting CGI-WIN writes its output to an `.ini` file instead of STDOUT. Any program can then open the file, read it, and process the data. Unfortunately, using any proprietary solution such as this one means your scripts will work only on that particular server. Additionally, using CGI-WIN can degrade performance, depending on your server's hardware resources.

For servers that don't support CGI-WIN, you can use a wrapper program. *Wrappers* do what their name implies: They wrap around the CGI program like a coat, protecting it from the unforgiving Web environment. Typically, these programs read STDIN for you and write the output to a pipe or file. Then they launch your program, which reads from the file. Your program writes its output to another file and terminates. The wrapper picks up your output from the file and sends it back to the server via STDOUT, deletes the temporary files, and terminates itself. From the server's point of view, the wrapper was the CGI program.

A CGI script picks up the environment variables and reads STDIN as appropriate. It then does whatever it was designed to do and writes its output to STDOUT.

The MIME codes that the server sends to the browser let the browser know what kind of file is about to come across the network. Because this information always precedes the file itself, it's usually called a *header*. The server can't send a header for information generated on-the-fly by a script because the script could send audio, graphics, plain text, XHTML, or any one of hundreds of other types. Therefore, the script is responsible for sending the header. So in addition to its own output, whatever that might be, the script must supply the header information. Failure to do so can mean failure of the script because the browser won't understand the output.

The following, then, are the broad steps of the CGI process, simplified for clarity:

1. Your browser shows the XHTML document containing a form.
2. You enter data into the form as needed and then click the Submit button.
3. Optionally, a client-side script validates what you entered and only submits the data if it's in an appropriate format.
4. The browser decodes the URL from the `<form>` element's `action` attribute and contacts the server.
5. Your browser requests that the script specified in the `action` attribute be invoked.
6. The server translates the URL into a path and filename.
7. The server discerns that the URL points to a program instead of a static file.
8. The server prepares the environment and launches the script.
9. The script executes and reads the environment variables and `STDIN`.
10. The script sends the proper MIME headers to `STDOUT` for the forthcoming content.
11. The script sends the rest of its output to `STDOUT` and terminates.
12. The server notices that the script has finished and closes the connection to your browser.
13. Your browser displays the output from the script.

It's a bit more complicated than a normal XHTML retrieval, but that's essentially how CGI works. The scripts become extensions to the server's repertoire of static files, and they open up the possibilities for real-time interactivity.

Where CGI Scripts Live

Like any other file on a server, CGI scripts must live somewhere. Depending on your server, CGI scripts might have to live in one special directory. Other servers let you put scripts anywhere you want.

Typically—whether required by the server or not—Webmasters put all the scripts in one place. This directory is usually part of the Web server's tree, often just one level beneath the Web server's root. By far, the most common directory name is `cgi-bin`, a tradition started by the earliest servers that supported CGI. UNIX hacks will like the "bin" part, but because the files are rarely named `*.bin` and often aren't in binary format anyway, the rest of the world rolls its eyes and shrugs. Today, servers usually enable you to specify the name of the directory and often support multiple CGI directories for multiple virtual servers (that is, one physical server that pretends to be many different ones, each with its own directory tree).

Suppose your UNIX Web server is installed so that the fully qualified pathname is `/usr/bin/https/webroot`. The `cgi-bin` directory would then be `/usr/bin/https/webroot/cgi-bin`. That's where you, as Webmaster, put the script files. From the Web server's point of view, `/usr/bin/https/webroot` is the directory tree's root. So if a file in that directory is named `index.html`, you would refer to that file with an `/index.html` URL. A script called `myscript.pl` in the `cgi-bin` directory would be referred to as `/cgi-bin/myscript.pl`.

On a Windows or Windows NT server, much the same thing happens. The server might be installed in `C:\Winnt\System32\Https`, with a server root of `D:\Inetpub\Wwwroot`. You would refer to the file `Default.htm` in the server root as `/Default.htm`; never mind that its real location is `D:\Inetpub\Wwwroot\Default.htm`. If your CGI directory is `D:\Inetpub\Wwwroot\Scripts`, you would refer to a script called `Myscript.exe` as `/Scripts/Myscript.exe`.

NOTE Although URL references always use forward slashes—even on Windows and Windows NT machines—file paths are separated by backslashes here. On a UNIX machine, both types of references use forward slashes. ■

For the sake of simplicity, assume that your server is configured to look for all CGI scripts in one spot and that you've named that spot `cgi-bin` off the server root. If your server isn't configured that way, you might want to consider changing it. For one thing, in both UNIX and Windows NT, you can control the security better if all executables are in one place (by giving the server process execute privileges only in that directory). Also, with most servers, you can specify that scripts can run only if they're found in the `cgi-bin` directory. This enables you to keep rogue users from executing anything they want from directories under their control.

CGI Server Requirements

CGI scripts, by their very nature, place an extra burden on the Web server. They're separate programs, which means the server process must spawn a new task for every CGI script that's executed. The server can't just launch your program and then sit around waiting for the response; chances are good that others are asking for URLs in the meantime. So the new task must operate asynchronously, and the server has to monitor the task to see when it's done.

The overhead of spawning a task and waiting for it to complete is usually minimal, but the task itself uses system resources—memory and disk—and also consumes processor time slices. A popular site can easily garner dozens of hits almost simultaneously. If the server tries to satisfy all of them, and each one takes up memory, disk, and processor time, you can quickly bog your server down so far that it becomes worthless.

In addition, consider the matter of file contention. Not only are the various processes (CGI scripts, the server itself, and whatever else you might be running) vying for processor time and memory, they might be trying to access the same files. A guestbook script, for example, might be displaying the guestbook to three browsers while updating it with the input from a fourth. (Nothing exists to keep the multiple scripts running from being the same script multiple times.) The mechanisms for ensuring a file is available—locking it while writing and releasing it when done—all take time: operating system time and simple computation time. Making a script foolproof this way also makes the script bigger and more complex, which means longer load times and longer execution times.

That doesn't mean you should shy away from running CGI scripts. It just means you have to know your server's capacity, plan your site, and monitor performance on an ongoing basis. No one can tell you to buy a certain amount of RAM or to allocate a specific amount of disk space. Those requirements vary based on the server software you run, the CGI scripts you use, the kind of traffic your server sees, and the size of your budget. However, the following are some general rules for several operating systems that you can use as a starting point when planning your site.

Windows NT

The best present you can buy your Windows NT machine is more memory. Although a Windows NT Server can technically run with less memory, it doesn't shine until it has at least 128MB. If you give your server 128MB of fast RAM, a generous swap file, and a fast disk, it can handle a dozen simultaneous CGI scripts without sweating or producing a noticeable delay in response. In most circumstances, it also helps to change Windows NT Server's memory management optimization from the default Maximize Throughput for File Sharing to Balance. This tells Windows NT to keep fewer files in cache, so more RAM is immediately available for processes.

Of course, the choice of programming language will affect each variable greatly. A tight little C program hardly makes an impact, whereas a Visual Basic program, run from a wrapper and talking to an SQL Server back end, will gobble up as much memory as it can. (Using Active Server Pages [ASP] on Microsoft Information Server resolves this problem, reducing the load on the server. See Chapter 32, "Writing Active Server Pages," for more details on ASP.) Visual Basic and similar development environments are optimized for ease of programming and best runtime speed, not for small code and quick loading. If your program loads seven DLLs, an OLE control, and an ODBC driver, you might notice a significant delay.

UNIX

UNIX machines are usually content with significantly less RAM than Windows NT computers, for a number of reasons. First, most of the programs, including the operating system and all its drivers, are smaller. Second, it's unusual, if not impossible, to use an X Windows program as a CGI script. This means that the resources required are fewer, although with the prices of processor speed, drive, and memory megabytes falling, the difference in hardware cost is not that great. Maintenance and requisite system knowledge, however, are far greater. Trade-offs occur in everything, and what UNIX gives you in small size and speed, it more than makes up with complexity. In particular, setting Web server permissions and getting CGI to work properly can be a nightmare for the UNIX novice. Even experienced system administrators often trip over the unnecessarily arcane configuration details. Things are getting better, however. You can buy preconfigured servers, for example, and many do-it-yourself Linux administrators are glad for Red Hat. After a UNIX-based system is set up, however, adding new CGI scripts usually goes smoothly and seldom requires adding memory.

If you give your UNIX computer 64MB of RAM and a reasonably fast hard disk, it will run quickly and efficiently for any reasonable number of hits. (Of course, you might not want to skimp on RAM when memory prices are low.) Database queries will slow it down, the same as they would if the program weren't CGI. Due to UNIX's multiuser architecture, the number of logged-on sessions (and what they're doing) can significantly affect performance. It's a good idea to let your Web server's primary job be servicing the Web rather than the users. Of course, if you have capacity left over, no reason exists not to run other daemons, but it's best to choose processes that consume resources predictably so that you can plan your site.

A large, popular site—one that receives several hits each minute, for example—requires more RAM, the same as on any platform. The more RAM you give your UNIX system, the better it can cache, and therefore, the faster it can satisfy requests.

CGI Script Structure

When your script is invoked by the server, the server passes information to the script via environment variables and, in the case of the HTTP `POST` method, via `STDIN`. `GET` and `POST` are the two most common request methods you'll encounter, and probably the only ones you'll need. The *request method* tells your script how it was invoked; based on that information, the script can decide how to act. The request method is passed to your script using the environment variable (see "Standard CGI Environment Variables" later in this chapter) called, appropriately enough, `REQUEST_METHOD`.

- `GET` is a request for data, the same method used for obtaining static documents. The `GET` method sends request information as parameters tacked onto the end of the URL. These parameters are passed to your CGI program in the environment variable `QUERY_STRING`.

If your script is called `myprog.exe`, for example, and if you invoke it from a link with the form

```
<a href="cgi-bin/myprog.exe?lname=blow&fname=joe">Click here</a>
```

the `REQUEST_METHOD` will be the string `GET`, and the `QUERY_STRING` will contain `lname=blow&fname=joe`.

The question mark separates the name of the script from the beginning of the `QUERY_STRING`. On some servers the question mark is mandatory, even if no `QUERY_STRING` follows it. On other servers, a forward slash might be allowed instead of or in addition to the question mark. If the slash is used, the server passes the information to the script using the `PATH_INFO` variable instead of the `QUERY_STRING` variable.

- A `POST` operation occurs when the browser sends data from a fill-in form to the server. With `POST`, the `QUERY_STRING` might or might not be blank, depending on your server.

  The data from a `POST`ed query gets passed from the server to the script using `STDIN`. Because `STDIN` is a stream and the script needs to know how much valid data is waiting, the server also supplies another variable, `CONTENT_LENGTH`, to indicate the size in bytes of the incoming data. The format for `POST`ed data is

  ```
  variable1=value1&variable2=value2&etc
  ```

  Your program must examine the `REQUEST_METHOD` environment variable to know whether to read `STDIN`. The `CONTENT_LENGTH` variable is typically useful only when the `REQUEST_METHOD` is `POST`.

URL Encoding

The HTTP 1.0 specification calls for URL data to be encoded in such a way that it can be used on almost any hardware and software platform. Information specified this way is called URL-encoded; almost everything passed to your script by the server will be URL-encoded.

Parameters passed as part of `QUERYSTRING` or `PATHINFO` will take the form `variable1=value1&variable2=value2` and so forth, for each variable defined in your form.

Variables are separated by the ampersand. If you want to send a real ampersand, it must be *escaped*—that is, encoded as a two-digit hexadecimal value representing the character. Escapes are indicated in URL-encoded strings by the percent (`%`) sign. Thus, `%25` represents the percent sign itself. (25 is the hexadecimal representation of the ASCII value for the percent sign.) All characters above 127 (7F hexidecimal) or below 33 (21 hexidecimal) are escaped by the server when it sends information to your CGI program. This includes the space character, which is escaped as `%20`. Also, the plus sign (+) needs to be interpreted as a space character.

Before your script can deal with the data, it must parse and decode it. Fortunately, these are fairly simple tasks in most programming languages. Your script scans through the string looking for an ampersand. When it is found, your script chops off the string up to that point and calls it a variable. The variable's name is everything up to the equal sign in the string; the variable's value is everything after the equal sign. Your script then continues parsing the original string for the next ampersand, and so on, until the original string is exhausted.

After the variables are separated, you can safely decode them, as follows:

1. Replace all plus signs with spaces.
2. Replace all %## (percent sign followed by two hexidecimal digits) with the corresponding ASCII character.

It's important that you scan through the string linearly rather than recursively because the characters you decode might be plus signs or percent signs.

When the server passes data to your form with the `POST` method, check the environment variable called `CONTENT_TYPE`. If `CONTENT_TYPE` is `application/x-www-form-urlencoded`, your data needs to be decoded before use.

The basic structure of a CGI application is straightforward: initialization, processing, output, and termination. Because this section deals with concepts, flow, and programming discipline, it will use pseudocode rather than a specific language for the examples.

Ideally, a script follows these steps in this order (with appropriate subroutines for `do-initialize`, `do-process`, and `do-output`):

1. The program begins.
2. The program calls `do-initialize`.
3. The program calls `do-process`.
4. The program calls `do-output`.
5. The program ends.

Initialization

The first thing your script must do when it starts is determine its input, environment, and state. Basic operating-system environment information can be obtained the usual way: from the system Registry in Windows NT, from standard environment variables in UNIX, from `.ini` files in Windows, and so forth.

State information comes from the input rather than the operating environment or static variables. Remember, each time CGI scripts are invoked, it's as if they've never been invoked before. The scripts don't stay running between calls. Everything must be initialized from scratch, as follows:

1. Determine how the script was invoked. Typically, this involves reading the environment variable `REQUEST_METHOD` and parsing it for the word `GET` or the word `POST`.

NOTE Although GET and POST are the only currently defined operations that apply to CGI, you might encounter other less frequent request methods like HEAD and PUT. Your code should check explicitly for GET and POST and refuse anything else because of the difficulty that can occur when trying to retrieve the submitted data. Don't assume that if the request method isn't GET then it must be POST, or vice versa. ■

2. Retrieve the input data. If the method was GET, you must obtain, parse, and decode the QUERYSTRING environment variable. If the method was POST, you must check QUERYSTRING and also parse STDIN. If the CONTENT_TYPE environment variable is set to application/x-www-form-urlencoded, the stream from STDIN needs to be decoded, too.

Listing 28.8 shows the initialization phase in pseudocode.

Listing 28.8 Initializing Your CGI Script (Shown in Pseudocode)

```
retrieve any operating system environment values desired
allocate temporary storage for variables
if environment variable REQUEST_METHOD equals "GET" then
   retrieve contents of environment variable QUERY_STRING;
   if QUERY_STRING is not null, parse it and decode it;
else if REQUEST_METHOD equals "POST" then
   retrieve contents of environment variable QUERY_STRING;
   if QUERY_STRING is not null, parse it and decode it;
   retrieve value of environment variable CONTENT_LENGTH;
   if CONTENT_LENGTH is greater than zero, read CONTENT_LENGTH
   ➥bytes from STDIN;
   parse STDIN data into separate variables;
   retrieve contents of environment variable CONTENT_TYPE;
   if CONTENT_TYPE equals application/x-www-form-urlencoded
   then decode parsed variables;
else if REQUEST_METHOD is neither "GET" nor "POST then
   report an error;
   deallocate temporary storage;
   terminate
end if
```

Processing

After initializing its environment by reading and parsing its input, the script is ready to get to work. What happens in this section is much less rigidly defined than during initialization. During initialization, the parameters are known (or can be discovered), and the tasks are more or less the same for every script you'll write. The processing phase, however, is the heart of your script, and what you do here depends almost entirely on the script's objectives.

1. Process the input data. What you do here depends on your script. You can ignore all the input and just output the date, for example, spit back the input in neatly formatted XHTML, find information in a database and display it, or do something never thought of before. Processing the data means, generally, transforming it somehow. In classical data-processing terminology, this is called the transform step because in batch-oriented processing, the program reads a record, applies some rule to it (transforming it), and then writes it back out. CGI programs rarely, if ever, qualify as classical data processing, but the idea is the same. This is the stage of your program that differentiates it from all other CGI programs, where you take the inputs and make something new from them.
2. Output the results. In a simple CGI script, the output is usually an HTTP header and some XHTML. More complex scripts might output graphics, graphics mixed with text, or all the information necessary to call the script again with some additional information. A common and rather elegant technique is to call a script once using `GET`, which can be done from a standard `<a>` element. The script "senses" that it was called with `GET` and creates an XHTML form on-the-fly, complete with hidden variables and code necessary to call the script again, this time with `POST`.

Row, Row, Row Your Script

In the UNIX world, a *character stream* is a special kind of file. `STDIN` and `STDOUT` are character streams by default. The operating system helpfully parses streams for you, making sure that everything going through is proper 7-bit ASCII or an approved control code.

Seven-bit? Yes. For XHTML, this doesn't matter. However, if your script sends graphical data, using a character-oriented stream means instant death. The solution is to switch the stream over to binary mode. In Perl, you do this using `binmode`; in C, you do this with the `setmode` function: `setmode(fileno(stdout), O_BINARY)`. You can change horses in midstream with the complementary `setmode(fileno(stdout), O_TEXT)`. A typical graphics script outputs the headers in character mode and then switches to binary mode for the graphical data.

In the Windows NT world, streams behave the same way for compatibility reasons. A nice simple `\n` in your output is converted to `\r\n` for you when you write to `STDOUT`. This doesn't happen with regular Windows NT system calls, such as `WriteFile()`; you must specify `\r\n` explicitly if you want a `CRLF` (carriage return-line feed).

Those who speak mainly UNIX frown at the term *CRLF*, whereas those who program on other platforms might not recognize `\n` or `\r\n`. `\r` is how C programmers specify a carriage return (CR) character. `\n` is how C programmers specify a line feed (LF) character. (That's `Chr(10)` for `LF` and `Chr(13)` for `CR` to those of use who have a `Chr()` function to call up characters by their ASCII values.)

Alternative words for character mode and binary mode are *cooked* and *raw*, respectively, although these terms more generally mean processed and unprocessed as well. Whatever words you use and whatever platform, another problem occurs with streams: by default, they're buffered. *Buffered* means that the operating system hangs on to the data until a line-terminating character is seen, the buffer fills up, or the stream is closed. This means that if you mix buffered `printf()` statements with unbuffered `fwrite()` or `fprintf()` statements, things will probably come out jumbled even though they might all write to `STDOUT`. The `printf()` statement writes buffered to the stream; file-oriented routines output directly. The result is an out-of-order mess.

You can lay the blame for this at the feet of backward compatibility. Beyond the existence of many old programs, streams have no reason to default to buffered and cooked. These should be options that you turn on when you want them, not that you turn off when you don't. Fortunately, you can get around this problem with the statement `setvbuf(stdout, NULL, _IONBF, 0)`, which turns off all buffering for the `STDOUT` stream.

Another solution is to avoid mixing types of output statements; even so, that won't make your cooked output raw, so it's a good idea to turn off buffering anyway. Many servers and browsers are cranky and dislike receiving input in dribs and drabs.

Listing 28.9 shows a pseudocode representation of a simple processing phase whose objective is to have the browser display all the environment variables gathered in the initialization phase.

This has the effect of creating a simple XHTML document containing a bulleted list. Each item in the list is a variable, expressed as `name=value`.

Listing 28.9 A Pseudocode Script to Show Variables Gathered During Initialization

```
output header "content-type: text/html\n"
output required blank line to terminate header "\n"
output "<html>"
output "<head><title>Variable Report</title></head>"
output "<body bgcolor=\"#ffffff\">"
output "<h1>Variable Report</h1>"
output "<ul>"
for each variable known
   output "<li>"
   output variable-name
   output "="
   output variable-value
loop until all variables printed
output "</ul>"
output "</body>"
output "</html>"
```

Troubleshooting Tip

If your document displays without explicit error but is empty, make sure you included a blank line following the header line(s) at the beginning of the `.cgi` script, before the output for the body of your document. Sometimes you might even need to use two blank lines to get your document content to show.

Troubleshooting Tip

If your script shows in the browser instead of its output, your script is not being executed. There are several possible causes for this. One is that your server might not be properly configured for CGI. Another is that your script might be in the wrong directory. Your scripts might need to be in a designated CGI script directory, often called `cgi-bin`. Finally, your script's filename might not have the proper filename extension for your server's configuration. This extension is usually `.cgi`, `.plx`, or `.pl`. In short, check your filename and location and your server's CGI-related configuration values.

Termination

Termination is nothing more than cleaning up after yourself and quitting. If you've locked any files, you must release them before letting the program end. If you've allocated memory, semaphores, or other objects, you must free them. Failure to do so might result in a "one-shot wonder" of a script: one that works only the first time. Worse yet, your script might hinder—or even break—the server itself or other scripts by failing to free up resources and release locks.

On some platforms, most noticeably Windows NT, and to a lesser extent, UNIX, your file handles and memory objects are closed and reclaimed when your process terminates. Even so, it's unwise to rely on the operating system to clean up your mess. For instance, under Windows NT, the behavior of the file system is undefined when a program locks all or part of a file and then terminates without releasing the locks.

Make sure your error-exit routine, if you have one (and you should), knows about your script's resources and cleans up just as thoroughly as the main exit routine does.

Planning Your Script

Now that you've seen a script's basic structure, you're ready to learn how to plan a script from the ground up:

1. Take your time defining the program's task. Think it through thoroughly. Write it down and trace the program logic. When you're satisfied that you understand the input, output, and the transform process you'll have to do, proceed.

2. Order a pizza and a good supply of your favorite beverage, lock yourself in for the night, and come out the next day with a finished program. This sounds cute, but it is oddly good advice. Sometimes, it seems as if more bugs stem from interruptions while programming—which cause loss of concentration—than from any other source. And while you're sequestered, don't forget to document your code as you write it.
3. Test, test, test. Use every browser known to mankind and every sort of input you can think of. Especially test for the situations in which users enter 32KB of data in a 10-byte field (using `maxsize` within your `<input />` element does not protect you from receiving more input than expected), or they enter control codes where you're expecting plain text.
4. Document the program as a whole—not just the individual steps within it—so that others who have to maintain or adapt your code will understand what you were trying to do.

Step 1, of course, is this section's topic, so we'll look at that process in more depth:

- If your script will handle form variables, plan out each one: its name, expected length, and data type.
- As you copy variables from `QUERY_STRING` or `STDIN`, check for proper type and length. A favorite trick of UNIX and Windows NT hackers is to overflow the input buffer purposely. Because of the way some scripting languages (notably sh and bash) allocate memory for variables, this sometimes gives the hacker access to areas of memory that should be protected, enabling them to place executable instructions in your script's heap or stack space.
- Use sensible variable names. A pointer to the `QUERY_STRING` environment variable should be called something such as `pQueryString`, not `p2`. This not only helps debugging at the beginning but also makes maintenance and modification much easier. No matter how brilliant a coder you are, chances are good that a year from now you won't remember that `p1` points to `CONTENT_TYPE` and `p2` points to `QUERY_STRING`.
- Distinguish between *system-level parameters* that affect how your program operates and *user-level parameters* that provide instance-specific information. In a script to send email, for example, don't let the user specify the IP number of the SMTP host. This information shouldn't even appear on the form in a hidden variable. It's instance-independent and should therefore be a system-level parameter. In Windows NT, store this information in the Registry or an `.ini` file. In UNIX, store it in a configuration file or system environment variable.
- If your script will *shell out* to the system to launch another program or script, don't pass user-supplied variables unchecked. Especially in UNIX systems, where the `system()` call can contain pipe or redirection characters, leaving variables unchecked can spell disaster. Clever users and malicious hackers can copy sensitive information or destroy data this way. If you can't avoid `system()` calls altogether, plan for them carefully.

Define exactly what can get passed as a parameter and know which bits will come from the user. Include an algorithm to parse for malicious character strings such as `rm -f` or `delete *.*` and exclude them.

- If your script will access external files, plan how you'll handle concurrency. You might lock part or all of a data file, you might establish a semaphore, or you might use a file as a semaphore. If you take chances, you'll be sorry. Never assume that because your script is the only program to access a given file that you don't need to worry about concurrency. Five copies of your script might be running at the same time, satisfying requests from five users.
- If you lock files, use the least-restrictive lock required. If you're only reading a data file, lock out writes while you're reading and release the file immediately afterward. If you're updating a record, lock just that one record (or byte range). Ideally, your locking logic should immediately surround the actual I/O calls. Don't open a file at the beginning of your program and lock it until you terminate. If you must do this, open the file but leave it unlocked until you're actually about to use it. This will enable other applications or other instances of your script to work smoothly and quickly.
- Prepare graceful exits for unexpected events. If, for example, your program requires exclusive access to a particular resource, be prepared to wait a reasonable amount of time and then back out gracefully. Never code a *wait-forever* call. When your program dies from a fatal error, make sure that it reports the error first. Error reports should use plain, sensible language. When possible, also write the error to a log file so the system administrator knows about it.
- If you're using a GUI language (for example, Visual Basic) for your CGI script, don't let untrapped errors result in a message box onscreen. This is a server application; chances are excellent that no one will be around to notice and clear the error, and your application will hang until the next time an administrator chances by. Trap all errors! Work around those you can live with and treat all others as fatal.
- Write pseudocode for your routines at least to the point of general logical structure before firing up the editor. It often helps to build stub routines so that you can use the actual calls in your program while you're still developing. A *stub routine* is a quick and dirty routine that doesn't actually process anything; it just accepts the inputs the final routine will be expecting and outputs a return code consistent with what the final routine would produce.
- For complex projects, a data flow chart can be invaluable. Data flow should remain distinct from logic flow; your data travels in a path through the program and is "owned" by various pieces along the way, no matter how it's transformed by the subroutines.
- Try to encapsulate private data and processing. Your routines should have a defined input and output: one door in, one door out, and you know who's going through the door. How your routines accomplish their tasks isn't any of the calling routine's business. This is called the *black box* approach. What happens inside the box can't be

seen from the outside and has no effect on it. A properly encapsulated lookup routine that uses flat file tables, for example, can be swapped for one that talks to a relational back-end database without changing any of the rest of your program.

- Document your program as you go along. Self-documenting code is the best approach, with generous use of comments and extra blank lines to break up the code. If you use sensible, descriptive names for your variables and functions, half your work is already done. But good documentation doesn't just tell *what* a piece of code does; it tells *why*. "Assign value of `REQUEST_METHOD` to pRequestMethod," for example, tells what your code does. "Determine if you were invoked by `GET` or `POST`" tells why you wrote that bit of code and, ideally, leads directly to the next bit of code and documentation: "If invoked via `GET`, do this," or "If invoked via `POST`, do this."
- Define your output beforehand as carefully as you plan the input. Your messages to the user should be standardized. For instance, don't report a file-locking problem as `Couldn't obtain lock. Please try again later`, and report a stack overflow error as `ERR4332`. Your success messages should be consistent as well. Don't return `You are the first visitor to this site since 1/1/96` one time and `You are visitor number 2 since 01-01-96` the next.

  If you chart your data flow and group your functions logically, each type of message will be produced by the appropriate routine for that type. If you hack the code with error messages and early-out success messages sandwiched into your program's logic flow, you'll end up with something that looks inconsistent to the end user and looks like a mess to anyone who has to maintain your code.

Standard CGI Environment Variables

The following is a brief overview of the standard environment variables you're likely to encounter. Each server implements the majority of them consistently, but variations, exceptions, and additions exist. In general, you're more likely to find a new, otherwise undocumented variable omitted rather than a documented variable. The only way to be sure, however, is to check your server's documentation.

This section is taken from the NCSA specifications (see Figure 28.1) and is the closest thing to "standard" as you'll find. The following environment variables are set each time the server launches an instance of your script and are private and specific to that instance:

- **`AUTH_TYPE`**—If the server supports basic authentication and if the script is protected, this variable provides the authentication type. The information is protocol and server-specific; for example, `BASIC`.

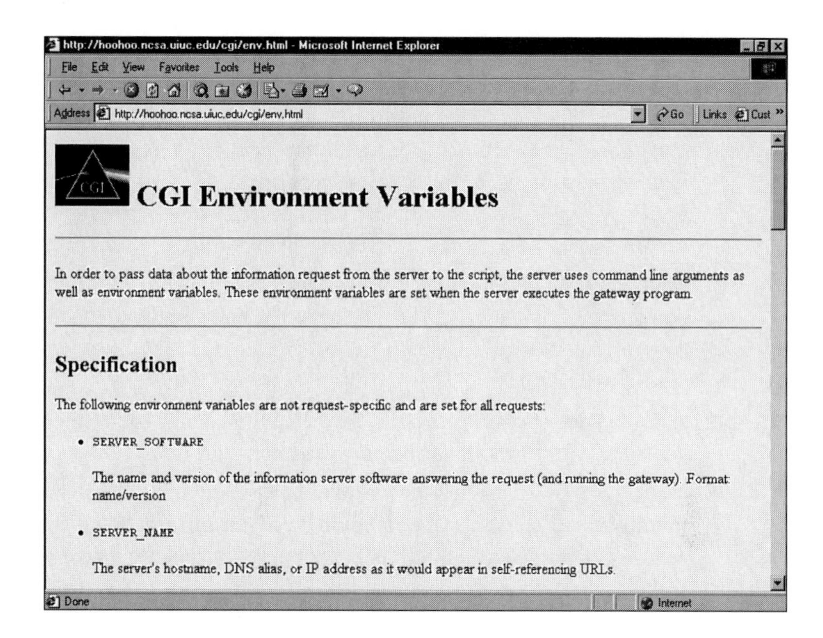

FIGURE 28.1
NCSA maintains a listing of the standard CGI environment variables.

- `CONTENT_LENGTH`—If the request includes data using the `POST` method, this variable is set to the length of valid data supplied in bytes through `STDIN`; for example, `72`.
- `CONTENT_TYPE`—If the request includes data, this variable specifies the type of data as a MIME header; for example, `application/x-www-form-urlencoded`.
- `GATEWAY_INTERFACE`—Provides the version number of the CGI interface supported by the server in the format `CGI/version-number`; for example, `CGI/1.1`.
- `HTTP_ACCEPT`—Provides a comma-delimited list of MIME types that are acceptable to the client browser; for example, `image/gif`, `image/x-xbitmap`, `image/jpeg`, `image/pjpeg`, and `*/*`. This list actually comes from the browser itself; the server just passes it on to the CGI script.
- `HTTP_USER_AGENT`—Supplies the name, possibly including a version number or other proprietary data, of the client's browser, such as `Mozilla/4.7 (WinNT; I)`.
- `PATH_INFO`—Shows any extra path information supplied by the client, tacked onto the end of the virtual path. This is often used as a parameter to the script. For example, with the URL `http://www.yourcompany.com/cgi-bin/myscript.pl/dir1/dir2`, the script is `myscript.pl` and the `PATH_INFO` is `/dir1/dir2`.

- **PATH_TRANSLATED**—Supported by only some servers, this variable contains the translation of the virtual path to the script being executed (that is, the virtual path mapped to a physical path). If, for example, the absolute path to your Web server root is `/usr/local/etc/httpd/htdocs` and your `cgi-bin` folder is in the root level of your Web server (that is, `http://www.mycorp.com/cgi-bin`), a script with the URL `http://www.mycorp.com/cgi-bin/search.cgi` would have the `PATH_TRANSLATED` variable set to `/usr/local/etc/httpd/htdocs/cgi-bin/search.cgi`.
- **QUERY_STRING**—Shows any extra information supplied by the client, tacked onto the end of a URL and separated from the script name with a question mark; for example, `http://www.yourcompany.com/hello.html?name=joe&id=45` yields a `QUERY_STRING` of `name=joe&id=45`.
- **REMOTE_ADDR**—Provides the IP address of the client making the request. This information is always available; for example, `199.1.166.171`.
- **REMOTE_HOST**—Furnishes the resolved host name of the client making the request; for example, `dial-up102.abc.def.com`. Often, this information is unavailable for one of two reasons: Either the caller's IP is not properly mapped to a host name via DNS or the Webmaster at your site has disabled IP lookups. Webmasters often turn off lookups because they mean an extra step for the server to perform after each connect, and this slows down the server.
- **REMOTE_IDENT**—If the server and client support RFC 931, this variable contains the identification information supplied by the remote user's computer. Very few servers and clients still support this protocol, and the information is almost worthless because the user can set the information to be anything he wants. Don't use this variable even if it's supported by your server.
- **REMOTE_USER**—If `AUTH_TYPE` is set, this variable contains the username provided by the user and validated by the server. Note that `AUTH_TYPE` and `REMOTE_USER` are only set after a user has successfully authenticated (usually via a username and password) his identity to the server. Hence, these variables are useful only when restricted areas have been established and then only in those areas.
- **REQUEST_METHOD**—Supplies the method by which the script was invoked. Only `GET` and `POST` are meaningful for scripts using the HTTP/1.0 protocol.
- **SCRIPT_NAME**—This is the name of the script file being invoked. It's useful for self-referencing scripts. For example, scripts use this information to generate the proper URL for a script that gets invoked using `GET`, only to turn around and output a form that, when submitted, reinvokes the same script using `POST`. By using this variable instead of hard-coding your script's name or location, you make maintenance much easier; for example, `/cgi-bin/myscript.exe`.
- **SERVER_NAME**—Your Web server's host name, alias, or IP address. It's reliable for use in generating URLs that refer to your server at runtime; for example, `www.yourcompany.com`.

- **SERVER_PORT**—The port number for this connection; for example, `80`.
- **SERVER_PROTOCOL**—The name/version of the protocol used by this request; for example, `HTTP/1.0`.
- **SERVER_SOFTWARE**—The name/version of the HTTP server that launched your script, for example, `HTTPS/1.1`.

CGI Script Portability

CGI programmers face two portability issues: platform independence and server independence. *Platform independence* is the capability of the code to run without modification on a hardware platform or operating system different from the one for which it was written. *Server independence* is the capability of the code to run without modification on another server using the same operating system.

Platform Independence

The best way to keep your CGI script portable is to use a commonly available language and avoid platform-specific code. It sounds simple, but in practice, this means using either C or Perl and not doing anything much beyond formatting text and outputting graphics.

This leaves Visual Basic, AppleScript, and UNIX shell scripts out. However, platform independence isn't the only criterion to consider when selecting a CGI platform. The speed of coding, the ease of maintenance, and the capability to perform the chosen task should also be considered.

Certain types of operations aren't portable. If you develop for 16-bit Windows, for instance, you'll have great difficulty finding equivalents on other platforms for the VBX and DLL functions you use. If you develop for 32-bit Windows NT, you'll find that all your asynchronous Winsock calls are meaningless in a UNIX environment. If your shell script does a `system()` call to launch `grep` and pipe the output back to your program, you'll find nothing remotely similar in the Windows NT environment unless you add a Windows NT version of `grep` to the system. And AppleScript is good only on Macintoshes.

If one of your mandates is the capability to move code among platforms with a minimum of modification, you'll probably have the best success with C. Write your code using the standard functions from the ANSI C libraries and avoid making other operating system calls. Unfortunately, following this rule will limit your scripts to very basic functionality. If you wrap your platform-dependent code in self-contained routines, however, you minimize the work needed to port from one platform to the next. As you saw in the section "Planning Your Script," when talking about encapsulation, a properly designed program can have any module replaced in its entirety without affecting the rest of the program. Using these guidelines, you might have to replace a subroutine or two, and you'll certainly have to recompile; however, your program will be portable.

Perl scripts are easier to maintain than C programs, mainly because no compile step is used. You can change the program quickly when you figure out what needs to be changed. And there's the rub: Although learning to write simple Perl is easier than learning C for many people, Perl has many obscure subtleties, and the libraries tend to be much less uniform—even between versions on the same platform—than do C libraries. You pay for all that wonderful string-processing and pattern-handling power. Also, Perl for Windows NT is fairly new and still quirky, although the most recent versions are much more stable. And in fairness to Perl, Win32 is not the only compiler or interpreter to be quirky on a relatively new operating system such as Windows NT 4.0 and now Windows 2000.

Server Independence

Far more important than platform independence is server independence. Server independence is fairly easy to achieve, but for some reason, it seems to be a stumbling block to beginning script writers. To be server independent, your script must run without modification on any server using the same operating system. Only server-independent programs can be useful as shareware or freeware, and without a doubt, server independence is a requirement for commercial software.

Most programmers think of obvious issues, such as not assuming that the server has a static IP address. The following are some other rules of server independence that, although obvious once stated, nevertheless get overlooked time and time again:

- **Don't assume your environment**—For example, just because the temp directory was `C:\Temp` on your development system, don't assume that it will be the same wherever your script runs. Never hard-code directories or filenames. This goes double for Perl scripts, where this travesty of proper programming happens most often. If your Perl script to tally hits needs to exclude a range of IP addresses from the total, don't hard code the addresses into the program and say, "Change this line" in the comments. Use a configuration file.
- **Don't assume privileges**—On a UNIX machine, the server (and therefore your script) might run as the user `nobody`, as `root`, or as any privilege level in between. On a Windows NT machine, too, CGI programs usually inherit the server's security attributes. Check for access rights and examine return codes carefully so you can present intelligible error information to the user in case your script fails because it can't access a resource. Some Windows NT servers enable you to specify a user account for CGI programs that is separate from the user account for the Web server. Microsoft's IIS does this and goes one step beyond: For CGI programs with authentication, the CGI runs in the security context of the authenticated user.
- **Don't assume consistency of CGI variables**—Some servers pass regular environment variables (for instance, `PATH` and `LIB` variables) along with CGI environment variables; however, the ones they pass depend on the runtime environment. Server configuration can also affect the number and the format of CGI variables. Be prepared for environment-dependent input and have your program act accordingly.

- **Don't assume version-specific information**—Test for it and include workarounds or sensible error messages telling the user what to upgrade and why. Both server version and operating system version can affect your script's environment.
- **Don't assume LAN or WAN configurations**—In the Windows NT world, the server can be Windows NT Workstation or Windows NT Server; it might be standalone, part of a workgroup, or part of a domain. DNS (Domain Name Services) might not be available; lookups might be limited to a static hosts file. In the UNIX world, don't assume anything about the configurations of daemons, such as `inetd`, `sendmail`, or the system environment, and don't assume directory names. Use a configuration file for the items that you can't discover with system calls, and give the script maintainer instructions for editing it.
- **Don't assume the availability of system objects**—As with privilege level, check for the existence of such objects as databases, messaging queues, and hardware drivers, and output explicit messages when something can't be found or is misconfigured. Nothing is more irritating than downloading a new script, installing it, and getting only `Runtime error #203` for the output.

CGI Libraries

When you talk about CGI libraries, two possibilities exist: First, you can use libraries of code you develop and want to reuse in other projects. Second, you can avail yourself of publicly available libraries of programs, routines, and information.

Personal Libraries

If you follow the advice given earlier in this chapter in the "Planning Your Script" section about writing your code in a black box fashion, you'll soon discover that you're building a library of routines that you'll use over and over. After you determine how to parse out URL-encoded data, for instance, you don't need to do it again. And when you have a basic `main()` function written, it will probably serve for every CGI program you ever write. This is also true for generic routines, such as querying a database, parsing input, and reporting runtime errors.

- How you manage your personal library depends on the programming language you use. With C and assembler, you can precompile code into actual `.Lib` files, with which you can then link your programs. Although possible, this likely is overkill for CGI, and it doesn't work for interpreted languages, such as Perl and Visual Basic. (Although Perl and VB can call compiled libraries, you can't link with them in a static fashion the way you can with C.) The advantage of using compiled libraries is that you don't have to recompile all your programs when you make a change to code in the library. If the library is loaded at runtime (a DLL), you don't need to change anything. If the library is linked statically, all you need do is relink.

- Another solution is to maintain separate source files and include them with each project. You might have a single, fairly large file that contains the most common routines, but put seldom used routines in files of their own. Keeping the files in source format adds a little overhead at compile time but not enough to worry about, especially when compared to the time savings you gain by writing the code only once. The disadvantage of this approach is that when you change your library code, you must recompile all your programs to take advantage of the change.
- Nothing can keep you from incorporating public-domain routines into your personal library, either. As long as you make sure that the copyright and license allow you to use and modify the source code without royalties or other stipulations, then you should strip out the interesting bits and toss them into your library.
- Well-designed and well-documented programs provide the basis for new programs. If you're careful to isolate the program-specific parts into subroutines, you can leverage an entire program's structure for your next project.
- You can also develop platform-specific versions of certain subroutines and, if your compiler will allow it, automatically include the correct ones for each type of build. At the worst, you'll have to manually specify which subroutines you want.

NOTE The key to making your code reusable is to make it as generic as possible. Don't make it so generic that, for example, a currency printing routine needs to handle both yen and dollars, but make it generic enough that any program that needs to print out dollar amounts can call that subroutine. As you upgrade, swat bugs, and add capabilities, keep each function's inputs and outputs the same, even when you change what happens inside the subroutine. This is the black box approach in action. By keeping the calling convention and the parameters the same, you're free to upgrade any piece of code without fear of breaking older programs that call your function. ■

- Another technique to consider is using function stubs. Suppose you decide that a single routine to print both yen and dollars is actually the most efficient way to go, but you already have separate subroutines, and your old programs wouldn't know to pass the additional parameter to the new routine. Rather than going back and modifying each program that calls the old routines, just "stub out" the routines in your library so the only thing they do is call the new, combined routine with the correct parameters. In some languages, you can do this by redefining the routine declarations; in others, you actually need to code a call and pay the price of some additional overhead. But even so, the price is far less than that of breaking all your old programs.

Public Libraries

The Internet is rich with public-domain sample code, libraries, and precompiled programs. Although most of what you'll find is UNIX-oriented (because it has been around longer), no shortage exists of routines for Windows NT.

The following is a list of some of the best sites on the Internet with a brief description of what you'll find at each site. This list is far from exhaustive. Hundreds of sites are dedicated to or contain information about CGI programming. Hop onto your Web browser and visit your favorite search engine, telling it to search for "CGI" or "CGI libraries." The following sites are among the more useful:

- **http://www.worldwidemart.com/scripts/**—The justifiably famous Matt's Script Archive. Look here first for tested, practical scripts in Perl and C for many common business uses.
- **http://www.ics.uci.edu/pub/websoft/libwww-perl/**—This is the University of California's public offering, libwww-perl. Based on Perl version 5.003, this library contains many useful routines. If you plan to program in Perl, this library is worth the download just for ideas and techniques.
- **http://www.w3.org/CGI/**—The W3C standards organization CGI site. W3C is always worth a periodic visit.
- **http://www.itm.com/cgicollection/**—A vast collection of CGI scripts that you can use and learn from. It covers CGI security and contains tutorials and other examples.
- **http://www-genome.wi.mit.edu/WWW/tools/scripting/cgi-utils.html**— `cgi-utils.pl` is an extension to `cgi-lib.pl` from Lincoln D. Stein at the Whitehead Institute, MIT Center for Genome Research.
- **http://www-genome.wi.mit.edu/ftp/pub/software/WWW/cgi_docs.html**—`cgi.pm` is a Perl 5 library for creating forms and parsing CGI input.
- **http://www-genome.wi.mit.edu/WWW/tools/scripting/CGIperl/**—This is a useful list of Perl links and utilities.
- **http://www.boutell.com/gd/**—A C library for producing GIF images on-the-fly, gd enables your program to create images complete with lines, arcs, text and multiple colors, and to cut and paste from other images and flood fills, which get written out to a file. Your program can then suck this image data in and include it in your program's output. Although these libraries are difficult to master, the rewards are well worth it. Many map-related Web sites use these routines to generate map location points on-the-fly.
- **http://www.boutell.com/cgic/**—A CGI library providing an easier method to parse CGI input using C.
- **http://stein.cshl.org/WWW/software/GD/GD.html**—GD.pm is a Perl wrapper and extender for gd.
- **http://www.iserver.com/cgi/library.html**—This is Internet Servers Inc.'s wonderful CGI library. Among the treasures here, you'll find samples of imagemaps, building a Web index, server-push animation, and a guest book.
- **http://www.wdvl.com/Vlib/Providers/**—This collection of links and utilities will help you build an editor, use C++ with predefined classes, join a CGI programmer's mailing list, and best of all, browse a selection of Clickables, Plug and Play CGI Scripts.

- `http://www.greyware.com/greyware/software/`—Greyware Automation Products provides a rich list of shareware and freeware programs for Windows NT. Of special interest are the free SSI utilities and the CGI-wrapper program, CGIShell, which enables you to use Visual Basic, Delphi, or other GUI programming environments with the freeware EMWAC HTTP server.
- `http://www.bhs.com/`—Although not specifically geared to CGI, the Windows NT Resource Center, sponsored by Beverly Hills Software, provides some wonderful applications, some of which are CGI-related. In particular, you'll find EMWAC's software, Perl for Windows NT and Perl libraries, and SMTP mailers.
- `http://website.oreilly.com/`—Bob Denny, author of WebSite, has probably done more than any other individual to popularize HTTP servers on the Windows NT platform. At this site, you'll find a collection of tools, including Perl for Windows NT, VB routines for use with the WebSite server, and other interesting items.
- `ftp://ftp.ncsa.uiuc.edu/Web/httpd/Unixncsa_httpd/cgi`—NSCA's CGI Archive.
- `http://www.cgi-resources.com/`—The CGI Resource Index is another good CGI site.
- `http://www.perl.com/perl/faq/`—The Perl Language Home Page's list of Perl FAQs. Check out the rest of the site while you're there.
- `http://www.w3.org/Security/Faq/www-security-faq.html`—Frequently asked questions about CGI security issues.

The Future of CGI Scripting

The tips, techniques, examples, and advice in this book will enable you to create your own scripts immediately. You should be aware, however, that the server-side programming world is in a constant state of change, more so perhaps than most of the computer world. Fortunately, most servers will stay compatible with existing standards, so you won't have to worry about your scripts not working. Here's a peek at other *CGI-like* options available for programming interactive sites. None of these will ever eliminate the need for CGI, but they do provide other alternatives that might work better for you based on your hardware configuration, your server software, and your programming background.

FastCGI

FastCGI, created by Open Market Inc., extends the capabilities of CGI while removing the overhead associated with executing CGI scripts. Much like CGI, FastCGI is a non-proprietary system in which scripts run continuously in the background, handling requests as needed.

Like CGI, FastCGI is language independent. You can create scripts in the language that you are most comfortable with. Scripts created with FastCGI run separately from the Web server maintaining the security associated with CGI.

NOTE The Apache Web server is one of the most-used Web servers that supports the FastCGI specification. If you're interested in FastCGI and Apache, you should also check out mod_perl, which will greatly increase the speed of CGI scripts. ■

FastCGI also uses distributed computing. Instead of serving documents and executing CGI scripts on one machine, you can use multiple machines sharing the load. To learn more about FastCGI, visit `http://www.fastcgi.com/`. This site contains additional information on the FastCGI specification, along with examples on how to convert your current CGI applications to take advantage of the FastCGI specification.

Java Servlets

Java Servlets were created to eliminate the problems that currently exist when using Java as CGI applications. Normally server-side Java applications require the use and overhead of the Java Virtual Machine. Each time a server-side Java application runs, the virtual machine needs to be loaded as well. Also, server-side Java applications have difficulty accessing environmental variables, which are commonly used in CGI scripting. Java servlets reduce these problems. Sun Microsystems has developed a platform that includes an API that enables Java applications to act as CGI applications. Of course, your applications are not limited to serving requests from the Web; they can access existing sockets, protocols created by the developer, or both.

▶ To find out more information on Java and building Java applications, **see** Chapter 35, "Introduction to Java"

Created applications that use the Java Server API are commonly known as servlets. *Servlets* are server-side applets. The difference between server-side applets and client-side applets, however, is that servlets do not use a user interface like that associated with client-side Java applets.

Servlets extend the traditional functionality of Web servers. Even so, servlets are not confined to the world of the Web. When a connection is made to the servlet, the servlet can create a connection between a client-side applet and a servlet, which communicate using a custom protocol with a new connection.

NOTE Java servlets work with many Web servers, including Sun's Java Web server, the Apache Web server using the `mod_jserv` module, and Microsoft's Web server (IIS) using Allaire's JRun. ■

You can run servlets continuously in the background or dynamically load them in a running server (if the server allows this function). You can also execute them either from a local disk or from the network. As such, a new servlet does not have to be executed for every request, thus greatly reducing the load of the server. The Web server calls the servlet, which in turn, responds to the request. Lastly, servlets don't need to be running in a Web server environment. The servlet API was designed so that servlets can run in conjunction with other types of servers as long as those servers can be accessed via the Net.

To learn more about Java servlets and Java programming, consult any of the following sites:

- **http://jserv.java.sun.com/products/java-server/servlets/environments.html**—Lists various Web servers that allow the use of Java servlets.
- **http://www.javasoft.com/products/java-server/servlets/index.html**—The Java servlet white paper and the Servlet Development Kit can be found at this site.

Server-Side JavaScript

Just as Java has been used to run on the server side, Netscape, using LiveWire, has created an environment to do the same thing with JavaScript. JavaScript as a server-side application can be used to extend the capabilities of the server. By using JavaScript, the Web server can do more without calling external programs. This makes it easier for Web developers to add features to their pages where the browser is used in conjunction with the application running on the server while reducing the load on the Web server. Netscape maintains a substantial amount of documentation on using server-side JavaScript at its DevEdge site. The URL is `http://developer.netscape.com/tech/javascript/index.html?content=/tech/javascript/ssjs/ssjs.html`.

▶ For more information on JavaScript, **see** Chapter 18, "Introduction to JavaScripting"

Active Server Pages

When Microsoft announced it was getting into the Web server business, no one was terribly surprised to learn that they intended to incorporate a variant of Visual Basic or that they wanted everyone else to incorporate Visual Basic, too. VBScript, similar to a subset of Visual Basic, has been useful on the Internet Explorer browser, especially with ActiveX controls. Server-side VBScript is an integral part of Microsoft's Active Server Page (ASP) technology built in to Internet Information Server. ASP scripts enable you to issue commands to the Internet Server Applications Programming Interface (ISAPI) that is part of Microsoft's Internet Information Server (IIS). ISAPI is a collection of programming "hooks" that help you do common server-side tasks such as opening a connection to a data source or writing data to a text file. ASPs relieve you of many of the burdens of traditional CGI programming and allow you to go almost immediately to writing code for the processing you want to happen. You can read more about Active Server Pages in Chapter 32, "Writing Active Server Pages."

Allaire ColdFusion

Allaire's ColdFusion application development platform is another way to use a server's Applications Programming Interface (API) to dynamically generate XHTML pages. You issue commands to the ColdFusion Application Server via tag-based instructions embedded into your XHTML code. These instructions are parsed out and processed by the Application Server. ColdFusion is able to work with many local and remote services such as ODBC and OLE data sources, mail servers, FTP servers, other HTTP servers, and the Web server's file system. You can get an introduction to the ColdFusion development environment by reading Chapter 33, "Using ColdFusion." ●

CHAPTER 

Server-Side Includes

by Eric Ladd

In this chapter

What Are Server-Side Includes?

A Web server normally doesn't look at the contents of the files that it passes along to browsers. It checks security—that is, it makes sure that the caller has the right to see the contents of the files—but otherwise it just hands over the file.

A Web page is often more than one document. The most common addition is an inline graphic or two, plus a background graphic. When a browser first receives a page, it scans the page, determines whether more parts exist, and sends out requests for the remaining parts. This scanning and interpretation process is called *parsing*, and it normally happens on the client's side of the connection.

Under certain circumstances, though, you can instruct the server to parse the document before it ever gets to the client. Instead of blindly handing over the document without knowing the contents, the server can interpret the document first. When this parsing occurs on the server's side of the connection, the process is called a *server-side include (SSI)*.

Why *include*? The first use of server-side parsing was to allow files to be included along with the one being referenced. Programmers love abbreviations, and SSI was established quickly. Changing the term later, when other capabilities also became popular, seemed pointless.

If you are the Webmaster for a site, you might be responsible for 50, 100, or 250 pages. Because you're a conscientious Webmaster, you include your email address at the bottom of each page so that people can tell you about any problems. But what happens when your email address changes? Without SSI, you must edit 50, 100, or 250 pages individually.

With SSI, however, you can include your email address on each page. Your email address actually resides in one spot—say, a file called `webmastermail.txt` somewhere on your server—and each page uses an SSI instruction to include the contents of this file. Then, when your email address changes, all you have to do is update `webmastermail.txt` with the new information. All 250 pages referencing it will have the new information automatically and instantly.

SSI can do more than include files. You can use special commands to include the current date and time. Other commands let you report the size of a file or the date that a file was last modified. Yet another command lets you execute a subprogram (similar to CGI) and incorporate its output right into the flow of the text.

NOTE The hallmark of SSI generally is that the end result is text. If you implement an SSI page hit counter, for example, it would report the hits using text, not inline graphical images. From your browser's point of view, the document is all text, with nothing odd about it. SSI works without the browser's consent, participation, or knowledge. The magic is that the text is generated on the fly by SSI, not hard-coded when you created the XHTML file.

SSI Specification

Unfortunately, no formal set of specifications for SSI applies to all HTTP servers. NCSA SSI documentation is available (see Figure 29.1) at `http://hoohoo.ncsa.uiuc.edu/docs/tutorials/includes.html`, but the syntax and usage given apply only to NCSA-style Web servers, such as the Apache Web server. Even so, most Web servers follow the basic rules outlined by NCSA, and usually there are only minor variances from the basic rules. We'll cover the rules that apply to the NCSA's documentation because they'll probably be compatible with the Web server that you are using.

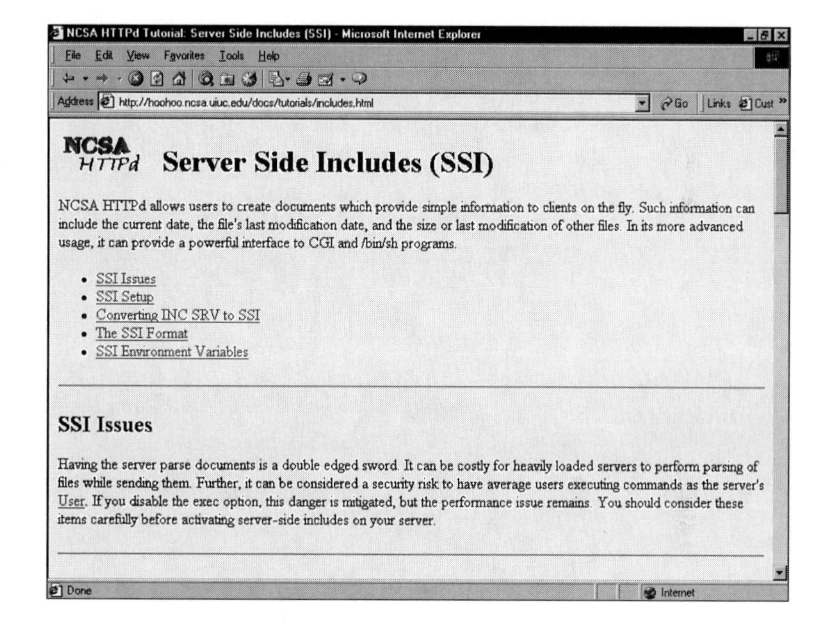

FIGURE 29.1
The venerable NCSA Web site can help you get started with server-side includes.

One of the things that makes SSI a challenge to master is that it is implemented slightly differently on different HTTP servers. The following are some specific points along this line:

- Unlike many protocols, options, and interfaces, SSI isn't governed by an Internet Request for Comment (RFC) or other standard. Each server manufacturer is free to implement SSI on an ad hoc basis, including whichever commands suit the development team's fancy and using whatever syntax strikes it as reasonable.
- No one can give you a list of commands and syntax rules that apply in all situations. Most servers follow NCSA's specification up to a point. Although you might not find the exact commands, you can probably find functions similar to those in NCSA's arsenal.
- Because SSI isn't defined by a standard, server developers tend to modify their implementations of SSI more frequently than they modify other things.

- The only way to determine which SSI functions your server supports and which syntax your server uses for each command is to find and study your server's documentation. This chapter shows you the most common functions on the most common servers, and you'll probably find that the syntax is valid in most cases. However, the only authority is your particular server's documentation, so get a copy and keep it handy as you work through this chapter.

Configuring SSI

Although plenty of SSI frequently asked questions sheets are available on the Internet, most of them are not that detailed. Configuring SSI to work on NCSA or Apache remains a common stumbling block. Other servers are a little easier to use. In addition to the NCSA site previously given, the following is one of the better sites for configuration information; it relates to the popular Apache server (see Figure 29.2): `http://www.apache.org/docs/mod/mod_include.html`.

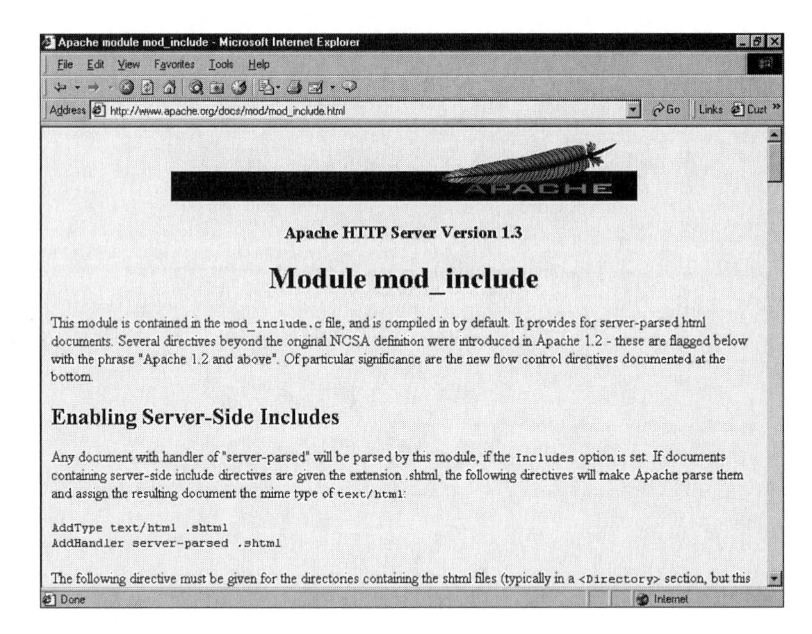

FIGURE 29.2
You'll want to bookmark Apache.org's documentation on server-side includes if you are deploying an Apache server.

On most servers, SSI must be "turned on" before it will work. By default, SSI is not enabled. This is for your protection because mismanaged SSI can be a huge security risk. For example, what if you give any user on the system privileges to run any program or read any file anywhere on the server? Maybe nothing bad would happen, but that's not the safe way to bet. Additionally, server administrators prefer to leave SSI turned off to reduce the processing load on the server. It takes more computing power to serve a page when you ask the server to parse the document requested.

In an NCSA or Apache (UNIX) environment, you enable SSI by editing the configuration files. You must have administrative privileges on the server to edit these files, although you can probably look at them with ordinary user privileges.

You must change the following directives to enable SSI on NCSA or Apache servers:

- **The `Options` directive**—Used to enable SSI for particular directories. Edit `access.conf` and add `Includes` to the `Options` lines for the directories in which you want SSI to work. If a line reads `Options All`, SSI is already enabled for that directory. If it reads anything else, you must add `Includes` to the list of privileges on that line. Note that adding this line enables SSI in whatever directory you select and all subdirectories under it. So, if you add this line to the server root section, you effectively enable SSI in every directory on the server.
- **The `AddType` directive**—Used to designate the MIME type for SSI files. For example, use this line to enable parsing for all files ending with `.shtml`:

  ```
  AddType text/x-server-parsed-html .shtml
  ```

  This information is normally stored in `srm.conf`. Also use this line if you want to allow the `exec` command to work:

  ```
  AddType application/x-httpd-cgi .cgi
  ```

  Specifying `.cgi` here means that all your SSI scripts must have that extension. Most `srm.conf` files already have these two lines, but they are commented out. Just skip down to the bottom of the file and either uncomment the existing lines or add them manually.

Learning to find the configuration files for your server, and to use the `Options` and `AddType` directives, is all you need to do to edit the configuration files.

Enabling SSI on Windows NT machines is usually a matter of naming your XHTML files correctly and clicking a check box somewhere in the Configuration dialog box. Process Software's Purveyor server uses `.htp` as the default filename extension for parsed files. Most other servers emulate NCSA and use `.shtml` instead. However, changing the extension is usually simple. Hunt up the MIME Types dialog box and add a MIME type of `text/x-server-parsed` for whichever filename extension you want. (As always, check your particular server's documentation to find out whether this technique works.) The latest version of Microsoft's Internet Information Server (IIS) also requires you to give the account under which the Web server runs Full Control permission to the directory where your SSI files are stored through a Windows Access Control List.

One last note on configuration: Most servers enable you either to require that all SSI executables be located in your `cgi-bin` or `scripts` directory, or to require this by default. If your server doesn't require this behavior by default, find the documentation to learn how to enable it. If the only programs that can be run are located in a known, controlled directory, the chances for errors (and hacking) are greatly reduced.

Using SSI in XHTML

Now that your server (or talked your system administrator into doing it for you), you're ready to learn how to use SSI. What you've done already is by far the hardest part. From here on, you simply need to find the syntax in your particular server's documentation and try things out.

NOTE Of special interest at this point is the one thing that all SSI implementations have in common: All SSI commands are embedded within regular XHTML comments.

Having embedded commands makes it easy to implement SSI while still making the XHTML portable. A server that doesn't understand SSI passes the commands to the browser, and the browser ignores them because they're formatted as comments. A server that does understand SSI, however, does not pass the commands to the browser. Instead, the server parses the XHTML code from the top down, executing each comment-embedded command and replacing the comment with the output of the command.

This process is not as complicated as it sounds. You will go through some step-by-step examples later in this chapter, but first you'll examine XHTML comments.

XHTML Comment Syntax

Because anything not tagged in XHTML is considered displayable text, comments must be tagged like any other element. Elements are always marked with angle brackets—the less-than sign (<) and greater-than sign (>)—and a keyword, which may be as short as a single letter. For example, the familiar line break element, `<br />`, is *empty*, so no closing tag is necessary. *Nonempty* elements, such as `<a href="...">...</a>`, enclose displayable information, or "content," between the opening and closing tags.

The comment tag is empty and is of this form:

```
<!-- comment text here -->
```

NOTE Although many servers and browsers can understand the nonstandard `<!-- comment text here>` syntax, the remaining ones want the comment to end with `-->`, as required by the XHTML specifications. Why? This lets you comment out sections of XHTML code, including lines containing < and > symbols. Although not all servers and browsers require comments to end with `-->`, all of them will understand the syntax. Therefore, you're better off following the standard and surrounding your comments with `<!--` at the front and `-->` at the end.

In summary, an XHTML comment is anything with the format `<!-- comment text here -->`. Browsers know to ignore this information, and servers don't even see it unless SSI is enabled.

Turning Comments into Commands

What happens to comments when SSI is enabled? The server looks for comments and examines the text inside them for commands. The server distinguishes comments that are really SSI commands from comments that are just comments by following a simple convention: Inside the comment, all SSI commands start with a pound sign (`#`).

Therefore, all SSI commands begin with `<!--#`, followed by an instruction that is meaningful to your server. Typically, each server supports a list of keywords, and it expects to find one of these keywords immediately following the pound sign. After the keyword are any parameters for the command—with syntax that varies both by command and by server—and then the standard comment closing (`-->`).

Syntax of SSI Commands

Most SSI commands have this form:

```
<!--#command parameter="value" -->
```

Here, `command` is a keyword indicating what the server is supposed to do, and `parameter` is the user-defined value for that command.

Note that the first space character is after the `command` keyword. Most servers refuse to perform SSI if you don't follow this syntax exactly. SSI syntax is among the fussiest you'll encounter. For example, Microsoft's Internet Information Server (IIS) recognizes the following command, but only in lowercase text:

```
<!--#include file="fname.inc" -->
```

Different versions of IIS also gave new users problems with syntax peculiarities and restrictions. For example, some versions of IIS reportedly required an extra bang at the end of the comment tag:

```
<!--#include file="fname.inc" --!>
```

And, for some versions, files containing SSI had to end in the `.stm` extension—except for Active Server Page (`.asp`) files. The ASP DLLs introduced with IIS 3.0 and higher offer better SSI support, but only for ASP files.

Another implementation variation to watch for is that various servers have rules about which kinds of files can be included and what the default file extension is. Some servers can include only files with a `.txt` or `.inc` extension, and yet others allow only an `.stm` extension.

The important thing to remember is that SSI syntax is highly idiosyncratic. Each server is different, and each server is fussy. Read the documentation!

Common SSI Commands

You can use SSI commands for a variety of tasks, including inserting (echoing) a value into the document, running a program, inserting the contents of a file into the document, setting the way file sizes appear, inserting the hit count or a file size into the document, and more. The following sections provide step-by-step examples of SSI commands in action.

NOTE Apache has expanded its Web server to use Extended Server-Side Includes (XSSI). XSSI provides additional functionality to SSI, including the use of condition statements. For more information, see `http://www.apache.org/docs/mod/mod_include.html`.

Most other servers support all the commands listed here or a variant command to accomplish the same task.

echo

The following is the syntax for `echo`:

```
The current date is <!--#echo var="DATE_LOCAL" -->
```

This syntax expands to something like the following when executed by an NCSA or Apache server:

```
The current date is 30 Nov 2000 17:05:13 GMT-6
```

The command is `echo`, the parameter is `var` (short for *variable*), and the value is `DATE_LOCAL`, which is a variable defined by the NCSA server that represents the local time on the server. When the server processes this line, it sees that the command requires it to echo (print) something. The `echo` command takes only one parameter, the keyword `var`, which is followed by a value specifying which variable you want to be echoed.

Most servers let you echo at least one subset of the standard CGI variables, if not all of them. You can usually find some special variables that are available only to SSI. `DATE_LOCAL` is one of them.

Again on the NCSA or Apache server, you can change the time format using the SSI `config` command, as follows:

```
<!--#config timefmt="format string" -->
```

Substitute a valid time format string for `"format string"` in the preceding example. The syntax of the format string is compatible with the string that you pass to the UNIX `strftime()` system call. For example, `%a %d %b %y` gives you `Thu 30 Nov 00`.

Here are some other useful variables that you can echo:

```
You are calling from <!--#echo var="REMOTE_ADDR" -->
```

This outputs a line like this:

```
You are calling from 38.247.88.150
```

Recall that `REMOTE_ADDR` is the CGI environment variable that stores the IP address of the user's machine.

▶ To learn more about environment variables, **see** "Standard CGI Environment Variables," **p. 744**

Here's another example:

```
This page is <!--#echo var="DOCUMENT_NAME" -->
```

This yields a line resembling this:

```
This page is /whatever/ssitest.shtml
```

Spend some time learning which variables your server lets you echo and the syntax for each. Related commands, such as the `config timefmt` command, often affect the way that a variable is printed.

include

The `include` command typically takes one of two parameters, `file` or `virtual`, with a single parameter specifying which file to include. Using the `file` attribute, the included file must be something relative to, but not above, the current directory. Thus, `../` is disallowed, as is any absolute path, even if the `httpd` server process would normally have access there. The `virtual` attribute enables you to include any file relative to the document root. For example, `/otherdir/file.html` can be included as long as the Web server can access the file.

A typical use for the `include` command is a closing tag line at the bottom of a page. Let's say that you're working in the directory `/home/susan`, and you create a simple text file called `email.html`:

```
Click <a href="mailto:susan@susan.com">here</a> to send me email.
```

Next, you create `index.shtml`, which is the default page for `/home/susan`, as follows:

```
<html>
<head><title>Susan's Home Page</title></head>
<body>
<h1>Susan's Home Page</h1>
Hi, I'm Susan.  <!--#include file="email.html"-->
See you later!
</body>
</html>
```

When `index.shtml` appears, the contents of `email.html` are inserted, resulting in the following being sent to the browser:

```
<html>
<head><title>Susan's Home Page</title></head>
<body>
<h1>Susan's Home Page</h1>
Hi, I'm Susan.  Click <a href="mailto:susan@susan.com">here</a>
to send me email.  See you later!
</body>
</html>
```

You can use the `email.html` file in as many other files as you want, limiting the places where you need to change Susan's email address to exactly one.

exec

You can turn off the `exec` command on some servers while leaving other SSI functions enabled. If you are the system administrator of your server, study your setup and security arrangements carefully before enabling `exec`.

`exec` is a very powerful and almost infinitely flexible command. An SSI `exec` is very much like regular CGI call in that it spawns a subprocess and lets it open files, provide output, and do just about anything else that an executable can do.

NOTE On Netscape and NCSA servers, your SSI executable must be named `*.cgi` and probably will have to live in a centrally managed `cgi-bin` directory. (The Apache server gives you a bit more flexibility, enabling you to control the extensions of programs used for SSI.) Check your particular server's documentation and your system setup to find out. Again, keep the documentation handy—you'll need it again in just a moment.

The `exec` command typically takes one attribute—most frequently called `cgi`, but also `exe`, `script`, and `cmd` on various servers. Some servers let you specify two different ways to execute programs. For example, `<!--#exec cgi` or `<!--#exec exe` usually means to launch a program and treat it just like a CGI program. `<!--#exec cmd` usually means to launch a shell script (called a *batch file* in the Microsoft world). Shell scripts are often, but not always, treated specially by the server. In addition to launching the shell or command processor and passing the script name as the parameter, the server often forges the standard MIME headers, relieving the script of that duty. You have only one way of knowing how your server handles this process: If you haven't found your server's documentation yet, stop right now and get it. There are no rules of thumb, no standards, and no rational ways to figure out the syntax and behavior.

Here's a trivial example of using a shell script on a UNIX platform to add a line of text. Start with a file called `myfile.shtml`, which contains the following somewhere in the body:

```
Now is the time
<!--#exec cgi="/cgi-bin/whatever.cgi" -->
to come to the aid of their country.
```

Then create the shell script `whatever.cgi` and place it in the `/cgi-bin` directory:

```
#!/bin/sh
echo "for all good persons"
```

When you then access `myfile.shtml`, you see the following:

```
Now is the time for all good persons to come to the aid of their country.
```

Note that this example assumes that you have configured your server to require that SSI scripts live in the `/cgi-bin` subdirectory, and that you have designated `.cgi` as the correct extension for scripts. Additionally, these scripts will run with the same permission as the user the server process runs under.

NOTE Some implementations of SSI enable you to include command-line arguments. Sadly, NCSA isn't one of them (although Apache is). Each server has its own way of handling command-line arguments, of course. Consult your trusty documentation yet again to find out whether—and how—your server allows this feature.

Other Commands

Your server probably supports as many as a dozen commands in addition to the three covered in the preceding sections. Following are some of the most common, with a brief explanation of each:

- **`config errmsg="message text"`**—Controls which message is sent back to the client if the server encounters an error while trying to parse the document.
- **`config timefmt="format string"`**—Sets the format for displaying time and date information from that point in the document on.
- **`sizefmt`**—Format varies widely among servers. This command controls how file sizes appear—as bytes, formatted bytes (1,234,567), kilobytes (1234K), or megabytes (1M).
- **`fsize file="filespec"`**—Reports the size of the specified file.
- **`flastmod file="filespec"`**—Reports the last modification date of the specified file.
- **`counter type="type"`**—Displays the count of hits to the server as of that moment.

Sample SSI Programs

This section presents the complete C code for several useful SSI programs. Some of them are platform-independent; others use some special features in the Windows NT operating system.

SSIDump

The `SSIDump` program is a handy debugging utility that dumps the SSI environment variables and command-line arguments back to the browser (see Listing 29.1).

Listing 29.1 *ssidump.c*—SSI Program for Dumping SSI Environment Variables

```
// SSIDUMP.C
// This program dumps the SSI environment variables
// to the screen.  The code is platform-independent.
// Compile it for your system and place it in your
```

Listing 29.1 Continued

```
// CGI-BIN directory.

#include <windows.h>  // only required for Windows machines
#include <stdio.h>

void main(int argc, char * argv[]) {

     // First declare our variables.  This program
     // only uses one, i, a generic integer counter.

     int i;

     // Print some nice-looking header
     // information.  Note that unlike a CGI
     // program, there is no need to include the
     // standard HTTP headers.

     printf("<H1>SSI Environment Dump</H1>\n");
     printf("<B>Command-Line Arguments:</B>\n");

     // Now print the command-line arguments.
     // By convention, arg[0] is the path to this
     // program at run-time.  args[1] through
     // arg[argc-1] are passed to the program as
     // parameters.  Only some servers will allow
     // command-line arguments.  We'll use a nice
     // bulleted list format to make it readable:

printf("<ul>\n");
     for (i = 0; i < argc; i++) {
          printf("<li>argv[%i]=%s\n",i,argv[i]);
     }
     printf("</ul>\n");

     // Now print out whatever environment variables
     // are visible to us.  We'll use the bulleted
     // list format again:

     printf("<b>Environment Variables:</b>\n<ul>\n");
     i = 0;
     while (_environ[i])
{
          printf("<li>%s\n",_environ[i]);
          i++;
}
     printf("</ul>\n");

     // Flush the output and we're done

     fflush(stdout);
     return;
}
```

RQ

The `RQ` program hunts up a random quotation or other bit of text from a file and outputs it. The quotation file uses a simple format: Each entry must be contiguous but can span any number of lines. Entries are separated by a single blank line. Listing 29.2 is a sample quotation file. The entries were chosen randomly by `RQ` itself.

Listing 29.2 *Rq.txt*—Sample Text File for Use with the *RQ* Program

```
KEEPING THIS A HAPPY FILE:
* All entries should start flush-left.
* Entries may be up to 8K in length.
* Entries must be at least one line.
* Entries may contain 1-9999 lines (8K max).
* Line length is irrelevant; CRs are ignored.
* Entries are separated by ONE blank line.
* The last entry must be followed by a blank line, too.
* The first entry (these lines here) will never get picked,
* so we use it to document the file.
* Length of the file doesn't change retrieval time.
* Any line beginning with "-" it is treated as a byline.
* It must be the last line in the block, otherwise the
* quotation might get cut off.
* You can use XHTML formatting tags.

Drunk is feeling sophisticated when you can't say it.
-Anon

What really flatters a man is that you think him worth
flattery.
-George Bernard Shaw

True patriotism hates injustice in its own land more
than anywhere else.
-Clarence Darrow

If by "fundies" we mean "fanatics," that's okay with
me, but in that case shouldn't we call them fannies?
-Damon Knight

My <I>other</I> car is <I>also</I> a Porsche.
-Bumper Sticker

The death sentence is a necessary and efficacious means for
the Church to attain its ends when rebels against it disturb
the ecclesiastical unity, especially obstinate heretics who
cannot be restrained by any other penalty from continuing to
disturb ecclesiastical order.
-Pope Leo XIII
```

Note that although the preceding sample file has text quotations in it, you can just as easily use RQ for random links or graphics. For random links or graphics, leave off the bylines and use the standard <a> element. You can even use RQ for single words or phrases used to complete a sentence in real time. For example, the phrases in parentheses can come from an RQ file to complete this sentence: "If you don't like this page, you're (a pusillanimous slug) (a cultured person) (pond scum) (probably dead) (quite perceptive) (drunk)."

NOTE RQ has security precautions built in. It does not read from a file that's located anywhere other than the same directory as RQ itself or a subdirectory under it. This precaution prevents malicious users from misusing RQ to read files elsewhere on the server. It looks for two periods in case the user tries to evade the path requirement by ascending the directory tree. It checks for a double backslash in case it finds itself on an NT server and the user tries to slip in a UNC file specification. Finally, it checks for a colon in case the user tries to specify a drive letter. If RQ finds any of these situations, it writes out an error message and dies.

RQ can accept the name of a quotation file from a command-line argument. If you're running RQ on a server that doesn't support command-line arguments, or if you leave the command-line arguments off, RQ tries to open `Rq.txt` in the same directory that it's in. You can have multiple executables, each reading a different file, simply by having copies of RQ with different names. RQ looks for its executable name at runtime, strips the extension, and adds `.txt`. So, if you have a copy of RQ named RQ2, it opens `Rq2.txt`.

Listing 29.3 shows the code for the `rq.c` program.

Listing 29.3 ***rq.c*—A Simple Random Quotation Script Used as an SSI**

```
// RQ.C
// This program reads a text file and extracts a random
// quotation from it.  If a citation line is found, it
// treats it as a citation; otherwise, all text is treated
// the same.  XHTML tags may be embedded in the text.

// RQ is mostly platform-independent.  You'll have to change
// path element separators to the correct slash if you
// compile for UNIX.  There are no platform-specific system
// calls, though, so a little bit of customization should
// enable the code to run on any platform.

#include <windows.h>  // only required for Windows
#include <stdio.h>
#include <stdlib.h>
#include <io.h>

char     buffer[16000];     // temp holding buffer

void main(int argc, char * argv[]) {
     FILE         *f;          // file-info structure
```

Listing 29.3 Continued

```
fpos_t          fpos;          // file-pos structure
long            flen;          // length of the file
char            fname[80];     // the file name
long            lrand;         // a long random number
BOOL            goodpos;       // switch
char            *p;            // generic pointer
char            *soq;          // start-of-quote pointer
char            *eoq;          // end-of-quote pointer

// Seed the random number generator

srand(GetTickCount());

// Set all I/O streams to unbuffered

setvbuf(stdin,NULL,_IONBF,0);
setvbuf(stdout,NULL,_IONBF,0);

// Open the quote file

// If a command-line argument is present, treat it as
// the file name.  But first check it for validity!

if (argc > 1) {
     p = strstr(argv[1],"..");
     if (p==NULL) p = strstr(argv[1],"\\\\");
     if (p==NULL) p = strchr(argv[1],':');

     // If .., \\, or : found, reject the filename
     if (p) {
          printf("Invalid relative path "
                 "specified: %s",argv[1]);
          return;
     }

     // Otherwise append it to our own path
     strcpy(fname,argv[0]);
     p = strrchr(fname,'\\');
     if (p) *p = '\0';
     strcat(fname,"\\");
     strcat(fname,argv[1]);

} else {

     // No command-line parm found, so use our
     // executable name, minus our extension, plus
     // .txt as the filename

     strcpy(fname,_pgmptr);
     p = strrchr(fname,'.');
```

Listing 29.3 Continued

```
          if (p) strcpy(p,".txt");
     }

     // We have a filename, so try to open the file

     f = fopen(fname,"r");

     // If open failed, die right here

     if (f==NULL) {
          printf("Could not open '%s' for read.",fname);
          return;
     }

     // Get total length of file in bytes.
     // We do this by seeking to the end and then
     // reading the offset of our current position.
     // There are other ways of getting this
     // information, but this way works almost
     // everywhere, whereas the other ways are
     // platform-dependent.

     fseek(f,0,SEEK_END);
     fgetpos(f,&fpos);
     flen = (long) fpos;

     // Seek to a random point in the file.  Loop through
     // the following section until we find a block of text
     // we can use.

     goodpos = FALSE;          // goes TRUE when we're done

     while (!goodpos) {

          // Make a random offset into the file.  Generate
          // the number based on the file's length.

          if (flen > 65535) {
               lrand = MAKELONG(rand(),rand());
          } else {
               lrand = MAKELONG(rand(),0);
          }

          // If our random number is less than the length
          // of the file, use it as an offset.  Seek there
          // and read whatever we find.

          if (lrand < flen) {
               fpos = lrand;
               fsetpos(f,&fpos);
               if (fread(buffer, sizeof(char),
```

Listing 29.3 Continued

```
                    sizeof(buffer),f) !=0 ) {
                    soq=NULL;
                    eoq=NULL;
                    soq = strstr(buffer,"\n\n");
                    if (soq) eoq = strstr(soq+2,"\n\n");
                    if (eoq) {
                         // skip the first CR
                         soq++;
                         // and the one for the blank line
                         soq++;
                         // mark end of string
                         *eoq='\0';
                         // look for citation marker
                         p = strstr(soq,"\n-");
                         // if found, exempt it & remember
                         if (p) {
                              *p='\0';
                              p++;
                         }
                         // print the quotation
                         printf(soq);
                         if (p)
                         // and citation if any
                         printf("<br><cite>%s</cite>",p);
                         // exit the loop
                         goodpos=TRUE;
                    }
               }
          }
     }

     fclose(f);
     fflush(stdout);
        return;
}
```

XMAS

The XMAS program (see Listing 29.4) prints out the number of days remaining until Christmas. It recognizes Christmas Day and Christmas Eve as special cases, and it solves the general case problem through brute force. You can certainly find more elegant and efficient ways to calculate elapsed time, but this method doesn't rely on any platform-specific date/time routines.

Listing 29.4 ***xmas.c*—A Simple SSI Script That Counts Down the Days Until Christmas**

```
// CHRISTMAS.C
// This program calculates the number of days between
// the time of invocation and the nearest upcoming 25
// December.  It reports the result as a complete sentence.
// The code is platform-independent.


#include <windows.h>     // only required for Windows
#include <stdio.h>
#include <time.h>

void main() {

     // Some variables, all self-explanatory

     struct tm     today;
     time_t        now;
     int           days;

     // Get the current date, first retrieving the
     // Universal Coordinated Time, then converting it
     // to local time, stored in the today tm structure.

     time(&now);
     today = *localtime(&now);
     mktime(&today);

     // month is zero-based (0=jan, 1=feb, etc);
     // day is one-based
     // year is one-based
     // so Christmas Eve is 11/24

     // Is it Christmas Eve?

     if ((today.tm_mon == 11) && (today.tm_mday==24)) {
          printf("Today is Christmas Eve!");

     } else {

          // Is it Christmas Day?

          if ((today.tm_mon == 11) && (today.tm_mday==25)) {
               printf("Today is Christmas Day!");

          } else {

               // Calculate days by adding one and comparing
               // for 11/25 repeatedly
```

Listing 29.4 Continued

```
                days =0;
                while ( (today.tm_mon  != 11) |
                        (today.tm_mday != 25) )
                {
                     days++;
                     today.tm_mday = today.tm_mday + 1;
                     mktime(&today);
                }

                // Print the result using the customary
                // static verb formation

                printf("There are %i days until Christmas."
                       ,days);
           }
      }

      // Flush the output and we're done

      fflush(stdout);
      return;
}
```

HitCount

The HitCount program creates that all-time favorite, a page's hit count. The output is a cardinal number (1, 2, 3, and so on) and nothing else. HitCount works only on Windows NT. See Listing 29.5 for the C source code.

Listing 29.5 *hitcount.c*—A Counter Script Used as an SSI

```
// HITCOUNT.C
// This SSI program produces a cardinal number page hit
// count based on the environment variable SCRIPT_NAME.

#include <windows.h>
#include <stdio.h>
#define  ERROR_CANT_CREATE "HitCount:  Cannot open/create registry key."
#define  ERROR_CANT_UPDATE "HitCount:  Cannot update registry key."
#define  HITCOUNT "Software\\Greyware\\HitCount\\Pages"

void main(int argc, char * argv[]) {
     char     szHits[33];     // number of hits for this page
     char     szDefPage[80];  // system default pagename
     char     *p;             // generic pointer
     char     *PageName;      // pointer to this page's name
     long     dwLength=33;    // length of temporary buffer
     long     dwType;         // registry value type code
```

Listing 29.5 Continued

```
long     dwRetCode;      // generic return code from API
HKEY     hKey;           // registry key handle

// Determine where to get the page name.  A command-
// line argument overrides the SCRIPT_NAME variable.

if ((argc==2) && ((*argv[1]=='/') | (*argv[1]=='\\')))
     PageName = argv[1];
else
     PageName = getenv("SCRIPT_NAME");

// If invoked from without SCRIPT_NAME or args, die

if (PageName==NULL)
{
     printf("HitCount 1.0.b.960121\n"
            "Copyright (c) 1995,96 Greyware "
            "Automation Products\n\n"
            "Documentation available online from "
            "Greyware's Web server:\n"
            "http://www.greyware.com/"
            "greyware/software/freeware.htp\n\n");
}
else
{

     // Open the registry key

     dwRetCode = RegOpenKeyEx (
          HKEY_LOCAL_MACHINE,
          HITCOUNT,
          0,
          KEY_EXECUTE,
          &hKey);

     // If open failed because key doesn't exist,
     // create it

     if ((dwRetCode==ERROR_BADDB)
          || (dwRetCode==ERROR_BADKEY)
          || (dwRetCode==ERROR_FILE_NOT_FOUND))
          dwRetCode = RegCreateKey(
               HKEY_LOCAL_MACHINE,
               HITCOUNT,
               &hKey);

     // If couldn't open or create, die

     if (dwRetCode != ERROR_SUCCESS) {
          printf (ERROR_CANT_CREATE);
```

Listing 29.5 Continued

```
        } else {

            // Get the default page name

            dwLength = sizeof(szDefPage);
            dwRetCode = RegQueryValueEx (
                hKey,
                "(default)",
                0,
                &dwType,
                szDefPage,
                &dwLength);

            if ((dwRetCode == ERROR_SUCCESS)
                && (dwType == REG_SZ)
                && (dwLength > 0)) {
                szDefPage[dwLength] = Ô\0';
            } else {
                strcpy(szDefPage,"default.htm");
            }

            // If current page uses default page name,
            // strip the page name

            _strlwr(PageName);
            p = strrchr(PageName,'/');
            if (p==NULL) p = strrchr(PageName,'\\');
            if (p) {
                p++;
                if (stricmp(p,szDefPage)==0) *p = '\0';
            }

            // Get this page's information

            dwLength = sizeof(szHits);
            dwRetCode = RegQueryValueEx (
                hKey,
                PageName,
                0,
                &dwType,
                szHits,
                &dwLength);

            if ((dwRetCode == ERROR_SUCCESS)
                && (dwType == REG_SZ)
                && (dwLength >0)) {
                szHits[dwLength] = '\0';
            } else {
                strcpy (szHits, "1");
            }
```

Listing 29.5 Continued

```
                // Close the registry key

                dwRetCode = RegCloseKey(hKey);

                // Print this page's count

                printf("%s",szHits);

                // Bump the count by one for next call

               _ltoa ((atol(szHits)+1), szHits, 10);

                // Write the new value back to the registry

                dwRetCode = RegOpenKeyEx (
                     HKEY_LOCAL_MACHINE,
                     HITCOUNT,
                     0,
                     KEY_SET_VALUE,
                     &hKey);

                if (dwRetCode==ERROR_SUCCESS) {
                     dwRetCode = RegSetValueEx(
                          hKey,
                          PageName,
                          0,
                          REG_SZ,
                          szHits,
                          strlen(szHits));
                     dwRetCode = RegCloseKey(hKey);
                } else {
                     printf(ERROR_CANT_UPDATE);
                }
           }
      }
      fflush(stdout);
      return;
}
```

HitCount takes advantage of one of NT's unsung glories, the system registry. Counters for other platforms need to worry about creating and updating a database file, file locking, concurrency, and a number of other messy issues. HitCount uses the hierarchical registry as a database, letting the operating system take care of concurrent access.

CAUTION

Although it's true that you can access the registry programmatically, you should also give the registry the respect it deserves and make sure that any program that can alter the registry has the proper security implemented to prevent a hacker from making deleterious registry changes.

HitCount is actually remarkably simple compared to other counters. It uses the SCRIPT_NAME environment variable to determine the name of the current page. Therefore, you have no worries about passing unique strings as parameters. HitCount takes the page name and either creates or updates a registry entry for it. The information is always available and can be rapidly accessed.

HitCount, like the other samples in this chapter, is freeware from Greyware Automation Products (http://www.greyware.com/, see Figure 29.3). You can find more extensive documentation online at its site. The code is unmodified from the code distributed by Greyware for a good reason: Registry keys are named, so having multiple versions of the software running around loose with different key names just wouldn't do. Therefore, the code retains the key names for compatibility.

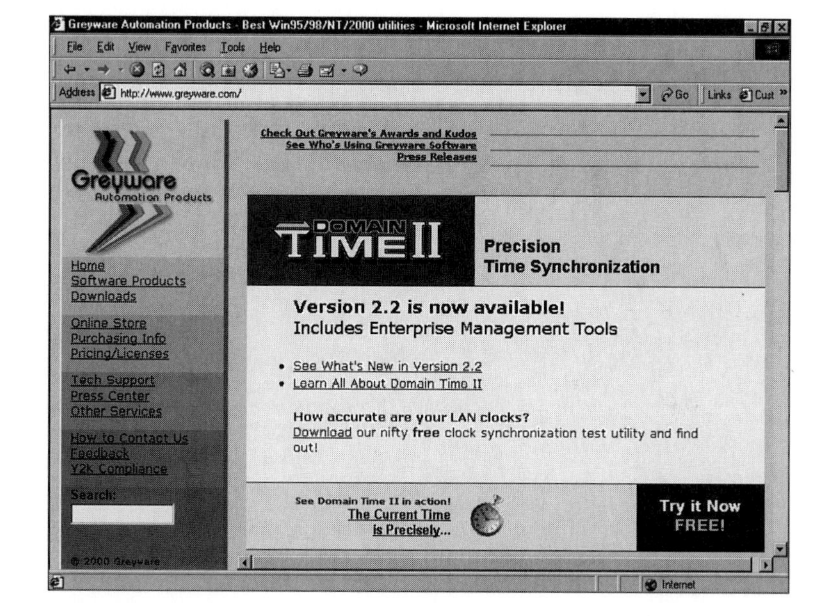

FIGURE 29.3
Greyware Automation Products makes many useful SSI programs available to the Web community.

The only bit of configuration that you might need to do is if your server's default page name isn't default.htm. In that case, add this key to the registry before using HitCount for the first time:

```
HKEY_LOCAL_MACHINE
    \Software
        \Greyware
            \HitCount
                \Pages
```

After you create the key, add a value under Pages. The name of the value is (default), and its type is REG_SZ. Fill in the name of your system's default page; case doesn't matter.

HitCount uses this information to keep from falsely distinguishing between a hit to `http://www.yourserver.com/` and one to `http://www.yourserver.com/default.name`. Some Web servers would report these two as different URLs in the `SCRIPT_NAME` environment variable, even though they refer to the same physical page. By setting the default in the registry, you tell HitCount to strip off the page name, if found, thus reconciling any potential problems before they arise. The default is `default.htm`, so you need to set this value only if your SSI pages use a different name.

HitCntth

HitCntth is a variation of HitCount. Its output is an ordinal number (1st, 2nd, 3rd, and so on). You probably understand the name by now: HitCntth provides the HitCount-th number.

HitCntth is designed to work alongside HitCount. It uses the same registry keys, so you can switch from one format to the other without having to reset the counter or worry about duplicate counts. See the HitCount documentation for configuration details.

Creating an ordinal takes a bit more work than printing a cardinal number because the English method of counting is somewhat arbitrary. HitCntth looks for exceptions and handles them separately, and then throws a *th* on the end of anything left over. Otherwise, the function is identical to HitCount. Listing 29.6 shows the source code for HitCntth.

Listing 29.6 *hitcntth.c*—A Counter Script That Provides the Count Using Ordinal Numbers

```
// HITCNTTH.C
// This SSI program produces an ordinal number page hit
// count based on the environment variable SCRIPT_NAME.

#include <windows.h>
#include <stdio.h>
#define   ERROR_CANT_CREATE "HitCntth:  Cannot open/create registry key."
#define  ERROR_CANT_UPDATE "HitCntth:  Cannot update registry key."
#define  HITCOUNT "Software\\Greyware\\HitCount\\Pages"

void main(int argc, char * argv[]) {
     char     szHits[36];       // number of hits for this page
     char     szDefPage[80];    // system default pagename
     char     *p;               // generic pointer
     char     *PageName;        // pointer to this page's name
     long     dwLength=36;      // length of temporary buffer
     long     dwType;           // registry value type code
     long     dwRetCode;        // generic return code from API
     HKEY     hKey;             // registry key handle


     // Determine where to get the page name.  A command-
     // line argument overrides the SCRIPT_NAME variable.
```

Listing 29.6 Continued

```
    if ((argc==2) && ((*argv[1]=='/') | (*argv[1]=='\\')))
         PageName = argv[1];
    else
         PageName = getenv("SCRIPT_NAME");

    // If invoked from without SCRIPT_NAME or args, die
    if (PageName==NULL)
    {
         printf("HitCntth 1.0.b.960121\n"
                "Copyright (c) 1995,96 Greyware "
                "Automation Products\n\n"
                "Documentation available online from "
                "Greyware's Web server:\n"
                "http://www.greyware.com/"
                "greyware/software/freeware.htp\n\n");
    }
    else
    {

         // Open the registry key

         dwRetCode = RegOpenKeyEx (
              HKEY_LOCAL_MACHINE,
              HITCOUNT,
              0,
              KEY_EXECUTE,
              &hKey);

         // If open failed because key doesn't exist,
         // create it

         if ((dwRetCode==ERROR_BADDB)
              || (dwRetCode==ERROR_BADKEY)
              || (dwRetCode==ERROR_FILE_NOT_FOUND))
              dwRetCode = RegCreateKey(
                   HKEY_LOCAL_MACHINE,
                   HITCOUNT,
                   &hKey);

         // If couldn't open or create, die

         if (dwRetCode != ERROR_SUCCESS) {
              printf (ERROR_CANT_CREATE);
         } else {
              // Get the default page name
              dwLength = sizeof(szDefPage);
              dwRetCode = RegQueryValueEx (
                   hKey,
                   "(default)",
                   0,
```

Listing 29.6 Continued

```
          &dwType,
          szDefPage,
          &dwLength);
     if ((dwRetCode == ERROR_SUCCESS)
          && (dwType == REG_SZ)
          && (dwLength > 0)) {
          szDefPage[dwLength] = '\0';
     } else {
          strcpy(szDefPage,"default.htm");
     }

     // If current page uses default page name,
     // strip the page name

    _strlwr(PageName);
     p = strrchr(PageName,'/');
     if (p==NULL) p = strrchr(PageName,'\\');
     if (p) {
          p++;
          if (stricmp(p,szDefPage)==0) *p = '\0';
     }

     // Get this page's information

     dwLength = sizeof(szHits);
     dwRetCode = RegQueryValueEx (
          hKey,
          PageName,
          0,
          &dwType,
          szHits,
          &dwLength);
     if ((dwRetCode == ERROR_SUCCESS)
          && (dwType == REG_SZ)
          && (dwLength >0)) {
          szHits[dwLength] = '\0';
     } else {
          strcpy (szHits, "1\0");
     }

     // Close the registry key

     dwRetCode = RegCloseKey(hKey);

     // Check for special cases:
     // look at count mod 100 first

     switch ((atol(szHits)) % 100) {
          case 11:     // 11th, 111th, 211th, etc.
               printf("%sth",szHits);
               break;
```

Listing 29.6 Continued

```
                case 12:     // 12th, 112th, 212th, etc.
                     printf("%sth",szHits);
                     break;
                case 13:     // 13th, 113th, 213th, etc.
                     printf("%sth",szHits);
                     break;
                default:
                     // no choice but to look at last
                     // digit
                     switch (szHits[strlen(szHits)-1]) {
                          case '1':     // 1st, 21st, 31st
                               printf("%sst",szHits);
                               break;
                          case '2':     // 2nd, 22nd, 32nd
                               printf("%snd",szHits);
                               break;
                          case '3':     // 3rd, 23rd, 36rd
                               printf("%srd",szHits);
                               break;
                          default:
                               printf("%sth",szHits);
                               break;
                     }
           }
           // Bump the count by one for next call
          _ltoa ((atol(szHits)+1), szHits, 10);

           // Write the new value back to the registry
           dwRetCode = RegOpenKeyEx (
                HKEY_LOCAL_MACHINE,
                HITCOUNT,
                0,
                KEY_SET_VALUE,
                &hKey);
           if (dwRetCode==ERROR_SUCCESS) {
                dwRetCode = RegSetValueEx(
                     hKey,
                     PageName,
                     0,
                     REG_SZ,
                     szHits,
                     strlen(szHits));
                dwRetCode = RegCloseKey(hKey);
           } else {
                printf(ERROR_CANT_UPDATE);
           }
      }
   }
   fflush(stdout);
   return;
}
```

FirstHit

FirstHit is a companion program for HitCount or HitCntth. It tracks the date and time of the first hit to any page. FirstHit uses the same registry scheme as HitCount or HitCntth, but it stores its information in a different key. You must set the `(default)` page name here, too, if it's something other than `default.htm`. The proper key is as follows:

```
HKEY_LOCAL_MACHINE
    \Software
        \Greyware
            \FirstHit
                \Pages
```

You might notice a pattern in several areas. First, all these programs use the registry to store information. Second, they use a similar naming scheme, a hierarchical one. Third, they share great quantities of code. Some of these functions can be moved into a library—and probably should be.

You use FirstHit typically right after using HitCount. To produce the line `You are visitor 123 since Fri 19 Sep 1997 at 01:13` on your server, your source would look like this:

```
You are visitor <!--#exec exe="cgi-bin\hitcount" --> since
<!--#exec exe="cgi-bin\firsthit" -->.
```

Listing 29.7 shows the source code. It's no more complicated than HitCount or HitCntth, and it writes to the registry only the first time that any page is hit. Thereafter, it just retrieves the information that it wrote before.

Listing 29.7 ***firsthit.c*—Provides Information on When the File Was First Hit**

```
// FIRSTHIT.C
// This SSI program keeps track of the date and time
// a page was first hit.  Useful in conjunction with
// HitCount or HitCntth.

#include <windows.h>
#include <stdio.h>
#define  ERROR_CANT_CREATE "FirstHit:  Cannot open/create registry key."
#define  ERROR_CANT_UPDATE "FirstHit:  Cannot update registry key."
#define  FIRSTHIT "Software\\Greyware\\FirstHit\\Pages"
#define  sdatefmt "ddd dd MMM yyyy"

void main(int argc, char * argv[]) {
     char     szDate[128];      // number of hits for this page
     char     szDefPage[80];    // system default pagename
     char     *p;               // generic pointer
     char     *PageName;        // pointer to this page's name
     long     dwLength=127;     // length of temporary buffer
     long     dwType;           // registry value type code
     long     dwRetCode;        // generic return code from API
     HKEY     hKey;             // registry key handle
```

Listing 29.7 Continued

```
SYSTEMTIME st;              // system time
char     szTmp[128];        // temporary string storage

// Determine where to get the page name.  A command-
// line argument overrides the SCRIPT_NAME variable.

if ((argc==2) && ((*argv[1]=='/') | (*argv[1]=='\\')))
     PageName = argv[1];
else
     PageName = getenv("SCRIPT_NAME");

// If invoked from without SCRIPT_NAME or args, die
if (PageName==NULL)
{
     printf("FirstHit 1.0.b.960121\n"
            "Copyright (c) 1995,96 Greyware "
            "Automation Products\n\n"
            "Documentation available online from "
            "Greyware's Web server:\n"
            "http://www.greyware.com/"
            "greyware/software/freeware.htp\n\n");
}
else
{
     // Open the registry key
     dwRetCode = RegOpenKeyEx (
          HKEY_LOCAL_MACHINE,
          FIRSTHIT,
          0,
          KEY_EXECUTE,
          &hKey);

        // If open failed because key doesn't exist,
     // create it
     if ((dwRetCode==ERROR_BADDB)
          || (dwRetCode==ERROR_BADKEY)
          || (dwRetCode==ERROR_FILE_NOT_FOUND))
          dwRetCode = RegCreateKey(
               HKEY_LOCAL_MACHINE,
               FIRSTHIT,
               &hKey);

     // If couldn't open or create, die
     if (dwRetCode != ERROR_SUCCESS)
     {
          strcpy(szDate,ERROR_CANT_CREATE);
     }
     else
     {
          // Get the default page name
```

Listing 29.7 Continued

```
dwLength = sizeof(szDefPage);
dwRetCode = RegQueryValueEx (
     hKey,
     "(default)",
     0,
     &dwType,
     szDefPage,
     &dwLength);
if ((dwRetCode == ERROR_SUCCESS)
     && (dwType == REG_SZ)
     && (dwLength > 0)) {
     szDefPage[dwLength] = '\0';
} else {
     strcpy(szDefPage,"default.htm");
}

// If current page uses default page name,
// strip the page name
_strlwr(PageName);
p = strrchr(PageName,'/');
if (p==NULL) p = strrchr(PageName,'\\');
if (p) {
     p++;
     if (stricmp(p,szDefPage)==0) *p = '\0';
}

// Get this page's information
dwLength = sizeof(szDate);
dwRetCode = RegQueryValueEx (
     hKey,
     PageName,
     0,
     &dwType,
     szDate,
     &dwLength);
if ((dwRetCode == ERROR_SUCCESS)
     && (dwType == REG_SZ)
     && (dwLength >0)) {
     szDate[dwLength] = '\0';
} else {
     GetLocalTime(&st);
     GetDateFormat(
          0,
          0,
          &st,
          sdatefmt,
          szTmp,
          sizeof(szTmp));
     sprintf(
          szDate,
          "%s at %02d:%02d",
```

Listing 29.7 Continued

```
                    szTmp,
                    st.wHour,
                    st.wMinute);
                 // Write the new value back to the
                // registry
                dwRetCode = RegOpenKeyEx (
                    HKEY_LOCAL_MACHINE,
                    FIRSTHIT,
                    0,
                    KEY_SET_VALUE,
                    &hKey);
                if (dwRetCode==ERROR_SUCCESS)
                {
                    dwRetCode = RegSetValueEx(
                        hKey,
                        PageName,
                        0,
                        REG_SZ,
                        szDate,
                        strlen(szDate));
                    dwRetCode = RegCloseKey(hKey);
                }
                else
                {
                    strcpy(szDate,ERROR_CANT_UPDATE);
                }
            }

            // Close the registry key
            dwRetCode = RegCloseKey(hKey);
        }
        printf("%s",szDate);
    }

    fflush(stdout);
    return;
}
```

LastHit

LastHit is yet another Windows NT SSI program. It tracks visitor information (date, time, IP number, and browser type). Like FirstHit, LastHit uses the same registry scheme as HitCount or HitCntth, but it stores its information in its own key. You must set the `(default)` page name here, too, if it's something other than `default.htm`. The proper key is as follows:

```
HKEY_LOCAL_MACHINE
    \Software
        \Greyware
            \LastHit
                \Pages
```

LastHit isn't actually related to HitCount or FirstHit, other than by its common code and its nature as an SSI program. LastHit tracks and displays information about the last visitor to a page. Each time the page is hit, LastHit displays the information from the previous hit and then writes down information about the current caller for display next time.

The source code for LastHit is a little more complicated than FirstHit's, as Listing 29.8 shows. It uses a subroutine. If nothing else, these programs should demonstrate how easily SSI lets you create dynamic documents.

Listing 29.8 ***lasthit.c*****—Provides Information on the Last Person Who Accessed the Page**

```
// LASTHIT.C
// This SSI program tracks visitors to a page, remembering
// the most recent for display.

#include <windows.h>
#include <stdio.h>
#define  ERROR_CANT_CREATE "LastHit:  Cannot open/create registry key."
#define  ERROR_CANT_UPDATE "LastHit:  Cannot update registry key."
#define  LASTHIT "Software\\Greyware\\LastHit\\Pages"

// This subroutine builds the info string about the
// current caller.  Hence the name.  It uses a pointer
// to a buffer owned by the calling routine for output,
// and gets its information from the standard SSI
// environment variables. Because "standard" is almost
// meaningless when it comes to SSI, the program
// gracefully skips anything it can't find.

void BuildInfo(char * szOut) {
     SYSTEMTIME   st;
     char         szTmp[512];
     char         *p;

     szOut[0]='\0';

     GetLocalTime(&st);
     GetDateFormat(0, DATE_LONGDATE, &st, NULL, szTmp, 511);
     sprintf(szOut,
          "Last access on %s at %02d:%02d:%02d",
          szTmp,
          st.wHour,
          st.wMinute,
          st.wSecond);

     p = getenv("REMOTE_ADDR");
     if (p!=NULL) {
          szTmp[0] = '\0';
          sprintf(szTmp,"<br>Caller from %s",p);
```

Listing 29.8 Continued

```
          if (szTmp[0] != '\0') strcat(szOut,szTmp);
     }
     p = getenv("REMOTE_HOST");
     if (p!=NULL) {
          szTmp[0] = '\0';
          sprintf(szTmp," (%s)",p);
          if (szTmp[0] != '\0') strcat(szOut,szTmp);
     }
     p = getenv("HTTP_USER_AGENT");
     if (p!=NULL) {
          szTmp[0] = '\0';
          sprintf(szTmp,"<br>Using %s",p);
          if (szTmp[0] != '\0') strcat(szOut,szTmp);
     }
}

void main(int argc, char * argv[]) {
     char      szOldInfo[512];
     char      szNewInfo[512];
     char      szDefPage[80];
     char      *p;
     char      *PageName;      // pointer to this page's name
     long      dwLength=511;   // length of temporary buffer
     long      dwType;         // registry value type code
     long      dwRetCode;      // generic return code from API
     HKEY      hKey;           // registry key handle

     // Determine where to get the page name.  A command-
     // line argument overrides the SCRIPT_NAME variable.

     if ((argc==2) && ((*argv[1]=='/') | (*argv[1]=='\\')))
          PageName = argv[1];
     else
          PageName = getenv("SCRIPT_NAME");

     // If invoked from without SCRIPT_NAME or args, die
     if (PageName==NULL)
     {
          printf("LastHit 1.0.b.960121\n"
                 "Copyright (c) 1995,96 Greyware "
                 "Automation Products\n\n"
                 "Documentation available online from "
                 "Greyware's Web server:\n"
                 "http://www.greyware.com/"
                 "greyware/software/freeware.htp\n\n");
     }
     else
     {

          // Build info for next call

          BuildInfo(szNewInfo);
```

Listing 29.8 Continued

```
// Open the registry key

dwRetCode = RegOpenKeyEx (
     HKEY_LOCAL_MACHINE,
     LASTHIT,
     0,
     KEY_EXECUTE,
     &hKey);

// If open failed because key doesn't exist,
//create it

if ((dwRetCode==ERROR_BADDB)
     || (dwRetCode==ERROR_BADKEY)
     || (dwRetCode==ERROR_FILE_NOT_FOUND))
     dwRetCode = RegCreateKey(
          HKEY_LOCAL_MACHINE,
          LASTHIT,
          &hKey);

// If couldn't open or create, die

if (dwRetCode != ERROR_SUCCESS) {
     printf (ERROR_CANT_CREATE);
} else {

     // Get the default page name
     dwLength = sizeof(szDefPage);
     dwRetCode = RegQueryValueEx (
          hKey,
          "(default)",
          0,
          &dwType,
          szDefPage,
          &dwLength);
     if ((dwRetCode == ERROR_SUCCESS)
          && (dwType == REG_SZ)
          && (dwLength > 0)) {
          szDefPage[dwLength] = '\0';
     } else {
          strcpy(szDefPage,"default.htm");
     }

     // If current page uses default page name,
     // strip the page name
     _strlwr(PageName);
     p = strrchr(PageName,'/');
     if (p==NULL) p = strrchr(PageName,'\\');
     if (p) {
          p++;
          if (stricmp(p,szDefPage)==0) *p = '\0';
     }
```

Listing 29.8 Continued

```
            // Get this page's information
            dwLength = sizeof(szOldInfo);
            dwRetCode = RegQueryValueEx (
                hKey,
                PageName,
                0,
                &dwType,
                szOldInfo,
                &dwLength);
            if ((dwRetCode == ERROR_SUCCESS)
                && (dwType == REG_SZ)
                && (dwLength >0)) {
                szOldInfo[dwLength] = '\0';
            } else {
                strcpy (szOldInfo, szNewInfo);
            }

            // Close the registry key
            dwRetCode = RegCloseKey(hKey);

            // Print this page's info
            printf("%s",szOldInfo);


            // Write the new value back to the registry
            dwRetCode = RegOpenKeyEx (
                HKEY_LOCAL_MACHINE,
                LASTHIT,
                0,
                KEY_SET_VALUE,
                &hKey);
            if (dwRetCode==ERROR_SUCCESS) {
                dwRetCode = RegSetValueEx(
                    hKey,
                    PageName,
                    0,
                    REG_SZ,
                    szNewInfo,
                    strlen(szNewInfo));
                dwRetCode = RegCloseKey(hKey);
            } else {
                printf(ERROR_CANT_UPDATE);
            }
        }
    }
    fflush(stdout);
    return;
}
```

Server Performance Considerations

Real-time programs can affect server performance. SSI doesn't bring anything new to the table in that regard.

In general, SSI programs tend to be less of a drain on the server than full-fledged CGI. SSI programs are usually small—they only have to produce text, after all—and seldom do much of any significance with files. Page hit counters that rely on generating inline graphics put far more stress on a server than an SSI counter does.

Still, a dozen—or a hundred—instances of your SSI program running at once can steal memory and processor slices needed by the server to satisfy client requests. Imagine that you are the Webmaster of a large site. On each of the 250 pages for which you're responsible, you include not one, but all the SSI examples in this chapter. Each page hit would produce seven separate processes, each of which must jostle with the others in resource contention. In a worst-case scenario, with 100 pages being hit per minute, you would have 700 scripts running each minute, 10 or more simultaneously, at all times. This kind of load would seriously affect your server's capability to do anything else.

You won't find much difference among platforms either. Some SSI utilities run more efficiently in UNIX, others work better under Windows NT, and, in the end, everything balances out. Programs that use the NT registry have a distinct advantage over programs that hit the file system to save data. The registry functions as a back-end database—always open and always ready for queries and updates. The code for handling concurrency is already loaded and running as part of the operating system, so your program can be smaller and tighter. However, pipes and forks tend to run more efficiently under some flavors of UNIX, so if your program does that sort of thing, you are better off in that environment.

Don't pick your server operating system based on which SSI programs you plan to run. If you run into performance problems, adding RAM usually gives your server the extra resources that it needs to handle the load imposed by SSI.

TIP For more information on server-side includes, direct your browser to `http://dir.yahoo.com/Computers_and_Internet/Software/Internet/World_Wide_Web/Servers/Server_Side_Scripting/Server_Side_Includes__SSI_/`.

CHAPTER 30

Server-Side Security Issues

by Eric Ladd

In this chapter

Scripts Versus Programs

Shell scripts, Perl programs, and C executables are the most common forms that a CGI script takes, and each has advantages and disadvantages when security is taken into account. No single language is the best; depending on other considerations such as speed and reuse, each has a place. Nonetheless, there are some common elements to most server-side programs, including the following:

- Although shell CGI programs are often the easiest to write, it can be difficult to fully control them because they usually do most of their work by executing other, external programs. This can lead to several possible pitfalls because your CGI script instantly inherits any of the security problems that those called programs have. The common UNIX utility `awk` has some fairly restrictive limits on the amount of data it can handle, for example, and your CGI program will be burdened with all those limits as well.
- Perl is a step up from shell scripts. It has many advantages for CGI programming and is fairly secure. But Perl can offer CGI authors just enough flexibility to lull them into a false peace of mind. Perl is interpreted, for example, and this makes it easier for bad user data to be included as part of the code.
- A third language option is C. Although C is popular for many uses, it's because of this popularity that many of its security problems are well known and can be exploited fairly easily. For example, C is bad at string handling; it does no automatic allocation or clean up, leaving coders to handle everything on their own. Many C programmers, when dealing with strings, set up a predefined space and hope that it is big enough to handle whatever the user enters. Robert T. Morris, the author of the infamous Internet Worm, exploited such a weakness in attacking the C-based `sendmail` program, overflowing a buffer to alter the stack and gain unauthorized access. The same can happen to your CGI program.

NOTE The National Institute of Standards and Technology maintains a very good site that documents security holes and how to work around them. You can visit the Computer Security Resource Center at `http://csrc.ncsl.nist.gov/`. ■

CGI Security Issues: Recognizing Problems and Finding Solutions

Almost all CGI security holes come from interaction with the user. By accepting input from an outside source, a simple, predictable CGI program suddenly takes on any number of new dimensions, each of which might have the smallest crack through which a hacker can slip. It is interaction with the user—through XHTML forms or file paths—that gives CGI scripts their power but also makes them the most potentially dangerous part of running a Web server.

CAUTION

Writing secure CGI scripts is largely an exercise in creativity and paranoia. You must be creative to think of all the ways that users, either innocently or otherwise, can send you data that has the potential to cause trouble. And you must be paranoid because, somehow, users will try every one of them.

Two Roads to Trouble

When users visit and interact with your Web site, they can cause headaches in two ways. One is by not following the rules, by bending or breaking every limit or restriction you've tried to build into your pages; the other is by doing just what you've asked them to do. Stating each case a little more specifically:

- Most CGI scripts act as the back end to XHTML forms, processing the information entered by users to provide some sort of customized output. Therefore, most CGI scripts are written to expect data in a specific format. They rely on input from the user matching the information that the form was designed to collect. This, however, isn't always the case. A user can get around these predefined formats in many ways, sending your script seemingly random data. Your CGI programs must be prepared for it.
- Secondly, users can send a CGI script exactly the type of data it expects, with each field in the form filled in, in the format you expect. This type of submission can be from an innocent user interacting with your site as you intended, or it can be from a malevolent hacker using his knowledge of your operating system and Web server software to take advantage of common CGI programming errors. Although these attacks occur less frequently, they tend to be more dangerous and the harder to detect.

Form Data: The Most Common Security Hole

Users are an unruly lot, and they're likely to find a handful of ways to send data that you never expect—even ways that you think are impossible. All your scripts must take this into account. For example, each of the following situations—and many more like them—are possible:

- The selection from a group of radio buttons or `<select>` element might not be one of the choices offered in the form. The options in the `<select name="opinion">` element might be `"yes"` and `"no"`, for example, but the URL returned to the server can be `http://www.yourdomain.com/cgi-bin/fileproc.cgi?opinion=maybe`. The user might have edited the URL to include nearly any string.
- The length of the data returned from a text field might be longer than what is allowed by the `maxlength` attribute. As in the previous example, the user might have edited the URL to include a string of nearly any length. If your form has a text field `<input name="city" type="text" maxlength="15" />`, for example, the URL returned to the server might be `http://www.yourdomain.com/cgi-bin/yourprog.pl/city=El+Pueblo+de+Nuestra+Senora+la+Reina+de+los+Angeles+de+Porciuncula`.

- The names of the fields themselves might not match what you specified in the form. If your survey form has three named fields: `q1`, `q2`, and `q3`, for example, you might still get a URL returned to the server ending in `?you_are=hacked`.
- Using hidden fields in your form provides no assurances that someone cannot read that value within the `<input />` element. Also, anyone viewing a form can view the source, and all form elements are displayed. They can edit the XHTML code and enter their own values.

Where Bad Data Comes From

These situations can arise in several ways—some innocent, some not. For example, your script can receive data that it doesn't expect because somebody else wrote a form (that requests input completely different from yours) and accidentally pointed the form's `action` attribute to your CGI script. Perhaps they used your form as a template and forgot to edit the `action` attribute's URL before testing it. This would result in your script getting data that it has no idea what to do with, possibly causing unexpected and potentially dangerous behavior.

Or the user might have accidentally (or intentionally) edited the URL to your CGI script. When a browser submits form data to a CGI program, it appends the data entered into the form onto the CGI's URL (for `get` methods). The user can easily modify the data being sent to your script by typing in the browser's Address bar.

Finally, an ambitious hacker might write a program that connects to your server over the Web and pretends to be a Web browser. This program, however, can do things that no true Web browser would do, such as send 100MB of data to your CGI script. What would a CGI script do if it didn't limit the amount of data it read from a `post` method because it assumed that the data came from a small form? It would probably crash and maybe crash in a way that would allow access to the person who crashed it.

Fighting Bad Form Data

You can fight the unexpected input that can be submitted to your CGI scripts in several ways—you should use any or all of them when writing CGI:

- Your first line of defense against bad form data should be the judicious use of client-side JavaScript to scan the values being provided by the user. This way, you can abort the submission of the form if you think there's a problem, and the potentially malicious data will never even be sent to the server. By not submitting the form, you also have the added advantage of not exposing the query string to a would-be hacker.

  ▶ To learn more about JavaScript and forms, **see** Chapter 21, "Using JavaScript to Create Smart Forms"

- Next, your CGI script should set reasonable limits on how much data it will accept, both for the entire submission and for each `name/value` pair in the submission. If your CGI script reads the `post` method, for instance, check the size of the `content_length` environment variable to make sure that it's something you can reasonably expect. Although most Web servers set an arbitrary limit on the amount of data that will be passed to your script via `post`, you might want to limit this size further. For example, if the only input your CGI script is designed to accept is a person's first name, it might be a good idea to return an error if `CONTENT_LENGTH` is more than, say, 100 bytes. No reasonable first name will be that long, and by imposing the limit, you've protected your script from blindly reading anything that gets sent to it.

NOTE In most cases, you don't have to worry about limiting the data submitted through the `get` method. `get` is usually self-limiting and won't deliver more than approximately 1KB of data to your script. The server automatically limits the size of the data placed into the `QUERY_STRING` environment variable, which is how `get` sends information to a CGI program.

Of course, hackers can easily circumvent this built-in limit by changing the `method` attribute of your form from `"get"` to `"post"`. At the very least, your program should check that data is submitted using the method you expect; at most, it should handle both methods correctly and safely.

▶ For more about working with CGI variables, **see** "Standard CGI Environment Variables," **p. 744**

- Next, make sure your script knows what to do if it receives data that it doesn't recognize. If, for example, a form asks that a user select one of two radio buttons, the script shouldn't assume that just because one isn't clicked, the other is. The following Perl code makes this mistake:

```
if ($form_Data{"radio_choice"} eq "button_one")
{
       # Button One has been clicked
}
else
{
       # Button Two has been clicked
}
```

- Your CGI script should anticipate unexpected or "impossible" situations and handle them accordingly. The preceding example is pretty innocuous, but the same assumption elsewhere can easily be dangerous. An error should be printed instead, as follows:

```
if ($form_Data{"radio_choice"} eq "button_one")
{
       # Button One selected
}
```

```
elsif ($form_Data{"radio_choice"} eq "button_two")
{
       # Button Two selected
}
else
{
       # Error
}
```

Of course, an error might not be what you want your script to generate in these circumstances. Overly picky scripts that validate every field and produce error messages on even the slightest unexpected data can turn users off.

TIP The balance between safety and convenience for the user is important. Don't be afraid to consult with your users to find out what works best for them.

- Having your CGI script recognize unexpected data, throw it away, and automatically select a default is a possibility, too. The following is C code that checks text input against several possible choices, for example, and sets a default if it doesn't find a match. You can use this to generate output that might better explain to the user what you expect.

```
/* Notes for non-C programmers:                                    */
/* Contrary to what its name implies,                             */
/*   the C string comparison function strcmp used below          */
/*   returns 0 (false) when its two arguments match and          */
/*   returns nonzero (true)_when its two arguments differ.       */
/*   A better name might be strDIFF.                               */
/* In C, "&&" is logical AND.                                      */
/*                                                                  */
/* If the help_Topic is not any of the three choices given...   */
if ((strcmp(help_Topic,"how_to_order.txt")) &&
 (strcmp(help_Topic,"delivery_options.txt")) &&
 (strcmp(help_Topic,"complaints.txt")))
{
       /* then set help_Topic to the default value here          */
       strcpy(help_Topic,"help_on_help.txt");
}
```

- However, your script might try to do users a favor and correct any mistakes rather than send an error or select a default. If a form asks users to enter the secret word, your script can automatically strip off any whitespace characters from the input before doing the comparison, such as the following Perl fragment:

```
# Remove whitespace by replacing it with an empty string
$user_Input =~ s/\s//g;
if ($user_Input eq $secret_Word)
{
        # Match!
}
```

TIP Although it's nice to try to catch the users' mistakes, don't try to do too much. If your corrections aren't really what users wanted, they'll be annoyed.

CAUTION

You should also be aware that trying to catch every possible user-entry error will make your code huge and nearly impossible to maintain. Don't over-engineer.

- Finally, you might choose to go the extra mile and have your CGI script handle as many different forms of input as it can—for example, malicious code that spoofs a browser's request to a server. Although you can't possibly anticipate everything that can initiate a CGI program, often several common ways exist to do a particular thing, and you can check for each.

Just because the form you wrote uses the `post` method to submit data to your CGI script, for example, that doesn't mean the data will come in that way. Rather than assuming that the data will be on standard input (`stdin`) where you're expecting it, you can check the `REQUEST_METHOD` environment variable to determine whether the `get` or `post` method was used and read the data accordingly. A truly well-written CGI script will accept data no matter what method was used to submit it and will be made more secure in the process. Listing 30.1 shows an example in Perl.

Troubleshooting

If your script returns an error, there are five usual causes. The first is that your script is not returning the proper `Content-type`. The second might be that your server is not properly set up to handle CGI scripts. The third is that the script named in the form's `action` attribute is not in your CGI-enabled directory, usually called `cgi-bin`. The fourth is that the path given in the form's `action` attribute is misspelled, or the filename is misspelled. Check the spelling of the filename and path. The fifth cause is that the filename and path are correct but the filename does not end in the proper extension (such as `.cgi` or `.plx` or `.pl`) for your server configuration.

Although you will usually get this error when the form is `method="post"`, a user can cause this error to occur in a form with `method="get"` by editing your page in his browser and substituting `"post"` for `"get"`.

Listing 30.1 *Cgi_read.pl*—Reading Form Input

```
# Takes the maximum length allowed as a parameter
# Returns 1 and the raw form data, or "0" and the error text
sub cgi_Read
{
      local($input_Max) = 1024 unless $input_Max = $_[0];
      local($input_Method) = $ENV{'REQUEST_METHOD'};

      # Check for each possible REQUEST_METHODs
      if ($input_Method eq "GET")
      {
            # "GET"
            local($input_Size) = length($ENV{'QUERY_STRING'});

            # Check the size of the input
            return (0, "Input too big") if ($input_Size > $input_Max);

            # Read the input from QUERY_STRING
            return (1,$ENV{'QUERY_STRING'});
      }
      elsif ($input_Method eq "POST")
      {
            # "POST"
            local($input_Size) = $ENV{'CONTENT_LENGTH'};
            local($input_Data);

            # Check the size of the input
            return (0,"Input too big") if ($input_Size > $input_Max);

            # Read the input from stdin
            return (0,"Could not read STDIN") unless
            ➥(read(STDIN,$input_Data,$input_Size));

            return (1,$input_Data);
      }

      # Unrecognized METHOD
      return (0,"METHOD not GET or POST");
}
```

TIP Many existing CGI programming libraries already offer good built-in security features. Rather than write your own routines, you might want to rely on some of the well-known, publicly available functions.

Don't Trust Path Data

Another type of data the user can alter is the PATH_INFO server environment variable. This variable is filled with any path information that follows the script's filename in a CGI URL. For example, if sample.sh is a CGI shell script, the URL http://www.yourserver.com/cgi-bin/sample.sh/extra/path/info will cause /extra/path/info to be placed in the PATH_INFO environment variable when sample.sh is run.

If you use this PATH_INFO environment variable, you must be careful to completely validate its contents. Just as form data can be altered in any number of ways, so can PATH_INFO—accidentally or on purpose. A CGI script that blindly acts on the path file specified in PATH_INFO can enable malicious users to wreak havoc on the server.

If a CGI script is designed to print out the file that's referenced in PATH_INFO, for example, a user who edits the CGI URL can read almost any file on your computer, as in the following script:

```
#!/bin/sh

# Send the header
echo "Content-type: text/html"
echo ""

# Wrap the file in some XHTML
echo "<html><head><title>File</title></head><body>"
echo "Here is the file you requested:<pre>\n"
cat $PATH_INFO
echo "</pre></body></html>"
```

Although this script works fine if the user is content to click only predefined links—for example, http://www.yourserver.com/cgi-bin/showfile.sh/public/faq.txt—a more creative (or spiteful) user could use it to receive *any* file on your server. If she were to jump to http://www.yourserver.com/cgi-bin/showfile.sh/etc/passwd, the preceding script would happily return your machine's password file, something you do not want to happen.

A much safer course is to use the PATH_TRANSLATED environment variable. It automatically appends the contents of PATH_INFO to the root of your server's document tree, which means that any file specified by PATH_TRANSLATED is probably already accessible to browsers and, therefore, safe. If your document root is /usr/local/etc/htdocs, for example, and PATH_INFO is /etc/passwd, then PATH_TRANSLATED is /usr/local/etc/htdocs/etc/passwd.

NOTE In one case, however, files that might not be accessible through a browser can be accessed if `PATH_TRANSLATED` is used within a CGI script. The `.htaccess` file, which can exist in each subdirectory of a document tree, controls who has access to the particular files in that directory. It can be used, for example, to limit the visibility of a group of Web pages to company employees. Whereas the server knows how to interpret `.htaccess` and thus knows how to limit who can and who can't see these pages, CGI scripts don't have this same capability. A program that uses `PATH_TRANSLATED` to access arbitrary files in the document tree might accidentally override the protection provided by the server. Thus, you might want to avoid using `PATH_TRANSLATED` altogether. ■

Handling Filenames

Filenames, for example, are simple pieces of data that might be submitted to your CGI script and cause endless amounts of trouble if you're not careful (see Figure 30.1).

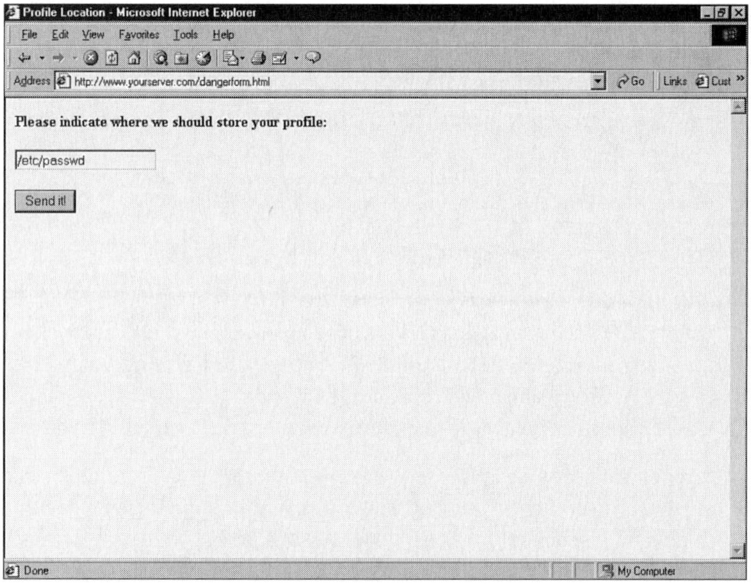

FIGURE 30.1
Depending on how well the CGI script is written, the Webmaster for this site can get into big trouble.

Any time you try to open a file based on a name supplied by the user, you must rigorously screen that name for any number of tricks that can be played. If you ask the user for a filename and then try to open whatever was entered, a number of problems might occur:

- For example, what if the user enters a name that has path elements in it, such as directory slashes and double dots? Although you expect a simple filename—for example, `File.txt`—you can end up with `/file.txt` or `../../../file.txt`. Depending on how your Web server is installed and what you do with the submitted filename, you can be exposing any file on your system to a clever hacker.

- Furthermore, what if the user enters the name of an existing file or one that's important to the running of the system? What if the name entered is `/etc/passwd` or `C:\WINNT\SYSTEM32\KERNEL32.DLL`? Depending on what your CGI script does with these files, they might be sent out to the user or overwritten with garbage.
- Under Windows NT, if you don't screen for the backslash character (`\`), you might enable Web browsers to gain access to files that aren't even on your Web server through Universal Naming Convention (UNC) filenames. If the script that's about to run in Figure 30.2 doesn't carefully screen the filename before opening it, it might give the Web browser access to any machine in the domain or workgroup.

FIGURE 30.2
Opening a UNC filename is one possible security hole that gives hackers access to your entire network.

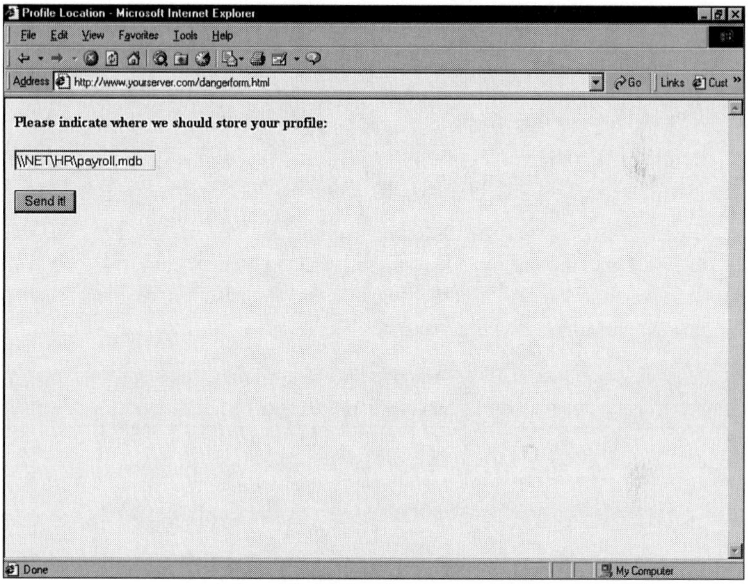

- What might happen if the user puts an illegal character in a filename? Under UNIX, any filename beginning with a period (.) becomes invisible. Under Windows, both slashes (/ and \) are directory separators. It's possible, if the filename begins with the pipe (|), to write a Perl program carelessly and allow external programs to be executed when you thought you were only opening a file. Even control characters (the Escape key or the Return key, for example) can be sent to you as part of filenames if the user knows how. (See "Where Bad Data Comes From," earlier in this chapter.)

NOTE Worse yet, in shell script, the semicolon ends one command and starts another. If your script is designed to `cat` the file the user enters, a user might enter `file.txt;rm -rf/` as a filename, causing `File.txt` to be returned and, consequently, the entire hard disk to be erased, without confirmation. ■

Verifying That Input Is Legitimate

To avoid all the dangers associated with bad input and close all the potential security holes, you should screen every filename the user enters. You must make sure that the input is only what you expect.

The best way to do this is to compare each character of the entered filename against a list of acceptable characters and return an error if they don't match. This is much safer than trying to maintain a list of all the illegal characters and comparing against that—it's too easy to accidentally let something slip through.

The following code snippet is an example of how to do this comparison in Perl. It allows any letter of the alphabet (upper- or lowercase), any number, the underscore, and the period. It also checks to make sure that the filename doesn't start with a period. Thus, this fragment doesn't allow slashes to change directories, semicolons to put multiple commands on one line, or pipes to play havoc with Perl's `open()` call.

```
if (($file_Name =~ /[^\w\.]/) || ($file_Name =~ /^\./)){
      # File name contains an illegal character or starts with a period
}
```

TIP

When you have a commonly used test, such as the previous code, it's a good idea to make it into a subroutine so you can call it repeatedly. This way, you can change it in only one place in your program if you think of an improvement.

Continuing that thought, if the subroutine is used commonly among several programs, it's a good idea to put it into a library so that any improvements can be instantly inherited by all your scripts.

CAUTION

Although the previous code snippet filters out most bad filenames, your operating system might have restrictions it doesn't cover. Can a filename start with a digit, for example? With an underscore? What if the filename has more than one period, or if the period is followed by more than three characters? Is the entire filename short enough to fit within the restrictions of the file system?

You must constantly ask yourself these kinds of questions. The most dangerous thing you can do when writing CGI scripts is rely on the users to follow instructions. They won't. It's your job to make sure they don't get away with it.

Handling XHTML

Another type of seemingly innocuous input that can cause you endless trouble is receiving XHTML when you request text from the user. The following code snippet is a Perl fragment that customizes a greeting to whomever has entered a name in the `$user_Name` variable; for example, John Smith (see Figure 30.3).

```
print("<html><head><title>greetings!</title></head><body>\n");
print("Hello, $user_Name!  It's good to see you!\n");
print("</body></html>\n");
```

FIGURE 30.3
When the user enters what you requested, everything works well.

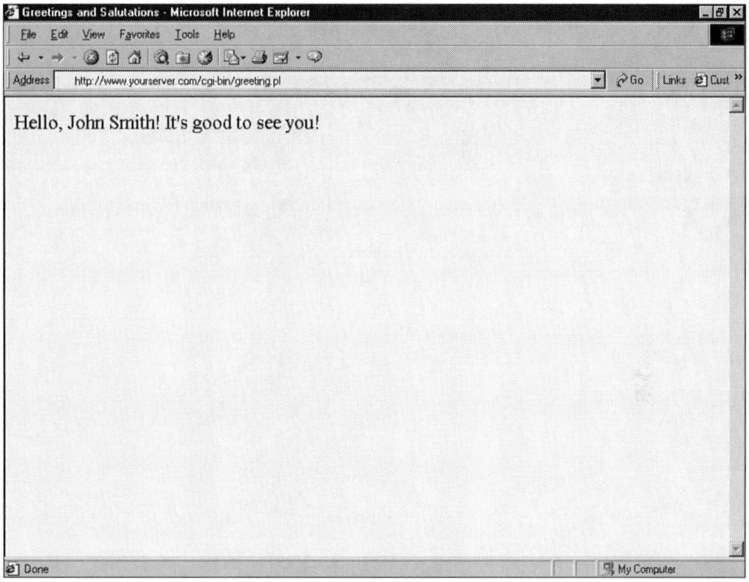

But imagine if, rather than entering only a name, the user types <hr /><h1><p align="center">Jane Smith</p></h1><hr />. The result would be Figure 30.4—probably not what you wanted.

FIGURE 30.4
Entering XHTML when a script expects plain text can change a page in unexpected ways.

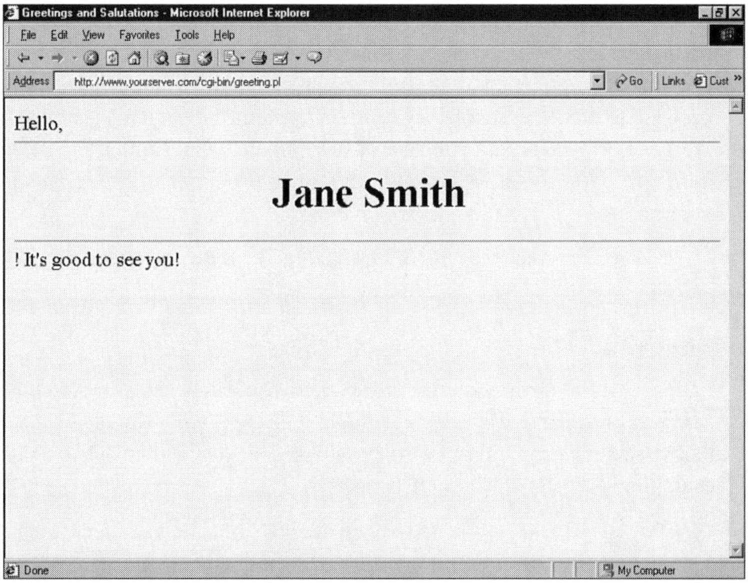

Or what if `Mystery Guest<form><select>` was entered as the user's name in a guest book? The `<select>` tag would cause the Web browser to ignore everything between it and a nonexistent `</select>`, including any names that were added to the list later. Even if 10 people signed the guest book shown in Figure 30.5, only the first four appear because the fourth name contains a `<form>` and a `<select>` tag.

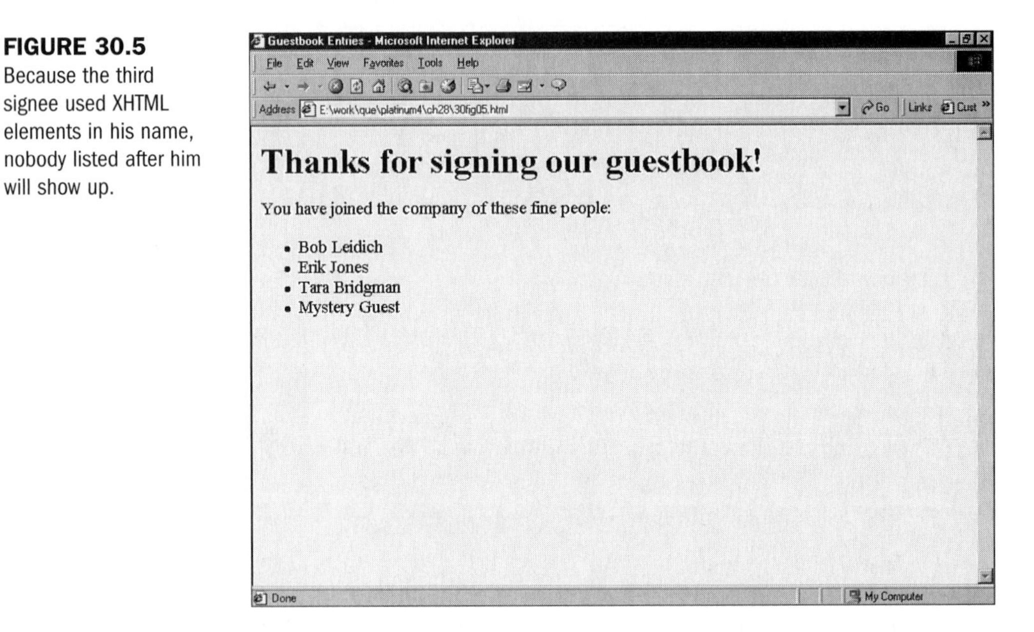

FIGURE 30.5
Because the third signee used XHTML elements in his name, nobody listed after him will show up.

But even more dangerous than entering simple XHTML, a malicious hacker might enter a server-side include directive instead. If your Web server is configured to obey server-side includes, a user might type `<!--#include file="/etc/passwd" -->` instead of his name to get your machine's password file. And probably worst of all, a hacker might input `<!--#exec cmd="rm -rf /" -->`, and the innocent code in the snippet shown before would proceed to delete almost everything on your hard disk. This is a primary example of why Web servers should not run as *root* (the Super User). Running the Web server under a nonprivileged user is the best way to reduce problems in case someone does find a hole in your script.

▶ To learn more about Server-Side Include directives, **see** "Common SSI Commands," **p. 761**

CAUTION

Server-side includes are often disabled because of how they can be misused. Although much more information is available in Chapter 29, "Server-Side Includes," you might want to consider this option to truly secure your site against this type of attack.

Two solutions exist to the problem of the user entering XHTML rather than flat text:

- The quick-and-dirty solution is to disallow the less than (<) and greater than (>) symbols. Because all XHTML elements must be contained within these two characters, removing them (or returning an error if you encounter them) is an easy way to prevent HTML from being submitted and accidentally returned. The following line of Perl code erases the characters:

```
$user_Input =~ s/<>//g;
```


- The more elaborate solution is to translate the two characters into their XHTML *entities* or *escape codes*. The following code does this by globally substituting < for the less than symbol and > for the greater than symbol:

```
$user_Input =~ s/</&lt;/g;
$user_Input =~ s/>/&gt;/g;
```

Handling External Processes

Another area in which you must be careful is how your CGI script interfaces user input with any external processes. Because executing a program outside your CGI script means you have no control over what it does, you must do everything you can to validate the input you send to it before the execution begins.

For example, shell scripts often make the mistake of concatenating a command-line program with form input and then executing them together. This works fine if the user has entered what you expected, but additional commands might be sneaked in and unintentionally executed.

The following fragment of shell script commits this error:

```
FINGER_OUTPUT='finger $USER_INPUT'
echo $FINGER_OUTPUT
```

If the user politely enters the email address of a person to finger, everything works as it should. But if he enters an email address followed by a semicolon and another command, that command is executed as well. If the user enters `webmaster@www.yourserver.com;rm -rf /`, you're in considerable trouble because this command will delete all your files.

CAUTION

You also must be careful to screen all the input you receive—not just form data—before using it in the shell. Web server environment variables can be set to anything by a hacker who has written his own Web client and can cause just as much damage as bad form data.

If you execute the following line of shell script, thinking that it will add the referer to your log, you might be in trouble if `HTTP_REFERER` has been set to `;rm -rf /;echo "Ha ha"`.

```
echo $HTTP_REFERER >> ./referer.log
```

Even if a hidden command isn't placed into user data, innocent input might give you something you don't expect. The following line, for instance, creates an unexpected result—a listing of all the files in the directory—if the user input is an asterisk:

```
echo "Your input: " $USER_INPUT
```

When sending user data through the shell, as both of these code snippets do, it's a good idea to screen it for shell meta-characters. Such characters include the semicolon (which allows multiple commands on one line), the asterisk and the question mark (which perform file globbing), the exclamation point (which, under `csh`, references running jobs), the back quote (which executes an enclosed command), and so on. Like filtering filenames, maintaining a list of allowable characters is often easier than trying to catch each character that should be disallowed. The following Perl fragment crudely validates an email address:

```
if ($email_Address ~= /[^a-zA-Z0-9_\-\+\@\.])
{
      # Illegal character!
}
else
{
      system("finger $email_Address");
}
```

If you decide that you must allow shell meta-characters in your input, there are ways to make their inclusion safer. Although you might be tempted to put quotation marks around user input that hasn't been validated to prevent the shell from acting on special characters, this almost never works. Look at the following:

```
echo "Finger information:<hr><pre>"
finger "$USER_INPUT"
echo "</pre>"
```

Although the quotation marks around `$USER_INPUT` will prevent the shell from interpreting, for example, an included semicolon that would enable a hacker to piggyback a command, this script still has several severe security holes. For instance, the input might be `` `rm -rf /` ``, with the back quotes causing the hacker's command to be executed before `finger` is even considered.

A better way to handle special characters is to escape them so that the shell takes their values without interpreting them. By escaping the user input, all shell meta-characters are ignored and treated instead as just more data to be passed to the program.

The following line of Perl code does this for all nonalphanumeric characters:

```
$user_Input =~ s/([^w])/\\\1/g;
```

Now, if this user input were appended to a command, each character—even the special characters—would be passed through the shell to `finger`.

In general, validating user input—not trusting anything sent to you—will make your code easier to read and safer to execute. Rather than trying to defeat a hacker after you're already running commands, give data the once-over at the door.

Handling Internal Functions

With interpreted languages, such as a shell or Perl, the user can enter data that will actually change your program–data that cause errors that aren't present if the data is correct. If user data is interpreted as part of the program's execution, anything he enters must adhere to the rules of the language or cause an error.

For example, the following Perl fragment might work fine or might generate an error, depending on what the user enters:

```
if ($search_Text =~ /$user_Pattern/)
{
      # Match!
}
```

In Perl, the `eval()` operator exists to prevent this. `eval()` allows for runtime syntax checking and determines whether an expression is valid Perl. The following code is an improved version of the preceding code:

```
if (eval{$search_Text =~ /$user_Pattern/})
{
      if ($search_Text =~ /$user_Pattern/)
      {
            # Match!
      }
}
```

Unfortunately, most shells (including the most popular, `/bin/sh`) have no easy way to detect errors such as this one, which is another reason to avoid them.

Guarding Against Loopholes When Executing External Programs

When executing external programs, you must also be aware of how the user input you pass to those programs will affect them. You can guard your own CGI script against hacker tricks, but it's all for naught if you blithely pass anything a hacker might have entered to external programs without understanding how those programs use that data.

Many CGI scripts send email to a particular person, for instance, containing data collected from the user by executing the `mail` program.

This can be dangerous because `mail` has many internal commands, any of which can be invoked by user input. If you send text entered by the user to `mail`, for example, and that text has a line that starts with a tilde (~), `mail` interprets the next character on the line as one of the many commands it can perform. `~r /etc/passwd`, for example, will cause your machine's password file to be read by `mail` and sent off to whomever the letter is addressed to, perhaps even the hacker.

In this example, rather than using `mail` to send email from UNIX machines, you should use `sendmail`, the lower-level mail program that lacks many of `mail`'s features. But, of course, you should also be aware of `sendmail`'s commands so those can't be exploited.

As a general rule, when executing external programs, you should use the one that fits your needs as closely as possible, without any frills. The less an external program can do, the less it can be tricked into doing.

CAUTION

You must be careful that the address you pass to the mail system is a legal email address when using `mail` and `sendmail`. Many mail systems treat an email address starting with a pipe (|) as a command to be executed, opening a huge security hole for any hacker who enters such an address.

Again, always validate your data!

Another example that demonstrates you must know your external programs well to use them effectively is `grep`. Most people will tell you that you can't get into much trouble with `grep`. However, `grep` can be fooled fairly easily, and how it fails is illustrative. The following code is an example: It's supposed to perform a case-sensitive search for a user-supplied term among many files:

```
print("The following lines contain your term:<hr /><pre>");
$search_Term =~ s/([^\w])/\\$1/g;
system("grep $search_Term /public/files/*.txt");
print("</pre>");
```

This all seems fine, unless you consider what happens if the user enters `-i`. It's not searched for, but functions as a switch to `grep`, as would any input starting with a dash. This causes `grep` either to hang while waiting for the search term to be typed into standard input, or to error out when anything after the `-i` is interpreted as extra switch characters. This, undoubtedly, isn't what you wanted or planned. In this case, it's not dangerous, but in other cases it might be.

A harmless command doesn't exist, and each must be carefully considered from every angle. You should be as familiar as possible with every external program your CGI script executes. The more you know about the programs, the more you can do to protect them from bad data, both by screening that data and by disabling options or disallowing features.

Security Beyond Your Own

`sendmail` has an almost legendary history of security problems. Almost from the beginning, hackers have found clever ways to exploit `sendmail` and gain unauthorized access to the computers that run it.

But `sendmail` is hardly unique. Dozens—if not hundreds—of popular, common tools have security problems, with more being discovered each year.

The point is that it's not only the security of your own CGI script that you must worry about, but the security of all the programs your CGI script uses. Knowing `sendmail`'s full range of documented capabilities is important, but perhaps more important is knowing capabilities that are not documented because they probably aren't intended to exist.

Keeping up with security issues in general is a necessary step to maintain the ongoing integrity of your Web site. One of the easiest ways to do this is on Usenet, in the newsgroups `comp.security.announce` (where important information about computer security is broadcast) and `comp.security.unix` (which has a continuing discussion of UNIX security issues). A comprehensive history of security problems, including attack-prevention software, is available through the Computer Emergency Response Team (CERT) at `http://www.cert.org`.

Inside Attacks: Precautions with Local Users

A common mistake in CGI security is to forget local users. Although people browsing your site over the Web usually won't have access to security considerations, such as file permissions and owners, local users of your Web server do, and you must guard against these threats even more than those from the Web.

CAUTION

Local system security is a big subject, and almost any reference on it will give you good tips on protecting the integrity of your machine from local users. As a general rule, if your system as a whole is safe, your Web site is safe, too.

The CGI Script User

Most Web servers are installed to run CGI scripts as a special user. This is the user that *owns* the CGI program while it runs, and the permissions granted limit what the script can do.

Under UNIX, the server itself usually runs as *root* to enable it to use socket port 80, and then changes to another nonprivileged user. Thus, when the server executes a CGI program, it does so as an innocuous user, such as the commonly used *nobody*, and the capability to configure this behavior is available on many servers. It is dangerous to run CGI scripts as root! The less powerful the user, the less damage a runaway CGI script can do.

Setuid and ACL Dangers

You should also be aware if the *setuid bit* is set on your UNIX CGI scripts. If enabled, no matter what user the server runs programs as, it will execute with the permissions of the file's owner. This, of course, has major security implications—you can lose control over which user your script runs as.

Fortunately, the setuid bit is easy to disable. Executing `chmod a-s` on all your CGI scripts will guarantee that it's turned off, and your programs will run with the permissions you intended.

Of course, in some situations you might want the setuid bit set; for example, if your script needs to run as a specific user to access a database. In this case, you should make doubly sure that the other file permissions on the program limit access to it to those users you intend.

A similar situation can occur under Windows NT. Microsoft's Internet Information Server (IIS) normally runs CGI scripts with the access control list (ACL) of `IUSR_computer`. However, by editing a Registry entry, IIS can be set to run scripts as `SYSTEM`. `SYSTEM` has much wider permissions than `IUSR_computer` and can cause correspondingly more damage if things go wrong. You should make sure that your server is configured the way you intend.

TIP Microsoft recommends that CGI scripts (`.pl`, `.dll`, `.exe`, and `.cmd` files), ASP pages, and included files (`.incl`, `.shtm`, and `.shtml` files) be given Execute permission for Everyone and Full Control permission for System and Administrators. Static content files (`.htm`, `.html`, `.txt`, `.gif`, `.jpg`) should be given Read permission for Everyone and Full Control permission for System and Administrators.

Additionally, you should put each type of content into its own folder so that it's easier for you to set the access permissions.

Community Web Servers

Another potential problem with the single, common user that Web servers execute scripts as is that a single human being is not necessarily always in control of the server. If many people share control of a server, each can install CGI scripts that run as, for example, the *nobody* user. This enables any of these people to use a CGI program to gain access to parts of the machine that they might be restricted from, but that *nobody* is allowed to enter.

Probably the most common solution to this potential security problem is to restrict CGI control to a single individual. Although this might seem reasonable in limited circumstances, it's often impossible for larger sites. Universities, for example, have hundreds of students, each of whom wants to experiment with writing and installing CGI scripts.

Using CGIWrap

A better solution to the problem of deciding which user a script runs as when multiple people have CGI access is CGIWrap. CGIWrap is a simple wrapper that executes a CGI script as the user who owns the file instead of the user whom the server specifies. This simple precaution leaves the script owner responsible for the damage it can do.

If the user Joanne, for instance, owns a CGI script that's wrapped in CGIWrap, the server will execute the script with Joanne's permissions. In this way, CGIWrap acts like a setuid bit but has the added advantage of being controlled by the Web server rather than the operating system. Therefore, anybody who sneaks through any security holes in the script will be limited to whatever Joanne herself can do—the files she can read and delete, the directories she can view, and so on.

Because CGIWrap puts CGI script authors in charge of the permissions for their own scripts, it can be a powerful tool not only to protect important files owned by others, but also to motivate people to write secure scripts. The realization that only their files would be in danger can be a powerful persuader to script authors.

CGI Script Permissions

You should also be aware of which users own CGI scripts and what file permissions they have. The permissions on the directories that contain the scripts are also very important.

If, for example, the `cgi-bin` directory on your Web server is world writeable, any local user can delete your CGI script and replace it with another. If the script itself is world writeable, anybody can modify the script to do anything they want.

Look at the following innocuous UNIX CGI script:

```
#!/bin/sh
# Send the header
echo "Content-type: text/html"
echo ""
# Send some XHTML
echo "<html><head><title>Fortune</title></head>
echo "<body>Your fortune:<hr /><pre>"
fortune
echo "</body></html>"
```

Now imagine if the permissions on the script allowed a local user to change the program to the following:

```
#!/bin/sh
# Send the header
echo "Content-type: text/html"
echo ""
# Do some damage!
rm -rf /
echo "<html><head><title>Got you!</title></head><body>"
echo "<h1>Ha ha!</h1></body></html>"
```

The next user to access the script over the Web would cause huge amounts of damage, even though that person had done nothing wrong. Checking the integrity of user input over the Web is important, but even more so is making sure that the scripts themselves remain unaltered and unalterable.

Troubleshooting

If you get an `Error 500: Bad Script Request` message when attempting to run your CGI script, you might have been too conservative in setting permissions. A CGI script must be executable. You can test your scripts beforehand by running them from the command line—the script should at least run. If your operating system is UNIX or UNIX-like, you can use `chmod -x` to set the file's permissions.

Local File Security

Equally important is the integrity of the files that your scripts create on the local hard disk. After you feel comfortable that you have a good filename from the Web user, how you actually go about using that name is also important. Depending on which operating system your Web server is running, permissions and ownership information can be stored on the file along with the data inside it. Users of your Web server might cause havoc depending on how various permission flags are set.

You should be aware, for example, of the permissions you give a file when you create it. Most Web server software sets the *umask*, or permission restrictions, to 0000, which means that it's possible to create a file that anybody can read or write. Although the permissions on a file probably don't make any difference to people browsing on the Web, people with local access can take advantage of loose restrictions. You should always specify the most conservative permissions possible while still allowing your program the access it needs when creating files.

TIP Specifying permissions is a good idea not only for CGI programs, but for all the code you write.

The simplest way to make sure that each `file-open` call has a set of minimum restrictions is to set your script's `umask`. `umask()` is a UNIX call that restricts permissions on every subsequent file creation. The parameter passed to `umask()` is a number that's "masked" against the permissions mode of any later file creation. A `umask` of `0022` causes any file created to be writeable only by the user, no matter what explicit permissions are given to the group and other users during the actual open.

But even with the `umask` set, you should create files with explicit permissions, just to make sure that they're as restrictive as possible. If the only program that will ever be accessing a file is your CGI script, only the user that your CGI program runs as should be given access to the file: permissions 0600. If another program needs to access the file, try to make the owner of that program a member of the same group as your CGI script so that only group permissions need to be set: permissions 0660. If you must give the world access to the file, make it so the file can only be read, not written to: permissions 0644.

Make Smart Use of HTTP Logs

Your HTTP server logs act as a security camera that document an attacker's activities. Thus, you will want to have your logs as detailed as possible so you can chase down as much information as possible about a potential hacker. The W3C extended log format enables you to capture a wealth of information about each HTTP transaction, so you should enable this feature if it's available on your server. IIS users will find a W3C Extended Log File Format option when they activate logging for a site.

TIP Another log file suggestion is to make sure that the log files have the proper permissions set so that an attacker cannot attempt to delete the logs. For an IIS server, this means read, write, and change permission for the Everyone group and Full Control for the System and Administrators groups.

Remove Sample Scripts

Sample scripts and applications that come bundled with your server make good targets for hackers because they can be assured that every server of that type will have the same vulnerability. For example, the application development platform ColdFusion installs a documentation directory called CFDOCS under the HTTP root directory. One security weakness with ColdFusion involved the exploitation of content in the CFDOCS directory.

On an IIS server, you might want to consider deleting or disabling the following pre-installed applications:

- IIS Samples, stored in the `c:\inetpub\iissamples` directory
- IIS Documentation, stored in the `c:\winnt\help\iishelp` directory
- Data Access Components, stored in the `c:\program files\common files\system\msadc` directory

Use Explicit Paths

Finally, a local user can attack your Web server in one last way—by fooling it into running an external program that he wrote instead of what you specified in your CGI script. The following is a simple program that shows a Web surfer a bit of wisdom from the UNIX `fortune` command:

```
#!/bin/sh
# Send the header
echo "Content-type: text/html"
echo ""
# Send the fortune
echo "<html><head><title>Fortune</title></head><body>"
echo "You crack open the cookie and the fortune reads:<hr /><pre>"
fortune
echo "</pre></body></html>"
```

This script seems harmless enough. It accepts no input from the user, so he can't play any tricks on it that way. Because it's run only by the Web server, the permissions on the script itself can be set to be very restrictive, preventing a trouble-minded local user from changing it. And, if the permissions on the directory in which it resides are set correctly, not much can go wrong, right?

Not so! The previous code snippet calls two commands, `echo` and `fortune`. Because these scripts don't have explicit paths specifying where they are on the hard disk, the shell uses the `PATH` environment variable to search for them, and this can be dangerous. If, for example, the `fortune` program was installed in `/usr/games`, but `PATH` listed, say, `/tmp` before it, then any program that happened to be named "fortune" and resided in the temporary directory would be executed instead of the true `fortune`.

This program can do anything its creator wants, from deleting files to logging information about the request and then passing the data on to the real `fortune`—leaving the user and you none the wiser.

You should always specify explicit paths when running external programs from your CGI scripts. The `PATH` environment variable is a great tool, but it can be misused the same as any other.

Using Others' CGI Scripts

Many helpful archives of CGI scripts are available free on the Web, and each is stuffed with dozens of useful, valuable programs. However, before you start haphazardly downloading all these gems and blindly installing them on your server, you should pause and consider two things:

- Does the script come with source code?
- Do you know the language the program is written in well enough to really understand what it does?

If the answer to either question is no, you could be opening yourself up to a huge con game, doing the hacker's work for him by installing a potentially dangerous CGI program on your own server. It's like bringing a bomb into your house because you thought it was a blender.

These *Trojan horse* scripts—so named because they contain hidden dangers—might be wonderful time savers, doing exactly what you need and functioning perfectly, until a certain time is reached or a certain signal is received. Then, they will spin out of your control and execute planned behavior that can range from the silly to the disastrous.

Examining External Source Code

Before installing a CGI program that you didn't write, you should take care to examine it closely for any potential dangers. If you don't know the language of the script or if its style is confusing, you might be better off looking for a different solution. Look, for example, at this Perl fragment:

```
system("cat /etc/passwd") if ($ENV{"PATH_INFO"} eq "/send/passwd");
```


This single line of code can be hidden among thousands of others, waiting for its author or any surfer to enter the secret words that cause it to send him your password file.

If your knowledge of Perl is shaky, if you didn't take the time to completely review the script before installing it, or if a friend assured you that he's running the script with no problems, you can accidentally open your site to a huge security breach—one that you might not know about. The most dangerous Trojan horses won't even let you know that they've gone about their work. They will continue to work correctly, silently sabotaging all your site's security.

Guarding Against Precompiled C CGI Scripts

Occasionally, you might find precompiled C CGI scripts on the Web. These are even more dangerous than prewritten programs that include the source. Because precompiled programs don't give you any way of discovering what's actually going on, their "payload" can be much more complex and much more dangerous.

A precompiled program, for instance, might take the effort not only to lie in wait for some hidden trigger, but also to inform the hacker-cum-author where you installed it! A cleverly written CGI program might mail its author information about your machine and its users every time the script is run, and you would never know because all that complexity is safely out of sight behind the precompiled executable.

Reviewing CGI Library Scripts

Full-blown CGI scripts aren't the only things that can be dangerous when downloaded off the Web. Dozens of handy CGI libraries are available as well, and they pose the same risks as full programs. If you never bother to look at what each library function does, you might end up writing the program that breaks your site's security.

All a hacker needs is for you to execute one line of code that he wrote, and you've allowed him entry. You should review—and be sure that you understand—every line of code that will execute on your server as a CGI script. Remember, always look a gift horse in the mouth!

The Extremes of Paranoia and the Limits of Your Time

Although sight-checking all the code you pull off the Web is often a good idea, it can take huge amounts of time, especially if the code is complex or difficult to follow. At some point, you might be tempted to throw caution to the wind and hope for the best, installing the program and firing up your browser. The reason you downloaded a CGI program in the first place was to save time. Right?

If you do decide to give your paranoia a rest and run a program that you didn't write, reduce your risk by getting the CGI script from a well-known and highly regarded site.

The NCSA httpd, for example, is far too big for the average user to go over line by line, but downloading it from its home site at `http://www.ncsa.uiuc.edu/` is as close to a guarantee of its integrity as you're likely to get. In fact, anything downloaded from NCSA will be prescreened for you.

CHAPTER 31

Survey of Web Databases

by Eric Ladd

In this chapter

Understanding Database Design

In this chapter, you'll take a look at three kinds of databases: flat file, DBM, and relational. You'll build a different database using each type of database so that you can see the differences among the three methods of storing information. The three methods used here require little or no money to use and build. Nearly everyone can work with databases, and most database applications—free or commercial—operate on the same basic principles.

The most difficult and daunting task is how to go about designing your database to store and retrieve information. What would happen if you wanted to upgrade your database or if you needed to insert additional information (fields or tables, for example) to your database? How will your chosen database platform perform as traffic to your site increases? Is it easy to design a database with your chosen platform or will you need to invest in some data modeling tools to help you out? All these factors need to be considered when designing your database.

Why Access a Database?

Most likely, your organization already has an existing database in which it has stored information about its products, its customers, and other aspects of business life. You might want to allow your customers to see some of this information, or you might even want to make the information in the database available to your workers stationed away from the office. If so, you would have to create XHTML documents that contain all this information several times, which can be a tedious task if you're part of a large organization. Integrating the Web with your databases can save you tremendous amounts of time in the long run, especially when it comes to maintaining that information. As long as you keep your database current, all your Web pages will be current as well.

Another good reason to use the World Wide Web to access your database is that any Web browser that supports forms can access information from the database—no matter which platform is being used. This enables you to create gateways to your databases that you or your co-workers can access from anywhere.

Database Access Limitations

Consider the following sequence of events:

1. Person one accesses the database for editing.
2. Next, person two comes along and does the same thing.
3. Person one makes changes and saves that information to the database.
4. Person two saves information as well, possibly writing over what person one just saved.
5. A short time later, person one is wondering what happened to his or her data.

The browser and the server communicate via HTTP, which is a stateless protocol. Except in certain instances with certain products, the browser makes a request, the server processes the query and sends the result back to the browser, and the connection is closed. This creates a problem with databases because a connection to a database is usually constant. Normally, someone accesses the database, which keeps a connection open, locking a record if any editing is performed, and closes the connection only when the person is finished. Accessing a database doesn't work the same way when you're using a CGI script.

NOTE Application Programming Interfaces (APIs) have been created to alleviate the problem with stateless connections. You must use proprietary software to use these APIs, but they are well worth it. For example, writing Active Server Pages allows you to tap into the Internet Server Applications Programming Interface (ISAPI) that is available as part of Microsoft's Internet Information Server (IIS).

Accessing a database using a Java client/server application can also eliminate the problems associated with stateless connections. ■

Two ways exist to handle the overwriting problem described previously. The first method involves keeping track of all entries with a time stamp. This enables both entries to be maintained by the database, without the possibility of either person's entry being overwritten.

Another solution is to only provide information from the database and not allow someone on the Web to edit, remove, or insert information to the database. Although this limits some of the possibilities for having the database on the Web, it also alleviates some of the security problems.

NOTE With the exception of ODBC for Windows NT and a few other proprietary methods, no official standard exists that you can use to connect to a database. If you create a script to access one type of database, that same script won't necessarily work on a different database—even if the query used was the same. Because of this restriction, you might be required to learn a lot about each database application that you come across. ■

Security Issues

A major problem with having Web users access your database is that your database program trusts your CGI script. That is, your database must accept commands from your CGI script, and your CGI script must perform queries based on what you want to provide to those on the Web. This can lead to problems if an ill-intentioned user gains access to a script and is able to edit your database.

In addition, most databases require the use of a password. Because your CGI script stores user information in the database as well as retrieves information from the database, your script needs to have the password to access your database. You must ensure that others within your organization and outside your organization cannot read your script.

Creating and Using Flat File Databases

Flat file databases are about the easiest databases you can create. To create a small ASCII text database, you need nothing more than a language with which to program and a text editor.

A flat file database consists mainly of lines of text, in which each line is its own entry. If you have more than one field for each record, the records are usually separated by a *delimiter*. No special technique is used to index the database. Therefore, flat file databases usually are relatively small (about 1,000–2,000 records). The larger the database, the longer it takes to perform queries to it.

In a flat file database, each record is contained on its own line. The number of fields in each record is completely up to you, but some sort of delimiter usually separates them. Often commas or tabs are used to delimit a record. A record containing, for example, a name, email address, home phone, work phone, and country might look like this:

```
Jane Doe,jdoe@yourcompany.com,555-5555,555-5566,USA
```

It doesn't matter which delimiter you use, but you want to ensure that the delimiter (in this case, a comma) isn't going to be used anywhere in each field. An address might contain commas and can present problems when retrieving information; for example:

```
Jane Doe,123 Main Street, Suite 125,Anywhere, NY, 12345
```

In the example, the street address would become two separate fields ("123 Main Street" and "Suite 125") when it was meant to be one ("123 Main Street, Suite 125"). You would either have to use a different delimiter, or your script would have to detect any instance of the delimiter when receiving information to add to the database. The latter can be easily accomplished using Perl, with something like

```
$incoming{'address'} =~ s/,/ /g;   #Replace any commas with a space
```

No matter what delimiter you use, it is always good practice to check the information coming in to ensure that it complies with your database structure.

You can build your database using any text editor or spreadsheet that will export a delimited text file (such as Microsoft Excel). After the database has been created, you can add, remove, and browse information within the database.

Adding Information

In a flat file database, nothing exists to check and ensure that the data you are receiving is the data that you are expecting. As stated previously, you must check to ensure that the new information doesn't contain the delimiter you are using. When writing your script, you will also have to ensure that you are getting what you need. If you are expecting a name, then you might want to ensure that you are not receiving an email address. A database is only as good as the information contained in it. Incorrect information can create problems.

Adding information to a flat file database is easy, no matter which programming language you use. The basic idea is that you want to append a new record to the end of the database. Rarely do you find that you have to place a new record somewhere in the middle of the database. If you would like to display your listing in a numerical or alphabetical order, you can easily sort the contents of the database any time you read from the database.

Using Perl, only a few lines of code are needed to add a new entry to a flat file database. If you need to store a name, address, city, and state, this could be easily accomplished with the following:

```
open(FILE, ">>database.txt");
print FILE "$name|$address|$city|$state\n";
close(FILE);
```

With Perl, you open the file using `">>"`, which appends the information to whatever already exists. Next, using the `FILE` filehandle, you add information using a pipe (`|`) for the delimiter, and then you finish your entry by printing a newline.

NOTE Although Perl was used in the example, you can easily perform the same operation using any other programming language. The functions might work differently, but the programming concept is the same. Perl is used here because it is easy to read and to follow and because Perl is widely available for various platforms. ■

Of course, you will want to ensure that you were able to successfully open the database and that the program produced an error if you could not.

Removing Information

Although adding information is crucial to any database application, so is the capability to remove any old information from the database. No matter which programming language is used, removing information is relatively easy. The basic idea is to read the database into an array and then print the database back out to the file, excluding the records that you do not want to keep.

Again, using Perl, it takes only a few lines of code to accomplish this task. If `$remove_key` contained the string "smith," then Listing 31.1 would remove any instance of "smith."

Listing 31.1 Searching Through a Database and Removing a Record

```
open(FILE, "database.txt"); @lines = <FILE>; close(FILE);
open(FILE, ">database.txt");
foreach $line (@lines) {
  print FILE "$line" unless $line =~ /$remove_key/i; }
close(FILE);
```

If you have a database containing information about people and need to remove an entry with the name "John Smith," you must ensure that your script only removes the "John Smith" that you no longer want. Often, you find that more than one person has the same name. The following code stores the text `"smith"` in the variable `$remove_key`. Next, write everything back into the database unless any record matches `"smith"`:

```
$remove_key = "smith";
print FILE "$line" unless $name =~ /$remove_key/i;
```

This could remove any entry such as "John Smith," "Jill Smithy," and "Jennifer Wilsmithmire." When deleting information from a database, you need to be as specific as possible so you don't remove any records that you want to keep.

Browsing the Database

Now that you have the capability to add and remove entries to the database, you need to create a script that enables you to display the contents of your database.

If the database is expected to be small, the easiest thing to do is to display all entries, formatting each record as you deem fit. With Perl, you read the database into an array and then print each line, as shown in Listing 31.2. Each field is provided within the record by using a comma as the delimiter.

Listing 31.2 Printing the Contents of a Flat File Database

```
open(FILE, "database.txt");
@lines = <FILE>;
close(FILE);
foreach $line (@lines) {
$line =~ s/\n//g;
($name, $address, $city, $state) = split(/,/, $line);
print "$name - $address - $city - $state<br>\n";
}
undef $lines;
```

Sometimes, displaying the database in its entirety isn't visually appealing. Looking for one specific entry in a list of 200 records, for example, is daunting. The best solution is to allow the visitor to enter a keyword and list only those entries that match the keyword. You can allow queries against specific fields or against the entire record.

As shown, flat file databases are handy and simple to use. Of course, using flat file databases is economical, as well, because they don't cost a penny. If your database is going to be relatively small, using flat file databases can provide a professional look and dynamic content without any expenses.

Performance Issues

Flat files are convenient and easy to get started, but they can become quite cumbersome after only a few hundred records. A Perl script could certainly still tear through a flat file that large, but you would find it tedious to open the file and work with it in a text editor.

Another problem with flat files is that the search time increases as the number of records increases. For example, in a flat file with 500 records, you would, on average, have to search through 250 records to find the one you want. Measured over the course of a day on a busy Web site, this can impair the performance of your server significantly.

DBM Databases

Most UNIX systems have some kind of DBM database. DBM is a set of library routines that manages data files consisting of key and value pairs. The DBM routines control how users enter and retrieve information from the database. Although it isn't the most powerful mechanism for storing information, using DBM is a faster method of retrieving information than using a flat file. Because most UNIX sites use one of the DBM libraries, the tools you need to store your information to a DBM database are readily available.

Almost as many flavors of the DBM libraries exist as there are UNIX systems. Although most of these libraries are not compatible with each other, they all basically work the same way. This section explores each DBM flavor to give you a good understanding of their differences. Afterward, you'll create an address book script, which should give you an idea of how DBM databases work.

A list follows of some of the most popular DBM libraries available:

- **DBM**—DBM stores the database in two files. The first has the extension `.Pag` and contains the bitmap. The second, which has the extension `.Dir`, contains the data.
- **NDBM**—NDBM is much like DBM with a few additional features; it was written to provide better storage and retrieval methods. Also, NDBM enables you to open many databases, unlike DBM, in which you are allowed to have only one database open within your script. Like DBM, NDBM stores its information in two files using the extensions `.Pag` and `.Dir`.
- **SDBM**—SDBM comes with the Perl archive, which has been ported to many platforms. Therefore, you can use DBM databases as long as a version of Perl exists for your computer. SDBM was written to match the functions provided with NDBM, so portability of code shouldn't be a problem. Perl is available on just about all popular platforms.

- **GDBM**—GDBM is the GNU version of the DBM family of database routines.

  GDBM also enables you to cache data, reducing the time that it takes to write to the database. The database has no size limit; its size depends completely on your system's resources. GDBM database files have the extension `.Db`. Unlike DBM and NDBM, both of which use two files, GDBM uses only one file.
- **Berkeley db**—The Berkeley db expands on the original DBM routines significantly. The Berkeley db uses hashed tables the same as the other DBM databases, but the library also can create databases based on a sorted balanced binary tree (`BTREE`) and store information with a record line number (`RECNO`). The method that you use depends completely on how you want to store and retrieve the information from a database. Berkeley db creates only one file, which has no extension.

If you can't find a particular DBM database on your system, search the Web for DBM databases.

Writing to a DBM Database

Perl provides the capability to work with a DBM database as if it were an associative array. This enables you to manipulate a DBM database using Perl with very little difficulty. Library files for C exist for using DBM databases as well, making a DBM database with C simplistic (see the UNIX db man page). Unfortunately, the "how-to" of using DBM databases isn't well documented, and trying to figure out how to use DBM databases can be a daunting task.

In actuality, using DBM databases is simple and much easier than using flat file databases. Adding an entry, for example, requires only a couple of lines in Perl. Perl provides various modules, depending on which DBM database you are using, including one called `AnyDBM_File.pm`, which covers all the common DBM databases. The full documentation on `AnyDBM` can be found at

`http://www.perl.com/CPAN-local/doc/manual/html/lib/AnyDBM_File.html`

DBM databases store information using a key and a value. The contents of each key cannot be repeated, although the value can. Therefore, treat the contents of each key the same. Because the key cannot be duplicated, you want to figure out which information that you want to store would be unique. For a simple phone book, the email address would make a good unique identifier because some names are common (look in your local phone book and see how many occurrences of "James Smith" you find).

For the value, you can store either one field or multiple fields using a delimiter, such as those used when accessing a flat file database. Using the email address as the key, you could store the name, work phone, and home phone in the value. The following is an example:

```
use AnyDBM_File;
$database=tie(%db, 'NDBM_File', "database", O_RDWR|O_CREAT, 0666);
$db{'jdoe@yourcompany.com'} = "Jane Doe,555-5555,555-6666";
untie %db;
undef $database;
```

As you can see, the key contains an email address, and the value contains the name and phone numbers—using a comma to delimit the record. With these few lines, the DBM database now contains a new entry.

Reading from a DBM Database

To retrieve information from a database, all you have to do is create a loop that reads the contents of the database and separates the value of each key at the colon. In your script, the following starts the loop that accomplishes this:

```
while (($key,$value)= each(%db)) {
```

Within the loop, the value of each key is split and assigned to the array `part`. When that is done, you can format the result in any manner you choose. In Listing 31.3, you will see the name to be printed as part of a `mailto:` anchor, using each entry's email address if it was entered.

Listing 31.3 Reading Records and Displaying Content from a DBM Database

```
use AnyDBM_File;
$database=tie(%db, 'NDBM_File', "database", O_RDWR|O_CREAT, 0666);
while (($key,$value)= each(%db)) {
  ($name, $work_phone, $home_phone) = split(/,/, $value);
  print "Name: $name\n";
  print "Email: $key\n";
  print "Work Phone: $work_phone\n";
  print "Home Phone: $home_phone\n";
}
untie %db;
undef $database;
```

You could print out only those entries matching a query by matching a query against the value of each record. Also, if you know the email address you are looking for, you can retrieve the associated information by reading only that record (see Listing 31.4).

Listing 31.4 Accessing a Specific Record Without Reading the Whole Database

```
use AnyDBM_File;
$database=tie(%db, 'NDBM_File', "database", O_RDWR|O_CREAT, 0666);
if ($db{'jdoe@yourcompany.com'}) {
  $value = $db{'jdoe@yourcompany.com'};
  ($name, $work_phone, $home_phone) = split(/,/, $value);
  print "Name: $name\n";
  print "Email: jdoe@yourcompany.com\n";
  print "Work Phone: $work_phone\n";
```

Listing 31.4 Continued

```
  print "Home Phone: $home_phone\n";
}
untie %db;
undef $database;
```

Searching a DBM Database

If your database starts to get large, it's convenient to provide a means by which visitors to your site can search for a specific keyword. Performing a search works much the same as displaying the whole database, except that rather than immediately displaying each entry, you check it first to see whether it matches the keyword entered by the visitor. If the keyword matches the key, you print the line; otherwise, you skip ahead and check the next entry (see Listing 31.5).

Listing 31.5 Matching Fields and Queries Limits Information Returned to the Visitor

```
$database=tie(%db, 'NDBM_File', "database", O_READ, 0660);
while (($key,$value)= each(%db)) {
  if ($key =~ /$query/i) {
    ($name, $work_phone, $home_phone) = split(/,/, $value);
    print "Name: $name\n";
    print "Email: $email\n";
    print "Work Phone: $work_phone\n";
    print "Home Phone: $home_phone\n";
  }
}
```

Now that you have seen how DBM databases work, you can take the same concepts from these scripts and apply them to something different. You could use them in a bookmark's script for example, in which you can store information for all your favorite Web sites or in a proper address book that stores the names, addresses, and phone numbers of all your customers. You can also create a database that stores names and email addresses and use it as a mailing list, providing friends and customers news about you or your organization.

Relational Databases

Most relational database servers consist of a set of programs that manage large amounts of data, offering a rich set of query commands that help manage the power behind the database server. These programs control the storage, retrieval, and organization of the information within the database. This information can be changed, updated, or removed after the support programs or scripts are in place.

Unlike DBM databases, relational databases don't link records together physically like the DBM database does by using a key/value pair. Instead, they provide a field in which information can be matched, and the results can be sent back to the person performing the query, as if the database were organized that way.

Relational databases store information in tables. A table is similar to a smaller database that sits inside the main database. Each table can usually be linked with the information in other tables to provide a result to a query. Figure 31.1 illustrates how this information could be tied together.

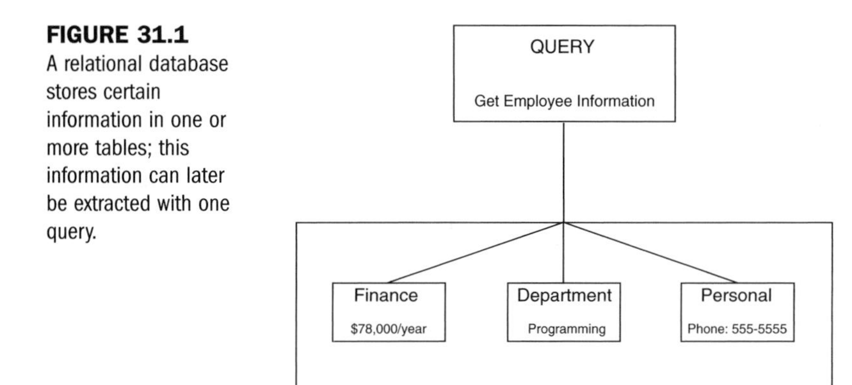

FIGURE 31.1
A relational database stores certain information in one or more tables; this information can later be extracted with one query.

Figure 31.1 depicts a query that requests employee information from a database. To get a complete response, information is retrieved from three tables, each of which stores only parts of the information requested. In the figure, information about the person's pay rate is retrieved, and departmental information and personal information are retrieved from other tables. This can produce a complete query response with an abundant amount of information on an individual.

Introduction to Database Design

Relational databases consist of tables, which then break down into records (looking horizontally across the table) and fields (looking vertically down the table). The tables hold all information that is stored in the database, and each table contains one or more records. A record contains one or more fields, grouping the fields for a specific entry. A field is given a specific data type, which specifies what kind of information is to be stored in that field. For example, a field might contain a date, a number, a set of characters, and so on.

NOTE Tables are formally called *relations*, records are called *tuples*, and fields are called *attributes*. More often, you will hear a record being called a row and a field being called a column. The rows and columns seem to be the most used when talking among database developers. ■

As stated, each table consists of columns and rows. The columns identify the data by a name, and the rows store information relevant to that name. Take a look at the following example:

Name	Extension	Email
Jane Doe	8756	`jdoe@yourcompany.com`
Fred Smith	4683	`fsmith@yourcompany.com`

The column heads give a name to each item below them. Information within a table is stored in much the same way.

If you add more tables to the database, you could have something that looks like the following:

Name	PayRate
Jane Doe	$3,500/month
Fred Smith	$2,800/month

You could have department information as well:

Name	Department	Tardy Record
Jane Doe	IT	1
Fred Smith	Personnel	3

With this information, you can perform a query to get a complete look at an individual.

When designing a database, you need to decide which tables you require and which data each table will contain. You also need to decide how each table will work with other tables.

You need to decide which bits (*entities*) of information you want to store and how this information is related to other entities. The usual technique, when designing a database, is to draw a graphical display of the database. This drawing is called an Entity-Relationship (E-R) diagram. In Figure 31.2, you can see that each box corresponds to a table. Each line in the box represents a specific field. When required, each box is connected to another where an entity is related to an entity in another table.

The purpose of having relational databases is to limit the amount of repetitive information contained in the database. After someone's address is entered in one table, for example, you should never have to provide an address in any other table.

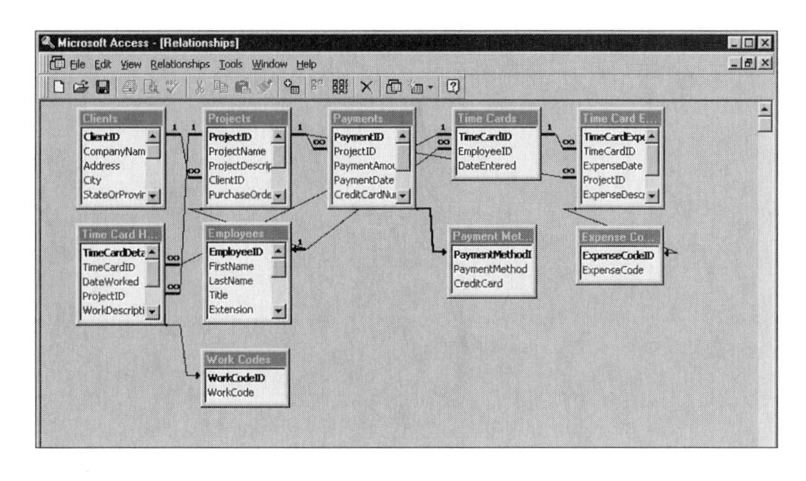

FIGURE 31.2
An E-R diagram shows how the information in various tables is to be related.

Making SQL Queries

Structured Query Language (SQL) is a language that provides a user interface to relational database management systems (RDBMS). Originally developed by IBM in the 1970s, SQL is the de facto standard for storing and retrieving information for relational databases, as well as being an ISO and ANSI standard. SQL's purpose is to provide a language, easily understandable by humans, that interfaces with relational databases.

When adding, removing, and retrieving information from SQL databases, you perform what is called a *query*. A query is a command that is sent to the database, telling the database engine what to do to manipulate the contents of a database.

One example of a query is provided here using the `select` command. The `select` command enables you to specifically define which information you want retrieved from the database. You can be as broad or as specific as you want when retrieving information from the database.

```
select * from personal where Name='Jane Doe'
```

This would pull up all information on Jane Doe from the table named personal. You could even be more specific, pulling only certain parts from each table:

```
select finance.Name, department.Name, department.Tardy
       from department,finance
       where deaprtment.Tardy > 5 AND finance.Name = department.Name
```

Many commands are used to query a database, providing you with quite a bit of power when working with a relational database. Most relational-database servers use basic commands such as `select`, but there are minor differences. It is best to check the documentation provided with your database-management system for a complete list of commands and the proper syntax for each command.

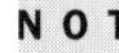

NOTE You can teach yourself the basics of ANSI SQL using the tutorial found at `http://w3.one.net/~jhoffman/sqltut.htm`. ■

Debugging Database Applications

One of the biggest problems when dealing with databases on the Web is trying to fix any problems that might occur when you are writing your script. You can have problems because of a bug in your script or because of an improper query.

The best way to see whether the problem lies within your script is to create a copy of the script that includes dummy variables—variables that contain information as if a visitor actually entered something into a form. Using the previous scripts, for example, you can create a set of variables that mimics information that a visitor might have entered:

```
$contents{'fname'} = "John";
$contents{'lname'} = "Doe";
```

After you have the dummy variables set, you can execute your script using the command line

```
% /usr/bin/perl phone.pl
```

Perl reports any problems with your script if you have programmed any code improperly.

To figure out what might be wrong with your SQL query, you can usually use the console interface provided with your database server. If you construct the query with the console interface and everything works fine, then look at your script and see if an error can be produced there.

TIP Last, try to keep things simple and build up from what you know works. At first, create a script that contains the query you need to perform, making sure that you use the `Content-type: text/plain`. This will enable you to make sure that your script is providing a proper query. If all goes well, access your database using the same query from the command line. If the query produces the proper results, you can move on and try to access your script through the Web server. If you are having problems here, make sure that you have specified the `Content-type` before anything is sent out to the server. This is probably one of the biggest problems with any script. An error occurs and your script sends information back to the Web server without specifying the `Content-type`.

Database Considerations

It is an appealing idea to take information that is stored in your database and allow those visiting your site to access it. Not only can it save you the time of reentering all that data to create an XHTML document, but it also can enable you to use your database to create Web pages that change the moment the information in your database changes.

Integrating your existing databases with the Web enables you to create Internet and intranet applications that can be beneficial to the customers visiting your site and to those within your organization who need up-to-date information.

For customers, a database enables them to place orders and purchase goods that you have for sale. Most businesses take customer information and store that information in a database whenever an order is placed. This enables you to keep track of who ordered what, when items were shipped, how much and by what method they paid, as well as the personal information used to ship each item.

The old method of purchasing goods on the Web was to take an order through a form and then email the order to the appropriate person. This person would enter the customer and order information into the database, and at that point any online order would be processed as expected.

Integrating your database with the Web removes the "middle man." Each order can be placed in the database and processed from that point, lessening the chances of lost paperwork or misdirected email.

You can use the information that already exists in your databases to create up-to-date Web documents. These documents can be used to provide a product listing in which visitors can select the items they want to purchase. The information in your databases can also be used to provide support.

For intranet purposes, you can provide your employees with information no matter where they are or what platform they are using. Many businesses have employees working in the field who need to quickly access company information. Direct access to a database of information enables your employees to be more efficient. Providing information via the Web even enables access to a database that wouldn't normally be accessible over a network. Accessing a database also eliminates the need for specific (often custom) client software that must be installed and maintained on the PC of everyone who's going to access the database.

All the databases and database tools described in the balance of this chapter can be used for these purposes, although some are better suited for a particular task than others.

Which database is best suited for your needs depends on how much you are willing to pay for a database and the tools needed to create dynamic Web pages. How much horsepower you are going to need to serve your customers will also have to be considered:

- The smaller databases available, such as Access and mSQL, work well and are within the budget of most small businesses. Even so, they wouldn't be able to handle one hundred thousand or more queries a day.
- Database engines such as SQL Server, Oracle, and Sybase are better suited for larger companies and those companies that receive a large number of queries each day. At the same time, these database systems would be overkill for a business that sells only a handful of goods and that receives a few hundred queries a day.

You often must consider the database a company is already using. Many companies have spent a lot of time training their employees to use a particular database, or they have spent a lot of money on a database that has worked well for them for years. At times, you will have to convince a company to change its database to something more Web worthy. First, you need to find out whether tools exist that can help a company use its existing database and whether the database it currently has is well within the bounds of the company's particular needs.

Not too long ago, it was difficult to create Web pages based on information from a database. Now, so much support is available that trying to figure out which way to go can be an intimidating task. The rest of this chapter briefly covers the favorite databases available and the gateways used to access and place that information on the Web.

Databases Available

In this section, you take a quick look at the most commonly used databases on the Web and where you can look for further information and support.

Oracle

Oracle is one of the largest database developers in the world. Oracle provides databases for Windows NT and various flavors of UNIX and has created its own set of tools called the Oracle Web Developer Suite. This suite integrates the Oracle8 Server, Oracle WebServer, Designer/2000, and the Developer/2000 kit, along with additional kits. With the Web Developer Suite, you can get your database information on the Web in minutes using a graphical point-and-click environment. With some additional time, you can make your Web site more interactive, storing and retrieving information with the Oracle database. A storefront, where you can sell goods or provide up-to-date product support, makes good use of the Oracle Web Developer Suite.

For more information on Oracle and how you can use Oracle with the World Wide Web, visit `http://www.oracle.com/tools/webdb/`.

Sybase

Sybase's Enterprise Application Server is the cornerstone of its Internet products. Provided with the Enterprise Application Server are tools that can be used to produce dynamic Web pages from the information data in your database. Sybase's newest product to help build Web applications is called PowerDesigner.

Enterprise Application Server allows you to develop Web applications in PowerBuilder. With PowerBuilder, you can create programs that easily integrate with the database, enabling those new to the environment to perform advanced queries. To learn more about how you can use Sybase and its supporting tools to Web-enable your data, direct your browser to `http://www.sybase.com/products/internet/`.

mSQL

mSQL (short for "mini-SQL") is a mid-sized relational database server for UNIX; it is much more affordable than the commercial relational database servers available on the market. Written by David Hughes, it was created to enable users to experiment with SQL queries and relational databases. It is free for noncommercial use (nonprofit, schools, and research organizations); for individual and commercial use, there is a modest fee per server. To get information on the current release and pricing of mSQL, consult the following URL: `http://www.Hughes.com.au/`.

Informix

Informix has grown up quite a bit. Originally called Illustra, Informix has been completely revamped and now has several complementary tools to help with the design and integration of database information with the Web environment. Currently, the Informix Internet Foundation.2000 is Informix's flagship Internet product offering.

To learn more about Informix and its product offerings, visit the Informix Web site at `http://www.informix.com/`.

Microsoft SQL Server

Microsoft released its own relational database server as a part of its BackOffice suite. Microsoft is trying to compete heavily with Oracle and Sybase by providing its own set of development tools and products to get database-driven information on the Web.

Microsoft SQL Server works well with any Web development tool that complies with Microsoft's ODBC standard. Even so, Microsoft has been working hard to tie SQL Server, Microsoft Internet Information Server, and Microsoft Internet Explorer together to provide one environment for those providing Web content and those who come to your site. Active Server Page scripts provide a simple way to pose queries to your SQL Server database and incorporate the results into a dynamically generated Web page.

You can learn all about Microsoft's most recent release of SQL Server (SQL Server 2000) at `http://www.microsoft.com/sql/`.

NOTE SQL Server 2000, in beta 2 at the time of this writing, should be in its release version in the last quarter of 2000. ■

FoxPro

Microsoft's Visual FoxPro has been a favorite for Web programmers, mostly because of its long time in the database community and its third-party support. FoxPro, available for MS-DOS, Macintosh, and some flavors of UNIX, is an Xbase database system that is widely used for smaller business and personal database applications. To find out more about FoxPro, direct your browser to `http://msdn.microsoft.com/vfoxpro/?RLD=196`.

Microsoft Access

Microsoft Access is a relational database management system that is part of the Microsoft Office suite. Access is frequently used as a server-side Web database because so many people develop databases in Access on their desktops and then want to Web-enable those databases. Access performs well on the Web up to a point, but after you have a threshold number of records in the database or too many concurrent users trying to hit your database, things will break down and you should consider upgrading to SQL Server. However, for small, read-only databases, Access does just fine as a server-side database format.

The Microsoft Access home page at `http://www.microsoft.com/office/access/default.htm` can provide you with a complete description of the capabilities of Access both on and off the Web.

MySQL

Developed by T.c.X, MySQL (pronounced My Ess Que Ell) was created to handle large amounts of data. MySQL provides a robust SQL engine comparable to the major commercial database servers. MySQL is a moderately priced platform (around $170) that can be accessed using Perl, ODBC, C, and Tcl. It enables you to provide database-generated Web content. For more information, visit `http://www.mysql.com/`.

Database Tools

Now that you have taken a look at the various databases available, it's time to take a look at the third-party tools that help you create applications to tie your databases to the Web.

Some of the tools work with only one specific database; other tools work with a couple of different databases; and some tools work with most databases available. Which tool you use depends on several factors:

- *Which database are you using?* Strange as it might seem, companies sometimes purchase a development tool that is not compatible with their existing database format. Most of the time, they purchased a particular tool because they liked that tool's features or ease of use. They didn't realize that some of the tools work with specific databases. You will want to know which tools work with each particular database. MsqlPerl doesn't work at all with Microsoft Access, for example, and Oracle can't be used with web.sql.
- *Which platform are your database and Web servers running on?* On Windows NT, you have the capability to use the ODBC driver to access a database, making programming Web/database applications easier. This doesn't help much, however, if your company's relational database server is on a UNIX machine. If you are programming the database application on a UNIX machine, it doesn't help if the database server is on a Windows NT box. How you go about programming your database application depends on what platform your Web server is running on, what platform your database is on, and what tools you have at your disposal.
- *How do you want to access a database (using CGI or a proprietary API)?* Portability used to be the biggest concern when constructing a database application for the Web. Now it isn't. Because of the ease of use with most proprietary APIs, they have become commonplace but might create problems if the technology changes drastically in the future. Web database tools such as ColdFusion Studio (see Figure 31.3) or Microsoft Visual Interdev provide a bit more flexibility when porting scripts or applications to be used with different databases. Other tools are limited and restrictive.

FIGURE 31.3
ColdFusion Studio supports the development of any text-based file including HTML, JavaScript, Cascading Style Sheets, Active Server Pages, and ColdFusion templates.

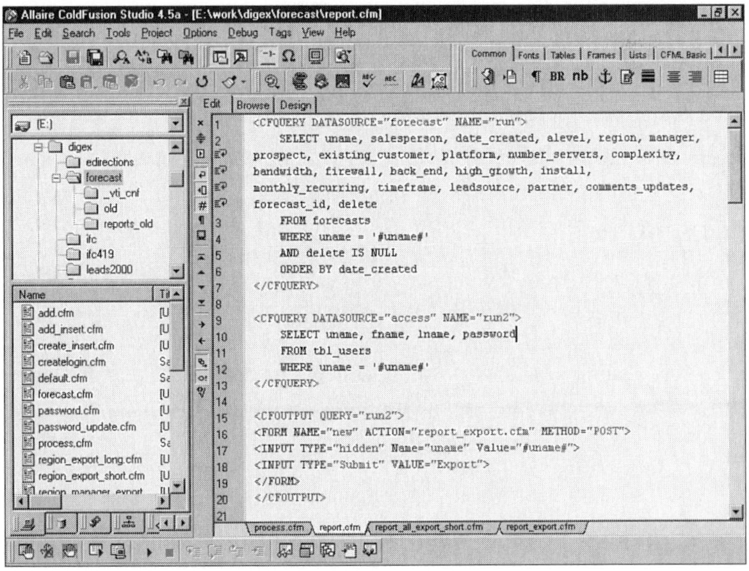

- *How much money is your company willing to spend?* This might not be a major consideration for most larger companies, but smaller businesses must watch their IT budgets closely. If you weigh the tools available with how much money a company is willing to spend, you will most likely be able to create a rock-solid application for even the most frugal company.

With these ideas in mind, take a look at the tools available, as described in the next sections, and see which Web database tool will suit your needs.

PHP

PHP (originally called PHP/FI) was developed by Rasmus Lerdorf, who needed to create a script that enabled him to log visitors to his page. The script replaced a few other smaller ones that were creating a load on Lerdorf's system. This script became PHP, which is an acronym for Lerdorf's Personal Home Page tools. Lerdorf later wrote a script that enabled him to embed commands within an XHTML document to access a relational database. PHP grew into a small language that enables developers to embed commands within their XHTML pages instead of running multiple smaller scripts to do the same thing. PHP is actually a CGI program written in C that can be compiled to work on any UNIX or Windows NT system. The embedded commands are parsed by the PHP script, which then prints the results through another XHTML document. PHP is browser-independent because the script is processed through the PHP executable that is on the server. For those using Apache, a module is provided that enables you to parse PHP embedded XHTML files without having to directly call the PHP parser.

PHP can be used to integrate MySQL along with Oracle, Sybase, mSQL, and any database using ODBC on Windows NT to dynamically create XHTML documents. It's fairly easy to use and quite versatile. A full set of documentation can be found on the PHP Web site at `http://www.php.net/`.

▶ To learn the basics of authoring PHP scripts, **see** Chapter 34, "Using PHP"

ColdFusion

Allaire created ColdFusion as a system that enables you to embed scripts within an XHTML document. The ColdFusion Application Server processes the scripts and then returns the information within the XHTML template the scripted instructions were embedded in. Allaire wrote ColdFusion to work with just about every Web server available for Windows NT, Solaris, and Linux and to integrate with just about every ODBC-compliant relational database engine.

The ColdFusion 4.5 release is a full-blown application development environment that enables you to communicate with many available network services including mail, FTP, HTTP, directory, and file servers. The ColdFusion Markup Language (CFML) has more than 80 basic instructions and more than 200 built-in functions to aid you in your development.

▶ For more information on developing ColdFusion applications, **see** Chapter 33, "Using ColdFusion"

W3-mSQL

W3-mSQL was created by David Hughes, the creator of mSQL, to simplify accessing an mSQL database from within your Web pages. It works as a CGI script that parses your Web pages. The script reads your document, performs any queries required, and sends the result back out to the server to the visitor. W3-mSQL is much like PHP/FI but on a smaller scale. W3-mSQL makes it easy for you to create Web documents that contain information based on what is in your database.

To learn more about W3-mSQL, consult David Hughes' Web site at `http://www.hughes.com.au/`.

Microsoft's Active Server Pages

Active Server Pages (ASP) enable you to produce dynamic content with the use of ActiveX on the server (MS Internet Information Server). Commonly, VBScript is used to write ASP applications, but JScript and Perl are also used. Using VBScript, you can easily write applications that access a database, enabling you to provide dynamic content based on the information in the database.

▶ For more information, **see** Chapter 32, "Writing Active Server Pages"

CHAPTER 32

Writing Active Server Pages

by Joe O'Donnell and Eric Ladd

In this chapter

Introduction to VBScript

When deploying a Web site with Microsoft's Internet Information Server (IIS), it is convenient to use Active Server Pages (ASPs) to dynamically generate content, rather than keeping it all in static files. ASPs are XHTML templates that have server-side scripts built into them. These scripts are parsed out and executed by the IIS server, and the scripts' output very often produces the dynamic content.

IIS supports a server-side object model that makes writing ASPs a relatively straightforward task. However, to manipulate these server-side objects, you must use an object-oriented scripting language. IIS supports scripts written in both JScript (Microsoft's variant of ECMAScript) and VBScript. VBScript tends to be easier to learn and frees up the beginner from some of the syntactic burden that comes along with JScript. Thus, this chapter first focuses on the basics of VBScript and then goes on to show you how to write Active Server Pages using VBScript.

Like JavaScript, Microsoft's Visual Basic Scripting Edition (VBScript) enables you to embed commands into an XHTML document. When a user of a compatible Web browser (primarily Internet Explorer) downloads your page, your VBScript commands are loaded by the Web browser along with the rest of the document and are run in response to any of a series of events. Again, like JavaScript, VBScript is an *interpreted* language; Internet Explorer interprets the VBScript commands when they are loaded and run. They do not first need to be *compiled* into executable form by the Web author who uses them.

VBScript is a fast and flexible subset of Microsoft's Visual Basic and Visual Basic for Applications languages, and is designed to be easy to program in and quick in adding active content to XHTML documents. The language elements are mainly ones that should be familiar to anyone who has programmed in just about any language: `If...Then...Else` blocks and `Do`, `While`, and `For...Next` loops, and a typical assortment of operators and built-in functions. The first half of this chapter takes you to the heart of the VBScript language and shows you examples of how to use it to add interaction and increased functionality to your Web pages. Then, in the second part of the chapter, you'll learn how to use VBScript on the server side to create applications using Active Server Pages.

VBScript Identifiers

An *identifier* is a unique name that VBScript uses to identify a variable, method, or object in your program. As with other programming languages, VBScript imposes some rules on what names you can use. All VBScript names must start with an alphabetic character, and they can contain both uppercase and lowercase letters and the digits 0 through 9. They can be as long as 255 characters, although you probably don't want to go much more than 32 or so for readability's sake.

Unlike JavaScript, which supports two ways for you to represent values in your scripts (literals and variables), VBScript has only variables. The difference in VBScript, therefore, is one of usage. If you want to use a constant value in your VBScript programs, set a variable equal to a value and don't change it. This discussion continues to refer to literals and variables as distinct entities, although they are interchangeable.

Literals and variables in VBScript are all of type `variant`, which means that they can contain any type of data that VBScript supports. It is usually a good idea to use a given variable for one type and explicitly convert its value to another type as necessary. The following are some of the types of data that VBScript supports:

- **Integers**—These types can be 1, 2, or 4 bytes in length, depending on how big they are.
- **Floating point**—VBScript supports single- and double-precision floating point numbers.
- **Strings**—Strings can represent words, phrases, or data, and they are set off by double quotation marks.
- **Booleans**—Booleans have a value of either `True` or `False`.
- **Objects**—A VBScript variable can refer to any object within its environment.

Objects, Properties, Methods, and Events in VBScript

Before you proceed further, you should take some time to review some terminology. VBScript follows much the same object model and uses many of the same terms as JavaScript. In VBScript, as in JavaScript—and in any object-oriented language, for that matter—an *object* is a collection of data and functions that have been grouped together. An object's data is known as its *properties*, and its functions are known as its *methods*. An *event* is a condition to which an object can respond, such as a mouse click or other user input. The VBScript programs that you write use properties and methods of objects, both those that you create and those objects provided by the Web browser, its plug-ins, ActiveX controls, Java applets, and so on.

TIP The following is a simple guideline: An object's properties are the information that it knows; its methods are how it can act on that information; and events are what it responds to.

NOTE A very important–and a little confusing–thing to remember is that an object's methods are *also* properties of that object. An object's properties are the information that it knows. The object certainly knows about its own methods, so those methods are properties of the object right along with its other data.

Using Built-In Objects and Functions

Individual VBScript elements are objects. Literals and variables are objects of type `variant`, which can be used to hold data of many types. These objects also have associated methods—ways of acting on the different data types. VBScript also enables you to access a set of useful objects that represent the Web browser, the currently displayed page, and other elements of the browsing session.

You access objects by specifying their names. The active document object, for example, is named `document`. To use `document`'s properties or methods, you add a period (.) and the name of the method or property that you want. For example, `document.title` is the `title` property of the `document` object.

Using Properties

Every object has properties, even literals. To access a property, use the object name followed by a period and the property name. To get the length of a string object named `address`, you can write the following:

```
address.length
```

You get back an integer that equals the number of characters in the string. If the object that you are using has properties that can be modified, you can change them in the same way. To set the `color` property of a house object, just write the following:

```
house.color = "blue"
```

You can also create new properties for an object by naming them. Assume, for example, that you define a class called `customer` for one of your pages. You can add new properties to the `customer` object as follows:

```
customer.name = "Jim O'Donnell"
customer.address = "1757 P Street NW"
customer.zip = "20036-1303"
```

Because an object's methods are properties, you can easily add new properties to an object by writing your own function and creating a new object property using your own function name. If you want to add a `Bill` method to your `customer` object, you can write a function named `BillCustomer` and set the object's property as follows:

```
customer.Bill = BillCustomer;
```

To call the new method, you write the following:

```
customer.Bill()
```

VBScript Language Elements

Although VBScript is not as flexible as C++ or Visual Basic, it is quick and simple. Because it is easily embedded in your Web pages, adding interactivity or increased functionality with a

VBScript is easy—a lot easier than writing a Java applet to do the same thing. (Although, to be fair, you *can* do a lot more with Java applets.) This section covers some of the nuts and bolts of VBScript programming.

A full language reference for VBScript, as well as Microsoft's tutorial for VBScript programming, can be found at the Microsoft Windows Script Technologies Web site at `http://msdn.microsoft.com/scripting/` (see Figure 32.1).

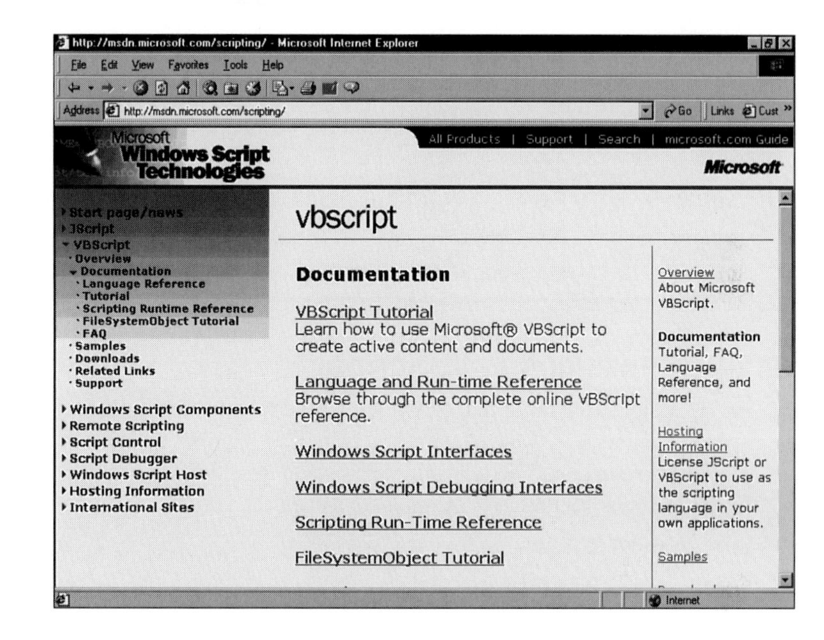

FIGURE 32.1
Consider bookmarking Microsoft's online documentation for the VBScript language.

VBScript Variables

All VBScript variables are of the type `variant`, which means that they can be used for any of the supported data types. Table 32.1 summarizes the types of data that VBScript variables can hold.

Table 32.1 Data Types That VBScript Variables Can Contain

Type	Description
empty	Uninitialized; is treated as 0 or the empty string, depending on the context
null	Intentionally contains no valid data
Boolean	`True` or `False`
byte	Integer in the range –128 to 127
integer	Integer in the range –32,768 to 32,767

Table 32.1 Continued

Type	Description
long	Integer in the range –2,147,483,648 to 2,147,483,647
single	Single-precision floating point number in the range –3.402823E38 to –1.401298E-45 for negative values, and 1.401298E-45 to 3.402823E38 for positive values
double	Double-precision floating point number in the range –1.79769313486232E308 to –4.94065645841247E-324 for negative values, and 4.94065645841247E-324 to 1.79769313486232E308 for positive values
date	Number that represents a date between January 1, 100, to December 31, 9999
string	Variable-length string up to approximately two billion characters in length
object	Any object
error	Error number

Forming Expressions in VBScript

An *expression* is anything that can be evaluated to get a single value. Expressions can contain string or numeric variables, operators, and other expressions, and they can range from simple to quite complex. The following expression uses the assignment operator (more on operators in the next section), for example, to assign the result `3.14159` to the variable `pi`:

```
pi = 3.14159
```

By contrast, the following is a more complex expression whose final value depends on the values of the two Boolean variables `Quit` and `Complete`:

```
(Quit = True) And (Complete = False)
```

Using VBScript Operators

Operators do just what their name suggests: They operate on variables or literals. The items that an operator acts on are called its *operands*. Operators come in the following two types:

- **Unary**—These operators require only one operand, and the operator can come before or after the operand. The `Not` operator, which performs the logical negation of an expression, is a good example.
- **Binary**—These operators need two operands. The four math operators (+ for addition, - for subtraction, ? for multiplication, and / for division) are all binary operators, as is the = assignment operator that you saw earlier.

Assignment Operators Assignment operators take the result of an expression and assign it to a variable. One feature that VBScript has that most other programming languages do not is the capability to change a variable's type on the fly. It is possible to use the same variable for string and numerical values within the same script. In most other languages, this would cause a runtime error; because VBScript variables can be any type, however, it is possible.

The assignment operator, `=`, assigns the value of an expression's right side to its left side. In the preceding example, the variable `pi` gets the floating point value `3.14159` or the Boolean value `False` after the expression is evaluated.

Math Operators The previous sections gave you a sneak preview of the math operators that VBScript furnishes. As you might expect, the standard four math functions (addition, subtraction, multiplication, and division) work the same as they do on an ordinary calculator and use the symbols `+`, `-`, `?`, and `/`.

VBScript supplies three other math operators:

- `\`—The backslash operator divides its first operand by its second, after first rounding floating-point operands to the nearest integer; it returns the integer part of the result. For example, `19 \ 6.7` returns `2` (6.7 rounds to 7, 19 divided by 7 is a little over 2.71, the integer part of which is 2).
- `Mod`—This operator is similar to `\` in that it divides the first operand by its second, again after rounding floating-point operands to the nearest integer; it returns the integer remainder. Therefore, `19 Mod 6.7` returns `5`.
- `^`—This exponent operator returns the first operand raised to the power of the second. The first operand can be negative only if the second, the exponent, is an integer.

Comparison Operators Comparing the value of two expressions to see whether one is larger, smaller, or equal to another is often necessary. VBScript supplies several comparison operators that take two operands and return `True` if the comparison is true and `False` if it is not. Table 32.2 shows the VBScript comparison operators.

Table 32.2 VBScript Comparison Operators

Operator	Read It As	Returns True When
=	equals	The two operands are equal.
<>	does not equal	The two operands are unequal.
<	less than	The left operand is less than the right operand.
<=	less than or equal to	The left operand is less than or equal to the right operand.
>	greater than	The left operand is greater than the right operand.
>=	greater than or equal to	The left operand is greater than or equal to the right operand.

You can also use the comparison operators on strings; the results depend on standard lexicographic ordering (ordering by the ASCII values of the string characters).

Thinking of the comparison operators as questions may be helpful. When you write this, you are really saying, "Is the value of variable x greater than or equal to 10?":

```
(x >= 10)
```

The return value answers the question True or False.

Logical Operators Comparison operators compare quantity or content for numeric and string expressions, but sometimes you need to test a logical value—whether a comparison operator returns True or False, for example. VBScript's logical operators enable you to compare expressions that return logical values. The following are VBScript's logical operators:

- **And**—The And operator returns True if both its input expressions are true. If the first operand evaluates to False, And returns False immediately, without evaluating the second operand. The following is an example:

```
x = True And True       ' x is True
x = True And False      ' x is False
x = False And True      ' x is False
x = False And False     ' x is False
```

- **Or**—This operator returns True if either of its operands is true. If the first operand is true, || returns True without evaluating the second operand. The following is an example:

```
x = True Or True        ' x is True
x = True Or False       ' x is True
x = False Or True       ' x is True
x = False Or False      ' x is False
```

- **Not**—This operator takes only one expression and returns the opposite of that expression. Thus, Not True returns False, and Not False returns True.
- **Xor**—This operator, which stands for "exclusive or," returns True if either, but not both, of its input expressions is True, as in the following:

```
x = True Xor True       ' x is False
x = True Xor False      ' x is True
x = False Xor True      ' x is True
x = False Xor False     ' x is False
```

- **Eqv**—This operator, which stands for "equivalent," returns True if its two input expressions are the same—either both True or both False. The statement x Eqv y is equivalent to Not (x Xor y).

- `Imp`—This operator, which stands for "implication," returns `True` according to the following:

```
x = True Imp True      ' x is True
x = False Imp True     ' x is True
x = True Imp False     ' x is False
x = False Imp False    ' x is True
```

NOTE Note that the logical implication operator `Imp` is the only logical operator for which the order of the operands is important.

Note that the `And` and `Or` operators don't evaluate the second operand if the first operand provides enough information for the operator to return a value. This process, called *short-circuit evaluation*, can be significant when the second operand is a function call.

NOTE Note that all six of the logical operators can also operate on non-Boolean expressions. In this case, the logical operations described previously are performed bitwise, on each bit of the two operands. Consider this example of the two integers 19 (00010011 in binary) and 6 (00000110):

```
19 And 6 =   2 (00000010 in binary)
19 Or 6  =  23 (00010111 in binary)
Not 19   = -20 (11101100 in binary)
```


String Concatenation The final VBScript operator is the string concatenation operator `&`. Although you can also use the addition operator `+` to concatenate strings (returning a string made up of the original strings joined together), using `&` is preferred because it is less ambiguous.

Testing Conditions in VBScript

VBScript provides one control structure for making decisions—the `If...Then...Else` structure. To make a decision, you supply one or more expressions that evaluate to `True` or `False`. Which code is executed depends on what your expressions evaluate to.

The simplest form of `If...Then...Else` uses only the `If...Then` part. If the specified condition is `true`, the code following the condition is executed; if not, that code is skipped. In the following code fragment, for example, the message appears only if the variable `x` is less than `pi`:

```
If (x < pi) Then document.write("x is less than pi")
```

You can use any expression as the condition. Because you can nest and combine expressions with the logical operators, your tests can be pretty sophisticated. Also, using the multiple statement character, you can execute multiple commands, as in the following:

```
If ((test = True) And (x > max)) Then max = x : test = False
```

The `Else` clause enables you to specify a set of statements to execute when the condition is false. In the same single-line form shown in the preceding line, your new line appears as follows:

```
If (x > pi) Then test = True Else test = False
```

A more versatile use of the `If...Then...Else` allows multiple lines and multiple actions for each case. It looks something like the following:

```
If (x > pi) Then
    test = True
    count = count + 1
Else
    test = False
    count = 0
End If
```

Note that with this syntax, additional test clauses using the `ElseIf` statement are permitted. For example, you could add one more clause to the preceding example:

```
If (x > pi) Then
    test = True
    count = count + 1
ElseIf (x < -pi) Then
    test = True
    count = count - 1
Else
    test = False
    count = 0
End If
```

Executing VBScript Loops

If you want to repeat an action more than one time, VBScript provides a variety of constructs for doing so. The first, called a `For...Next` loop, executes a set of statements some number of times. You specify three expressions: an *initial* expression, which sets the values of any variables that you need to use; a *final value*, which tells the loop how to see when it is done; and an *increment* expression, which modifies any variables that need it. The following is a simple example:

```
For count = 0 To 100 Step 2
    document.write("Count is " & CStr(count) & "<br />")
Next
```

NOTE The `Cstr` function converts a numerical value into a string.

In this example, the expressions are all simple numeric values—the initial value is `0`, the final value is `100`, and the increment is `2`. This loop executes 51 times and prints out a number each time.

The second form of loop is the `While...Wend` loop. It executes statements as long as its condition is true. You can rewrite the first `For...Next` loop, for example, as follows:

```
count = 0
While (count <= 100)
    document.write("Count is " & CStr(count) & "<br />")
    count = count + 2
Wend
```

The last type of loop is the `Do...Loop`, which has several forms that test the condition either at the beginning or at the end of the loop. The test can either be a `Do While` or `Do Until`, and can occur at the beginning or end of the loop. If a `Do While` test is done at the beginning, the loop executes as long as the test condition is true, similar to the `While...Wend` loop. The following is an example:

```
count = 0
Do While (count <= 100)
    document.write("Count is " & CStr(count) & "<br />")
    count = count + 2
Loop
```

An example of having the test at the end, as a `Do...Until`, can also yield equivalent results. In that case, the loop looks like the following:

```
count = 0
Do
    document.write("Count is " & CStr(count) & "<br />")
    count = count + 2
Loop Until (count > 100)
```


One other difference between these two forms is that when the test is at the end of the loop, as in the second case, the commands in the loop are executed at least one time. If the test is at the beginning, that is not necessarily the case.

Which form you prefer depends on what you are doing. `For...Next` loops prove useful when you want to perform an action a set number of times. Although `While...Wend` and `Do...Loop` loops can be used for the same purpose, they are best when you want to keep doing something as long as a particular condition remains true.

NOTE The `For...Next` and `Do...Loop` loops also have a way to exit the loop from inside—the `End For` and `End Do` statements, respectively. Normally, these tests would be used as part of a conditional statement, such as the following:

```
For i = 0 To 100
    x = UserFunc()
    document.write("x[" & CStr(i) & "] = " & CStr(x) & "<br />")
    If (x > max) End For
Next
```

Using Other VBScript Statements

This section provides a quick reference to some of the other VBScript statements. The following formatting is used:

- All VBScript keywords are in a `monospace` font.
- Words in *`monospace italic`* represent user-defined names or statements.
- Any portions enclosed in square brackets (`[` and `]`) are optional.
- Portions enclosed in braces (`{` and `}`) and separated by a vertical bar (`|`) represent an option, of which one must be selected.
- The word `statements...` indicates a block of one or more statements.

The *Call* Statement

The `Call` statement calls a VBScript `Sub` or `Function` procedure, as follows:

Syntax:

```
Call MyProc([arglist])
```

or

```
MyProc [arglist]
```

Note that `arglist` is a comma-delimited list of zero or more arguments to be passed to the procedure. When the second form is used, omitting the `Call` statement, the parentheses around the argument list, if any, must also be omitted.

The *Dim* Statement

The `Dim` statement is used to declare variables and also to allocate the storage necessary for them. If you specify subscripts, you can also create arrays.

Syntax:

```
Dim varname[([subscripts])][,varname[([subscripts])],...]
```

The *Set* Statement

The `Set` statement is used to create and name an object. This is particularly useful in an Active Server Page script where you frequently must create server-side objects to help you accomplish certain tasks.

Syntax:

```
Set objname = function_to_create_object
```

The *Function* and *Sub* Statements

The `Function` and `Sub` statements declare VBScript procedures. The difference is that a `Function` procedure returns a value, and a `Sub` procedure does not. All parameters are passed to functions *by value*—the function gets the value of the parameter but cannot change the original value in the caller.

Syntax:

```
[Static] Function funcname([arglist])
    statements...
    funcname = returnvalue
End
```

and

```
[Static] Sub subname([arglist])
    statements...
End
```

Variables can be declared with the `Dim` statement within a `Function` or `Sub` procedure. In this case, those variables are local to that procedure and can be referenced only within it. If the `Static` keyword is used when the procedure is declared, all local variables retain their value from one procedure call to the next.

The *On_Error* Statement

The `On Error` statement is used to enable error handling.

Syntax:

```
On Error Resume Next
```

`On Error Resume Next` enables execution to continue immediately after the statement that provokes the runtime error. Alternatively, if the error occurs in a procedure call after the last executed `On Error` statement, execution commences immediately after that procedure call. This way, execution can continue despite a runtime error, enabling you to build an error-handling routine inline within the procedure. The most recent `On Error Resume Next` statement is the one that is active, so you should execute one in each procedure in which you want to have inline error handling.

VBScript Functions

VBScript has an assortment of intrinsic functions that you can use in your scripts. The VBScript documentation on the Microsoft Web site contains a full reference for these functions. Table 32.3 shows the functions that exist for performing different types of operations. (Because you can use some functions for several types of operations, they appear multiple times in the table.)

Table 32.3 VBScript Functions

Type of Operation	Function Names
Array operations	IsArray, LBound, UBound
Conversions	Abs, Asc, AscB, AscW, Chr, ChrB, ChrW, Cbool, CByte, CDate, CDbl, CInt, CLng, CSng, Cstr, DateSerial, DateValue, Hex, Oct, Fix, Int, Sgn, TimeSerial, TimeValue
Dates and times	Date, Time, DateSerial, DateValue, Day, Month, Weekday, Year, Hour, Minute, Second, Now, TimeSerial, TimeValue
Input/output	InputBox, MsgBox
Math	Atn, Cos, Sin, Tan, Exp, Log, Sqr, Randomize, Rnd
Objects	IsObject
Strings	Asc, AscB, AscW, Chr, ChrB, ChrW, Instr, InStrB, Len, LenB, LCase, UCase, Left, LeftB, Mid, MidB, Right, RightB, Space, StrComp, String, LTrim, RTrim, Trim
Variants	IsArray, IsDate, IsEmpty, IsNull, IsNumeric, IsObject, VarType

Active Server Pages and the Active Server Platform

The Active Server Platform refers to Microsoft's take on server-side application development. As with the Active Desktop, you can author on the server side with three standard components: XHTML, scripting, and software components, such as Java applets and ActiveX server components. This enables you to leverage your client-side development skills to start building dynamic applications on your server.

In addition, you can take advantage of a number of Microsoft server technologies and services, such as Transaction Server, Merchant Server, Proxy Server, and so on, to implement specialized business solutions. Microsoft's server technology is tightly integrated with Windows NT operating system and Internet Information Server (IIS). As a result, your Active Platform solution will benefit from the operating system's services and features. Your Web application, for example, can inherit Windows NT's built-in security mechanism.

The Active Server Page (ASP) is primary means of dynamically generating Web pages on the Active Server Platform. The chief ingredients in any ASP are scripted instructions embedded in an XHTML document. When a browser requests a file containing an Active Server Page document, the server parses out and executes the scripted instructions. Any XHTML output from the script is inserted back into the document in place of the original script code. The result is a pure XHTML page that is sent back to the browser.

NOTE ASPs are not precompiled. Rather, they are interpreted when they are requested by a browser. IIS does cache interpreted ASPs so that later requests can occur more quickly.

To execute a script on the server, you must include the `runat="server"` attribute inside your `<script>` element. The code is as follows:

```
<script language="VBScript" runat="server">
...
</script>
```

`<SCRIPT>` tags without this attribute define scripts that are to run on the client side. Listing 32.1 shows some script code that will execute on the client. Notice the line of code that displays a message box. Because the script will execute on the client, displaying a message box is meaningful.

Listing 32.1 A Client-Side Script

```
<script language="VBScript">
<!--
Option Explicit

Dim validCreditCardNumber

Sub Submit_OnClick
validCreditCardNumber = True
Call CheckCreditCardNumber(CreditCardNumberField.Value,
"Please enter your credit card number.")
If validCreditCardNumber then
Msgbox "Thank you for your order"
End if
End Sub

</script>
```

If you tried to execute the same script on the server, displaying a message box would be meaningless because no user interface exists on the server. As a result, the server will bypass the line of code that displays the message box.

The server-side scripts that you embed inside XHTML code should reside in a text file with the extension `.asp`. An XHTML file is a text file that the browser can render on the client machine. The XHTML file has the extension `.htm` or `.html`. Similarly, an ASP file is a text file that the IIS will process on the server. Within an ASP file, you integrate server components through your scripted instructions. Microsoft recommends using VBScript or JScript as your default ASP scripting language.

TIP If you are an experienced C++ or Java programmer, you will find JavaScript or JScript easy to learn. If you are an experienced Visual Basic programmer, you will probably find VBScript easier to use. If you don't have experience with any of these languages, you will likely find VBScript easier to pick up than JScript.

Listing 32.2 shows an example of an ASP file done with VBScript, the scripting language discussed in the first portion of this chapter.

Listing 32.2 A Sample ASP File

```
<html>
<head>
<title>Hello World in ASP</title>
</head>
<body bgcolor="white">
<%

' ASP script begins

sub HelloWorld()
        dim Greeting
        Greeting = "Hello, World!"
        Response.Write(Greeting)
End sub

%>

<%

'Calling ASP subroutine

Call HelloWorld

%>

</body>
</html>
```

As you can see, this ASP file includes both traditional XHTML and scripted instructions. Note that all script code is enclosed within the `<% %>` containers.

You read earlier than ASPs may be written in VBScript or JScript. The essential similarity between these two languages is that both are object-oriented. You need to write ASPs in an object-oriented language because Microsoft has developed an extensive object model for the

Active Server environment. The only way to manipulate these objects is with an object-oriented language.

Some of the objects available in the Active Server environment are special-purpose objects that you create only when you need them. Others are always available during the processing of any ASP. The objects that are always available are frequently called the *intrinsic* ASP objects. The next section discusses the five intrinsic objects and tells how you use each to accomplish many basic tasks in ASP development.

Intrinsic Active Server Page Objects

The Active Server object model provides for five intrinsic objects:

- **`Application`**—The `Application` object manages application-level information. This generally refers to global quantities that are common to all users.
- **`Session`**—The `Session` object tracks individual user sessions within your Web application. A session object is ideal for programming constructs such as shopping carts, in which each user needs his or her own unique place to store information.
- **`Server`**—The `Server` object enables you to treat the server itself as an object and to control aspects of its behavior.
- **`Response`**—The `Response` object holds the HTTP response that will ultimately be sent back to the browser.
- **`Request`**—The `Request` object holds all the information that the browser handed over to the HTTP server when the ASP was invoked. This includes things such as form data, query string parameters, and cookies.

As in any object model, each intrinsic object has its own properties and methods that you can use while writing your code. The next five sections look at each of the intrinsic objects in detail and show you how their properties and methods are commonly used.

The *Response* Object

The `Response` object is essentially the "staging area" where you are building the response to be delivered back to the requesting browser. This may compel you to think of just the XHTML code that will go back to the browser, but it is actually more than that. The `Response` object lets you specify content in the HTTP response header, thereby enabling you to do things such as place cookies and perform redirects.

The next three sections examine three common tasks that you do using the `Response` object:

- Dynamically writing out XHTML code
- Instructing the browser to load a new page
- Writing a cookie to the user's browser

Following these sections is a brief listing of the remaining properties and methods of the `Response` object, so that you may have a complete understanding of its structure.

Dynamically Writing XHTML Code Probably the most common reason to appeal to the `Response` object is to dynamically write some content into the document that you're preparing for the browser. To do this, you use the `Write()` method of the `Response` object, as follows:

```
<% Response.Write(string) %>
```

The string that you write out can take on many forms. For example, you can pass a string literal directly to the method:

```
<% Response.Write("<h1>Hello, World!</h1>") %>
```

You can also appeal to one of VBScript's built-in functions for a value:

```
<% Response.Write("<b>Today is " & Date & ".</b>") %>
```

Note how the `Date` function is not inside double quotes. This is true of any value being taken from memory, whether a variable value or the result of a function call. Also note the use of the ampersand (`&`) operator to represent string *concatenation* (joining two or more smaller strings into a single string).

`Response.Write()` gets used so frequently that it has a shortcut notation. The equals sign (`=`) in front of a variable or function call instructs the script interpreter to write out the value of that variable or function into the `Response` object. Thus, the last line of code above could also be written as this:

```
<b>Today is <% =Date %>.</b>
```

Note that the parts of the message that are always the same are now outside the ASP code containers, and only the call to the `Date` function is inside the containers. Using the equals sign as a shortcut for `Response.Write()` is good only in this kind of situation, when you need to go quickly into ASP mode to drop in the value of a dynamic quantity and then jump right back to the supporting static content.

Doing a Redirect The `Redirect` method of the `Response` object is used to instruct the browser to load a URL different from the one that it requested. This is useful in a situation in which you detect that a user is trying to access a page in your application without properly authenticating. When this happens, you can redirect the user to a login page, rather than presenting the page requested.

The `Redirect` method has the following syntax:

```
Response.Redirect(URL)
```

Here, `URL` is the new URL to load. When you issue a `Response.Redirect()` instruction, the server will send a redirect command to the browser as part of the HTTP header of the response. It is important to realize that no other header information or XHTML code can be sent to the browser in the event of a redirect. This can create difficulty in an ASP, as in the following example:

```
<html>
<head>
<title>Redirect Document</title>
</head>
<body>
<%
   if Request.Cookies("login") <> 1 then
    Response.Redirect("login.html")
   else
     Response.Write("Authentication confirmed")
   end if
%>
</body>
</html>
```

The `If...Then` statement checks the value of a cookie named login to see if it has a value of 1. If it does have a value of 1, the user has been previously authenticated and does not need to be sent to the login page. However, if the cookie has a value other than 1, you need to redirect the user to the page login.html so that he or she can provide an appropriate username and password. Unfortunately, by the time the `Redirect` method kicks in, you have already begun to send some XHTML code to the browser (the `<html>`, `<head>`, and `<title>` elements), and the HTTP header was sent on ahead of that code. Thus, it isn't possible to incorporate the `Redirect` command into the HTTP header.

What you must do in this situation is to buffer the contents of the `Response` object so that the code is not sent right away. The `Response` object has a property called `Buffer` that, when set to `True`, will hold the XHTML code in the `Response` object and will wait for your explicit instructions to send the code on to the browser. This gives you the flexibility that you need to do the redirect, if necessary. Thus, the previous code can be modified to this:

```
<%
   Response.Buffer = True
%>
<html>
<head>
<title>Redirect Document</title>
</head>
<body>
<%
   if Request.Cookies("login") <> 1 then
      Response.Redirect("login.html")
   else
      Response.Write("Authentication confirmed")
   end if
%>
</body>
</html>
<%
   Response.End()
%>
```

The first thing to do is to turn on buffering before sending any output back to the browser. If the `If...Then` statement is processed and a redirect is necessary, the buffered output will be thrown away in favor of sending the redirect instruction to the browser. Otherwise, we continue to build out the XHTML code for the resulting page. The `Response.End()` command tells ASP that we are done creating the output and that it's okay to send it along to the browser.

NOTE In ASP 3.0, `Response.Buffer` has a value of `True` by default. If you're using an earlier version, the default value is `False`, so you will need to explicitly set it to `True` to buffer your output.

The `Response` object has two other methods that can be useful when buffering is active:

- **Clear**—Issuing a `Response.Clear()` instruction empties any XHTML output that has accumulated in the buffer. The `Clear` instruction will not erase any part of the HTTP header, though.
- **Flush**—`Response.Flush()` sends any accumulated output on to the browser and allows the ASP script to continue adding more output to the `Response` object. This is useful when you are building a long page and want to send part of it on to the user so that he or she is not kept waiting too long.

Placing a Cookie The example in the previous section used an HTTP cookie, and you might have found yourself wondering how the cookie got there in the first place. When you place a cookie, you are presenting the browser with a name/value pair that you want it to "remember" for you and to hand back to you as part of each subsequent request. To place a cookie using ASP, you need to appeal to the `Cookies` collection of the `Response` object. In the ASP object model, a *collection* is a set of related name/value pairs stored together.

For example, to place the cookie named login in the previous example, you would issue this instruction:

```
Response.Cookies("login") = 1
```

The name of the cookie (login) acts as an index of the `Cookies` collection. The 1 on the right side of the equals sign indicates the value of the cookie.

Cookies are often stored with "freshness dating" that tells the browser when it can discontinue retaining the name/value pairs held. To specify an expiration date for the login cookie, you could add the following line of code:

```
Response.Cookies("login").Expires = #Now + 7#
```

This sets the cookie named login to expire seven days from the current time.

NOTE If you don't specify an `Expires` property for a cookie, the cookie will expire when the browser holding the cookie shuts down.

NOTE Remember that HTTP limits you to placing not more than 20 cookies on a browser. Each cookie also cannot exceed 4KB in length.

CAUTION

If you're using ASP 3.0, you can write cookies anywhere in your ASP code because the `Response` is buffered automatically. If you're using an earlier version of ASP, you will have to either place the cookies before generating any XHTML output, or buffer the `Response` so that the cookie information can still be incorporated into the HTTP header.

Other Properties and Methods of the *Response* Object To round out your study of the `Response` object, this section walks you through the other properties and methods of the object. Although they may not be as high-profile as the ones you learned about in the previous sections, each has its place and can be extremely useful in the right situation.

In addition to `Buffer`, the `Response` object also has the following properties:

- **`Expires`**—By using the `Expires` property, you can control the amount of time before the browser will remove the page from its cache. The syntax for using the `Expires` property is this:

  ```
  Response.Expires = number
  ```

  Here, `number` equals the number of minutes that you want the browser to keep the page active within its cache.
- **`ExpiresAbsolute`**—The `ExpiresAbsolute` property specifies the exact date and time when the browser should remove the page from its cache. The syntax for using the `ExpiresAbsolute` property is this:

  ```
  Response.ExpiresAbsolute = #[date][time]#
  ```
- **`IsClientConnected`**—The `IsClientConnected` property tells you if the client was disconnected since the last time the Web server sent data to the browser. The syntax for using the `IsClientConnected` property is this:

  ```
  Response.IsClientConnected
  ```
- **`Status`**—The `Status` property controls the status line that the Web server will return. The syntax for using the `Status` property is this:

  ```
  Response.Status = StatusCodeAndMessage
  ```

  Here, `StatusCodeAndMessage` includes the status code and description. HTTP status codes and messages include strings such as "200 OK" or "404 Not Found".
- **`PICS`**—By using the `PICS` property, you can control the rating values of the PICS-label field. PICS is a standard by which authors can voluntarily rate their pages for lewdness,

violence, or other potentially objectionable content. The syntax for using the `PICS` property is this:

```
Response.PICS(PicsLabelString)
```

Here, `PicsLabelString` is the formatted PICS label.

NOTE To learn more about `PICS`, direct your browser to `http://www.w3.org/PICS/`.

- **`ContentType`**—The `ContentType` property indicates the MIME type of the content that the Web server will send to the browser. The syntax for using the `ContentType` property is this:

  ```
  Response.ContentType = [ContentType]
  ```

  Here, `ContentType` is a valid content type. Examples of valid content types are image/gif, image/jpeg, text/html, and so on.
- **`CharSet`**—The `CharSet` property controls the character set of the content type that the browser will display. The syntax is this:

  ```
  Response.CharSet(CharSetName)
  ```

  Here, `CharSetName` is a valid character set name. Character set names are specified as ISO standards such as "ISO-8869-1," which is the standard Latin character set.
- **`CacheControl`**—The `CacheControl` property is set to `Public` to allow proxy server caching, or `Private` to disallow proxy server caching. The syntax is this:

  ```
  Response.CacheControl = "Private"
  ```

The following are the remaining methods of the `Response` object:

- **`BinaryWrite`**—By using the `BinaryWrite` method, you can send binary information, such as dynamically generated image data, to the client. The `BinaryWrite` method's syntax is this:

  ```
  Response.BinaryWrite(binarydata)
  ```

- **`AppendToLog`**—The `AppendToLog` method enables you to store information in the Web server's log file. As a result, you can use the `AppendToLog` method and the log file for debugging and tracking purposes. The `AppendToLog` method's syntax is this:

  ```
  Response.AppendToLog(string)
  ```

  Here, `string` is the string that you will record to the log file.
- **`AddHeader`**—`AddHeader` adds information to the existing HTTP header. The `AddHeader` method's syntax is this:

  ```
  Response.AddHeader(header_name, header_value)
  ```

  Here, `header_name` is the name of the header, and `header_value` is the header's value.

The *Request* Object

The `Request` object bundles information that came from the browser as part of the HTTP request that invoked the processing of an ASP. The `Request` object organized the information into five different collections, making it easy for you to access any part of the request. These collections include the following:

- **`Form`**—The `Form` collection is extremely useful because it enables you to retrieve information that the user enters through an XHTML form. Recalling that each form field has a unique name, the syntax for using the `Form` collection is this:

  ```
  Request.Form("fieldname")
  ```

  Here, `fieldname` is the name of the form field. When you appeal to the `Request` object in this way, ASP returns the value associated with the specified form field. For example, this line prints out a custom greeting to the user:

  ```
  Response.Write("Hello, " & Request.Form("FirstName") & "!")
  ```

- **`QueryString`**—Sometimes data is passed to the server as part of the URL. The data occurs in name/value pairs and is separated from the rest of the URL by a question mark. In these instances, the data after the question mark is called the query string.

  By using the `QueryString` collection, you can access data passed on the query string. The syntax for using the `QueryString` collection is this:

  ```
  Request.QueryString("variablename")
  ```

  Here, `variablename` is the URL variable's name. When a specific variable name is used as an index into the `QueryString` collection, the value of that variable is returned.

- **`Cookies`**—The `Cookies` collection of the `Request` object lets you retrieve the value of any cookies that the browser handed to the server as part of the HTTP request. The syntax for using the `Cookies` collection is this:

  ```
  Request.Cookies("cookiename")
  ```

  Here, `cookiename` is the cookie's name. Using `Request.Cookies` in this way returns the value of the cookie that you name.

- **`ServerVariables`**—The `ServerVariables` collection enables you to access values of server environment variables. The syntax for using the `ServerVariables` collection is this:

  ```
  Request.ServerVariables("variablename")
  ```

  Here, `variablename` is the server variable's name. Table 32.4 lists the server variables and what their associated values mean.

Table 32.4 The Server Variables

Variable Name	Description
AUTH_TYPE	Specifies the server's authentication method
AUTH_PASSWORD	Specifies the password that the user entered within the client browser
CONTENT_LENGTH	Returns the content's length
CONTENT_TYPE	Returns the content's data type
GATEWAY_INTERFACE	Returns the version of the server's CGI specification
HTTP_<HeaderName>	Returns information contained within <HeaderName>
LOGON_USER	Specifies the NT login account that made the request
PATH_INFO	Specifies the server's path information
PATH_TRANSLATED	Returns a translated version of PATH_INFO
QUERY_STRING	Returns the query string contained within the URL
REMOTE_ADDR	Specifies the client machine's IP address
REMOTE_HOST	Specifies the requesting host's name
REQUEST_METHOD	Returns the method initiating the request
SCRIPT_NAME	Specifies the executing script's virtual path
SERVER_NAME	Returns the server's hostname, DNS alias, or IP address
SERVER_PORT	Returns the server's port number on which the request is made
SERVER_PORT_SECURE	Returns a 1 if the request is made on the server's secure port, and returns 0 if unsecured
SERVER_PROTOCOL	Returns the requesting protocol's name and version
SERVER_SOFTWARE	Returns the HTTP server's name and version
URL	Returns the URL's base portion

NOTE If you've done any CGI programming, you'll recognize the variables in Table 32.4 as the CGI environment variables.

- **ClientCertificate**—The ClientCertificate collection of the Request object holds the information from the browser's digital certificate, if one was presented. To reference the ClientCertificate collection, you use the following syntax:

  ```
  Request.ClientCertificate("key")
  ```

  Here, key is one of the certificate keys. The different types of certificate keys are shown in Table 32.5.

Table 32.5 Client Certificate Keys

Key	Description
`Certificate`	Contains the entire certificate in ASN.1 format
`SerialNumber`	Indicates the certificate's serial number
`ValidFrom`	Specifies when the certificate takes effect
`ValidUntil`	Specifies when the certificate expires
`Issuer`	Indicates who issued the certificate
`Subject`	Holds the contents of the certificate's subject line

In addition, the `Request` object includes the following property and method:

- **`TotalBytes`**—The `TotalBytes` property tells you the total number of bytes in the HTTP request. You can reference this value as follows:

  ```
  Request.TotalBytes
  ```

- **`BinaryRead`**—By using the `BinaryRead` method, the Web server can read binary information that the client sends through a `POST` request. The `BinaryRead` method's syntax is this:

  ```
  BinaryArray = Request.BinaryRead(count)
  ```

  Here, `BinaryArray` is the binary array that the `BinaryRead` method will create, and `count` is the total number of bytes to be read.

NOTE You cannot reference `Request.Form` after performing a `Request.BinaryRead`. Similarly, after you do a `Request.BinaryRead`, you cannot reference the `Request.Form` collection.

The *Server* Object

The ASP `Server` object lets you manage the server itself as an object. One of the most common things to do with the `Server` object is to use its `CreateObject` method to instantiate new server-side objects as you need them. For example, the following line of code creates an Active Data Object of type `Connection` that can be used to establish a link to a server-side data source:

```
Set dbConn = Server.CreateObject("ADODB.Connection")
```

`dbConn` is the name of the `Connection` object, but you are free to name your objects whatever you like. The string "ADODB.Connection" passed to the `CreateObject` method is called a *class string*, and it tells the method which kind of object it should create.

Another common reason to use the `Server` object is to set the amount of time that an ASP script has to run. The `ScriptTimeOut` property of the `Server` object has a default value of 30 seconds, but you are welcome to change that to a higher or lower value as needed. To reset the timeout value to 10 seconds, for example, you would issue the following command:

```
Server.ScriptTimeOut = 10
```

NOTE ASPs typically execute on a time scale measured in milliseconds, so 30 seconds may seem like an eternity compared to the time actually needed. It's fine to set `ScriptTimeOut` to a lower value, but don't set it too low either. Establishing a connection to a busy data source, for example, may take a few seconds, so you should be sure that you have specified a sufficiently generous timeout value to allow those types of operations to happen.

The `Server` object also has the following methods that are useful in certain situations:

- **`MapPath`**—The `MapPath` method maps a physical or virtual path to a directory on the server. The `MapPath` method's syntax is this:

  ```
  Server.MapPath("path")
  ```

  Here, `path` is the virtual or physical directory.

- **`HTMLEncode`**—Sometimes you need to include HTML reserved characters such as the less than (<) or greater than (>) symbols in your output. In these cases, you must use the characters' entities (`<` for less than and `>` for greater than) instead of the characters themselves. The `HTMLEncode` method scans a string for any reserved characters and replaces them with their corresponding entities. The method's syntax is as follows:

  ```
  Server.HTMLEncode("string")
  ```

  Here, `string` is the string to be HTML-encoded.

- **`ULREncode`**—When passing data as part of the URL, you need to do some encoding to the data first. Specifically, you must convert all space characters to plus signs (+), and you must convert all nonalphanumeric characters to their hexadecimal escape codes (for example, an exclamation point (`!`) becomes `%21`). By using the `URLEncode` method, you can encode a string using these URL encoding methods. The `URLEncode` method's syntax is this:

  ```
  Server.URLEncode("string")
  ```

  Here, `string` is the string to be encoded.

- **`GetLastError`**—The `GetLastError` method returns a reference to the most recent error object generated during the processing of an ASP. ASP error objects contain specifics about the error, including error code, description, and line number.

- **`Execute`**—The `Server` object's `Execute` method transfers processing to a second ASP. When the second ASP finishes processing, control returns to just after the call to the `Execute` method in the first ASP. The `Execute` method's syntax is this:

  ```
  Server.Execute("URL")
  ```

  Here, `URL` is the URL of the second ASP.

- **`Transfer`**—The `Transfer` method transfers processing control to a second ASP script. Unlike the `Execute` method, however, control does not pass back to the first ASP when the second ASP finishes.

  ```
  Server.URLEncode( string )
  ```

  Here, `URL` is the URL of the second ASP.

The *Application* Object

The ASP `Application` object is used for storing global quantities within an application. For example, every user of an application would most likely work against the same data source, so it would be reasonable to set up an application variable called `DataSourceName` and set that equal to the name of the data source that the application is to work with. This would be especially advantageous if you had to switch to a different data source later. In that case, all you would have to do is change the value of the application variable instead of making edits in all your individual ASP files.

You define an application variable as follows:

```
Application("variablename") = value
```

Once defined, the application variable becomes part of `Contents` collection of the `Application` object. You can access a variable value through the `Contents` collection by referencing the following quantity:

```
Application.Contents("variablename")
```

Here, `variablename` is the name of the desired application variable. If you need to remove an application variable from the `Application` object, you can apply the `Remove` method to the `Contents` collection as follows:

```
Application.Contents.Remove("variablename")
```

TIP You can remove all application variables by using the `RemoveAll` method:

```
Application.Contents.RemoveAll()
```

NOTE If you are concerned about two or more users accessing the Application object at the same time (an issue called concurrency), you can restrict access to just the currently running ASP by applying the Lock method to the Application object:

```
Application.Lock()
```

When you're ready to release the lock on the Application object, you can appeal to the Unlock method:

```
Application.Unlock()
```

The Application object is a little different from the other intrinsic objects that you've studied so far in that it also has event handlers associated with it. An application's OnStart event occurs when the very first user hits the very first page of an application. You can use the OnStart event handler to detect this event and execute some scripted instructions that initialize the variables and objects that the application needs to run. Similarly, the application OnEnd event detects the shutdown of the application and enables you to do housekeeping chores such as destroy application level objects to free up the memory that they consume. The application OnEnd event occurs after all user sessions have terminated.

OnStart and OnEnd scripts are defined in special file called the global.asa file. The global.asa file resides in an application's root directory and applies to all subdirectories below the root. A typical global.asa file might look like the following:

```
<%
Sub Application_OnStart()
   Application("DataSourceName") = "webstorefront"
   Set Application("dbConn") = Server.CreateOnject("ADODB.Connection")
End Sub

Sub Application_OnEnd()
   Set Application("dbConn") = Nothing
End Sub
%>
```

In this example, the OnStart script defines an application variable called DataSourceName and sets it equal to webstorefront. Then it creates an application-level ADO Connection object that can be used to connect to the data source. The OnEnd script destroys the application-level connection object so that the memory it consumes can return to the server's pool of available resources.

The *Session* Object

All users get an ASP Session object assigned to them when they hit the application for the very first time. Session objects are for tracking individual behavior as a user moves through the application. This makes them ideal for implementing a shopping cart for an electronic commerce site (because every user wants his or her own unique cart) or for tracking which banner ads have been presented to a user (so that you can finely control which users see a particular banner).

The `Session` object is structured very much like the `Application` object in that you can store variables on it, and those values become part of a `Contents` collection belonging to the `Session` object. You define a session variable as follows:

```
Session("variablename") = value
```

Like `Application`, the `Session` object also takes the `Contents.Remove("variablename")` and `Contents.RemoveAll()` methods to remove a particular session variable or all session variables, respectively. Alternatively, you can apply the `Abandon()` method to a `Session` object to destroy the object and its contents.

NOTE If you issue a `Session.Abandon()` instruction as part of an ASP script, the `Session` object is not destroyed until the script has finished processing. This means that you can still access the contents of the `Session` object throughout the entire script.

Another similarity between the `Application` and `Session` objects is that both have `OnStart` and `OnEnd` event handlers. A session's `OnStart` event occurs when any user hits the application for the first time, and its `OnEnd` event occurs when the timeout period has elapsed or when the `Abandon` method is used. You can associate scripts with each of these events in the `global.asa` file in the same way you did with application `OnStart` and `OnEnd` events. For example, the `global.asa` file that you saw in the previous section could be expanded to the following:


```
<%
Sub Application_OnStart()
   Application("DataSourceName") = "webstorefront"
   Set Application("dbConn") = Server.CreateOnject("ADODB.Connection")
End Sub

Sub Application_OnEnd()
   Set Application("dbConn") = Nothing
End Sub

Sub Session_OnStart()
   Session("ShoppingCart") = ""  'Empty cart initially
   Set Session("BrowsCap") = Server.CreateObject("MWSC.BrowserType")
End Sub

Sub Session_OnEnd()
   Set Session("BrowsCap") = Nothing
End Sub
%>
```

In this new `global.asa` file, each new `Session` object has a variable on it called `ShoppingCart` that is initially set to the empty string to indicate that the cart is empty. The `Session` object also has a *browser capabilities* object stored on it. The browser capabilities object lets you do a server-side detection of what browser the user is running. When you know which browser is in use, you can generate code appropriate to that browser. When the session ends, the browser capabilities object is destroyed to free up the memory it consumes.

In addition to the methods and event handlers discussed previously, the `Session` object has four properties:

- **CodePage**—The `CodePage` property is set equal to the numeric code that represents the character set to be used to display the page. For example, a code page of `1252` is used for American English. The syntax for the `CodePage` property is this:

  ```
  Session.CodePage = CodePageNumber
  ```

  Here, `CodePageNumber` is a valid code page number.
- **`LCID`**—The `LCID` property gives you control over the locale identifier to use for your output. The locale identifier expresses the location of the user and can be used to guide functions such as `FormatCurrency`, which have to use different symbols when displaying currency amounts (`$` for dollars, `£` for pounds, and so on). The locale identifier can also influence the display of dates and times, which also vary from location to location.
- **`SessionID`**—When a new user initiates a session with your Web application, the Web server automatically generates a `SessionID` for the user's session. The `SessionID` values that the server uses are unique as long as the application's `Application` object persists. If you shut down the application and then restart, it is possible to get `SessionID` values that were assigned in a previous incarnation of the application. For this reason, it is not a good idea to use `SessionID` values as primary key values in a relational database table.
- **`TimeOut`**—The `TimeOut` property represents the amount of time that the user session will remain active before the Web server closes the `Session` object. The syntax for using the `TimeOut` property is this:

  ```
  Session.Timeout = TimeoutDuration
  ```

  Here, `TimeoutDuration` is specified in minutes. The default timeout is 20 minutes.

The intrinsic objects that you have examined in the previous five sections—`Application`, `Session`, `Server`, `Response`, and `Request`—are available to you during the processing of any ASP script. No special action is required to create any of these objects.

The ASP object model does support other types of objects beyond these five, but to use them, you must create them first. The next three sections of the chapter look at three different classes of objects that you must create yourself:

- **Active Data Object (ADO)**—You create an ADO object whenever you need to establish a connection with and pose a query to a data source on the server.
- **Scripting objects**—The ASP scripting objects include a `Dictionary` object, where you can store key/value pairs for later lookup, and the `FileSystemObject` object, which gives you access to the server's file system
- **Component objects**—Some ASP component objects are provided by Microsoft, and others can be purchased from third-party vendors. Each object performs a particular task, such as sending out an email message or tracking which banner ads a user has seen.

Using the Active Data Object

The Active Data Object (ADO) is based on OLE DB, a C++ based applications programming interface (API). OLE DB refers to Microsoft's database connectivity approach based on object linking and embedding. Because the technology is based on C++, its API is object-oriented. ADO is similar to Microsoft's Data Access Object (DAO) and Remote Data Object (RDO). However, Microsoft designed ADO specifically with Internet-based applications in mind.

ADO enables you to add database connectivity to your ASP applications. Four main types of ADO objects enable you to communicate with and handle data from a database:

- **Connection**—An ADO `Connection` object enables you to set up an open pipe into a system data source. When the pipe is open, you can send queries down the pipe and receive data from the database back through it.
- **Command**—The ADO `Command` object is used to issue a command to a database. Typically, the command is to execute a stored procedure that is part of the database.
- **Recordset**—An ADO `Recordset` object holds the data that is returned in response to a SQL `SELECT` query.
- **Error**—An ADO `Error` object captures any information about any errors that occur during a database query.

Of these objects, the two that are most frequently used are `Connection` and `Recordset`, so those will be examined first.

ADO *Connection* Objects

To create an instance of the ADO `Connection` object, you use the `Server` object's `CreateObject` method. The following line of code shows an example of creating a database connection:

```
Set dbConn = Server.CreateObject("ADODB.Connection")
```

This command creates a `Connection` object named `dbConn`. At this point, the object exists, but it does not yet have a purpose. What you need to do next is to direct the object to establish a connection with a Windows system data source. You accomplish this by using the `Open` method of the `Connection` object, as follows:

```
dbConn.Open("dsn=sales")
```

After this command executes, the `Connection` object has an open connection into the data source named sales.

NOTE If your data source is password-protected, you can incorporate the necessary username and password right into the `Open` method. For example, if your username was webapp and your password was hardtoguess, then you could change the previous line of code to this:

```
DbConn.Open("dsn=sales; uid=webapp; pw=hardtoguess")
```

The parameter passed to the `Open` method is often referred to as the *connection string*.

With the connection to the data source now open, you are free to send SQL statements to the database. You do this by using the `Execute` method of the `Connection` object. For example, you might do a `DELETE` query that looks like the following:

```
dim SQL
SQL = "DELETE FROM Products WHERE ProductID = " & Request.Form("ProductID")
dbConn.Execute(SQL)
```

TIP The advantage to storing a dynamically constructed SQL statement in its own variable is that you can print out the value of that variable to the browser screen to help you diagnose any syntax errors. If you were getting a syntax error in the previous code, you could simply add this command just before the `Execute` method so that the SQL statement would be displayed on the browser screen:

```
Response.Write(SQL)
```

Similarly, you might do an `UPDATE` query as follows:

```
dim SQL
SQL = "UPDATE Products SET Price = " & Request.Form("price")
SQL = SQL & "WHERE ProductID = " & Request.Form("ProductID")
dbConn.Execute(SQL)
```

Where things get interesting is when you do a SQL `SELECT` statement. In this case, you expect to get some number of records back from the database in response to your query. When the results come back from the query, they are stored in an ADO `Recordset` object. Because you'll want to refer to the data in the `Recordset` object, it is important that you give it a name when it is created. You can do that by modifying the `Execute` command as follows:

```
Set myRS = dbConn.Execute("SELECT Name,Price,InventoryLevel
➥FROM Products ORDER BY Name")
```

The results coming back from the query are automatically stored in a `Recordset` object, and that object is given the name `myRS` by the previous statement. When the recordset has a name, it becomes a simple matter to access the data within it.

Working with Recordsets

The most common thing to do with a recordset is to use the data that it contains to dynamically construct a Web page. You do this by setting up a VBScript `while` loop that systematically moves through the recordset and prints out data from each record as it goes. For example, using the recordset defined at the end of the previous section, you could create a bulleted list of the products in the database, as follows:

```
<ul>
<%
   myRS.MoveFirst()
   while not myRS.EOF
      Response.Write("<li>" & myRS("Name") & "</li>")
      MyRS.MoveNext()
   Wend
%>
</ul>
```

The MoveFirst() method moves the recordset's pointer to the first record in the recordset (the pointer indicates which record is the current record that you're focused on). Next, a while loop is set up to run until the end of the recordset is reached. This is controlled by using the recordset's EOF property. EOF is a Boolean property that has a value of TRUE when the pointer has moved passed the last record in the recordset; it is FALSE otherwise.

NOTE Even though the acronym EOF might make you think of an "End of File" marker, it's important to realize that the recordset is not a file. Rather, it is a construct that exists only in the server's memory.

TIP The EOF property, together with the BOF property, give you a simple way to test to see whether any records were returned. Consider the following code:

```
<%
   if myRS.EOF And myRS.BOF then
      Response.Write("No records found!")
   end if
%>
```

IF EOF and BOF are both TRUE, then you must be simultaneously at the beginning and at the end of the recordset. The only way this is possible is if the recordset contains no records.

Once inside the loop, the Response.Write instruction takes care of writing out the necessary list item to the browser. Note how you reference a quantity in the recordset by indexing the recordset with the name of a database field (myRS("Name")). The MoveNext method advances the pointer to the next record in the recordset when you're done writing out data to the browser.

CAUTION

Don't forget the MoveNext() instruction! Without it, you can never advance to the end of the recordset, and you'll end up in an infinite loop.

Looping over a recordset is a very handy way to generate a lot of XHTML code that would be tedious to create by hand. Suppose, for example, that you wanted to generate a table of all your products and their prices. If you have 50 products in your database, that's 50 table rows that you must create and maintain. With ASP, all you need to do is query the product names and prices out of the database table and use a while loop to print them all out. Listing 32.3 shows you how to accomplish this.

Listing 32.3 Building a Table from Data in a Recordset

```
<%
   Set dbConn = Server.CreateObject("ADODB.Connection")
   dbConn.Open("dsn=sales")
   Set myRS = dbConn.Execute("SELECT Name,Price FROM Products ORDER BY Name")
%>
```

Listing 32.3 Continued

```
<html>
<head>
<title>Product Names and Prices</title>
</head>

<body>

<p>A table of our products and their prices appears below:</p>

<table>

<tr><th>Product Name</th><th>Price</th></tr>

<%
   myRS.MoveFirst()
   while not myRS.EOF
%>

      <tr>
      <td><% =myRS("Name") %></td>
      <td><% =myRS("Price") %></td>
      </tr>

<%
      myRS.MoveNext()
   wend
%>

</table>

</body>

</html>

<%
   myRS.Close()
   dbConn.Close()
   Set myRS = Nothing
   Set dbConn = Nothing
%>
```

Note at the end of the listing that both the `Recordset` and `Connection` objects are closed with the `Close` method and then are set to `Nothing`. This is a good memory-management practice that frees up the resources that those objects were consuming while they existed.

One other popular XHTML construct that you can generate from a recordset is a select list in a form. In this case, you use the loop to create the `<option>` elements that comprise the list. Listing 32.4 illustrates how this is done.

Listing 32.4 Building a Select List from Data in a Recordset

```
<%
   Set dbConn = Server.CreateObject("ADODB.Connection")
   dbConn.Open("dsn=sales")
   Set myRS = dbConn.Execute("SELECT ProductID,Name
   ➥FROM Products ORDER BY Name")
%>

<html>
<head>
<title>Pick a Product!</title>
</head>

<body>

<p>Select a product from the list below to see more detail on that product.</p>

<form action="detail.asp" method="post">

<select name="product" size="1">

<%
   myRS.MoveFirst()
   while not myRS.EOF
%>

      <option value="<% =myRS("ProductID") %>"><% =myRS("Name") %>

<%
      myRS.MoveNext()
   wend
%>

</select>
<br />
<input type="submit" value="Get Product Detail" />

</form>

</body>

</html>

<%
   myRS.Close()
   dbConn.Close()
   Set myRS = Nothing
   Set dbConn = Nothing
%>
```

Note in this case that the name of the product is displayed in the list, but it is the product's primary key value that is passed to the next ASP page. This facilitates a rapid lookup of the product detail information.

ADO *Command* Objects

ADO `Command` objects are chiefly used to trigger stored procedures, but they can be used to issue SQL statements as well. To create an ADO `Command` object, you appeal to the `CreateObject` method of the `Server` object:

```
Set dbCmd = Server.CreateObject("ADODB.Command")
```

After the `Command` object is created, you need to set two properties for it to do its job. The first is the `ActiveConnection` property, which you set equal to the name of the data source where the stored procedure resides. Then you set the `CommandText` property equal to the name of the stored procedure that you want to run:

```
dbCmd.ActiveConnection = "dsn=sales"
dbCmd.CommandText = "PurgeOldProducts"
```

After these properties are set, you apply the `Execute` method to the `Command` object to trigger the stored procedure:

```
dbCmd.Execute()
```

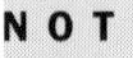

NOTE If you want to use a `Command` object to do a SQL statement, then you set the `CommandText` property equal to the SQL statement that you want to execute.

ADO *Error* Objects

Even the best ASP programmer makes an occasional typo when writing in a SQL statement, and that typo results in a SQL syntax error when you try to execute the query. When any kind of error occurs that involves an ADO object, information about that error is captured in an ADO `Error` object. An ADO `Error` object has many properties that describe the nature of the error to you:

- **`Description`**—An English-language description of why the error occurred.
- **`NativeError`**—The platform-specific code for the error. Each database platform has its own codes for each type of error. By knowing the error code for your database platform, you can then look up the error code in your documentation.
- **`Number`**—A unique identifier for the `Error` object.
- **`Source`**—The name of the object or application that brought about the error.

Each `Error` object, in turn, becomes part of the `Errors` collection. The `Errors` collection has a `Count` property that you can check to see if any errors have occurred. Listing 32.5 shows you how to loop through the `Errors` object, printing out details from each individual `Error` object as you go.

Listing 32.5 Printing Out the Details About ADO Errors

```
<%
   'If an error occurs, continue on to the next statement
   On Error Resume Next

   Set dbConn=Server.CreateObject("ADODB.Connection")
   dbConn.Open("sales")
   Set myRS=dbConn.Execute("SELECT RepName FROM Reps WHERE RepID = 8")

   'If any errors occurred, display them
   If dbConn.Errors.Count > 0 Then
      For i = 0 to dbConn.Errors.Count-1
         Response.Write("<p>Error Number: "
         ➥& dbConn.Errors(i).Number & "<br />")
         Response.Write("Error Code: "
         ➥& dbConn.Errors(i).NativeError & "<br />")
         Response.Write("Description: "
         ➥& dbConn.Errors(i).Description & "</p>")
         Response.Write("<hr />")
      Next
   End If

   myRS.Close()
   dbConn.Close()
   Set myRS = Nothing
   Set dbConn = Nothing
%>
```


Note the use of `On Error Resume Next`, which tells the script interpreter to proceed to the next statement in the event of an error.

Using the ASP Scripting Objects

Beyond the intrinsic objects and the ADO object, there is another class of ASP objects called the *scripting objects*. These objects are supported by the `scrrun.dll` file that comes as part of your IIS server.

The *Dictionary* Object

There are two major types of scripting object. The first is the `Dictionary` object, which lets you store key/value pairs. After the key/value pairs are stored, you can then look up values by searching for the associated keys in the `Dictionary` object. As an example of why you might need a `Dictionary` object, consider that states are often stored in a database table according to their two-letter abbreviations, but you may want to spell out the full state name as part of your output. In this case, you could set up a `Dictionary` object that maps state abbreviations (the keys) to the full state names (the values). Then, when you need to change an abbreviation to the full name, you just look up the abbreviation in the `Dictionary` object and use the value associated with it.

You create a `Dictionary` object by appealing to the `CreateObject` method of the `Server` object. The class string for a `Dictionary` object is `"Scripting.Dictionary"`, as shown here:

```
Set states = Server.CreateObject("Scripting.Dictionary")
```

After the object is created, you must store key/value pairs in it to make it useful. You can accomplish this by using the `Add` method to place each pair. For the state dictionary described, you would use statements such as the following:

```
States.Add "AK","Alaska"
States.Add "AL","Alabama"
States.Add "AR","Arkansas"
...
States.Add "WY","Wyoming"
```

After the `Dictionary` object is established, you can then look up the value associated with a particular key by appealing to the objects `Item` collection. When you index the `Item` collection with a key, you get the associated value returned to you.

Listing 32.6 shows how you might use the states `Dictionary` object to translate state abbreviations.

Listing 32.6 Translating State Abbreviations with a *Dictionary* Object

```
<%

   'Create the dictionary object and set up the keys and values

   Set states = Server.CreateObject("Scripting.Dictionary")
   states.Add "AK","Alaska"
   states.Add "AL","Alabama"
   states.Add "AR","Arkansas"
   ...
   states.Add "WY","Wyoming"

   'Now query out a customers from a selected state
   Set dbConn = Server.CreateObject("ADODB.Connection")
   dbConn.Open("customers")
   myQuery = "SELECT * FROM Customers
   ➥WHERE State = '" & Request.Form("state") & "'"
   Set myRS = dbConn.Execute(myQuery)

%>

<html>

<head>
<title>All Customers from
<% =states.Item(Trim(Request.Form("state"))) %></title>
</head>
```

Listing 32.6 Continued

```
<body>
<h1>Customers from <% =states.Item(Trim(Request.Form("state"))) %></h1>

<ul>

<%
   myRS.MoveFirst()
   while not myRS.EOF
      Response.Write("<li>" & myRS("Name") & "</li>")
      MyRS.MoveNext()
   wend

   myRS.Close()
   dbConn.Close()
   Set myRS = Nothing
   Set dbConn = Nothing

%>

</ul>

</body>

</html>
```


NOTE It would be a maintenance headache to build a `Dictionary` object into every ASP file, so programmers usually incorporate them by means of a server-side include (SSI). You can read more about SSIs in Chapter 29, "Server-Side Includes."

The *FileSystemObject* Object

The other type of scripting object is the `FileSystemObject` object, or FSO. An FSO enables you to access the server's file system and read from or write to any text file on the server. The various methods of the FSO enables you to do all the common file operations, such as copy, move, rename, and delete. Additionally, the FSO supports a special kind of object called a `TextStream` object. You can think of a `TextStream` object as an open pipe into a text file on the server. The pipe is bidirectional, meaning that you can read data from the file and write data to the file through the same pipe.

A common use of the FSO is to create a delimited text file containing data from one of your data sources. Desktop applications such as Microsoft Word and Excel are quite adept at reading in data in a delimited format, so Web programmers are frequently asked to provide data this way.

The first step in creating the delimited text file is to query out the data that has to go into the file and get it into a `Recordset` object. After you have done that, you create an FSO as follows:

```
Set myFSO = Server.CreateObject("Scripting.FileSystemObject")
```

This leaves you with an FSO named `myFSO`. To this object, you then apply the `CreateTextFile` method to create the `TextStream` object:

```
Set targetFile = myFSO.CreateTextFile("c:\datafiles\customers.txt")
```

After the `TextStream` is open, you are then free to loop over the recordset and write data to the file as you go. Listing 32.7 provides you with the complete details.

Listing 32.7 Writing Data to a Delimited Text File

```
<%

   'Query out a customer data
   Set dbConn = Server.CreateObject("ADODB.Connection")
   dbConn.Open("customers")
   myQuery = "SELECT * FROM Customers ORDER BY Zip"
   Set myRS = dbConn.Execute(myQuery)

   'Now set up the TextStream object
   Set myFSO = Server.CreateObject("Scripting.FileSystemObject")
   Set targetFile = myFSO.CreateTextFile("c:\datafiles\customers.txt")

   'Loop over the Recordset and write to the file as you go
   myRS.MoveFirst()
   while not myRS.EOF
      fileline = myRS("Name") & "," & myRS("Company")
      ➥& "," & myRS("Address") & ","
      fileline = fileline & myRS("City") & ","
      ➥& myRS("State") & "," & myRS("Zip")
      targetFile.WriteLine(fileline)
      myRS.MoveNext()
   wend

   'Housekeeping chores
   targetFile.Close()
   myRS.Close()
   dbConn.Close()
   Set myFSO = Nothing
   Set myRS = Nothing
   Set dbConn = Nothing

%>

<html>

<head>
<title>Text file created!</title>
```

Listing 32.7 Continued

```
</head>

<body>

<h1>Text file created!</h1>

</body>

</html>
```

The result of executing this ASP script would be a comma-delimited text file found at `c:\datafiles\customers.txt` on the server's hard drive. The delimited data is sorted in ZIP Code order, making it perfectly suited for generating a mail merge.

Using ASP Components

Yet another class of ASP object is an *ASP component.* Microsoft furnishes you with support for several component objects, including these:

- Browser Capabilities
- Ad Rotator
- Content Linking
- Content Rotator
- Page Counter
- Permission Checker

Because browsers are familiar to most people, this section considers the Browser Capabilities component in some detail.

The Browser Capabilities component enables you to detect the type of client browser accessing your Web site. To create an instance of the Browser Capabilities component, you use the `Server` object's `CreateObject` method. The following code shows an example of creating an instance of the Browser Capabilities component:

```
Set bc = Server.CreateObject("MSWC.BrowserType")
```

You can use the Browser Capabilities component along with the `browscap.ini` file to determine the type of browser and its capabilities. The `browscap.ini` file contains information about the different industry-standard browsers. An excerpt from a typical `browscap.ini` file follows:

```
[Mozilla/4.7]
browser=Mozilla
version=4
```

```
majorver=4
minorver=7
frames=TRUE
JavaScript=TRUE
VBScript=FALSE
...
```

If the client browser does not support ActiveX controls, for example, you can decide to send alternative content to that browser instead of an ActiveX control. By using the Browser Capabilities component, you can design your Web site irrespective of the browser that the visitors to your site will use. This way, your target audience will not be limited by the type of browser.

Once instantiated, a Browser Capabilities object has properties whose values tell you what the target browser is capable of processing. The key properties of a Browser Capabilities object are outlined in Table 32.6.

Table 32.6 Properties of a Browser Capabilities Object

Property	Description
`BackgroundSounds`	Whether the browser supports background sounds
`Browser`	The name of the browser ("Mozilla" for Netscape Navigator, "Explorer" for Microsoft Internet Explorer, and so on)
`Cookies`	Whether the browser supports cookies
`Frames`	Whether the browser supports frames
`JavaScript`	Whether the browser supports JavaScript
`Majorver`	Browser's major version number
`Minorver`	Browser's minor version number
`Tables`	Whether the browser supports tables
`VBScript`	Whether the browser supports VBScript
`Version`	Browser's complete version number

Suppose, for example, that you have a frames and nonframes version of your site, and you want to direct the user to the appropriate one. You could then use the Browser Capabilities component as follows:

```
if bc.frames then
   Response.Redirect("frameshome.html")
else
   Response.Redirect("nonframeshome.html")
end if
```

Extending ASP with Third-Party Components

As powerful as it is, there are some things that ASP cannot do with the objects that it supports. One example is the capability to send email messages—a fairly common task to be done on a busy, modern Web site. Another is the capability to upload a file. Job sites invite users to upload their resumes all the time, so you need some way to handle these files when they are submitted.

In these cases, you can check on the Web to see if there is a third-party component to help you out. A number of software vendors will sell you a `.dll` file that supports a particular type of ASP object. When you install that `.dll` file on your server, you are then free to use that object in your ASP scripts.

A popular third-party component is ASPMail from ServerObjects, Inc. (`www.serverobjects.com`). With ASPMail installed on your server, you can create a mail object and fill out the mail message by setting the various properties of the object. When you've finished composing the message, you would apply a method to send the email.

NOTE You receive full documentation of the objects, their properties, and their methods after you purchase the third-party component. ■

There are other component object vendors as well. To sample the offerings of a few more, direct your browser to one of the following sites:

- `http://www.aspstudio.com/`
- `http://www.aspalliance.com/components/`
- `http://www.aspxtras.com/`

Putting It All Together: A Simple ASP Application

In the first part of this chapter, you read about VBScript and how you could use it to create client-side scripts. Then you learned quite a bit about Active Server Page applications and some of the built-in objects and components that support ASP development. Now it is time to join these two bodies of knowledge by looking at a short ASP application developed in VBScript. Suppose that your company is running a Web-based marketing campaign. You have sent mailers to your clients assigning a unique promotional identifier to each one, and inviting them to check out the promotion on your site. At your site, you will verify their contact information, ask them a few marketing questions, and then thank them for their participation. A back-end data source named promotion holds the current contact information and promotion IDs for each of your clients.

To begin the application, you need to prompt your client for his or her promotion ID. A simple XHTML form will suffice for this. What's unique in this case is that the `action` attribute of the `<form>` element will point to the ASP file `promo1.asp`, not at a CGI program. Listing 32.8 shows one possible way to code the form.

Listing 32.8 Form to Prompt User for Promotion ID

```
<html>
<head>
<title>Your Company: Marketing Promotion</title>
</head>
<body bgcolor="white">
<blockquote>
<p>Please enter your ID number below and
click the "Enter Promotion" button.</p>
<form action="promo1.asp" method="post">
<input type="text" name="ID" size="10" /><br />
<input type="submit" value="enter promotion" />
</form>
</body>
</html>
```

Next, you must create the file `promo1.asp` that will use the ID number entered by the user to query your promotion data source and present the information found in a second XHTML form, where the user can confirm his or her information and then answer your marketing questions. You also need to be prepared to handle the cases in which the ID entered is not a valid one and the database query returns no results. In Listing 32.9, both the confirmation form and the error messages are handled by VBScript subroutines called by the main VBScript code block. Figure 32.2 shows the response to a valid ID number.

Listing 32.9 Code Listing for *promo1.asp*

```
<%
dim error
dim ID
error=""

if Not(IsNumeric(request.form("ID"))) then   'ID Not Numeric - stop
   call sub_error                           ' call error and don't come back
else
   ID = Request.Form("ID")                  ' ID Fine, continue

' Create Connection
set dbConn = Server.CreateObject("ADODB.Connection")
dbConn.Open("promotion")

' Build SQL statement
SQL = "Select * "
SQL = SQL & "FROM Clients "
SQL = SQL & "WHERE ClientID = " & ID
```

Listing 32.9 Continued

```
' Execute Query
Set RS = dConn.Execute(SQL)

if (RS.EOF) AND (RS.BOF) then    ' No record exists, print error
    call sub_empty
else
    call sub_Confirm
end if

' Clean Up RecordSets for Better
' memory management
RS.Close()
Set RS=Nothing
dbConn.Close()
Set dbConn = Nothing

end if   ' Else from Login Error

' BEGIN SUBPROCEDURES

' Sub ERROR:  Provide user with message stating that entered ID is
' invalid, provide link to return to main page and start again

Sub sub_error
%>
<html><head><title>Invalid ID Number</title></head>
<body bgcolor="white">
<h1>Invalid ID Number</h1>
<p>The ID number you entered is not valid.  Please click the Continue
button below and re-enter the number from the letter you received in the
 mail.</p>
<form action="index.html" method="post">
<input type="submit" value="Continue" />
</form>
</body></html>
<%
end sub

' Sub empty:  Tells user no matching records were found and reprompts for
 promotion ID number.
Sub sub_empty
%>
<html><head><title>No Matches Found</title></head>
<body bgcolor="white">
<h1>No Matches Found</h1>
<p>No records in our database matched the ID number you entered.  Please
click the Continue button below and re-enter the number from the letter
you received in the mail.</p>
<form action="index.html" method="post">
<input type="submit" value="Continue" />
```

Listing 32.9 Continued

```
</form>
</body></html>
<%
end sub

' Sub Confirm:  Provide user with current data from database and
' allow user to update/modify information.

sub sub_confirm
%>
<html><head><title>Contact Information</title></head>
<body bgcolor="white">
<p>Please review the information below, making corrections where necessary.
 Click the "Continue" button when you're finished.</p>

<form action="promo2.asp" method="post">
<table>
  <tr>
   <td><b>First Name</b></td>
   <td><input type="text" name="firstname" value="<%=RS("firstname")%>"
        size="35" /></td>
  </tr>
  <tr>
   <td><b>Last Name</b></td>
   <td><input type="text" name="lastname" value="<%=RS("lastname")%>"
        size="35" /></td>
  </tr>
  <tr>
   <td><b>Title</b></td>
   <td><input type="text" name="title"
    value="<%=RS("title")%>" size="35" /></td>
  </tr>
  <tr>
   <td><b>Company</b></td>
   <td><input type="text" name="company" value="<%=RS("company")%>"
       size="35" /></td>
  </tr>

<%if (not isempty(RS("address2"))) then%>
  <tr>
   <td rowspan="2" valign="top"><b>Address</b></td>
   <td><input type="text" name="address1" value="<%=RS("address1")%>"
        size="35" /></td>
  </tr>
  <tr>
   <td><input type="text" name="address2" value="<%=RS("address2")%>"
        size="35" /></td>
  </tr>
<%else%>
  <tr>
```

Listing 32.9 Continued

```
    <td rowspan="2" valign="top"><b>Address</b></td>
    <td><input type="text" name="address1" value="<%=RS("address1")%>"
         size="35" /></td>
   </tr>
   <tr>
    <td><input type="text" name="address2" value=""
         size="35" /></td>
   </tr>
<%end if%>
  <tr>
    <td><b>City</b></td>
    <td><input type="text" name="city" value="<%=RS("city")%>" size="35" />
    </td>
   </tr>
   <tr>
    <td><b>State</b></td>
    <td><input type="text" name="state" value="<%=RS("state")%>" size="35" />
    </td>
   </tr>
   <tr>
    <td><b>Zip Code</b></td>
    <td><input type="text" name="zip" value="<%=RS("zip")%>" size="35" />
    </td>
   </tr>
   <tr>
    <td><b>phone</b></td>
    <td><input type="text" name="phone" value="<%=RS("phone")%>"
size=35></td>
   </tr>
   <tr>
    <td><b>Fax</b></td>
    <td><input type="text" name="fax" value="<%=RS("fax")%>" size="35" />
    </td>
   </tr>
   <tr>
   <td><b>Email</b></td>
    <td><input type="text" name="email" value="<%=RS("email")%>" size="35" />
    </td>
   </tr>
   <tr>
    <td colspan="2"><hr noshade="noshade" width="100%" /></td>
   </tr>
   <tr>
    <td colspan="2"><b>Are you a decision maker for
     technology purchases?</b></td>
   </tr>
   <tr>
     <td><input type="radio" name="decide" value="1" />
         Yes</td>
     <td><input type="radio" name="decide" value="0" />
```

Listing 32.9 Continued

```
        No</td>
  </tr>
  <tr>
    <td colspan="2"><b>How much will you spend on new
     equipment this year?</b>
    </td>
  </tr>
  <tr>
    <td colspan="2"><input type="text" name="amount" /></td>
  </tr>
  <tr>
    <td colspan="2"><input type="submit" name="Continue" /></td>
  </tr>
</table>
<input type="hidden" name="id" value="<%=id%>" />
</form>
</body>

</html>
<%
end sub
%>
```

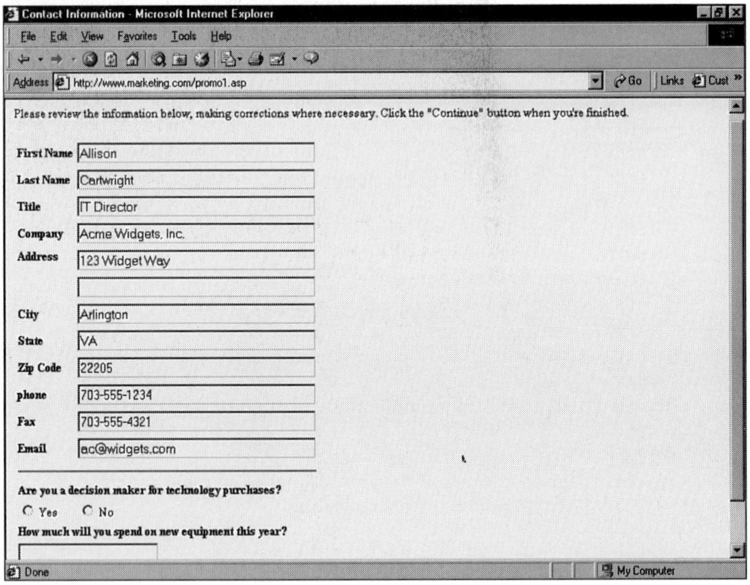

FIGURE 32.2
If a user's ID number is found in the database, you present him with his information as it currently exists and invite him to update it.

Note the use of many of the things you've seen so far in this chapter:

- VBScript for validation of the form input and general control of the processing through `If...then...else` type statements

- Use of the `Request` object to get the form data submitted by the user
- Use of the ADO component to initiate a query against the database
- Referencing an ADO `Recordset` object to get the values of the fields returned in the query

Users entering a valid ID into the initial form will now see their current contact information displayed in an HTML form that they can update, if required. Then, after they click the Continue button, the ASP `promo2.asp` is launched to process the submitted form data. `promo2.asp`, shown in Listing 32.10, builds the SQL statement to update the database with the submitted information and then presents a thank-you message to the user (see Figure 32.3).

Listing 32.10 Code Listing for *promo2.asp*

```
<%
dim ID
dim FirstName
dim LastName
dim Title
dim Company
dim Address1
dim Address2
dim City
dim State
dim Zip
dim Phone
dim Fax
dim Email
dim Decide
dim Amount

FirstName = Request.Form("FirstName")
LastName  = Request.Form("LastName")
Title     = Request.Form("Title")
Company   = Request.Form("Company")
Address1  = Request.Form("Address1")
Address2  = Request.Form("Address2")
City      = Request.Form("City")
State     = Request.Form("State")
Zip       = Request.Form("Zip")
Phone     = Request.Form("Phone")
Fax       = Request.Form("Fax")
Email     = Request.Form("Email")
Decide    = Request.Form("Decide")
Amount    = Request.Form("Amount")
ID        = Request.Form("ID")

' Build SQL statement

SQL = "UPDATE  Clients "
SQL = SQL & "SET FirstName='" & FirstName  & "',LastName='" & LastName
```

Listing 32.10 Continued

```
SQL = SQL & ",Title= '" & Title & "',Company='" & Company & "',"
SQL = SQL & "Address1='" & Address1 & "',Address2='" & Address2 &"',"
SQL = SQL & "City='" & City & "',State='" & State & "',"
SQL = SQL & "Zip='" & Zip & "',Phone='" & Phone & "',"
SQL = SQL & "Fax='" & Fax & "',Email='" & Email & "',"
SQL = SQL & "Decide='" & Decide & "',"
SQL = SQL & "Amount='" & Amount
SQL = SQL & "WHERE ClientID = " & ID

' Execute Query - execute the update

Set dbConn = Server.CreateObject("ADODB.Connection")
dbConn.Open("promotion")
Set RS = dbConn.Execute(SQL)

' Clean Up RecordSets for Better
 ' memory management
RS.Close()
Set RS=Nothing
dbConn.Close()
Set dbConn = Nothing

%>

<html>
<head>
<title>Information Updated!</title>
</head>
<body bgcolor="white">
<h2>Thank you, <%=FirstName%></h2>
<p>Thanks for participating in our survey.  We look forward to
supporting you in the future.</p>
</body>
</html>
```

Again, the ASP file uses the `Request` object and the ADO component to take the user's input, compose a SQL statement that will update the user's record, and then perform the update.

Now that you have seen some of the basics of VBScript and ASP development, it would not be hard to extend this sample application to include greater functionality, such as assigning a client ID number to someone who does not have one or doing some basic error-checking. Additionally, you should be able to easily adapt the approaches used in this example to build other ASP applications for your Web site. For more information on ASP development, consult the ASP developer resource site found at `http://www.learnasp.com/`.

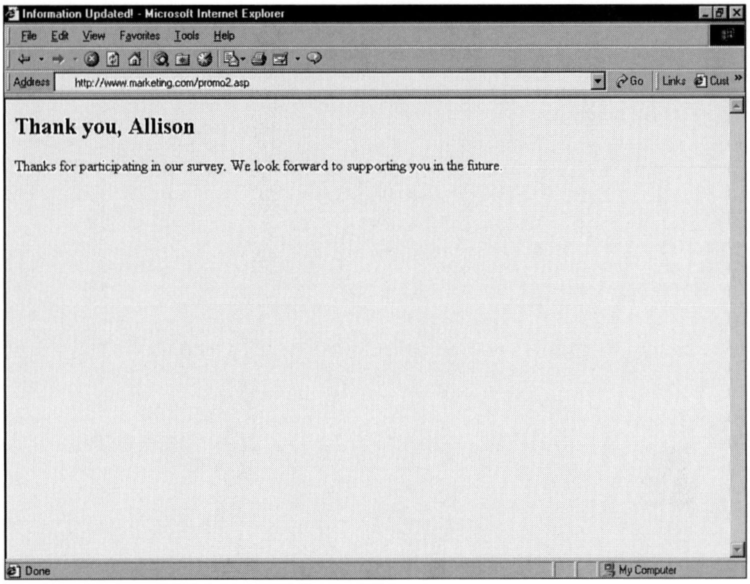

FIGURE 32.3
A second ASP takes care of updating the database and presenting a closure message to the user.

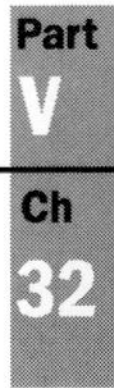

33

Using ColdFusion

by Eric Ladd

In this chapter

What Is ColdFusion?

As the Web has become more pervasive in the business world, developers have come under increased pressure to build applications that support their companies' mission-critical business functions. As with any Web-based deliverable, these applications need "to be done yesterday" and also are expected to scale effortlessly with the growth of the business. These stringent requirements have compelled developers to seek development environments in which they can quickly build, test, and deploy the applications their companies need.

Allaire's ColdFusion—currently in version 4.5—continues to be a favorite application-development platform among Web programmers who need to rapidly deploy complex, interactive sites. Figure 33.1 shows an overview of how ColdFusion works with your Web server.

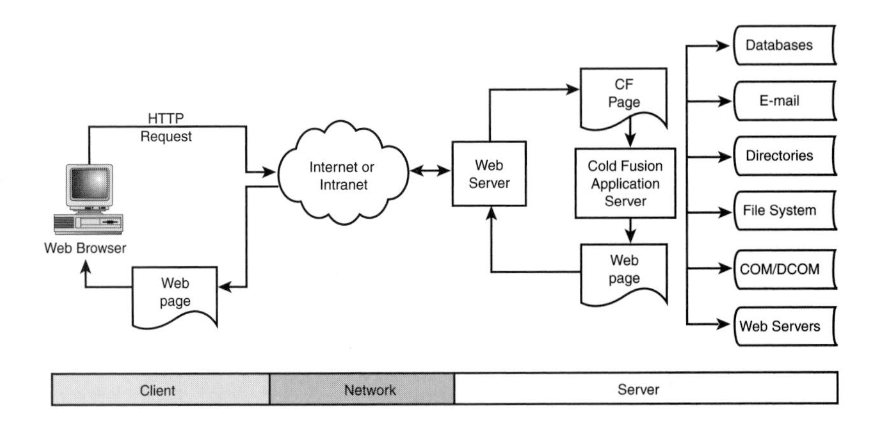

FIGURE 33.1
Requests for ColdFusion templates are handed off to the ColdFusion Application Server, which processes the embedded programming instructions and generates the XHTML page that is delivered to the browser.

The following are the major steps in the delivery of a ColdFusion-based page:

1. A user requests a file containing ColdFusion code (called a ColdFusion *template*) or submits a form that has a ColdFusion template as its action attribute. ColdFusion templates end in the extension `.cfm`.
2. The Web server hands the template over to the ColdFusion Application Server for processing.
3. The ColdFusion Application Server parses out the programmatic instructions, makes all necessary calls to other services on the network (database servers, mail servers, directory servers, and so on), performs any required data manipulation, and then prepares an XHTML document as its response to the HTTP server.
4. The XHTML document is returned to the Web server which, in turn, sends it to the user's browser.

You give instructions to the ColdFusion Application Server through the ColdFusion Markup Language (CFML), a tag-based language that you embed inside XHTML code to produce a

ColdFusion template. In addition to the tags, CFML features scores of useful built-in functions that make it easy to handle data structures such as queries, arrays, strings, lists, dates, and variables.

In addition to its capability to interact with ODBC-compliant databases, ColdFusion extends its usefulness with the capability to interact with other services running on your server. These include

- The local file system
- Other HTTP servers
- FTP servers
- Mail servers
- Lightweight Directory Access Protocol (LDAP) directory servers
- Verity search engine collections
- Java applets
- COM/DCOM objects

Thus, it becomes easy to perform basic tasks common to many Web-based applications. In an electronic commerce application, for example, you could gather a user's purchases as he or she shops, storing them as an HTTP cookie or as a ColdFusion session variable. At checkout time, you appeal to the cookie or session variable for the user's purchases and present them for confirmation. Then you collect the user's credit card information, stashing that in your customer database, and email a receipt confirming the purchase. All these steps are simple to implement using ColdFusion.

This chapter introduces you to the ColdFusion application-development environment. The major components of this environment include

- The ColdFusion Application Server, which can be installed on Windows NT/98/2000, Solaris, or Linux platforms
- The ColdFusion Administrator, a browser-based interface that enables you to configure the ColdFusion Application Server
- ColdFusion Studio, a useful tool for authoring ColdFusion templates

Over the course of this chapter, you'll also learn about many of the useful CFML tags and functions that make Web-based application development with ColdFusion a straightforward and enjoyable task.

NOTE A single chapter cannot do justice to the power and utility of the ColdFusion development environment. For a fuller treatment, beginners should consult Ben Forta's popular book, The ColdFusion 4.0 Web Application Construction Kit. Developers with some experience are advised to read Advanced ColdFusion 4.0 Application Development, also by Ben Forta. Both are published by Que.

What Else Do I Need to Know to Develop ColdFusion Applications?

Understanding the ColdFusion development environment and mastering CFML are two important steps in becoming proficient in developing ColdFusion applications. However, to do serious application development, you should also be versed in the following skills:

- **XHTML**—CFML instructions are embedded inside XHTML code, so to excel at ColdFusion development, you need to truly understand XHTML and be able to work with raw XHTML code.
- **Relational database design**—You should have a command of data modeling theory and know how to express your model in terms of fields and tables in a relational database.
- **Structured Query Language (SQL)**—SQL (pronounced "sequel") is the language used to search, insert data into, update data in, or delete data from a backend database. You can find an excellent SQL tutorial on the Web at `w3.one.net/~jhoffman/sqltut.htm`.
- **JavaScript**—You can combine JavaScript and ColdFusion to produce applications more powerful and flexible than those you could create with ColdFusion alone. For example, client-side JavaScript that validates form data before it is submitted frees up the ColdFusion Application Server from having to do the same task. Thus, your server has more resources to dedicate to the tasks that it absolutely has to do.

You will most definitely need to have a basic understanding of XHTML, SQL, and relational database design to become a competent ColdFusion developer. After you feel well-grounded in these basics, you can then move on to building JavaScript-enabled ColdFusion applications. But knowing JavaScript is not an absolute prerequisite for being able to develop with ColdFusion.

Installing the ColdFusion Application Server

As noted earlier in this chapter, the ColdFusion Application Server can run on both Windows NT/98/2000, Solaris, and Linux platforms. On a Windows server, ColdFusion is compatible with the following kinds of HTTP servers:

- Netscape servers, such as FastTrack or Enterprise
- Microsoft servers, such as Internet Information Server (IIS), Peer Web Services, or Personal Web Server (PWS)
- O'Reilly WebSite Pro
- Apache for Windows NT

If you're installing ColdFusion on a Solaris machine, it will need to be running with one of the following Web servers:

- Apache
- Netscape Enterprise or FastTrack servers

Although there are many LINUX distributors, Allaire will only support ColdFusion installed on RedHat Linux, version 6.0 or higher, running the Apache Web server.

NOTE Allaire has also released the Enterprise edition of its ColdFusion Application Server for HP-UX platform.

NOTE Earlier versions of ColdFusion for Solaris were the Windows NT version of ColdFusion running on top of a Windows NT emulation layer—a fact that contributed to slower performance of ColdFusion on Solaris machines. Developers will be happy to know that ColdFusion for both Solaris and Linux now runs natively.

Installing ColdFusion on any platform is fairly straightforward. On a Windows machine, you are walked through the process by several dialog boxes that prompt you for the directory location, the Web server, and the password information. If you're doing a Solaris or Linux installation, you'll find that all you need to do is launch the installation file and respond to the few questions you are asked during the install. In either case, it's important to make sure your HTTP service is installed and running before you attempt the ColdFusion installation.

After you've installed the application server, you can immediately check to see if it's working properly by accessing the ColdFusion Getting Started page at `http://127.0.0.1/CFDOCS/index.htm`. There you will find links to an application in which you can test your installation, as well as links to help and documentation in HTML format (see Figure 33.2).

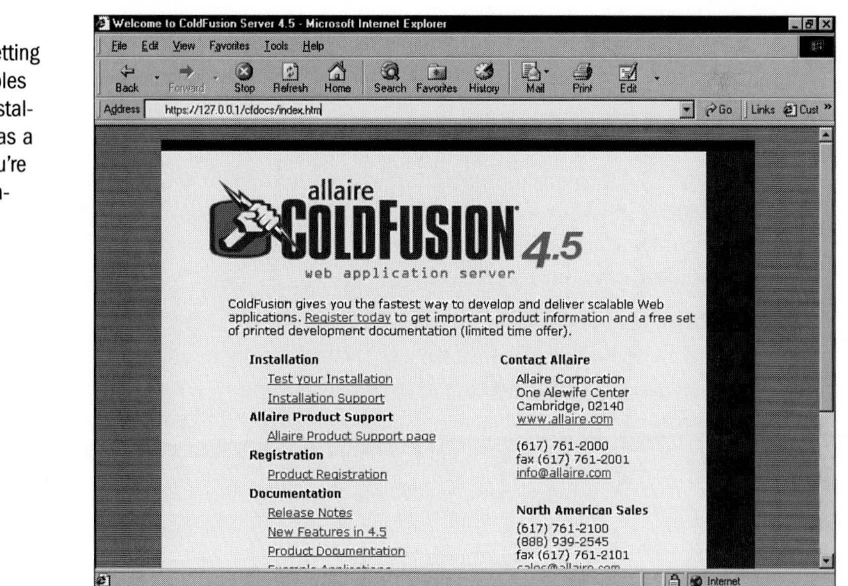

FIGURE 33.2
The ColdFusion Getting Started page enables you to test your installation and serves as a reference while you're developing applications.

NOTE The IP address `127.0.0.1` is reserved for addressing the Web server running on the local machine.

With the ColdFusion Application Server installed, you can configure the server using the ColdFusion Administrator. The many functions of the Administrator are discussed in the next section.

TIP Be sure to write down the ColdFusion Administrator and ColdFusion Studio passwords you specify during the installation. If you forget them, you'll need to repeat the installation.

Using the ColdFusion Administrator

A lot is going on behind the scenes within the ColdFusion development environment, and you can orchestrate all aspects of this activity through the ColdFusion Administrator. Specifically, you can do things such as

- Stop and start the ColdFusion Application Server
- Create and configure data sources
- Restrict the use of potentially harmful CFML tags
- Activate debugging messages that make it easier to troubleshoot your applications
- Specify how and where the ColdFusion Application Server should log certain events
- Configure the ColdFusion Application Server to work with an email server
- Create searchable Verity collections
- Install custom CFML tags
- Register Java applets

To access the ColdFusion Administrator, access the URL `http://127.0.0.1/CFIDE/administrator/index.cfm` and enter the Administrator password you specified during the installation of the ColdFusion Application Server. After you're authenticated, you'll see a screen such as the one in Figure 33.3.

The main administrator page is split into two frames. The left frame contains links that enable you to quickly navigate to the major parts of the Administrator. The right frame displays the settings that you can change within a given part. The next several sections of this chapter walk you through the various parts of the Administrator and point out the ColdFusion environment parameters that you can control through the Administrator.

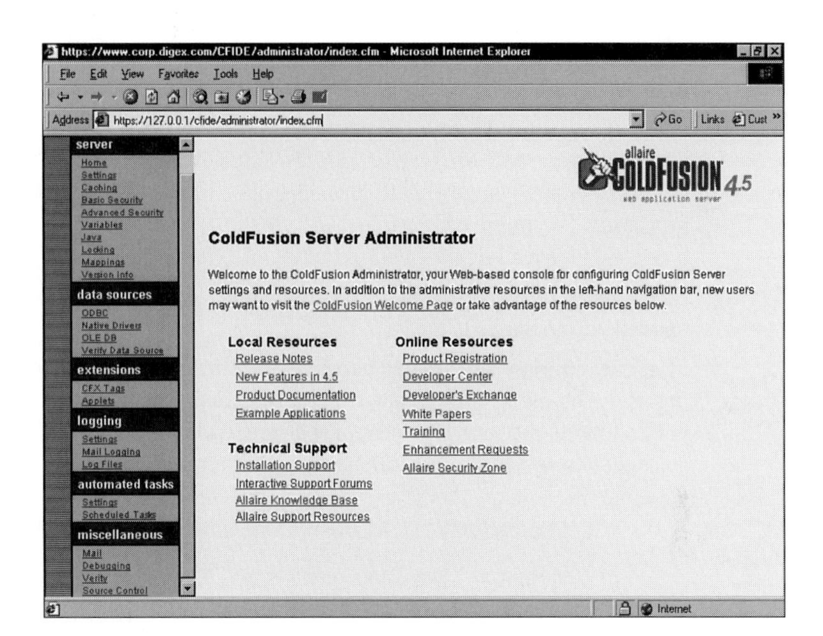

FIGURE 33.3
You can control the ColdFusion development environment through a browser-based interface.

Configuring the ColdFusion Application Server

If you click the Settings link in the left frame, you'll see the configuration options shown in Figure 33.4. These include

- **Number of simultaneous requests**—You can enhance the application server's performance by limiting the number of requests that it can simultaneously process. Any requests beyond this limiting number are queued in memory and processed in the order in which they are received.

TIP A good rule of thumb is to make the maximum number of simultaneous requests equal to the number of processors on your server.

- **Request timeout**—You can specify a certain number of seconds after which the processing of a template will time out. This helps to avoid infinite loops or other programming glitches that might bog down your server.

NOTE Even if you specify a timeout value, you should keep in mind that users can override this value by adding a `RequestTimeOut` parameter to the URL of the ColdFusion template that they are calling. If you have the timeout set to 30 seconds, for example, a user could circumvent this by entering a URL such as

```
http://www.cfserver.com/template.cfm?RequestTimeOut=300
```

The `RequestTimeOut` parameter passed with the URL increases the timeout value for that request to 300 seconds instead of the 30 seconds that you specified in the Administrator.

- **Server restart**—The ColdFusion Application Server can restart itself if a threshold number of requests are unresponsive or if requests are terminating abnormally.
- **Whitespace suppression**—Previous versions of ColdFusion have put in whitespace characters where CFML instructions are parsed out of the template. This often made for cumbersomely large HTML files generated as a result of the template being processed. By suppressing whitespace, ColdFusion consolidates all whitespace down to a single character, allowing your resulting HTML file to transfer and load more quickly.
- **Strict attribute validation**—If you check this option, ColdFusion will not permit any extraneous attributes in a CFML tag.
- **Missing template and error handlers**—In the event that a user requests a template that is not on the server or that an error occurs during the processing of a template, you can direct the user to a customized page that alerts them to the problem. This is analogous to setting up a custom 404 page on an HTTP server.

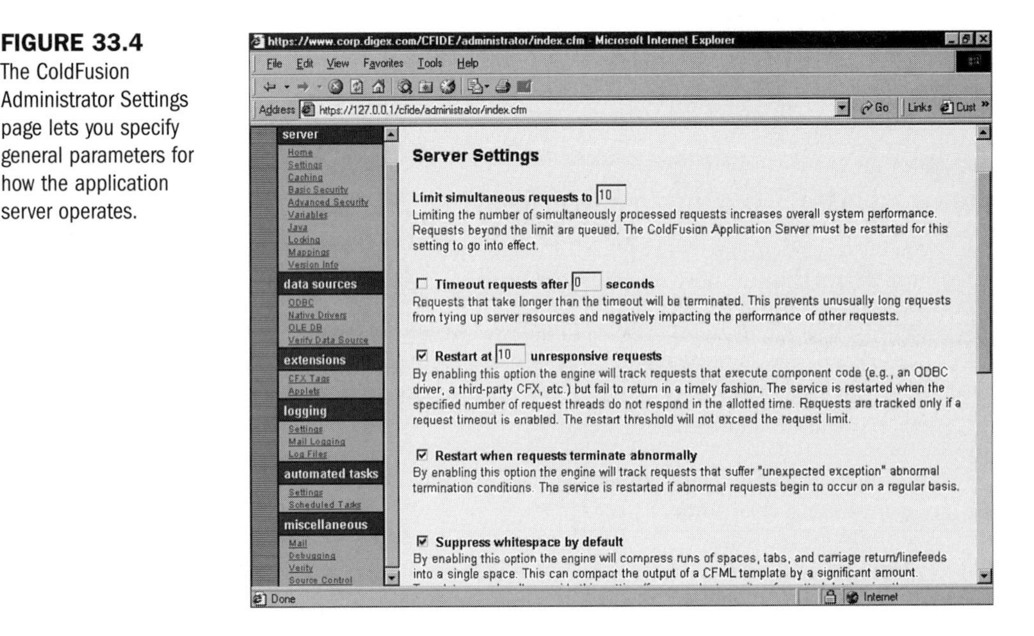

FIGURE 33.4
The ColdFusion Administrator Settings page lets you specify general parameters for how the application server operates.

Setting Up Data Sources

ColdFusion can communicate with databases on the same server or, in some cases, on a remote server, provided a data source is available that "points to" the database. ColdFusion can work with Open Database Connectivity (ODBC) data sources and Object Linking and Embedding (OLE DB) data sources.

If you click the ODBC link, you'll see a screen like the one shown in Figure 33.5. This is where you create, modify, test, and delete ODBC data sources. These data sources are pointers to database files, together with specifications on how ColdFusion should interact with the database.

> **TIP** Clicking the Verify All button in the upper-right part of the screen tests the connection to all your ODBC data sources.

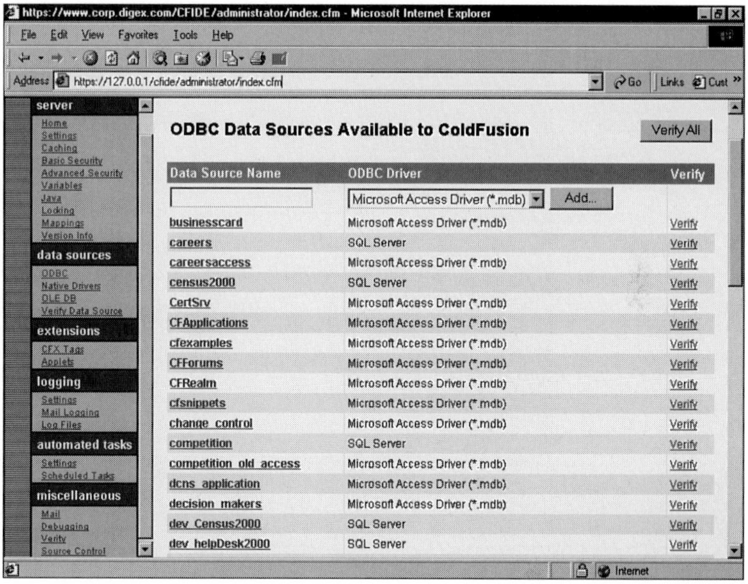

FIGURE 33.5
You specify which databases ColdFusion is able to use and how it should connect to those databases in the ODBC Data Sources section of the ColdFusion Administrator.

On the initial page of the ODBC Data Sources section, you'll see a list of all the available data sources and which kind of ODBC driver is being used to access the data source. Additionally, each data source has a Verify link next to it. When you click a Verify link, ColdFusion tests its connection to that data source and lets you know whether the test succeeded or failed. If the test failed, check to make sure the data source is configured to work with the proper database and, in the case of SQL Server or Oracle databases, make certain that those services are up and running properly.

To create a new ODBC data source, follow these steps:

1. Type the name of the data source into the text field at the top of the Data Source Name column.
2. Select which kind of ODBC driver you want to use from the drop-down list at the top of the ODBC Driver column. The list of ODBC drivers available depends on your operating system. If you're using a Windows machine, you'll see drivers for all the Microsoft database formats (Access, SQL Server, FoxPro, Excel), as well as Oracle drivers and any other drivers you might have installed yourself. On a Solaris or Linux machine, you will not find drivers for the Microsoft database formats.

3. Click Add to create the data source. The right frame changes to show you the Edit ODBC Data Source page similar to the one you see in Figure 33.6.

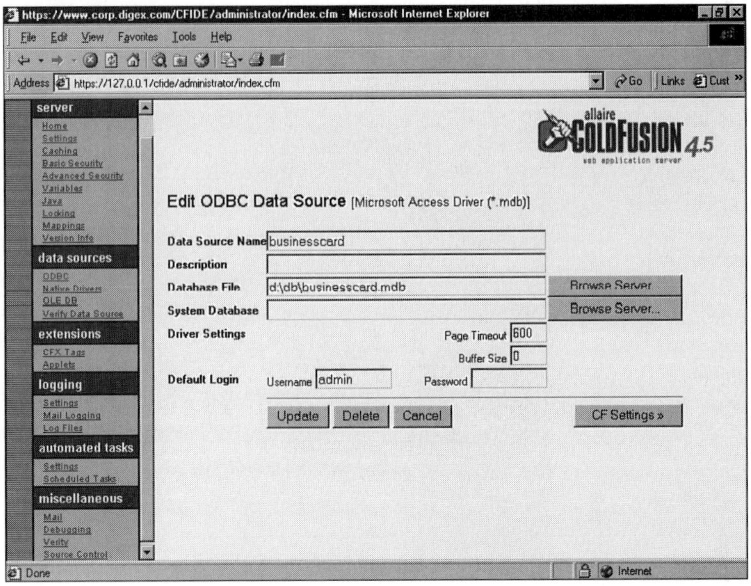

FIGURE 33.6
When setting up a data source, you must give it a name, specify the location of the database file, and set other driver-specific parameters.

NOTE The Edit ODBC Data Source page will look slightly different for each kind of ODBC driver because each driver has its own specific parameters that need to be set.

4. Fill in the information requested on the Edit ODBC Data Source page, making sure to specify the drive and directory path to the database file in the Database File field. ColdFusion comes with a Java applet that enables you to browse the drives and directories until you find the file you want.
5. At this point, you have two options. You can click the Update button to create the data source and return to the initial data source page, or you can click the CF Settings button to reveal a more detailed version of the Edit ODBC Data Source page (see Figure 33.7).
6. Choose values for the ColdFusion settings to associate with the data source. This includes values for the login timeout (how long ColdFusion will try to connect to the data source), how many simultaneous connections to allow to the database, a special username and password for ColdFusion to use when logging into the database, whether to maintain a connection to the database between requests, and any restrictions on SQL operations done against the database.

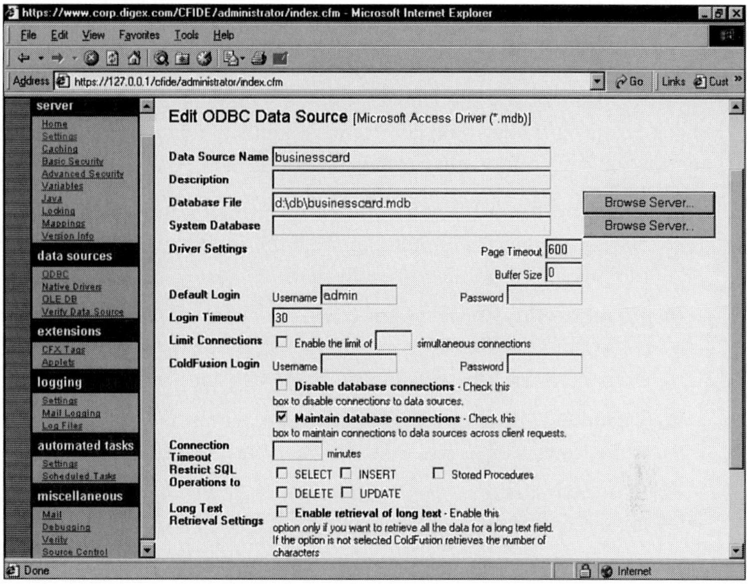

FIGURE 33.7
You can also configure how ColdFusion interacts with the data source when you create it.

Don't maintain connections to the database if you frequently have to upload updated copies of the database. If ColdFusion maintains the connection, it keeps a lock on the database file and you can't overwrite it with the new file without stopping the ColdFusion service.

7. Click the Update button (not visible in Figure 33.7) to create the data source and return to the main data source page.

To edit an existing data source, click its name from the main data source page. This will take you to a page that looks almost like the one you saw in Figure 33.6. From there, you can edit the data source's properties or click the CF Settings button to get an expanded edit page that is similar to what you saw in Figure 33.7. When you're finished making your changes, click the Update button to save them.

If you need to delete a data source, click the data source's name to go to the edit page, and then click the Delete button.

CAUTION

After you delete a data source, it is no longer available to any of your ColdFusion applications. Before deleting a data source, make sure none of your applications contain references to it.

Also, keep in mind that deleting a data source is not the same as deleting a database file. If you want to delete the database file, you'll need to do that through your operating system's file interface.

Using Debugging

ColdFusion's debugging feature is invaluable when you're troubleshooting an application. Figure 33.8 shows you the Debug Settings section of the ColdFusion Administrator. The check boxes on the left side control what kinds of debugging messages you get from the server. You can choose any combination of

- **Enabling the NT Performance Monitor (Windows servers only)**—The Windows NT Performance Monitor can track the ColdFusion Application Server's usage of system resources if this box is checked.
- **Enabling the CFML stack trace**—If checked, ColdFusion captures information about the tag or tags that were executing when a structured exception occurred. Structured exceptions are set up using the `<CFCATCH>` tag.
- **Variables**—If checked, you get a list of all form, URL, cookie, and CGI environment variables as well as the values of each variable.
- **Processing time**—Knowing the total processing time for a request can help you determine if changes to your code are making it more efficient or if they are impairing performance. The detail view can show you how much time was dedicated to each template in a request that involves more than one template.
- **SQL and data source name**—In the event of a query error, ColdFusion shows you the SQL statement and the target data source that caused the error.
- **Query information**—ColdFusion can tell you the processing time, how many records were returned, and what SQL statement was used for each query in the request.
- **Template path information**—Some server administrators consider it a security risk to include the path to an erroneous template in an error message. If you share the same concerns, you can disable the display of the template path by unchecking this box.

ColdFusion appends debugging information to the bottom of the XHTML page it generates in response to a browser's request. As you can see in Figure 33.9, the debugging information is rendered in a monospace font, so it's easy to pick out from the rest of the document.

One nice feature about ColdFusion debugging information is that you can restrict the delivery of the information to a specific set of IP addresses but not to every user. Thus, if you and/or your development team all have fixed IP addresses, you can insert these addresses into the IP Address listing you see in Figure 33.8. That way, your developers will see debugging messages but regular application users will not.

TIP

If your IP addresses are dynamically assigned, you might want to do your ColdFusion development and testing on a separate server and then port the finished application to a production server when you are done. You can then turn on debugging for the development server without restricting the output to specific IP addresses, and your developers will still be able to get debugging feedback.

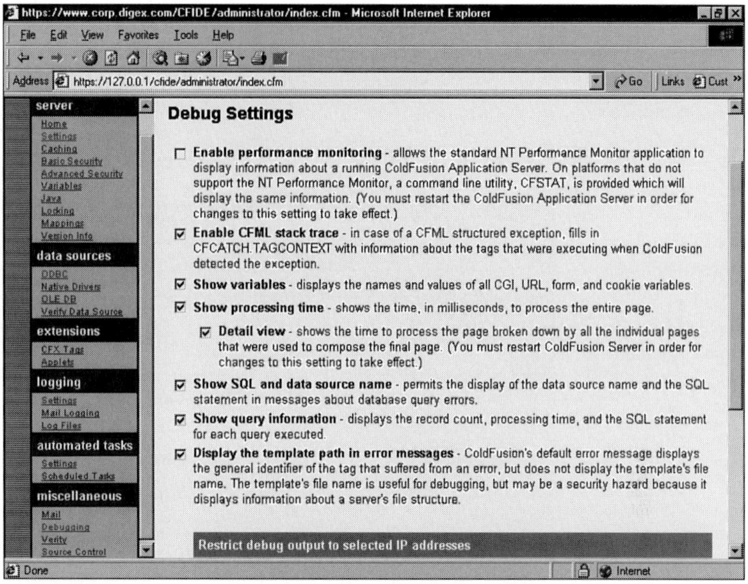

FIGURE 33.8
You can choose which kinds of debugging messages you want displayed during application development and testing.

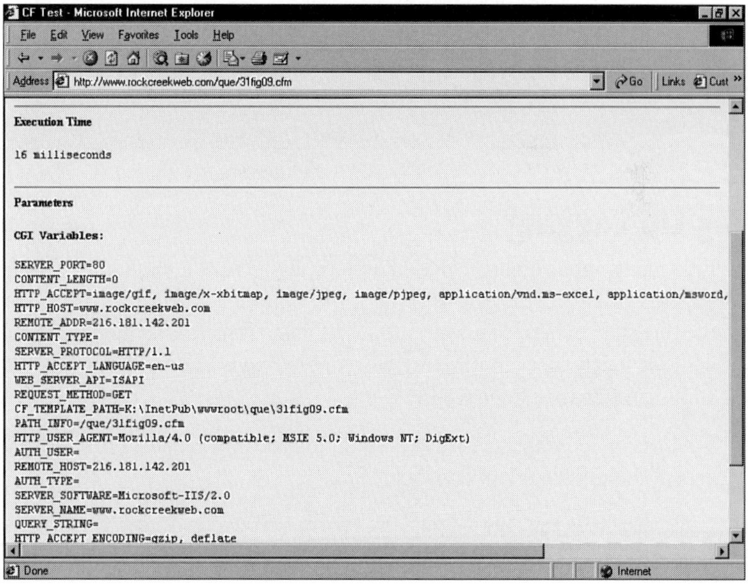

https://www.corp.digex.com/CFIDE/administrator/index.cfm - Microsoft Internet Explorer
File Edit View Favorites Tools Help
Address https://127.0.0.1/cfide/administrator/index.cfm Go Links Cust

server
Home
Settings
Caching
Basic Security
Advanced Security
Variables
Java
Locking
Mappings
Version Info
data sources
ODBC
Native Drivers
OLE DB
Verify Data Source
extensions
CFX Tags
Applets
logging
Settings
Mail Logging
Log Files
automated tasks
Settings
Scheduled Tasks
miscellaneous
Mail
Debugging
Verity
Source Control

Debug Settings

Enable performance monitoring - allows the standard NT Performance Monitor application to display information about a running ColdFusion Application Server. On platforms that do not support the NT Performance Monitor, a command line utility, CFSTAT, is provided which will display the same information. (You must restart the ColdFusion Application Server in order for changes to this setting to take effect.)

Enable CFML stack trace - in case of a CFML structured exception, fills in CFCATCH.TAGCONTEXT with information about the tags that were executing when ColdFusion detected the exception.

Show variables - displays the names and values of all CGI, URL, form, and cookie variables.

Show processing time - shows the time, in milliseconds, to process the entire page.

Detail view - shows the time to process the page broken down by all the individual pages that were used to compose the final page. (You must restart ColdFusion Server in order for changes to this setting to take effect.)

Show SQL and data source name - permits the display of the data source name and the SQL statement in messages about database query errors.

Show query information - displays the record count, processing time, and the SQL statement for each query executed.

Display the template path in error messages - ColdFusion's default error message displays the general identifier of the tag that suffered from an error, but does not display the template's file name. The template's file name is useful for debugging, but may be a security hazard because it displays information about a server's file structure.

Restrict debug output to selected IP addresses

Done Internet

FIGURE 33.9
Debugging information always appears at the end of the ColdFusion page.

CF Test - Microsoft Internet Explorer
File Edit View Favorites Tools Help
Address http://www.rockcreekweb.com/que/31fig09.cfm Go Links Cust

Execution Time

16 milliseconds

Parameters

CGI Variables:

```
SERVER_PORT=80
CONTENT_LENGTH=0
HTTP_ACCEPT=image/gif, image/x-xbitmap, image/jpeg, image/pjpeg, application/vnd.ms-excel, application/msword,
HTTP_HOST=www.rockcreekweb.com
REMOTE_ADDR=216.181.142.201
CONTENT_TYPE=
SERVER_PROTOCOL=HTTP/1.1
HTTP_ACCEPT_LANGUAGE=en-us
WEB_SERVER_API=ISAPI
REQUEST_METHOD=GET
CF_TEMPLATE_PATH=K:\InetPub\wwwroot\que\31fig09.cfm
PATH_INFO=/que/31fig09.cfm
HTTP_USER_AGENT=Mozilla/4.0 (compatible; MSIE 5.0; Windows NT; DigExt)
AUTH_USER=
REMOTE_HOST=216.181.142.201
AUTH_TYPE=
SERVER_SOFTWARE=Microsoft-IIS/2.0
SERVER_NAME=www.rockcreekweb.com
QUERY_STRING=
HTTP_ACCEPT_ENCODING=gzip, deflate
```

Done Internet

Using ColdFusion with a Mail Server

You can send email messages from your ColdFusion applications after you have ColdFusion configured to work with your mail server. Figure 33.10 shows the Mail portion of the

ColdFusion Administrator, which you can call up by clicking the Mail link in the left frame. Here you can tell the ColdFusion Application Server the name or IP address of your mail server, which server port it should use (typically port 25), and a connect timeout value. You can also verify the connection to your mail server by clicking the Verify button near the bottom of the Mail Server Connection Settings page.

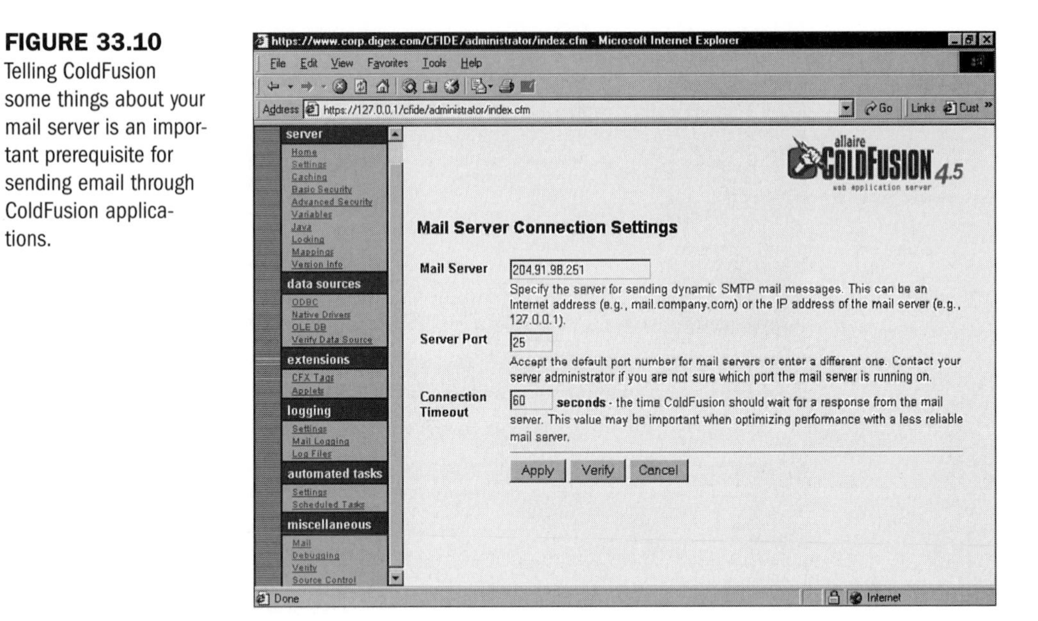

FIGURE 33.10
Telling ColdFusion some things about your mail server is an important prerequisite for sending email through ColdFusion applications.

Setting Up Logging

Like many applications, ColdFusion logs any errors it encounters while processing your templates. Under the Logging section of the ColdFusion Administrator, you can tell ColdFusion the directory where you want the ColdFusion logs stored, and you can provide an email address for the server administrator so that users can mail any error occurrences to the administrator (see Figure 33.11).

ColdFusion classifies errors according to type and creates different log files for each type of error. The different log files include

- `application.log`—Logs any errors that occur during the processing of a template.
- `executive.log`—Records errors detected by the ColdFusion Executive (the overarching ColdFusion service).
- `mail.log`—Logs any errors that occur during interactions with mail servers.
- `rdsservice.log`—The Remote Data Server (RDS) service allows developers using ColdFusion Studio to create and maintain files on the server without an FTP connection. RDS can also be used to examine data sources on the remote server. Any RDS errors are recorded in the `rdsservice.log` file.

- **`scheduler.log`**—The ColdFusion Scheduler is responsible for making sure that templates scheduled to be run at specific times are actually processed. `scheduler.log` contains any error messages generated by the Scheduler.
- **`server.log`**—Records any errors encountered by the ColdFusion Application Server.
- **`webserver.log`**—Logs any HTTP errors that occur during a request for a ColdFusion template.

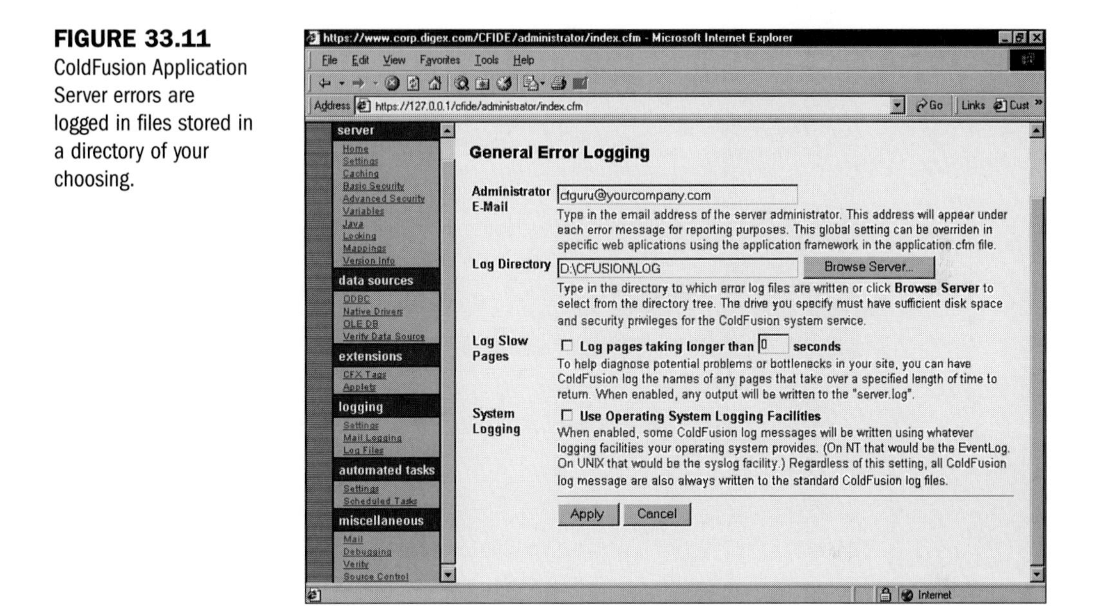

FIGURE 33.11
ColdFusion Application Server errors are logged in files stored in a directory of your choosing.

A special Mail Logging link lets you log mail server error messages by their severity (Information, Warning, or Error), and you can choose to log the content of every email that ColdFusion sends.

> **TIP** If you opt to log all email messages, make sure you archive the contents of the file periodically so it doesn't become too large and unmanageable.

Restricting Potentially Harmful Tags

Some CFML tags can manipulate files, Registry settings, and other critical system resources. An ill-intentioned user could exploit these tags to upload content to, modify content on, or delete content from your server. To prevent this from happening, you can choose to enable or disable these tags from the Basic Security section of the ColdFusion Administrator. As you can see in Figure 33.12, you can activate the `<CFCONTENT>`, `<CFDIRECTORY>`, `<CFFILE>`, `<CFOBJECT>`, `<CFREGISTRY>`, `<CFADMINSECURITY>`, and `<CFEXECUTE>` tags by checking the box next to each one.

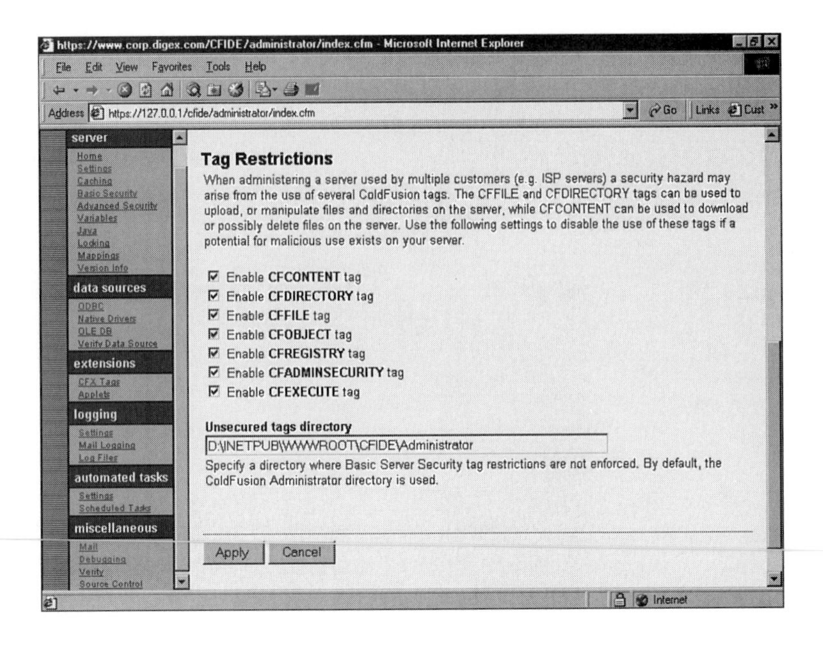

FIGURE 33.12
If you're administering a ColdFusion server and are concerned about file security, you will probably want to disable the file-related CFML tags.

NOTE You can also change your ColdFusion Administrator and ColdFusion Studio passwords on the Basic Security page. ■

Using Custom Tags

Another of ColdFusion's many great features is that you can develop your own tags when existing CFML tags won't do the job. Custom ColdFusion tags can be developed in CFML or in more complicated programming languages such as C++ or Java. After you have developed a custom tag, you need to register it with the ColdFusion Administrator. To do this, click the CFX Tags link, enter the tag's name in the text field you see under the Registered CFX Tags heading in Figure 33.13, choose which language the tag is written in, and then click the Add button. You then need to specify a few additional pieces of information, such as the supporting DLL file, procedure, whether to keep the DLL loaded in memory, and a description of the tag.

NOTE All custom tags that you write in C++ or Java must begin with CFX_. Custom tags written in CFML begin with CF_ and can reside in the same directory as your other application templates. ■

FIGURE 33.13
All custom tags must be registered with the ColdFusion Administrator before you can use them.

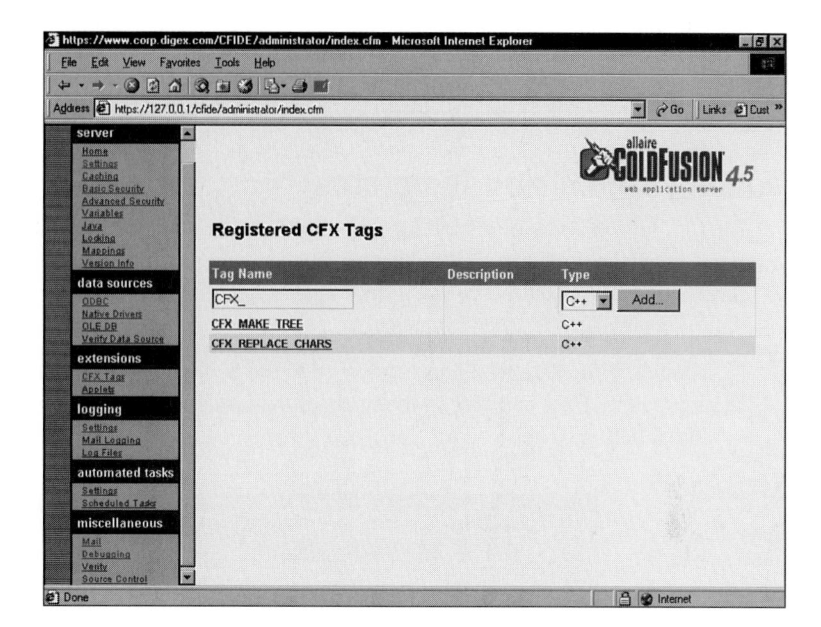

Setting Up Mappings

Sometimes it's much easier to set up a logical path or *alias* to a long directory path than to type out that path again and again. You can do this through the ColdFusion Administrator's Mappings page (see Figure 33.14). To set up a directory mapping, enter the logical path in the first text field, enter the actual directory path into the second text field, and then click the Add Mapping button.

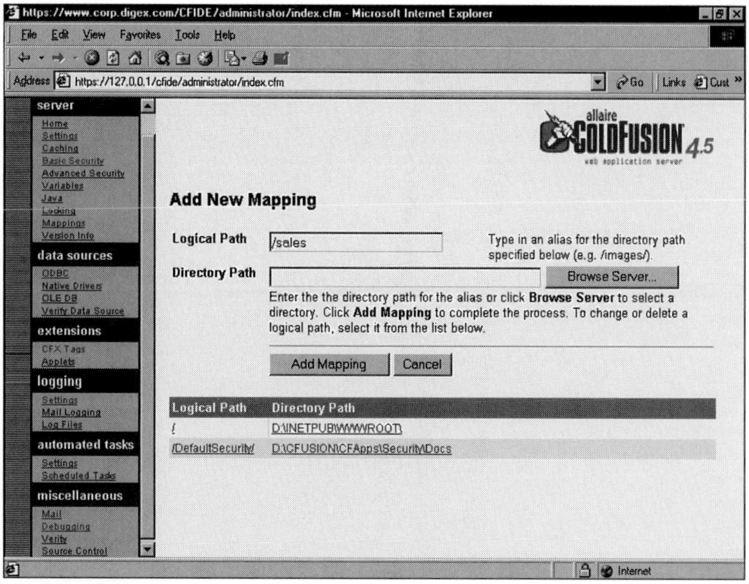

FIGURE 33.14
You can shorten long, tedious directory paths by setting up aliases in the ColdFusion Administrator.

TIP It's easier to use the built-in Java applet to browse the server when specifying the directory path. It also reduces the chance of your making a mistake while typing in the path.

Scheduling ColdFusion Templates

The ColdFusion Scheduler submits templates for processing at intervals you specify. This might be useful, for example, when reporting to management. You could write a template that queries out your e-commerce site's sales figures from the previous day and puts them in a summary email to the Sales Manager.

To schedule a template, you first need to go to the Scheduler page of the ColdFusion Administrator. There you type in the name of the task you want to schedule and click the Add New Task button. When you do, you'll see a screen similar to the one shown in Figure 33.15.

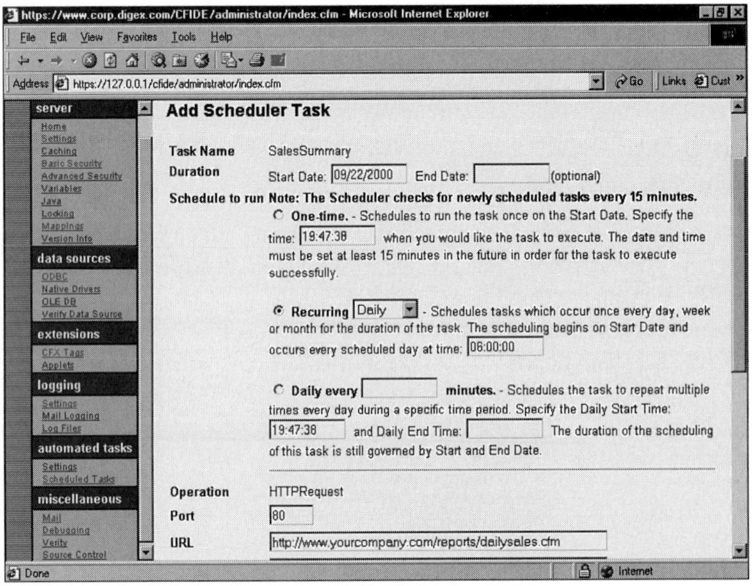

FIGURE 33.15
ColdFusion templates can be run automatically according to schedules that you create.

When scheduling the task, you will have to provide information such as

- Start and end dates for the task (ColdFusion will assume no end date if none is specified)
- The frequency of the task (once, daily, every 45 minutes, and so on)
- The URL of the template and any login and proxy information needed to invoke the template
- Where to write the output from the template, should you choose to record it

After you have all the scheduling parameters entered, click the Create button to schedule the task. If you need to modify the task later on, click the task name from the main Tasks page and make the edits on the Edit Scheduler Task page (which looks exactly like the page in Figure 33.15). When you're done making your changes, click the Update button to apply them.

CAUTION

After you create a scheduled task, the ColdFusion Scheduler might require up to 15 minutes to recognize and incorporate the task into its master schedule. You can reduce this time by clicking the Settings link under the Automated Tasks heading and changing the Scheduler Refresh Interval to a value less than the default 15 minutes.

NOTE Tasks are automatically deleted after the end date specified in the task duration has passed. If you did not specify an end date, you can delete the task by going to the Edit Scheduler Task page and clicking the Delete button.

Using the Verity Search Engine

ColdFusion comes bundled with a version of the popular Verity search engine, making it easy to set up searchable sets of documents. In Verity vernacular, these sets of documents are called *collections*, and you can create your own collections from the ColdFusion Administrator's Verity page (see Figure 33.16).

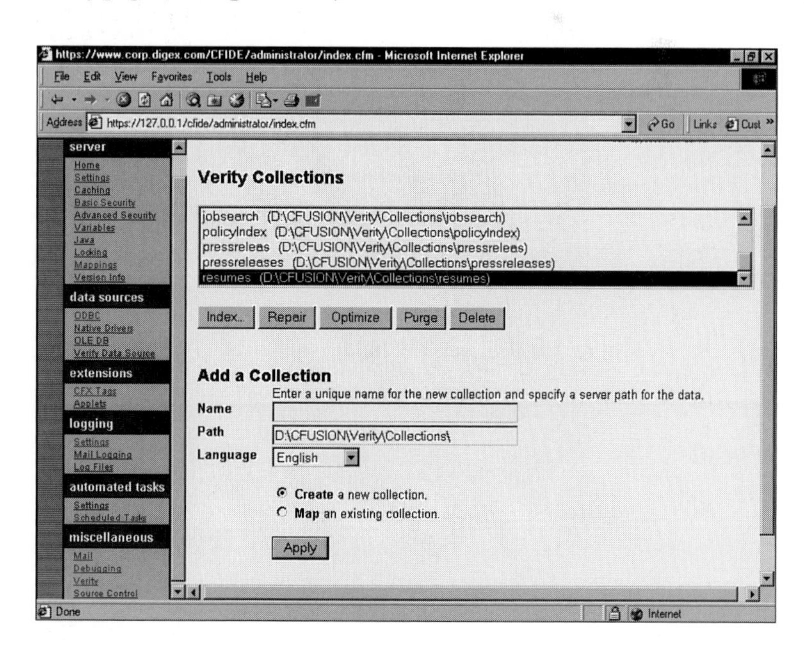

FIGURE 33.16
Verity collections are groups of searchable documents that you can access through ColdFusion.

The Verity page is divided into two parts. The top part shows any existing Verity collections and enables you to perform different operations on those collections. The most common task is to index a collection. When you click the Index button, you get the option of specifying (by file extension) which type of files you want to index, the directory you want to index, and whether you want to recursively index subdirectories. When Verity indexes a collection, it examines the contents of each file and builds a database to support search engine queries against those files.

NOTE Not only can Verity index commonly used text-based files (`.html`, `.cfm`, `.txt`, `.rtf`), but it can also index Adobe Acrobat PDF files and files generated by popular desktop software applications such as Microsoft Office.

The lower part of the Verity page enables you to create a new Verity collection. To do this, you type in a name for the collection, specify the directory where ColdFusion should store the collection, and provide a language context for the collection.

Registering Applets

ColdFusion works well with Java applets, but only after you register the applet with the ColdFusion Administrator. To do this, click the Applet link in the Administrator to reveal the screen shown in Figure 33.17. Then type in a name for the applet, click the Register New Applet button, and provide the information requested about the applet.

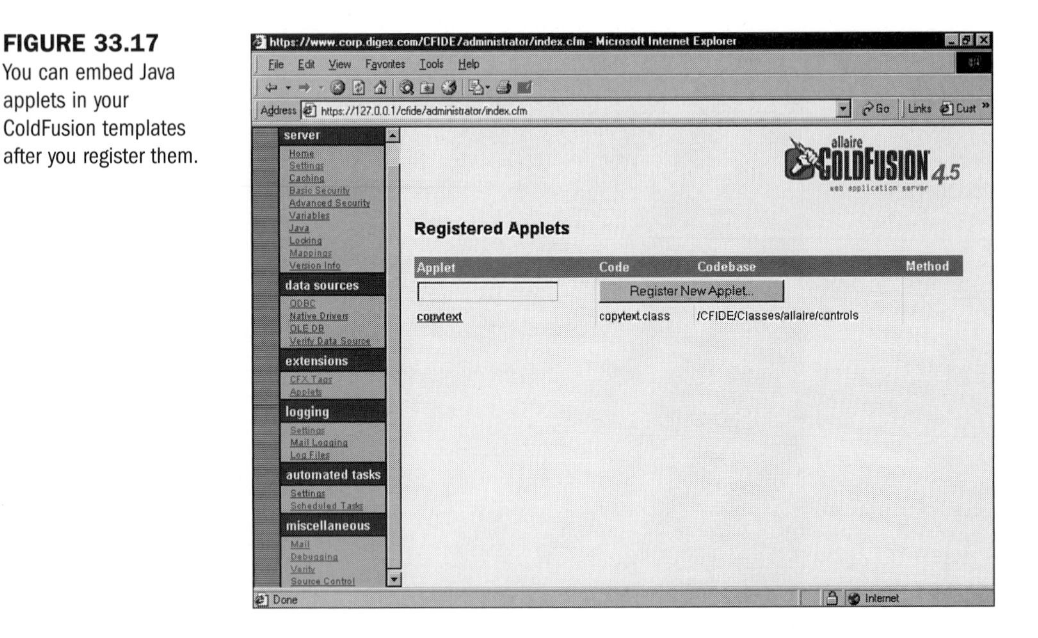

FIGURE 33.17
You can embed Java applets in your ColdFusion templates after you register them.

The information you have to provide when registering a new applet might look familiar to you if you use the XHTML `<applet>` element a lot. The values for the `code`, `codebase`, `method`, `height`, `width`, `vspace`, `hspace`, and `align` attributes are exactly what you would put in the corresponding fields on the registration page. ColdFusion uses this information to write out an `<applet>` element for you. The text entered in the Java Not Supported Message is exactly what you might specify in an `alt` attribute, except what you enter through the ColdFusion Administrator can be marked up with XHTML code.

In the applet parameters section, you can specify the parameter/value pairs that get passed to the applet. This is analogous to using the `<param>` element to pass parameters to an applet placed with the `<applet>` element.

The ColdFusion Markup Language

Now that you are familiar with the basics of ColdFusion administration, you can begin to learn the ColdFusion Markup Language (CFML)—the language used to develop ColdFusion applications. Two important things to remember about CFML are

- CFML code is located in the same file as XHTML code.
- CFML is a tag-based language, so if you're comfortable with XHTML, it will be easier to pick up CFML.

As you read earlier, CFML also comes with more than 200 functions for processing specific data structures. These functions are used within tags and make ColdFusion application development that much easier.

The next two major sections look at the most useful CFML tags and functions in the context of common tasks you would need to code when developing a ColdFusion application. Documentation covering every CFML tag and function can be found in ColdFusion's built-in help and reference material (`http://127.0.0.1/CFDOCS/index.htm`) or in the Help section of the ColdFusion Studio Resource Tab.

▶ To learn more about ColdFusion Studio, **see** "Using ColdFusion Studio," **p. 944**

CFML Tags

CFML tags are similar to XHTML elements in that

- They can occur as standalone tags or in an opening tag/closing tag pair.
- They have attributes that modify the effect of the tag.

One thing common to all CFML tags is that the keyword for each tag always begins with the letters `CF`. This is especially important to remember because some CFML tags, such as

<CFFORM> and <CFTABLE>, would be reduced to regular XHTML tags if you left the CF off the keywords.

The next several sections examine many of the useful tags that make up CFML, including

- Assigning values to ColdFusion variables with <CFSET> and printing their values with <CFOUTPUT>
- Querying, inserting, updating, and deleting records in a database using <CFQUERY>
- Implementing conditional logic with <CFIF>
- Creating looping constructs with <CFLOOP>
- Sending email using <CFMAIL>
- Using several other useful tags such as <CFINCLUDE>, <CFLOCATION>, <CFCOOKIE>, <CFTRANSACTION>, and <CFFORM>

Setting Variables and Displaying Their Values

In any programming language, it is common to create named areas in memory called *variables* and store key values there for reference during the execution of the program. ColdFusion is no different in this regard and enables you to create variables of many types, including

- Numeric
- Strings
- Boolean (TRUE or FALSE)
- Date/Time
- Lists (items delimited by commas or another character of your choosing)
- Arrays
- Queries

Each type of variable is instantiated by the <CFSET> tag. <CFSET> is a standalone tag with the following syntax:

```
<CFSET variable = value>
```

Some sample variable assignments might look like this:

```
<CFSET sorted = FALSE>
<CFSET total = 0>
<CFSET name = "Allaire">
<CFSET today = DateFormat(Now(),'mm/dd/yy')>
<CFSET flavors = "Vanilla,Chocolate,Strawberry">
```

NOTE The `Now()` function fetches the system date and time, and the `DateFormat` function applies the mm/dd/yy format to the date.

You also use `<CFSET>` to update the value of an existing variable. For example,

```
<CFSET total = total + item_cost>
```

takes the value currently stored in the variable `total`, adds `item_cost` to that amount, and then stores the result back in the variable `total`.

Creating arrays and queries requires a few other ColdFusion functions in addition to the `<CFSET>` tag because these data structures are more complex than the other variable types. To create an array, you first have to use the `ArrayNew()` function:

```
<CFSET planets = ArrayNew(1)>
```

NOTE The number you pass to the `ArrayNew()` function specifies how many indexes the array is to have. ColdFusion arrays can have up to three indexes.

Also, ColdFusion array indexes start at the value 1. This is different from languages such as JavaScript, in which array indexes beginning at 0.

With the array declared, you can then use `<CFSET>` to assign values to the array:

```
<CFSET planets[1] = "Mercury">
<CFSET planets[2] = "Venus">
<CFSET planets[3] = "Earth">
...
<CFSET planets[9] = "Pluto">
```


Query variables are structured much like a query result set in memory. In fact, after you've defined a query variable, you can use it just as you would if it were generated by a call to a database, meaning you can loop over the query variable with `<CFLOOP>` or output the contents of the query variable using `<CFOUTPUT>`.

To establish the query variable, you use the ColdFusion `QueryNew()` function:

```
<CFSET contact_info = QueryNew("Name,Address,City,State,Zip")>
```

The quoted list of values you pass to the `QueryNew()` function is the column names you want to use in the query. With the query created, you can add empty rows to the query so you can populate it with data. You do this with the `QueryAddRow()` function. Because you have to call this function from within a tag, you most commonly see `QueryAddRow` used as follows:

```
<CFSET temp = QueryAddRow(contact_info,20)>
```

The number following the name of the query indicates how many blank rows to add to the query. If you don't specify a value, ColdFusion assumes you just want to insert one row. If successful, the `QueryAddRow()` function returns a value of `TRUE`, and this is what is assigned to the variable `temp`. Otherwise, `temp` ends up being set to `FALSE`.

Finally, to place values into the individual cells of the query, you use the `QuerySetCell()` function. `QuerySetCell()` is used in a `<CFSET>` tag in much the same way as `QueryAddRow()`. For example, the code

```
<CFSET temp = QuerySetCell(contact_info,"City","Alexandria",12)>
```

places the value `"Alexandria"` in the City column of the 12th row of the query variable `contact_info`. If no row number is specified, ColdFusion inserts the value into the last row. If the insert is successful, `temp` takes on a value of `TRUE`; otherwise, `temp` is set to `FALSE`.

When it comes time to print the value of a ColdFusion variable on an HTML page, you need to know two things:

- You must use the `<CFOUTPUT>` tag.
- You must enclose the name of the variable in pound signs (#) to indicate to ColdFusion that it should replace the variable name with its value.

To illustrate what can happen if you miss one or the other, consider the following code:

```
<CFSET job = "Web Programmer">
<CFOUTPUT>job</CFOUTPUT><P>
#job#<P>
<CFOUTPUT>#job#</CFOUTPUT>
```

When ColdFusion processes this code, it produces the HTML page you see in Figure 33.18. In the first line, you just see the word `"job"` because no # signs tell ColdFusion to replace the variable with its value. You see `#job#` on the second line because ColdFusion will only do variable value substitution inside of `<CFOUTPUT>` and `</CFOUTPUT>` tags. The third line reads `Web Programmer` because both the `<CFOUTPUT>` tag and the # signs are used.

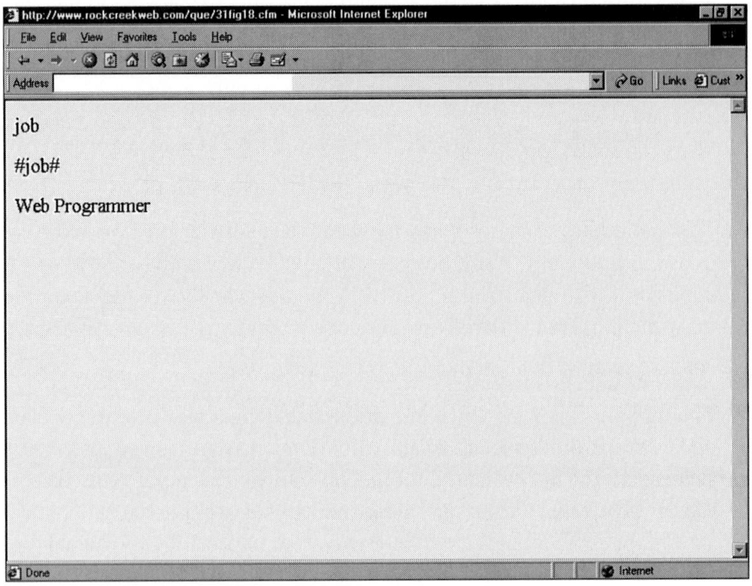

FIGURE 33.18
Getting ColdFusion to output variable values can be tricky initially.

CAUTION

Be careful when using hexadecimal color triplets because the pound sign (#) that precedes them can confuse the ColdFusion Application Server when it parses the file. As long as you keep the color triplets outside of any CFML container tags, your code should be parsed without any problems.

A useful variant of the <CFOUTPUT> tag is to use its QUERY attribute to make the output loop over an entire query result set. If you have done a query to retrieve course and instructor names, for example, you could print them all out in a table using the following code:

```
<table border="1">
<tr><th>Course</th><th>Instructor</th></tr>
<CFOUTPUT QUERY="classes">
<tr><td>#CourseName#</td><td>Prof. #FacultyName#</td></tr>
</CFOUTPUT>
</table>
```

In this case, the variables CourseName and FacultyName are column names from the database containing the course and faculty member names. When flanked with # signs and enclosed in <CFOUTPUT> and </CFOUTPUT> tags, the values of these variables are printed instead. And because you used the QUERY attribute of the <CFOUTPUT> tag, ColdFusion automatically loops over the entire query set and produces a table row for each course and faculty name. Imagine how long it would take you to code such a table for a schedule of 30 classes! With ColdFusion, you can produce the output table with just a few lines of code.

Sometimes query result sets can be rather long, and it's helpful to limit the amount of output the user gets at one time. To assist with this, you can use the MAXROWS attribute of the <CFOUTPUT> tag to specify a maximum number of rows from the result set that the tags should loop over. You might set MAXROWS to 20, for example, so a user only sees, at most, 20 records at a time.

You can also control the record where the output begins by using the <CFOUTPUT> tag's START attribute. This enables you to set up a link to see the next 20 records. Just pass the value of the last record printed, add one to it, and set the START attribute equal to that value.

Performing Database Operations

ColdFusion's strength lies in its capability to communicate with databases and retrieve, store, update, or delete records in those databases. Regardless of the type of database operation you're doing, you use the <CFQUERY> and </CFQUERY> tags to enclose the SQL statement that does the operation. The next four sections look at how to use <CFQUERY> for the basic operations of retrieving, inserting, updating, and deleting.

Retrieving Database Records Querying a database to find records that match specific search criteria is probably the most popular of the fundamental database operations. ColdFusion makes each part of this task easy—from incorporating search criteria entered on an XHTML form into the SQL statement, to performing the actual query, to receiving and printing out the results of the query in XHTML format.

Suppose you are assigned to create an intranet page for your company's sales force that prints a list of your clients in a state that the user can specify. To begin, you set up a form that asks the user for which state they want a list. The XHTML for that form might look like this:

```
<form action="statelist.cfm" method="post">
<b>Show me clients in the following state:</b><br>
<select name="state">
<option value="AL">Alabama
<option value="AK">Alaska
<option value="AR">Arkansas
...
<option value="WY">Wyoming
</select>
<input type="Submit" value="Generate List"/>
</form>
```

This produces a drop-down list of all the states. The user chooses one of them and then clicks the Generate List button to submit the request to the server. Seeing an `action` attribute that ends in `.cfm` (the file extension for ColdFusion templates), the server hands over the template and the form data to the ColdFusion Application Server for processing.

The challenge now is to write the template called `statelist.cfm` so that it does two things:

- Queries the database for clients located in the state the user selects
- Produces an XHTML page that displays the client listing

Both of these are easy to accomplish with CFML. First, you need to write a query that pulls client information based on the selected state. You can do this with the following code:

```
<CFQUERY DATASOURCE="clients" NAME="ByState">
SELECT company, city
FROM Clients
WHERE state = '#Form.state#'
</CFQUERY>
```

Note first that `<CFQUERY>` takes a few attributes. The `DATASOURCE` attribute is mandatory and should be set equal to the name of a data source you set up in the ColdFusion Administrator. The `NAME` attribute is also required and enables you to assign a unique name to the query so you can reference the results set by that name.

Next, note the `WHERE` clause in the SQL statement. Instead of a specific state's name, you see `#Form.state#`. ColdFusion treats submitted form data as an object that you can reference by the name Form. To key in on a particular form field, you can say `Form.field_name`. That's why you see `Form.state` in the sample code—it references the state field of the form that was submitted. By enclosing `Form.state` in # signs, you instruct ColdFusion to substitute the value it finds at `Form.state`. So in this case, if the user chose the state of California, the resulting SQL statement (after ColdFusion substitutes the value) would be

```
SELECT company, city, state
FROM Clients
WHERE state = 'CA'
```

In response to this SQL statement, the database would return the company name and city of each client in the state of California and store the result set under the name "ByState". You can then use the <CFOUTPUT> tag with the QUERY attribute to produce a table that prints out the entire list of clients. The complete listing for this template is shown in Listing 33.1.

Listing 33.1 *statelist.cfm* Code Listing

```
<CFQUERY DATASOURCE="clients" NAME="ByState">
SELECT company, city
FROM Clients
WHERE state = '#Form.state#'
</CFQUERY>

<html>

<head>
<title>Client Listing for <CFOUTPUT>#Form.state#</CFOUTPUT></title>
</head>

<body bgcolor="white">

<h1>Client Listing for <CFOUTPUT>#Form.state#</CFOUTPUT></h1>

<p><CFOUTPUT>#ByState.RecordCount#</CFOUTPUT> records found</p>

<table>
<tr><th>Company</th><th>Location</th></tr>
<CFOUTPUT QUERY="ByState">
<tr><td>#company#</td><td>#city#, #Form.state#</td></tr>
</CFOUTPUT>
</table>

</body>

</html>
```


NOTE A query's RecordCount property contains the number of records found when performing the query. You can access the value by referencing query_name.RecordCount, but be sure to enclose it in # signs and <CFOUTPUT> tags if you want to write its value into your resulting XHTML document.

This short template file should begin to give you an inkling of ColdFusion's power. In just a few lines of code, you have taken the form input, used it to dynamically build a SQL statement, passed the SQL statement to a database engine, retrieved the query results, and an XHTML table that presents the results in a readable format. If you've ever coded any CGI programs in a language such as Perl, think about how much code you would need to replicate the same functionality and compare it to Listing 33.1. You will very likely conclude that ColdFusion wins hands down in terms of power and efficiency.

NOTE Always use `method="post"` with a form that uses a ColdFusion template as its `action` attribute. Otherwise, the form data will be passed on the URL, in which case you would have to reference the URL object to get the submitted values.

Inserting Records into a Database Another common database operation is to insert a new record into a database table. Suppose, for example, you were gathering subscription information for an email-based newsletter. You would need to collect the subscriber's name and email address so that you could send the newsletter whenever it is published. In support of this, you could write a form similar to the following:

```
<form action="subscribe.cfm" method="post">
<b>Name: </b>
<input type="text" name="subscriber_name" size="20"/>
<br />
<b>E-mail: </b>
<input type="text" name="subscriber_email" size="20"/>
<br />
<input type="submit" value="Sign me up!"/>
</form>
```

After you write the form, you need to write the ColdFusion template named `subscribe.cfm`. The important thing for this template to do is to insert the name and email address information into the database, but it would also be nice if the user received some kind of confirmation message to let them know that the subscription has been entered.

To handle the insertion of the new record, you can use the following code:

```
<CFQUERY DATASOURCE="newsletter" NAME="NewSubscriber">
INSERT
INTO Subscribers (name,email)
VALUES ('#Form.subscriber_name#','#Form.subscriber_email#')
</CFQUERY>
```

Note in the `VALUES` specification that you reference the `subscriber_name` and `subscriber_email` fields of the submitted form, and that by enclosing them in # signs, you instruct ColdFusion to substitute the values passed in those fields. Thus, the resulting SQL statement for a user named Mabel Anderson with email address `manderson@isp.net` would look like this:

```
INSERT
INTO Subscribers (name,email)
VALUES ('Mabel Anderson','manderson@isp.net')
```

You can round out the template with some kind of message back to the user that repeats her information and confirms the insertion of her record into the database. Listing 33.2 shows one possible way of accomplishing this.

Listing 33.2 ***subscribe.cfm*** **Code Listing**

```
<CFQUERY DATASOURCE="newsletter" NAME="NewSubscriber">
INSERT
INTO Subscribers (name,email)
VALUES ('#Form.subscriber_name#','#Form.subscriber_email#')
</CFQUERY>

<html>

<head>
<title>Subscription Confirmation</title>
</head>

<body bgcolor="white">

<h1>Thank you, <CFOUTPUT>#Form.subscriber_name#</CFOUTPUT></h1>

<p>Your subscription has been entered and will be sent to you each
month at <CFOUTPUT>#Form.subscriber_email#</CFOUTPUT>.</p>

</body>

</html>
```

If you're not that comfortable with SQL `INSERT` statements, ColdFusion can relieve you of some of the burden with the `<CFINSERT>` tag. `<CFINSERT>` automatically generates the SQL call to insert submitted form data into a database—all you need to provide is the data source name and the name of the table where the data should be inserted. The one catch, however, is that the names of the form fields and the names of the corresponding columns in the database have to be an *exact match*. Looking back at the form that collects subscriber information, you can see that the form field names are `subscriber_name` and `subscriber_email`. However, the SQL in the earlier Listing 33.2 tells you that the column names you're inserting into are `name` and `email`. The names of the form fields and columns are different in this case, so you are not set up properly to use `<CFINSERT>`. If you abbreviated the form field names to `name` and `email`, then you would be able to successfully use `<CFINSERT>`. In that case, you could replace the `<CFQUERY>` code with

```
<CFINSERT DATASOURCE="newsletter" TABLENAME="subscribers">
```

and achieve the same result.

NOTE <CFINSERT> also takes the FORMFIELDS attribute, which is set equal to the names of the fields you want to insert. If FORMFIELDS is not specified, ColdFusion tries to insert every form field that was submitted.

Updating an Existing Database Record A third common database operation is to make a change to an existing record or records. Again, the <CFQUERY> tag plays a pivotal role in doing the update.

For this example, suppose that you are a developer for a credit card company that wants to Web-enable many of its customer service functions. The function you are tasked with coding is the change of address. As part of this function, you have to code the following form to collect the new address information:

```
<form action="updateaddr.cfm" method="post">
<p>Please enter your credit card number:</p>
<input type="text" name="card_number" size="20"/>

<p>Please enter your new address below:</p>
Street:
<input type="text" name="new_street" size="20"/>
<br/>
City:
<input type="text" name="new_city" size="20"/>
<br/>
State:
<input type="text" name="new_state" size="2"/>
<br/>
Zip:
<input type="text" name="new_street" size="20"/>
<br/>
<input type="submit" value="Update my Address"/>
</form>
```

In addition to the new address information, you also have to ask for something to uniquely identify the customer. In this case, you could use the credit card number itself, provided you knew that each customer has a unique number (this might not be true for a husband and wife with a joint account). In other situations, you would need to use the customer's primary key value from the database table that holds customer data.

Now you need to write the template updateaddr.cfm to do the update operation and display a confirmation message so that customers know their information was changed. To do the update, you would again use the <CFQUERY> tag:

```
<CFQUERY DATASOURCE="customers" NAME="updateAddr">
UPDATE Contact_Info
SET street='#Form.new_street#',city='#Form.new_city#',
   state='#Form.new_state#',zip='#Form.new_zip#'
WHERE customer_ID = '#Form.card_number#'
</CFQUERY>
```

The SQL UPDATE command is used to do the update, and you can see how each field is being set equal to the new values submitted on the form. The WHERE clause is important in the SQL statement because it restricts the update to the record belonging to the user with the credit card number entered on the form. Without the WHERE clause, the street, city, state, and zip columns of *every record in the database* would have been updated to reflect the new address information! The moral of the story is this: When doing updates, make sure that you are keying in on the record or records that require the updates by using the WHERE clause in your SQL statement. Otherwise, your updates will be made globally—usually with disastrous results.

Unique Record Identifiers

In relational database theory, the column that uniquely identifies a record in a table is called the table's *primary key*. The table is indexed by the primary key values, so searching by the primary key value is typically rapid and efficient. In the credit card example shown previously, you could conceivably use the customer's credit card number as a primary key, but primary keys are usually shorter than a 16-digit credit card number. In fact, primary keys are usually numeric fields that are automatically incremented each time a new record is inserted into the database. This ensures that each primary key is unique.

Tables in a well-designed relational database usually contain pointers to records in other tables. You might have a table, for example, where you store all transactions posted for an electronic commerce site. You know that a customer is associated with that transaction, but rather than put the customer's name and address into the transaction table, you can include the primary key of the customer's entry in your customer information table. That way, if you need that customer's contact information, you can use the primary key for the contact information table to do a quick query into that table and retrieve the information. When you use a primary key from one table as a pointer in a second table, you are said to be putting a *foreign key* into the second table.

Listing 33.3 shows one possible way to code the template updateaddr.cfm so that it does the update and notifies the user about the change.

Listing 33.3 *updateaddr.cfm* Code Listing

```
<CFQUERY DATASOURCE="customers" NAME="updateAddr">
UPDATE Contact_Info
SET street='#Form.new_street#',city='#Form.new_city#',
   state='#Form.new_state#',zip='#Form.new_zip#'
WHERE customer_ID = '#Form.card_number#'
</CFQUERY>

<html>

<head>
<title>Address Updated</title>
</head>
```

Listing 33.3 Continued

```
<body bgcolor="white">

<h1>Address Updated</h1>

<p>We have updated your address information as you requested.</p>

<p>Your monthly bill will now be sent to:</p>
<blockquote>
<CFOUTPUT>
#Form.new_street#<br/>
#Form.new_city#, #Form.new_state# #Form.new_zip#
</CFOUTPUT>
</blockquote>

</body>

</html>
```

Just as you could use `<CFINSERT>` instead of `<CFQUERY>` to do a database insert, you can use the `<CFUPDATE>` tag to do an update. `<CFUPDATE>` works much the same way as `<CFINSERT>`—you specify the data source and table names and ColdFusion writes the SQL code to do the update. Again, you have to make sure that the form field names and the database column names are the same, or the tag won't work.

Deleting Database Records The fourth common database operation you can do with the `<CFQUERY>` tag is delete records from a database. Like updating, deleting is something that you have to do selectively because after a record is gone, there's no getting it back. This means you will almost always want to use a `WHERE` clause in your SQL `DELETE` statements so you don't do a wholesale deletion of all the records in a table.

NOTE One way to delete records without really losing any information is to do what's called a *logical* or *soft delete*. This involves adding a Boolean field to your database table, so if the field is set to `TRUE`, the record is considered to be deleted and not included in any query results. With such a field in place, all you have to do to "delete" a record is to update it so the field has a value of `TRUE`. Similarly, you can "undelete" the record by setting the Boolean field to `FALSE`. Regardless of the value of the Boolean field, the record information is still in the database and could be retrieved by the database administrator if it became necessary.

Another technique to preserve deleted records is to write a copy of the record into an archival database before deleting it. This is fairly easy to do, but it does mean you have to manage the archival database pretty closely so that it doesn't become too large.

Suppose you maintain a comments page on your personal Web site and you want to remove any comments that are more than 30 days old. You can accomplish this by setting up a template with the following `<CFQUERY>` tag:

```
<CFQUERY DATASOURCE="feedback" NAME="PurgeOldComments">
DELETE
FROM Comments
WHERE entry_date < #CreateODBCDate(Now() - CreateTimeSpan(30,0,0,0))#
</CFQUERY>
```

The SQL statement is fairly straightforward except for what you see in the `WHERE` clause. Recall that the `Now()` function grabs the current system date and time. The `CreateTimeSpan()` function creates a date differential that you can add or subtract from a valid date. In this example, this function is used to create a differential of 30 days, 0 hours, 0 minutes, and 0 seconds, and then that differential is subtracted from the current date. The result is the date from 30 days ago.

The `CreateODBCDate()` function is then applied so date is in the appropriate format for doing a comparison. Now the `entry_date` value of the comment is checked to see if it's "less than" (occurred before) the current date minus 30 days. If it is, the comment is deleted by the `DELETE` statement.

This is a good example of a maintenance query that you can automate to keep your site fresh. You could set up a task in the Scheduler that submits the template once a day, and ColdFusion will then automatically remove any old comments for you. If you want to know which comments were deleted, you could retrieve the delete candidates first with a `SELECT` statement, output them with a `<CFOUTPUT>` tag, and then do the delete query. The Scheduler enables you to capture the template's output in an XHTML file that you can review each morning to see which comments have been deleted. Listing 33.4 shows the ColdFusion code that accomplishes this.

Listing 33.4 Automatic Deletion of Old Comments

```
<CFQUERY DATASOURCE="feedback" NAME="GetDeleteCandidates">
SELECT visitor,comment
FROM Comments
WHERE entry_date < #CreateODBCDate(Now() - CreateTimeSpan(30,0,0,0))#
</CFQUERY>

<html>

<head>
<title>Deleted Comments</title>
</head>

<body bgcolor="white">

<p>
<b>The following comments have been deleted:</b>
</p>

<table>
```

Listing 33.4 Continued

```
<tr><th>Visitor Name</th><th>Comment</th></tr>
<CFOUTPUT QUERY="GetDeleteCandidates">
<tr><td>#visitor#</td><td>#comment#</td></tr>
</CFOUTPUT>
</table>

</body>

</html>

<CFQUERY DATASOURCE="feedback" NAME="PurgeOldComments">
DELETE
FROM Comments
WHERE entry_date < #CreateODBCDate(Now() - CreateTimeSpan(30,0,0,0))#
</CFQUERY>
```

NOTE The delete query in Listing 33.4 could have occurred before the HTML output section. After you have the delete candidate information stored in the query named `GetDeleteCandidates`, it doesn't matter where in the template you do the deletion.

Using Decision Statements

Conditional logic is another basic component of any programming language, and ColdFusion enables you to build conditional processing into your applications with the `<CFIF>` tag. Instead of taking a particular attribute, the `<CFIF>` tag has to contain one of ColdFusion's eight decision operators:

- `IS`, `EQ` (equality)
- `IS NOT`, `NEQ` (inequality)
- `GREATER THAN`, `GT`
- `LESS THAN`, `LT`
- `GREATER THAN OR EQUAL TO`, `GTE`, `GE`
- `LESS THAN OR EQUAL TO`, `LTE`, `LE`
- `CONTAINS` (substring operator)
- `DOES NOT CONTAIN`

Each of these operators evaluates to a Boolean `TRUE` or `FALSE` value. If the operator evaluates to `TRUE`, the code between the `<CFIF>` and `</CFIF>` tags is executed. Otherwise, the code is ignored.

TIP Many of the decision operators can be abbreviated to a more compact form. For example, you can abbreviate `LESS THAN` to `LT` and `GREATER THAN OR EQUAL TO` to `GE`.

You can expand your programming logic by using the <CFELSE> and <CFELSEIF> tags inside a <CFIF> and </CFIF> tag pair. <CFELSE> enables you to define a block of code to execute if the condition in the <CFIF> tag evaluates to FALSE. For example:

```
<CFQUERY DATASOURCE="customers" NAME="GetCustomers">
SELECT name, phone
FROM Customers
WHERE city = 'Springfield'
</CFQUERY>

<CFIF GetCustomers.RecordCount IS NOT 0>
   <h1>Customers Living in Springfield</h1>
   <table border="1">
   <tr><th>Name</th><th>Phone Number</th></tr>
   <CFOUTPUT QUERY="GetCustomers">
   <tr><td>#name#</td><td>#phone#</td></tr>
   </CFOUTPUT>
   </table>
<CFELSE>
   <h1>No customers in Springfield</h1>
</CFIF>
```

After doing the query named GetCustomers, ColdFusion checks to see how many records were returned. If the number of records is not zero, ColdFusion prints out a table of the names and phone numbers of the records selected in the query. Otherwise, the number of query results was zero, so ColdFusion outputs a message saying that no customers were found.

TIP It's helpful to indent code inside <CFIF>, <CFELSE>, <CFELSEIF>, and </CFIF> tags because it makes troubleshooting the code much easier.

In addition to the <CFELSE> tag, you can also place as many <CFELSEIF> tags as you want between the <CFIF> and </CFIF> tags. <CFELSEIF> is used to test other conditions if the condition in the <CFIF> tag evaluates to FALSE. Suppose, for example, you had a string variable named residence that could take on one of four values. You could use the following code to do conditional processing based on the four values:

```
<CFIF residence IS "apartment">
   <b>Please enter your monthly rent: </b>
<CFELSEIF residence IS "condo">
   <b>Please enter your total monthly mortgage payment + condo fee: </b>
<CFELSEIF residence IS "home">
   <b>Please enter your total monthly mortgage payment: </b>
<CFELSEIF residence IS "other">
   <b>Please enter your monthly housing expense: </b>
</CFIF>
<input type="text" name="housing_expense"/>
```

Technically, if you were absolutely sure that residence could only take on values of "apartment", "condo", "home", or "other", you could change the <CFELSEIF residence IS

"other"> tag to a <CFELSE> tag because that would be the only possibility left at that point in the processing.

Variables referenced inside the <CFIF> or <CFELSEIF> instructions should not be enclosed in # signs. That would actually slow down the processing of the code.

The <CFIF> tag is also flexible enough to work with other constructs that evaluate to either TRUE or FALSE. These include

- **Compound decision operators**—You can join decision operators with logical ANDs and ORs to produce more complex decision criteria. For example:

  ```
  <CFIF (Sex IS "Male") AND (Age GE 16)>
     <b>You must register with the Selective Service.</b>
  </CFIF>
  ```

  It's a good idea to group each individual condition in parentheses so it's easier to troubleshoot the expression later.

- **Negation operator**—You can also use the NOT operator to logically negate one of the decision operators:

  ```
  <CFIF NOT(Age GE 21)>
     <b>You are not old enough to drink.</b>
  </CFIF>
  ```

- **Boolean variables**—You can also use Boolean variables in place of a decision operator in a <CFIF> tag. This is useful when the variable is a flag in the program. In the following example, a set of names taken from a query is printed out in a comma-delimited list. Each name from the query needs a comma and a space in front of it, except for the first name printed. You can control this by introducing the printed_one flag, which has a value of TRUE if the first item in the list has been printed.

  ```
  <CFSET printed_one = FALSE>
  <CFOUTPUT QUERY="names">
  <CFIF printed_one>
     , #name#
  <CFELSE>
     #name#
     <CFSET printed_one = TRUE>
  </CFIF>
  </CFOUTPUT>
  ```

- **Numeric variables**—ColdFusion interprets a zero as a Boolean FALSE and any positive values as a Boolean TRUE. This provides for a useful shortcut in some situations. For example, in the earlier code listing where the results of a query were printed out if at least one record was found, this line could be changed

```
<CFIF GetCustomers.RecordCount IS NOT 0>
```

to

```
<CFIF GetCustomers.RecordCount>
```

If the RecordCount is non-zero, it's interpreted as a Boolean `TRUE`, and the records will be displayed.

- **CFML functions**—Many of the ColdFusion functions evaluate to values of `TRUE` or `FALSE`. Any of these functions is valid to use inside the `<CFIF>` tag. The `IsNumeric()` function, for example, checks a variable to see whether it is a number. You can use `IsNumeric()` together with a `<CFIF>` tag to do some basic data checking as follows:

```
<CFIF NOT(IsNumeric('Form.price'))>
   The price you entered is not valid.
</CFIF>
```

Using Looping Constructs

Looping enables you to execute a set of instructions again and again until a certain condition is met. ColdFusion loops are implemented with the `<CFLOOP>` tag and can be one of four types:

- Looping over an index
- Looping while a specified condition is `TRUE`
- Looping over a query result set
- Looping over the items in a list

Each type of loop is considered in the following five sections.

NOTE You can also loop over a COM/DCOM collection object, but this type of object is a bit too advanced for an introductory discussion on ColdFusion looping. For more details, consult Chapter 12, "Extending ColdFusion with COM/DCOM," in *Ben Forta's Advanced ColdFusion 4.0 Application Development.*

CAUTION

Whenever you're doing any kind of looping, make sure that you have a reasonable `Request Timeout` value set in the ColdFusion Administrator. This prevents an infinite loop from consuming all your server's resources and crashing it.

Looping Over an Index When looping over an index variable, you need to specify the name of the variable, the initial value of the variable, and the terminating value of the variable. This is done in the `<CFLOOP>` tag with the `INDEX`, `FROM`, and `TO` attributes, respectively. Each of these attributes is required when looping over an index. `<CFLOOP>` can also take the optional `STEP` attribute, which you can use to specify the value by which the index variable should change after each pass through the loop. The default value of `STEP` is `1`, which means that the loop index is increased by 1 after each iteration.

NOTE This type of ColdFusion loop is equivalent to a `for-next` loop in other programming languages.

As a simple example of index-based looping, consider the following code:

```
<CFIF (Form.value GE 1) AND (Form.value LE 9)>
   <CFLOOP INDEX="count" FROM="1" TO="#Form.value#">
      <CFOUTPUT>#count#. #planets[count]#<br/></CFOUTPUT>
   </CFLOOP>
</CFIF>
```

NOTE As illustrated in the `<CFLOOP>` tag above, # signs are necessary around a variable name when you are using that variable to supply the value of an attribute of an CFML tag.

This code takes a value specified by the user through an XHTML form and checks to make sure that the value is between 1 and 9. If it is, a loop is used to print out the elements of the array called *planets*, beginning with the first element and ending with the element the user specified through the form. If a user entered the value `6` on the form, ColdFusion would generate the output you see in Figure 33.19.

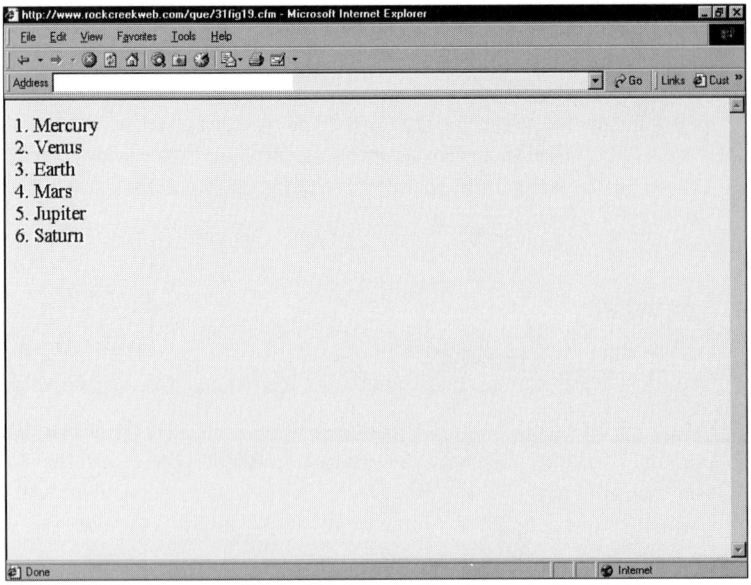

FIGURE 33.19
Index-based loops are useful for referencing arrays.

Looping While a Condition Is *TRUE* You can also loop based on the value of one of the ColdFusion decision operators by using the `CONDITION` attribute of the `<CFLOOP>` tag. As long as the condition is `TRUE`, the loop continues to iterate. When the condition becomes `FALSE`, the loop terminates.

The following code illustrates a conditional loop:

```
<CFIF (IsNumeric('Form.value')) AND (Form.value GE 1)>
   <CFSET count = 1>
   <CFLOOP CONDITION="count LE Form.value">
      <CFOUTPUT>#count#<br/></CFOUTPUT>
      <CFSET count = count + 1>
   </CFLOOP>
</CFIF>
```

This code produces the output you see in Figure 33.20. After checking to make sure that a user's form input is a numeric value that is greater than 1, ColdFusion enters a loop and prints out the values between 1 and the value entered by the user.

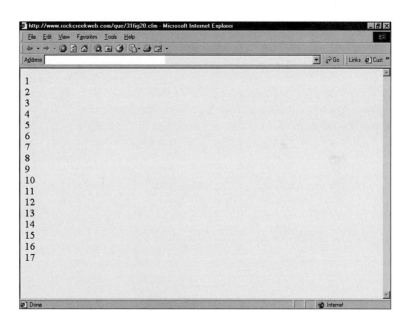

FIGURE 33.20
Conditional looping enables you to repeat a set of CFML or XHTML instructions as long as the looping condition is `TRUE`.

NOTE Remember when you use conditional looping, it's up to you to manage the variables in the condition so that it eventually evaluates to `FALSE` and exits the loop.

Looping Over Query Results Looping over a query result set is a useful capability in many settings. You've already seen how you can use `<CFOUTPUT>` with the `QUERY` attribute to loop over and print out a query result set. This gives you a convenient way to incorporate the results of a query into the Web page you're producing. However, you are limited as to what tags you can use while using <CFOUTPUT> to loop over a query. Specifically, you can only use the following tags inside of a <CFOUTPUT>:

- <CFOUTPUT> (provided the outermost <CFOUTPUT> tag has a GROUP attribute, which allows you to group the output according to values of selected database fields)
- <CFIF>
- <CFELSEIF>
- <CFELSE>

Using any other CFML tag inside a <CFOUTPUT> tag will result in a syntax error. Thus, you need the capability to do a more general loop over a query set as well. This is where <CFLOOP> with the QUERY attribute comes into play. When you use the <CFLOOP> tag, there are no restrictions on which tags you use inside the <CFLOOP>.

As an example of a situation in which you might <CFLOOP> over a query, consider the following: Suppose you have a Web-based sales system that tracks referrals to your company, and you want to count how many referrals you received each week for a given year. You could then use the following code to accomplish that:

```
<CFQUERY DATASOURCE="sales" NAME="GetReferrals">
SELECT ReferralID,EnterDate
FROM Referrals
WHERE EnterDate BETWEEN #ParseDateTime('01/01/00')# AND
#ParseDateTime('12/31/00')#)
ORDER BY EnterDate
</CFQUERY>

<!--- Initialize the counting array --->

<CFSET weekcount = ArrayNew(1)>
<CFLOOP FROM="1" TO="53" INDEX="i">
    <CFSET weekcount[i] = 0>
</CFLOOP>

<CFLOOP QUERY="GetReferrals">
    <CFSET weekcount[Week(EnterDate)] = weekcount[Week(EnterDate)] + 1>
</CFLOOP>

<h2>All referrals counted!</h2>
```

In this example, first all the referrals and the date each was entered into the database (EnterDate) is queried out. Then a one-dimensional array called weekcount is established, and all its values are set to 0 using an indexed loop from 1 to 53. Finally, <CFLOOP> is done over the query results, and the array element whose index corresponds to the week during the year when the referral was made is incremented. The CFML function Week() takes a date as input and returns a number between 1 and 53 that indicates which week during the year the given date occurs.

NOTE When looping over a query result set, you don't necessarily have to loop over the entire set. You can use the STARTROW and ENDROW attributes of the <CFLOOP> tag to specify starting and ending rows for the looping.

Looping Over a List ColdFusion lists are collections of items separated by some kind of delimiter character. The default delimiter is a comma, but you can choose any other delimiter you'd like as well. ColdFusion enables you to loop over the items in a list by using the <CFLOOP> tag with the LIST and INDEX attributes. LIST is set equal to the list you want to loop over. INDEX specifies the name of the "holding variable" that takes on the values of the individual list items as the loop progresses.

As a simple example of looping over a list, consider the following example:

```
<CFSET xfiles = "Mulder,Scully,Cigarette Smoking Man,Black Oil Aliens">
<p>Who is your favorite X-Files character?</p>
<form action="favchar.cfm" method="post">
<CFLOOP LIST="#xfiles#" INDEX="character">
   <CFOUTPUT>
   <input type="radio" name="favorite" value="#character#"/> #character#<br/>
   </CFOUTPUT>
</CFLOOP>
<input type="submit" value="Register my Favorite"/>
</form>
```

This code produces a set of four radio buttons—one for each *X-Files* character in the list. Note how the INDEX variable character is used to populate the value attribute of the <input/> element as well as to produce the text that appears next to the radio button.

NOTE To change the list delimiter from a comma to another character, you use the ListChangeDelims() function. The syntax of this function is explained in the "CFML Functions" section later in this chapter.

TIP If you want to loop over a one-dimensional array, you can use the ArrayToList() function to convert the array into a list and then loop over the list.

Breaking Out of a Loop You can break out of a loop before it would ordinarily terminate by using the <CFBREAK> tag. Suppose, for example, you were using a loop to look for the first non-zero element of a list:

```
<CFLOOP LIST="0,0,4,7,0,9,0" INDEX="value">
   <CFIF value IS NOT 0>
      <CFSET magic = value>
      <CFBREAK>
   </CFIF>
</CFLOOP>

<p>The first non-zero value is <CFOUTPUT>#magic#</CFOUTPUT>.</p>
```

On each pass through the loop, the variable value takes on the next value of the next list item. The <CFIF> tag checks to see if the current value is non-zero. If it is, it sets magic equal to that value and then breaks out of the loop because there is no point in continuing the search. Thus, the loop stops after its third iteration (when it encounters the value of 4) rather than looping through all seven values.

Sending an Email Message

When you read about the ColdFusion Administrator, you learned that ColdFusion can interface with an electronic mail server to send email messages. But all you could do through the Administrator was tell ColdFusion which mail server to use. When it comes time to actually compose and send a message, you need to use the <CFMAIL> tag. <CFMAIL> is a container tag, which means that there is a companion </CFMAIL> closing tag. You place the contents of the message you want to send between these two tags, as follows:

```
<CFMAIL>
... message to send ...
</CFMAIL>
```

The message doesn't have to be plain text. In fact, it often includes ColdFusion variables. As long as the variable names are enclosed in # signs, ColdFusion replaces the variable name with its value as it composes the message.

Certainly more components are part of an email than the body of the message, and ColdFusion enables you to handle these other message components through attributes of the <CFMAIL> tag. Following is a complete list of the <CFMAIL> tag's attributes:

- **TO**—Set equal to the email address of the recipient of the message.
- **FROM**—Set equal to the name or the email address of the sender.
- **SUBJECT**—Specifies the subject of the message.
- **CC**—Set equal to a list of email addresses that should receive a copy of the message.
- **BCC**—Set equal to a list of email addresses that should receive a "blind carbon copy" of the message (addresses of the blind carbon copy recipients are not visible to the primary recipients of the message).
- **MIMEATTACH**—Set equal to the path of a file that you want to attach to the message.

NOTE If you want to attach more than one file to an email message, you should use the <CFMAILPARAM> tag instead. <CFMAILPARAM> takes the FILE attribute that is set equal to the path of the file that you want to attach. <CFMAILPARAM> tags are placed between the <CFMAIL> and </CFMAIL> tags, and you are free to use as many <CFMAILPARAM> tags as you need.

- **QUERY**—Denotes a query to use to generate the message. The query information can be used in one of two ways. You can loop over the query set and generate a separate email for each record in the set, or you can send the results of the entire query in a single message.

- **STARTROW**—If a QUERY attribute is given, you can start processing it in a row other than the first row by setting STARTROW equal to the row where the processing should commence.
- **MAXROWS**—If you're looping over a query and want to limit the number of messages you're sending, you can set MAXROWS equal to the maximum number of messages to send.
- **GROUP**—Specifies the query column to use when grouping records. This is only applicable when sending an entire set of query results in a single message.
- **TYPE**—If you know your recipients are using mail readers that are capable of parsing HTML-based email, you can set TYPE="HTML" so that the message is sent in HTML format.

NOTE Even if you're writing XHTML in your email message, a mail client capable of rendering HTML 4.0 should be able to handle it.

- **SERVER**—By default, ColdFusion uses the server specified in the Mail section of the ColdFusion Administrator. You can override this choice of server by specifying a different mail server with the SERVER attribute.
- **PORT**—ColdFusion automatically uses the port set up in the ColdFusion Administrator (which is almost always port 25). Should you need to direct a mail message to a different port, you can specify the port number with the PORT attribute of the <CFMAIL> tag.
- **TIMEOUT**—If specified, the TIMEOUT attribute overrides the timeout set up in the ColdFusion Administrator.

The capability to dynamically generate and send email messages enables you to add many useful features to your ColdFusion applications. You could do the following, for example, on an electronic commerce site:

- Send email to customers who make purchases from your site, confirming their order and thanking them for shopping with you. This can be sent right away so customers feel they are getting an immediate response from you.
- Send status messages to customers as their orders are filled. This enables you to inform them when their orders are shipped, if an item has to be back-ordered, and when they can expect to receive their orders.
- Send follow-up messages to assess satisfaction and to notify customers about upcoming specials.

Indeed, you could create and maintain an entire mailing list using ColdFusion. Subscribers could add themselves to the database and post messages to the list through XHTML forms.

Then, when it's time to send a message to the list, you would query the list of recipients to get everyone's email address:

```
<CFQUERY DATASOURCE="mailinglist" NAME="GetAddresses">
SELECT name, emailaddress
FROM Subscribers
</CFQUERY>
```

Then you can use <CFMAIL> with the QUERY attribute to send a submitted message to each member of the list:

```
<CFMAIL QUERY="GetAddresses" TO="#name#" FROM="Mailing List Admin"
  SUBJECT="#Form.subject#">
#Form.message#
</CFMAIL>
```

How ColdFusion Handles the Message Text

The content you place between the <CFMAIL> and </CFMAIL> tags is what ColdFusion uses to generate the body of the email message. An important thing to keep in mind is that ColdFusion might insert blank lines into the message where it has parsed out any CFML tags it encounters. Consider the following code, for example:

```
<CFMAIL TO="#email#" FROM="confirm@yourserver.com"
  SUBJECT="Address Confirmation" QUERY="GetAddressInfo">
Your name and address are shown below.  If any of this information
is incorrect, please reply to this message with the correct information.

#GetAddressInfo.name#
#GetAddressInfo.address1#
<CFIF GetAddressInfo.address2 IS NOT "">#GetAddressInfo.address2#</CFIF>
#GetAddressInfo.city#, #GetAddressInfo.state# #GetAddressInfo.zip#
</CFMAIL>
```

Notice in the body of the message that a <CFIF> tag checks the value of GetAddressInfo.address2 to see if it is not blank. If it isn't, then ColdFusion outputs its value. If it is, then ColdFusion parses out the entire line and keeps going. Unfortunately, this produces a blank line in the resulting email and the recipient sees something like

```
Your name and address are shown below. If any of this information
is incorrect, please reply to this message with the correct information.

John Doe
123 Main Street

New York, NY 10033
```

To avoid this problem, you can compose a string that contains the contents of the message, and then place the variable containing the string between the <CFMAIL> and </CFMAIL> tags. The trick to doing this is to account for breaks to a new line, but ColdFusion makes this fairly easy with the Chr() function. In the following code, the concatenation of Chr(13) and Chr(10) produces the carriage returns in the message. The ampersand (&) operator concatenates the strings.

```
<CFSET message = GetAddressInfo.name & Chr(13) & Chr(10)>
<CFSET message = message & GetAddressInfo.address1 & Chr(13) & Chr(10)>
<CFIF GetAddressInfo.address2 IS NOT "">
 <CFSET message = message & GetAddressInfo.address2 & Chr(13) & Chr(10)>
</CFIF>
<CFSET message = message & GetAddressInfo.city & ", " &
 GetAddressInfo.state & " " & GetAddressInfo.zip>

<CFMAIL TO="#email#" FROM="confirm@yourserver.com"
  SUBJECT="Address Confirmation" QUERY="GetAddressInfo">
Your name and address are shown below.  If any of this information
is incorrect, please reply to this message with the correct information.

#message#
</CFMAIL>
```

Other Useful CFML Tags

More than 70 CFML tags are available, and to fully describe them all would require several chapters. The tags you have read about so far form the core of most ColdFusion applications, but many others deserve mention. This section briefly surveys some of the other CFML tags that are popular with developers.

These tags include

- **<CFABORT>**—If ColdFusion encounters the <CFABORT> tag, it stops processing the template at that point and sends whatever XHTML it has generated to the server. <CFABORT> is useful when you're doing server-side error checking on form data:

```
<CFIF NOT(IsNumeric('Form.age'))>
   <h1>Invalid age</h1>
   <p>Please use your browser's Back button
    and enter a valid age on the form.</p>
   <CFABORT>
</CFIF>
...
```

- **<CFLOCATION>**—<CFLOCATION> enables you to put redirects into your applications. It takes the URL attribute, which is set equal to the URL of the page where you want to redirect your users. You might do some queries to insert some information into one of your data sources, for example, and redirect the user back to the main page of your site with the following code:

```
<CFQUERY DATASOURCE="info" NAME="add">
INSERT
INTO Transactions (Item_number,quantity)
VALUES (#Form.item_number#, #Form.quantity#)
</CFQUERY>
...
<CFLOCATION URL="index.cfm">
```

- **<CFCOOKIE>**—If you need to write a cookie to a user's browser, you can do so easily with the <CFCOOKIE> tag. <CFCOOKIE> has two required attributes: NAME, which is set equal to the name of the cookie, and VALUE, which is set equal to the cookie's value. Additionally, you can use the EXPIRES attribute to specify the cookie's expiration date and the SECURE attribute to require secure transmission of the cookie. For example:

  ```
  <CFCOOKIE NAME="ID" VALUE="#User_ID#" EXPIRES="01/01/01" SECURE="YES">
  ```

  You can also specify the domain for which the cookie is valid with the DOMAIN attribute and the paths on the server to which the cookie applies with the PATH attribute.

NOTE If you do not specify an EXPIRES attribute in the <CFCOOKIE> tag, the cookie you place will be eliminated when the user's browser shuts down.

- **<CFTRANSACTION>**—Data integrity is important on transaction-oriented databases in which several users might be accessing the database at any given time. Suppose you have the following three queries that insert a new record in the Customers table, query the Customers table for the primary key of the record that was just inserted, and then insert that primary key value into the Orders table:

  ```
  <CFQUERY DATASOURCE="store" NAME="InsertInfo">
  INSERT
  INTO Customers (name,address,city,state,zip,phone)
  VALUES ('#Form.name#','#Form.address#','#Form.city#','#Form.state#',
  '#Form.zip#', '#Form.phone#')

  </CFQUERY>

  <CFQUERY DATASOURCE="store" NAME="GetPrimaryKey">
  SELECT MAX(CustomerID) as pk
  FROM Customers
  </CFQUERY>

  <CFQUERY DATASOURCE="store" NAME="InsertPrimaryKey">
  INSERT
  INTO Orders (CustomerID)
  VALUE (#GetPrimaryKey.pk#)
  </CFQUERY>
  ```

  These queries will work just fine, so long as no other queries are processed between them. Suppose, for example, that immediately after the contact information for customer A is inserted, contact information for customer B is also inserted. Then, when ColdFusion queries the database for customer A's primary key, it really gets customer B's primary key and customer B is then associated with customer A's order in the Orders table. This creates the potential for erroneous orders throughout your entire electronic commerce application and sows the seeds for some pretty unhappy customers.

Fortunately, you can eliminate this problem by wrapping queries that should occur together in `<CFTRANSACTION>` and `</CFTRANSACTION>` tags. Queries grouped this way are treated as a single entity, and ColdFusion won't attempt any other queries until those in the `<CFTRANSACTION>` have finished.

- **`<CFFORM>`**—CFML has some souped-up versions of the XHTML form tags that enable you to automatically build JavaScript into your pages to check for required fields and for appropriate formatting of input items such as phone numbers and zip codes. To use these tags, you have to use `<CFFORM>` and `</CFFORM>` tags where you would normally use `<form>` and `</form>` elements. After you've declared your intention to build a ColdFusion form, you can use tags such as `<CFINPUT>` for text fields, `<CFSELECT>` for drop-down lists, `<CFSLIDER>` for a Java-based slider control, `<CFTREE>` for a Java-based tree control, and `<CFGRID>` for a Java-based spreadsheet-like control.

  The automated JavaScript comes into play when you use attributes such as `REQUIRED` or `VALIDATE` in the CFML form tags. For example, the tag

  ```
  <CFINPUT TYPE="TEXT" NAME="fax" REQUIRED="YES" VALIDATE="telephone">
  ```

  sets up a text input field rigged with JavaScript that checks to make sure the user entered a value into the field (`REQUIRED="YES"`) and that what was entered is in a United States telephone number (XXX-XXX-XXXX) format (`VALIDATE="telephone"`).

Of all the available CFML tags, you have only read about slightly less than one-third of them here. But these should be enough to get you started with ColdFusion application development. Remember the online documentation that comes with ColdFusion and ColdFusion Studio contains full documentation on all the CFML tags in the event that you need to look up one of them.

CFML Functions

If you thought more than 70 was a lot of CFML tags, you'll be overwhelmed by the number of CFML functions—over 250! Although that might seem like a huge number of new things to learn, you should make your best effort to get as familiar with as many of the CFML functions as you can. By using the built-in functions, you can accomplish critical tasks quickly and efficiently instead of trying to write your own tags to do the same work (which is almost always less efficient).

In reading about CFML tags, you were introduced to a few of the CFML functions as well. This section reviews several more of the key CFML functions. To help you understand them a little better, they are grouped as follows:

- String functions
- Formatting functions
- Array functions

- List functions
- Date and time functions
- Math functions
- Query functions
- Two other useful functions: `IsDefined()` and `URLEncodedFormat()`

As you read about these functions, try to focus on developing an awareness of the functions and what they do. You can always look up the details of the syntax later.

String Functions

CFML comes with a wealth of functions that make string manipulation a breeze. In fact, CFML string functions comprise one of the largest classes of CFML functions. The following list summarizes some of the more commonly used string functions:

- **`Asc(str)`**—Returns the ASCII numeric value of the first character of `str`.
- **`Chr(val)`**—Returns the character with the ASCII value equal to `val`. `val` must therefore be an integer between 0 and 255.
- **`CJustify(str,len)`**—Centers `str` in a field of length `len`.
- **`Compare(str1,str2)`**—Does a case-sensitive comparison of `str1` and `str2`, returning `-1` if `str1` is less than `str2`, `0` if the strings are equal, and `1` if `str1` is greater than `str2`.
- **`CompareNoCase(str1,str2)`**—Does a case-insensitive comparison of `str1` and `str2`, returning `-1` if `str1` is less than `str2`, `0` if the strings are equal, and `1` if `str1` is greater than `str2`.
- **`Find(str1,str2,start)`**—Returns the position in `str2` where there is an occurrence of `str1`. The case-sensitive search begins at the first character unless you specify a different value with the `start` parameter. The function returns `0` if no occurrence of `str1` is found.
- **`FindNoCase(str1,str2,start)`**—Returns the position in `str2` where there is an occurrence of `str1`. The case-insensitive search begins at the first character unless you specify a different value with the `start` parameter. The function returns `0` if no occurrence of `str1` is found.
- **`Insert(str1,str2,pos)`**—Inserts `str1` into `str2` at position `pos`. If `pos` is `0`, the function concatenates `str1` and `str2`.
- **`LCase(str)`**—Converts `str` to lowercase.
- **`Left(str,pos)`**—Returns the leftmost `pos` characters from `str`.
- **`Len(str)`**—Returns the number of characters in `str`.
- **`LTrim(str)`**—Removes any leading spaces from `str`.
- **`Mid(str,start,num)`**—Extracts `num` characters from `str`, starting at position `start`.

- **REFind(rexpr,str,start)**—Returns the position of an occurrence of the regular expression `rexpr` in `str`, beginning its search at position `start`.
- **Replace(str1,str2,str3,scope)**—Replaces occurrences of `str2` in `str1` with `str3`. `scope` controls how many replacements should be made (“one” or “all”).
- **RERplace(str1,rexpr,str2,scope)**—Replaces occurrences of the regular expression `rexpr` in `str1` with `str2`. `scope` controls how many replacements should be made (“one” or “all”).
- **Reverse(str)**—Reverses the order of the characters in `str`.
- **Right(str,pos)**—Returns the rightmost `pos` characters from `str`.
- **RJustify(str,len)**—Right justifies `str` in a field of length `len`.
- **RTrim(str)**—Removes trailing spaces from `str`.
- **UCase(str)**—Converts `str` to uppercase.

Formatting Functions

ColdFusion can do some of the preparatory work that needs to be done before displaying a value. Following are some of the more popular CFML formatting functions:

- **DateFormat(date,mask)**—Formats `date` according to the specified mask. A `mask` of `'mm/dd/yy'`, for example, would yield a date in the form 11/30/00.
- **DollarFormat(number)**—Returns `number` formatted as a dollar amount with a dollar sign, decimal point, and commas where necessary.
- **HTMLEditFormat(HTMLcode)**—Removes reserved characters within the string `HTMLcode` and replaces them with their escaped values. The less than sign (<), for example, would be replaced with `<`.
- **NumberFormat(number,mask)**—Returns `number` formatted according to the specified `mask`. For example, a mask of '_,___.__' would produce a number in the form `1,000.00`.
- **ParagraphFormat(str)**—Removes consecutive carriage return and line feed characters from `str` and replaces them with `<p>` elements.
- **TimeFormat(time,mask)**—Formats `time` according to the specified `mask`. A mask of `'hh:mm:ssTT'`, for example, produces a time in the form `07:25:00AM`.

Array Functions

Arrays are convenient ways to store related information for quick reference throughout your template. You create an array with the `ArrayNew` function. For example

```
<CFSET stats = ArrayNew(2)>
```

creates a new, two-dimensional array. This means the array will have two subscripts: `stats[subs1][subs2]`. ColdFusion supports one-, two-, and three-dimensional arrays.

NOTE One-dimensional arrays are essentially the same as a ColdFusion list.

CFML comes with a large number of functions to handle array manipulation. These include

- **`ArrayAppend(arr,element)`**—Adds `element` to the end of the array `arr`. Returns a value of `TRUE` if successful.
- **`ArrayAvg(arr)`**—Returns the average value of the elements in the array `arr`.
- **`ArrayClear(arr)`**—Clears all elements from the array `arr`. Returns a value of `TRUE` if successful.
- **`ArrayDeleteAt(arr,index)`**—Removes the element at position `index` from the array `arr`. Returns a value of `TRUE` if successful.
- **`ArrayInsertAt(arr,index,element)`**—Inserts `element` into the array `arr` at position `index`. Returns a value of `TRUE` if successful.
- **`ArrayIsEmpty(arr)`**—Returns `TRUE` if `arr` has no elements or `FALSE` if `arr` has at least one element.
- **`ArrayLen(arr)`**—Returns the length of the array `arr`.
- **`ArrayMax(arr)`**—Returns the maximum value in the array `arr`.
- **`ArrayMin(arr)`**—Returns the maximum value in the array `arr`.
- **`ArrayPrepend(arr,element)`**—Adds `element` at the front of the array `arr`. Returns a value of `TRUE` if successful.
- **`ArrayResize(arr,min_size)`**—Resizes the array `arr` to have at least `min_size` elements.
- **`ArraySort(arr,type,order)`**—Sorts the array `arr` according to the `type` of sort specified (`"numeric"`, `"text"`, or `"textnocase"`). The sort `order` can be ascending (`"asc"`) or descending (`"desc"`). Returns a value of `TRUE` if successful.
- **`ArraySum(arr)`**—Returns the sum of the elements in the array `arr`.
- **`ArrayToList(arr,del)`**—Converts the array `arr` to a list with the delimiter character `del`.
- **`IsArray('variable')`**—Returns `TRUE` if `variable` is an array.

List Functions

ColdFusion lists are delimited sets of items. The default delimiter is a comma (,), but you can use any other character you would like to delimit your lists.

The same as with arrays, CFML comes with many functions that support rapid processing of lists. Some of the key CFML list functions follow. In each case, `del` represents the list delimiter. If no delimiter is specified, ColdFusion uses the comma as the delimiter character. Following is a list of the more frequently used list functions:

- **ListAppend(lst,item,del)**—Adds item to the end of the list lst.
- **ListChangeDelims(lst,new_del,del)**—Replaces all delimiters in the list lst with new_del.
- **ListContains(lst,str,del)**—Returns the position of the first item in the list lst that contains str as a substring. The substring search is case sensitive.
- **ListContainsNoCase(lst,str,del)**—Returns the item number of the first item in the list lst that contains str as a substring. The substring search is not case sensitive.
- **ListDeleteAt(lst,pos,del)**—Deletes the item at position pos from the list lst.
- **ListFind(lst,item,del)**—Returns the position of the first instance of item in the list lst. Search is case sensitive.
- **ListFindNoCase(lst,item,del)**—Returns the position of the first instance of item in the list lst. Search is not case sensitive.
- **ListFirst(lst,del)**—Returns the first item from the list lst.
- **ListGetAt(lst,pos,del)**—Returns the item at position pos from the list lst.
- **ListInsertAt(lst,pos,item,del)**—Inserts item at position pos of the list lst.
- **ListLast(lst,del)**—Returns the last item from the list lst.
- **ListLen(lst,del)**—Returns the number of items in the list lst.
- **ListPrepend(lst,item,del)**—Adds item to the front of the list lst.
- **ListRest(lst,del)**—Returns all items in the list lst except for the first one.
- **ListSetAt(lst,pos,item,del)**—Sets the value of the item at position pos in the list lst to item.
- **ListToArray(lst,del)**—Converts the list lst to a one-dimensional array.

Date and Time Functions

Handling date and time variables can be somewhat tricky, especially when you're using the SQL calls, in which case they have to be in a format that ODBC can interpret correctly. CFML supports a number of functions that operate on date and time variables. The following list provides a sampling of these functions. If you specify a year quantity less than 100, it is interpreted as a twentieth century value.

- **CreateDateTime(year,month,day,hour,minute,second)**—Creates a date/time variable with the value corresponding to the year, month, day, hour, minute, and second information provided.
- **CreateODBCDateTime(year,month,day,hour,minute,second)**—Creates a date/time variable in ODBC format with the value corresponding to the year, month, day, hour, minute, and second information provided. You should use ODBC-formatted dates in your SQL statements.

- **`DateCompare(datetime1,datetime2)`**—Compares `datetime1` and `datetime2` and returns `-1` if `datetime1` is less than `datetime2`, `0` if `datetime1` equals `datetime2`, and `1` if `datetime1` is greater than `datetime2`.
- **`Day(date)`**—Returns the day of the month (1–31) on which that `date` falls.
- **`Hour(date)`**—Returns the hour (0–23) specified by `date`.
- **`IsDate('variable')`**—Returns `TRUE` if `variable` is a valid date/time variable or `FALSE` if `variable` is not.
- **`IsLeapYear(year)`**—Returns `TRUE` if `year` is a leap year or `FALSE` if `year` is not.
- **`Minute(date)`**—Returns the value of the minutes (0–59) specification in the variable `date`.
- **`Month(date)`**—Returns the numeric value of the month (1–12) in the variable `date`.
- **`Now()`**—Returns the current system date and time.

TIP The `Now()` function makes it easy to timestamp database transactions.

- **`ParseDateTime(str)`**—Converts the string `str` to a valid date/time variable.
- **`Second(date)`**—Returns the value of the seconds (0–59) specification in the variable `date`.
- **`Week(date)`**—Returns the numerical week of the year (1–53) during which `date` occurs.
- **`Year(date)`**—Returns the value of the year specification in the variable `date`.

Math Functions

You might not need to do much mathematical computation as part of your ColdFusion applications, but CFML includes a large library of math functions for you to use when the need arises. Some of these include

- **`Abs(num)`**—Returns the absolute value of `num`.
- **`Ceiling(num)`**—Returns the closest integer bigger than `num`.
- **`DecrementValue(num)`**—Subtracts 1 from the value of `num`.
- **`IncrementValue(num)`**—Adds 1 to the value of `num`.
- **`Int(num)`**—Returns the closest integer smaller than `num`.
- **`Log(num)`**—Returns the natural logarithm of `num`.
- **`Log10(num)`**—Returns the base 10 logarithm of `num`.
- **`Max(num1,num2)`**—Returns the larger of `num1` and `num2`.
- **`Min(num1,num2)`**—Returns the smaller of `num1` and `num2`.
- **`pi()`**—Returns the value of the constant pi, 3.14159265358979. pi represents the ratio of the circumference of a circle to its diameter.
- **`Rand()`**—Returns a random number between 0 and 1.

- **RandRange(num1,num2)**—Returns a random number between `num1` and `num2`.
- **Round(num)**—Rounds `num` to the closest integer.
- **Sgn(num)**—Returns `-1` if `num` is negative, `0` if `num` is zero, and `1` if `num` is positive.
- **Sqr(num)**—Returns the positive square root of `num`.

Two Other Useful Functions

Two other valuable functions should be part of your basic ColdFusion awareness:

- **IsDefined('variable')**—Returns `TRUE` if `variable` is defined and `FALSE` if it isn't defined.
- **URLEncodedFormat(str)**—Converts `str` so it can be passed to the next template as a `URL` variable.

`IsDefined()` is ideal for handling radio button and check box form controls. The problem with both of these controls is that no name/value pairs are passed for them if nothing is selected. In the following set of check boxes, for example,

```
<b>Additional Pizza Toppings</b><br/>
<input type="text" name="toppings" value="Pepperoni"/> Pepperoni<br/>
<input type="text" name="toppings" value="Mushrooms"/> Mushrooms<br/>
<input type="text" name="toppings" value="Pineapple"/> Pineapple<br/>
<input type="text" name="toppings" value="Onions"/> Onions<br/>
<input type="text" name="toppings" value="Anchovies"/> Anchovies<br/>
```

a user might not select any of them. You could check for this in the template that processes the pizza order form as follows:

```
<CFIF IsDefined('Form.toppings')>
    ... extra topping processing code ...
<CFELSE>
    <p>You did not select any extra toppings.</p>
</CFIF>
```

If the user does select extra toppings, `Form.toppings` is defined and ColdFusion executes the block of code that processes the user's selections.

TIP By naming all the check boxes with the same `NAME` attribute, any selected check box values are passed to ColdFusion as a list. If a user selects pepperoni, onions, and anchovies, for example, the value of `Form.toppings` would be `"Pepperoni,Onions,Anchovies"`, and you could process the toppings like so:

```
<CFIF IsDefined('Form.toppings')>
    <p>You requested the following additional toppings:</p>
   <ul>
   <CFLOOP LIST="#Form.toppings#" INDEX="top">
      <CFOUTPUT><li>#top#</li></CFOUTPUT>
   </CFLOOP>
   </ul>
<CFELSE>
   <p>You did not select any extra toppings.</p>
</CFIF>
```

The `URLEncodedFormat()` function is essential if you plan to pass strings of data on a URL. Recall that the browser encodes form data before sending it, doing things such as replacing spaces with plus signs (+) and replacing special characters with hexadecimal escape codes. To have to do this conversion yourself would be nightmarish, but thankfully the `URLEncodedFormat()` function spares you the agony.

`URLEncodedFormat()` is especially useful when you are setting up links that users can click to invoke other templates. For example:

```
<CFQUERY DATASOURCE="sales" NAME="GetAll">
SELECT ID, region
FROM Territories
</CFQUERY>

<b>Please click a region's ID number for more information.</b>
<br/>
<table>
<tr><th>ID</th><th>Region</th></tr>
<CFOUTPUT QUERY="GetAll">
<tr>
<td>
<a href="regiondetail.cfm?region=#URLEncodedFormat(region)#">#ID#</a>
</td>
<td>#region#</td>
</tr>
</CFOUPTUT>
</table>
```

If `region` had the value `Central Region`, for example, it would need to be converted to `Central+Region` before passing it on the URL for the `regiondetail.cfm` template. In this code example, the `URLEncodedFormat()` function takes care of this conversion for you.

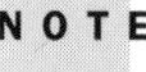

If you're familiar with JavaScript, the `URLEncodedFormat` function does the same thing as the JavaScript `escape()` function.

Using ColdFusion Studio

As you've seen throughout this chapter, CFML code coexists in the same file as XHTML code. Therefore, ColdFusion templates have to be plain text files, just as XHTML documents are. So technically, all you need to write ColdFusion templates is an editor that can write out plain text files. This means you could compose your templates using Notepad, Microsoft Word, or any XHTML authoring tool that enables you to edit the raw code.

Although any text editor is fine, you should seriously consider using Allaire's ColdFusion Studio—currently in version 4.5—as your development tool of choice for ColdFusion templates. Based on the popular authoring program HomeSite, ColdFusion Studio comes with many helpful features that directly support you as you write CFML code. This section of the chapter introduces you to ColdFusion Studio and how to use Studio to make your development work much less tedious.

NOTE ColdFusion Studio is not yet writing true XHTML code, but it can be configured to write code that is very close to compliant. For example, you can set up Studio so that all tags are in lowercase—something you need for proper XHTML.

The ColdFusion Studio Interface

Figure 33.21 shows the ColdFusion Studio user interface. The interface is toolbar oriented, and you have the option of displaying any or none of the toolbars. Additionally, you can customize many of the toolbars to include only the buttons you use frequently or buttons that you create.

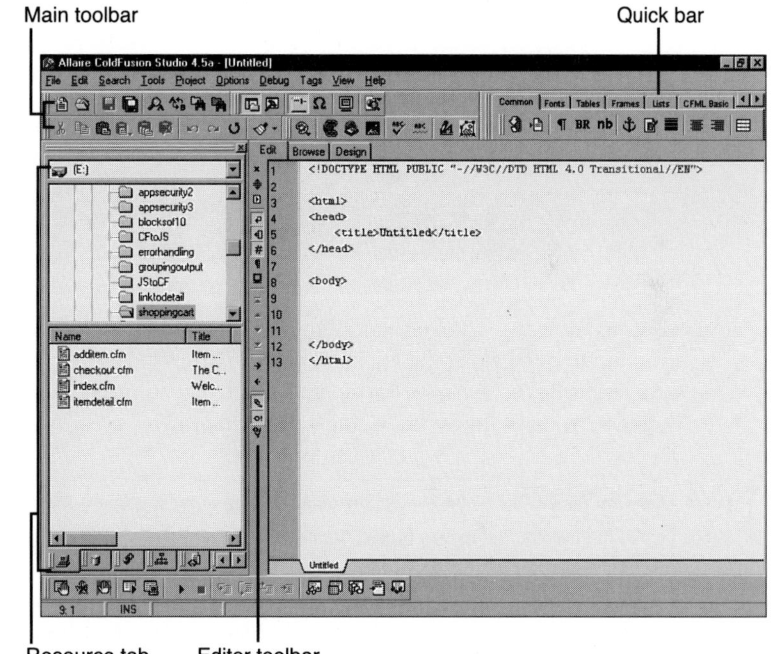

FIGURE 33.21 The ColdFusion Studio user interface strongly resembles that of HomeSite.

The major components of the interface include

- **Main Toolbar**—The Main Toolbar contains buttons for common file-related tasks such as opening, saving, and printing, and editing tasks such as cut, copy, and paste. Buttons also launch Studio's verification tools: a link checker, an HTML validator, and a spell checker.

- **QuickBar**—The QuickBar plays host to several tabs (all of which you can display or hide easily), including Common, Fonts, Tables, Frames, Lists, Forms, CFML, Script, and Active Server Pages (ASP). Each tab, in turn, contains buttons that place XHTML and CFML tags into your documents. By putting the tags into logical grouping on the tabs, it becomes easy to switch back and forth between sets of buttons as you need them.

To show or hide toolbars on the QuickBar, press Shift+F8 to open the Customize dialog box (see Figure 33.22). In the Visible Toolbars window, you will see all the available toolbars. To include a toolbar on the QuickBar, make sure the box next to the desired toolbar is checked.

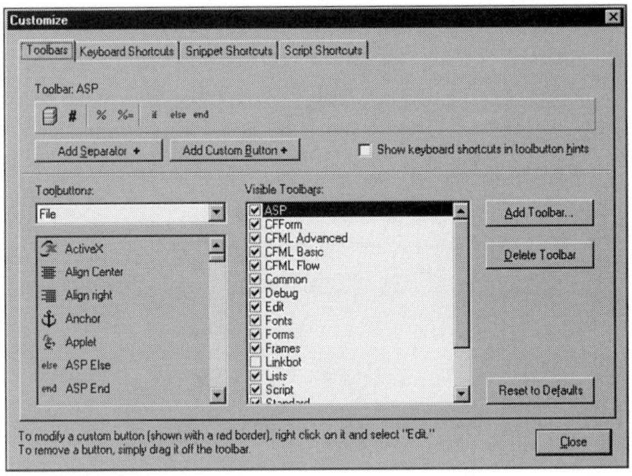

FIGURE 33.22
You can configure the QuickBar to display only the toolbars you use regularly.

- **Editor Toolbar**—The behavior of the editing window is controlled by the Editor Toolbar (located along the left side of the editing window). Buttons on this toolbar control properties such as word wrapping, block indenting, and numbering lines of code. In addition, you can toggle the window between browser preview mode and edit mode and between full-screen and partial-screen modes.

TIP ColdFusion error diagnostic messages usually refer to a line number where it has detected the error, so it's helpful to have line numbering turned on in the editing window.

The remaining buttons on the Editor Toolbar support what Allaire calls Studio's What-You-See-Is-What-You-Need (WYSIWYN) feature. This includes Tag Completion (a container tag's closing tag automatically appears when you finish typing in the opening tag), Tag Tips (pop-up messages that show all the possible attributes permitted by the tag's syntax), and Tag Insight (which provides a drop-down list of attributes the tag can take, enabling you to easily choose the ones you want). Figure 33.23 shows the Tag Insight in action.

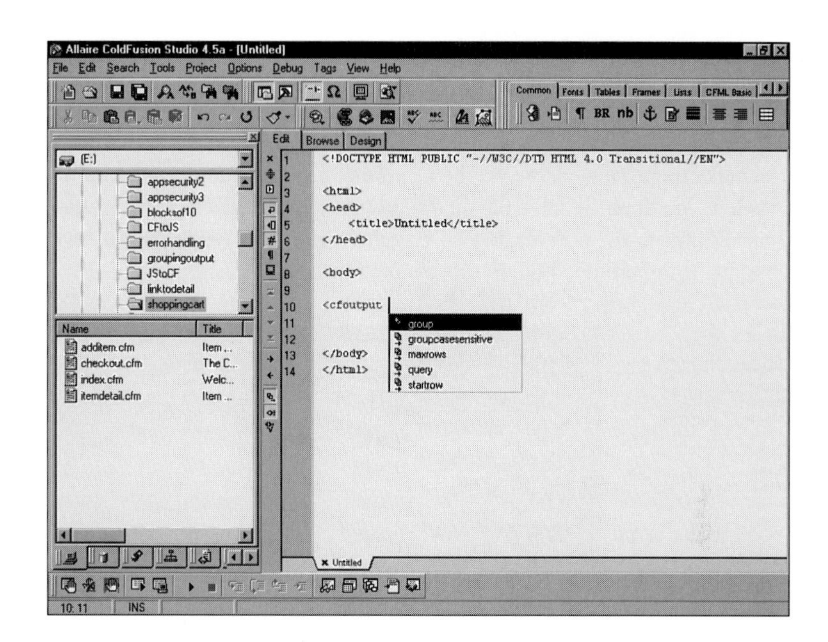

FIGURE 33.23
With Tag Insight activated, you can select which attributes you want to place inside a tag from a context-sensitive list.

NOTE With some practice, most users adjust to the WYSIWYN features and are able to develop more rapidly. If you find the features more of a hindrance, you can suppress them by deselecting their buttons on the Edit Toolbar.

- **Resource Tab**—The Resource Tab typically appears to the left of the edit window, although you can change its position easily enough. The Resource Tab is itself tabbed to give you access to local and remote disk drives, ColdFusion data sources on remote servers, groups of related templates called *projects*, tag *snippets* (chunks of reusable code), and the full set of ColdFusion and ColdFusion Studio documentation in HTML format.

Using the Resource Tab

The Resource Tab is an incredibly useful window to access many of the resources developers need while creating a ColdFusion application. This section takes a closer look at the tabs on the Resource Tab and what they let you access.

The tab you see open in Figure 33.21 is the Files Tab. When this tab is selected, the Resource Tab is divided into two windows. In the upper window, you can navigate drives and folders on your machine. As you change from one folder to another, the files in that folder appear in the lower window. Having the list of files at your disposal is very valuable. You can double-click a file to open it, drag and drop an HTML file or a ColdFusion template into the edit window to set up a link to it, or drag and drop an image file into the edit window to place the image in your document.

If you open the drop-down list over the upper window, you'll notice that one of the options is Allaire FTP & RDS. Choosing this option presents you with a list of remote servers like the one you see in Figure 33.24. ColdFusion Studio enables you to work with remote servers via standard FTP or by a Remote Data Server (RDS) connection. When you use RDS, you are connecting to the server via the ColdFusion service. Regardless of how you're connected, when you double-click a file on a remote server, the file is downloaded to your machine and presented in the edit window so you can work on it. When you save your changes, Studio uploads the modified file to the remote machine.

FIGURE 33.24
There's no need to use a separate FTP client because ColdFusion Studio has one built in.

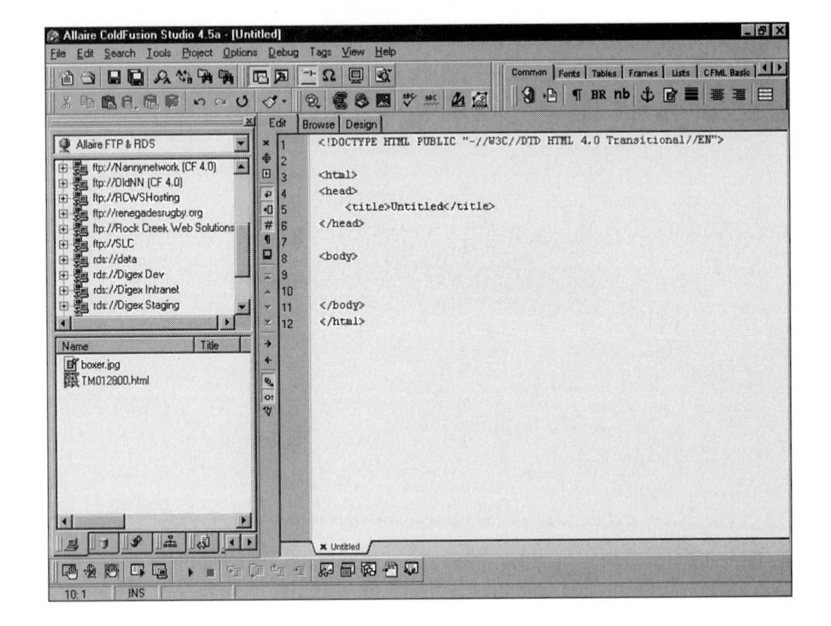

NOTE To set up a new remote server profile, right-click the Allaire FTP & RDS entry at the top of the tree listing the servers, and choose Add FTP Server or Add RDS Server as needed.

CAUTION

If you don't save frequently, your FTP connection might time out, and you'll have to reconnect to the remote server.

The Database Tab enables you to access the system data sources on a remote server that's running ColdFusion. This can be incredibly valuable during development, especially when writing queries. Each data source on the server is presented in a tree structure that you can expand to display the tables, views, and queries stored in the corresponding database file. You can also expand a given table to display the database columns that compose the table. Studio shows you not only the name of the column, but its type and length as well (see Figure 33.25). Double-clicking a database table prompts Studio to download a copy of the table.

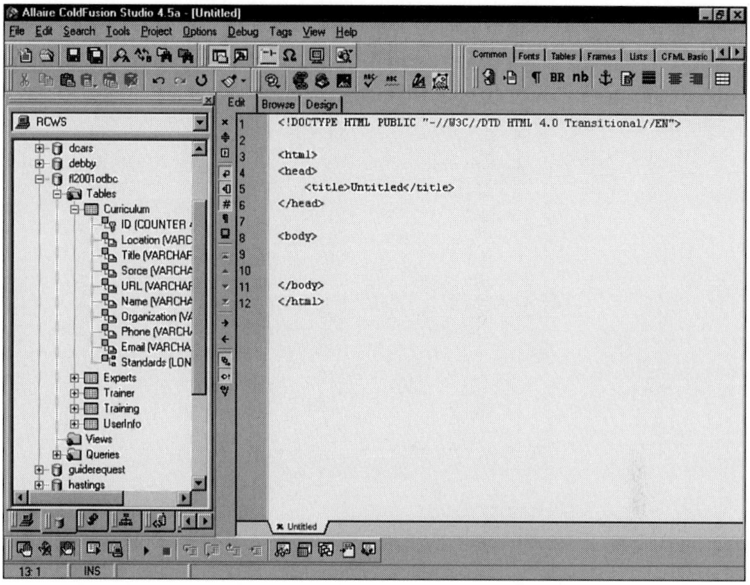

FIGURE 33.25
By connecting to a remote ColdFusion server through the Database Tab, you can view the tables, fields, and queries available under each data source on the server.

Projects are groups of related files stored together. For example, you can group all the templates that support a single application into a project. After they are grouped, you can open, close, and save all the files simultaneously. Furthermore, you can do search and replace operations across all the files, making it simple to deploy global changes in your applications. You can access the projects you've created through the Projects Tab on the Resources Tab.

The Snippets Tab enables you to set up folders to hold frequently used blocks of code (see Figure 33.26). This is an excellent place to store code for things such as standard headers and footers, common form controls (for example, a drop-down list of all 50 states—something that is painful to type out each time you need it!), and client-side image maps.

Finally, the Help Tab gives you access to complete documentation on all CFML tags and functions, explanations of how to use and customize ColdFusion Studio, references for HTML and Cascading Style Sheets, and information on how to contact Allaire for technical support.

Using Special ColdFusion Studio Tools

In addition to the excellent tag support provided by the Tag Toolbar and the easy access to resources through the Resource Tab, ColdFusion Studio also comes with a few other useful tools. This section takes a brief look at three of them: the Tag Chooser, the Expression Builder, and the SQL Builder.

The Tag Chooser Figure 33.27 shows the Tag Chooser, which you can activate by pressing Ctrl+E. Within the Chooser, all HTML and CFML tags are stored in an easy-to-navigate tree structure that enables you to zero in on the tags you want quickly. As you move through the tree structure, the various tags available are displayed in the right side of the Chooser. To insert one of the tags into your document, click it and then click the Select button in the lower right.

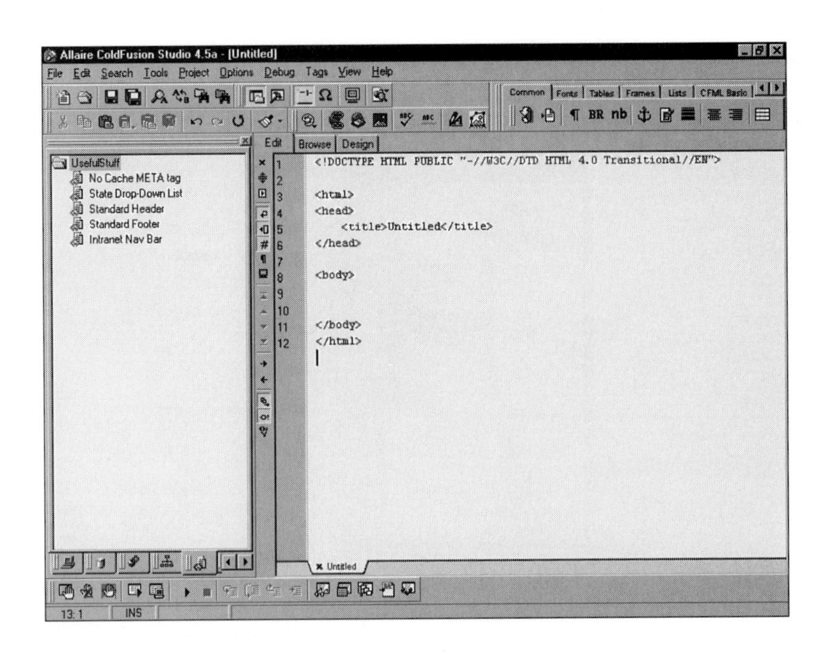

FIGURE 33.26
The Snippets Tab is like a big clipboard where you can store chunks of code that you use frequently.

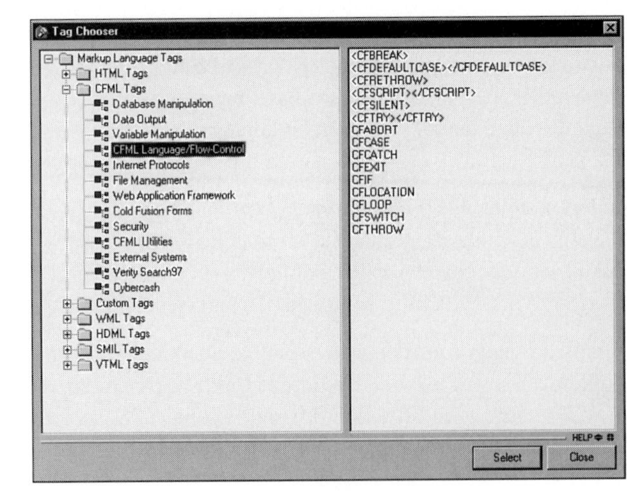

FIGURE 33.27
If you don't like using the toolbars, the Tag Chooser can put all the HTML and CFML tags at your fingertips.

The Expression Builder You launch the ColdFusion Studio Expression Builder by pressing Ctrl+Shift+E. The Expression Builder is useful in two ways. First, it is helpful when you're building complicated expressions that involve ColdFusion functions. You can see the expression in the window at the top of the Builder and make edits to it there as necessary (see Figure 33.28).

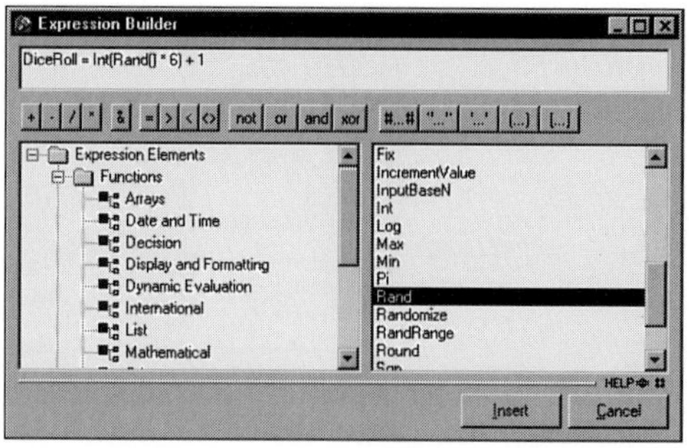

FIGURE 33.28
Can't remember one of the CFML list functions? Look it up through the Expression Builder.

The other useful feature of the Expression Builder is that it catalogs all CFML functions, constants, operators, and variables in the tree you see on the left side of the builder. By navigating the tree, you can easily look up one of the CFML functions that are otherwise too numerous to commit to memory. As you move through the tree, the available functions, constants, operators, and variables are displayed in the right side of the Builder. After you're done composing your expression, clicking the Insert button places it into your template.

The SQL Builder If you need to use a query stored in one of your data sources or if you need to construct a new query, you can choose the Insert SQL Statement option under the Tools menu to open the window you see in Figure 33.29. From this window, you can connect to one of the ColdFusion servers that Studio is configured to work with and navigate to the Queries subtree of the data source you're using. From there you can choose one of the queries and insert it directly into your template.

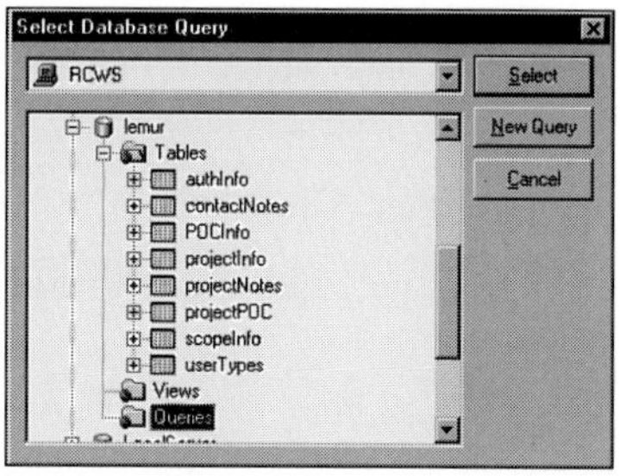

FIGURE 33.29
ColdFusion Studio can easily grab a pre-existing query from one of your data sources.

If you need to compose a brand new query, you can click the New Query button you see in Figure 33.29 to launch the Query Builder you see in Figure 33.30. The Query Builder gives you a visual environment in which to construct your query. You can open as many tables as you need in the Query Builder window and do joins on the tables by dragging the joining fields from one table to another. As you do, the corresponding SQL statement is constructed at the bottom of the Query Builder. When you're done building the query and click the Close (X) button, the Query Builder gives you the option to insert the SQL statement directly into your template.

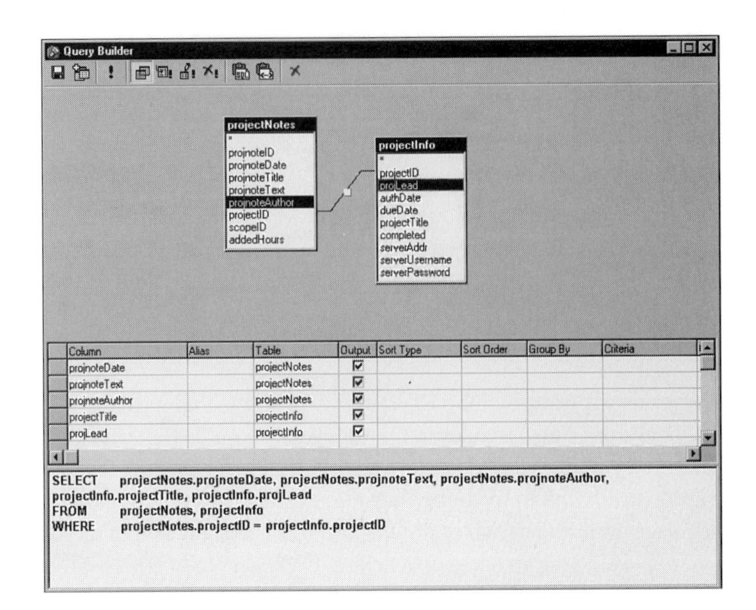

FIGURE 33.30
The ColdFusion Studio Query Builder is similar to the Microsoft Query Builder and can place the SQL statements you build directly into your template file.

Putting It All Together: A Sample ColdFusion Application

This chapter has reviewed many of the basics of setting up and using ColdFusion and has shown you some short examples to illustrate various tags and how they work. To truly appreciate ColdFusion, however, you need to see it put to work over the course of several templates to create an integrated application. This final section of the chapter looks at how you can use ColdFusion to quickly put up a simple electronic storefront.

The storefront site is comprised of four templates. These are

- `index.cfm`—This template initializes the user's shopping cart and presents a list of products to choose from.
- `itemdetail.cfm`—After the user selects an item, this template presents the details about the selected product and gives the user the option to put one or more of that item in his shopping cart.
- `additem.cfm`—This template adds the item to the user's shopping cart and then allows the user to continue shopping or to proceed to the checkout.
- `checkout.cfm`—This template summarizes the contents of the user's cart and presents the total amount of the purchase.

Additionally, the following is assumed to be true:

- All items for sale are stored in a database table called Items. Any information needed about an item can be queried out of the Items table.

- To maintain the user's shopping cart, two key pieces of information must be stored: what items are in the cart and how many of each item. This is accomplished by maintaining two ColdFusion lists—one for the primary key values of the selected items and one for the respective quantities of those items.

  Additionally, these lists will be stored as HTTP cookies placed on the user's browser. Alternatively, the lists could be stored in hidden form fields or by using ColdFusion session variables (a server-side construct for storing state information).

The following four sections show you the source code for each of the templates and explain what the code is doing to support the storefront.

The Initial Page

Listing 33.5 shows the source code for the initial page `index.cfm`. The first task is to do a query that grabs all the item names and primary key values from the database, ordering the results alphabetically by item name. Then the shopping cart is set up using the `<CFCOOKIE>` instructions. The two lists—`qtylist` and `itemlist`—are both empty initially.

Next, a simple form is generated that allows the user to select an item and proceed to a page that gives the details about that item. Note that the drop-down list in the form is dynamically generated using the `<CFOUTPUT>` tag with the `QUERY` attribute. Note also that the primary key value of the item is passed when the form is submitted, rather than the name of the item. This is because the item detail must be queried out in the next template, and the query is most rapidly done by looking up the item by its primary key value.

Listing 33.5 *index.cfm* Code Listing

```
<cfquery datasource="sales" name="GetAllItems">
SELECT ItemID,ItemName
FROM Items
ORDER BY ItemName
</cfquery>

<!--- Initialize the shopping cart - both lists are empty. --->

<cfcookie name="qtylist" value="">
<cfcookie name="itemlist" value="">

<html>

<head>
<title>Welcome to our Online Catalog</title>
</head>

<body bgcolor="white">

<h1>Thanks for shopping with us!</h1>
```

Listing 33.5 Continued

```
<p>Please choose an item to inspect in greater detail:</p>

<form action="itemdetail.cfm" method="post">

<select name="item" size="1">

<cfoutput query="GetAllItems">
    <option value="#ItemID#">#ItemName#
</cfoutput>

</select>
<br/>

<input type="SUBMIT" value="View Item Detail">

</form>

</body>

</html>
```

The Item Detail Page

When the form on `index.cfm` submits, it invokes the template `itemdetail.cfm` and passes the value of the form field `item` to that template. Listing 33.6 contains the source code for `itemdetail.cfm`. In this template, all the information in the database about the selected item is queried out first. Note that the SQL statement is partially dynamic because the value of a form field is used in the `WHERE` clause.

With the detail about the selected item in hand, you can go about the task of building a page that displays the detail about the item. Place the item name and price in headings near the top of the page and drop in a picture of the item by using an `<img/>` element whose `src` attribute is dynamically determined. After the full description of the item, you can present a form field into which the user can type in the quantity of the item to buy. The item's primary key value is stored in a hidden form field so it can be passed along to the `additem.cfm` template, which adds the item to the shopping cart.

Listing 33.6 *itemdetail.cfm* Code Listing

```
<cfquery datasource="sales" name="GetItemDetail">
SELECT *
FROM Items
WHERE ItemID = #Form.item#
</cfquery>

<html>
```

Listing 33.6 Continued

```
<head>
<title>Item Detail: <cfoutput>#GetItemDetail.ItemName#</cfoutput></title>
</head>

<body bgcolor="white">

<cfoutput query="GetItemDetail">

<h2>#ItemName#</h2>
<h2>#DollarFormat(ItemPrice)#</h2>

<img src="#ItemPhoto#" align="right" alt="Photo of #ItemName#"/>

<p>#ItemDescription#</p>

<br clear="all"/>

<form action="additem.cfm" method="post">
Quantity: <input type="text" name="quantity" size="3" value="1"/><br/>
<input type="hidden" name="ItemID" value="#ItemID#"/>
</cfoutput>

<input type="Submit" value="Add Item to Cart">

</form>

</body>

</html>
```


Updating the Cart and Choosing the Next Step

The template `additem.cfm` (see Listing 33.7) has two major tasks. The first is to add the appropriate quantity and item primary key values to the lists that maintain the shopping cart information. This is accomplished by the two `<CFCOOKIE>` instructions near the top of the file. The `ListAppend` function is used to tack on the specified quantity to the `qtylist` cookie and to tack on the primary key of the selected item to the `itemlist` cookie.

The second task is to allow the user to choose another item to look at in detail or to proceed to the checkout counter. To let the user pick another item, you just regenerate the drop-down list created in the template `index.cfm`. If the user chooses an item from this list, the form submits back to `itemdetail.cfm` and a new detailed information page is created. If the user clicks the Proceed to Checkout button, `checkout.cfm` is invoked.

Listing 33.7 *additem.cfm* Code Listing

```
<!--- Update the lists with the new quantity and ItemID --->
<cfcookie name="qtylist" value="#ListAppend(Cookie.qtylist,Form.quantity)#">
<cfcookie name="itemlist" value="#ListAppend(Cookie.itemlist,Form.ItemID)#">

<cfquery datasource="sales" name="GetAllItems">
SELECT ItemID,ItemName
FROM Items
ORDER BY ItemName
</cfquery>

<html>

<head>
<title>Item Added to Cart</title>
</head>

<body bgcolor="white">

<h1>Thank You!</h1>

<p>We have added <cfoutput>#Form.quantity# of item number
#Form.ItemID#</cfoutput> to your shopping cart.</p>

<p>Please choose another item to inspect or move on to
the checkout counter.</p>

<form action="itemdetail.cfm" method="POST">

<select name="item" size="1">

<cfoutput query="GetAllItems">
    <option value="#ItemID#">#ItemName#
</cfoutput>

</select>

<input type="submit" value="View Item Detail"/>

</form>

<p><hr/></p>

<form action="checkout.cfm" method="POST">

<input type="submit" value="Proceed to Checkout">

</form>

</body>

</html>
```

The Checkout Counter

The final template `checkout.cfm` (see Listing 33.8) is tasked with presenting a summary listing of the user's purchases and the grand total of the purchase. To accomplish this, one of the two lists used to maintain the shopping cart is looped over. However, you do this as an indexed loop running from a value of `1` and ending when the index variable reaches the value equal to the length of the lists. This allows you to more easily draw information out of both lists.

The first thing to do is check to make sure there is actually something in the shopping cart by using a `<CFIF>` tag. If `ListLen(Cookie.qtylist)` is non-zero, then there is at least one item in the cart and you can proceed with the summary table. If it is zero, the user is notified that she is trying to check out without any items in the shopping cart.

To create the summary table, first initialize a variable called `total` to zero and set up a row of headers for an XHTML table. Then you dynamically generate the rows of the table by using `<CFLOOP>` to systematically move through the values in the `qtylist` and `itemlist` cookies. The cookies contain the primary keys and quantities of each item, so you need to query the database each time through the loop to get the name and price of the item for display in the table. Also, each time through the loop, you should add to the value of `total` so you keep a running track of what the entire purchase is going to cost. Finally, after the loop is finished, add one final row to the table that prints the grand total of the user's purchase.

Listing 33.8 *checkout.cfm* Code Listing

```
<html>

<head>
<title>The Checkout Line</title>
</head>

<body bgcolor="white">

<h1>Checkout</h1>

<cfif ListLen(Cookie.qtylist)>

    Here's a summary of what's in your cart:<p>

    <cfset total = 0>

    <table>

    <tr>
    <th>Item Number</th><th>Item Name</th><th>Quantity</th>
    <th>Unit Price</th><th>Extended Price</th></tr>

    <!--- Loop over both lists simultaneously --->
```

Listing 33.8 Continued

```
    <cfloop index="count" from="1" to="#ListLen(Cookie.qtylist)#">

        <cfquery datasource="sales" name="GetItemInfo">
        SELECT ItemName,ItemPrice
        FROM Items
        WHERE ItemID = #ListGetAt(Cookie.itemlist,count)#
        </cfquery>

        <cfoutput>
        <tr>
        <td>#ListGetAt(Cookie.itemlist,count)#</td>
        <td>#GetItemInfo.ItemName#</td>
        <td>#ListGetAt(Cookie.qtylist,count)#</td>
        <td>#DollarFormat(GetItemInfo.ItemPrice)#</td>
        <td>#DollarFormat(GetItemInfo.ItemPrice *
         ➥ListGetAt(Cookie.qtylist,count))#</td>
        </tr>
        </cfoutput>

        <cfset total = total + (getiteminfo.itemprice *
         ➥ListGetAt(Cookie.qtylist,count))>

    </cfloop>

    <tr>
    <td colspan="4" align="right"><b>Grand Total</b></td>
    <td><cfoutput>#DollarFormat(total)#</cfoutput></td>
    </tr>

    </table>

<cfelse>

    <p><b>You didn't buy anything yet!</b></p>

</cfif>

</body>

</html>
```

This simple example was meant to show you what you can accomplish with only a few short ColdFusion templates. The electronic storefront created in the example is rather basic, but could be easily expanded to include features you see on popular e-commerce sites, such as the ability to modify quantities when reviewing the shopping cart and to collect credit card information. ColdFusion's power and flexibility make it fairly straightforward to meet these or any other requirements you might come up against in your experience as a Web applications programmer. ●

Using PHP

by Eric Ladd

In this chapter

PHP: A New Server-Side Scripting Alternative

ColdFusion and Active Server Pages are widely used server-side scripting platforms that earned their popularity, in part, by being deployable on the Windows NT operating system. Indeed, ASP is a native Microsoft technology, so it should come as no surprise that ASP cultivated its following by tapping into the huge Windows NT user base. Allaire initially deployed ColdFusion in a Windows environment but later expanded its horizons to include the Solaris (from Sun Microsystems) and, most recently, the Linux operating systems.

Does this mean that during all that time, developers working with UNIX platforms only had Perl to work with? Definitely not. The open source community has been steadily providing us with high-quality software—the Linux operating system and the Apache Web server being two good examples—for years now. Apache's popularity has helped to boost the notoriety of a new server-side scripting paradigm called *PHP*. PHP is similar in concept to ColdFusion and ASP in that script instructions are embedded within an XHTML template. These instructions are parsed out and processed by a special program running on the Web server. The XHTML output from these instructions is incorporated back into the XHTML template, and the finished document is sent on to the browser. What is different about PHP is the specifics of the scripting language. However, if you have programming experience in a UNIX-shell scripting language, JavaScript, or C, you will probably find PHP easy to learn and enjoyable to use.

This chapter introduces you to PHP, tells how you can get it installed and running on your Web server, and shows how you can begin writing server-side PHP scripts. Additionally, you will learn how to make database queries through your PHP scripts. Although it is true that PHP is best known for working with an open source database platform called MySQL, it currently can talk to any ODBC-compliant data source as well. This is especially valuable when deploying PHP in a Windows environment, where ODBC is the principal interface between programs and databases.

NOTE Entire books have been written about PHP, so you will no doubt want to have other reference material available to you after you finish this chapter. A good place to start is on the Web, at `http://www.php.net/`. You can download the PHP script processor from here, as well as complete an online PHP programming tutorial (see Figure 34.1). ■

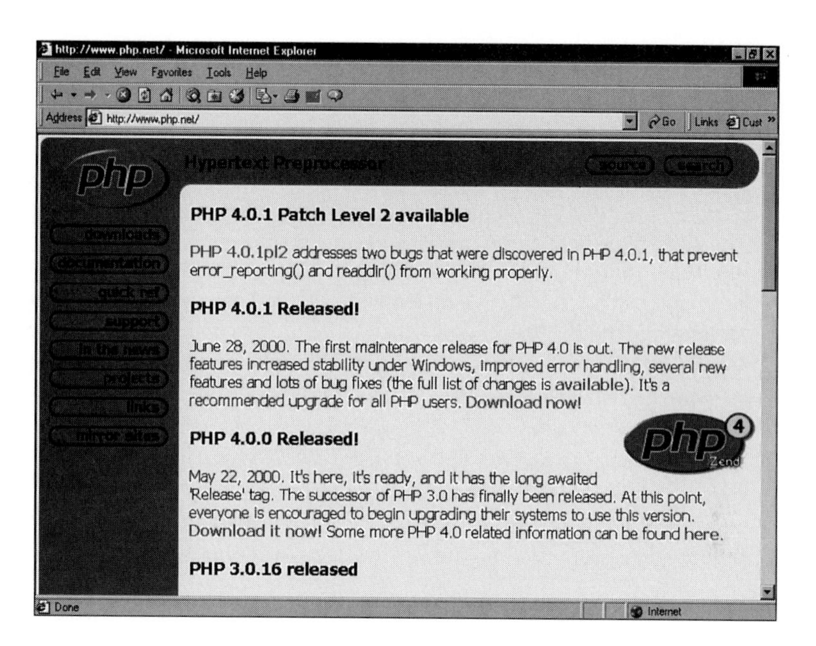

FIGURE 34.1
www.php.net is the official site for the PHP downloads and documentation.

What Is PHP?

PHP is a special scripting language used to dynamically generate Web documents. PHP can be traced back to a developer named Rasmus Lerdorf, who developed a set of macro commands and a parser to interpret them. The commands were for common elements on Web pages at the time—page counters, guest books, and so on. Lerdorf named his language "Personal Home Page Tools," which was later abbreviated to PHP. Later he added the capability to handle data from HTML forms (form interpreter), and PHP/FI was born.

PHP/FI was released into the open source community, where it was met with great enthusiasm and the desire to keep adding to its capabilities. Over time, PHP added the capability to perform common server-side tasks such as sending an email message or placing an HTTP cookie. Additionally, it was ported to multiple platforms (not just the Linux environment, where it was nurtured) and was refitted to work with different kinds of databases. In May 2000, PHP4 was released to the world, and it included a souped-up parsing engine called Zend. Given the fervor over PHP and the energy of the open source software community, enhancements to PHP should continue to come fast and furiously.

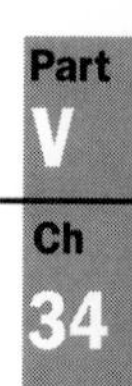

One of PHP's greatest features for many Web server administrators is that it is free: It doesn't cost you a penny to download and install the PHP engine on your Web server. Additionally, PHP is fairly easy to learn, so there's not a huge investment to make in training, either. Books like this one, online tutorials, and busy newsgroups are all places you can go to learn more about PHP programming. Thus, for Web shops with budgetary constraints, PHP is often the best way to build a dynamically generated site at a bare minimum of expense.

PHP is not without its drawbacks though. A major one is that PHP is not a supported product like ColdFusion is, so there's no technical support line you can call if you run into trouble. Members of the PHP community tend to be pretty good about helping each other out, so you can usually find a solution to your problem by checking out a newsgroup or posting a question to a mailing list.

NOTE Developers who work on open source software would never actually charge for their products, but they are not averse to accepting donations to help defray their operating costs. If PHP has worked out well for you, you might want to consider a small contribution to help advance the cause. For more information, consult `http://www.php.net/funding.php3`. ■

Which Servers Support PHP Scripts?

One of the first questions people have about PHP is, "Can it run on my server?" Now that PHP has been ported to the Windows operating systems, the odds are very good that the answer to that question is "Yes." The next two sections look at the basics of installing PHP in both the Windows and UNIX operating systems, and they examine which Web servers PHP can work with in those environments.

Windows

Even though PHP has its heritage in a Linux environment, the sheer number of Windows users made it inevitable that PHP would eventually be supported in Windows. To install PHP for Windows, you need to download the compiled Win 32 binaries that support PHP processing from `http://www.php.net/downloads.php`, and extract binaries from the compressed file in a directory such as `C:\PHP`. You'll note that the `.dll` files that support PHP commands all begin with the php_ prefix.

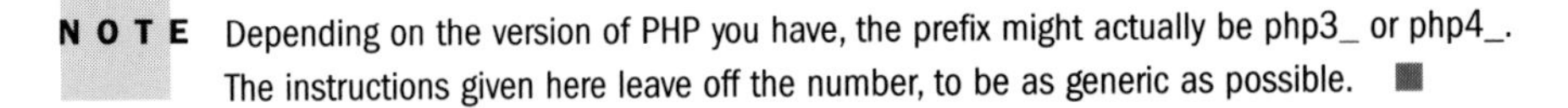
NOTE Depending on the version of PHP you have, the prefix might actually be php3_ or php4_. The instructions given here leave off the number, to be as generic as possible. ■

Next you'll need to move the `php.ini-dist` file to your Windows root directory: `C:\Windows` for Windows 98 and `C:\WINNT` for Windows NT users. After you move the file, rename it to `php.ini`. This is your initialization file for the PHP service.

You next must make some edits inside the `php.ini` file. Specifically, you should do the following:

1. Modify the `extension_dir` entry to point to the directory where the binaries reside (`C:\PHP`, if that's what you chose).
2. Modify the `doc_root` entry to point to the root directory of your Web service (for example, `C:\InetPub\WWWRoot` for a Windows NT system).
3. Uncomment the lines corresponding to the modules that you want to be available when PHP starts up. These lines are of the form `extension=php_*.dll`.
4. If you are using Personal Web Server (PWS) or Internet Information Server (IIS), a special `.dll` file supports a browser capabilities object. This object uses a file called `browscap.ini` to determine what types of code (JavaScript, VBScript, frames, and so on) a browser can handle. PHP can tap into the `browscap.ini` file as well, provided that you tell it where to find the file. The `browscap.ini` file is typically located in the `C:\Winnt\System32\Inetsrv` directory for an IIS machine, and in the `C:\Windows\System\Inetsrv` directory for a PWS server.

The PHP online documentation details what needs to be done next for three different Windows-based Web servers: PWS, IIS, and Apache. For the server that you have installed on your machine, follow the instructions in the appropriate section.

Personal Web Server To get PHP to work with PWS, follow these steps:

1. Open the Windows registry and add a new script mapping for the file extension that you want to use for PHP documents (generally `.php`). You do this by first adding a new string value here:

   ```
   HKEY_LOCAL_MACHINE/System /CurrentControlSet/Services/W3Svc/
   ➥Parameters/ScriptMap
   ```

   You should associate the string value (which should be the file extension) with the path to the PHP executable file (most likely `C:\PHP\php.exe`).
2. Add a key under `HKEY_CLASSES_ROOT`. Set the key equal to file extension that you used previously, and then give it a default value of `phpfile`.
3. Add another new key under `HKEY_CLASSES_ROOT` for `phpfile`, and give it a default value of `PHP Script`.
4. Right-click on the `phpfile` key, and add a new key below it called `Shell`.
5. Right-click on the `Shell` key, and add a new key below it called `Open`.
6. Right-click on the `Open` key, and add a new key below it called `Command`.
7. Give the `Command` key a default value of `C:\PHP\php.exe -q %1` (assuming that `C:\PHP` is the directory where the PHP executable lives).
8. Exit the Registry Editor.

Internet Information Server For IIS 4 and above, follow these steps to get PHP working:

1. Open the Microsoft Management Console (MMC), and select the Web site or application where you want PHP to be active.
2. Right-click on the site or application, and call up its Properties dialog box.
3. Click the Configuration button, and select the Application Mappings tab.
4. Choose to add a new mapping. For the `Executable` entry, type in `C:\PHP\php.exe %s %s` (assuming that you put the PHP executable in `C:\PHP`).
5. For the extension, provide the file extension that you want to use to designate a PHP script (most likely `.php`).
6. Return to the MMC, and set up the Web site or application's root directory to have execute access.
7. Close out of MMC, and give the I_USR_servername account the appropriate permissions to access the `C:\PHP` directory using the Windows NT Explorer.

Apache To get PHP running with an Apache server, you need to edit your `httpd.conf` file to include the following lines:

```
ScriptAlias /php/ "c:/PHP/"
AddType application/x-httpd-php .php
Action application/x-httpd-php "/php/php.exe"
```

Note that with Apache, the usual Windows backslashes (`\`)must be converted to forward slashes (`/`).

UNIX

If you're lucky, you have a UNIX system in which PHP comes preconfigured and ready to go. Red Hat Linux is now bundling its Linux operating system with PHP preconfigured to work with the Apache server.

If you're downloading PHP for UNIX and need to install it from scratch, you will need to compile the code because your downloaded files will contain just the source code, not the binary executable files. The steps will vary based on which flavor of UNIX you are running, but they will go more or less as follows:

1. Decompress the archived file by typing `gunzip php-4.0.x.tar.gz`. This will produce a `.tar` file.
2. Untar the `.tar` file by typing `tar -xvf php-4.0.x.tar`. This will create a `/usr/local/php` directory containing all the necessary files.
3. Type `./setup` to begin the PHP installation. You will be asked to respond to several questions.
4. Assuming that you choose to set up PHP as a CGI extension, you will need to compile the CGI executable. Do this by typing `make` at the command prompt.

5. Copy the binary file into your server's /cgi-bin/ directory.
6. Copy the file php.ini-dist to the /cgi-bin/ directory, and rename it php.ini.

Finally, if you're using the Apache Web server, you need to add the following to your httpd.conf file:

```
AddType application/x-httpd-php .php
Action application/x-httpd-php /cgi-bin/php
```

NOTE Apache is, by far, the most popular Web server for UNIX environments, but other UNIX Web servers are available. To see if your server supports PHP, consult the documentation at http://www.php.net/ and your own server's documentation. ■

Writing PHP Code

With PHP up and running on your server, you are ready to begin writing PHP scripts. All you need to do this is a simple text editor, such as Notepad in Windows or vi on a UNIX machine.

Basic Syntax Rules

You read earlier that PHP code coexists with XHTML code in the same file. The PHP instructions are parsed out and executed by the PHP scripting engine. To make it easy for the scripting engine to find your PHP code, you must enclose it in special delimiters. These take this form:

```
<?php
   ... PHP code ...
?>
```

TIP If you're an astute XML developer, you might be wondering whether the PHP code delimiters might conflict with an XML processing instruction. XML processing instructions are enclosed by the <? and ?> delimiters. You can prevent a conflict between these two languages by setting the short_tags entry in your php.ini file to 0.

A very basic PHP command is echo, which is used to write output into the resulting XHTML page. Thus, the quintessential first script that every programmer writes would look like the following in PHP:

```
<html>
<head>
<title>Hello, World! (PHP style)</title>
</head>
<body>

<?php
```

```
    // Say hello to everyone ...
    echo "<h1>Hello, World!</h1>\n";

?>

</body>
</html>
```

In this code, the double forward slashes (//) designate a PHP comment. The echo command prints out your greeting as a level one heading and also includes a \n character. This is to break to the next line before putting in the </body> tag in the code being generated. The semicolon at the end of the command separates the command from the one that follows it, if one exists. When you request this PHP script from your Web server, the source code delivered to the browser will look like this:

```
<html>
<head>
<title>Hello, World! (PHP style)</title>
</head>
<body>
<h1>Hello, World!</h1>
</body>
</html>
```

This will produce the screen that you see in Figure 34.2.

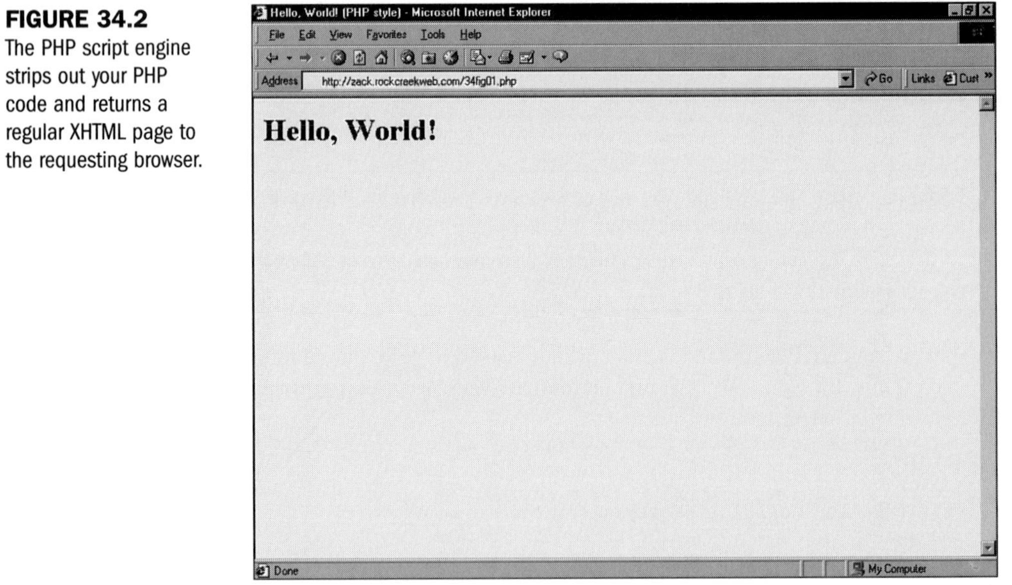

FIGURE 34.2
The PHP script engine strips out your PHP code and returns a regular XHTML page to the requesting browser.

TIP Don't forget to use `\n`! The screen in Figure 34.2 would look the same even if you had left off the `\n` instruction, so it's easy to fall into the habit of leaving these off. However, including the `\n` at the end of each `echo` command helps to make the XHTML source code more readable when you do a View Source. This can be helpful when debugging complex XHTML constructs such as forms and tables.

PHP Variables

As a language, PHP possesses the capability to handle variables. *Variables* are a named chunk of memory in which you can store a particular literal value until you need it at a later time. PHP variables can be of one of two types: scalar and array. A *scalar* variable can take on only one value, whereas an *array* can hold multiple values.

A PHP scalar variable must begin with the dollar sign character (`$`), followed by its name. The name can be any meaningful combination of letters, numbers, and the underscore character (_), although the name should not begin with a numeric character. Scalar variables have values assigned to them by using the equals sign (=), as follows:

```
<?php
   $language = "PHP";
?>
```

In this code, the scalar `$language` has a *string* value. Strings are combinations of letters, numbers, and other characters, enclosed in either double quotes (") or single quotes ('). Scalar variable can also be of type `integer` (number with no decimal part) or `floating point` (number with a decimal part).

NOTE Variable names in PHP are case-sensitive. ■

PHP Operators

When you start getting values into arrays, you'll end up wanting to manipulate them, and that's where the PHP operators come in. For integer and floating-point variables, you have all the common mathematical functions at your disposal:

```
<?php
  $x = 9;
  $y = 4;

  $z = $x + $y;    // $z = 13 (addition)
  $z = $x - $y;    // $z = 5 (subtraction)
  $z = $x * $y;    // $z = 36 (multiplication)
  $z = $x / $y;    // $z = 2.25 (division)
?>
```

PHP also supports the modulus operator (%), which tells you the remainder you get when dividing one value into another:

```
<?php
  $x = 9;
  $y = 4;

  // 9 divided by 4 is 2 with
  // a remainder of 1.

  $z = $x % $y;    // $z = 1

?>
```

PHP supports addition for string variables as well, a process usually called *concatenation*. Concatenation is represented by the dot (.) operator. The following code is a variation on the "Hello, World!" example that uses concatenation:

```
<html>
<head>
<title>Hello, World! (PHP style)</title>
</head>
<body>

<?php

  $x = "<h1>Hello, ";
  $y = "World!</h1>";

  $z = $x . $y  // Concatenate the strings

  echo $z;

?>

</body>
</html>
```

Regardless of their data types, you often need to compare two variables. PHP provides several operators to help you do this. Table 34.1 details each comparison operator.

Table 34.1 PHP Comparison Operators

Operator	Function
==	Tests to see whether the variables are equal to each other
!=	Tests to see whether the variables are not equal to each other
>	Tests to see whether one variable is greater than the other
<	Tests to see whether one variable is less than the other
>=	Tests to see whether one variable is greater than or equal to the other
<=	Tests to see whether one variable is less than or equal to the other

In each case, a comparison operator returns a value of True or False, depending on the results of the test. For example, the following code would display a value of False (because 21 does not equal 12), followed by a value of True (because 21 is greater than or equal to 12) on a new line:

```
<html>
<head>
<title>PHP Comparison Operators</title>
</head>
<body>

<?php

  $x = 21;
  $y = 12;

  echo $x == $y;
  echo "<br />";
  echo $x >= $y;

?>

</body>
</html>
```

Because the comparison operators return Boolean values, you may need to use these values to perform some Boolean arithmetic. The Boolean arithmetic operators are shown in Table 34.2.

Table 34.2 PHP Boolean Arithmetic Operators

Operator	Function
&&	Logical AND. (Both values must be True for the whole expression to be True.)
||	Logical OR. (At least one of the values must be True for the whole expression to be True.)
!	Logical NOT. (This negates the Boolean value.)

PHP Decision Structures

The PHP comparison operators probably have their greatest utility in helping to make decisions about what to do during the course of the script processing. The most basic way to make a decision in a PHP script is to use an if statement. An if statement includes a Boolean condition and an associated block of code. If the condition evaluates to True, the block of code is executed. If the condition is False, the code is skipped. Take a look at this example:

```
<html>
<head>
```

```
<title>A PHP if Statement</title>
</head>
<body>

<?php

  $age = 26;

  if ($age >= 18) {
    echo "Be sure to register to vote!";
  }

?>

</body>
</html>
```

Note that the condition is enclosed in parentheses. Also, even though this is typically thought of as an if-then sort of rule, the word ***then*** does not appear in the code. The curly brackets (`{` and `}`) are used to contain the block of code to execute when the condition is `True`.

The `if` statement by itself is somewhat limiting because you can take action only if the associated condition is `True`. Fortunately, you can extend the `if` statement by adding an `else` clause that lets add a block of code to execute if the condition evaluates to `False`.

```
<html>
<head>
<title>A PHP if-else Statement</title>
</head>
<body>

<?php

  $age = 26;

  if ($age >= 18) {
    echo "Be sure to register to vote!";
  } else {
    echo "Ah well ... no good choices anyway!";
  }

?>

</body>
</html>
```

The `else` clause immediately follows the block of code to execute if the condition is `True`. You place the block of code to execute if the condition is `False` right after the `else`. Note that this code block is also contained in curly brackets.

PHP Looping Structures

Most programming languages provide support for the iterative execution of a set of instructions. This is commonly called *looping*. PHP includes commands to implement two frequently used kinds of loops: the `for` loop and the `while` loop.

A `for` loop counts through a set of values, processing the instructions inside the loop once for each time that it counts. To set up a `for` loop in any language, you must provide starting and ending values for the loop, how much the loop counter should increase or decrease from one iteration to the next, and a block of code to execute. In PHP, you assemble this information as follows:

```
for (initial value; stopping condition; increment) {
  ... code to execute ...
}
```

The `initial value` is where you specify the starting value of the counter. The `stopping condition` is a Boolean condition that is evaluated after each iteration of the loop. If the condition is `True`, the loop continues for another iteration. If it's `False`, the loop terminates. The `increment` specifies how the counter should change after an iteration of the loop. A typical loop might look like this:

```
<html>
<head>
<title>Generating Perfect Squares with a Loop</title>
</head>
<body>

<p>Here are some perfect squares:</p>

<ul>

<?php

  for ($i=1; $i<=10; $i++) {
    $square = $i * $i;
    echo "<li> $square\n";
  }

?>

</ul>

</body>
</html>
```

The counter variable in this case is `$i`, and it has an initial value of 1. As long as `$i` is less than or equal to 10, the loop will continue to execute, and we add 1 to the value of the counter after each iteration of the loop.

NOTE `$i++` is a shorthand way of saying `$i = $i + 1`. You can also do a shorthand decrement by using `$i--`.

A PHP `while` loop has the following structure:

```
while (condition) {
   ... code to execute ...
}
```

The code inside the loop will continue to execute as long as the loop condition evaluates to `True`. The condition is evaluated before the loop begins and is evaluated again before continuing to the next iteration of the loop; when it becomes `False`, the loop terminates. Consider this example:

```
<html>
<head>
<title>Even Numbers between a Value and its Square</title>
</head>
<body>

<?php

  $yournumber = 7;

?>

<p>Here are the even numbers between your number and its square:</p>

<ul>

<?php

  $j = $yournumber;
  $square = $j * $j;

  while ($j <= $square) {
    if ($j % 2 == 0) {
      echo "<li>$j";
      $j = $j + 1;
    }
  }

}

?>

</ul>

</body>
</html>
```

In the case of the chosen number being 7, the script would print out a bulleted list of all even numbers between 7 and 49 (7 squared).

NOTE Normally, you would not hard-code a user's guess into the script, as in the previous example. Very soon you will learn how to use data submitted on an XHTML form in your PHP scripts. ■

CAUTION

In any programming language, `while` loops tend to have a higher risk of incidence of an infinite loop. Make sure that the condition in your `while` loop will eventually become `False`.

PHP Functions

PHP has a large number of built-in functions that perform many common programming tasks. The following list outlines some of the types of functions that PHP supports:

- Apache-specific functions
- Database-specific functions (MySQL, mSQL, Informix, SQL Server)
- Network service-specific functions (mail, FTP, LDAP, ODBC)
- Mathematical functions
- String functions
- PDF functions
- File system functions
- XML parser functions
- Session maintenance functions

NOTE A full set of documentation for all classes of functions and the functions within each class can be found at `http://www.php.net/manual/html/funcref.html`. ■

One example of a useful built-in function is the PHP `Header()` function. `Header()` is used to add a line to the HTTP header, a block of information that arrives at the browser before your XHTML content. HTTP headers can tell a browser what type of file it is about to receive, what cookies it should write, and a host of other bits of information. Occasionally, the header is used to do an HTTP redirect, which refers to sending the user off to a different URL than the one requested. You can do an HTTP redirect in an PHP script as follows:

```
<?php
   Header("Location: new_url");
?>
```

Here, `new_url` is the URL that the user's browser should load instead of the one requested.

NOTE When you do a redirect, the only thing sent to the browser is the HTTP header with the redirect instruction. It's not possible to display any content before the redirect, or any other header-based instruction, occurs. ■

In addition to the built-in functions, you can define your own functions. A user-defined function has this form:

```
function myfunction ($arg1, $arg2, ..., $argn) {
   ... code to execute ...
}
```

As an example of a user-defined function, consider the following code:

```
<html>
<head>
<title>Your Very Own Factorial Function</title>
</head>
<body>

<?php

  function myfactorial ($x) {

  $f = 1;
  for ($k=1; $k <= $x; $k++) {
    $f = $f * $k;
  };
  return $f
}

  $yournumber = 4;

  echo "The factorial of $yournumber is:<br />";
  echo myfactorial($yournumber)

?>

</ul>

</body>
</html>
```

The second `echo` command makes the call to the function named `myfactorial`, passing it the value stored in `$yournumber`. The function uses a `for` loop to compute the factorial value and then uses the `return` command to hand back the result.

NOTE Arguments passed to a function are passed by value, meaning that if you change the value of the argument inside the function, it does not change the value of the argument outside the function. If you want to pass arguments by reference, in which case changes inside the function also change the value outside the function, you should precede the argument to be passed by reference with an ampersand character (&). ■

Doing Common Web Tasks with PHP

So far, you have seen the basics of the PHP language, but what you're probably most interested in knowing is how to use it in the context of a Web-based application or a dynamic Web site. The next few sections show you how PHP is useful in several situations that crop up during dynamic Web development. In each case, PHP makes it simple to complete the task at hand.

Responding to a Form Submission The cornerstone of a dynamic Web site is the capability to interact with a user by means of an XHTML form. You collect information from users through a form, and the browser bundles the data collected and sends it along to the server when the form is submitted. Consider the form produced by the XHTML code here:

```
<html>

<head>
<title>Survey Form</title>
</head>

<body bgcolor="white">

<h1>Survey Form</h1>

<p>Thanks for taking the time to fill out our survey.
Please answer the questions below and hit the Submit Form!
button.</p>
<table>
<form action="surveyresponse.php" method="post">
<tr>
<td><b>First Name:</b></td>
<td><input type="TEXT" name="fname" size="20" /></td>
</tr>
<tr>
<td><b>Last Name:</b></td>
<td><input type="TEXT" name="lname" size="20" /></td>
</tr>
<tr>
<td><b>Age:</b></td>
<td><input type="TEXT" name="age" size="20" /></td>
</tr>
<tr>
<td><b>College Graduate?</b></td>
<td><input type="RADIO" name="college" value="1" checked="checked" /> Yes
```

```
<input type="RADIO" name="college" value="0" /> No</td>
</tr>
<tr>
<td colspan="2" align="CENTER"><input type="SUBMIT" value="Submit Form!" />
<input type="RESET" value="Clear Form!" /></td>
</tr>
</form>
</table>

</body>

</html>
```

The form asks the user for his or her first name, last name, age, and college graduation status. Each of these quantities is associated with a unique form field name: `fname`, `lname`, `age`, and `college`, respectively.

When a form is submitted to a PHP script for processing, the PHP engine automatically stores the form data in an associative array called `$HTTP_POST_VARS`, if `method="post"` is used, or `$HTTP_GET_VARS`, if `method="get"` is used. An associative array is one that you index by a keyword rather than by a number. In the case of these associative arrays, the keywords that you use to index them are the names of the form fields. When you index the array with a form field name, you get back the data that was submitted in that form field.

The previous form uses `method="post"`, so you would appeal to the `$HTTP_POST_VARS` array to get the data submitted in the form. Thus, you could build a simple confirmation page as follows:

```
<html>

<head>
<title>Thanks!</title>
</head>

<body bgcolor="white">

<?php

  echo "<h1>Thank you, $HTTP_POST_VARS['fname']!</h1>"

?>

<p>Thank you for completing our survey.  To ensure accuracy,
please check that the information below is correct.</p>


<table>
<tr>
<td><b>First Name:</b></td>
<td>
```

```
<?php

  echo $HTTP_POST_VARS['fname']

?>
</td>
</tr>

<tr>
<td><b>Last Name:</b></td>
<td>

<?php

  echo $HTTP_POST_VARS['lname']

?>
</td>
</tr>

<tr>
<td><b>Age:</b></td>
<td>

<?php

  echo $HTTP_POST_VARS['age']

?>
</td>
</tr>

<tr>
<td><b>College Grad:</b></td>
<td>

<?php

  if ($HTTP_POST_VARS['college'] == 1) {
    echo "Yes";
  } else {
    echo "No";
  }

?>
</td>
</tr>

</table>

</body>

</html>
```

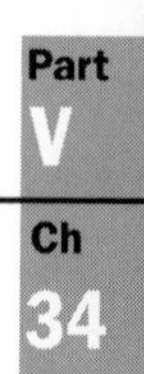

Note that the array index is enclosed in square brackets (`[` and `]`) and is also quoted. You can use either single or double quotes, although single quotes were used here because the first instance of indexing the array was within double quotes already.

TIP When you pass form data by `method="get"`, the data is passed on the URL. Because `$HTTP_GET_VARS` retrieves form data passed by `method="get"`, it stands to reason that you can also use it to retrieve the value of URL parameters that you create yourself.

Using Environment Variables When a browser and a server first begin to communicate, they exchange a great deal of information about each other. The server stores all this information in what are called ***environment variables***. For a listing of the various environment variable names and their meanings, refer to Table 32.4 in Chapter 32, "Writing Active Server Pages," or to the section noted in the cross-reference.

▶ For a list of the environment variable names and their meanings, **see** "Standard CGI Environment Variables," **p. 744**

PHP supports a function called `getenv()` that you can use to retrieve the value of an environment variable. If you pass the `getenv()` function the name of the environment variable that you want, it will return the value of that variable to you. This means that you can reprise the old "Big Brother" trick that showed up on some Web pages a number of years ago—trying to make users feel like you are spying on them by telling them what their IP addresses are—as follows:

```
<html>

<head>
<title>We see you!</title>
</head>

<body bgcolor="white">

<?php

  $yourIP = getenv("REMOTE_ADDR");

  echo "<h1>Hello!</h1>\n";
  echo " I see your IP address is <b>$yourIP</b>.";

?>

</body>

</html>
```

Sending an Email The PHP `mail()` function makes sending an email message a very simple matter. The syntax of the `mail()` function is this:

```
mail("recipient_address", "subject", "body", "headers")
```

This makes it easy to set up a feedback form on your Web site. First, have the user fill out the following form:

```
<html>

<head>
<title>Feedback</title>
</head>

<body bgcolor="white">

<h1>Tell us what you think!</h1>

<p>Please type in your email address and comments below
and click the Send! button.</p>
<table>
<form action="feedback.php" method="post">
<tr>
<td><b>Your Address:</b></td>
<td><input type="TEXT" name="from" size="20" /></td>
</tr>
<tr valign="top">
<td><b>Comments:</b></td>
<td><textarea name="comments" rows="10" cols="20></textarea></td>
</tr>
<tr>
<td colspan="2" align="CENTER"><input type="SUBMIT" value="Send!" />
<input type="RESET" value="Clear Form!" /></td>
</tr>
<input type="hidden" name="to" value="webmaster@yourcompany.com" />
<input type="hidden" name="subject" value="Web site comments" />
</form>
</table>

</body>

</html>
```

Then you could process their submission with the following PHP script:

```
<?php

  $to = $HTTP_POST_VARS["to"];
  $subj = $HTTP_POST_VARS["subject"];
  $body = $HTTP_POST_VARS["comments"]
  $header = "From: " . $HTTP_POST_VARS["from"];

  mail($to, $subj, $body, $header);

?>

<html>
```

```
<head>
<title>Thanks</title>
</head>

<body bgcolor="white">

<h1>Thank you!</h1>

<p>We value your feedback and will get back to you soon!</p>

</body>

</html>
```

Placing a Cookie The PHP `setcookie()` function lets you write an HTTP cookie to a user's browser. The function has the following syntax:

```
setcookie("name", "value", "expiration_date")
```

A convenient way to set the expiration date is with the PHP `time()` function. By setting the expiration to the value of `time()` plus an additional number of seconds, you can specify whatever expiration time you'd like. For example, you might place a cookie on a user's browser after that user successfully logs in to the application, and have the cookie expire at the end of the work day (eight hours later). There are 3600 seconds in an hour, so you could use the following instruction to place the cookie:

```
setcookie("loggedin", "true", time()+28800)
```

After you've placed a cookie, the browser will hand the cookie's name and value back to your server on each subsequent request. To get at the value of a particular cookie, you can use the `$HTTP_COOKIE_VARS` associative array. When you index the array with the name of the desired cookie, PHP will hand you back the value associated with that cookie. Thus, you could check to make sure that a user is logged in as follows:

```
<?php
  if ($HTTP_COOKIE_VARS["loggedin"] != "true") {
    Header("Location: loginpage.html");
  }
?>
```

Database Access with PHP

Most high-end Web sites have some kind of database behind them, helping to power the dynamic nature of the site. PHP has been capable of working with back-end databases for quite some time. Initially, it worked only with open source databases such as MySQL and mSQL, but now it can work with ODBC-compliant databases as well. This means that you can now Web-enable your Microsoft Access, Microsoft SQL Server, and Oracle databases using PHP.

This section examines how to pose queries to databases using PHP and how to dynamically build a Web page using the results from those queries. In particular, you will learn about the built-in functions that enable PHP to communicate with the following types of databases:

- MySQL
- Microsoft SQL Server
- Oracle

Additionally, you will see how to get PHP to communicate with any ODBC-compliant data source on your system.

NOTE PHP supports functions for communicating with other database platforms, including mSQL, Sybase, Informix, and PostgreSQL. If you are using one of these databases, consult the PHP documentation for the appropriate functions. Even though they might not share the same names as the functions that you read about here, many of them behave similarly. ■

Connecting to MySQL Databases

MySQL is a freely available relational database management system from MySQL AB in Stockholm, Sweden. You can learn more about MySQL and download a copy of it at `http://www.mysql.com/`.

PHP has a number of functions that let you work directly with MySQL databases, but by using just a few of the basic ones, you can be issuing queries to your MySQL database in no time. The first of these functions is `mysql_connect()`, which is used to open a connection to the MySQL server. The function has the following syntax:

```
$dbconnection = mysql_connect(host, username, password);
```

For example, if your MySQL server were running on a machine named WebDB, and the username and password to log in to the server were webapp and Ix87lwz, you would issue the following command to establish a connection to the server:

```
$dbconnection = mysql_connect("WebDB", "webapp", "Ix87lwz");
```


Because it may be possible that the connect instruction fails, it's a good idea to use the PHP `die()` function in conjunction with the `mysql_connect()` command. The `die()` function presents the user with an error message in the event of a connection failure:

```
$dbconnection = mysql_connect("WebDB", "webapp", "Ix87lwz")
➥or die("Could not connect to MySQL server!");
```

The MySQL server is responsible for administering many individual databases, so your next step is to select one of them. You can accomplish this by using the `mysql_select_db()` function. `mysql_select_db()` takes two arguments: the name of the database that you want to open, and the variable that you set up to represent the connection. If your target database is named onlinestore and you use the connection created previously, you would issue this command:

```
$targetdb = mysql_select_db("onlinestore", $dbconnection)
➥or die("Could not open database \"onlinestore\"");
```

NOTE The character sequence \" instructs PHP to print out the double quote character, rather than interpreting the double quote as the end of the string. ■

With the connection open, you are now ready to send a SQL statement to the database. SQL `SELECT`, `INSERT`, or `DELETE` statements are similar in that they don't retrieve records from the database. For statements like these, you first store the statement in a variable:

```
$sql = "UPDATE Products SET Price = 34.99 WHERE ProductID = 817";
```

Then you send the statement to the database using the `mysql_query()` function:

```
$queryresults = mysql_query($sql, $dbconnection)
➥or die("Could not perform database update");
```

In the case of a `SELECT` statement, you must be able to get at the records that come back from the query and incorporate them into the Web page that you're building. The steps to do the query are similar to those that you take for any of the other types of SQL statements:

```
$sql = "SELECT Name, Price FROM Products ORDER BY Name";
$queryresults = mysql_query($sql, $dbconnection)
➥or die("Could not perform database query");
```

The records that came back from the query are now stored in the variable called `$queryresults`. To get at the data in the records, you use the `mysql_fetch_array()` function to grab a row and place the data from the row into an array. For example, the following command grabs the first record from the results and stores them in an array called `$dbrec`:

```
$dbrec = mysql_fetch_array($queryresults)'
```

You index the array `$dbrec` by using the field names that you queried out of the database in your `SELECT` statement—in this case, `Name` and `Price`.

```
echo "The first product is $dbrec['Name'] and its price is \$$dbrec['Price'].";
```

A much more useful thing to do is to set up a loop that will move through the records in `$queryresults`, printing them out as you go. To do this, you can use the following `while` loop:

```
while ($dbrec = mysql_fetch_array($queryresults)) {
  echo " The product $dbrec['Name'] costs \$$dbrec['Price'].<br />";
}
```

Having the capability to loop over the query results is handy for creating XHTML constructs such as tables or lists that have a repetitive structure. For example, to generate a select list of all the products, you could use the following code:

```
<form action="productdetail.php" method="post">
<p>Please select a product to inspect in more detail:</p>
<select name="product" size="1">
<?php
```

```
$dbconnection = mysql_connect("WebDB", "webapp", "Ix87lwz")
➥or die("Could not connect to MySQL server!");
$targetdb = mysql_select_db("onlinestore", $dbconnection)
➥or die("Could not open database \"onlinestore\"");

$sql = "SELECT Name, Price FROM Products ORDER BY Name";
$queryresults = mysql_query($sql, $dbconnection)
➥or die("Could not perform database query");

while ($dbrec = mysql_fetch_array($queryresults)) {
  echo "<option>$dbrec['Name']</option>";
}
?>

</select>
<br />
<input type="submit" value="Show Product Detail" />

</form>
```

Similarly, you could generate a table by creating individual table rows inside the loop, or you could generate a list by creating `<li>` elements inside the loop.

When you're done with the MySQL database connection, you should take care of a few housekeeping chores. The first is to free up the system resources being used to maintain the connection and the query results that you create using it. Then you must close the connection itself. You can do this easily with the `mysql_free_result()` and `mysql_close()` functions, respectively. Adding these functions to the previous code yields the following:

```
<form action="productdetail.php" method="post">
<p>Please select a product to inspect in more detail:</p>
<select name="product" size="1">
<?php

$dbconnection = mysql_connect("WebDB", "webapp", "Ix87lwz")
➥or die("Could not connect to MySQL server!");
$targetdb = mysql_select_db("onlinestore", $dbconnection)
➥or die("Could not open database \"onlinestore\"");

$sql = "SELECT Name, Price FROM Products ORDER BY Name";
$queryresults = mysql_query($sql, $dbconnection)
➥or die("Could not perform database query");

while ($dbrec = mysql_fetch_array($queryresults)) {
  echo "<option>$dbrec['Name']</option>";
}

// Housekeeping chores
mysql_free_result($queryresults);
mysql_close($dbconnection);
```

```
?>

</select>
<br />
<input type="submit" value="Show Product Detail" />

</form>
```

TIP If you use mSQL as your database platform, the PHP functions for opening a connection, selecting a database, issuing a query, and so on are virtually the same as they are for MySQL databases. The chief difference is that the function names start with the msql_ prefix instead of mysql_.

Connecting to Microsoft SQL Server Databases

If you're running PHP scripts on a Microsoft server, you may very well need to connect to Microsoft SQL Server databases. PHP is capable of working with SQL Server, and the functions that you use bear a striking resemblance to those used to work with MySQL databases. These functions include the following:

- **`mssql_connect()`**—Establishes a connection to the SQL Server service
- **`mssql_select_db()`**—Chooses a SQL Server database to work with
- **`mssql_query()`**—Sends a SQL statement to the selected database
- **`mssql_fetch_array()`**—Converts a record returned from a `SELECT` query to a PHP associative array
- **`mssql_freeresult()`**—Gives back the memory being used by the connection and the set of records generated
- **`mssql_close()`**—Closes the recordset

Because the functions are so similar to those for MySQL, this section looks at how you can generate a table with your results, rather than a select list. All the concepts are the same—only the prefixes on the function names have changed.

To begin, you first open a connection to the SQL Server service, choose a database, and perform the query. This can be handled by the following code:

```
$dbconnection = mssql_connect("MSSQLDB", "webapp", "di9jd7")
➥or die("Could not connect to SQL Server!");
$targetdb = mssql_select_db("employees", $dbconnection)
➥or die("Could not open database \"employees\"");

$sql = "SELECT LastName, FirstName, Salary FROM Employees ORDER BY LastName";
$queryresults = mssql_query($sql, $dbconnection)
➥or die("Could not perform database query");
```

With the results stored in the `$queryresults` variable, you can set up a `while` loop to systematically print the results into table rows. But first, you need to start the table and put a row of headers over your data. If you prefer to keep everything in terms of PHP code, you could use the following:

```
echo "<table border=\"1\">";
echo "<tr><th>Employee</th><th>Salary</th></tr>";
while ($dbrec = mssql_fetch_array($queryresults)) {
  echo "<tr><td>$dbrec['LastName'], $dbrec['FirstName']</td>
  ➥<td>$dbrec['Salary']</td></tr>";
}
echo "</table>";
```

Alternatively, you could leave the static parts of the table as XHTML and just dynamically generate the rows:

```
<table border="1">
<tr><th>Employee</th><th>Salary</th></tr>

<?php

$dbconnection = mssql_connect("MSSQLDB", "webapp", "di9jd7")
➥or die("Could not connect to SQL Server!");
$targetdb = mssql_select_db("employees", $dbconnection)
➥or die("Could not open database \"employees\"");

$sql = "SELECT LastName, FirstName, Salary FROM Employees ORDER BY LastName";
$queryresults = mssql_query($sql, $dbconnection)
➥or die("Could not perform database query");

while ($dbrec = mssql_fetch_array($queryresults)) {
  echo "<tr><td>$dbrec['LastName'], $dbrec['FirstName']</td>
➥<td>$dbrec['Salary']</td></tr>";
}

?>

</table>
```

Regardless of your table generation approach, you should still give back the memory that you used to generate the records and close the connection. Adding the `mssql_freeresult()` and `mssql_close()` functions to the previous code as follows will take care of that final task.


```
<table border="1">
<tr><th>Employee</th><th>Salary</th></tr>

<?php

$dbconnection = mssql_connect("MSSQLDB", "webapp", "di9jd7")
➥or die("Could not connect to SQL Server!");
$targetdb = mssql_select_db("employees", $dbconnection)
➥or die("Could not open database \"employees\"");
```

```
$sql = "SELECT LastName, FirstName, Salary FROM Employees ORDER BY LastName";
$queryresults = mssql_query($sql, $dbconnection)
➥or die("Could not perform database query");

while ($dbrec = mssql_fetch_array($queryresults)) {
  echo "<tr><td>$dbrec['LastName'], $dbrec['FirstName']</td>
➥<td>$dbrec['Salary']</td></tr>";
}

mssql_freeresult($queryresults);
mssql_close($dbconnection);

?>

</table>
```

Connecting to Oracle Databases

PHP supports several functions that can assist you in connecting to an Oracle 7 or 8 database. Many of the concepts are the same as for MySQL and SQL Server databases, but the function names are somewhat different.

To begin working with an Oracle database, you need to open a connection to the Oracle server. You accomplish this by using the `OCILogon()` function. `OCILogon()` expects a valid username and password that it can use to log into Oracle; it also needs the name of a database. A typical `OCILogon()` call looks like this:

```
$dbconnection = OCILogon("webapp", "wQp509I", "marketing");
```

NOTE Sometimes the database name is set through an environment variable called `ORACLE_SID`. In this case, the third argument of the `OCILogon()` function becomes optional. ■

With the connection in place, your next step is to parse and execute your SQL statement. The `OCIParse()` and `OCIExecute()` functions handle these tasks, respectively. Take a look at this example:

```
$sql = "SELECT LastName, FirstName, Company FROM Leads ORDER BY LastName";
$parsedsql = OCIParse($dbconnection, $sql)
➥or die("Unable to parse SQL statement");
OCIExecute($parsedsql) or die("Unable to execute query");
```

The byproduct of the `OCIExecute()` command is a set of records that came back from the query. You can get at the data in these records by using the `OCIFetch()`, `OCINumCols()`, and `OCIResult()` functions. `OCIFetch()` grabs a row from the set of records and places it in a results buffer. The `OCINumCols()` function tells you how many columns of data are in the buffer, enabling you to set up a loop to print them out. The `OCIResult()` function actually grabs the data from the buffer and makes it available for inclusion on the Web page that you're building. You can make the three functions work together as follows:

```
while (OCIFetch($parsedsql)) {
  // Find out how many columns of data
  $columns = OCINumCols($parsedsql);
  // Now set up a for loop to print the data
  for ($k = 0; $k < $columns; $k++) {
    $value = OCIResult($parsedsql, $k);
    echo "$value<br />";
  }
}
```

This code prints each piece of data in the query results on its own line. What you're more likely to do is print the results into an XHTML table. To do this, you would modify the code as follows:

```
echo "<table border=\"1\">";
echo "<tr><th>Last Name</th><th>First Name</th><th>Company</th></tr>";
while (OCIFetch($parsedsql)) {
  // Find out how many columns of data
  $columns = OCINumCols($parsedsql);
  echo "<tr>";
  // Now set up a for loop to print the data
  for ($k = 0; $k < $columns; $k++) {
    $value = OCIResult($parsedsql, $k);
    echo "<td>$value</td>";
  }
  echo "</tr>";
}
echo "</table>"
```

When you have your data from the query printed out, you can use the `OCIFreeStatement()` and `OCILogoff()` functions to free up the memory that you've used and close the connection to Oracle. Modifying the previous table code to include these steps, you have the following lines:

```
echo "<table border=\"1\">";
echo "<tr><th>Last Name</th><th>First Name</th><th>Company</th></tr>";
while (OCIFetch($parsedsql)) {
  // Find out how many columns of data
  $columns = OCINumCols($parsedsql);
  echo "<tr>";
  // Now set up a for loop to print the data
  for ($k = 0; $k < $columns; $k++) {
    $value = OCIResult($parsedsql, $k);
    echo "<td>$value</td>";
  }
  echo "</tr>";
}
echo "</table>"
```

```
// Housekeeping chores
OCIFreeStatement($parsedsql);
OCILogoff($dbconnection);
```

Connecting to ODBC Data Sources

Many people use Microsoft Access as their Web database of choice, though more for convenience than for Access's capability to handle the volume of activity that a high-end Web site can generate. Access databases are commonly accessed via Open Database Connectivity (ODBC) rather than connecting directly to the database file. When you set up an Access database in ODBC, you are creating what is called an ODBC *data source*. Just as it can do with many database platforms, PHP can work with ODBC data sources through a number of built-in functions.

NOTE It's also possible to set up Microsoft SQL Server and Oracle databases as ODBC data sources. For these platforms, though, it makes more sense to use the functions specially designed to work with them. ■

To do queries against ODBC data sources, you first must open a connection to the data source. The `odbc_connect()` function helps you do this. `odbc_connect()` expects three arguments: the data source name and the username and password required to log in to the data source.

```
$dbconnection = odbc_connect("dsn=library","webapp","weu8ude")
➥or die("Unable to connect to ODBC data source");
```

With the connection established, there is a two-step process for sending a SQL statement down the connection. The first step is to prepare the SQL statement, and the second is to execute it. These tasks are handled by the `odbc_prepare()` and `odbc_execute()` functions, respectively.

```
$sql = "SELECT Author,Title,ISBN FROM Books WHERE Topic = 'Internet'";
$preppedsql = odbc_prepare($dbconnection,$sql)
➥or die("Unable to prepare SQL statement");
$queryresults = odbc_execute($preppedsql)
➥or die("Unable to execute SQL statement");
```

At this point, `$queryresults` is holding the data that came back from the query. You might think that the next step is to set up a loop to print out the data, but PHP spares you from having to do that in this case. Here, you can use the `odbc_result_all()` function to create an XHTML table that summarized the data that came back from the query. `odbc_result_all()` takes two arguments: the set of query results and a string that specifies any attributes that you want to put in the `<table>` tag:

```
odbc_result_all($queryresults,"border=\"1\"");
```

NOTE Some ODBC-related functions will let you loop over the records to create structures other than tables. These include `odbc_fetch_into()`, `odbc_num_fields()`, and `odbc_result()`. You use these functions in the same way that you saw the `OCIFetch()`, `OCINumCols()`, and `OCIResult()` functions used in the Oracle section. ■

After you have used the query results, you need to take care of the housekeeping steps that return resources back to the server. The functions that do this for an ODBC data source connection are `odbc_free_result()` and `odbc_close()`:

```
odbc_free_result($queryresults);
odbc_close($dbconnection);
```

The Future of PHP

PHP is currently at version 4 and shows no sign of slowing down. The community of PHP users is growing rapidly, and those community members are eagerly pushing the language to include new capabilities. Some of the things that PHP can do for you that were not covered in this chapter include these:

- Implement basic HTTP authentication to protect resources on your server
- Read from and write to files on your server
- Handle files uploaded through an XHTML form
- Monitor user behavior through session tracking

The PHP Manual, found at `http://www.php.net/manual/html/`, can give you the details on how to implement some of these more advanced functions. As you continue working with PHP, you will no doubt want to bookmark this site as both a reference and a way to keep abreast of the PHP's rapid evolution. ●

Java 2

Introduction to Java

by Mike Morgan

In this chapter

What Is Java?

When you write in most programming languages, you need to decide which processor and operating system your finished program is intended to run on. Then you include specific function calls to a library associated with the operating system of that target platform. If you're writing for a Windows environment, for example, you might refer to the Microsoft Foundation Classes. If your target machine is a Macintosh, you'll call functions in the Mac OS Toolbox. Figure 35.1 illustrates this process.

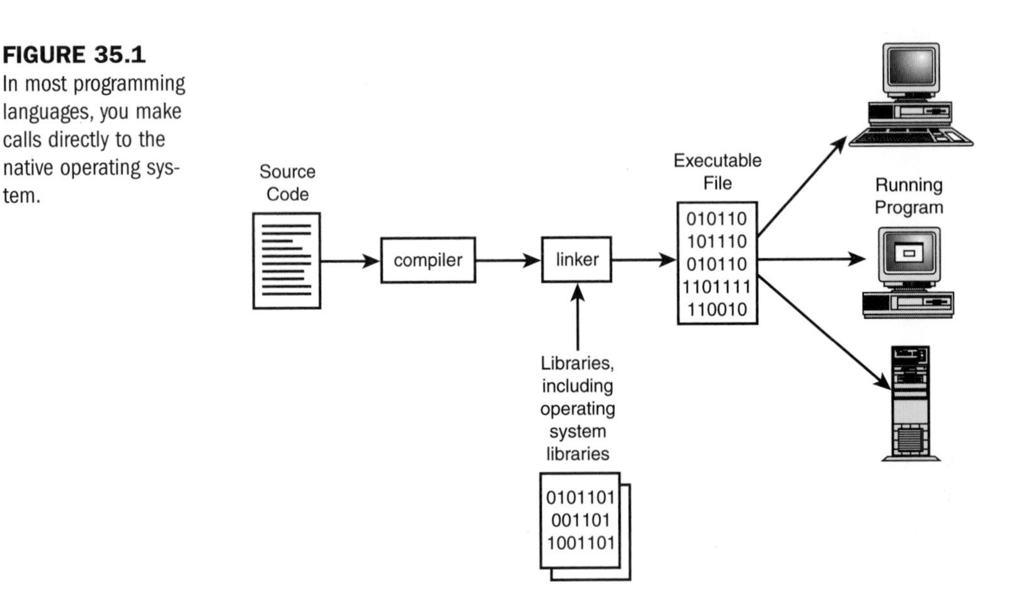

FIGURE 35.1
In most programming languages, you make calls directly to the native operating system.

When you're ready to test your program, you send your source code through a *compiler* that transforms it into a set of native instructions for whatever processor your target machine uses. Windows usually runs on an Intel processor such as a Pentium, for example, and Macs typically use PowerPC processors.

When you write Java, you don't need to think about calls to Windows, the Mac OS, or other operating system libraries. Java contains its own libraries—called *packages*—that are platform independent.

Similarly, you aren't concerned with whether the finished product will run on an Intel Pentium, an IBM PowerPC, or a Sun SPARC processor. The Java compiler doesn't generate native instructions. Instead, it writes *bytecodes* for a machine that doesn't physically exist—the *Java Virtual Machine*, or *JVM*.

NOTE The Java compiler generates files of bytecodes–instructions for the Java Virtual Machine (JVM). Because the JVM has been ported to nearly every kind of computer, these files of bytecodes serve as cross-platform applications. ■

Because the JVM doesn't really exist in the physical sense, it's natural to wonder how the Java code runs. Sun (and others) have implemented a software version of the JVM for most common platforms. When you load the file of bytecodes (called a *class file*) onto the target machine, it runs on the JVM on that machine. The JVM reads the class file and does the work specified by the original Java. Figure 35.2 illustrates how the Java compiler, the class file, and the JVM interact.

FIGURE 35.2

The output of the Java compiler is interpreted by the JVM on each specific platform.

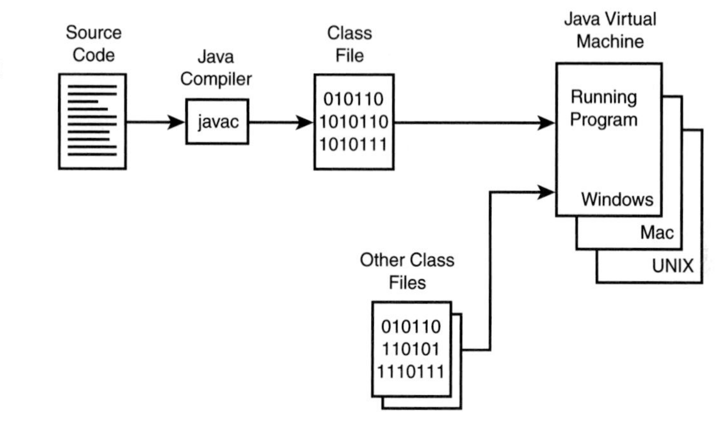

Because the JVM is easy to port from one machine to another, you can expect that any new processor or operating system will soon have an implementation of the JVM. After you've written Java code that runs on one machine, you can run it on any common platform.

NOTE The JVM is part of a larger collection of software on the end user's machine that's called the *Java Runtime Environment*, or *JRE*. Browser vendors such as Microsoft and Netscape include a JRE in their Web browsers. If you want end users to be able to run Java applications, you need to make sure they have a JRE. You get a JRE in your Software Development Kit; end users can download the JRE separately.

Understanding Applications

If all you could do with Java was write portable applications, it would still be an important development. In 1993, however, Sun noticed that the Internet was gaining in popularity, and it began to position Java to run inside *Web browsers*. Standalone Java programs are known as *applications*, and programs that run with the help of a Web browser are known as *applets*. We'll talk about applications in this section and get to applets later in this chapter.

In most languages, the "finished product" is an executable file of native binary instructions. In the DOS and Windows environments, these files have the suffix `.exe`, which is easily recognizable. In a graphical user environment, such as Mac OS or Windows, you can double-click the application's icon to run the program.

Java is a little different. Because the class files contain bytecodes for the JVM, you must launch an implementation of the JVM to run the application. The Java Software Development Kit (SDK) includes a Java interpreter called `java` that implements the JVM. To run an application named `myApp` on the JVM, you go to the command prompt and type

```
java myApp
```

TIP

The Mac OS doesn't have a command prompt. To run an application on the Mac, drag the icon of the class file onto the icon of the Java interpreter.

If you want to deliver an application to an end user, don't ask him to go to the command prompt. Write a batch file that launches the Java interpreter and starts the application. Have the end user double-click the batch file, the same way he would start any other application.

Who Needs Applets?

Modern Web browsers, such as Netscape Navigator and Microsoft Internet Explorer, are highly capable programs with a rich set of features. Why would anyone need to extend the browser through applets?

Many Web designers want to go beyond simple displays of static content. They want dynamic or "live" pages that are capable of interacting with the user. Often the best way to add dynamic content is to write a program, yet the Hypertext Markup Language (HTML) that is used to write Web pages has no programming capability at all.

Both the Netscape and Microsoft browsers support scripting languages such as JavaScript. Those languages enable you to attach functions to HTML elements such as buttons, but you don't have complete control over the appearance of the user interface. You also cannot use these scripting languages to reconnect the client machine to the network, so you cannot write true client/server programs. Sometimes you need a solution that is more powerful than these scripting languages, or you need a solution that doesn't depend on a particular browser. For those times, a Java applet is ideal.

You place a Java applet on your Web page by using the HTML `<APPLET>` tag. Because Java runs on any popular platform, applets appear and work as expected as long as the visitor to the site is using one of the Java-capable browsers.

What Makes Java Different from Other Languages?

Sun boasts that Java is a concurrent, object-oriented programming language with client/server capabilities. In this section, we'll take that claim apart and examine each of Java's major distinctive qualities.

Java Is a Programming Language The world of software today is similar in many ways to the way things were in the late 1970s. In those days, PCs had just come out, and the available software lagged far behind the demand. However, nearly every model of PC shipped with a BASIC interpreter. Thousands of people who did not consider themselves professional programmers—teachers, life insurance agents, bankers—learned BASIC and began to write programs. Often they would share their programs by floppy disk or, later, by electronic bulletin boards—and the shareware industry was born.

Like SmallTalk, C, and C++ (and unlike BASIC), Java is designed for use by professional programmers. Today the Hypertext Markup Language (HTML) and the scripting languages, such as Netscape's JavaScript, occupy the niche formerly held by BASIC. Many nonprogrammers cannot write Java applets, but they can use applets written by others to add life to their Web pages. Often they use Netscape LiveConnect, an integration technology based on JavaScript, to stitch Web pages, Java applets, and browser plug-ins together.

TIP After you've learned Java, you might also want to learn how nonprogrammers can use your applets in their Web pages. Read Part III, "JavaScript," to learn this powerful scripting language. Then read the section "Netscape's LiveConnect" in Chapter 23, "Using JavaScript to Control Web Browser Objects" to learn how to integrate JavaScript with Java applets.

However, this section is about Java. Unlike JavaScript, Java was designed for the experienced programmer. If you're a professional programmer, you should have little trouble learning Java. If you don't have prior experience with the object-oriented techniques, you'll want to brush up on the object-oriented concepts.

TIP For more information on the object-oriented methods, see *Java 2 for Professional Developers* (Sams, 1999). Chapter 6, "Object-Oriented Analysis," and Chapter 7, "Object-Oriented Design and Programming with Java," will get you up to speed on the latest techniques.

If you're not a programmer but you're prepared to work hard, you can use Java to learn how to program. You'll want to refer to some of the basic programming concepts described in *Using Java 1.2* (Que, 1998), Appendix A, "Introduction to Programming."

Java Is Object Oriented In general, software engineers engage in five activities during the development of software:

- **Analysis**—The process of identifying user requirements.
- **Design**—The process of developing a solution to the user's needs and requirements.
- **Implementation**—Coding the design in a computer language such as Java.
- **Test**—Ensuring that the finished software satisfies the requirements.
- **Maintenance**—Fixing latent defects, adding new features, and keeping the software up to date with its environment (such as operating systems and database managers).

During object-oriented analysis, you are encouraged to view the application domain as a set of related classes. In a transportation application, for example, there might be a class called `Truck`. When the application runs, it typically makes ***instances*** of these classes. You might build a fleet of trucks based on the class `Truck`.

During initial object-oriented design, you identify all the classes, typically arranging them in a hierarchy. Figure 35.3 illustrates where the `Truck` class might fall in a transportation hierarchy. You also identify methods and data that should be associated with each instance. Figure 35.4 illustrates one way of recording this information during the design activity.

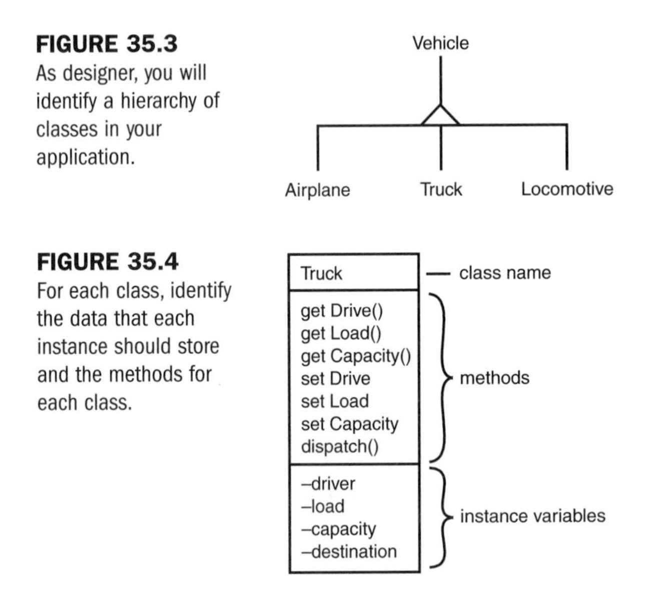

FIGURE 35.3
As designer, you will identify a hierarchy of classes in your application.

FIGURE 35.4
For each class, identify the data that each instance should store and the methods for each class.

After you've identified and described each class, you need to design the code for each method. Some designers prefer to write simple diagrams to show how each method should be written. Others prefer to write ***pseudocode***, a loose method of coding that is intended to be read by humans rather than by the compiler.

Object-oriented languages were introduced as early as 1967. During 1983, Bjarne Stroustrup of AT&T Bell Laboratories introduced a version of the popular C programming language that supported classes. This "C with classes" went on to become C++, the most popular object-oriented language ever—possibly the most popular computer programming language ever.

The people at Sun Microsystems who designed Java were C++ programmers. They understood the features of C++ that made it a good language. They also understood its limitations. In designing Java, they copied C++ syntax and reused the best pieces of C++'s design, including the fact that it makes it easy to code object-oriented designs.

Java Supports the Client/Server Model One of the design goals of C (and later, C++) was to keep platform-specific capabilities out of the core language. Thus, in C and C++, nothing exists in the language itself that enables you to output any information. Instead, you call a library routine—`printf()`—or write to standard out (called `cout` in C++).

Java has adopted this aspect of C++'s design and has extended the standard libraries to include network communications. In Java, for example, you can open a connection to a Web page or other Internet application and read or write data, in much the same way as a C or C++ programmer reads or writes to the local terminal. This design decision makes it easy to write Internet-aware applications in Java. In fact, HotJava, the Java-aware Web browser written by Sun, is written entirely in Java.

Java Supports Concurrency In the real world, different objects do their work simultaneously. In a computer—at least, in a computer with a single processor—only one set of instructions can be executing at once. To help programmers build applications that more accurately reflect the way the real world works, operating system developers introduced *multitasking*. In a multitasking operating system, two or more applications can share a single processor, with each having the illusion that it has the processor to itself.

Each such application (often called a *process*) has its own protected part of memory where it stores its data. In most operating systems, one process cannot accidentally interfere with another process. In fact, these operating systems include special function calls (called *Inter-Process Communication*, or *IPC*) that enable one process to send or receive data from another.

At the operating-system level, a significant amount of work is required to start a process or to switch from one process to another. Programmers asked for, and got, a "lightweight process" called a *thread*. In general, threads don't offer the bulletproof protection of processes, but they can be started and used more quickly.

The biggest problem with processes and threads is that these facilities are offered by the operating system. If you write a program to run in a Windows NT environment, you'll have to modify the parts that start and control processes and threads if you port the code to UNIX, for example. In some operating systems, such as older versions of Microsoft Windows, the facilities for multitasking are primitive.

Sun's solution was to make threads a part of the language itself. Thus, if you write a multi-threaded Java application, that application will run on any supported platform, including Windows, UNIX, and Mac OS. Furthermore, because Java's object-oriented model restricts the way one application can communicate with another, Java threads have some of the same safeguards as processes, with little of the overhead.

▶ To learn more about Java threads, **see** "Adding Animation," **p. 1139**

Suppose, for example, you wanted to explore what happens in a particular Web application when many users access the same page at the same time. In a multitasking operating system such as UNIX, you might write an application that makes several copies of itself. (In UNIX, such a process is called *forking*; in Windows NT, it's called *spawning*.) In Java, you can write an application that reads the number of simultaneous connections from the command line, opens the specified number of threads, reads the same Web page in each thread, and reports any errors—in just 22 lines of code.

Java Has a Strong Security Model

Java's designers have always been able to boast that their language was among the most secure. The latest release, in SDK 1.3, has several enhancements to Java's security model. See Chapter 40, "Security," to learn how Java provides security—particularly for network applications. The next section, "What's New in Java 2?," tells you more about those security enhancements.

What's New in Java 2?

To write Java you need a text editor, a Java compiler, and a Java runtime environment. The easiest way to get a Java compiler and runtime environment is to download Sun's Java Software Development Kit (SDK). The SDK also includes a variety of tools—it's a "must-have" item for any Java developer. (You'll have to supply your own text editor; Window's WordPad and NotePad are both acceptable.)

TIP After you've learned Java, you might want to look at some of the integrated development environments (IDEs) being offered by Borland, WebGain, and others. These environments typically enable you to write Java faster, although not all of them give you access to the latest Java features.

Sun continues to improve Java and periodically issues a new version of the SDK. The latest version, SDK 1.3, was released to the general public on May 8, 2000. SDK 1.3 introduces a large number of new APIs and includes some updated tools. This section reviews the new features in SDK 1.3 (Standard Edition).

NOTE In December 1998, Sun released the Java 2 Platform and renamed the Java Development Kit (JDK), calling it the Java 2 (Standard Edition) Software Development Kit (SDK). You'll still see some references on the Web to the JDK, but the official name of the latest version is the Java 2SE SDK version 1.3. In this book, this software is referred to simply as "the SDK." ■

Java Naming and Directory Interface

The Java Naming and Directory Interface (JNDI) has been around for a while as a standard extension. Starting with SDK 1.3, Sun is adding JNDI to the Java 2 platform.

JNDI is Sun's solution to the fact that naming and directory services vary from one operating system or service provider to another. For example, a file on a UNIX machine might be named `/usr/michmor/addresses`. The same file, stored on a Windows machine, might be named `C:\My Documents\AddressBook.txt`.

Other popular naming systems include the Domain Naming Service (DNS) and the Lightweight Directory Access Protocol (LDAP). DNS maps domain names such as `mcp.com` to IP addresses such as 204.95.224.200. LDAP provides organizational directory lookup services. For examples of LDAP servers, visit the Address Book in Netscape Communicator and look at properties of the various directories listed.

JNDI allows your Java programs to look up objects by name or to search a directory. For example, if your program's environment contained the necessary context information (such as a reference to a file system), your program might include the following lines:

```
Context theContext = new InitialContext(theEnvironment);

File theFile = (File) theContext.lookup("AddressBook.txt");
```

The first line builds the context; the second line looks up an object based on its name and casts the object as a Java `File` object.

Remote Method Invocation

As your programs grow in complexity, you'll want to build complex systems with executing modules on several different computers. If all the modules are written in Java, you can use Java's Remote Method Invocation (RMI) feature to allow objects on one machine to run code on a different machine.

Of course, often you'll want your Java program to invoke features in a remote non-Java program. Java fully supports the Internet IntraORB Protocol (IIOP), which allows heterogeneous communications of this sort.

In SDK 1.3, Sun has made several enhancements to the RMI mechanism and its supporting tools. It has also added IIOP to the list of communications protocols available to RMI programmers. By using the new RMI-IIOP capability, you can use the straightforward methods in RMI to communicate with non-Java objects.

Applet Deployment Enhancements

One shortcoming of applets is that the entire set of class files must be downloaded from the server before the applet can run. As applets become larger and more sophisticated, the download time increases. To deal with this problem, SDK 1.3 includes a powerful caching mechanism. This caching mechanism works with the Java plug-in, a Sun-supplied JVM that can be installed into the Netscape or Microsoft browsers.

To run your applet in the plug-in, use the `<OBJECT>` tag rather than the `<APPLET>` tag. In the `<OBJECT>` syntax, include lines like

```
<PARAM NAME="cache_option" VALUE="...">
```

and

```
<PARAM NAME="cache_archive" VALUE="...">
```

Use the `cache_option` parameter to specify whether the applet should be cached in the browser cache, the plug-in cache, or not at all (requiring the applet to always be reloaded from the server). Use the `cache_archive` parameter to list the files that are to be cached.

NOTE SDK 1.3 also supports JAR indexing. You can divide your functionality across several different Java Archives (JARs). Only the JARs you actually need are downloaded to the client. See `http://java.sun.com/j2se/1.3/docs/guide/jar/jar.html#JAR Index` for details.

Security Enhancements

Recall from earlier in this chapter, in the section titled "Java Has a Strong Security Model," that tight security is one of Java's distinctions. It's not surprising that SDK 1.3 includes some major improvements in security. These changes include improved support for X.509v3 certificates. You can use the latest industry-standard encryption technology to sign the Java Archives in which you distribute your classes. The new SDK includes new features, such as the new `java.security.interfaces.RSAKey` class, to make working with certificates and public keys safer and easier. This section describes these certificates and explains their benefits.

Certificate Interfaces and X.509v3 Implementation Not so long ago, the only way for a server to identify a client was to ask the user for a username and password. If the username and password matched those stored in the password file, the server granted the user access.

Several problems exist with password-based authentication. First, the password often has to travel over a non-secure network. If an adversary is able to "sniff" the username and password from the Net, he can masquerade as a valid user.

Another problem is that most users access more than one system and have more than one username and password. Users find it difficult to keep these names and passwords straight, so they either write the names and passwords down or use the same name and password on every system. Either solution is subject to abuse.

A better solution is for the user to generate a special kind of cryptographic key, called a public/private key pair. These keys work together—if you encrypt something with my public key, only a person with my private key can decrypt it. If I keep my private key secret, you can be sure that I'm the only one who can read your message.

In an ideal world, we could all post our public keys on servers somewhere and begin to communicate securely with each other. That practice is subject to abuse, too—an opponent could put a public key on the server with my name on it. If my opponent can trick you into using the bogus key, she will be able to read messages intended for me. (This strategy is a variation of the "man in the middle" attack described later in Chapter 40, in the section titled "How Java Provides Security Over the Internet.")

The solution is simple—I generate my public/private key pair, making sure I keep my private key secret. I send my public key to a "public key certifying authority," which requires that I prove my identity. After I've satisfied the certifying authority that I am who I say I am, it signs my key with *its* private key. Now anyone who wants to be sure that a public key with my name on it really belongs to me can check the signature of the certifying authority. If you find that the signature is valid, and you're satisfied with the authority's policy for checking my identity, then you can trust my public key.

The combination of a public key, identifying information, and a certification authority's signature is called a *certificate*. The current generation of the standard for certificates is *X.509v3*.

Version 1.3 of the SDK includes new APIs for parsing certificates and maintaining local databases of X.509v3 certificates.

Issuing and Managing Certificates Version 1.3 of the SDK also includes tools to help you manage X.509v3 certificates. Within your company, for example, you might decide to issue certificates to your employees. The Java `keytool`, which was introduced in SDK 1.2, enables each user to generate a public/private `keypair`. The user can also use `keytool` to generate his or her own certificate (although the certificate is to a slightly older standard—X.509v1).

TIP If you plan to issue your own certificates, you'll need a certificate server. Visit the Netscape site (`http://home.netscape.com/comprod/server_central/product/certificate/index.html`) and learn about Netscape's Certificate Server, part of the SuiteSpot family of servers.

You use `jarsigner` in combination with your certificate to digitally sign Java Archives (JARs).

TIP If you've been using `javakey` from JDK 1.1 or earlier, replace it with `keytool` and `jarsigner`. The older tool, `javakey`, is now obsolete.

You can write an external security configuration file that specifies your machine's security policy. The easiest way to write such a file is to use Sun's *policytool*, also a part of the SDK.

Network Enhancements

Sun has always maintained that "the network is the computer." If Java is the computer language, then Java needs advanced network capabilities. Basic TCP/IP sockets have been available in Java since its earliest days. With SDK 1.3, Sun is adding powerful low-level features that make it easier to write sophisticated client/server systems:

- Java now supports TCP half-close sockets with the new methods `shutdownInput()` and `shutdownOutput()` in classes `java.net.Socket` and `java.net.SocketImpl`.
- You can add keepalive behavior to sockets by using the new `setKeepAlive(Boolean on)` method in `java.net.Socket`. There's an analogous `get` method, `getKeepAlive()`.
- Class `java.net.URL` and its related classes now include improved methods to parse out the components of a URL.
- SDK 1.3 provides client-side support for HTTP 1.1.

Reflection Enhancements

Reflection is the capability to examine an object at runtime to discover its fields, methods, and attributes. Code that uses reflection can become unmanageably complex if you have to support many different types of objects.

In SDK 1.3, Sun added the capability to build dynamic proxy classes at runtime. These proxy classes serve as a bridge between your program and the objects you're examining. They can provide a consistent set of capabilities, simplifying your code.

For example, suppose you build an `Employee` class, generate a few thousand employees, and save them in an object-oriented database. Sometime later your organization decides to record the information about each employee's car, and you modify the `Employee` class, adding methods `getCar()` and `setCar()`. When you read an employee's record in from the database, you choose to use reflection to discover whether this employee is a "new" employee, with car information, or an "old" employee, with no such information on file.

Over time, you might add many new capabilities to the `Employee` class, without necessarily updating the information on each employee in the database. Rather than have a complex piece of code that examines each record to see what capabilities it has, you might opt to have your user interface interact with a proxy object that matches the newest `Employee` specification. Then, if a particular method is not supported, the proxy could return default information such as "Not on file."

Object Serialization Enhancements

From time to time, you'll want to write an instance of an object to a serial stream such as a network socket or a disk file. In SDK 1.3, this capability (called object serialization) is up to 20% faster. Sun has also overcome certain limits—for example, strings longer than 64KB can now be serialized.

JAR Enhancements

The JAR format is becoming increasingly important, especially with the new Extensions Framework. Sun has introduced policies and mechanisms, for example, for handling dependencies on extensions and other classes distributed as JAR files.

With SDK 1.2, Sun has enhanced the command-line tool used to manage JARs. It also has enhanced the API that enables Java programs to read and write JAR files.

Java Foundation Classes

Like C and C++, most of the features of Java are not in the language itself, but in the libraries (which are called *packages* in Java). The first releases of Java came with some simple libraries (such as the Abstract Windowing Toolkit) that served to whet developers' appetites. SDK 1.3 comes bundled with a set of packages—the Java Foundation Classes, or JFC—that include an improved user interface.

Swing Package The first versions of the SDK supported a graphical user interface through a package called the *Abstract Windowing Toolkit* (AWT). In newer versions, Sun has introduced the *Swing* package, which includes and expands upon the AWT. Swing contains many more components than those in the AWT, so you can build more sophisticated interfaces. More importantly, Swing implements the Lightweight User Interface Framework, which includes "pluggable look and feel." This feature means that an end user who prefers the look of Sun's Motif interface can have that look, even though you, the developer, might prefer the basic Java interface. (Swing is introduced in Chapter 37, "User Input and Interactivity with Java.")

The Abstract Windowing Toolkit Although much of Sun's attention has been focused on the newer Swing components, it certainly isn't ignoring the parent AWT classes. Here's a partial list of AWT enhancements appearing in SDK 1.3:

- Multiple monitor support
- Improved test capability through the new `java.awt.Robot` class
- Improved performance when calling the `paint()` method (by coalescing overlapping regions to be repainted)
- Improved control over print job and page attributes
- An AWT native interface, making it easier to integrate native rendering engines into Java programs

Java 2D In SDK 1.2, Sun extended the AWT package to include a set of tools for dealing with two-dimensional drawings and images. These extensions included provision for color-spaces (`java.awt.color`), text (`java.awt.font`), line art (`java.awt.geom`), and printing (`java.awt.print`). Now, in SDK 1.3, Sun has added several new capabilities, including

- Multiple monitor support
- Portable Network Graphics (PNG) format support
- Dynamic font loading
- Improved paragraph balancing and hyphenation

Accessibility Many users who are visually impaired use screen readers to read HTML pages to them. Other people who have limited vision need to display text in large fonts to read the information comfortably. In the past, Sun has been criticized because Java applets displayed only a graphical image, inaccessible to visually impaired users. Starting in SDK 1.2, Sun addressed these concerns by adding specific provisions for accessibility. These provisions, in the package `java.awt.accessibility`, ensure that your programs will work well with screen readers, screen magnifiers, and speech recognition systems—a group of hardware and software products collectively known as *assistive technology*.

In SDK 1.3, Sun has gone further to ensure accessibility of Java programs. For example, Swing icons in SDK 1.3 implement a new interface—AccessibleIcon—that allows assistive technology to get information about the icon.

Drag and Drop Sun has committed itself to supporting drag-and-drop data transfer between Java and native applications, as well as between Java applications and within a single Java application. The Java drag-and-drop interface was in its infancy when SDK 1.2 was released. With SDK 1.3, Sun has improved the handling of native text. If you're careful to manage non-Java data types, you can use drag and drop to transfer data into and out of your Java Virtual Machine.

Collections Enhancements

Sun is gradually improving the set of collection classes shipped with the SDK. Version 1.3 included seven concrete classes, as well as a variety of algorithms and abstract classes. SDK 1.3 adds three convenience implementations: `singletonList`, `singletonMap`, and `EMPTY_MAP`. The two `singleton` implementations (along with `singletonSet`, which was introduced in SDK 1.2) are useful when you know that a method will return only a single object. `EMPTY_MAP` is a useful constant corresponding to an empty map.

When discussing collection classes it's useful to know a bit about data structures. Table 35.1 summarizes the key characteristics of three important kinds of collection. These collections can be implemented in any of several data structures. A *hash table* is a highly efficient structure that can look up most items in one step. Large hash tables can require a significant amount of memory.

Table 35.1 Fundamental Collections

Name	Ordered?	Duplicate Values Allowed?
`Set`	no	no
`List`	yes	yes
`Map`	no	yes

An *array* is an efficient structure, although adding or deleting entries can be difficult if you're also trying to preserve order.

A *tree* structure maintains order naturally. One of the most common kinds of tree—a balanced binary tree—is particularly efficient when you need fast lookup.

The seven concrete classes are

- **`HashSet`**—A set implemented in a hash table.
- **`ArrayList`**—A list implemented in a resizable array.
- **`LinkedList`**—A useful starting point if you want to build a deque or queue class.
- **`Vector`**—A variant of the `ArrayList`.
- **`HashMap`**—A map implemented in a hash table.
- **`TreeMap`**—A map implemented by a balanced binary tree.
- **`Hashtable`**—A variant of `HashMap`.

Audio Enhancements

The earliest releases of Java did not include much provision for sound—a serious shortcoming for a language so well suited for multimedia. Sun quickly closed this gap. The latest version of the SDK offers the best sound support yet.

SDK 1.3 contains a reference implementation of a new, higher-quality sound engine that supports the capture, processing, and playback of MIDI files as well as traditional sounds (such as `.au`, `.wav`, and `.aiff` formats). Prior to SDK 1.3, applets didn't require any special permission to access the system's audio resources. That policy has changed in SDK 1.3—the Java Sound APIs check `javax.sound.sampled.AudioPermission`. Your applet will need to secure the appropriate `AudioPermission` before it can use Java Sound.

Performance Enhancements

When the subject of Java comes up, someone always points out that native code runs about 20 times faster than Java. Although that figure might have been true at one time, Sun has been working hard to close the gap. The greatest successes came from the use of Just-in-Time (JIT) compilers, but Sun has also introduced an improved JVM with runtime optimization. This JVM is called HotSpot. The client version of this technology is included in SDK 1.3. The server version is included in the Solaris and Linux versions of the SDK 1.3.

TIP HotSpot doesn't ship with the Windows SDK, but it's available as a separate download for Windows at `http://java.sun.com/products/hotspot/2.0/download.html`.

NOTE If your application needs true native speed but you still want to work in Java, consider one of the new compilers that generate native code. Just remember that you'll lose many of the benefits of the JRE when you compile your Java as a native application.

Improvements in *java.lang, java.util., and *java.math*** `java.lang` now has both a `Math` and a `StrictMath` class. `Math` is generally faster but might yield slightly different results across JVM implementations. `StrictMath` is guaranteed to be consistent across implementations, at a small performance cost.

A new Timer API (`java.util.Timer` and `java.util.TimerTask`) has been added to improve animation and the human interface.

`java.math.BigInteger` has been re-implemented in pure Java. The previous implementation used some native code to get a performance boost—the new Java implementation is as much as five times faster than the old native implementation.

HotSpot Technology HotSpot 2.0 is a next-generation JVM with the capability to optimize the stream of bytecodes at runtime. Separate versions are available for servers and clients. Whether you use the server or client version, this JVM is the fastest JVM delivered by Sun. It boasts a smaller RAM footprint, faster startup time, and virtually pauseless garbage collection. ●

CHAPTER 36

Developing Java Applets

by Mike Morgan

In this chapter

Basic Language Constructs

This section introduces Java language basics that will aid you in the creation of applets. Tables 36.1 through 36.4 summarize Java's basic language constructs. Table 36.1 shows the data types available for variables and constants. Table 36.2 shows the operators available for manipulating those variables and constants. Table 36.3 shows the major statements of the language, used for controlling the flow of execution through the program. The last table, Table 36.4, shows three ways to add comments to your program.

Table 36.1 Basic Language Constructs (Java Types)

Type	Example	Notes
`boolean`	`boolean flag = false;`	A Java `boolean` is just `true` or `false`. It cannot be cast to `char` or `int`.
`char`	`char c[] = {'A','\uu42','C'};`	A Java `char` is a 16-bit Unicode character. Use the Java `String` class to manage Unicode strings.
`byte`	`byte b = 0x7f;`	8-bit signed integer (–127 .. 127).
`short`	`short s = 32767;`	16-bit signed integer (–32,768 .. 32,767).
`int`	`int i = 2;`	32-bit signed integer.
`long`	`long l = 2L;`	64-bit signed integer. Use the suffix `L` for a `long` (decimal) literal.
`float`	`float x = 2.0F;`	32-bit IEEE754 number. Use the suffix `F` for a `float` literal.
`double`	`double d = 2.0;`	64-bit IEEE754 number (15 significant digits).

NOTE Some languages, such as JavaScript and Visual Basic, are weakly typed—they enable the programmer to make new variables on-the-fly and to freely interchange numbers, text, or other values.

Java is a *strongly typed* language. The programmer must explicitly declare the "type" of each variable. You can't arbitrarily mix or inter-convert types.

To deal with strong typing, focus on classes rather than primitive datatypes. By thinking at this higher level—the class level—you will need fewer primitive types and they will be less likely to interact with each other in troublesome ways. In addition, you will end up with simpler, more robust programs.

The operators in Table 36.2 are arranged in order of precedence. The compiler will treat the expression `2 + 2 * 2 ^ 2` as `2 + (2 * (2 ^ 2))`, for example, executing `2 XOR 2` first, `2 *` the result next, and so on.

Table 36.2 Basic Language Constructs (Java Operators)

Operator	Description
.	Member selection
[]	Array subscript
()	Parentheses/function call
++, --	Auto-increment/auto-decrement
*, /, %	Arithmetic: multiply, divide, modulo
+, -,	Arithmetic: add, subtract
<<, >>, >>>	Bitwise: shift left, arithmetic shift right, and logical shift right
<=, <, >, >=	Equality: less than or equal to, less than, greater than, greater than or equal to
==, !=	Equality: equal to, not equal to
&, |, ^, ~	Bitwise: AND, OR, Exclusive Or (XOR), and NOT
&&, ||, !	Logical: AND, OR, and NOT
? :	Conditional expression
=	Simple assignment
*=, /=, %=, +=, -=, &=, |=, ^=, <<=, >>=, >>>=	Assignment with operation

TIP In your own Java programs, use parentheses liberally. Compare how much easier it is to read `2 + (2 * (2 ^ 2))` than `2 + 2 * 2 ^ 2`. Not only is the first version clearer, but using parentheses rather than relying on the default precedence hierarchy will also help you avoid a common source of defects.

Table 36.3 Basic Language Constructs (Control Flow)

Construct	Example
`if...then...else`	`if (i >= theSalesGoal) { ... }`
`for`	`for (i = 0; i < MAXITEMS; i++) {...}`
`while`	`while (i < theSalesGoal) { ... }`
`do...while`	`do { ... } while (i < theSalesGoal);`
`switch (...) case`	`switch (i) { case FIRST: ... break; ...}`
`break`	`while (i < theSalesGoal) { if (i==10) break;...}`
`continue`	`while (i < theSalesGoal) { if (i==10) continue; ... }`
`labeled break`	`while (i < theSalesGoal) { if (i==10) break my_label;...}`

Table 36.4 Basic Language Constructs (Java Comments)

Comment style	Format	Notes
C comments	`/* ... */`	Can span multiple lines
C++ comments	`// ...`	Comment stops at the end of the line: less prone to error
javadoc comments	`/** ... */`	Appropriate for header comments: automatically generates program documentation

NOTE Sun's official Java documentation, including reference manuals and language tutorials, can be found at `http://java.sun.com/docs/index.html`.

NOTE Even the best programmers often allow their documentation to drift out of date. Use `javadoc`, a tool supplied in your SDK, to automatically build documentation from your source files. Javadoc will copy information in `Javadoc` comments (`/** . . . */`) into the documentation.

Leveraging Java Classes and Packages

Although operators and data types are obviously very important in Java, *classes* are where the real action is.

A class is a group of objects with similar properties (attributes), common behavior (operations), common relationships to other objects, and common semantics. An object, on the other hand, is an *instance* of a class, dynamically created by the program during runtime. In other words, classes *define* objects; *objects*, on the other hand, are specific, concrete instances of a class.

NOTE In most languages, you can place related routines or classes into a library. Java is no exception—here libraries are called *packages*. You'll learn more about packages when you build an applet later in this chapter.

This discussion is continued later in this chapter. For now, however, it is time to get on with the fun stuff: coding and running a Java applet!

Installing the SDK

Many excellent, graphical tools for developing Java applets are on the market. These tools are called Integrated Development Environments, or IDEs. For professional development, you'll probably want one of these tools. Regardless of which IDE you or your company choose, you should still be familiar with Sun's command-line SDK tools. Several reasons for this are

- Periodically uploading and installing Sun's current SDK is the best way to keep up to speed with all the latest Java APIs.
- The SDK is an excellent "reference platform" to make sure your code is portable to as wide an audience as possible.
- The SDK is easy to install; it doesn't take an excessive amount of disk space; it contains some excellent tools; and it is absolutely free.

NOTE You can download a free copy of the latest Java SDK at `http://java.sun.com/`.

Minimum Requirements

Sun has targeted Java to run on any machine. It has focused its SDK development efforts on a smaller group. This section describes the minimum hardware and operating system requirements needed for the SDK.

Your Computer Although Java runs on nearly every computer, the Java 2 SDK (Standard Edition) itself runs on fewer machines. The following is the list of hardware and operating system combinations supported by Sun:

- Microsoft Windows 95, 98, NT 4.0, or 2000, on Intel
- Sun Solaris 8, 7, and 2.6 on SPARC or x86
- Linux kernel v 2.2.5 and glibc v2.1 on Intel

Sun recommends that you run the SDK on a Pentium 166MHz or better, with 32MB to 48MB. The higher memory is particularly important if you're using the Java plug-in. If the plug-in is starved for memory, it will use virtual memory on the hard drive, which has a tremendously negative impact on performance.

If you need to run the SDK but don't have Windows, Solaris, or Linux, don't despair. Many hardware vendors have ported the entire SDK to their machines. See the comments on "Other SDKs," later in this section.

Disk Space A typical copy of the SDK installer requires about 30MB. The installer will expand into a set of files about twice its size. Thus, you should budget around 65MB to get started. (You can delete the installer itself after you're done if you need to free up the space.)

You'll also want to allow another 120MB for the documentation. If you're tight on space, you can use the online version, but it's slower than a local copy.

NOTE Windows users need to be running Windows 95, Windows NT, or higher to develop Java applets because Java requires a 32-bit operating system and long, case-sensitive filenames.

Other SDKs

If you're not using a common operating system such as Sun's Solaris or Microsoft's Windows NT, don't worry. Even though a Sun SDK might not be available for your computer, you still might be able to develop Java programs. Check with your computer vendor to see if it has ported the SDK to your operating system.

IBM, for example, has released versions of the SDK for AIX (IBM's version of UNIX), OS/400 (which runs on the popular AS/400), and OS/390 (a mainframe operating system).

NOTE Find out which operating systems support Java by running the Sun Web application at `http://java.sun.com/cgi-bin/java-ports.cgi`. Note that not all operating systems that support Java support an SDK. Note, too, that these versions usually will be at least one generation behind the latest Sun SDK. ■

Downloading to Windows, Step by Step

This section describes the process of downloading Sun's SDK to your desktop computer. This example assumes you use a Windows system—other operating systems work similarly.

Connecting to JavaSoft The easiest way to find the current SDK is to start at `http://java.sun.com/`. Choose the Products and APIs link on the left side of the page, and then follow the link to Java 2 Platform, Standard Edition (which takes you to `http://java.sun.com/j2se/`).

TIP If you want to be sure to have access to the latest versions of the SDK, consider downloading public betas. Learn more about beta software at `http://developer.java.sun.com/` by registering as a member of the Java Developer Connection (JDC). Membership is free.

Downloading the SDK After you're on the download page, note the version number; make sure you're getting the version you expect. Figure 36.1 shows the download section of the J2SE release.

Follow the link to the J2SE SDK, and look for the Download Now! link. In this example, that link points to `http://java.sun.com/j2se/1.3/download-windows.html`.

TIP From the download page, you'll find links to various text files, including a README file, a list of changes, and a list of features supported in this version of the SDK. Use the README file to get an overview of the download and installation process.

You might want to print out the README file because some of the recommendations about setting environment variables can get tricky. If you don't get them right, you'll get errors when you try to use the SDK tools.

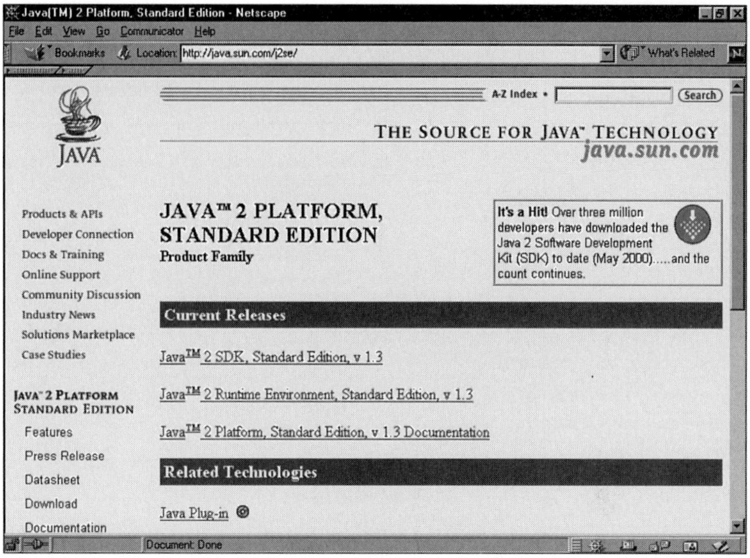

FIGURE 36.1
Start your download by selecting the version of the SDK.

Below the download section for the SDK, you'll see options for the documentation and other software. You can download either the documentation or the SDK first—this example starts with the SDK itself. When you're done, come back to this page and follow the same procedures to download the documentation.

Before leaving this page, scroll down to the end. Sun has put many useful links on this page, including links to Java tutorials, documentation, and the Developer Connection. Consider bookmarking this page, so you'll always have the latest information on Java.

Choose whether you want to download the software as one large bundle or as multiple disk-sized pieces, and then click the Continue button. The license agreement for the SDK appears. Read the license agreement; if you want the SDK, you must accept the agreement.

NOTE Note that the license agreement prohibits you from distributing the SDK. If you develop a Java applet, you might not need to send the end user anything. Most browsers contain a Java Runtime Environment (JRE). Alternatively, you can ask the end user to install Sun's Java plug-in for Netscape Navigator or Microsoft Internet Explorer. That way you can be sure the user has the latest JVM.

If you want to distribute a standalone application, you can download the Java Runtime Environment (JRE) from Sun and bundle it with your application, or you can instruct the user how to get the JRE directly. ■

After you navigate the license agreement, you finally arrive at the download page itself. Figure 36.2 shows this page. Note that you can download the SDK either from Sun's FTP server or via HTTP. If your network connection permits you to use FTP, do so; it's faster and more reliable. If you must, use HTTP.

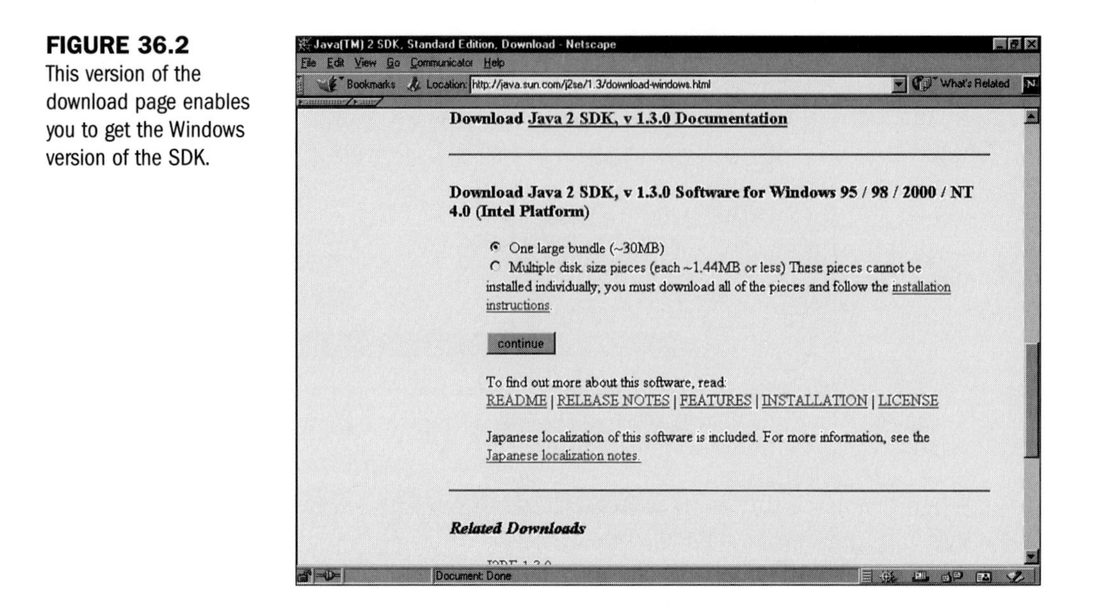

FIGURE 36.2
This version of the download page enables you to get the Windows version of the SDK.

You can download the installation kit into any convenient directory; the installer will place the components into the proper directories.

Be sure to note the name of the file you're downloading—it's given at the top of the download page. Some network connections change the name of the downloaded file to match the name of the page from which it is downloaded. If your software makes this mistake, switch the name back to the one given by Sun before continuing the installation process.

Installing the SDK The SDK installer for Windows is an executable archive. Double-click this file to start the installation process. Follow the instructions to make the SDK directory.

NOTE You should unpack both the documentation and the SDK into the same directory. The documentation installer will make a docs folder in the SDK directory. Sun's links are designed to look for the documentation in that folder. ■

When you finish installation, feel free to delete the installer programs for both the SDK and the documentation. You won't need them again unless you have to reinstall the software.

NOTE As you explore your SDK and third-party products, you might run across zip files such as `lib/classes.zip`. Don't unzip these files–they are designed to be read directly by the Java runtime environment. In the Java 2SDKs, these zip files are being replaced by Java Archives, or JAR files, which serve the same purpose but aren't likely to be confused with zip archives. ■

Setting Environment Variables Java uses the CLASSPATH environment variable to tell it where to look for Java classes. As a developer, you'll want to add new class libraries to the CLASSPATH variable.

If you've installed the SDK in the default location for your platform, the SDK tools will find the lib directory without searching `CLASSPATH`. You'll still need to set `CLASSPATH` if you install third-party programs.

To see if `CLASSPATH` is set on a Windows machine, type `set` at the command prompt. If you find that `CLASSPATH` is set, you can clear it by typing `set CLASSPATH=`. Of course, if you set `CLASSPATH` in a startup file such as `Autoexec.bat`, you'll want to remove that entry to permanently unset `CLASSPATH`.

On a Windows 95 or 98 machine, you can edit the `CLASSPATH` entry in the `Autoexec.bat` file. A typical entry might read

```
SET CLASSPATH=.;C:\jdk1.3\lib;
```

On a Windows NT or 2000 machine, use the System Control panel and this step-by-step procedure:

1. From the Start menu, choose Settings, Control Panel, as shown in Figure 36.3.

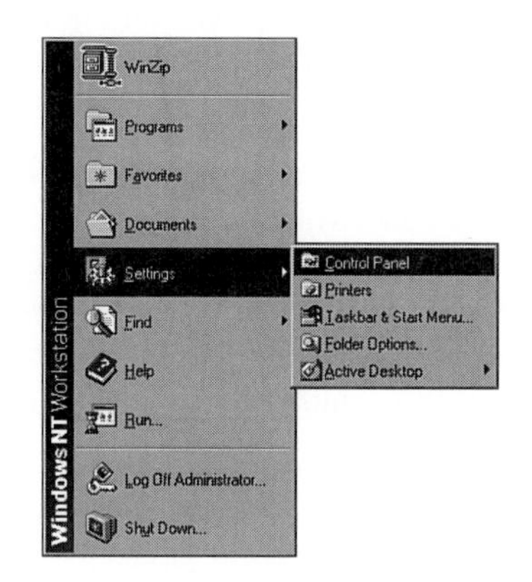

FIGURE 36.3
On a Windows NT machine, set up your environment variables through the System control panel.

2. In the resulting folder, locate the System Control Panel and double-click it.
3. In the System Properties dialog box, choose the Environment tab, shown in Figure 36.4.
4. Select the `CLASSPATH` variable in the upper window (marked System Variables). When you click the variable name, the variable and its current value appear in the edit fields at the bottom of the dialog box.
5. Add the path of your library directories to the value of `CLASSPATH`.

When you're working in your development directory (described in the next section), you'll find it useful to be able to refer to the tools by name rather than having to specify the full path. Thus, you will prefer to type `javac myClass.java` rather than `C:/JDK1.3/bin/javac myClass.java`.

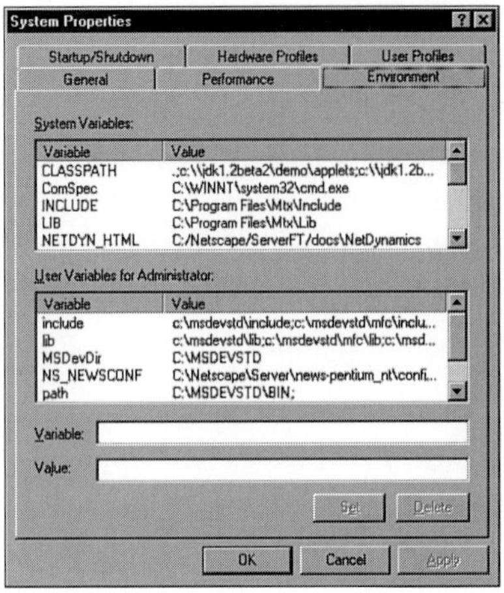

FIGURE 36.4
In the System Properties dialog box, select the Environment tab to change the CLASSPATH variable.

The solution is to set the PATH variable. Include the bin directory of your SDK in the PATH so that the operating system can find the SDK tools. You can set the PATH variable in the same way you set the CLASSPATH variable.

Setting Up a Development Directory You can place a development directory anywhere you like on your hard drive. (Remember to set the PATH variable so you don't have to type the full path to every SDK tool.) You might store code for the Model 1000 project in C:\Projects\Model1000\ on a Windows machine, for example, or /home/myname/projects/model1000/ under UNIX. If you're using a development environment, such as WebGain VisualCafé or Borland JBuilder, follow the instructions that came with your tools to set up a development directory.

As you gain experience in Java, you'll undoubtedly develop several libraries of classes (called packages). You can add these libraries to your CLASSPATH variable, or wrap your calls to Java tools in a batch file or shell script that sets its own version of CLASSPATH. To compile all the Java programs in the current directory on a Windows machine, for example, you can type

```
javac -classpath .;C:\usr\local\classes\;
➥C:\projects\model1000\java\lib\classes.zip *.java
```

To avoid retyping this long line each time you need to compile, put this line into a batch file. If you name the file compile.bat, for example, you now only need to type compile to invoke the javac compiler on all Java files. (If you're using UNIX, you can get the same effect by using a shell script.)

Testing Your Installation To test your SDK installation, go to a command prompt. (On a UNIX system, go to a shell prompt.) Change to your development directory and type javac—the name of the Java compiler.

You should get a usage message back telling you about the dozen or so options available. If you get a message complaining that the command or program doesn't exist, check your `PATH` variable and make sure it includes the `bin` subdirectory of your SDK directory. Thus, if you placed the SDK in a directory called `JDK1.3`, make sure your `PATH` variable includes `JDK1.3/bin` (or `JDK1.3\bin` in Windows).

If you have an older version of Java on your machine and have changed your environment variables to point to SDK 1.3, type `java -version` to make sure you've correctly set the `PATH`. If you don't see a message showing version 1.3, double-check your environment variables. Remember that you might have to close and reopen the command prompt window (in Windows NT and 2000) or reboot (in Windows 95 or 98) for the new environment variables to be set. In UNIX, you'll need to rerun your shell script.

Building an Applet

To build an applet, you need to have the SDK installed. After that's done, you'll follow a four-step process.

To build a Java application:

1. Enter the code into a text file.
2. Compile all classes by using `javac`.
3. Write an HTML file that loads the applet.
4. Load the HTML file by using your Web browser.

This section covers the first two steps. The next section, "Running the Applet," describes the last two steps.

Writing the Code

Use any text editor to make a program source file, as shown in Listing 36.1. Complete source code for each of these programs is included on the Web site.

Listing 36.1 *HelloApplet.java*—Start by Importing Sun's Classes

```
import java.applet.Applet;
import java.awt.Graphics;

public class HelloApplet extends Applet
{
  public void paint(Graphics theGraphics)
  {
    theGraphics.drawString("Hello, World!", 0, 50);
  }
}
```

Java is an object-oriented language, and the engineers at Sun have written a complete applet that you can use as a starting point. As you'll see in a moment, all you have to do is build a class that inherits from `java.applet.Applet`, and then override any methods in `Applet` that don't meet your requirements. This code is covered in detail later in this section—for now, just type in the code or copy it from the Web site.

NOTE You must use a text editor that supports long, case-sensitive filenames.

The versions of Notepad, WordPad, and Edit that come with Windows 95 or higher work fine. Microsoft Word 95 or higher also works. Older versions of Word for 16-bit Windows do not work.

Be sure, too, to save your file as plain text. If you save the file as a word processing document, the compiler won't be able to process it.

Your Java source file must have the same name as the public class. That is, you must name this file `HelloApplet.java`, which corresponds to the public class `HelloApplet`.

Furthermore, the capitalization also must match exactly. If your class is named `HelloApplet` (capital `H`, capital `A`) but your source file is named `helloapplet.java`, the program will not compile.

Compiling the Applet

Open a command prompt window. Make sure you're in your development directory and then type `javac HelloApplet.java`. Remember that the filename must match the name of the class exactly—including capitalization. Even on a Windows system, which typically is case-insensitive, you must type the filename the way the compiler expects to see it. Four outcomes are possible whenever you run `javac`:

- *The command interpreter cannot find* `javac`*.* Check your `PATH` variable to make sure the `bin` subdirectory of your `JDK` folder is in the path.
- *The compiler returns without comment.* Your code has compiled successfully.
- *Your compiler emits one or more warnings.* You should examine the warning to see if you've made a coding error.
- *Your compiler emits one or more errors.* You have made a coding error.

You must eliminate the causes for all compiler errors before you can run the applet. You should strive to eliminate all warnings as well. Although your program might run, warnings are an indication that you might have made a mistake. You should almost always be able to rewrite the code to eliminate the warnings.

Occasionally, you might get a warning that tells you that you are using a deprecated method. Rerun the compiler with the `-deprecated` switch to find out the exact problem. *Deprecated methods* are those that are still supported but are no longer recommended—they might be removed completely in some future release. When writing new code, you should eliminate all deprecated calls.

After your code has compiled successfully, it's time to load the applet into a Web page.

▶ For more about the `Graphics` class, **see** "Displaying Graphics," **p. 1108**

Running the Applet

If you were writing an application, you could invoke the Java interpreter from the command line to run the class. An applet, however, requires a browser environment, so you'll have to write some HTML to display the applet.

Writing the HTML

Listing 36.2 shows a simple Web page that includes the `HelloApplet` applet. This Web page will work with the appletviewer—you'll want to improve the HTML by adding a head, title, background color, and perhaps some text before you use it on your Web site.

Listing 36.2 *helloApplet.html*—You Must Write an HTML File to Test an Applet

```
<HTML>
<BODY>
<APPLET CODE="HelloApplet.class" WIDTH="200" HEIGHT="200">
</APPLET>
</BODY>
</HTML>
```

TIP Your HTML source file is not subject to the same strict rules about long filenames and case sensitivity as your Java source files. The file here is called `helloApplet.html`. You can pretty much name yours anything you want, provided it has an `.htm` or `.html` suffix.

NOTE You can ensure that the user is running your applet in the latest version of Java by configuring your HTML pages to use the Sun Java plug-in at `http://java.sun.com/products/plugin/`. There's a copy of this plug-in in your SDK. See `http://java.sun.com/products/plugin/`*`currentVersion`*`/docs/tags.html#Any` to learn how to convert <APPLET> tags to JavaScript that will load the plug-in correctly on either a Microsoft or a Netscape browser. (In this URL, replace *`currentVersion`* with the current version number, such as 1.3.) You can convert your pages automatically by using Sun's Java Plug-In HTML Converter, described at `http://java.sun.com/products/plugin/features.html`. ■

Getting Started Quickly with a Simple <*Applet*> Tag The <APPLET> tag shown earlier in Listing 36.2 is about as simple as an <APPLET> tag can get. You must include the CODE attribute to tell the browser which class to load. You need to specify the height and width of the graphical space so the browser can allocate it. Other than that, everything in this tag is defaulted.

Note that you must close the applet tag with </APPLET>. If you forget the closing tag, the appletviewer will be confused.

Using the Full <*Applet*> Tag From time to time, you might need to add other elements to the <APPLET> tag. Listing 36.3 shows a more complete example.

Listing 36.3 *bigApplet.html*—More Attributes, Parameters, and Even HTML in the <*APPLET*> Tag

```
<HTML>
<BODY>
<APPLET CODEBASE="http://myserver.mydomain.com/applets">
CODE="SomeApplet.class" WIDTH="200" HEIGHT="200"
ALT="A simple applet" NAME="hello"
ALIGN="Center" VSPACE="2" HSPACE="2">
<PARAM NAME="Auto" VALUE="True">
<PARAM NAME="Interface" VALUE="Full">
Your browser doesn't understand Java. If you had a Java-enabled
➥browser you'd see something like this:<BR>
<IMG SRC="applet.gif" ALT="Image of Applet" HEIGHT="200" WIDTH=
➥"200">
You can get a Java-aware browser from
<A HREF="http://home.netscape.com/">Netscape Communications</A>.
</APPLET>
</BODY>
</HTML>
```

In this version of the <APPLET> tag, a CODEBASE has been specified where the browser should look for the class file. (By default, the browser asks for the applet from the same server and directory that provided the HTML page.) This version also includes some descriptive text about the applet (in ALT) and a NAME (for use by other applets or by JavaScript).

▶ For an example of JavaScript that communicates with an applet, **see** "Java to JavaScript Communication," **p. 582**

The final set of attributes, ALIGN, VSPACE, and HSPACE, provides alignment and vertical and horizontal spacing.

Following the opening <APPLET> tag, you can place parameters (in <PARAM> tags). Give each parameter a name and a value; the applet will be able to read the parameters.

It's a good idea to make your applets customizable with parameters. Parameterized applets are more useful as components.

TIP Try to avoid having required parameters—if someone else uses your applet on his Web page, he might not know how to use all the parameters. Your applet should behave in a reasonable manner with no parameters at all.

You can make your applet more usable by implementing the `getParameterInfo()` method, which enables a tool such as `AppletViewer` to find out about the parameters you support.

Before you close the `<APPLET>` tag, you can include some HTML. This HTML will only be displayed if the browser did not understand the `<APPLET>` tag, so you should display a message telling the user what she is missing. The HTML in Listing 36.3 (lines 9 through 13) tells the user about the problem, puts up a graphic showing what the applet looks like, and then offers a link to the Netscape site so the user can download Netscape Communicator.

Running Your Applet with *AppletViewer*

To start `AppletViewer`, type `appletViewer HelloApplet.html` at the command line. Figure 36.5 shows the applet in action. It doesn't do much, but it works!

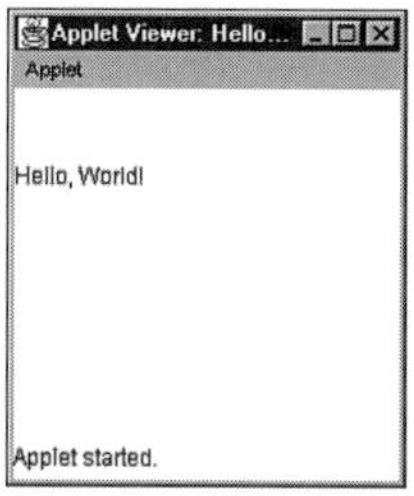

FIGURE 36.5
The fastest and easiest way to test an applet is with the `AppletViewer`.

Seeing Your Applet in a Web Browser

Eventually you'll want your applet to appear on a Web page. Figure 36.6 shows `HelloApplet` viewed with Microsoft Internet Explorer. Figure 36.7 shows the same applet in Netscape Navigator.

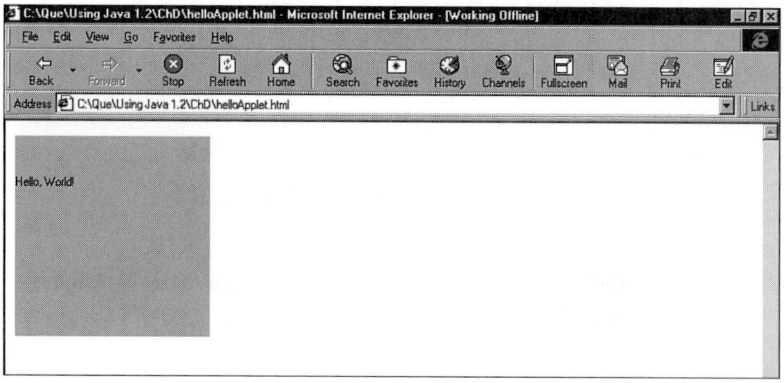

FIGURE 36.6
Microsoft displays a gray rectangle to show the applet's reserved space.

FIGURE 36.7
Netscape displays the applet against a transparent background.

TIP Even an applet as simple as this one can look different when run on different Web browsers.

Depending on how widely you expect your applets to be circulated, it is usually a good idea to have several browsers (on different machines with different resolutions and different operating systems) and several different versions handy for testing.

To ensure that users are using Sun's version of the Java Virtual Machine (rather than one written by the browser vendor), script your pages so they load Sun's plug-in. That way you won't have as much variation from one machine to another.

Troubleshooting

If all doesn't go well when you compile and load your applet, double-check your `CLASSPATH` variable. The most common problem new Java programmers experience is an incorrect `CLASSPATH` variable. If either your compiler or interpreter complains about missing classes, make sure every class archive is listed in `CLASSPATH`. If your class files are "loose" files in a directory, list the directory. If they're archived into a `.zip` file or `.jar` file, you should name the archive in `CLASSPATH`. You shouldn't have much trouble with `HelloApplet`, but it does need to find Sun's `Applet` and `Graphics` classes.

NOTE If you want to know more about how the browser calls the various methods of your applet, look at "Life Cycle of an Applet," later in this chapter.

Stepping Through the Code

This section steps through the code for the `HelloApplet` class to show why each line is written the way it is. Even though only one executable statement exists (in line 8), this tiny program illustrates many of the principles you'll use in writing any Java applet:

- The class is declared to be `public`.
- The class contains a member named `paint()`.
- `paint()` is declared to be `public` and to return `void`.

Importing Packages

The first two lines of `HelloApplet.java` tell the compiler to use class definitions from two specific packages: `java.applet` and `java.awt`. (AWT stands for the Abstract Windowing Toolkit.) Specifically, these directives tell the compiler to use the `Applet` object from `java.applet` and the `Graphics` object from `java.awt`.

The `import` statement is a shorthand notation. You could have written

```
public class HelloApplet extends java.applet.Applet
```

and

```
public void paint (java.awt.Graphics theGraphics)
```

but most programmers prefer the aesthetics of `import`. If you had planned to use many classes from `java.applet` or `java.awt`, you could have written

```
import java.applet.*;
import java.awt.*;
```

to give the compiler permission to use any class from those packages. In practice, this asterisk notation is used frequently, although you lose the immediate capability to identify where a class is defined. Those who don't know Java well wouldn't know whether the `Graphics` class was part of `java.applet` or `java.awt`.

NOTE If two classes in different packages have the same name, you can run into problems if you use the asterisk (`*`) notation on both packages. To make sure you get the class you want, fully qualify it in your code or in the `import` statement. ■

Extending *Applet*

The most powerful statement in `HelloApplet` is in the class definition `HelloApplet extends Applet`. That one statement says that your little class, `HelloApplet`, inherits all the methods and variables of Sun's much larger class, `Applet`. `Applet` already knows how to communicate with the Web browser. It knows how to communicate with the graphical interface inside the browser window. It even knows how to redraw its content (although that content is empty). What it doesn't know is how to do any work. By extending `Applet`, you get a complete applet—ready to go. All you have to do is add content.

What's a *public* Class?

Java provides several levels of access—`public`, `protected`, `private`, and a default. Anyone can access classes and members that are `public`. When you write an applet, you need to declare the applet's class as `public` so the Java environment can find it and run its methods.

Using *Applet's paint* Method

An applet draws into a graphical space provided by the Web browser. Whenever that space is covered (by another window) or disappears (because the user has minimized the window) it becomes invalid. When it becomes visible again, the applet must repaint itself. In fact, internally, `Applet` calls a method called `repaint()`. That `repaint()` method, in turn, calls `paint()`. To draw something into the applet's graphical space, you need to do the work in `paint()`.

The graphical space allocated for you by the browser is represented by a `Graphics` object, so you begin the `paint()` method by accepting that `Graphics` object (which is called `theGraphics`).

The `Graphics` class supports over three dozen public methods, including `drawLine()`, `draw3DRect()`, and `fillArc()`. Because you want to put a `String` into the graphic, the method you're interested in is `drawString()`. `drawString()` takes three parameters—the `String` you want to draw, and the x and y coordinates where you want to start drawing. The coordinates `0` and `50` have been chosen to start the `String` against the left margin, down a bit from the top.

NOTE The `paint` method is one of several methods that the browser calls. You can get sophisticated behavior from your applet by overriding other methods, such as `start()` and `init()`. More detail is given in the next section, "Life Cycle of an Applet."

Life Cycle of an Applet

You've seen `Applet`'s `paint()` method. As you might guess, repainting the screen is only one part of an applet's life cycle. This section shows the various stages of an applet's life and suggests various tasks you might want to undertake at each step. To see these steps in action, compile `LifeCycle.java` given in Listing 36.4. You can construct an HTML file based on the pattern given in `HelloApplet.html`—just change the name of the class file.

Listing 36.4 *LifeCycle.java*—Stages in the Life of an Applet

```
import java.applet.Applet;
import java.awt.Graphics;

public class LifeCycle extends Applet
{
  public LifeCycle()
  {
    System.out.println("Constructor running...");
  }
  public void init()
  {
    System.out.println("This is init.");
```

Listing 36.4 Continued

```
    }
    public void start()
    {
      System.out.println("Applet started.");
    }
    public void paint(Graphics theGraphics)
    {
      theGraphics.drawString("Hello, World!", 0, 50);
      System.out.println("Applet just painted.");
    }
    public void stop()
    {
      System.out.println("Applet stopped.");
    }
    public void destroy()
    {
      System.out.println("Applet destroyed.");
    }
  }
```

If you run the LifeCycle applet from the appletviewer, you'll receive standard out messages in the command prompt window. If you're using a Web browser, you can open the Java console. To open the Java console in Netscape Communicator, for example, choose Communicator, Tools, Java Console. Figure 36.8 shows the console in action.

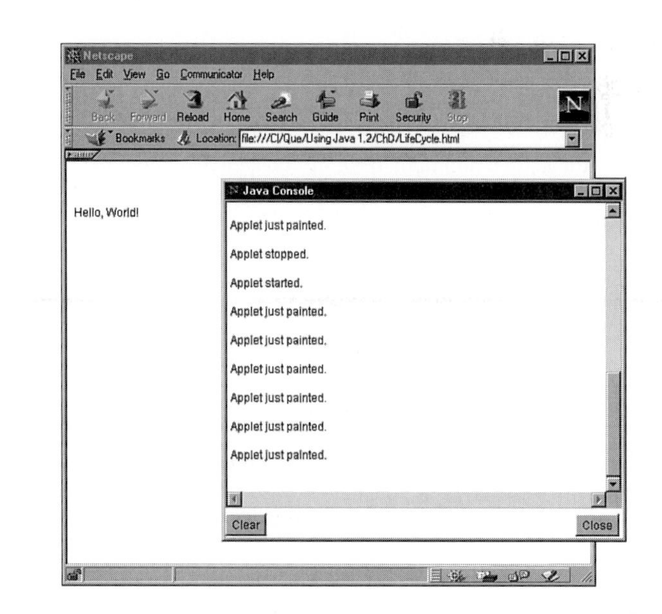

FIGURE 36.8
You can write to the Java console to help debug your applets.

TIP You can type commands into Navigator's Java console. Enter a question mark (`?`) to see a list of commands. If you enter nine (`9`) you'll put the console in maximum debugging mode—it will show you all kinds of information about your running applet.

Constructor

Every class has a constructor—you'll spot it because it has the same name as the class. You can put initialization code in the constructor. Restrict yourself to code that should be run only once during the life of the applet.

CAUTION

Not all browsers load and unload applets in the same way. For best results, put once-only code into `init()` rather than the constructor.

init()

When the browser sees an `<APPLET>` tag, it instructs the Java class loader to load the specified class. The Java environment in the browser makes an instance of the class (by calling its constructor). It then calls the `init()` method of the instance. The `init()` method is the best place to put code that should run only once during your applet's lifetime. Experiment with the LifeCycle applet in different browsers to see the circumstances under which the constructor and `init()` are called.

start() and *stop()*

After your applet is loaded and initialized, the Java environment calls `start()`. If the user leaves the page or minimizes it, the applet's `stop()` method is called. The `start()` method will be called again when the user returns to the page.

If your applet should take special action when the user enters or leaves the page, place the code for those actions in `start()` or `stop()`.

paint()

The Java environment calls `paint()` whenever it suspects that the applet's graphic space might have been obscured. As a result, `paint()` gets called far more often than you might expect. Experiment with the LifeCycle applet in various browsers to see when `paint()` gets called. Design your applets so that `paint()` is as efficient as possible—this method is where your program will spend much of its time.

destroy()

Put up Navigator's Java Console, open a page with the LifeCycle applet on it, and exit Navigator. If you watch the console closely, you'll see LifeCycle's "destroy" message just before the console itself disappears. In general, browsers will try to keep applets around (at least in their stopped state) as long as they can. When the browser's memory is full, or when the user exits the browser, the applet's resources are released. Just before the browser destroys the applet's memory, it calls `destroy()`. Use `destroy()` to release any resources your applet might have acquired.

Where's the Destructor? If you're experienced in C++, you might be puzzled by Java's lack of a destructor. Java relies on garbage collection—you don't have to explicitly delete objects. Nevertheless, your C++ habits will stand you in good stead—most programmers prefer to release resources as soon as they know they're done with them. The code you put into `destroy()` should, therefore, resemble code you might write in a C++ destructor; look through your constructor and `init()` code, identify any resources (such as object references) you acquired, and release them. If your applet acquired other resources during its lifetime (such as nodes on a linked list), release them by setting the references to `null`.

You get a similar effect by writing a `finalize()` method. The garbage collector calls an object's `finalize()` method just before the object's memory is reclaimed. If you have a sophisticated applet with more than one class, you might want to write a `finalize()` method for each class that needs to dispose of resources. You can then use `finalize()` to dispose of system resources or perform other cleanup, and use `destroy()` to wrap up the applet itself.

Troubleshooting *HelloApplet*

Even with an applet as simple as this, several things could go wrong:

- **`javac: Bad command or filename error`**—This message means that you didn't install the SDK correctly.

  If you are sure that you installed the SDK, all you need to do is set your DOS `PATH`. The easiest way to fix this problem is to make sure `PATH` and `CLASSPATH` are correctly defined in `AUTOEXEC.BAT` and then reboot your PC. The following is a sample `AUTOEXEC` entry:

  ```
  PATH=c:\windows;c:\windows\command;c:\jdk1.3\bin
  CLASSPATH=c:\jdk1.3\lib;.
  ```

  Remember to use the Control Panel if you're using Windows NT or a shell script if you're on a UNIX system. You might need to restart your shell or command prompt window for this change to take effect. If you've changed `AUTOEXEC.BAT`, you need to run that batch file or reboot the machine.

- **Extraneous `thread applet-HelloApplet.class find class HelloApplet` messages**—This message means that `CLASSPATH` is not defined correctly. The solution is the same as for the preceding problem: Double-check your definitions for `PATH` and `CLASSPATH` and reboot your PC.

  `CLASSPATH` consists of a list of directory paths in which appletviewer looks for Java classes. Each different pathname is separated by a semicolon. Make sure that the current directory (represented by a dot) is in your `CLASSPATH` list.

- **`HelloApplet.java:26: Class gelloApplet not found in type declaration`**—This message or any similar-sounding compiler error probably means you mistyped something.

  Carefully double-check every place in the program where you meant to type the name in question (here, `HelloApplet`). Be sure each occurrence matches exactly (including capitalization—Java is case sensitive).

  In this case, you carefully double-check your program and discover that you typed `gelloApplet` rather than `HelloApplet`. It compiles correctly after you make this correction.

- **`HelloApplet.java:24: Warning: Public class HelloApplet must be defined in a file called HelloApplet.java`**—The name of your Java source file must match the name of your public Java class exactly.

  For the sample program, this requirement means the class needs to be called `HelloApplet`, the source file needs to be called `HelloApplet.java`, and the HTML `<APPLET>` tag needs to specify `HelloApplet.class`, or your program will neither compile cleanly nor execute.

  To fix this problem, carefully double-check everything for exact spelling and capitalization, and then compile again.

- **Nothing happens**—If you are running Microsoft Internet Explorer and you see the HTML, but not your applet, your browser probably is not configured to run Java. In IE 5, choose Tools, Internet Options, Security, and specify Internet, Custom Level. Make sure Java is enabled—the default is High Security, which works well.

Sample Applets

Sometimes programming is better "caught than taught." This section shows three fairly advanced applets—each uses techniques that haven't been described in detail in this book. If you have a programming background, most of the logic of these applets should be clear; look in the Java documentation for details about the API. If you want a more detailed treatment of Java programming, read *Special Edition Using Java 2, Standard Edition* (Que, 2000).

SystemInfo

The applet in Listing 36.5 demonstrates how to build several "cards" of data into an applet. The file defines three classes:

- **`LabelField`**—A derivative of `Panel` that knows how to lay out its data and a label.
- **`SystemInfo`**—The applet class itself, which reads various system properties and displays them on the "cards" of a `CardLayout`.
- **`ButtonAction`**—An "inner class" of `SystemInfo` that responds to clicks on the applet's two buttons.

Figure 36.9 shows the applet in action.

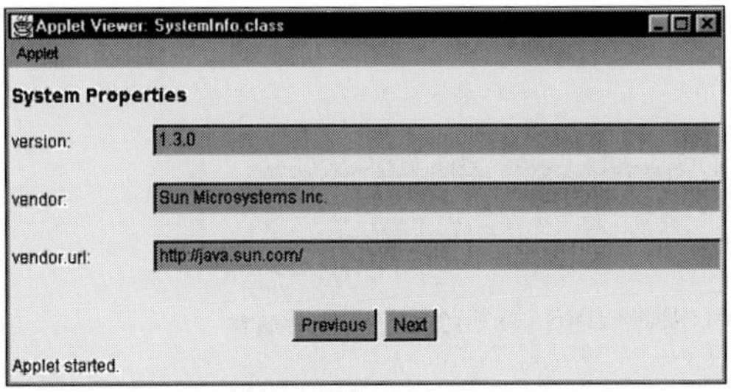

FIGURE 36.9
The first card of `SystemInfo`.

Listing 36.5 *SystemInfo.java*—This Applet Displays Several "Cards" of Information

```
import java.applet.Applet;
import java.awt.Panel;
import java.awt.GridLayout;
import java.awt.BorderLayout;
import java.awt.CardLayout;
import java.awt.Label;
import java.awt.Button;
import java.awt.Font;
import java.awt.TextField;
import java.awt.Dimension;
import java.awt.event.ActionListener;
import java.awt.event.ActionEvent;

class LabelField extends Panel {
  int fLabelWidth;
  Label fLabel;
  TextField fField;

  public LabelField(int theLabelWidth, String theLabel, String theValue) {
    this.fLabelWidth = theLabelWidth;
    add(this.fLabel = new Label(theLabel));
```

Listing 36.5 Continued

```
    add(this.fField = new TextField(theValue));
    fField.setEditable(false);
  }
  public void doLayout() {
    Dimension theDimension = getSize();
    Dimension theLabelSize = fLabel.getPreferredSize();
    Dimension theFieldSize = fField.getPreferredSize();
    fLabel.setBounds(0, 0, fLabelWidth, theLabelSize.height);
    fField.setBounds(fLabelWidth + 5, 0, theDimension.width -
      (fLabelWidth + 5), theFieldSize.height);
  }
}

public class SystemInfo extends Applet {
  CardLayout fCardLayout;
  Panel fPanel;
  Button fNextButton;
  Button fPrevButton;

  public void init() {
  Font theFont = new Font("Helvetica", Font.BOLD, 14);
  setLayout(new BorderLayout());
  add("South", fPanel = new Panel());

  fNextButton = new Button("Next");
  fPrevButton = new Button("Previous");
  ButtonAction aButtonAction = new ButtonAction();

  fNextButton.addActionListener(aButtonAction);
  fPrevButton.addActionListener(aButtonAction);

  fPanel.add(fPrevButton);
  fPanel.add(fNextButton);

  add("Center", fPanel = new Panel());
  fPanel.setLayout(fCardLayout = new CardLayout());

  try {
    Panel aPanel = new Panel();
    aPanel.setLayout(new GridLayout(0, 1));
    aPanel.add(new Label("System Properties")).setFont(theFont);
    aPanel.add(new LabelField(100, "version:",
      System.getProperty("java.version")));
    aPanel.add(new LabelField(100, "vendor:",
      System.getProperty("java.vendor")));
    aPanel.add(new LabelField(100, "vendor.url:",
    ➥System.getProperty("java.vendor.url")));
    fPanel.add("system", aPanel);

    aPanel = new Panel();
```

Listing 36.5 Continued

```
      aPanel.add(new Label("Java Properties")).setFont(theFont);
      aPanel.setLayout(new GridLayout(0, 1));
      aPanel.add(new LabelField(100, "class version:",
        System.getProperty("java.class.version")));
      fPanel.add("java", aPanel);

      aPanel = new Panel();
      aPanel.setLayout(new GridLayout(0, 1));
      aPanel.add(new Label("OS Properties")).setFont(theFont);
      aPanel.add(new LabelField(100, "OS:",
      ➥System.getProperty("os.name")));
      aPanel.add(new LabelField(100, "OS Arch:",
      ➥System.getProperty("os.arch")));
      aPanel.add(new LabelField(100, "OS Version:",
      ➥System.getProperty("os.version")));
      fPanel.add("os", aPanel);

      aPanel = new Panel();
      aPanel.setLayout(new GridLayout(0, 1));
      aPanel.add(new Label("Misc Properties")).setFont(theFont);
      aPanel.add(new LabelField(100, "File Separator:",
        System.getProperty("file.separator")));
      aPanel.add(new LabelField(100, "Path Separator:",
        System.getProperty("path.separator")));
      aPanel.add(new LabelField(100, "Line Separator:",
        System.getProperty("line.separator")));
      fPanel.add("sep", aPanel);
    } catch (SecurityException e) {
        System.out.println("Security Exception: " + e);
      }
    }

    class ButtonAction implements ActionListener {

      public void actionPerformed (ActionEvent theEvent) {
        Object anObject = theEvent.getSource();
        if (anObject == fNextButton)
          fCardLayout.next(fPanel);
        else if (anObject == fPrevButton)
          fCardLayout.previous(fPanel);
      }
    }
  }
```

The Great Thread Race

Java enables your applet (or application) to have more than one thread of control. *TRaceApplet*, shown in Listing 36.6, starts several "racing" threads and shows them moving across the screen. You can use this applet to test your Web browser to see how well it shares time between threads of different priorities. (Most Web browsers do a poor job in this area—you shouldn't rely on relative priorities between threads for any critical feature.) Note, too, that this program has a `main()` method and can be run as an application as well as an applet.

Listing 36.6 ***TRaceApplet.java*****—This Program Sets Up the User Interface and Starts the Race**

```
import java.applet.Applet;
import java.awt.Graphics;
import java.awt.GridLayout;

public class TRaceApplet extends Applet implements Runnable,
➥TSuspendable
{
  private TRacer fRacers[];
  static private short fRacerCount = 0;
  private Thread fThreads[];
  static private Thread fMonitorThread;
  static private boolean fInApplet = true;
  private boolean fThreadSuspended = false;
  static private java.awt.Frame fFrame = null;
  private TWindowAdapter fWindowAdapter = null;

  public void init()
  {
    if (fInApplet)
    {
      String theParameter = getParameter("NUMBER");
      if (theParameter == null)
        fRacerCount = 0;
      else
        fRacerCount = Short.parseShort(theParameter);
    }
    if (fRacerCount <= 0)
      fRacerCount = 2;
    if (fRacerCount > Thread.MAX_PRIORITY -
    ➥Thread.MIN_PRIORITY + 1)
      fRacerCount = (short)(Thread.MAX_PRIORITY -
      ➥Thread.MIN_PRIORITY + 1);

    if (!fInApplet)
      fWindowAdapter = new TWindowAdapter();

    // have one column, with one row per Racer
    setLayout(new GridLayout(fRacerCount, 1));

    // initialize the fRacers and fThreads arrays
    fRacers = new TRacer[fRacerCount];
    fThreads = new Thread[fRacerCount];
```

Listing 36.6 Continued

```
    for (short i=0; i<fRacerCount; i++)
    {
      fRacers[i] = new TRacer("Racer# " + i, this);

      // scale the image so that all of the racers will fit
      fRacers[i].setSize(getSize().width,
      ➥getSize().height/fRacerCount);
      add(fRacers[i]);
    }
  }

  public void start()
  {
    // set up our own "monitor" thread
    fMonitorThread = new Thread(null, this,
    ➥"Monitor Thread");
    fMonitorThread.start();
  }

  public void stop()
  {
    fMonitorThread = null;
  }

  public void run()
  {
    if (fMonitorThread == Thread.currentThread())
    {
      TMouseAdapter aMouseAdapter = new TMouseAdapter();
      for (short i=0; i<fRacerCount;i++)
      {
        // this version of the Thread constructor specifies a
        ➥Runnable target
        fThreads[i] = new Thread(fRacers[i]);

        // should guarantee that the high-number thread wins
        fThreads[i].setPriority(Thread.MIN_PRIORITY+i);
        fThreads[i].start();
        fRacers[i].addMouseListener(aMouseAdapter);
      }
      synchronized (fMonitorThread)
      {
        fMonitorThread.notify();
      }
    }

    // now the world knows that all the racers are running
    while (fMonitorThread == Thread.currentThread())
    try
    {
      fMonitorThread.sleep(100);
```

Listing 36.6 Continued

```
      synchronized(fMonitorThread)
      {
        while (fThreadSuspended)
        {
          fMonitorThread.wait();
        }
        synchronized(this)
        {
          notifyAll();
        }
      }
    } catch (InterruptedException e)
    {
      System.err.println("The monitor thread was interrupted
      ➥while sleeping.");
      System.exit(1);
    }
  }

  public String[][] getParameterInfo()
  {
   short theMaximumNumberOfThreads =
  ➥(short)(Thread.MAX_PRIORITY - Thread.MIN_PRIORITY + 1);
   String theParameterInfo[][] =
   {
     {"NUMBER",    "1-"+theMaximumNumberOfThreads,
     ➥"number of racers"},
   };
   return theParameterInfo;
  }

  public String getAppletInfo()
  {
    String theAppletInfo = "Author: Michael L. Morgan\nDate:
    ➥19 March 98\nInspired by the Great Thread Race
    ➥(Special Edition Using Java, Que, 1996, p. 551)";
    return theAppletInfo;
  }

  public boolean isSuspended()
  {
    return fThreadSuspended;
  }

  public static void main(String argv[])
  {
    fInApplet = false;

    //look for the number of racers on the command line
    if (argv.length>0)
```

Listing 36.6 Continued

```
    try {
      fRacerCount = Short.parseShort(argv[0]);
    } catch (NumberFormatException e)
    {
      fRacerCount = 5;
    }

    fFrame = new java.awt.Frame("Racing Threads");

    TRaceApplet theRace = new TRaceApplet();
    fFrame.setSize(400,200);
    fFrame.add(theRace, java.awt.BorderLayout.CENTER);
    fFrame.show();
    theRace.init();

    // be sure to wait until after init() to hook up listener
    fFrame.addWindowListener(theRace.fWindowAdapter);
    fFrame.pack();
    theRace.start();

    // don't pass here till all racers are started
    synchronized (fMonitorThread)
    {
      try {
        fMonitorThread.wait();
      } catch (InterruptedException e)
      {
        System.err.println("Main thread interrupted while
        ➥waiting for racers to start.");
        System.exit(1);
      }
    }
    System.out.println("And they're off!");

    // wait till all the racers are finished
    for (short i=0; i<fRacerCount; i++)
    try
    {
      theRace.fThreads[i].join();
    } catch (InterruptedException e)
    {
      System.err.println("The monitor thread was interrupted
      ➥while waiting for the other threads to exit.");
    }
    System.exit(0);
  }

  class TWindowAdapter extends java.awt.event.WindowAdapter
  {
    public void windowClosing(java.awt.event.WindowEvent
```

Listing 36.6 Continued

```
      ➥anEvent)
      {
        fFrame.setVisible(false);
        fFrame.dispose();
        System.exit(0);
      }
    }
    class TMouseAdapter extends java.awt.event.MouseAdapter
    {
      public synchronized void mousePressed(
      ➥java.awt.event.MouseEvent anEvent)
      {
        anEvent.consume();
        fThreadSuspended = !fThreadSuspended;
        if (!fThreadSuspended)
          synchronized (fMonitorThread)
          {
            fMonitorThread.notifyAll();
          }
      }
    }
  }
```

TIP

Whenever possible, include code such as `main()` in your own applets. This is shown in `TRaceApplet` beginning about 2/3 into the listing with

```
public static void main(String argv[])
```

and ending with

```
System.exit(0);
   }
```

When you include code such as this, you can run your program either as an applet or as an application. You'll want to run as an application when you regression test, or if you later reuse the code outside of a browser environment.

Note that `TRaceApplet` supports parameters from the HTML `<PARAM>` tag. Lines 21 through 28 (as follows) look for a parameter named `NUMBER`.

```
  String theParameter = getParameter("NUMBER");
  if (theParameter == null)
    fRacerCount = 0;
  else
    fRacerCount = Short.parseShort(theParameter);
}
if (fRacerCount <= 0)
  fRacerCount = 2;
```

If the parameter is found, it is used as the number of racers (`fRacerCount`). If it can't be found, if it is unreadable, or if it is less than or equal to zero, the program defaults to two racers.

How is the HTML author to know that this applet supports this parameter? Many browsers can call the `getParameterInfo()` method. `TRaceApplet` implements this method in lines 114 through 124 (as follows).

```
public String[][] getParameterInfo()
{
 short theMaximumNumberOfThreads =
 ➥(short)(Thread.MAX_PRIORITY - Thread.MIN_PRIORITY + 1);
 String theParameterInfo[][] =
 {
   {"NUMBER",    "1-"+theMaximumNumberOfThreads,
 ➥"number of racers"},
 };
 return theParameterInfo;
}
```

If the user requests this information, the program returns the parameter name, type, and range. Figure 36.10 shows how `AppletViewer` handles this request.

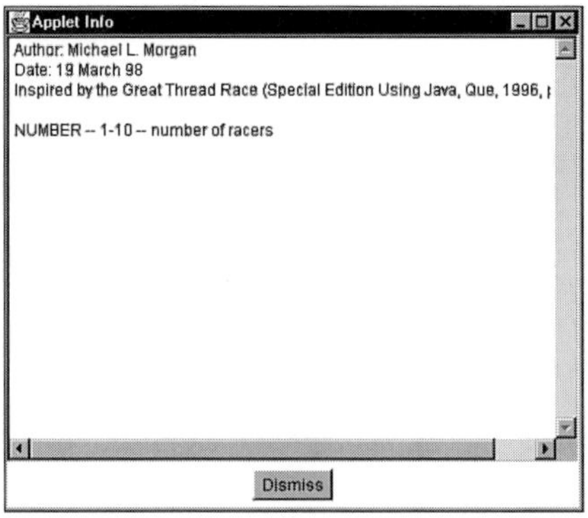

FIGURE 36.10
Choose Info from the Applet menu in `AppletViewer` to see the applet and parameter information.

Listing 36.7 shows an HTML file that takes advantage of this feature.

Listing 36.7 *autogen_Race1.html*—This HTML Was Originally Written by Visual Café

```
<HTML>
<HEAD>
<TITLE>Autogenerated HTML</TITLE>
</HEAD>
<BODY>
```

Listing 36.7 Continued

```
<APPLET CODE="TRaceApplet.class" WIDTH=430 HEIGHT=270>
<PARAM NAME="NUMBER" VALUE="5">
</APPLET>
</BODY>
</HTML>
```

`TRaceApplet` requires two additional files: `TRacer.java`, which contains the class definition for the racer itself, and `TSuspendable.java`, an interface that supports pausing and unpausing the race with a mouse click. These files appear in Listings 36.8 and 36.9, respectively.

Listing 36.8 *TRacer.java—TRacer* Is a Runnable Canvas and Responsible for Its User Interface

```
import java.awt.Graphics;
import java.awt.Color;

public class TRacer extends java.awt.Canvas implements
➥Runnable
{
  private short fPosition = 0;
  private String fName;
  static private final short kNumberOfSteps = 1000;
  TSuspendable fAncestor;

  public TRacer(String theName, TSuspendable theAncestor)
  {
    fName = new String(theName);
    fAncestor = theAncestor;
  }

  public TRacer(String theName)
  {
    fName = new String(theName);
    fAncestor = null;
  }

  public synchronized void paint(Graphics g)
  {
    g.setColor(Color.black);
    g.drawLine(0,getSize().height/2, getSize().width,
    ➥getSize().height/2);
    g.setColor(Color.red);
    g.fillOval(fPosition*getSize().width/kNumberOfSteps, 0,
   ➥15, getSize().height);
  }

  public void run()
  {
```

Listing 36.8 Continued

```
    while (fPosition < kNumberOfSteps)
    {
      fPosition++;
      repaint();
      try
      {
        Thread.currentThread().sleep(10);
        if (fAncestor != null)
        {
          synchronized (fAncestor)
          {
            if (fAncestor.isSuspended())
              fAncestor.wait();
          }
        }
      } catch (InterruptedException e)
      {
        System.err.println("Thread " + fName + " interrupted.");
        System.exit(1);
      }
    }
    System.out.println("Thread " + fName + " has finished
    ➥the race.");
  }

  public static void main(String argv[])
    {
      java.awt.Frame theFrame = new java.awt.Frame("One Racer");
      TRacer aRacer = new TRacer("Test");
      theFrame.setSize(400,200);
      theFrame.add(aRacer, java.awt.BorderLayout.CENTER);
      theFrame.show();
      aRacer.paint(theFrame.getGraphics());
      theFrame.pack();
      aRacer.run();
      System.exit(0);
    }
}
```

Listing 36.9 ***TSuspendable.java*****—Use This Interface to Ensure That the Ancestor Is Suspendable**

```
public interface TSuspendable
{
  public boolean isSuspended();
}
```

Recall (lines 79 and 80 of `TRaceApplet.java` follow) that the highest-numbered thread should always win:

```
// should guarantee that the high-number thread wins
fThreads[i].setPriority(Thread.MIN_PRIORITY+i);
```

As Figures 36.11 and 36.12 show, you can't count on the priority mechanism to function as expected. In `AppletViewer`, threads 2, 3, and 4 have a decided advantage over threads 0 and 1, but little difference exists within each group. Figure 36.12 shows that Netscape Navigator (a component of Netscape Communicator) ignores priority completely.

FIGURE 36.11
This version of the Great Thread Race is running on the SDK 1.3 `AppletViewer`.

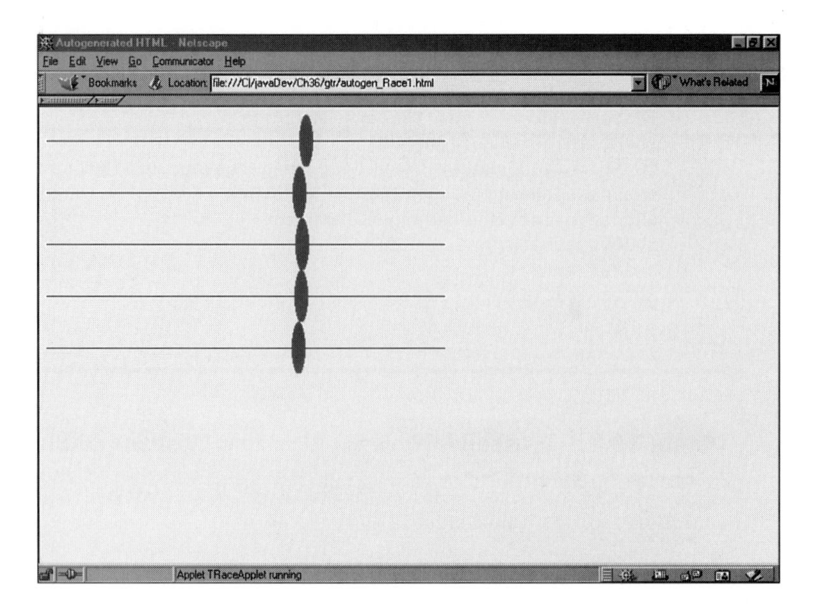

FIGURE 36.12
When run in Navigator 4.72, thread priority seems to have no effect.

Working with a Relational Database

Sun supports an interface to relational databases called JDBC. The simple demo described in this section uses JDBC to connect to a relational database and, on command, executes a query against the database and returns the results.

If you have an ODBC-compliant database such as Microsoft Access available, you can build and run applications such as bookQueryApplet, shown in Listing 36.10. This program opens an existing database (`bookWholesale.mdb`).

NOTE Before you run the program, use your ODBC Control Panel to make a new ODBC source. Name it booksWholesale and point it to the `bookWholesale.mdb` file.

Listing 36.10 *bookQueryApplet.java*—Test Program Opens a Database and Reads Data Interactively

```
import java.awt.*;
import java.applet.Applet;
import java.sql.*;

public class bookQueryApplet extends Applet
{
  // declare a few objects to be global
  Connection theConnection = null;
  Statement theStatement = null;
  Button theCheckDatabaseButton = null;
  List theBooksList = null;

  public void init()
  {
    // put up some controls
    setLayout(null);
    setSize(400,400);
    theCheckDatabaseButton = new java.awt.Button("Check database");
    theCheckDatabaseButton.setBounds(48,192,360,32);
    theCheckDatabaseButton.setFont(new Font("Dialog", Font.BOLD, 18));
    add(theCheckDatabaseButton);

    Label theBooksInDatabaseLabel =
    ➥new java.awt.Label("Books in Database");
    theBooksInDatabaseLabel.setBounds(24,12,360,32);
    theBooksInDatabaseLabel.setFont(new Font("Dialog",
    ➥Font.BOLD, 18));
    add(theBooksInDatabaseLabel);

    theBooksList = new java.awt.List(0, false);
    theBooksList.setBounds(30, 60, 329, 103);
    theBooksList.setFont(new Font("Dialog", Font.BOLD, 14));
    add(theBooksList);
```

Listing 36.10 Continued

```
    // connect to the database
    setupDatabase();

    //register listeners
    MyActionListener theListener = new MyActionListener();
    theCheckDatabaseButton.addActionListener(theListener);
  }

  public void destroy()
  {
    try {
      if (theStatement != null)
        theStatement.close();
      if (theConnection != null)
        theConnection.close();
    } catch (SQLException se) {
      System.err.println("SQL Exception: " + se.getMessage());
    }
  }

  void setupDatabase()
  {
    // Load the driver
    Class theDriver = sun.jdbc.odbc.JdbcOdbcDriver.class;

    // Open the connection
    try {
      theConnection =
        DriverManager.getConnection("jdbc:odbc:booksWholesale");
      theStatement = theConnection.createStatement();
    } catch (SQLException se) {
      System.err.println("SQL Exception: " + se.getMessage());
    }
  }

  public static void main(String args[])
  {
    // run a test routine
    System.out.println("Starting");
    bookQueryApplet theApplet = new bookQueryApplet();
    System.out.println("setting up database");
    theApplet.setupDatabase();
    System.out.println("setup done");
    try {
      ResultSet theResults = theApplet.theStatement.executeQuery(
        "SELECT title, retailPrice FROM books,
        ➥publishers WHERE publisher = publishers.ID AND
```

Listing 36.10 Continued

```
        ➥publishers.Imprint = 'Que'");
      while (theResults.next())
      {
        String theTitle = theResults.getString("title");
        float thePrice = theResults.getFloat("retailPrice");
        System.out.println(theTitle + " " + thePrice);
      }
    } catch (SQLException se) {
      System.err.println("SQL Exception: " + se.getMessage());
    } finally {
      theApplet.destroy();
      System.out.println("exiting");
    }
    System.exit(0);
  }

  class MyActionListener implements java.awt.event.ActionListener
  {
    public void actionPerformed(java.awt.event.ActionEvent theEvent)
    {
      Object anObject = theEvent.getSource();
      if (anObject == theCheckDatabaseButton)
        theCheckDatabaseButton_Action(theEvent);
    }

    void theCheckDatabaseButton_
    ➥Action(java.awt.event.ActionEvent theEvent)
    {
      theBooksList.removeAll();
      try {
        ResultSet theResults = theStatement.executeQuery(
          "SELECT title, retailPrice FROM books, publishers
          ➥WHERE publisher = publishers.ID AND
          ➥publishers.Imprint = 'Que'");
        while (theResults.next())
        {
          String theTitle = theResults.getString("title");
          float thePrice = theResults.getFloat("retailPrice");
          System.out.println(theTitle + " " + thePrice);
          theBooksList.add(theTitle + " " + thePrice);
        }
      } catch (SQLException se) {
        System.err.println("SQL Exception: " + se.getMessage());
      }
    }
  }
}
```

Figure 36.13 shows `bookQueryApplet` in action.

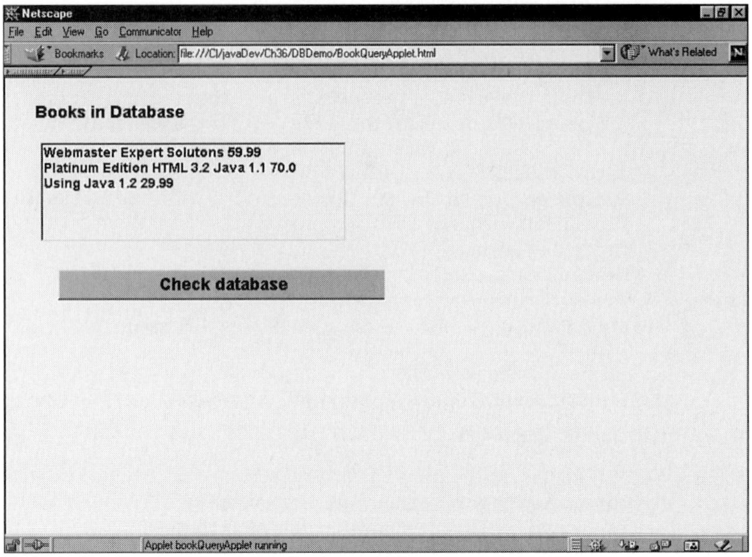

FIGURE 36.13
`bookQueryApplet` reads data from an ODBC database such as Access.

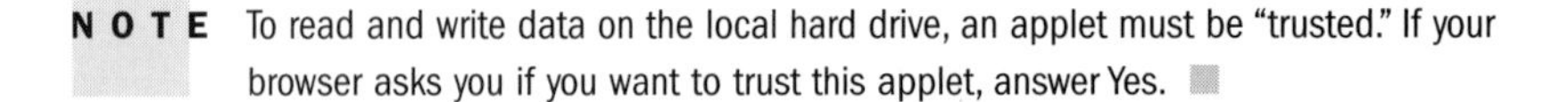

NOTE To read and write data on the local hard drive, an applet must be "trusted." If your browser asks you if you want to trust this applet, answer Yes.

HelloApplet as a Standalone Application

Recall that the first applet example (`HelloApplet`) ran in a Graphical User Interface (GUI) provided by the Web browser. You don't need to limit your Java GUI programming to writing applets that run only inside Web pages—you can write a standalone application with its own graphical environment.

It is often more appropriate—or more convenient—to write a standalone Java application. A *servlet*—a Java program that runs on your Web server—is one example of a Java application; it runs in the environment of a Web server such as Sun's Java Server. The `HelloGUI` program described here is another example.

Writing the Standalone Application

It is not much work at all to convert an applet into a standalone Java application. To do so, follow these steps:

1. A standalone application does not subclass `Applet`. Change this. Usually, your application's main class will be `Frame` instead:

   Applet version:

   ```
   public class HelloApplet extends Applet
   ```

   Standalone version:

   ```
   public class HelloGUI extends Frame
   ```

2. Delete the line `import java.applet.Applet`. Replace it with either `import java.awt.Frame` or `import java.awt.*`.

3. A Java applet overrides the `init ()` method. A standalone application doesn't use `init()`. Instead, when the Java interpreter (java) runs an application, it looks for a public static void method named `main()`.

   Move all the code from the old `init()` into `main()` or into the `Frame`'s constructor. Suppose, for example, you had written

   ```
   public void init ()
   {
     f = new Font ("Helvetica", Font.BOLD, 24);
   }
   ```

   In the standalone version, you would write

   ```
   // main: application initialization code goes here
   public static void main (String[] args)
   {
      Frame theFrame = new HelloGUI ();
      theFrame.setTitle ("Hello World!");
      theFrame.setSize (250, 100);
      f = new Font ("Helvetica", Font.BOLD, 24);
      theFrame.show ();
    }
   ```

4. Delete your applet's `init()` method.

5. A standalone application typically needs to do a little more setup work: organize its frame layout, set the window title, and so on, as shown in step 3 of this list.

6. Finally, you need to run your standalone application by using the SDK `java` interpreter rather than the appletviewer or a Web browser.

Listing 36.11 shows a completed Java application.

Listing 36.11 ***HelloGUI.java*—A Simple Standalone Java Application**

```
/**
 * HelloGUI: Standalone Java application
 *
 * NOTES:
 * Compare this standalone Java application
 *    with "HelloApplet" applet.
 *
 * @version 1.0, DATE: 07.07.98
 * @author Mike Morgan
 */
import java.awt.*;              // User Interface components

public class HelloGUI extends Frame
{
  private static Font f;

  private void drawCenteredString (Graphics g, String s)
  {
    Dimension d = getSize ();
    FontMetrics fm = getFontMetrics (f);
    int x =
      (d.width - fm.stringWidth (s)) / 2;
    int y =
      d.height -
        ( (d.height - fm.getHeight ()) / 2 );

    g.drawString (s, x, y);
  }

  // paint: window refresh code goes here
  public void paint (Graphics g)
  {
    g.setFont (f);
    g.setColor (Color.red);
    drawCenteredString (g, "Hello from Java!");
  }

  // main: application initialization code goes here
  public static void main (String[] args)
  {
     Frame theFrame = new HelloGUI ();
     theFrame.setTitle ("Hello World!");
     theFrame.setSize (250, 100);
     f = new Font ("Helvetica", Font.BOLD, 24);
     theFrame.show ();
   }
}
```

The biggest practical difference between applets running on a Web page and standalone applications is that the application can generally be "trusted" and allowed to do more: open files, establish TCP/IP connections with arbitrary computers, and so on. Applets, on the other hand, are restricted from doing anything that might compromise the security of the user's computer. The restricted environment that Java-enabled browsers set up for applets to run in is called a "sandbox."

▶ To learn more about the sandbox, **see** "Executable Content and Security," **p. 1178**

Compiling and Running the Standalone Application

You can compile and run the standalone application from the command line:

```
javac HelloGUI.java
java HelloGUI
```

If you run this application with the Java interpreter, the output will look like what you saw earlier in this chapter in Figure 36.5.

NOTE If you look carefully at `HelloGUI`, you will see that a new method is there that was not in the applet version: `drawCenteredString()`. This code illustrates how you can use `getSize()` if you ever need to find out the height and width of your "Component" (here, a `Frame`).

`drawCenteredString()` also introduces `FontMetrics` objects and shows how you can use them.

CHAPTER 37

User Input and Interactivity with Java

by Mike Morgan

In this chapter

Interacting with People by Using Java

User interaction with your programs is by far the most important aspect of creating Java applets and applications. If your interface is bad, people won't want to use your program. Come up with an intuitive interface, however, and you could have the next "killer" app. But keep in mind that building those awesome interfaces requires you to start with some foundation.

The Java foundation is discussed in this chapter. Learning about the different tools at your disposal enables you to build intuitive interfaces that empower your users.

The Abstract Windowing Toolkit

The Abstract Windowing Toolkit (AWT) was Java's primary user interface component package in JDK 1.0 and 1.1. You can still use the AWT, but now Sun has also introduced a new package code-named Swing. These packages contain all the programming tools you need to interact with the user. This section describes the now-classic AWT tools; the next section describes Swing.

The AWT contains many familiar user interface elements. Figure 37.1 shows a Java applet with a sample of some of the components of the AWT.

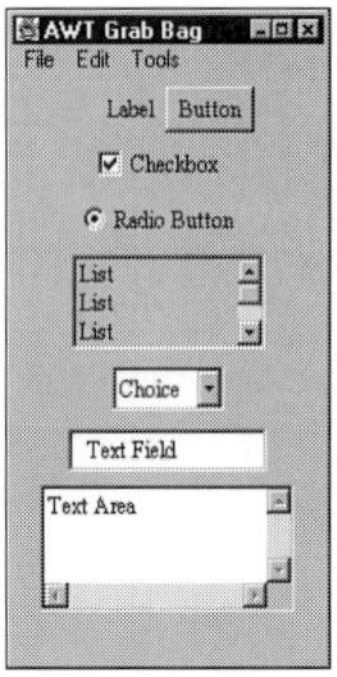

FIGURE 37.1
The AWT features many familiar components.

Figure 37.2 shows a portion of the AWT's inheritance hierarchy.

The original AWT in version 1.0 of the JDK did its work by instantiating *peer objects* from the native operating system. Suppose you asked Java to put a button on the screen, for example, and then ran your application on a Windows machine. The Java runtime would handle your request by asking Windows to make a new button. After that, your Java object and the corresponding Windows object would communicate about mouse clicks and other events for the button to behave as you expected. As you'll see, you now have the choice of using these heavyweight peer components or, through Swing, using a completely different approach.

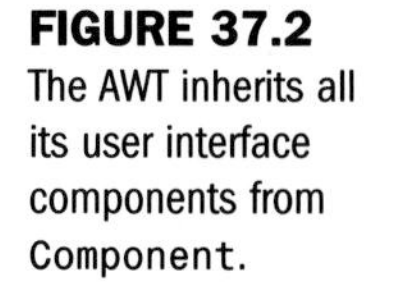

FIGURE 37.2
The AWT inherits all its user interface components from `Component`.

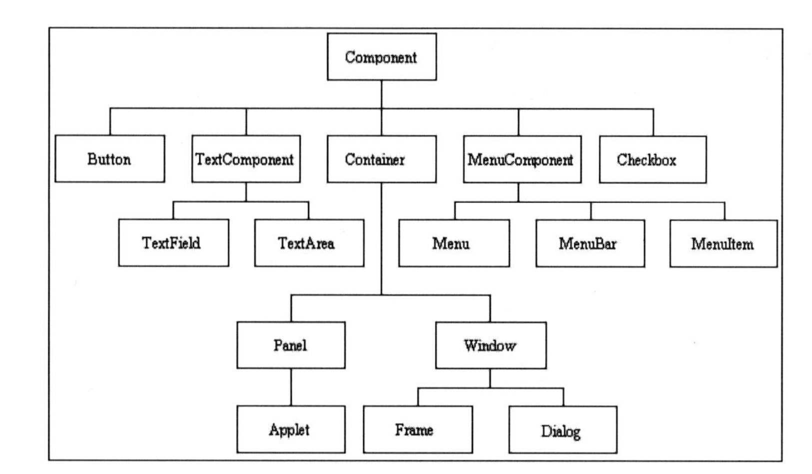

Java Foundation Classes and the Swing Components

Starting in JDK 1.1, Sun made substantial changes to the user interface components. Figure 37.3 illustrates the current state of affairs. The original AWT from JDK 1.0 is gone; in its place is the AWT that was introduced in JDK 1.1, as well as a new interface called Swing. *Swing* is a specialization of the AWT. Swing components are derived from `javax.swing.Jcomponent`, which is derived from `java.awt.Container`. Java user interface classes that do their work through peer objects are still available; they're called ***heavyweight components*** now. As you might guess, there are also ***lightweight components*** that don't tie you to the peer objects of the native operating system. Instead, they support ***pluggable look-and-feel***, enabling an end user to select from a Windows, Macintosh, Sun Motif, or native Java appearance (among others).

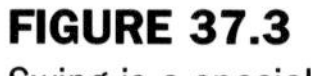

FIGURE 37.3
Swing is a specialized derivation of the AWT.

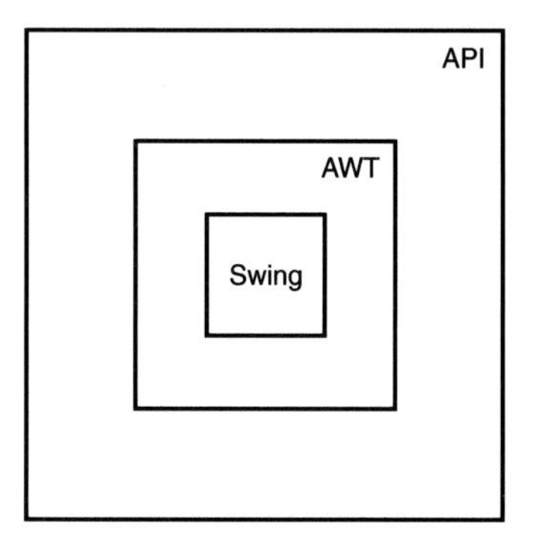

NOTE In addition to Swing and its pluggable look-and-feel, the JFC offers printing capability, clipboard data transfer, improved accessibility for people with disabilities, and much more. It's a major upgrade and well worth the time it takes to learn it.

Using the Abstract Windowing Toolkit

As a platform-neutral language, Java makes many of the details of graphical user interface (GUI) programming invisible, but they don't go away. As you saw in Chapter 36, "Developing Java Applets," you can build a simple applet with a GUI interface in just 10 lines of code. It takes just a few more lines to add a `main()` routine and a standalone `Frame`, enabling the applet to double as a GUI application. (Listing 37.1 shows such a program.)

Listing 37.1 ***HelloApplication.java*—You Can Write an Applet That Will Also Run as an Application**

```
import java.applet.*;
import java.awt.*;
import java.awt.event.*;

public class HelloApplication extends Applet {
  public static void main(String[] args) {
    HelloApplicationFrame theApplication =
      new HelloApplicationFrame("Hello Application");
    theApplication.setSize(200,200);
    theApplication.show();
  }

  public void paint(Graphics theGraphics) {
    theGraphics.drawString("Hello, World!", 0, 50);
  }
}

class HelloApplicationFrame extends Frame {
  private HelloApplication fApplet;

  public HelloApplicationFrame(String name) {
    super(name);
    addWindowListener(new HelloWindowAdapter());
    fApplet = new HelloApplication();
    fApplet.init();
    fApplet.start();
    add(fApplet);
  }
  class HelloWindowAdapter extends WindowAdapter {
    public void windowClosing(WindowEvent e) {
      fApplet.stop();
      fApplet.destroy();
      System.exit(0);
    }
  }
}
```

In this first section, you'll learn how this program works; then you can use it as the foundation for building more sophisticated user interfaces with the AWT.

To learn more about programs that can run both as an application and as an applet, compile `HelloApplication.java` and experiment with it in both environments. (To use `HelloApplication` as an applet, you'll need an HTML file. The one in Listing 37.2 works well.) Figure 37.4 shows this program in action.

Listing 37.2 *HelloApplication.html*—Use This HTML to View the *HelloApplication* Applet

```
<HTML>
<BODY>
<APPLET CODE="HelloApplication.class"
  WIDTH="200" HEIGHT="200">
</APPLET>
</BODY>
</HTML>
```

FIGURE 37.4
`HelloApplication` can be run as an applet or as an application.

Understanding Components and Containers

You can write a one-line `main()` method and get a command-line application started. To build a GUI program, however, someone must provide a place in which to draw. (In GUI programs, all elements of the interface are drawn—even text.) If you're writing an applet, the browser is responsible for that detail. If you want your program to function as an application, you must do that work yourself.

If you're coming to Java from another language such as C++ or C, some of the object-oriented terminology might seem strange. A *method* is a function that is associated with a class. An *object* is an instance of a class. Unlike C++, where `main` is a function, Java's `main` is a method on the application's class.

In AWT, the "place in which to draw" is called a *container*, and is derived from the Java `java.awt.Container` class. The elements of the user interface itself are called *components*—they all derive from `java.awt.Component`. Some of the components supplied with the AWT include

- `java.awt.Button`
- `java.awt.Canvas`

- `java.awt.Checkbox`
- `java.awt.Choice`
- `java.awt.Container`
- `java.awt.Label`
- `java.awt.List`
- `java.awt.Scrollbar`
- `java.awt.TextComponent`
- `java.awt.Composite`

Most of these components provide familiar functionality. A `Button`, for example, works the way you expect buttons to work in any GUI. The classes `Canvas` and `Composite` enable you to use drawing primitives to build a custom GUI component. What's most significant about this list is that it includes `java.awt.Container`, which means you can build a new drawable area and add it to an existing `Container`. The AWT supplies a variety of subclasses of `Container`, including `Panel`, `ScrollPane`, and `Window`.

`Window`, in turn, has two subclasses in the AWT: `Dialog` and `Frame`. (Each of those classes has further subclasses, but they're not a concern right now.) To add a GUI to an application, you must supply a top-level `Frame` into which the application can add `Components`, as is done in line 18 of Listing 37.1:

```
class HelloApplicationFrame extends Frame
```

NOTE If you run `HelloApplication` as an application, you invoke `main()`, which starts by making a new `HelloApplicationFrame`, and then transfers control to it. If you load `HelloApplication` as an applet, the browser and the Java runtime work together to make a new frame inside the browser window. Then the Java runtime calls the applet's `init()`, `start()`, and `paint()` methods.

Introducing the JDK 1.1 Delegation Event Model

Much of the work of writing a user interface has to do with communication. If the operating system detects a key being pressed or a mouse button coming up, it must notify the right application. The application, in turn, needs to find out which components are interested in that activity and send them a message. Starting with JDK 1.1, Sun introduced a new way of communicating information about events: the *delegation event model*. Prior to JDK 1.1 the model was, well, different. Don't worry about how the user interface worked in JDK 1.0—it's gone for good. Do be aware that the mechanism did change; if you have occasion to read old code or you have old books on Java, don't copy the way they do things. Its use is discouraged in JDK 1.1 or later because it doesn't support some of the newest features (such as Java's component model, JavaBeans). When you write code for use with SDK 1.3, you should use the new (JDK 1.1) event model.

NOTE JavaBeans is an advanced topic not covered in this book. To learn more about Beans, see Chapters 19 and 20 of *Using Java 1.2* (Que, 1998), or read *Sams Teach Yourself JavaBeans in 21 Days* (Sams, 1997).

So how does the delegation event model work? Every element of communication between the GUI and the program is defined as an *event*. Application classes register their interest in particular events from particular components by asking the component to add its *listener* to a list. When the event occurs, the event source notifies all registered listeners.

Two kinds of events exist: low-level events and semantic events. All of them are derived from `java.awt.AWTEvent`. A low-level event is concerned with the physical aspects of the user interface—mouse clicks, key presses, and so on. Semantic events are based on low-level events. To choose a menu item, for example, a user might click the menu bar, and then click a menu item. To "click" means to press the mouse button down and then release it. This series of low-level events (mouse-down on the menu bar, mouse-up on the menu bar, mouse-down on the menu item, and mouse-up on the menu item) is combined into one semantic event.

Class `ComponentEvent` includes a special type of event that is not used with the delegation event model: `PaintEvent`. A `PaintEvent` signals that the operating system wants to redraw a portion of the user interface. A component must override `paint()` or `update()` to make sure it handles the `PaintEvent` correctly.

Look at line 23 of Listing 37.1:

```
addWindowListener(new HelloWindowAdapter());
```

This line is part of `HelloApplicationFrame`'s constructor. As the new `Frame` is being built, this line tells the `Frame` that it is interested in certain events. Rather than notify it directly, however, the constructor tells it to send the notifications to an *adapter*—a convenience class that handles only one kind of event. Our adapter is called `HelloWindowAdapter`—it's an instance of `WindowAdapter`, which is interested in `WindowEvents`. When the frame sends a `WindowEvent`, `HelloWindowAdapter` looks to see if the message is `windowClosing`. If it isn't, `HelloWindowAdapter` ignores it, but if it is, the program starts the process of shutting down.

Because `HelloApplication` is written as both an applet and an application, it begins its shutdown by calling the methods a browser calls when it wants to shut down an applet—`stop()` and `destroy()`. Finally it calls `exit()`, ending the application and enabling the `Frame` to close.

Class `AWTEvent` also includes semantic events:

- **`ActionEvent`**—Notifies your program about component-specific actions such as button clicks
- **`AdjustmentEvent`**—Tells you that a scrollbar has been adjusted
- **`ItemEvent`**—Notifies your program when the user interacts with a choice, list, or check box
- **`TextEvent`**—Tells you when the user changes text in a `TextArea` or `TextField` component

NOTE Many user actions, such as mouse clicks, send events at both the low level and the semantic level. If you move your mouse onto a button and click the mouse button, you'll get a series of `MouseEvents`: one for when the mouse enters the component, one for the button press, one for the button release, and one for the click itself. You'll also get a single `ActionEvent` from the button saying that it was clicked. Unless you need fine-grained control of the user interface, listen for semantic events.

Drawing and Adding—Constructing the User Interface

In Listing 37.1, the applet's `paint` method was implemented by calling `drawString()` on the `Graphics` object. The `drawString()` method is one of the drawing primitives that has been available in Java from its earliest days. `Graphics`' drawing methods also include

- `draw3DRect()`
- `drawArc()`
- `drawBytes()`
- `drawChars()`
- `drawImage()`
- `drawLine()`
- `drawOval()`
- `drawPolygon()`
- `drawPolyline()`
- `drawRect()`
- `drawRoundRect()`

`Graphics` also supports a whole range of `fill...`, `get...`, and `set...` methods. Much of the time, however, you're less interested in the image that appears onscreen than in the controls, such as `Buttons` and `TextFields` (which are implemented as `Components`). To add controls to your `Container`, you call the `Container`'s `add()` method. See line 27 of Listing 37.1:

```
add(fApplet);
```

Listing 37.3 shows a more elaborate version of Listing 37.1. In this program, you see more AWT components at work: a `Button`, a `TextField`, a `Checkbox`, a `Choice`, and several `Labels`.

TIP You might have noticed that the AWT doesn't include *radio buttons*—a group of buttons designed so that, at most, one selection is active. To make radio buttons, just build a `CheckboxGroup`—it's documented in the SDK documentation.

Listing 37.3 *HelloPlus.java*—This Version of the Application/Applet Has Some Working AWT Components

```
import java.applet.*;
import java.awt.*;
import java.awt.event.*;

public class HelloPlus extends Applet {
  private Button fButton;
  private TextField fTextField;
  private Label fLabelForTextField;
  private Checkbox fCheckbox;
  private OKDialog fDialog;
  private Label fLabelForChoice;

  public static void main(String[] args) {
    HelloApplicationFrame theApplication =
      new HelloApplicationFrame("Hello Application");
    theApplication.setSize(200,200);
    theApplication.show();
  }

  public void init() {
    add (new Label("Hello, World!"));

    fTextField = new TextField("TextField");
    add(fTextField);
    fLabelForTextField = new Label("Your text is TextField");
    add(fLabelForTextField);

    setBackground(java.awt.Color.red);
    fButton = new Button("White");
    fButton.setBackground(java.awt.Color.white);
    add(fButton);

    fCheckbox = new Checkbox("Checkbox");
    add(fCheckbox);
    fDialog = OKDialog.makeDialog("You clicked the checkbox!");
    Choice theChoice = new Choice();
    theChoice.addItem("Choice Item 1");
    theChoice.addItem("Choice Item 2");
    theChoice.addItem("Choice Item 3");
    add(theChoice);
    fLabelForChoice = new Label("You haven't chosen anything");
    add(fLabelForChoice);

    fButton.addActionListener(new ActionListener(){
      public void actionPerformed(ActionEvent e) {
        if (fButton.getLabel() == "White") {
          setBackground(java.awt.Color.white);
          fButton.setLabel("Red");
        }
```

Listing 37.3 Continued

```
        else {
          setBackground(java.awt.Color.red);
          fButton.setLabel("White");
        }
        Component theComponents[] = getComponents();
        try {
          if (theComponents.length == 0)
            throw (new AWTException("Cannot find the components"));
        } catch (AWTException theException) {
          System.err.println("Exception: " + theException.getMessage());
          theException.printStackTrace();
          System.exit(1);
        }
        for (short theIndex = 0;
             theIndex < theComponents.length; theIndex++)
               getComponent(theIndex).setBackground(getBackground());
        if (fButton.getLabel() == "White")
          fButton.setBackground(java.awt.Color.white);
        else
          fButton.setBackground(java.awt.Color.red);
      }
    });

    fTextField.addActionListener(new ActionListener() {
      public void actionPerformed(ActionEvent e) {
         fLabelForTextField.setText("Your text is " +
                                    fTextField.getText());
      }
    });

    fCheckbox.addItemListener(new ItemListener(){
      public void itemStateChanged(ItemEvent e) {
        if (fCheckbox.getState())  // the box is checked
          fDialog.show();
        else
          fDialog.setVisible(false);
      }
    });

    theChoice.addItemListener(new ItemListener() {
      public void itemStateChanged(ItemEvent e) {
        try {
          Object theSelectedItem[] =
            e.getItemSelectable().getSelectedObjects();
          if (theSelectedItem.length != 1)
            throw(
              new AWTException(
                "Number of selected items in choice is " +
                                 theSelectedItem.length));
          fLabelForChoice.setText("Your choice is " +
```

Listing 37.3 Continued

```
              theSelectedItem[0]);
          } catch (AWTException theException) {
            System.err.println("Exception: " + theException.getMessage());
            theException.printStackTrace();
            System.exit(1);
          } // end catch
        } // end method
      }); // end addItemListener
  } // end init

} // end HelloPlus

class HelloApplicationFrame extends Frame {
  private HelloPlus fApplet;

  public HelloApplicationFrame(String name) {
    super(name);
    addWindowListener(new HelloWindowAdapter());
    fApplet = new HelloPlus();
    fApplet.init();
    fApplet.start();
    add(fApplet);
  }

  // We're still within HelloApplicationFrame;
  // these adapters are inner classes
  class HelloWindowAdapter extends WindowAdapter {
    public void windowClosing(WindowEvent e) {
      fApplet.stop();
      fApplet.destroy();
      System.exit(0);
    }
  } // end inner class HelloWindowAdapter
} // end HelloApplicationFrame

class OKDialog extends Dialog {
  private Button fOKButton;
  static private Frame fFrame;

  private OKDialog(Frame theParent, String theMessage) {
    super(theParent, true); // call Dialog's modal constructor
    fOKButton = new Button("OK");
    add(fOKButton, BorderLayout.CENTER );
    Label theMessageLabel = new Label(theMessage);
    add (theMessageLabel, BorderLayout.NORTH );
    pack();

    fOKButton.addActionListener(new ActionListener(){
      public void actionPerformed(ActionEvent e) {
        setVisible( false );
      }
```

Listing 37.3 Continued

```
      }
      );

    } // end constructor

    static public OKDialog makeDialog(String theMessage) {
      if (fFrame == null)
        fFrame = new Frame();
      OKDialog theResult = new OKDialog(fFrame, theMessage);
      fFrame.setSize(theResult.getSize().width,
                     theResult.getSize().height);
      return theResult;
    }
  } // end OKDialog class
```

If you compile `HelloPlus.java` and run it as an application or as an applet, your screen will resemble Figure 37.5. This section describes how the code in `HelloPlus.java` works.

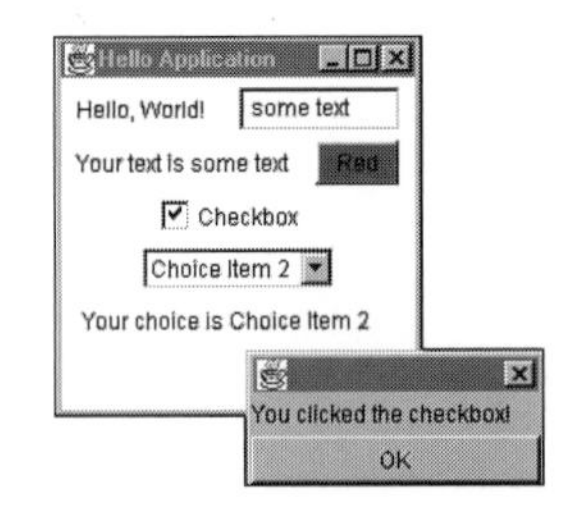

FIGURE 37.5
By default, `HelloPlus` fills a 200×200 pixel panel.

The first difference you'll notice between `HelloPlus` and `HelloApplication` is that several data members have been added to the class: `fButton`, `fTextField`, and so on. Often you'll need to refer to user-interface components during the life of the program—it's convenient to have all the components available as class members. (If you don't want to carry these references around in the class, you don't have to—`theChoice` is an example of a user interface component that is not referenced as an instance variable.)

The biggest area of change is in `init()`. `init()` is used to build the user interface—that way, the components are added to the applet when it's running as an applet, and the application frame when it's running as an application.

Understanding *fTextField* and *fLabelForTextField* `init()` is started by adding the ubiquitous Hello, World! label. Then a new `TextField` is instantiated and added to the interface. This is followed with a new `Label`, which is likewise added to the interface. Now go down to lines 72 through 77:

```
fTextField.addActionListener(new ActionListener() {
       public void actionPerformed(ActionEvent e) {
```

```
        fLabelForTextField.setText("Your text is " +
                                   fTextField.getText());
    }
  });
```

Here's a construct you haven't seen before. Because a `TextField` was added, you can get a semantic event—the `ActionEvent`—which has only one method: `actionPerformed()`. Although the action differs from one component to the next, the method for listening to these events is the same. You don't need an adapter because there's only one method in the event. Instead, you can declare a new `ActionListener` and define it right here inside `addActionListener()`. In this case, the body of the method is quite simple:


```
fLabelForTextField.setText("Your text is " +
                           fTextField.getText());
```

When you change the text in the text field and press Enter, the Java runtime sends an `ActionEvent` to your listening program, which changes the text in `fLabelForTextField`.

TIP The components in `HelloPlus.java` don't need adapters because their events have only one method. If you want to receive events with more than one method, consider using adapters–abstract classes that implement an interface and "stub out" the methods.

Understanding *fButton* This version of the program starts with a red background on the frame and a white button labeled White. When you click the button, it sends an `ActionEvent` to the listening program. The definition of the listener starts at line 43 of Listing 37.3:

```
fButton.addActionListener(new ActionListener(){
      public void actionPerformed(ActionEvent e) {
        if (fButton.getLabel() == "White") {
          setBackground(java.awt.Color.white);
          fButton.setLabel("Red");
        }
        else {
          setBackground(java.awt.Color.red);
          fButton.setLabel("White");
        }
        Component theComponents[] = getComponents();
        try {
          if (theComponents.length == 0)
            throw (new AWTException("Cannot find the components"));
        } catch (AWTException theException) {
          System.err.println("Exception: " + theException.getMessage());
          theException.printStackTrace();
          System.exit(1);
        }
        for (short theIndex = 0;
             theIndex < theComponents.length; theIndex++)
               getComponent(theIndex).setBackground(getBackground());
        if (fButton.getLabel() == "White")
          fButton.setBackground(java.awt.Color.white);
```

```
        else
          fButton.setBackground(java.awt.Color.red);
      }
    });
```

The button click is handled in three steps:

1. Change the `Container`'s background and the label of the button to reflect the `Container`'s new state.
2. Step through each `Component` in the `Container`, setting its background to match the background of the `Container`.
3. Because step 2 changed the background of the button, change it back to match the button's label.

Understanding *fCheckbox* and *fDialog* The `Checkbox`, named `fCheckbox`, is added in the same way as the other components you've seen, but there is something different—a new `Dialog`. The plan is to have a modal dialog box come up whenever the end user checks the `Checkbox`, so you have to go through a couple of extra steps to make this work.

NOTE Unlike `Button` and `TextField`, a `Checkbox` doesn't send an `ActionEvent`. Instead, it sends an `ItemEvent`. The principle is the same as the `ActionEvent`, however—you just instantiate a new `ItemListener`.

If you examine the documentation for class `Dialog`, you'll see that all its constructors need an owner—a `Frame` or another `Dialog` that serves as the parent of the new `Dialog` in the `Window` hierarchy. If you're writing a pure application, you can use the application's `Frame` as the owner of the `Dialog`. In this case, the program can be called as either an applet or an application. An `Applet` is a `Panel`, not a `Frame`, so it must start up its own `Frame` to serve as the parent.

At the bottom of the `HelloPlus.java` listing, you'll see a definition of class `OKDialog`. After the constructor (which is private), you'll see a `makeDialog()` factory method:

```
static public OKDialog makeDialog(String theMessage) {
    if (fFrame == null)
      fFrame = new Frame();
    OKDialog theResult = new OKDialog(fFrame, theMessage);
    fFrame.setSize(theResult.getSize().width,
                   theResult.getSize().height);
    return theResult;
  }
} // end OKDialog class
```

NOTE A factory method returns a new object based on an existing object. For example, `java.awt.geom.Arc2D` supports `makeBounds()`, a factory method that returns a new `Rectangle2D` based on the bounding rectangle of the arc.

The class OKDialog has a static Frame member fFrame. When makeDialog() is first called, it instantiates a new Frame and assigns it to fFrame. Next, makeDialog() instantiates a new OKDialog, using fFrame as the parent. It scales the Frame to the same size as the OKDialog and returns a reference to the OKDialog for use by the calling class.

The OKDialog constructor instantiates a button and a label, adds them to the dialog, and then calls pack() to shrink the dialog window down to a size that contains the components. The listener attached to the dialog's button makes the dialog window invisible.

NOTE You might have noticed that the calls to add() in OKDialog() include strings. For example, the message label is added by this line:

```
add(theMessageLabel, BorderLayout.NORTH);
```

These strings are part of the BorderLayout, which is described in the next section.

Understanding *theChoice* In Java, a Choice is a pop-up list that displays one item at a time. This code includes a Choice (called theChoice—it's a local variable, not an instance variable) and a matching Label. Then an ItemListener is added. When the ItemListener gets an itemStateChanged() event, getItemSelectable() is used to get a reference back to theChoice and then call getSelectedObjects() to get an array of selected items. If theChoice is working correctly, you should be able to get back only a single item. (An exception is thrown if that condition doesn't hold.) Finally, fLabelForChoice is modified to reflect the user's choice.

Working with Layouts

Recall that several of the sample applets shown in Chapter 36 use layout managers such as CardLayout or GridLayout to manage the placement of components on the screen. You can see the effect of a layout manager by resizing the HelloPlus window. Figure 37.6 shows a maximized window in which the components have room to spread out; in Figure 37.7, the window is tall and narrow—the components appear one above the other.

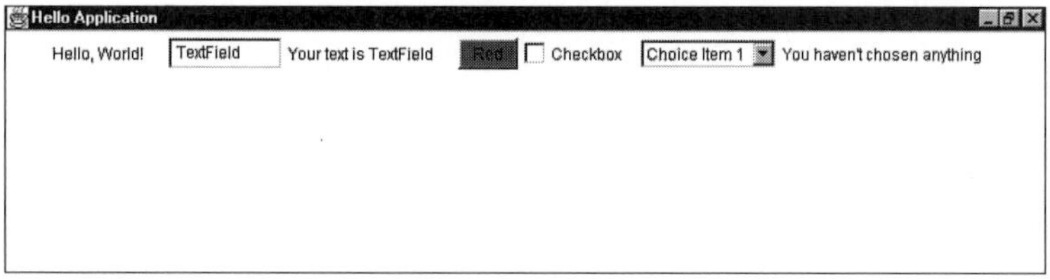

Hello Application

Hello, World! TextField Your text is TextField Red Checkbox Choice Item 1 You haven't chosen anything

FIGURE 37.6
When the components have enough room, they're laid out one beside the other.

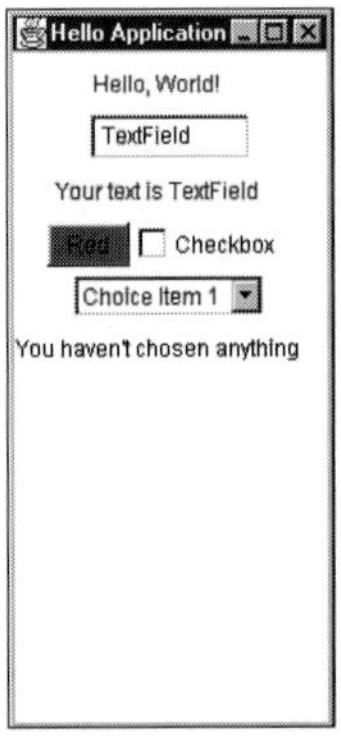

FIGURE 37.7
When the window is narrow, the components flow one above the next.

You don't have to worry about the precise location of every component or whether the user is working on a 640×480 screen or an older Macintosh with a 9-inch monitor. That's because every Java window has an associated `LayoutManager`. If you don't specify the manager, Java supplies one for you. This section walks you through the standard layouts:

- **`FlowLayout`**—The components are added left to right, top to bottom. This layout is the default layout for `Panel` and its derived classes, including `Applet`.
- **`GridLayout`**—Similar to `FlowLayout`, but each component gets an equal-sized cell.
- **`BorderLayout`**—Divides the container into five areas: North, South, East, West, and Center. This layout is the default layout for `Windows` (except special-purpose `Windows` such as `FileDialog`).
- **`CardLayout`**—Used to display one component at a time, like a stack of index cards.
- **`GridBagLayout`**—A flexible (and complicated) layout used when none of the other layout managers will do.

NOTE By default, Java supplies a layout manager for every new `Container`. It's possible to turn it off (by calling `setLayout(null)`) and then use absolute positioning to lay out your components. That's a poor idea, however–your application won't display correctly on different-sized monitors.

TIP If you find that none of the standard layout managers meet your needs, you can make your own implementation of `LayoutManager2`. (`LayoutManager`, a simpler class, doesn't support a `constraints` object, so it's less useful.)

Using *FlowLayout*

Figures 37.6 and 37.7 showed how `HelloPlus.java` looks when you use the default layout for `Panel`, `FlowLayout`. (Recall that an applet is a kind of panel.) If you're happy with this design—all the components laid out left to right, top to bottom, with each component taking up whatever amount of space it requires—you don't have to do anything. Just call `add()` to place each component into the `Container`.

If you're working in a `Window` where the default layout is `BorderLayout`, you'll need to change the layout manager if you want a `FlowLayout`. Just write

```
setLayout(new FlowLayout());
```

before you `add()` any components.

Using *GridLayout*

Figure 37.8 shows how HelloPlus looks in a `GridLayout`. A `GridLayout` is similar to a `FlowLayout`, but each component gets the same size cell as all the others. To apply a `GridLayout` to `HelloPlus`, add this line to the top of `init()`:

```
setLayout(new GridLayout(rows, columns));
```

where `rows` gives the number of rows and `columns` gives the number of columns. If you set either value to zero, Java will use as many of that dimension as necessary to display all the components in the layout.

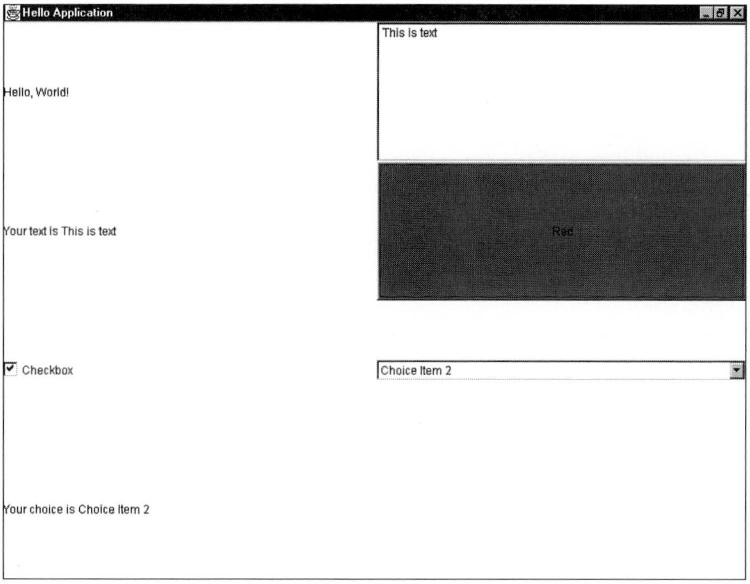

FIGURE 37.8
This grid was produced with `rows=0` and `columns=2`.

NOTE If you specify both the number of rows and the number of columns and then add more components than the product of those two numbers, the layout manager will behave as though you had specified a zero for the number of columns. I don't recommend that you rely on this feature–it's not documented, so Sun could change the behavior in the future.

Using *BorderLayout*

`BorderLayout` is particularly appropriate when you have one large component and several smaller ones because you can place the large component in the center position. Figure 37.9 illustrates the general design of `BorderLayout`, and Figure 37.10 shows `HelloPlus.java` in this layout.

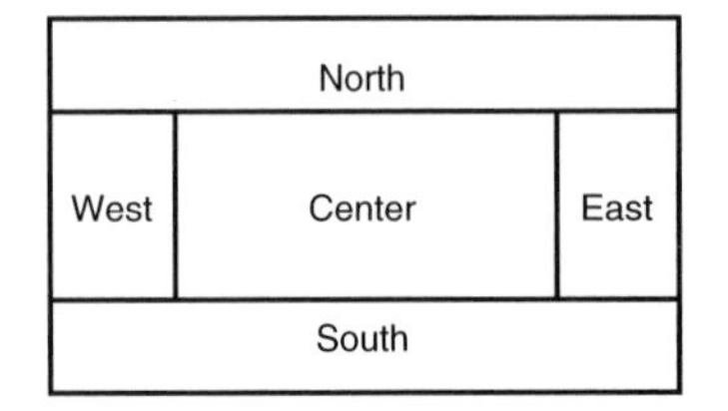

FIGURE 37.9 Think of `BorderLayout` as a compass, with the largest component in the center.

FIGURE 37.10 You must put some components into panels to lay out more than five components in a `BorderLayout`.

To modify `HelloPlus.java` to use a `BorderLayout`, you need to make three changes:

- Set the layout to `BorderLayout` in `init()`.
- Assemble some of the components into groups on `Panels`.
- Change `add()` so that it passes the location `String`.

Here's a code snippet that shows these changes in **bold**:

```
public void init() {
    setLayout(new BorderLayout());

    add (new Label("Hello, World!"), BorderLayout.NORTH);

    Panel theWestPanel = new Panel();
    fTextField = new TextField("TextField");
    theWestPanel.add(fTextField);
    fLabelForTextField = new Label("Your text is TextField");
    theWestPanel.add(fLabelForTextField);
    add(theWestPanel, BorderLayout.WEST);

    setBackground(java.awt.Color.red);
    fButton = new Button("White");
    fButton.setBackground(java.awt.Color.white);
    add(fButton, BorderLayout.CENTER);
```

```
fCheckbox = new Checkbox("Checkbox");
add(fCheckbox, BorderLayout.EAST);
fDialog = OKDialog.makeDialog("You clicked the checkbox!");

Panel theSouthPanel = new Panel();

Choice theChoice = new Choice();
theChoice.addItem("Choice Item 1");
theChoice.addItem("Choice Item 2");
theChoice.addItem("Choice Item 3");
theSouthPanel.add(theChoice);
fLabelForChoice = new Label("You haven't chosen anything");
theSouthPanel.add(fLabelForChoice);
add(theSouthPanel, BorderLayout.SOUTH);
```


TIP At some point you'll change the layout and discover that your components are no longer visible. The reason is that you *must* use the two-parameter version of `add()` when you add components to a `BorderLayout`. Double-check the `Constraint`, too—the only valid `Constraints` are `BorderLayout`.NORTH, SOUTH, EAST, WEST, and CENTER. If you leave off the `Constraint` or mistype it, you might not see your component.

Using *CardLayout*

Figure 37.11 shows how `HelloPlus.java` looks when you switch to `CardLayout`. Like `BorderLayout`, you must do more than just call `setLayout()`. `CardLayout` shows one component at a time; you call `next()` and `previous()` to move from one card to another. In the design shown in Figure 37.11, there's a `BorderLayout` for the application, and then a `CardLayout` in a `Panel` in the South position to hold the contents. Two buttons are in a `Panel` in the North position; by clicking those buttons you can issue calls to `next()` and `previous()`. The code changes from HelloPlus are

```
public void init() {

    setLayout(new BorderLayout());
    Panel theControls = new Panel();
    Button thePreviousButton = new Button("Previous");
    theControls.add(thePreviousButton);
    Button theNextButton = new Button("Next");
    theControls.add(theNextButton);

    add(theControls, BorderLayout.NORTH);

    fContents = new Panel();
    fContents.setLayout(new CardLayout());

    fContents.add (new Label("Hello, World!"), "Hello");

    Panel theTextPanel = new Panel();
    fTextField = new TextField("TextField");
```

```
theTextPanel.add(fTextField);
fLabelForTextField = new Label("Your text is TextField");
theTextPanel.add(fLabelForTextField);
fContents.add(theTextPanel, "Text");

setBackground(java.awt.Color.red);
fButton = new Button("White");
fButton.setBackground(java.awt.Color.white);
fContents.add(fButton, "Button");

fCheckbox = new Checkbox("Checkbox");
fContents.add(fCheckbox, "Checkbox");
fDialog = OKDialog.makeDialog("You clicked the checkbox!");

Panel theChoicePanel = new Panel();
Choice theChoice = new Choice();
theChoice.addItem("Choice Item 1");
theChoice.addItem("Choice Item 2");
theChoice.addItem("Choice Item 3");
theChoicePanel.add(theChoice);
fLabelForChoice = new Label("You haven't chosen anything");
theChoicePanel.add(fLabelForChoice);
fContents.add(theChoicePanel, "Choice");

add(" fContents, BorderLayout.SOUTH);

theNextButton.addActionListener(new ActionListener() {
  public void actionPerformed(ActionEvent e) {
    CardLayout theLayout = (CardLayout) fContents.getLayout();
    theLayout.next(fContents);
}});

thePreviousButton.addActionListener(new ActionListener() {
  public void actionPerformed(ActionEvent e) {
    CardLayout theLayout = (CardLayout) fContents.getLayout();
    theLayout.previous(fContents);
}});
```

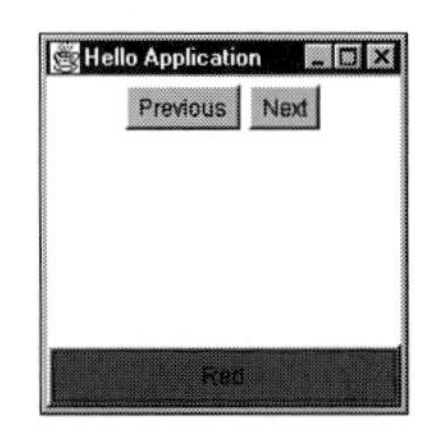

FIGURE 37.11
You can use `CardLayout` to simulate a deck of index cards, with one card showing at a time.

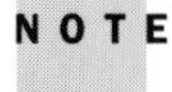

NOTE In addition to `next()` and `previous()`, the `CardLayout` supports `first()`, `last()`, and `show()`. The latter enables you to display a card by name.

Using *GridBagLayout*

Although you can control such factors as alignment and horizontal and vertical gap in the other layout managers, the `GridBagLayout` gives you the ultimate in flexibility. At its simplest, `GridBagLayout` works much like a grid, except that it puts each component in a cell of its preferred size. The total area that a component occupies is called its *display area*. You specify suggestions—called `GridBagConstraints`—that further control how the layout will appear.

The `GridBagConstraints` class has several variables to control the placement of a component:

- `gridx` and `gridy` are the coordinates of the cell where the next component should be placed. (If the component occupies more than one cell, these coordinates are for the upper-left cell of the component.) The upper-left corner of the `GridBagLayout` is at 0,0. The default value for both `gridx` and `gridy` is `GridBagConstraints.RELATIVE`, which for `gridx` means the cell to the right of the last component that was added; for `gridy` it means the cell just below the last component added.
- `gridwidth` and `gridheight` tell how many cells wide and how many cells tall a component should be. The default for both `gridwidth` and `gridheight` is 1. If you want this component to be the last one on a row, use `GridBagConstraint.REMAINDER` for the `gridwidth`. (Use this same value for `gridheight` if this component should be the last one in a column.) Use `GridBagConstraint.RELATIVE` if the component should be the next-to-last component in a row or column.
- `fill` tells the `GridBagLayout` what to do when a component is smaller than its display area. The default value, `GridBagConstraint.NONE`, causes the component size to remain unchanged. `GridBagConstraint.HORIZONTAL` causes the component to be widened to take up its whole display area horizontally while leaving its height unchanged. `GridBagConstraint.VERTICAL` causes the component to be stretched vertically while leaving the width unchanged. `GridBagConstraint.BOTH` causes the component to be stretched in both directions to completely fill its display area.
- `ipadx` and `ipady` tell the `GridBagLayout` how many pixels to add to the size of the component in the x and y direction. The pixels are added on both sides of the component, so an `ipadx` of 4 causes the size of a component to be increased by 4 on the left and also 4 on the right. Remember, the component size grows by twice the amount of padding because the padding is added to both sides. The default for both `ipadx` and `ipady` is 0.
- `insets` is an instance of an `Insets` class and indicates how much blank space to leave between the borders of a component and the edges of its display area. The `Insets` class has separate values for the top, bottom, left, and right insets.
- `anchor` is used when a component is smaller than its display area. It indicates where the component should be placed within the display area. The default value is `GridBagConstraint.CENTER`, which indicates that the component should be in the center of the display area. The other values are all compass points:

GridbagConstraints.NORTH, GridBagConstraints.NORTHEAST, GridBagConstraints.EAST, GridBagConstraints.SOUTHEAST, GridBagConstraints.SOUTH, GridBagConstraints.SOUTHWEST, GridBagConstraints.WEST, and GridBagConstraints.NORTHWEST. As with the BorderLayout class, NORTH indicates the top of the screen; EAST is to the right.

- weightx and weighty are used to set relative sizes of components. A component with a weightx of 2.0, for example, takes up twice the horizontal space of a component with a weightx of 1.0. Because these values are relative, no difference exists between all components in a row having a weight of 1.0 or a weight of 3.0. You should assign a weight to at least one component in each direction; otherwise, the GridBagLayout squeezes your components toward the center of the container.

Figure 37.12 shows HelloPlus.java laid out using a GridBagLayout. The following code produced this layout:

```
public void init() {
    GridBagLayout theGridBag = new GridBagLayout();
    setLayout(theGridBag);
    GridBagConstraints theConstraints =
      new GridBagConstraints();

    // have all components expand to their largest size
    theConstraints.fill = GridBagConstraints.BOTH;

    // set the first label to span a row
    theConstraints.gridwidth = GridBagConstraints.REMAINDER;
    theConstraints.weightx = 1.0;

    Label theHelloLabel = new Label("Hello, World!", java.awt.Label.CENTER);
    theGridBag.setConstraints(theHelloLabel, theConstraints);
    add(theHelloLabel);

    // the text field and its label are a row
    theConstraints.gridwidth = GridBagConstraints.RELATIVE;
    theConstraints.weightx = 1.0;
    fTextField = new TextField("TextField");
    theGridBag.setConstraints(fTextField, theConstraints);
    add(fTextField);
    fLabelForTextField = new Label("Your text is TextField");
    theConstraints.gridwidth = GridBagConstraints.REMAINDER;
    theConstraints.weightx = 0.0;
    theGridBag.setConstraints(fLabelForTextField, theConstraints);
    add(fLabelForTextField);

    // make the button double-height
    setBackground(java.awt.Color.red);
    theConstraints.gridwidth = 1;
    theConstraints.gridheight = 2;
    theConstraints.weightx = 0.0;
    theConstraints.weighty = 1.0;
```

```
fButton = new Button("White");
theGridBag.setConstraints(fButton, theConstraints);
fButton.setBackground(java.awt.Color.white);
add(fButton);

// let the checkbox end its own row
theConstraints.gridwidth = GridBagConstraints.REMAINDER;
theConstraints.gridheight = 1;
fCheckbox = new Checkbox("Checkbox");
theConstraints.weightx = theConstraints.weighty = 0.0;
theGridBag.setConstraints(fCheckbox, theConstraints);
add(fCheckbox);
fDialog = OKDialog.makeDialog("You clicked the checkbox!");

// and the choice and corresponding label span another row
Choice theChoice = new Choice();
theChoice.addItem("Choice Item 1");
theChoice.addItem("Choice Item 2");
theChoice.addItem("Choice Item 3");
theConstraints.gridwidth = GridBagConstraints.RELATIVE;
theConstraints.weightx = 1.0;
theGridBag.setConstraints(theChoice, theConstraints);
add(theChoice);
fLabelForChoice = new Label("You haven't chosen anything");
theConstraints.gridwidth = GridBagConstraints.REMAINDER;
theConstraints.weightx = 0.0;
theGridBag.setConstraints(fLabelForChoice, theConstraints);
add(fLabelForChoice);
```

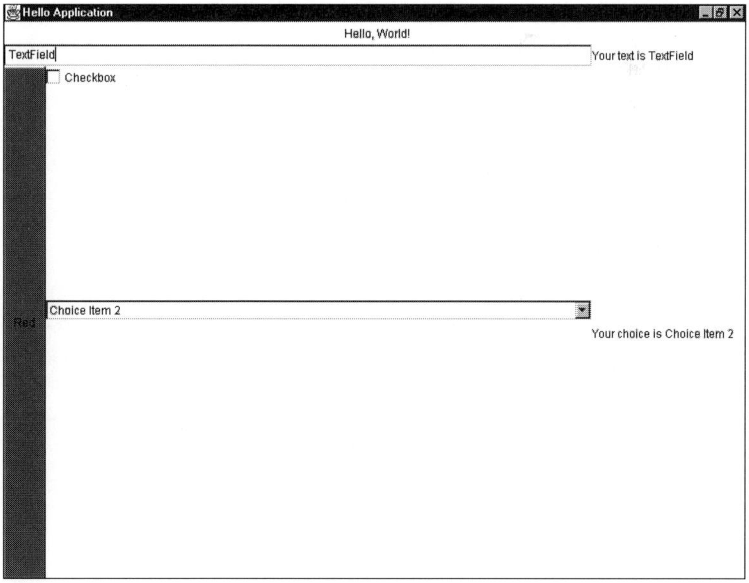

FIGURE 37.12 Use the data members of the `GridBagConstraint` to set up each row of a `GridBagLayout`.

As you can see, most of the changes have to do with manipulating the data members of the `GridBagConstraint` as you move from row to row and cell to cell.

Adding Menus to Frames

You first saw a frame in Listing 37.1. You can attach a `MenuBar` class to a frame to provide drop-down menu capabilities. To make a menu bar and add it to a frame, write

```
MenuBar myMenuBar = new MenuBar();
myFrame.setMenuBar( myMenuBar );
```

After you have a menu bar, you can add menus to it. The following code fragment makes a menu called File and adds it to the menu bar:

```
Menu fileMenu = new Menu( "File" );
myMenuBar.add( fileMenu );
```

Some windowing systems enable you to make menus that stay up after you release the mouse button. These are referred to as *tear-off* menus. You can specify that a menu is a tear-off menu when you make it:

```
// true indicates it can be torn off
Menu tearOffMenu = new Menu( "Tear Me Off", true );
```

In addition to adding submenus, you will want to add menu items to your menus. ***Menu items*** are the parts of a menu the user actually selects. Menus are used to contain menu items as well as submenus. The File menu on many systems, for example, contains menu items such as New, Open, Save, and Save As. You can add menu items to a menu in two ways. You can add an item name by writing

```
// Add an "Open" option to the file menu
fileMenu.add( "Open" );
```

You can also add an instance of a `MenuItem` class to a menu:

```
// Make a "Save" menu item
MenuItem saveMenuItem = new MenuItem( "Save" );

// Add the "Save" option to the file menu
fileMenu.add( saveMenuItem );
```

You can enable and disable menu items by using the `setEnabled` method. When you disable a menu item, it still appears on the menu, but it usually appears in gray (depending on the windowing system). You cannot select disabled menu items. This is the format for `setEnabled`:

```
// Disable the save option from the file menu
saveMenuItem.setEnabled( false );

// Enable the save option again
saveMenuItem.setEnabled( true );
```

In addition to menu items, you can add submenus and menu separators to a menu. A separator is a line that appears on the menu to separate sections of the menu. To add a separator, just call the `addSeparator` method:

```
fileMenu.addSeparator();
```

To add a submenu, make a new instance of a menu and add it to the current menu:

```
Menu printSubmenu = new Menu( "Print" );
fileMenu.add( printSubmenu );
printSubmenu.add( "Print Preview" );
        // Add print preview as option on Print menu
printSubmenu.add( "Print Document" );
        // Add print document as option on Print menu
```


You can also add special check box menu items. These items function like check box buttons. The first time you select one, it becomes checked or "on." The next time you select it, it becomes unchecked or "off." The code to add a check box menu item is

```
CheckboxMenuItem autoSaveOption = new CheckboxMenuItem( "Auto-save" );
fileMenu.add( autoSaveOption );
```

You can check to see whether a check box menu item is checked with `getState`:

```
if ( autoSaveOption.getState() )
{
     // autoSaveOption is checked, or "on"
}
else
{
     // autoSaveOption is off
}
```

You can set the current state of a check box menu item with `setState`:

```
autoSaveOption.setState( true );
```

Typically, menus are added to a menu bar in a left-to-right fashion. Some windowing systems, such as Microsoft Windows, have a special Help menu that is on the far right of a menu bar. You can add such a menu to your menu bar with the `setHelpMenu` method:

```
Menu helpMenu = new Menu();
myMenuBar.setHelpMenu( helpMenu );
```

Using AWT Menus Whenever a menu item is selected, it generates an `ActionEvent`. Just add an `ActionListener` for each menu item to handle events.

Listing 37.4 shows an application that sets up a simple File menu with New, Open, and Save menu items, a check box called Auto-Save, and a Print submenu with two menu items on it.

Listing 37.4 *MenuApplication*—Add Menus and Menu Items to a Menu in a Frame

```
import java.awt.*;
import java.applet.*;

public class MenuApplication extends Frame {
  public static void main( String[] args ) {
    new MenuApplication();
  }

  public MenuApplication() {
    //  Construct the Frame
    super( "Menu Example" );

    // Add the menu bar
    MenuBar theMenuBar = new MenuBar();
    setMenuBar( theMenuBar );

    // Make the file menu and add it to the menubar...
    Menu aFileMenu = new Menu( "File" );
    theMenuBar.add( aFileMenu );

    // Add the New and Open menuitems
    aFileMenu.add( new MenuItem( "New" ) );
    aFileMenu.add( new MenuItem( "Open" ) );

    // Add a (disabled) Save menuitem
     MenuItem theSaveMenuItem = new MenuItem( "Save" );
     theSaveMenuItem.setEnabled( false );
     aFileMenu.add( theSaveMenuItem );

    // Add an Auto-Save checkbox, followed by a separator
    aFileMenu.add( new CheckboxMenuItem( "Auto-Save" ) );
    aFileMenu.addSeparator();

    // Add the Print submenu
    Menu thePrintSubmenu = new Menu( "Print" );
    aFileMenu.add( thePrintSubmenu );
    thePrintSubmenu.add( "Print Preview" );
    thePrintSubmenu.add( "Print Document" );

    // Resize the frame before it can be shown
    setSize( 300, 200 );

    // Make the frame appear on the screen
    show();
  }
}
```

Figure 37.13 shows the output from the `MenuApplication` program, with the Print Document option in the process of being selected.

FIGURE 37.13
The AWT provides several popular menu features, including checked menu items, disabled menu items, and separators.

AWT Dialogs

Like frames, dialogs are windows. Unlike frames, dialogs are designed to be pop-up windows that are not quite as flexible as frames. Dialogs are used for things such as "Are you sure you want to quit?" pop-ups, better known as message boxes. You can set a dialog to be either modal or non-modal. The term *modal* means the dialog box blocks input to other windows while it is being shown. This technique is useful for dialogs in which you want to stop everything and get a crucial question answered, such as "Are you sure you want to quit?" An example of a non-modal dialog box is a control panel that changes settings in an application while the application continues to run.

Making Dialogs To make a dialog, you first must have a frame. A dialog cannot belong directly to an applet. However, an applet can instantiate a frame to which the dialog can then belong. You must specify whether a dialog is modal or non-modal when you instantiate it; you cannot change its modality after it has been built. The following example makes a modal dialog whose parent is `myFrame`:

```
// true means model dialog
Dialog myDialog = new Dialog( myFrame, true );
```

You can also give a dialog a title:

```
Dialog myDialog = new Dialog( myFrame, "A Non-Modal Dialog", false );
```

NOTE Because a dialog cannot belong directly to an applet, your use of dialogs might be somewhat limited. One solution is to make a dummy frame as the dialog's parent. Unfortunately, you cannot make modal dialogs this way because only the frame and its children would have their input blocked—the applet would continue on its merry way. A better solution is to use the technique shown in `HelloPlus.java` (Listing 37.3) in which you make a standalone application using frames and then have a "bootstrap" applet make a frame and run the real applet in it.

After you have instantiated a dialog, you can make it visible using the `show` method:

```
myDialog.show();
```

Dialog Features The `Dialog` class has several methods in common with the `Frame` class:

```
void setResizable( boolean );
boolean isResizable();
void setTitle(String);
String getTitle();
```

In addition, the `isModal` method returns `true` if the dialog is modal.

A Reusable OK Dialog Box Listing 37.5 shows the `OKDialog` class that provides an OK dialog box that displays a message and waits for you to click OK.

Listing 37.5 *OKDialog*—Pop Up a Simple Dialog Box with an OK Button

```
import java.awt.*;
import java.awt.event.*;

public class OKDialog extends Dialog {
  protected Button  fOKButton;
  protected static Frame  fFrame;

  public OKDialog( Frame theParent, String theMessage )
  {
    super( theParent, true );    // Call the parent's constructor

    // This Dialog box uses the GridBagLayout.
    GridBagLayout theGridBagLayout = new GridBagLayout();
    GridBagConstraints theConstraints = new GridBagConstraints();

    // Make the OK button and the message to display
    fOKButton = new Button( "OK" );
    Label aMessageLabel = new Label( theMessage );

    fOKButton.addActionListener(new ActionListener() {
      public void actionPerformed(ActionEvent e) {
        setVisible ( false );
        if (fFrame != null)
         fFrame.setVisible( false );
      }
    });

    setLayout( theGridBagLayout );

    // The message should not fill, it should be centered within this area,
with
    // some extra padding.  The gridwidth of REMAINDER means this is the only
    // thing on its row, and the gridheight of RELATIVE means there should only
    // be one thing below it.
    theConstraints.fill = GridBagConstraints.NONE;
    theConstraints.anchor = GridBagConstraints.CENTER;
    theConstraints.ipadx = 20;
    theConstraints.ipady = 20;
    theConstraints.weightx = 1.0;
    theConstraints.weighty = 1.0;
    theConstraints.gridwidth = GridBagConstraints.REMAINDER;
    theConstraints.gridheight = GridBagConstraints.RELATIVE;
    theGridBagLayout.setConstraints( aMessageLabel, theConstraints );
    add( aMessageLabel );

    // The button has no padding, no weight, takes up minimal width, and
    // is the last thing in its column.
    theConstraints.ipadx = 0;
```

Listing 37.5 Continued

```
    theConstraints.ipady = 0;
    theConstraints.weightx = 0.0;
    theConstraints.weighty = 0.0;
    theConstraints.gridwidth = 1;
    theConstraints.gridheight = GridBagConstraints.REMAINDER;
    theGridBagLayout.setConstraints( fOKButton, theConstraints );
    add( fOKButton );

    // Pack is a special window method that makes the window take up the
minimum
    // space necessary to contain its components.
    pack();
  }



  // Shortcut to make a frame automatically
  public static void makeOKDialog( String theDialogString ) {
    if ( fFrame == null )
      fFrame = new Frame( "Dialog" );
    OKDialog theOKDialog = new OKDialog( fFrame, theDialogString );

    // Shrink the frame to just fit the dialog
    fFrame.setSize( theOKDialog.getSize().width, theOKDialog.getSize().height
);

    theOKDialog.show();
  }
}
```

The `DialogApplet` in Listing 37.6 pops up an `OKDialog` whenever a button is pressed.

Listing 37.6 ***DialogApplet.java*—Test Your New *OKDialog* with This Applet**

```
import java.awt.*;
import java.awt.event.*;
import java.applet.*;

public class DialogApplet extends Applet {
  protected Button fLaunchButton;

  public void init() {
    fLaunchButton = new Button( "Show OK Dialog" );
    add( fLaunchButton );
    fLaunchButton.addActionListener( new ActionListener() {
      public void actionPerformed( ActionEvent e ) {
        doLaunchClicked(); } } );
  }

  public void doLaunchClicked() {
    OKDialog.makeOKDialog( "Press OK to dismiss this dialog" );
  }
}
```

Figure 37.14 shows the `DialogApplet` with the OK dialog popped up.

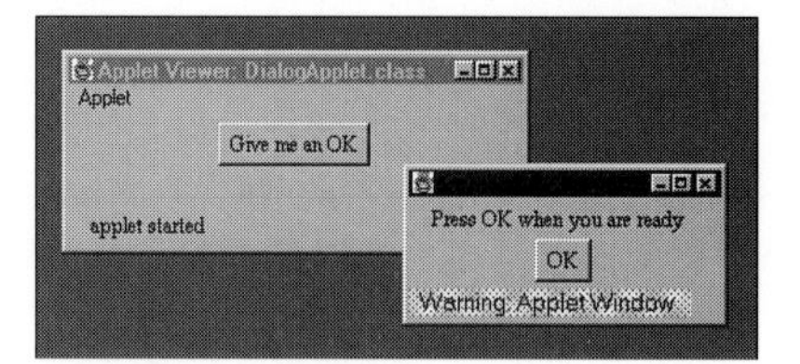

FIGURE 37.14
The `OKDialog` class makes a pop-up dialog box with an OK button.

The Swing Architecture

When Java was first introduced, the only graphical user interface (GUI) available was the Abstract Windowing Toolkit (AWT). Recall from the first section of this chapter, "Interacting with People by Using Java," that AWT components are considered to be "heavyweight" in that each Java component has a peer object from the native GUI.

Sun also offers "lightweight" components that don't have a peer object. Instead, they offer "pluggable look-and-feel." If the end user is running a Windows machine but prefers the look-and-feel of Sun's Motif interface, for example, the user can select that interface in the running application. When Sun developed these lightweight components, it did so as part of a project called "Swing," so the lightweight user interface components are usually called Swing components.

Swing components are one part of the Java Foundation Classes (JFC). Figure 37.15 illustrates the relationship of the AWT and the Swing components to the JFC.

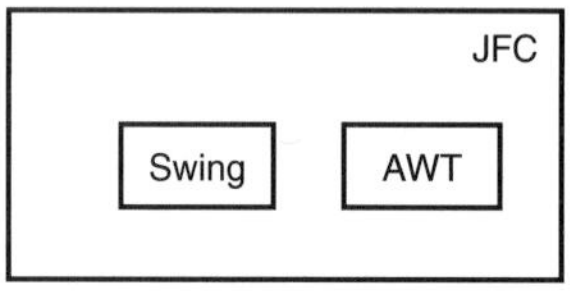

JFC
Swing AWT

FIGURE 37.15
The Swing components are the lightweight user-interface components of the JFC.

NOTE Many of the Swing components are derived from their AWT counterparts. Most developers, however, reserve the term "AWT component" for the heavyweight components, and refer to the components in `javax.swing` as "Swing components."

Understanding the JFC

Although the JFC was released well before SDK 1.2, Sun didn't make a big deal about it. Most of Sun's description of the new JFC has centered on Swing, so many people have the idea that Swing is all there is to the JFC and that the JFC came out as part of SDK 1.2. The link is so strong that Sun unofficially called JFC 1.1 "Swing 1.0."

In fact, the JFC includes

- The lightweight user-interface components (code-named Swing)
- The delegation event model
- Printing capability
- Clipboard data transfer
- Better integration with system colors
- Mouseless operation
- Drag-and-drop operation
- Better support for assistive technology for people with disabilities
- Improved 2D graphics operations

NOTE Before JFC was developed, Netscape developed a set of classes called the Internet Foundation Classes, or IFC. Microsoft has also developed the Application Foundation Classes, or AFC. Netscape has announced that the JFC supersedes the IFC, leaving Microsoft and Sun to battle it out.

A Short Tour of Swing

Sun supplies Swing in 17 packages:

- **`javax.swing`**—Components, adapters, default component models, and interfaces.
- **`javax.swing.border`**—The Border interface and classes, which define specific border-rendering styles.
- **`javax.swing.colorchooser`**—Classes and interfaces used by the `JColorChooser` component.
- **`javax.swing.event`**—Swing-specific event types and listeners.
- **`javax.swing.filechooser`**—Classes and interfaces used by the `JFileChooser` component.
- **`javax.swing.plaf`**—The interface and abstract classes that Swing uses to provide its pluggable look-and-feel (PLAF) capabilities.
- **`javax.swing.plaf.basic`**—User interface objects built according to the Basic look-and-feel—the default look-and-feel of Swing components.
- **`javax.swing.plaf.metal`**—The user interface objects built according to the "metal" look-and-feel, a platform-independent look-and-feel introduced in SDK 1.2.
- **`javax.swing.multi`**—The multiplexing user interface classes that enable you to make components from different factory classes.
- **`javax.swing.table`**—The Swing `Table` class and its kin.

- **javax.swing.text**—Support for the Swing document framework.
- **javax.swing.text.html**—The class `HTMLEditorKit` and supporting classes for creating HTML text editors.
- **javax.swing.text.html.parser**—The default HTML parser, along with support classes.
- **javax.swing.text.rtf**—The class `RTFEditorKit` for creating Rich-Text Format text editors.
- **javax.swing.tree**—Classes and interfaces for dealing with `javax.swing.JTree`.
- **javax.swing.undo**—Support classes for implementing undo and redo.
- **javax.accessibility**—Support for working with assistive technology to make Java programs accessible for people with disabilities.

NOTE Swing is an emerging technology–not all Java-compatible browsers understand Swing. Furthermore, Swing is independent of the SDK, so Swing components are not necessarily released on the same schedule as SDK updates. If you plan to use Swing components in your applets, design your HTML to use the Java plug-in–don't rely on the browser vendor to support Swing in its JVM.

Swing was first released as a separate set of classes that worked with JDK 1.1. Swing was not actually part of JDK 1.1 but had to be downloaded and installed separately. Swing remained a separate set of classes through much of the SDK 1.2 beta process. Now, however, Swing is fully integrated into SDK 1.3. Be sure to get the most up-to-date version of Swing by downloading the release version of Java 2 at `http://java.sun.com/j2se/`.

TIP Before you begin to develop with Swing components, make sure you can run an existing Swing-based application. Remember that you'll have to use Sun's Java plug-in to take advantage of the latest Swing classes. Sun includes SwingSet, an overview of the Swing components, in the SDK. If you installed your copy of the SDK in the default location (`/jdk1.3`), you'll find it in `jdk1.3/demo/jfc/SwingSet2/`. Open `SwingSet2Plugin.html` in your browser. Make sure it loads and runs without errors.

Swing Component APIs

With the AWT, you can choose buttons, labels, lists, and a few other user-interface components. With the Swing components, Sun provides a richer interface, more akin to the full range available in Microsoft Foundation Classes or the Macintosh Toolbox. More than twice as many Swing components are available as AWT components. The Swing components include

- Labels
- Bordered panes

- Progress bars
- ToolTips
- Buttons
- Radio buttons
- Check boxes
- Toolbars
- Sliders
- Combo boxes
- Menus
- Trees
- Scrollbars
- List boxes
- Tabbed panes
- Tables

All these components are lightweight—instead of building a peer component from the native operating system, they look for a library of pluggable look-and-feel classes. Three complete PLAF libraries come with the Windows version of SDK 1.3:

- **Windows**—A look-and-feel strongly resembling Windows 95 and above
- **Motif**—A look-and-feel based on Sun's own Motif interface
- **Metal**—A platform-independent look-and-feel derived from the Basic PLAF

NOTE Sun has released a Macintosh look-and-feel, but it doesn't include it in the Windows SDK. Sun is careful not to risk copyright infringement by making a vendor's look-and-feel outside its own operating system. The exception, of course, is its own Motif look-and-feel, derived from Sun's own Solaris operating system. Use the Java look-and-feel, called Metal, if you want your application or applet to look the same on every platform.

Most of Sun's demo applets enable you to change the look-and-feel from a control at runtime. Figure 37.16 shows SimpleExample, one of the examples in the Metal look-and-feel. To run this example, navigate to `JAVA_HOME/demo/jfc/SimpleExample` and type

```
java -jar SimpleExample.jar
```

Compare Figure 37.16 with Figure 37.17. Figure 37.16 shows SimpleExample with the Metal look-and-feel. By choosing the Windows radio button, you can switch SimpleExample to the Windows look-and-feel, shown in Figure 37.17. Similarly, you can use the Motif look-and-feel, shown in Figure 37.18.

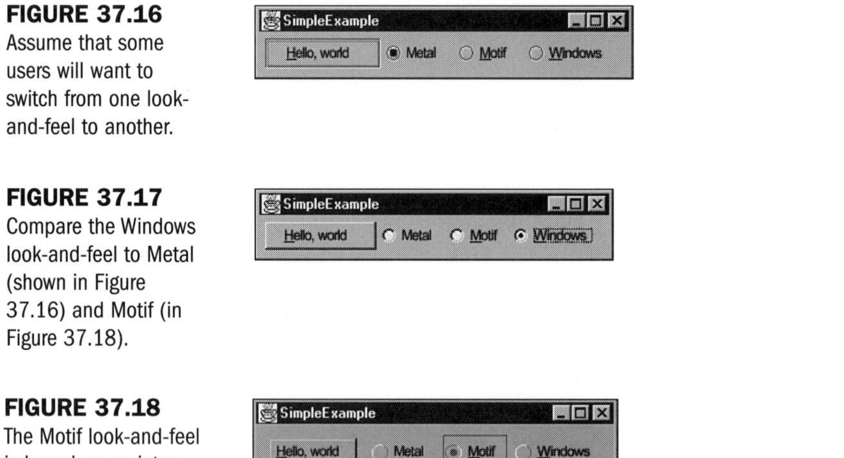

FIGURE 37.16
Assume that some users will want to switch from one look-and-feel to another.

FIGURE 37.17
Compare the Windows look-and-feel to Metal (shown in Figure 37.16) and Motif (in Figure 37.18).

FIGURE 37.18
The Motif look-and-feel is based on an interface Sun designed to its UNIX operating system, Solaris.

NOTE Pluggable Look-and-Feel (PLAF) is here to stay. Use the SwingSet to explore all three PLAFs, as well as others that will become available in the future. Remember that the decision about which look-and-feel to use is left to the user. Strive to make sure your design looks good in all available PLAFs.

Using the *TPanelTester* Application

The examples in this section are based on subclasses of the Swing panel component, `JPanel`. To run the various panels, you need an application to display the panel. Listing 37.7 shows a generic panel tester.

Listing 37.7 ***TPanelTester.java*****—Change the Name in This Panel Tester to Match the Panel Under Test**

```
import javax.swing.*;

public class TPanelTester extends JFrame {
  public TPanelTester() {
    super("Panel Tester");

    // change TLabelPanel to match the name of the panel under test
    JPanel thePanelUnderTest = new TLabelPanel();
    setContentPane(thePanelUnderTest);
  }
```

Listing 37.7 Continued

```
  public static void main(String[] args) {
    JFrame theFrame = new TPanelTester();
    theFrame.addWindowListener(new java.awt.event.WindowAdapter() {
      public void windowClosing(java.awt.event.WindowEvent e)
        {System.exit(0);}
      });
    theFrame.pack();
    theFrame.setVisible(true);
  }
}
```


Using *JPanel*

You first looked at panels earlier in this chapter in the AWT discussion. A `JPanel` is a lightweight version of `Panel`; it is used in most of the examples in this section.

NOTE In Chapter 38, "Graphics and Animation," you'll learn how to reduce flicker with double buffering. Double buffering is built into `JComponent`; check the documentation for the `setDoubleBuffered()` method.

Working with Icons

In the AWT discussion, you learned that subclasses of `java.awt.Container` can contain `java.awt.Components`, and that `Containers` themselves are `Components`. This hierarchy enables you to add `Panels` to `Frames`, for example. All the Swing components are derived from `JComponent`, which is a `java.awt.Container`. This design means that every `JComponent` can contain other components, either AWT or Swing. Therefore, you can add a graphical icon to a `JButton`, a `JLabel`, or another Swing component. Swing provides `Icon` as an interface; to implement it you must provide a `paintIcon()` method, a `getIconWidth()` method, and a `getIconHeight()` method. The `paintIcon()` method is

```
paintIcon(Component c, Graphics g, int x, int y);
```

where `x` and `y` specify the drawing origin; the drawing itself happens in `Graphics g`. You can use the `Component` to get properties such as the foreground or background color—in practice, the `Component` parameter is usually ignored.

NOTE In theory, any `JComponent` can contain either AWT or Swing components. Unfortunately, the words "in theory" often translate into "not really." Some programmers report that they have had difficulty mixing classic AWT components with Swing components. If you want to try, go ahead–you've been warned.

Swing provides one `Icon` class for you—`ImageIcon`, used to display images. Listing 37.8 is an example of an Icon.

Listing 37.8 ***TBigBlackDot.java*—You Can Add This Icon to Swing Buttons and Labels**

```
public class TBigBlackDot implements javax.swing.Icon {
  public void paintIcon(java.awt.Component c,
                        java.awt.Graphics g, int x, int y) {
    g.setColor(java.awt.Color.black);
    g.fillOval(x, y, getIconWidth(), getIconHeight());
  }
  public int getIconWidth() {
    return 100;
  }
  public int getIconHeight() {
    return 100;
  }
}
```

Adding an Instance of *JLabel*

A label enables you to place static text onto the screen. You looked at `Label` in the AWT discussion earlier in this chapter. The Swing `JLabel` improves upon `java.awt.Label` by enabling you to add an icon and giving you better control over the position of the text. Listing 37.9 shows a `JLabel` in action on a `JPanel`.

Listing 37.9 ***TLabelPanel.java*—This Panel Contains a Label with a *TBigBlackDot* Icon**

```
public class TLabelPanel extends javax.swing.JPanel {
  public TLabelPanel() {
    javax.swing.JLabel theLabel =
      new com.sun.java.swing.JLabel("Example of BigBlackDot");

    // we don't have to settle for plain vanilla text
    java.awt.Font theBigBoldFont =
      new java.awt.Font("Serif",
                        java.awt.Font.BOLD,
                        32);
    theLabel.setFont(theBigBoldFont);

    // now add an icon
    javax.swing.Icon aDot = new TBigBlackDot();
    theLabel.setIcon(aDot);
    theLabel.setPreferredSize(new
      java.awt.Dimension(600, 150));

    // place the text to the right of the icon
    theLabel.setHorizontalAlignment(javax.swing.JLabel.RIGHT);
```

Listing 37.9 Continued

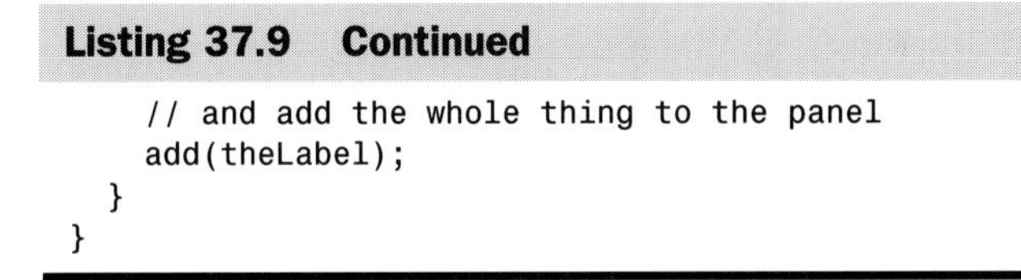

```
        // and add the whole thing to the panel
        add(theLabel);
    }
}
```

Figure 37.19 shows an instance of `TLabelPanel`.

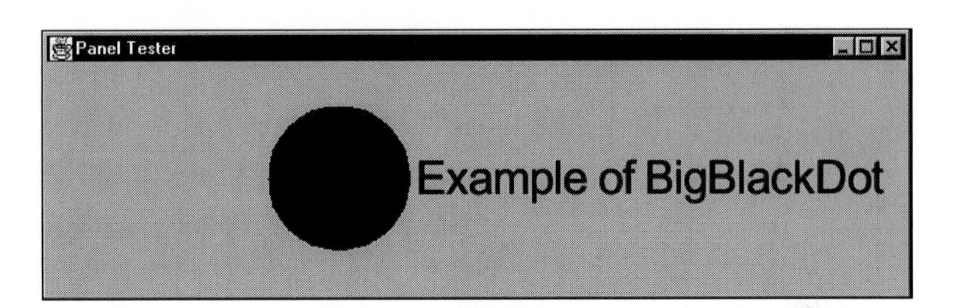

FIGURE 37.19 You can add icons to a `JLabel` and control the text's position and appearance.

Using *JButton*

`JButton` behaves much like `Button`; you add it to a `JPanel` and listen for its action with an `ActionListener`.

> **TIP** By default, a new `JButton` has the same background color as the container. Some developers don't like this design and prefer that it stand out more. Consider adding a line such as
>
> ```
> theButton.setBackground(SystemColor.control );
> ```
>
> to make the button highly visible.

As with `JLabel`, you can add an icon to `JButton` by calling the `setIcon()` method.

> **TIP** Several Swing components, including `JButton`, are derived from `AbstractButton`. Review the documentation for `AbstractButton`—you'll find methods that allow you to enable and disable the button, control the internal alignment, and associate an accelerator key with the button.

Adding an Instance of *JCheckBox*

Recall from the earlier section of this chapter, "Using the Abstract Windowing Toolkit," that you can implement check boxes with `java.awt.Checkbox`. You implemented radio buttons by placing the check box into a `CheckboxGroup`. In Swing, the concept of a radio button is handled explicitly—Swing has its own `JRadioButton` class with an associated `ButtonGroup`. You use `JCheckBox` just to implement check boxes.

NOTE `JCheckBox` has its own icons to signify the selected and unselected states. If you prefer, you can make your own icons and use them in `setIcon()` and `setSelectedIcon()`.

Using *JRadioButton*

To make a group of radio buttons, make instances of `JRadioButton` and add them to a `ButtonGroup`. Listing 37.10 shows an example of some radio buttons.

Listing 37.10 ***TDoseNotGivenPanel.java*—This Panel Contains a Group of Radio Buttons**

```
public class TDoseNotGivenPanel extends javax.swing.JPanel {
  public TDoseNotGivenPanel() {

    // make room for a label and four buttons
    setLayout(new java.awt.GridLayout(5, 1));

    javax.swing.ButtonGroup aReason =
      new javax.swing.ButtonGroup();
    javax.swing.JLabel theLabel =
      new javax.swing.JLabel("Dose not given because");
    theLabel.setFont(new java.awt.Font("SansSrif",
                                    java.awt.Font.BOLD, 14));
    add(theLabel);

    javax.swing.JRadioButton thePatientNotAvailableButton =
      new javax.swing.JRadioButton("Patient not available");
    thePatientNotAvailableButton.setHorizontalAlignment(
      javax.swing.AbstractButton.LEFT);

    thePatientNotAvailableButton.setSelected(true); //default
    add(thePatientNotAvailableButton);
    aReason.add(thePatientNotAvailableButton);

    javax.swing.JRadioButton thePatientOffWardButton =
      new javax.swing.JRadioButton("Patient off ward");
    thePatientOffWardButton.setHorizontalAlignment(
      javax.swing.AbstractButton.LEFT);

    add (thePatientOffWardButton);
    aReason.add(thePatientOffWardButton);

    javax.swing.JRadioButton thePatientRefusedButton =
      new javax.swing.JRadioButton("Patient refused dose");
    thePatientRefusedButton.setHorizontalAlignment(
      javax.swing.AbstractButton.LEFT);

    add (thePatientRefusedButton);
    aReason.add(thePatientRefusedButton);
```

Listing 37.10 Continued

```
      javax.swing.JRadioButton thePatientExpelledDoseButton =
        new javax.swing.JRadioButton("Patient expelled dose");
      thePatientExpelledDoseButton.setHorizontalAlignment(
        javax.swing.AbstractButton.LEFT);

      add (thePatientExpelledDoseButton);
      aReason.add(thePatientExpelledDoseButton);
    }
  }
```


Figure 37.20 shows the `JPanel` that results from the code in Listing 37.10.

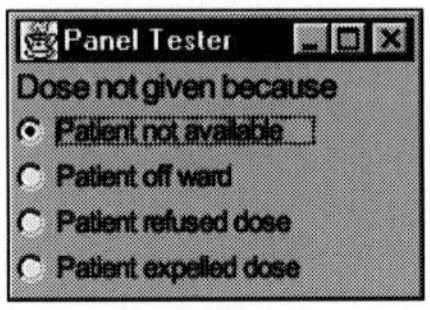

FIGURE 37.20
Use a `ButtonGroup` to implement a set of radio buttons.

Panel Tester
Dose not given because
Patient not available
Patient off ward
Patient refused dose
Patient expelled dose

Remembering State with *JToggleButton*

`JToggleButton` is the parent class of both `JCheckBox` and `JRadioButton`, but it's a concrete class that you can use in your design. When unselected, a `JToggleButton` is indistinguishable from a `JButton`. When someone clicks it, it goes to its selected state and stays there. (By default, it looks like a pushbutton that's locked in the "Down" state.)

Managing Text

Swing's `JTextComponent` gives you more than what's expected from a simple field or text area. Its methods include

- `copy()`
- `cut()`
- `paste()`
- `getSelectedText()`
- `getSelectionStart()`
- `getSelectionEnd()`
- `getText()`
- `setText()`
- `setEditable()`
- `setCaretPosition()`

Figure 37.21 illustrates the inheritance hierarchy that derives from `javax.swing.text.JTextComponent`.

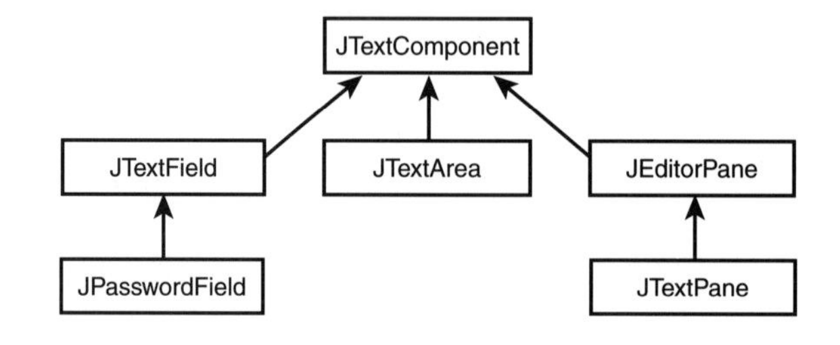

FIGURE 37.21
Each member of the `JTextComponent` family supports the methods of a simple text editor.

`JTextField` and `JTextArea` resemble their AWT counterparts, but `JeditorPane` and its subclass, `JtextPane`, are new. They implement a complete text editor; you can format text and embed images. Words will wrap where you expect them to, based on their current font, size, and style. `TProgressNotePanel`, a class used in a pharmacy application, is shown in Listing 37.11. Figure 37.22 shows the `TProgressNotePanel` itself.

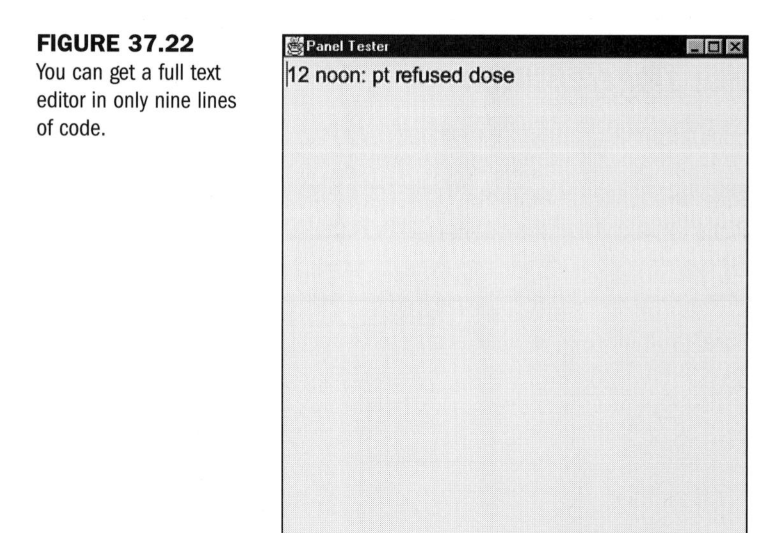

FIGURE 37.22
You can get a full text editor in only nine lines of code.

TIP When a user enters a password or other sensitive information, the information should not be visible on the screen. Use `JPasswordField` instead of `JTextField` to ensure privacy. Use `setEchoChar()` if you want to override the default echo character, asterisk (`*`).

Listing 37.11 *TProgressNotePanel.java*—Nurses Enter Progress Notes to Report Significant Events in Patient Care

```
public class TProgressNotePanel extends javax.swing.JPanel
{
  public TProgressNotePanel() {
    setLayout(new java.awt.BorderLayout());
    setPreferredSize(new java.awt.Dimension(400,400));
    javax.swing.JTextPane theText = new javax.swing.JTextPane();

    javax.swing.text.MutableAttributeSet theAttributes =
      new javax.swing.text.SimpleAttributeSet();
    javax.swing.text.StyleConstants.setFontFamily(theAttributes,
                                                   "Serif");
    javax.swing.text.StyleConstants.setFontSize(theAttributes, 18);
    javax.swing.text.StyleConstants.setBold(theAttributes, true);
    theText.setCharacterAttributes(theAttributes, false);

    add(theText, java.awt.BorderLayout.CENTER);
  }
}
```

Giving Feedback with *JProgressBar*

In Chapter 38, you'll learn about starting up more than one independent thread of control. Sometimes you'll want a thread running in the background while the user goes on with other work. You can put up a progress bar to report on the progress in that thread and, if you like, enable the user to control that thread. Listing 37.12 and Figure 37.23 show one way to use a `JProgressBar`.

▶ To learn more about threads, **see** "Adding Animation" **p. 1139**

Listing 37.12 *TBackgroundPanel.java*—Use a *JProgressBar* to Report the Progress of a Thread

```
import javax.swing.*;
public class TBackgroundPanel extends JPanel {
  private Thread fThread;
  private Object fLock;
  private boolean fNeedsToStop = false;
  private JProgressBar fProgressBar;
  private JButton fStartButton;
  private JButton fStopButton;

  public TBackgroundPanel() {
    fLock = new Object();
    setLayout(new java.awt.BorderLayout());
    add(new JLabel("Status"), java.awt.BorderLayout.NORTH);
```

Listing 37.12 Continued

```
    fProgressBar = new JProgressBar();
    add(fProgressBar, java.awt.BorderLayout.CENTER);
    JPanel theButtons = new JPanel();

    fStartButton = new JButton("Start");
    fStartButton.setBackground(java.awt.SystemColor.control);
    theButtons.add(fStartButton);
    fStartButton.addActionListener(new java.awt.event.ActionListener() {
      public void actionPerformed(java.awt.event.ActionEvent e) {
        startTheThread();
      }
    });
    fStopButton = new JButton("Stop");
    fStopButton.setBackground(java.awt.SystemColor.control);
    theButtons.add(fStopButton);
    fStopButton.addActionListener(new java.awt.event.ActionListener() {
      public void actionPerformed(java.awt.event.ActionEvent e) {
        stopTheThread();
      }
    });
    add(theButtons, java.awt.BorderLayout.SOUTH);
  }

  public void startTheThread() {
    if (fThread == null)
      fThread = new TBackgroundThread();
    if (!fThread.isAlive())
    {
      fNeedsToStop = false;
      fThread.start();
    }
  }

  public void stopTheThread() {
    synchronized(fLock) {
      fNeedsToStop = true;
      fLock.notify();
    }
  }

  // inner class, so it has access to private members of panel
  class TBackgroundThread extends Thread {
    public void run() {
      // run at a low priority; after all, we _
      // are_ a background thread
      Thread.currentThread().setPriority(Thread.MIN_PRIORITY);
      int theMinimum = 0;
      int theMaximum = 100;
      fProgressBar.setValue(theMinimum);
      fProgressBar.setMinimum(theMinimum);
     fProgressBar.setMaximum(theMaximum);
```

Listing 37.12 Continued

```
        for (int i=0; i<theMaximum; i++) {
          fProgressBar.setValue(i);

          // do the real work of the background thread
          // here

          synchronized(fLock) {
            if (fNeedsToStop)
              break;
            try {
              fLock.wait(100);
            } catch (InterruptedException e) {
              // ignore the exception
            }
          }
        }
        // clue the garbage collector that we're done with the thread
        fThread = null;
      }
    }
  }
```


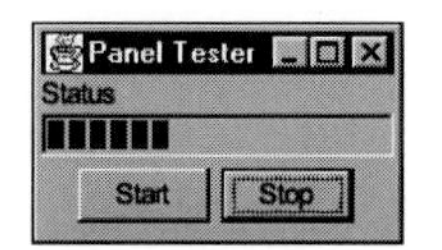

FIGURE 37.23 For a nice touch, enable the user to start and stop the work of the background thread.

TBackgroundPanel is a generic JPanel that can be used to display and control a background thread. The class has six instance variables:

- **Thread fThread**—The background thread itself; see "Adding Animation" in Chapter 38 to learn more about threads.
- **Object fLock**—A simple object used to synchronize the foreground and background threads.
- **boolean fNeedsToStop**—A bit of shared data that tells the background thread that the foreground thread wants it to stop.
- **JProgressBar fProgressBar**—The Swing progress bar.
- **JButton fStartButton and JButton fStopButton**—The controls to start and stop the background thread.

The TBackgroundPanel constructor builds the user interface, including the pair of buttons that communicates with the background thread. The listeners are designed to start and stop the thread by calling TBackgroundPanel's methods startTheThread() and stopTheThread().

The class `TBackgroundThread` is an inner class, so it has access to all the instance variables of `TBackgroundPanel`. Like most threads, it has only one method: `run()`.

When the user clicks `fStartButton`, `startTheThread()` instantiates a new `TBackgroundThread` and tells it to `start()`. When the thread starts, its `run()` method immediately sets the priority to the minimum value; the user interface has a higher priority, so the application feels responsive to the user. The `TBackgroundThread` sits in a tight loop doing whatever work it does—that work has been left as a comment in this version. You could download a file, query a database, or do anything else that takes so much time that you don't want the user to have to wait.

As it runs, `TBackgroundThread` continually reports its status to `fProgressBar`. Then it checks the state of `fNeedsToStop`. If the user has clicked `fStopButton`, `fNeedsToStop` is true and `run()` breaks out of its loop.

TIP The Boolean variable `fNeedsToStop` is shared between the two threads. If you're not careful, it's possible that both threads could be using the variable at once. To prevent this, use the `Object fLock` as a semaphore so that only one thread can work with `fNeedsToStop` at a time.

Adding Toolbars and ToolTips

It's easy to add toolbars and ToolTips to your Swing components. If you have a `JButton` named `fButton`, just write

```
fButton.setToolTipText("This is the tooltip");
```

to add a ToolTip to the button. You can use this technique on any `JComponent`.

A `JToolBar` is another `JComponent`. You can write code such as the following to build a toolbar:

```
JToolBar theToolBar = new JToolBar();
JButton aButton = new JButton("One");
theToolBar.add(aButton);
JButton anotherButton = new JButton("Two");
theToolBar.add(anotherButton);
```

TIP You can add `JButtons` and other components to your toolbar; use an `ActionListener` to handle mouse clicks, the same as you would with any other button. `ActionListeners` are part of the delegation event model described earlier in this chapter in the section, "Using the Abstract Windowing Toolkit."

The Long-Awaited Tabbed Pane

The Windows32 user interface (implemented in Windows 95 and above) includes a tabbed pane, which is commonly used throughout Windows applications. Unfortunately, the AWT interface did not include a tabbed pane—early Java programmers often cobbled one together by using the `CardLayout`.

Now, with Swing, you get your own `JTabbedPane`. You can add one to a `BorderLayout` with just a few lines of code, as shown in Listing 37.13.

Listing 37.13 *TTabbedPanel.java*—Add Tabs to a *JTabbedPanel*

```
import javax.swing.*;
public class TTabbedPanel extends JPanel
{
  private JTabbedPane fTabbedPane;
  public TTabbedPanel() {
    setLayout (new java.awt.BorderLayout());
    fTabbedPane = new JTabbedPane();
    fTabbedPane.addTab("One", null, makePane("One"));
    fTabbedPane.addTab("Two", null, makePane("Two"));
    fTabbedPane.addTab("Three", null, makePane("Three"));
    fTabbedPane.setSelectedIndex(0);
    add (fTabbedPane, java.awt.BorderLayout.CENTER);
  }
  protected JPanel makePane(String theString) {
    // customize makePane to display the exact info you want
    // on each panel
    JPanel thePanel = new JPanel();
    thePanel.setBackground(java.awt.SystemColor.control);
    thePanel.add(new JLabel(theString));
    return thePanel;
  }
}
```


Other Swing Components

Swing is a huge component library; in addition to the components described here, `JSliders`, `JComboBoxes`, `JLists`, and many other widgets are included. A `JSlider` resembles a `JScrollBar`, but you can add major and minor tick marks and display a border around the slider. A `JComboBox` resembles the AWT's `Choice` component but has more capability. (You can use a `JComboBox` to supply a list of default choices, for example, and then enable the users to enter their own values if none of the defaults are appropriate.) Use `JList` the same as you would use `List` in the AWT. You can listen for `ListSelectionEvents`, the same as you do other events—just add a `ListSelectionListener`.

Unlike its AWT counterpart, `JList` doesn't support scrolling directly. That's not a problem, however—just add it to a `ScrollPane` or `JScrollPane` to restore that capability.

Writing Swing Applets

Swing introduces a new class—JApplet—that is derived from Applet. Many of the new methods you'll find in JApplet have to do with accessibility for people with disabilities. The other new capability is called JRootPane.

JRootPane enables you to place contents into one of several layers. In order from front (closest to user) to back (farthest from user) the layers are

- **glassPane**—A JComponent that fills the entire viewable area of the JRootPane. By default, the glassPane is not visible.
- **layeredPane**—A subclass of JComponent designed to hold dialog boxes, menu pop-ups, and other components that should appear to be floating between the user and the content.
- **menubar**—An optional component; if present, it appears anchored to the top of the JRootPane.
- **contentPane**—The JComponent where most of the contents will be drawn.

Using the *contentPane* To add components to a JApplet, you should usually add them to the contentPane. Instead of writing

```
theApplet.add(theComponent);
```

as you would in AWT, write

```
theApplet.getContentPane().add(theComponent);
```

Working with the *JLayeredPane* By placing most of your components in the contentPane (which is farthest away from the user), you make it possible to add special components, such as menu pop-ups or dialog boxes, in a layer closer to the user (such as the layeredPane).

NOTE By default, the contentPane has a BorderLayout layout manager.

If you plan to use the layeredPane, be sure to read the SDK documentation on javax.swing.JLayeredPane. This class–a layer in itself–supports six distinct layers internally: from back to front, the FRAME_CONTENT_LAYER, the DEFAULT_LAYER, the PALETTE_LAYER, the MODAL_LAYER, the POPUP_LAYER, and the DRAG_LAYER. In addition, you can make up layers of your own.

Adding Menus to *JApplets* If you've worked with the AWT, you know that you cannot easily add menus to an applet. AWT menus must be attached to a frame, but an applet is a panel. With JApplet, you can set a JMenuBar on the JRootPane. It will be positioned along the upper edge of the JApplet's JRootPane. (You can see this menu bar in /jdk1.3/demo/jfc/SwingSet2/SwingSet2Plugin.html).

Drawing on the *glassPane* The glassPane is closest to the user. If you need to draw something that should appear in front of *all* components, including dialog boxes, menu pop-ups, and other components on the layeredPane, add it to the glassPane.

If you use the `glassPane`, remember to make it visible. It is not visible by default. In a `JApplet`, for example, you might write

getGlassPane.setVisible(TRUE);

Using Swing-Specific Layouts

In addition to the AWT layouts that you saw in earlier examples in this chapter, Swing comes with four layouts of its own:

- **`ScrollPaneLayout`**—Built into the `ScrollPane` component.
- **`ViewportLayout`**—Built into the `Viewport` component.
- **`BoxLayout`**—Built into the `Box` component, but also available as an option in other components.
- **`OverlayLayout`**—A layout manager in which every component is added on top of every previous component.

Taking Advantage of *ScrollPaneLayout* in *JScrollPanes*

You'll never need to instantiate a `ScrollPaneLayout`. Instead, just make a new `JScrollPane`. You'll get the nine areas associated with the `ScrollPaneLayout` automatically:

- **A `JViewport`, in the center**—Use it for your contents.
- **Two `JScrollBars`**—One for horizontal scrolling, the other for vertical scrolling.
- **Two `JViewPorts`**—One for row headers, the other for column headers.
- **Four `Components`**—One for each corner.

NOTE `ScrollPaneLayout` includes named constants to make it easy for you to refer to the parts of the layout. The corners, for example, are named `LOWER_LEFT_CORNER`, `LOWER_RIGHT_CORNER`, `UPPER_LEFT_CORNER`, and `UPPER_RIGHT_CORNER`.

Each `JViewport` has its own layout manager, the `ViewportLayout`.

Working with *ViewportLayout* and *OverlayLayout*

Like the `ScrollPaneLayout`, you don't need to make your own `ViewportLayout`; you get it automatically with every `Viewport`. Just add a component to the `Viewport`—the `ViewportLayout` will position it based on the properties of your `Viewport`.

The `OverlayLayout` positions each component over the top of the others. The size of the complete layout is the size of the largest component.

Using *Box* and *BoxLayout*

The `BoxLayout` resembles the AWT `FlowLayout`, except that you can specify the axis—either x or y. Unlike `GridLayout`, each component can occupy a different size cell. To use the `BoxLayout` in the y axis, write

```
setLayout(new BoxLayout(this, BoxLayout.Y_AXIS));
```

Figure 37.24 illustrates a `BoxLayout` in the y axis.

FIGURE 37.24
This `BoxLayout` is set up for the y axis and has three components.

TIP If you plan to use `BoxLayout`, just subclass `Box` rather than `JPanel`. `BoxLayout` is the default layout manager for `Box` and provides several methods that give you detailed control over the layout.

Swing Listeners and Events

Recall from the earlier sections of this chapter, "Using the Abstract Windowing Toolkit" and "The Swing Architecture," that one of the distinctions of the JFC is the delegation event model. Although the AWT components can still use the now-deprecated JDK-1.0 model for communicating about actions, Swing components use only the delegation event model. In fact, Swing takes the delegation event model to new heights, based on the *Model-View-Controller* (MVC) design pattern.

NOTE To learn more about MVC, see Chapter 13 of *Using Java 1.2* (Que, 1998).

Understanding Swing Events

Earlier in this chapter, in "Using the Abstract Windowing Toolkit," you learned about the delegation event model and about low-level and semantic events. Swing has its own `event` package for Swing-specific events. Use the `javax.swing.event` package for the event listeners and the events themselves; the event sources are the Swing components. The following is a list of the Swing event classes—`DocumentEvent` is an interface—and their meanings.

NOTE Many Swing events, such as those that refer to the "model," assume that you're using the MVC pattern. Read the Swing documentation on MVC or Chapter 13 of *Using Java 1.2* before attempting to use these Swing events.

- `AncestorEvent`—Ancestor has been added, moved, or removed.
- `ChangeEvent`—A component has had a state change.
- `DocumentEvent`—A document has had a state change.
- `ListDataEvent`—Contents of a list have changed, or an interval has been added or removed.
- `ListSelectionEvent`—The selection on a list has changed.
- `MenuEvent`—A menu item has been selected or posted, deselected, or canceled.
- `TableColumnModelEvent`—The model for a table column has changed.
- `TableModelEvent`—The model for a table has changed.
- `TreeExpansionEvent`—A tree node has been expanded or collapsed.
- `TreeModelEvent`—A tree model has changed.
- `TreeSelectionEvent`—The selection in a tree has changed status.

NOTE Sun divides events into two categories: semantic events and low-level events. Usually you'll get a better, more portable interface by listening for semantic events such as the `ActionEvent`. If you need special behavior, however, you can listen for low-level events such as mouse clicks and key presses. Refer to Listing 36.6–`TRaceApplet.java`–Chapter 36 to see how to use low-level events. Line 72 (copied here) constructs a new `TMouseAdapter`:

```
TMouseAdapter aMouseAdapter = new TMouseAdapter();
```

That adapter is defined in lines 202 to 215 (shown here). When the adapter "hears" a mouse press, it consumes the event (line 207–copied here)

```
anEvent.consume();
```

and toggles `fThreadSuspended`; if the thread was suspended, it is now unsuspended, and vice versa. Here's the code that puts it all together:

```
class TMouseAdapter extends java.awt.event.MouseAdapter
{
  public synchronized void mousePressed(
  ➥java.awt.event.MouseEvent anEvent)
  {
    anEvent.consume();
    fThreadSuspended = !fThreadSuspended;
    if (!fThreadSuspended)
      synchronized (fMonitorThread)
      {
        fMonitorThread.notifyAll();
      }
  }
}
```

▶ To learn more about TRaceApplet.java, **see** "Sample Applets," **p. 1030**

Drag and Drop

In the latest version of the SDK, all drag-and-drop (DnD) operations (for both Swing and AWT components) are supported through the interface `java.awt.dnd`. Listing 37.14 shows a typical DnD program.

NOTE When a class implements an interface, the class must provide an implementation of every method in the interface. To implement a drag-and-drop target, a class must implement `DropTargetListener`. As shown in Listing 37.14, most of the work is done in `dragEnter()` and `drop()`.

Listing 37.14 ***DnDTest.java*—An Implementation of a *DropTargetListener***

```
import java.awt.*;
import java.awt.dnd.*;
import java.awt.datatransfer.*;
import java.awt.event.*;
import java.io.*;

public class DnDTest extends Frame implements DropTargetListener {

  DropTarget fTarget;
  TextArea fTextArea;

  public DnDTest () {
    fTextArea = new TextArea("Grab some text and \npull it over here!");
    fTarget = new DropTarget(fTextArea, DnDConstants.ACTION_COPY, this);
    fTarget.setActive (true);
    add ("Center", fTextArea);
    enableEvents(AWTEvent.WINDOW_EVENT_MASK);
  }

  public static void main (String args[]) {
    DnDTest theFrame = new DnDTest();
    theFrame.setSize (400, 200);
    theFrame.setVisible (true);
  }

 // required methods in DropTargetListener

  public  void dragEnter (DropTargetDragEvent dtde) {
    System.out.println ("dragEnter");

    // use the DropTargetDragEvent to find out what flavors are offered
    DataFlavor df[] = dtde.getCurrentDataFlavors();
    for (int i = 0; i < df.length; i++)    {
      if (df[i].isMimeTypeEqual ("text/plain")) {
```

Listing 37.14 Continued

```
        // if the flavor is plain text, accept the drag
        dtde.acceptDrag (DnDConstants.ACTION_COPY);
        return;
      }
    }
    // otherwise reject this drag
    dtde.rejectDrag ();
  }

  public  void dragOver (DropTargetDragEvent dtde) {

    // dragOver is called repeatedly while the cursor is over
    // the target. Uncomment the println to see how often this
    // method is called.
    //System.out.println ("dragOver");
  }

  public void dropActionChanged(DropTargetDragEvent dtde) {
    System.out.println("dropActionChanged");
  }

  public  void dragScroll (DropTargetDragEvent dtde) {
    System.out.println ("dragScroll");
  }

  public  void dragExit (DropTargetEvent dte) {
    System.out.println ("dragExit");
  }

  public  void drop (DropTargetDropEvent dtde) {
    dtde.acceptDrop (DnDConstants.ACTION_COPY);
    System.out.println ("dropped");
    Transferable theTransferable = dtde.getTransferable();
    DataFlavor df[] = dtde.getCurrentDataFlavors();
    Object theObject = null;

    try {

      // search through the flavor looking for plain text
      // when you find it get the associated data and stuff
      // it into the Object.
      for (int i = 0; i < df.length; i++)    {
        if (df[i].isMimeTypeEqual ("text/plain")) {
          theObject = theTransferable.getTransferData(df[i]);
        }
      }

      // if the data comes from outside the JVM, it comes in
      // on an InputStream. Read in the stream.
      if (theObject != null && theObject instanceof InputStream) {
        InputStream theInputStream = (InputStream) theObject;
```

Listing 37.14 Continued

```
          StringBuffer theStringBuffer = new StringBuffer();
          byte[] aBuffer = new byte[64];
          int theCount = theInputStream.read(aBuffer);
          while (theCount != -1) {
            // keep stuffing data into the string buffer
            theStringBuffer.append (new String (aBuffer, 0, theCount));
            theCount = theInputStream.read(aBuffer);
          }
          // We've read in all the data. Now let's use it
          theInputStream.close();
          fTextArea.setText (theStringBuffer.toString());
        }
      } catch (Exception e) {
      e.printStackTrace();
      } finally {
        try {
          fTarget.getDropTargetContext().dropComplete(true);
        } catch (Exception ignore) {}
      }
    }

  // let's handle a click on the window's close box
    protected void processWindowEvent (WindowEvent e) {
      if (e.getID() == WindowEvent.WINDOW_CLOSING)
        System.exit(0);
      super.processWindowEvent (e);
    }
  }
```

Compile `DnDTest` and run it from the command line (by typing `java DnDTest`). Open a text editor or other native application that's DnD-capable and drag some text onto the Java application. Your Java program detects the drag event over the `DropTarget` (called a `DropTargetDragEvent`) and calls `dragEnter()`. Because the incoming data is plain text, `dragEnter()` accepts the drag—the user sees the default cursor showing a drag-copy in progress. If the user moves the cursor out of the target area, the program calls `dragExit()`. If the user drops the transferred object over the target, your program calls `drop()`. In this case, `DnDTest` extracts the plain text from the transferred flavor and places it in the `TextArea`.

Your Java program can be a source for a drag-and-drop operation as well as being a target. Your source should implement `DragGestureListener` so that Java recognizes a click-and-drag action as the start of a drag and drop. The source should also implement `DragSourceListener`, although you won't need its methods unless you want a special effect.

`DragGestureListener` requires that you implement only one method: `dragGestureRecognized()`. In this method, you should determine what data is to be transferred, and then package that data into a flavor. If your interface stores data in a `Vector` called `fModel`, for example, and the user has selected `theItem`, you might write:

```
Transferable theTransferable = null;
theTransferable = (Transferable) fModel.elementAt(theItem);
DataFlavor theFlavors[] = theTransferable.getTransferDataFlavors();
try {
  theDragGestureEvent.startDrag(DragSource.DefaultCopyDrop,
                               theTransferable,
                               this);
  } catch (InvalidDnDOperationException e) {
    System.out.println("Invalid Drag and Drop operation: " + e);
  }
```


DragSourceListener requires that you implement five methods:

- dragDropEnd()
- dragEnter()
- dragExit()
- dragOver()
- dropActionChanged()

Unless you need a special effect, you can stub out all these methods. Now when you start a drag, dragGestureRecognized() runs, stuffs the data into one or more flavors, and attaches the array of flavors to the DragGestureEvent. When the cursor enters a drop target, your program examines the array of flavors; if it finds one that it can accept, it accepts the drag. Finally, when the user drops the transferred object, your program reads out the data from the flavor and puts it to work in the target.

Using Swing Event Listeners

Like their AWT counterparts, Swing event listeners are interfaces. Unlike AWT, Sun hasn't yet implemented many adapter classes, so usually you'll need to override every listener method to implement a listener. To implement an AncestorListener (which has three methods), for example, you might write

```
public class myAncestorListener implements AncestorListener {
  public void ancestorAdded(AncestorEvent e) {
    // ignore this one
  }
  public void ancestorRemoved(AncestorEvent e) {
    // don't care about this one either
  }
  public void ancestorMoved(AncestorEvent e) {
    // do something in this case
    Here is code to handle the case of a moving ancestor
  }
}
```

NOTE In GUI jargon, an *ancestor* is a member of the path of containers that goes back to the root window. If you put a JPanel into a frame, then put a JLabel on the JPanel, and finally put an icon in the JLabel, then the JLabel, the JPanel, and the frame are all ancestors of the icon. ■

Understanding Swing Event Sources

Swing events originate in the Swing components. A list showing which events come from which sources follows. (Remember the component hierarchy—an event sent by a `JComponent` is sent by every class that derives from `JComponent`.)

- **`ActionEvent`**

  `AbstractButton`

  `DefaultButtonModel`

  `JDirectoryPane`

  `JTextField`

  `Timer`

- **`AdjustmentEvent`**

  `JScrollBar`

  `Spinner`

- **`AncestorEvent`**—`JComponent`
- **`CellEditorEvent`**—`DefaultCellEditor`
- **`ChangeEvent`**

  `AbstractButton`

  `DefaultBoundedRangeModel`

  `DefaultButtonModel`

  `DefaultCaret`

  `DefaultSingleSelectionModel`

  `FontChooser.Patch`

  `JProgressBar`

  `JSlider`

  `JTabbedPane`

  `JViewport`

  `StandardDialog`

  `StyleContext`

- **`DocumentEvent`**—`AbstractDocument`
- **`ItemEvent`**

  `AbstractButton`

  `DefaultButtonModel`

  `JComboBox`

- **ListDataEvent**—AbstractListModel
- **ListSelectionEvent**

  DefaultListSelectionModel

  JList
- **MenuEvent**—JMenu
- **PropertyChangeEvent**

  AbstractAction

  DefaultTreeSelectionModel

  DirectoryModel

  JComponent

  TableColumn
- **TableColumnModelEvent**—DefaultTableColumnModel
- **TableModelEvent**—AbstractTableModel
- **TreeExpansionEvent**—DefaultTreeModel
- **TreeSelectionEvent**

  DefaultTreeSelectionModel

  JTree
- **VetoableChangeEvent**—JComponent
- **WindowEvent**—JPopupMenu

Of course, you still have access to events sent by AWT components:

- **ComponentEvent**—From Component
- **FocusEvent**—From Component
- **KeyEvent**—From Component
- **MouseEvent**—From Component
- **MouseMotionEvent**—From Component
- **ContainerEvent**—From Container
- **WindowEvent**—From Window ●

CHAPTER 38

Graphics and Animation

by Mike Morgan

In this chapter

Displaying Graphics

Colorful graphics and animation can change a dull, static, and gray Web page into an exciting and interesting place to visit. Java provides a wide range of tools for building and displaying graphics. These tools are found in Swing (package `javax.swing*`), the Abstract Windowing Toolkit (AWT) package (`java.awt`), and especially in the Graphics2D class (`java.awt.Graphics2D`). Most of what you need is part of the AWT. In fact, the majority of Java's graphics methods are contained in the `Graphics` class.

▶ For more information on the AWT, **see** "Using the Abstract Windowing Toolkit," **p. 1054**

▶ For more information on Swing, **see** "The Swing Architecture," **p. 1080**, and "Swing Component APIs," **p. 1082**

Using Java's *Graphics* Class

Java's `Graphics` class provides methods for manipulating several graphics features, including the following:

- Drawing graphics primitives
- Displaying colors
- Displaying text
- Displaying images
- Creating flicker-free animation

The following sections discuss all these graphics features and show how to implement them in Java applets. Along the way, you will acquire a complete understanding of the `Graphics` class and its methods.

You can find Java's `Graphics` class in the `java.awt` (the Java Abstract Window Toolkit) package. Be sure to properly import the `Graphics` class when you use it in your code. Include the following line at the beginning of your file:

```
import java.awt.Graphics;
```

NOTE The `Graphics` class is a nice class with plenty of capabilities. To graphics professionals, however, `Graphics` seems a bit anemic. More mature GUI platforms, such as Windows 95 and the Macintosh, support features that are not present in `Graphics`.

If you need to go beyond `Graphics`, take a look at `java.awt.Graphics2D`, a richer, two-dimensional graphics class. It's described later in this chapter, in the section titled "Using the 2D API." ■

Using Java's Coordinate System

You display the various graphics you produce—lines, rectangles, images, and so on—at specific locations in an applet or application window. A simple Cartesian (x, y) coordinate system defines each location within a Java window, as shown in Figure 38.1. The upper-left corner of a window is its origin (0, 0). Point x increases by the number of screen pixels that you move to the right of the left edge of an applet's window. The number of pixels you move down from the top of a window is y.

FIGURE 38.1
Java's graphics coordinate system increases from left to right and from top to bottom.

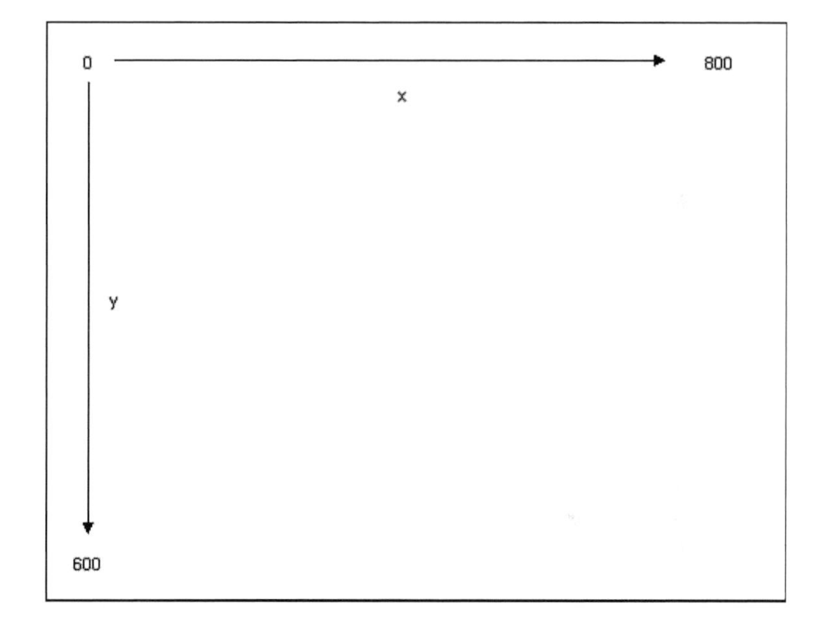

Displaying Graphics Primitives

The Java `Graphics` class provides you with methods that make it easy to draw two-dimensional graphics primitives. You can draw any two-dimensional graphics primitive, including

- Lines
- Rectangles
- Ovals
- Arcs
- Polygons

The following sections explain how to draw these graphics primitives.

Drawing Lines

Perhaps the simplest graphics primitive is a line. The Java `Graphics` class provides a single `drawLine()` method for drawing lines. The complete definition of the `drawLine()` method is

```
public abstract void drawLine(int  x1, int  y1, int  x2,  int  y2)
```

The `drawLine()` method takes two pairs of coordinates—x1, y1 and x2, y2—and draws a line between them.

The applet in Listing 38.1 uses the `drawLine()` method to draw some lines. Figure 38.2 shows the output from this applet.

NOTE If you're following along building these examples, remember that you'll have to write an HTML file with an `APPLET` tag that references `DrawLine.class`. See Chapter 36, "Developing Java Applets," if you need a review of this technique. ■

Listing 38.1 *DrawLines.java*—Use Graphics Primitives to Display Two Lines

```
import java.awt.Graphics;

public class DrawLines extends java.applet.Applet
{
   public void paint(Graphics g)
   {
     g.drawLine(0, 0, 400, 200);
     g.drawLine(20, 170, 450, 270);
   }
}
```

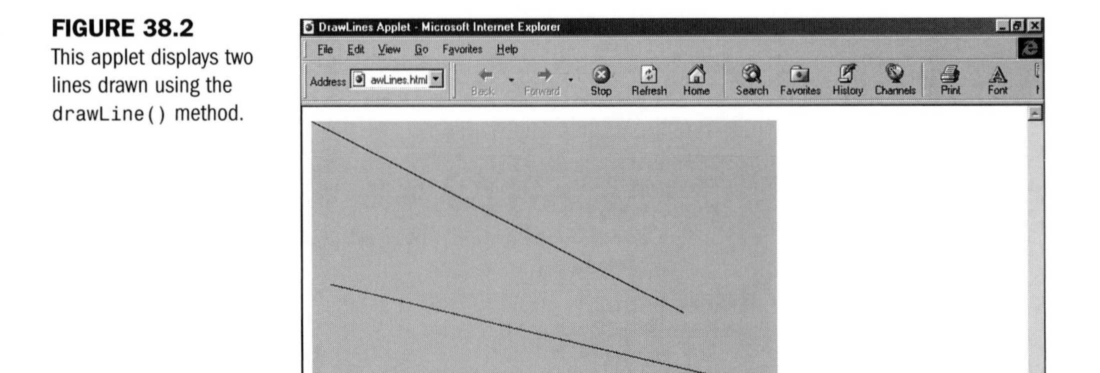

FIGURE 38.2
This applet displays two lines drawn using the `drawLine()` method.

Drawing Rectangles, Ovals, and Other Shapes

The Java `Graphics` class provides six methods for drawing rectangles: `drawRect()`, `fillRect()`, `drawRoundRect()`, `fillRoundRect()`, `draw3DRect()`, and `fill3DRect()`. You can use these methods to draw and fill three designs of rectangles.

To draw a simple rectangle using the `drawRect()` method, use this definition:

```
public void drawRect(int  x, int  y, int  width, int  height)
```

Pass the x and y applet window coordinates of the rectangle's upper-left corner along with the rectangle's width and height to the `drawRect()` method. Assume, for example, that you want to draw a rectangle that is 300 pixels wide (width = 300) and 170 pixels high (height = 170). You also want to place the rectangle with its upper-left corner 150 pixels to the right of the left edge of the applet's window (x = 150) and 100 pixels down from the window's top edge (y = 100). You would write

```
g.drawRect(150, 100, 300, 170);
```

Use the `fillRect()` method if you want to draw a solid rectangle. The complete definition of the `fillRect()` method follows:

```
public abstract void fillRect(int  x, int  y, int  width,  int  height)
```

As you can see, the `fillRect()` method takes the same parameters as the `drawRect()` method.

The Java `Graphics` class also provides two methods for drawing rectangles with rounded corners. The `drawRoundRect()` and `fillRoundRect()` methods are similar to the `drawRect()` and `fillRect()` methods except that they take two extra parameters: the `arcWidth` and `arcHeight` parameters. Their complete definitions are

```
public abstract void drawRoundRect(int  x, int  y, int  width,
➥int  height, int  arcWidth, int  arcHeight)

public abstract void fillRoundRect(int  x, int  y, int  width,
➥int height, int  arcWidth,  int  arcHeight)
```

The `arcWidth` and `arcHeight` parameters determine how the corners will be rounded. Using an `arcWidth` of 10 results in including the leftmost 5 pixels and the rightmost 5 pixels of each horizontal side of a rectangle in the rectangle's rounded corners. Similarly, using an `arcHeight` of 8 includes the topmost 4 pixels and the bottommost 4 pixels of each vertical side of a rectangle in the rectangle's rounded corners.

The syntax for the `draw3DRect()` and `fill3DRect()` methods is similar to the `drawRect()` and `fillRect()` methods except that they have an extra parameter added to the end of their parameter lists. It is a Boolean parameter that results in a raised rectangle effect when set to `true`. If it is set to `false`, the face of the rectangle shows a sunken effect.

NOTE The three-dimensional rectangles discussed here do not actually exist as three-dimensional objects. A shadow effect is used to give the illusion that they are three dimensional. This effect consists of a relatively dark color along two adjacent sides of a rectangle and a light color along the opposite two sides. Java assumes the light source to be from the upper-left corner of the screen. ■

NOTE Sun has developed a set of classes for writing true 3D objects. Learn more about the Java 3D classes on this Web page at `http://java.sun.com/products/java-media/3D/`; download the classes and documentation from `http://java.sun.com/products/java-media/3D/download.html`. You'll also need OpenGL on your machine. If you don't already have this software, visit `http://www.opengl.org/`—it's available free for most operating systems.

For still more info on Java 3D, check out the white papers and sample code at `http://java.sun.com/products/java-media/3D/collateral/j3d_api/j3d_api_1.html`. After you've installed Java 3D, try the spectacular spinning cube demo called `HelloUniverse.java`. It's available here, or on your hard drive at *JAVA_HOME*`/demo/java3d/HelloUniverse/`. ■

TIP Three-dimensional rectangles typically look best when their color matches the background color. Three-dimensional effects depend on several aspects of your system, including your computer graphics and color capabilities and the browser you use. If your 3D effects are less than satisfactory, try using different colors. Color manipulation using Java is covered in detail later in this chapter in the section titled "Displaying Colors."

The Java `Graphics` class provides two methods for drawing ovals or circles: the `drawOval()` and `fillOval()` methods. These methods are similar to their `Rectangle` counterparts and are fully described in the Java 2 documentation.

NOTE A circle is an oval with its width equal to its height. ■

An *arc* is a segment of the line that forms the perimeter of an oval. Two `Graphics` class methods are provided for drawing arcs: the `drawArc()` and `fillArc()` methods. Their complete definitions are as follows:

```
public abstract void drawArc(int  x, int  y, int  width,
➥int  height, int  startAngle, int  arcAngle)

public abstract void fillArc(int  x, int  y, int  width,
➥int  height, int  startAngle, int  arcAngle)
```

Use the first four parameters just as you do with the oval methods. In fact, you are drawing an invisible oval and the arc is a segment of the oval's perimeter defined by `startAngle` and `arcAngle`, the last two parameters.

The `startAngle` parameter defines where your arc starts along the invisible oval's perimeter. In Java, angles are set around a 360° circle as follows:

- 0° is at 3 o'clock.
- 90° is at 12 o'clock.
- 180° is at 9 o'clock.
- 270° is at 6 o'clock.

The `arcAngle` parameter defines the distance, in degrees, that your arc traverses along the invisible oval's perimeter. Angles are positive in the counterclockwise direction and negative in the clockwise direction.

Notice that the last parameter is given in the angle traversed and not the angle at which the arc ends. Therefore, if you want an arc that starts at 45° and ends at 135°, you must provide a `startAngle` parameter value of 45° and an `arcAngle` parameter value of 90°.

NOTE When you use a negative `arcAngle` parameter value, the arc sweeps clockwise along the invisible oval's perimeter. ■

Using the `fillArc()` method results in a filled, pie-shaped wedge defined by the center of the invisible oval and the perimeter segment traversed by the arc.

Drawing Polygons

The Java `Graphics` class provides four methods for building polygons: two versions of the `drawPolygon()` method and two versions of the `fillPolygon()` method. Each has two methods so that you can either pass two arrays containing the x, y coordinate of the points in the polygon, or you can pass an instance of a `Polygon` class. The `Polygon` class is defined in the `java.awt` package.

Making a Polygon by Passing Coordinate Arrays First look at how to make a polygon by using two arrays. The full definitions of the `drawPolygon()` and `fillPolygon()` methods for using arrays are

```
public abstract void drawPolygon(int  xPoints[], int yPoints[],
➥int  nPoints)
```

```
public abstract void fillPolygon(int  xPoints[], int  yPoints[],
➥int  nPoints)
```

The DrawPoly applet in Listing 38.2 draws a polygon using an array of x coordinates (`xCoords`) and an array of y coordinates (`yCoords`). Each x, y pair, the first x (50) and the first y (100) pair, for example, defines a point on a plane (50, 100). Use the `drawPolygon` method to connect each point to the following point in the list. The first pair is (50, 100) and connects by a line to the second pair (200, 0), and so on. The `drawPolygon` method's third parameter, `nPoints`, is the number of points in the polygon and should equal the number of pairs in the `x` and `y` arrays. Figure 38.3 shows the `DrawPoly` applet's output.

Listing 38.2 *DrawPoly.java*—This Applet Draws Polygons Based on Arrays of Coordinates

```
import java.awt.Graphics;

public class DrawPoly extends java.applet.Applet
{
   int xCoords[] = { 50, 200, 300, 150, 50 };
   int yCoords[] = { 100, 0, 50, 300, 200 };

   int xFillCoords[] = { 450, 600, 700, 550, 450 };

   public void paint(Graphics g)
   {
     // Draw the left polygon.
     g.drawPolygon(xCoords, yCoords, 5);
     // Draw the right filled polygon.
     g.fillPolygon(xFillCoords, yCoords, 5);
   }
}
```

FIGURE 38.3
Draw polygons using x and y arrays.

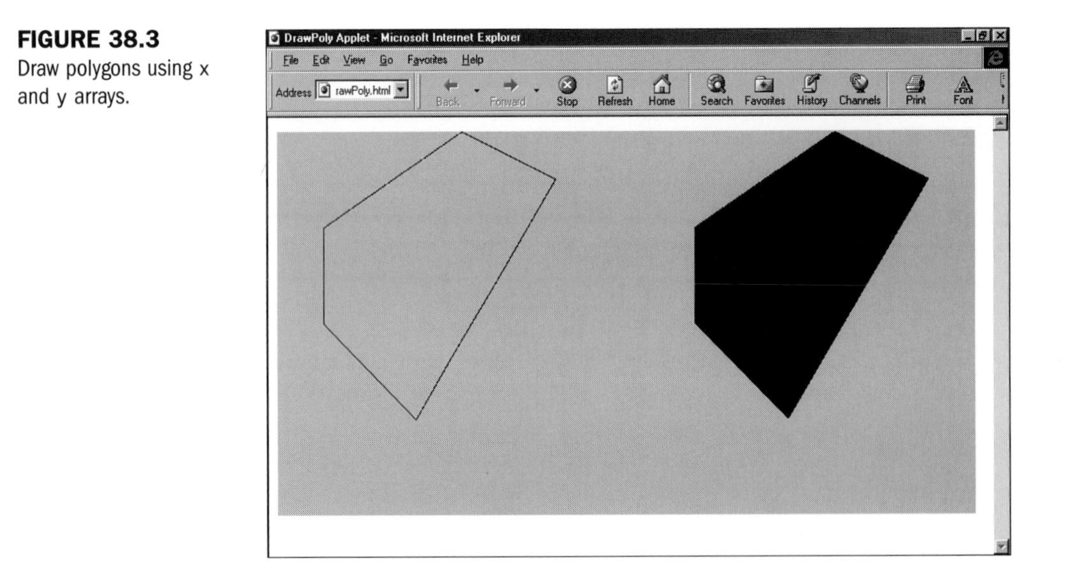

TIP The applets in this chapter assume that you have a graphics resolution of at least 800 pixels across by 600 pixels top to bottom (800×600). If your monitor displays a smaller number of pixels (640×480, for example), you can either use your browser's scrollbars to see the rest of the applet window, or you can change some of the coordinates in the example so they are no larger than your largest screen coordinates.

Using Java's *Polygon* Class The Java `Polygon` class provides features that often make it the most convenient way to define polygons. The `Polygon` class provides the two constructors, defined as follows:

```
public Polygon()
public Polygon(int  xpoints[], int  ypoints[], int  npoints)
```

These constructors enable you to either instantiate an empty polygon or instantiate a polygon by initially passing an array of x and an array of y numbers and the number of points made up of the x and y pairs. If you do the latter, the parameters are saved in the following `Polygon` class fields:

```
public int xpoints[]
public int ypoints[]
public int npoints
```

Regardless of whether you started with an empty polygon, you can add points to it dynamically by using the `Polygon` class `addPoint()` method, defined as follows:

```
public void addPoint(int  x, int  y)
```

The `addPoint()` method automatically increments the `Polygon` class number of points field, named `npoints`.

The `Polygon` class includes two other methods: the `getBounds()` and `contains()` methods, defined as follows:

```
public Rectangle getBounds()
public Boolean contains(Point p)
public boolean contains(int  x, int  y)
```

You can use the `getBounds()` method to determine the minimum-sized rectangle that can completely surround the polygon in screen coordinates. The `Rectangle` object returned by `getBounds()` contains variables indicating the x, y coordinates of the rectangle along with the rectangle's width and height.

You determine whether a point is contained within the polygon or is outside it by calling the `contains` methods with the `Point`, or the x, y coordinate of the point.

Use the `Polygon` class in place of the `x` and `y` arrays for either the `drawPolygon()` or `fillPolygon()` method as indicated in their definitions, shown here:

```
public void drawPolygon(Polygon  p)
public void fillPolygon(Polygon  p)
```


Displaying Colors

Remember when you were in elementary school and the teacher showed you how to make green by combining yellow and blue paint? Forget all that—those techniques applied to pigments on paper, in which colors are made by subtracting colors from the white light falling on the paper. Most of the graphics you make in Java must look good on a computer screen—an additive process based on the primary colors red, green, and blue. Common combinations are

- Red and green, which results in yellow when the colors are bright and in brown when the colors are less intense
- Green and blue, resulting in cyan
- Red and blue, resulting in magenta

Black is formed by the absence of all light, and white is formed by the combination of all the additive primary colors. In other words, red, blue, and green, transmitted in equal amounts, result in white (or, if the colors are less intense, gray).

NOTE The color effects of subtractive pigments and directly transmitted (additive) light are closely related. Each color pigment absorbs light, but not all of it. The color of a pigment is due to the wavelength of the light that the pigment does not absorb–and, therefore, the light that the pigment reflects. Because the absence of pigments results in all wavelengths of light being reflected, the result is white. This effect is the same as the transmission of all the additive primary colors of light. In contrast, all the colored pigments mixed together absorb all light. This effect is equivalent to the color black resulting from the absence of light. ■

Java uses the RGB (Red, Green, and Blue) color model. You define the colors you want by indicating the amount of red, green, and blue light that you want to transmit to the viewer. You can do this either by using integers between 0 and 255 or by using floating-point numbers between 0.0 and 1.0. Table 38.1 indicates the red, green, and blue amounts for some common colors. Note that you don't always have to specify the RGB values—the `Color` class includes some named colors, such as `red`, `blue`, and `white`, as shown in the first column of Table 38.1.

Table 38.1 Common Colors and Their RGB Values

Color Name	Red Value	Green Value	Blue Value
`Color.black`	0	0	0
`Color.blue`	0	0	255
`Color.cyan`	0	255	255
`Color.darkGray`	64	64	64
`Color.gray`	128	128	128
`Color.green`	0	255	0
`Color.lightGray`	192	192	192
`Color.magenta`	255	0	255
`Color.orange`	255	200	0
`Color.pink`	255	175	175
`Color.red`	255	0	0
`Color.white`	255	255	255
`Color.yellow`	255	255	0

You must import the Color class to use a Color class constant, but you don't need to make a new Color object. Just type the class name followed by the dot operator followed by the color name. For example, you can write the following to get a yellow oval:

```
g.setColor(Color.yellow);
g.fillOval(50, 50, 200, 200);
```

NOTE Although the Graphics class uses an informal version of the RGB model, the Graphics2D class is based on a proposed standard called sRGB. For more information, see "Using the 2D API" later in this chapter, or visit the standard's Web site, http://www.w3.org/pub/WWW/Graphics/ Color/sRGB.html. ■

Java's Graphics class provides two methods for manipulating colors: the getColor() and setColor() methods. Their full definitions are

```
public abstract Color getColor()
public abstract void setColor(Color  c)
```

The getColor() method returns the Graphics object's current color encapsulated in a Color object, and the setColor() method sets the Graphics object's color by passing it a Color object.

Using Java's *Color* Class

The Color class is defined in the java.awt package and has seven constructors. One constructor enables you to instantiate a Color object using explicit red (r), green (g), and blue (b) integers between 0 and 255:

```
public Color(int  r, int  g, int  b)
```

The second constructor is similar to the first. Instead of integer values, it uses floating-point values between 0.0 and 1.0 for red (r), green (g), and blue (b):

```
public Color(float  r, float  g, float  b)
```

The third constructor enables you to make a Color using red, green, and blue integers between 0 and 255, but you combine the three numbers into a single, typically hexadecimal, value (rgb):

```
public Color(int  rgb)
```

In the 32-bit rgb integer, bits 16 through 23 (8 bits) hold the red value, bits 8 through 15 (8 bits) hold the green value, and bits 0 through 7 (8 bits) hold the blue value. The highest 8 bits, bits 24 through 32, are not manipulated. You usually write rgb values in hexadecimal notation so it's easy to see the color values. A number prefaced with 0x is read as hexadecimal. For example, 0xFFA978 would give a red value of 0xFF (255 decimal), a green value of 0xA9 (52 decimal), and a blue value of 0x78 (169 decimal).

In addition to these three constructors, Java 2 supports three more versions that allow you to specify a value for the alpha channel. The alpha value specifies the transparency of the color.

Although sRGB is the default `ColorSpace` for the `Color` class, you can change to a different `ColorSpace` by calling this constructor:

```
Color(ColorSpace cspace, float[] components, float alpha)
```

For example, if you want to make a `Color` object that works well for printing, you might specify the CMYK `ColorSpace`, and pass the four-color components in the `float` array.

After you make a `Color` object, set a `Graphics` object's drawing color by using its `setColor` method. The default drawing color for `Graphics` objects is black. The `ColorPlay` applet in Listing 38.3 gets the graphics context's default color and assigns it to the `defaultColor` variable by passing the color value encapsulated in a `Color` object. A new `Color` object is built by using a hexadecimal value and is assigned to the `newColor` variable. You can draw a filled circle on the left using `newColor` and another on the right using the `defaultColor` variable. Figure 38.4 shows the resulting output.

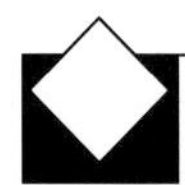

Troubleshooting

How do you return to the original color assigned to your program's `Graphics` object?

It's a good policy to always save the color assigned to your program's `Graphics` object to a `Color` object variable before you assign it a new color. That way you can reassign the original color to the `Graphics` object after the program is finished using the new color.

Listing 38.3 *ColorPlay.java*—Setting the Color Affects All Subsequent Drawings

```
import java.awt.Graphics;
import java.awt.Color;

public class ColorPlay extends java.applet.Applet
{
   public void paint(Graphics g)
   {
     // Assign the red Color object to newColor.
     Color newColor = new Color(0xFFA978);
     // Assign Graphic object's current color to default Color.
     Color defaultColor = g.getColor();
     // Draw a red oval 200 pixels wide and 200 pixels
     //  high with the upper left corner of its
     //  enclosing rectangle at (50, 50).
     g.setColor(newColor);
     g.fillOval(50, 50, 200, 200);
     // Draw an oval 200 pixels wide and 200 pixels
     //  high with the upper left corner of its
     //  enclosing rectangle at (300, 50) in the
     //  default color.
     g.setColor(defaultColor);
     g.fillOval(300, 50, 200, 200);
   }
}
```

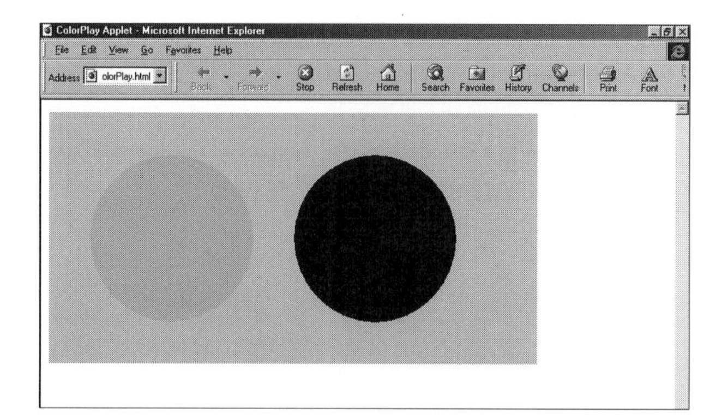

FIGURE 38.4
Make color graphics by changing the graphics context's current color using the `setColor` method.

Displaying Text

Java's `Graphics` class provides seven methods related to displaying text. Before plunging into the various aspects of drawing text, however, you should be familiar with the following common terms for fonts and text:

- **Baseline**—The imaginary line that the text rests on.
- **Descent**—The distance below the baseline that a particular character extends. The letters *g* and *j,* for example, extend below the baseline.
- **Ascent**—The distance above the baseline that a particular character extends. For example, the letter *d* has a higher ascent than the letter *x*.
- **Leading**—The space between a line of text's lowest descent and the following line of text's highest ascent. Without leading, the letters *g* and *j* would touch the letters *M* and *h* on the next line.

Figure 38.5 illustrates the relationships among descent, ascent, baseline, and leading.

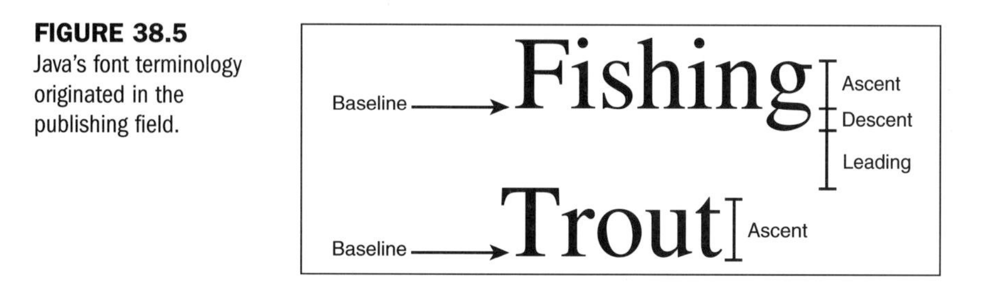

FIGURE 38.5
Java's font terminology originated in the publishing field.

> **CAUTION**
>
> The term *ascent*, as used in Java, is slightly different from the way the term is used in the publishing world. The publishing term *ascent* refers to the distance from the top of a letter such as x to the top of a character such as d. In contrast, the Java term *ascent* refers to the distance from baseline to the top of a character.

NOTE You might hear the terms *proportional* and *fixed* associated with fonts. Characters in a proportional font take up only as much space as they need. In a fixed font, every character takes up the same amount of space.

Most of the text in this book is in a proportional font. Compare the width of the letters in a word in a proportional font with the letters of the same word in a fixed font:

FIXIM

`FIXIM` ■

One simple way to display text in Java is to draw from an array of bytes representing ASCII characters or from an array of 16-bit Unicode characters. You can use an array of ASCII codes when you use the `drawBytes()` method, or you can use an array of characters when you use the `drawChars()` method. Both of these methods are available in Java's `Graphics` class. They are defined as

```
public void drawBytes(byte  data[], int  offset, int  length,
➥int  x, int  y)
public void drawChars(char  data[], int  offset, int  length,
➥int  x, int  y)
```

The `offset` parameter refers to the position of the first character or byte in the array to draw. This is most often 0 because you will usually want to draw from the beginning of the array. The `length` parameter is the total number of bytes or characters in the array. The x coordinate is the integer value that represents the beginning position of the text, in number of pixels, from the left edge of the applet's window. The y coordinate is distance, in pixels, from the top of the applet's window to the text's baseline.

NOTE The numbers used in the byte array, `bytesToDraw`, are base-10 ASCII codes. They are the numbers that most computer systems use to represent letters. (Java uses the 16-bit Unicode, but for the common characters and punctuation marks of English, the Unicode codes are identical to the ASCII codes.) You could use any base for these numbers, including the popular hexadecimal. ■

Java provides another object type, the `String` object, which is similar to the array objects that are used in `drawBytes` and `drawChars`. It is, however, more convenient for manipulating text.

Using Java's *String* Class

The Java `Graphics` class provides a method for displaying text by drawing a string of characters. The `drawString` method shown here takes a `String` object as a parameter:

```
public abstract void drawString(String  str, int  x, int  y)
```

If you put double quotation marks around a string, Java automatically makes a `String` object. You then pass an x coordinate—the integer value that represents the beginning position of the text in number of pixels from the left edge of the applet's window—and pass a y coordinate—the distance in pixels from the top of the applet's window to the text's baseline.

CAUTION

For security reasons, Java's strings are *immutable*—after you make one, you cannot change it. When you manipulate it (for example, by extracting substrings) the Java runtime makes a new string. All this building and releasing of string storage can have an impact on performance.

TIP If your program manipulates passwords, store them as a `char` array rather than as a `String` object. After you've used the password, overwrite it, minimizing the time the password is in memory.

Using Java's *Font* Class

You might find that the default font you have been working with so far is not very interesting. Fortunately, you can select from many fonts. Java's `Graphics` class provides the `setFont()` method, defined here, so that you can change your text's font characteristics:

```
public abstract void setFont(Font  font)
```

The `setFont` method takes a `Font` object as its argument. Java provides a `Font` class that gives you a lot of text-formatting flexibility. The `Font` class provides two constructors. The first is

```
public Font(String  name, int  style, int  size)
```

Pass the name of the font, surrounded by double quotation marks, to the `name` parameter. The availability of fonts varies from system to system, so make sure that the user has the font you want. You can check the availability of a font by using the `Toolkit` class `getFontList` method defined here:

```
public abstract String[] getFontList()
```

The second constructor is

```
Public Font(Map attributes)
```

To use this constructor, build a `Map` object with keys selected from the `TextAttribute` class. If you leave an attribute undefined, the constructor will take that attribute's default value.

Troubleshooting

How do you avoid demanding the use of a font in your program that a user does not have?

Always query for the available fonts by using the `GraphicsEnvironment.getAvailableFontFamilyNames()` method. This method returns an array of `Strings`—the names of the font families available on the user's machine. If the font you had planned to use isn't named in the array, your program can either pick a similar font family or display the list of names and ask the user to select one. This dynamic method of using fonts is the best policy for distributed computing software such as Java programs.

Typically, you don't import the `Toolkit` class. Instead, you use the `Applet` class `getToolkit()` method (which is inherited from the `Component` class), defined as follows:

```
public Toolkit getToolkit()
```

You use the style parameter to set the font style. Bold, italic, plain, as well as the combination (bold and italic) are available. The Font class provides three class constants: Font.BOLD, Font.ITALIC, and Font.PLAIN, which you can use in any combination to set the font style. To set a font to bold, for example, pass Font.BOLD to the style parameter. If you want to display a bold italic font, you pass Font.BOLD + Font.ITALIC to Font class's style parameter.

Finally, you set the point size of the font by passing an integer to the Font class's size parameter. The point size is a printing term. When printing on a printer, an inch has 100 points, but this does not necessarily apply to screen fonts. Just as in your word processor, a typical point size value for printed text is 12 or 14. The point size does not indicate the number of pixels high or wide; it is a relative term. A point size of 24 is twice as big as a point size of 12.

All this information is pulled together in the ShowFonts applet, shown in Listing 38.4. Figure 38.6 shows the output from the ShowFonts applet.

Listing 38.4 *ShowFonts.java*—Use This Simple Applet to Display the Variety of Fonts Available

```
import java.awt.Graphics;
import java.awt.Font;

public class ShowFonts extends java.applet.Applet
{
   public void paint(Graphics g)
   {
     String fontList[];
     int startY = 15;

     // Get the list of fonts installed on
     //  this computer.
     fontList = getToolkit().getFontList();

     // Go through the list of fonts and draw each
     //  to the applet window.
     for (int i=0; i < fontList.length; i++)
     {
        // Draw font name in plain type.
        g.setFont(new Font(fontList[i], Font.PLAIN, 12));
        g.drawString("This is the " + fontList[i] + " font.",
       ➥5, startY);
        startY += 15;

        // Draw font name in bold type.
        g.setFont(new Font(fontList[i], Font.BOLD, 12));
        g.drawString("This is the bold "+ fontList[i] + " font.",
       ➥5, startY);
        startY += 15;

        // Draw font name in italic type.
        g.setFont(new Font(fontList[i], Font.ITALIC, 12));
        g.drawString("This is the italic " + fontList[i] + " font.",
       ➥5, startY);
        startY += 20;
```

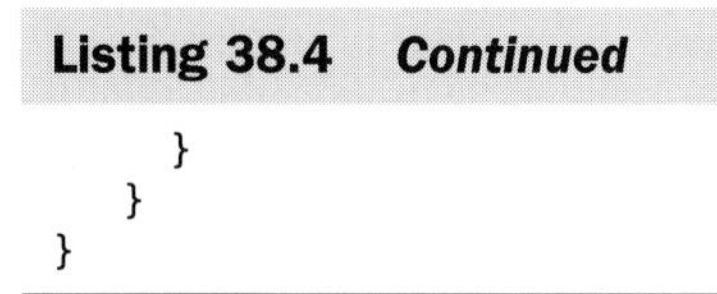

Listing 38.4 Continued

```
        }
      }
  }
```

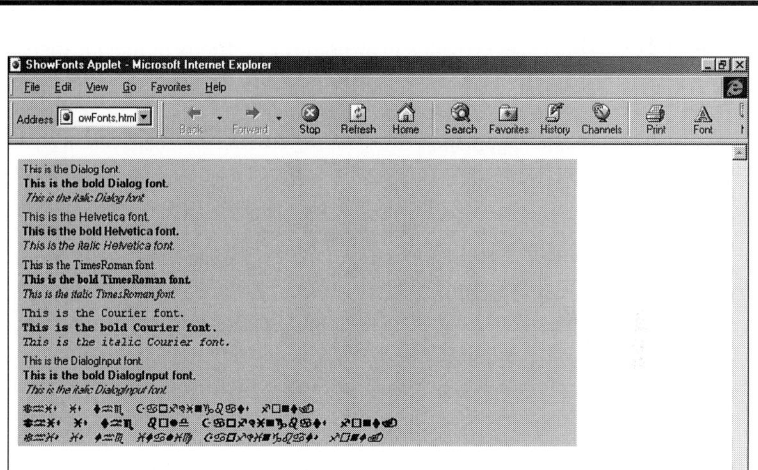

FIGURE 38.6
Java provides many fonts and font styles.

Displaying Images

To use Java to display images, you must first get the image, and then you must draw it. The Java `Applet` class provides methods for getting images, and the Java `Graphics` class provides methods for drawing them.

Java's `Applet` class provides two `getImage()` methods, listed here:

```
public Image getImage(URL  url)
public Image getImage(URL  url, String  name)
```

In the first method listed, you provide a `URL` class. You can just type the URL surrounded by double quotation marks, or you can create a URL object and then pass it to the `getImage()` method. If you do the latter, be sure to import the `URL` class. The `URL` class is part of the `java.net` package.

Whichever way you pass the URL, the first method takes the whole path, including the filename of the image itself. Because images are usually aggregated into a single directory or folder, it is usually handier to keep the path and filename separate.

The second method takes the URL path to the image as the `url` parameter, and it takes the filename—or even part of the path and the filename—as a string enclosed by double quotation marks and passed to the `name` parameter.

The `Applet` class provides two particularly useful methods, the `getDocumentBase()` and `getCodeBase()` methods, as follows:

```
public URL getDocumentBase()
public URL getCodeBase()
```

The `getDocumentBase()` method returns a `URL` object containing the path to where the HTML document resides that displays the Java applet. Similarly, the `getCodeBase()` method returns a `URL` object that contains the path to where the applet is running the code. Using these methods makes your applet flexible. You and others can use your applet on different servers, directories, or folders.

Java's `Graphics` class provides `drawImage()` methods to use for displaying images. The most basic method is listed here:

```
public abstract boolean drawImage(Image  img, int  x, int  y,
➥ImageObserver  observer)
```

The first parameter, `img`, takes an `Image` object. Often, you will get an `Image` object by using the `getImage()` method, as discussed previously. The second, `x`, and third, `y`, parameters set the position of the upper-left corner of the image in the applet's window. The last parameter, `observer`, takes an object that implements the `ImageObserver` interface. This design enables your code to make decisions based on an image's loading status. It is usually enough to know that the `Applet` class inherits the `ImageObserver` interface from the `Component` class. Just passing the applet itself (`this`) as the `observer` parameter is usually sufficient. You might use an alternative object with an `ImageObserver` interface if you are tracking the asynchronous loading of many images.

Troubleshooting

The image doesn't load into the applet. What do you do?

Make sure the image is in the proper folder or directory—either in the same place as the Java code or in the same place as the HTML document, depending on the method your program uses. See the section, "Loading Images Over the Web," later in this chapter, if the problem is due to slow or faulty network connections.

With other graphics primitives, such as `drawLine`, the primitive was called from inside the applet's `paint` method. Putting actions not directly related to putting something onscreen inside your applet's `paint()` method is poor coding practice. Every time your applet's window needs updating, the `paint` method is called. If you include the call to `getImage` inside `paint`, the applet is forced to reload the image every time your applet's window is refreshed. You should override the `init()` method to take actions such as loading images that are done only one time, at the beginning of the applet's life. The `init()` method takes no arguments and returns `void`.

Another version of the `drawImage()` method is similar to the one you already have seen and used, but it includes two additional parameters. These enable you to determine the size of the image displayed in an applet window. This version of the `drawImage()` method is as follows:

```
public abstract boolean drawImage(Image  img, int  x, int  y,
          int  width, int  height, ImageObserver  observer)
```

The `width` and `height` parameters take the width and height, in pixels, of the display area for the image regardless of the image's native size. You can stretch and shrink an image by using these parameters; the actual disk size of the image remains the same.

CAUTION

Changing the size of the image at runtime can degrade the quality of your image. For best results, use your graphics tools to scale the image to the desired size, and don't attempt to use Java for further scaling.

Putting It All Together—The Art Display Applet

Now that you've seen how the various graphics primitives work, you can put them together to build a graphics-intensive applet. Suppose an art dealer has hired you to build a Web site that displays pieces of art online. In addition to showing the art, the dealer wants to allow customers to select a frame and matte. You might write the HTML shown in Listing 38.5.

Listing 38.5 *Frames.html*—The User Chooses a Frame, Matte, and Piece of Art to Display

```
<HTML>
<HEAD><TITLE>Demo of Frames</TITLE></HEAD>
<SCRIPT LANGUAGE="JavaScript">
<!--
  // set the applet's frame property based on the value selected
  function setFrame(theObject)
  {
    //alert("got: " + theObject.options[theObject.selectedIndex].value);
    document.theImage.setFrame(theObject.
    ➥options[theObject.selectedIndex].value);
  }

  // set the applet's matte property based on the value selected
  function setMatte(theObject)
  {
    //alert("got: " + theObject.options[theObject.selectedIndex].value);
    document.theImage.setMatte(theObject.
    ➥options[theObject.selectedIndex].value);
  }

  // set the applet's image property based on the value selected
  function setImage(theObject)
  {
    //alert("got: " + theObject.options[theObject.selectedIndex].value);
    document.theImage.setImage(theObject.
    ➥options[theObject.selectedIndex].value);
  }
//-->
</SCRIPT>
```

Listing 38.5 Continued

```
<BODY>
<FORM NAME="imageForm">
<TABLE>
<TR>
  <TD><BIG>Frame</BIG></TD>
  <TD><BIG>Matte</BIG></TD>
  <TD><BIG>Picture</BIG></TD>
</TR><TR>
  <TD>
  <SELECT onChange="setFrame(this);">
    <OPTION>--choose a frame material--
    <OPTION VALUE="#FFCC99">Light Wood
    <OPTION VALUE="#993300">Dark Wood
    <OPTION VALUE="#FFCC00">Gold Metal
    <OPTION VALUE="#C0C0C0">Silver Metal
  </SELECT>
  </TD><TD>
  <SELECT onChange="setMatte(this);">
    <OPTION>--choose a matte material--
    <OPTION VALUE="#FFFFFF">White
    <OPTION VALUE="#DDDDDD">Light Gray
    <OPTION VALUE="#999999">Dark Gray
    <OPTION VALUE="#000000">Black
  </SELECT>
  </TD><TD>
  <SELECT NAME="thePicture" onChange="setImage(this);">
    <OPTION VALUE="">--choose a picture--
    <OPTION VALUE="mike.jpg">Mike
  </SELECT>
  </TD></TR>
</TABLE>
</FORM>
<APPLET NAME="theImage" CODE="TImage.class" WIDTH="500" HEIGHT="300">
</APPLET>
</BODY>
</HTML>
```

Understanding the HTML Form

This HTML displays a form that has three `<SELECT>` items. The first allows the user to specify a frame color, the second allows the user to specify the matte color, and the third allows the user to select a piece of art.

NOTE You might be wondering whether it's necessary to hard-code the names of the works of art. It's not. You could write a servlet to generate `Frames.html` dynamically. The servlet would build the third `<SELECT>` based on the contents of the directory on the server. You'll hear more about servlets in Chapter 41, "Server-Side Java." ■

Calling the Applet from JavaScript

When the user changes a selection, the appropriate `set . . .` method is called, in turn calling the corresponding method in the applet. For example, `setFrame` calls

```
document.theImage.setFrame(theObject.
➥options[theObject.selectedIndex].value);
```

▶ If you're not familiar with <SELECT>, **see** "Creating Forms," **p. 234**

▶ For more information about using JavaScript to process a change in a <FORM> element, **see** "Dynamic HTML Events and the event Object," **p. 633**

Note that the applet is named with the following:

```
<APPLET NAME="theImage" CODE="TImage.class" WIDTH="500" HEIGHT="300">
```

You can refer to the applet by name and call its methods by using LiveConnect. The `onChange` handler in each `<SELECT>` passes the `<SELECT>` object itself (`this`). You read out the index of the selected menu item, and then use it to extract the appropriate `option`. Each `option` has a `value`, given in the HTML by the `<OPTION VALUE=". . .">` attribute. By the time you're ready to call the applet, you have a color string such as `"#FFCC99"` (for the frame and the matte) or a filename (such as `mike.jpg`) for the artwork.

▶ To learn more about Netscape's LiveConnect (which also works in the Microsoft browser), **see** "Netscape's LiveConnect," **p. 578**

Walking Through the Applet

Because you're directly calling the applet, your applet must support the methods `setFrame(String)`, `setMatte(String)`, and `setImage(String)`. The complete code for the applet appears in Listing 38.6.

Listing 38.6 *TImage.java*—This Applet Displays a Piece of Art, Complete with Frame and Matte

```
import java.awt.Graphics;
import java.awt.Image;
import java.awt.Color;
import java.awt.image.ImageObserver;
import java.awt.Rectangle;

public class TImage extends java.applet.Applet
{
  String fImageName = "";
  boolean fScalingComplete = false;
  Image fImage = null;
  Color fFrameColor = null;
  Color fMatteColor = null;
```

Listing 38.6 Continued

```
Rectangle fBounds = null;
int SCALE_FACTOR = 100;
int FRAME_THICKNESS = 10;
int MATTE_THICKNESS = 30;

public void init()
{
  setFrame("#000000");
  setMatte("#FFFFFF");
  setImage("logo.jpg");
}

public void setFrame(String theColor)
{
  fFrameColor = getColorFromHex(theColor);
  repaint();
}

public void setMatte(String theColor)
{
  fMatteColor = getColorFromHex(theColor);
  repaint();
}

public void setImage(String theImageName)
{
  //System.out.println("setting image to " + theImageName + ".");
  fImageName = theImageName;
  fScalingComplete = false;

  //System.out.println("in setImage, codebase is " + getCodeBase());
  //System.out.println("in setImage, fImageName is " + fImageName + ".");
  if (fImageName != null && fImageName.length() != 0)
  {
    //System.out.println("About to get original image: " +
   ➥getCodeBase() + ":" + fImageName + ".");
    fImage = getImage(getCodeBase(), fImageName);
    if (fImage != null)
      ;//System.out.println("Got " + fImage.toString());
    else
      System.out.println("getImage failed");
  }
  else
    System.out.println("in setImage, fImageName is null or has zero length");
  if (fImage != null)
  {
    //System.out.println("in setImage, preparing to scaleDown");
    Scaler theScaler = new Scaler();
    int theWidth = fImage.getWidth(theScaler);
    int theHeight = fImage.getHeight(theScaler);
```

Listing 38.6 Continued

```
      //System.out.println("Image is " + theWidth + " x " + theHeight + ".");
      fBounds = getBounds();
      //System.out.println("Bounds are " + fBounds.width +
      ➥" x " + fBounds.height + ".");

      if (theWidth != -1 && theHeight != -1)
      {
        fImage = setImage(new Rectangle(theWidth, theHeight));
        //System.out.println("painting synchronously");
        repaint();
      }
      // else control passes to imageUpdate;
    }
    else
      System.out.println("in setImage, theImage is null");

  }

  public void paint(Graphics g)
  {
    //System.out.println("Painting . . .");

    // don't allow the full-size image to paint
    if (fImage != null && fScalingComplete)
    {
      //System.out.println(" the image " + fImage.toString());
      int theImageWidth = fImage.getWidth(this);
      int theImageHeight = fImage.getHeight(this);

      // center the image
      int theXCoord = fBounds.width/2 - theImageWidth/2;
      int theYCoord = fBounds.height/2 - theImageHeight/2;

      // draw the frame

      // three-D rectangles usually look best against a matching background
      setBackground(fFrameColor.brighter());
      g.setColor(fFrameColor);
      g.fill3DRect(theXCoord - MATTE_THICKNESS - FRAME_THICKNESS,
                   theYCoord - MATTE_THICKNESS - FRAME_THICKNESS,
                   theImageWidth + 2*MATTE_THICKNESS + 2*FRAME_THICKNESS,
                   theImageHeight + 2*MATTE_THICKNESS + 2*FRAME_THICKNESS,
                   true);

      // draw the matte
      g.setColor(fMatteColor);
      g.fillRect(theXCoord - MATTE_THICKNESS,
                 theYCoord - MATTE_THICKNESS,
                 theImageWidth + 2*MATTE_THICKNESS,
                 theImageHeight + 2*MATTE_THICKNESS);
```

Listing 38.6 Continued

```
      g.drawImage(fImage, theXCoord, theYCoord, this);
    }
  }

  // compute a rectangle that maps a large rectangle (such as an image)
  // into a small rectangle (such as the clip rectangle of a Graphics object
  private Rectangle scaleDown(Rectangle theLargeRectangle,
  ➥Rectangle theSmallRectangle)
  {
    Rectangle theResult = null;
    int theNewHeight = Integer.MAX_VALUE;
    int theNewWidth = Integer.MAX_VALUE;
    int theRatio = Integer.MAX_VALUE;
    if ((theSmallRectangle.width > theLargeRectangle.width) &&
        (theSmallRectangle.height > theLargeRectangle.height))
    {
      //System.out.println("In scaleDown, no scaling required.");
      theResult = theLargeRectangle; // it fits!
    }
    else
    {
      // scale the height; see if the width fits
      //System.out.println("Scaling height: " +
      ➥theSmallRectangle.height + ":" +
      //                                        theLargeRectangle.height +
➥".");
      theRatio = (SCALE_FACTOR  * theSmallRectangle.height) /
      ➥theLargeRectangle.height;
      //System.out.println("Ratio is " + theRatio + ".");

      // use fixed-point with a scaling factor
      if ( theRatio < SCALE_FACTOR )
      {
        //System.out.println("Scaling down by height; ratio is 1:" + theRatio);
        theNewHeight = theSmallRectangle.height;
        theNewWidth = (theLargeRectangle.width * theRatio)/SCALE_FACTOR;
      }
      if (theNewWidth > theSmallRectangle.width)
      {
        //System.out.println("Scaling width:" + theSmallRectangle.width + ":" +
        //                                  theLargeRectangle.width + ".");
        theRatio = (SCALE_FACTOR * theSmallRectangle.width) /
        ➥theLargeRectangle.width;
        //System.out.println("Scaling down by width; ratio is 1:" + theRatio);
        theNewWidth = theSmallRectangle.width;
        theNewHeight = (theLargeRectangle.height * theRatio)/SCALE_FACTOR;
      }
      theResult = new Rectangle(theNewWidth, theNewHeight);
    }
    return theResult;
  }
```

Listing 38.6 Continued

```
private Image setImage(Rectangle theImageRectangle)
{
  Image theResult = null;
  //System.out.println("Calling setImage with width: " +
  ➥theImageRectangle.width +
  //                    ", height: " + theImageRectangle.height);
  //System.out.println("bounds wd:" + fBounds.width + " ht:" +
  ➥fBounds.height + ".");
  Rectangle theNewRectangle = scaleDown(theImageRectangle, fBounds);
  //System.out.println("in setImage(rect), scaled down to " +
  ➥theNewRectangle.width + " x " +
  //                     theNewRectangle.height + ".");
  //System.out.println("setImage(r) about to scale down " +
  ➥fImage.toString());
  theResult = fImage.getScaledInstance(theNewRectangle.width,
                                       theNewRectangle.height,
                                       Image.SCALE_DEFAULT);
  //System.out.println("The scaled down image is " + theResult.toString());
  fScalingComplete = true;
  return theResult;
}

private Color getColorFromHex(String theColor)
{
  Color theResult = null;

  // skip the leading '#'
  String theRed = theColor.substring(1,3);
  String theGreen = theColor.substring(3,5);
  String theBlue = theColor.substring(5,7);
  //System.out.println("getColorFromHex has R: " + theRed + " G: " +
  ➥theGreen + " B: " + theBlue + ".");
  int r = Integer.parseInt(theRed, 16);
  int g = Integer.parseInt(theGreen, 16);
  int b = Integer.parseInt(theBlue, 16);
  theResult = new Color(r, g, b);
  return theResult;
}

private class Scaler implements ImageObserver
{
  public boolean imageUpdate(Image theImage, int theInfoFlags, int x,
  ➥int y, int width, int height)
  {
    boolean theResult = false; // don't need more info
    //System.out.println("Someone called Scaler.imageUpdate; width is " +
    //                    width + " height is " + height + ".");
    if (((theInfoFlags & ImageObserver.ABORT) == ImageObserver.ABORT) ||
        ((theInfoFlags & ImageObserver.ERROR) == ImageObserver.ERROR))
      theResult = false; // bail out
```

Listing 38.6 Continued

```
        else
          if ((theInfoFlags & ImageObserver.ALLBITS) == ImageObserver.ALLBITS)
          {
            fImage = setImage(new Rectangle(width, height));
            //System.out.println("About to paint asynchronously");
            repaint();
          } else
          {
            //System.out.println("Waiting for image width and height.");
            theResult = true;
          }
        return theResult;
      }
    }
  }
```

Several advanced concepts are demonstrated in this code. The following sections walk through it method by method.

Understanding *init* and *paint* When the applet is first loaded the browser calls `init`, which, in turn, sets the frame and matte colors to default colors and loads the `logo.jpg` image. For review, here's `init`:

```
public void init()
{
  setFrame("#000000");
  setMatte("#FFFFFF");
  setImage("logo.jpg");
}
```

You'll look at `setFrame`, `setMatte`, and `setImage` in just a moment. For now, look at the next method called by the browser: `paint`.

```
public void paint(Graphics g)
{
  //System.out.println("Painting . . .");

  // don't allow the full-size image to paint
  if (fImage != null && fScalingComplete)
  {
    //System.out.println(" the image " + fImage.toString());
    int theImageWidth = fImage.getWidth(this);
    int theImageHeight = fImage.getHeight(this);

    // center the image
    int theXCoord = fBounds.width/2 - theImageWidth/2;
    int theYCoord = fBounds.height/2 - theImageHeight/2;

    // draw the frame
```

```
// three-D rectangles usually look best against a matching background
    setBackground(fFrameColor.brighter());
    g.setColor(fFrameColor);
    g.fill3DRect(theXCoord - MATTE_THICKNESS - FRAME_THICKNESS,
                 theYCoord - MATTE_THICKNESS - FRAME_THICKNESS,
                 theImageWidth + 2*MATTE_THICKNESS + 2*FRAME_THICKNESS,
                 theImageHeight + 2*MATTE_THICKNESS + 2*FRAME_THICKNESS,
                 true);

    // draw the matte
    g.setColor(fMatteColor);
    g.fillRect(theXCoord - MATTE_THICKNESS,
                 theYCoord - MATTE_THICKNESS,
                 theImageWidth + 2*MATTE_THICKNESS,
                 theImageHeight + 2*MATTE_THICKNESS);

    g.drawImage(fImage, theXCoord, theYCoord, this);
  }
}
```


This method examines the state of various instance variables such as `fImage` and `fScalingComplete`. If it finds them in their default state, it exits without drawing anything. After `fImage` points to an image and `fScalingComplete` is true, `paint` proceeds into three sections, each of which concludes with a `draw . . .` primitive. The first section draws a filled 3D rectangle in the current frame color. Note that the final parameter of `fill3Drect` is `true`, which gives the rectangle an embossed appearance. The second section builds a slightly smaller `Rectangle` in the matte color. The final section concludes with `drawImage`—it simply draws the current piece of art.

Understanding *setFrame* and *setMatte* Recall that `init` called `setFrame`, `setMatte`, and `setImage`. The first two of these methods are fairly simple. They take one parameter—a string of the form `"#rrggbb"` where `rr`, `gg`, and `bb` stand for the red, green, and blue components of the color. They pass the parameter to `getColorFromHex`, which extracts the three-color components, converts them into hexadecimal numbers, and builds a new `Color` object based on the `String`. Here, for review, is `getColorFromHex`:

```
  private Color getColorFromHex(String theColor)
  {
    Color theResult = null;

    // skip the leading '#'
    String theRed = theColor.substring(1,3);
    String theGreen = theColor.substring(3,5);
    String theBlue = theColor.substring(5,7);
    //System.out.println("getColorFromHex has R: " + theRed + " G: " +
    ➥theGreen + " B: " + theBlue + ".");
    int r = Integer.parseInt(theRed, 16);
    int g = Integer.parseInt(theGreen, 16);
    int b = Integer.parseInt(theBlue, 16);
```

```
    theResult = new Color(r, g, b);
    return theResult;
  }
```

CAUTION

If the HTML <SELECT> tag doesn't have a well-formed color string in the `VALUE` attribute, the `parseInt` method will throw an `Exception` and the applet won't run. When you test in Sun's AppletViewer, you'll see these errors reported in the command prompt window. If you're testing in a browser, open the Java Console to see messages that are written to `System.error` or `System.out`.

Walking Through *setImage*

The most complex of the three `set . . .` methods is `setImage`. Let's go through it a few lines at a time:

```
public void setImage(String theImageName)
  {
    //System.out.println("setting image to " + theImageName + ".");
    fImageName = theImageName;
    fScalingComplete = false;

    //System.out.println("in setImage, codebase is " + getCodeBase());
    //System.out.println("in setImage, fImageName is " + fImageName + ".");
    if (fImageName != null && fImageName.length() != 0)
    {
      //System.out.println("About to get original image: " + getCodeBase() +
      ➥":" + fImageName + ".");
      fImage = getImage(getCodeBase(), fImageName);
      if (fImage != null)
        ;//System.out.println("Got " + fImage.toString());
      else
        System.out.println("getImage failed");
    }
    else
      System.out.println("in setImage, fImageName is null or has zero length");
    if (fImage != null)
    {
      //System.out.println("in setImage, preparing to scaleDown");
      Scaler theScaler = new Scaler();
      int theWidth = fImage.getWidth(theScaler);
      int theHeight = fImage.getHeight(theScaler);

      //System.out.println("Image is " + theWidth + " x " + theHeight + ".");
      fBounds = getBounds();
      //System.out.println("Bounds are " + fBounds.width + " x " +
      ➥fBounds.height + ".");

      if (theWidth != -1 && theHeight != -1)
      {
        fImage = setImage(new Rectangle(theWidth, theHeight));
```

```
          //System.out.println("painting synchronously");
          repaint();
        }
        // else control passes to imageUpdate;
      }
      else
        System.out.println("in setImage, theImage is null");

  }
```

One of the tasks of `setImage` is to scale the image to fit into the space allocated by the browser. The browser allocates drawing space for the applet in accordance with the `WIDTH` and `HEIGHT` attributes in the `APPLET` tag—in this case, 500×300 pixels.

TIP If your images are too large to fit into the space you've reserved, use a graphics tool such as Adobe PhotoShop to change the image size. Companies like Adobe have invested heavily in algorithms that change image size with little loss of quality. The `scaledown` code in this applet only serves as a backup, in case the image doesn't fit.

Many of the methods in the `Image` class are asynchronous—that is, there might be a delay while the method is processed. One parameter of these asynchronous methods is an `ImageObserver`. An `ImageObserver` class was built right into the applet—it's called `Scaler`. Note that `Scaler` implements the `ImageObserver` interface—you'll look at interfaces in the next section, "Adding Animation."

With an instance of `Scaler` at hand, ask the `Image` for its height and width. Because these values won't be available until the image is loaded, tell the `Image` to notify `theScaler` when the data is available. `SetImage`, meanwhile, goes on to get the size of the graphical space (`getBounds`). Because this size won't change for the life of the applet and it's used frequently, store it in instance variables.

Although the height and width are unknown, `Image` sets their values to –1. If the image has previously loaded and the height and width are available, proceed with painting the image. Otherwise, that step is deferred until the asynchronous methods call us back.

Using a Callback Method Recall that `theScaler` was specified to handle callbacks from `fImage`. An `imageObserver` has only one required method: `imageUpdate`. The Java environment will call this method when the `Image` needs attention. Here's the `imageUpdate`:

```
public boolean imageUpdate(Image theImage, int theInfoFlags, int x, int y,
➥int width, int height)
{
  boolean theResult = false; // don't need more info
  //System.out.println("Someone called Scaler.imageUpdate; width is " +
  //                    width + " height is " + height + ".");
  if (((theInfoFlags & ImageObserver.ABORT) == ImageObserver.ABORT) ||
     ((theInfoFlags & ImageObserver.ERROR) == ImageObserver.ERROR))
    theResult = false; // bail out
```

```
    else
      if ((theInfoFlags & ImageObserver.ALLBITS) == ImageObserver.ALLBITS)
      {
        fImage = setImage(new Rectangle(width, height));
        //System.out.println("About to paint asynchronously");
        repaint();
      } else
      {
        //System.out.println("Waiting for image width and height.");
        theResult = true;
      }
    return theResult;
}
```

This method returns a Boolean—whenever you determine that you have all the information needed about the image, you return `false`.

CAUTION

If you intend to display the image, don't return `false` from `imageUpdate` until you have all the scanlines. Otherwise the image is incomplete and won't display.

The Java environment passes an `int`—`theInfoFlags`—to tell you what information is available about the `Image`. You can read `theInfoFlags` by masking out certain class constants. First, check to make sure there hasn't been a problem (`ImageObserver.ERROR`) or that the user hasn't cancelled the loading process (`ImageObserver.ABORT`).

After `ImageObserver.ALLBITS` is set, you can proceed to use the image. Before displaying the image, scale it to fit the available space. Just call a different version of `setImage`—one that takes the width and height of the image as a parameter (in a `Rectangle`). This version of `setImage` returns an `Image` (which might have been scaled down), which you use as the new `fImage`.

NOTE Note that `Scaler` was written right inside the class definition for `TImage`. That approach makes `Scaler` an inner class of `TImage`—all of `TImage`'s class and instance variables are available in `Scaler`. ■

Understanding *setImage(Rectangle)* Most of the work of `setImage` is done by calling `scaleDown`, which you'll look at in a moment. After `scaleDown` gives you an image that fits into the `fBounds` rectangle, call `Image.getScaledInstance` to make a new (scaled) version of the image. Here's `setImage`:

```
private Image setImage(Rectangle theImageRectangle)
{
  Image theResult = null;
  //System.out.println("Calling setImage with width: " +
  ➥theImageRectangle.width +
```

```
  //                    ", height: " + theImageRectangle.height);
  //System.out.println("bounds wd:" + fBounds.width + " ht:" +
  ➥fBounds.height + ".");
  Rectangle theNewRectangle = scaleDown(theImageRectangle, fBounds);
  //System.out.println("in setImage(rect), scaled down to " +
  ➥theNewRectangle.width + " x " +
  //                     theNewRectangle.height + ".");
  //System.out.println("setImage(r) about to scale down " +
  ➥fImage.toString());
  theResult = fImage.getScaledInstance(theNewRectangle.width,
                                       theNewRectangle.height,
                                       Image.SCALE_DEFAULT);
  //System.out.println("The scaled down image is " + theResult.toString());
  fScalingComplete = true;
  return theResult;
}
```


TIP If you expect that you will routinely be changing image size, you can choose a scaling algorithm other than `Image.SCALE_DEFAULT`. For example, you can choose a high-speed algorithm (and sacrifice quality). Because it's expected that the user will usually make the image size fit the `fBounds` rectangle, just use `Image.SCALE_DEFAULT`.

How Does *scaleDown* Work? The last step in preparing the image for display is to scale it down to the size of the space reserved in the browser. Use the method `scaleDown` to compute the new `Rectangle` size:

```
private Rectangle scaleDown(Rectangle theLargeRectangle,
➥Rectangle theSmallRectangle)
{
  Rectangle theResult = null;
  int theNewHeight = Integer.MAX_VALUE;
  int theNewWidth = Integer.MAX_VALUE;
  int theRatio = Integer.MAX_VALUE;
  if ((theSmallRectangle.width > theLargeRectangle.width) &&
      (theSmallRectangle.height > theLargeRectangle.height))
  {
    //System.out.println("In scaleDown, no scaling required.");
    theResult = theLargeRectangle; // it fits!
  }
  else
  {
    // scale the height; see if the width fits
    //System.out.println("Scaling height: " +
    ➥theSmallRectangle.height + ":" +
    //
    ➥theLargeRectangle.height + ".");
    theRatio = (SCALE_FACTOR  * theSmallRectangle.height) /
    ➥theLargeRectangle.height;
    //System.out.println("Ratio is " + theRatio + ".");

    // use fixed-point with a scaling factor
```

```
      if ( theRatio < SCALE_FACTOR )
      {
        //System.out.println("Scaling down by height; ratio is 1:" + theRatio);
        theNewHeight = theSmallRectangle.height;
        theNewWidth = (theLargeRectangle.width * theRatio)/SCALE_FACTOR;
      }
      if (theNewWidth > theSmallRectangle.width)
      {
        //System.out.println("Scaling width: " +
        ➥theSmallRectangle.width + ":" +
        //
        ➥theLargeRectangle.width + ".");
        theRatio = (SCALE_FACTOR * theSmallRectangle.width) /
        ➥theLargeRectangle.width;
        //System.out.println("Scaling down by width; ratio is 1:" + theRatio);
        theNewWidth = theSmallRectangle.width;
        theNewHeight = (theLargeRectangle.height * theRatio)/SCALE_FACTOR;
      }
      theResult = new Rectangle(theNewWidth, theNewHeight);
    }
    return theResult;
  }
```

Most of the time, you hope that the "large rectangle" (which represents the image) is actually smaller than the "small rectangle." If that's the case, just return the large rectangle.

If the image doesn't fit, determine whether you need to scale down the height or width more. Arbitrarily, scale the large rectangle down so that the height fits into the small rectangle. Then, check to see if the scaled width fits. If it doesn't, repeat the process, this time scaling down the width. Either way, you now have a new height and width—use those values to make a new `Rectangle` and return it.

NOTE In some languages, such as C++, the programmer is responsible for deallocating memory. If you're experienced in those languages, you might have wondered who will ultimately release the memory associated with the new `Rectangle`. In Java, you don't have to worry about deallocation–the Java environment has a garbage collector that will free the space when it's no longer needed. ■

After `scaleDown` has run, it returns a `Rectangle` guaranteed to fit the image into the space reserved in the browser. `SetImage` (called from `theScaler`) scales the image. When `theScaler` calls `repaint`, `paint` accesses the scaled image (which is referenced by `fImage`). Because `drawImage` is asynchronous, you need to specify an `ImageObserver`. You don't need any special handling this time, so use the applet itself (`this`) as the `ImageObserver`. Figure 38.7 shows the finished product.

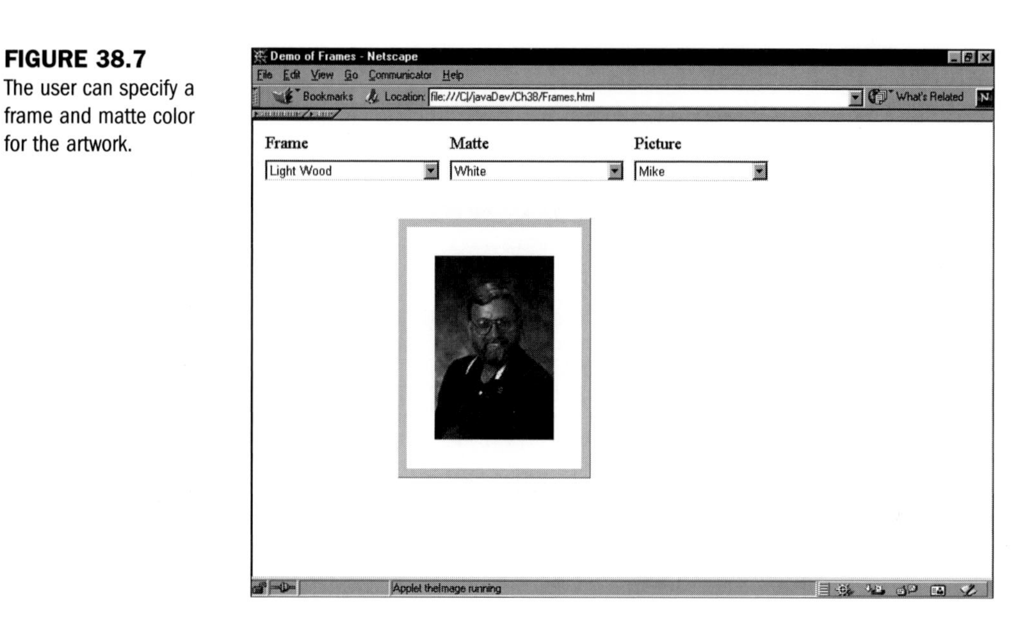

FIGURE 38.7
The user can specify a frame and matte color for the artwork.

Adding Animation

As you develop your user interfaces—particularly user interfaces for applets—you might find a need for animation. The previous section explored `drawImage()`; it is the graphical analog of `drawString()` that you've been using for a while. Listing 38.7 illustrates an animation technique you might consider using.

Listing 38.7 ***Animation1.java*****—This Applet Loads and Displays a Series of Images in Rapid Succession**

```
import java.awt.*;
import java.applet.Applet;

public class Animation1 extends Applet implements Runnable {
    int fFrame = -1;
    int fDelay;
    Thread fThread;
    Image[] fEarth;

    public void init() {
      fEarth = new Image[30];
      String theString;
      int theFramesPerSecond = 10;

      //load in the images
      for (int i=1; i<=30; i++)
      {
      System.err.println("Starting load from " +
         getCodeBase() +
```

Listing 38.7 Continued

```
          " of ./Earth" + i +".gif");
           fEarth[i-1] = getImage (getCodeBase(),
                                   "./Earth"+i+".gif");
      }
//How many milliseconds between frames?
      theString = getParameter("fps");
      try {
        if (theString != null) {
            theFramesPerSecond = Integer.parseInt(theString );
        }
      } catch (NumberFormatException e) {}
      fDelay = (theFramesPerSecond > 0) ?
               (1000 / theFramesPerSecond) : 100;
    }

    public void start() {
      // start a new thread for the animation
      if (fThread == null) {
          fThread = new Thread(this);
      }
      fThread.start();
    }

    public void stop() {
      // stop the animation thread
      fThread = null;
    }

    public void run() {
      // run at a low priority; animation is second-place to content
      Thread.currentThread().setPriority(Thread.MIN_PRIORITY);
      long theStartTime = System.currentTimeMillis();

      //Here comes the show.
      while (Thread.currentThread() == fThread) {

        //Advance the frame.
        fFrame++;

        //Display it.
        repaint();

        //Delay depending on how far we are behind.
        try {
             theStartTime += fDelay;
             Thread.sleep(Math.max(0,
                                   theStartTime-
                          System.currentTimeMillis()));
        } catch (InterruptedException e) {
                 break;
        }
    }
  }
```

Listing 38.7 Continued

```
//Draw the current frame
  public void paint(Graphics g) {
    g.drawImage(fEarth[fFrame % 30], 0, 0, this);
  }
}
```

This applet works, but it suffers from two problems. First, the animation is far from smooth. Even when the images are loading from the local hard drive, there is a certain jerkiness as the frames change. Second, if you load this applet over the network, the animation might begin before all the image files have finished loading, resulting in an ugly half-drawn frame. Both of these problems will be solved in the next two sections.

You can use this applet, `Animation1.java`, as the basis for building a smooth, flicker-free animation applet.

Notice that this applet implements an interface called `Runnable`. `Runnable` enables the applet to start a new *thread* of control so the animation can proceed independently of the user interface.

NOTE Java interfaces are Sun's solution to multiple inheritance. A class can only subclass one base class, but it can implement as many interfaces as you like. When you subclass a class (such as `Applet`), you can override as many or as few of the class's methods as you like. When you implement an interface, you must provide an implementation for every method in the interface. ■

The list of instance variables includes a reference to the animation thread (`fThread`) and a reference to the array of images. This examples uses 30 frames of the revolving Earth, so this array is called `fEarth`.

In `init()`, loop from `1` to `30`, loading the images of Earth. (They're stored in files named `Earth1.gif` through `Earth30.gif`.)

Next, look for an applet `<PARAM>` called `fps` (frames per second). If you find it, attempt to parse it into a number. If you don't find it or if you can't read it, use 10 frames per second as the basis for calculating the delay between calls to `paint()`.

When the browser first shows the applet, it calls `init()` followed by `start()`. The browser will call `stop()` if the user iconifies the browser window or moves to a different page. You handle `start()` by checking to see whether the animation thread has already been set up. If it hasn't, you instantiate it. In either case, you `start()` the thread and destroy it in `stop()`.

The required method of `Runnable` is `run()`. The Java runtime environment calls this method whenever time is available to run your thread. Your version of `run()` starts by setting the animation thread's priority to a low value because any user interaction should take precedence over the animation. Then, you step through the frames, repaint on each loop, and delay as necessary to match the desired frame rate.

Finally, the work is done in `paint()` itself (as it is in most graphics-intensive applets). You draw the current frame onto the screen.

Loading Images Over the Web

As you experiment with this code, you'll discover that it sometimes jerks a bit. This happens when the image doesn't load fast enough to support the animation, particularly when someone is loading this applet over the Internet.

A simple fix to this problem requires only six lines of code. You add an instance of the `MediaTracker` class to your applet. The `MediaTracker` knows which images are already loaded into memory and can prevent you from using an image that has not been fully loaded. Follow these steps to add a `MediaTracker` to any animation project:

1. Add a `MediaTracker` as an instance variable:

```
MediaTracker fTracker;
```

2. In `init()`, instantiate a new `MediaTracker`:

```
fTracker = new
MediaTracker( this );
```

3. As each image is loaded, place it under the control of the `MediaTracker`:

```
fTracker.addImage ( fEarth[i], 0 );
```

   The second parameter to this method, `0`, is an ID number that will be used to refer to this set of images.

4. Before the `while` loop in `run()`, call `waitForID()`:

```
try {
  fTracker.waitForID( 0 );
} catch (InterruptedException e) {
  return;
}
```

5. Before using the images in `paint()`, double-check that they're loaded:

```
if (fTracker.checkID( 0 ))
```

Fighting Flicker

You might have also noticed an annoying flicker in your animation program. This flicker occurs because a delay exists between the start of `paint()` and the time the image is actually loaded from the disk. (The flicker is even worse if you're loading images over a slow Internet connection.) You can eliminate the flicker by preloading the image into memory—a technique called *double buffering*. Like the `MediaTracker` technique, double buffering requires only a few lines of code. Follow these steps to add double buffering:

1. Add an offscreen buffer and its graphics context to the list of instance variables:

   ```
   Image fOffScreenImage;
   Graphics fOffScreenGraphics;
   ```

2. In `init()`, instantiate the offscreen buffer and paint it blue:

   ```
   fOffScreenImage = createImage( getSize().width, getSize().height);
   fOffScreenGraphics = fOffScreenImage.getGraphics();
   fOffScreenGraphics.setColor(Color.blue);
   fOffScreenGraphics.fillRect(0, 0, getSize().width, getSize().height);
   ```

3. Override `update()`, which is responsible for clearing the background and calling `paint()`:

   ```
   public void update( Graphics g ) {
     fOffScreenGraphics.setColor(Color.blue);
     fOffScreenGraphics.clearRect(0, 0, getSize().width, getSize().height);
     fOffScreenGraphics.fillRect(0, 0, getSize().width, getSize().height);
     paint(g);
   }
   ```

4. Modify `paint()` so that it updates the offscreen image and draws the onscreen image from the offscreen image:

   ```
   fOffScreenGraphics.drawImage(fEarth[i], 0, 0, this);
   g.drawImage(fOffScreenImage, 0, 0, this);
   ```

Listing 38.8 shows the revised animation applet, with double buffering and a `MediaTracker`. You can use an HTML file to put the two applets up side-by-side, as a before-and-after demonstration. For smoothest performance, however, put Animation2 on a Web page without Animation1 so its thread doesn't compete with Animation1's thread.

Figure 38.8 shows a screen shot of an HTML page that illustrates all three versions of this applet—the original `Animation1.java`, a version with a `MediaTracker`, and a version that adds double buffering.

TIP AppletViewer's performance with animation is sometimes poor. Use a Web browser such as Netscape Navigator (part of Netscape Communicator) to view these applets.

Listing 38.8 *Animation2.java*—This Version of the Animation Applet Is Noticeably Smoother and Flicker-Free

```
import java.awt.*;
import java.applet.Applet;
```

Listing 38.8 Continued

```
public class Animation2 extends Applet implements Runnable {
    int fFrame = -1;
    int fDelay;
    Thread fThread;
    Image[] fEarth;
    MediaTracker fTracker;
    Image fOffScreenImage;
    Graphics fOffScreenGraphics;

    public void init() {
      fEarth = new Image[30];
      String theString;
      int theFramesPerSecond = 10;
      fTracker = new MediaTracker( this );
      fOffScreenImage = createImage(getSize().width,
                                    getSize().height);
      fOffScreenGraphics = fOffScreenImage.getGraphics();

      // fill the offsceen buffer with blue
      fOffScreenGraphics.setColor(Color.blue);
      fOffScreenGraphics.fillRect(0, 0,
                     getSize().width, getSize().height);

      //load in the images
      for (int i=1; i<=30; i++)
      {
         fEarth[i-1] = getImage (getCodeBase(),
                                 "./Earth"+i+".gif");
         fTracker.addImage(fEarth[i-1], 0);
      }

      //How many milliseconds between frames?
      theString = getParameter("fps");
      try {
        if (theString != null) {
            theFramesPerSecond = Integer.parseInt(theString );
        }
      } catch (NumberFormatException e) {}
      fDelay = (theFramesPerSecond > 0) ?
               (1000 / theFramesPerSecond) : 100;
    }

    public void start() {
      // start a new thread for the animation
      if (fThread == null) {
          fThread = new Thread(this);
      }
      fThread.start();
    }
```

Listing 38.8 Continued

```
  public void stop() {
    // stop the animation thread
    fThread = null;
  }

  public void run() {
    // run at a low priority; animation is second-place to content
    Thread.currentThread().setPriority(Thread.MIN_PRIORITY);
    long theStartTime = System.currentTimeMillis();

    //Here comes the show.
    try {
     fTracker.waitForID(0);
    } catch (InterruptedException e) {
      System.err.println("Interrupted Exception: " + e.getMessage());
      e.printStackTrace();
      return;
    }
    while (Thread.currentThread() == fThread) {

      //Advance the frame.
      fFrame++;

      //Display it.
      repaint();

      //Delay depending on how far we are behind.
      try {
           theStartTime += fDelay;
           Thread.sleep(Math.max(0,
                                theStartTime-
                         System.currentTimeMillis()));
      } catch (InterruptedException e) {
               break;
      }
  }
}

public void update( Graphics g) {

    // fill the offsceen buffer with blue
    fOffScreenGraphics.setColor(Color.blue);
    fOffScreenGraphics.clearRect(0, 0,
                   getSize().width, getSize().height);
    fOffScreenGraphics.fillRect(0, 0,
                   getSize().width, getSize().height);
    paint(g);
}

//Draw the current frame
```

Listing 38.8 Continued

```
    public void paint(Graphics g) {
      if (fTracker.checkID( 0 )) {
        fOffScreenGraphics.drawImage(fEarth[fFrame % 30], 0, 0, this);
        g.drawImage(fOffScreenImage, 0, 0, this);
      }
    }
  }
```

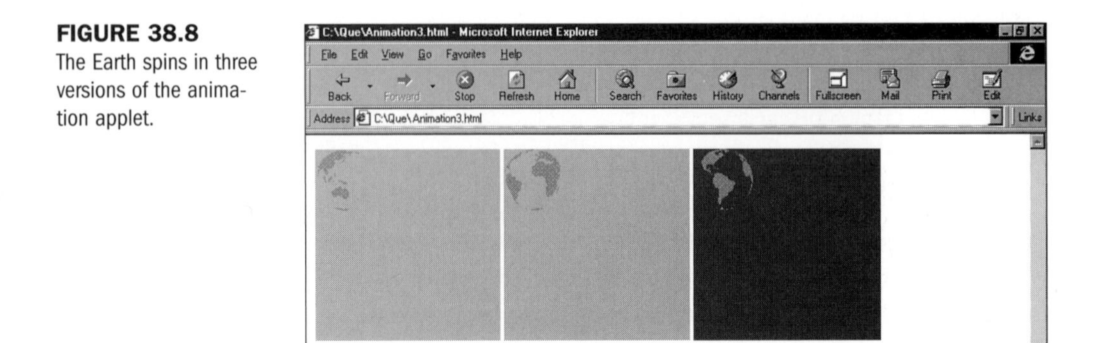

FIGURE 38.8
The Earth spins in three versions of the animation applet.

TIP Animations with many frames of large images can take a long time to load. Consider putting a notice to the user in the applet, or even displaying a progress bar while the images are downloaded.

Using the 2D API

From its earliest days, Java has included a nice graphics class called `java.awt.Graphics`. To graphics professionals, however, `Graphics` left some features to be desired. More mature GUI platforms, such as Windows 95 and above and the Macintosh, support features that are not present in `Graphics`.

Now, in Java 2, all that has changed. Sun has provided a much richer, two-dimensional graphics class called `java.awt.Graphics2D`. This section describes the major improvements available in `Graphics2D`. Listing 38.9 shows a demonstration program, `PathsFill.java`, that shows how to display shapes by using `Graphics2D`. The `PathsFill` class is a type of canvas, so `Graphics2D` is able to draw on it by casting the `Graphics` parameter to `paint()` as `Graphics2D`. The class also contains a `main()` method, enabling you to run it from the command line. Compile `PathsFill.java` by typing

```
javac PathsFill.java
```

and run it by typing

```
java PathsFill
```

at the command line. You should see a spiral of shapes in a variety of colors.

NOTE `Graphics2D` is an abstract class—you must either subclass it yourself or rely on Sun's subclasses to actually draw anything. ■

TIP If you're a member of Sun's Java Developer Connection, you can read technical articles such as, "New Color Classes: A Programmer's Palette of Color," by Monica Pawlan at `http://developer.java.sun.com/developer/technicalArticles/Media/ColorClasses/index.html`. The extended example in this section, Listing 38.9, is drawn from another of Pawlan's articles, at `http://developer.java.sun.com/developer/technicalArticles/Media/Simple2D/index.html`.

Listing 38.9 *PathsFill.java*—This Program Demonstrates the Major Capabilities of *Graphics2D*

```
import java.awt.*;
import java.awt.event.*;
import java.awt.geom.*;

public class PathsFill extends Canvas {

    public PathsFill() {
        setBackground(Color.cyan);
    }

    public void paint(Graphics g) {
        int n = 0;
        Dimension theSize = getSize();

        Graphics2D g2;
        g2 = (Graphics2D) g;
        g2.setRenderingHints(Graphics2D.ANTIALIASING,
        ➥Graphics2D.ANTIALIAS_ON);

        GeneralPath p = new GeneralPath(1);
        p.moveTo( theSize.width/6, theSize.height/6);
        p.lineTo(theSize.width*5/6, theSize.height/6);
        p.lineTo(theSize.width*5/6, theSize.height*5/6);
        p.lineTo( theSize.width/6, theSize.height*5/6);
        p.closePath();

        g2.setColor(Color.blue);
        g2.draw(p);
```

Listing 38.9 Continued

```
        AffineTransform at = new AffineTransform();
        at.scale(.5, .5);
        at.translate(theSize.width/2, theSize.height/2);
        g2.setTransform(at);
        g2.setColor(Color.red);
        g2.fill(p);

        Color colorArray[] = new Color[10];
        colorArray[0] = Color.blue;
        colorArray[1] = Color.green;
        colorArray[2] = Color.magenta;
        colorArray[3] = Color.lightGray;
        colorArray[4] = Color.pink;
        colorArray[5] = Color.white;
        colorArray[6] = Color.yellow;
        colorArray[7] = Color.black;
        colorArray[8] = Color.gray;
        colorArray[9] = Color.orange;

        for(n = 0;  n < 10; n++){
                at.scale(.9, .9);
                at.rotate(15, theSize.width/2, theSize.height/2);
                g2.setTransform(at);
                g2.setColor(colorArray[n]);
                g2.fill(p);
        }

    }

    public static void main(String s[]) {
      WindowListener l = new WindowAdapter() {
        public void windowClosing(WindowEvent e)
        ➥{System.exit(0);}
        public void windowClosed(WindowEvent e)
        ➥{System.exit(0);}
        };
        Frame f = new Frame("Simple 2D Demo ...");
        f.addWindowListener(l);
        f.add("Center", new PathsFill());
        f.pack();
        f.setSize(new Dimension(500,500));
        f.show();
    }
}
```

Understanding Coordinate Spaces

Graphics display is an interesting problem because not all graphics devices have the same coordinate system or resolution. This problem is compounded for Java, which has staked its reputation on being the "Write Once, Run Anywhere" language. To live up to this name, Sun needed a way for designers to produce graphics that look good regardless of the device's characteristics.

In some cases, you might want to write a program that enables a user to draw—and then play back—that file of captured points. If the playback device has different characteristics than the one on which the original drawing was captured, a potential for error exists.

Sun solved this problem by introducing a *user coordinate space*, also known in some of Sun's documentation as *user space*.

Using Transforms To actually display a `Graphics2D` object on a device, you must transform the object from user space to a specific *device space*. Although you can apply a transform at any time, you'll start with a default transform that is selected for you based on the target of your `Graphics2D` object.

All transforms from user space to device space share three characteristics:

- The origin is in the upper-left corner of the target space (such as a screen or printed page).
- Increasing numbers in the x dimension move to the right.
- Increasing numbers in the y dimension move down.

If you specify a screen or an image buffer as the target for your drawing, you'll get the identity transform. If your target is a printer or other high-resolution device, you'll get a default transform of 72 user-space coordinates per device inch.

Understanding Rendering

NOTE You can use the `Graphics2D` class without understanding how the class places your shape, text, or image on the screen. If you're building sophisticated graphics that can be rendered on different devices (such as monitors and printers), you need to know the basics of both coordinate spaces and color spaces. If you'd like, skip this section while you're learning to use `Graphics2D`, and then return here when you're ready to build a sophisticated graphic. ■

Rendering is the mechanism by which the graphics object is made to appear on the output device. With `Graphics2D`-based objects, rendering proceeds in four conceptual steps. (Because of optimization, Sun does not guarantee that each step will be performed each time an image is rendered—it guarantees only that the finished graphic will appear as though it has gone through all four rendering steps.)

The four steps are

1. Determining where to render.
2. Constraining the current rendering operation to the current clip.

3. Determining what colors to render.
4. Applying the colors to the destination drawing space.

By understanding how the Graphics2D class processes each step, you'll be better equipped to produce high-quality graphics.

Determining Where to Render a Shape The first step in rendering is to determine the area of the screen, printed page, or other output device that is affected by the rendering operation. Graphics2D objects can be either shapes, text, or images. If the object is a shape, the "where to render" question is answered by computing the outline of the shape. If the object is text, Graphics2D computes the outline of the text by using information about the font. In the case of an image, the class computes a bounding box into which the image is rendered. This section provides details on how each of these three kinds of objects is rendered.

In Listing 38.9, for example, you see the lines

```
Graphics2D g2;
g2 = (Graphics2D) g;
```

where g is the Graphics object passed in as the parameter of paint(). Next, the program constructs a new shape inside a GeneralPath:

```
GeneralPath p = new GeneralPath(1);
p.moveTo( theSize.width/6, theSize.height/6);
p.lineTo(theSize.width*5/6, theSize.height/6);
p.lineTo(theSize.width*5/6, theSize.height*5/6);
p.lineTo( theSize.width/6, theSize.height*5/6);
p.closePath();
```

Finally, the author uses the new shape

```
g2.draw(p);
...
g2.fill(p);
...
for (n=0; n < 10; n++) {
  at.scale(.9, .9);
  at.rotate(15, theSize.width/2, theSize.height/2);
  g2.setTransform(at);
  ...
  g2.fill(p);
}
```

where at is an AffineTransform, described later.

When the object is a shape, as it is in this case, the Graphics2D class determines where to render it by following a four-step procedure to compute the outline of the shape:

1. Compute a stroke to fill based on the shape.
2. Transform the shape from user space into device space.

3. Call `Shape.getPathIterator()` to extract the outline of the shape. (The outline is an instance of class `PathIterator`, which can contain curved segments.)
4. If the `Graphic2D` object cannot handle the curved segments in the `PathIterator`, it calls an alternative version of `Shape.getPathIterator()` that accepts a `flatness` parameter. This alternative version only returns straight line segments.

The shape's outline will be rendered by using an implementation of the `java.awt.Stroke` interface. To make an ellipse, you might write

```
draw(Ellipse2D.Float(10.0, 10.0, 150.0, 100.0));
```

but the `Graphics2D` class will implement that call as

```
BasicStroke theStroke = new BasicStroke();
theStroke.createStrokedShape(new Ellipse2D.Float(10.0, 10.0, 150.0, 100.0);
```

`BasicStroke` is a class that implements `Stroke`. Figure 38.9 illustrates the concept of a mitre limit, the part of `BasicStroke` that determines whether two lines are joined when they pass close to each other.

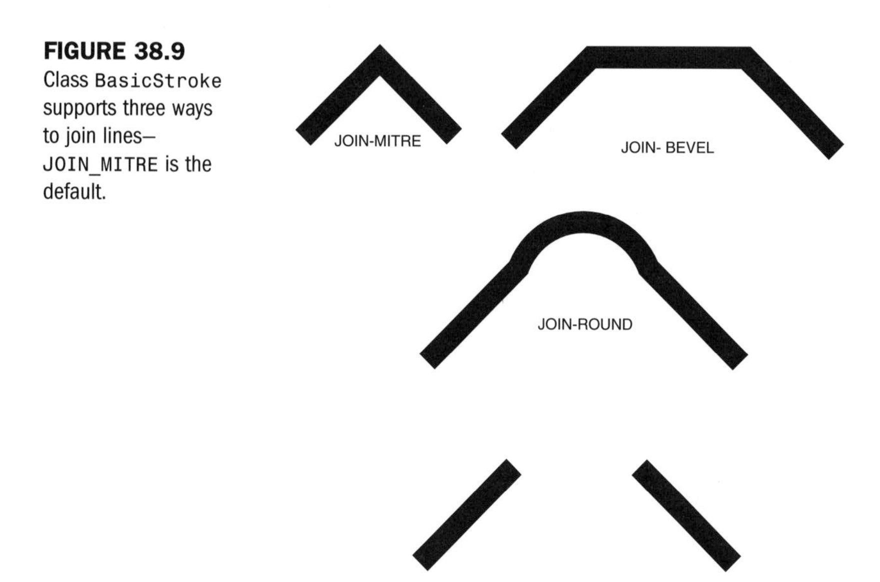

FIGURE 38.9
Class `BasicStroke` supports three ways to join lines—`JOIN_MITRE` is the default.

NOTE `BasicStroke`'s default constructor specifies a line width of 1.0, a `CAP_SQUARE` style at the ends of lines, a `JOIN_MITRE` style where lines come together, a mitre limit of 10.0, and no dashing. (A mitre limit is the limit at which to trim the mitre join where two lines come together.) ■

`Ellipse2D` is an abstract shape; `Ellipse2D.Float` is a concrete class that accepts floating-point coordinates.

To transform the shape into device space, `Graphics2D` calls the currently defined transform. Transforms are instances of class `AffineTransform`, which supports the following types of transform:

- **`GENERAL_ROTATION`**—Rotation through an arbitrary angle.
- **`GENERAL_SCALE`**—Scale by arbitrary factors in x and y.
- **`GENERAL_TRANSFORM`**—Arbitrary conversion of the input coordinates.
- **`IDENTITY`**—The output is identical to the input.
- **`QUADRANT_ROTATION`**—Rotation through a multiple of 90 degrees.
- **`TRANSLATION`**—The graphic is moved in the x and y dimensions.
- **`UNIFORM_SCALE`**—The graphic is scaled uniformly in both dimensions.

In Listing 38.9 you see the lines that set up and use an `AffineTransform`:

```
AffineTransform at = new AffineTransform();
at.scale(.5, .5);
at.translate(theSize.width/2, theSize.height/2);
g2.setTransform(at);
```

and later

```
for(n = 0;  n < 10; n++){
  at.scale(.9, .9);
  at.rotate(15, theSize.width/2, theSize.height/2);
  g2.setTransform(at);
  . . .
}
```

Determining Where to Render Text If the `Graphics2D` represents text rather than a shape, it is rendered by using *glyphs*—integer codes used by fonts to represent text graphically. If the text is in a string, the string is sent to the current font, which is asked to compute a `java.awt.font.GlyphSet` based on the font's default layout.

If the text is in a `StyledString`, the `StyledString` itself computes the `GlyphSet` based on its own font attributes.

If the text is already a `GlyphSet`, this step is skipped.

After `Graphics2D` has a `GlyphSet`, it asks the current font to convert the glyphs to shapes. It then starts the process of rendering the shapes, as described earlier in this section.

Determining Where to Render an Image If the `Graphics2D` is an image (as indicated by a call to the `drawImage()` method), the class computes a bounding rectangle for the image in a local coordinate system called *image space*. If the programmer has specified a transform, that transform is used to convert the bounding rectangle from image space coordinates to user space coordinates. If the programmer doesn't supply a transform, an identity transform is used.

The bounding rectangle—now in user coordinate space—is transformed again, into device space.

Constraining the Graphic with *Clip* `Graphics2D` inherits `getClip()` and `setClip()` methods from its base class, `Graphics`. You can use `setClip()` to limit the rendering to a specified rectangle. You specify the `clipRect` in user space—`Graphics2D` transforms it into device space by using the current transform.

TIP If you have a complex graphic or animation in which performance is important, you can improve performance by limiting the rendering area with `setClip()`.

After `Graphics2D` has computed the rendering region (for either a graphic, text, or an image) it applies the `clipRect` to define the region that will actually be rendered.

Determining the Colors If the `Graphics2D` object is an image, the class samples the colors in the image based on the current transform. (If you specify an image transform, that transform is also applied during color sampling.)

For text and graphic instances of `Graphics2D`, the class looks at the current `Paint` implementation. You set the `Paint` instance by calling `Graphics2D.setPaint()`. `Paint` itself is an interface; Sun has provided `GradientPaint` and `TexturePaint` to enable you to implement special effects. A gradient is a smooth transition from one color to another, whereas a texture repeats an image over and over, like a tile pattern. To fill a circle with a gradient, you might write code like that shown in Listing 38.10.

Listing 38.10 *Gradient.java*—This Applet Draws a Circle with a Cyclic Gradient from Red to White

```
import java.applet.Applet;
import java.awt.Graphics;
import java.awt.geom.Ellipse2D;
import java.awt.geom.Ellipse2D.Double;
import java.awt.Color;
import java.awt.Graphics2D;
import java.awt.GradientPaint;

public class Gradient extends java.applet.Applet
{
   public void paint(Graphics g)
   {
      Graphics2D g2 = (Graphics2D)g;
      Ellipse2D theEllipse = new Ellipse2D.Double(50, 50, 200, 200);
      GradientPaint theGradient =
        new GradientPaint(75, 75, Color.white,
                          100, 100, Color.red, true);
      g2.setPaint(theGradient);
      g2.fill(theEllipse);
   }
}
```

Instead of a `Paint`-based object, you can set a `Color`. `PathsFill`, in Listing 38.9, uses this approach. You'll notice lines such as

```
g2.setColor(Color.blue);
```

and

```
g2.setColor(Color.red);
```

Whether you've provided a `Paint` object or a `Color` object, `Graphics2D` uses it to obtain a `PaintContext`—a specific mapping of colors and textures into device space—and is now ready to apply the colors.

Applying the Colors `Graphics2D` objects are drawn on a `java.awt.Composite` object. The `Composite` interface contains predefined rules to combine the source with colors that have already been drawn.

NOTE Sun provides one example of a `Composite`-based class: `AlphaComposite`. This class implements a set of blending and transparency rules based on T. Porter and T. Duff's paper, "Compositing Digital Images," SIGGRAPH 84, 253-259. Read the API documentation on `AlphaComposite` to see the essence of these rules. ■

Dealing with Compatibility Issues

Not only does Sun have to deal with a range of device compatibility, it also has had to ensure that changes in Java 2 don't break the `Graphics` API of JDK 1.1. To help your `Graphics2D` objects deal with the range of rendering environments they might encounter, use `Graphics2D.setRenderingHints()`. This method accepts hints that you might want to add to improve the performance and appearance of your graphics.

Suppose, for example, that you know an image contains a number of diagonal lines that would benefit from antialiasing. You might specify `ANTIALIASING_ON`—at runtime, the environment and the device driver would negotiate whether to actually make the antialiasing pass. If you've specified `RENDER_SPEED`, the device driver can ignore the `ANTIALIASING_ON` directive entirely, but for `RENDER_QUALITY`, the driver can use the best antialiasing algorithm at its disposal, even though that algorithm might require extra time.

The hint list includes the following:

- **`ANTIALIASING ON` and `ANTIALIASING_OFF`**—Control whether an extra step is applied for smoothing jagged edges.
- **`RENDER_SPEED` and `RENDER_QUALITY`**—Control whether the rendering algorithm should optimize for performance or appearance.

Notice the line in Listing 38.9 that sets these hints:

```
g2.setRenderingHints(Graphics2D.ANTIALIASING,
➥Graphics2D.ANTIALIAS_ON);
```

Java Resources on the Web

The Java language is continually being upgraded. New packages and versions are being released at a rapid pace. Many of these new features will increase the power and ease of Java graphics and animation programming. Continue to increase your Java graphics and animation knowledge and programming skills by keeping up with the latest developments over the Web.

The most important Web site is the Java home page provided by JavaSoft—the Java development branch of the Sun Corporation. The Java home page is at `http://java.sun.com/`.

Use the Search feature at the top of the page (or go to `http://search.java.sun.com/`) and enter terms such as "graphics" or "animation" to see the latest information. You can also keep informed about the latest Java developments and software release dates at this Web site and download the latest production-quality Java development software. (For access to pre-release versions of the software, join the Java Developer Connection—it's free—at `http://developer.java.sun.com/`.)

While browsing the JavaSoft site, you'll want to visit `http://java.sun.com/products/java-media/2D/samples/index.html`—as the URL suggests, that page shows sample code using the features of the new SDK 1.3.

In addition to the JavaSoft site, you can find some excellent central Java news-gathering sources on the Web. These also include reviews, tutorials, and other useful information. The best of these includes JavaWorld at `http://www.javaworld.com/`.

For example, they have archives of articles on graphics at `http://www.javaworld.com/javaworld/topicalindex/jw-ti-graphics.html`. Go to `http://www.javaworld.com/javaworld/topicalindex/jw-ti-animation.html` for information on animation.

You can download sample programs and tutorials from the Java archive at Gamelan (`http://www.gamelan.com/`) and the Java library at `http://www.developer.com/`. Graphics information is at `http://www.developer.com/directories/pages/dir.java.programming.graphics.html`. ●

CHAPTER 39

Network Programming

by Mike Morgan

In this chapter

Java Simplifies Network Programming

Not so long ago, programming network applications in any language was an ordeal. Sometimes it involved writing specialized system software that talked directly to network drivers—or even the network cards themselves. Programming IPX/SPX applications in DOS or Windows once required the programmer to write software interrupt handlers. With Java, however, writing some kinds of network applications is as easy as using `println()`.

The thing that makes network programming in Java easier is encapsulation. Java hides the difficult, low-level network programming from you. This design enables you to concentrate on your application, not on the communications. In older systems, many steps were required to talk over a network. You had to

- Initialize the network card
- Set up buffers for inbound and outbound packets
- Create callback routines for the networking driver to notify you of data
- Write low-level (sometimes assembler!) code to talk with the network driver

If it sounds like it was a lot of work—it was! On the other hand, programming the network in Java is relatively easy. Just instantiate a `Socket` class and you are on your way. But more on that later.

This chapter discusses the network classes in Java (in the `java.net` package). These classes make writing programs for communication over the Internet, intranets, or even local area networks easier than in any other language you're likely to use.

How Do Java Programs Communicate with the Outside World?

Java's network classes use streams for their underlying communications. A *stream* is a path of communication between a source of information and a destination. For this example, the Java program is at one end of the stream. If you're the source, the stream is an output stream. If you're the destination, the stream is called an input stream.

Readers and *writers* are analogous to streams, except that streams are based on bytes and readers and writers are based on chars. In older languages, such as C and C++, this distinction is not important. In Java, however, a char is a 16-bit entity designed to hold Unicode characters.

You used an output stream without realizing it when you wrote `System.out.println("Hello, world!")`. Streams enable you to communicate with files, printers, the screen, and the network. Streams, readers, and writers are all part of the `java.io` package. You can find complete documentation on each class, interface, and method in your SDK `/docs` directory. (If you accept the defaults during installation, you'll find the documentation in `/jdk1.3/docs`.) You'll also need to import `java.io.*` or specify `java.io` as part of the class name in your code.

Connecting to the Internet: The *URL* Class

Back in Chapter 36, "Developing Java Applets," you learned how to write a tiny Java program—`HelloWorld.java`—with only one executable statement. People have been writing tiny programs that write information to the screen ever since there were computer screens. One of the features that makes Java exciting is that you can connect to the Internet with a program that's not much more complex than `HelloWorld.java`.

NOTE For years, Sun has been telling us that "the network is the computer," and its design of Java reflects that philosophy. Java is the only major language that enables you to connect your program to the Internet in just one line of code, as shown in line 38 of Listing 39.1 (the entire listing appears in the next section):

```
URL theURL = new URL(theURLString);
```

Using *showDocument()* to Change Web Pages

Listing 39.1 shows `HelloNet.java`, a simple applet that connects you to a new Web page.

Listing 39.1 *HelloNet.java*—This Simple Applet Connects to Three URLs

```
import java.awt.*;
import java.net.*;
import java.applet.Applet;
import java.awt.event.*;
public class HelloNet extends Applet
{
  public void init()
  {
    setLayout(new GridLayout(3,1));
    Button theBookSiteButton = new Button("Platinum Edition");
    theBookSiteButton.addActionListener(new ActionListener(){
      public void actionPerformed(ActionEvent e) {
        linkTo("http://www.mcp.com/info/0-7897/0-7897-2473-1");
      }
    });
    add(theBookSiteButton);

    Button theMCPButton = new Button("Macmillan Computer Publishing");
    theMCPButton.addActionListener(new ActionListener(){
      public void actionPerformed(ActionEvent e) {
        linkTo("http://www.mcp.com/");
      }
    });
    add(theMCPButton);

    Button theJavaSoftButton = new Button("JavaSoft");
    theJavaSoftButton.addActionListener(new ActionListener(){
      public void actionPerformed(ActionEvent e) {
```

Listing 39.1 Continued

```
        linkTo("http://java.sun.com/");
      }
    });
    add(theJavaSoftButton);
  }

  public void linkTo(String theURLString)
  {
    try {
      URL theURL = new URL(theURLString);
      getAppletContext().showDocument(theURL, "_top");
    } catch (MalformedURLException e) {
      System.err.println("Bad URL: " + theURLString);
    }
  }
}
```

Most of this applet is familiar to you by now. (If you're new to the Abstract Windowing Toolkit, take a look at Chapter 37, "User Input and Interactivity with Java.") This applet has three buttons, each with a Web destination name. When you click a button, it fires the `linkTo()` method. This code is where the new Web-specific information appears.

First, a new `URL` object is made from the `String`. If the `URL` constructor cannot make sense out of `theURLString`, it throws `MalformedURLException`. Given a valid URL, `linkTo()` now transfers control to the browser's `AppletContext` and asks it to show the specified URL in the browser's topmost window.

TIP If your applet is buried inside an HTML frame, the `showDocument(String)` page will also appear inside that frame. When you're linking to a page outside your site, you generally want the new content to appear on a page by itself, not inside the frame. You can get the desired behavior by adding `"_top"`, as shown in this line in the `linkTo` method:

getAppletContext().showDocument(theURL, "_top");

This code has only three executable lines per button and three executable lines in `linkTo()`. Of course, it takes advantage of the fact that it's running inside a Web browser. The browser supplies the `AppletContext` and actually fetches the document specified by the URL.

NOTE If you plan to display HTML pages inside a standalone application (rather than in an applet) you're essentially writing a Web browser. Consider saving some time by using Sun's HotJava HTML component, a JavaBean that addresses this need. You'll find the latest licensing information at `http://java.sun.com/products/hotjava/index.html#bean`.

Calling Back the Server with *openStream()*

From within either an applet or an application, you can open a connection to a URL and read back the contents. The basic mechanism is a URL method called `openStream()`:

```
try {
  DataInputStream theData =
    new BufferedReader(new
      InputStreamReader(theURL.openStream()));
  String aLine;
  while ((aLine = theData.readLine()) != null) {
    System.out.println(aLine);
  }
} catch (IOException e) {
  System.err.println("IOException: " + e.getMessage());
} finally {
  theData.close();
}
```

The fourth line uses `openStream()` to retrieve the `InputStream`. `URL.openStream()` is really shorthand for

```
theURL.openConnection().getInputStream();
```

but most programmers will appreciate the shorter version.

Also in the first line, the `InputStream` is wrapped first in an `InputStreamReader` (to bridge between the byte-oriented world of streams and the char-oriented world of readers). Then the `InputStreamReader` is wrapped in a `BufferedReader` for efficiency—to read the stream a buffer at a time, rather than a byte at a time!

Finally, `theData.readLine()` is called successively, bringing in lines of data from the server. For this simple code snippet, you just send the data back out to standard out.

If anything goes wrong, throw an `IOException` somewhere in there and catch it on the way out. Whether an exception is thrown or not, the `finally` clause is always executed, closing the stream.

CAUTION

If you compile the `URL.openStream()` code into an applet and attempt to fetch data from some Web server, it probably won't work. Most browsers include a `SecurityManager` that reports a `SecurityException` as soon as you attempt to contact a host other than the one you were downloading from. To make this code work in an applet, either restrict yourself to connecting only to the applet's home server or negotiate higher rights with the browser's `SecurityManager`.

▶ To learn more about applet security, **see** "Executable Content and Security," **p. 1178**

How the *URL* Class Works

The `URL` class contains constructors and methods for managing a URL—an object or service on the Internet, which uses the Transmission Control Protocol, or TCP. TCP requires two pieces of information: the IP address and the port number. So how is it possible that when you type

```
http://www.mcp.com/
```

you get Macmillan's home page?

First, Macmillan has registered its name, enabling `www.mcp.com` to be assigned an IP address (`63.69.110.193`). This address is resolved by using your system's domain name resolution service.

Now what about the port number? If not specified, the server's default port is used—for the Web, that's port 80.

The `URL` class supports six constructor variations:

```
public URL(String spec) throws MalformedURLException;
public URL(String protocol, String host, int port, String file) throws
➥MalformedURLException;
public URL(String protocol, String host, int port, String file,
➥URLStreamHandler handler) throws MalformedURLException;
public URL(String protocol, String host, String file) throws
➥MalformedURLException;
public URL(URL context, String spec) throws MalformedURLException;
public URL(URL context, String spec, URLStreamHandler handler) throws
MalformedURLException;
```

Therefore, you can specify each piece of the URL, as in `URL("http","www.mcp.com",80,"index.html")`, or enable the defaults to take over, as in `URL("http://www.mcp.com/")`, letting Java figure out all the pieces.

CAUTION

A malicious user could design a URL with resources that the code would not normally have access to (such as a file on the local file system). That user could then specify a stream handler that gets bytes from some legitimate source and writes them to an unauthorized location, tricking the system into making a new `java.security.ProtectionDomain` that has an unauthorized `CodeSource`. For this reason, Sun restricts your ability to specify your own stream handler.

If you use one of the constructor forms that accepts a `URLStreamHandler`, and if the handler is not null and a security manager is present, then the runtime environment calls the security manager's `checkPermission` method, passing a `NetPermission("specifyStreamHandler")` permission. If that access isn't permitted by the current security policy, the constructor throws a `SecurityException`.

The Java Socket Classes

Java, of course, was developed by Sun. Sun earned its reputation as a leading developer of UNIX workstations—much of the Internet runs on Sun servers. It's not surprising, therefore, that Java is designed from the ground up as a networking language. This overview shows how Java makes network programming easier by encapsulating connection functionality in *socket classes*:

- `Socket` is the basic object in Internet communication and supports the TCP/IP protocol. The Transmission Control Protocol/Internet Protocol (TCP/IP) is a reliable stream network connection. The `Socket` class provides methods for stream I/O, which make reading from and writing to `Socket` easy.
- `ServerSocket` is an object used by Internet server programs for listening to client requests. `ServerSocket` does not actually perform the service; instead, it creates a `Socket` object on behalf of the client. The communication is performed through that object.
- `DatagramSocket` is an object that uses the *User Datagram Protocol* (UDP). Datagram sockets are technically unreliable because no connection is involved. You send them out hoping they reach their destination, but you have no guarantee that any receiver is even listening. In addition, the networking software will not guarantee the delivery of UDP packages. However, communication using datagram sockets is faster because no connection is made between the sender and receiver. Think of UDP as a telegram, sent out in the hope that it will be delivered. TCP, in contrast, is more like a telephone call—you know the message is delivered because you delivered it yourself, through a connection. Streaming audio and video often use UDP, trading off occasional data loss in favor of high performance.
- `SocketImpl` is an abstract class that enables you to implement your own flavor of data communication. As with all abstract classes, you subclass `SocketImpl` and implement its methods, as opposed to instantiating `SocketImpl` itself.

How the Internet Uses Sockets

You can think of an Internet server as a set of sockets, each of which provides capabilities called *services*. Examples of services are electronic mail, *Telnet* for remote login, and the *File Transfer Protocol* (FTP) for transferring files around the network. If the server to which you are attached is a Web server, then you can retrieve Web pages as well.

Ports and Services

Each service is associated with a *port*. A port is a numeric address through which service requests (such as asking for a Web page) are processed. On a UNIX system, the particular services provided are listed in the `/etc/services` file. Here are a few lines from a typical `/etc/services` file:

```
daytime     13/udp
ftp         21/tcp
telnet      23/tcp      telnet
smtp        25/tcp      mail
www         80/tcp
```

The first column displays the system name of the service (such as `daytime`). The second column displays the port number and the protocol, separated by a slash (as in `13/udp`). The third column displays an alias to the service, if any. For example, SMTP (the Simple Mail Transfer Protocol), also known as *mail*, provides the email service.

Mapping Java Sockets to Internet Sockets

Sockets are based on a client/server model. One program (the server) provides the service at a particular IP address and port. The server listens for service requests, such as requests for Web pages, and fills the order. Any program that wants to be serviced (a client, such as a Web browser) needs to know the IP address and port to communicate with the server.

An advantage of the socket model over other forms of data communication is that the server doesn't care where the client requests come from. As long as the client is sending requests according to the TCP/IP protocol, the requests will reach the server—provided the server is up and the Internet isn't too busy. What the particular server program does with the request is another matter.

This design also means that the client can be any type of computer. No longer are you restricted to UNIX, Macintosh, DOS, or Windows platforms. Any computer that supports TCP/IP can talk to any other computer that supports it through this socket model. This design is a potentially revolutionary development in computing. Instead of maintaining armies of programmers to *port* a system from one platform to another, you write it one time—in Java. Any computer with a Java Virtual Machine can run it.

NOTE You might have read about the lawsuit between Sun and Microsoft. Sun alleged that Microsoft's implementation of the Java Virtual Machine failed to comply with Sun's standards, as their license required. On January 24, 2000, the court granted a preliminary injunction against Microsoft, referring to "Microsoft's...false and misleading statements to the developer community." Microsoft now refers to its software as the Microsoft Virtual Machine. For both sides of the argument, see `http://java.sun.com/lawsuit/index.html` and `http://www.microsoft.com/java/issues/sunsuit.htm`.

Java socket classes fit nicely into this picture. You implement a server by creating subclasses of `Thread` and overriding the `run()` method. The Java Virtual Machine can then perform the thread management without any help from the program. Thus, with a few lines of code, you can write a server that can handle as many data communication sessions as you want. And data transmission is just a matter of calling the `Socket` methods. This technique is demonstrated in the next section.

Writing Your Own Client and Server

Applets are restricted from connecting to just any Web server. They can only connect back to the server from which they were downloaded. If you want to give an applet access to the rest of the Internet, you'll need to place a server on the same machine that hosts the applet. You can use a commercial server such as a File Transfer Protocol (FTP) server, or you can write your own special-purpose server.

When you write a server, you write a program that opens a socket (typically on a well-known port number) and waits for some client to connect. The client calls in from some unused port number (called an *ephemeral port*). As soon as the client and the server connect, it's common for the server to propose that the conversation continue on a different port. This design frees up the well-known port number to handle a new connection. Table 39.1 shows some common well-known port numbers. These services are offered both on TCP ports and on UDP ports. The RFC column refers to the Internet Request for Comments document, where you'll find the specification for the service.

NOTE You can download any RFCs that you want to read from `ftp://ds.internic.net/rfc/`. Check the login message you get when you connect—FTP sites are on each continent. If you're not on the East Coast of North America, one might be closer to you than `ds.internic.net`.

Table 39.1 Common Internet Services and Their Port Numbers

Service Name	TCP Port	UDP Port	RFC	Description
echo	7	7	862	Server returns whatever the client sends.
discard	9	9	863	Server discards whatever the client sends.
daytime	13	13	867	Server returns the time and date in a human-readable format.
chargen	19		864	TCP server sends a continual stream of characters until the client terminates the connection.
chargen		19	864	UDP server sends a datagram containing a random number of characters each time the client sends a datagram.
time	37	37	868	Server returns the time as a 32-bit binary number—the number of seconds since midnight on January 1, 1900, UTC.

NOTE TCP/IP port numbers are managed by the Internet Assigned Numbers Authority (IANA). IANA has specified that well-known port numbers are always between 1 and 1023. A Telnet server listens on TCP port 23, for example, and the Trivial File Transfer Protocol (TFTP) server listens on UDP port 69. Most TCP/IP implementations allocate ephemeral port numbers between 1,024 and 5,000, but that design isn't specified by IANA.

Java provides two kinds of sockets: client sockets, implemented in the `Socket` class, and server sockets, implemented in the `ServerSocket` class.

Understanding the Client *Socket* Class

To connect to a host, your client program should include a line such as

```
Socket theConnection = new Socket(hostname, portNumber);
```

(Remember the security restrictions that apply to applets.)

▶ To learn more about the restrictions browsers place on applets, **see** "Executable Content and Security," **p. 1178**

The `Socket` constructor throws an `IOException` if it has a problem. Otherwise, you can presume that the `Socket` is open and ready for communication:

```
BufferedReader theReader = new BufferedReader(
  new InputStreamReader(theConnection.getInputStream()));
BufferedWriter theWriter = new BufferedWriter(
  new OutputStreamWriter(theConnection.getOutputStream()));
```

Now you can read and write `theReader` and `theWriter` in the usual fashion. When you're done with `theConnection`, call

```
theConnection.close();
```

This step also closes all the streams, readers, and writers you have associated with this `Socket`.

Understanding *ServerSockets*

If you choose to write a server, you'll need to write a `ServerSocket`. Such a socket binds a specified port. To bind port 8000, for example, you write

```
ServerSocket theServerConnection = new ServerSocket(8000);
```

When you install a server, it's a good idea to check `/etc/services` to make sure the port number is free. Likewise, after you choose a port number, add a corresponding entry in `/etc/services` to notify other programmers who might want to add a server to this machine.

This code tells the underlying operating system that you intend to offer a service on port 8000. (You aren't listening to that port quite yet.) If the runtime environment is able to bind to the specified port, it does so and sets the allowable backlog to a default of 50. (This means that after you have 50 pending requests to connect, all subsequent requests are refused. You can specify a different backlog value in the `ServerSocket` constructor.) If the runtime environment cannot bind to the port (which happens if the port is already allocated to another service), you'll get an `IOException`.

After you've bound the port, you can attach the port and start listening for connections by calling `accept()`:

```
Socket aSocket = theServerConnection.accept();
```

When the connection is made, `accept()` unblocks and returns a `Socket`. You can open streams, readers, and writers on the `Socket` the same as you did from the client program.

Using Client and Server Sockets

Listing 39.2 shows a server framework. This simple server sets up the `ServerSocket`, and then implements four steps:

1. Waits for a client to connect.
2. Accepts the client connection.
3. Sends a message to the client.
4. Tears down the connection.

Listing 39.2 *TServer.java*—Use This Framework as the Basis for Your Own Server

```
import java.net.*;
import java.io.*;

public class TServer extends Thread {
  private static final int PORTNUMBER = 8013;
  private ServerSocket fServerSocket;

  public TServer() {
    super("TServer");
    try {
      fServerSocket = new ServerSocket(PORTNUMBER);
      System.out.println("TServer up and running...");
    } catch (IOException e) {
      System.err.println("Exception: couldn't make server socket.");
      System.exit(1);
    }
  }
```

Listing 39.2 Continued

```
  public void run() {
    Socket theClientSocket;

    while (true) {

      // wait for a client to connect
      if (fServerSocket == null)
        return;
      try {
        theClientSocket = fServerSocket.accept();

        // accept the client connection

        // send a message to the client
        PrintWriter theWriter = new PrintWriter(new
          OutputStreamWriter(theClientSocket.getOutputStream()));
        theWriter.println(new java.util.Date().toString());

        // force the writer to write
        theWriter.flush();

        // tear down the connection
        theWriter.close();
        theClientSocket.close();
      } catch (IOException e) {
        System.err.println("Exception: " + e.getMessage());
        System.exit(1);
      }
    }
  }

  public static void main(String[] args) {
    TServer theServer = new TServer();
    theServer.start();
  }
}
```

Listing 39.3 shows a client designed to work with the server in Listing 39.2. This client has four steps:

1. Connect to the server.
2. Wait for a message.
3. Display the message to the user.
4. Tear down the connection.

Listing 39.3 *TClient.java*—This Class Helps You Design Your Client Program

```
import java.net.*;
import java.io.*;

public class TClient {
  private static final int PORTNUMBER = 8013;
  public static void main(String args[]) {
    Socket theSocket;
    BufferedReader theReader;
    String theAddress = "";

    // check the command line for a host address
    if (args.length != 1) {
     System.out.println("Usage: java TClient <address>");
     System.exit(1);
    }
    else
      theAddress = args[0];

    // connect to the server
    try {
      theSocket = new Socket(theAddress, PORTNUMBER);
      theReader =
        new BufferedReader(new
           InputStreamReader(theSocket.getInputStream()));

      // wait for a message

      String theLine;
      int c;
      while ((theLine = theReader.readLine()) != null) {

        // show the message to the user
        System.out.println("Server: " + theLine);
        break;
      }

      // Tear down the connection
      theReader.close();
      theSocket.close();
    } catch (IOException e) {
      System.err.println("Exception: " + e.getMessage());
    }
  }
}
```


NOTE As long as you keep the server on the machine that hosts your applet, you can put the code from Listing 39.3 into an applet. Just move the code in `main()` into `init()`. You don't have to look for the server's address in a parameter. Just use the `Applet` method `getCodeBase()`; it returns the complete URL of the applet itself.

To test this code, first start the server:

```
java TServer
```

Now run the client in a different command prompt window by entering this line:

```
java TClient "localhost"
```

Note that `"localhost"` is a common name for a TCP/IP machine to use for itself—this invocation specifies that the server is running on the same machine as the client. We could also have used `127.0.0.1`, the local loopback address. When you start the client, it contacts the server and responds by reporting the date and time:

```
Server: someDateandTime
```

To fault-isolate between the client and the server, use your computer's Telnet client to access the server by port number. Figure 39.1 shows this step. If you're able to connect and the server works as you expect, you have a problem with your client. Otherwise, you have a problem with the server.

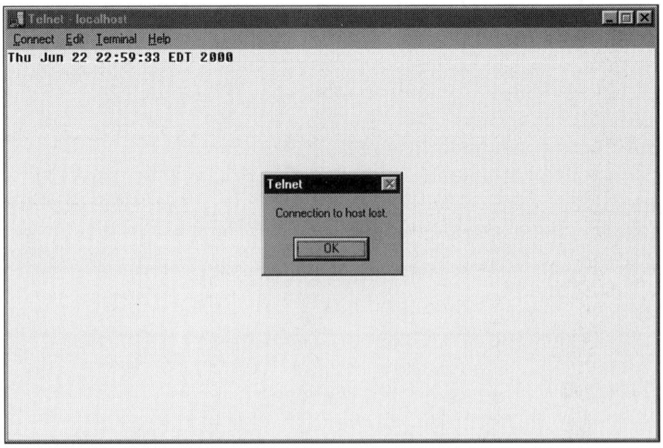

FIGURE 39.1
Use your platform's Telnet client to attempt to connect to your new server's well-known port.

Communicating with Datagram Sockets

Communicating using datagram sockets is simpler than using the TCP-based sockets (`Socket` and `ServerSocket`) that you used for the `TServer`. Communication is also faster because no connection overhead exists. There is also no attempt to send packets again if an error occurs, and there's no concern with sequencing multiple packets, as occurs in TCP/IP transmissions.

A datagram packet is sent as an array of bytes to a receiving program, presumably listening at a particular IP address and port. If the receiving program gets the datagram and wants to send a reply, it becomes the sender, addressing a datagram back to a known IP address and port. The conversation style is a bit like those two-way radios in airplanes in which the pilot sends a message, says "Over," and waits for the controller to respond.

You might use datagram socket communication if you are writing an interactive game—returning a small piece of information such as the time. In such a case, you don't want the overhead of establishing a connection, or perhaps you don't need a connection because the communication takes place locally.

Sending a Datagram Packet

Listing 39.4 shows a prototype program for sending a datagram packet. It sends a 27-byte message ("I'm a datagram and I'm O.K.") to the IP address mapped to `"localhost"` at port number 6969. When you try this, use an IP address and port that you know is available. These values should work on most machines.

Listing 39.4 *DatagramSend.java*—A Prototype Program to Transmit a Datagram Packet

```
import java.net.*;
import java.net.*;
import java.io.IOException;

public class DatagramSend {
  static final int PORT = 6969;

  public static void main( String args[] ) throws Exception {
    String theStringToSend = "I'm a datagram and I'm O.K.";
    byte[] theByteArray = new byte[ theStringToSend.length() ];
    theByteArray = theStringToSend.getBytes();

    // Get the IP address of our destination...
    InetAddress theIPAddress = null;
    try {
      theIPAddress = InetAddress.getByName( "localhost" );
    } catch (UnknownHostException e) {
      System.out.println("Host not found: " + e);
      System.exit(1);
    }

    // Build the packet...
    DatagramPacket thePacket = new DatagramPacket( theByteArray,
      theStringToSend.length(),
      theIPAddress,
      PORT );

    // Now send the packet
    DatagramSocket theSocket = null;
    try {
      theSocket = new DatagramSocket();
    } catch (SocketException e) {
        System.out.println("Underlying network software has failed: " + e);
        System.exit(1);
```

Listing 39.4 Continued

```
    }
    try {
      theSocket.send( thePacket );
    } catch (IOException e) {
      System.out.println("IO Exception: " + e);
    }
    theSocket.close();
    }
}
```

You must use only one socket: the `DatagramSocket`. There is no concept of the server listening for client requests. The idea is to establish a `DatagramSocket` object and then send and receive messages. The messages are sent in a `DatagramPacket` object. An additional object—`InetAddress`—is needed to construct the IP address to send the packet.

The `DatagramSend` class has only one method—`main()`—so it is a standalone Java program. This demonstration program sends only one message. You can, of course, modify `main()` to pass any message to any IP address and port.

The `DatagramPacket` constructor used here has the following four arguments:

- **`theByteArray`**—An array of `bytes` containing the message to send
- **`theStringToSend.length()`**—The length of the string you are going to send
- **`theIPAddress`**—The `InetAddress` object containing the resolved IP address of your destination
- **`PORT`**—An integer specifying the port number

Another form of the constructor requires only the first two arguments. It is designed for local communication when the IP address and port are already known. You'll see it in action in the following section, "Receiving a Datagram Packet."

You first build a string (`theStringToSend`) that contains the string you want to send. Then you create a `byte` array that is as long as your string by using the `String` class's `length()` method. The `PORT` constant is used to store the port number, 6969.

The `getBytes()` instance method of the `java.lang.String` class converts strings into `byte` array form. You store this in your `byte` array `theByteArray`.

The `getByName()` method of `InetAddress` converts a string into an Internet address in the form that the `DatagramPacket` constructor accepts. In this case, the string is a simple one: `localhost`.

Next, an instance of `DatagramSocket` is constructed with no arguments, meaning that Java will attempt to use any available port. Finally, the packet is sent using the `send()` method of the `DatagramSocket`.

Receiving a Datagram Packet

The packet is on its way, so it's time to receive it. Listing 39.5 shows the receiving program.

Listing 39.5 *DatagramReceive.java*—A Prototype Program to Receive a Datagram Packet

```
import java.net.*;

public class DatagramReceive {
  static final int PORT = 6969;
  public static void main( String args[] ) throws Exception {
    String theReceiveString;
    byte[] theReceiveBuffer = new byte[ 2048 ];

    // Make a packet to receive into...
    DatagramPacket theReceivePacket =
      new DatagramPacket( theReceiveBuffer, theReceiveBuffer.length );

    // Make a socket to listen on...
    DatagramSocket theReceiveSocket = new DatagramSocket( PORT );

    // Receive a packet...
    theReceiveSocket.receive( theReceivePacket );

    // Convert the packet to a string...
    theReceiveString =
      new String( theReceiveBuffer, 0, theReceivePacket.getLength() );

    // Print out the string...
    System.out.println( theReceiveString );

    //  Close the socket...
    theReceiveSocket.close();
    }
}
```

The `DatagramReceive` class, like the `DatagramSend` class, uses the `DatagramSocket` and `DatagramPacket` classes from `java.net`. First, make a buffer large enough to hold the message. The buffer in this example (`theReceiveBuffer`) is a 2KB array. Your buffer size might vary. Just make sure it will hold the largest packet you will receive.

You then make a new datagram packet. Note that the receive program already knows its IP address and port, so it can use the two-argument form of the constructor. The new `DatagramSocket` is set up to receive data at port 6969.

The `receive()` method of `Datagram` receives the packet as a `byte` array. The `String` (`theReceiveString`) is constructed out of the `byte` array and is displayed on the user's screen. Finally, the socket is closed—a good practice, freeing memory rather than waiting for Java's garbage collection.

TIP

Here's another way to get the IP address of the host on which you are running: Call the `getLocalHost()` and `getAddress()` methods of the class `java.net.InetAddress`. First, `getLocalHost()` returns an `InetAddress` object. Then you use the `getAddress()` method, which returns a `byte` array consisting of the four bytes of the IP address. Here's an example:

```
InetAddress theLocalIPAddress = InetAddress.getLocalHost();
byte[] theLocalIPAddressDecoded = theLocalIPAddress.getAddress();
```

If the IP address of the machine on which your program is running is `221.111.112.23`, `getAddress` will populate `theLocalIPAddressDecoded` array like this:

```
theLocalIPAddressDecoded[0] = 221
theLocalIPAddressDecoded[1] = 111
theLocalIPAddressDecoded[2] = 112
theLocalIPAddressDecoded[3] = 23
```

To test `DatagramSend` and `DatagramReceive`, open two command prompt windows. In one, start `DatagramReceive`; the program will wait for the message to arrive. Now start `DatagramSend` in the other window—if all goes well, both programs will exit, and you'll get the message "I'm a datagram and I'm O.K." in the receiver's window.

Customized Network Solutions

The Internet provides no transactional security whatsoever, nor do the socket-oriented communications methods discussed so far verify whether any particular request for reading or writing data is coming from a source that should have such access. To do this, you need a customized network protocol.

These protocols sit as a layer between your network protocol (that is, TCP/IP) and your application. They encrypt outgoing packets and decrypt incoming packets while verifying that you are still talking to the sender you think you are talking to.

To address these issues, Netscape developed the Secure Sockets Layer (SSL) protocol, and it has matured into the industry standard for secure Internet communication. SSL is a protocol that resides between the services—such as Telnet, FTP, and HTTP—and the TCP/IP connection sessions that are described in this chapter. SSL checks that the client and server networks are valid, provides data encryption, and ensures that the message does not contain any embedded commands or programs. SSL would thus provide for secure transactions to occur across the Internet.

▶ To learn more about security protocols, **see** Chapter 30, "Server-Side Security Issues"

In your organization, you might want to provide a firewall between the public and private areas of your networks. Therefore, for a number of reasons, you might need more protection for your network than TCP/IP provides.

Java provides a set of methods called `SocketImpl`, an abstract class, for implementing either of these strategies. To use it, you create a subclass and implement its methods, such as connecting to the server, accepting client requests, getting file information, writing to local files, and so on. Even if you have never written your own server or a custom socket class, it's nice to know that it's possible with Java.

Will Security Considerations Disable Java Applets?

Imagine a world in which Java applets on any network can set up client/server communications of the type discussed in this chapter. Perhaps an applet on your network can call a method in an applet on someone else's network or remotely run a program on that other network. An applet connects to a quote server, for example, determines that the price of a certain stock has reached the target price, and then connects to a user's machine on a network, displaying a message and requesting permission to buy. Or perhaps the applet can run an Excel spreadsheet macro to update the portfolio every 10 minutes. Many powerful applets could be written.

With this power comes potential danger. How can you prevent the applet from deleting files or downloading unauthorized data? In this world of distributed objects, tension exists between enabling more capabilities for an applet and fear of unwanted use. This tension is why the debate on object access is fierce. The main stage is a standard called *Common Object Request Broker Architecture*, or CORBA.

NOTE You can get an overview of CORBA online and learn more about writing Java programs that can interface with object request brokers at `http://www.vex.net/~ben/corba/`.

Untrusted applets loaded from a network cannot load libraries on the local machine, nor can they define native method calls. They cannot start programs, so they cannot run the DOS `dir` command or other commands that would find out the names of files on the client. In addition, network applets cannot make network connections except to the machine from which they were loaded.

NOTE These limitations apply only to applets loaded from a network. Locally loaded applets have fewer restrictions. See Sun's Security FAQ at `http://java.sun.com/sfaq/` for details.

▶ To learn more about Java security protocols, **see** "Executable Content and Security," **p. 1178**

The debate between power and security seems to be veering toward the security side. An example is a "bug" that Drew Dean, Ed Felten, and Dan Wallach of Princeton University found in an old version of Netscape Navigator (version 2.0) running a Java applet. They tricked the domain name server (DNS—the program that resolves host names, such as `www.mcp.com`, into IP addresses) into disguising their origin. They made DNS believe they were actually from another computer, and then they were able to breach security on it. Netscape acknowledged the situation and quickly provided an update (version 2.01) that provided closer control over how an IP address is resolved.

Another security flaw was found in Internet Explorer version 3.0. It allowed a Web site or Webmaster to place a Windows 95 shortcut on your system. This shortcut could be any kind of command to run a program or even format your hard disk.

More recently, sites around the world have been plagued by viruses spread through email, especially Microsoft Outlook and its scripting language, VBScript. These situations have caused a stir in the Internet community. Concerns about Internet security are rampant. Many users and developers have also raised concerns about restricting applet access to the point where the usefulness of the applications is diminished.

Starting with JDK 1.2, you can attach a digital signature to your applets before they are distributed. This approach ensures the user that he is getting the applet he wants.

▶ To learn more about signed applets, **see** "Signing Your JARs," **p. 1205**

Using Network Communications in Applets

Recall from "Writing Your Own Client and Server," earlier in this chapter, that you can write your own server or use a commercial server to communicate with your applets. You'll find a collection of servers written in Java at `http://www.developer.com/directories/pages/dir.java.net.server.html`.

You can review the applets at `http://www.developer.com/directories/pages/dir.java.net.html` to get an idea of what other developers are doing with network programming. You'll find a set of classes, for example, that gives you access to your SMTP (email) server at `http://www.savarese.org/oro/software/NetComponents.html`.

The Gamelan page `http://www.developer.com/directories/pages/dir.java.net.intertools.html` also lists several Telnet clients and an FTP client, all written as applets. ●

CHAPTER 40

Security

by Mike Morgan

In this chapter

Executable Content and Security

Java has changed the face of the Web from a static publishing medium to an interactive application development platform by providing executable "live" content embedded in HTML documents. This is a frightening thought to many system administrators. After all, it's bad enough that people can download software that might contain viruses that could damage their machines. How can the network stay secure with programs coming in and running on the host machines all on their own? Malicious code such as the "LoveBug" virus has made us all wonder, what is to keep somebody from reading sensitive data, wiping out hard drives, setting up back doors to the network, or something worse? Fortunately, the folks at Sun gave this matter some thought and designed Java with security in mind from the ground up, starting with the language and continuing on through the compiler, compiled code, and runtime environment.

To understand Java's preventative measures, this chapter starts by reviewing the special security concerns that apply to interactive content. Then it covers the types of attacks that unscrupulous programmers attempt and the kinds of security issues that relate to a well-intentioned but poorly written program. You'll also learn about the security features of the Java language, the Java compiler, and the Java Virtual Machine. Finally, you'll hear about the remaining open issues related to Java security and what you can (and can't) do about them, as well as the Security API implemented in Java 2.

This section discusses how interactivity on the Web has evolved and how security issues have changed with each new technique. The section then focuses on how live content, executing on host machines, poses the most challenging security issues of all.

The general security issues that relate only to executable content on the Web are discussed, as opposed to other means of interactivity. From there, the issues are outlined and possible attack scenarios are illustrated.

Interactivity Versus Security

A direct correlation exists between interactivity and security: The greater the level of interactivity, the greater the security risk.

The Internet enables information to be spread, but this capability is also what makes it potentially dangerous. This risk is especially high when the information is executable code, such as Java. An image or other non-program file cannot execute instructions on your machine, and so is inherently safer than a Java applet (or ActiveX control). As you will see, this relationship between interactivity and security is true on the server side as well as the client side.

Step back to the basic building block of the Web—HTTP. *HTTP*, the *Hypertext Transfer Protocol*, is the protocol of the Web. It is a simple, stateless protocol. When an HTTP server receives a request for a file, it hands that file over. No interaction occurs between the server and client beyond the call and response. An HTTP server is similar to a television transmitter, and an HTTP client is similar to a television. A television is a receiver that receives signals from a transmitter. The only real difference between the way television transmitters and HTTP servers interact with televisions and HTTP clients is that instead of broadcasting, the server is responding to individual requests. The HTTP server is sending out whatever was specifically requested by an HTTP client and not just pumping out information to everyone. HTTP is a fairly secure protocol on both the client and server sides. The server controls what files and information the client has access to by choosing what it serves. The client is open to very little risk, except maybe being overloaded by too much data from the server, but the operating system on the client side usually prevents that. Although this protocol is quite reliable and more interactive than television, it is still a relatively passive medium.

Of course, the basic HTTP protocol leaves much to be desired in the way of interactivity, and people had to really fight it to build compelling, interactive content. Still, interactivity techniques were developed. The most popular of these have been the combination of forms and CGI programs.

The use of forms and CGI is still relatively secure on the client side, but significantly less so for the server. The process works like this: The browser on the client side receives an HTML form document. The form can contain HTML combo boxes, radio buttons, check boxes, and text fields as well as buttons to post the form data. An end user fills out the form and submits its contents to the server. Form contents are submitted by passing them as an argument to a program that executes on the server. Most often, this program is a CGI (Common Gateway Interface) program. It can be written in any language that executes on the server and commonly consists of a UNIX shell script, a C program, or a PERL script. The CGI program parses up the parameter string supplied by the client and uses the data. The CGI program can store the data in a local database, email it, and so forth. The CGI program is responsible for all access to the server. No direct access to the server by the client ever occurs. This arrangement presents a server-side security risk because badly behaved CGI programs can damage a server by depleting system resources, corrupting files, or doing anything else an executable program is capable of doing.

Although Active Server Pages and other non-CGI server-side scripting methods were not mentioned in the preceding discussion, the security issues are much the same.

▶ For more information on CGI programs and security, **see** Chapter 30, "Server-Side Security Issues"

The next logical step in the evolution of interactivity on the Web was client-side executable content. This sort of content actually existed before Java in the form of helper apps and plug-ins. Through the use of helper apps—and helper apps that execute right in the browser, called *plug-ins*—it is possible to view and interact with Web content by using code that executes on your own machine. You need to download and install the helper software first (assuming it is available for your platform) and get the content later. The content is not executable but contains information about itself that tells the browser what program to use to interact with it. This is accomplished by use of a MIME (Multipurpose Internet Mail

Extensions) type. This model allows a security risk on the client that is worse than the Java model because no limits are imposed on the application running on the client. The person using the helper application must trust that it won't do any harm. The content (images, sounds, and movies) is not executable, and an end user must explicitly install the viewer software. Hence, no more risk exists than in installing any other kind of application.

What about the Java model? It is a big step forward for interactivity, which would typically cause security concerns. If the client can download executable code without knowing exactly what it does, what's to prevent a malicious Java programmer from writing an applet that wipes out the user's hard drive, infects files with viruses, steals private information, or crashes the machine? The remainder of this section describes these risks in more detail and talks about how these security risks have been closed in Java.

The Security Problem

How is network-distributed dynamic executable content any different from software installed and running on a local machine? A piece of software needs to be able to access all the system resources within the limits of the operating system. It typically needs to save files, read information, and access the system's memory. Although defects exist in software as well as malicious attacks, the person installing the software generally makes a decision to trust the person who wrote the software. This approach is the traditional software model.

An application arriving over a network must also be able to make use of system resources to function. The only difference is that executable content arriving in a Web page does not need to be installed first. The user might not even know from where it is coming. If the applet needs access to key system resources, it will contact the browser and ask for special access. Typically, the browser responds by displaying a special dialog box, asking the user if she is willing to trust this applet. If the code was written by a malicious programmer who wanted to damage the end user's machine or violate that user's security, and if the end user was willing to grant that live content all the same freedoms a regular local application would have, the user would have no warning and no protection.

How do you allow for a useful applet and maintain a level of trust? It doesn't make sense to completely restrict outside programs from doing anything on the local machine. Such an approach severely limits the functionality of the network application. A better strategy is to develop limitations that hinder the malicious behavior but allow the freedom to do the things that need to be done. Six steps define this strategy:

1. Determine in advance all potential malicious behavior and attack scenarios.
2. Reduce all potential attack scenarios to a basic set of behaviors.
3. Design a programming language and architecture that does not allow the basic set of behaviors that forms the basis for attack. Hopefully, this disallows the malicious behavior.

4. Prove that the language and architecture are secure against the intended attack scenarios.
5. Allow executable content using only this secure architecture.
6. Design the language and architecture to be extensible so new attack scenarios can be dealt with as they are discovered and new countermeasures can be retrofitted into the existing security measures.

Java was designed with each of these steps in mind, and it addresses most, if not all, of these points. Before exploring Java's security architecture, the next section discusses the types of potential attack scenarios.

Potential Attack Scenarios

An adversary might try to perpetrate two basic categories of attack. The first of these is the security breach; the second is the nuisance attack. Some examples of nuisance attacks are as follows:

- Application starts a process that hogs all system resources and brings all computer use to a halt.
- Application locks the browser by attacking it internally.
- Application interferes with or reassigns the browser's Domain Name Service (DNS) server. Such an attack can prevent the user from loading documents and possibly cause a security breach if the user were on as the privileged superuser (called root in UNIX and Administrator in Windows NT).
- Application searches and destroys other applications by interfering with some specific process. Someone has written a Java applet, for example, that kills any other Java applets that try to load.
- Application displays obscene pictures or profanity.
- Application deletes or damages files on your computer.

These types of attacks might not necessarily open you up to a security breach because they do not leak private information about your company or yourself to any unauthorized third party. They can, however, make your computing experience unpleasant and even damage your computer's operating system or files. The goal of these attacks is to wreak havoc of one type or another.

The other, more serious, types of attacks are security breaches, where somebody attempts to gain private or sensitive information about you or your business. More strategies are used to accomplish this than can be covered in a single chapter of a book. You'll find full coverage of the subject in *Internet Security Professional Reference, Second Edition* (New Riders, 1997) and

Maximum Security, Second Edition (Sams, 1998). A few of the major strategies that people might try include

- Installing a back door into your network for future unauthorized access
- Accessing confidential files on the network and giving them to an unauthorized third party
- Usurping your identity and impersonating you or your computer to carry out attacks on other computers

NOTE For a different sort of overview of computer security, read *Tangled Web: Tales of Digital Crime from the Shadows of Cyberspace* (Que, 2000). You can read about this book online at `http://www.mcp.com/detail.cfm?item=078972443X`.

The Java Approach to Security

Not only is Java a programming language, it also is a cross-platform operating environment—the Java Virtual Machine (JVM). The JVM is separate and independent of Java, the language. The Java Software Development Kit (SDK) also includes a compiler (javac) for the Java language that produces *bytecodes* for the JVM. The JVM could run bytecodes compiled from any language, not only Java, and the `.class` files that make up Java objects could be created by any compiler that targeted the Java Virtual Machine. Security needs to be implemented separately on each of these fronts: in the language, the compiler, and the Virtual Machine.

The Java programming language is more secure than other languages because it is designed to be

- Portable
- Secure
- Object oriented
- Network aware
- Extensible

Many of these requirements affect the way security is implemented in the language, the compiler, and the Virtual Machine. The portability requirement, for example, means that Java cannot rely on any security measures built into an operating system because it needs to run on any system.

Defending Against Attacks from Network Software

If you're going to design a language that makes it easy for programmers to send their work to end users, you have to deal with an unpleasant reality: Not all programmers are as nice as you are. In fact, a few twisted people write programs that are positively malicious.

Trojan horse programs pretend to be useful applications, but when they run, they carry out some hidden (and generally malicious) operation. *Viruses* attach themselves to other programs or to files that support executable content, such as Word documents or email messages. As part of their function, they copy themselves to other programs or files. As these files spread around the network, more and more machines are affected. At some point, the virus delivers its payload, which might be anything from a mischievous message on the screen to actually deleting data.

Two lines of defense prevent programs such as Trojan horses and viruses from being spread. First, you can enable the developer to "sign" the program with a signature that can't be forged. If the signature is valid, the program does not have any viruses or other code that was added after the programmer finished the program. (of course, a malicious programmer can still sign a virus-laden document.) Second, you can design the language in such a way that certain operations, such as reading from or writing to the local hard drive, are prohibited. Although these operations might be useful to some programs, they are also exploited by malicious programmers.

Modern browsers allow end users to download executable content in the form of Java applets and as ActiveX controls. Both Java and ActiveX give the programmer a way to digitally sign the program so the end user can be confident that the code he is downloading is actually the program the programmer wrote. Java differs from ActiveX, however, in that Java prevents the programmer from doing things on the client's machine that might be used by a virus or a Trojan horse.

If you have a signed program that can do anything it likes to the end user's machine, you have a serious vulnerability. Not every malicious operation is immediately obvious. If a malicious program starts deleting files off your hard drive, you'll probably notice. But will you notice if it goes through your Web browser's disk cache looking up confidential information from your intranet?

Even if you detect a malicious program at work, you might not be able to identify which program is doing the work. In fact, there's no guarantee that the problem-causing program came to you over the Internet. Some security experts have reported that more viruses are loaded from CD-ROMs than from the Internet.

So the best that an electronic signature can guarantee is that if you detect something going wrong, the problem was caused by something you downloaded, and if you know which downloaded program caused the problem, you have someone to blame.

Many security experts—not to mention users—would prefer that the problem never occur in the first place. That's the Java approach—deny the malicious programmer any opportunity to write a virus or a Trojan horse in the first place.

NOTE As an applet developer, you should become familiar with the security capabilities offered by Java. Visit the Security Frequently Asked Questions page at `http://java.sun.com/sfaq/` to get the latest reports on Java security. Visit `http://java.sun.com/security/` for an overview of Java security.

To ensure security, Java designers implemented a mechanism called the *sandbox*. The sandbox ensures that untrusted (and possibly malicious) Java applets are allowed access to only a limited set of capabilities on the end user's machine.

NOTE The comments here about security are directed at applets, not applications. An end user can run an applet by downloading a Web page, so applets need tight security. End users must install applications explicitly, so applications are allowed to exercise capabilities that are denied to applets.

This section describes the three major mechanisms that implement the sandbox:

- JVM-level checks
- Language-level safeguards
- The *JavaSecurity* interface

JVM-Level Checks

Suppose you've written a Java applet and have compiled it into a class file. You use this applet on your Web page; when an end user who uses a Java-aware browser downloads this page, he also downloads the applet. To ensure that the applet cannot access system-level resources such as the hard drive, the Java Virtual Machine (JVM) that is built into the browser performs several checks.

NOTE Java applets can run either in the browser's own JVM or in Sun's Java plug-in. If the HTML author used the `<APPLET>` tag, the browser itself attempts to load the applet. If the browser sees an `<OBJECT>` or `<EMBED>` tag, it will use the plug-in. The comments in this section about the browser's JVM also apply to the plug-in's JVM.

First, the JVM includes a *class loader*, which is responsible for finding and downloading all the classes used by the applet. Second, before the class file is allowed to execute, the *bytecode verifier* tests the contents of the class file. Third, the class runs under the supervision of the JVM *Security Manager* (implemented in `java.lang.SecurityManager`). Figure 40.1 illustrates how these three components work together.

These three mechanisms work together to ensure that

- Only the proper classes are loaded.
- Each class is in the proper format.
- Untrusted classes are not allowed to execute dangerous instructions.
- Untrusted classes are not allowed to access system resources.

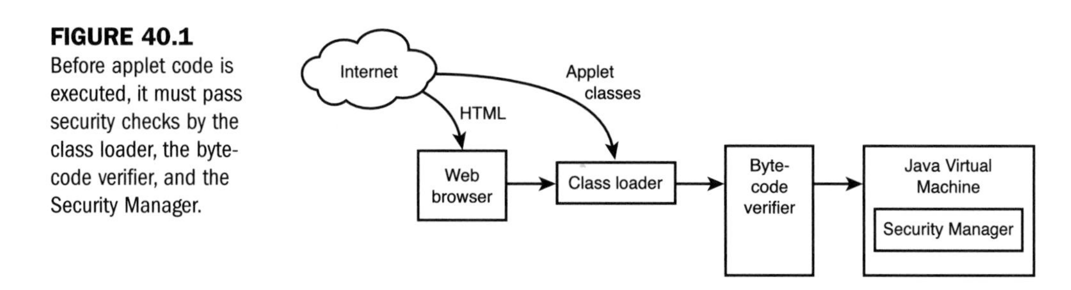

FIGURE 40.1
Before applet code is executed, it must pass security checks by the class loader, the byte-code verifier, and the Security Manager.

Understanding the Class Loader When a Java-aware browser sees the <APPLET> tag, it invokes the class loader and asks the class loader to load the specified applet. The class loader defines a ***namespace*** associated with that particular Web page. Classes loaded as part of this applet are not allowed to access classes outside the applet (although they can access classes that form part of the standard Java libraries). Figure 40.2 illustrates the class loader's namespaces.

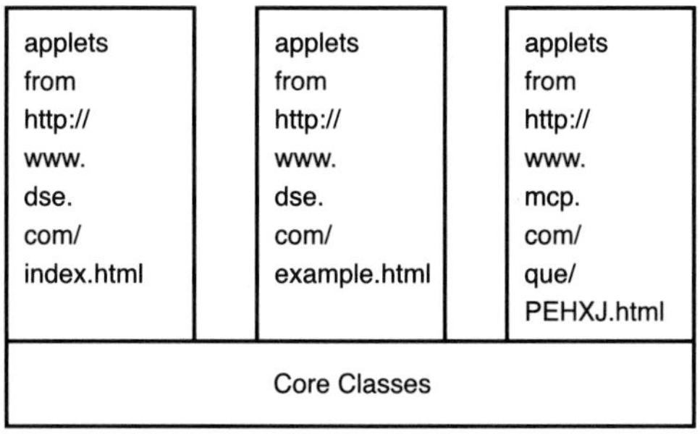

applets from http://www.dse.com/index.html

applets from http://www.dse.com/example.html

applets from http://www.mcp.com/que/PEHXJ.html

Core Classes

FIGURE 40.2
The Java class loader uses namespaces to isolate one applet from another.

The security provided by a class loader is only as good as the class loader itself. If the class loader was built by Sun or is based on Sun's template, it should provide the safeguards described here. Sun's model class loader contains checks to make sure the applet does not install its own class loader, for example, or call methods that are used solely by the class loader. If the browser vendor has not followed Sun's guidelines, the class loader might have security holes.

NOTE Any application designer can write his own class loader. End users should not trust a class loader unless they trust the application developer. ■

Security Afforded by the Bytecode Verifier After a class is loaded (by the class loader), it is inspected by the bytecode verifier. The bytecode verifier includes a sophisticated theorem prover that ensures the applet does not forge pointers, circumvent access restrictions, or convert objects illegally. Just as the class loader's namespace mechanism ensures that one applet cannot interfere with another, the bytecode verifier ensures that an applet cannot wreak havoc within its own namespace. The bytecode verifier also checks for stack overflow or underflow—a traditional way malicious programmers have breached system security. You'll hear more about the bytecode verifier later in this chapter, in the section "The Security of Compiled Code."

Working with the JVM's Security Manager The final set of checks at the JVM level is made by the JVM's Security Manager. The Security Manager watches out for "dangerous" operations—those that could be exploited by a malicious programmer. The Security Manager must agree any time the applet attempts to access any of the following:

- Network communications
- Protected information (including the hard drive or personal data)
- Operating-system level programs and processes
- The class loader
- Libraries of Java classes (known as *packages*)

The Security Manager is also responsible for preserving thread integrity. That is, code in one group of threads cannot interfere with code in another group of threads, even if the two groups have the same parent applet.

▶ To learn more about threads, **see** "Adding Animation," **p. 1139**

Language-Level Safeguards

Many languages, such as SmallTalk, enable the programmer to easily convert objects of one sort to objects of another. This *loose typing* enables programmers to get code up and running quickly, but also opens opportunities for the malicious programmer (in addition to leaving opportunities for software defects).

Strongly typed languages such as Ada are somewhat more difficult to use, but they generally result in programs with fewer defects and tighter compiled code. For this reason, loosely typed languages are popular for prototyping, and strongly typed languages are often used for production code.

C and C++ offer a combination of typing methods. The language presents itself as being strongly typed—the compiler needs to be able to determine the type of each object—but the programmer can override a type and coerce an object of one type into a different type. This override mechanism is called *casting*. To cast an object of type `Book` to be of type `Volume`, you could write

```
Volume myVolume = (Volume) aBook;
```

The Java approach to typing is based on the older C and C++ languages. Java's approach provides three security benefits:

- Objects cannot be cast to a subclass without an explicit runtime check.
- All references to methods and variables are checked to make sure the objects are of the correct type.
- Integers cannot be converted into objects, and objects cannot be converted to integers.

In general, much of C and C++'s strength comes from the capabilities of those languages to use *pointers*—variables that hold memory addresses of other data. Although you'll sometimes see descriptions of Java that claim the language has no pointers, the fact is that nearly everything in Java is a pointer—they're just not accessible by the user. The reason pointers are "invisible" is that the Java designers removed the capability to point a pointer to an arbitrary location. This capability, often used by C and C++ programmers, is called *pointer arithmetic*—the capability to modify a pointer so it points to a new location. Pointer arithmetic enables a malicious C or C++ programmer to access anything within the program's range of allowable addresses (called the *address space*). In some operating systems, and on some processors, each program has access to the entire machine's address space. On those systems, a malicious programmer can use pointer arithmetic to wreak havoc in other programs.

NOTE If you're an experienced C or C++ programmer, you might ask, "Won't I miss pointer arithmetic?" Most pointer arithmetic is used to get efficient access to character strings or other arrays. Java supports strings and arrays as explicit classes, with efficient methods to get at their contents. If you use these built-in methods, chances are you'll never miss pointer arithmetic.

Another technique commonly used by malicious programmers is to deliberately overflow an array. Suppose a programmer defines an array of characters named `myString` to have 128 bytes. The locations `myString[0]` through `myString[127]` are reserved for use by the program. By accessing `myString[128]` and beyond, the program is reading and writing outside its assigned bounds. You can get away with that in C or C++, but in Java, array accesses are checked at runtime. The program will not be allowed to access `myString[]` outside the range 0 to 127. Not only does this bounds-checking close a security hole; it also prevents one common source of program defects.

Strings are also immutable—after you've made a character string, no one can change it (although you can extract substrings and put them together to make new strings). By requiring that strings be immutable, Java's designers closed another security hole and prevented still more common programming errors.

CAUTION

Because strings are immutable, string manipulation can be time-consuming. Many Java programmers avoid this problem by using the class `StringBuffer` instead of `String`. `StringBuffer` still has some built-in security: If you append too many characters and overflow the internal buffer, the class automatically allocates more space.

In addition to strong typing and overflow protection, Sun's engineers also took advantage of the object-oriented nature of the language itself to add security. With the exception of the primitive types, everything in Java is derived from basic objects. This strict adherence to object-oriented methodology means that all the theoretical benefits of object-oriented programming (OOP) are realized in Java. These include

- Encapsulation of data within objects
- The capability to inherit from existing secure objects
- Controlled access to data structures via public methods only, so no operator overloading occurs

Every Java object has a unique hash code associated with it. This feature enables the current state of a Java program to be fully inventoried at any time, enabling the Java Virtual Machine to watch for unauthorized objects.

How Java Provides Security Over the Internet

Because of the protection of the JVM and the language itself, most users can run most applets and be confident that the applet will "play in its own sandbox" without interfering with system resources on the end user's machine. Sometimes, however, you need to write an applet that accesses those system resources, and the end user is willing to trust that you won't damage her system or steal confidential information.

The problem is that an end user downloading your applets over the Internet could be duped into running malicious applets written by someone else. Figure 40.3 illustrates the problem, known as the "man-in-the-middle" attack.

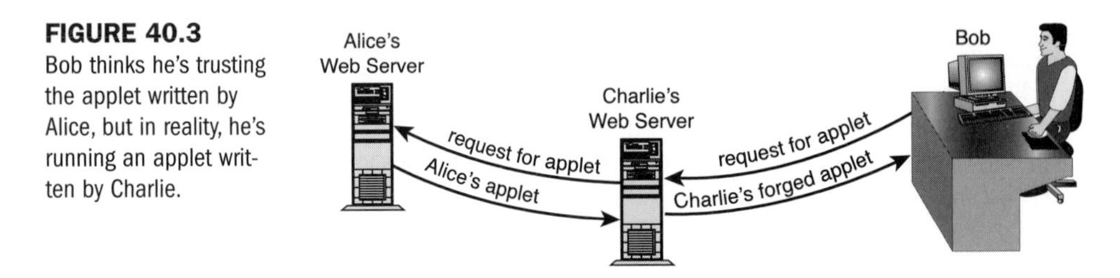

FIGURE 40.3
Bob thinks he's trusting the applet written by Alice, but in reality, he's running an applet written by Charlie.

In this example, Bob thinks he has connected to Alice's server. His browser downloaded a Web page that included an applet. In reality, Charlie has programmed his server to intercept the applet on its way to Bob and substitute Charlie's version of the applet. Although Bob thinks he's trusting Alice's applet, in reality he has opened his system to a malicious applet written by Charlie.

NOTE For a technical description of how a man-in-the-middle attack applies to the Web, read this paper on Web spoofing developed by the Secure Internet Programming team at Princeton University at `http://www.cs.princeton.edu/sip/pub/spoofing.html`.

The solution to this problem is offered by an applet-level security mechanism called the JavaSecurity API. (An API is an *Application Programming Interface*—a way for a library developer to give the programmer access to a set of features.)

One of the capabilities offered in the JavaSecurity API is *digital signing*. To use this capability, bundle your Java class files and any related files that your applet needs into a *Java archive* (JAR). Then electronically sign the JAR file. When the end user retrieves the JAR from your server, he can verify your signature. If a man in the middle attempts to substitute a different applet, the signature will not verify and the end user will be warned about the forgery.

NOTE Learn more about the Java archive format at `http://java.sun.com/products/jdk/1.3/docs/guide/jar/jarGuide.html`. Here you'll learn how to reference a JAR in the `<APPLET>` tag instead of a class file.

Applets Versus ActiveX Controls

The only serious competitor to Java applets is offered by Microsoft and is called ActiveX controls. ActiveX controls are an Internet version of an older standard, called OCX controls. These controls can be written in any language and can do anything that anyone can do in that language. No technical reason prevents an ActiveX programmer from writing a Trojan horse that deletes every file on your hard drive or that copies confidential information back to the Internet. Microsoft has tried to address this problem by encouraging ActiveX developers to use their code-signing facility, making ActiveX controls proof against man-in-the-middle attacks.

Sun's approach, with Java, is different, with security checks built into the language itself. As you'll see, Sun also supports signed applets, which the end user might choose to trust.

The Microsoft Way

Microsoft's approach means that every ActiveX control functions like a trusted Java applet. Because most end users will not want to download unsigned ActiveX controls, no equivalent exists to the untrusted applet, in which security is ensured by the Java sandbox.

If an end user chooses to trust all ActiveX controls, sooner or later the end user's machine might fall victim to an attack. With most attacks, it might be difficult to determine which ActiveX control was responsible. An ActiveX control could replace a system file such as `move.exe`, for example, and then alter itself so the malicious part of the ActiveX control was deleted. The next time the end user attempts to move a file, the Trojan horse version of `move.exe` runs, accomplishing the malicious programmer's objective. Even if the end user detects the problem, it will be difficult to trace the problem back to the specific ActiveX control.

NOTE Microsoft's side of the applet versus ActiveX argument is that Java represents a "lowest common denominator." Microsoft casts the argument not as "Java versus ActiveX" but as "PCs versus Sun." They also point to `http://www.webfayre.com/pendragon/jpr/index.html`, which benchmarks Java performance on a number of different machines. (Windows JVMs running on high-speed Pentiums outperform all other platforms.)

Java Browser Restrictions

Sun recommends that browser vendors limit applets by enforcing three rules. These rules are enforced by the Sun code licensed by major browser vendors, such as Netscape Communications and Microsoft, as well as by the Sun Java plug-in:

- Untrusted applets cannot access the local hard drive.
- All standalone windows put up by untrusted applets are labeled as such. Figure 40.4 shows such a window.

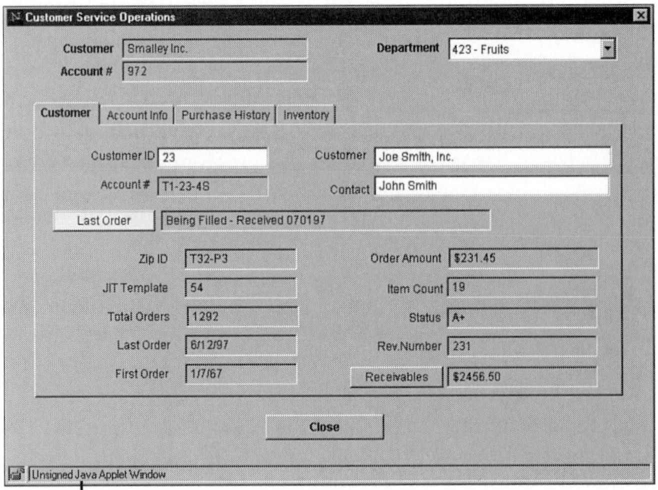

FIGURE 40.4
The browser warns the user if a window was opened by an untrusted applet.

Warning supplied by browser

- Untrusted applets can only establish a network connection back to the server from which they were loaded.

The first rule closes most security holes. If an applet cannot read the local hard drive, it cannot access most confidential information. If it cannot write the hard drive, it cannot plant viruses or Trojan horses.

The second rule makes it less likely that the user will inadvertently enter confidential information (such as a credit card number) into an untrusted applet.

The third rule prevents someone from accessing non-local hard drives, such as those on a local area network or intranet. Like the first rule, this provision closes many opportunities the malicious programmer might have for stealing confidential information or for planting malicious programs.

NOTE Sun provides sample applets at `http://java.sun.com/sfaq/#examples` to test your browser's security. Your browser should catch security exceptions when you attempt to run these applets from the Internet. You shouldn't get exceptions when you run `http://java.sun.com/sfaq/example/getOpenProperties.html`, which demonstrates the 10 system properties untrusted applets are allowed to read, or `http://java.sun.com/sfaq/example/myWindow.html`, which opens a standalone window (although you should see the "Untrusted Applet" message).

Note that Sun recommends somewhat tighter restrictions for applets downloaded from the Web versus those loaded from the local file system. For full details see `http://java.sun.com/sfaq/`.

Although no one has suggested that it's impossible to build malicious applets—someone is probably working on one right now—Sun has certainly gone to great lengths to make it difficult. If someone wants to attack your system, it's far easier for them to attack through a mechanism such as an ActiveX control than through a Java applet. As long as most users are downloading both, malicious programmers will continue to favor ActiveX controls.

NOTE If you're responsible for security at your organization, you should get familiar with the services of the Computer Emergency Response Team (CERT) Coordination Center (`http://www.cert.org/`). CERT will keep you up-to-date on known security holes and fixes.

The Security of Compiled Code

The Java compiler checks Java code for security violations. It is a thorough, stringent compiler that enforces the restrictions previously listed. However, it is possible that Java code could be compiled with a "fixed" compiler that allows illegal operations. This is where the Java class loader and bytecode verifier come into play. Various types of security are enforced by the runtime system on compiled code.

Java *.class* File Structure

Java applets and applications are made up of `.class` files that are compiled bytecode. All public classes used in a Java applet or application reside in their own separate `.class` file. They might be transferred over the network a file at a time or bundled into a `.zip` or `.jar` file. The `.class` file is a series of bytes. Longer values are formed by reading two or four of these bytes and joining them together. Each `.class` file contains

- A magic constant
- Major and minor version information
- The constant pool
- Information about the class
- Information about each of the fields and methods in the class
- Debugging information

The *constant pool* is how constant information about the class is stored. This information can be any of the following:

- A Unicode string
- A class or interface name
- A reference to a field or method
- A numeric value
- A constant string value

As previously mentioned, all references to variables and classes in the Java language are done through symbolic names, not pointers. This is true in the `.class` file as well. Elsewhere in the `.class` file, references to variables, methods, and objects are accomplished by referring to indices in this constant pool. Security is thus maintained inside the `.class` file.

NOTE Each method can have multiple code attributes. The `CODE` attribute signifies Java bytecode, but other code attributes, such as `SPARC-CODE` and `386-CODE`, allow for a machine code implementation of the method. This technique allows for faster execution, but such native code cannot be verified to be secure.

The class loader of most current Java implementations, including Sun's own HotJava browser, considers any code that comes from a remote source to be potentially hostile and will not use any native code contained in a Java `.class` file unless the user designates the applet as "trusted." Some of these browsers will run native code loaded from local `.class` files, however.

More About Bytecodes

In addition to the actual bytecodes that execute a method, the CODE attribute also supplies other information about the method. This information is for the memory manager, the bytecode verifier, and the JVM's exception handling mechanism:

- Maximum stack space used by the method.
- Maximum number of registers used by the method.
- Bytecodes for executing the method.
- Exception handler table. This is a lookup table for the runtime system that provides an offset to where the exception handler is found for code within a starting and ending offset.

Six primitive types are available in the JVM:

- 32-bit integer (integers)
- 64-bit integer (long integers)
- 32-bit floating point numbers (single float)
- 64-bit floating point numbers (double float)
- Pointers to objects and arrays (handles)
- Pointers to the virtual machine code (return addresses)

The Java VM also recognizes several array types:

- Arrays of each of the primitive types (except return addresses)
- Arrays of Booleans, bytes (8-bit integers), shorts (16-bit integers), and Unicode characters

In the case of an array of handles, an additional type field indicates the class of object that the array can store.

Each method has its own expression-evaluation stack and set of local registers. The registers must be 32 bit and hold any of the primitive types other than the double floats and the long integers. These are stored in two consecutive registers, and the JVM instructions—*opcodes*—address them using the index of the lower-numbered register.

The JVM instruction set provides opcodes that operate on various data types and can be divided into several categories:

- Pushing constants onto the stack
- Accessing and modifying the value of a register
- Accessing arrays
- Stack manipulation

- Arithmetic, logical, and conversion instructions
- Control transfer
- Function return
- Manipulating object fields
- Method invocation
- Object creation
- Type casting

The bytecodes consist of a one-byte opcode followed by zero or more bytes of additional operand information. With two exceptions, all instructions are fixed length and based on the opcode.

The Bytecode Verifier

The bytecode verifier is the last line of defense against a bad Java applet. This is where the classes are checked for integrity, where the compiled code is checked for its adherence to the Java rules, and where a misbehaving applet is most likely caught. If the compiled code was created with a "fixed" compiler to get around Java's restrictions, it will still fail the verifier's checks and be stopped. The bytecode verifier is one of the most interesting parts of the Java security mechanism because of the way it is designed to be thorough and general at the same time. The bytecode verifier does not have to work only on code created by a Java compiler, but on any bytecodes created for a JVM, so it needs to be general. However, it also needs to catch all exceptions to the rules laid out for a Java applet or application and must, therefore, be thorough.

All bytecode goes through the bytecode verifier, which makes four passes over the code.

Pass 1 is the most basic pass. The verifier makes sure that the following criteria are met:

- The `.class` file conforms to the format of a `.class` file.
- The magic constant at the beginning is correct.
- All attributes are of the proper length.
- The `.class` file does not have any extra bytes, nor too few.
- The constant pool does not have any unrecognized information.

Pass 1 finds any corrupt `.class` files from a faulty compiler and also catches `.class` files that were damaged in transit. Assuming everything goes well, you get to the second pass.

Pass 2 adds a little more scrutiny. It verifies almost everything without actually looking at the bytecodes themselves. Some of the things for which Pass 2 is responsible are

- Ensuring that final classes are not subclassed and that final methods are not overridden
- Checking that every class (except `Object`) has a superclass

- Ensuring that the constant pool meets certain constraints
- Checking that all field references and methods in the constant pool have legal names, classes, and a type signature

On Pass 2, everything needs to look legal—that is, at face value all the classnames appear to refer to classes that really exist, rules of inheritance aren't broken, and so on. It does not check the bytecodes themselves; this task is left up to further passes. Passes 3 and 4 check to see if the fields and methods actually exist in a real class and if the types refer to real classes.

On Pass 3, the actual bytecodes of each method are verified. Each method undergoes dataflow analysis to ensure that the following conditions are met:

- The stack is always the same size and contains the same types of objects.
- No registers are accessed unless they are known to contain values of a specific type.
- All methods are called with the correct arguments.
- All opcodes have appropriate type arguments on the stack and in the registers.
- Fields are modified with values of the appropriate type.

The verifier ensures that the exception handler offsets point to legitimate starting and ending offsets in the code. It also makes sure the code does not end in the middle of an instruction.

Pass 4 occurs as the code actually runs. During Pass 3, the bytecode verifier does not load any classes unless it must check its validity. This approach makes the bytecode verifier more efficient. On Pass 4, the final checks are made the first time an instruction referencing a class executes. The verifier then does the following:

- Loads in the definition of the class (if not already loaded)
- Verifies that the currently executing class is allowed to reference the given class

Likewise, the first time an instruction calls a method or accesses or modifies a field, the verifier does the following:

- Ensures that the method or field exists in the given class
- Checks that the method or field has the indicated signature
- Checks that the currently executing method has access to the given method or field

Namespace Encapsulation Using Packages

Java classes are defined within packages that give them unique names. The Java standard for naming packages is the domain the package originates from, but in reverse order. If your domain is `yourdomain.com`, your classes should be in the `com.yourdomain` package.

What is the advantage to using packages? With packages, a class arriving over the network is distinguishable, and therefore, cannot impersonate a trusted local class.

Runtime Linking and Binding

The exact layout of runtime resources is one of the last things done by the JVM. Java uses *dynamic linking*—linking and binding during runtime. This technique prevents an unscrupulous programmer from making assumptions about the allocation of resources or using this information to attack security.

Security in the Java Runtime System

Classes can be treated differently when loaded locally rather than over a network. One of these differences is how the class is loaded into the runtime system. The default way for this to happen is to load the class from a local `.class` file. Any other way of retrieving a class requires the class to be loaded with an associated `ClassLoader`. The `ClassLoader` class is a subtype of a standard Java object that has the methods to implement many of the security mechanisms discussed so far. Many of the attack scenarios that have been used against Java have involved getting around the `ClassLoader`.

The `ClassLoader` comes into play after Pass 3 of the bytecode verifier as the classes are actually loaded on Pass 4. The `ClassLoader` is fairly generic because it does not know for certain that it is loading classes written in Java. It could be loading classes written in C++ and compiled into bytecodes.

The `ClassLoader`, therefore, has to check general rules for consistency within `ClassFiles`. If a class fails these checks, it isn't loaded and an attack on an end user's system fails. It is an important part of the Java security system.

Automatic Memory Management and Garbage Collection

In C or C++, the programmer is responsible for allocating and deallocating memory and needs to keep track of the pointers to all the objects in memory. This design can result in memory leaks, dangling pointers, null pointers, and other defects that are difficult to find and fix. Additionally, leaving memory management up to the programmer can allow for mischief. Manual allocation and deallocation of memory opens the door for unauthorized replication of objects, impersonation of trusted objects, and attacks on data consistency. By having automatic memory management, Java gets around these problems and, at the same time, makes life easier for the programmer.

The following example shows how a programmer might go about impersonating a trusted class (for instance, the `ClassLoader`) if Java did not have automatic deallocation of memory. First, the program would create a legitimate object of class `MyFakeClassLoader` and make a reference to that object. Now, with a little sleight of hand and knowledge of how allocation and deallocation work, the programmer removes the object from memory but leaves the reference. He or she then instantiates a new instance of `ClassLoader`, which happens to be the exact same size, in the same memory space, and *voila*! The pointer now refers to the other class, and the programmer has access to methods and variables that are supposed to be private. This scenario is not possible in Java because of the automatic memory management. The Java automatic memory management system doesn't allow manual manipulation of references.

The *SecurityManager* Class

The Java security model is open to extension when new holes are found. A key to this is the `SecurityManager` class. This class is a generic class for implementing security policies and providing security wrappers around other parts of Java. Although not a comprehensive list, this class contains methods to

- Check to prevent the installation of additional `ClassLoaders`
- Check whether a `.class` file can be read by the Java Virtual Machine
- Check whether native code can be linked in
- Check whether a file can be written to
- Check whether a network connection can be created
- Check whether a certain network port can be listened to for connections
- Check whether a network connection can be accepted
- Check whether a certain package can be accessed
- Check whether a new class can be added to a package
- Verify security of a native OS system call
- Prevent a new Security Manager from being created

For a complete list of permissions, along with a description of the risks associated with each permission, read `JAVA_HOME/docs/guide/security/permissions.html`.

As you might guess from the preceding list, the names of many of the methods in the `java.lang.SecurityManager` class begin with `check`. All but one of these `checkXXX` methods return if all is well or throw a `SecurityException` if there is a problem. Only `checkTopLevelWindow` returns a value—a Boolean.

To check to see whether the local `SecurityManager` will grant a permission, include code such as this in your program:

```
SecurityManager secMgr = System.getSecurityManager();
if (secMgr != null) {
    secMgr.checkXXX( arguments go here,... );
}
```

Everything discussed so far in this section has been about Java as a whole. The language has no pointers whether you are working with applets or applications. The bytecode verifier and class loading mechanisms still apply. Applications in Java function like any other applications in any full-featured language, including direct memory access through use of native code. Some limitations on applets exist, however, that do not apply to applications.

Time-Tested Applet Security

Java would not have made the splash that it did only by being cross platform and object oriented. It was the Internet and applets that put it on the cover of *Time* magazine. The Internet is also where the biggest risks come for Java applets.

Applets are limited Java programs—extended from class `Applet`—that execute within the user's Web browser. Applets usually load from remote machines and are subject to severe limitations on the client machine.

Recall (from "Applets Versus ActiveX Controls," earlier in this chapter) that untrusted applets arriving on the client machine are subject to the local machine's security policy. This policy is specified in `JAVA_HOME/jre/lib/security/java.policy`. By default, the following file system and network restrictions apply to untrusted applets:

- Cannot read or write files on the local file system.
- Cannot create, copy, delete, or rename files or directories on the local file system.
- Can only connect to the machine from which they originally came. The machine is identified by the URL specified in the `APPLET` tag in the HTML document or in the `CODEBASE` parameter of the `APPLET` tag. The machine identifier cannot be a numeric IP address.
- Cannot call external programs.
- Cannot manipulate Java threadgroups other than their own.
- Cannot run outside the Java Virtual Machine's memory area.

NOTE This default set of restrictions on the applet can vary from one machine to another. All these apply, for instance, when using Java 1.1 or older (for example, in Netscape Navigator 2.0). If you want to know of detailed limitations for a particular browser, go to the applicable Web site and get the most up-to-date information. For the Microsoft Internet Explorer, check `http://www.microsoft.com/windows/ie/security/default.asp/`, and for the Netscape Navigator, check `http://home.netscape.com/browsers/index.html`. If you need to have a consistent security model no matter where your applet runs, consider designing your Web pages to load Sun's Java plug-in instead of relying on the browser's JVM.

▶ For more information on the Java plug-in, **see** "Running the Applet," **p. 1021**

CAUTION

Many JVMs have a default security policy that includes the line

```
permission java.lang.RuntimePermission "stopThread";
```

In the SDK 1.3 `java.policy` file, Sun cautions users to either remove or restrict this permission. The unrestricted permission to stop threads could be exploited by an unscrupulous programmer to wreak havoc on the user's system.

For more detail, visit `http://java.sun.com/j2se/1.3/docs/guide/misc/threadPrimitiveDeprecation.html`.

Some system information is available to applets, however. Access to this information depends on the specific Java implementation. A method of the `System` object is called `getProperty`. By calling `System.getProperty(String key)`, an applet can learn about its environment. The information generally available to the applet is as follows:

- **`java.version`**—The version of Java currently running.
- **`java.vendor`**—The name of the vendor responsible for this specific implementation of Java.
- **`java.vendor.URL`**—The URL of the vendor listed in `java.vendor`.
- **`java.class.version`**—The Java class version number.
- **`os.name`**—The name of the operating system.
- **`os.arch`**—The architecture of the operating system.
- **`file.separator`**—The file separator (for example, `/`).
- **`path.separator`**—The path separator (for example, :).
- **`line.separator`**—The line separator (for example, `CRLF`).

Applets can also retrieve the version, vendor, and name of the JVM and the associated language and JVM specifications.

Other pieces of information that are not available by default are

- **`java.home`**—The Java home directory.
- **`java.class.path`**—The Java class path.
- **`user.name`**—The logon name of the current user.
- **`user.home`**—The location of the user's home directory.
- **`user.dir`**—The user's current directory.

NOTE There's a list of system properties in the SDK documentation, under `System.getProperties`. You can also use `System.getProperties` or `System.getProperty` to retrieve environment variables that might have been set outside the Java environment.

Making and Using Signed Applets

Starting in JDK 1.1, Sun introduced several new APIs to the core set of Java APIs. Two of these classes are `Security` and `SignedObject`. These classes provide for digital signatures and message digests (in accordance with the industry standard X.509v3). These signatures are based on `public/private` key pairs.

To sign your applets or to prepare your system to use signed applets, you need the *jar*, *keytool*, *jarsigner*, and *appletviewer* tools included with SDK 1.3. You make and access Java archives with jar, make keys with keytool, sign archives with jarsigner, and test and develop using the appletviewer mini-browser.

Before getting started, you might want to see what happens when an applet throws a security exception. Sun provides a harmless sample applet that does just that. You can try it by running

```
appletviewer http://java.sun.com/security/signExample/writeFile.html
```

at a command prompt.

Digital Signature Enhancements in Java 2

As you've seen throughout this chapter, tight security is one of Java's distinctive features. It's not surprising that Java 2 includes features to ensure a secure environment, especially for applets. These features include

- **Policy-based access control**—The capability to grant rights to software is based on an external configuration file named `java.policy`.
- **Support for X.509v3 certificates**—You can use the latest industry-standard encryption technology to sign the Java archives in which you distribute your classes.
- **Security utilities**—These tools allow you to manage certificates and write your security policy file.

This section describes each of these capabilities.

Policy-Based Access Control

If you've used any modern multiuser operating system, you're familiar with the concept of permissions. The owner of a file can grant other users (or programs) the right to read, write, or execute a file. Processes take on the rights of the person who started them—although some users will choose to restrict the rights of programs they launch. (For example, on UNIX systems, someone with `root` authority often starts Web servers but the servers run as the nonprivileged user `nobody`.)

Beginning with Java 2, Java developers have similar choices with their applications and applets—although the level of control is finer-grained than that offered by many operating systems.

Computer resources include files, directories, hosts, and ports. The person responsible for a computer that will be running Java can set up a *security policy* that specifies who is allowed to access each resource. Access includes read and write permission (for files and directories) and connect permission (for hosts and ports). The security policy is specified in an external security configuration file, `java.policy`.

When a Java class is loaded, the JVM examines the security policy currently in effect. If the code is signed, permissions can be granted on the basis of the identity of the signer. Permissions can also be granted based on the location of the class file. (A file loaded from the local host might be given more access, for example, than one loaded from the Internet.)

Certificate Interfaces and X.509v3 Implementation

Not so long ago, the only way for a server to identify a client was to ask the user for a username and password. If the username and password matched those stored in the password file, the server granted the user access.

Several problems occur with password-based authentication. First, the password often has to travel over a non-secure network. If an adversary is able to "sniff" the username and password from the Net, she will be able to masquerade as a valid user.

Another problem is that most users access more than one system and have more than one username and password. Users find it difficult to keep these names and passwords straight, so they either write down the names and passwords or use the same name and password on every system. Either solution is subject to abuse.

A better solution is for the user to generate a special kind of cryptographic key, called a public/private key pair. These keys work together—if you encrypt something with another user's public key, only that user with his private key can decrypt it. If that user keeps his private key secret, you can be sure that he's the only one who can read your message.

In an ideal world, everyone could post their public keys on servers somewhere and begin to communicate securely with each other. That practice is subject to abuse, too—an opponent could put a public key on the server with my name on it. If your opponent can trick another user into using the bogus key, he will be able to read messages intended for you. (This strategy is a variation of the man-in-the-middle attack described earlier in this chapter, in "The Java Approach to Security.")

The solution is simple—you generate your public/private key pair, making sure to keep your private key secret. You send your public key to a "public key certifying authority," which requires that you prove your identity. Each certifying authority posts a Certification Practice Statement (CPS) formally describing the documentation they require in order to confirm your identity. For example, Verisign's CPS is online at `http://www.verisign.com/repository/CPS/`. After you've satisfied the certifying authority that you are who you say you are, the authority signs your key with *its* private key. Now any user who wants to be sure that a public key with your name on it really belongs to you can check the signature of the certifying authority. If the signature is valid, and the user is satisfied with the certifying authority's policy for checking your identity, then the user can trust your public key.

The combination of a public key, identifying information, and a certification authority's signature is called a *certificate.* The current generation of the standard for certificates is *X.509v3.* For more information about certificates and public-key encryption, see the section, "Signing Your JARs," later in this chapter.

Java 2 includes APIs for parsing certificates and maintaining local databases of X.509v3 certificates.

New Security Tools

Java 2 also includes tools to help you manage X.509v3 certificates. Within your company, for example, you might decide to issue certificates to any employee. The Java *keytool* enables each user to generate a public/private keypair. The user can also use keytool to generate his or her own certificate (although the certificate is to a slightly older standard—X.509v1).

NOTE If you plan to issue your own certificates, you'll need a Certificate Server. Visit the Netscape site and learn about Netscape's Certificate Server, part of the SuiteSpot family of servers, at `http://home.netscape.com/certificate/v1.0/index.html`.

You use *jarsigner* in combination with your certificate to digitally sign Java archives (JARs).

TIP If you've been using javakey from JDK 1.1 or earlier, replace it with keytool and jarsigner. javakey is now obsolete.

You can write an external security configuration file that specifies your machine's security policy. The easiest way to write such a file is to use Sun's *policytool.* Policytool is documented at `JAVA_HOME/docs/tooldocs/solaris/policytool.html` (for Solaris) and `JAVA_HOME/docs/tooldocs/win32/policytool.html` (for Windows).

Making a JAR

In the earliest days of Java, it was common to write simple applets that had only a single class file. More sophisticated applets might have dozens of class files as well as supporting files such as images and sounds. It became common to use the popular archive format, `.zip`, to bundle class files together. The Java Virtual Machine can read the `.zip` format, so it's not necessary to unzip these files.

Unfortunately, many users automatically unzip any arriving `.zip` file, breaking the applet. In Java 2, Sun provides tools for working with the Java archive format, JAR. A JAR file is still a

.zip file, but includes a special manifest file to identify its contents. By using a suffix that is more clearly Java related, Sun has decreased the likelihood that end users will extract the files from the archive.

You can place all the files associated with an applet into a JAR file and write

```
<APPLET CODE="TMyApplet.class"
  ARCHIVE="MyArchive.jar, AnotherArchive.jar"
  WIDTH="200" HEIGHT="200">
</APPLET>
```

This bit of code tells the browser to download the two JARs named `MyArchive.jar` and `AnotherArchive.jar`. The browser can expect that the components of `TMyApplet` will all be found in those two JARs. Furthermore, if the browser already has a current copy of both of those JAR files in its cache, it might be able to skip the download and load the applet right away. Figure 40.5 illustrates how the class files for `TMyApplet` are distributed across the two JAR files.

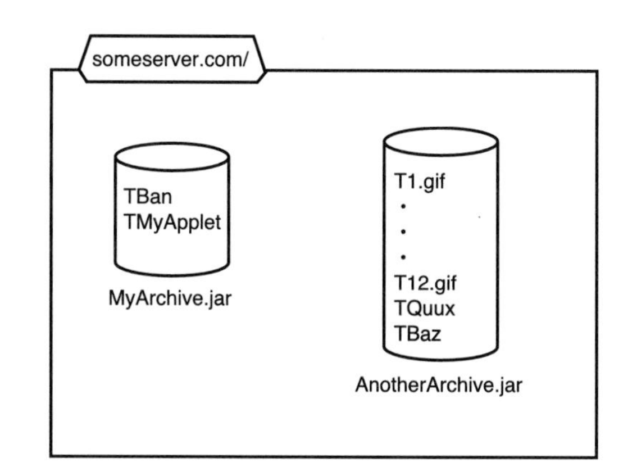

FIGURE 40.5
You can store the files of an applet in one or more JAR files.

NOTE If your applet uses files that aren't in the JAR file, the Web browser will go back to the Web server and look in the current `CODEBASE` directory for the missing files.

As an applet developer, you get six benefits from JARs:

- **Improved download efficiency**—You need only one HTTP transfer per JAR instead of one per class file.
- **Improved file storage**—A JAR stores the class files in one compressed file instead of leaving them "loose" in the directory.
- **Improved security**—You can sign JAR files digitally, giving the end user a guarantee that the file has not been tampered with since you signed it. If the end user trusts you, he might be willing to give your signed applet access to the hard drive or other sensitive resources.

- **Platform independence**—JAR files are based on PKZIP, a popular DOS compression utility, but they can be built and stored on any computer platform.
- **Backward compatibility**—A JAR file doesn't care what kind of files you put into it. You can take a JDK 1.0 applet and store its class files in a JAR file. As long as the user's browser understands how to read JAR files, she will be able to download and run the applet.
- **Extensibility**—Sun acknowledges that Internet technology in general—and Java technology in particular—is still in a state of flux. They've provided some hooks in the JAR specification for future growth, so that future developers can extend it as demands change.

Although you can use PKZIP-based tools to make and change JARs, Sun provides a tool specifically designed for the task. This utility is called *jar*—Sun has versions for all supported platforms.

Suppose you have the directory structure shown in Figure 40.6: several `.class` files plus an `images` directory. You could use the jar utility to put all these into a new JAR file named `MyApplet.jar`.

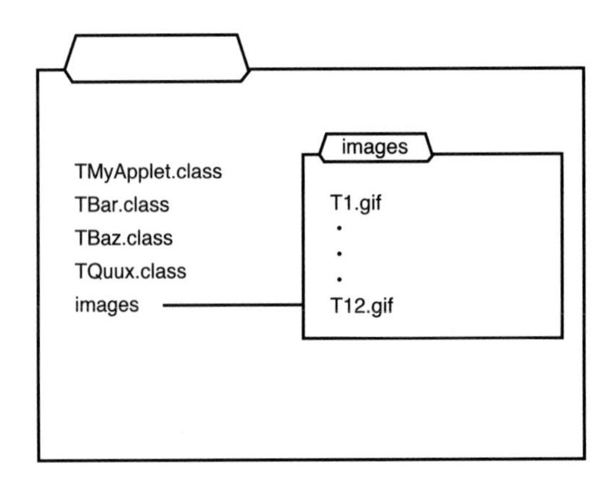

FIGURE 40.6
This directory contains a typical set of files for an applet or application.

The general format for the `jar` command line is

```
jar options filenames
```

NOTE The name for Sun's Java archive format is not accidental. Sun's jar utility is consciously modeled on a UNIX utility called "tar" (for tape archiver). The tar utility is used by UNIX users for building a variety of archives (not just those on tape) in much the same way as PKZIP and WinZip are used by MS-DOS and Windows users.

The first file named in the `filenames` list is the name of the archive. The use of any remaining files named in this list is given in the options list:

- `c`—Makes a new archive.
- `m`—Uses an external manifest file, named as the second file in the `filenames` list.
- `M`—Specifies not to make a manifest file for this archive.
- `t`—Lists the contents of this archive.
- `x`—Extracts the files named in the `filenames` list; if none, extracts all the files in the archive.
- `f`—Specifies that the archive is named as the first file in the `filenames` list.
- `v`—Specifies that the utility should produce verbose information while it performs the actions described by the other options.
- `0`—Stores files in the archive without using compression.

NOTE Unlike other utilities with which you might be familiar, jar doesn't require that you use `/` or `-` in front of the options.

To make your new archive, write

```
jar cf MyApplet.jar *.class images/*.gif
```

If you had prepared a manifest file in the text file `MyApplet.MF`, you would write

```
jar cfm MyApplet.jar MyApplet.MF *.class images/*.gif
```

CAUTION

A package name such as `com.mcp.que.platinumHTMLXMLJava.chapter40` means that the class file is located in the `com/mcp/que/platinumHTMLXMLJava/chapter40` directory underneath one of the directories named in the `CLASSPATH` environment variable. Be sure to place these class files into the proper directory before installing them into the JAR, or the JVM won't be able to find the class file.

You can examine a JAR file by using any PKZIP-compatible tool, including the jar utility itself. To get a listing of the files in `MyApplet.jar`, type

```
jar tf MyApplet.jar
```

Suppose you want to make a copy of a file that's come to you in a JAR file. Use the `x` option. To read the manifest file out of `MyApplet.jar`, for example, type

```
jar xf MyApplet.jar MyApplet.MF
```

Signing Your JARs

Regardless of what your JAR file contains, there are times when you want to be able to prove to the person using it that you are, indeed, the originator, and that no one has tampered with the contents after you made the JAR. If your JAR contains an applet, this need is particularly critical because, without such proof, applets are left in an untrusted state and will have no access to the hard drive or operating system services on the machine to which they're downloaded.

You can provide this guarantee by digitally signing your JAR. To understand how to set up a digital signature, you need to understand a little about cryptography.

Understanding Public Key Encryption

Many years ago encryption was the province of the military and the diplomats. You kept messages secret by combining the message with a secret piece of information called a *key*. The receiver needed a copy of the key. With the key and the proper equipment, anyone could decrypt a message. Figure 40.7 illustrates one of these old systems.

FIGURE 40.7

Old-style encryption systems were based on secret keys.

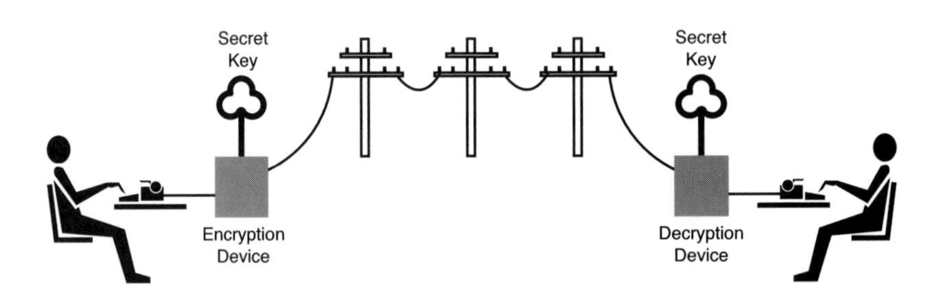

Introducing Public Key Technology In more recent days, cryptographers have invented *public key encryption*. A public key encryption system is based on two pieces of information, or keys. These keys come in pairs—they must be used together. One of these keys is secret and is kept under tight security by the owner. The other is public and can be distributed widely. Figure 40.8 illustrates how a public key encryption system works.

FIGURE 40.8
Public key encryption is based on the fact that no one can read a message that was signed with one key unless he has the other key.

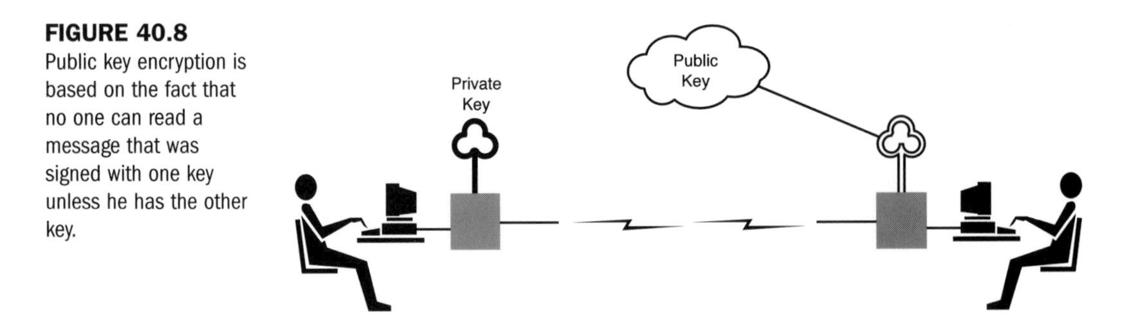

Suppose you want to send a message (which could be a JAR file) and be able to assure the person receiving the message that the message is really from you and hasn't been tampered with. You would start by encrypting the message with your private key. Because only you have your private key—you're being very careful to keep it secret—only you could have produced this encrypted file. Your public key is well known—assume the recipient already has a copy. When the recipient receives your message, she attempts to decrypt the message by using your public key. Remember that these keys work together—only one key can successfully decode a message encrypted by your private key. If the recipient is able to decrypt the message with your public key, she can safely assume that you signed it.

CAUTION

You should never send your private key out over the Internet. Most of the time, it never needs to leave your computer. When you generate it, choose a good long (multiword) passphrase that no one else is likely to guess, but that you're certain to remember.

Why Do You Need a Certificate? A flaw is present in this system—it requires that your public key be well known and that the recipient already have a copy. That's not true—the recipient doesn't necessarily know you, and she probably doesn't have a copy of your public key. You could send one by email, but then how could the recipient know that *that* message didn't come from someone impersonating you?

The solution is to have your public key embedded in a message that is signed by someone both you and the recipient trust. Such a message is called a *digital certificate*. The current standard version is X.509 version 3, so these certificates are often called *X.509v3 certificates*. (Commercially, they're sometimes called "digital IDs.") The "someone" both parties trust is called a *Certification Authority*, or CA. If both you and the recipient work for the same company, or if the recipient trusts my employer, you might present a certificate signed by my company CA. If the two parties have no other relationship, you might present a certificate signed by a public Certification Authority, such as Verisign (`http://www.verisign.com/`). If the recipient is the trusting sort, she might even accept a certificate you signed yourself—a self-certifying certificate.

NOTE Although Certification Authorities and X.509v3 certificates are emerging as the de facto standard, other systems are available. Phil Zimmermann's PGP (Pretty Good Privacy) software, for example, is based on a "web of trust," in which you are invited to trust an unknown person because people whom you know and trust either vouch for the unknown person or they vouch for people who vouch for the unknown person, and so on. Learn more about PGP online at `http://www.pgp.com/` and `http://www.pgpi.com/`.

Why Do You Need a Message Digest Algorithm? Another flaw is present in this system. Computationally, it's inefficient to encrypt a large file, such as a JAR file, with a private key. Actual public key encryption systems don't try to do this—instead, they apply an efficient algorithm called a *message digest* algorithm to produce a long number—one that is virtually unique to this message. Then they encrypt only the message digest itself.

One of the most common message digest algorithms is called the Secure Hash Algorithm, or SHA-1; one of the most common public key encryption algorithms is called the Digital Signature Algorithm (DSA). The rest of this section shows you how to sign JAR files with an SHA1/DSA-based signature.

TIP If you want to know more about SHA-1 and DSA (or other message digest and digital signature algorithms you might choose), read `JAVA_HOME/docs/guide/security/CryptoSpec.html#AppA`.

The Java Utilities In addition to the jar utility, you'll need two tools to sign JARs:

- **keytool**—Used to produce public/private keypairs and certificates. For complete documentation on keytool, see `docs/guide/security/spec/security-spec.doc6.html#27533` in your SDK directory.
- **jarsigner**—Used to actually sign the JARs, based on your certificate. For complete documentation on jarsigner, see `file:///C%7C/jdk1.3/docs/guide/security/spec/security-spec.doc6.html#21611` in the SDK directory on your hard drive.

TIP Both keytool and jarsigner are designed to be run from the command line—they're wrappers around the Java classes that implement keys, certificates, and signatures. Sun provides a tool for users to use in setting their security policy—called policytool—that has a graphical interface.

Signing a JAR—Step-by-Step Here's a step-by-step procedure for signing your JAR files. The remainder of this section describes each of these steps in detail.

1. Generate a keypair.
2. Obtain a certificate for your keypair.
3. Distribute your certificate so people will know that you're the person behind the trusted applet.
4. Use your certificate to sign your JAR.

Figure 40.9 illustrates this process.

If you've already generated a keypair and obtained a certificate through another means (such as Netscape Navigator and the Netscape Certificate Server or Verisign, Inc.), you can skip the first two steps and go right to jarsigner. In the rest of this section, it's assumed that you're starting from scratch. In the first step, you generate a keypair and a self-signed certificate. In the second step, you send off a Certificate Signing Request to the CA of your choice.

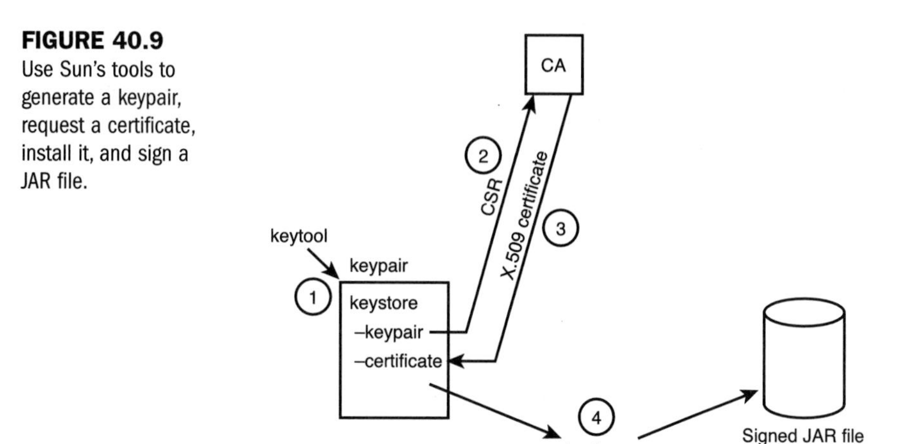

FIGURE 40.9
Use Sun's tools to generate a keypair, request a certificate, install it, and sign a JAR file.

CAUTION

You could use a self-signed certificate to claim you were anyone. Sophisticated users will often ignore such certificates. For serious work on the Internet, consider having your certificate generated by a reputable firm such as Verisign (`http://www.verisign.com/`).

Generating a Keypair

Sun provides the utility keytool to administer databases of keys and certificates for use by the utility jarsigner. You can get basic usage information by typing

```
keytool -help
```

at the command prompt.

To generate a new key you might type

```
keytool -genkey -alias mike
```

This line tells the keytool to generate a new key to be stored under the name "mike."

NOTE Not enough information is in this line for keytool to generate a new key. It needs a Distinguished Name, a passphrase for the password itself, and a passphrase for the keystore. It will prompt you for any required fields you fail to specify.

When you generate a new keypair, you can include the following options:

- **`-v`**—Produces verbose information.
- **`-alias alias`**—Specifies a common name to be associated with this key.
- **`-keyalg keyalg`**—Specifies the algorithm to be used for generating the key.

- **`-keysize keysize`**—Specifies the size of the key, in bits.
- **`-sigalg sigalg`**—Specifies the algorithm to be used for preparing a message digest.
- **`-dname distinguishedName`**—Specifies your personal Distinguished Name, which usually includes your organization and country.

TIP The X.500 Distinguished Name uses commas to separate the fields. If one of your fields contains a comma, escape it with a \ character.

- **`-keypass keypass`**—Specifies the passphrase for this key. If you don't provide one, you'll be prompted for it. The tool requires that the passphrase be at least six characters long—for better security, make yours much longer than that.
- **`-keystore keystore`**—Specifies the location where the keys will be stored.

NOTE If you allow keytool to put your keys in the default file, it will build a keystore in a file named `.keystore` in your home directory. On a Windows system, your "home directory" is the concatenation of the `HOMEDRIVE` and `HOMEPATH` environment variables. If they're not defined or they don't constitute a valid path, the keystore is put in the SDK installation directory.

- **`-storepass storepass`**—Specifies the passphrase for the keystore.

The default key size is 1,024 bits and uses a key algorithm of DSA. Your Distinguished Name should follow the format

```
CN=Common Name OU=Organizational Unit ORG=Organization C=Country
```

For example, my Distinguished Name is

```
CN=Michael L Morgan OU=Software Engineering ORG=DSE Inc C=US
```

CAUTION

If you default your Distinguished Name, it will prompt you for your state and locality, which are usually unnecessary.

`-alias` refers to a shorter name by which you will know this Distinguished Name. For example, I might write

```
keytool -genkey -alias Mike Morgan
➥-dname CN=Michael L Morgan OU=Software Engineering
➥ORG=DSE Inc C=US
➥-keypass A password for Platinum Edition
```

CAUTION

Don't enter your passphrases as parameters or embed them in scripts—wait and let the system prompt you for them. When you enter them, keytool will echo the characters. Make sure no one can see you when you type in this information.

By default, keytool wraps the public key into a self-signed X.509v1 certificate (but not the newer X.509v3). The two formats (X.509v1 and X.509v3) are similar—most end users who know the difference won't care whether you're using v1 or v3, but they might hesitate before accepting a self-signed certificate. If you want an X.509v3 certificate, you'll have to go to a public Certification Authority such as Verisign or obtain your own Certificate Server.

NOTE If you've worked with JARs in an earlier release of the JDK, you'll have seen a utility called javakey. That program is now obsolete–stick with keytool and jarsigner.

Obtaining a Certificate

After you've generated your keypair, you need to generate a Certificate Signing Request, or CSR, and send that CSR to the Certificate Authority (CA) of your choice—either a public CA or your own organization's CA.

NOTE You can learn how to get your keypair certified by Verisign from its Web site, `http://www.verisign.com/`. You'll need to be able to prove to them that you are who you say you are, and you'll pay a small fee.

To learn more about the Netscape Certificate Server, visit `http://home.netscape.com/certificate/v1.0/index.html`.

To generate a Certificate Signing Request (CSR), type

```
keytool -csr
```

Just as with `-genkey`, the program will prompt you for any required parameters you omit. You might want to use one or more of the following options:

- **`-v`**—Generates verbose output.
- **`-alias alias`**—Specifies the alias of the key you want to certify. The default is `mykey`.
- **`-sigalg sigalg`**—Specifies the signing algorithm to be used. The default is DSA with SHA-1.
- **`-file csr_file`**—Specifies the file into which the CSR should be written.
- **`-keypass keypass`**—Specifies the passphrase for this key.
- **`-keystore keystore`**—Specifies the file where the keys are stored.
- **`-storepass storepass`**—Specifies the passphrase of the keystore.

After you've generated the CSR, send it to your CA following the instructions it gives you. (CAs generally accept CSRs by email, although some prefer that you copy the CSR and paste it into an HTML form.) After the CA follows its certificate-signing policy to verify your identify (and, in the case of a commercial CA, after it has received payment), the CA will issue you a certificate. This certificate might come by email, or you might be sent to a Web page to pick it up. Either way, get it into a file by itself and type

```
keytool -import
```

TIP If your certificate comes by email, mail headers and footers might be on the message. The part of the message you want to copy into a file is the part bounded by `BEGIN CERTIFICATE` and `END CERTIFICATE`.

Some other parameters for the `import` option that you might find useful are

- **`-v`**—To get a verbose output.
- **`-alias alias`**—The common name of the person associated with this certificate.
- **`-file cert_file`**—The name of the file where the certificate is stored.

CAUTION

Do not use the `-noprompt` option of keytool. Require the keytool to show you the certificate–satisfy yourself that it's not a forgery. You can call the CA and read them the certificate's message digest (it's called the fingerprint) if you want to be sure.

TIP Your CA will probably send you a copy of its certificate so you can verify the signature on your certificate. Install its certificate too, but first, double-check the CA's fingerprint to make sure no one has forged its certificate.

Distributing Your Certificate

Now that you have a signed certificate, let people know it exists so they can get your public key. They'll use this key to verify messages and applets from you. You might type

```
keytool -export -alias mike -file filename
```

You can also specify a filename in the `-file` parameter. The utility will copy your certificate to the designated `filename`. Distribute that certificate to people who might use your signed applet—they should verify your signature on the certificate before they put a strange applet to work on their machines.

Using jarsigner to Sign a JAR File

After you have a public/private keypair and an X.509 certificate that attests to its authenticity, you're able to digitally sign your JAR files. Sun provides the jarsigner utility for this purpose.

NOTE The version of jarsigner that is distributed with Java 2 can only sign JAR files that have been built with Sun's jar utility.

In addition to signing JAR files, jarsigner can also verify the integrity of a signed JAR. Just run it with the `-verify` option.

NOTE If you previously used javakey (the forerunner of keytool), you'll have to get a new keypair and certificate. jarsigner has no backward compatibility with the javakey database.

The simplest way to use jarsigner is to type

```
jarsigner MyJarFile.jar mike
```

jarsigner will sign the specified jar with the private key stored under the certificate alias "mike." In this case jarsigner will use the default keystore (`.keystore` in your `home` directory) and will prompt you for the passphrases to the keystore and the certificate. The output will be written to the file named `MyJarFile.jar`, overwriting the original file. You can specify more information on the command line:

```
jarsigner -keystore C:\JDK\projects\.keystore -signedjar
➥MySignedJarFile.jar MyJarFile.jar mike
```

This tells jarsigner to sign the file `MyJarFile.jar` by using the certificate associated with the alias `mike`. The keystore is located at `C:\JDK\projects\.keystore`. The output is written to `MySignedJarFile.jar`, and the original file (`MyJarFile.jar`) is left unchanged.

NOTE When you sign a JAR with jarsigner, it computes a message digest of the JAR file (using either the MD5 or the SHA-1 algorithm, depending on your certificate) and then encodes that message digest by using your private key. It writes two new files—a signature file with an .SF suffix and a signature block file with a .DSA or .RSA suffix—into the JAR file. The base name used in these two files is based on the alias you used to sign the file.

Working with Encryption from Inside Your Program

You can write Java to do everything done in the previous section from the command line. Look at the documentation in `java.security` and its subpackages, `java.security.cert`, `java.security.interfaces`, and `java.security.spec`. These packages provide you with such classes as `KeyPairGenerator`, `Signature`, and `MessageDigest`, and the interface `Key`.

You can read more about the Java 2 security architecture in your SDK documentation at `docs/guide/security/spec/security-spec.doc.html`. You also can get detailed information about using the jar and javakey tools in the SDK 1.3 documentation.

NOTE You can read more about Java 2 security features, including the Java Security API and related classes, at Sun's `http://java.sun.com/products/jdk/1.3/docs/guide/security/index.html` Java 2 security site.

Open Issues on Security

In the case of Java, the security is only as good as its runtime implementation. Holes have been found and fixed in various implementations, but these same issues might arise again in future implementations as Java is ported to other platforms. After all, each version of the JVM needs to be written in a platform-specific programming language, such as C, and can have its own flaws and weaknesses.

Aside from that, many types of malicious behavior are difficult (if not impossible) to avoid. No matter what is done to the Java security model, for instance, it will not stop someone from putting rude or obscene material in an applet or starting long, resource-intensive processes. Such actions are not defects but will continue to be nuisances.

For links to and discussions of current problems and a chronology of security-related bugs, see the Java Security FAQ at `http://java.sun.com/sfaq/index.html`. Every implementation of Java has its own open issues, and Sun's is no exception. The best thing to do is stay on top of the issues for the implementation you are using.

Further References on Java and Security

The following references can help you keep up with the changing world of Java security. It is by no means a comprehensive list, but it should get you started on researching the topic further and give you some valuable starting places from which to continue your research.

- Usenet:

  `alt.2600`

  `comp.risks`

  `comp.lang.java.*` (especially `comp.lang.java.security`)

  `comp.infosystems.www.*`

- WWW:

  Sun's Java Security site, with a wealth of links about Java security bug chronology, the Applet Security FAQ, Security API information, applet and code signing, JDK 1.3 features, JDK 1.3 security documentation, the Java security model, Java cryptographic architecture, the Java Security Q&A archives, the Java Cryptography Extension (JCE) to the JDK 1.3, and more. Highly recommended:

  `http://java.sun.com/security/index.html`

  Slides from a presentation by Li Gong, Sun's Java security architect, at JavaOne 1997, on the future and direction of Java security:

  `http://java.sun.com/javaone/sessions/slides/TT03/TT03.zip`

The Java Security Q&A archives:

`http://java.sun.com/security/hypermail/java-security-archive/index.html`

The Java Security FAQ:

`http://java.sun.com/sfaq/index.html`

Sun's recommendations for security policies:

`http://java.sun.com/security/policy.html`

Sun's *Jar Guide*, about using the JAR file format and tools:

`http://java.sun.com/products/jdk/1.3/docs/guide/jar/jarGuide.html`

Netscape Navigator Security FAQ:

`http://developer.netscape.com:80/support/faqs/champions/security.html`

"Java Security," the December 1995 classic paper by Joseph A. Bank, MIT:

`http://www-swiss.ai.mit.edu/~jbank/javapaper/javapaper.html` ●

CHAPTER 41

Server-Side Java

by Mike Morgan

In this chapter

Servlet Overview and Architecture

So far, you've looked at Java applets—where the Java runs in the user's browser—and Java applications—where the program runs in a standalone JVM. In this chapter, you'll learn about Java programs that are designed to run on the same machine as the Web server.

If a visitor to your Web site is to install a Java application, he must first obtain a JVM (possibly in Sun's Java Runtime Environment, or JRE). Then the user must download the application's installation package and run the installer. Although this process is relatively painless, it's still much more work than, say, running an applet.

NOTE You can simplify the process of installing applications by packaging them with a double-clickable installation program such as InstallAnywhere from ZeroG software. Check it out at `http://www.zerog.com/`.

If you include an applet on your Web page, you must deal with the various versions. Netscape Communicator 4.7 supports only Java 1.1. Microsoft no longer claims to even offer Java—it offers the Microsoft Virtual Machine, which runs a language that strongly resembles Java. To run Java 2 in an applet, you'll have to convert your applet and ask the end user to install the Java plug-in.

The good news is that the plug-in is bundled with the SDK 1.3. The bad news is that some users will balk at installing yet another plug-in. Some users, of course, have browsers that don't even support plug-ins—if you're designing a Web site for WebTV or Lynx users, applets are not an option.

Java programs designed to run on the server are called *servlets*. These programs have advantages and disadvantages compared with applets. Because they aren't running on the client's machine, they don't have direct access to the user's screen—you can't draw anything. On the other hand, code running on the server has direct access to email servers, databases, and other enterprise resources. Figure 41.1 illustrates how a user interacts with a servlet.

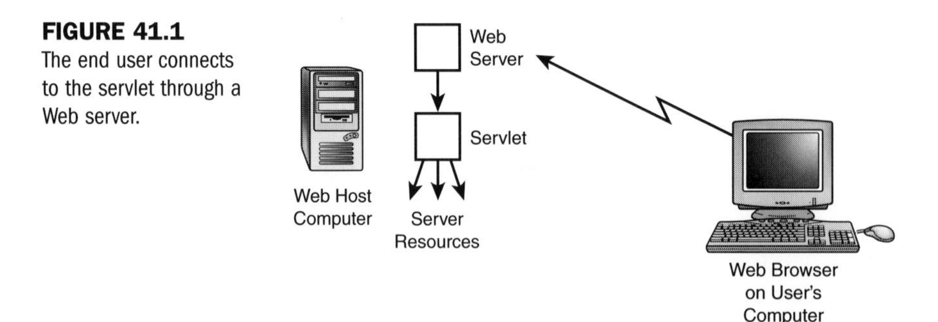

FIGURE 41.1
The end user connects to the servlet through a Web server.

You might use servlets to implement an online storefront. Because it has direct access to the database, the servlet could generate Web pages that appear to be from a catalog. You could also use servlets to Web-enable a legacy application. The servlet would receive information from an HTML form. When the user `POST`s the form, the servlet forwards that information to the legacy code, and then sends the legacy application's response back to the browser in HTML.

Why Run Java on the Server?

Web developers have been providing server-based designs for storefronts and other applications from the earliest days of the Web. This section describes several alternatives to servlets and the strengths and weaknesses of each.

Servlets Versus CGI The earliest server-based solution was the Common Gateway Interface, or CGI. This technology is still popular—writing a simple Perl script, following the CGI rules, and installing the finished script on your Web server is easy.

▶ To learn more about CGI programming, **see** "How CGI Works," **p. 726**

CGI has three limitations compared to servlets:

- Most languages that are used for CGI scripts (such as Perl) are general-purpose languages. You must write your own interface to read data from the browser and to write out a new Web page.
- Many languages that are popular for CGI (again, including Perl) are interpreted languages—they are inherently slower than a compiled language. Java is mostly compiled, and the interpreter—the JVM—is highly optimized.
- Each CGI request requires the server software to generate an entirely new process. (This process is known as *forking* in UNIX and *spawning* in Windows.) This process is time-consuming and uses large amounts of the server's memory.

TIP If, after everything said here, you decide to use CGI, check out `mod_perl` from the Apache Software Foundation. `mod_perl` is integrated into the Apache server, so it gives you greater control of processes than does "plain" Perl. See `http://perl.apache.org/faq/#What_is_mod_perl_` for details.

Server-Side JavaScript Server-Side JavaScript (SSJS) is an elegant server-side solution. Netscape provides a version of its popular JavaScript language that takes advantage of the server's special capabilities. The language is tailored for use on servers and is compiled, not interpreted. SSJS also executes inside the server process's address space, avoiding the computationally expensive fork.

JavaScript was developed by Netscape Communications; only Netscape supports this technology. If you want to use SSJS, you have no choice but to use the Netscape Enterprise server. If your project requires platform independence, SSJS isn't an option.

NOTE Although Microsoft doesn't support SSJS *per se*, they allow you to use virtually any language to write Active Server Pages. In fact, their Internet Information Server comes preconfigured to run JScript–Microsoft's counterpart to JavaScript. For details on this capability, visit `http://www.microsoft.com/ NTServer/web/deployment/planguide/WebSerScript.asp`.

Finally, SSJS is a cousin to JavaScript, described in Part III, "JavaScript." Recall from that section that JavaScript is designed to be used by people who are not professional programmers. JavaScript is missing some powerful language capabilities. Although the amateur might never miss them, serious programmers soon run into the limits of JavaScript.

Microsoft's Active Server Pages Like Netscape, Microsoft developed a proprietary scripting language. Microsoft calls its language VBScript, after its popular product, Visual Basic. You can embed VBScript (or scripts in a few other languages) into a Web page and arrange to have that code executed when the page is downloaded. This solution is called Active Server Pages, or ASP, and runs on the Microsoft Internet Information Server. In addition to the performance problem associated with interpreted code, ASPs tie you to a single-vendor solution.

Proprietary APIs In addition to scripting languages such as SSJS or VBScript, you can also write server extensions in a high-level programming language such as C++. These server extensions run in the same address space as the server—you avoid the delay associated with forking a new process for every request.

To communicate with the server, you use the server vendor's proprietary interface. For example, Netscape offers the Netscape Server Application Programming Interface (NSAPI) and Microsoft has the Information Server API (ISAPI). Other server vendors have similar solutions.

There are two reasons to hesitate before using one of these APIs. The first is the obvious one: They are proprietary. Like SSJS and ASPs, you tie yourself to one vendor when you choose its technology.

The second problem is more subtle. By running inside the server's process, these proprietary APIs open you up to yet another problem. If the server extension malfunctions, the entire server could crash.

Reasons to Choose Java As an alternative to CGI scripts, SSJS, or ASP, Sun offers Java servlets. Servlets offer six advantages over the other server-side technologies:

- **Efficiency**—The servlet loads and initializes only once. After that, each request calls the same method (`service`).
- **Persistence**—After the servlet is loaded, it remains in memory. You can take advantage of this fact to retain information from one service request to the next. For example, you might load information from a database on the first service request and refresh only periodically.
- **Portability**—After all, they are written in Java!

- **Robustness**—Unlike SSJS, VBScript, or Perl, Java is a complete programming language with full access to the network, the file system, databases, and distributed objects. You can write a more powerful program in Java than in any of the other languages commonly used for server extensions.
- **Extensibility**—Because Java is an object-oriented language, you can build specialized versions of Java classes. That's as true for servlets as it is for other classes.
- **Security**—Like all Java programs, servlets can take advantage of the services of the Java Security Manager and other security-related classes.

TIP As a servlet developer, you'll benefit from subscribing to the servlet-interest mailing list. Send email to `listserv@java.sun.com`. In the message body, write `subscribe` *`yourlastname yourfirstname`*. You can also review archived messages at `http://archives.java.sun.com/archives/servlet-interest.html`.

The Servlet Classes

To write servlets, you'll need to add two packages to your development environment:

- **`javax.servlet`**—This package contains the class `javax.servlet.GenericServlet` as well as the three interfaces that this class implements.
- **`javax.servlet.http`**—This package contains `javax.servlet.http.HttpServlet`, which extends `javax.servlet.GenericServlet`.

You'll get these two packages (as well as a package for Java Server Pages, described later in this chapter) in Java Servlet Development Kit (JSDK), which you can download free from `java.sun.com`. Although you can write applets with just these two packages, you'll need a compatible server or servlet engine to run them. You'll learn where you can get those tools later in this chapter, in the section "Configuring Your Development Environment."

NOTE You'll want the latest JSDK to build servlets. For convenience, download the JSWDK–that version includes the JSDK as well as the packages and documentation on Java Server Pages (JSP) from `http://java.sun.com/products/servlet/index.html`.

Java servlets don't have a `main` method. When the server first loads them, it calls their `init` method. After the server is loaded and has had an opportunity to initialize itself, it sits in memory waiting for the server to receive a request for its services. The server then calls the servlet's `service` method.

In `HttpServlet`—the kind you'll be implementing to provide Web services—the service method looks up the HTTP method the browser used. This method is almost always either `GET` or `POST`. `HttpServlet`'s `service` method then dispatches either `doGet` or `doPost`. (Methods for other HTTP mechanisms, such as `PUT` and `TRACE`, are also available if you want to use them.)

When the server calls `GenericServlet`, it passes two objects to `service`. The first object, `ServletRequest`, contains the data sent from the browser to the server. The second object, `ServletResponse`, allows the servlet to pass information (such as HTML) back to the browser.

TIP If you're an advanced developer, you could write an applet and servlet that work together as a pair. The applet would have a direct connection to the user's screen and could carry out special interface instructions passed to it from the servlet through `ServletResponse`.

When you choose to extend `HttpServlet`, `service` is ready-made. The server passes it an `HttpServletRequest` and accepts an `HttpServletResponse` in return. You'll look at these two objects in more detail later in this chapter, in the section titled "The Life Cycle of a Servlet."

Configuring Your Development Environment

The end user needs a compatible Web browser to run applets. To run servlets, you'll need a Web server that knows how to invoke the JVM. Most of the popular Web servers support servlets, either directly or through third-party add-ons.

Choosing a Server

Your choice of a server will be determined by many factors. Most of the servers you're likely to choose will support servlets. Check their documentation to ensure that you'll get the capabilities that you want.

If you're looking for a free server where you can learn about servlets, consider downloading the servlet container Jakarta Tomcat from Apache. The Apache Software Foundation (`www.apache.org`) is the same group that developed the popular Apache Web server. Jakarta Tomcat is the reference implementation for the Java Servlet API 2.2. If you can get your servlet running under Tomcat, you should be able to follow your vendor's instructions and install it in a commercial server.

NOTE A *servlet container* is a runtime shell that manages and invokes servlets on behalf of users. Tomcat is a servlet container with a Java Server Pages (JSP) environment. You'll learn about JSP later in this chapter, in "Implementing Servlets Using JSP." ■

TIP Servlet containers are showing up in more and more products. If you're considering solving a problem with Java, check `http://java.sun.com/products/servlet/industry.html` to see if there's a servlet engine for your environment.

Downloading and Installing Tomcat

Start at `http://jakarta.apache.org/tomcat/index.html` to read about the Tomcat portion of the Jakarta project. Follow the link to download binaries for your platform. Unless you need the very latest features, stick with the more stable release builds. The other builds—milestone builds and nightly builds—often have unidentified defects. Likewise, unless you're working on an unsupported platform, there's little benefit in downloading and compiling the source code.

Tomcat binaries are available for both UNIX and Windows. When you unpack the binaries, you'll find a `Jakarta-tomcat` directory with five subdirectories: `lib`, `doc`, `bin`, `conf`, and `src`. For the simplest installation, leave the configuration files at their default settings and run `bin/Tomcat start`. If you do want to customize Tomcat, examine the files in the `doc` directory—in addition to the README file and a FAQ, there's a complete user guide and application developer's manual there.

TIP Tomcat's startup script expects to find an environment variable—`TOMCAT_HOME`—set to the `Jakarta-tomcat` directory. If you start Tomcat by using `bin/Tomcat start`, the script will attempt to determine `TOMCAT_HOME` and will set it before invoking `startup`.

Running Tomcat as a Standalone Server When your Web server is written in Java, you can make the servlet container an integral part of the server. Sun's Java Web Server product (`http://www.sun.com/software/jwebserver/index.html`) has such a container.

In addition to its capabilities as a servlet container, Tomcat is a standalone Web server written in Java. If you start Tomcat (by running `bin/Tomcat start`) with its default configuration, it will launch a Web server that listens to port 8080 on the local machine.

Using Tomcat with a Server Although standalone Tomcat might be quite satisfactory for use on your desktop testing servlets, you'll want to improve its performance if you place it in a production environment. You can get that improvement by allowing a highly optimized Web server, such as the commercial Microsoft and Netscape products, handle all requests for static Web pages. The server then calls the servlet container only when the user requests a servlet.

TIP If you're using a commercial server such as the Netscape/iPlanet Enterprise server, you don't have to use Tomcat. Check your server's documentation to see whether it supports servlets. If you're considering adding a third-party servlet container, check out the Usenet newsgroup `comp.lang.java.programmer` to learn from others' experiences.

In addition to its standalone configuration, you can use Tomcat 3.1 with several popular Web servers, including

- Apache, version 1.3 or later
- Microsoft Internet Information Server, version 4.0 or later

- Microsoft Personal Web Server, version 4.0 or later
- Netscape Enterprise Server, version 3.0 or later

Note that the most recent versions of the Netscape Enterprise server are available through iPlanet at `http://www.iplanet.com/products/infrastructure/web_servers/index.html`.

Follow the instructions that come with your server and with Tomcat to integrate Tomcat into your Web server. For example, if you plan to run your Web site on the Apache server, open `src/doc/uguide/tomcat_ug.html` in `TOMCAT_HOME` and scroll down to "Setting Tomcat to Cooperate with the Apache Web Server." Look in `src/doc` to find documentation on integrating Tomcat with the Microsoft and Netscape browsers.

The Life Cycle of a Servlet

This section assumes that you've downloaded Sun's JSDK and installed and started Apache's Jakarta Tomcat. If you're using a different server you might need to modify these instructions somewhat, but the principles of servlet operation remain the same.

For the latest documentation on application development under Tomcat, read `TOMCAT_HOME/src/doc/appdev/index.html`. That manual shows you how to use the Java-centric build environment, Ant, to manage your servlet development.

NOTE If you're serious about developing software, take the time to download the complete Ant installation kit, which includes developer documentation, at `http://jakarta.apache.org/tomcat/jakarta-tomcat/src/doc/appdev/index.html`.

You'll also want a source code control system (SCCS). This software ensures that only one programmer is modifying a source file at any one time. Even if you're the only developer on the project, use a SCCS to maintain your version history. One of the most popular SCCSs is the Concurrent Version System (CVS). The source code is available for free at `http://www.cvshome.org/`. Windows binaries for cvs.exe version 1.10.5 are at `ftp://ftp.cvshome.org/pub/cvs-1.10.5/windows/cvs.exe`.

Compiling and Installing the Servlet For this example, the build process will be run by hand. The code in Listing 41.1 demonstrates the life cycle of a servlet. In Chapter 42, "Java and XML," you'll see a servlet that actually implements a real-world application.

Listing 41.1 ***HelloServlet.java*—The Life Cycle of a Servlet**

```
import java.io.PrintWriter;
import java.io.IOException;
import java.util.Enumeration;
import javax.servlet.ServletConfig;
```

Listing 41.1 Continued

```
import javax.servlet.ServletException;
import javax.servlet.http.HttpServlet;
import javax.servlet.http.HttpServletRequest;
import javax.servlet.http.HttpServletResponse;

public class HelloServlet extends HttpServlet {
    public void init(ServletConfig theConfiguration)
      throws ServletException {
      super.init(theConfiguration);
    }

    public void doGet(HttpServletRequest theRequest,
                      HttpServletResponse theResponse)
      throws IOException, ServletException {

    theResponse.setContentType("text/html");
    PrintWriter aWriter = theResponse.getWriter();

    aWriter.println("<HTML>");
    aWriter.println("<HEAD>");
    aWriter.println("<TITLE>Demo Servlet Page</TITLE>");
    aWriter.println("</HEAD>");
    aWriter.println("<BODY>");
    aWriter.println("<H1>Demo Servlet</H1>");
    aWriter.println("<P>Hello, World! from a servlet<BR>");
    aWriter.println("Here are the headers from this request:</P>");
    Enumeration theHeaders = theRequest.getHeaderNames();
    while (theHeaders.hasMoreElements()) {
        String aHeader = (String) theHeaders.nextElement();
       aWriter.println("<P>" + aHeader + " is " +
         theRequest.getHeader(aHeader) + "</P>");
        }
    aWriter.println("</BODY>");
    aWriter.println("</HTML>");
    aWriter.close();
    }

  public String getServletInfo() {
    return "HelloServlet, by Mike Morgan";
  }
}
```


Make sure your `CLASSPATH` includes `servlet.jar`, and then compile `HelloServlet.java`.

After you have the `HelloServlet.class` file, you need to package it into a Web Application Archive. This format has been standardized in Servlet API 2.2, so you can use this package on any Web server that conforms to that standard.

First, decide on a "context" for your Web application. The application in this example is named Hello. Find your Web server's document root and make a new directory named `Hello`.

(If you're using the default configuration for Tomcat, the document root is at TOMCAT_HOME/webapps/.)

Inside the Hello directory, create a subdirectory called WEB-INF. In that directory, make two subdirectories. Name the first classes and the second lib. Copy your HelloServlet.class file into classes. This is the directory where you place "loose" class files. If the application required any JAR files, they would be put into the lib directory.

If this application required any HTML files (or JSP files, which are discussed in the next section), they would be placed in the Hello directory.

Now restart your server. The server looks for Web application directories in the document root when it starts up. It should detect the new context and make it available to users. Point your browser to http://localhost:8080/Hello/servlet/HelloServlet. You should see a page similar to the one shown in Figure 41.2.

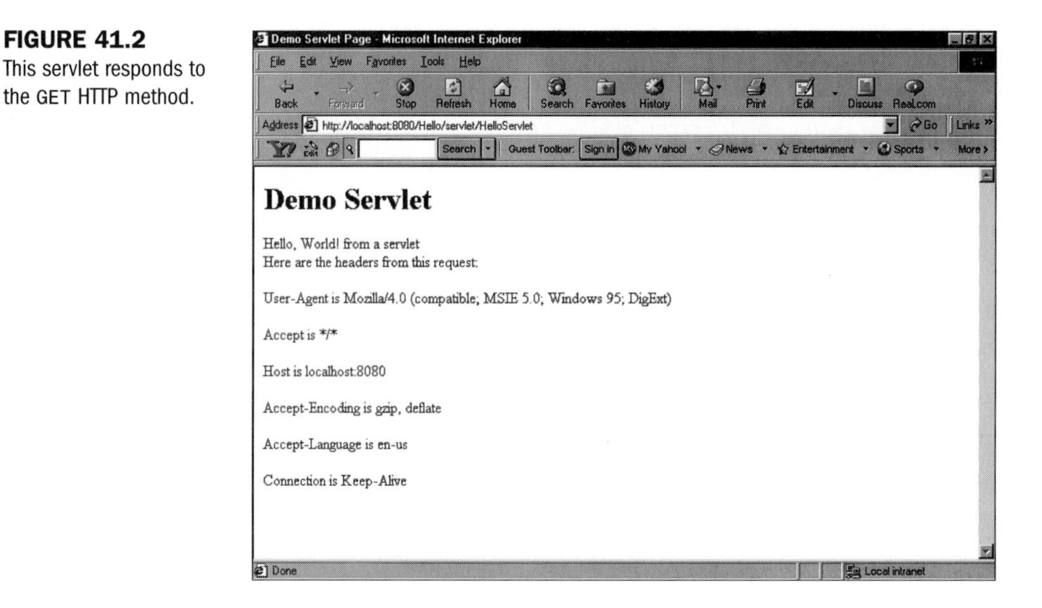

FIGURE 41.2
This servlet responds to the GET HTTP method.

Although this process works, an important step was left out. The "Web Application Deployment Descriptor"—an XML file that describes the application to the server—was never specified. You should name this file web.xml and place it in the WEB-INF directory. Listing 41.2 shows an example of this file. For a complete specification of this file, download a copy of the Servlet Specification (version 2.2) from Sun's Java site (http://java.sun.com/products/servlet/download.html#specs), and read Chapter 13, "Transforming XML—XSLT."

Listing 41.2 *web.xml*—Place a *web.xml* File in the *WEB-INF* Directory

```
<!DOCTYPE web-app PUBLIC "-//Sun Microsystems, Inc.//DTD Web Application
2.2//EN" "http://java.sun.com/j2ee/dtds/web-app_2_2.dtd">

<web-app>

    <!-- General description of your web application -->

    <display-name>My Web Application</display-name>
    <description>
      Describe your Web application here.
    </description>

    <!--Define as many parameters as you like, including zero.
       You can read the parameters in your program.
       The server administrator sets parameters in order to
       tailor the behavior of your servlet. -->

    <context-param>
      <param-name>someParameter</param-name>
      <param-value>theValue</param-value>
      <description>
        What does this parameter represent?
      </description>
    </context-param>

    <servlet>
      <servlet-name>theServletName</servlet-name>
      <description>
        Describe your servlet here.
      </description>
      <servlet-class>com.yourCompany.yourPackage.YourServlet</servlet-class>
      <init-param>
        <param-name>someParameter</param-name>
        <param-value>someValue</param-value>
      </init-param>
      <!-- once again, you can have as many init-params as you like,
      ➥including zero -->
      <!-- Load this servlet at server startup time -->
      <load-on-startup>5</load-on-startup>
    </servlet>

    <!--You can define other servlets that are part of this
    ➥same application. -->

    <servlet-mapping>
      <servlet-name>theServletName</servlet-name>
      <!--specify a pattern that should be referred to this servlet -->
      <url-pattern>*.do</url-pattern>
    </servlet-mapping>
```

Listing 41.2 Continued

```
    <session-config>
      <!-- How long to wait before the session times out -->
      <!-- 30 minutes -->
      <session-timeout>30</session-timeout>
    </session-config>

</web-app>
```

If you haven't done so already, open the JSDK or JSWDK documentation on the `javax.servlet` APIs. The JSWDK path is `jswdk-1.0.1\webpages\docs\api\index.html`.

Instantiation and Destruction If the `<load-on-startup>` tag is present in the `web.xml` file, the servlet will load when the application starts up. The value is typically a small positive integer giving the order in which this particular servlet should load (compared to others in the application). Lower numbers load before higher numbers. If you don't specify `<load-on-startup>`, the servlets in the application don't load in any specific order.

As soon as the servlet loads, the server calls the `init` method (if it's present). Use the `init` method to set up resource allocations that span the life of the servlet. When the servlet is unloaded, the corresponding method, `destroy`, is called. Typically, you will release resources in `destroy` that were allocated in `init`.

Recall the `init` method from Listing 41.1:

```
public void init(ServletConfig theConfiguration)
  throws ServletException {
  super.init(theConfiguration);
}
```

Here you're saving `theConfiguration` so you can access its members later in the servlet. The easiest way for an `HttpServlet` to do this is to pass the `ServletConfig` to its parent, a `GenericServlet`.

When `init` is called, the Web server passes in a `ServerContext` object as part of the `ServerConfig`. The `ServerContext` object gives you access to other resources that are part of the same Web application. For example, suppose your Web application connects to a relational database through the Java Database Connectivity (JDBC) package. Setting up JDBC connections can be computationally expensive. You might opt to make a pool of connections so that each servlet in the application would have high-performance, prebuilt database connections. You might specify that one servlet loads first (`<load-on-startup>1</load-on-startup>`). In that servlet, you could set up the pool:

```
public void init(ServletConfig theConfiguation)
  throws ServletException {
  super.init(theConfiguration);
```

```
ConnectionPool thePool = new ConnectionPool();
  . . . configure and initialize the ConnectionPool . . .

  ServletContext theContext = getServletContext();
  theContext.setAttribute("CONNECTION_POOL", thePool);
}
```

Now other servlets in the application can take advantage of the prebuilt connections. In those other servlets, you would write

```
ConnectionPool thePool =
  (ConnectionPool) getServletContext().
    getAttribute("CONNECTION_POOL");
```

Remember that resources allocated in `init` should be released in `destroy`. To complete this example, you might write

```
public void destroy() {
  ServletContext theContext = getServletContext();
  ConnectionPool thePool =
    (ConnectionPool) theContext.getAttribute("CONNECTION_POOL");

  if (thePool != null) {
    thePool.emptyPool();
    theContext.removeAttribute("CONNECTION_POOL");
  } else {
    System.err.println(("ConnectionPoolServlet: destroy() cannot
    ➥get a reference to CONNECTION_POOL");
}
```

The *doGet* Method When a Web browser contacts a server and requests service from a servlet, the server transfers control to the servlet's `service` method. If the servlet is derived from `HttpServlet`, `service` examines the HTTP request type (for example, `GET`, `POST`, `OPTIONS`, `TRACE`) and dispatches the appropriate handler. If the request type is `GET` or `HEAD`, it calls `doGet`.

Recall from Listing 41.1 that `doGet` takes two parameters—an `HttpServletRequest` and an `HttpServletResponse`. Because you usually intend to send HTML back to the browser, your first line in `doGet` is

```
theResponse.setContentType("text/html");
```

This line forces the `HttpServletResponse`'s content header to the specified MIME type.

The `HttpServletResponse` also includes a reference to a `PrintWriter` that will write data back to the browser. The second line of `doGet` gets a local reference to that `PrintWriter`:

```
PrintWriter aWriter = theResponse.getWriter();
```

From here, use your `PrintWriter` to send HTML back to the browser. If you need to read information from the `HttpServletRequest`, you can use any of several methods, including

- **`getAuthType`**—Checks whether the user had to present authorization credentials (such as a password) to access the servlet.
- **`getCookies`**—Reads back the array of Cookie objects the browser provided.
- **`getDateHeader`**—Gets the value of an HTTP header such as Last-Modified.
- **`getHeader`**—Gets the value of an HTTP header `String` such as Accept-Language.
- **`getHeaderNames`**—Gets an enumeration of all the headers this request contains.

NOTE The HTTP/1.1 specification contains a complete list of headers (in Section 14) and request types (in Section 9). Find this at `ftp://ftp.isi.edu/in-notes/rfc2616.txt`.

In addition to the `HttpServletRequest` methods, you can also use methods of its parent class, `ServletRequest`. Those methods include `getParameterNames` and `getParameter`, which you can use to read back the values of an HTML form.

The *doPost* Method In an HTML form, you specify the `METHOD` by which the value of the form element will be sent back to the form processor. If you write

```
<FORM ACTION="servlet/ProcessingServlet" METHOD="GET">
```

the field names and values are appended to the URL as a `QUERY_STRING`. If, instead, you write

```
<FORM ACTION="servlet/ProcessingServlet" METHOD="POST">
```

the names and values are passed back to the server in the request itself. `POST` is usually more appropriate for form data, especially when the data can be lengthy.

Suppose you have the HTML form shown in Listing 41.3.

Listing 41.3 *registration.html*—Submitting Information Using the *GET* Method

```
<HTML>
  <HEAD>
    <TITLE>A Simple Form</TITLE>
  </HEAD>
  <BODY>
    <H1>A Simple Form</H1>
    <FORM ACTION="servlet/ProcessingServlet" METHOD="GET">
      <TABLE>
        <TR>
          <TD>
            Name:
          </TD>
          <TD>
            <INPUT TYPE="Text" NAME="UserName">
          </TD>
        </TR>
```

Listing 41.3 Continued

```
          <TR>
            <TD>
              Student ID:
            </TD>
            <TD>
              <INPUT TYPE="Text" NAME="StudentID">
            </TD>
          </TR>
          <TR>
            <TD>
              Academic Program:
            </TD>
            <TD>
              <SELECT NAME="Program">
                <OPTION>Ph.D, Communication
                <OPTION>Ph.D, Leadership
                <OPTION>Juris Doctor
                <OPTION>M.A., Communication
                <OPTION>Master of Business Administration
              </SELECT>
            </TD>
          </TR>
        </TABLE>
        <INPUT TYPE="Reset" VALUE="Clear">
        <INPUT TYPE="Submit" VALUE="Submit">
      </FORM>
    </BODY>
  </HTML>
```

The finished form appears in Figure 41.3.

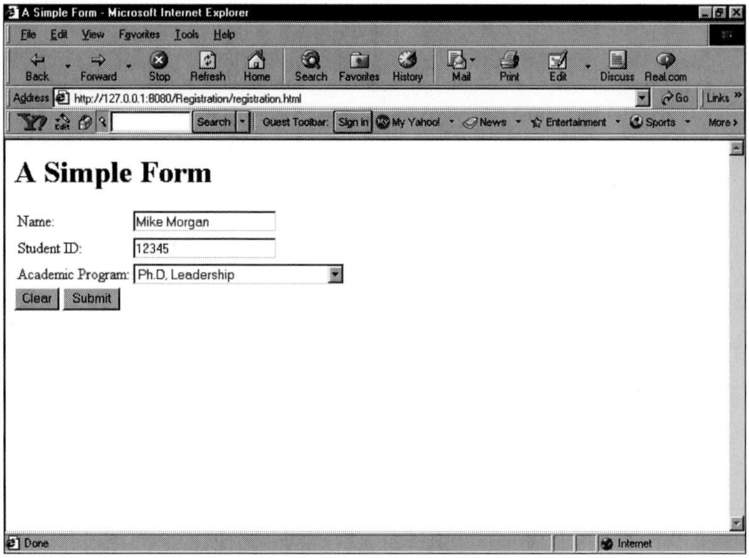

FIGURE 41.3
This form collects registration information.

Because `METHOD` is `"GET"`, if you fill out the form and click Submit you'll see a URL like this one:

```
http://127.0.0.1:8080/Registration/servlet/ProcessingServlet?
➥UserName=Mike+Morgan&StudentID=12345&Program=Ph.D%2C+Leadership
```

If you change the `METHOD` to `POST`, the fields and values are no longer visible in the URL but they're still passed to the servlet. In either case, you can read the values out by using the `getParameter` method of the `HttpServletRequest` object. Listing 41.4 shows the code for the servlet.

Listing 41.4 *ProcessingServlet.java*—Accepting Parameters Using Either *GET* or *POST*

```
import java.io.PrintWriter;
import java.io.IOException;
import java.util.Enumeration;
import javax.servlet.ServletConfig;
import javax.servlet.ServletException;
import javax.servlet.http.HttpServlet;
import javax.servlet.http.HttpServletRequest;
import javax.servlet.http.HttpServletResponse;

public class ProcessingServlet extends HttpServlet {
    public void init(ServletConfig theConfiguration)
      throws ServletException {
      super.init(theConfiguration);
    }

    public void doGet(HttpServletRequest theRequest,
                      HttpServletResponse theResponse)
      throws IOException, ServletException {
        doPost(theRequest, theResponse);
    }

    public void doPost(HttpServletRequest theRequest,
                       HttpServletResponse theResponse)
      throws IOException, ServletException {

    theResponse.setContentType("text/html");
    PrintWriter aWriter = theResponse.getWriter();

    aWriter.println("<HTML>");
    aWriter.println("<HEAD>");
    aWriter.println("<TITLE>Registration Confirmation</TITLE>");
    aWriter.println("</HEAD>");
    aWriter.println("<BODY>");
    aWriter.println("<H1>Registration Confirmation</H1>");
    aWriter.println("<P>Here is the information you provided:</P>");
    aWriter.println("<TABLE>");
      Enumeration theParameters = theRequest.getParameterNames();
```

Listing 41.4 Continued

```
        String theParameter = null;
        while (theParameters.hasMoreElements()) {
          theParameter = (String)theParameters.nextElement();
          aWriter.println("<TR><TD>" + theParameter + "</TD><TD>" +
            theRequest.getParameter(theParameter) + "</TD></TR>");
        }
        aWriter.println("</TABLE>");
      aWriter.println("</BODY>");
      aWriter.println("</HTML>");
      aWriter.close();
      }
      public String getServletInfo() {
        return "ProcessingServlet, by Mike Morgan";
    }
  }
```

Notice that a `doGet` method was written and a `doPost` was called. Even though you might prefer that the HTML author use the `POST` method, the servlet now handles either option. Figure 41.4 shows the result of submitting the form when the method is `POST`.

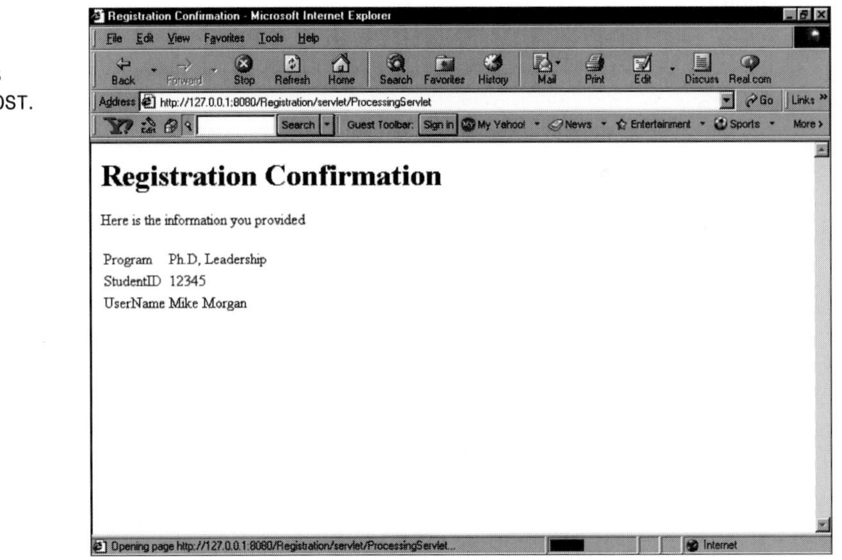

FIGURE 41.4 Look closely at the URL—this form was submitted using `POST`.

If you wanted to build an actual registration system, you could extend this servlet so that it read and wrote a database using JDBC. You might also add additional servlets to allow a student to register in courses, check to make sure the student's account is up to date, and allow the student to pay his or her tuition.

TIP A more complete servlet application will be developed in the next chapter. If you want even more examples of servlets in action, read James Goodwill's book, *Developing Java Servlets* (Sams, 1999).

Implementing Servlets Using JSP

As you've seen, servlets are well suited to function as form processors. You write an HTML form, submit it using GET or POST, and process the results in the servlet. Alas, all those lines like

```
aWriter.println("<HTML><HEAD><TITLE>Some title</TITLE></HEAD>");
```

can get tedious. Sun has mixed HTML and Java in the same file to combat this problem. The solution is called Java Server Pages, or JSP. Listing 41.5 shows a small JSP file.

Listing 41.5 *demo.jsp*—This JSP Compiles into a Servlet When First Accessed

```
<HTML>
<HEAD><TITLE>Demo JSP</TITLE></HEAD>
<BODY>
<%@ page contentType="text/html" %>
<% out.println("Hello, world! from a JavaServer Page"); %>
</BODY>
</HTML>
```

To install and run a JSP in Jakarta Tomcat, make a new directory under the server's document root and put the JSP file into a jsp folder in the new directory. (Don't forget to restart Tomcat so it finds the new application.) If you put the JSP file into TOMCAT_HOME/webapps/jspDemo/jsp, the URL of the page is http://127.0.0.1:8080/jspDemo/jsp/demo.jsp.

JSP Basics

Before looking at advanced JSP techniques, let's examine what happens when you request http://127.0.0.1:8080/jspDemo/jsp/demo.jsp. If you're following along on your server, you'll notice that the code ran, even though you never explicitly invoked the compiler. That's because the JSP specification requires the JSP container (in this case, Jakarta Tomcat) to compile the JSP into a servlet if it detects that the source code has changed since the last compilation. This design gives you the option of working directly on the source during development, and then deploying the JSP either in its source form or as a compiled servlet in a Web Application Archive.

Look again in the TOMCAT_HOME directory. You'll see that the server has built a new directory called work. Inside work, you'll see a directory for each JSP file. The page you've just been working on is in `localhost_8080%2FjspDemo`. Here you'll see the servlet source file and the compiled class file. Listing 41.6 shows the source file that Tomcat generated.

Listing 41.6 *_0002fjsp_0002fdemo_0002ejspdemo_jsp_1.java*—Tomcat Generates All This from One Tiny JSP

```
package jsp;

import javax.servlet.*;
import javax.servlet.http.*;
import javax.servlet.jsp.*;
import javax.servlet.jsp.tagext.*;
import java.io.PrintWriter;
import java.io.IOException;
import java.io.FileInputStream;
import java.io.ObjectInputStream;
import java.util.Vector;
import org.apache.jasper.runtime.*;
import java.beans.*;
import org.apache.jasper.JasperException;

public class _0002fjsp_0002fdemo_0002ejspdemo_jsp_1 extends HttpJspBase {

    static {
    }
    public _0002fjsp_0002fdemo_0002ejspdemo_jsp_1( ) {
    }

    private static boolean _jspx_inited = false;

    public final void _jspx_init() throws JasperException {
    }

    public void _jspService(HttpServletRequest request,
    ➥HttpServletResponse  response)
        throws IOException, ServletException {

        JspFactory _jspxFactory = null;
        PageContext pageContext = null;
        HttpSession session = null;
        ServletContext application = null;
        ServletConfig config = null;
        JspWriter out = null;
        Object page = this;
        String  _value = null;
        try {

            if (_jspx_inited == false) {
                _jspx_init();
                _jspx_inited = true;
            }
```

Listing 41.6 Continued

```
                _jspxFactory = JspFactory.getDefaultFactory();
                response.setContentType("text/html");
                pageContext = _jspxFactory.getPageContext(this, request, response,
                "", true, 8192, true);

                application = pageContext.getServletContext();
                config = pageContext.getServletConfig();
                session = pageContext.getSession();
                out = pageContext.getOut();

                // HTML // begin [file="C:\\jsp\\demo.jsp";from=(0,0);to=(3,0)]
                    out.write("<HTML>\r\n<HEAD><TITLE>Demo JSP</TITLE>
                    ➥</HEAD>\r\n<BODY>\r\n");
                // end
                // HTML // begin [file="C:\\jsp\\demo.jsp";from=(3,35);to=(4,0)]
                    out.write("\r\n");
                // end
                // begin [file="C:\\jsp\\demo.jsp";from=(4,2);to=(4,56)]
                     out.println("Hello, world! from a JavaServer Page");
                // end
                // HTML // begin [file="C:\\jsp\\demo.jsp";from=(4,58);to=(7,0)]
                    out.write("\r\n</BODY>\r\n</HTML>\r\n");
                // end

            } catch (Exception ex) {
                if (out.getBufferSize() != 0)
                    out.clearBuffer();
                pageContext.handlePageException(ex);
            } finally {
                out.flush();
                _jspxFactory.releasePageContext(pageContext);
            }
        }
    }
```

So when you first request a JSP, the JSP container translates the `.jsp` into a servlet. Then it calls javac and compiles the servlet. Finally, the servlet container loads the servlet (calling `init`), runs the servlet's `service` method, and passes in the browser's request and response objects. On subsequent calls, the server can skip nearly all those steps, transferring control directly to the servlet's `service` method.

If you want a better idea of how this code works, examine the JSP Specification (`ftp://ftp.java.sun.com/pub/jsp/11final-87721/jsp1_1-spec.pdf`) and API documentation (in your JSWDK directory, in `webpages/docs/api/javax/servlet/jsp/package-summary.html`). The rest of this section concentrates on how to build JSPs, not on the servlets that are generated from them.

Directives Look again at Listing 41.5. You'll see that only two lines are not standard HTML. The first of these lines is an example of the `page` directive. Directives provide information that is independent of the request. The complete list appears in Section 2.7 of the JSP 1.1 specification.

The `page` directive provides information to the JSP container about the characteristics of the HTML page it is to generate. The `page` directive supports such attributes as `language` (for the scripting language), `extends`, `import`, `errorPage`, and, of course, `contentType`. Thus, you could write

```
<%@ page import="edu.regent.syllabusGenerator.Module" errorPage="/oops.jsp" %>
```

On this page, the defaults reign. The language is "java," the page participates in an HTTP session, the page has a buffer of at least 8KB, the buffer will flush automatically when it is filled, the content type is `"text/html"`, and the author asserts that the Java will be threadsafe. If the code on this page throws an exception, the server will load the JSP specified in `errorPage`, in this case, `"/oops.jsp"`.

You must use the following syntax to specify a directive:

```
<%@ directive attributes %>
```

The spaces after the at sign and before the final percent sign are significant.

In addition to the `page` directive, JSP also supports an `include` directive and a `taglib` directive. Use the `include` directive when you want to embed static data into the page. For example, you can write

```
<%@ include file="copyright.html" %>
```

The `taglib` directive enables you to extend the set of tags that are understood by the JSP container. You'll learn about this technique later in this chapter.

Actions Unlike directives, actions usually depend on the contents of the request object and directly affect the response object. To write actions, you'll need to gain access to these two objects by means of implied objects.

Implied Objects You can code JSPs as though you had already declared some useful objects:

- **`request`**—The request, passed in from the `service` method.
- **`response`**—The response, providing a connection back to the user's browser.
- **`pageContext`**—An encapsulation of implementation-dependent features.
- **`session`**—The HTTP session object.
- **`application`**—The servlet context object (from `getServletConfig(). getContext()`).
- **`out`**—A reference to the response object's output stream.

- **config**—The `ServletConfig` for this page.
- **page**—The instance of this page's implementation class; comparable to `this` in conventional Java classes.

Using JavaBeans

JavaBean technology is an important part of the Java world. You can use conventional JavaBeans in a development environment to add special graphical components to an applet. Enterprise JavaBeans encapsulate business logic for the "middleware" of a three-tier application.

In JSP, beans are used to make large amounts of functionality available to the JSP. Listing 41.7 shows a simple bean that stores the names of the eight academic schools at Regent University (`http://www.regent.edu/`).

Listing 41.7 ***SchoolBean.java*****—This Bean Stores the Names of Schools in a Vector**

```
import java.util.*;

public class SchoolBean {
  private Vector fList = new Vector(8);
  private int fIndex = 0;

  public SchoolBean() {
    fList.addElement(new String("Business"));
    fList.addElement(new String("Communication"));
    fList.addElement(new String("Divinity"));
    fList.addElement(new String("Education"));
    fList.addElement(new String("Government"));
    fList.addElement(new String("Law"));
    fList.addElement(new String("Leadership"));
    fList.addElement(new String("Psychology"));
  }

  public String getList() {
    return (String)fList.elementAt(fIndex);
  }

  public boolean hasMoreElements() {
    return (! (++fIndex >= fList.size()));
  }

  public void reset() {
    fIndex = 0;
  }

  // test routine
  public static void main (String[] args) {
```

Listing 41.7 Continued

```
    SchoolBean theTester = new SchoolBean();
    while (theTester.hasMoreElements()) {
      System.out.println("School of " + theTester.getList());
    }
  }
}
```

This bean is compiled and moved into the `CLASSPATH`. Now you can build a JSP such as the one shown in Listing 41.8.

Listing 41.8 *SchoolBeanDemo.jsp*—A JSP Author Can Use a Bean Without Knowing Java

```
<HTML>
<HEAD><TITLE>School Bean Demo</TITLE></HEAD>
<BODY>
<H1>The Schools of <A HREF=http://www.regent.edu/>Regent University</A></H1>

<jsp:useBean id='RegentBean' scope='page' class='SchoolBean'
➥type="SchoolBean" />
<% while (RegentBean.hasMoreElements()) {
%>
    <jsp:getProperty name="RegentBean" property="list"/><BR>
<%
   }
%>

</BODY>
 </HTML>
```

In this code, `jsp:useBean` is invoked to make a new instance of the `SchoolBean`. This new instance is named `RegentBean`. Because the list has multiple elements—in bean terms it is an indexed property—use the Boolean method `hasMoreElements` to iterate over the entire `Vector`. Each time through the loop, use `jsp:getProperty` to retrieve the current value of `list`. Figure 41.5 shows the result of running this JSP.

Although this code works, it is a bit messy. It's preferable to avoid exposing the iteration mechanism to the HTML/JSP author. Way back in JSP 0.92, there were special tags such as `DISPLAY` and `LOOP` to handle this issue. In JSP 1.1, you have a more general mechanism—the ability to develop your own tag library.

NOTE There's a great interest among developers in having some standard tags, similar to `DISPLAY` and `LOOP` in JSP 0.92. This site was developed by a group working on such a standard tag library. You are invited to join in at `http://java.sun.com/aboutJava/communityprocess/jsr/jsr_052_jsptaglib.html`. ■

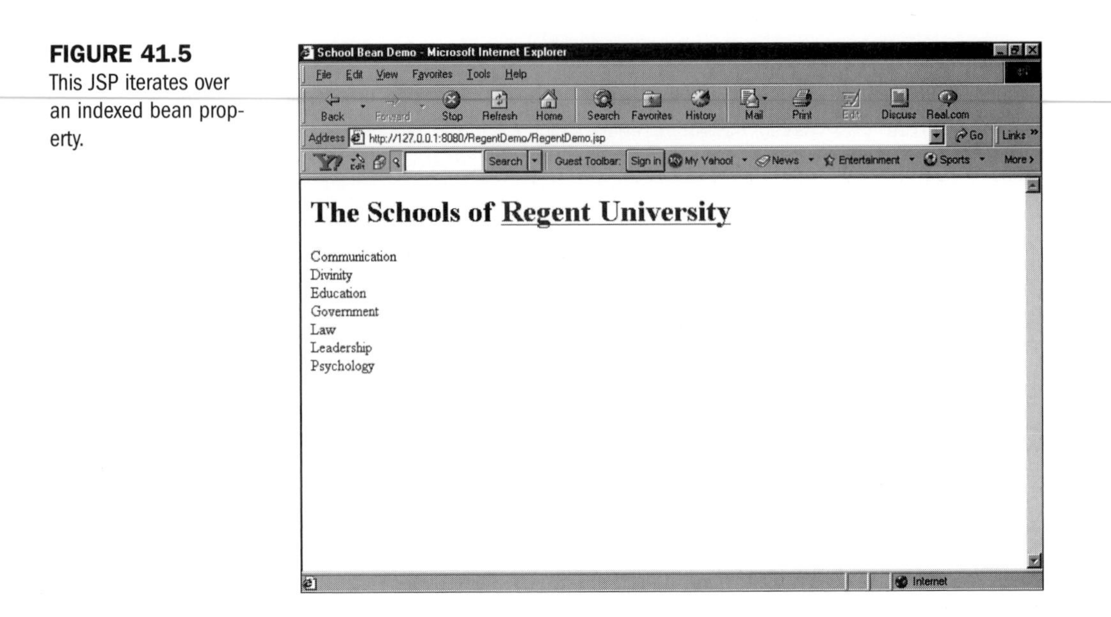

FIGURE 41.5
This JSP iterates over an indexed bean property.

Extending the Tag Library

Although Sun has built some common functions into JSP 1.1 (for example, `useBean` and `getProperty`), you'll undoubtedly find things you want to do that aren't directly supported by the standard. You can always break out into Java, as was done in Listing 41.8. If you want a cleaner way, or if you want to make it easier for JSP authors to build their pages without knowing Java, consider adopting a custom tag library.

For example, a database expert could write a tag library that gave access to a relational database. A Web page author could use those tags to build a JSP, without knowing much about either Java or relational databases.

Using the *taglib* Directive To add custom tags to a JSP, make sure you include the `taglib` directive in the file. The `taglib` directive has the following form:

```
<%@ taglib uri="someIdentifier" prefix="somePrefix" %>
```

For example, you could write

```
<%@ taglib uri="http://www.regent.edu/taglib/" prefix="ru" %>
```

to add a tag library developed at Regent University. To use these tags, specify the prefix:

```
<ru:searchDatabase query="SELECT * FROM STUDENTS WHERE SEMESTER=0"/>
```

NOTE Begin to acclimate yourself to the XML tag style. If a tag doesn't have a matching closing tag, add a "/" at the end of the tag.

You quickly and easily can develop tags that have no body, but only attributes. Tags with a body require somewhat more work. The most complex tags are those that must maintain a context, such as tags that imply iteration.

NOTE To get started quickly, use the sample tag libraries in the Jakarta project as examples at `http://jakarta.apache.org/taglibs/`.

Building and Using Tag Handlers In this section, you'll build a tag handler class and hook it up to a JSP.

Begin with the code in Listing 41.9. Note that the class implements `Tag`, which comes from `javax.servlet.jsp.tagext` in the latest `servlet.jar` (`servlet_2_2`). To implement that interface, you need to override six methods:

- **`doStartTag`**—Processes the opening of the custom tag.
- **`doEndTag`**—Processes the closing of the tag.
- **`release`**—Where you would usually clean up any resources.
- **`setPageContext`**—Used by the container to pass in the context.
- **`setParent`**—Used by the container to tell you which tag you're in.
- **`getParent`**—Used by the container to find out where you fit in the hierarchy.

Listing 41.9 ***RegentUniversity.java*—This Tag Class Generates "Regent University"**

```
import javax.servlet.jsp.*;
import javax.servlet.jsp.tagext.*;

public class RegentUniversity implements Tag {
  private PageContext fPageContext;
  private Tag fParent;

  // respond to the starting tag by skipping any body
  public int doStartTag() throws javax.servlet.jsp.JspException {
    return SKIP_BODY;
  }

  // use the occasion of the ending tag to pump out our contents
  public int doEndTag() throws javax.servlet.jsp.JspException {
    try {
      fPageContext.getOut().write("Regent University");
    } catch (java.io.IOException ioe) {
      throw new JspException("IO Error: " + ioe.getMessage());
    }
    // evaluate the rest of the page
    return EVAL_PAGE;
  }
```

Listing 41.9 Continued

```
// clean up here as necessary
  public void release() {
  }

  // the JSP container will call this method
  public void setPageContext(final javax.servlet.jsp.PageContext
  ➥thePageContext) {
    fPageContext = thePageContext;
  }

  // the JSP container will call this method
  public void setParent(final javax.servlet.jsp.tagext.Tag theParent) {
    fParent = theParent;
  }

  public javax.servlet.jsp.tagext.Tag getParent() {
    return fParent;
  }
}
```

In this code, you've specified that when you see the closing tag, you'll write out "Regent University."

Next, write a tag description file, shown in Listing 41.10. This file announces that the tags in this library will be known by the short name `ru` and provides a pointer to the JAR file where the classes are stored. (In this case, of course, you'll have only one class in the JAR.) For demo purposes, leave the JAR file on your local server. If you were deploying this library, you would want to place `mytags.jar` on some publicly accessible server.

The `<tag>` tag maps between the name you'll use in the JSP and the name of the class. It also informs the parser that it is an error for this tag to have body content. You have three choices here. If `<bodycontent>` is `empty`, any content raises an error. If it's `tagdependent`, the content (if any) is handled by the tag handler. Specifying `jsp` means that the JSP container handles the body if it's present.

Listing 41.10 *taglib.tld*—An XML File Describing the New Tag

```
<?xml version="1.0" encoding="ISO-8859-1" ?>
<!DOCTYPE taglib PUBLIC "-//Sun Microsystems, Inc.//DTD JSP Tag
➥Library 1.1//EN"
 "http://java.sun.com/j2ee/dtds/web-jsptaglibrary_1_1.dtd">
<taglib>
  <tlibversion>1.0</tlibversion>
  <jspversion>1.1</jspversion>
  <shortname>ru</shortname>
  <uri>http://127.0.0.1:8080/taglibDemo/lib/mytags.jar</uri>
  <info>A Demo Tag Library</info>
```

Listing 41.10 Continued

```
  <tag>
    <name>Regent</name>
    <tagclass>RegentUniversity</tagclass>
    <bodycontent>empty</bodycontent>
    <info>The University name</info>
  </tag>
</taglib>
```

Next, assemble the class file and the TLD file into a JAR. Put the TLD into the subdirectory `META-INF`, and then run the jar program from the command line:

```
jar cvf mytags.jar RegentUniversity.class META-INF\taglib.tld
```

Place the JAR file in your Web server's document root hierarchy. If you're using Tomcat, you might put it into `TOMCAT_HOME\webapps\taglibDemo\lib`. Then, in `TOMCAT_HOME\webapps\taglibDemo`, you would put a JSP file such as the one in Listing 41.11.

Listing 41.11 *taglibDemo.jsp*—Calling the Custom Tag

```
<%@ taglib uri="http://127.0.0.1:8080/taglibDemo/lib/mytags.jar" prefix="ru" %>
<HTML>
<HEAD><TITLE>Tag Demo</TITLE></HEAD>
<BODY>
<H1>Welcome to <ru:Regent/></H1>
</BODY>
</HTML>
```

You'll recognize the `taglib` directive from the earlier discussion. It tells the JSP container to load `mytags.jar` and to use that library for custom tags that begin with `ru`. Finally, use the custom tag named `Regent` inside your `<H1>` HTML tag.

Going Further with Tag Extension Regent University is composed of eight schools. Suppose you wanted to have a custom tag called `welcome` that accepted a parameter. In your JSP file, you would write

```
<ru:welcome school="School of Business">
```

You can easily add parameters to your tags. In the Java file for the class, add a `school` string. Then add a new method—`setSchool`—that accepts a string and assigns it to the class member. Change the `doEndTag` method so that it includes the `school` string in its output.

The biggest change is in `taglib.tld`. You'll want to add these lines right before `</tag>`:

```
<attribute>
  <name>school</name>
  <required>false</required>
  <rtexprvalue>false</rtexprvalue>
</attribute>
```

These lines tell the JSP container that your tag accepts a parameter named `school`. It's optional, so you might want to set up a reasonable default value in the Java code.

For even more ideas on work you can do with custom tag libraries, see the JSP specification. ●

Java and XML

In this chapter

Reading XML Documents

If you've read Part II, "XML," you know that XML is a wonderful language that lets you develop documents in a platform- and vendor-neutral format. Likewise, if you've been reading the other chapters here in Part VI "Java 2," you know that Java is a platform-independent programming language. Although the language was developed by Sun, the list of licensees reads like a veritable "who's who" of computing. So, it should come as no surprise that many people believe that Java and XML were made for each other. You can write Java to run on nearly any computing platform. On that platform, the program can read XML documents and use them as input. The program can allow the user to edit the document or even transform the document itself.

The points of this chapter are illustrated by developing a small Java servlet that allows users to edit files, and then writes those files out as HTML. Before you get to the application, however, you need to look at the fundamentals of working with XML in Java.

Parsing and Navigating XML

Recall from Chapter 12, "Parsing and Navigating XML—SAX, DOM, XPath, XPointer, and XLink," that XML documents are supposed to be well-formed, making them easy to read into a program. The Java community has developed two main parsing technologies: the Simple API for XML, or SAX, and the Document Object Model, or DOM. In this section, you'll look at the strengths and weaknesses of these two parsing technologies. You'll see how to use both SAX and DOM parsers. Finally, you'll look at some high-level APIs that simplify the use of SAX and DOM.

SAX Recall that SAX is a serial parsing technique—the parser begins at the top of the file and reads sequentially tag by tag. As the programmer, you register handlers that are interested in certain events—a particular content element, for example, or an error. During the course of parsing, these events occur and your handler is called.

▶ For an introduction to SAX, **see** "SAX—the Simple API for XML," **p. 336**

The serial nature of SAX parsing is both a blessing and a curse. Because you are processing the data as it's read, there's no need to maintain the whole document in memory. Programs that use SAX tend to be faster and use less memory than programs that use the other major parsing technology, DOM. On the other hand, the fact that you never have the entire document in memory makes it difficult to write the document back to the filesystem. If you're writing an XML editor, for example, SAX just isn't an option.

To use SAX, you must first have a SAX parser. Several vendors offer such parsers; this example uses the Apache Xerces parser because it's available for free (see Listing 42.1).

NOTE You can download many useful pieces of XML-related software from Apache (`http://xml.apache.org/`), including the Xerces-Java parser. ■

Listing 42.1 ***SAXParserDemo.java*—This Parser Reports Its Progress**

```
import java.io.IOException;

import org.xml.sax.Attributes;
import org.xml.sax.ContentHandler;
import org.xml.sax.ErrorHandler;
import org.xml.sax.Locator;
import org.xml.sax.SAXException;
import org.xml.sax.SAXParseException;
import org.xml.sax.XMLReader;
import org.xml.sax.helpers.XMLReaderFactory;

public class SAXParserDemo {
  public void doParse( String theURI ) {
    System.out.println("Parsing XML File: " + theURI + "\n\n");
    ContentHandler theContentHandler = new TContentHandler();
    ErrorHandler theErrorHandler = new TErrorHandler();

    try {
      XMLReader theParser =
        XMLReaderFactory.createXMLReader(System.getProperty("parserClass"));
      theParser.setContentHandler(theContentHandler);
      theParser.setErrorHandler(theErrorHandler);
      theParser.setFeature("http://xml.org/sax/features/validation", false);
      theParser.setFeature("http://xml.org/sax/features/namespaces", true);


      theParser.parse( theURI );
    } catch (IOException ioe) {
      System.out.println("Error reading URL: " + ioe.getMessage());
    } catch (SAXException se) {
      System.out.println("Error in parsing: " + se.getMessage());
    }
  }

  public static void main( String[] args ) {
    if (args.length != 1) {
      System.out.println("Usage: java SAXParserDemo [XML URI]");
      System.exit(0);
    }

    String aURI = args[0];
    SAXParserDemo theParserDemo = new SAXParserDemo();
    theParserDemo.doParse( aURI );
  }
  class TContentHandler implements ContentHandler {
    private Locator fLocator;

    public void setDocumentLocator(Locator theLocator) {
      System.out.println("   * setDocumentLocator() called");
      fLocator = theLocator;
    }
```

Listing 42.1 Continued

```
  public void startDocument() throws SAXException {
    System.out.println("Parsing begins  . . .");
  }

  public void endDocument() throws SAXException {
    System.out.println(". . . Parsing ends");
  }

  public void processingInstruction(String theTarget, String theData)
    throws SAXException {
    System.out.println("PI: Target:" + theTarget + " and Data:" +
      theData);
  }

  public void startPrefixMapping(String thePrefix, String theURI)
    throws SAXException {
    System.out.println("Mapping starts for prefix " + thePrefix +
      " mapped to URI " + theURI);
  }

  public void endPrefixMapping(String thePrefix) throws SAXException {
    System.out.println("Mapping ends for prefix " + thePrefix);
  }

  public void startElement(String theNamespaceURI, String theLocalName,
    String theRawName, Attributes theAttributes) throws SAXException {
    System.out.print("startElement: " + theLocalName);
    if (!theNamespaceURI.equals("")) {
      System.out.println(" in namespace " + theNamespaceURI + " (" +
        theRawName + ")");
    } else {
      System.out.println(" has no associated namespace.");
    }
    for (int i=0; i<theAttributes.getLength(); i++)
      System.out.println(" Attribute: " + theAttributes.getLocalName(i) +
        "=" + theAttributes.getValue(i));
  }

  public void endElement(String theNamespaceURI, String theLocalName,
                         String theRawName) throws SAXException {
     System.out.println("endElement: " + theLocalName + "\n");
  }

  public void characters(char[] theChars, int theStart, int theEnd)
    throws SAXException {
    String aString = new String(theChars, theStart, theEnd);
    System.out.println("characters: " + aString);
  }

  public void ignorableWhitespace(char[] theChars, int theStart,
    int theEnd) throws SAXException {
```

Listing 42.1 Continued

```
      String aString = new String(theChars, theStart, theEnd);
      System.out.println("ignorableWhiteSpace: [" + aString + "]");
    }

    public void skippedEntity(String aName) throws SAXException {
      System.out.println("Skipping entity " + aName);
    }
  }

  class TErrorHandler implements ErrorHandler {
    public void warning( SAXParseException exception ) throws SAXException {
      System.out.println("**Parsing Warning**\n" +
                         "  Line:    " + exception.getLineNumber() + "\n" +
                         "  URI:     " + exception.getSystemId() + "\n" +
                         "  Message: " + exception.getMessage());
      throw new SAXException("Warning encountered");
    }

    public void error( SAXParseException exception ) throws SAXException {
      System.out.println("**Parsing Error**\n" +
                         "  Line:    " + exception.getLineNumber() + "\n" +
                         "  URI:     " + exception.getSystemId() + "\n" +
                         "  Message: " + exception.getMessage());
      throw new SAXException("Error encountered");
    }

    public void fatalError( SAXParseException exception ) throws SAXException {
      System.out.println("**Parsing Fatal Error**\n" +
                         "  Line:    " + exception.getLineNumber() + "\n" +
                         "  URI:     " + exception.getSystemId() + "\n" +
                         "  Message: " + exception.getMessage());
      throw new SAXException("Fatal Error encountered");
    }
  }
}
```

Make sure your SAX parser is in the CLASSPATH. If you're using Xerces, you could place the parser in your development directory, and type

```
javac -classpath ./xerces_1_0_3.jar SAXParserDemo.java
```

to compile. Before you can test this program, you'll need some XML. Listing 42.2 shows a sample document that describes a course at the School of Business at Regent University (http://www.regent.edu/).

NOTE If you're testing with Listing 42.2, omit (or comment out) the line

```
<Regent:Policies>&RegentAcademicPolicies;</Regent:Policies>
```

near the bottom of the file. Read the detailed description of this code for an explanation of how to get this line to work. ■

Listing 42.2 *test1.xml*—A University Course Described in XML

```
<?xml version="1.0"?>

<Regent:Course xmlns:Regent="http://www.regent.edu/syllabi/course/">
 <Regent:ID>BUSN 620</Regent:ID>
 <Regent:Name>Ideas, Customers, and Competition</Regent:Name>
 <Regent:Contents>
  <Regent:Section focus="Ideas">
   <Regent:Heading>Ideas, Innovations and Opportunities</Regent:Heading>
   <Regent:Module objectives="5">Conceiving an Idea</Regent:Module>
   <Regent:Module objectives="3">Strategic Fit</Regent:Module>
   <Regent:Module objectives="3">Strategic Choice and Process</Regent:Module>
   <Regent:Module objectives="4">Researching an Idea</Regent:Module>
  </Regent:Section>

  <Regent:Section focus="Competition">
   <Regent:Heading>Industry Analysis</Regent:Heading>
   <Regent:Module objectives="2">Building an Industry Analysis</Regent:Module>
   <Regent:Module objectives="3">Strategic Fit</Regent:Module>
  </Regent:Section>

  <Regent:Section focus="Customers">
   <Regent:Heading>Market Feasibility</Regent:Heading>
   <Regent:Module objectives="3">Understanding Customer Segments and Buyer
   ➥Behavior</Regent:Module>
   <Regent:Module objectives="3">Understanding Channels of Sales and
   ➥Distribution</Regent:Module>
  </Regent:Section>


  <Regent:Section focus="Feasibility">
   <Regent:Heading>Operations and Production Feasibility</Regent:Heading>
   <Regent:Module objectives="2">Internal Capabilities and
   ➥Assessment</Regent:Module>
   <Regent:Module objectives="3">Strengths, Weaknesses, Opportunities, and
   ➥Threats</Regent:Module>
  </Regent:Section>

  <Regent:Section focus="Feasibility">
   <Regent:Heading>Financial Feasibility</Regent:Heading>
   <Regent:Module objectives="3">Sales, Revenues, and Expense
   ➥Forecasts</Regent:Module>
 </Regent:Section>

 <Regent:SectionBreak/>

  <Regent:Section focus="Feasibility">
   <Regent:Heading>Reporting Your Findings, Conclusions, and
   ➥Recommendations</Regent:Heading>
   <Regent:Module objectives="1">Feasibility Study Presentation</Regent:Module>
   <Regent:Module objectives="3">Feasibility Report Development and
```

Listing 42.2 Continued

```
    ➥Peer Review</Regent:Module>
   </Regent:Section>
  </Regent:Contents>

  <Regent:Policies>&RegentAcademicPolicies;</Regent:Policies>

 </Regent:Course>
```

This document announces that it describes a `Course` in the `Regent` namespace. After announcing the course ID and Name, it describes the `Contents` as a series of `Sections`. Each `section` has a `focus`, a `Heading`, and one or more `Modules`. Each `module` has zero or more `objectives`.

Just prior to the last section, the instructor identifies a `SectionBreak`, as the course begins to refocus on student assessment. This course description concludes with an XML entity—`&RegentAcademicPolicies;`—that contains "boilerplate" information about grading and participation policies.

In Listing 42.1, the parser was told that validation wasn't wanted

```
theParser.setFeature("http://xml.org/sax/features/validation", false);
```

but that the parser should be aware of the namespace:

```
theParser.setFeature("http://xml.org/sax/features/namespaces", true);
```

Later in this section, you'll turn on validation.

To run the demo code, you need to specify some vendor's parser in the System properties. You can do this on the command line. If you're using the Xerces parser and if you've placed it into the same directory as the class file, type:

```
java -classpath .;./xerces_1_0_3.jar -DparserClass=
➥org.apache.xerces.parsers.SAXParser SAXParserDemo test1.xml
```

Let's walk through the code in Listing 42.1, and look at how it processes the XML document from Listing 42.2. Starting in the `main` method, after a quick usage check, a new instance of the demo class is made, and the URI specified on the command line is run.

All the parsing is done inside the `doParse` method. One of the first things you do in `doParse` is instantiate the parser itself. Because you plan to use the Xerces parser, you could write

```
//import org.xml.sax.helpers.XMLReaderFactory;
import org.apache.xerces.parsers.SAXParser;
      . . .
      XMLReader theParser = new SAXParser();
```

This design is poor, however. You might want to distribute the class file (but not the Java source). Class users should be able to decide for themselves whether they want to use the Xerces parser or a parser from some other vendor. Instead, you'll specify the name of the parser class in a System property. That way the class user tells the program where to look for the parser. Instead of coding the `SAXParser` explicitly, you write:

```
XMLReader theParser =
XMLReaderFactory.createXMLReader(System.getProperty("parserClass"));
```

Then, on the command line, this property is passed:

```
-DparserClass=org.apache.xerces.parsers.SAXParser
```

Recall from the discussion earlier that SAX parsers proceed tag by tag through the XML file. When they find certain events such as content or errors, they pass control to the appropriate handler. The handler classes are registered in the lines

```
theParser.setContentHandler(theContentHandler);
theParser.setErrorHandler(theErrorHandler);
```

As the last step before parsing, you tell the parser that you don't want it to validate the XML document—assuming the document is already valid—but you do want it to recognize the namespace you're using. (Later in this section, you'll learn more about validating parsers.)

When you call `theParser.parse( theURI );`, the parser goes to work, reading through the file. As it processes content, it calls the appropriate method in the `ContentHandler`. If it finds an error, it calls either `warning`, `error`, or `fatalError` in the `ErrorHandler`. Let's concentrate on methods in the `ContentHandler`.

Here are the first few lines of the program's output, interspersed with comments:

```
Parsing XML File: test1.xml
```

From the `setDocumentLocator` method:

```
* setDocumentLocator() called
```

The `Locator` keeps track of the parser's progress, in case the callback method needs to access the actual XML. You can use the `Locator` to get the row number and column number where the parser is currently reading.

The `startDocument` method announces that the document has been opened:

```
Parsing begins  . . .
```

Because you told the parser to respect namespaces, it pulls out the `Regent` name from the `Course` element:

```
Mapping starts for prefix Regent mapped to URI
➥http://www.regent.edu/syllabi/course/
startElement: Course in namespace http://www.regent.edu/syllabi/course/
➥(Regent:Course)
```

This element has no characters associated with it, but the next element—`ID`—does:

```
characters:

startElement: ID in namespace http://www.regent.edu/syllabi/course/ (Regent:ID)
characters: BUSN 620
```

```
endElement: ID

characters:
```

Scroll down to the bottom of the program's output. Here you'll see that the parser encounters a fatal error. Remember that errors are handled by the `ErrorHandler`, so your own method—`fatalError`—writes this output:

```
startElement: Policies
 in namespace http://www.regent.edu/syllabi/course/ (Regent:Policies)
**Parsing Fatal Error**
  Line:    49
  URI:     file:/C:/javaDev/Ch42/SAX/test1.xml
  Message: The entity "RegentAcademicPolicie" was referenced, but not declared.
Error in parsing: Fatal Error encountered
```

To eliminate this error, you need to declare the entity. The right place to do this is in the DTD, but a DTD hasn't been associated with this document yet. You can fix that by adding this line at the top of the XML file, where the new line is shown in bold:

```
<?xml version="1.0"?>

<!DOCTYPE Regent:Course SYSTEM "DTD\Regent1.dtd">
```

Now, inside the development directory, you make a new directory (`DTD`) and add `Regent1.dtd` to that directory. Listing 42.3 shows a minimal DTD that contains just the entity.

Listing 42.3 *Regent1.dtd*—A DTD Defining an Entity

```
<!ENTITY RegentAcademicPolicies SYSTEM
  "http://www.regent.edu/syllabi/docs/academicPolicies.xml">
```

When this entity is read, it tells the parser to load the file `academicPolicies.xml` at the specified URL. That file can be arbitrarily large and can contain detailed information about grading, academic honesty, and other academic policies.

TIP If you have only a small piece of text to include, don't bother referencing a URI. Just place the text into the entity itself, like this:

```
<!ENTITY RegentCopyright
  "Copyright 2000, Regent University. All Rights Reserved">
```

The Regent DTD is still far from complete. Later in this section, you'll see how to use a validating parser to completely check the XML document against a full DTD.

DOM In the previous section, you used SAX to parse your document. Recall from that discussion that SAX uses memory efficiently by reading the XML document one tag at a time. As the document is read, the parser calls your `ContentHandler` to process the tags.

> **CAUTION**
> As you use DOM with larger and larger documents, your programs will require greater amounts of memory. Always think ahead to the ways in which users will use your programs; if the memory requirements are too great, consider redesigning the program so you don't have to parse too many nodes at once—or find a way to use SAX.

If you want to read the entire document into memory so you can access any part of it randomly, you can't use SAX. The alternative is to use a DOM (Document Object Model) parser. Listing 42.4 illustrates how you might use such a parser.

Listing 42.4 ***DOMParserDemo.java*—Load and Print the Entire Document from Memory**

```
import java.io.IOException;
import org.xml.sax.SAXException;
import org.apache.xerces.parsers.DOMParser;
import org.w3c.dom.Document;
import org.w3c.dom.DocumentType;
import org.w3c.dom.NamedNodeMap;
import org.w3c.dom.Node;
import org.w3c.dom.NodeList;

public class DOMParserDemo {
  public void doDemo( String theURI ) {
    System.out.println("Parsing XML File: " + theURI);
    System.out.println(); System.out.println();
    DOMParser theParser = new DOMParser();
    try {
      theParser.parse( theURI );
      Document theDocument = theParser.getDocument();
      printNode(theDocument, "");
    } catch (IOException ioe) {
      System.out.println("Error reading URI: " + ioe.getMessage());
    } catch (SAXException se) {
      System.out.println("Error in parsing: " + se.getMessage());
    }
  }

  public static void main(String[] args) {
    if (args.length != 1) {
      System.out.println("Usage: java DOMParserDemo [XML URL]");
      System.exit(0);
    }
    String theURI = args[0];
    DOMParserDemo theParserDemo = new DOMParserDemo();
    theParserDemo.doDemo( theURI );
  }

  public void printNode(Node theNode, String indent) {
    switch (theNode.getNodeType()) {
      case Node.DOCUMENT_NODE:
```

Listing 42.4 Continued

```
    System.out.println("<xml version=\"1.0\">");

    // leave a bit more white space, for neatness
    System.out.println();
    NodeList theNodes = theNode.getChildNodes();
    if (theNodes!= null) {
      for (int i=0; i< theNodes.getLength(); i++) {
        printNode(theNodes.item(i), "");
      }
    }
    break;
  case Node.ELEMENT_NODE:
    String theName = theNode.getNodeName();
    System.out.print(indent + "<" + theName);
    NamedNodeMap theAttributes = theNode.getAttributes();
    for (int i=0; i< theAttributes.getLength(); i++) {
      Node theCurrentNode = theAttributes.item(i);
      System.out.print(" " + theCurrentNode.getNodeName() +
                       "=\"" + theCurrentNode.getNodeValue() +
                       "\"");
    }
    System.out.println(">");

    NodeList theChildren = theNode.getChildNodes();
    if (theChildren != null) {
      for (int i=0; i< theChildren.getLength(); i++) {
        printNode(theChildren.item(i), indent + "  ");
      }
    }
    // make sure we have an open line before closing
    System.out.println();
    System.out.println(indent + "</" + theName + ">");
    break;
  case Node.TEXT_NODE:
  case Node.CDATA_SECTION_NODE:

    // only print non-whitespace
    String thePrintableText = theNode.getNodeValue().trim();
    if (thePrintableText.length() != 0)
      System.out.print(indent + thePrintableText);
    break;
  case Node.PROCESSING_INSTRUCTION_NODE:
    System.out.println("<?" + theNode.getNodeName() +
                       " " + theNode.getNodeValue() +
                       "?>");
    break;
  case Node.ENTITY_REFERENCE_NODE:
    System.out.println(indent + "&" + theNode.getNodeName() + ";");
    break;
  case Node.DOCUMENT_TYPE_NODE:
```

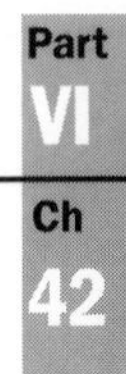

Listing 42.4 Continued

```
          DocumentType docType = (DocumentType)theNode;
          System.out.print("<!DOCTYPE " + docType.getName());
          if (docType.getPublicId() != null) {
            System.out.print(" PUBLIC \"" +
              docType.getPublicId() + "\" ");
          } else {
            System.out.print(" SYSTEM ");
          }
          System.out.println("\"" + docType.getSystemId() + "\">");
          break;
      }
    }
  }
```

Let's walk through this code as it handles the current version of the test XML document (which now references a small DTD that defines the entity).

NOTE You might have noticed that the DOM parser throws `org.xml.sax.SAXException`. That's not a mistake. DOM parsers typically use an underlying SAX architecture to read the document, even though they're reading it into memory. ■

Execution begins with `main`; after checking to make sure that there's exactly one parameter, the program makes a new instance of `DOMParserDemo`, and then asks that object to "`doDemo`." After you are into `doDemo`, you make a new instance of `org.apache.xerces. parsers.DOMParser` and ask it to parse your document. Unlike SAX, which calls `ContentHandlers` as it parses, the DOM parser parses the file into a memory-resident data structure, and then makes the entire document available. To retrieve the document from the Xerces parser, you use the method `getDocument`.

NOTE Class `DOMParserDemo` is hard-coded to use the Xerces parser. A better design would be to allow the user to specify the parser class at runtime, as was done in the SAX example. That design doesn't work as well with DOM, because the methods to parse the document and retrieve the parsed document aren't standardized. Because you have to hard-code the methods to retrieve the document (in this case, `parse` and `getDocument`), you might as well hard-code the parser class. ■

With the document in hand, you can examine any part of it—you don't have to read it in sequential order. For the purposes of this demo, it is just printed back out. Later in this chapter, you'll look at a more complete example based on JDOM.

The `printNode` method takes two parameters—a reference to the node of the document, and a string of blanks. By adding blanks to the string as you descend into the document, a "pretty-printed" version of the XML document is generated.

`printNode` handles seven types of document node:

- **`DOCUMENT_NODE`**—The top level of the document; you respond by printing out the XML version (which isn't accessible directly from the node) and then recursively call `printNode` on each of the nodes of the document.
- **`ELEMENT_NODE`**—This node is associated with a tag. You print out the name and value of each attribute of the tag, and then recursively call `printNode` on each of the child nodes. You add two blank spaces to the `indent` String, to support pretty-printing.
- **`TEXT_NODE` and `CDATA_SECTION_NODE`**—Recall (from "XML Document Fundamentals" in Chapter 11, "Creating XML Files for Use") that you can "hide" data from the parser by placing it in a `CDATA` section. Whether the text is inside `CDATA` or just the text of a tag, you'll print it out.
- **`PROCESSING_INSTRUCTION_NODE`**—If the XML node is a PI, you report its name and value.
- **`ENTITY_REFERENCE_NODE`**—The test document contains one entity—`RegentAcademicPolicies`. When you recognize an entity, print out its name.
- **`DOCUMENT_TYPE_NODE`**—This node is associated with the `<!DOCTYPE>` tag. You print out the public or system ID, as appropriate.

When you run `DOMParserDemo` with your test document (which includes a reference to a small DTD that defines the entity), you see output like this:

```
Parsing XML File: test1.xml

<xml version="1.0">

<!DOCTYPE Regent:Course SYSTEM "DTD\Regent1.dtd">
<Regent:Course xmlns:Regent="http://www.regent.edu/syllabi/course/">
  <Regent:ID>
    BUSN 620
  </Regent:ID>
  <Regent:Name>
    Ideas, Customers, and Competition
  </Regent:Name>
  <Regent:Contents>
    <Regent:Section focus="Ideas">
      <Regent:Heading>
        Ideas, Innovations and Opportunities
      </Regent:Heading>
      <Regent:Module objectives="5">
        Conceiving an Idea
      </Regent:Module>
      <Regent:Module objectives="3">
        Strategic Fit
      </Regent:Module>
      <Regent:Module objectives="3">
        Strategic Choice and Process
```

```
    </Regent:Module>
    <Regent:Module objectives="4">
      Researching an Idea
    </Regent:Module>

  </Regent:Section>
  <Regent:Section focus="Competition">
    <Regent:Heading>
      Industry Analysis
    </Regent:Heading>
    <Regent:Module objectives="2">
      Building an Industry Analysis
    </Regent:Module>
    <Regent:Module objectives="3">
      Strategic Fit
    </Regent:Module>

  </Regent:Section>
  <Regent:Section focus="Customers">
    <Regent:Heading>
      Market Feasibility
    </Regent:Heading>
    <Regent:Module objectives="3">
      Understanding Customer Segments and Buyer Behavior
    </Regent:Module>
    <Regent:Module objectives="3">
      Understanding Channels of Sales and Distribution
    </Regent:Module>

  </Regent:Section>
  <Regent:Section focus="Feasibility">
    <Regent:Heading>
      Operations and Production Feasibility
    </Regent:Heading>
    <Regent:Module objectives="2">
      Internal Capabilities and Assessment
    </Regent:Module>
    <Regent:Module objectives="3">
      Strengths, Weaknesses, Opportunities, and Threats
    </Regent:Module>

  </Regent:Section>
  <Regent:Section focus="Feasibility">
    <Regent:Heading>
      Financial Feasibility
    </Regent:Heading>
    <Regent:Module objectives="3">
      Sales, Revenues, and Expense Forecasts
    </Regent:Module>

  </Regent:Section>
  <Regent:SectionBreak>
```

```
</Regent:SectionBreak>
    <Regent:Section focus="Feasibility">
      <Regent:Heading>
        Reporting Your Findings, Conclusions, and Recommendations
      </Regent:Heading>
      <Regent:Module objectives="1">
        Feasibility Study Presentation
      </Regent:Module>
      <Regent:Module objectives="3">
        Feasibility Report Development and Peer Review
      </Regent:Module>

    </Regent:Section>

  </Regent:Contents>
  <Regent:Policies>
    &RegentAcademicPolicies;

  </Regent:Policies>

</Regent:Course>
```

Even though a validating parser hasn't been used—you'll learn about that technology later in this section—the parser still requires that the entity be defined.

JAXP In the discussions of SAX and DOM, you learned the strengths and weaknesses of each. SAX is fast and doesn't require much memory. DOM gives you random access to the document but isn't completely standardized (and you don't have the luxury of an `XMLReaderFactory` class). Sun has come up with a set of classes that defines an abstraction layer between your code and the DOM and SAX parsers. This layer enables you to access parsers without writing vendor-specific code. The solution is called the Java API for XML Parsing, or JAXP.

To make and use a DOM parser with JAXP, you write

```
DocumentBuilderFactory theFactory =
  DocumentBuilderFactory.newInstance();
DocumentBuilder theParser = theFactory.newDocumentBuilder();
Document theDocument = theParser.parse( theURI );
```

`DocumentBuilderFactory` and `DocumentBuilder` are part of the `javax.xml.parsers` package—JAXP. Sun has donated JAXP to the Apache Xerces project, and the two are being merged. You can get the latest information from `http://xml.apache.org/xerces-j/index.html`, or download JAXP with the Xerces `xml-contrib` module.

NOTE You can use JAXP with either SAX or DOM parsers. The analogous SAX classes are `javax.xml.parsers.SAXParserFactory` and `javax.xml.parsers.SAXParser`. ■

Although each JAXP implementation has a default parser, you can override the default at runtime by specifying a value for the system property; for DOM, it's javax.xml.parsers.DocumentBuilderFactory; for SAX, it's javax.xml.parsers.SAXParserFactory. You can set system properties by using the -D option to the java interpreter (as you did in running the SAXParserDemo). You also can read properties from a property file and set them by using System.setProperty. Starting with SDK 1.3, you also can use the Extension Mechanism (JAVA_HOME/ docs/guide/extensions/ spec.html) to specify properties in a JAR file.

JDOM Note that in JAXP, DocumentBuilder and SAXParser are abstract—that's why factory classes had to be used to get instances of the parser. Many programmers would prefer a simpler implementation, with concrete parser classes that they can instantiate directly. Brett McLaughlin and Jason Hunter (both of K&A Software) have addressed this need by offering a Java representation of an XML document, called JDOM (http://www.jdom.org/).

NOTE The developers of JDOM intend to make a stable version of the reference implementation of JDOM available on their Web site in both binary and source form. The latest version, however, is available only by CVS. Get the CVS command line program from http://www.cvshome.org. (Binaries for Windows are available at ftp://ftp.cvshome.org/pub/cvs-1.10.5/ windows/.) Then use it to download the JDOM classes:

```
cvs -d :pserver:anonymous@cvs.jdom.org:/home/cvspublic login
password: anonymous

cvs -d :pserver:anonymous@cvs.jdom.org:/home/cvspublic co jdom
```

After you have the JDOM classes, invoke build (in Windows) or sh build.sh (in UNIX or Linux) from the JDOM root directory. This script will generate jdom.jar in the JDOM/build directory. It puts the API documentation into JDOM\build\apidocs\index.html. ■

To parse an XML document with a SAX parser by using JDOM, you import the JDOM classes and write

```
SAXBuilder theBuilder = new SAXBuilder();
Document theDocument = theBuilder.build ( theXMLFile );
```

The analogous code for a DOM parser is

```
DOMBuilder theBuilder = new DOMBuilder();
Document theDocument = theBuilder.build ( theXMLFile );
```

After you have a JDOM Document, you can access its components in much the same way as you did with DOM (although the JDOM API is simpler). For example, to step through the first-level elements in a document, write

```
Element theRootElement = theDocument.getRootElement();
java.util.List theElements = theRootElement.getChildren();
Iterator i = theElements.iterator();
```

```
while (i.hasNext()) {
  Element theCurrentElement = (Element) i.next();
  System.out.println("The element is named " + theCurrentElement.getName();
}
```

JDOM isn't designed to be a complete API—McLaughlin and Hunter have stated that their intent is that it "…solve 80% (or more) of Java/XML problems with 20% (or less) of the effort." If you're able to design your program around JDOM, you'll nearly always have fewer lines of source than a similar program written using direct access to the SAX or DOM parsers. You'll look at a JDOM-based application later in this chapter, in "Java and XML in Action."

Using a Validating Parser

In the examples you've been given so far, the document being parsed has been assumed to be well-formed and valid. If that assumption breaks down, you might have runtime errors. Rather than writing extensive error-checking code, a better design is to validate the XML.

▶ To learn more about the differences between a document being "well-formed" and being "valid," **see** "Document Type Definitions (DTDs)," **p. 370**

TIP In most applications, your XML document will be written once and read many times. Because a validating parser runs more slowly than a non-validating parser, you might want to design your application so the writer validates the XML, and the readers can assume that the XML documents are valid.

Recall (from Chapter 14, "Constraining XML—DTDs and XML Schemas") that you can ensure the XML is well-formed and valid either by specifying a Document Type Definition (DTD) or by using an XML Schema. In this section, you'll learn how to ensure the validity of an XML document with Java with DTDs.

NOTE Apache has started to add support for XML Schema to Xerces. Check the Xerces-Java site (`http://xml.apache.org/xerces-j/schema.html`) for the latest info. ■

In `SAXParserDemo` (refer to Listing 42.1) and `DOMParserDemo` (refer to Listing 42.4), the presence of the `RegentAcademicPolicies` entity forced a reference to a tiny DTD (refer to Listing 42.3) to be added to the test document. That DTD included only the entity definition. Now you can expand that DTD to completely describe the `Regent:Course` document. Listing 42.5 shows a complete DTD.

Listing 42.5 ***Regent2.dtd*—This DTD Describes the Test XML Document**

```
<!ELEMENT Regent:Course (Regent:ID, Regent:Name, Regent:Contents,
➥Regent:Policies)>
<!ATTLIST Regent:Course
  xmlns:Regent CDATA #REQUIRED
```

Listing 42.5 Continued

```
>
<!ELEMENT Regent:ID (#PCDATA)>
<!ELEMENT Regent:Name (#PCDATA)>
<!ELEMENT Regent:Contents ((Regent:Section+) | (Regent:Section+,
➥Regent:SectionBreak?)+)>
<!ELEMENT Regent:Section (Regent:Heading?, Regent:Module+)>
<!ATTLIST Regent:Section
      focus CDATA #IMPLIED
>
<!ELEMENT Regent:Heading (#PCDATA)>
<!ELEMENT Regent:Module (#PCDATA)>
<!ATTLIST Regent:Module
      objectives CDATA #REQUIRED
>
<!ELEMENT Regent:SectionBreak EMPTY>
<!ELEMENT Regent:Policies (#PCDATA)>
<!ENTITY RegentAcademicPolicies SYSTEM "policies.txt">
<!ENTITY RegentCopyright "Copyright 2000, Regent University.
➥All Rights Reserved">
```

To “turn on” validation in a SAX 2.0 parser, set this feature before calling `parse`:

```
theParser.setFeature("http://xml.org/sax/features/validation", true);
```

If you make this change and compile and run the `SAXParserDemo`, you'll get this obscure error message:

```
Document root element "Regent:Course", must match DOCTYPE root "Regent:Course".
```

What's going on here? Under XML 1.0, parsers cannot distinguish between a namespace prefix and an element name. The validating parser looks at the DTD and expects to find a `Regent:Course` object as the root. Because the `namespaces` feature is on—in fact, it's on by default, even if you don't specify it—the parser has already stripped off the prefix `Regent`. The solution is to explicitly turn off the `namespaces` feature:

```
theParser.setFeature("http://xml.org/sax/features/namespaces", false);
```

Now compile and run the code. Make sure the test document includes the line

```
<!DOCTYPE Regent:Course SYSTEM "DTD\Regent2.dtd">
```

and the XML should validate without error.

Transforming XML Documents

Recall (from Chapter 15, “Formatting and Displaying XML”) that you can use the Extensible Stylesheet Language (XSL) to describe the ways in which XML documents can be formatted. In this chapter, a particular XSL Transformation (XSLT) engine is used to generate both PDF and XHTML from the Regent `Course` document. Listing 42.6 shows the style sheet used for this example.

Listing 42.6 *Regent.xsl*—Generate HTML from a *Course* Document

```
<?xml version="1.0"?>

<xsl:stylesheet xmlns:xsl="http://www.w3.org/1999/XSL/Transform"
                xmlns:Regent="http://www.regent.edu/syllabi/course/"
                version="1.0"
>

<xsl:template match="Regent:Course">
  <HTML>
    <HEAD>
      <TITLE>
        <xsl:value-of select="Regent:ID" />:
        <xsl:value-of select="Regent:Name" />
      </TITLE>
    </HEAD>
    <BODY>
      <H1 ALIGN="Center">
        <xsl:value-of select="Regent:ID" />:
        <xsl:value-of select="Regent:Name" />
        Syllabus
      </H1>
      <HR />
      <xsl:apply-templates select="*[not(self::Regent:ID)]
      ➥[not(self::Regent:Name)]" />
    </BODY>
  </HTML>
</xsl:template>

<xsl:template match="Regent:Contents">
  <TABLE BORDER="1">
    <TR BGCOLOR="#9999FF"><TH>Section</TH><TH>Modules</TH></TR>
    <xsl:for-each select="Regent:Section">
      <TR BGCOLOR="#FFFF00">
        <TD>
          <xsl:value-of select="Regent:Heading" />
          (<xsl:value-of select="@focus" /> focus)
        </TD>
        <TD>
          <UL>
            <xsl:for-each select="Regent:Module">
              <LI><xsl:value-of select="self::*" /></LI>
            </xsl:for-each>
          </UL>
        </TD>
      </TR>
    </xsl:for-each>
  </TABLE>
</xsl:template>

<xsl:template match="Regent:Policies">
  <xsl:copy-of select="self::*" />
</xsl:template>

</xsl:stylesheet>
```

Using an XSLT to Write HTML After you have an XML document and a corresponding style sheet, you can use an XSLT processor to transform the XML. Recall (from the XML chapters) that you used Instant Saxon as an XSLT processor.) Because the next example hooks up Apache's Cocoon framework, Apache's Xalan XSLT processor is used here to manually test the style sheet. (You can choose another XSLT processor if you prefer.)

NOTE Download the Cocoon servlet from the Apache site at `http://xml.apache.org/`. It includes the Xalan JAR. ■

Make sure both the Xalan and Xerces JARs are in your `CLASSPATH`. (These files will have version numbers in their names, such as `xalan_1_0_1.jar` and `xerces_1_0_3.jar`.) Then go to the command prompt and type

```
java org.apache.xalan.xslt.Process -IN test2.xml -XSL Regent.xsl
➥-OUT test2.html
```

Xalan parses the style sheet. Then it parses the XML document. Finally, it applies the style sheet to the document to generate HTML. Listing 42.7 shows the code Xalan generates. Figure 42.1 shows this Web page in Netscape Navigator.

Listing 42.7 ***test2.html*—Xalan Generates HTML from XML Based on an XSL Style Sheet**

```
<HTML xmlns:Regent="http://www.regent.edu/syllabi/course/">
<HEAD>
<TITLE>BUSN 620:
        Ideas, Customers, and Competition</TITLE>
</HEAD>
<BODY>
<H1 ALIGN="Center">BUSN 620:
        Ideas, Customers, and Competition
        Syllabus
      </H1>
<HR>
<TABLE BORDER="1">
<TR BGCOLOR="#9999FF">
<TH>Section</TH><TH>Modules</TH>
</TR>
<TR BGCOLOR="#FFFF00">
<TD>Ideas, Innovations and Opportunities
          (Ideas focus)
        </TD><TD>
<UL>
<LI>Conceiving an Idea</LI>
<LI>Strategic Fit</LI>
<LI>Strategic Choice and Process</LI>
<LI>Researching an Idea</LI>
</UL>
```

Listing 42.7 Continued

```
</TD>
</TR>
<TR BGCOLOR="#FFFF00">
<TD>Industry Analysis
          (Competition focus)
        </TD><TD>
<UL>
<LI>Building an Industry Analysis</LI>
<LI>Strategic Fit</LI>
</UL>
</TD>
</TR>
<TR BGCOLOR="#FFFF00">
<TD>Market Feasibility
          (Customers focus)
        </TD><TD>
<UL>
<LI>Understanding Customer Segments and Buyer Behavior</LI>
<LI>Understanding Channels of Sales and Distribution</LI>
</UL>
</TD>
</TR>
<TR BGCOLOR="#FFFF00">
<TD>Operations and Production Feasibility
          (Feasibility focus)
        </TD><TD>
<UL>
<LI>Internal Capabilities and Assessment</LI>
<LI>Strengths, Weaknesses, Opportunities, and Threats</LI>
</UL>
</TD>
</TR>
<TR BGCOLOR="#FFFF00">
<TD>Financial Feasibility
          (Feasibility focus)
        </TD><TD>
<UL>
<LI>Sales, Revenues, and Expense Forecasts</LI>
</UL>
</TD>
</TR>
<TR BGCOLOR="#FFFF00">
<TD>Reporting Your Findings, Conclusions, and Recommendations
          (Feasibility focus)
        </TD><TD>
<UL>
<LI>Feasibility Study Presentation</LI>
<LI>Feasibility Report Development and Peer Review</LI>
</UL>
</TD>
</TR>
</TABLE>
```

Listing 42.7 Continued

```
<Regent:Policies>This is our grading policy.
This is our policy on academic honesty.

</Regent:Policies>
</BODY>
</HTML>
```

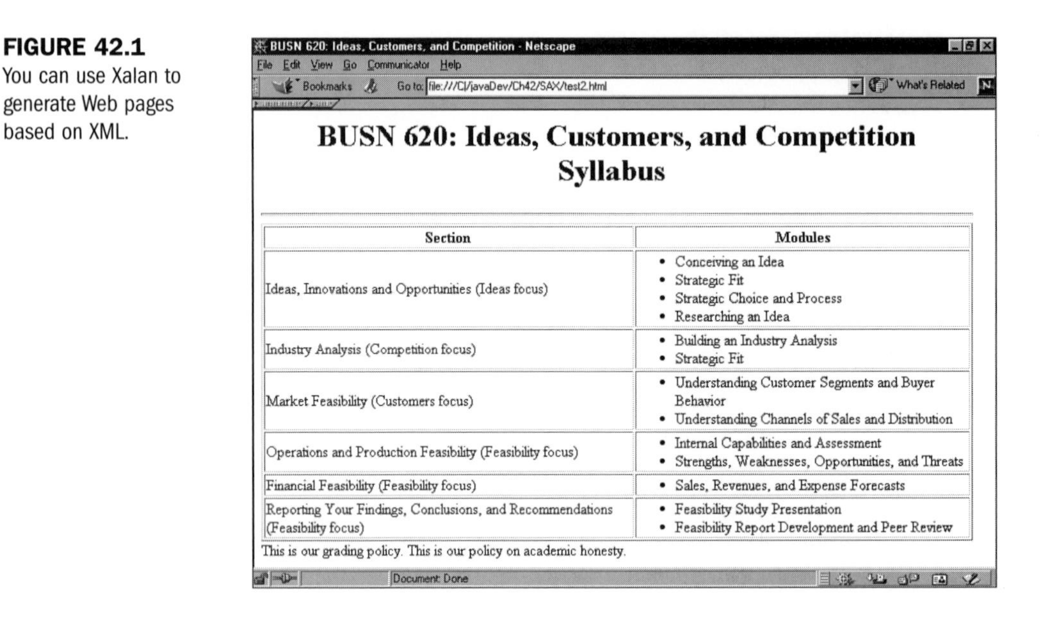

FIGURE 42.1
You can use Xalan to generate Web pages based on XML.

Automatically Transforming XML into HTML Although it's nice to be able to transform XML into other formats such as HTML, you don't want to rerun Xalan from the command prompt every time the XML changes. There is a better way. Apache provides a Web publishing framework (Cocoon) that will run Xalan automatically to transform XML into the desired format.

Download Cocoon from `http://xml.apache.org/`. To integrate Cocoon with Tomcat, copy the Cocoon, Xerces, Xalan, and FOP JAR files to the `Tomcat /lib` directory. Next, open the Tomcat startup script and update the `CLASSPATH`. (On Windows, the script is in `TOMCAT_HOME/bin/tomcat.bat`; on UNIX, it's in `TOMCAT_HOME/bin/tomcat.sh`.) Find the line that reads

```
set CLASSPATH=%TOMCAT_HOME%\classes
```

Immediately below that line add

```
rem Cocoon classes and libraries
set CLASSPATH=%CLASSPATH%;%TOMCAT_HOME%\lib\xerces_1_0_3.jar
```

```
set CLASSPATH=%CLASSPATH%;%TOMCAT_HOME%\lib\xalan_1_0_1.jar
set CLASSPATH=%CLASSPATH%;%TOMCAT_HOME%\lib\fop_0_12_1.jar
set CLASSPATH=%CLASSPATH%;%TOMCAT_HOME%\lib\cocoon.jar
```

(Of course, by the time you read this book Apache might have newer versions of these files.)

NOTE If you're on a UNIX machine, these lines should be of the form

`CLASSPATH=${CLASSPATH}:${TOMCAT_HOME}/lib/xerces_1_0_3.jar`

and so forth. ■

Be sure to place these Cocoon classes before the rest of Tomcat's classes. If Java finds `xml.jar` before it finds Cocoon's classes, Cocoon won't work because Tomcat's version of `xml.jar` doesn't yet support SAX 2 and DOM Level 2.

Next, copy the `cocoon.properties` file from the Cocoon home directory to `TOMCAT_HOME/conf`. In that same directory, open `web.xml` and add these lines to the `<web-app>` tag:

```
<!--Added the following servlet in order to support Cocoon-->
<servlet>
  <servlet-name>
    org.apache.cocoon.Cocoon
  </servlet-name>
  <servlet-class>
    org.apache.cocoon.Cocoon
  </servlet-class>
  <init-param>
    <param-name>
      properties
    </param-name>
    <param-value>
      TOMCAT_HOME/conf/cocoon.properties
    </param-value>
  </init-param>
</servlet>
<servlet-mapping>
  <servlet-name>
    org.apache.cocoon.Cocoon
  </servlet-name>
  <url-pattern>
    *.xml
  </url-pattern>
</servlet-mapping>
<!--End Cocoon support-->
```

(Replace *TOMCAT_HOME* with the absolute path to the Tomcat root directory, or use a path relative to `TOMCAT_HOME/webapps/ROOT/`.)

This entry tells Tomcat to call Cocoon whenever a user requests a file with file extension `.xml`. Finally, restart Tomcat. You should now be able to retrieve `http://localhost:8080/Cocoon.xml`, shown in Figure 42.2. (Note that the filename is case sensitive, even under Windows.)

FIGURE 42.2
Retrieve `Cocoon.xml` to test your new installation of Cocoon.

To use Cocoon to automatically transform the test XML document into XHTML, make a new directory inside `TOMCAT_HOME/Webapps`. For purposes of this example, call it `XSLDemo`. Inside the new directory, copy the test document (`test2.xml`), the DTD folder (with `Regent2.dtd` inside), and the `policies.txt` file (because an entity that requires this file is being used).

Next, make an XSL directory inside the new directory. Copy `Regent.xsl` into XSLDemo but change its name to `Regent.html.xsl` (to signify that this style sheet transforms Regent `course` documents into HTML). Later, you'll add another style sheet to generate PDF.

If you used a relative pathname to `cocoon.properties` in `conf/web.xml`, you'll need to ensure that that path is valid for XSLDemo as well. For example, if you choose to put `cocoon.properties` into `webapps/ROOT/`, you'll also need a copy in `webapps/XSLDemo`.

Finally, open `test2.xml` and add these two lines, right after the initial `<?xml version="1.0"?>`:

```
<?xml-stylesheet href="XSL\Regent.html.xsl" type="text/xsl"?>
<?cocoon-process type="xslt"?>
```

You'll need to restart Tomcat again so that it finds the new directory. After restarting, you can point your browser into the new directory and open `test2.xml`. Tomcat sees the `.xml` file extension and transfers control to Cocoon. Cocoon opens the XML file and sees the PIs telling it to use the `XSL\Regent.html.xsl` style sheet. Directives in the `cocoon.properties` file tell Cocoon to use Xalan to transform documents. It runs Xalan and sends the output back to your browser. The result is the same page you saw earlier in Figure 42.1.

Automatically Transforming XML into PDF As you saw in Chapter 15, you can also use XSL to transform XML into non-HTML formats. Listing 42.8 shows a style sheet that generates Adobe Acrobat's Portable Document Format (PDF) from Regent `Course` documents.

Listing 42.8 *Regent.fo.xls*—Generate PDF from the *Course* XML

```
<?xml version="1.0"?>

<xsl:stylesheet version="1.0"
  xmlns:xsl="http://www.w3.org/1999/XSL/Transform"
  xmlns:fo="http://www.w3.org/1999/XSL/Format"
  xmlns:Regent="http://www.regent.edu/syllabi/course/"
>

  <xsl:template match="Regent:Course">
    <xsl:processing-instruction name="cocoon-format">
      type="text/xslfo"
    </xsl:processing-instruction>
    <fo:root xmlns:fo="http://www.w3.org/1999/XSL/Format">
      <fo:layout-master-set>
        <fo:simple-page-master
          page-master-name="right"
          margin-top="75pt"
          margin-bottom="25pt"
          margin-left="100pt"
          margin-right="50pt">
          <fo:region-body margin-bottom="50pt"/>
          <fo:region-after extent="25pt"/>
        </fo:simple-page-master>
        <fo:simple-page-master
          page-master-name="left"
          margin-top="75pt"
          margin-bottom="25pt"
          margin-left="50pt"
          margin-right="100pt">
          <fo:region-body margin-bottom="50pt"/>
          <fo:region-after extent="25pt"/>
        </fo:simple-page-master>
      </fo:layout-master-set>

      <fo:page-sequence>
        <fo:sequence-specification>
          <fo:sequence-specifier-alternating
            page-master-first="right"
            page-master-odd="right"
            page-master-even="left"/>
        </fo:sequence-specification>

        <fo:static-content flow-name="xsl-after">
```

Listing 42.8 Continued

```
            <fo:block text-align-last="centered" font-size="10pt">
              <fo:page-number/>
            </fo:block>
          </fo:static-content>

          <fo:flow>
            <xsl:apply-templates/>
          </fo:flow>
        </fo:page-sequence>

      </fo:root>
    </xsl:template>

    <xsl:template match="Regent:ID">
      <fo:block font-size="36pt" text-align-last="centered"
      ➥space-before.optimum="24pt">
        <xsl:apply-templates/>
      </fo:block>
    </xsl:template>

    <xsl:template match="Regent:Name">
      <fo:block font-size="24pt" space-before.optimum="24pt"
      ➥text-align="centered">
        <xsl:apply-templates/>
      </fo:block>
    </xsl:template>

    <xsl:template match="Regent:Section">
      <xsl:apply-templates/>
    </xsl:template>

    <xsl:template match="Regent:Heading">
      <fo:block font-size="18pt" space-before.optimum="18pt"
      ➥text-align="centered">
        <xsl:apply-templates/>
      </fo:block>
    </xsl:template>

    <xsl:template match="Regent:Module">
      <fo:block font-size="12pt" space-before.optimum="12pt"
      ➥text-align="justified">
        <xsl:apply-templates/>
      </fo:block>
    </xsl:template>

    <xsl:template match="Regent:Policies">
      <fo:block font-size="10pt" space-before.optimum="10pt"
      ➥text-align="justified">
        <xsl:apply-templates/>
      </fo:block>
    </xsl:template>
</xsl:stylesheet>
```

To use this style sheet, change the style sheet directive in the XML document to

```
<?xml-stylesheet href="XSL/Regent.fo.xsl" type="text/xsl" ?>
```

and request `http://localhost:8080/XSLDemo/test2.xml` again. Figure 42.3 shows the resulting PDF file.

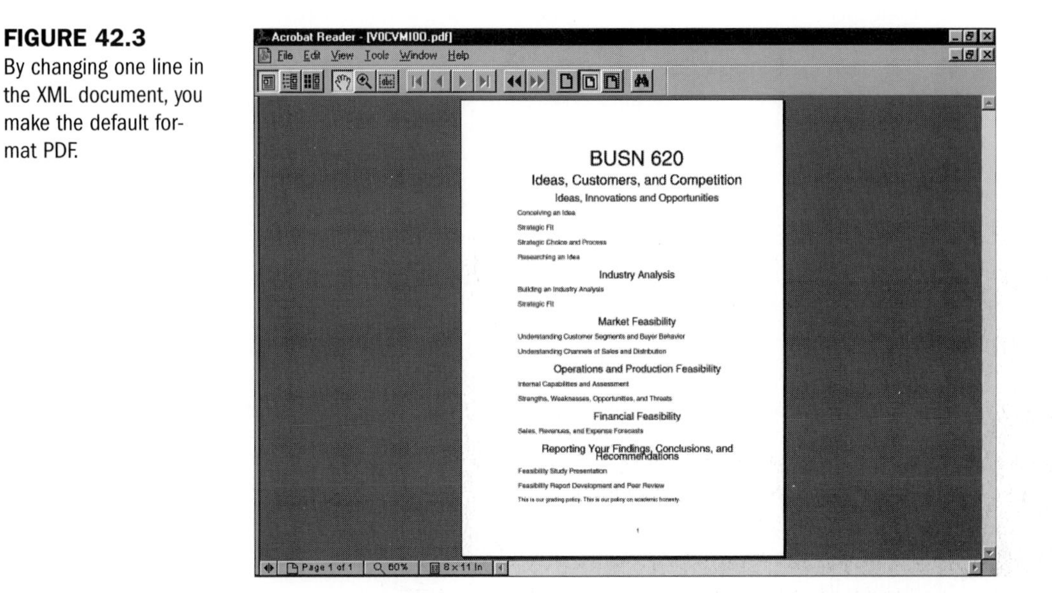

FIGURE 42.3
By changing one line in the XML document, you make the default format PDF.

Java and XML in Action

This section describes a prototype of an application developed for Regent University's School of Business (`http://www.regent.edu/acad/schbus/`).

The Project

As you've already seen, Regent University's School of Business divides each course into a series of sections, each of which is divided into modules. Each module, in turn, has one or more learning objectives, and requires various resources such as texts, journal articles, and computer files.

A syllabus describes a particular course being offered in a particular semester. One syllabus can cover multiple course offerings. Each offering is led by a faculty member, who might be assisted by other faculty who are specialists in the module topics.

Designing the Data Representation As software engineers, you can capture requirements in a variety of notations. Most commonly the Unified Modeling Language, or UML, is used (`http://www.rational.com/uml/`).

NOTE For a description of how you might use UML to describe Web applications (including XML-based applications), read these white papers at Rational's UML Resource Center: `http://www.rational.com/products/whitepapers/101066.jsp`.

For the syllabus generator, DTD notation is used to quickly capture a rough description of the concepts associated with Regent syllabi, courses, and other resources:

```
<!ELEMENT Regent:Syllabus (Regent:Course,
                           Regent:Offering+,
                           Regent:Policy*,
                           Regent:Procedure*,
                           Regent:Copyright,
                           Regent:ContactInfo,
                           Regent:LastUpdatedDate)>
<!ATTLIST Regent:Syllabus
          semester (Fall | Winter | Summer) #REQUIRED
>
<!ELEMENT Regent:Course (Regent:CatalogID,
                         Regent:Contents,
                         Regent:Policy*,
                         Regent:Procedure*)>
<!ELEMENT Regent:CatalogID (Regent:Subject, Regent:CourseNumber)>
<!ELEMENT Regent:Subject (#PCDATA)>
<!ELEMENT Regent:CourseNumber (#PCDATA)>
<!ELEMENT Regent:Contents (Regent:Objective+, Regent:Overview,
➥Regent:Section+)>
<!ELEMENT Regent:Objective (Regent:Paragraph+)>
<!ELEMENT Regent:Overview (Regent:Paragraph+)>
<!ELEMENT Regent:Paragraph (#PCDATA)>
<!ELEMENT Regent:Offering (Regent:OfferingID, Regent:Instructor+)>
<!ELEMENT Regent:OfferingID (#PCDATA)>
<!ELEMENT Regent:Instructor (Regent:Name, Regent:Email, Regent:Phone,
➥Regent:FAX)>
<!ELEMENT Regent:Name (#PCDATA)>
<!ELEMENT Regent:Email (#PCDATA)>
<!ELEMENT Regent:Phone (#PCDATA)>
<!ELEMENT Regent:FAX (#PCDATA)>
<!ELEMENT Regent:Section (Regent:Heading, Regent:Module+)>
<!ELEMENT Regent:Heading (Regent:SectionID, Regent:Title)>
<!ELEMENT Regent:Module (Regent:Title,
                         Regent:Objective+,
                         Regent:Instructor,
                         Regent:Prerequisite*,
                         Regent:Overview,
                         Regent:ResourceReference,
                         Regent:Assignment*,
                         Regent:InstructorsConclusion?,
                         Regent:AssessmentTool?,
                         Regent:ForFurtherStudy?)>
<!ELEMENT Regent:Prerequisite (#PCDATA)>
<!ELEMENT Regent:Assignment (Regent:Title,
                             Regent:Deadline?,
```

```
                              Regent:Activity+,
                              Regent:Points>
<!ELEMENT Regent:Activity (Regent:RefersToObjective,
                             Regent:Motivation,
                             Regent:EstimatedDuration,
                             Regent:Description)>
<!ELEMENT Regent:RefersToObjective (Regent:Objective)>
<!ELEMENT Regent:Motivation (#PCDATA)>
<!ELEMENT Regent:EstimatedDuration (#PCDATA)>
<!ELEMENT Regent:Description (Regent:Paragraph+)>
<!ELEMENT Regent:Points (#PCDATA)>
<!ELEMENT Regent:InstructorsConclusion (Regent:Paragraphs+)>
<!ELEMENT Regent:ResourceReference (Regent:Resource, Regent:ResourcePortion)>
<!ELEMENT Regent:Resource (Regent:ResourceName, Regent:Citation,
➥Regent:Source*, Regent:Price)>
<!ELEMENT Regent:ResourcePortion (#PCDATA)>
<!ATTLIST Regent:ResourcePortion
          type (book, URL, computerFile, other) #REQUIRED,
          required (true | false) #REQUIRED
>
<!ELEMENT Regent:ResourceName (#PCDATA)>
<!ELEMENT Regent:Citation (Regent:Author, Regent:Publisher, Regent:Year,
➥Regent:ISBN>
<!ELEMENT Regent:Source (#PCDATA)>
<!ELEMENT Regent:Price (#PCDATA)>
<!ELEMENT Regent:AssessmentTool (Regent:Paragraph+)>
<!ELEMENT Regent:ForFurtherStudy (Regent:Paragraph+)>
<!ELEMENT Regent:Procedure (Regent:Title, Regent:Paragraph+_)>
<!ELEMENT Regent:Procedure (Regent:Title, Regent:Paragraph+_)>
<!ELEMENT Regent:ContactInfo (#PCDATA)>
<!ELEMENT Regent:LastUpdatedDate (#PCDATA)>
<!ENTITY RegentContactInfo SYSTEM "contactInfo.xml">
<!ENTITY RegentRequiredResourcesPolicy SYSTEM "requiredResources.xml">
<!ENTITY RegentCopyright "Copyright 2000, Regent University.
➥All Rights Reserved">
```

Taking Advantage of Industry Standards Whenever possible, use an industry standard rather than writing your own DTD from scratch. The emerging standard for course content packaging is being developed by the IMS Global Learning Consortium, Inc. (`http://www.imsproject.org/content/packaging/`). Because both courses and modules are "packages" in the sense of the specification, you can use the IMS XML bindings to capture the course and module descriptions.

The IMS design represents resources in a Package Interchange File, or PIF. The PIF contains a manifest describing the contents, and also can contain the physical files holding the resource's content. The manifest contains sections on metadata (data about the data), the organization of the resource (such as a table of contents), resource descriptions and, when necessary, submanifests.

The following code is a sample manifest describing BUSN 620 and its associated sections, modules, and other resources. This course description addresses many of the course-related requirements captured in the syllabus DTD—you'll need to define a `syllabus` document, but it can refer to an IMS-compliant `course` (which, in turn, can refer to `modules` and `resources` represented in IMS notation).

```
<?xml version="1.0"?>
<manifest identifier="MANIFEST1" xmlns="http://www.imsproject.org/content">
  <metadata>
    <schema>IMS Content</schema>
    <schemaversion>1.0</schemaversion>
    <record xmlns="http://www.imsproject.org/metadata">
      <metametadata>
        <metadatascheme>IMS:1.1</metadatascheme>
        <!-- English as default metadata language. -->
        <language>en_US</language>
      </metametadata>
      <general>
        <title>
          <langstring lang="en_US">BUSN 620</langstring>
        </title>
        <catalogentry>
          <catalogue>Regent University</catalogue>
            <entry>
              <langstring>BUSN 620</langstring>
            </entry>
        </catalogentry>
        <language>en_US</language>
        <description>
          <!--English description-->
          <langstring lang="en_US">
            Ideas, Customers and Competition
          </langstring>
        </description>
        <keywords>
          <!--English Keywords, unordered list-->
          <langstring lang="en">entrepreneuring</langstring>
          <langstring lang="en">business plan</langstring>
          <langstring lang="en">feasibility plan</langstring>
        </keywords>
        <structure>
          <langstring lang="en">Hierarchical</langstring>
        </structure>
        <aggregationlevel>3</aggregationlevel>
      </general>
      <lifecycle>
        <version>
          <langstring lang="en">1.0</langstring>
        </version>
        <status>
          <langstring lang="en">Final</langstring>
        </status>
        <contribute>
          <role>
```

```
      <langstring lang="en">Manager</langstring>
    </role>
    <centity>
      <vcard>
        BEGIN:VCARD
        FN:Dr. Ken Burger
        ORG:Regent University
        EMAIL;INTERNET:kenburg@regent.edu
        LABEL;QUOTED-PRINTABLE:1000 Regent University Drive,
        ➥Virginia Beach, VA 23464
        TEL;VOICE:757 226 4423
        TEL;FAX: 757 226 4369
        END:VCARD
      </vcard>
    </centity>
    <date>
      <datetime>2000-05-22</datetime>
    </date>
  </contribute>
</lifecycle>
<technical>
  <format>
    <langstring lang="en">XML 1.0</langstring>
  </format>
  <size>21,480</size>
  <location type="URI">http://www.regent.edu/syllabi/course/
  ➥schbus/busn620.xml"></location>
  <requirements>
    <type>
      <langstring lang="en">Binding</langstring>
    </type>
    <name>
      <langstring lang="en">XML</langstring>
    </name>
    <minimumversion>1.0</minimumversion>
    <maximumversion>5.2</maximumversion>
  </requirements>
  <installationremarks>
    <langstring lang="en">Download</langstring>
  </installationremarks>
  <otherplatformrequirements>
    <langstring lang="en">
      Requires web browser for rendering
    </langstring>
  </otherplatformrequirements>
  <duration/>
</technical>
<educational>
  <learningresourcetype>
    <langstring lang="en">Course</langstring>
  </learningresourcetype>
  <interactivitylevel>3</interactivitylevel>
  <semanticdensity>2</semanticdensity>
```

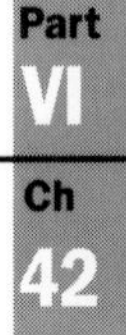

```
            <intendedenduserrole>
              <langstring lang="en">Student</langstring>
            </intendedenduserrole>
            <learningcontext>
              <langstring lang="en">Business Graduate</langstring>
            </learningcontext>
            <typicalagerange>
              <langstring lang="en">18-99</langstring>
            </typicalagerange>
            <description>
              <langstring lang="en">Interactive course for use in small groups
              ➥</langstring>
            </description>
            <language>en_US</language>
          </educational>
          <rights>
            <cost>
            <langstring lang="en">yes</langstring>
            </cost>
            <copyrightandotherrestrictions>
              <langstring lang="en_US">yes</langstring>
            </copyrightandotherrestrictions>
          </rights>
        </record>
      </metadata>
      <organizations default="TOC1">
        <tableofcontents identifier="TOC1" title="default">
          <item identifier="Section 1" identifierref=" BUSN620s01"
           title="Ideas, Innovations, and Opportunities" isvisible="1">
            <item identifier="Module 1" identifierref="BUSN620m01"
             title="Conceiving an Idea" isvisible="1">
              <item identifier="Resource 1" identifierref="JonesGeorgeandHill"
               title="Contemporary Management" isvisible="1">
              </item>
              <item identifier="Resource 2" identifierref="Bible"
               title="Holy Bible, any translation" isvisible="1">
              </item>
              <item identifier="Resource 3" identifierref="Drucker85"
               title="Innovation and Entrepreneurship: Practice and Principles"
               ➥isvisible="1">
              </item>
              <item identifier="Resource 4" identifierref="Wujec95"
               title="Five Star Mind: Games and Exercises to Stimulate Your
               ➥Creativity and Imagination" isvisible="1">
              </item>
            </item>
            <item identifier="Module 2" identifierref="BUSN620m02"
             title="Strategic Fit" isvisible="1">
             . . . other resources omitted . . .
            </item>
            <item identifier="Module 3" identifierref="BUSN620m03"
             title="Strategic Choice and Process" isvisible="1">
             . . . other resources omitted . . .
```

```
          </item>
          <item identifier="Module 4" identifierref="BUSN620m04"
           title="Researching an Idea" isvisible="1">
           . . . other resources omitted . . .
          </item>
        </item>
        <item identifier="Section 2" identifierref="BUSN620s02"
          title="Industry Analysis" isvisible="1"/>
          . . . modules and resources omitted . . .
        </item>
        <item identifier="Section 3" identifierref="BUSN620s03"
          title="Market Feasibility" isvisible="1"/>
          . . . modules and resources omitted . . .
        </item>
        <item identifier="Section 4" identifierref="BUSN620s04"
          title="Operations and Product Feasibility" isvisible="1"/>
          . . . modules and resources omitted . . .
        </item>
        <item identifier="Section 5" identifierref="BUSN620s05"
          title="Financial Feasibility" isvisible="1"/>
          . . . modules and resources omitted . . .
        </item>
        <item identifier="Section 6" identifierref="BUSN620s06"
          title="Reporting Your Findings, Conclusions, and
          ➥Recommendations" isvisible="1"/>
          . . . modules and resources omitted . . .
        </item>
      </tableofcontents>
    </organizations>
    <resources>
      <resource identifier=" BUSN620m01" type="webcontent"
      ➥href="BUSN620m01main.html">
        <metadata>
          <record xmlns="http://www.imsproject.org/metadata">
            <general>
              <title>
                <langstring lang="en_US">Conceiving an Idea</langstring>
              </title>
            </general>
          </record>
        </metadata>
        <file href="busn620m01main.html"/>
      </resource>
      . . . other resources omitted . . .
    </resources>
  </manifest>
```

The `Regent:syllabus` data will be designed so that it references the IMS `manifest` of a course. That design allows you to leverage the thinking that's already gone into designing course content packaging. As the standard becomes popular, Regent will be able to exchange course data with other schools.

Like many schools, Regent uses a computer-mediated learning environment as a "virtual classroom." This environment supplements the physical classroom (for those classes taught on campus) and *becomes* the classroom for distance education courses. Regent's vendor for the virtual classroom is Blackboard, Inc. (`http://www.blackboard.com/`). Because Blackboard participates in the IMS project, it's likely that one day the manifests for courses and other resources designed for syllabi will plug directly into the virtual classroom. Figure 42.4 shows BUSN 620 in Regent's virtual classroom.

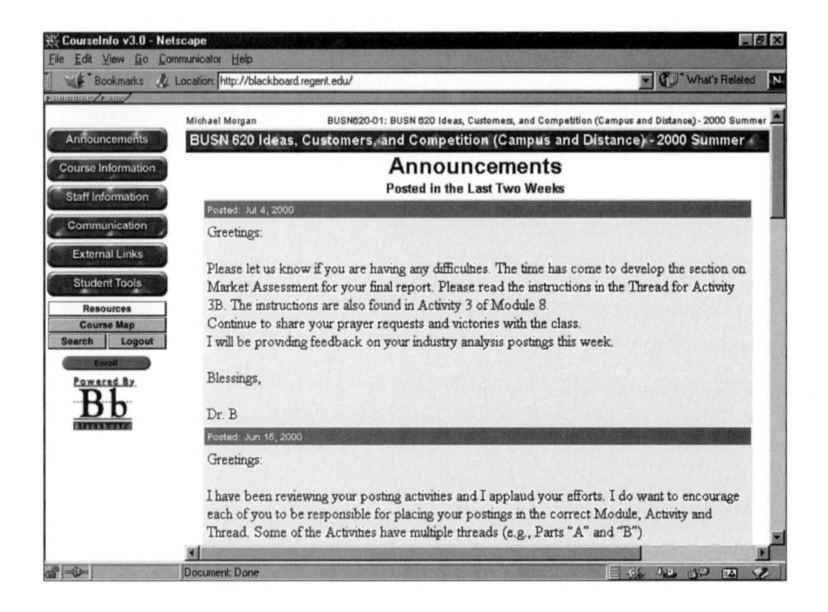

FIGURE 42.4
Regent University uses Blackboard as a virtual classroom.

Designing the Syllabus Editor

The School of Business wants all its faculty members to design and edit syllabi. There are three approaches you might take to implement the editor in Java. First, you could build an application and distribute it to each faculty member. Second, you could build an applet. Third, you could keep the functionality on the server and implement the editor as a servlet.

As you've seen, each course consists of several modules. Each module might reference various resources that can be shared across modules and courses. Because all this information needs to be shared among the course developers, you should keep the manifests on a server rather than on the developer's own computer.

Although you could build an applet that would allow you to edit a file locally and then return it to the server, that design seems unnecessarily complex. The best choice is to build a servlet that allows the faculty member to open, view, and change XML documents. When the professor has built the syllabus, he or she notifies the dean's office, where a clerk can run the XSLT processor, generating the HTML syllabus. The clerk proofs the syllabus, and then posts it to the public server where students can see it.

In Chapter 41, "Server-Side Java," you learned that you can run a Java program on the server that sends HTML (including HTML forms) and receives user data by either GET or POST. Course manifests and other resource descriptions will be kept in directories on the server's hard drive. This servlet design allows the user to request a file from the hard drive via GET. When the servlet processes doGet, it parses the XML file and uses the resulting document to build an HTML form. The end user is free to submit the form (via POST). The doPost method updates the document in memory, and then writes the document back to the hard drive.

Note that this design has a serious flaw—if two users request the same resource at the same time, their respective POSTs can overwrite each other. For the syllabus generator this problem is minor—each resource has one faculty member who is responsible for updating it. As the product grows, you might want to add some code to "lock" the resource, or even unpack the XML data into a relational database.

Building a *Module* Class

For a clean design, each major concept (for example, syllabus, course, module) will be encapsulated in its own class. Listing 42.9 shows the Module class with some representative methods for reading and writing metadata. Note that a considerable amount of work has been avoided by reusing the IMS classes. These classes are available as part of Sun's IMS toolkit (LOM-IMS XML Toolkit 1.0), available at http://www.imsproject.org/tools/sun.html. This toolkit allows you to easily build relatively sophisticated objects that conform to the IMS specification.

For example, most strings in IMS objects are stored as imsLangStrings, an array that can hold a string in up to eight different languages. By using the Sun toolkit, you can build such a string by writing

```
imsLangString[] theTitle = new imsLangString[2];
theTitle[0] = new imsLangString("Hello", "en");
theTitle[1] = new imsLangString("Bonjour", "fr");
```

Because many toolkit methods (and the corresponding IMS objects) expect a single imsLangString rather than an array, you can write

```
imsExampleElement someElement = new imsExampleElement
➥(new imsLangString(theTitle));
```

When the time comes to output this string, you'll get

```
<TITLE>
  <LANGSTRING LANG="en">Hello</LANGSTRING>
  <LANGSTRING LANG="fr">Bonjour</LANGSTRING>
</TITLE>
```

Listing 42.9 *Module.java*—This Class Encapsulates a Course Module

```
import java.io.FileInputStream;
import java.io.InputStream;
import java.io.IOException;
import java.util.List;
import java.util.HashSet;
import java.util.StringTokenizer;

import ims.imsMaster;
import ims.imsMetaMetaData;
import ims.imsGeneral;
import ims.imsLifeCycle;
import ims.imsTechnical;
import ims.imsRights;
import ims.imsClassification;
import ims.imsLangString;
import ims.imsCatalogEntry;
import ims.imsContribute;
import ims.imsVCard;
import ims.imsDateTime;

import org.jdom.Document;
import org.jdom.Element;
import org.jdom.JDOMException;
import org.jdom.Namespace;
import org.jdom.input.SAXBuilder;
import org.jdom.NoSuchChildException;
import org.jdom.NoSuchAttributeException;

/**
  * <B><CODE>Module</CODE></B> is a utility class that
  * loads Module information.
  *
  * @author
  *  <A HREF="mailto:michmor@regent.edu">Mike Morgan</A>
  * @version 1.0
  */
public class Module extends imsMaster {
  private InputStream fInputStream;
  private Document fDoc;

  private imsMetaMetaData fMetaMetaData;
  private imsGeneral fGeneral;
  private imsLifeCycle fLifeCycle;
  private imsTechnical fTechnical;
  private imsRights fRights;
  private imsClassification[] fClassification;

  /**
   * <P>Set a filename to read module information from</P>
   *
```

Listing 42.9 Continued

```
 * @param theFilename <CODE>String</CODE> name of Module file.
 */
public Module(String theFilename) throws IOException {
  this(new FileInputStream(theFilename));
}

/**
 * <P>Set a stream to read module information from</P>
 *
 * @param in <CODE>InputStream</CODE> to read Module information from.
 */
public Module(InputStream theInputStream) throws IOException {
  fInputStream = theInputStream;
  parseModule();
}

private void parseModule() throws IOException {
  try {
    // use JDOM to set up SAX builder with default parser
    // we assume that any document already written has been validated,
    // so we don't validate here. This saves time.
    SAXBuilder theBuilder = new SAXBuilder(false);

    // get the Module Document
    fDoc = theBuilder.build(fInputStream);

    // for demo and testing purposes, print out what we read

    // get root element
    Element theRoot = fDoc.getRootElement();

    // set up a default namespace for modules
    Namespace theNamespace = Namespace.getNamespace(
    ➥"http://www.imsproject.org/metadata/");

    // report out what we're about to do
    System.out.println("Parsing root element " + theRoot.getName());

    java.util.List nestedElements = theRoot.getChildren();
    for (int i=0; i<nestedElements.size(); i++) {
      Element oneLevelDeep = (Element)nestedElements.get(i);
      System.out.println("Element " + oneLevelDeep.getName() +
                         " contains " + oneLevelDeep.getContent());
      java.util.List twoLevelsDeep = oneLevelDeep.getChildren();
      for (int j=0; j<twoLevelsDeep.size(); j++) {
        Element theChildElement = (Element)twoLevelsDeep.get(j);
        System.out.println("  Element " + theChildElement.getName() +
                           " contains " + theChildElement.getContent());
      }
    }
```

Listing 42.9 Continued

```
        // parse out metametadata
        Element theMetaMetaData = theRoot.getChild("METAMETADATA", theNamespace);
        String theScheme = theMetaMetaData.getChild("METADATASCHEME",
        ➥theNamespace).getContent();
        String theLanguage = theMetaMetaData.getChild("LANGUAGE",
        ➥theNamespace).getContent();
        fMetaMetaData = new imsMetaMetaData(theScheme, theLanguage);

        System.out.println("metadata parsed");

        // parse out general data
        Element theGeneralData = theRoot.getChild("GENERAL", theNamespace);

        System.out.println("got generalData root");

        //Title is stored in an imsLanguageString, with provision for
        ➥multiple languages
        imsLangString theTitle =
          getIMSLangString(theGeneralData, "TITLE", theNamespace);
        if (theTitle == null)
          theTitle = new imsLangString("Untitled", "en-US");

        System.out.println("Title is " + theTitle.string[0]);

        String theAggregationLevel;
        try {
          theAggregationLevel =
            theGeneralData.getChild("AGGREGATIONLEVEL",
            ➥theNamespace).getContent();
        } catch (NoSuchChildException nsce) {
          theAggregationLevel = "2"; // when it doubt, it's a module
        }

        System.out.println("AggregationLevel is " + theAggregationLevel);

        List theCatalogEntryElements = theGeneralData.getChildren(
        ➥"CATALOGENTRY", theNamespace);
        imsCatalogEntry[] theCatalogEntries = null;
        if (theCatalogEntryElements.size() != 0)
          theCatalogEntries = new imsCatalogEntry[
          ➥theCatalogEntryElements.size()];
System.out.println("Found " + theCatalogEntryElements.size() +
➥" catalog entries.");

        for (int i=0; i<theCatalogEntryElements.size(); i++) {
System.out.println("Processing catalog entry " + i);
          Element theElement = (Element)theCatalogEntryElements.get(i);
          Element theCatalog = theElement.getChild("CATALOGUE", theNamespace);
System.out.println("Catalog name is " + theCatalog.getContent());
          imsLangString theEntry =
            getIMSLangString(theElement, "ENTRY", theNamespace);
```

Listing 42.9 Continued

```
    theCatalogEntries[i] = new imsCatalogEntry(theCatalog.getContent(),
    ➥theEntry);
  }

  System.out.println("Catalog entries parsed");

  String theGeneralLanguage[] = null;
  List theGeneralLanguages = theGeneralData.getChildren("LANGUAGE",
  ➥theNamespace);
  theGeneralLanguage = new String[theGeneralLanguages.size()];
  for (int i=0; i<theGeneralLanguages.size(); i++) {
    Element theElement = (Element)theGeneralLanguages.get(i);
    theGeneralLanguage[i] = theElement.getContent();
  }
  if (theGeneralLanguage == null) {
    theGeneralLanguage = new String[1];
    theGeneralLanguage[0] = "en-US"; // when it doubt, it's English
  }

  System.out.println("General language is " + theGeneralLanguage[0]);

  //Description is stored in a multiple imsLanguageStrings, with provision
  ➥for multiple languages
  imsLangString[] theDescription =
    getIMSLangStringArray(theGeneralData, "DESCRIPTION", theNamespace);
  if (theDescription == null) {
    theDescription = new imsLangString[1];
    theDescription[0] = new imsLangString("None", "en-US");
  }
  System.out.println("Description is " + theDescription[0].string[0]);
  System.out.println("Description has been parsed");

  //Keywords are stored in a multiple imsLanguageStrings, with provision
  ➥for multiple languages
  imsLangString[] theKeywords =
    getIMSLangStringArray(theGeneralData, "KEYWORDS", theNamespace);
  if (theKeywords == null) {
    theKeywords = new imsLangString[1];
    theKeywords[0] = new imsLangString("None", "en-US");
  }
  System.out.println("First keyword is " + theKeywords[0].string[0]);


  //The COVERAGE tag is currently being developed by IMS. Use is
  ➥experimental.
  //Coverage is stored in an imsLanguageString, with provision for multiple
  ➥languages
  imsLangString[] theCoverage =
    getIMSLangStringArray(theGeneralData, "COVERAGE", theNamespace);
  if (theCoverage == null) {
```

Listing 42.9 Continued

```
        theCoverage = new imsLangString[1];
        theCoverage[0] = new imsLangString("None", "en-US");
      }

      System.out.println("Coverage is " + theCoverage[0].string[0]);

      //Structure is stored in an imsLanguageString, with provision for
      ➥multiple languages
      imsLangString theStructure =
        getIMSLangString(theGeneralData, "STRUCTURE", theNamespace);
      if (theStructure == null)
        theStructure = new imsLangString("None", "en-US");

      System.out.println("Structure is " + theStructure.string[0]);

      fGeneral = new imsGeneral(theTitle, theCatalogEntries,
      ➥theGeneralLanguage, theDescription,
        theKeywords, theCoverage, theStructure, theAggregationLevel);

      System.out.println("Loaded fGeneral");

      // parse out lifecycle data
      Element theLifeCycleData = theRoot.getChild("LIFECYCLE", theNamespace);

      System.out.println("got lifecycle root");

      //Status is stored in an imsLanguageString, with provision for multiple
      ➥languages
      imsLangString theStatus =
        getIMSLangString(theLifeCycleData, "STATUS", theNamespace);
      if (theStatus == null)
        System.out.println("Status is null");
      else
        System.out.println("Status is " + theStatus.string[0]);

      //Version is stored in an imsLanguageString, with provision for multiple
      ➥languages
      imsLangString theVersion =
        getIMSLangString(theLifeCycleData, "VERSION", theNamespace);
      if (theVersion == null)
        theVersion = new imsLangString("None", "en-US");

System.out.println("Version is " + theVersion.string[0]);

      List theContributorElements = theLifeCycleData.getChildren("CONTRIBUTE",
      ➥theNamespace);
      imsContribute[] theContributors = null;
System.out.println("Looking for Contributor elements");
      if (theContributorElements.size() != 0)
        theContributors = new imsContribute[theContributorElements.size()];
```

Listing 42.9 Continued

```
System.out.println("Found " + theContributorElements.size() + " contributor
➥entries.");

      for (int i=0; i<theContributorElements.size(); i++) {
System.out.println("Processing contributor entry " + i);
        Element theElement = (Element)theContributorElements.get(i);
        imsLangString theRole = getIMSLangString(theElement, "ROLE",
        ➥theNamespace);

System.out.println("Role is " + theRole.string[0]);

        imsDateTime theDateTime = null;
        try {
          Element theDateElement = theElement.getChild("DATE", theNamespace);
          Element theDateTimeElement = theDateElement.getChild("DATETIME",
          ➥theNamespace);
          String theDateTimeString = theDateTimeElement.getContent();
System.out.println("DateTime string is " + theDateTimeString);
          imsLangString theDescriptionString = getIMSLangString(theDateElement,
          ➥"DESCRIPTION", theNamespace);
if (theDescriptionString != null)
  System.out.println("D/T Description is " + theDescriptionString.string[0]);
else
  System.out.println("No D/T Description found.");
          if (theDescriptionString != null)
            theDateTime = new imsDateTime(theDateTimeString,
            ➥theDescriptionString);
          else
            theDateTime = new imsDateTime(theDateTimeString);
        } catch (NoSuchChildException nsce) {
          System.out.println("No DATETIMEs found.");
        }

        imsVCard[] theVCards = null;
        List theCEntityElements = theElement.getChildren("CENTITY",
        ➥theNamespace);
System.out.println("Looking for CENTITYs.");
        if (theCEntityElements.size() != 0) {
          theVCards = new imsVCard[theCEntityElements.size()];
System.out.println("Found " + theCEntityElements.size() + " CEntities.");
          for (int j=0; j<theCEntityElements.size(); j++) {
            Element theCEntityElement = (Element)theCEntityElements.get(j);
            String theAddress = "";
            String theEmail = "";
            String theFN = "";
            String theOrg = "";
            String thePhone = "";
            try {
              Element theVCardElement = theCEntityElement.getChild("VCARD",
              ➥theNamespace);
```

Listing 42.9 Continued

```
System.out.println("Processing vCard " + j);
              String theVCardString = theVCardElement.getContent();
              StringTokenizer theTokenizer =
                new StringTokenizer(theVCardString, ":\n");
              while (theTokenizer.hasMoreTokens()) {
                String theToken = theTokenizer.nextToken().trim();
                String theValue = theTokenizer.nextToken().trim();
                System.out.println("VCard token " + theToken + "=" + theValue);
                if (theToken.equals("LABEL;QUOTED-PRINTABLE"))
                  theAddress = theValue;
                else
                if (theToken.equals("EMAIL;INTERNET"))
                  theEmail = theValue;
                else
                if (theToken.equals("FN"))
                  theFN = theValue;
                else if (theToken.equals("ORG"))
                  theOrg = theValue;
                else if (theToken.equals("TEL;VOICE"))
                  thePhone = theValue;
              }
              theVCards[j] = new imsVCard(theFN, theOrg, theEmail,
              ➥theAddress, thePhone);
            } catch (NoSuchChildException nsce) {
              System.out.println("No vCard inside this CENTITY");
            }
          }
        }
System.out.println("About to add contributor " + i);
        theContributors[i] = new imsContribute(theRole, null, theDateTime);
      }
      if (theStatus == null)
        fLifeCycle = new imsLifeCycle(theVersion, theContributors);
      else
        fLifeCycle = new imsLifeCycle(theVersion, theStatus, theContributors);
System.out.println("Added new imsLifeCycle");

    } catch (JDOMException jde) {
      throw new IOException(jde.getMessage());
    }
  }


  public imsLangString getIMSLangString(Element theElement, String theName,
  ➥Namespace theNamespace) {
    imsLangString theResult = null;
    System.out.println(">>>getIMSLangString: looking for " + theName);
    imsLangString[] theIntermediateResults = getIMSLangStringArray(theElement,
    ➥theName, theNamespace);
    if (theIntermediateResults != null)
```

Listing 42.9 Continued

```
      theResult = new imsLangString(theIntermediateResults);
    return theResult;
  }

  public imsLangString[] getIMSLangStringArray(Element theElement,
  ➥String theName, Namespace theNamespace) {
    imsLangString[] theResult = null;
    System.out.println(">>>getIMSLangStringArray looking for " + theName);
    try {
        Element theStringElement = theElement.getChild(theName, theNamespace);
        System.out.println(">>>getIMSLangStringArray  found a " + theName);
        List theStrings = theStringElement.getChildren();
        theResult = new imsLangString[theStrings.size()];
        System.out.println(">>>getIMSLangStringArray  found " +
        ➥theStrings.size() + " children.");
        for (int i=0; i<theStrings.size(); i++) {
          System.out.println(">>>getIMSLangStringArray :
          ➥processing child " + i);
          Element aLangString = (Element)theStrings.get(i);
          try {
            theResult[i] =
              new imsLangString(aLangString.getContent(),
                                aLangString.getAttribute("lang").getValue());
            System.out.println(">>>getIMSLangStringArray : child is " +
            ➥aLangString.getContent() +"; lang= " +
            ➥aLangString.getAttribute("lang").getValue());
          } catch (NoSuchAttributeException nsae) {
            theResult[i] = new imsLangString(aLangString.getContent());
            System.out.println(">>>getIMSLangStringArray : no lang;
            ➥content is " + aLangString.getContent());
          }
        }
      } catch (NoSuchChildException nsce) {
        System.out.println(">>>getIMSLangStringArray: no such children");
        theResult = null;
      }
    return theResult;
  }

  public String getMetaDataScheme() {
    return fMetaMetaData.scheme;
  }

  public String getMetaDataLanguage() {
    return fMetaMetaData.language;
  }

  public String getAggregationLevel() {
    return fGeneral.aggregationlevel;
  }
```

Listing 42.9 Continued

```
    public String getTitle() {
      // when in doubt, just return the first element
      return getTitle(0);
    }

    public String getTitle(int theIndex) {
      String[] theTitle = fGeneral.title.string;
      return theTitle[theIndex];
    }

    public String getStructure() {
      String[] theStructure = fGeneral.structure.string;
      return theStructure[0];
    }

    public HashSet getCatalogEntries() {
      HashSet theResult = new HashSet(fGeneral.catalogentry.length);
      for (int i=0; i<fGeneral.catalogentry.length; i++)
        theResult.add(fGeneral.catalogentry[i].catalogue + " " +
                      fGeneral.catalogentry[i].entry.string[0]);
      return theResult;
    }

    public String getLanguage() {
      return fGeneral.language[0];
    }

    public HashSet getDescription() {
      HashSet theResult = new HashSet(fGeneral.description.length);
      for (int i=0; i<fGeneral.description.length; i++)
        theResult.add(fGeneral.description[i].string);
      return theResult;
    }

    public HashSet getKeywords() {
      HashSet theResult = new HashSet(fGeneral.keywords.length);
      for (int i=0; i<fGeneral.keywords.length; i++)
        theResult.add(fGeneral.keywords[i].string);
      return theResult;
    }

    public HashSet getCoverage() {
      HashSet theResult = new HashSet(fGeneral.coverage.length);
      for (int i=0; i<fGeneral.coverage.length; i++)
        theResult.add(fGeneral.coverage[i].string);
      return theResult;
    }
  }
```

A test routine is needed to tell us if the `Module` class is working correctly. Listing 42.10 provides such a tester.

Listing 42.10 *moduleTester.java*—It's Good Practice to Build Some "Scaffolding" Like This Tester

```
import java.io.IOException;

public class moduleTester  {
  public static void main(String[] args) {
      try {
        Module theModule =
          new Module( args[0]);
        System.out.println(theModule.getMetaDataScheme());
        System.out.println(theModule.getMetaDataLanguage());
        System.out.println(theModule.getAggregationLevel());
        System.out.println(theModule.getTitle());
        // add other accessor methods as desired
      } catch (IOException ioe) {
        System.out.println("Error: Unable to parse module: " +
          ioe.getMessage());
      }
  }
}
```

doGet—Reading and Displaying XML

Listing 42.11 shows the servlet and its `doGet` method. When the user requests that the servlet open a document, the servlet generates an HTML form such as the one shown in Figure 42.5.

Listing 42.11 *moduleEditorServlet.java*—This Servlet Shows the Basics of Opening and Parsing an XML Document

```
import java.io.IOException;
import java.io.File;
import java.io.PrintWriter;
import java.util.HashSet;
import java.util.Iterator;

import javax.servlet.ServletException;
import javax.servlet.http.HttpServlet;
import javax.servlet.http.HttpServletRequest;
import javax.servlet.http.HttpServletResponse;

public class moduleEditorServlet extends HttpServlet {
  // hard code directory during development; in production
  // code, set this item from a system property
  private final String theDirectory =
    "C:/javaDev/Ch41/editor/moduleEditor/modules/BUS620";
```

Listing 42.11 Continued

```
// this value is hardcoded in the prototype, and becomes the SELECT choice
// in production code.
private final String theModuleFilename =
  "C:\\javaDev\\Ch42\\editor\\moduleEditor\\modules\\BUS620\\BUS620m01.xml";

public void doGet(HttpServletRequest req,
                  HttpServletResponse res)
  throws ServletException, IOException {
  res.setContentType("text/html");
  PrintWriter out = res.getWriter();

  out.println("<HTML><HEAD>");
  out.println("<TITLE>Module Editor Servlet</TITLE>");
  out.println("</HEAD><BODY>");

  // read out the list of modules
  File theModuleDirectory = null;
  try {
  // during testing, we'll hardcode the path to the
    // XML document. On deployment, we'll allow the
    // user to choose a module from this menu.
    theModuleDirectory = new File(theDirectory);
    if (!theModuleDirectory.isDirectory() ||
        !theModuleDirectory.canRead())
      throw (new IOException());

    out.println("<H1>Module Editor Servlet</H1>");
    out.println("<FORM>");
    out.println("<H2>Module</H2>");
    out.println("<SELECT NAME=\"Module\">");

    String[] theFileNames = theModuleDirectory.list(new XMLFilter());
    if (theFileNames.length == 0)
      out.println("<OPTION>None");
    else
      for (int i=0; i<theFileNames.length; i++)
        out.println("<OPTION>" + theFileNames[i]);

    out.println("</SELECT>");

    try {
      // here's the hard-coded test module
      Module theModule =
        new Module(theModuleFilename);
      out.println("<H2>Scheme</H2>");
      out.println("<INPUT TYPE=\"text\" NAME=\"scheme\" VALUE=" +
        theModule.getMetaDataScheme() + ">");
      out.println("<H2>Language</H2>");
      out.println("<INPUT TYPE=\"text\" NAME=\"language\" VALUE=" +
        theModule.getMetaDataLanguage() + ">");
```

Listing 42.11 Continued

```
out.println("<H2>Aggregation Level</H2>");
out.println("<SELECT NAME=\"AggregationLevel\">");
String theAggregationLevel = theModule.getAggregationLevel();
if (theAggregationLevel.equals("0"))
  out.println("<OPTION VALUE=\"0\" SELECTED>Raw data");
else
  out.println("<OPTION VALUE=\"0\">Raw data");
if (theAggregationLevel.equals("1"))
  out.println("<OPTION VALUE=\"1\" SELECTED>Lesson");
else
  out.println("<OPTION VALUE=\"1\">Lesson");
if (theAggregationLevel.equals("2"))
  out.println("<OPTION VALUE=\"2\" SELECTED>Module");
else
  out.println("<OPTION VALUE=\"2\">Module");
if (theAggregationLevel.equals("3"))
  out.println("<OPTION VALUE=\"3\" SELECTED>Course");
else
  out.println("<OPTION VALUE=\"3\">Course");
out.println("</SELECT>");
out.println("See Appendix E of <A HREF=\"http://www.adlnet.org/Scorm/
➥docs/SCORM_2.doc\" TARGET=\"_blank\">the SCORM reference</A>.");


out.println("<H2>Structure</H2>");
out.println("<SELECT NAME=\"Structure\">");
String theStructure = theModule.getStructure();
if (theStructure.equals("Collection"))
  out.println("<OPTION SELECTED>Collection");
else
  out.println("<OPTION>Collection");
if (theStructure.equals("Mixed"))
  out.println("<OPTION SELECTED>Mixed");
else
  out.println("<OPTION>Mixed");
if (theStructure.equals("Linear"))
  out.println("<OPTION SELECTED>Linear");
else
  out.println("<OPTION>Linear");
if (theStructure.equals("Hierarchical"))
  out.println("<OPTION SELECTED>Hierarchical");
else
  out.println("<OPTION>Hierarchical");
if (theStructure.equals("Network"))
  out.println("<OPTION SELECTED>Network");
else
  out.println("<OPTION>Network");
if (theStructure.equals("Branched"))
  out.println("<OPTION SELECTED>Branched");
else
  out.println("<OPTION>Branched");
```

Listing 42.11 Continued

```
        if (theStructure.equals("Parceled"))
          out.println("<OPTION SELECTED>Parceled");
        else
          out.println("<OPTION>Parceled");
        if (theStructure.equals("Atomic"))
          out.println("<OPTION SELECTED>Atomic");
        else
          out.println("<OPTION>Atomic");
        out.println("</SELECT>");
        out.println("See Paragraph 1.8 of <A HREF=\"http://www.imsproject.org/
        ➥metadata/mdinfov1p1.html\" TARGET=\"_blank\">
        ➥the IMS Meta-Data Information Model</A>.");

        out.println("<HR>");

        HashSet theCatalogEntries = theModule.getCatalogEntries();
        Iterator theEntriesIterator = theCatalogEntries.iterator();
        int i=0;
        if (theCatalogEntries.size() != 0)
          out.println("<H2>Catalog Entries</H2>");
        while (theEntriesIterator.hasNext())
          out.println("<INPUT TYPE=\"text\" NAME=\"CatalogEntry\"" + i++ +
          ➥" VALUE=\"" +
                      theEntriesIterator.next() + "\" SIZE=\"25\"><BR>");

      } catch (IOException ioe) {
        out.println("<H1>Error: Unable to parse module</H1>");
        out.println("<P>" + ioe.getMessage() + "</P>");
      }

      out.println("</FORM>");

    } catch (NullPointerException npe) {
      out.println("<H1>Error: Null pointer for module directory</H1>");
    } catch (IOException ioe) {
      if (theModuleDirectory.isDirectory())
        out.println("<H1>Error: Cannot read directory " +
          theModuleDirectory.getPath() + "</H1>");
      else
        out.println("<H1>Error: " + theModuleDirectory.getPath() +
                    " is not a directory.</H1>");
    }

    out.println("</BODY></HTML>");
    out.close();
  }
  /**
   *<B><CODE>XMLFilter</CODE></B> is an inner class. It's
   * single method, <CODE>accept</CODE>, returns true if
   * the file is a directory or has an XML suffix.
```

Listing 42.11 Continued

```
 *
 * @version 1.0
 */
class XMLFilter implements java.io.FilenameFilter {
  public boolean accept(File theDirectory, String theFilename) {
    boolean theResult = false;
    File theFile = new File(theDirectory, theFilename);
    theResult = theFile.isDirectory();
    if (!theResult)
      theResult = theFilename.substring(theFilename.length() - 4).
      ➥equals(".xml");
    return theResult;
  }
 }
}
```

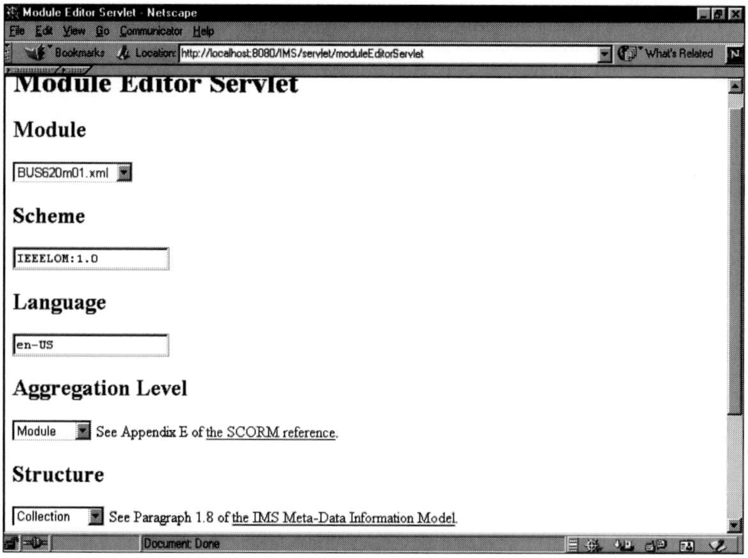

FIGURE 42.5
Running doGet produces an HTML form.

doPost—Editing XML

To allow the user to change and save module information, a `doPost` method must be added to the `moduleEditorServlet` class:

```
public void doPost(HttpServletRequest theRequest,
                   HttpServletResponse theResponse)
  throws ServletException, IOException {

  // make sure the user hasn't waited too long
  // and allowed the reference to become invalid
  if (theModule == null)
    theModule = new Module(theModuleFilename);
```

```
    String theScheme =
      theRequest.getParameterValues("scheme")[0];
    if ((theScheme != null) && (!theScheme.equals(""))) {
      theModule.setMetaDataScheme( theScheme );
    }
    // . . . add other elements of the module . . .
    // write out the document to the file
    theModule.saveDocument(theModuleFilename);

    // finally, tell the user everything worked
    theResponse.setContentType("text/html");
    PrintWriter out = theResponse.getWriter();
    out.println("<HTML><HEAD>");
    out.println("<TITLE>Module Updated</TITLE>");
    out.println("</HEAD><BODY>");
    out.println("<H1>Changes saved</H1>");

    // run the new file through the validator, just to be sure
    SAXBuilder theBuilder = new SAXBuilder( true );
    try {
      Document theDocument = theBuilder.build ( theModuleFilename );
    } catch (JDOMException jde) {
      out.println("<P>Error validating document: " + jde.getMessage() + "</P>");
    }
    out.println("<A HREF=\"moduleEditorServlet\">Edit another module");
    // add other links here as desired
    out.println("</BODY></HTML>");
    out.close();
  }
```

Mutator methods must be added for each `Module` data member that you want to change. For example, you could write `setMetaDataScheme` like this:

```
public void setMetaDataScheme( String theNewScheme ) {
  fMetaMetaData.scheme = theNewScheme;
}
```

You also need to add the `saveDocument` method to the `Module` class:

```
import org.jdom.output.XMLOutputter;
. . .
public synchronized void saveDocument( OutputStream out )
  throws IOException {
  try {
    // set up a default namespace for modules
    Namespace theNamespace = Namespace.getNamespace(
    ➥"http://www.imsproject.org/metadata/");

    // the JDOM document was loaded in the parse method and is saved
    ➥in a variable called fDoc.
    Element theRoot = fDoc.getRootElement();

    // update each field
    theRoot.getChild("METAMETADATA", theNamespace).
      getChild("METADATASCHEME", theNamespace).setContent(getMetaDataScheme());
    // . . . repeat for other fields . . .
```

```
    } catch (JDOMException jde) {
      throw new IOException(jde.getMessage());
    }

    // finally, write the finished document back out to the filesystem
    XMLOutputter theOutputter = new XMLOutputter();
    TheOutputter.output(fDoc, out);
  }
```

Because you've already updated the data members, `saveDocument` only has to copy this data into `fDoc` and write it out to the filesystem.

If it's possible for the user to make a change that results in an invalid document, consider implementing an "undo" capability: Write `fDoc` to a temporary file or stream, parse the document with a validating parser, throw an exception if the document isn't valid, and give the user a chance to fix the mistake. Avoid committing invalid documents to the filesystem where they might be read by non-validating parsers.

Using Xalan to Generate HTML

You can write XSL style sheets to transform the XML documents of this application into HTML. When the prototype is fielded, the School of Business wants to have a clerk run the XSLT processor and perform a quality check on the resulting Web pages. He can open the pages in a Web page editor, correct any formatting or layout errors, and save the finished documents to the public server. Figure 42.6 shows the course syllabus for BUSN 620. As the school gains confidence in the system, this clerk's function could be taken over by a Web publishing framework such as Cocoon.

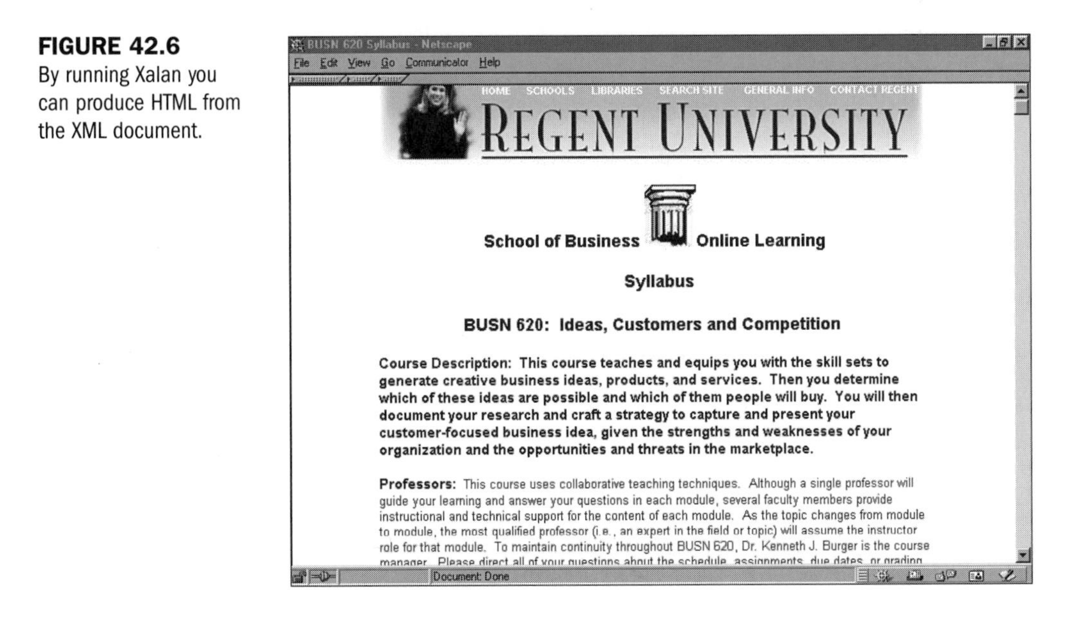

FIGURE 42.6
By running Xalan you can produce HTML from the XML document.

Writing Extensible Server Pages

In Chapter 41 you looked at Java Server Pages (JSPs). As you might have noticed, JSPs solve one problem while making another. They provide a nice mechanism for generating dynamic content but they force you to embed stylistic tags inside the source code, tightly coupling content and presentation.

Separating Content from Presentation

As you've seen in this chapter, XML provides an excellent way to separate content and presentation. Instead of writing JSPs, we can write Extensible Server Pages (XSPs) that read XML documents and generate HTML based on an XSL style sheet. Like JSPs, XSPs can contain Java code that is compiled when the document is first loaded.

NOTE You can read more about XSP on Apache's Cocoon site at `http://xml.apache.org/cocoon/xsp.html`. ■

Storing Content and Logic in an XML Document Listing 42.12 shows an example XSP—the content portion of the XSP.

Listing 42.12 ***test3.xml*—This Test Document Includes a Dynamically Generated Date**

```
<?xml version="1.0"?>

<?cocoon-process type="xsp"?>
<?cocoon-process type="xslt"?>
<?xml-stylesheet href="XSL/Regent2.html.xsl" type="text/xsl"?>

<xsp:page
     language="java"
     xmlns:xsp="http://www.apache.org/1999/XSP/Core"
>

<xsp:logic>
   private String showDate() {
     String theResult = "";
     java.text.SimpleDateFormat theFormatter
       = new java.text.SimpleDateFormat ("MMM dd, yyyy");
     Date today = new Date();
     theResult = theFormatter.format(today);
     return theResult;
   }
</xsp:logic>

   <Course>
    <ID>BUSN 620</ID>
    <Name>Ideas, Customers, and Competition</Name>
    <GeneratedOnDate><xsp:expr>showDate()</xsp:expr></GeneratedOnDate>
   </Course>
</xsp:page>
```

To add Java to a document (making it an XSP), add the following lines, as shown previously in Listing 42.12:

```
<?cocoon-process type="xsp"?>
```

To tell Cocoon to run the XSP processor (which will invoke the Java compiler), add

```
<xsp:page
      language="java"
      xmlns:xsp="http://www.apache.org/1999/XSP/Core"
>
. . .
</xsp:page>
```

making the root document an `xsp:page`,

```
<xsp:logic> . . . </xsp:logic>
```

to add Java as needed, and

```
<xsp:expr> . . . </xsp:expr>
```

to embed Java values into the content. (Other XSP tags are described at `http://xml.apache.org/cocoon/xsp.html`.)

Putting Presentation Information into a Style Sheet In this case, the date was placed into a new tag—`<GeneratedOnDate>...</GeneratedOnDate>`, and the template was added to the style sheet:

```
<xsl:template match="GeneratedOnDate">
  <P ALIGN="Center">
    <SMALL>
      This dynamic document was generated on <xsl:value-of select="self::*"/>.
    </SMALL>
  </P>
  <HR />
</xsl:template>
```

Figure 42.7 shows the resulting Web page.

Separating Logic from Content

Just as you built a custom tag library in Chapter 41, you can build a tag library for use in XSP documents. This technique allows you to separate the logic that is used to generate dynamic content from the content itself. With an appropriate library you could write

```
<GeneratedOnDate><Regent:showDate/></GeneratedOnDate>
```

Details of this technique are given on the XSP Web page (`http://xml.apache.org/cocoon/xsp.html`).

FIGURE 42.7
Write your documents as XSPs to add dynamic content with Java.

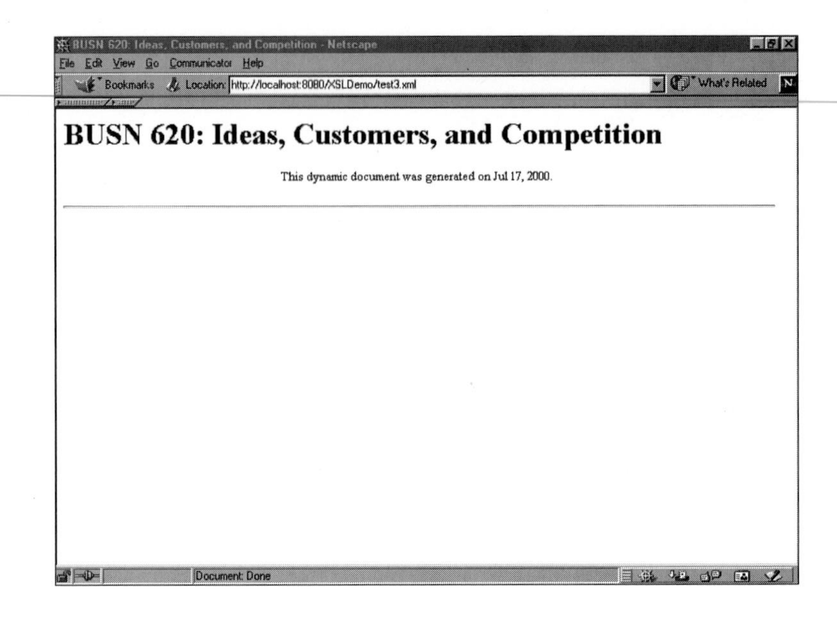

Appendixes

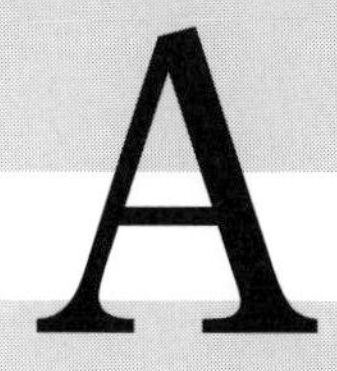

JavaScript Language Reference

How This Reference Is Organized

The first part of this reference is organized by object, with properties and methods listed by the object to which they apply. It covers most of the objects included in the Document Object Model supported by the most common versions of JavaScript. The second part covers independent functions in JavaScript not connected with a particular object, as well as operators in JavaScript.

Note that at the time of this writing, at least five "current" versions of JavaScript are extant. The standard for JavaScript is the ECMA standard ECMA-262. Netscape has JavaScript 1.3 (release) and 1.5 (beta, in the preview release of Navigator 6). Microsoft has the two releases (5.1 and 5.5) versions of its own JavaScript implementation, JScript. In this appendix, the most common and useful elements of each of these versions will be covered.

A Note About JavaScript Implementations

The various implementations of JavaScript are designed to interface seamlessly with Netscape Navigator and Microsoft Internet Explorer. New features have been introduced in various areas of the language model, including but not limited to the following:

- Events
- Objects
- Properties
- Methods

The latest versions of Netscape Navigator and Internet Explorer have been coded to support these new features, but earlier versions have not. Backward compatibility is, therefore, an issue. The following codes are used next to section headings to indicate where objects, methods, properties, and event handlers are implemented:

- **2**—Netscape Navigator 2
- **3**—Netscape Navigator 3
- **4**—Netscape Navigator 4
- **I**—Microsoft Internet Explorer 4 and later

Other than the `layer` object that follows, it is pretty safe to assume that everything discussed in this appendix will work in Netscape Navigator 6 and later and Microsoft Internet Explorer 5 and later. The `layer` object was implemented in Netscape Navigator 4 to support Netscape's proprietary `<layer>` element. When the `<layer>` element was not selected by the W3C for the Document Object Model standard, Netscape dropped support for it in later versions of its browser.

NOTE All the JavaScript information referenced in this appendix is client-side JavaScript; server-side JavaScript is not covered.

The *anchor* Object [2|3|4|I]

The `anchor` object reflects an HTML anchor.

Properties

- **`name`**—A string value indicating the name of the `anchor`. (Not 2|3.)

The *applet* Object [3]

The `applet` object reflects a Java applet included in a Web page with the `<applet>` element.

Properties

- **`name`**—A string reflecting the `name` attribute of the `<applet>` element.

The *area* Object [3]

The `area` object reflects a clickable area defined in an imagemap; `area` objects appear as entries in the `links` array of the `document` object.

Properties

- **`hash`**—A string value indicating an anchor name from the URL.
- **`host`**—A string value reflecting the host and domain name portion of the URL.
- **`hostname`**—A string value indicating the host, domain name, and port number from the URL.
- **`href`**—A string value reflecting the entire URL.
- **`pathname`**—A string value reflecting the path portion of the URL (excluding the host, domain name, port number, and protocol).
- **`port`**—A string value indicating the port number from the URL.
- **`protocol`**—A string value indicating the protocol portion of the URL, including the trailing colon.
- **`search`**—A string value specifying the query portion of the URL (after the question mark).
- **`target`**—A string value reflecting the `target` attribute of the `<area>` element.

Methods

- **getSelection**—Gets the current selection and returns this value as a string.

Event Handlers

- **onClick**—Specifies JavaScript code to execute when the user clicks the area.
- **onDblClick**—Specifies JavaScript code to execute when the user double-clicks the area. (Not implemented on Macintosh.) (4)
- **onKeyDown**—Specifies JavaScript code to execute when the user presses a specific key. (4)
- **onKeyPress**—Specifies JavaScript code to execute when the user holds down a specific key. (4)
- **onKeyUp**—Specifies JavaScript code to execute when the user releases a specific key. (4)
- **onMouseOut**—Specifies JavaScript code to execute when the mouse moves outside the area specified in the `<area>` element.

New Properties with JavaScript 1.2 and Later

`type`	Indicates a MouseOut event.
`target`	Indicates the object to which the event was sent.
`layer[n]`	Where `[n]` represents *x* or *y*, as in `layerx` or `layery`, used (with `page[n]` and `screen[n]`) to describe the cursor location when the `MouseOut` event occurred.
`page[n]`	Where `[n]` represents *x* or *y*, used (with `layer[n]` and `screen[n]`) to describe the cursor location when the `MouseOut` event occurred.
`screen[n]`	Where `[n]` represents *x* or *y*, used (with `layer[n]` and `page[n]`) to describe the cursor location when the `MouseOut` event occurred.

- **onMouseOver**—Specifies JavaScript code to execute when the mouse enters the area specified in the `<area>` element.

New Properties with JavaScript 1.2 and Later

`type`	Indicates a `MouseOver` event.
`target`	Indicates the object to which the event was sent.
`layer[n]`	Where `[n]` represents *x* or *y*, used (with `page[n]` and `screen[n]`) to describe the cursor location when the `MouseOver` event occurred.

`page[n]`	Where `[n]` represents *x* or *y*, used (with `layer[n]` and `screen[n]`) to describe the cursor location when the `MouseOver` event occurred.
`screen[n]`	Where `[n]` represents *x* or *y*, used (with `layer[n]` and `page[n]`) to describe the cursor location when the `MouseOver` event occurred.

The *array* Object [3|4|I]

The `array` object provides a mechanism for creating arrays and working with them. New arrays are created with `arrayName = new Array()` or `arrayName = new Array(arrayLength)`.

Properties

- **`length`**—An integer value reflecting the number of elements in an array.
- **`prototype`**—Used to add properties to an `array` object.

Methods

- **`concat(arrayname)`**—Combines elements of two arrays and returns a third, one level deep, without altering either of the derivative arrays. (Netscape Navigator 4.0 only; is not in the ECMAScript standard.)
- **`join(string)`**—Returns a string containing each element of the array, separated by `string`. (Not I.)
- **`reverse()`**—Reverses the order of an array. (Not I.)
- **`slice(arrayName, beginSlice, endSlice)`**—Extracts a portion of some array and derives a new array from it. The `beginSlice` and `endSlice` parameters specify the target elements at which to begin and end the slice. (Netscape Navigator 4.0 and Internet Explorer 4 and higher only.)
- **`sort(function)`**—Sorts an array based on function, which indicates a `function` defining the sort order. `function` can be omitted, in which case the sort defaults to dictionary order. Note: `sort` now works on all platforms.

The *button* Object [2|3|I]

The `button` object reflects a push button from an HTML form in JavaScript.

Properties

- `enabled`—A Boolean value indicating whether the button is enabled. (Not 2|3.)
- `form`—A reference to the `form` object containing the button. (Not 2|3.)
- `name`—A string value containing the name of the button element.
- `type`—A string value reflecting the `TYPE` attribute of the `<input/>` element. (Not 2|I.)
- `value`—A string value containing the value of the button element.

Methods

- `click()`—Emulates the action of clicking the button.
- `focus()`—Gives focus to the button. (Not 2|3.)

Event Handlers

- `onMouseDown`—Specifies JavaScript code to execute when a user presses a mouse button.
- `onMouseUp`—Specifies JavaScript code to execute when the user releases a mouse button.
- `onClick`—Specifies JavaScript code to execute when the button is clicked.
- `onFocus`—Specifies JavaScript code to execute when the button receives focus. (Not 2|3.)

The *checkbox* Object [2|3|I]

The `checkbox` object makes a check box in an HTML form available in JavaScript.

Properties

- `checked`—A Boolean value indicating whether the check box element is checked.
- `defaultChecked`—A Boolean value indicating whether the check box element was checked by default (that is, it reflects the `checked` attribute).
- `enabled`—A Boolean value indicating whether the check box is enabled. (Not 2|3.)
- `form`—A reference to the `form` object containing the check box. (Not 2|3.)
- `name`—A string value containing the name of the check box element.
- `type`—A string value reflecting the `TYPE` attribute of the `<input/>` element. (Not 2|I.)
- `value`—A string value containing the value of the check box element.

Methods

- **`click()`**—Emulates the action of clicking the check box.
- **`focus()`**—Gives focus to the check box. (Not 2|3.)

Event Handlers

- **`onClick`**—Specifies JavaScript code to execute when the check box is clicked.
- **`onFocus`**—Specifies JavaScript code to execute when the check box receives focus. (Not 2|3.)

The *combo* Object [I]

The `combo` object reflects a combo field in JavaScript.

Properties

- **`enabled`**—A Boolean value indicating whether the combo box is enabled. (Not 2|3.)
- **`form`**—A reference to the `form` object containing the combo box. (Not 2|3.)
- **`listCount`**—An integer reflecting the number of elements in the list.
- **`listIndex`**—An integer reflecting the index of the selected element in the list.
- **`multiSelect`**—A Boolean value indicating whether the combo field is in multiselect mode.
- **`name`**—A string value reflecting the name of the combo field.
- **`value`**—A string containing the value of the combo field.

Methods

- **`addItem(index)`**—Adds an item to the combo field before the item at `index`.
- **`click()`**—Simulates a click on the combo field.
- **`clear()`**—Clears the contents of the combo field.
- **`focus()`**—Gives focus to the combo field.
- **`removeItem(index)`**—Removes the item at `index` from the combo field.

Event Handlers

- **`onClick`**—Specifies JavaScript code to execute when the mouse clicks the combo field.
- **`onFocus`**—Specifies JavaScript code to execute when the combo field receives focus.

The *date* Object [2|3|I]

The `date` object provides mechanisms for working with dates and times in JavaScript. Instances of the object can be created with the following syntax:

```
newObjectName = new Date(dateInfo)
```

Here, `dateInfo` is an optional specification of a particular date and can be one of the following:

```
"month day, year hours:minutes:seconds"
```

```
year, month, day
```

```
year, month, day, hours, minutes, seconds
```

The latter two options represent integer values.

If no `dateInfo` is specified, the new object represents the current date and time.

Properties

- **`prototype`**—Provides a mechanism for adding properties to a `date` object. (Not 2.)

Methods

- **`getDate()`**—Returns the day of the month for the current `date` object as an integer from 1 to 31.
- **`getDay()`**—Returns the day of the week for the current `date` object as an integer from 0 to 6 (0 is Sunday, 1 is Monday, and so on).
- **`getHours()`**—Returns the hour from the time in the current `date` object as an integer from 0 to 23.
- **`getMinutes()`**—Returns the minutes from the time in the current `date` object as an integer from 0 to 59.
- **`getMonth()`**—Returns the month for the current `date` object as an integer from 0 to 11 (0 is January, 1 is February, and so on).
- **`getSeconds()`**—Returns the seconds from the time in the current `date` object as an integer from 0 to 59.
- **`getTime()`**—Returns the time of the current `date` object as an integer representing the number of milliseconds since January 1, 1970 at 00:00:00.
- **`getTimezoneOffset()`**—Returns the difference between the local time and GMT as an integer representing the number of minutes.
- **`getYear()`**—Returns the year for the current `date` object as a two-digit integer representing the year minus 1900.

- **`parse(dateString)`**—Returns the number of milliseconds between January 1, 1970 at 00:00:00 and the date specified in `dateString`, which should take the following format (not I):

  ```
  Day, DD Mon YYYY HH:MM:SS TZN
  Mon DD, YYYY
  ```

- **`setDate(dateValue)`**—Sets the day of the month for the current `date` object. `dateValue` is an integer from 1 to 31.
- **`setHours(hoursValue)`**—Sets the hours for the time for the current `date` object. `hoursValue` is an integer from 0 to 23.
- **`setMinutes(minutesValue)`**—Sets the minutes for the time for the current `date` object. `minutesValue` is an integer from 0 to 59.
- **`setMonth(monthValue)`**—Sets the month for the current `date` object. `monthValue` is an integer from 0 to 11 (0 is January, 1 is February, and so on).
- **`setSeconds(secondsValue)`**—Sets the seconds for the time for the current `date` object. `secondsValue` is an integer from 0 to 59.
- **`setTime(timeValue)`**—Sets the value for the current `date` object. `timeValue` is an integer representing the number of milliseconds since January 1, 1970 at 00:00:00.
- **`setYear(yearValue)`**—Sets the year for the current `date` object. `yearValue` is an integer greater than 1900.
- **`toGMTString()`**—Returns the value of the current `date` object in GMT as a string using Internet conventions in the following form:

  ```
  Day, DD Mon YYYY HH:MM:SS GMT
  ```

- **`toLocaleString()`**—Returns the value of the current `date` object in the local time using local conventions.
- **`UTC(yearValue, monthValue, dateValue, hoursValue, minutesValue, secondsValue)`**—Returns the number of milliseconds since January 1, 1970 at 00:00:00 GMT. `yearValue` is an integer greater than 1900. `monthValue` is an integer from 0 to 11. `dateValue` is an integer from 1 to 31. `hoursValue` is an integer from 0 to 23. `minutesValue` and `secondsValue` are integers from 0 to 59. `hoursValue`, `minutesValue`, and `secondsValue` are optional. (Not I.)

The *document* Object [2|3|I]

The `document` object reflects attributes of an HTML document in JavaScript.

Properties

- **`alinkColor`**—The color of active links as a string or a hexadecimal triplet.
- **`anchors`**—Array of `anchor` objects in the order they appear in the HTML document. Use `anchors.length` to get the number of anchors in a document.
- **`applets`**—Array of `applet` objects in the order they appear in the HTML document. Use `applets.length` to get the number of applets in a document. (Not 2.)
- **`bgColor`**—The color of the document's background.
- **`cookie`**—A string value containing cookie values for the current document.
- **`domain`**—A string value indicating the server for the current document.
- **`embeds`**—Array of `plugin` objects in the order they appear in the HTML document. Use `embeds.length` to get the number of plug-ins in a document. (Not 2|I.)
- **`fgColor`**—The color of the document's foreground.
- **`forms`**—Array of form objects in the order the forms appear in the HTML file. Use `forms.length` to get the number of forms in a document.
- **`images`**—Array of image objects in the order they appear in the HTML document. Use `images.length` to get the number of images in a document. (Not 2|I.)
- **`lastModified`**—String value containing the last date of the document's modification.
- **`linkColor`**—The color of links as a string or a hexadecimal triplet.
- **`links`**—Array of link objects in the order the hypertext links appear in the HTML document. Use `links.length` to get the number of links in a document.
- **`location`**—A string containing the URL of the current document. Use `document.URL` instead of `document.location`. This property is expected to disappear in a future release.
- **`referrer`**—A string value containing the URL of the calling document when the user follows a link.
- **`title`**—A string containing the title of the current document.
- **`URL`**—A string reflecting the URL of the current document. Use instead of `document.location`. (Not I.)
- **`vlinkColor`**—The color of followed links as a string or a hexadecimal triplet.

Event Handlers

- **`onDblClick`**—Specifies JavaScript code to execute when the user double-clicks the area. (Not implemented on Macintosh; Netscape Navigator 4.0 only.) (4)
- **`onKeyDown`**—Specifies JavaScript code to execute when the user presses a specific key. (Netscape Navigator 4.0 only.) (4)

- **onKeyPress**—Specifies JavaScript code to execute when the user holds down a specific key. (Netscape Navigator 4.0 only.) (4)
- **onKeyUp**—Specifies JavaScript code to execute when the user releases a specific key. (Netscape Navigator 4.0 only.) (4)
- **onMouseDown**—Specifies JavaScript code to execute when a user presses a mouse button.
- **onMouseUp**—Specifies JavaScript code to execute when a user releases a mouse button.

Methods

- **captureEvents()**—Used in a window with frames (along with `enableExternalCapture`), it specifies that the window will capture all specified events. New in JavaScript 1.2 and later.
- **clear()**—Clears the document window. (Not I.)
- **close()**—Closes the current output stream.
- **open(mimeType)**—Opens a stream that allows `write()` and `writeln()` methods to write to the document window. `mimeType` is an optional string that specifies a document type supported by Netscape Navigator or a plug-in (for example, `text/html` or `image/gif`).
- **releaseEvents(eventType)**—Specifies that the current window must release events (in contrast to capturing them) so that these events can be passed to other objects, perhaps further on in the event hierarchy. New in JavaScript 1.2 and later.
- **routeEvent(event)**—Sends or routes an event through the normal event hierarchy.
- **write()**—Writes text and HTML to the specified document.
- **writeln()**—Writes text and HTML to the specified document followed by a newline character.

The *fileUpload* Object [3]

Reflects a file upload element in an HTML form.

Properties

- **name**—A string value reflecting the name of the file upload element.
- **value**—A string value reflecting the file upload element's field.

The *form* Object [2|3|I]

The `form` object reflects an HTML form in JavaScript. Each HTML form in a document is reflected by a distinct instance of the `form` object.

Properties

- **`action`**—A string value specifying the URL to which the form data is submitted.
- **`elements`**—Array of objects for each form element in the order in which they appear in the form.
- **`encoding`**—String containing the MIME encoding of the form as specified in the `enctype` attribute.
- **`method`**—A string value containing the method of submission of form data to the server.
- **`name`**—A string value reflecting the name of the form element.
- **`target`**—A string value containing the name of the window to which responses to form submissions are directed.

Methods

- **`reset()`**—Resets the form. (Not 2.)
- **`submit()`**—Submits the form.

Event Handlers

- **`onReset`**—Specifies JavaScript code to execute when the form is reset. (Not 2.)
- **`onSubmit`**—Specifies JavaScript code to execute when the form is submitted. The code should return a `true` value to allow the form to be submitted. A `false` value prevents the form from being submitted.

The *frame* Object [2|3|I]

The `frame` object reflects a frame window in JavaScript.

Properties

- **`frames`**—An array of objects for each frame in a window. Frames appear in the array in the order in which they appear in the HTML source code.
- **`parent`**—A string indicating the name of the window containing the frame set.
- **`self`**—An alternative for the name of the current window.
- **`top`**—An alternative for the name of the topmost window.
- **`window`**—An alternative for the name of the current window.

Methods

- **`alert(message)`**—Displays `message` in a dialog box.
- **`blur()`**—Removes focus from the frame. (Not 2.)

- **`clearInterval(intervalID)`**—Cancels timeouts created with the `setInterval` method. New in JavaScript 1.2 and later.
- **`clearTimeout(name)`**—Cancels the timeout with the name `name`.
- **`close()`**—Closes the window.
- **`confirm(message)`**—Displays `message` in a dialog box with OK and Cancel buttons. Returns `true` or `false` based on the button clicked by the user.
- **`focus()`**—Gives focus to the frame. (Not 2.)
- **`open(url,name,features)`**—Opens `url` in a window named `name`. If `name` doesn't exist, a new window is created with that name. `features` is an optional string argument containing a list of features for the new window. The feature list contains any of the following name-value pairs separated by commas and without additional spaces:

`toolbar=[yes,no,1,0]`	Indicates whether the window should have a toolbar.
`location=[yes,no,1,0]`	Indicates whether the window should have a location field.
`directories=[yes,no,1,0]`	Indicates whether the window should have directory buttons.
`status=[yes,no,1,0]`	Indicates whether the window should have a status bar.
`menubar=[yes,no,1,0]`	Indicates whether the window should have menus.
`scrollbars=[yes,no,1,0]`	Indicates whether the window should have scrollbars.
`resizable=[yes,no,1,0]`	Indicates whether the window should be resizable.
`width=pixels`	Indicates the width of the window in pixels.
`height=pixels`	Indicates the height of the window in pixels.

- **`print()`**—Prints the contents of a frame or window. This is the equivalent of the user clicking the Print button in Netscape Navigator. New in JavaScript 1.2 and later.
- **`prompt(message,response)`**—Displays `message` in a dialog box with a text entry field with the default value of `response`. The user's response in the text entry field is returned as a string.
- **`setInterval(function, msec, [args])`**—Repeatedly calls a function after the period specified by the `msec` parameter. New in JavaScript 1.2 and later.
- **`setInterval(expression, msec)`**—Evaluates `expression` after the period specified by the `msec` parameter. New in JavaScript 1.2 and later.
- **`setTimeout(expression,time)`**—Evaluates `expression` after `time`; `time` is a value in milliseconds. The timeout can be named with the following structure:

```
name = setTimeOut(expression,time)
```

Event Handlers

- **onBlur**—Specifies JavaScript code to execute when focus is removed from a frame. (Not 2.)
- **onFocus**—Specifies JavaScript code to execute when focus is placed in a frame. (Not 2.)
- **onMove**—Specifies JavaScript code to execute when the user moves a frame. (Netscape Navigator 4.0 only.)
- **onResize**—Specifies JavaScript code to execute when a user resizes the frame. (Netscape Navigator 4.0 only.)

The *function* Object [3]

The `function` object provides a mechanism for indicating JavaScript code to compile as a function. This is the syntax to use the `function` object:

```
functionName = new Function(arg1, arg2, arg3, ..., functionCode)
```

This is similar to the following:

```
function functionName(arg1, arg2, arg3, ...) {
   functionCode
}
```

In the former, `functionName` is a variable with a reference to the function, and the function is evaluated each time it's used instead of being compiled once.

Properties

- **arguments**—An integer reflecting the number of arguments in a function.
- **prototype**—Provides a mechanism for adding properties to a `function` object.

The *hidden* Object [2|3|I]

The `hidden` object reflects a hidden field from an HTML form in JavaScript.

Properties

- **name**—A string value containing the name of the hidden element.
- **type**—A string value reflecting the `type` property of the `<input/>` element. (Not 2|I.)
- **value**—A string value containing the value of the hidden text element.

The *history* Object [2|3|I]

The `history` object enables a script to work with the Netscape Navigator browser's history list in JavaScript. For security and privacy reasons, the actual content of the list isn't reflected into JavaScript.

Properties

- **`length`**—An integer representing the number of items on the history list.

Methods

- **`back()`**—Goes back to the previous document in the history list.
- **`forward()`**—Goes forward to the next document in the history list.
- **`go(location)`**—Goes to the document in the history list specified by `location`, which can be a string or integer value. If it's a string, it represents all or part of a URL in the history list. If it's an integer, `location` represents the relative position of the document on the history list. As an integer, `location` can be positive or negative.

The *image* Object [3]

The `image` object reflects an image included in an HTML document.

Properties

- **`border`**—An integer value reflecting the width of the image's border in pixels.
- **`complete`**—A Boolean value indicating whether the image has finished loading.
- **`height`**—An integer value reflecting the height of an image in pixels.
- **`hspace`**—An integer value reflecting the `hspace` attribute of the `<img/>` element.
- **`lowsrc`**—A string value containing the URL of the low-resolution version of the image to load.
- **`name`**—A string value indicating the name of the `image` object.
- **`prototype`**—Provides a mechanism for adding properties as an `image` object.
- **`src`**—A string value indicating the URL of the image.
- **`vspace`**—An integer value reflecting the `vspace` attribute of the `<img>` element.
- **`width`**—An integer value indicating the width of an image in pixels.

Event Handlers

- **onAbort**—Specifies JavaScript code to execute if the attempt to load the image is aborted. (Not 2.)
- **onError**—Specifies JavaScript code to execute if an error occurs while loading the image. Setting this event handler to null suppresses error messages if an error occurs while loading. (Not 2.)
- **onKeyDown**—Specifies JavaScript code to execute when the user presses a specific key. (Netscape Navigator 4.0 only.) (4)
- **onKeyPress**—Specifies JavaScript code to execute when the user holds down a specific key. (Netscape Navigator 4.0 only.) (4)
- **onKeyUp**—Specifies JavaScript code to execute when the user releases a specific key. (Netscape Navigator 4.0 only.) (4)
- **onLoad**—Specifies JavaScript code to execute when the image finishes loading. (Not 2.)

The *layer* Object [4]

The `layer` object is used to embed layers of content within a page; they can be hidden or not hidden. Either type is accessible through JavaScript code. The most common use for layers is in developing Dynamic HTML (DHTML). With layers, you can create animation or other dynamic content on a page by cycling through the layers you have defined.

Properties

- **above**—Places a layer on top of a newly created layer.
- **background**—Used to specify a tiled background image of the layer.
- **below**—Places a layer below a newly created layer.
- **bgColor**—Sets the background color of the layer.
- **clip(left, top, right, bottom)**—Specifies the visible boundaries of the layer.
- **height**—Specifies the height of the layer, expressed in pixels (integer) or by a percentage of the instant layer.
- **id**—Previously called `name`. Used to name the layer so that it can be referred to by name and accessed by other JavaScript code.
- **left**—Specifies the horizontal positioning of the top-left corner of the layer; used with the `Top` property.
- **page[n]**—Where `[n]` is *x* or *y*. Specifies the horizontal (*x*) or vertical (*y*) positioning of the top-left corner of the layer, in relation to the overall enclosing document. (Note: This is different from the `left` and `top` properties.)

- **parentLayer**—Specifies the layer object that contains the present layer.
- **src**—Specifies HTML source to be displayed with the target layer. (This source also can include JavaScript.)
- **siblingAbove**—Specifies the layer object immediately above the present one.
- **siblingBelow**—Specifies the layer object immediately below the present one.
- **top**—Specifies the vertical positioning of the top-left corner of the layer. (Used with the `Left` property.)
- **visibility**—Specifies the visibility of the layer. Three choices are possible: `show` (visible), `hidden` (not visible), and `inherit` (layer inherits the properties of its parent).
- **width**—Specifies the width of the layer. Used for wrapping procedures; that is, the width denotes the boundary after which the contents wrap inside the layer.
- **z-index**—Specifies the Z-order (or stacking order) of the layer. Used to set the layer's position within the overall rotational order of all layers. Expressed as an integer. (Used where there are many layers.)

Events

- **onBlur**—Specifies JavaScript code to execute when the layer loses focus.
- **onFocus**—Specifies JavaScript code to execute when the layer gains focus.
- **onLoad**—Specifies JavaScript code to execute when a layer is loaded.
- **onMouseOut**—Specifies JavaScript code to execute when the mouse cursor moves off the layer.

Properties

`type`	Indicates a `MouseOut` event.
`target`	Indicates the object to which the event was sent.
`layer[n]`	Where `[n]` represents *x* or *y*, used (with `page[n]` and `screen[n]`) to describe the cursor location when the `MouseOut` event occurred.
`page[n]`	Where `[n]` represents *x* or *y*, used (with `layer[n]` and `screen[n]`) to describe the cursor location when the `MouseOut` event occurred.
`screen[n]`	Where `[n]` represents *x* or *y*, used (with `layer[n]` and `page[n]`) to describe the cursor location when the `MouseOut` event occurred.

- **`onMouseover`**—Specifies the JavaScript code to execute when the mouse cursor enters the layer.

New Properties with JavaScript 1.2 and Later

`type`	Indicates a `MouseOver` event.
`target`	Indicates the object to which the event was sent.
`layer[n]`	Where `[n]` represents *x* or *y*, used (with `page[n]` and `screen[n]`) to describe the cursor location when the `MouseOver` event occurred.
`page[n]`	Where `[n]` represents *x* or *y*, used (with `layer[n]` and `screen[n]`) to describe the cursor location when the `MouseOver` event occurred.
`screen[n]`	Where `[n]` represents *x* or *y*, used (with `layer[n]` and `page[n]`) to describe the cursor location when the `MouseOver` event occurred.

Methods

- **`captureEvents()`**—Used in a window with frames (along with `enableExternalCapture`), it specifies that the window will capture all specified events. New in JavaScript 1.2 and later.
- **`load(source, width)`**—Alters the source of the layer by replacing it with HTML (or JavaScript) from the file specified in `source`. Using this method, you also can pass a width value (in pixels) to accommodate the new content.
- **`moveAbove(layer)`**—Places the layer above `layer` in the stack.
- **`moveBelow(layer)`**—Places the layer below `layer` in the stack.
- **`moveBy(x,y)`**—Alters the position of the layer by the specified values, expressed in pixels.
- **`moveTo(x,y)`**—Alters the position of the layer (within the containing layer) to the specified coordinates, expressed in pixels.
- **`moveToAbsolute(x,y)`**—Alters the position of the layer (within the page) to the specified coordinates, expressed in pixels.
- **`releaseEvents(eventType)`**—Specifies that the current window should release events instead of capturing them so that these events can be passed to other objects, perhaps further on in the event hierarchy. New in JavaScript 1.2 and later.
- **`resizeBy(width,height)`**—Resizes the layer by the specified values, expressed in pixels.

- **`resizeTo(width,height)`**—Resizes the layer to the specified height and size, expressed in pixels.
- **`routeEvent(event)`**—Sends or routes an event through the normal event hierarchy.

The *link* Object [2|3|I]

The `link` object reflects a hypertext link in the body of a document.

Properties

- **`hash`**—A string value containing the anchor name in the URL.
- **`host`**—A string value containing the hostname and port number from the URL.
- **`hostname`**—A string value containing the domain name (or numerical IP address) from the URL.
- **`href`**—A string value containing the entire URL.
- **`pathname`**—A string value specifying the path portion of the URL.
- **`port`**—A string value containing the port number from the URL.
- **`protocol`**—A string value containing the protocol from the URL (including the colon, but not the slashes).
- **`search`**—A string value containing any information passed to a `get` CGI-BIN call (such as any information after the question mark).
- **`target`**—A string value containing the name of the window or frame specified in the `target` attribute.

Event Handlers

- **`moveMouse`**—Specifies the JavaScript code to execute when the mouse pointer moves over the link. (Not 2|3.)
- **`onClick`**—Specifies the JavaScript code to execute when the link is clicked.
- **`onDblClick`**—Specifies the JavaScript code to execute when the user double-clicks the area. (Not implemented on Macintosh; Netscape Navigator 4.0 only.) (4)
- **`onKeyUp`**—Specifies the JavaScript code to execute when the user releases a specific key. (Netscape Navigator 4.0 only.) (4)
- **`onKeyPress`**—Specifies the JavaScript code to execute when the user holds down a specific key. (Netscape Navigator 4.0 only.) (4)
- **`onKeyDown`**—Specifies the JavaScript code to execute when the user presses a specific key. (Netscape Navigator 4.0 only.) (4)

- **`onMouseDown`**—Specifies JavaScript code to execute when a user presses a mouse button. (JavaScript 1.2 and later and Netscape Navigator 4.0 only.) (4)
- **`onMouseOut`**—Specifies JavaScript code to execute when the user moves the mouse cursor out of an object. (JavaScript 1.2 and later and Netscape Navigator 4.0 only.) (4)

  New Properties with JavaScript 1.2 and Later

`type`	Indicates a `MouseOut` event.
`target`	Indicates the object to which the event was sent.
`layer[n]`	Where `[n]` represents *x* or *y*, used (with `page[n]` and `screen[n]`) to describe the cursor location when the `MouseOut` event occurred.
`page[n]`	Where `[n]` represents *x* or *y*, used (with `layer[n]` and `screen[n]`) to describe the cursor location when the `MouseOut` event occurred.
`screen[n]`	Where `[n]` represents *x* or *y*, used with `layer[n]` and `page[n]`) to describe the cursor location when the `MouseOut` event occurred.

- **`onMouseUp`**—Specifies the JavaScript code to execute when the user releases a mouse button.
- **`onMouseOver`**—Specifies the JavaScript code to execute when the mouse pointer moves over the hypertext link.

  New Properties with JavaScript 1.2 and Later

`type`	Indicates a `MouseOver` event.
`target`	Indicates the object to which the event was sent.
`layer[n]`	Where `[n]` represents *x* or *y*, used (with `page[n]` and `screen[n]`) to describe the cursor location when the `MouseOver` event occurred.
`page[n]`	Where `[n]` represents *x* or *y*, used (with `layer[n]` and `screen[n]`) to describe the cursor location when the `MouseOver` event occurred.
`screen[n]`	Where `[n]` represents *x* or *y*, used (with `layer[n]` and `page[n]`) to describe the cursor location when the `MouseOver` event occurred.

The *location* Object [2|3|I]

The `location` object reflects information about the current URL.

Properties

- **`hash`**—A string value containing the anchor name in the URL.
- **`host`**—A string value containing the hostname and port number from the URL.
- **`hostname`**—A string value containing the domain name (or numerical IP address) from the URL.
- **`href`**—A string value containing the entire URL.
- **`pathname`**—A string value specifying the path portion of the URL.
- **`port`**—A string value containing the port number from the URL.
- **`protocol`**—A string value containing the protocol from the URL (including the colon, but not the slashes).
- **`search`**—A string value containing any information passed to a `get` CGI-BIN call (such as information after the question mark).

Methods

- **`reload()`**—Reloads the current document. (Not 2|I.)
- **`replace(url)`**—Loads `url` over the current entry in the history list, making it impossible to navigate back to the previous URL with the Back button. (Not 2|I.)

The *math* Object [2|3|I]

The `math` object provides properties and methods for advanced mathematical calculations.

Properties

- **`E`**—The value of Euler's constant (roughly 2.718) used as the base for natural logarithms.
- **`LN10`**—The value of the natural logarithm of 10 (roughly 2.302).
- **`LN2`**—The value of the natural logarithm of 2 (roughly 0.693).
- **`LOG10E`**—The value of the base-10 logarithm of e (roughly 0.434).
- **`LOG2E`**—The value of the base 2 logarithm of e (roughly 1.442).
- **`PI`**—The value of π; used to calculate the circumference and area of circles (roughly 3.1415).
- **`SQRT1_2`**—The value of the square root of one-half (roughly 0.707).
- **`SQRT2`**—The value of the square root of two (roughly 1.414).

Methods

- **abs(number)**—Returns the absolute value of number. The absolute value is the value of a number with its sign ignored—for example, abs(4) and abs(-4) both return 4.
- **acos(number)**—Returns the arc cosine of number in radians.
- **asin(number)**—Returns the arc sine of number in radians.
- **atan(number)**—Returns the arc tangent of number in radians.
- **atan2(number1,number2)**—Returns the angle of the polar coordinate corresponding to the Cartesian coordinate (number1,number2). (Not I.)
- **ceil(number)**—Returns the next integer greater than number; in other words, rounds up to the next integer.
- **cos(number)**—Returns the cosine of number, which represents an angle in radians.
- **exp(number)**—Returns the value of E to the power of number.
- **floor(number)**—Returns the next integer less than number; in other words, rounds down to the nearest integer.
- **log(number)**—Returns the natural logarithm of number.
- **max(number1,number2)**—Returns the greater of number1 and number2.
- **min(number1,number2)**—Returns the smaller of number1 and number2.
- **pow(number1,number2)**—Returns the value of number1 to the power of number2.
- **random()**—Returns a random number between zero and 1 (at press time, this method was available only on UNIX versions of Netscape Navigator 2.0).
- **round(number)**—Returns the closest integer to number; in other words, rounds to the closest integer.
- **sin(number)**—Returns the sine of number, which represents an angle in radians.
- **sqrt(number)**—Returns the square root of number.
- **tan(number)**—Returns the tangent of number, which represents an angle in radians.

The *mimeType* Object [3]

The mimeType object reflects a MIME type supported by the client browser.

Properties

- **description**—A string containing a description of the MIME type.
- **enabledPlugin**—A reference to plugin object for the plug-in supporting the MIME type.

- **`suffixes`**—A string containing a comma-separated list of file suffixes for the MIME type.
- **`type`**—A string value reflecting the MIME type.

The *navigator* Object [2|3|I]

The `navigator` object reflects information about the version of browser being used.

Properties

- **`appCodeName`**—A string value containing the code name of the client (for example, "Mozilla" for Netscape Navigator).
- **`appName`**—A string value containing the name of the client (for example, "Netscape" for Netscape Navigator).
- **`appVersion`**—A string value containing the version information for the client in the following form:

  ```
  versionNumber (platform; country)
  ```

  For example, Navigator 4.73 for Windows 98 (English version) would have an `appVersion` property with the value "4.73 – (Win98; U)".
- **`language`**—Specifies the translation of Netscape Navigator (a read-only property). New in JavaScript 1.2 and later.
- **`mimeTypes`**—An array of `mimeType` objects reflecting the MIME types supported by the client browser. (Not 2|I.)
- **`platform`**—Specifies the platform for which Netscape Navigator was compiled (for example, Win32, MacPPC, UNIX). New in JavaScript 1.2 and later.
- **`plugins`**—An array of `plugin` objects reflecting the plug-ins in a document in the order of their appearance in the HTML document. (Not 2|I.)
- **`userAgent`**—A string containing the complete value of the user-agent header sent in the HTTP request. The following contains all the information in `appCodeName` and `appVersion`:

  ```
  Mozilla/4.73 - (Win98; U)
  ```

Methods

- **`javaEnabled()`**—Returns a Boolean value indicating whether Java is enabled in the browser. (Not 2|I.)

- **preference(preference.Name, setValue)**—In signed scripts, this method enables the developer to set certain browser preferences. Preferences available with this method are the following:

general.always_load_images	true/false value that sets whether images are automatically loaded.
security.enable_java	true/false value that sets whether Java is enabled.
javascript.enabled	true/false value that sets whether JavaScript is enabled.
browser.enable_style_sheets	true/false value that sets whether style sheets are enabled.
autoupdate.enabled	true/false value that sets whether autoinstall is enabled.
network.cookie.cookieBehavior	(0,1,2) value that sets the manner in which cookies are handled. There are three parameters: 0 accepts all cookies; 1 accepts only those that are forwarded to the originating server; 2 denies all cookies.
network.cookie.warnAboutCookies	true/false value that sets whether the browser will warn on accepting cookies.

The *option* Object [3]

The option object is used to create entries in a select list by using the following syntax:

```
optionName = new Option(optionText, optionValue, defaultSelected, selected)
```

Then the following line is used:

```
selectName.options[index] = optionName.
```

Properties

- **defaultSelected**—A Boolean value specifying whether the option is selected by default.
- **index**—An integer value specifying the option's index in the select list.
- **prototype**—Provides a mechanism to add properties to an option object.
- **selected**—A Boolean value indicating whether the option is currently selected.
- **text**—A string value reflecting the text displayed for the option.
- **value**—A string value indicating the value submitted to the server when the form is submitted.

The *password* Object [2|3|I]

The `password` object reflects a password text field from an HTML form in JavaScript.

Properties

- **`defaultValue`**—A string value containing the default value of the password element (such as the value of the `VALUE` attribute).
- **`enabled`**—A Boolean value indicating whether the password field is enabled. (Not 2|3.)
- **`form`**—A reference to the `form` object containing the password field. (Not 2|3.)
- **`name`**—A string value containing the name of the password element.
- **`value`**—A string value containing the value of the password element.

Methods

- **`blur()`**—Emulates the action of removing focus from the password field.
- **`focus()`**—Emulates the action of focusing in the password field.
- **`select()`**—Emulates the action of selecting the text in the password field.

Event Handlers

- **`onBlur`**—Specifies JavaScript code to execute when the password field loses focus. (Not 2|3.)
- **`onFocus`**—Specifies JavaScript code to execute when the password field receives focus. (Not 2|3.)

The *plugin* Object [2|3|I]

The `plugin` object reflects a plug-in supported by the browser.

Properties

- **`description`**—A string value containing the description supplied by the plug-in.
- **`filename`**—A string value reflecting the filename of the plug-in on the system's disk.
- **`name`**—A string value reflecting the name of the plug-in.

The *radio* Object [2|3|I]

The `radio` object reflects a set of option or "radio" buttons (named because, like preset buttons on a radio, only one of them can be selected at a time) from an HTML form in

JavaScript. To access individual radio buttons, use numeric indexes starting at zero. Individual buttons in a set of radio buttons named `testRadio`, for example, could be referenced by `testRadio[0]`, `testRadio[1]`, and so on.

Properties

- **`checked`**—A Boolean value indicating whether a specific radio button is checked. Can be used to select or deselect a button.
- **`defaultChecked`**—A Boolean value indicating whether a specific radio button was checked by default (that is, it reflects the `checked` attribute). (Not I.)
- **`enabled`**—A Boolean value indicating whether the radio button is enabled. (Not 2|3.)
- **`form`**—A reference to the `form` object containing the radio button. (Not 2|3.)
- **`length`**—An integer value indicating the number of radio buttons in the set. (Not I.)
- **`name`**—A string value containing the name of the set of radio buttons.
- **`value`**—A string value containing the value of a specific radio button in a set (that is, it reflects the `value` attribute).

Methods

- **`click()`**—Emulates the action of clicking a radio button.
- **`focus()`**—Gives focus to the radio button. (Not 2|3.)

Event Handlers

- **`onClick`**—Specifies the JavaScript code to execute when a radio button is clicked.
- **`onFocus`**—Specifies the JavaScript code to execute when a radio button receives focus. (Not 2|3.)

The *regExp* Object [3|I]

The `regExp` object is relevant to searching for regular expressions. Its properties are set before or after a search is performed. They don't generally exercise control over the search itself, but instead articulate a series of values that can be accessed throughout the search.

Properties

- **`input`**—The string against which a regular expression is matched. New in JavaScript 1.2 and later.
- **`multiline [true, false]`**—Sets whether the search continues beyond line breaks on multiple lines (`true`) or not (`false`). New in JavaScript 1.2 and later.

- **`lastMatch`**—Indicates the characters last matched. New in JavaScript 1.2 and later.
- **`lastParen`**—Indicates the last matched string that appeared in parentheses. New in JavaScript 1.2 and later.
- **`leftContext`**—Indicates the string just before the most recently matched Regular Expression. New in JavaScript 1.2 and later.
- **`rightContext`**—Indicates the remainder of the string, beyond the most recently matched Regular Expression. New in JavaScript 1.2 and later.
- **`$1,..$9`**—Indicates the last nine substrings in a match; those substrings are enclosed in parentheses. New in JavaScript 1.2 and later.

The Regular Expression Object [3|I]

The Regular Expression (`RegExp`) object contains the pattern of a Regular Expression.

Parameters

- **`regexp`**—Specifies the name of the Regular Expression object. New in JavaScript 1.2 and later.
- **`pattern`**—Specifies the text of the Regular Expression. New in JavaScript 1.2 and later.

Flags

- **`g`**—Specifies that during the Regular Expression search, the match (and search) should be global.
- **`gi`**—Specifies that during the Regular Expression search, case is ignored and during the Regular Expression search, the match (and search) should be global.
- **`i`**—Specifies that during the Regular Expression search, case is ignored (that is, the search is not case sensitive).

Properties

- **`global [true,false]`**—Sets the `g` flag value in code, such as whether the search is global (`true`) or not (`false`). New in JavaScript 1.2 and later.
- **`ignoreCase [true,false]`**—Sets the `i` flag value in code, such as whether the search is case sensitive (`true`) or not (`false`). New in JavaScript 1.2 and later.
- **`lastIndex`**—(Integer value) Indicates the index position at which to start the next matching procedure (for example, `lastIndex == 2`). New in JavaScript 1.2 and later.
- **`source`**—(Read-only) Contains the pattern's text. New in JavaScript 1.2 and later.

Methods

- **`compile`**—Compiles the Regular Expression. This method is usually invoked at script startup, when the Regular Expression is already known and will remain constant. New in JavaScript 1.2 and later.
- **`exec(str)`**—Executes a search for a Regular Expression within the specified string (`str`). New in JavaScript 1.2 and later. Note: It uses the same properties as the `RegExp` object.
- **`test(str)`**—Executes a search for a Regular Expression and a specified string (`str`). New in JavaScript 1.2 and later. Note: It uses the same properties as the `RegExp` object.

The *reset* Object [2|3|I]

The `reset` object reflects a reset button from an HTML form in JavaScript.

Properties

- **`enabled`**—A Boolean value indicating whether the reset button is enabled. (Not 2|3.)
- **`form`**—A reference to the `form` object containing the reset button. (Not 2|3.)
- **`name`**—A string value containing the name of the reset element.
- **`value`**—A string value containing the value of the reset element.

Methods

- **`click()`**—Emulates the action of clicking the reset button.
- **`focus()`**—Specifies the JavaScript code to execute when the reset button receives focus. (Not 2|3.)

Event Handlers

- **`onClick`**—Specifies the JavaScript code to execute when the reset button is clicked.
- **`onFocus`**—Specifies the JavaScript code to execute when the reset button receives focus. (Not 2|3.)

The *screen* Object [4|I]

The `screen` object describes (or specifies) the characteristics of the current screen.

Properties

- **`availHeight`**—Specifies the height of the screen in pixels (minus static display constraints set forth by the operating system). New in JavaScript 1.2 and later.
- **`availWidth`**—Specifies the width of the current screen in pixels (minus static display constraints set forth by the operating system). New in JavaScript 1.2 and later.
- **`colorDepth`**—Specifies the number of possible colors to display in the current screen. New in JavaScript 1.2 and later.
- **`height`**—Specifies the height of the current screen in pixels. New in JavaScript 1.2 and later.
- **`pixelDepth`**—Specifies the number of bits (per pixel) in the current screen. New in JavaScript 1.2 and later.
- **`width`**—Specifies the width of the current screen in pixels. New in JavaScript 1.2 and later.

The *select* Object [2|3]

The `select` object reflects a selection list from an HTML form in JavaScript.

Properties

- **`length`**—An integer value containing the number of options in the selection list.
- **`name`**—A string value containing the name of the selection list.
- **`options`**—An array reflecting each of the options in the selection list in the order they appear. The `options` property has its own properties:

`defaultSelected`	A Boolean value indicating whether an option was selected by default (that is, it reflects the `selected` attribute).
`index`	An integer value reflecting the index of an option.
`length`	An integer value reflecting the number of options in the selection list.
`name`	A string value containing the name of the selection list.
`selected`	A Boolean value indicating whether the option is selected. Can be used to select or deselect an option.
`selectedIndex`	An integer value containing the index of the currently selected option.
`text`	A string value containing the text displayed in the selection list for a particular option.
`value`	A string value indicating the value for the specified option (that is, it reflects the `VALUE` attribute).

- **`selectedIndex`**—Reflects the index of the currently selected option in the selection list.

Methods

- **`blur()`**—Removes focus from the selection list. (Not 2|3.)
- **`focus()`**—Gives focus to the selection list. (Not 2|3.)

Event Handlers

- **`onBlur`**—Specifies the JavaScript code to execute when the selection list loses focus.
- **`onChange`**—Specifies the JavaScript code to execute when the selected option in the list changes.
- **`onFocus`**—Specifies the JavaScript code to execute when focus is given to the selection list.

The *string* Object [2|3|I]

The `string` object provides properties and methods for working with string literals and variables.

Properties

- **`length`**—An integer value containing the length of the string expressed as the number of characters in the string.
- **`prototype`**—Provides a mechanism for adding properties to a `string` object. (Not 2.)

Methods

- **`anchor(name)`**—Returns a string containing the value of the string object surrounded by an `A` container element with the `name` attribute set to `name`.
- **`big()`**—Returns a string containing the value of the string object surrounded by a `big` container element.
- **`blink()`**—Returns a string containing the value of the string object surrounded by a `blink` container element.
- **`bold()`**—Returns a string containing the value of the string object surrounded by a `b` container element.
- **`charAt(index)`**—Returns the character at the location specified by `index`.
- **`charCodeAt(index)`**—Returns a number representing an ISO-Latin-1 codeset value at the instant `index`. (Netscape Navigator 4.0 and later only)

- **`concat(string2)`**—Combines two strings and derives a third, new string. (Netscape Navigator 4.0 and later only.)
- **`fixed()`**—Returns a string containing the value of the string object surrounded by a `fixed` container element.
- **`fontColor(color)`**—Returns a string containing the value of the string object surrounded by a `font` container element with the `color` attribute set to `color`, which is a color name or an RGB triplet. (Not I.)
- **`fontSize(size)`**—Returns a string containing the value of the string object surrounded by a `fontsize` container element with the size set to `size`. (Not I.)
- **`fromCharCode(num1, num2, …)`**—Returns a string constructed of ISO-Latin-1 characters. Those characters are specified by their codeset values, which are expressed as `num1`, `num2`, and so on.
- **`indexOf(findString,startingIndex)`**—Returns the index of the first occurrence of `findString`, starting the search at `startingIndex`, which is optional; if it's not provided, the search starts at the start of the string.
- **`italics()`**—Returns a string containing the value of the string object surrounded by an `I` container element.
- **`lastIndexOf(findString,startingIndex)`**—Returns the index of the last occurrence of `findString`. This is done by searching backward from `startingIndex`. `startingIndex` is optional and is assumed to be the last character in the string if no value is provided.
- **`link(href)`**—Returns a string containing the value of the string object surrounded by an `A` container element with the `href` attribute set to `href`.
- **`match(regular_expression)`**—Matches a Regular Expression to a string. The parameter `regular_expression` is the name of the Regular Expression, expressed either as a variable or a literal.
- **`replace(regular_expression, newSubStr)`**—Finds and replaces `regular_expression` with `newSubStr`.
- **`search(regular_expression)`**—Finds `regular_expression` and matches it to some string.
- **`slice(beginSlice, [endSlice])`**—Extracts a portion of a given string and derives a new string from that excerpt. `beginSlice` and `endSlice` are both zero-based indexes that can be used to grab the first, second, and third character, and so on.
- **`small()`**—Returns a string containing the value of the string object surrounded by a `SMALL` container element.
- **`split(separator)`**—Returns an array of strings created by splitting the string at every occurrence of `separator` (not 2|I). `split` has additional functionality in JavaScript 1.2

and later and for Netscape Navigator 4.0 and later. That new functionality includes the following elements:

regex and fixed string splitting	You can now split the `string` by both Regular Expression argument and fixed string.
limit count	You can now add a limit count to prevent including empty elements within the string.
whitespace splitting	The capability to split on a whitespace (including any whitespace, such as space, tab, newline, and so on).

- **`strike()`**—Returns a string containing the value of the `string` object surrounded by a `STRIKE` container element.
- **`sub()`**—Returns a string containing the value of the `string` object surrounded by a `SUB` container element.
- **`substr(start, [length])`**—Used to extract a set number (length) of characters within a string. Use `start` to specify the location at which to begin this extraction process. New in JavaScript 1.2 and later.
- **`substring(firstIndex,lastIndex)`**—Returns a string equivalent to the substring beginning at firstIndex and ending at the character before `lastIndex`. If `firstIndex` is greater than `lastIndex`, the string starts at `lastIndex` and ends at the character before `firstIndex`.
- **`sup()`**—Returns a string containing the value of the `string` object surrounded by a `SUP` container element.
- **`toLowerCase()`**—Returns a string containing the value of the `string` object with all characters converted to lowercase.
- **`toUpperCase()`**—Returns a string containing the value of the `string` object with all characters converted to uppercase.

The *submit* Object [2|3|I]

The `submit` object reflects a submit button from an HTML form in JavaScript.

Properties

- **`enabled`**—A Boolean value indicating whether the submit button is enabled. (Not 2|3.)
- **`form`**—A reference to the `form` object containing the submit button. (Not 2|3.)
- **`name`**—A string value containing the name of the submit button element.
- **`type`**—A string value reflecting the `type` attribute of the `<input/>` element. (Not 2|I.)
- **`value`**—A string value containing the value of the submit button element.

Methods

- **click()**—Emulates the action of clicking the submit button.
- **focus()**—Gives focus to the submit button. (Not 2|3.)

Event Handlers

- **onClick**—Specifies the JavaScript code to execute when the submit button is clicked.
- **onFocus**—Specifies the JavaScript code to execute when the submit button receives focus. (Not 2|3.)

The *text* Object [2|3|I]

The `text` object reflects a text field from an HTML form in JavaScript.

Properties

- **defaultValue**—A string value containing the default value of the text element (that is, the value of the `VALUE` attribute).
- **enabled**—A Boolean value indicating whether the text field is enabled. (Not 2|3.)
- **form**—A reference to the `form` object containing the text field. (Not 2|3.)
- **name**—A string value containing the name of the text element.
- **type**—A string value reflecting the `type` attribute of the `<input/>` element. (Not 2|I.)
- **value**—A string value containing the value of the text element.

Methods

- **blur()**—Emulates the action of removing focus from the text field.
- **focus()**—Emulates the action of focusing in the text field.
- **select()**—Emulates the action of selecting the text in the text field.

Event Handlers

- **onBlur**—Specifies the JavaScript code to execute when focus is removed from the field.
- **onChange**—Specifies the JavaScript code to execute when the content of the field is changed.
- **onFocus**—Specifies the JavaScript code to execute when focus is given to the field.
- **onSelect**—Specifies the JavaScript code to execute when the user selects some or all of the text in the field.

The *textarea* Object [2|3|I]

The `textarea` object reflects a multi-line text field from an HTML form in JavaScript.

Properties

- **`defaultValue`**—A string value containing the default value of the textarea element (that is, the value of the `value` attribute).
- **`enabled`**—A Boolean value indicating whether the textarea field is enabled. (Not 2|3.)
- **`form`**—A reference to the `form` object containing the textarea field. (Not 2|3.)
- **`name`**—A string value containing the name of the textarea element.
- **`type`**—A string value reflecting the type of the `textarea` object. (Not 2|I)
- **`value`**—A string value containing the value of the textarea element.

Methods

- **`blur()`**—Emulates the action of removing focus from the textarea field.
- **`focus()`**—Emulates the action of focusing in the textarea field.
- **`select()`**—Emulates the action of selecting the text in the textarea field.

Event Handlers

- **`onBlur`**—Specifies the JavaScript code to execute when focus is removed from the field.
- **`onChange`**—Specifies the JavaScript code to execute when the content of the field is changed.
- **`onFocus`**—Specifies the JavaScript code to execute when focus is given to the field.
- **`onKeyDown`**—Specifies the JavaScript code to execute when the user presses a specific key. (Netscape Navigator 4.0 only.) (4)
- **`onKeyUp`**—Specifies the JavaScript code to execute when the user releases a specific key. (Netscape Navigator 4.0 only.) (4)
- **`onKeyPress`**—Specifies the JavaScript code to execute when the user holds down a specific key. (Netscape Navigator 4.0 only.) (4)
- **`onSelect`**—Specifies the JavaScript code to execute when the user selects some or all of the text in the field.

The *window* Object [2|3|I]

The `window` object is the top-level object for each `window` or `frame` and the parent object for the `document`, `location`, and `history` objects.

Properties

- **`defaultStatus`**—A string value containing the default value displayed in the status bar.
- **`frames`**—An array of objects for each frame in a window. Frames appear in the array in the order in which they appear in the HTML source code.
- **`innerHeight()`**—Specifies the vertical size of the content area (in pixels). New in JavaScript 1.2 and later.
- **`innerWidth()`**—Specifies the horizontal size of the content area (in pixels). New in JavaScript 1.2 and later.
- **`length`**—An integer value indicating the number of frames in a parent window. (Not I.)
- **`name`**—A string value containing the name of the window or frame.
- **`opener`**—A reference to the `window` object containing the `open()` method used to open the current window. (Not 2|I.)
- **`pageXOffset`**—Specifies the current *x* position of the viewable window area (expressed in pixels). New in JavaScript 1.2 and later.
- **`pageYOffset`**—Specifies the current *y* position of the viewable window area (expressed in pixels). New in JavaScript 1.2 and later.
- **`parent`**—A string indicating the name of the window containing the frameset.
- **`personalbar [visible=true,false]`**—Represents the Directories bar in Netscape Navigator and whether it's visible. New in JavaScript 1.2 and later.
- **`scrollbars [visible=true,false]`**—Represents the scrollbars of the instant window and whether they are visible. New in JavaScript 1.2 and later.
- **`self`**—An alternative for the name of the current window.
- **`status`**—Used to display a message in the status bar; it's done by assigning values to this property.
- **`statusbar=[true,false,1,0]`**—Specifies whether the status bar of the target window is visible.
- **`toolbar=[true,false,1,0]`**—Specifies whether the toolbar of the target window is visible.
- **`top`**—An alternative for the name of the topmost window.
- **`window`**—An alternative for the name of the current window.

Methods

- **alert(message)**—Displays message in a dialog box.
- **back()**—Sends the user back to the previous URL stored in the history list. (Simulates a user clicking the Back button in Netscape Navigator.) New in JavaScript 1.2 and later.
- **blur()**—Removes focus from the window. On many systems, it sends the window to the background. (Not 2|I.)
- **captureEvents()**—Used in a window with frames (along with enableExternalCapture), it specifies that the window will capture all specified events.
- **clearInterval(intervalID)**—Cancels timeouts created with the setInterval method. New in JavaScript 1.2 and later.
- **clearTimeout(name)**—Cancels the timeout with the name name.
- **close()**—Closes the window. (Not I.)
- **confirm(message)**—Displays message in a dialog box with OK and Cancel buttons. Returns true or false based on the button clicked by the user.
- **disableExternalCapture()**—Prevents the instant window with frames from capturing events occurring in pages loaded from a different location. New in JavaScript 1.2 and later.
- **enableExternalCapture()**—Enables the instant window (with frames) to capture events occurring in pages loaded from a different location. New in JavaScript 1.2 and later.
- **find([string], [true, false], [true, false])**—Finds string in the target window. There are two true/false parameters: The first specifies the Boolean state of case sensitivity in the search; the second specifies whether the search is performed backward. New in JavaScript 1.2 and later.
- **focus()**—Gives focus to the window. On many systems, it brings the window to the front. (Not 2|I.)
- **forward()**—Sends the user to the next URL in the history list. (Simulates a user clicking the Forward button in Netscape Navigator.) New in JavaScript 1.2 and later.
- **home()**—Sends the user to the user's Home Page URL. (For example, in a default configuration of Netscape Navigator, it sends the user to http://home.netscape.com.) New in JavaScript 1.2 and later.
- **moveBy(horizontal, vertical)**—Moves the window according to the specified values horizontal and vertical. New in JavaScript 1.2 and later.
- **moveTo(x, y)**—Moves the top-left corner of the window to the specified location; x and y are screen coordinates. New in JavaScript 1.2 and later.
- **navigator(url)**—Loads url in the window. (Not 2|3.)
- **open(url,name,features)**—Opens url in a window named name. If name doesn't exist, a new window is created with that name. features is an optional string argument

containing a list of features for the new window. The feature list contains any of the following name/value pairs separated by commas and without additional spaces (not I):

`toolbar=[yes,no,1,0]`	Indicates whether the window should have a toolbar.
`location=[yes,no,1,0]`	Indicates whether the window should have a location field.
`directories=[yes,no,1,0]`	Indicates whether the window should have directory buttons.
`status=[yes,no,1,0]`	Indicates whether the window should have a status bar.
`menubar=[yes,no,1,0]`	Indicates whether the window should have menus.
`scrollbars=[yes,no,1,0]`	Indicates whether the window should have scrollbars.
`resizable=[yes,no,1,0]`	Indicates whether the window should be resizable.
`width=pixels`	Indicates the width of the window in pixels.
`alwaysLowered=[yes,no,1,2]`	Indicates (if `true`) that the window should remain below all other windows. (This feature has varying results on varying window systems.) New in JavaScript 1.2 and later. Note: The script must be signed to use this feature.
`alwaysRaised=[yes,no,1,2]`	Indicates (if `true`) that the window should always remain the top-level window. (This feature has varying results on varying window systems.) New in JavaScript 1.2 and later. Note: The script must be signed to use this feature.
`dependent[yes,no,1,2]`	Indicates that the current child window will die (or close) when the parent window does. New in JavaScript 1.2 and later.
`hotkeys=[yes,no,1,2]`	Indicates (if `true`) that most hot keys are disabled within the instant window. New in JavaScript 1.2 and later.
`innerWidth=pixels`	Indicates the width (in pixels) of the instant window's content area. New in JavaScript 1.2 and later.
`innerHeight=pixels`	Indicates the height (in pixels) of the instant window's content area. New in JavaScript 1.2 and later.
`outerWidth=pixels`	Indicates the instant window's horizontal outside width boundary. New in JavaScript 1.2 and later.
`outerHeight=pixels`	Indicates the instant window's horizontal outside height boundary. New in JavaScript 1.2 and later.

`screenX=pixels`	Indicates the distance that the new window is placed from the left side of the screen (horizontally). New in JavaScript 1.2 and later.
`screenY=pixels`	Indicates the distance that the new window is placed from the top of the screen (vertically). New in JavaScript 1.2 and later.
`z-lock=[yes,no,1,2]`	Indicates that the instant window does not move through the cycling of the z-order; that is, it doesn't rise above other windows, even if activated. New in JavaScript 1.2 and later. Note: The script must be signed for this feature to work.
`height=pixels`	Indicates the height of the window in pixels.

- **`print()`**—Prints the contents of a frame or window. It's the equivalent of the user pressing the Print button in Netscape Navigator. New in JavaScript 1.2 and later.
- **`prompt(message,response)`**—Displays `message` in a dialog box with a text entry field with the default value of `response`. The user's response in the text entry field is returned as a string.
- **`releaseEvents(eventType)`**—Specifies that the current window should release events instead of capturing them, so that these events can be passed to other objects, perhaps further on in the event hierarchy. New in JavaScript 1.2 and later.
- **`resizeBy(horizontal, vertical)`**—Resizes the window, moving from the bottom-right corner. New in JavaScript 1.2 and later.
- **`resizeTo(outerWidth, outerHeight)`**—Resizes the window, using `outerWidth` and `outerHeight` properties. New in JavaScript 1.2 and later.
- **`routeEvent(event)`**—Sends or routes an event through the normal event hierarchy. New in JavaScript 1.2 and later.
- **`scrollBy(horizontal, vertical)`**—Scroll the viewing area of the current window by the specified amount. New in JavaScript 1.2 and later.
- **`scrollTo(x, y)`**—Scrolls the current window to the specified position, calculated in `x,y` coordinates, starting at the top-left corner of the window. New in JavaScript 1.2 and later.
- **`setInterval(function, msec, [args])`**—Repeatedly calls a function after the period specified by the `msec` parameter. New in JavaScript 1.2 and later.
- **`setInterval(expression, msec)`**—Evaluates `expression` after the period specified by the `msec` parameter. New in JavaScript 1.2 and later.

- **`setTimeout(expression,time)`**—Evaluates `expression` after `time`, which is a value in milliseconds. The timeout can be named with the following structure:

  ```
  name = setTimeOut(expression,time)
  ```

- **`stop()`**—Stops the current download. It's the equivalent of the user pressing the Stop button in Netscape Navigator.

Event Handlers

- **`onBlur`**—Specifies the JavaScript code to execute when focus is removed from a window. (Not 2|I.)
- **`onDragDrop`**—Specifies the JavaScript code to execute when the user drops an object onto the window. (Netscape Navigator 4.0 and later only.) (4.0)
- **`onError`**—Specifies the JavaScript code to execute when a JavaScript error occurs while loading a document. It can be used to intercept JavaScript errors. Setting this event handler to `null` effectively prevents JavaScript errors from being displayed to the user. (Not 2|I.)
- **`onFocus`**—Specifies the JavaScript code to execute when the window receives focus. (Not 2|I.)
- **`onLoad`**—Specifies the JavaScript code to execute when the window or frame finishes loading.
- **`onMove`**—Specifies the JavaScript code to execute when the user moves a window. (Netscape Navigator 4.0 only.)
- **`onResize`**—Specifies the JavaScript code to execute when a user resizes the window.
- **`onUnload`**—Specifies the JavaScript code to execute when the document in the window or frame is exited.

Independent Functions, Operators, Variables, and Literals

The following subsections describe the functions, operators, variables, and literals that are built in to JavaScript, without being attached to a specific JavaScript object.

Independent Functions

- **escape(character)**—Returns a string containing the ASCII encoding of character in the form %xx; xx is the numeric encoding of the character. (2|3|I)
- **eval(expression)**—Returns the result of evaluating expression, which is an arithmetic expression. (2|3|I)
- **isNaN(value)**—Evaluates value to see if it's NaN. Returns a Boolean value. (2|3|I) (On UNIX platforms, not 2.)
- **parseFloat(string)**—Converts string to a floating-point number and returns the value. It continues to convert until it hits a non-numeric character and then returns the result. If the first character can't be converted to a number, the function returns NaN (zero on Windows platforms). (2|3|I)
- **parseInt(string,base)**—Converts string to an integer of base base and returns the value. It continues to convert until it hits a non-numeric character and then returns the result. If the first character can't be converted to a number, the function returns NaN (zero on Windows platforms). (2|3|I)
- **toString()**—This is a method of all objects. It returns the object as a string or returns "[object type]" if no string representation exists for the object. (2|3) (Note: In JavaScript 1.2 and later, it converts objects and strings into literals.)
- **unescape(string)**—Returns a character based on the ASCII encoding contained in string. The ASCII encoding should take the form "%integer" or "hexadecimalValue". (2|3|I)
- **untaint(propertyName)**—Removes tainting from propertyName. (3)

Statements

- **break**—Terminates a while or for loop and passes program control to the first statement following the loop. (2|3|4) (Note: In JavaScript 1.2 and later, break has the added functionality of being able to break out of labeled statements.)
- **comment**—Used to add a comment within the script. This comment is ignored by Netscape Navigator. Comments in JavaScript work similarly to those in C. They are enclosed in a /* (start), */ (end) structure. (2|3|4)
- **continue**—Terminates execution of statements in a while or for loop and continues iteration of the loop. (2|3|4) (Note: In JavaScript 1.2 and later, continue has added functionality that enables you to continue within labeled statements.)
- **do while**—Sets up a loop that continues to execute statements and code until the condition evaluates to false. New in JavaScript 1.2 and later.

- **export**—Used with the `import` statement. In secure, signed scripts, it enables the developer to export all properties, functions, and variables to another script. New in JavaScript 1.2 and later.
- **for([initial-expression]; [condition]; [incremental-expression];))**—Specifies the opening of a for loop. The arguments are these: initialize a variable (`initial-expression`), create a condition to test for (`condition`), and specify an incrementation scheme (`incremental-expression`). (2|3|4)
- **for…in**—Imposes a variable to all properties of an object and executes a block of code for each. (2|3|4)
- **function [name]()**—Declares a function so that it can be referred to or reached by event handlers (or other processes). (2|3|4)
- **if…else**—A structure used to test whether a certain condition is `true`. `If…else` blocks can contain nested statements and functions (and call them) if a condition is either `true` or `false`. (2|3|4)
- **import**—Used with the `export` statement. In secure, signed scripts, it enables the developer to import all properties, functions, and variables from another script. New in JavaScript 1.2 and later.
- **label (labeled statements)**—Statement that creates a label or pointer to code elsewhere in the script. By calling this label, you redirect the script to the labeled statement.
- **new**—Creates an instance of a user-defined object. (It can also be used to create an instance of built-in objects, inherent to JavaScript, such as new `Date`.) (2|3|4)
- **return [value]**—Specifies a value to be returned by a given function. For example, return x returns the variable value associated with *x*. (2|3|4)
- **switch**—Evaluates an expression and attempts to match it to a `case` pattern or label. If the expression matches the `case`, trailing statements associated with that label are executed. New in JavaScript 1.2 and later. (Operates similarly to the `switch` statement in C shell syntax.)
- **this**—A statement used to refer to a specific object, as shown in this example: [2|3|4]

  ```
  onClick = 'javascript:my_function(this.form)'
  ```
- **var [name]**—Declares a variable by `name`. (2|3|4)
- **while**—Statement that begins a `while` loop. `while` loops specify that as long as (while) a condition is `true`, execute some code. (2|3|4)
- **with**—Statement that sets the value for the default object; a method that's similar to creating a global variable with a function. (2|3|4)

Operators

- **Assignment Operators**—See Table A.1. (2|3|I)

Table A.1 Assignment Operators in JavaScript

Operator	Description
=	Assigns the value of the right operand to the left operand.
+=	Adds the left and right operands and assigns the result to the left operand.
-=	Subtracts the right operand from the left operand and assigns the result to the left operand.
*=	Multiplies the two operands and assigns the result to the left operand.
/=	Divides the left operand by the right operand and assigns the value to the left operand.
%=	Divides the left operand by the right operand and assigns the remainder to the left operand.

- **Arithmetic Operators**—See Table A.2. (2|3|I)

Table A.2 Arithmetic Operators in JavaScript

Operator	Description
+	Adds the left and right operands.
-	Subtracts the right operand from the left operand.
*	Multiplies the two operands.
/	Divides the left operand by the right operand.
%	Divides the left operand by the right operand and evaluates to the remainder.
++	Increments the operand by one (can be used before or after the operand).
–	Decreases the operand by one (can be used before or after the operand).
-	Changes the sign of the operand.

- **Bitwise Operators**—Bitwise operators deal with their operands as binary numbers but return JavaScript numerical value. (See Table A.3.) (2|3|I)

Table A.3 Bitwise Operators in JavaScript

Operator	Description
AND (or &)	Converts operands to integers with 32 bits, pairs the corresponding bits, and returns one for each pair of ones. Returns zero for any other combination.

Table A.3 Continued

Operator	Description
OR (or |)	Converts operands to integers with 32 bits, pairs the corresponding bits, and returns one for each pair when one of the two bits is one. Returns zero if both bits are zero.
XOR (or ^)	Converts operands to integer with 32 bits, pairs the corresponding bits, and returns one for each pair when only one bit is one. Returns zero for any other combination.
<<	Converts the left operand to an integer with 32 bits and shifts bits to the left the number of bits indicated by the right operand. Bits shifted off to the left are discarded, and zeros are shifted in from the right.
>>>	Converts the left operand to an integer with 32 bits and shifts bits to the right the number of bits indicated by the right operand. Bits shifted off to the right are discarded, and zeros are shifted in from the left.
>>	Converts the left operand to an integer with 32 bits and shifts bits to the right the number of bits indicated by the right operand. Bits shifted off to the right are discarded, and copies of the leftmost bit are shifted in from the left.

- **Logical Operators**—See Table A.4. (2|3|I)

Table A.4 Logical Operators in JavaScript

Operator	Description
&&	Logical AND. Returns `true` when both operands are true; otherwise, it returns `false`.
||	Logical OR. Returns `true` if either operand is true. It returns `false` only when both operands are false.
!	Logical NOT. Returns `true` if the operand is false and `false` if the operand is true. This is a unary operator and precedes the operand.

- **Comparison Operators**—See Table A.5. [2|3|I]

Table A.5 Logical (Comparison) Operators in JavaScript

Operator	Description
==	Returns `true` if the operands are equal.
!=	Returns `true` if the operands are not equal.
>	Returns `true` if the left operand is greater than the right operand.
<	Returns `true` if the left operand is less than the right operand.

Table A.5 Continued

Operator	Description
>=	Returns `true` if the left operand is greater than or equal to the right operand.
<=	Returns `true` if the left operand is less than or equal to the right operand.

- **Conditional Operators**—Conditional expressions take one form:

  ```
  (condition) ? val1 : val2
  ```

  If `condition` is true, the expression evaluates to `val1`; otherwise, it evaluates to `val2`. (2|3|I)

- **String Operators**—The concatenation operator (+) is one of two string operators. It evaluates to a string combining the left and right operands. The concatenation assignment operator (+=) is also available. (2|3|I)
- **The `typeof` Operator**—The `typeof` operator returns the type of its single operand. Possible types are `object`, `string`, `number`, `boolean`, `function`, and `undefined`. (3|I)
- **The `void` Operator**—The `void` operator takes an expression as an operand but returns no value. (3)
- **Operator Precedence**—JavaScript applies the rules of operator precedence as follows (from lowest to highest precedence):

  Comma (,)

  Assignment operators (=, +=, -=, *=, /=, %=)

  Conditional (? :)

  Logical OR (||)

  Logical AND (&&)

  Bitwise OR (|)

  Bitwise XOR (^)

  Bitwise AND (&)

  Equality (==, !=)

  Relational (<, <=, >, >=)

  Shift (<<, >>, >>>)

  Addition/subtraction (+, -)

  Multiply/divide/modulus (*, /, %)

  Negation/increment (!, -, ++, —)

  Call, member ((), [])

B

General Reference Resource

The Web as a Resource

One of the greatest advantages of the World Wide Web is the amount of information it makes available 24 hours a day, 7 days a week. This appendix contains a selection of Internet addresses covering the information contained within this book. It is divided according to the six parts of the book: XHTML, XML, JavaScript, Dynamic HTML, Server-Side Processing, and Java 2.

If you've spent any time Web surfing in the last few years, you know that Web site URLs are not the most stable things. Keep this in mind when perusing the URLs for the resources mentioned here. If you try a URL such as

`http://developer.netscape.com/docs/examples/javascript/formval/overview.html`

and it no longer works, your best bet is to instead go to the "root" URL

`http://developer.netscape.com`

and try to find the material you want from there.

NOTE **Site:** Macmillan USA

`http://www.mcp.com`

Don't forget one of the main URLs associated with this book. Use the ISBN (0-7897-2473-1) to link to this book's Web page and download the sample code listings in this book.

Part I, "XHTML"

Site: W3C XHTML 1.0 Main Page

`http://www.w3.org/TR/xhtml1/`

Consult the W3C page for the most up-to-date status of XHTML. Here you will find links to the most current version of the standard and any versions prior to that.

Site: W3C Web Accessibility Initiative

`http://www.w3.org/WAI/`

The World Wide Web Consortium's Web Accessibility Initiative (WAI) seeks to ensure that all Web-based technologies and standards include features that make content accessible to persons with disabilities.

Site: The Browser-Safe Color Palette

`http://www.lynda.com/hex.html`

Lynda Weinman explains the notion of the "browser-safe" color palette. The palette is made up of colors that will be rendered the same way on Macintosh and Windows platforms, so you can be assured that all users will see the exact same thing.

Site: HTML TIDY

`http://www.w3.org/People/Raggett/tidy/`

HTML Tidy can also give you suggestions on where you need to improve your coding.

Site: Boutell.Com, Inc.

`http://www.boutell.com/`

Download Mapedit, WWW Imagemap Software here. Mapedit is available for all Windows platforms, Macintosh, and many kinds of UNIX, including Linux.

Site: W3C Scalable Vector Graphics

`http://www.w3.org/Graphics/SVG/`

You can keep pace with the development of SVG by periodically visiting the W3C Web site.

Site: MNG Documentation

`http://www.libpng.org/pub/mng/mngdocs.html`

A proposal is under development for a format called MNG that will support storage of multiple images and, therefore, animation. You can track the progress of this effort by regularly visiting this site.

Site: Portable Network Graphics

`http://www.libpng.org/pub/png/`

For the latest about PNG, including documentation of the standard, sample images, and a list of PNG-compliant software, consult this PNG home page.

Site: Jakob Nielsen's Alertbox

`http://www.useit.com/alertbox/9612.html`

Web usability guru Jakob Nielsen explains the advantages and disadvantages of using frames in his highly readable "Alertbox" column, "Why Frames Suck (Most of the Time)."

Site: CSS2 Specification

`http://www.w3.org/TR/1998/REC-CSS2-19980512`

The next standard—Cascading Style Sheets, level 3—is in the works. However, you can read about the current CSS level 2 standard here.

Site: Webreview.com

`http://www.webreview.com/pub/guides/style/style.html`

For an interesting article about Cascading Style Sheets, read Eric Meyer's article, "Browser Compatibility Charts."

Site: HTTP—Hypertext Transfer Protocol

`http://www.w3.org/Protocols`

Check out this site if you're interested in the technical specifications of HTTP, both current and future.

Part II, "XML"

Site: Learning XML

`http://www.learningXML.com`

Keep up to date with the XML Specifications and these XML resources at author Andrew Watt's Web site.

W3C Recommendations

Site: W3C—XML

`http://www.w3.org/XML/`

The W3C is constantly revising and updating drafts and specifications for XML and XML-related protocols and tools. Find the latest working drafts and recommendations here.

Site: W3C Technical Documents

`http://www.w3c.org/TR/`

At the time of this writing, a complete list of public World Wide Web Consortium technical documents can be found here.

General XML Resources

Site: XMLHack

`http://www.xmlhack.com`

This general XML site is one of the most useful for up-to-the-minute XML news.

XML Mailing Lists

Site: Mailing Lists for XML Developers

`http://metalab.unc.edu/xml/mailinglists.html`

Check out the number of lists to which you can subscribe for XML information and updates. Don't omit to scroll farther down the page because it is possible to subscribe to many of the XML mailing lists from that one Web page. A nice touch.

XML Job Sites

Site: Dice.com

`http://www.dice.com`

If you are thinking seriously about developing professional skills in XML, take time to browse around XML job sites, look at the skills you have now, and think how you can make the move to the necessary skill set. This is one of the most useful sites for XML and other IT jobs.

XML Tutorials

Site: W3Schools

`http://www.w3schools.org`

Some of the general XML sites contain links to XML tutorials. Check out the W3C's tutorial sites to see what they have available.

XML Tools

Site: XMLSpy

`http://www.xmlspy.com`

This is a full-featured XML editor with combined style sheet facilities and so on. Further details, including a demo download, are available here.

Site: XMLWriter

`http://xmlwriter.com`

XMLWriter is a useful but less fully featured XML editor.

XSLT Resources

Site: XSLT.com

`http://www.xslt.com`

At the time of this writing relatively few XSLT sites exist on the Web. However, check out this site for information, updates, tutorials, and more.

Site: Robin Cover's Pages

`http://oasis-open.org/cover/xsl.html`

Robin Cover has a densely packed page of information and XSL links, as well as further links to other more general XML material.

Site: Microsoft's XSL Developer's Guide

`http://msdn.microsoft.com/xml/XSLGuide/default.asp`

Microsoft has a useful section on XSL on its Web site. I repeat here my earlier caution about the past non-compliance of Microsoft's XSL with the W3C Recommendation. It is getting better, but you need to exercise care in judging whether it is now good enough for your purpose.

XPath

Site: Arbortext

`http://www.arbortext.com/Think_Tank/Norm_s_Column/Issue_One/Issue_One.html`

Here is a useful introductory tutorial on XPath by Norman Walsh of Arbortext.

Scalable Vector Graphics

Site: W3C SVG Conformance Test Suite

`http://www.w3.org/Graphics/SVG/Test/20000608/toc-ps.html`

`http://www.w3.org/Graphics/SVG/Test/svg-manual-r200.html`

In June 2000 the W3C SVG Working Group released the first version of a test suite for Scalable Vector Graphics. These links provide the initial version of the test suite and the manual for the test suite.

Site: Adobe

`http://www.adobe.com/svg/main.html`

The Adobe Web site has an interesting section devoted to Scalable Vector Graphics. The SVG Zone has a download for an SVG Viewer from Adobe and also some basic tutorial material. Adobe is clearly aiming to use SVG in a substantive way with Adobe's vector drawing package Illustrator in version 9 and beyond.

Site: Concordia University

`http://indy.cs.concordia.ca/svg/main.html`

Concordia University in Montreal has a site with various SVG examples and SVG links.

Site: Corel

`http://venus.corel.com/nasapps/DrawSVGDownload/index.html`

Corel has a filter for CorelDRAW 9 downloadable here.

Site: eGroups.com

`http://www.egroups.com/group/svg-developers/`

Among the large number of mailing lists on eGroups.com is one devoted to SVG. eGroups has recently been taken over by Yahoo!, so the URL might be liable to change.

Site: Alphaworks

http://www.alphaworks.ibm.com/

IBM has produced an SVG viewer available from the IBM Alphaworks Web site.

Site: Jasc Software—PaintShop Pro

http://www.jasc.com/psp7.asp?

The producers of PaintShop Pro have announced the beta of PaintShop Pro version 7.

Part III, "JavaScript"

The House of JOD Web Sites

Site: The House of JOD

http://jim.odonnell.org

Check out author Jim O'Donnell's Web page.

Site: The House of JOD Platinum Support Page

http://jim.odonnell.org/phtml4/

Contains sample code listings from the JavaScript and Dynamic HTML parts of this book. This site is organized hierarchically.

Microsoft Web Sites

Site: Microsoft Developer's Network Web Site

http://msdn.microsoft.com

This is Microsoft Developer's main Web site.

Site: Microsoft Internet Explorer Developer Center

http://msdn.microsoft.com/ie/

The main Microsoft Internet Explorer Developer's Web site.

Site: Microsoft Windows Script Technologies

http://msdn.microsoft.com/scripting/

This site discusses all Microsoft scripting technologies. In addition to JScript (Microsoft's JavaScript-compatible language), the site also discusses Visual Basic Script (VBScript), the Windows Script Host, and other scripting topics.

Netscape Web Sites

Site: DevEdge Online

`http://developer.netscape.com`

This is Netscape Developer's main Web site.

Site: JavaScript Documentation

`http://developer.netscape.com/docs/manuals/index.html?content=javascript.html`

Find all the documentation for Netscape's client- and server-side JavaScript language.

Site: JavaScript Sample Code

`http://developer.netscape.com/docs/examples/index.html?content=javascript.html`

Use this library of sample code that uses Netscape JavaScript.

Site: Sample Code for Form Validation

`http://developer.netscape.com/docs/examples/javascript/formval/overview.html`

This site contains the JavaScript code and sample Web page for form validation. This works with versions of Netscape Navigator 2 and higher.

Site: Form Validation with JavaScript 1.2 Regular Expressions

`http://developer.netscape.com/docs/examples/javascript/regexp/overview.html`

This site contains JavaScript code and a sample Web page for form validation. It uses regular expression support in Netscape Navigator 4 and higher to create faster, smaller scripts.

Site: Persistent Client State HTTP Cookies

`http://home.netscape.com/newsref/std/cookie_spec.html`

This site describes Web browser cookies. It contains good reference information only.

Site: Cookie Recipes Client-Side Persistent Data by Danny Goodman

`http://developer.netscape.com/viewsource/index_frame.html?content=archive/`
`➥goodman_cookies.html`

Goodman describes Web browser cookies and how to set and use them from JavaScript. This is a good all-around site to learn how to access and use cookies from JavaScript.

Site: Setting and Reading Cookies Using JavaScript

`http://developer.netscape.com/docs/examples/javascript/cookies/cookie.html`

This site contains a sample HTML document showing how to set and read cookies using JavaScript.

Site: JavaScript `RegExp` Object Documentation

`http://developer.netscape.com/docs/manuals/js/client/jsref/regexp.htm`

Learn how to use regular expressions using the JavaScript `RegExp` object.

Site: JavaScript and Plug-In Interaction Using Client-Side LiveConnect

`http://developer.netscape.com/docs/technote/javascript/liveconnect/`
`➥liveconnect_rh.html`

This site describes how to use JavaScript to interact with other Web browser technologies in Netscape Navigator.

Site: JavaScript Calling a Java Applet

`http://developer.netscape.com/docs/technote/javascript/liveconnect/Fade.html`

Go to this site for a LiveConnect JavaScript to Java communication example.

Site: Communication Between JavaScript and LiveAudio Plug-In

`http://developer.netscape.com/docs/technote/javascript/liveconnect/`
`➥js_plugin.html`

This site contains a LiveConnect JavaScript to Plug-In communication example.

World Wide Web Consortium Web Sites

Site: World Wide Web Consortium (W3C) Home Page

`http://www.w3c.org`

This is the home page of one of the foremost groups involved in setting Internet standards.

Site: W3C Document Object Model (DOM) Working Group Web Site

`http://www.w3c.org/DOM/`

Check out the main page for the W3C Working Group on the specification of the Document Object Model.

Site: W3C DOM Requirements Document

`http://www.w3.org/TR/DOM-Requirements/`

This document is for groups such as Microsoft, Netscape, and other developers. It details the W3C's requirements for the various levels of their Document Object Model standard.

Site: W3C DOM Level 1 Recommendation

`http://www.w3.org/TR/REC-DOM-Level-1/`

This is the final Recommendation of the W3C for their Level 1 Document Object Model standard. It covers the object model of the pre-Dynamic HTML Web browsers (version 3 of Internet Explorer and Navigator).

Site: W3C DOM Level 2 Candidate Recommendation

`http://www.w3.org/TR/DOM-Level-2/`

Read the Candidate Recommendation of the W3C for their Level 2 Document Object Model standard, the W3C Recommendation for the object model that includes capabilities usually referred to as "Dynamic HTML."

ECMA Web Sites

Site: ECMA Home Page

`http://www.ecma.ch`

This is the home page of one of the groups involved in setting Internet standards.

Site: ECMAScript Language Specification

`http://www.ecma.ch/ecma1/stand/ECMA-262.HTM`

Read the standard for Web browser scripting languages. Both Microsoft and Netscape claim ECMAScript compliance; not surprisingly, there are still incompatibilities in the two.

Internet Engineering Task Force Web Sites

Site: Internet Engineering Task Force (IETF) Home Page

`http://www.ietf.cnri.reston.va.us/home.html`

The IETF is another group involved in setting Internet standards.

Site: HyperText Transfer Protocol

`http://www.ietf.cnri.reston.va.us/html.charters/http-charter.html`

This page describes the IETF's work of the HyperText Transfer Protocol (HTTP) Working Group.

Site: HTTP State Management Mechanism

```
http://www.ietf.cnri.reston.va.us/internet-drafts/
➥draft-ietf-http-state-man-mec-12.txt
```

This is a draft of the specification for HTTP state management (cookie). If this URL doesn't work, use the link for the IETF HTTP Working Group.

Simon Tneoh Chee-Boon's Web Sites

Site: Simon Tneoh Chee-Boon's Home Page

`http://www.tneoh.zoneit.com`

Mr. Chee-Boon maintains a collection of Web pages with examples of all sorts of Web technologies and techniques.

Site: Credit Card Number Validator

`http://www.tneoh.zoneit.com/javascript/cardobject.html`

Read and study Mr. Chee-Boon's JavaScript code for performing credit-card evaluation.

Cookie Central Web Site

Site: Cookie Central Web Site

`http://www.cookiecentral.com/`

This Web site is "dedicated to provide full information upon Internet Cookies."

Part IV, "Dynamic HTML"

Microsoft Web Sites

Site: Microsoft Internet Explorer 4 Demos

`http://www.microsoft.com/ie/ie40/demos/`

Here are some demo Web pages for Internet Explorer. These are set up for Internet Explorer 4 but still apply to version 5 and higher.

Site: Microsoft Typography Web Site

`http://www.microsoft.com/typography/`

This site includes information about Microsoft typography, including their downloadable font technology.

Netscape Web Sites

Site: Navigator 4 Dynamic HTML Developer Central

`http://developer.netscape.com/tech/dynhtml/`

This is a repository of information for Netscape's Dynamic HTML for Navigator 4.

Site: W3C DOM Developer Central

`http://developer.netscape.com/tech/dom/`

This is a repository of information for Netscape's Dynamic HTML for Navigator 6.

Site: The Ultimate JavaScript Client Sniffer

`http://developer.netscape.com/docs/examples/javascript/browser_type.html`

This site provides Netscape's JavaScript code for determining browser vendor, version, and operating system with JavaScript.

Site: Cross-Browser DHTML Technote: API For Setting CSSP Properties from JavaScript

`http://developer.netscape.com/docs/technote/dynhtml/csspapi/csspapi.html`

Find information on the Netscape developer site for cross-browser compatible ways to access style sheet properties in Internet Explorer and Navigator 4.

World Wide Web Consortium Web Sites

Site: W3C Style Sheet Working Group Web Site

`http://www.w3.org/Style/`

This is the main page for the W3C Working Group on the specification for style sheets.

Dynamic HTML Zone Web Sites

Site: Macromedia Dynamic HTML Web Site

`http://www.dhtmlzone.com`

Use this support site to produce Dynamic HTML Web sites.

Site: Cross-Browser Dynamic HTML by Kevin Lynch

`http://www.dhtmlzone.com/articles/dhtml.html`

Read this article on the Dynamic HTML Zone discussing techniques for producing cross-browser compatible Dynamic HTML Web pages. Techniques focus on Internet Explorer and Navigator 4 (not Navigator 6).

CNET Builder.com Web Sites

Site: CNET Builder.com Web Site

`http://www.builder.com`

This is a general resource with information for Web developers.

Site: Writing Cross-Browser Dynamic HTML by David Boles and Rachael Ann Siciliano

`http://www.builder.com/Authoring/Dhtml/`

Boles and Siciliano provide many useful cross-browser Dynamic HTML tips. This article also includes some discussion of both Navigator 4 and Navigator 6, as well as Internet Explorer.

Site: Dynamic Duo Cross-Browser Dynamic HTML Web Site

`http://www.dansteinman.com/dynduo/`

This site includes a tutorial and library with JavaScripts for cross-browser Dynamic HTML; it does not cover Navigator 6.

Site: Dynamic Drive Web Site

`http://www.dynamicdrive.com/`

This is a great source of free JavaScripts for implementing Dynamic HTML effects on your Web pages. It also contains a collection of scripts, marked for the browser on which they work; many are cross-browser compatible (though primarily between Internet Explorer and Navigator 4 rather than 6).

Part V, "Server-Side Processing"

Site: W3C—CGI

`http://www.w3.org/CGI/`

NCSA Software Development maintains the CGI specification. You'll find the specification at the World Wide Web Consortium's CGI pages.

Site: Boutell.com

`http://www.boutell.com/cgic`

For CGI programming in C, a helpful library called `cgic` can be found here.

Site: Matt's Script Archive, Inc.

`http://www.worldwidemart.com/scripts/`

Find the justifiably famous Matt's Script Archive here. Look here first for tested, practical scripts in Perl and C for many common business uses.

Site: WWW Protocol Library for Perl

`http://www.ics.uci.edu/pub/websoft/libwww-perl/`

This is the University of California's public offering. Based on Perl version 5.003, this library contains many useful routines. If you plan to program in Perl, this library is worth the download just for ideas and techniques.

Site: The CGI Collection

`http://www.itm.com/cgicollection/`

Here is a vast collection of CGI scripts that you can use and learn from. It covers CGI security and contains tutorials and other examples.

Site: cgi-utils.pl

`http://www-genome.wi.mit.edu/WWW/tools/scripting/cgi-utils.html`

cgi-utils.pl is an extension to cgi-lib.pl from Lincoln D. Stein at the Whitehead Institute, MIT Center for Genome Research.

Site: CGI.pm—a Perl 5 CGI Library

`http://www-genome.wi.mit.edu/ftp/pub/software/WWW/cgi_docs.html`

CGI.pm is a Perl 5 library for creating forms and parsing CGI input.

Site: Index of `/WWW/tools/scripting/CGIperl`

`http://www-genome.wi.mit.edu/WWW/tools/scripting/CGIperl/`

This is a useful list of Perl links and utilities.

Site: Boutell.com—gd 1.8.3

`http://www.boutell.com/gd/`

A C library for producing GIF images on-the-fly, gd enables your program to create images complete with lines, arcs, text, and multiple colors, and to cut and paste from other images and flood fills, which get written out to a file. Your program can then suck this image data in and include it in your program's output. Although these libraries are difficult to master, the rewards are well worth it. Many map-related Web sites use these routines to generate map location points on-the-fly.

Site: Boutell.com—cgic

`http://www.boutell.com/cgic/`

This CGI library provides an easier method to parse CGI input using C.

Site: GD.pm

`http://stein.cshl.org/WWW/software/GD/GD.html`

GD.pm is a Perl wrapper and extender for gd.

Site: Internet Servers Inc.

`http://www.iserver.com/cgi/library.html`

This is Internet Servers Inc.'s wonderful CGI library. Among the treasures here you'll find samples of image maps, building a Web index, server-push animation, and a guest book.

Site: Web Developer's Virtual Library

`http://www.wdvl.com/Vlib/Providers/`

This collection of links and utilities will help you build an editor, use C++ with predefined classes, join a CGI programmer's mailing list, and best of all, browse a selection of clickables—Plug-and-Play CGI scripts.

Site: Greyware Automation Products

`http://www.greyware.com/greyware/software/`

Greyware Automation Products provides a rich list of shareware and freeware programs for Windows NT. Of special interest are the free SSI utilities and the CGI-wrapper program, CGIShell, which enables you to use Visual Basic, Delphi, or other GUI programming environments with the freeware EMWAC HTTP server.

Site: BHS.com

`http://www.bhs.com/`

Although not specifically geared toward CGI, the Windows NT Resource Center, sponsored by Beverly Hills Software, provides some wonderful applications, some of which are CGI-related. In particular, you'll find EMWAC's software, Perl for Windows NT and Perl libraries, and SMTP mailers.

Site: O'Reilly WebSite

`http://website.oreilly.com/`

Bob Denny, author of WebSite, has probably done more than any other individual to popularize HTTP servers on the Windows NT platform. At this site, you'll find a collection of tools, including Perl for Windows NT, VB routines for use with the WebSite server, and other interesting items.

Site: NCSA's CGI Archive

`ftp://ftp.ncsa.uiuc.edu/Web/httpd/Unixncsa_httpd/cgi`

Here is the NCSA's CGI Archive.

Site: CGI Resource Index

`http://www.cgi-resources.com/`

The CGI Resource Index is another good CGI site.

Site: Perl Language Home Page

`http://www.perl.com/perl/faq/`

The Perl Language Home Page's list of Perl FAQs. Check out the rest of the site while you're there.

Site: CGI FAQ

`http://www.w3.org/Security/Faq/www-security-faq.html`

Frequently asked questions about CGI security issues.

Site: NCSA Server-Side Includes

`http://hoohoo.ncsa.uiuc.edu/docs/tutorials/includes.html`

NCSA SSI documentation is available here, but the syntax and use given applies only to NCSA-style Web servers such as the Apache Web server.

Site: Apache HTTP Server Version 1.3

`http://www.apache.org/docs/mod/mod_include.html`

Apache has expanded its Web server to use Extended Server-Side Includes (XSSI). XSSI provides additional functionality to SSI, including the use of condition statements.

Site: CERT

`http://www.cert.org`

A comprehensive history of security problems, including attack-prevention software, is available through the Computer Emergency Response Team (CERT).

Site: NCSA

`http://www.ncsa.uiuc.edu/`

The NCSA httpd, for example, is far too big for the average user to go over line by line, but downloading it from its home site is as close to a guarantee of its integrity as you're likely to get. In fact, anything downloaded from NCSA will be prescreened for you.

Site: Introduction to SQL

`http://w3.one.net/~jhoffman/sqltut.htm`

You can teach yourself the basics of ANSI SQL using the tutorial found here.

Site: Oracle

`http://www.oracle.com/tools/webdb/`

Check out this site for more information on Oracle and how you can use Oracle with the World Wide Web.

Site: Sybase

`http://www.sybase.com/products/internet/`

Learn more about how you can use Sybase and its supporting tools to Web-enable your data.

Site: Hughes Technology

`http://www.Hughes.com.au/`

Written by David Hughes, this site was created to enable users to experiment with SQL queries and relational databases. It is free for noncommercial use (nonprofit, schools, and research organizations); for individual and commercial use, there is a modest fee per server.

Site: Informix

`http://www.informix.com/`

To learn more about Informix and its product offerings, visit the Informix Web site.

Site: Microsoft—SQL Server 2000

`http://www.microsoft.com/sql/`

You can learn all about Microsoft's most recent release of SQL Server (SQL Server 2000).

Site: FoxPro

`http://msdn.microsoft.com/vfoxpro/?RLD=196`

Look here to find out more about FoxPro.

Site: Microsoft Access

`http://www.microsoft.com/office/access/default.htm`

The Microsoft Access home page can provide you with a complete description of the capabilities of Access both on and off the Web.

Site: MySQL

`http://www.mysql.com/`

Find out anything you need to know about MySQL.

Site: Microsoft—VBScript

`http://msdn.microsoft.com/scripting/`

Microsoft's tutorial for VBScript programming can be found at the Microsoft Windows Script Technologies Web site.

Site: More Component Object Vendors

`http://www.aspstudio.com/ http://www.aspalliance.com/`
`➥components/ http://www.aspxtras.com/`

There are other component object vendors as well. To sample the offerings of a few more, direct your browser to one of these sites.

Site: Learn ASP

`http://www.learnasp.com/`

For more information on ASP development, consult the ASP developer resource site found here.

Site: PHP.net

`http://www.php.net/`

Entire books have been written about PHP, so you will no doubt want to have other reference material available after you finish this chapter. A good place to start is on the Web. You can download the PHP script processor for here, as well as complete an online PHP programming tutorial.

Site: PHP.net—Downloads

`http://www.php.net/downloads.php`

To install PHP for Windows, you need to download the compiled Win 32 binaries that support PHP processing.

Site: PHP Manual—Function Reference

`http://www.php.net/manual/html/funcref.html`

A full set of documentation for all classes of functions and the functions within each class can be found here.

Site: Allaire

`http://www.allaire.com/`

Learn more about Allaire's Web development products, including ColdFusion, HomeSite, and Jrun.

Part VI, "Java 2"

Site: Sun Microsystems—Java

`http://java.sun.com/`

Download a free copy of the latest Java SDK.

Site: Sun Microsystems—Downloads

`http://java.sun.com/j2se/1.3/download-windows.html`

Sun maintains a list of IDEs known to be compatible with Java 2.

Site: Java2 Information

`http://java.sun.com/products/jdk/1.2/java2.html`

Learn more about the various versions of the Java 2 platform.

Site: JNDI Tutorial

`http://java.sun.com/products/jndi/tutorial/index.html`

Sun provides a comprehensive online tutorial on JNDI.

Site: Applet Caching

`http://java.sun.com/j2se/1.3/docs/guide/misc/appletcaching.html`

Visit to learn more about the applet-caching feature.

Site: Java 2 Security Enhancements

`http://java.sun.com/j2se/1.3/docs/guide/security/enhancements.html`

Look here for a detailed description of the SDK 1.3 security enhancements.

Site: Swing Enhancements

`http://java.xun.com/j2se/1.3/docs/guide/swing/SwingChanges.html`

SDK 1.3 includes a significant list of enhancements to Swing. If you've used Swing from SDK 1.2 or before, be sure to look over the new capabilities.

Site: AWT Capabilities

`http://java.sun.com/j2se/1.3/docs/guide/awt/enhancements.html`

SDK 1.3 includes a significant list of enhancements to AWT. If you've used AWT from SDK 1.2 or before, be sure to look over the new capabilities listed here.

Site: AWT Native Interface

`http://java.sun.com/j2se/1.3/docs/guide/awt/AWT_Native_Interface.html`

If you're porting a legacy application into Java—especially one that relies on a native high-performance rendering engine—visit this URL and learn how to get the best of both worlds.

Site: Java 2 SDK—Accessibility

`http://java.sun.com/j2se/1.3/docs/guide/access/`

Make sure your Java programs are accessible; this Web page contains information about the utilities Sun added in SDK 1.3 to enable Java to work with assistive technology.

Site: Java Sound

`http://java.sun.com/products/java-media/sound/index.html`

Java Sound has its own home page. If you plan to use Java to capture, process, or play audio, visit this URL.

Site: HotSpot

`http://java.sun.com/features/1999/04/hotspot.html`

Learn what HotSpot technology can do for your project.

Index

Symbols

A

B

C

D

F

G

H

I

M

N

O

P

Q-R

S

T

U

W

X-Z